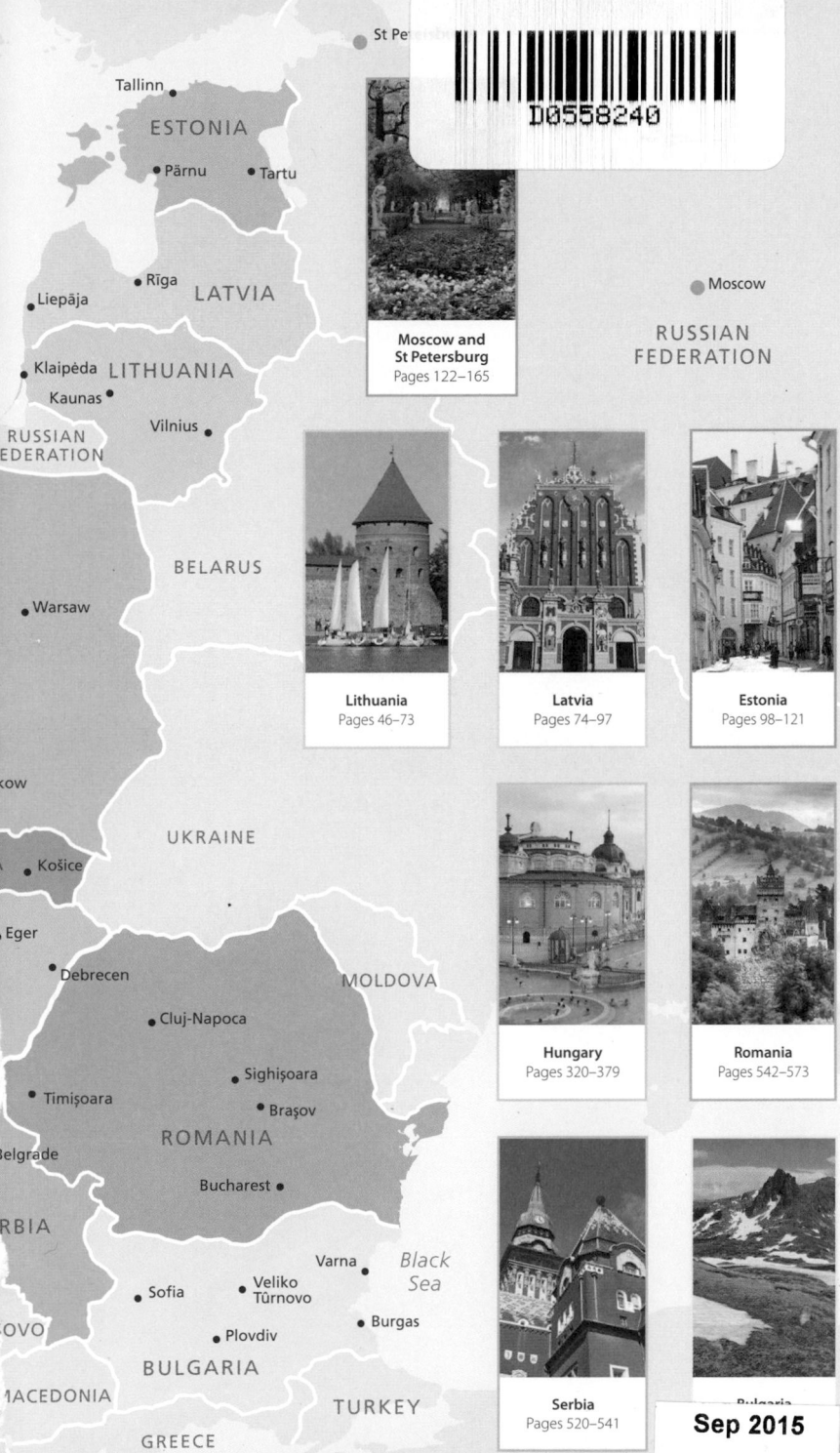

Tallinn

ESTONIA

Pärnu • Tartu

Rīga

Liepāja

LATVIA

Klaipėda LITHUANIA

Kaunas

Vilnius

RUSSIAN
FEDERATION

BELARUS

Warsaw

**Moscow and
St Petersburg**
Pages 122–165

Moscow

RUSSIAN
FEDERATION

Lithuania
Pages 46–73

Latvia
Pages 74–97

Estonia
Pages 98–121

UKRAINE

Košice

Eger

Debrecen

MOLDOVA

Cluj-Napoca

Sighişoara

Timişoara

Braşov

ROMANIA

Belgrade

Bucharest

RBIA

Varna

Black
Sea

Sofia

Veliko
Tŭrnovo

Burgas

OVO

Plovdiv

BULGARIA

MACEDONIA

TURKEY

GREECE

Hungary
Pages 320–379

Romania
Pages 542–573

Serbia
Pages 520–541

Bulgaria

Sep 2015

EYEWITNESS TRAVEL

EASTERN AND CENTRAL EUROPE

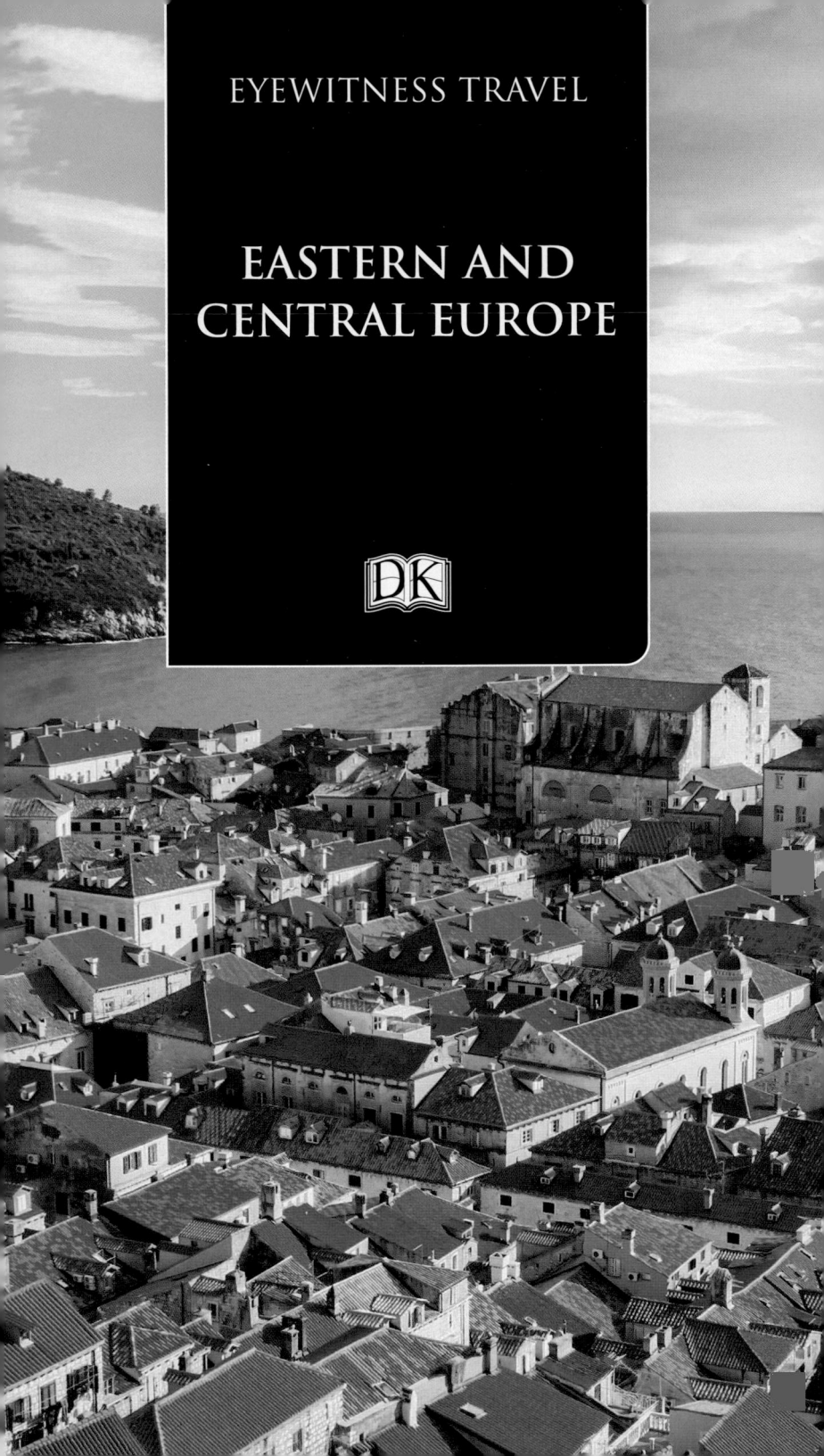

EYEWITNESS TRAVEL

EASTERN AND CENTRAL EUROPE

LONDON, NEW YORK,
MELBOURNE, MUNICH AND DELHI
www.dk.com

Managing Editor Aruna Ghose

Senior Editorial Manager Savitha Kumar

Senior Design Manager Priyanka Thakur

Project Editor Arundhti Bhanot

Project Designer Mathew Kurien

Editors Jyoti Kumari, Parvati M. Krishnan, Jayashree Menon, Beverly Smart

Designers Kaberi Hazarika, Rajnish Kashyap, Saroj Patel, Neha Sethi

Senior Cartographic Manager Uma Bhattacharya

Senior Cartographer and Assistant Manager Suresh Kumar

Cartographer Mohammad Hassan

DTP Designers Rakesh Pal, Azeem Siddiqui

Senior Picture Research Coordinator Taiyaba Khatoon

Main Contributors
Jonathan Bousfield, Matthew Willis

Main Photographer
Jonathan Smith

Illustrators
Chinglemba Chingtham, Surat Kumar Mantoo, Arun Pottirayil, T. Gautam Trivedi

Printed and bound in China
First American Edition, 2010

15 16 17 18 10 9 8 7 6 5 4 3 2 1

Published in the United States by Dorling Kindersley Publishing, Inc.,
345 Hudson Street, New York 10014

Reprinted with revisions 2012, 2015

A catalog record for this book is available from the Library of Congress.

ISSN 1542-1554

ISBN 978-1-46542-704-5

MIX
Paper from
responsible sources
FSC
www.fsc.org   FSC™ C018179

Front cover main image: View of Kotor along the St Giovanni trail, Montenegro

◀ Classic red-tiled rooftops in the Old Town, Dubrovnik, Croatia

Forested hills, Western Tatras, Slovakia

Contents

Stained-glass window at the State Jewish Museum, Vilnius

Embroidered hood of Bishop Trzebicki's cope, Cathedral Museum, Krakow

View of Drava riverfront, Maribor, Slovenia

Russian coat of arms, Peter and Paul Fortress, St Petersburg

Trakai Island Castle, Lithuania *(see pp60–61)*

HOW TO USE THIS GUIDE

This travel guide helps you to get the most from your visit to Eastern and Central Europe, providing detailed practical information and expert recommendations. *Eastern and Central Europe at a Glance* gives an overview of some of the main attractions and a brief history. There are three sightseeing chapters, covering four,

five and seven countries each. Chapters start with a historical portrait and a map of the region. The main sightseeing section then follows, with maps of the main cities. For each country there are sections on practical and travel information, shopping and entertainment, followed by listings of recommended hotels and restaurants.

Eastern and Central Europe Map

The coloured map on the inside front cover indicates the 14 country and 3 city chapters in this guide.

1 At a Glance
The map here highlights the most interesting cities, towns and sights in the countries covered by each of the guide's three sections, such as South Eastern Europe.

A locator map shows where the region lies in relation to the countries around it.

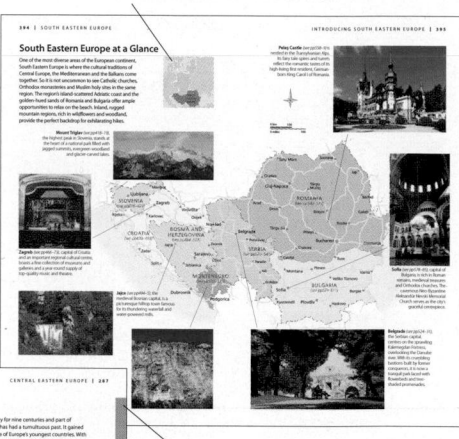

Each country chapter has colour-coded thumb tabs.

2 Country Introduction
This section gives the reader an insight into the country's history, geography and culture. A chart lists the key dates and events in the country's history.

Sights at a Glance lists the numbered sights in the chapter.

3 Country Map
For easy reference, sights in each country are numbered and plotted on a map. The black bullet numbers indicate the order in which the sights are covered in the chapter.

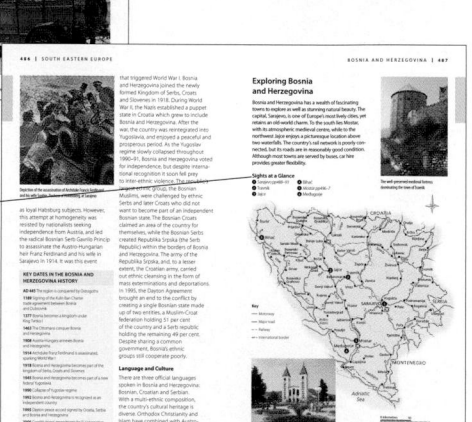

4 Street-by-Street Map
This gives a bird's-eye view of interesting and important parts of each sightseeing area.

A suggested route takes in some of the area's most fascinating and attractive streets.

Numbers correspond to each sight's position on the country map and its place in the chapter.

6 Major Sights
Historic buildings are dissected to reveal their interiors, while museums have colour-coded floorplans to help one find the most important exhibits.

Stars indicate the features that no visitor should miss.

5 Detailed Information
Cities, towns and other sights are described individually. Entries appear in the same order as the numbering on the country map.

A Visitors' Checklist gives all the practical information needed to plan one's visit.

7 Practical Information
This section covers topics such as visas, security, travel, shopping and entertainment. The larger countries are covered in greater detail.

Directory boxes give contact information for the services and venues mentioned in the text.

Climate charts are provided for each country.

VISITING EASTERN AND CENTRAL EUROPE

DISCOVERING EASTERN AND CENTRAL EUROPE

Discovering the great cities of Eastern and Central Europe offers an insight into their countries. In each destination, the visitor will get a real flavour of the history, culture, character and cuisine of the nation. Each of the following 10 itineraries offers a one-day exploration of some of Central and Eastern Europe's most beguiling cities,

combining the must-visit sights with a wealth of local colour and charm. The ten cities described here only represent a small selection of the exciting urban destinations that Eastern and Central Europe has to offer; the capital cities, not covered in the itineraries below, make equally enticing targets for travel.

Vienna

- Take a stroll around the streets of Old Vienna.
- Watch the elegant horses of the Spanish Riding School.
- Enjoy the panorama from Vienna's famous Ferris wheel.

Morning

Start at the landmark **Stephansdom** (p386) cathedral then wander around the pedestrianized streets of Old Vienna. Take a stroll along Kärntnerstrasse, the city's main shopping street, and check for tickets for a performance at the **Spanish Riding School** (p384), held most days at 11am. Finish the morning at **The Hofburg Complex** (pp382–4), the imperial palace of the Habsburgs. Opt for a tour of the opulent State Apartments, before stopping for lunch in one of the many typical Viennese cafés nearby.

Prague

- Tour Prague Castle, a Gothic gem.
- Watch the Town Hall Clock strike the hour on Old Town Square.
- Cross the statue-studded Charles Bridge.

Morning

Begin the day by admiring the medieval and Baroque buildings lining the **Old Town Square** (p244). Be at **Town Hall Clock** (p245) on the hour, when its chimes are accompanied by a parade of mechanical figures. The pretty

Kinský Palace (p242) features ancient art in the shadow of the spire-topped **Church of Our Lady Before Týn** (p246). Head north into Josefov, Prague's former Jewish quarter, and take an evocative stroll through the **Old Jewish Cemetery** (p250).

Afternoon

Cross **Charles Bridge** (pp240–41), lined with statues of saints, to the Malá Strana quarter. Make your way up **Nerudova Ulice** (p236) to Hradčany Hill, taking a tour of the Gothic architectural wonder **St Vitus's Cathedral** (pp232–3) and the **Old Royal Palace** (p230). Be sure to visit the quaint **Golden Lane** (p231), or Zlatá Ulička. Spend the evening in Malá Strana.

Spectacular interiors of the Kunsthistorisches Museum in Vienna

Afternoon

Walk a city block from the Hofburg to the **MuseumsQuartier Wein** (*p385*), a superb cultural complex that contains the Leopold Museum, home to an unmissable collection of Klimts and Schieles, Next door is the **Kunsthistorisches Museum** (*p385*), boasting hall after hall of old masters. Finally, ride Vienna's swift and efficient metro to take some fresh early-evening air in Prater park, and take a spin on the famous giant Ferris wheel.

Krakow

- Admire the Gothic spires, murals and altars of St Mary's Church.
- Gaze upon the graves of Poland's medieval kings at Wawel Cathedral.
- Soak up Krakow's multicultural history in the Kazimierz quarter.

Morning

Start with a circuit of the **Main Market Square** (*pp186–7*) before exploring the covered stalls of the Renaissance **Cloth Hall** (*p187*). Climb the **City Hall Tower** (*p187*) for great views, before joining the crowds milling around the foot of the Mickiewicz Statue. Head next for the sumptuously-decorated **Church of St Mary** (*pp188–9*): arrive at 11:50am to observe the ritual unveiling of **Veit Stoss's altar** (*p189*). The cafés and restaurants surrounding the square ensure that you're spoilt for choice when it comes to lunch.

Afternoon

Walk south along Grodzka street to **The Wawel** (*pp190–91*), site of **Krakow Cathedral** (*pp192–3*) and the **Wawel Royal Castle** (*p193*). Take a tour of the state apartments or chose between several history museums in the castle complex. Reserve the afternoon for exploring **Kazimierz District** (*pp194–5*) the former Jewish quarter and now a bohemian hotspot, its atmospheric squares and piazzas filled with bars and restaurants.

Dubrovnik

- Walk the full circuit of Dubrovnik's perfectly preserved medieval walls.
- Stroll down Stradun, the pedestrianized main street.
- Ascend by cable car to Mt Srđ to enjoy a stunning panorama of the city.

Morning

Start with a tour of the **city walls** (*p434*), a popular destination that can get crowded later in the day. Follow this with a stroll along the **Stradun** (*p435*), the Old Town's main street and the site of many of its cafés. At the eastern end of Stradun, **St Blaise's Church** (*p438*) honours the city's patron saint. Visit the nearby **Dominican Monastery** (*p440*) for quiet cloisters and Renaissance paintings.

Afternoon

The former **Rector's Palace** (*p438*) houses an intriguing museum filled with artworks. Also, nearby is the **Cathedral** (*pp438–9*), its treasury packed full of intriguing relics. Behind the cathedral, lie some of the Old Town's most atmospheric alleyways, perfect for leisurely strolling. Early evening is a good time to ride the cable car to Mt Srđ, the mountainous ridge that overlooks Dubrovnik to the north.

Loggia in the Rector's Palace in Dubrovnik, Croatia

The imposing Kalemegdan Fortress in Belgrade

Belgrade

- Retrace Belgrade's turbulent history from the ramparts of Kalemegdan Fortress.
- Admire the Ottoman-influenced furnishings of the Palace of Princess Ljubica.
- Wine and dine along Skadarlija Street, long-time haunt of artists.

Morning

Start at Terazije, the traffic intersection at the heart of Belgrade, before taking a stroll along Knez Mihailova, a pedestrianized street lined with historic buildings. Detour west to admire the icon-filled **Orthodox Cathedral** (*p529*) before enjoying the oriental-style interiors of the **Palace of Princess Ljubica** (*p529*). Spend the rest of the morning exploring the vast, park-like **Kalemegdan Fortress** (*pp526–7*), filled with bastions and towers.

Afternoon

Leave Kalemegdan via the **Ethnographic Museum** (*p528*), a great place to learn about Serbian folk culture. Visit the **Vuk and Dositej Museum** (*p528*), a well-preserved Ottoman-style house, before proceeding to the lively café-lined Trg Republike. Spend the evening in **Skadarlija** (*p529*), the cobbled street where Belgrade's bohemian scene once held sway.

Opulent interior of the Palace of Parliament, Bucharest

Bucharest

- Learn about Romania's rich cultural heritage at the National History Museum.
- Be amazed by the vast, Neo-Baroque Palace of Parliament.
- Tour the shops and cafés of Strada Lipscani in the historical centre.

Morning
Begin the day at Piaţa Revoluţiei, the set-piece square where crowds famously heckled the communist dictator, Nicolae Ceauşescu in December 1989. Head down Calea Victoriei, Bucharest's main shopping street to the **National History Museum** (p550), rich in ancient and medieval treasures. Cross the Dimboviţa river and reach the colossal **Palace of Parliament** (pp548–9), the famously megalomaniac project begun by Ceauşescu. Next, visit the **National Museum of Contemporary Art** (p548) in the palace's northern wing.

Afternoon
Cross the river again and dive into Bucharest's historical centre, explore Strada Lipscani, a pedestrianized warren of streets dating back to medieval times and today filled with fashionable shops. The richly ornamented **Old Court Church** (p550), and mural-filled **Stavropoleos Church** (p550) are surviving monuments. Spend the evening in Strada Lipscani.

Rīga

- Explore the tragic side of Latvian history at the Museum of the Occupation.
- Enjoy stunning views from the towering belfry of St Peter's Church.
- Gaze in awe at the Dome Cathedral, an outstanding example of red-brick Baltic Gothic architecture.

Morning
At the heart of Rīga's Old Town is **Town Hall Square** (pp82–3), overlooked by the fancy Gothic brickwork of the **House of the Blackheads** (p84). The nearby **Museum of the Occupation** (p84) will tell you everything you need to know about Latvia's suffering under both Nazis and Communists. Next, take the lift up the belfry of **St Peter's Church** (p84) for a birds-eye view of the

Relaxing in the Town Hall Square in the Old Town, Rīga

city centre. From here stroll along Skārņu iela, one of the Old Town's best-preserved medieval streets, before taking lunch in one of the nearby restaurants.

Afternoon
Follow Šķūņu iela to Cathedral Square, dominated by the impressively capacious **Dome Cathedral** (p80). Continue along Pils iela to **Rīga Castle** (pp80–81), home to the Latvian History Museum, a well-presented guide to national culture. Take time to wander the maze of alleys around Maza Pils iela, lined with medieval merchants' houses, before emerging at the **Swedish Gate** (p81). Wind up with a walk through the belt of parkland east of the Old Town.

Tallinn

- Join the milling crowds in Town Hall Square, one of Europe's best-preserved medieval marketplaces.
- Admire Gothic art in the medieval Niguliste Church.
- Enjoy lakes, meadows and tree-shaded avenues in the grounds of Kadriorg Palace.

Morning
The obvious place to start exploring Tallinn's charming Old Town is **Town Hall Square** (pp104–5), a delightful cobbled space surrounded by medieval merchants' houses. Climb the **Town Hall Tower** (p106) to enjoy sweeping views of the

Colourful buildings line the Town Hall Square in Tallinn

Old Town and its surroundings. Next, head for the venerable **Niguliste Church** (p107), home to a unique collection of Gothic altar paintings. From here ascend the steep, winding Luhike Jalg to Toompea or Castle Hill, where the multi-domed **Alexander Nevsky Cathedral** (p109) presides over a knot of quiet, walkable streets.

Afternoon
Descend from Toompea for a spot of lunch in one of the Old Town's many restaurants before heading northeast along Pikk, one of the Old Town's most representative streets. Peek inside the **Holy Spirit Church** (p106) before admiring the Renaissance portals of the **House of the Blackheads** (p107). Exit the Old Town at **Fat Margaret Tower** (p108), and take a tram to **Kadriorg Palace** (p109) and its extensive park. Consider a visit to **Kadriorg's Kumu Art Museum** (p109), a spectacularly modern building showcasing the best of Estonian art.

The magnificent golden dome of St Issac's Cathedral visible from the Moyka river

National Gallery (p328) contains a stunning collection of artworks from medieval times to modern.

Afternoon
Descend from Buda and cross to the Pest side of the river via the Chain Bridge. Walk along the Danube riverbank to café-filled **Vigadó Square** (p339) before taking a leisurely stroll along **Váci Utca** (p339), central Pest's most famous shopping and promenading street. Walk along Múzeum Körút to get a flavour of 19th-century Pest, visiting the **Hungarian National Museum** (p340) for a thorough run-down of Hungarian culture. Finish up at the Art Nouveau-styled **Museum of Applied Arts** (p340) before exploring the restaurants of Ráday utca.

Budapest

- **Explore the romantic backstreets of old Buda.**
- **Survey the century-spanning art collections of the Hungarian National Gallery.**
- **Window-shop your way along Váci utca, Budapest's most animated downtown area.**

Morning
Take the Sikló funicular to the hilltop settlement of Buda, packed with historic buildings and evocative Baroque-era streets. Admire the richly decorated interior of the **Mátyás Church** (pp330–31) before checking out the sweeping views of Pest from the nearby bastions. From here it's a short stroll to the former **Royal Palace** (pp326–7) with its ornamental gateways, courtyards and gardens. Inside the palace, the **Hungarian**

The striking Gothic exterior of the Mátyás Church in Budapest, Hungary

St Petersburg

- **Admire the opulent interiors and art collections of the Hermitage Museum.**
- **Get your photograph taken next to the Bronze Horseman, famous statue of Peter the Great.**
- **Take a boat ride across the River Neva to the Peter and Paul Fortress.**

Morning
Head to **Palace Square** (p147), a huge space surrounded by Baroque and Rococo facades. Next, visit **The Winter Palace** (pp154–5), home to **The Hermitage** (pp148–9) – with its stunning state rooms and an art collection ranging from Leonardo da Vinci to Matisse. Walk along the Neva riverbank past the **Admiralty** (p146) building to reach the **Bronze Horseman** (p146), the landmark equestrian statue of Peter the Great.

Afternoon
Follow **Malaya Morskaya Ulitsa** (p147) then the banks of the Moyka river to reach the **Pushkin House Museum** (p157), filled with the poet's personal effects. Next, take a ferry across the River Neva to the **Peter and Paul Fortress** (pp144–5). You'll need the rest of the afternoon to explore this walled naval fort with its glittering Baroque cathedral, well-preserved ramparts and numerous museum collections.

Putting Eastern and Central Europe on the Map

The continent of Europe covers a total surface area of 10.4 million square km (4 million square miles) and stretches east as far as the Ural Mountains in the Russian Federation. This guide covers 14 countries, 10 of which belong to the European Union (EU), as well as the cities of Vienna, Moscow and St Petersburg. The featured countries are shown on this map in bright green. The principal international airports and major road links are also shown here, while the European rail network is shown on the inside back cover.

Torsby Gävle
Örebro
SWEDEN Stockholm
Jönköping Norrköping
Värnamo
Ljungby
Kalmar
Baltic Sea
Malmö

Hamburg Gdynia Koszalin Gdańsk
NETHERLANDS Oldenburg Szczecin Bydgoszcz
Amsterdam Braunschweig Toruń
Brussels Antwerpen Dortmund Berlin Włocławek
BELGIUM Köln Poznań POLAND
Zielona Góra Kalisz Łódź
LUX. GERMANY Leipzig Legnica Wrocław
Frankfurt Karlovy Vary Opole
Luxembourg Mainz Prague Ostrava Kraków
Paris Metz Plzeň CZECH Olomouc
Karlsruhe REPUBLIC
Strasbourg Nürnberg České Budějovice Brno SLOVAKIA
FRANCE Mulhouse *Danube*
Dijon Zürich Munich Vienna Bratislava
Beaune Bern Innsbruck Esztergom
Geneva SWITZ. Chur AUSTRIA Győr Budapest
Lyon Graz Veszprém Kecskemét
ITALY Keszthely HUNGARY
Milan Ljubljana Maribor Pécs
Genoa Venice SLOVENIA Varaždin
Nice Bologna Zagreb Osijek
Pisa Florence Pula Rijeka Novi Sad
Banja Luka
Mediterranean Sea CROATIA Zadar BOSNIA AND
Corsica Bastia Trogir Split HERZEGOVINA
Civitavecchia *Adriatic Sea* Mostar Sarajevo
Bonifacio Pescara MONTENEGRO
Porto Torres Olbia Rome Dubrovnik
Sardinia Foggia Podgorica
Naples Bari ALBANIA

For keys to symbols *see back flap*

PRACTICAL INFORMATION

The countries in Eastern and Central Europe have undergone a great transformation since the collapse of Communism in 1990. Some states have adapted quickly to the change and are now active members of the European Union (EU), while others continue to wrestle with serious economic and political problems. As a result, the quality of tourist facilities varies greatly throughout the region. Accommodation and public transport are well organized and reliable in North Eastern Europe. In the southeast, on the other hand, travel may be slower and standards less predictable. However, with an impressive diversity of history, culture and folklore to discover, Eastern and Central Europe makes for a rich and enjoyable travel experience.

When to Go

The best time to visit Eastern and Central Europe depends on the visitor's itinerary. However, most people prefer spring and summer, from April to September. Stretching from the Baltic Sea in the north to the Mediterranean Sea in the south, the region has a wide variety of climates. Summers in North Eastern Europe can be cool and rainy, while in South Eastern Europe they can be unbearably hot, especially in big cities. The Adriatic coast, with its hot, dry summers and relatively mild winters, has the balmiest climate, but crowds can be a drawback in the peak season of July and August, making May, June and September better times to visit.

Elsewhere in South Eastern Europe, long, hot summers and long, cold winters are the usual trends. The mountains of Slovenia, Slovakia, Romania and Bulgaria provide ideal conditions for skiing, with a season that runs from mid-December to late March.

Winters in the north of the region, near the Baltic coast, can be long, cold and dark. During the depths of winter the sun sets at 3–4pm, and daytime temperatures rarely rise above 0° C (32° F). Summertime, on the other hand, offers the prospect of long daylight hours in St Petersburg and the northern Baltic States.

Visitors should bear in mind that August is a busy month in all parts of Eastern and Central Europe, when most Europeans take their vacations.

Time Zones

The countries covered in this guide sit across three time zones. Poland, the Czech Republic, Slovakia, Hungary, Austria, Slovenia, Croatia, Bosnia and Herzegovina, Montenegro and Serbia are all on Central European Time (CET), which is one hour ahead of Greenwich Mean Time (GMT) and 6 hours ahead of New York. Lithuania, Latvia, Estonia, Romania and Bulgaria are on East European Time (EET), which is 2 hours ahead of GMT and 7 hours ahead of New York. The Russian cities of Moscow and St Petersburg are on Moscow Standard Time (MST), which is 3 hours ahead of GMT and 8 hours ahead of New York.

In Europe, the clocks go forward by one hour in late March and go back by one hour in late October.

Documentation

Of the 16 countries included in this guide, 12 (Lithuania, Latvia, Estonia, Poland, the Czech Republic, Slovakia, Hungary, Austria, Slovenia, Croatia, Romania and Bulgaria) are members of the European Union (EU). EU citizens can visit all of these countries with a valid identity card. Citizens of the United States, Canada, Japan, New Zealand, Norway and Switzerland can also enter these countries with a valid passport.

All of the EU members listed above, except Romania and Bulgaria, are signatories of the Schengen Agreement. Borders between Schengen zone countries are open, and once inside the Schengen zone, identity documents do not usually need to be shown when crossing a common frontier. However, visitors should always keep their identity documents handy just in case random checks are made.

In the rest of Eastern Europe, entry requirements differ from country to country. Visitors from the EU, US, Canada, Australia and New Zealand can enter Bosnia and Herzegovina, Serbia and Montenegro on the production of a valid passport. Citizens of other countries, however, should check current regulations before they travel.

Russia requires almost all foreign visitors to purchase a visa before travel, which usually involves applying in person or through a travel agent to the local Russian embassy or consulate several weeks before the trip. For visitors who want to include Moscow and St Petersburg in their itinerary, it is advisable to plan this part of the trip well in advance.

Student Cards

Various bus and rail tickets offer discounts on European travel (see pp22–3), but, in addition to these, students with a recognized student card may be eligible for a wider range of discounts. The best card is the International Student Identity Card (ISIC), which gives discounts on all kinds of goods and transport as well as cheaper admission to many museums, galleries and other sights. Most students can obtain this card from their educational establishment at home, but it can also be obtained abroad from an ISIC issuing office or from branches of STA travel (see p21). For US students, this card also includes some medical cover.

Customs and Duty-Free

Duty-free allowances are not available to visitors travelling from one EU country to another. However, duty-free goods can be purchased on entry or exit from the EU as a whole. The allowances are as follows: tobacco (200 cigarettes, 50 cigars or 250 g/ 9 oz of loose tobacco); alcohol (1 litre/2 pints of strong spirits, 2 litres/4 pints of alcohol under 22 per cent proof, and 2 litres/4 pints of wine); coffee (500 g/18 oz) and perfume (60 ml/0.1 pint).

When returning to their home country, visitors may be asked to declare any items purchased abroad and pay duty on any amount that exceeds their home country's allowance; the scope of these allowances will vary from one country to another.

Value Added Tax

In both EU member-states and most other countries in Eastern and Central Europe, all goods and services (except certain items such as food and children's clothing) are subject to Value Added Tax (VAT), which is included in most prices. Visitors may claim a refund on this tax if they are neither citizens of the EU nor of the particular country they are visiting, but it can be a lengthy process.

The easiest way to do this is to shop at places displaying the "Euro Free Tax" sign, although the stores that offer this service may be expensive or sell only luxury goods. Visitors need to show their passport to the shop assistant and complete a form, after which VAT will be deducted from the bill. In certain countries, visitors need to keep their receipts and VAT forms and present them at a tax refund desk with their unopened purchases when they leave the country. These forms will be processed and a refund is eventually sent to their home address.

Personal Security

Although Eastern and Central Europe is a relatively safe region in which to travel, visitors should always take certain precautions. Pickpocketing and petty theft are by far the biggest threats to visitors, although these are more common in some countries than in others – specific information is given in the practical and travel information section of each country chapter.

The safest way of carrying money is in the form of traveller's cheques. Visitors should have their belongings adequately insured before leaving home and not leave them unattended. In the event of a robbery, it should be reported immediately to the local police and a copy of the report acquired. Visitors are advised to keep their valuables well concealed, especially in crowded areas or on public transport. If driving, it is safer to leave the car in a car park rather than on the street.

Insurance and Medical Treatment

Travel insurance is essential to cover any loss or damage to possessions and for unexpected medical and dental treatment. Many major credit cards offer some insurance if travellers purchase their flight tickets or holiday package through them, so it is advisable to check before buying a separate policy. If possible, it is better to buy a policy that pays for medical treatment on the spot, rather than one that reimburses later. Most general insurance policies do not cover potentially hazardous outdoor activities such as climbing, skiing and scuba diving, although these can be included at an extra cost.

Facilities for the Disabled

Conditions for disabled travellers are improving rapidly throughout Eastern and Central Europe, how-ever facilities can vary drastically from one country to the next. In some cities, pavements, tourist attractions such as museums and public transport have been adapted for wheelchair users, while elsewhere much of this work still remains to be done. In general terms, the cities of South Eastern Europe lag behind those of Central and North Eastern Europe in serving disabled travellers. Not all destinations provide adapted accommodation for those with special needs; wheelchair users should plan their itinerary carefully and much in advance.

Recommended Hotels and Restaurants

The hotel and restaurant options in this guide have been selected across a wide range of prices and locations. The hotel listings have been chosen for their excellent facilities and good value, and vary from luxury retreats to boutique hotels, humble B&Bs and historic lodgings. Similarly the selected restaurants adhere to a criterion of great food and atmosphere. These include restaurants specialising in regional cuisine. For the best of each country, look out for entries designated as DK Choices. Each of these has one or more exceptional features, such as stunning location, a compelling history or a special ambience.

Conversion Chart

The metric system is used throughout Eastern and Central Europe.

Imperial to Metric

1 inch = 2.54 centimetres
1 foot = 30 centimetres
1 mile = 1.6 kilometres
1 ounce = 28 grams
1 pound = 454 grams
1 US pint = 0.47 litre
1 UK pint = 0.55 litre
1 US gallon = 3.8 litres
1 UK gallon = 4.6 litres

Metric to Imperial

1 millimetre = 0.04 inch
1 centimetre = 0.4 inch
1 metre = 3 feet 3 inches
1 kilometre = 0.6 mile
1 gram = 0.035 ounce
1 kilogram = 2.2 pounds
1 litre = 2.1 US pints
1 litre = 1.76 UK pints

Communications and Money

Communications in Eastern and Central Europe have improved vastly over the last two decades, and all countries in the region now have reliable postal services and extensive mobile phone networks. There is also a growing number of hotels and cafés which offer Internet services. Of the currencies in use in Eastern and Central Europe, some, such as the euro, can be purchased from banks in any country, while others are difficult to obtain until arrival. Credit cards are widely accepted throughout the region and ATM cash machines are not hard to find.

Telephones

Mobile (cell) phone coverage extends across the region. Not all mobile phones, however, work everywhere. Visitors should check with their service provider before travelling to ensure that their mobile phone works abroad. Also, most US mobile phones do not work in Europe and vice versa, but visitors can buy phones that work in both continents.

Public telephone booths are becoming less common in Eastern and Central Europe, although they can still be found in the centre of towns and cities. Some public telephones are coin-operated, although most now accept phone cards, which can be bought from newspaper kiosks and post offices.

Mail Services

Mail services are generally efficient, with letters and cards typically taking 5 days to reach Western Europe and 7 days to reach North America or Australasia. Services do vary across the region, however, and in some areas such as Serbia, Bulgaria and Russia, they may be slower. If the visitor's itinerary involves moving through countries rather than staying long-term at a particular address, they can still receive mail by using the poste restante system. This can be set up at main post offices in large towns. Travellers should ask for any mail to be sent "care of" poste restante at the main post office in the town in question. They will need to show their identity cards or passports to collect their mail. Mail from overseas is usually kept for one month.

Internet Cafés

Most towns and cities in Eastern and Central Europe will have a handful of Internet cafés offering computer access, scanning, printing and, frequently, cheap international telephone calls as well. An increasing number of city-centre cafés offer free wireless Internet to their customers. In addition, many hotels and hostels now offer wireless or cable Internet access to their guests. Many have a computer in the lobby which guests can use.

Changing Money

The majority of countries in Eastern and Central Europe have their own currency and, in most cases, visitors will need to change money every time they cross a border.

Money can usually be changed at banks, post offices, exchange bureaus *(bureaux de change)* and hotel reception desks. Banks and post offices are often open only from Monday to Friday (sometimes with the addition of a few hours on Saturday morning). Exchange bureaus are more likely to stay open at evenings and weekends. Those located at airports, railway stations and border crossings generally offer poor rates, so it is usually best to change only a small amount here and then proceed elsewhere to change the bulk of your spending money at a better rate. Many bureaus only offer advantageous rates on larger sums of money and apply a different rate of exchange to smaller transactions. Reception desks at hotels usually offer the worst rates of exchange and should only be used if other options are unavailable.

ATM cash machines are distributed widely throughout Eastern and Central Europe. Those visitors with a card belonging to a global network (Plus, Visa, Maestro, Cirrus or MasterCard) can withdraw cash anywhere, but a small fee will be charged for each ATM transaction carried out abroad. It is always a good idea to carry more than one card when travelling, in case one of them is refused or retained by an ATM due to a banking error. Although traveller's cheques remain the safest way to carry money, they are increasingly uncommon; trying to cash them in a bank can be a tedious and time-consuming process since cashiers are often unfamiliar with them.

International Dialling Codes

The list below gives the international dialling codes for the countries covered in this guide. When calling from the US and Canada, prefix all numbers by "011"; from Australia by "0011"; from New Zealand by "00". When calling from within Europe, use the "00" prefix. If unsure, call international directory enquiries.

• Austria	43		• Lithuania	70
• Bosnia and Herzegovina	387		• Montenegro	82
• Bulgaria	359		• Poland	48
• Croatia	381		• Romania	40
• Czech Republic	420		• Russia	7
• Estonia	372		• Serbia	81
• Hungary	36		• Slovakia	21
• Latvia	371		• Slovenia	86

The Euro

The euro (the common European Union currency) has so far been adopted by five of the countries in this guide: Austria, Estonia, Slovenia, Slovakia and, despite not yet being an EU member, Montenegro. Several other countries in the region are planning to adopt the euro in the future, although this may take several years.

In countries outside the euro zone, the euro is sometimes accepted by hotels, restaurants and shops in big resorts, but it is always better to carry local currency in case it is not. The price of accommodation and transport is frequently quoted in euros in order to make it easier for visitors to calculate their expenditure, but actual payment is usually made in the local currency.

Bank Notes

Euro banknotes have seven denominations. The €5 note (grey in colour) is the smallest, followed by the €10 note (pink), €20 note (blue), €50 note (orange), €100 note (green), €200 note (yellow) and €500 note (purple). All notes feature the stars of the European Union.

5 euros

10 euros

20 euros

50 euros

100 euros

200 euros

500 euros

2 euros

1 euro

50 cents

20 cents

10 cents

Coins

The euro has eight coin denominations: 1 euro and 2 euros; 50 cents, 20 cents, 10 cents, 5 cents, 2 cents and 1 cent. The 2- and 1-euro coins are both silver and gold in colour. The 50-, 20- and 10-cent coins are gold. The 5-, 2- and 1-cent coins are bronze.

5 cents

2 cents

1 cent

Eastern and Central Europe by Air

With a good network of international flights, the whole of Eastern and Central Europe is easily accessible by air. Most European nations have well-respected national carriers operating flights to Western Europe as well as North America. With the recent addition of budget airlines offering "no frills" flights in the area, several new destinations have opened up, resulting in an increase in the number of flights within countries in the region. Competition between various airlines ensures that air fares are relatively low, especially for travellers who book ahead over the Internet. Package tours and travel agencies help keep costs down as well and ensure great trips.

Flying to Eastern and Central Europe

Visitors travelling from a major international airport will find that a significant number of cities in Eastern and Central Europe are served by direct flights. National carriers offering direct flights from North America include **Austrian Airlines** to Vienna, **CSA Czech Airlines** to Prague, **LOT Polish Airlines** to Warsaw and Krakow and **Aeroflot** to Moscow. **Malév Hungarian Airlines** also flies from major cities in Europe and the US.

Most of the major North American airlines such as **Delta**, **Air Canada**, **American** and **Continental** offer one-stop flights to the region in conjunction with their European partner airlines, usually involving a change of flight in a city in Western Europe. From Australasia, **Qantas** and Air New Zealand offer one- or two-stop flights to the region in partnership with other airlines.

The biggest choice of flights is offered by airports in the UK and Ireland, and travellers from North America and Australasia may find it convenient to break their journey there before proceeding to Eastern and Central Europe. National carriers connect London directly with most of the capital cities in the region.

In addition, budget airlines such as **easyJet**, **Ryanair** and **Wizzair** fly direct from London and other regional UK and Irish airports to several destinations in the region. Capitals such as Warsaw, Prague, Budapest and Rīga are well covered, along with a host of regional cities in Poland, the Adriatic resorts of Croatia, and a handful of destinations in Slovakia, Romania and Bulgaria. Travellers should bear in mind that flights with budget airlines do not provide passengers with much legroom and do not offer any complimentary food and drink.

Flight Times

As a rough guide, flights from New York to Eastern and Central Europe take between 8 and 9 hours. Flights from Sydney will involve at least one change and are likely to take 23 to 25 hours. From London, flights to Austria, the Czech Republic, Slovenia and Croatia take around 2 hours and 30 minutes; flights to Poland and the Baltic States take around 3 hours and 30 minutes; and flights to Romania and Bulgaria take around 4 hours.

Budget Travel Agencies

As a rule, European air fares are at their cheapest between November and March, with the exception of Christmas and Easter weeks. The high season is from June to mid-September. A "shoulder season" of moderate prices exists between these periods. It is always advisable to travel mid-week, when tickets are cheaper and airports less busy. Many of the cheapest fares from North America or Australasia involve flights with more than one stop en route and long stopovers. While this may be an economical way to travel, it can also be tiring; it is best to check timings carefully before booking.

Whichever season visitors travel, there are several ways of saving money on air fares. A good way of finding out about cheap fares is to contact a travel agency that specializes in budget travel, such as **STA Travel** or **Trailfinders** in the US and the UK respectively. Youngsters (under 25), students and senior citizens will usually find that they are eligible for reduced fares. Generally speaking, the cheapest are return (round-trip) tickets, which have fixed dates rather than an "open" return. Depending on the distance, round-the-world (RTW) tickets can sometimes work out cheaper than a standard long-haul return. These enable travellers to fly around the world on specified routes, providing they do not backtrack. The number of Eastern and Central European cities that feature in RTW tickets is relatively small, but it is always worth enquiring with established travel agents to see what is available.

Standby tickets are also economical, but visitors need to be flexible about the date and time of departure. Travelling this way may involve a wait of several days until a cancellation comes up.

Package Deals

One of the easiest ways to arrange a visit to Eastern and Central Europe is to opt for a package holiday. They normally include flights, transfers, accommodation and some-times, side trips and meals. Package trips often work out cheaper than if travellers were to book these deals separately. The downside is that such trips usually involve travelling in a group with a fixed itinerary, thereby cutting down on the independence of the visitor.

Several North American travel companies, including **Adventures Abroad**, **Gate 1** and **Tradesco**, offer week-long or 21-day holidays to the region, either focusing on one country or combining several in a busy itinerary.

Similar packages are offered by **Abercrombie & Kent**, which specializes in upmarket accommodation and is therefore slightly more expensive than the other operators. Those who specialize in Eastern and Central European destinations and provide the services of local guides include **Regent Holidays** in the UK, and **Gateway Travel** and **Contal Travel** in Australia.

Travellers who want to experience the great outdoors should consider adventure-holiday companies such as **Exodus** and **Explore**, which offer hiking and activity holidays with itineraries to suit all levels of fitness.

Fly-Drive

Many airlines and travel companies offer fly-drive packages, which combine flights and car rental. These deals are often worth considering, as they offer flexibility and save the effort of arranging for the two separately.

Internet Booking

The Internet has become a popular way of booking tickets. Many scheduled and budget airlines now offer their cheapest rates on the Internet, and these fares frequently undercut anything offered by the high-street travel agencies.

As well as checking individual airline websites, travellers should also browse the websites of Internet-based travel agents such as **Opodo**, **Expedia** and **Travelocity**. They are particularly useful for finding out the best deals on one-stop or two-stop flights to Eastern and Central Europe, which may involve more than one airline. These agents also offer bookings in select hotels, allowing visitors to sort out their flights and accommodation in one go. The US company **Europebyair** offers a FlightPass for non-European citizens, operating one-way flights between selected European cities for a reasonable price. Only a handful of East European airports are included in the FlightPass scheme, but it is still a useful way of getting around the vast European continent.

Flights Within Eastern and Central Europe

Travelling from one end of the region to the other can be time consuming for those who attempt to do it by road or rail. Fortunately, there is an extensive network of flights between the major capitals.

National carriers such as **CSA Czech Airlines** and **LOT Polish Airlines** offer the biggest choice of regional flights, with Prague, Budapest and Warsaw serving as the main hubs for their respective networks. Several budget airlines also operate regional flights, especially in the summer, when travellers from North Eastern Europe head for the Mediterranean and Black Sea beaches. The Latvian company **AirBaltic** has services linking the capitals of North Eastern Europe. In addition, the budget airline Wizzair offers summer flights from Poland and Hungary to the Bulgarian coast.

DIRECTORY

Flying to Eastern and Central Europe

Aeroflot
W aeroflot.ru

Air Canada
W aircanada.com

American
W aa.com

Austrian Airlines
W austrian.com

Continental
W continental.com

CSA Czech Airlines
W czechairlines.com

Delta
W delta.com

easyJet
W easyjet.com

LOT Polish Airlines
W lot.com

Qantas
W qantas.com.au

Ryanair
W ryanair.com

Wizzair
W wizzair.com

Budget Travel Agencies

STA Travel
W statravel.com

Trailfinders
W trailfinders.com

Package Deals

Abercrombie & Kent
Tel 800 554 7016 (US).
W abercrombie kent.com

Adventures Abroad
Tel 800 665 3998 (US),
0114 247 3400 (UK).
W adventures-abroad. com

Contal Travel
Tel 02 9212 5077 (Aus).
W contaltours.com.au

Exodus
Tel 020 8675 5550 (UK).
W exodus.co.uk

Explore
Tel 0845 013 1537 (UK).
W exploreworld wide. com

Gate 1
Tel 800 682 3333 (US).
W gate1travel.com

Gateway Travel
Tel 02 9745 3333 (Aus).
W russian-gateway. com.au

Regent Holidays
Tel 0845 277 3317 (UK).
W regent-holidays. co.uk

Tradesco
Tel 800 448 4321 (US).
W tradescotours.com

Internet Booking

Europebyair
W europebyair.com

Expedia
W expedia.com

Opodo
W opodo.com

Travelocity
W travelocity.com

Flying Within Eastern and Central Europe

AirBaltic
W airbaltic.com

Eastern and Central Europe by Train, Road and Ferry

Eastern and Central Europe is covered by an extensive and comprehensive rail network, but services vary in speed and comfort from one part of the region to another. Buses are a popular means of transport throughout, covering towns and villages that are not served by trains. Good-quality modern motorways connect the major cities but, away from the main routes, road surfaces can be poor. Boat trips are a great way to view the region's beautiful scenery, but can be expensive.

Trains and Tickets

The rail network in Eastern and Central Europe features every kind of train, at every speed. Among the fastest and most comfortable are the InterCity (IC) services, which link major centres and make few stops. Faster still are the Euro City (EC) international trains which connect big cities and may run through several countries en route. Most IC and EC routes are equipped with modern, air-conditioned carriages offering both first- and second-class seating.

Slightly slower are the regional express trains, which operate under different names in various countries. Slower still, regional passenger trains serve the local community and stop at all stations en route. These passenger trains only offer second-class seating and the carriages are frequently old and basic.

Tickets should be bought at the ticket counter in the station before boarding the train. Some stations have separate counters for domestic and international trains; it is best to confirm before queuing up. Many IC and EC trains offer seat reservations for a small extra cost. It is also advisable to check whether regional and international express services have buffet cars; many do not.

Train Routes

The best IC and EC services are in Central Europe, where all major capitals and regional cities are served by fast, punctual trains. Using the rail network to tour Austria, the Czech Republic, Slovakia, Poland, Hungary, Slovenia and northern Croatia is very convenient and problem-free.

However, in South Eastern Europe, services between the main cities in Bosnia and Herzegovina, Serbia, Romania and Bulgaria are relatively slow, and visitors might consider travelling by bus instead. In North Eastern Europe, the capital cities of Lithuania, Latvia and Estonia are only connected by bus.

Several railway journeys are worth making for the fantastic scenery along the route. The express train from Belgrade, in Serbia, to Bar, in Montenegro, passes through dramatic mountain terrain. Much slower, but equally delightful, is the Bulgarian narrow-gauge line from Bansko to Septemvri, which goes through a bewitching highland landscape. The rail routes connecting central Romanian towns such as Braşov, Sibiu and Sighişoara pass through some of Europe's loveliest rural countryside, while travelling from Vienna in Austria to the Slovenian capital Ljubljana or the Croatian capital Zagreb features some gorgeous subalpine terrain.

Information and Timetables

Most of the national rail companies in the region have websites with relevant timetable details. However, information is not always available in English, and international rail routes across the whole continent are not consistently covered.

The best source of information on international services is **German Railways (Deutsche Bahn)**, whose website provides a timetable for most destinations in Eastern and Central Europe. Excellent advice on trans-European travel can also be found on **The Man in Seat 61**, a website run by dedicated rail enthusiasts. In addition, **Thomas Cook** publishes a European Railway Timetable which covers all the main routes in Europe. This can be bought from branches of Thomas Cook in the UK, or purchased online.

Rail Passes for Non-Europeans

For non-Europeans, the cheapest way to explore the region by rail is to buy one of the many passes available from **Eurail**. For those travelling from North America or Australasia, it is cheaper to buy one before travelling. The official representative for Eurail in North America is **Railpass**. Eurail passes cover Austria, Bulgaria, the Czech Republic, Croatia, Hungary, Romania and Slovenia, but do not extend to Bosnia and Herzegovina, Estonia, Latvia, Lithuania, Montenegro, Serbia, Poland, Slovakia or Russia.

Several kinds of Eurail passes are available. Eurail Select covers unlimited first-class travel in a cluster of three to five countries of the visitor's choice, with passes valid for periods ranging from five days to two months. The Eurail Global pass covers first-class travel in the seven countries in Eastern and Central Europe mentioned above as well as in 14 countries in Western Europe, for periods ranging from 15 days to three months. The Eurail Youthpass is a cheaper, second-class version of the Global pass, available to those aged under 26.

Rail Passes for Europeans

For Europeans, the best option is the Inter-Rail pass, which can be purchased from **Rail Europe** or from the main train operators in individual countries. This pass covers 30 countries across

Europe, including most of the countries covered in this guide; Estonia, Latvia, Lithuania and Russia are the exceptions.

The pass comes in two versions – one for adults, and a less expensive one for travellers under the age of 26. It covers periods ranging from five days to one month. It is not valid for the country in which it is purchased, where full-price individual rail tickets must be bought.

Driving Permits

Visitors planning to drive in Eastern and Central Europe are advised to acquire an International Driving Permit (IDP) before they travel.

The IDP is not compulsory everywhere in the region, but regulations differ from one country to the next, and many of the region's car-hire companies require an IDP in addition to a national driving permit issued in the visitor's home country. The IDP is valid for one year and can be obtained from the national motoring organization in a traveller's home country.

Driving in Eastern and Central Europe

In Eastern and Central Europe, people drive on the right-hand side of the road and overtaking is from the left. Visitors should note that they are not allowed to overtake more than one car at a time. Distances are measured in kilometres. Speed limits are usually 120–130 kmph (75–80 mph) on motorways, 80–100 kmph (50–60 mph) on secondary roads, and 50 kmph (30 mph) in built-up areas, although there are differences from one country to the next.

Some countries charge toll fees on particular motorways, while others such as Austria and Slovenia charge a one-time fee which must be paid on entering the country. Elsewhere, the vast majority of roads are free. Petrol stations are common on motorways and main roads but are less frequent in rural areas. Unleaded fuel is available everywhere in most destinations. Driving at night can be dangerous in rural areas, where roads might be narrow and winding.

Car Rental

Car rental is a competitive business in the region, so prices are generally affordable. The biggest car rental companies are **Avis**, **Budget**, **Europcar**, **Hertz** and **Sixt**, all of which offer excellent services.

Travelling by Bus

Domestic bus services offer an alternative to trains throughout Eastern and Central Europe, and provide the only means of getting to those places that are not served by the rail network. Buses running between major cities are often fast and comfortable, and may also have air conditioning. However, rural services frequently make use of slow, ageing vehicles.

Most towns and cities have a central bus station where visitors can check information and purchase tickets. Advance reservations are advisable when travelling on major intercity routes at weekends or during the summer holiday period.

There is a wide network of international buses, especially in the Baltic States and in South Eastern Europe, where international trains are slow or infrequent. International bus services are run by several local companies, but the international operator **Eurolines** runs an extensive network of routes across the continent.

Travelling by Ferry

Ferries constitute a lifeline in countries such as Estonia and Croatia, where they provide the only access to many of the offshore islands. A ride on the ferry which runs along the Croatian coast from Rijeka to Dubrovnik is one of South Eastern Europe's classic journeys. For visitors travelling from Western Europe, one of the quickest ways to get there is to catch a ferry from Italy to Croatia. **Jadrolinija** and **SNAV** are the two biggest operators. Most ferries depart from the Italian port of Ancona, although there are services from Bari as well.

DIRECTORY

Information and Timetables

German Railways (Deutsche Bahn)
w bahn.de

The Man in Seat 61
w seat61.com

Thomas Cook
w thomascookpublishing.com

Rail Passes for Non-Europeans

Eurail
w eurail.com

Railpass
Tel 1 877 724 5727 (US).
w railpass.com

Rail Passes for Europeans

Rail Europe
Tel 08448 485 848 (UK).
w raileurope.co.uk

Car Rental

Avis
w avis.com

Budget
w budget.com

Europcar
w europcar.com

Hertz
w hertz.com

Sixt
w sixt.com

Travelling by Bus

Eurolines
Tel 0871 781 8178 (UK).
w eurolines.co.uk

Travelling by Ferry

Jadrolinija
Tel 385 51 666 111 (Cro).
w jadrolinija.hr

SNAV
Tel 39 71 207 6116 (Ita).
w snav.it

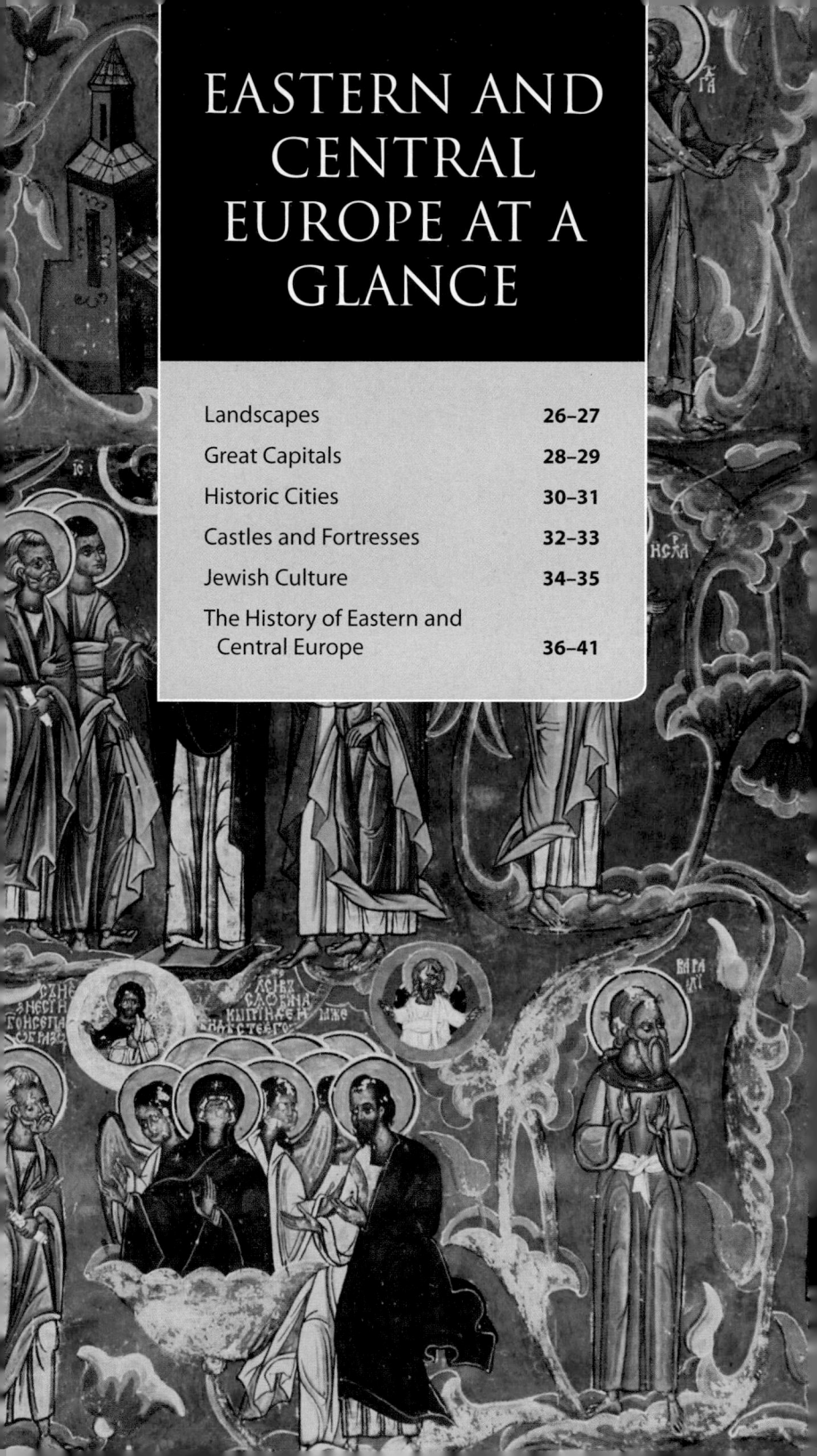

EASTERN AND CENTRAL EUROPE AT A GLANCE

Landscapes

A range of climatic and geological conditions has forged an impressive variety of landscapes in Eastern and Central Europe. Despite the impact of human activity, there are many areas of wilderness that remain intact. From the bogs of North Eastern Europe and the wetlands of the Danube delta to striking mountain ranges such as the Carpathians, stretching from the Czech Republic to Romania, the region's diverse landscapes offer endless opportunities for exploration.

Slovakia
Running along Slovakia's border with Poland, the Tatra Mountains *(see pp306–7)* feature towering peaks and deep blue lakes. At 2,655 m (8,711 ft), Gerlachovský Štít is the range's highest point.

Slovenia
Much of western Slovenia is made up of karst – dry limestone plateau dotted with caves. Caverns at Postojna *(see pp408–9)* and Škocjan *(see p410)* contain a spectacular array of stalagmites and stalactites.

Baltic Sea

POLAND

CZECH REPUBLIC

SLOVAKIA

Vienna ●

AUSTRIA

HUNGARY

SLOVENIA

CROATIA

BOSNIA AND HERZEGOVINA

SERBIA

MONTENEGRO

Croatia
Croatia's heavily indented Adriatic coast boasts stunning maritime scenery, with stark mountains overlooking turquoise seas. Charming stone-built villages and Mediterranean flora characterize the string of islands along its length.

Montenegro
The granite massif of Mount Durmitor offers some of the wildest landscapes in the western Balkans. The most dramatic feature is the Tara Gorge, hemmed in by jagged cliffs.

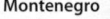

◄ Detail of biblical scenes painted on a monastery church wall in Bucovina, Romania

Latvia
Eastern Latvia's Gauja National Park
(see pp90–91) is dotted with green hills,
sandstone cliffs and riverside castles.
Highlights include the wildlife reserve
at Līgatne and the Iron-Age Latvian
village at Lake Āraiši.

St Petersburg

ESTONIA

RUSSIAN
FEDERATION

LATVIA

Moscow

LITHUANIA

Lithuania
Running parallel to the Baltic
coast, the Curonian Spit
(see pp66–7) is a thin sliver of
land formed by wind-blown
sand. Quaint fishing villages,
such as Nida, are bordered by
striking golden dunes.

0 kilometres   250

0 miles   250

Romania
With its heavy concen-
tration of marshes, lakes
and floodplains, the
reedy Danube delta
is a paradise for flocks
of migrating birds,
while attracting a
small population of
fishermen and farmers.

ROMANIA

Black
Sea

BULGARIA

Bulgaria
Some of Eastern Europe's most
exhilarating hiking terrain is found
in the Rila Mountains, where bare grey
summits loom over shimmering glacial
lakes. At 2,925 m (9,596 ft), Mt Musala
is Eastern Europe's highest peak.

Great Capitals

Until the 20th century, Eastern and Central Europe were characterized by powerful empires rather than independent nation states. These royal dynasties built magnificent cathedrals, palaces and castles to symbolize their greatness and assert their supremacy, giving rise to some of Europe's most impressive capital cities. Several imperial cities, including Vienna and Budapest, were repositories of a fascinating mix of cultures, reflecting the rich ethnic diversity of the local population.

0 km   250

0 miles   250

Prague
This remarkable city on the Vltava river has long been considered one of Europe's most magical capitals, boasting cobbled medieval alleys, soaring Gothic spires and lively squares.

Baltic Sea

POLAND

CZECH REPUBLIC

SLOVAKI

Vienna

Vienna
In terms of imperial grandeur, few cities can match Vienna, once capital of the Habsburg Empire and still the epitome of Central European style.

AUSTRIA

SLOVENIA

HUNGAR

CROATIA

BOSNIA AND HERZEGOVINA

SERBI

MONTENEGRO

Budapest
Straddling the Danube river, the Hungarian capital enjoyed something of an architectural golden age in the 19th century, endowing the city with an array of fine buildings.

Vilnius
The capital of the Grand Duchy of Lithuania, which stretched from the Baltic to the Black Sea in its 15th-century heyday, Vilnius is packed with grand architecture befitting its wide-ranging historical heritage.

Moscow
Capital of Russia since 1480, Moscow rose to become the nerve centre of the Tsarist Empire. Though displaced by St Petersburg from 1712–1918, this fascinating city remained the heartland of Russian Orthodox culture as is evident from the fine churches lining its central squares.

Warsaw
Elegant Neo-Classical Warsaw was almost completely destroyed by the Germans in 1944. Painstakingly reconstructed after World War II, today it is an enduring symbol of Polish national survival.

Historic Cities

Since time immemorial, Eastern Europe has been crossed by major trade routes to Russia, Central Asia and the Near East. Market towns grew rich from this commerce, and their streets and squares were lined with fine architecture. Some trading towns, such as Krakow in Poland, became, for a time, the seat of royal dynasties and the centre of political power before being sidelined by history. Others, notably the prominent Baltic ports of Rīga and Tallinn, spent centuries on the fringes of large empires before finally emerging as the capitals of independent states.

Krakow
The capital of Poland's medieval kings and the site of the biggest market square in Europe, Krakow is packed with buildings from the medieval and Renaissance periods.

Ljubljana
The Slovenian capital is rich in Baroque churches and red-tiled mansions. The tree-lined banks of the Ljubljanica river provide the perfect setting for a stroll.

Sarajevo
An important trading centre in the Ottoman Empire, Sarajevo has, over the centuries, been home to Muslim, Orthodox, Catholic and Jewish communities, all of whom have left their striking architectural imprint on the city.

Baltic Sea

POLAND

CZECH REPUBLIC

Vienna ● SLOVAKIA

AUSTRIA

HUNGARY

SLOVENIA CROATIA

BOSNIA AND HERZEGOVINA

SERBIA

MONTENEGRO

Dubrovnik
The Adriatic port of Dubrovnik, in Croatia, was an independent city-state that thrived on trade with the Ottoman Empire. The Baroque Old Town, surrounded by stout defensive walls, has been well preserved.

Tallinn
The Estonian capital is one of the best-preserved medieval cities in Europe. Its cobbled streets are lined with churches and guild halls built by Baltic merchants of the past.

St Petersburg

ESTONIA

RUSSIAN
FEDERATION

Moscow

LATVIA

ITHUANIA

Rīga
Rīga has been a major Baltic port since the 12th century. It still enjoys the reputation of a city driven by commerce and business, while wonderfully restored Gothic buildings add character to the city centre.

ROMANIA

0 km   250
0 miles   250

Black
Sea

BULGARIA

Plovdiv
Providing a useful lesson in Balkan history, Plovdiv boasts an impressive Roman amphitheatre and Ottoman mosques, as well as 19th-century mansions built by Bulgarian merchants.

Castles and Fortresses

The history of Eastern and Central Europe is one of shifting borders and military conquests. It is no surprise, therefore, that castles and fortresses are a ubiquitous feature of the landscape. Many of the castles became aristocratic residences once their military role was over and were often furnished lavishly by their owners. In modern times, a large number of the fortresses have been restored by governments eager to showcase their country's rich past. They now house some of the region's most prestigious museums, offering a good opportunity to understand the local history and culture.

0 km   250
0 miles   250

Malbork
A religious and political centre, Malbork Castle *(see p209)* was built to serve as the capital of the Teutonic knights, the Germanic crusaders who carved out an empire in North Eastern Europe. The castle contains an imposing medieval church.

Balti Sea

POLAND

CZECH REPUBLIC

SLOVAK

Vienna●

AUSTRIA

HUNGAR

SLOVENIA

CROATIA

BOSNIA AND HERZEGOVIN

MONTENEGR

Karlštejn
Residence of the Holy Roman Emperor Charles IV, Karlštejn Castle *(see pp256–7)* symbolizes the power and influence enjoyed by medieval Czech rulers. Paintings in the castle's chapel represent a high point of Gothic art.

Tvrđa
Built by the Austrians to serve as their military command centre in South Eastern Europe, the fort of Tvrđa *(see p476)* in Osijek is a virtual city-within-a-city. Complete with squares, mansions and churches, it is one of the best-preserved Baroque ensembles in the continent.

Trakai
Romantically situated on an island in the middle of a lake, Trakai Castle *(see pp60–61)* was the one-time residence of Grand Duke Vytautas the Great, who extended Lithuanian power as far as the Black Sea.

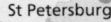
St Petersburg

ESTONIA

Moscow

LATVIA   **RUSSIAN**
                    FEDERATION

LITHUANIA

Bran
The captivating hilltop stronghold of Bran *(see pp556–7)* was built in the 14th century to defend Europe from the Turks. It was subsequently used as a holiday home by the Romanian royal family.

ROMANIA

Black Sea

ERBIA

BULGARIA

Tsarevets
A fortress that also served as Bulgaria's capital city, Tsarevets *(see pp600–601)* was home to the Bulgarian tsars from 1185 to 1393. It now plays host to a spectacular *son-et-lumiere* show on summer evenings.

Kalemegdan
Affording access to the Danube river, this medieval fortress *(see pp526–7)* was used by Serbian, Ottoman and Austrian rulers. It now serves as Belgrade's most popular park, offering sweeping views from its battlements.

Jewish Culture

One of the key heartlands of Jewish culture, Eastern and Central Europe was home to two main groups of Jewish communities. The first to arrive were the Ashkenazi, who emigrated from the Rhine valley from the 12th century onwards. They were followed by the Sephardic Jews, who, after being expelled from Spain in 1492, resettled in South Eastern Europe. Although over 90 per cent of the region's Jewish population perished during World War II, traces of their heritage can still be seen in the carefully preserved historic quarters of many European cities.

A 19th-century line engraving depicting the expulsion of Jews from Spain on the orders of King Ferdinand and Queen Isabella.

The old historic quarter of Třebíč *(see p274)*, in the Czech Republic, is a beautifully preserved example of one of the small towns once dominated by Jewish trading families.

Jewish Heritage

Eastern and Central Europe's rich Jewish heritage is evident in the large number of synagogues found across the region. Dating from the 1850s, Budapest's Great Synagogue (see p341) is a testament to the size and prestige of Hungary's Jewish community. Built in the Moorish Revival style, the interior features both Byzantine and Gothic elements.

Sofia Synagogue *(see p580)*, built in 1909 to serve the city's growing Jewish community, is an impressive combination of Oriental and Art Nouveau styles.

Tallinn's Beit Bella Synagogue, inaugurated in 2007, is the first synagogue to open in Estonia since the destruction of the earlier one during World War I. It hosts many concerts and events.

Vilnius's Choral Synagogue was the only one in the Lithuanian capital to survive World War II unscathed. It was completed in 1903 for a congregation that introduced choral singing into their religious services.

Language and Culture

The everyday language of North Eastern European Jewry was Yiddish. By the early 19th century, Vilnius had emerged as a centre of Jewish learning. The religious customs of the Litvaks, as Lithuanian Jews are known in Yiddish, were marked by a rigid analysis of the Talmud, the Jewish laws and traditions. However, any proliferation of Yiddish literature was cut short by the devastation of Jewish communities in World War II.

The Jewish Museum in Prague is spread between four historic synagogues. The museum's collections provide a fascinating insight into all aspects of Jewish culture.

The Sarajevo Haggadah, illustrating the Jewish Passover, is a beautifully illuminated manuscript produced by Sephardic Jews in 1350.

Vilnius was regarded as the European Jewry's most vibrant cultural centre. It was famous as a centre of study as well as of art and literature.

The Jewish Culture Festival in Krakow, held in June each year, features films, theatre, choral performances and traditional *klezmer* music, and is one of the biggest festivals of Jewish culture in the world.

Eminent Jews

Banned from taking up most professions until the late 19th century, Jews lived largely as traders. However, over time many gained recognition in the fields of art and literature.

Mark Rothko *(1903–70)*, a pioneer of brooding, meditative abstract art, was born in the Latvian city of Daugavpils. He later moved to New York.

Franz Kafka *(1883–1924)*, renowned for his surreal stories written in German, was part of a German-Jewish literary circle in Prague, where he spent most of his life.

Sigmund Freud *(1856–1939)*, the father of modern psychoanalysis, spent much of his life in Vienna until Hitler's invasion of Austria drove him to London.

The History of Eastern and Central Europe

In this timeline of the history of Eastern and Central Europe, important political and social events appear on the upper half of the page, while the lower half charts contemporary developments in art and architecture. This lower section focuses on buildings and works of art that illustrate major historical trends and can still be seen today. They are described in more detail in the main sightseeing sections of the book.

AD 101 Roman Emperor Trajan completes the conquest of Dacia (modern-day Romania)

From Prehistory to the Early Middle Ages

Civilization in Europe started in the southeast, with metalworking and clay-firing techniques developing in the Balkans before spreading to the rest of the continent. Much of Central and South Eastern Europe came under Roman rule, while the northeast remained isolated. The collapse of Rome and the period of great migrations changed the ethnic map of Europe and hastened the emergence of nation states such as Bulgaria, Serbia, Croatia, Hungary and Poland.

AD 45 Rome takes over Thrace (modern-day Bulgaria)

AD 276 Goths overrun Roman territories in the Balkans

168 BC Romans conquer Illyria (modern-day Croatia, Bosnia, Serbia and Montenegro)

700 BC Greeks establish colonies in the Adriatic Sea and the Black Sea

4500 BC Start of the Copper Age in South Eastern Europe

Prehistory				Roman Empire	
	4500 BC	3000 BC	1500 BC	AD 1	AD 200
Neolithic				Hellenistic and Roman	

4200 BC Gold and copper jewellery is made near Varna, Bulgaria *(see p602)*

2500 BC Sophisticated earthenware is produced in the Danube valley, most notably the Vučedol Dove *(see p473)* in present -day Croatia

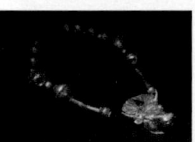

300 BC Thracian goldsmiths produce jewellery, ceremonial goblets and funeral masks *(see p580)*

AD 81 Construction of the Roman Amphitheatre at Pula, Croatia completed *(see p463)*

Art and Architecture

South Eastern Europe enjoyed long contact with Greek, Roman and Byzantine civilizations, which greatly enriched its art and culture over the centuries. The Romans were great admirers of the Greeks and the growth of the Roman Empire spread Greek aesthetics throughout Eastern Europe. North Eastern Europe, however, largely missed out on these cultural links until the region's gradual conversion to Christianity, when Western art and architecture made an impact.

AD 681 The Bulgars, under Khan Asparuh, migrate into the territory of modern-day Bulgaria

896 Magyars invade Central Europe, creating the state subsequently known as Hungary

AD 880 A Czech state emerges under the Přemyslid Dynasty with Prague at its centre

1091 The Croatian royal line dies out, leading to union with Hungary

1201 German crusaders found the city of Rīga, introducing several centuries of Teutonic rule in the Baltic States

AD 441 Huns invade the Balkans and Central Europe

966 Mieszko I creates the first unified Polish state, adopting Christianity at the same time

AD 500–600 Slavs migrate in large numbers from their homeland on the Polish-Ukrainian border, settling across much of Central and South Eastern Europe

AD 862 Byzantine monks Cyril and Methodius set out to convert Central-European Slavs to Christianity

1219 Danish King Valdemar II founds Tallinn, the future capital of Estonia

1001 Hungary accepts Christianity under Stephen, the country's first king

1228 Serbia emerges as a kingdom under Stefan Prvovenčani

After the Fall of Rome		Early Middle Ages	
AD 400	AD 600	AD 800	1000	1200

zantine

Byzantine and Romanesque

1270 Construction of the perfectly proportioned Gothic Old-New Synagogue *(see pp248–9)*, Prague

AD 550 Poreč's Basilica of Euphrasius *(see pp464–5)* decorated with captivating mosaics

850 The Rotunda of St Donat in Zadar *(see p458)* exemplifies the Romanesque style

1261 Teutonic knights build Bishop's Castle *(see p111)*

1240 Master Radovan carves the Romanesque portal of the Cathedral of St Lawrence *(see p456)*, Trogir

AD 305 Roman Emperor Diocletian builds the palace that still forms the centrepiece of the Croatian city of Split *(see pp446–9)*

1180 Studenica Monastery *(see p534)* founded by Serbian ruler Stefan Nemanja

The Age of Empires

The arrival of the Ottoman Turks had a lasting impact on Europe, wiping out the nation states of the Balkans and replacing them with a multinational empire. The main challenge to the Ottomans came from the Austrian Habsburg Dynasty, which won control of Czech and Hungarian territories before expanding south and east. For centuries, the dominant force in North Eastern Europe was the Polish-Lithuanian Commonwealth, but this was ultimately toppled by Russia, the rising power in the East.

1533 Ivan IV the Terrible becomes Grand Prince of Muscovy

1410 Polish and Lithuanian armies defeat the Teutonic knights at Grünwald

1526 Ottoman Turks defeat the Hungarians at the Battle of Mohács; the Hungarian crown falls to the Austrian Habsburg Dynasty

1349 Charles IV of Bohemia becomes Holy Roman Emperor, turning his capital Prague into a hub of politics, art and culture

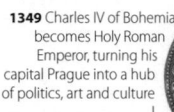

1415 Czech reformist theologian Jan Hus is burnt at the stake as a heretic, but his ideas inspire the development of Protestantism a century later

1569 Union of Lublin creates Polish-Lithuanian Commonwealth

1282 The Habsburg Dynasty establishes its first feudal holdings in Slovene lands

1331–55 Under Stefan Dušan, Serbia becomes the leading power in the Balkans

1431 Birth of Vlad II the Impaler, who leads Wallachian resistance against Ottoman expansion

1340 Ottoman Turks invade Thrace, gaining a foothold in Europe

1353–91 Bosnia becomes a regional power under King Tvrtko, then falls to the Ottoman Turks

1458-90 Reign of Mátyás Corvinus in Hungary

1463 The Ottomans conquer Bosnia and Herzegovina

Late Middle Ages				Reformation	
1350	1400	1450	1500	1550	
Gothic				Renaissance	

1380 Teutonic knights reconstruct Malbork Castle *(see p209)*, creating one of the great Gothic fortresses of North Eastern Europe

1477 Veit Stoss begins work on the altarpiece of the Church of St Mary, Krakow *(see pp188–9)*

1490s Bernt Notke creates the *Dance Macabre* for the Niguliste Church *(see p107)*

1499 John of Kastav fills St Trinity Church *(see p512)* with vivid late-Gothic frescoes

1420s Frescoes at the Manasija Monastery *(see p534)* mark the high point of Serbian religious art

1344 Work begins on St Vitus's Cathedral *(see pp232–3)*, Prague's distinctive landmark

1531 Construction of Gazi Husrev Bey's Mosque *(see p491)*, Sarajevo

Art and Architecture

In Central and North Eastern Europe, imperial courts and mercantile cities imported the very latest in Gothic, Renaissance and Baroque styles. In parts of the Balkan peninsula subject to Ottoman rule, however, artistic influences came from the East, and the region was almost totally excluded from the European art world.

1552 Moscow's St Basil's Cathedral *(see pp134–5)* built to celebrate the victories of Ivan the Terrible

1561 Construction of Stari most, the Old Bridge *(see p496)* in Mostar. Destroyed in 1993, it is reconstructed in 2004

1600 Prince Michael the Brave briefly unites Wallachia, Moldavia and Transylvania to form a state corresponding to modern Romania

1878 Austria-Hungary annexes Bosnia and Herzegovina

1877–8 Russia defeats Ottoman armies in Bulgaria; establishment of independent principality of Bulgaria

1867 The Habsburg Empire is divided into Austrian and Hungarian halves, and becomes the Austro-Hungarian Empire

1721 Sweden surrenders Estonia and Latvia to Peter the Great of Russia

1683 Ottoman Turks lay siege to Vienna but are beaten back by the combined armies of Austria and Poland

1829 Serbia is formally recognized as an independent principality

1812 Napoleon Bonaparte invades Russia but is defeated by the elements, losing most of his troops in a disastrous winter retreat

1629 Estonia passes into Swedish hands

1804 First Serbian Uprising begins the process of freeing Serbia from Ottoman control

		Age of Enlightenment		Industrial Revolution	
1600	**1650**	**1700**	**1750**	**1800**	**1850**
Baroque		Rococo	Neo-Classical	Realism and Impressionism	

1680s Austrian military architects begin construction of Tvrđa Fortress *(see p32)* in Osijek

1850–70 Bulgarian architecture blossoms with styles imported from both East and West

1716 Vienna's sublime Karlskirche *(see p387)* built by Fischer von Elach

1885 Neo-Gothic style reaches new heights in the form of the Hungarian Parliament building *(see pp336–7)*

1703 Peter the Great founds St Petersburg

1754 Francesco Bartolomeo Rastrelli begins construction of St Petersburg's Winter Palace *(see pp154–5)*

1897 Gustav Klimt and others form the Vienna Secession in a direct challenge to the established art world

The 20th Century to the Present

War and revolution destroyed the multinational empires of the 19th century, and after 1918, independent nation states were re-established throughout Eastern Europe. With the onset of World War II, however, the region was first conquered by Germany, then by Soviet Russia, which imposed Communist regimes on the seized territories. Communist rule collapsed in 1989 but the transition to democracy was not smooth everywhere; Yugoslavia, in particular, was riven by conflict before the emergence of new, internationally recognized states.

1918–19 The end of World War I brings independence for Estonia, Latvia, Lithuania, Poland, Czechoslovakia and Yugoslavia

1941 Germany mounts a surprise attack on the Soviet Union

1956 An anti-Communist uprising breaks out in Hungary but is crushed by Soviet tanks

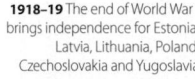

1939 Germany and the Soviet Union secretly agree to divide Poland between them, triggering World War II

1953 The death of Stalin eases political terror

1938 The Munich Agreement allows Germany to take hold of large parts of Czechoslovakia

1917 Revolution in Russia brings Lenin's Bolsheviks to power

1937–8 Stalin unleashes the Great Purge, killing an estimated 2 million citizens

1945 Collapse of Germany leaves the Soviet Union in control of Central and Eastern Europe

1914 Gavrilo Princip assassinates Austrian Archduke Franz Ferdinand in Sarajevo, sparking World War I

1924 Soviet leader Lenin dies; Stalin emerges as his successor

Age of Imperialism

1910	1920	1930	1940	1950	1960

Art Nouveau | **Art Deco and Modernism**

1915 Kazimir Malevich paints his most iconic work, *The Black Square*

1935–8 The Moscow Metro opens, featuring palatial stations, such as Arbatskaya and Komsomolskaya, full of mosaics and frescoes

1911 Completion of Municipal House *(see p252)* in Prague, a high point in Art Nouveau architecture

1907–11 Lithuanian painter Mikalojus Konstantinis Čiurlionis develops the quasi-mystical, Symbolist style

1961 Soviet cosmonaut Yuri Gagarin becomes the first man in space

1903–6 Mikhail Eisenstein designs Art Nouveau apartment blocks in Riga *(see pp78–9)*

1931 Alfons Mucha designs sumptuous stained-glass windows for St Vitus's Cathedral *(see pp232–3)* in Prague

1900–10 Rihard Jakopič, Ivan Grohar and Matej Šternen spearhead the Slovene Impressionist Movement *(see p405)*

1929 Slovene architect Jože Plečnik redesigns the riverside quarter in Ljubljana *(see pp402–403)*

Art and Architecture

Eastern European art was at the forefront of the Modernist movement in the early 20th century, before the combined effects of war and authoritarian rule disrupted its development. After the political changes of 1989, however, Eastern and Central Europe is gradually re-establishing its position at the heart of European culture.

1952 Work begins on Warsaw's Palace of Culture and Science *(see p183)*, Eastern Europe's best example of Stalinist Baroque

1989–90 Following the fall of the Berlin Wall, Communist regimes throughout Eastern Europe are replaced by democratic governments

1991 Slovenia and Croatia declare independence from Yugoslavia; fighting erupts between Croats and Serbs

1992 Bosnian Serb forces begin the siege of Sarajevo

1995 The Dayton Agreement brings to an end the wars in Croatia and Bosnia

1985 Mikhail Gorbachev becomes Soviet leader, launching a wave of reforms

1968 A period of liberalization in Czechoslovakia known as the "Prague Spring" ends with Soviet invasion

1999 Tension between Serbs and Albanians in Kosovo leads to the NATO bombing of Serbia

2004 Estonia, Latvia, Lithuania, Poland, Hungary, the Czech Republic, Slovakia and Slovenia join the European Union (EU)

1980 Strikes in Poland lead to the formation of the Solidarity Movement

2007 Romania and Bulgaria join the European Union

The European Union

| 1970 | 1980 | 1990 | 2000 | 2010 | 2020 |

Post-Modernism

1977 Invented by a local mathematician, the world's first Rubik's Cube goes on sale in Budapest

1984 In Belgrade, work commences on St Sava (see p531), the world's largest Orthodox church

2014 Croatia joins the EU, Russia annexes the Crimea.

2010 Polish president Lech Kaczyński and 95 others die in a plane crash

1983 Romanian President Ceaușescu orders the construction of the House of the People, now known as the Palace of Parliament (see pp548–9) in Bucharest

2006 Opening of Kumu Art Museum (see p108), Tallinn's ultra-modern art museum, designed by Finnish architect Pekka Vapaavuori

NORTH EASTERN EUROPE

North Eastern Europe at a Glance

Long fought over by Baltic, Teutonic, Scandinavian and Slavic warlords, North Eastern Europe presents a rich palette of ancient castles, imperial cities and stately churches. Cities such as St Petersburg in Russia and Vilnius in Lithuania once ruled over extensive multinational empires, while the Latvian and Estonian capitals, Rīga and Tallinn, stood at the heart of north-European trade routes. Today the region's cities are among the fastest developing on the European continent, blending thriving urban culture with stunning landscapes and an extraordinary wealth of historic architecture.

Saaremaa Island *(see pp110–11)*, the largest island in Estonia, offers a haunting mixture of reed-rimmed shores and juniper-covered heath, in addition to the majestic windmills that are its trademark.

Rundāle Palace *(see pp88–9)*, regarded as Latvia's most impressive surviving stately home, was designed by Italian architect Francesco Bartolomeo Rastrelli (1700–71). It features ornate rooms decorated in the Rococo style of the second half of the 18th century.

Tallinn
Paldiski
Haapsalu
Pärnu
Kuressaare

Baltic Sea

Gulf of Rīga

Ventspils
Rīga
Tukums
Pāvilosta
Jelgava
Liepāja

Telšiai
Šiaul
Palanga
LITHUANIA
(see pp46–73)
Klaipēda
Raseini
Šilutē
Jurbarkas
Kauna

0 kilometres 100
0 miles 100

Parnidis Dune towers over the fishing village of Nida, on the Curonian Spit *(see pp66–7)*. Spectacular views from the summit take in the Baltic Sea and the Curonian Lagoon, and stretch southwards to Kaliningrad.

◀ View of the impressive façade of the Great Kremlin Palace, Moscow

Moscow and St Petersburg
(see pp122–65)

St Petersburg

ESTONIA

RUSSIAN
FEDERATION

LATVIA

Moscow

LITHUANIA

BELARUS

The Hermitage *(see pp148–55)* houses the state rooms of the tsar's Winter Palace and has nearly three million exhibits ranging from fine arts to archaeological finds.

St Basil's Cathedral *(see pp131–5)* was built in 1555–61 for Ivan the Terrible. Pointed roofs, colourful domes and tiers of arched gables typify its stunning architectural diversity.

Jõhvi
Rakvere

Paide
Lake
Peipsi

ESTONIA
ee pp98–121)

Tartu
Viljandi

Võru

Valga

Alūksne
Smiltene

Ērgli
re
LATVIA
(see pp74–97)
Rēzekne

Jēkabpils

Krāslava
Daugavpils

nevežys
Utena

Ukmergė
onava

Vilnius

ruskininkai

Gauja National Park *(see pp90–91)* is one of the most attractive national parks in Latvia. Besides a compelling mix of natural landscapes and historic sites, it also offers an extensive range of outdoor activities, from canoeing to bobsledding.

Vilnius Cathedral *(see pp52–3)*, is a striking Neo-Classical edifice, with huge statues of saints Casimir, Stanislaus and Helena topping the pediment. Inside, a chapel dedicated to St Casimir (1458–84), patron saint of Lithuania, is filled with stunning Baroque stuccowork and statuary.

LITHUANIA

The largest of the three Baltic States and one of the hidden jewels of Europe, Lithuania takes pride in its relatively undiscovered landscape of clean lakes, ancient forests and coastal dunes. The capital Vilnius, which has a UNESCO-protected Old Town, combines the romance of breathtaking Baroque architecture with the modern trappings of 21st-century Europe.

Lithuania is blessed with an unblemished natural landscape of rolling hills, lakes and rivers. The eastern half of the country is known as the "highlands" and the west as the "lowlands", even though the terrain is almost universally flat.

Following a tumultuous history, the country is forging a positive political and cultural role for itself in the expanded European Union. Many of its fine historic buildings have survived, and folk culture colours every corner of the country.

History

At the beginning of the 13th century, Lithuanian tribes, such as the Samogitians (Žemaičiai) and Aukštaičiai, began to unite in the face of incursions by Germanic crusaders. In 1253, Duke Mindaugas (r. 1235–63) crowned himself king of the united tribes. However, his acceptance of Christianity enraged the Samogitians, who murdered him and reverted to paganism. In the 14th century, the Teutonic knights (German warrior-monks) returning from the Middle East joined the fight against the pagan Grand Duchy of Lithuania. In 1410, they were defeated at the Battle of Grünwald (Žalgiris) by the armies of Lithuania and Poland, which had forged an alliance by marriage in 1386. Fear of Russia led to closer ties between Lithuania and Poland and the creation of the Commonwealth of the Two Nations, cemented at the Union of Lublin in 1569. When King Sigismund Augustus died without an heir, the combined position of grand duke of Lithuania and king of Poland became an elected one. The aristocracy adopted the Polish language, and Lithuanian culture was marginalized.

Children playing in the sand dunes near Nida, Curonian Spit National Park

◀ Yachts moored near the enchanting red-brick Trakai Island Castle, Trakai

Detail from Jan Matejko's depiction of *Battle of Grünwald* (1878)

The 17th century was a disastrous period for Lithuania, characterized by misrule, plague and a calamitous invasion by the Russians. During the 18th century the Commonwealth gradually became a puppet state of tsarist Russia. In a series of partitions, its vast lands were divided between Russia, Prussia and Austria. By 1795, Poland and Lithuania had ceased to exist. Over 120 years of occupation followed, during which Russification led to the eradication of all traces of

KEY DATES IN LITHUANIAN HISTORY

AD 1236 Samogitian victory over German crusaders

1240 Duke Mindaugas unites Lithuania

1253 Duke Mindaugas crowned king

1386 Royal marriage unites Lithuania and Poland

1410 Battle of Grünwald destroys the Teutonic knights

1569 Union of Lublin creates Polish-Lithuanian Commonwealth

1655 Russian Army sacks Vilnius

1795 Final partition of the Commonwealth

1831 Rebellion against tsarist rule

1863 Lithuanian rebels persecuted by Russia

1918 Lithuania declares independence

1923 Lithuania reclaims Klaipėda

1926 President Smetona seizes power

1944 Soviets reoccupy Lithuania

1955 Partisan war against Soviet occupation dies away

1988 Sajūdis Movement founded

1990 Declaration of independence

2004 Lithuania joins NATO and becomes a member of the EU

2015 Lithuania adopts the Euro as the official currency and becomes the 19th member of the Eurozone

traditional Lithuania. Resistance simmered under the surface, and as World War I and the 1917 Russian Revolution destroyed the Tsarist Empire, a national council in Vilnius declared Lithuania independent on 16 February 1918. Between 1926 and 1940, under authoritarian Antanas Smetona, Lithuania enjoyed a period of growing prosperity. However, it was then occupied by the Red Army, ushering in a reign of terror defined by mass deportations and massacres that continued under the Nazis. The return of the Red Army in 1944 saw between 120,000 and 300,000 people deported to the Siberian gulags.

In 1988, a group of intellectuals founded the Sajūdis Movement to rally popular support for demonstrations and, on 11 March 1990, Lithuania declared its independence, prompting a fierce response by Soviet troops. Freedom was finally declared in August 1991. Several years of economic hardship followed, but membership of the EU and NATO has since brought far greater prosperity.

Language and Culture

Lithuanian belongs to the Baltic family of languages. While English is commonly used as a second language, German, Russian and Polish are also widely spoken. Lithuanians celebrate a host of festivals. Most of the year's events take place in summer when the country comes alive with music, dance and food festivals.

Exploring Lithuania

With its rich history and wealth of scenic beauty, Lithuania offers many attractions. Its capital Vilnius possesses one of Europe's finest Old Towns. While Vilnius and Kaunas are the most vibrant cities, the less-visited towns and villages, with their beautiful churches and farmsteads, and the coast, with its fascinating sandy dunes and beaches, also draw visitors. Trains are cheap, but not frequent, and there are few routes. The country's flat landscape makes it ideal for cycling.

Sights at a Glance

1 *Vilnius pp50–59*
2 *Trakai Castle pp60–61*
3 *Kaunas pp62–3*
4 *Klaipėda pp64–5*
5 *Curonian Spit National Park pp66–7*

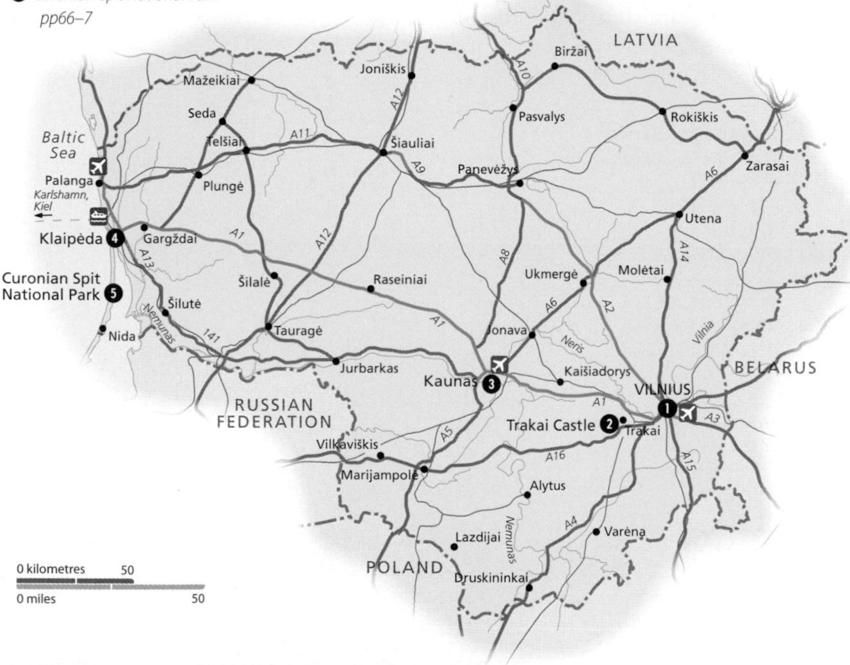

View of Upper Castle across the Neris river, Vilnius

Vast sand dunes, Curonian Spit National Park

Key

— Motorway
— Major road
— Railway
– – International border

For keys to symbols *see back flap*

❶ Vilnius

Whether viewed from one of the hills that overlook the Old Town or one of the many pavement cafés with tall spires rising all around, Vilnius is unmistakably a city of great beauty. The city, now home to 600,000 people, sustained a series of wars, invasions and fires between the early 17th and mid-18th centuries. Efforts to rebuild the city resulted in the rich offshoot of the Baroque style that is typical of Vilnius today. The Old Town, on the UNESCO World Heritage list since 1994, blends Gothic and Neo–Classical styles. The best places to begin a tour of the Old Town are Vilnius Cathedral in the north and the Gates of Dawn in the south. Vilnius University and its surrounding churches and courtyards are one of the city's finest architectural ensembles.

Sights at a Glance

① *Vilnius Cathedral pp52–3*
② Cathedral Square
③ Ducal Palace
④ Upper Castle
⑤ Applied Arts Museum
⑥ Vilnius University
⑦ St John's Church
⑧ Town Hall Square
⑨ Church of St Casimir
⑩ Gates of Dawn
⑪ State Jewish Museum
⑫ Holocaust Museum
⑬ The Museum of Genocide Victims

Outdoor cafés along a cobblestoned street, Old Town

Getting Around

Vilnius is a compact city that can easily be explored on foot. Walking is the best way to explore the Old Town. Cycling is another popular way of getting around the town centre, and the tourist office in the Old Town offers bicycles to rent. Outlying sites can be reached by bus, but others, located further away from the city centre, are more easily reached by car or taxi.

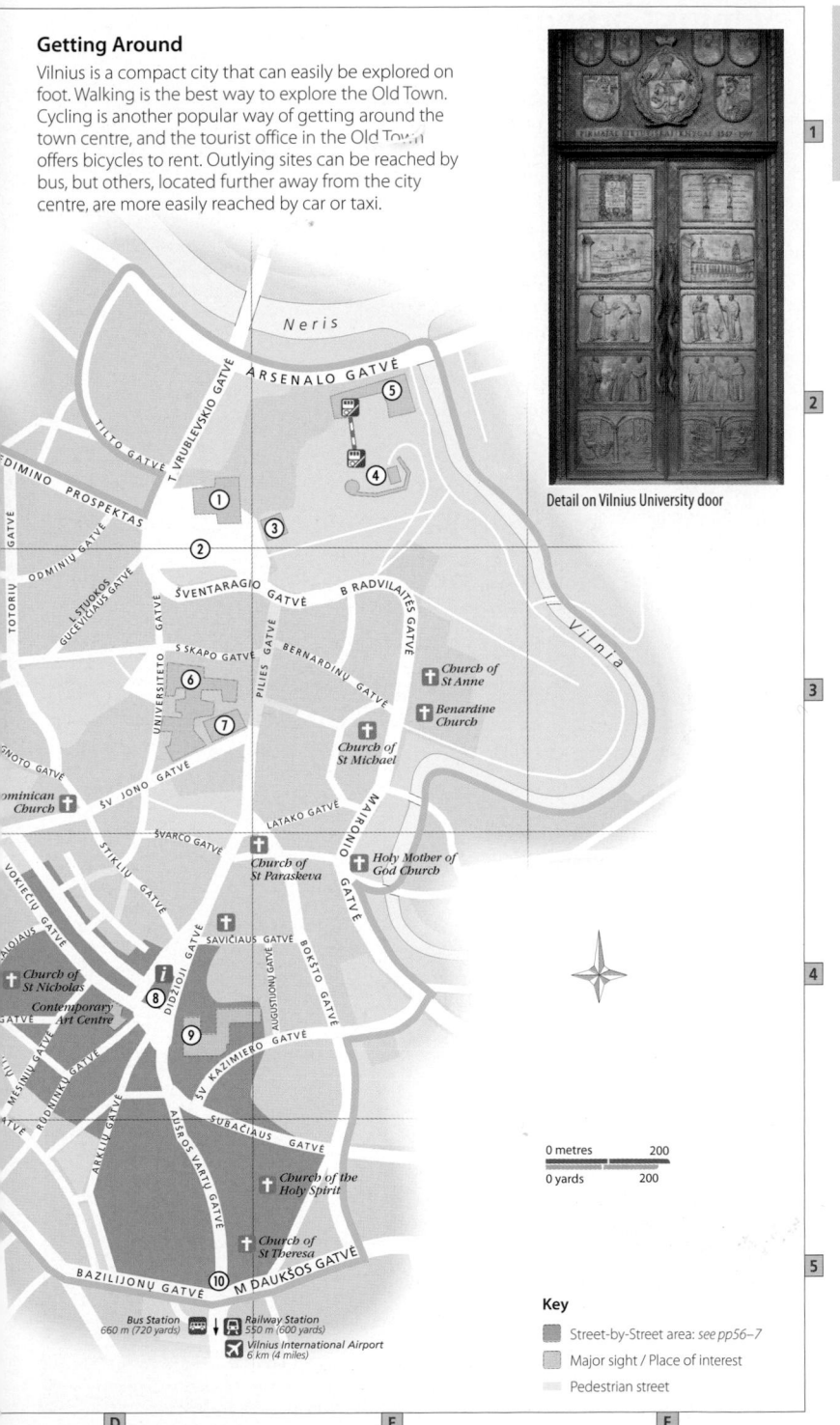

Detail on Vilnius University door

Key

Church of St Anne

Benardine Church

Church of St Michael

Church of St Paraskeva

Holy Mother of God Church

Dominican Church

Church of St Nicholas

Contemporary Art Centre

Church of the Holy Spirit

Church of St Theresa

Neris

Vilnia

Bus Station 660 m (720 yards)

Railway Station 550 m (600 yards)

Vilnius International Airport 6 km (4 miles)

0 metres 200
0 yards 200

Key

Street-by-Street area: *see pp56–7*

Major sight / Place of interest

Pedestrian street

For keys to symbols *see back flap*

① Vilnius Cathedral

Vilniaus arkikatedra bazilika

Having taken various guises since it was first built as a Christian church on the site of a pagan temple in 1251, Vilnius Cathedral today largely dates from the late 18th century. The young architect, Laurynas Stuoka-Gucevičius, brought the fashionable French Classicist style to Baroque Vilnius; his idea for the cathedral exterior and interior being a visual re-creation of a Greek temple. Vilnius Cathedral was closed by the Soviets in 1950 and initially mooted for use as a garage for truck repairs. In 1956, however, it opened as a picture gallery. It was eventually returned to the Catholic Church in 1988 and reconsecrated in 1989, a year before independence was declared.

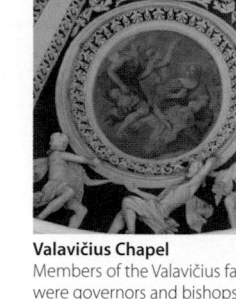

Valavičius Chapel
Members of the Valavičius family were governors and bishops of Vilnius. Their lavish chapel was built in the early 17th century.

Statue of St Helena

Stucco Sculpture
This sculpture depicting a bird sacrifice can be seen on the tympanum of the façade.

Main entrance

Wall Painting of the Crucifixion
The oldest surviving fresco in Lithuania, dating from the 14th century, can be found in the crypt. It was discovered in 1985.

Statue of Luke, the Evangelist
Of the statues of the Four Evangelists on the southern façade, the one of Luke's appears with a bull, a symbol of service and sacrifice.

High Altar
The marvellously intricate tabernacle door on the High Altar, which was created in the 1620s, is fashioned from gold and silver. Two biblical scenes, the *Last Supper* and *Christ Washing the Disciples' Feet*, are beautifully depicted on the panel.

VISITORS' CHECKLIST

Practical Information
Katedros aikštė. **Map** D2.
Tel (5) 261 0731. **Open** 7am–7pm daily. 🎦 mandatory to visit the crypt. Enquire at the souvenir shop at the north entrance for timings and fees. 🕁 8am, 5:30pm, 6:30pm daily, also 9am, 10am, 11:15am, 12:30pm Sun. 🎦

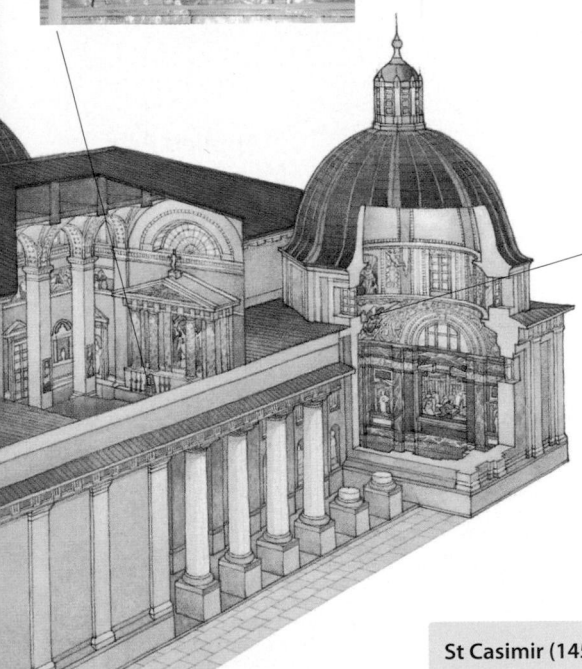

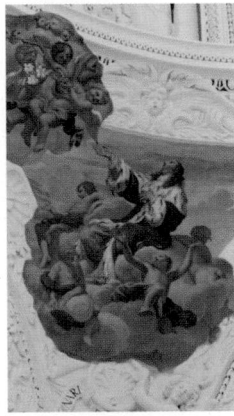

★ St Casimir's Chapel
Italian masters created this superb chapel, one of the major Baroque jewels of Vilnius, from 1623 to 1636. Its main highlights are the marble columns, magnificent stucco figures and colourful frescoes.

St Casimir (1458–84)

Casimir was the second son of King Casimir IV of Poland, whose siblings became kings and queens of European states through lineage and marriage. Pious Casimir shunned the luxuries of court life and would often go to the cathedral to pray. When he died of tuberculosis at the age of 25, it was rumoured that his coffin could cure the disease. A fresco in St Casimir's Chapel shows how a sick orphan, who prayed beneath the coffin, was miraculously cured.

Richly decorated altar of St Casimir's Chapel

★ Crypt
A sombre mausoleum holds the remains of two grand dukes and two wives of Sigismund Augustus (r. 1548–72), Gediminas' last descendant (r. 1316–41).

Vilnius Cathedral Belfry, Cathedral Square

② Cathedral Square
Katedros aikštė

Map D2 & D3. 🚌 10, 11, 33.

The paving stones around Cathedral Square show the outline of the wall around the Lower Castle, a defence that made Vilnius a 14th-century bastion against the crusades.

At the square's western end is the **Vilnius Cathedral Belfry**, which was originally part of the fortifications. There was also a western gate where Vilnius Cathedral stands today. The square's eastern end is dominated by a statue of the city's founder, Grand Duke Gediminas. Unveiled in 1996, it conveys his predilection for diplomacy over force. In the square's centre is a tile marked *stebuklas* (miracle), reputed to be the point from where the Baltic Way, the human chain linking Vilnius, Rīga and Tallinn in 1989, started. Locals believe that turning around on the tile three times makes wishes come true.

③ Ducal Palace
Valdovų Rūmai

Katedros 4. **Map** E2. **Tel** (5) 212 7476. 🚌 10, 11, 33. **Open** call in advance for timings. 📷 🌐 **valdovurumai.lt**

Situated on the left bank of Neris river, the Vilnius Castle Complex consists of the Ducal Palace and the Upper Castle. Vilnius Cathedral, the New Arsenal, the Royal Palace where the grand dukes of Lithuania resided and other buildings that stood at the foot of Castle Hill and survived the sieges of the 14th century are known as the Ducal Palace. In the 1520s, the palace was renovated in Renaissance style by Italian architects invited by Sigismund the Old (r. 1506–48). Destroyed by Russians in 1802, the Ducal Palace has been rebuilt to provide Vilnius with a symbol of past glories. The building holds a museum devoted to the courtly culture of Lithuania's grand dukes.

④ Upper Castle
Aukštutinė pilis

Arsenalo 5. **Map** E2. **Tel** (5) 261 7453. 🚌 10, 11, 33. **Open** May–Sep: 10am–7pm daily; Oct–Apr: 10am–5pm daily. 📷

The oldest part of the Vilnius Castle complex is the Upper Castle, also known as Gedimino pilies bokštas, built atop Gediminas Hill. The western tower, the only remaining part of this complex, which once included defensive structures, is today the symbol of independent Lithuania. The viewing platform at the top provides a panorama of the spires and rooftops of the Old Town to the south. A funicular from the courtyard of the Applied Arts Museum offers a ride to the Upper Castle.

The stone buildings of the western tower were built in 1419, and restored in the 1950s. According to legend, Grand Duke Gediminas dreamed of an iron wolf howling from the hills in the park. This, his pagan priest said, was a sign that a fortress should be built there. As a result, wooden upper and lower castles and another one on the adjacent hill were built.

⑤ Applied Arts Museum
Taikomosios dailės muziejus

Arsenalo gatvė 3a. **Map** E2. **Tel** (5) 262 8080. **Open** 11am–6pm Tue–Sat, 11am–4pm Sun. 📷

The 16th-century Old Arsenal houses the Applied Arts Museum, which hosts major state-sponsored exhibitions on topics relating mainly to the history of Lithuania, the Grand Duchy and sacred art.

One of the permanent exhibitions in the museum displays Lithuanian folk art from the 17th to the 19th centuries, illustrating the heavy impact that Christian

Western tower, the Upper Castle's lone surviving structure

Colourful interior of Littera, with its collection of books and study material, Vilnius University

themes had on traditional mediums such as sculpture. The collection includes wayside wooden crosses, shrines, saints and *rūpintojėlis* (Lithuanian local representations of a weary Christ holding his head in his right hand). Particularly illuminating is the work of Vincas Svirskis (1835–1916), a prolific craftsman who carved many shrines for farmsteads and villages in the Kėdainiai and Kaunas regions.

⑥ Vilnius University

Vilniaus universitetas

Universiteto 3. **Map** D3. **Tel** (5) 268 7001. **Open** 10am–5:30pm Mon–Sat. for prior booking call (5) 268 7298. **vu.lt**

The oldest university in Eastern Europe, Vilnius University was founded as a Jesuit College in 1568 before becoming a school of higher education in 1579. The current campus, constructed between the 16th and 18th centuries, is a combination of different architectural styles.

Lithuania's largest university, it has 13 courtyards and multiple buildings. The most impressive of its courtyards, the Great Courtyard has open galleries dating from the 17th century, which were later lined with dedications to professors. Accessed via a passage from the western side of the Great Courtyard, the Observatory Courtyard by contrast is a serene enclosed garden from which the observatory and its zodiac symbols can be seen.

Sarbievius Courtyard, the oldest part of the campus, is located north of the Great Courtyard and at its far end, is the bookshop **Littera**. Frescoes caricaturing professors and students decorate its interior. These were painted in 1978 by Lithuanian artist Antanas Kmieliauskas.

Façade of St John's Church and adjoining bell tower

⑦ St John's Church

Šv Jono bažnyčia

Universiteto 3/Šv Jono 12. **Map** D3. **Tel** (5) 611 795. **Open** 10am–5pm Mon–Sat. 6pm Mon–Sat, 11am Sun.

At the southern edge of the Vilnius University campus, the impressive façade of the Church of St John the Baptist and St John the Evangelist and the nearby bell tower dominate the Great Courtyard. The original Gothic church, built here in 1426, was reconstructed in 1749 in flamboyant Baroque by Jan Krzysztof Glaubitz (1700–67). He was the most influential of Vilnius's late-Baroque architects and one of the creators of the distinct school known as Vilnius Baroque.

The magnificent structure boasts an overwhelming four-tier façade made up of clusters of columns. The church has ten imposing altars that are interconnected. These faux marble altars with Corinthian columns illuminate the otherwise austere interior. Initially, there were 22 columns, most of which were removed during further rebuilding in the 19th century. At 68 m (223 ft), the bell tower, which was given two additional tiers by Glaubitz, is considered the tallest structure in the Old Town.

Street-by-Street: Town Hall Square to the Gates of Dawn

Lithuania's distinctive Baroque architecture, known as Vilnius Baroque, can be admired in the outstanding monuments clustered around the Church of St Casimir and the Gates of Dawn. The enchanting collection of towers and sculptures was built during the 17th and 18th centuries by Italian and Polish architects and their Polish-Lithuanian noble patrons. The buildings are elegantly designed, with symmetrical façades reflecting an unmistakable Italian influence. Nonetheless, the regal atmosphere, so unique to Vilnius, distinguishes this place from similar architectural areas of other European cities.

⑨ ★ **Church of St Casimir**
This church was the city's museum of atheism from 1963–91. The crown atop the central dome symbolizes St Casimir's royal lineage.

↖ Vilnius Cathedral

DIDŽIOJI GATVĖ

⑧ **Town Hall Square**
This busy square has the impressive Town Hall as its focal point. The hall's bold Classical portico was designed by the renowned Lithuanian architect, Laurynas Stuoka-Gucevičius.

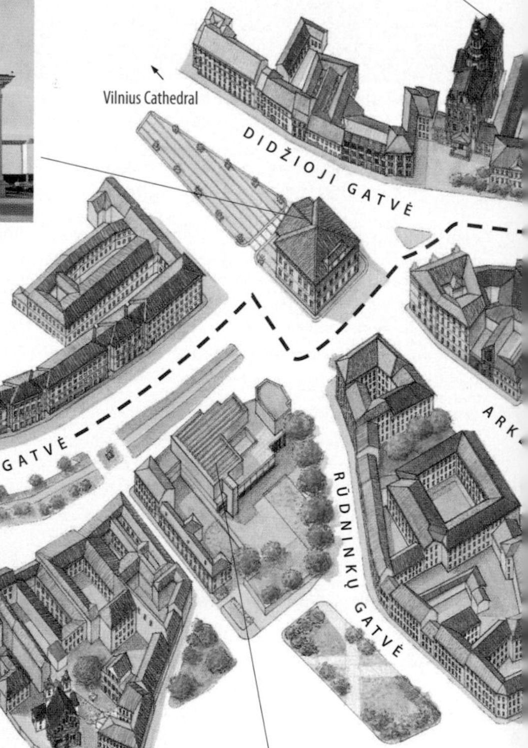

VOKIEČIŲ GATVĖ

RŪDNINKŲ GATVĖ

ARK

Key

— Suggested route

Vokiečių Gatvė
One of the city's oldest streets, Vokiečių resembles a park during the summer, with its outdoor cafés and a pleasant central tree-lined walkway.

Contemporary Art Centre, a Soviet-era building, is now a venue for groundbreaking art.

Šv Kazimiero Gatvė
Named after St Casimir, this narrow street snakes around the back of the church towards Užupis, a district filled with cafés and art galleries.

★ Church of St Theresa
Scenes from the life of St Theresa, revered for her mystical writings, adorn the vaulted nave of the church. The frescoes were painted in the late 18th century following a fire in the 17th-century church.

Church of the Holy Spirit

M AUŠROS GATVĖ

0 metres 100
0 yards 100

AUŠROS VARTŲ GATVĖ

BAZILIJONŲ GATVĖ

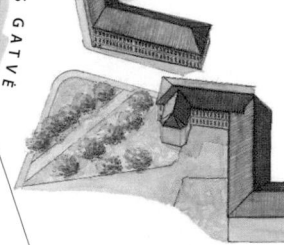

Basilian Gate

Basilian Monastery
The now dilapidated monastery complex was used as a prison to hold anti-Russian activists, including the poet Adam Mickiewicz, in the 1820s.

⑩ ★ Gates of Dawn
A pilgrimage site, this gateway to the Old Town protects a silver-covered painting of the Virgin Mary, said to have miraculous powers.

Nave and altar in the Church of St Casimir

⑧ Town Hall Square

Rotušės Aikštė

Didžioji 31. **Map** D4. Town Hall: **Tel** (5) 261 8007. 🛈 (5) 262 6470. **Open** 9am–6pm daily. 🎭 Kaziuko Crafts Fair (Mar). 🌐 **vilnius.lt**

Fully repaved in 2006, Town Hall Square was for centuries a marketplace and the centre of public life. It still bustles with activity, especially during the annual Kaziuko Crafts Fair, a festival of traditional arts and crafts marking St Casimir's Day, when stalls line the square. The main building of the square, the **Town Hall**, was earlier the site of a court; prisoners were marched from its cells to the square to be beheaded. The building was constructed at the end of the 18th century. Today, the Town Hall hosts cultural and social events through the year.

⑨ Church of St Casimir

Šv Kazimiero Bažnyčia

Didžioji 34. **Map** D4. **Tel** (5) 212 1715. 🕙 5:30pm Mon–Fri, 10:30am & noon Sun.

The first Baroque church of the city, St Casimir was destroyed by fire three times after being built by the Jesuits between 1604 and 1635, prompting extensive reconstruction led by the architect, mathematician and astronomer Tomas Žebrauskas (1714–58) in the 1750s. Much of the interior

was destroyed in 1812, when Napoleon's Army used the church as a granary. It became a Russian Orthodox church during the 19th century, when onion domes were added to it.

It served as a Lutheran church for the German Army during World War I, and was then returned to the Jesuits and restored in the 1920s. The central dome was rebuilt in 1942 and a crown was added. The Soviets used the church as a museum of atheism from 1963. It was reconsecrated in 1991 after heavy renovation.

⑩ Gates of Dawn

Aušros Vartai

Aušros vartų 12. **Map** D5. **Tel** (5) 212 3513. 🕙 9am, 6:30pm Mon–Fri. Chapel: 6am–9pm.

The Classical chapel of Gates of Dawn follows the centuries-old custom of having a chapel or a religious image in every gateway to safeguard a city from outside enemies and protect departing travellers. This is the only gateway from Vilnius' original defensive walls to have survived a series of attacks.

The focus of this chapel is *The Madonna of Mercy*, an image reputed to have miracle-working powers. It was painted on oak in the 1620s and encased in silver 150 years later. The miracles attributed to it were faithfully recorded by nuns at the neighbouring Carmelite convent. Hundreds of hearts of different sizes stand out on plates of silver around the painting.

The image was originally placed on the gate, in a recess, with shutters to protect it from the elements, but was shifted to a wooden chapel in the 17th century. The chapel that houses the image today dates from

The Madonna of Mercy, seen through the window of the Gates of Dawn

For hotels and restaurants see p72 and p73

Stained-glass window at the State Jewish Museum

1829, when it was rebuilt to replace an earlier Baroque version. A site of pilgrimage, it was one of the first stops made by Pope John Paul II when he visited Lithuania in 1993.

⑪ State Jewish Museum
Valstybinis Vilniaus Gaono Žydų Muziejus

Naugarduko 10/2. **Map** C3. **Tel** (5) 231 2357. **Open** 9am–5pm Mon–Thu, till 3:30pm Fri. 🦽 ✅ excursions of the museum & Vilnius Old Town offered. 🖥 **jmuseum.lt**

The hub of the city's now tiny Jewish community, this small museum displays copies of ghetto diaries and handwritten notes on the backs of cigarette packets about life in the ghetto, as well as items that remained from the museum that existed before World War II. Several objects that miraculously survived from the Great Synagogue, demolished by the Soviets, include a Ten Commandments bas-relief.

The building plays host to a newspaper in Lithuanian, English, Yiddish and Russian, *Jerusalem of Lithuania*. It is also the venue where groups, such as the Union of Former Ghetto and Concentration Camp Prisoners and the Union of Jewish War Veterans, meet.

⑫ Holocaust Museum
Holokausto Ekspozicija

Paménkalnio 12. **Map** B2 and C2. **Tel** (5) 261 6253. **Open** 9am–5pm Mon–Thu, 9am–4pm Fri, 10am–4pm Sun. 🦽 ✅ 🖥 **jmuseum.lt**

Also known as the Green House, this department of the State Jewish Museum reveals some of the horrors that befell the Jews of Lithuania during World War II. A display on Jewish life before the terror unfolded is followed by maps and photographs of how and where the Holocaust was executed. There are also descriptions of the harsh life in the ghettos and eyewitness accounts of the mass killings of 100,000 people in the forests of Paneriai, outside Vilnius.

⑬ The Museum of Genocide Victims
Genocido Aukų Muziejus

Aukų 2a. **Map** B2. **Tel** (5) 249 8156. **Open** 10am–6pm Wed–Sat, 10am–5pm Sun. 🦽 ✅ 📷 🖥 **genocid.lt**

Also known as the KGB Museum, the Museum of Genocide Victims was opened in 1992, on the first floor of the former KGB building. In the effectively designed display area, personal stories are used to reveal the regime of terror under the Soviet occupations of 1940–41 and 1944–91. The exhibits here chronicle Soviet repression in Lithuania, the cattle-car

Holocaust Museum, annexe of the State Jewish Museum

deportations to Siberia and the futile efforts of the Forest Brothers, who fought a guerrilla-style campaign against the Soviet regime with strong support from the locals. Underground, the cells that were in use right up until the late 1980s are even more overwhelming. They include the smaller cells used in winter with no glass in their windows and the floors covered with water, as well as an execution chamber displaying, under glass, the recently exhumed remains of victims of the era.

In 1997, the museum was taken over by the Genocide and Resistance Research Centre of Lithuania, a state institution dedicated to investigating atrocities that occurred in the country during the Nazi and Soviet occupations.

Exhibition of Lithuanian partisans at the Museum of Genocide Victims

❷ Trakai Castle

Trakų pilis

Located on one of the 21 islands in Lake Galvė in the peninsula town of Trakai, the castle was built as a seat of power during the reign of Vytautas the Great in the 13th century. Building was completed just before the Grand Duchy's crushing victory over the Teutonic knights at the Battle of Grünwald. As Vilnius grew in importance, Trakai lost its significance and was destroyed by the Cossacks during the 1655 Russian invasion. In the late 19th century, the elegiac island ruins captured the imagination of poets and painters during the National Revival. Oddly, it was the Soviet authorities who, in the 1950s, sanctioned the reconstruction of this monument to Lithuania's glorious past. It was completed in 1987.

Dry moat, separating the main castle from the outer courtyard

★ Lakeside Walk
One way to appreciate Trakai's idyllic lake-filled landscape and the scale of the castle's construction is to take the pretty walk that follows the shore of the island.

Yachts
Between May and October, yachts from the nearby Žalgiris Yacht Club are moored next to the castle. The boats can be hired by the hour, but charges vary.

Lake Galvė
This lake serves as a moat around the castle. Rowing boats and paddle boats can be hired along the quayside on the Lithuanian mainland for a spectacular view of the castle.

VISITORS' CHECKLIST

Practical Information
30 km (19 miles) W of Vilnius.
🛈 Vytauto gatvė 69, (528) 51 934.
Žalgiris Yacht Club: Žemaitės gatvė 3. **Tel** (528) 52 824. History Museum: Kęstučio gatvė 4. **Tel** (528) 53 946. **Open** May–Sep: 10am–7pm daily; Oct–Apr: 10am–5pm Tue–Sun (to 6pm Mar, Apr & Oct).
🏛 ⓦ trakaimuziejus.lt

Transport
🚌 from Vilnius. 🚆 from Vilnius.

KEY

① **A wooden footbridge** links Trakai to the castle.

② **The circular defence towers** have 4-m (13-ft) thick bases.

③ **The Ducal Palace's keep**, which is 30 m (100 ft) high, served as the residence of the grand duke.

④ **Dry moat**

★ **History Museum**
This museum showcases a wide array of weaponry as well as items found during excavations, including 16th-century tankards, tiles and coins.

Graves in the Karaim Cemetery, partially hidden by long grass

The Karaim of Trakai

A community of Turkic settlers practising a particular kind of Judaism, the Karaim, lend a distinctly exotic flavour to Trakai. Their ancestors were taken prisoners by Vytautas the Great when on a military venture to the Crimea in 1397, and they subsequently served as royal guards. The Karaim have maintained their customs and traditions. Their characteristic wooden houses, each typically with gable ends and three windows facing the street, their synagogue, or Kenesa, and the Karaim Museum are all on Karaimų gatvė, at Trakai's northern end. Their cemetery lies beside Lake Totoriskiai close to Lake Galvė.

❸ Kaunas

Lithuania's second largest city, Kaunas stands at the confluence of the Nemunas and Neris, the country's biggest rivers. A series of disasters hindered the city's development, including invasions by the Russians (1655), Swedes (1701) and Napolean (1812). Rapid growth in the 19th century culminated in Kaunas becoming the temporary capital of newly independent Lithuania in 1919. Later, the city suffered under Nazi and Soviet occupations. Today, Kaunas is a modern city with a boulevard and a host of museums. The main historic sights are located in its well-preserved Old Town.

View of the bridge over the Nemunas river leading to the Old Town

🏛 Old Town Hall
Rotušės aikštė.

Known locally as the "White Swan" and resembling a church with its single, tiered tower, the Old Town Hall (Kauno Rotušė) has been a marriage registry office since the 1970s. It continues to be a photogenic backdrop for newlyweds. Built in the mid-16th century, it has housed magistrates and the mayor, and has been used as an ammunition store, clubhouse, fire station, theatre and a subterranean prison. Town Hall Square, where it stands, was once a busy marketplace and is still the hub of the Old Town.

🏛 Church of the Holy Trinity
A. Jakšto gatvė 1. **Tel** (37) 323 734.
🕇 10am Sun.

Built for a Bernardine convent in the late 1620s, this church (Šventos Trejybės bažnyčia), with its blend of Renaissance and Gothic styles and its pastel colours brightens up the northwestern corner of the Town Hall Square. The interior was redesigned just before the outbreak of World War II.

🏛 Church of St George
Papilio gatvė 7. **Tel** (37) 224 659.
🕇 6pm Mon–Fri, 10:30am Sun.

This 15th-century Gothic church (Šv Jurgio bažnyčia) was destroyed twice by fire, by the Russians in the 17th century and in 1812 by Napoleon's soldiers. It was finally returned to the Bernardines in 1993.

🏛 Kaunas Castle
Pilies 17. **Tel** (37) 300 672.
Open 10:30am–1pm Mon–Fri.
📷 mandatory.

The ruins of Kaunas Castle (Kauno pilis) are a reminder of its strategic location, between the rivers Neris and Nemunas. Built in the 13th century, it was damaged by the Teutonic knights in 1362. Soon after its reconstruction, the knights were defeated by Lithuanians in the Battle of Grünwald in 1410. Thereafter the castle lost its significance as a military base and was used for administrative purposes. It functioned as a prison in the 18th century, but was restored in the 1920s.

🏛 Cathedral of Sts Peter and Paul
Vilniaus 1. **Tel** (37) 324 093. 🕇 7am, 8am, 6pm, 9am daily; 8am, 9am, 10:30am Sat & Sun, also noon Sun.

Several reconstructions have culminated in the Gothic and Renaissance exterior of this 15th-century cathedral (Šv apaštalų Petro ir Pauliaus arkikatedra bazilika). The late-Baroque interior, however,

The elegant Old Town Hall

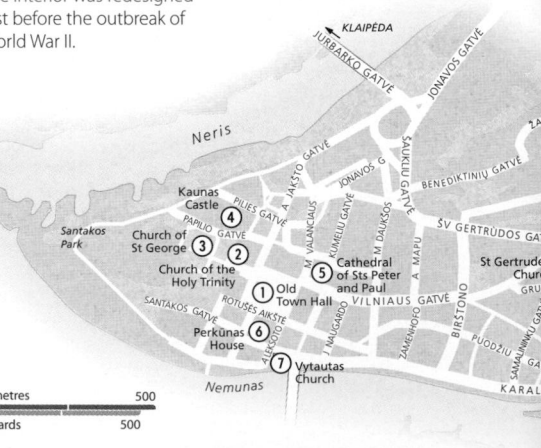

remains largely unchanged since 1800. The oldest painting in the cathedral, the *Suffering Mother of God*, is reputed to have miraculous powers.

🏠 Perkūnas House

Aleksoto 6. **Tel** (37) 641 44614. **Open** 2–5pm Fri, call to arrange a visit Mon–Thu. 📷

The red-brick Gothic building (Perkūno namai) was named after Perkūnas, the god of thunder. Dating from the early 1500s, it was initially a meeting house for members of the Hanseatic League. Bought by the Jesuits, the house was converted into a chapel before becoming a theatre and then a school. Later, during the Soviet period, it was used as a warehouse. It is now back with the Jesuits.

🏠 Vytautas Church

Aleksoto 3. **Tel** (37) 203 854. 🏛 6pm Tue–Fri, 10am & 6pm Sat–Sun, noon Sun.

This church (Vytauto bažnyčia) was built by Vytautas the Great after the Holy Roman Emperor decided in 1413 that the land on Nemunas river's right bank belonged to Lithuania's Grand Duchy. Used as an army storehouse by Napoleon, it was later converted to serve a Russian

The red-brick Vytautas Church, built by Vytautas the Great

congregation. After Lithuania's first independence in 1918, a reconstruction took place. In 1930, a medallion was placed in the church wall to commemorate the 500th anniversary of Vytautas's death.

🏠 Laisvės Aleja

This pedestrianized street, set in the heart of modern Kaunas, is also called Freedom Avenue. A monument outside the Music Theatre at Laisvės 4 marks where Romas Kalanta, a local student, set fire to himself on 14 May 1972. His suicide sparked student protests, which were suppressed.

The silver-blue onion domes of the Church of St Michael dominate the street's eastern end. Built in the early 1890s, it was originally Russian Orthodox, but later served as a German

Army church during World War I, and, soon after, became a Lithuanian Army church.

🏛 Mykolas Žilinskas Art Gallery

Nepriklausomybės 12. **Tel** (37) 322 788. **Open** 11am–5pm Tue–Sun. 🅿 📷

Named after the famous art connoisseur Mykolas Žilinskas, this gallery (Mykolo Žilinsko dailės galerija) houses the valuable art collection he donated to Kaunas in the 1970s. Besides paintings and porcelain from the 16th to the 20th centuries, including *The Crucifixion* by Rubens, the gallery also includes pre-war paintings and sculptures by Baltic artists.

🏛 M K Čiurlionis Art Museum

V Putvinskio 55. **Tel** (37) 229 475. **Open** 11am–5pm Tue–Sun. 🅿 📷

Housing the paintings of the Lithuanian artist Čiurlionis, this museum (M K Čiurlionio dailės muziejus) also offers an insight into the development of art in Lithuania. It is the country's biggest art gallery, with 335,000 exhibits. Artifacts from other cultures include pieces from ancient Egypt.

🏛 Devil's Museum

V Putvinskio 64. **Tel** (37) 221 587. **Open** Oct–May: 11am–5pm Tue–Sun; Jun–Sep: 10am–5pm Tue–Sun. 🅿 📷 🅿 📷

This museum's (Velnių muziejus) collection of representations of devils, demons and witches from Lithuania and around the world, was brought together by avid collector Antanas Žmuidzinavičius. A sculpture of Hitler and Stalin fighting over Lithuania in a pit of bones is grim, but most of the devils are shown with humour.

Kaunas Town Centre

① Old Town Hall
② Church of the Holy Trinity
③ Church of St George
④ Kaunas Castle
⑤ Cathedral of Sts Peter and Paul
⑥ Perkūnas House
⑦ Vytautas Church
⑧ Laisvės Aleja
⑨ Mykolas Žilinskas Art Gallery
⑩ M K Čiurlionis Art Museum
⑪ Devil's Museum

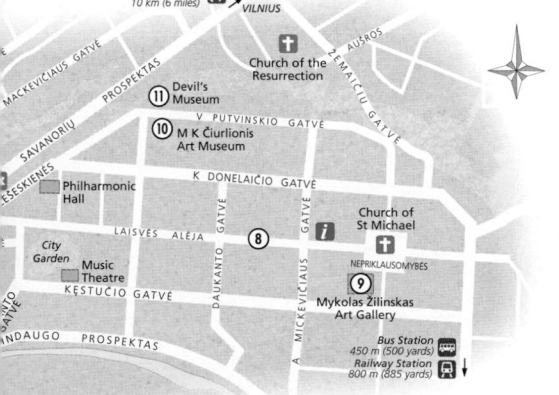

❻ Klaipėda

Founded in 1252 by the Livonian Order who built the city's first fortress, Klaipėda was the main trading port until 1629. The order named the city Memel after a river of the same name (Nemunas in Lithuanian). Briefly the capital of Prussia after the Napoleonic wars, Klaipėda remained an important port under Prussian control until World War I. However, in 1923, the Lithuanian Army claimed the city, renaming it Klaipėda. Despite serious damage during World War II and its status as a military-industrial centre during the Soviet years, this thriving city is Lithuania's third largest city and a major port today.

Cafés lining a pedestrian street in the Old Town

Ännchen of Tharau

Taravos anikė.

In front of the theatre in the **Theatre Square**, which is the heart of Klaipėda's Old Town, stands the statue *Ännchen of Tharau*. The statue is the focal point of the fountain dedicated to Simon Dach (1605–59), one of the city's eminent personalities. Born in Klaipėda, then known as Memel, Dach was a leading Prussian poet from the late 1630s until his death. He is well known throughout Germany for his songs, hymns and dialect poems. The statue was inspired by his poem *Ännchen of Tharau*, written in 1637.

The original statue, created in 1912, mysteriously vanished on the eve of World War II to make way for a statue of Adolf Hitler. On 23 March 1939, Hitler made a speech from the theatre balcony

Ännchen of Tharau in Theatre Square

behind its original location. In 1989, a replica of the original statue was placed in the middle of the fountain.

🏛 Castle Museum

Pilies 4. **Tel** (46) 313 323.
Open 10am–6pm Tue–Sat. 🅿

Housed in a 17th-century castle, this museum (Pilies muziejus) is one of modern Klaipėda's most recognized symbols. The castle was built on the foundations of the city's first fortress dating back to 1252. In 2002, an exhibition opened inside one of the ramparts, illustrating the development of the fortress and the city from the 13th to the 17th centuries. The exhibits include weapons, household articles, wooden tools and re-created models of the castle and the city in the 17th century.

A Renaissance-era gold ring encrusted with diamonds is the highlight here.

🏛 History Museum of Lithuania Minor

Didžioji vandens 6. **Tel** (46) 410 524.
Open 10am–6pm Tue–Sat. 🅿

Located inside one of the Old Town's loveliest buildings, this museum (Mažosios Lietuvos istorijos muziejus) paints an illuminating picture of the earliest inhabitants of the eastern region of Lithuania Minor. Coins, maps, clothes, old photographs and models give a glimpse of the lives of the local German- and Lithuanian-speaking communities before World War II. The highlight is a collection of photographs taken during Hitler's visit in 1939.

🏛 Blacksmiths' Museum

Šaltkalvių 2a. **Tel** (46) 410 526.
Open 10am–6pm Tue–Sat. 🅿 🅲

Black metal crosses, fences and cemetery gates are exhibited in a garden beside an old working smithy originally owned by Gustav Katzke, a metalwork artist of the early 20th century. Some of the crosses were rescued from destruction when the Sculpture Park replaced the city's main cemetery in the 1970s. Lithuania's cross-crafting tradition, in metal and in wood, was recognized by UNESCO in 2001.

Old wooden clock inside the Clock Museum

🏛 Clock Museum

Liepų 12. **Tel** (46) 410 413.
Open noon–5:30pm Tue–Sat, noon–4:30pm Sun. 🅿 🅲

From sundials to atomic clocks, this unique museum offers a fascinating insight into man's attempts to measure time. The

Clock Museum (Laikrodžių muziejus) was opened in 1984 inside a villa built in 1820 by John Simpson, an English merchant. Reconstructions of ancient calendars, sun, fire, water and sand clocks from around the world, and timepieces showing the changes in the faces and mechanisms of clocks dating back to the Renaissance, form the bulk of the exhibits.

The pleasant courtyard, featuring a large sundial, is a popular venue for music, dance and poetry evenings. The house next door was built by another English merchant, Mae Lean. In 1905, it was reconstructed in Art Nouveau style. The Neo-Gothic post office located close by is another striking building in the neighbourhood.

🏛 Picture Gallery and Sculpture Park

Liepų 33. **Tel** (46) 41 05 27. **Open** noon–6pm Tue–Sat, noon–5pm Sun. 🖼

The city's main state-run art gallery (Paveikslų galerija) is named after Pranas Domšaitis (1880–1965), a Lithuanian artist who was born near Königsberg and who settled in South Africa in 1949. Heavily influenced by the Norwegian Symbolist painter Edvard Munch, Domšaitis won recognition for his art in inter-war Germany and later in South Africa. The gallery exhibits 20th-century Lithuanian art as well as a permanent exhibition of works by Domšaitis.

Situated behind the gallery, the Sculpture Park (Skulptūrų parkas) is dedicated to Martynas Mažvydas (1510–63), the author of the first Lithuanian book. Until the 1970s, the site was reserved for the city's cemetery. Spread over nearly 10 ha (25 acres), the park is scattered with abstract and

intriguing sculptures by various artists, and new works are added to it each year.

Unique creations laid out in the Sculpture Park

Klaipėda Town Centre

① Ännchen of Tharau
② Castle Museum
③ History Museum of Lithuania Minor
④ Blacksmiths' Museum
⑤ Clock Museum
⑥ Picture Gallery and Sculpture Park

⑤ Curonian Spit National Park

Kuršių Nerijos Nacionalinis parkas

A narrow 98-km (61-mile) strip of land on the Baltic coast, the Curonian Spit was formed 5,000 years ago. Its landscape consists largely of pine forests, dunes and sandy beaches. The park's forests are rich in wildlife such as roe deer, elk, foxes and wild boars. The dunes that tower over the village of Nida fall like cliffs into the Curonian Lagoon. Entire villages have been buried beneath the shifting sands. The Curonian Spit National Park, covering most of the spit, was created in 1991 to preserve the dunes, lagoons and surrounding area, and has been a UNESCO World Heritage Site since 2000.

Key

🟥 Curonian Spit National Park

★ Nida
The highly characteristic red-and-blue fishermen's cottages in Nida have remained unchanged for centuries. Some old weather-beaten fishing boats lie in the gardens outside the cottages.

Baltic Beach
The entire length of the spit on the side of the Baltic Sea is one long sandy beach. Areas adjacent to the villages are popular in summer, but other parts are little visited. Throughout the spit, parking is allowed only at designated parking areas.

★ Parnidis Dune
Looming 52 m (171 ft) above Nida, Parnidis Dune offers great views and is one of the highest points on the spit. A sundial erected here in 1995 collapsed during a storm in 1999. Only a part of it has been reconstructed.

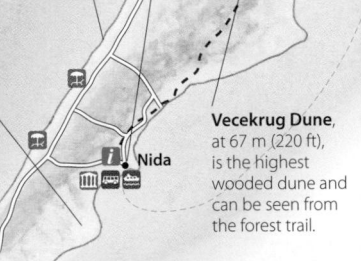

Vecekrug Dune, at 67 m (220 ft), is the highest wooded dune and can be seen from the forest trail.

For hotels and restaurants see p72 and p73

★ Hill of Witches
Comically demonic wooden statues lurk alongside a path through the pine forest behind Juodkrantė. The statues were set up by a group of local sculptors in the 1980s.

VISITORS' CHECKLIST

Practical Information
350 km (217 miles) W of Vilnius. Operators offer cruises in vessels, as well as in replicas of *kurėnas* (traditional fishing boats). Visitors can explore the Dead Dunes on the sightseeing trail of the Nagliai Natural Reserve. **i** Taikos 4, Nida, (469) 52 345. Bike rentals offered. **w** visitneringa.com

Transport
Naglių 18e, Nida, (469) 52 859. Naglių 14, Nida, (469) 51 101.

Dead Dunes
These once-shifting dunes are now held in place with vegetation and offer a sanctuary to birds, animals and plants. Apart from a scenic trail to the Naglių Dune, the area is out of bounds to visitors.

Forest Trails
It is possible to walk or cycle the entire length of the spit. The path takes visitors past isolated stretches of sandy beach and is lined with rich local flora.

Key
══ Main road
--- Trail
— — Ferry route

Juodkrantė

Nagliai Natural Reserve

Naglių Dune

ervalka

Shifting dunes

In the 17th century, when the Curonian Spit forests were cut down to fuel industry and constant military campaigns, the mountainous dunes were released. Carried by the Baltic winds, the sand started to shift up to 20 m (66 ft) a year in places, burying entire villages. It was only in the 19th century, when a vast number of trees were planted to reforest the area, that the moving dunes were stopped.

Parnidis Dune seen from the harbour at Nida

0 km   2
0 miles   2

For keys to symbols *see back flap*

Practical & Travel Information

After many years of being excluded from the tourist map of Europe, Lithuania is now drawing a large number of eager visitors. Tour operators are increasing in number and offer a great variety of packages to the region. Most airlines fly to Vilnius, which has direct connections with many European cities. Lithuania is not, however, covered by Eurail or InterRail, making travelling by train from Western Europe relatively expensive.

When to Visit

The best time to visit the country is from May to October, when the weather is generally pleasant and rarely cold. Nearly all the best festivals take place in summer, and some small museums and historic sights are only open between May and September. This is also the ideal time to explore the region's natural attractions, by visiting one of the many national parks or walking in the countryside. Autumn is often splendid in the Baltic States, but the weather can turn chilly as early as October.

Documentation

Citizens of EU member-states, the US, Canada, Australia and New Zealand can enter Lithuania for up to 90 days in a half-year period on presentation of a valid passport. Those wishing to stay beyond 90 days will need to apply for a national long-term visa or a residence permit.

Visitors from other countries should enquire about visa requirements at the relevant embassy or consulate before travelling. The official website of the Lithuanian Ministry of Foreign Affairs offers information on visa regulations. For detailed information on entry regulations and visa costs, visitors are advised to check the official website of the **European Commission**. EU citizens are not subject to customs regulations, provided they adhere to EU guidelines. All visitors should check for any customs duty or special permission required to export a cultural object before buying one.

Visitor Information

All cities and most major towns in Lithuania have a tourist information office, which is usually located in the town centre. The country's official tourism website lists all the tourist information centres across Lithuania. In the case of very small towns, the office may be situated in a museum or historic building. Tourist offices are usually open from 9am to 6pm on weekdays, but opening hours are more erratic in remote places and it is advisable to check in advance. Free brochures covering local and national sights are available at these offices. Lithuania also has tourist offices in London, Finland, Sweden and Russia.

Health and Security

Lithuania is generally a safe country to visit with instances of theft and mugging relatively rare. However, visitors should remain vigilant in Vilnius, particularly in and around the Old Town.

After years of underfunding *ligoninė* (Lithuanian hospitals) were in rather poor condition, although those in Kaunas and Vilnius have improved. Emergency treatment is free, but visitors should note that they will need to pay for medication and any subsequent medical treatment.

Facilities for the Disabled

Although there has been great improvement in recent years, Lithuania as a whole is not very well equipped in providing facilities for the disabled. The situation is best in Vilnius, where a large number of new buses and trolleybuses provide access for disabled people.

Banking and Currency

Banking hours in Lithuania vary, with branches operating from 8am to 5pm on weekdays. Banks in big trade centres are open on Saturdays from 8am to 3pm or 10am to 5pm. The national currency of Lithuania is the litas, which is usually abbreviated to Lt. One litas consists of 100 centai. However, from 1 Jan 2015, Lithuania is scheduled to adopt the Euro as the official currency. Foreign currency can be easily exchanged in banks or exchange bureaus. There is a wide network of ATMs across the country, most of which accept all major international credit and debit cards.

Communications

Lithuania has a highly developed communications network. Mobile phone usage is high and broadband Internet access is widespread. Public payphones only accept

The Climate of Lithuania

Lithuania has a temperate climate. The country usually gets its first snowfall in November. Winters are long, with temperatures dipping to -5° C (23° F). Summers generally last from mid-May to late August when temperatures average 18° C (64° F) in the capital city of Vilnius. Summer evenings are pleasant, with some short spells of rain.

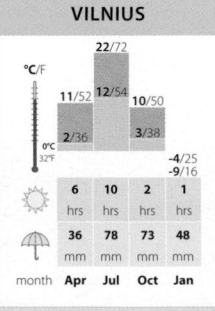

VILNIUS			
°C/F	22/72		
	11/52	12/54	10/50
	2/36		3/38
0°C 32°F			-4/25 -9/16
6 hrs	10 hrs	2 hrs	1 hrs
36 mm	78 mm	73 mm	48 mm
month Apr	Jul	Oct	Jan

taksofono kortelė (prepaid cards), which are available at newspaper kiosks and post offices. Mobile phone users can avoid roaming costs by using local SIM cards which are available at newspaper kiosks. *Paštas* (post offices) can be found almost everywhere in the country.

Arriving by Air

Lithuania is well connected to the rest of Europe and, via major European transport hubs such as London, Copenhagen and Amsterdam, to the rest of the world. Opened in 1944, **Vilnius Airport** is the arrival point for most flights. Services at the airport include car rental offices, currency exchange, cafés and newspaper kiosks, which also sell bus tickets.

Lithuania does not have a national carrier, although Latvia's **airBaltic** uses Vilnius airport as a hub. The airport is also used by about 15 other airlines, including **Lufthansa**, **Finnair**, **Czech Airlines** and **Austrian Airlines**. There are connections to almost all the capitals of Western Europe as well as many cities in former Soviet republics.

Kaunas Airport has a small number of scheduled international flights, and is served by low-cost operator **Ryanair** from the UK and Ireland. **Auracom** has information on airport bus services throughout the country.

Arriving by Sea

Lithuania's only commercial maritime harbour, **Klaipėda State Sea Port**, is linked by ferry to ports in Germany, Sweden and Denmark. There are connections to Kiel and Mukran in Germany, Copenhagen-Fredericia and Aabenraa-Aarhus in Denmark and Karlshamn in Sweden.

Rail Travel

The national rail network is run by **Lietuvos Geležinkeliai** (Lithuanian Railways). The main routes run from Vilnius to Šiauliai and Klaipėda; Vilnius to Visaginas, which passes Ignalina and Aukštaitija National Park; Šiauliai to Panevėžys and Rokiškis; and the speedy and regular Vilnius to Kaunas route. All train tickets must be purchased at the ticket desks in railway stations. At the larger railway stations it is possible to leave your baggage at the left luggage room for a small fee, or deposit the luggage in a self-service locker. Although the stations at Vilnius and Kaunas have been modernized, there is little emphasis on cleanliness and hygiene in other train stations.

Travelling by Bus

Lithuania has an extensive network of roads connecting the country to neighbouring countries and there are numerous crossing points, making it fairly simple to travel by bus to or from Estonia and Latvia. There are express passenger coaches from Vilnius to Rīga and Tallinn, as well as to other cities including Warsaw, Berlin, Prague, Vienna, Kaliningrad and Moscow. On the other hand, the journey from countries further west, such as Germany or the UK, is very long and the inconvenience is best avoided.

Travelling by Car

Roads in Lithuania are excellent by post-Soviet-era standards and present no special problems to drivers. There are no toll roads except through the Curonian Spit National Park.

Lithuanian regulations state that every car must carry a small fire extinguisher, a first-aid kit, a reflective warning triangle and reflective safety vest. It is mandatory for passengers to wear seat belts and motorists must use headlights at all times, both during the day and the night. The traffic police may not be able to speak fluent English but it can collect fines on the spot.

Driving while one is intoxicated is a punishable offence and local authorities sometimes use roadblocks and breath analyzer tests as enforcement tools.

DIRECTORY

Documentation

European Commission
w ec.europa.eu

Visitor Information

w tourism.lt

Embassies

Australia
Vilnius 23.
Tel (5) 212 3369.

Canada
Jogailos 4, Vilnius.
w canada.lt

United Kingdom
Antakalnio 2, Vilnius.
w britain.lt

United States
Akmenų 6, Vilnius.
w usembassy.lt

Emergency Numbers

Ambulance
Tel 03, 112.

Fire
Tel 01, 112.

Police
Tel 02, 112.

Arriving by Air

airBaltic
w airbaltic.com

Auracom
w airport-bus.lt

Austrian Airlines
w austrian.lt

Czech Airlines
w czechairlines.com

Finnair
w finnair.com

Kaunas Airport
Karmėlava, Kaunas.
w kaunas-airport.lt

Lufthansa
w lufthansa.com

RyanAir
w ryanair.com

Vilnius Airport
Raudūnios Kelias, Vilnius.
Tel (5) 273 9305.
w vilnius-airport.lt

Arriving by Sea

Klaipėda State Sea Port
w portofklaipeda.lt

Rail Travel

Lietuvos Geležinkeliai
w litrail.lt

Shopping & Entertainment

Souvenirs and gifts in Lithuania usually consist of traditional arts and handicrafts made from locally available materials such as amber, ceramic and wood. The shops and stalls of the Old Towns in the country's larger cities, as well as in the various resorts, are flooded with offerings of this kind. A variety of entertainment is on offer in Lithuania, although, outside Vilnius the options tend to be limited. Baroque and chamber music concerts are regularly performed in churches throughout the country.

Opening Hours

Most shops in city centres open at 10am and stay open until 7pm. Outside the city centre, shops remain open until 9pm or even 10pm. Food shops and supermarkets that are part of larger chains often open at 8am and close late in the evening. On Saturdays, many shops open until 4pm, and some in tourist areas and larger towns and cities are open on Sundays as well.

Markets

The most extraordinary market in Lithuania is **Gariūnai**, located next to Vilnius's towering water-heating facility. It sells everything from inexpensive clothes, shoes, toys, toiletries and cosmetics to food, gadgets and even cars. At the southern edge of the Old Town, near the bus and train stations, is **Halės Market**, which mostly stocks fresh fruit and vegetables, cheese, meat and cakes.

Traditional Crafts

Lithuanian craftsmen make all manner of objects out of wood; from handcarved spatulas and spoons to grotesque masks of devils and witches. A popular religious memento is the crucifix, which is commonly made out of wood. For the musically inclined, handcarved musical instruments, such as the alluring Lithuanian *kanklės*, or zither, make ideal gifts.

The most original items of clothing on offer are made of flax. Shirts and blouses, dresses and hand-crocheted hats are all widely available. The crafting of amber is an indisputable part of Lithuania's heritage and one to which its artisans apply great imagination. They fashion it into a wide range of objects, such as jewellery, lampshades and writing materials.

Black ceramics in the form of pots, jugs, cups and figures are among the specialities of the southern region of Lithuania, and are available throughout the country.

In Vilnius, traditional arts and crafts are most easily found along Pilies, Aušros Vartų and Didžioji streets. **Linen & Amber Studio**, a chain of gift shops, is one of the best places to find handicrafts made of flax and amber. For those interested in local textiles, a good destination is **Aukso Avis**. **Sauluva** stocks a reliable assortment of Lithuanian handicraft items made of wood, ceramic, amber and dried flowers.

Fine Art and Antiques

Vilnius offers an astonishing range of imaginative gift items in small art galleries such as **Rūtos Galerija**. Here quirky paintings, colourful plates designed with old photographs, vases with intricate patterns and decorative curios cover the gallery space. The **Artists' Union Exhibition Hall** has original artwork, hand-decorated cards and a fine range of Lithuanian and international art books, as well as works of the country's foremost sculptors, on display. The bohemian district of Užupis has a surfeit of art galleries, among which **Užupio Galerija**, selling metal and enamel pieces, is the most interesting.

Food and Drink

Traditional foods of all kinds are sold in Lithuanian shops, including *blynai* (a thin potato pancake with both sweet and savoury fillings), *spurgos* (doughnuts), smoked and steamed cheeses and a range of milk products. Smoked meats are usually sold as long, thick sausages or bound into balls. Forest berries and mushrooms can make unusual gifts, but visitors need customs clearance to carry them home. Some supermarkets have cafés offering a traditional Lithuanian meal of *cepelinai* (potato dumplings) as well as *kugelis* (baked potato pudding) and *vėdarai* (potato sausage).

Local favourites, such as *starka* (aged vodka), or *trejos devynerios* (herbal panacea), should not be missed. The best of the many varieties of *degtinė* (vodka) include Lithuania's excellent gold-topped vodkas, while the company Alita makes a popular brand of brandy. Švyturys Baltijos and the Švyturys Ekstra Draught are both very fine bottled beers.

Nightlife

Though a little quieter than other European capitals, Vilnius has an abundance of bars and clubs featuring a variety of music genres and both local and international DJs. The uproarious **Bix** is for heavy metal fans. A little more central are **Paparazzi**, popular for its friendly atmosphere and wide range of cocktails, and **Pabo Latino**, specializing in Latin beats. **Aula** hosts a number of live bands.

Club life is not limited to the capital. Klaipėda has an increasingly lively nightlife, with crowds flocking to the popular **Pabo Latino**. Some of the new bars in the Old Town even have casinos and restaurants. Kaunas has a mix of classy bars such as **Skliautai** in the Old Town and the hip and swinging club **Siena**, frequented by the young.

Theatre

Lithuanians are passionate about theatre. Productions by Oskaras Koršunovas and Eimuntas Nekrošius are highly recommended. The **Lithuanian National Drama Theatre** and the more avant-garde **State Small Theatre of Vilnius** provide pre-recorded English translations for some performances. The **Klaipėda State Drama Theatre**, which dates from 1819, is the most famous theatre outside Vilnius.

Live Music

With a small but fanatical following, jazz forms an inextricable part of the Lithuanian lifestyle. The **Holiday Inn Vilnius** hosts excellent jazz performances and both Vilnius and Kaunas have brilliant jazz festivals. **Kurpiai** in Klaipėda is best known for its jazz and blues concerts.

Several outstanding Lithuanian rock and pop performers play regularly at atmospheric venues such as **Tamsta Club**, **Brodvėjus** and the **Forum Palace** in Vilnius. International artistes tend to play at the modern **Siemens Arena** or the **Pramogų Arena**.

Folk festivals are often organized in the premises of Vilnius University.

Classical Music, Opera and Ballet

Vilnius has a good classical music scene. Both the **National Philharmonic** and the **Congress Palace** hold superb concerts. The innovative choreography of the **Anželika Cholina Dance Theatre** is popular with locals and visitors alike. The famous **National Opera & Ballet Theatre** is often packed to capacity. Theatres in Klaipėda and Kaunas organize regular classical music concerts and opera performances.

Music Festivals

Several music festivals have grown in popularity over the years. The magnificent Baroque Pažaislis Monastery complex, near Kaunas, forms the backdrop to the annual **Pažaislis Music Festival**. The **Edvard Grieg and M K Čiurlionis Festival**, hosted in Kaunas each spring, features classical music concerts. The **Muzikinis Pajūris** (Musical Seaside) festival of opera and symphony takes place every summer in Klaipėda.

DIRECTORY

Markets

Gariūnai
Vilnius–Kaunas Highway.

Halės Market
Pylimo and Bazilijonų street corner, Vilnius.

Traditional Crafts

Aukso Avis
Pilies 38, Vilnius.
Tel (5) 261 0421.

Linen & Amber Studio
Didžioji 5, Vilnius.
Tel (5) 262 4986.
W lgstudija.lt
(One of several branches).

Sauluva
Literatų 3, Vilnius.
Tel (8) 686 43906.
W sauluva.lt

Fine Art and Antiques

Artists' Union Exhibition Hall
Vokiečių 4/2, Vilnius.
Tel (5) 261 9516.
W galerija-lds.lt

Rūtos Galerija
Pranciškonų gatvė 8, Vilnius.
Tel (8) 685 80080.

Užupio Galerija
Užupio 3–I, Vilnius.
Tel (5) 231 2318.

Nightlife

Aula
Pilies 11, Vilnius.
Tel (5) 268 7173.

Bix
Etmonų 6, Vilnius.
Tel (5) 262 7791.

Pabo Latino
Trakų 3, Vilnius.
Tel (5) 262 1045.
Žvejų 4, Klaipėda.
Tel (46) 403 040.

Paparazzi
Totorių 1, Vilnius.
Tel (5) 212 0135.

Siena
Laisvės 93, Kaunas.
Tel (37) 424 424.

Skliautai
Aušros Vartų 11, Kaunas.
Tel (37) 411 955.

Theatre

Klaipėda State Drama Theatre
Manto 45, Klaipėda.
Tel (46) 314 453.
W kldteatras.lt

Lithuanian National Drama Theatre
Gedimino 4, Vilnius.
Tel (5) 262 1593.
W teatras.lt

State Small Theatre of Vilnius
Gedimino 22, Vilnius.
Tel (5) 249 9869.
W vmt.lt

Live Music

Brodvėjus
Vokiečių 4, Vilnius.
Tel (8) 652 57790.
W brodvejus.lt

Forum Palace
Konstitucijos 26, Vilnius.
Tel (5) 263 6666.
W forumpalace.lt

Holiday Inn Vilnius
Šeimyniškių 1, Vilnius.
Tel (5) 210 3000.
W holidayInnvilnius.lt

Kurpiai
Kurpių 1a, Klaipėda.
Tel (46) 410 555.

Pramogų Arena
Ažuolyno 9, Vilnius.
Tel (5) 242 4444.

Siemens Arena
Ozo 14, Vilnius.
Tel (5) 247 7576.
W siemens-arena.lt

Tamsta Club
Subačiaus 11, Vilnius.
Tel (5) 212 4498.
W tamstaclub.lt

Classical Music, Opera and Ballet

Anželika Cholina Dance Theatre
Šimulionio 4–103, Vilnius.
Tel (5) 6883 4181.

Congress Palace
Vilnius 6–14, Vilnius.
Tel (5) 261 8828.7.

National Opera & Ballet Theatre
Vienuolio 1, Vilnius.
Tel (5) 262 0727.

National Philharmonic
Aušros Vartų 5, Vilnius.
Tel (5) 266 5216.
W filharmonija.lt

Music Festivals

Edvard Grieg and M K Čiurlionis Festival
W kaunofilharmonija.lt

Muzikinis Pajūris
W muzikinis-teatras.lt

Pažaislis Music Festival
W pazaislis.lt

Where to Stay

Vilnius

Grybų Namai Ⓛⓣ
B&B **Map** D5
Aušros Vartų 3a, 01129
Tel *(5) 261 9695*
W grybashouse.com
Located near the Gates of Dawn, this is a family-run B&B in a lovely old house with vintage design touches. Fully equipped rooms with free Wi-Fi.

Litinterp Ⓛⓣ
B&B **Map** E3
Bernardinų 7, 01124
Tel *(5) 212 3850*
W litinterp.com
An excellent bargain with small but comfortable rooms in a typical Old Town alley setting. Breakfast delivered to the door.

DK Choice

Apia ⓁⓉⓁⓉ
B&B **Map** D3
Šv. Ignoto 12, 01144
Tel *(5) 212 3426*
W apia.lt
A charming B&B in a prime Old Town location, Apia has 11 individually decorated rooms done-up in warm and soothing colours, plenty of natural wood surfaces and a subtle mixture of rustic, vintage and contemporary furnishings. Top-floor rooms are atmospheric with sharply sloping attic ceilings.

Domus Maria ⓁⓉⓁⓉ
B&B **Map** D5
Aušros vartų 12, 01129
Tel *(5) 264 4880*
W domusmaria.lt
A complex of church buildings, beautifully converted into fully equipped suites with high ceilings. Centrally located in the Old Town.

Dvaras ⓁⓉⓁⓉ
Luxury **Map** D2
Tilto 3/1, 01101
Tel *(5) 210 7370*
W dvaras.lt
Located close to the Cathedral, this classy guesthouse with country-styled interiors features wooden floors and rustic textiles.

Narutis ⓁⓉⓁⓉⓁⓉ
Historic **Map** E3
Pilies 24, 01123
Tel *(5) 212 2894*
W narutis.com

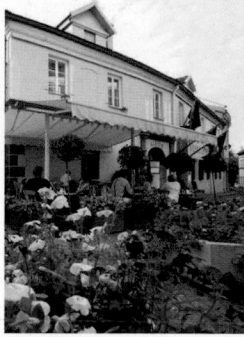

Visitors relax on the porch of Stikliai in Vilnius

Historic Old Town building with contemporary touches added to its original Gothic features. Elegantly furnished rooms.

Radisson Blu Astoria ⓁⓉⓁⓉⓁⓉ
Luxury **Map** D4
Didžioji 35/2, 01128
Tel *(5) 212 0110*
W radissonblu.com
Housed in an Old Town building that was once a bank, plush Astoria with its Art-Deco features, offers some of the finest accommodation in the city.

Stikliai ⓁⓉⓁⓉⓁⓉ
Luxury **Map** D4
Gaono 7, 01131
Tel *(5) 264 9595*
W stikliaihotel.lt
This opulent five-star hotel on a characterful Old Town street, boasts beautifully furnished rooms and attentive service.

Rest of Lithuania

CURONIAN SPIT: Ąžuolynas Ⓛⓣ
Resort
L Rėzos 54, Juodkrantė, 93101
Tel *(469) 53 310*
W hotelazuolynas.lt
This lagoon-facing resort hotel with neat en suites, also has tennis courts, a swimming pool, waterslide and fitness centre.

CURONIAN SPIT: Vila Banga ⓁⓉⓁⓉ
B&B
Pamario 2, Nida, 93124
Tel *(469) 51 139*
W nidosbanga.lt
Rooms that blend rustic ambience with modern facilities: this B&B, located close to the lagoon shore, is a fisherman's cottage with a traditional thatched roof.

Price Guide
Prices are based on one night's stay in high season for a standard double room, inclusive of service charges and taxes.

Ⓛⓣ	under 250 Lt
ⓁⓉⓁⓉ	250–500 Lt
ⓁⓉⓁⓉⓁⓉ	over 500 Lt

KAUNAS: Best Western Santakos ⓁⓉⓁⓉ
Historic
Gruodžio 21, 44293
Tel *(37) 302 702*
W santakahotel.eu
Set in an elegant, red-brick building in the Old Town, this hotel has plush rooms, a good restaurant, indoor pool and excellent service.

KAUNAS: Daugirdas ⓁⓉⓁⓉⓁⓉ
Luxury
Daugirdo 4, 44279
Tel *(37) 301 561*
W daugirdas.lt
A mix of modern and original red-brick Gothic architecture, this business hotel tastefully blends atmosphere and style.

KLAIPĖDA: Old Mill Hotel ⓁⓉⓁⓉ
Design
Žvejų 22, 91241
Tel *(46) 219 215*
W oldmillhotel.lt
Combining glass surfaces with traditional brick and timber, this hotel, located next to the swing bridge in the Old Port area, offers smart, modern rooms.

KLAIPĖDA: Radisson Blu ⓁⓉⓁⓉⓁⓉ
Luxury
Šiaulių 28, 92231
Tel *(46) 490 800*
W radissonblu.com/hotel-klaipeda
With rooms decorated in maritime style, the hotel offers a vast range of facilities including a fitness and wellness centre. Excellent service.

TRAKAI: Akmeninė Rezidencija ⓁⓉⓁⓉ
Resort
Bražuolės village, 21100
Tel *698 30 544*
W akmeninerezidencija.lt
Rustic-style getaway comprising five hotels and five apartments in cottages built in traditional style and set around a small lake. Saunas and restaurant also on site.

Where to Eat and Drink

Vilnius

Marceliukės Klėtis Ⓛ
Lithuanian
Tuskulėnų 35
Tel *(5) 272 5087*
Good place to try real Lithuanian fare such as *cepelinai* (meat-stuffed potato dumplings) and other staples. The menu gives dishes humourous titles.

DK Choice

Vieta Ⓛ
Vegetarian **Map** D3
Šv Ignoto 12
Tel *607 13 990* **Closed** *Sun*
An informal, vegetarian restaurant, 'The Place', offers creative cooking in a homely café environment. Its great value-for-money menus are chalked up daily based on fresh and seasonal availability. The only danger is of portions running out before the end of the evening. Fresh-juice cocktails and soya milk shakes are particularly good and there is a full choice of alcoholic drinks.

In Vino Ⓛ Ⓛ
International **Map** D5
Aušros Vartų 7, 01013
Tel *(5) 212 1210*
Popular wine bar with courtyard seating and Mediterranean tapas and soups of the day; many of these make for a perfect vegetarian lunch option too.

Sonnets Ⓛ Ⓛ
International **Map** E3
Bernardinų 8/8
Tel *(5) 266 5885*
Fine dining option in the snug bar-restaurant of the Shakespeare Hotel. Creative selection of French, Russian and Mediterranean cuisine. Impressive wine list.

Balzac Ⓛ Ⓛ Ⓛ
French **Map** D4
Savičiaus 7, 01127
Tel *614 89 223*
Unpretentious but classy French bistro offering a good balance of meat and seafood. Menu spans from highly affordable soups to deservedly expensive duck and game.

Brasserie de Verres en Vers Ⓛ Ⓛ Ⓛ
French **Map** D4
Didžioji 35/2
Tel *(5) 236 0840*

This elegant spot in the Astoria Hotel offers classic European and French cuisine with seafood well represented. The glass-enclosed terrace is great for people-watching.

Medininkai Ⓛ Ⓛ Ⓛ
International **Map** D5
Aušros Vartų 8, 01013
Tel *600 86 491*
The evocative brick-cellar-look and attractive courtyard provide the perfect ambience to enjoy the classic European cuisine served here with panache. Good wine list.

Sue's Indian Raja Ⓛ Ⓛ Ⓛ
Indian **Map** D3
Odminių 3, 01122
Tel *(5) 266 1888*
Long-standing Vilnius institution serving classy Indian food in elegant surroundings. The extensive menu covers pretty much everything in the genre, including seafood and vegetarian dishes.

Rest of Lithuania

CURONIAN SPIT: Kuršis Ⓛ
Lithuanian
Naglių 29, Nida
Tel *612 18 868*
Unpretentious place that serves consistently reliable Lithuanian food, including locally caught smoked fish, roast pike-perch, *šaltibarščiai* (cold beetroot soup) and potato pancakes.

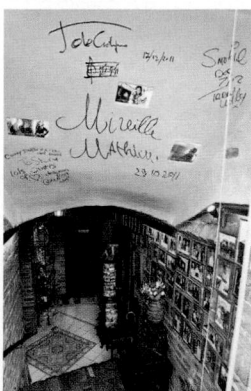

Warm and inviting interiors of Stora Antis, Klaipėda

CURONIAN SPIT: Vela Bianca Ⓛ Ⓛ
Italian
Rėzos 10, Juodkrantė
Tel *690 06 544*
Excellent Italian cuisine, including delicious desserts and an outstanding wine list, served in a glass-walled pavilion situated on the harbour front.

KAUNAS: Bernelių Užeiga Ⓛ Ⓛ
Lithuanian
Valančiaus 9
Tel *(37) 200 913*
Enjoy generous helpings of local Lithuanian fare served in this 18th-century building. Household knick-knacks used as decor to recreate the atmosphere of a traditional village tavern.

KAUNAS: Skliautas Ⓛ Ⓛ
Central European
Rotušės 26
Tel *(37) 206 843*
In an alley just off the main square this cult café with a natty clientele, serves a full menu of Lithuanian-Central European dishes, with plentiful soups and salads.

KLAIPĖDA: Ararat Ⓛ Ⓛ
Armenian
Liepų 48a
Tel *(46) 410 001*
The classy Armenian cuisine served in elegant dining rooms includes succulent grilled meats and delectable desserts. Do sample the Armenian wines and cognac.

KLAIPĖDA: Stora Antis Ⓛ Ⓛ
Central European
Tiltų 6
Tel *(46) 493 910*
Enjoy Lithuanian dumplings, Central European meat and fish dishes and famously delicious soups in this barrel-vault cellar, filled with household bric-a-brac.

TRAKAI: Senoji Kibininė Ⓛ
Lithuanian
Karaimų 65
Tel *(528) 55 865*
This wooden house is famous for its two Trakai specialities: *kibinai* (pasties stuffed with meat, usually lamb) and *čenakai* (stewed cabbage hotpot).

LATVIA

Lying between Lithuania and Estonia, Latvia is characterized by delightful forests and lakes, fascinating historical towns and dynamic cities, which are, by and large, under-explored. By contrast, the country's exciting capital, Rīga, draws hordes of Western Europeans all year round. The largest city in the Baltic region, Rīga revels in its cultural treasures and hedonistic nightlife.

Latvia's strategic geographical position prompted its more powerful neighbours to gain control over the region and largely decided the course of its history. A short period of self-determination in the early 20th century ended with occupation first by Nazi Germany and then twice by Soviet Russia. Independence was not restored until 1991. Nonetheless, a distinctive Latvian culture survived, assimilating foreign influences and still retaining a strong connection with nature. While still coming to terms with the legacies of the 20th century, today the country has a new confidence. Its historic cities have been restored, while rural areas are being developed for ecotourism.

History

Latvia's history is traditionally considered to begin with the advent of the Teutonic knights in 1201. Looking for conquests and converts in a pagan land, these German warrior-monks conquered Latvia and founded Rīga, which grew into an important centre for trade between the Baltic region and Western Europe. The beneficiaries of this growth were the Germans, while the Latvians were dispossessed and forced to become serfs.

The early 16th century saw Protestantism declared as the state religion. However, in 1561, Catholicism was established when Poland conquered Latvia during the Livonian Wars. The clash between the Protestant Swedes and Catholic Poles resulted in Swedish rule in northern Latvia for much of the 17th century. In 1710, during the Great Northern War, the Swedes surrendered Rīga to Peter the Great of Russia, ushering in 200 years of stability.

Bank of the Gauja river below Eagle Cliff, Gauja National Park

◀ Dutch Renaissance façade of the House of Blackheads, Rīga's Old Town

Independence Day celebrations, Rīga, 1933

When World War I broke out in 1914, Latvia became the main battleground between Germany and Russia. The Allied victory in 1918 forced the German troops to withdraw and Latvia was declared an independent nation. Despite the constantly changing governments that ruled until 1934, much was achieved during this period of independence. However, progress came to a halt with the Soviet invasion on 17 June 1940, which saw Latvians of influence either executed or deported to Siberia. The Germans invaded a year later, with brutal consequences for the Jewish community. The Soviets returned to eastern Latvia and Rīga as "liberators" in the autumn of 1944. Further deportations were carried out, and Russian numbers swelled, posing a serious threat to Latvian culture.

In 1988, new political groups began to emerge. The most forceful of these, the Popular Front of Latvia (PLF), demanded full independence and won the elections in 1990, provoking clashes with Soviet forces. Moscow's conservative Communists staged a coup against President Mikhail Gorbachev in August 1991, but it collapsed and Latvia finally found itself free. Since then governments have come and gone, but the beginning of the 21st century saw the effective integration of Latvia into Western Europe, particularly with its entry into the EU and NATO in 2004.

KEY DATES IN LATVIAN HISTORY

AD 1201 Rīga founded by Albrecht of Buxhoeveden

1282 Rīga joins a trading confederation of German port cities and merchants' associations

1372 German replaces Latin as official language

1561 Latvia occupied by Poland

1629 Sweden colonizes Latvia

1710 Rīga conquered by Peter the Great of Russia

1822 First Latvian newspaper printed

1850s National Awakening Movement formed

1905 Socialist revolution demands independence

1915 German troops enter Latvia

1918 Formal declaration of Latvian independence

1920 The Soviet Union recognizes Latvia's independence

1940 First Soviet occupation of Latvia

1941 Occupation by Nazi Germany

1944–91 Second Soviet occupation of Latvia

1988 Pro-independence Popular Front is formed

1989 Baltic Way demonstratation occured

1991 Latvian independence re-established

2004 Latvia joins NATO and the EU

2007 Valdis Zatlers sworn in as president

2014 Rīga is the European capital of culture

Language and Culture

Latvian is the official language of the people, although a sizeable Russian-speaking minority also exists.

Echoes of Latvia's pagan past remain to this day, most obviously in the celebration of Midsummer. The Latvian calendar is punctuated by festivities which mark the passing of seasons; many folk rituals are incorporated into Christian celebrations.

Exploring Latvia

Latvia is extremely visitor friendly. At its heart lies Rīga, the largest and most cosmopolitan city in the Baltic States. Strategically positioned on the Gulf of Rīga, it has a long history as a thriving mercantile centre. Beyond the capital, western Latvia enchants with its contrasts – dense forests and fertile plains, lively cities such as Liepāja and sleepy rural towns. Eastern Latvia, meanwhile, boasts some of the country's most popular attractions, such as the Gauja National Park. Most places of interest are connected by regular trains and buses, although public transport is less reliable for getting off the beaten track. Renting a vehicle is a good way to get around the country on a short trip.

Boats moored at a sailing club, Jūrmala

Key

— Motorway
— Major road
— Railway
-- International border

The Marble Hall in Rundāle Palace

0 km ———— 50
0 miles ———— 50

Sights at a Glance

1 Rīga pp78–85
2 Jūrmala
3 Kuldīga
4 Liepāja
5 Rundāle Palace pp88–9
6 Sigulda
7 Gauja National Park pp90–91
8 Cēsis

For keys to symbols see back flap

❶ Rīga

For many centuries Rīga was largely contained within the city walls on the bank of the Daugava river. Now known as the Old Town, this area contains most of the city's sites of interest. The main route through the tangle of picturesque streets and squares is Kaļķu iela, leading from the Stone Bridge (Akmens tilts) to Brīvības bulvāris and the Freedom Monument. When the city walls were removed in the mid-19th century, the space was developed into a ring of boulevards and parks. The main train and bus stations lie on the southeastern edge of this ring. To the north is the late 19th- and 20th-century extension of the city known as the Centre (Centrs), which includes some of Rīga's most impressive Art Nouveau architecture. Today the city is home to about 700,000 residents.

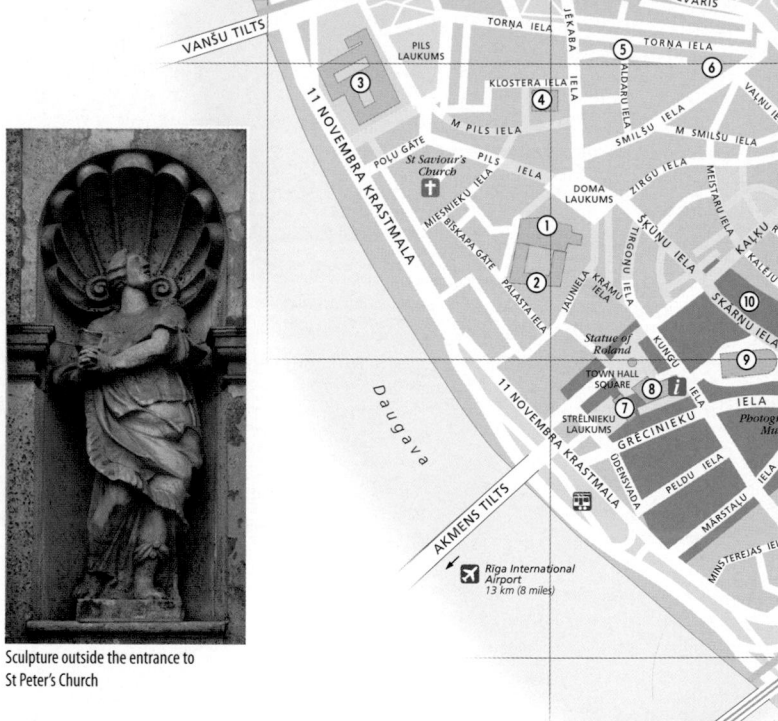

Sculpture outside the entrance to St Peter's Church

Getting Around

The best way to get around the Old Town is on foot: parking is expensive and there is no public transport available. The main Art Nouveau district is within walking distance of the Old Town, while a network of trams, trolleybuses and buses provides access to far-flung attractions. Taxis are also abundant on Town Hall Square (Rātslaukums). The main tourist information office here can offer advice on guided tours.

Greater Riga

Kiš́ecers

P1

Priedaine

Rīga

A10

A5

Riga International
Airport

0 km   5

0 miles   5

A7

A2

(12)

Lake
Jugla

P4

Ūlupji

Ulbroka

Daugava

A8   A7   A6

Baloži

Key

Area of the main map

ALDEMĀRA IELA

DZIRNAVU IELA

ELIZABETES

SKOLAS IELA

(11)

BAZNĪCAS IELA

IELA

ESPLANĀDE

BRĪVĪBAS GATVE

DZIRNAVU IELA

PAKA BULVĀRIS

Orthodox
Cathedral

BRĪVĪBAS BULVĀRIS

TĒRBATAS IELA

ELIZABETES IELA

LVĀRIS

VĒRMANES
PARK

MERĶELA IELA

Freedom
Monument

ĪVĪBAS BULVĀRIS

RAIŅA BULVĀRIS

K. BARONA IELA

ASPAZIJAS BULVĀRIS

IEKU

TRA IELA

RIDZENES IELA

VAĻŅU IELA

JU IELA

ĒJU IELA

Rīga Central
Railway Station
100 m (110 yards)

JU IELA

Autoosta
(Main Bus Station)
300 m (330 yards)

JANVĀRA IELA

Key

Street-by-Street area: *see pp82–3*

Major sight / Place of interest

Pedestrian street

Major Road

Railway

0 metres   200

0 yards   200

Sights at a Glance

① Dome Cathedral

② Museum of Rīga's History
  and Navigation

③ Rīga Castle

④ St James's Cathedral

⑤ Swedish Gate

⑥ Powder Tower

⑦ Museum of the Occupation
  of Latvia

⑧ House of Blackheads

⑨ St Peter's Church

⑩ Museum of Decorative Arts
  and Design

⑪ Museum of Jews in Latvia

⑫ Latvian Ethnographic
  Open-Air Museum

D   E   F

For keys to symbols *see back flap*

Impressive cross-vaulted gallery of the Dome Cathedral

① Dome Cathedral
Doma baznīca

Doma laukums 1. **Map** B3. **Tel** 6722 7573. **Open** May–Sep: 9am–6pm Sat–Tue, Thu, 9am–5pm Wed & Fri; Oct–Apr: 10am–5pm daily. **Closed** for special events. 🎧 🏛 10am Sun. **W** doms.lv

Founded as St Mary's by Bishop Albert von Buxhoeveden in 1211, the cathedral became one of the city's three seats of power along with the Town Hall and Rīga Castle. It gained its current name from the German word *dom* (cathedral) during the Reformation. The cathedral looks as if it has sunk, but in fact the land around it has been raised to keep out flood-water from the Daugava river.

One of the largest places of worship in the region, the cathedral has been altered over the years and its bulky structure exhibits a variety of styles. The altar alcove and the east wing crossing are Romanesque, with a cross-vaulted ceiling and rows of semi-circular windows. Simpler Neo-Gothic additions are characterized by pointed arches, large windows and lierne vaulting, while the eastern pediment and the steeple are in 18th-century Baroque style. The portal was added in the 19th century, followed by an Art Nouveau vestibule in the 20th century. Most of the interior's decor was destroyed during the Reformation, and it is now very

plain, except for the tombs of merchants and the 19th-century stained glass. The woodwork of the 17th-century pulpit is ornate, however, as is the organ case, which is Mannerist with Baroque and Rococo additions. The organ was built in Germany in 1884. In the summer it is possible to visit the cross-vaulted gallery of the Dome, the Romanesque cloister and courtyard.

② Museum of Rīga's History and Navigation
Rīga's vēstures un kuģniecības muzejs

Palasta iela 4. **Map** B3. **Tel** 6721 1358. **Open** May–Sep: 10am–5pm daily; Oct–Apr: 11am–5pm Wed–Sun. 🎧 🛇 **W** rigamuz.lv

Founded in 1773, this museum is the oldest in Rīga. Housed in an impressive building with tiled stoves and stained-glass windows, it is also one of the city's most interesting museums. The exhibition on navigation covers the maritime history of the city up until World War I, and includes several large models of ships and material on Krišjānis Valdemārs (1825–91), a key figure of the Latvian National Awakening. Other rooms cover everything from prehistory to independence, with an emphasis on the mid-19th to mid-20th centuries.

Model ship at the Museum of Rīga's History and Navigation

Highlights from the Middle Ages include the Madonna on a Crescent Moon, a sculpture of the patroness of the Great Guild (a union of Rīga merchants), which was taken to Germany during World War II and Big Kristaps, a large 16th-century statue of St Christopher.

③ Rīga Castle
Rīgas pils

Pils laukums 3. **Map** B3. Museum of Foreign Art: **Tel** 6722 6467. **Open** 11am–5pm Tue–Sun. 🎧 🛇 **W** vmm.lv
History Museum of Latvia: **Tel** 6722 1357. **Open** 11am–5pm Wed–Sun. 🎧 🛇

The city's original Livonian Order castle was destroyed by Rīga's citizens during a war against the Order lasting from 1297 to 1330. After losing, the townspeople were forced to build a new castle on the present site just outside the city. Continuing quarrels resulted in the Master of the Order leaving the capital, but Rīga Castle was destroyed by the citizens once more in 1484. They were defeated again and the next castle the townspeople were compelled to build forms the core of the current structure and was the headquarters of the Livonian Order until 1561. As well as being the official residence of Latvia's president, the building also earlier housed the **History Museum of Latvia** (Latvijas

Changing of the guard outside Rīga Castle in the Old Town

For hotels and restaurants see p96 and p97

vēstures muzejs), which featured religious sculpture, traditional regional costumes and consumer goods from the first period of independence in 1920. The **Museum of Foreign Art** (Ārzemju mākslas muzejs), which displays copies of Egyptian and Greek statues and has a collection of paintings was also part of the castle. However, an accidental fire in June 2013 destroyed the roof of the castle and it has been closed for renovation. Due to the ongoing reconstruction, the **History Museum of Latvia** has moved to Brivibas boulevard 32 while the **Museum of Foreign Art** has shifted to the Art Museum Rīga Bourse.

Entrance to the 13th-century St James's Cathedral

④ St James's Cathedral
Šv Jēkaba katedrāle

Jekaba iela 9. **Map** B3. **Tel** 6732 6419. **Open** Nov–Apr: 7am–6pm; May–Oct: 7am–7pm. 🕆 daily.

Sited outside the old city walls, St James's was built in 1225 to serve the surrounding villages. The church was renowned for having its bell hanging from a cupola, which is still visible on the southern side, although the bell has gone. It was rung to signal that an execution was taking place in the city, although another story insists that it was heard when unfaithful women passed by the church. The structure has been renovated several times and, today it is the seat of Rīga's Catholic archbishop.

⑤ Swedish Gate
Zviedru vārti

Between Torņa iela & Aldaru iela. **Map** C2.

The sole remnant of eight city gates, the Swedish Gate was built in 1698 during a period of Swedish rule in Rīga. It runs through the ground floor of the house at Torņa 11, and legend has it that the gate was created illegally by a wealthy merchant to give him direct access to his warehouse. More likely, it was built for the use of soldiers stationed at St James's Barracks. Today, the gate provides access between the popular strip of shops and bars on Torņa iela and the quieter, but pleasant, Aldaru iela. Newly-married couples include the gate on their tour of the city, as passing through it is said to bring good luck.

⑥ Powder Tower
Pulvertornis

Smilšu iela 20. **Map** C3. **Tel** 6722 8147. **Open** May–Sep: 10am–6pm Wed–Sun; Oct–Apr: 10am–5pm Wed–Sun. 🎨 donations. 📷 🅦 **karamuzejs.lv**

The cylindrical Powder Tower is all that remains from a total of 18 towers that were once part of the city's defences. Its 14th-century foundations are among the oldest in the city, but the rest of the structure dates from 1650, when it was rebuilt after being destroyed by the Swedish Army in 1621. The 2.5-m- (8-ft-) thick walls were intended to protect the gunpowder stored inside, after which the tower was named. Nine Russian cannonballs remain embedded in the walls as proof of its strength.

The tower was bought by a German student fraternity at the end of the 19th century, and in 1919, it housed a military museum reflecting on the then-recent fight for independence as well as on World War I. The annexe building was constructed from 1937 to 1940, but the Soviet occupation meant that it did not fulfil its function until several decades

Swedish Gate, built through the ground floor of an old house

later. From 1957, the tower housed the Museum of the Revolution in the Soviet Republic of Latvia.

The tower and the annexe are now home to the **Latvian War Museum** (Latvijas Kara muzejs). While the oldest exhibit – part of a cannon discovered during the 1930s – dates from the 15th century, the museum concentrates on 20th-century warfare. World War I is covered with displays of weapons, uniforms and propaganda posters.

Other rooms examine the role of Latvians in the Russian Revolution, the Latvian War of Independence, World War II and the Soviet occupation. Recent additions include a collection of 360 models of military machinery.

The Powder Tower, home to the Latvian War Museum, Rīga

Street-by-Street: Around Town Hall Square

Until a local government reform in 1877, the Town Hall Square (Rātslaukums) was Rīga's administrative centre. Built in 1334, the Town Hall was one of three pillars of power alongside Dome Cathedral and Rīga Castle, representing the interests of the city's residents. The square functioned as a marketplace and a site where festivals were held and executions carried out. The impressive step-gabled House of Blackheads has been completely rebuilt, while the Town Hall is a modern building behind a Neo-Classical façade. At the square's edge is a Soviet-era building housing the Museum of the Occupation of Latvia.

A roadside café in summer in the courtyard of St John's Church

Key

— Suggested route

Town Hall

Town Hall Square
Many of the square's elaborate buildings, destroyed by the Russians after World War II, have benefited from a restoration project tied to the city's 800th anniversary in 2001.

KAĻĶU IELA

KAĻĶU IELA

GRĒCINIEKU IELA

Statue of Roland
A legendary medieval figure and one of Charlemagne's knights, Roland became a symbol of the independence of cities from the local nobility.

Museum of the Occupation of Latvia

⑧ ★ **House of Blackheads**
Damaged by bombing in 1941, the ornate building was restored to its former glory during the 1990s.

⑦ ★ Museum of the Occupation of Latvia
This incongruous slab of concrete houses a chilling and detailed testament to the suffering of Latvians during the Soviet and Nazi occupations in the 20th century.

Konventa Sēta
The Convent Courtyard has been renovated and is now home to shops, galleries and a porcelain museum.

0 metres   100
0 yards   100

St John's Church

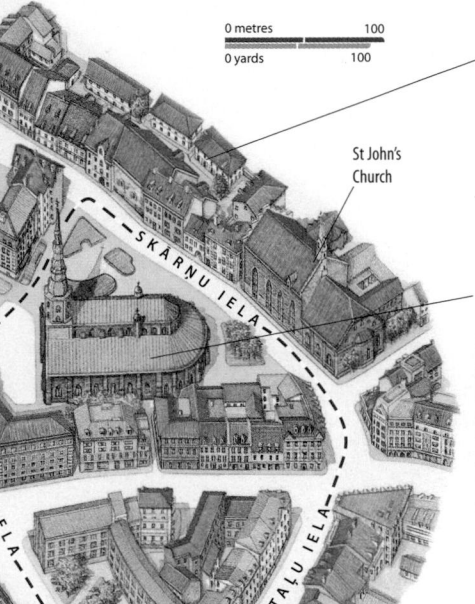

SKARŅU IELA

ŅU IELA

MĀRSTAĻU IELA

⑨ ★ St Peter's Church
This striking building has been destroyed and rebuilt several times over since its original 13th-century incarnation.

Photography Museum traces the development of photography from 1839 to 1941 through photographs and camera equipment.

Mentzendorff House
Constructed in 1695 to house an apothecary, this building is now a museum devoted to the life of Rīga's merchant class in the 17th and 18th centuries.

Dannenstern House
was the largest dwelling in 17th-century Rīga.

Textile artwork on display at the Museum of Decorative Arts and Design

⑦ Museum of the Occupation of Latvia
Latvijas okupācijas muzejs

Strēlnieku laukums 1. **Map** C4. **Tel** 6721 2715. **Open** May–Sep: 11am–6pm daily; Oct–Apr: 11am–5pm Tue–Sun. 🖼 donations. 🖼 🖼 **w** occupationmuseum.lv

This Soviet-era structure was built to house a museum in honour of the Latvian Riflemen, but since 1993 it has provided an account of the suffering of Latvians at the hands of Nazi Germany in World War II and under the Soviets. The collection includes eyewitness accounts and photographs of deportations and political represssion.

Temporary exhibitions are showcased at Raiņa bulvāris 7.

⑧ House of Blackheads
Melngalvju nams

Rātslaukums 6. **Map** C4. **Tel** 6704 4300. 🛈 Schwab House. **Open** 11am–5pm Tue–Sun. 🖼 🖼 🖼 🖼

The House of Blackheads was originally built in 1334 for the city's guilds, after the Livonian Order seized the existing guild buildings. Over time, a guild of unmarried foreign merchants, the Blackheads, became the sole occupants. Their name derives from their patron, St Maurice, and they were known for their riotous parties. The building was devastated by bombing in 1941 and the Soviet authorities demolished the remnants seven years later; the current structure

dates from 1999. Rooms that are open to the public include the Grand Hall and a concert hall.

⑨ St Peter's Church
Pēterbaznīca

Skārņu iela 19. **Map** C4. **Tel** 6722 9426. **Open** 10am–6pm Tue–Sun. 🖼 tower only. 🖼 except tower.

First mentioned in 1209, St Peter's Church was largely built by the Livs, Finnic people who settled along the Gulf of Rīga some 5,000 years ago. Sadly, none of the original wooden church remains, although parts of the walls date from the 13th century. The church, which had become Lutheran in 1523, was damaged by fire in 1721, when Peter the Great is said to have headed the failed efforts to rescue it. The church's steeple has been rebuilt many times. Reaching a height of 123 m (403 ft), it provides excellent views across the city.

Stone figure outside the entrance of St Peter's Church

⑩ Museum of Decorative Arts and Design
Dekoratīvās mākslas un dizaina muzejs

Skārņu iela 10/20. **Map** C3. **Tel** 6722 7833. **Open** 11am–5pm Tue–Sun. 🖼 🖼 🖼 **w** dlmm.lv

This museum is housed in the former St George's Church, Rīga's oldest surviving stone building. It was constructed as the chapel for Rīga's original Livonian Order castle in 1208, and became a separate church after the castle was destroyed in 1297. After the Reformation it was used as a warehouse.

The museum gives an overview of decorative arts from the 1890s to the present day. The ground floor hosts temporary exhibitions, while the first floor, covering the 1890s to the 1960s, is the most interesting part of the main collection. Highlights include a vast selection of painted ceramics and carpet designs by local graphic artist Jūlijs Madernieks (1870–1955).

⑪ Museum of Jews in Latvia
Muzejs Ebreji Latvijā

Skolas iela 6. **Map** D1. **Tel** 6728 3484. **Open** noon–5pm Mon–Thu, Sun. 🖼 donations.

Housed inside a Jewish cultural centre, this museum is based around the collections of two Holocaust survivors, Zalman Elelson and Marģers Vestermanis, which tell the story of the Jewish community in Latvia. Beginning with the first records of Jews in the 16th century, it progresses to photographs of early 20th-century family life. The focus, however, is on the horrific years of Nazi occupation. The museum has images of the Holocaust, including footage of the massacre of Jews on Liepāja Beach. A guidebook to Rīga's Jewish sites is available which lists the places from where the once-vibrant community was erased.

⑫ Latvian Ethnographic Open-Air Museum

Latvijas etnogrāfiskais brīvdabas muzejs

Occupying 86 ha (213 acres) of woodland on the shores of Lake Jugla on the city's eastern edge, this site includes over 118 homesteads, churches, windmills and other structures from across Latvia. Founded in 1924, the site is organized according to Latvia's administrative regions – Vidzeme, Kurzeme, Zemgale and Latgale – drawing attention to variations in building design and living arrangements in different parts of the country. With craftspeople working on site during the summer, and many buildings containing everyday artifacts, the museum offers an insight into 19th-century rural life.

VISITORS' CHECKLIST

Practical Information
220 km (137 miles) SW of Rīga.
🚍 87,000. **Map** F1. **Tel** 6799
4106. **Open** 10am–5pm daily.
🚻 🛒 🎁 Sun (Usma Church).
🌐 **brivdabasmuzejs.lv.**

Transport
🚌 1, 19, 28.

Dutch Windmill
Built in 1890, this windmill, from Latgale, has a movable "cap" including sails, a shaft and a gear wheel.

Vidzeme Spinning Wheel-Maker's Homestead

★ Kurzeme Peasants' Homestead
This wooden building with a reed-thatched roof is typical of 19th-century rural architecture in southwest Kurzeme.

Zemgale Peasants' Homestead
includes a dwelling-house, a bathhouse and a granary.

0 metres   100
0 yards   100

Entrance

★ Usma Church
Most wooden churches were replaced by stone buildings in the 19th century, making this a rare example.

Old Believers' House
Located in a Latgale village, the house exhibits a loom for weaving and a samovar used to boil water for tea.

Handicrafts
Handicraft displays include traditional wickerwork.

Kurzeme Fishermen's Village

❷ Jūrmala

20 km (12 miles) W of Rīga. 🏠 56,000.
🚂 from Rīga. *i* Lienes iela 5 Majori,
6714 7900. **W** jurmala.lv

Literally meaning "seaside" in Latvian, Jūrmala is an attractive stretch of beaches, small towns and pine forests alongside the Gulf of Rīga. During the 19th century, the area became famous for its medicinal mud and sulphur-rich spring water. Jūrmala soon grew into a popular resort and it became fashionable to own a summerhouse here. These wooden houses are still scattered across the area, standing alongside upmarket spas and modern guesthouses. Strict building regulations have helped preserve these 19th-century wooden summerhouses and restrict further building work in the area.

Forming the heart of Jūrmala is the pedestrianized strip of Jomas iela in the town of Majori. Lining the street are several outdoor cafés, shops, restaurants and hotels, including the Historicist-style Hotel Majori, built in 1925.

To the east of Majori, in Dzintari town, is the **Exhibition of Antique Machinery**, which displays a popular collection of old cars and radio sets.

Located west of Majori, in Dubulti town, **Aspazija House** is the last home of one of Latvia's most famous poets, Elza Rozenberga (1865–1943), who wrote under the pen

One of Jūrmala's many popular beaches

name "Aspazija". She was the wife of Jānis Rainis, considered Latvia's national poet by many. Now a branch of the Jūrmala Town Museum, the house has an interesting collection of manuscripts and photographs related to the couple.

🏛 **Exhibition of Antique Machinery**
Turaidas iela 11, Dzintari. **Tel** 2926 3329. **Open** 10am–5pm daily.

🏛 **Aspazija House**
Meierovica prosp 20, Dubulti.
Tel 6776 9445. **Open** 11am–5pm Tue–Sat. 🎫

❸ Kuldīga

150 km (93 miles) W of Rīga.
🏠 14,000. 🚌 *i* Baznīcas iela 5,
6332 2259. 🎪 Town Festival (mid-Jul).
W kuldiga.lv

With a well-preserved Old Town and an attractive location alongside the Venta river, Kuldīga is one of Latvia's most alluring provincial towns. It was founded in 1242 by the Livonian Order, who chose the site to capitalize on the river and land route linking Prussia with the lower Daugava valley.

In the 16th century, Kuldīga's castle was one of the residences of Duke Gothard Kettler and the town traded with Rīga and Jelgava. The streets near the attractive Old Town Hall Square, running alongside the Alekšupīte river, feature 17th- and 18th-century timber buildings. The Old Town also has a couple of

fine churches: St Catherine's (Šv Katrīnas baznīca) and the Holy Trinity (Šv Trīsvienības Katoļu baznīca). A short walk from Kuldīga is the **Venta Waterfall** (Ventas rumba), the widest in Europe. Close by is a 164-m- (538-ft-) long brick bridge, one of Europe's longest. Overlooking the Venta river is **Kuldīga District Museum** (Kuldīgas novada muzejs), best known for its collection of playing cards.

Environs
The **Riežupe Sand Caves** (Riežupes smilšu alas), 4 km (2 miles) north of Kuldīga, form the longest cave system in Latvia. A quarter of the 2-km (1-mile) site is open to visitors.

🏛 **Kuldīga District Museum**
Pils iela 5. **Tel** 6332 2364.
Open 11am–5pm Tue–Sun. 🎫

Venta Waterfall, stretching the width of the Venta river, Kuldīga

White-and-blue exterior of Aspazija House, Jūrmala

❹ Liepāja

Although Liepāja was officially declared a town in 1625, it expanded only in the early 19th century. The deepening of the ice-free port and the building of a railway link were followed, in 1890, by the foundation of a Russian naval port at the nearby town of Karosta. Today, Liepāja is Latvia's third largest city and boasts a vibrant cultural life. It is dotted with many interesting sights, most of which are located in its historic core. Many of the city's older buildings have been extensively restored.

VISITORS' CHECKLIST

Practical Information
220 km (137 miles) SW of Rīga.
🚇 87,000. 🅸 Rožu laukums 5/6,
6348 0808. 🅰 daily. 🎹 Piano
Star Festival (Mar), Baltic Beach
Party (Jul), International Organ
Music Festival (Sep).
🆆 liepaja.lv

Transport
✈ Cimdenieki, Lidostas iela 8.
🚆 Rīgas iela. 🚌 Rīgas iela.

🏛 Liepāja Museum
Kūrmājas prospekts 16/18.
Tel 6342 2327. **Open** 10am–6pm
Thu, Sat & Sun, 11am–7pm Fri.
🆆 liepajasmuzejs.lv

Set in a sculpture garden, the Liepāja Museum (Liepājas muzejs) is housed in an ornate early 20th-century building with an impressive galleried hall. The displays trace local history, with exhibits including the heads of stone cherubs from St Anne's Basilica, a series of pewter drinking vessels topped by human figures and the traditional costumes of the southern region of Kurzeme. The museum also includes a reconstruction of the workshop of the sculptor Mikelis Pankoks (1894–1983), who vanished in 1944 and was presumed dead. He had fled the country incognito, and ended his days in a Swiss mental hospital.

Wooden sculpture, Liepāja Museum

🚊 Liepāja Beach
The long, sandy Liepāja Beach (Liepājas pludmale), with its prestigious EU Blue Flag, is separated from the Old Town by the wooded Seaside Park (Jūrmalas parka). The nearby streets are lined with elegant timber buildings in the Art Nouveau style, many of which have been restored.

🏠 St Joseph's Cathedral
Rakstvežu iela 13. **Tel** 6342 9775.
Decorated inside with scenes from the Bible, St Joseph's Cathedral (Šv Jāzepa katedrāle) attained its current towering form in the 19th century. The congregation needed a larger church but had no land on which to build, so they expanded the existing building upwards.

🏛 Occupation Museum
K Ukstiņa iela 7/9. **Tel** 6342 0274.
Open 10am–6pm Thu, Sat & Sun,
11am–7pm Fri. 🖾

The Occupation Museum (Okupāciju režīmos) offers an absorbing account of the city's treatment at the hands of Nazi Germany and the Soviet Union, with notes available in English. Exhibits include photographs of people deported en masse by the Soviets in June 1941, everyday objects that were left behind and an account of the killing of the city's Jews and other "undesirables". At the end is a display about the events leading up to independence. The offices of the Popular Front, which was based in the building, have been left intact. Rooms upstairs house a unique exhibition of antique photographic equipment.

🏠 St Anne's Basilica
Veidenbauma iela 1. **Tel** 6342 3384.
First documented in 1508, the current Neo-Gothic structure of St Anne's Basilica (šv Annas baznīca) dates from the end of the 19th century. The interior is dominated by a huge Baroque altar, carved in 1697. The altar

painting depicts the Passion of Christ in three panels – with the Crucifixion at the bottom, the wrapping of his body in the centre and the Ascension at the top.

House of Craftsmen
Bāriņu 33. **Tel** 6342 3286.
Open 9am–5pm Mon–Fri. 🖾 🏠
With a wide variety of fine handicrafts on sale, the House of Craftsmen (Amatnieku namiņš) is a place where one can watch skilled artisans at work. The world's longest amber necklace, 123-m (404-ft) long and weighing 60 kg (132 lb), is also on display, along with photographs documenting its creation.

🏠 Holy Trinity Church
Baznīcas 1. **Tel** 2943 8050.
Open 10am–4pm daily.
🐦 donations. Organ recital (call for timings).

The modest exterior of the mid-18th-century Holy Trinity Church (Svētās Trīsvienības baznīca) belies one of the finest church interiors in the Baltic region, adorned with gilt detailing and woodcarvings. The church's organ, built in 1773, was the world's largest until 1912.

Beautifully carved Baroque altar, St Anne's Basilica, Liepāja

❺ Rundāle Palace

Rundāles pils

Designed by Francesco Bartolomeo Rastrelli, Rundāle Palace is one of the finest in the region. Work began in 1736 on a Baroque summer residence for Ernst Johann Biron, but was left unfinished when he was exiled. After Biron's return, the interiors were renovated in Rococo style. Biron's son removed most of the embellishments when he left in 1795, when Courland was annexed by Russia. Damaged in the 20th-century restoration begun in 1972, work is still in progress. The rooms have served as government offices, an elementary school and a granary.

Detail, Rose Room
Rococo touches such as fake marble, silver detailing and floral motifs adorn the room.

★ **Duke's Bedroom**
This room was the focal point of Biron's private apartments, which occupied the central block of the palace.

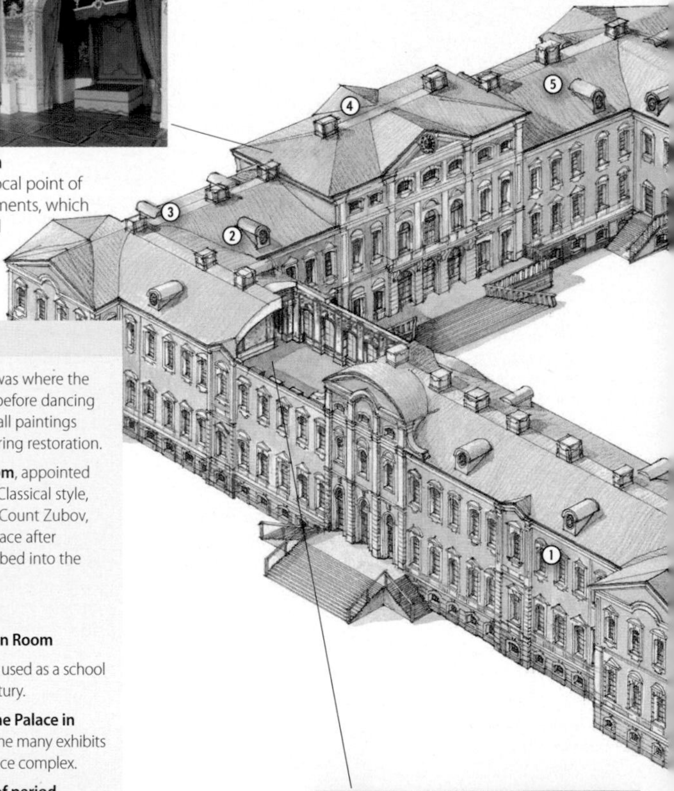

KEY

① **Grand Gallery** was where the guests would dine before dancing in the White Hall. Wall paintings were uncovered during restoration.

② **The Corner Room**, appointed in the Russian Neo-Classical style, reflects the taste of Count Zubov, who lived in the palace after Courland was absorbed into the Russian Empire.

③ **Rose Room**

④ **Duke's Reception Room**

⑤ **Marble Hall** was used as a school gym in the 20th century.

⑥ **Old photos of the Palace in Jelgava** are one of the many exhibits displayed in the palace complex.

⑦ **The exhibition of period clothes** in Room 107 mostly features items belonging to the duke's family.

⑧ **The Heraldic Lion**, the duke's emblem, is placed on the top of the gateposts.

⑨ **The Oval Porcelain Cabinet**, made by Johann Michael Graff, was designed to exhibit exquisite artifacts.

★ **Gold Hall**
The initials of the palace's owner, "EJ", can be seen amidst the ornate gilt scrolls. The hall has magnificent chandeliers and ceiling decoration.

Formal French-style gardens, re-created from the original plans

Duchess's Boudoir
The duchess could rest and receive visitors during the
day in her splendidly decorated boudoir, which has
now been restored. The duchess and other family
members lived in the west wing.

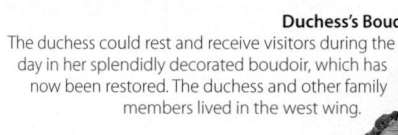

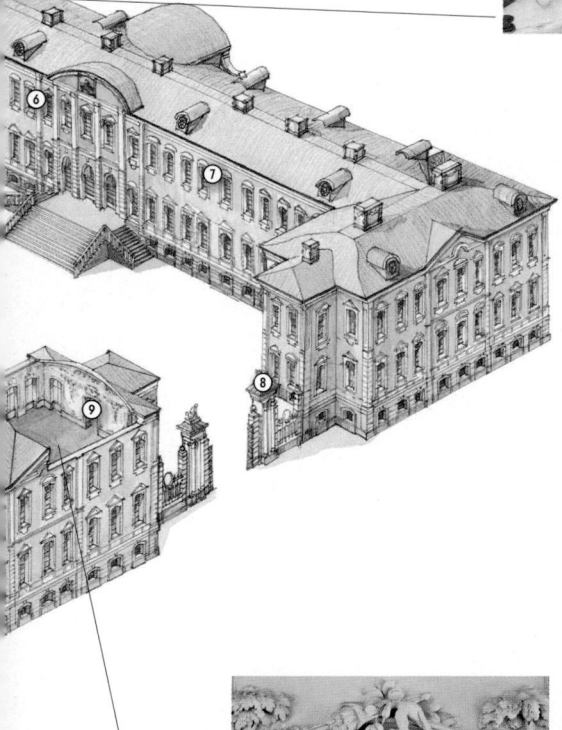

Ernst Johann Biron

The son of a minor landlord,
Ernst Johann Biron was
asked to leave the academy
in Königsberg (present-day
Kaliningrad in Russia) for bad
behaviour. Failing to establish
himself in the Russian court,
he returned to Jelgava, a town
in the Zemgale region, and
became close to the Duchess
of Courland, Anna Ivanovna. In
1730, Anna became empress
of Russia, and three years later
Biron was appointed Duke of
Courland. After his patron died
in 1740, Biron was sent into
exile, returning only in 1763.
A year later, Catherine II made
him duke once more but he
abdicated in 1769 in favour
of his son Peter.

Duke of Courland, Ernst Johann Biron
(1690–1772)

★ White Hall
This ballroom boasts a
parquet floor and lavish
stuccowork by German
sculptor Johann Michael
Graff. The restrained
colour scheme gives the
room its name.

❻ Sigulda

50 km (31 miles) NE of Rīga.
⏴ 15,000. 🚆 from Rīga. 🚌 from
Rīga. 🛈 Valdemāra iela 1a, 6797 1335.
🌐 **sigulda.lv**

A pretty town situated in the scenic woodland of Gauja National Park, Sigulda is a centre for outdoor activities and is often described as the Switzerland of the Vidzeme region. After the Brotherhood of the Sword subdued the Liv population in 1207, they gave the right bank of the Gauja river to the Bishop of Rīga and built their own castle on the left bank. The Brotherhood, renamed the Livonian Order, lost the town to the Poles in 1562, and it passed between the Poles and Swedes for 150 years, until

Ruins of the castle built by the Brotherhood of the Sword, Sigulda

it was taken by Russia in the Great Northern War (1700–21). The castle ruins are tucked away behind the 19th-century **New Castle** (Jaunā pils), which now houses city council offices and a restaurant. Close by is a Lutheran church and an impressive viewpoint called **Artists' Hill** (Gleznotāju kalns). Paths run through the woodland to Satzele Castle Mound, once a Liv fortress, and Peter's Cave on the bank of the Vējupīte river.

❼ Gauja National Park

Gauja nacionālā parka

Latvia's first national park was established in 1973, stretching for about 100 km (62 miles) along the Gauja River valley. Almost half of the park is forested, and it is home to about 900 plant, 149 bird and 48 mammal species. Boating and canoeing are great ways to see the caves, cliffs and ravines carved out by the river since the glaciers receded 12,000 years ago. In addition to its natural attractions, the area has some of Latvia's most fascinating historic sites, and been attracting visitors to its trails since the 19th century.

Key

🟩 Gauja National Park

Turaida Museum Reserve
The reserve comprises the extensively restored Turaida Castle, which houses historical exhibitions, and the grounds, with the outbuildings and a sculpture park.

KEY

① **Sigulda** offers a rare chance to experience the thrill of a world-class bobsleigh run at a reasonable price.

② **Zvārte Rock**, a 35-m (115-ft) high sandstone outcrop, boasts excellent views. It is locally believed to be a haunt of witches and demons.

❽ Cēsis

90 km (56 miles) NE of Rīga.
🚠 18,000. 🚉 from Rīga. 🚌 from
Rīga. ℹ️ Pils laukums 9, 6412 1815.
🌐 **cesis.lv**.

One of Latvia's oldest towns,
Cēsis has winding streets lined
with attractive wooden and
stone buildings. It became a
member of the Hanseatic
League in 1383 and grew into
an important trading centre.
The town served as the headquarters of the Brotherhood of
the Sword, and later the Livonian
Order, for much of the period
between 1237 and 1561. In
1577, Ivan the Terrible took Cēsis.
Further damage was inflicted
during the Great Northern War
and Cēsis also witnessed fierce

Row of wooden and stone houses in
the Old Town, Cēsis

fighting during the War of
Independence (1918–20). The
Cēsis castle complex is the
town's major attraction. Visitors
are given builders' helmets and
lanterns for the tour of the 15th-
to 16th-century towers of the

13th-century Old Castle. The
pink New Castle, built in 1777,
is home to the **Museum of Art
and History** (Cēsu vēstures un
mākslas muzejs). The highlight
is the well-presented "Treasures
of Cēsis" exhibition. Cēsis
Exhibition House (Cēsu izstāžu
nams), a renovated 18th-
century coach house, stands
on the square in front of the
New Castle.

To the north, the Castle Park
is a popular place to relax in
the summer. Other attractions
include the 19th-century Cēsis
Brewery, although the beer is
now brewed outside the town.

🏛 **Museum of Art and History**
Pils laukums 9. 🖼 includes access
to the Old and New Castles.

Cēsis

Once the seat of the German
crusaders, Cēsis is a romantic
town with a lakeside park.

CĒSIS

P14

Raiskums   Ciruliši

P20

Gauja

Āraiši

Amata

Kārļi   Drabeši

ajasmala   ②   Leriki

Līgatne

Līgatne

A2

Augšligatne

0 kilometres   5

0 miles   5

VISITORS' CHECKLIST

Practical Information
40 km (25 miles) NE of Rīga.
ℹ️ Gauja National Park Visitors'
Centre, Baznicas iela 7, Sigulda,
6797 4006. 🚣 guided canoe
trips organized by Campo in Rīga
(2922 2339) and Makars in
Sigulda (2924 4948). 🚠
🌐 **daba.gov.lv**

Transport
🚉 from Rīga. 🚌

Lake Āraiši
The remains of a rudimentary fortress were found on
the lake bed. A lakeside reconstruction re-creates life
here in the 9th and 10th centuries.

**Līgatne Education and
Recreation Centre**
This centre hosts wildlife,
such as brown bears and
European bison. Its footpaths
and motorable tracks wind past
the spacious animal enclosures.

Key
▬ Major road
═ Minor road
═ Other road
— Railway
-- Park boundary

For keys to symbols *see back flap*

Practical & Travel Information

Latvia offers a wealth of historic sights and cultural activities as well as stunning natural beauty. In recent years there has been a rapid increase in the number of European cities directly linked to Rīga, due mainly to the arrival of low-cost carriers which have raised the capital's profile as a destination for weekend breaks. For those who wish to avoid air travel, there are several sea routes from Scandinavia and Germany, besides comfortable trains and coaches. Travelling by car is also perfectly feasible.

When to Visit

The best time to visit Latvia is from May to October, when the weather is pleasantly warm and the days are longer. July and August are the warmest months and can also be the wettest. Winter is cold and dark with very few daylight hours, making it difficult for outdoor excursions. March, when the snow thaws, and November and December, when it starts to fall, are also best avoided.

Documentation

Citizens of EU member-states, the US, Canada, Australia and New Zealand, only need a valid passport for entry into Latvia for a period of up to 90 days within a half-year. Those wishing to stay beyond 90 days will need to apply for a national long-term visa or a residence permit. Visitors from other countries should enquire at their local Latvian embassy or consulate for visa requirements before travelling. The official website of the Latvian Ministry of Foreign Affairs offers information on visa regulations. EU citizens are not subject to customs regulations, provided they adhere to EU guidelines. Visitors should check for any customs duty or special permission required to export a cultural object before buying it. For detailed information on these guidelines, entrance regulations and visa charges, it is advisable to visit the official website of the European Commission.

Visitor Information

Practically every town and city in Latvia has a tourist office staffed by friendly English-speaking locals. These offices provide information about the major cities and towns, as well as on accommodation, entertainment venues, restaurants and historic sights. The tourist office in Rīga provides helpful city guides, free maps, brochures and regional tourism information.

Most offices are open from 9am to 6pm on weekdays and for shorter hours on Saturdays; some are also open on Sundays. In remote places, opening hours are more erratic. The Latvian Tourism Development Agency is the official tourism agency; its website lists all the tourist offices in the country. Information on tourism offices that represent this agency abroad can also be found on the website.

Health and Security

Emergency care in Latvia is provided free of charge to all foreigners who are treated in state hospitals. Standards are similar to those elsewhere in Europe. Pharmacies throughout Latvia are usually open from 8am to 7 or 8pm on weekdays and until 3 or 4pm on Saturdays. Rīga has a few 24-hour pharmacies.

Latvia is a safe country in which to travel, with very rare instances of theft and mugging. However, it is best to remain vigilant and to avoid carrying luxury items.

Facilities for the Disabled

In recent years public awareness about the needs of the disabled has improved significantly in Latvia. Most upmarket hotels and restaurants in the country take such needs into consideration, although public transport in Rīga has only a limited number of buses which provide wheelchair access.

Banking and Currency

Latvia replaced its previous currency, the lats, with the Euro on 1 January, 2014. Although most foreign currency can be exchanged at banks, exchange bureaus and upmarket hotels, euros and dollars are preferred. Traveller's cheques are accepted only in upmarket hotels and major banks.

There is a wide network of ATMs, mostly in the major towns and cities. Banks are generally open from 9am to 6pm on weekdays and 10am to 3pm on Sundays.

The Climate of Latvia

Latvia experiences a short summer, with July and August being the warmest months and subject to thunderstorms. Between May and September temperatures average between 14º C (57º F) and 22º C (72º F). Winter, between November and March, is extremely cold with temperatures rarely going above 4º C (39º F) and frequently dipping to freezing conditions.

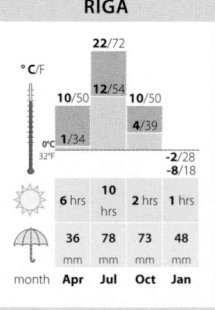

RĪGA

	Apr	Jul	Oct	Jan
°C/F	10/50	22/72	10/50	
	1/34	12/54	4/39	-2/28
				-8/18
sun (hrs)	6 hrs	10 hrs	2 hrs	1 hrs
rain (mm)	36 mm	78 mm	73 mm	48 mm
month	Apr	Jul	Oct	Jan

Communications

Latvia's telephone and postal networks are both reliable and efficient. Post offices provide a range of services at competitive postal rates. Payphone booths accept pre-paid phone cards, available at kiosks, post offices and supermarkets. Internet facilities are excellent in Rīga and most cafés and hotels have Wi-Fi access.

Arriving by Air

The majority of passengers arrive at **Rīga International Airport**, which is now connected to most European cities. The country's national carrier, **airBaltic**, was established in 1995 and offers some very affordable flights. Rīga is also served by other major airlines including **KLM**, **SAS**, **Lufthansa** and **Finnair**. Several low-cost carriers, such as **easyJet** from Berlin and **Ryanair** from Ireland and the UK, have also started services to the country.

There are few direct flights to Latvia from the US, New Zealand, Canada or Australia. Visitors from outside Europe usually need to change flights in London, Stockholm, Helsinki or Copenhagen.

Arriving by Sea

Travelling by ferry takes longer than air travel, although crossing the Baltic Sea has its own appeal and you may decide to include a leisurely sea crossing as part of your trip. Ferries operated by **Lisco** link the German port of Lübeck to Rīga, while **Tallink** connects Rīga to Stockholm (Sweden). The main **Ferry Terminal** can be reached by trams 5, 7 or 9 from the main bus terminal or outside the National Opera. **Terrabalt** connects Liepāja to Karlshamn (Sweden) and Rostock (Germany). Ventspils is served by **Scandlines** to Nynashamn (Sweden), Rostock and Karlshamn.

Rail Travel

The main railway station in Rīga is **Central Railway Station**, located southeast of the Old Town. From here international rail routes head east towards Moscow, Vitebsk, Odessa and St Petersburg. The most comfortable way to travel on most routes is by *kupeja* (four-bunk compartment). However, there are more luxurious two-bunk compartments on the trains serving Moscow.

Travelling by Coach

One of the best ways to travel between the three Baltic capitals is by coach. This costs less than travelling by air, although the difference is negligible, except during the peak season. International carriers such as **Ecolines** and **Eurolines** run services between Rīga and several other European cities. Rīga's main bus terminal, **Autoosta**, is five minutes south of the Old Town.

Travelling by Car

Since 2007, under the Schengen Agreement, there are no longer border controls between the Baltic States. Nevertheless, busy border crossings can take up to 20 minutes to negotiate. It is essential to carry the vehicle's registration document, a valid third-party insurance policy and either a European driving licence or an International Driving Permit. Vehicles must be in roadworthy condition and it is compulsory to have a first-aid kit, fire extinguisher and hazard-warning triangle. From December to March, winter tyres must be used, and drivers should fit spiked tyres between September and April.

DIRECTORY

Documentation
W am.gov.lv
W ec.europa.eu

Visitor Information
W latviatourism.lv
W liveriga.com/en/3613

Embassies and Consulates

Australia
Lienes iela 28, Rīga.
Tel 6722 4251.

Canada
Baznīcas iela 20/22, Rīga.
Tel 6781 3945.

France
Raina bulvāris 9, Rīga.
Tel 6703 6600.

United Kingdom
J Alunana iela 5, Rīga.
Tel 6777 4700.

United States
Raiņa bulvāris 7, Rīga.
Tel 6703 6200.

Emergency Numbers

Ambulance
Tel 03.

Fire
Tel 01.

Police
Tel 02.

Arriving by Air

airBaltic
W airbaltic.com.

easyJet
W easyjet.com

Finnair
W finnair.com

KLM
W klm.com

Lufthansa
W lufthansa.com

Ryanair
W ryanair.com

Riga International Airport
W riga-airport.com

SAS
W flysas.com

Arriving by Sea

Ferry Terminal
W freeportofriga.lv

Lisco
W lisco.lt

Scandlines
W scandlines.lt

Tallink
W tallink.com

Terrabalt
W terrabalt.lv

Rail Travel

Central Railway Station
W ldz.lv

Travelling by Coach

Autoosta
W autoosta.lv

Ecolines
W ecolines.ee

Eurolines
W eurolines.com

Shopping & Entertainment

Numerous shopping centres have opened throughout Latvia since 1991, although Rīga undoubtedly has the largest range of shopping options. This is particularly true when it comes to items likely to be of interest to visitors, although outside the capital it is usually possible to find typical handicrafts such as amber jewellery and embroidered knitwear. Latvia's major cultural events are also concentrated in Rīga, although the dynamic festival calendar provides plenty of reasons to explore other parts of the country. The city is also renowned for its energetic nightlife; clubs range from small and hip to huge and mainstream, and stay open throughout the night.

Opening Hours

Most shops in Latvia open around 10am. Small shops close around 6 or 7pm, while bigger malls and shopping centres usually stay open until 10pm. Many small shops remain closed on Sundays.

Markets

Most Latvian towns have regular or even daily markets, although they are rarely aimed at visitors and are most useful for everyday food shopping. Housed in five huge zeppelin hangars, Rīga's **Central Market** has most of its indoor space dedicated to food, while the stalls and kiosks outside sell CDs, clothes and electrical goods. Also of interest is the covered outdoor antiques and organic food market on the second and fourth Sunday of each month at Berga Bazārs.

Beyond the capital, markets such as the covered market hall in Liepāja, a throwback to the Soviet era, are very atmospheric. In the summer months, markets in Jūrmala sell souvenirs as well as fresh produce.

Handicrafts

Traditional Latvian handicrafts include handmade linen, amber jewellery, woodwork and knitwear embroidered with popular Latvian folk symbols. Motifs from nature, such as the sun, stars or trees, are commonly used among the repertoire of geometric designs found on many handcrafted goods. There are numerous souvenir shops in Rīga's Old Town stocking items such as linen and wooden toys. More authentic and unusual gifts can be found in **Grieži**, which also holds craft demonstrations. **Tine** boasts a wide range of souvenirs, while **Sāmsalas Kalēji** specializes in metalwork. Some shops also sell Russian goods such as *matryoshka* – wooden dolls of various sizes which are placed one inside another. Outside Rīga, a good place to find handicrafts is the branch of **Tornis** in the tower of Turaida Castle in Gauja National Park *(see pp90–91)*.

Art and Antiques

Antique shops in Latvia are well worth exploring. A licence, which is available at most shops, is usually required before genuine antiques can be exported. Rīga has a fine selection, including the upmarket **Doma Antikvariāts**, the busy **Retro A** and **Volmar**.

The best places to buy art are commercial art galleries. There are many galleries in Rīga and the tourist information office can provide an up-to-date list. **Māksla XO** is one of the most highly regarded, while **Art Nouveau Rīga**, a leading souvenir shop, offers attractive reproductions.

Amber

Amber is a popular Latvian souvenir, readily available in tourist areas and in some museum shops. Rīga has dozens of specialist shops such as **Amber Line**, **Dzintara Muzejs** and **Dzintara Galerija**. There are also several general souvenir shops selling more affordable items. However, buyers should be aware that not all amber on sale is genuine. Visitors spending a large sum of money on amber objects should ask for a certificate of authenticity.

Food and Drink

Laima chocolate is among the country's most popular buys, and the brand has a dedicated store in Rīga. Its upmarket rival, **Emihls Gustavs Chocolate**, has stores all over the city.

Another common gift is Rīga Black Balsam, a herbal liqueur taken neat or in cocktails. **Latvijas Balzams** is among the best places to buy it. Beer also makes a good gift. There are many varieties of traditional honey available in the **Latvijas Bite** shops, owned by the Latvian Association of Beekeepers.

Nightlife

With a wide range of bars and clubs, Rīga has a swinging nightlife. **Skyline Bar** in the Reval Hotel Latvija is a favourite, while **Rīgas Balzāms** is a popular place to try the eponymous drink in various cocktails. **I Love You** attracts a youthful local crowd, while **Sapņu Fabrika** offers rock to world music. The best-known nightclub, **Pulkvedim Neviens Neraksta**, draws a young and stylish clientele. Larger venues, such as **La Rocca** and the submarine-themed **Nautilus**, feature DJs at the weekend. Casinos with gaming tables include the **Tobago Casino Club** and **Casino Aladins**.

Outside the capital city, **Latvia's 1st Rock Café** and **Fontaine Palace**, both in Liepāja, are worth visiting.

Music, Theatre and Dance

Rīga has a thriving live-music scene. Major international artists perform at the **Arēna Rīga**. Local bands play at a host of smaller venues – **Kaļķu Vārti**, noted for booking some of the country's top artists; **Depo**, which features alternative music; **Sapņu Fabrika**, which offers a range of genres; and **Četri Balti Krekli**, with

Latvian music. The best blues venues in Rīga are the **Bīts Blūza Klubs**, **Hamlets** and **Carpe Diem** restaurant. The summer sees performances on Liepāja's open-air stage **Pūt Vējiņi**.

Some of the best classical music concerts take place at annual events such as the International Early Music Festival in Rundāle Palace *(see pp88–9)*. **Saulkrasti Jazz Festival** and the **International Music Festival** in Rīga are also important events. **Ave Sol** also hosts small classical concerts.

The **Latvian National Opera** is the venue for world-class performances of opera and ballet. The **Latvian National Theatre**, the **Dailes Theatre**, the **New Rīga Theatre** and the **Russian Drama Theatre** are some of the best places to see theatre in Latvian or Russian. The **Liepāja Theatre** in Liepāja produces expansive theatrical works. Rīga's most important theatre festival, **Homo Novus**, concentrates on experimental theatre and dance.

The **Latvian Music Information Centre** provides details of performances across the country. Bookings can be made at the venue or through ticket agencies such as **Biļešu Paradīze**. Tickets can also be booked online on the **Latvian Culture Vortal**, which has a nationwide calendar.

DIRECTORY

Markets

Central Market
Negu St 7, Rīga.
Tel 6722 9985.

Handicrafts

Grieži
Mazā miesnieku iela1.
Rīga. **Tel** 6750 7236.

Sāmsalas Kalēji
Laipu iela 6, Rīga.
Tel 6722 4496.

Tine
Vaļņu iela2, Rīga.
Tel 6721 6728.

Art and Antiques

Art Nouveau Rīga
Strēlnieku 9, Laipu 8, Rīga.
Tel 2836 7112.

Doma Antikvariāts
Doma laukums 1a, Rīga.
Tel 6781 4401.
W antikvariats.lv

Māksla XO
Skārņu 8, Rīga.
Tel 2948 2098.

Retro A
Tallinas 54, Rīga.
Tel 6731 5306.

Volmar
Šķūņu 6, Rīga.
Tel 6721 4278.

Amber

Amber Line
Torna 4, Rīga.
Tel 6732 5058.

Dzintara Galerija
Torņa iela 4, Rīga.
Tel 6732 5157.

Dzintara Muzejs
Kalēju iela 9/11, Rīga.
Tel 6708 7545.

Food and Drink

Emihls Gustavs Chocolate
Aspazijas bulvāris 24, Rīga.
W sokolade.lv

Laima
Ģertrūdes iela 6, Rīga.
W laima.lv

Latvijas Balzams
Audēju iela 8, Rīga.
Tel 6722 8814.

Latvijas Bite
Ģertrūdes iela 13, Rīga.
Tel 6727 9495.

Nightlife

Casino Aladins
Dzirnavu iela 57, Rīga.
Tel 2929 6060.

Fontaine Palace
Dzirnavu iela 4, Liepāja.
Tel 6348 8510.
W fontainepalace.lv

I Love You
Aldaru iela 9, Rīga.
Tel 6722 5304.
W iloveyou.lv

La Rocca
Brivibas iela 96, Rīga.
Tel 6750 6030.
W larocca.lv

Latvia's 1st Rock Café
Stendera 18/20, Liepāja.
Tel 6348 1555.
W pablo.lv

Nautilus
Kungu iela 8, Rīga.
Tel 6781 4455.
W nautilus.lv

Pulkvedim Neviens Neraksta
Peldu iela 26–28, Rīga.
Tel 6721 3886.
W pulkvedis.lv

Rīgas Balzāms
Torņa iela 4, Rīga.
Tel 6721 4494.

Sapņu Fabrika
Lāčplēša 101, Rīga.
Tel 6722 9045.
W sapnufabrika.lv

Skyline Bar
Reval Hotel Latvija,
Elizabetes iela 55, Rīga.
Tel 6777 2222.

Tobago Casino Club
Aspāzijas bulvāris 22, Rīga.
Tel 6722 5411.

Music, Theatre and Dance

Arēna Rīga
Skanstes iela 21, Rīga.
W arenariga.com

Ave Sol
Valdemāra Iela 5, Rīga.
Tel 6704 3631

Biļešu Paradīze
W bilesuparadize.lv

Bites Blūza Klubs
Dzirnavu iela 34a, Rīga.
W bluesclub.lv

Carpe Diem
Meistaru iela 10–12, Rīga.
W carpediem.lv

Četri Balti Krekli
Vecpilsētas iela 12, Rīga.

Dailes Theatre
Brīvības iela 75, Rīga.
W dailesteatris.lv

Depo
Vaļņu iela 32, Rīga.
W klubsdepo.lv

Hamlets
Jāņa sēta 5, Rīga.
Tel 6722 9938

Homo Novus
W theatre.lv

International Music Festival
W rigasritmi.lv

Kaļķu Vārti
Kaļķu iela 11a, Rīga.
W kalkuvarti.lv

Latvian Culture Vortal
W kultura.lv/en

Latvian Music Information Centre
W lmic.lv

Latvian National Opera
Aspāzijas bulvāris 3, Rīga.
W opera.lv

Latvian National Theatre
Kronvalda bulvāris 2, Rīga.
W teatris.lv

Liepāja Theatre
Teatra iela 4, Liepāja.
Tel 6340 7811.
W liepajasteatris.lv

New Rīga Theatre
Lāčplēša iela 25, Rīga.
W jrt.lv

Pūt Vējiņi
Peldu iela 57, Liepāja.
Tel 6342 4479.

Russian Drama Theatre
Kaļķu iela 16, Rīga.
W trd.lv

Saulkrasti Jazz Festival
W saulkrastijazz.lv

Where to Stay

Rīga

B&B Rīga €
B&B **Map** F2
Ģertrūdes iela 43, LV-1011
Tel *6727 8505*
🌐 bb-riga.lv
This family-run B&B, located in
the 19th-century part of town,
has tasteful en suites equipped
with TV and fridge.

Cinnamon Sally €
Hostel **Map** E3
Merķeļa iela 1, 3rd Floor, LV-1001
Tel *2204 2280*
🌐 cinnamonsally.com
On the 3rd floor of an apartment
block, this hostel has a homely
atmosphere and good social
areas. Choice of dorms and
private doubles.

Homestay €
B&B **Map** D3
Stockholmas iela 1, LV-1014
Tel *6755 3016*
🌐 homestay.lv
Family-run B&B in the leafy
suburb of Mežaparks. Cosy rooms
in a modern timber house. Just a
20-minute tram ride away from
the Centre.

Albert Hotel €€
Business **Map** D1
Dzirnavu iela 33, LV-1010
Tel *6733 1717*
🌐 alberthotel.lv
Just round the corner from the
celebrated Art Nouveau district,
this contemporary hotel offers
neat, comfortable en suites. Great
views from top-floor café too.

DK Choice

Hotel Centra €€
Boutique **Map** C4
Audēju iela 1, LV-1050
Tel *6722 6441*
🌐 hotelcentra.lv
A well-run boutique hotel,
the quiet and calm Centra is
located in the heart of Rīga's
nightlife district. Set in a
handsomely restored 19th-
century building the hotel
offers spacious rooms that
favour a clean, minimalist style.

Radi un Draugi €€
B&B **Map** C4
Mārstaļu iela 1/3, LV-1050
Tel *6782 0200*
🌐 hotelradiundraugi.lv
Centrally located hotel that offers
excellent value with its simple

Guests relax in the bright, colourful lounge
of Cinnamon Sally, Rīga

but comfortable rooms, friendly
service and decent breakfast.

Grand Palace €€€
Luxury **Map** B3
Pils iela 12, LV-1050
Tel *6704 4000*
🌐 grandpalaceriga.com
Elegant, upmarket hotel with
plush, superbly equipped rooms
and a range of facilities that
includes a gym, sauna and two
haute cuisine restaurants.

Hotel Bergs €€€
Design **Map** E2
Elizabetes iela 83/85, LV-1050
Tel *6777 0900*
🌐 hotelbergs.lv
The tasteful luxury suites at this
design-conscious hotel boast
chic contemporary fittings, sleek
bathrooms and fully equipped
kitchenettes.

Rest of Latvia

CĒSIS: Hotel Kolonna €€
Historic
Vienības laukums 1, LV-4101
Tel *6412 0122*
🌐 hotelkolonna.com
Dating from the 1930s, this
refurbished hotel in the centre of
town, offers plush rooms with
spacious bathrooms.

JŪRMALA: Jūrmala Spa €€€
Spa
Jomas iela 47/49, LV-2015
Tel *6778 4415*
🌐 hoteljurmala.com
Modern spa resort and
conference centre with swanky
rooms, offering a full range of spa
and beauty treatments. Located
on the main pedestrianized strip
near the golden beaches.

Price Guide

Prices are based on one night's stay in
high season for a standard double room,
inclusive of service charges and taxes.

€	under €75
€€	€75 to €150
€€€	over €150

KULDĪGA: Metropole €
Historic
Baznicas iela 11, LV-3301
Tel *6335 0588*
🌐 hotel-metropole.lv
Skillfully restored, 19th-century
building in the centre of the
historic little town. Tidy en suites
and a friendly ambience.

LIEPĀJA: Libava €€
Luxury
Vecā ostmala 29, LV-3401
Tel *6342 5318*
🌐 libava.lv
Canalside hotel providing an
affordable slice of luxury with
smart en suite rooms, a
basement spa centre and a
sofa-filled conservatory.

LIEPĀJA: Promenade €€€
Luxury
Vecā ostmala 40, LV-3401
Tel *6348 8288*
🌐 promenadehotel.lv
Superbly renovated red-brick
warehouse on a canalside
location. Offers luxurious rooms
with all mod cons and a classy
café-restaurant.

RUNDĀLE: Baltā Māja €
B&B
Pilsrundāle, LV-3921
Tel *6396 2140*
Located in what were previously
servants' quarters just outside
Rundāle Palace, this 8-room B&B
offers simple accommodation
with a rustic touch.

SIGULA: Hotel Sigulda €€
Historic
Pils iela 6, LV-2150
Tel *6797 2263*
🌐 hotelsigulda.lv
This historic building in the
leafy centre of town provides
smart, cosy rooms and an
indoor pool in its interesting
modern annexe.

SIGULDA: Spa Hotel Ezeri €€
Spa
Sigulda, LV-2150
Tel *6797 3009*
🌐 hotelezeri.lv
Out in the countryside with
well laid out Scandinavian-style
rooms, a spa centre, pools and a
pleasant restaurant.

For map references see pp78–9

Where to Eat and Drink

Rīga

Lido Atpūtas Centrs €
Latvian
Krasta iela 76, LV-1019
Tel *6750 4420*
Theme-park-cum-restaurant
with a wooden barn, windmill
and children's playground, serving
tasty, order-at-the-counter
Latvian staples.

Pelmeņi XL €
Russian **Map** C3
Kaļķu iela 7, LV-1050
Tel *6722 2728*
Enjoy *pelmeņi* (Russian pastry
parcels) stuffed with minced
meat, cabbage or cottage
cheese at this popular order-
at-the-counter café that also
serves soups and salads.

DK Choice

Ķiploku Krogs €€
International **Map** C3
Jēkaba iela 3/5, LV-1050
Tel *6721 1451*
Just as its name suggests 'Garlic
Tavern' features garlic in almost
every dish, including the ice
cream. The menu labels the
dishes that do not contain any.
The results are less gimmicky
than might be expected and
there are some very exciting
choices.

Pie Kristapa Kunga €€
Latvian
Baznīcas iela 27/29, LV-1010
Tel *6729 4898*
With wooden tables, medieval
fittings and old Rīga atmosphere,
Kristapa Kunga is spread over many
floors. Expect hearty meat and fish
dishes and great Latvian beers.

Čarlstons €€€
International
Blaumaņa iela 38, LV-1011
Tel *6777 0572*
High-end cuisine in informal
surroundings, with grilled steaks
forming the centrepiece of a menu
that also covers Mediterranean
seafood and superb desserts.

Neiburgs €€€
International **Map** C3
Jauniela 25, LV-1050
Tel *6711 5522*
Quality Latvian–European fare
in a beautifully light and airy
Art Nouveau building. Choose
between pastas, salads, roast
meat and fish dishes.

Restaurant Gutenbergs €€€
International **Map** B3
Doma Laukums 1, LV-1050
Tel *6781 4090*
Elegant restaurant in the
Gutenbergs Hotel serving
impeccable European
cuisine in a sophisticated
atmosphere.

Vincent's €€€
French **Map** E2
Elizabetes iela 19, LV-1000
Tel *6733 2634*
Adventurous international
dishes with a classic French
core is what the menu offers at
this elegant, upscale restaurant,
just a short walk from the Art
Nouveau district.

Rest of Latvia

CĒSIS: Café Popular €
Latvian
Vienibas laukums 1, LV-4101
Tel *6412 0122*
In the basement of the Kolonna
Hotel, an atmospheric café
serving salads, pancakes and
inexpensive main meals to a
devoted local following.

JŪRMALA: Villa Joma €€€
International
Jomas iela 90, LV-2015
Tel *6777 1999*
Located in the heart of Jūrmala
on the main promenade near the
beach, Joma offers a classy
Mediterranean–Middle Eastern
menu that includes plenty of
exquisitely prepared seafood.

KULDĪGA: Pagrabiņs €
Latvian
Baznīcas iela 5, LV-3301
Tel *6332 0034*
With traditional wood and stone
interiors and a small terrace that

Price Guide

Prices are based on a three-course meal
for one, half a bottle of wine, including
cover charge, service and tax.

€	under €20
€€	€20 to €40
€€€	over €40

overlooks a stream, this is a good
place for freshwater fish and
traditional Latvain pork staples.

LIEPĀJA: Pastnieka Māja €€
International
Brīvzemnieka iela 53, LV-3401
Tel *6340 7521*
A combination of traditional
Latvian fare and mainstream
European cuisine in a building
that mixes traditional timber
features with modern minimalist
design. Pleasant summer garden.

LIEPĀJA: Vēcais Kapteinis €€
Latvian
Dubelsteina iela 14, LV-3401
Tel *6342 5522*
Set in an old half-timbered
house with a nautical theme,
the lovely 'Old Captain' serves
meat and fish dishes of a
high standard.

SIGULDA: Kaķu Māja €
Latvian
Pils iela 8, LV-2150
Tel *2905 0104*
Great example of a Latvian
self-service café, with home-
style meat, fish and poultry
staples served up in big,
inexpensive portions. Try
the fresh cakes.

SIGULDA: Aparjods €€
International
Ventas iela 1a, LV-2150
Tel *6797 4414*
Right in the centre of town,
this restaurant with a farmhouse
theme, serves traditional Latvian
and classic European cuisine.

Attractive dining area at Neiburgs, Rīga

ESTONIA

Presenting a heady mix of medieval heritage and technological advancement, Estonia has rebuilt itself in the post-Soviet era, adapting to the demands of the modern world while preserving a distinct cultural identity. With its rich historic architecture, natural landscapes and dynamic culture, the country makes a significant impression on the ever-growing number of visitors that it attracts.

Estonia's tumultuous history has resulted from its geographical position as a crossroads between Eastern and Western Europe. With Russia dominating its eastern border, Scandinavia surrounding it to the north and west and the other two Baltic States to its south, Estonia was considered a prize strategic asset among the regional powers through the centuries.

After regaining independence from the Soviet Union in 1991, Estonia was left severely dilapidated. But persistent reforms by successive governments have helped to stabilize the economy. Although the rural areas still lag behind the cities in raising living standards, Estonia has grown into a major travel destination. Its pristine islands and traditional villages are as alluring as its capital Tallinn, a pulsating city with a medieval Old Town.

History

Historical references to Estonia date from the early 13th century, when the Teutonic knights arrived, introducing a new social order in which the Germans dominated for several centuries. A bitter struggle ensued that saw the destruction of Estonia's pagan culture and its replacement by a harsh feudal system. The Danes were also involved, taking control of northern Estonia before being pushed out by the Teutonic knights. The 16th century saw Estonia as the major battleground between Russia and Sweden in the Livonian Wars (1558–82). By 1629, the country was in Swedish hands. The Swedes achieved much over the next 50 years, including the introduction of schools and the establishment of Tartu University. Later, however, the Swedish kings seized German-owned estates, incurring the wrath of the Germans, who turned to Russia's Peter the

A group of Estonian folk dancers performing in traditional costume during a local festival

◀ Tourists exploring the Old Town in Tallinn

Depiction of the Siege of Narva, Livonian Wars

Great for help. In 1709, Peter defeated the Swedish King Charles XII, which consigned the country to tsarist rule for the next 200 years.

During World War I (1914–18), the prospect of Estonian independence seemed bleak. However, the 1917 Revolution that ended the tsarist regime in Russia encouraged Estonia to declare independence in February 1918, in Pärnu. Political stability proved difficult to establish, however; there were 20 coalition governments between 1919

KEY DATES IN ESTONIAN HISTORY

1219 Danes seize Tallinn

1227 Germans conquer all of Estonia

1558–83 Northern Estonia comes under Swedish rule, southern Estonia under Polish rule

1629 Estonia passes into Swedish hands

1709 Great Northern War between Charles XII of Sweden and Peter the Great results in Russian victory

1885 Russification of the Baltics begins

1918 Declaration of Estonian independence signed; Germany loses World War I

1920 Treaty of Tartu confirms Estonia's independence

1939 Molotov-Ribbentrop Pact puts Estonia under the influence of the USSR

1940 Soviet occupation begins

1941 German occupation begins

1944 Return of Soviet forces; Stalinist era begins

1953 Stalin dies

1989 Baltic Way demonstratation occured

1991 Estonia declares independence

2004 Estonia joins NATO and the EU

2011 Introduction of the euro

and 1933. In 1934, a prominent nationalist politician, Konstantin Päts, staged a coup.

He continued to rule until the Soviet invasion on 16 June 1940, which brought a brutal end to independent Estonia. The German invasion, which came a year later, was seen by many in Estonia as a liberation. In September 1944, the Red Army returned to Estonia, forcing the Nazis to surrender, and subjecting the country to almost five decades of Soviet rule.

From the 1960s, Estonia's link with the non-Soviet world began to grow. At the time of the collapse of the USSR in 1991, Estonians were better prepared for a capitalist economy than any of the other Soviet republics. Thirteen years after independence, entry into the EU in 2004 and NATO has further strengthened the economy.

Language and Culture

In general, Estonians are more strongly influenced by Scandinavian culture than by that of their Baltic neighbours. Finns and Estonians also share close linguistic links through the Finno-Ugric language family. The most important aspects of Estonian culture are distinctly pagan in origin, such as the Midsummer festival Jaanipaev (John's Day), characterized by drinking, dancing and revelry. Folk culture is central to national identity, and the All Estonian Song Festival, held every five years since 1869, remains an iconic occasion for the nation.

Exploring Estonia

Estonia offers an irresistible blend of cultural heritage and natural beauty. Walking is an ideal way to explore the country's historic towns. Highlights include the capital Tallinn, with its lovely Old Town dotted with church spires and fascinating museums, picturesque Pärnu, with its elegant 19th-century villas and long sandy beach, and the charming university town of Tartu. The best way of getting around the country is by road, as most sights are within a few hours' drive of each other. A well-developed bus system links all the major towns and cities. Estonia's largest island, Saaremaa, is well connected to the mainland by ferry.

View towards the Baltic Sea from St Olav's Church, Tallinn

Sights at a Glance

1. Tallinn pp102–109
2. Saaremaa Island pp110–11
3. Pärnu pp112–13
4. Tartu pp114–15

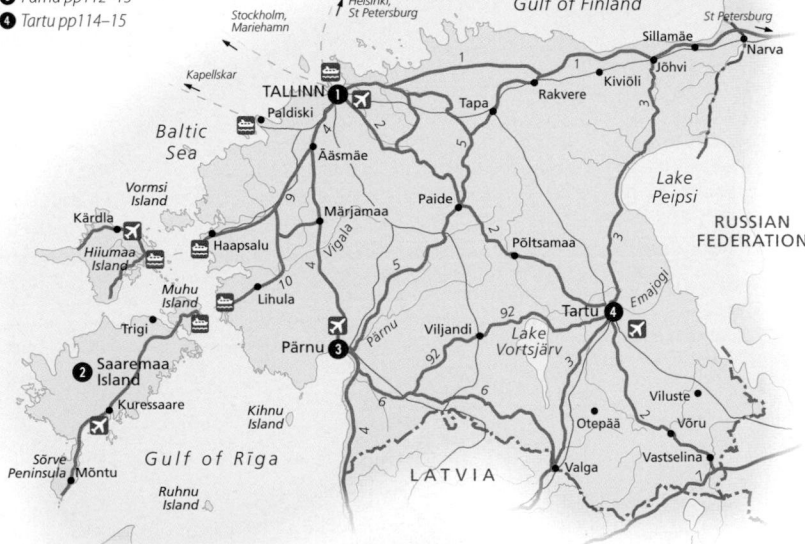

Elizabeth's Church, graced by an elegant spire, Pärnu

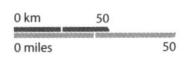

Key

— Motorway

— Major road

⸺ Railway

■ ■ International border

For keys to symbols see back flap

❶ Tallinn

Founded by the Danes at the beginning of the 13th century, Tallinn was for ages known by its Teutonic name, Reval. The city flourished in the 14th and 15th centuries, when it was one of the leading members of the powerful Hanseatic League. The brilliantly restored Old Town, a UNESCO World Heritage Site since 1997, is a living monument to this golden period of Tallinn's history. The vast majority of sights in the city are concentrated in and around Town Hall Square (Raekoja plats) and Toompea, in the medieval Old Town. Its winding cobbled streets are dotted with elegant back alleys, courtyards and spired churches, as well as fascinating museums that present the city's historic and cultural traditions. An architectural wonder, Tallinn has grown into a dynamic, chic and exciting city over the years, with a population of about 400,000 people.

Sights at a Glance

① Town Hall
② Holy Spirit Church
③ Great Guild Hall
④ Dominican Monastery
⑤ Niguliste Church
⑥ House of Blackheads
⑦ Estonian Museum of Applied
   Art and Design
⑧ St Olav's Church
⑨ Fat Margaret Tower
⑩ Toompea Castle
⑪ Alexander Nevsky Cathedral
⑫ Kadriorg Palace

Central Railway Station
150 m (170 yards)

TORNIDE VÄLJAK

Church of Transfigr of Our Le

SUUR-KLO

GUMNAASIUMI

NUNNE

RAHUKOHTU

KIRIKU PÕIK

TOOM-RÜÜTLI

KONTU

PIKK JALG

NUNNE

PIISKOPIAED

KIRIKU

Cathedral of
St Mary the Virgin

RATASKAEVU

DUN

KIRIKU PLATS

TOOMPEA

RUTU

TOOM-KOOLI

PIKK JALG

LÜHIKE JALG

NIGULISTI

⑤

⑩

LOSSI PLATS

⑪

LOSSI PLATS

TAANI KUNINGA GARDEN

RÜÜTLI

HARJU

FALGI TEE

KOMANDANDI TEE

RÜÜTLI

TOOMPEA

HARJUMÄGI

VABA
VÄL

KAARLI PUIESTEE

0 metres   200
0 yards   200

Key

▪ Street-by-Street area: *see pp104–105*
▫ Major sight / Place of interest
▬ Pedestrian street

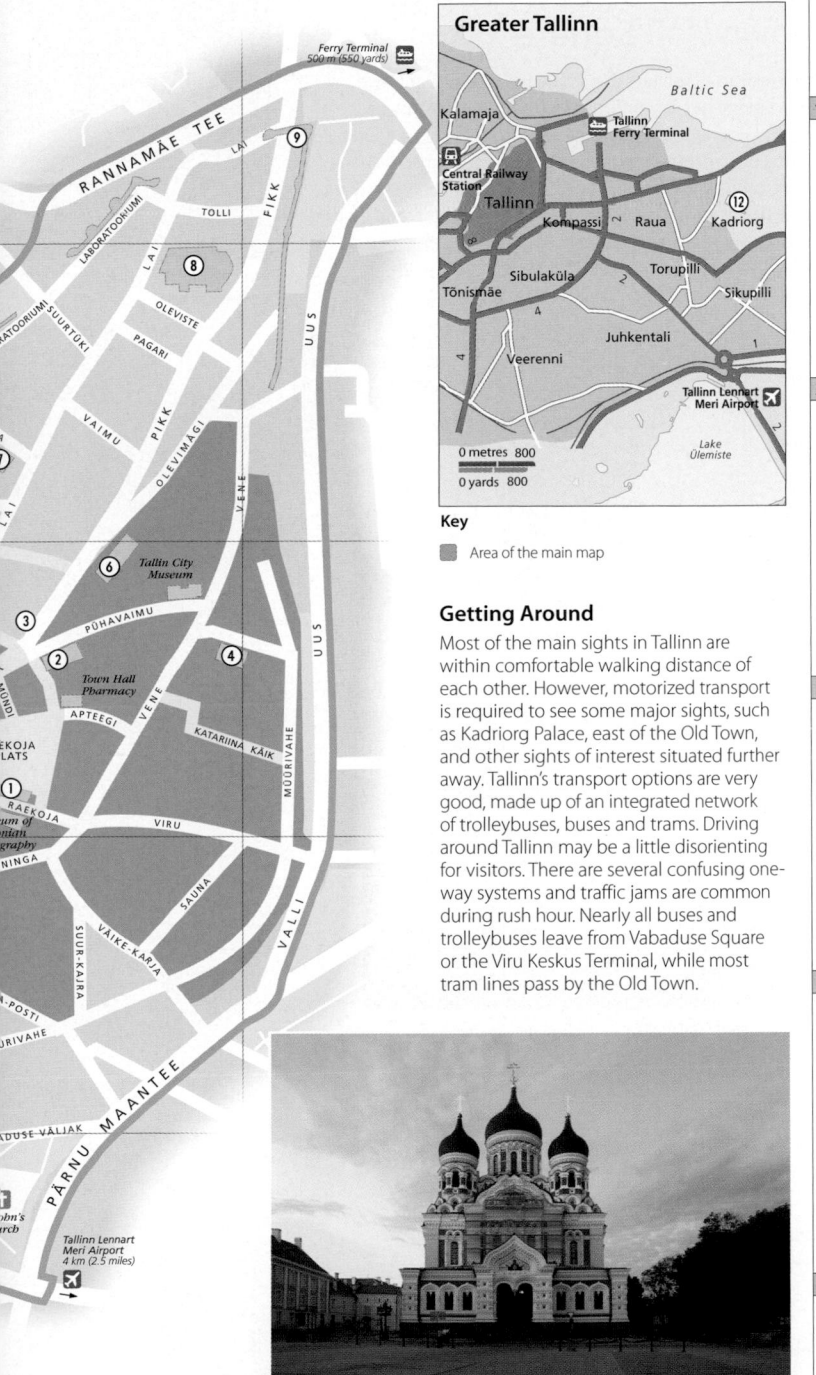

Greater Tallinn

Baltic Sea

Kalamaja

Tallinn
Ferry Terminal

Central Railway
Station

Tallinn

Kompassi   Raua   ⑫ Kadriorg

Sibulaküla   Torupilli

Tõnismäe   Sikupilli

Juhkentali

Veerenni

Tallinn Lennart
Meri Airport

Lake
Ülemiste

0 metres   800
0 yards   800

Key

☐ Area of the main map

Getting Around

Most of the main sights in Tallinn are within comfortable walking distance of each other. However, motorized transport is required to see some major sights, such as Kadriorg Palace, east of the Old Town, and other sights of interest situated further away. Tallinn's transport options are very good, made up of an integrated network of trolleybuses, buses and trams. Driving around Tallinn may be a little disorienting for visitors. There are several confusing one-way systems and traffic jams are common during rush hour. Nearly all buses and trolleybuses leave from Vabaduse Square or the Viru Keskus Terminal, while most tram lines pass by the Old Town.

The Neo-Byzantine Alexander Nevsky Cathedral in the Old Town, Tallinn

Street-by-Street: Around Town Hall Square

In the heart of Tallinn's Old Town, the magnificent Town Hall Square has for centuries served as a marketplace. Gently sloping, the cobblestoned square is surrounded by a ring of elegantly designed medieval buildings. The early 14th-century Town Hall is northern Europe's only surviving late-Gothic town hall. A meeting point for locals and visitors, the square captures the essence of the Old Town. In summer, it is filled with open-air cafés and restaurant tables.

Busy market in Town Hall Square, seen from the Town Hall tower

⑥ House of Blackheads was the meeting place for the Brotherhood of Blackheads.

Tallinn City Museum
Housed in a medieval merchants' house, this museum presents Tallinn's history through a variety of fascinating exhibits and artifacts.

★ Town Hall Pharmacy
Worth a visit just for its impressive interior, this long-running pharmacy also has a charming little museum displaying old curiosities.

Key

— Suggested route

0 metres	100
0 yards	100

② Holy Spirit Church
Regarded as one of Tallinn's most attractive churches, this splendidly preserved structure is a treasure trove of medieval and Renaissance features.

④ Dominican Monastery
Among Tallinn's oldest buildings, the monastery complex also includes an atmospheric museum which has some beautiful stone carvings.

Viru Street
One of the most famous in the Old Town, this busy street is packed with a variety of restaurants, bars, cafés and shops.

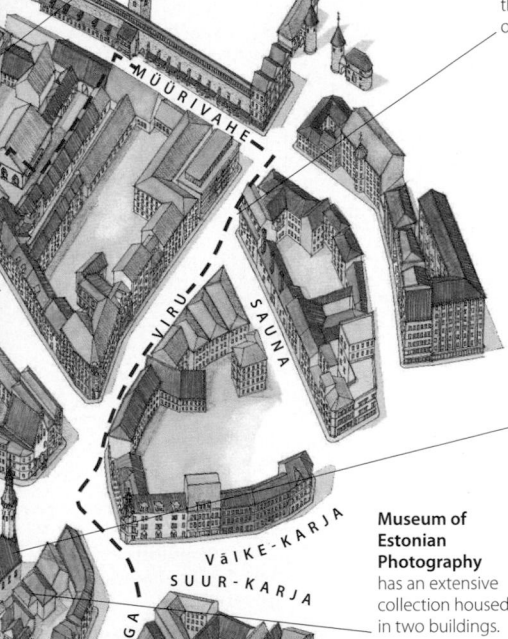

Museum of Estonian Photography has an extensive collection housed in two buildings.

① ★ Town Hall
Occupying pride of place in Town Hall Square, this imposing Gothic building has been the focus of civic life since the Middle Ages.

⑤ Niguliste Church
This remarkable Gothic church is now a Tallinn landmark boasting an excellent museum of religious art. The church holds organ recitals every weekend.

Outdoor tables of the cafés around Town Hall Square

① **Town Hall**
Tallinna raekoda

Raekoja plats 1. **Map** D3. **Tel** 645 7900.
5, 40. 1, 2, 3, 4. **Open** Jul–Aug:
10am–4pm Mon–Sat; Sep–Jun: by
appointment. **w tallinn.ee/raekoda**

One of the most revered symbols
of Tallinn, the Town Hall dates
back to 1404. Its steeply pitched
roof is supported by two tall
gables and a late-Renaissance
spire crowns the slender
octagonal tower. The windows
and crenellated parapet
complete the building's impressive appearance. Inside the
building, it is possible to see the
Citizens' Hall and the Council
Hall, although most visitors head
straight for the tower and the
115-step ascent to the top.
Facing the Town Hall is the Town
Hall Square *(see pp104–105)*, with
a vaulted arcade running along
its north façade. Small cafés put
out tables here in summer.

② **Holy Spirit Church**
Pühavaimu kirik

Pühavaimu 2. **Map** D3. **Tel** 646 4430.
5, 40. 1, 2, 3, 4. **Open** May–Sep:
9am–5pm Mon–Sat; Oct–Apr: 10am–
3pm Mon–Sat. 3pm (in English).
w eelk.ee/tallinna.puhavaimu

Considered one of the most
beautiful churches in Tallinn, the
Gothic building of the Holy Spirit
Church served as the Town Hall
chapel before being converted
into a church. Its whitewashed

exterior includes the oldest
public clock in Tallinn, with
carvings dating from 1684.
The stepped gable is topped
by a striking Baroque tower. The
spire was nearly destroyed by
fire in 2002, but was restored
within a year. Inside,
the church is a
treasure trove of
religious artifacts
and architecture,
from the magnificently
intricate Baroque
pews to the
Renaissance-era
pulpit. The sublime
altar triptych, *The
Descent of the Holy Ghost*
(1483), by Berndt Notke, is the
main highlight. The church
has a special place in Estonian
history, as the first sermons
in Estonian were delivered
here in 1535 following
the Reformation.

Clock at Holy
Spirit Church

③ **Great Guild Hall**
Suurgildi hoone

Pikk jalg 17. **Map** D3. **Tel** 641 1630.
5, 40. 1, 2, 3, 4. **Open** 11am–
6pm Thu–Tue. Estonian History
Museum: **Open** Check website for
timings. **w ajaloomuuseum.ee**

One of the most important
buildings in medieval Tallinn,
the Great Guild Hall was
constructed in 1417. It was
owned by a powerful union
of wealthy merchants and was
mainly used as a gathering
place for the members of the
Great Guild. The starting as
well as the end point of most
festive processions of Tallinn,
it was sometimes also rented
out for wedding parties and
court sessions.
 The late-Gothic building has
retained its original appearance
through the centuries, although
the windows were remodelled
in the 1890s. The
Great Guild Hall's
majestic interior
provides the perfect
setting for a branch
of the **Estonian
History Museum**.
The museum's
collection of
historical artifacts
covers Estonian
history from the Stone Age
to the mid-19th century in
fine detail. The exhibits,
which include everything
from jewellery to weaponry,
are accompanied by explana-
tory texts in Estonian, Russian
and English.

Altar of the Holy Spirit Church, Old Town

A passageway in the medieval Dominican Monastery

④ Dominican Monastery
Dominiiklaste klooster

Vene 16/18. **Map** D3. **Tel** 515 5489.
🚌 5, 40. 🚋 1, 2, 3, 4. **Open** May–Sep: 10am–6pm daily. Private tours are available year round. 🖼 🎧 tour offered to the monastery's inner chambers through the cloister. 🏛 Dominican Monastery Museum: **Open** mid-May–mid-Sep: 10am–6pm daily; winter: by appointment.
🖼 W **kloostri.ee**

Founded by Dominican monks in 1246, this monastery was a renowned centre of learning and thrived until the Reformation riots broke out in 1524. The Lutherans destroyed the monastery and forced the monks into exile. In 1531, a fire damaged most of the desecrated St Catherine's Church, the monastery's south wing.

After suffering neglect for four centuries, the ruined monastery was renovated in 1954. Today a serene cloister, its atmospheric passageways and a pretty inner garden draw visitors.

The star attraction, however, is the excellent **Dominican Monastery Museum**, with Estonia's largest collection of medieval and Renaissance stone carvings created by local stonemasons. One of the prominent works, a decorative relief of an angel on a triangular slab, is attributed to Hans von Aken, the popular 16th-century German Mannerist painter. The collection also includes carved 14th-century tombstones.

⑤ Niguliste Church
Niguliste kirik

Niguliste 3. **Map** C4. **Tel** 631 4330.
🚌 5, 40. **Open** 10am–5pm Wed–Sun. 🎫 tickets available until 4:30pm (call 644 9903 for bookings). 🎧 book in advance; extra charges for guided tours (up to 35 persons) in a foreign language. W **nigulistemuuseum.ee**

Dedicated to St Nicholas, Niguliste Church was built in the 13th century, although nearly all that remains today is from the 15th century. Most of Tallinn's medieval artworks were destroyed in the Reformation riots of 1524. However, according to legend, Niguliste Church escaped being ransacked due to the laudable efforts of the church warden, who sealed the door with melted lead. The church was restored during Soviet times after being damaged by Soviet air raids in World War II and since then has served as a museum.

Today, the building houses Tallinn's most impressive collection of medieval religious artworks. These include the detailed altarpiece, painted in 1482 by Herman Rode of Lübeck, showing scenes from the life of St Nicholas, as well as the beheading of St George, and *Dance Macabre*, a 15th-century frieze by the German painter and sculptor Bernt Notke, considered the church's finest object. Unfortunately only a fragment

Exterior of Niguliste Church, one of Tallinn's medieval treasures

Ornate front door of the Renaissance House of Blackheads

of the magnificent 30-m (98-ft) original remains. Organ and choral concerts are regularly held here at weekends.

⑥ House of Blackheads
Mustpeade maja

Pikk 26. **Map** D3. **Tel** 631 3199.
🚌 5, 40. 🚋 1, 2, 3, 4. **Open** only for chamber music concerts (call for timings & fill entry permit application on website) or by appointment.
W **mustpeademaja.ee**

This 15th-century Renaissance building was the meeting place of the Brotherhood of Blackheads, an association of unmarried merchants and shipowners, who could join the more powerful Great Guild upon marriage. The unusual name was inspired by the North African St Maurice, the organization's patron saint, whose image can be seen on the ornate front door of the building.

Unlike their counterparts in Rīga, the Tallinn Blackheads were obliged to defend the city in times of strife and proved themselves especially formidable adversaries during the Livonian Wars (*see p99*). However, in general, it seems that the wealthy Blackheads lived somewhat leisurely and hedonistic lives. The association survived until the Soviet invasion in 1940. Today, the House of Blackheads regularly hosts chamber music concerts in its elegant main hall.

⑦ Estonian Museum of Applied Art and Design

Eesti tarbekunsti ja disainimuuseum

Lai 17. **Map** D2. **Tel** 627 4600. 🚋 3.
🚌 1, 2. **Open** 11am–6pm Wed–Sun.
🅿 📷 🅦 etdm.ee

Housed in a converted 17th-century granary, the Estonian Museum of Applied Art and Design features the best in Estonian design from the early 20th century to the present day. The vast selection of exhibits is a splendid example of the nation's pride in applied arts. Many of the exhibits meld Scandinavian-style refinement with subtle Baltic irony to excellent effect. The furniture is especially eye-catching and a delight for art collectors. There are also some fine pieces of porcelain, dating from the 1930s to the 1960s by Adamson-Eric, one of the key figures of 20th-century Estonian art.

Since the museum opened in 1980 it has done a formidable job of promoting Estonian design at home and abroad. Be sure to pick up a copy of the map, which highlights some notable examples of Estonian design around Tallinn.

⑧ St Olav's Church

Oleviste kirik

Lai 50. **Map** D2. **Tel** 641 2241. 🚋 3.
🚌 1, 2. **Open** Apr–Oct: 10am–6pm
Tue–Sun. 🅿 ℹ 🅦 oleviste.ee

The 124-m (407-ft) spire of St Olav's Church is a major Tallinn landmark and the church holds a proud place in local history. Legend says that Tallinners wanted to build the tallest spire in the world to attract merchant ships and a complete stranger promised to help them. In return he wanted the people of the city to guess his name. When the church was nearing completion, the city fathers sent a spy to his home and found out his name. As he

The soaring spire of St Olav's Church looking out over the Baltic Sea

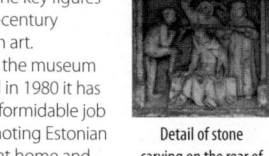
Detail of stone carving on the rear of St Olav's Church

was fixing the cross they called out "Olev" and he lost his balance and fell. In fact, the name of the church was a homage to King Olav II of Norway. The 159-m- (522-ft-) tall spire made the church the tallest building in the world in 1500 until a lightning strike burned it down in 1625. The church was struck by lightning six more times and burned down twice between 1625 and 1820. The original 16th-century structure of the church was renovated in the 19th century. St Olav's has an impressive vaulted ceiling and the church tower has a platform that offers breathtaking vistas of the city. The exterior rear wall features an elaborately carved 15th-century tombstone.

Metal ship replica on the entrance wall, Estonian Maritime Museum

⑨ Fat Margaret Tower

Paks Margareeta

Pikk 70. **Map** E1. **Tel** 641 1408.
🚋 3. 🚌 1, 2. **Open** 10am–6pm
Wed–Sun. 🅿 📷 call in advance.
ℹ Estonian Maritime Museum:
Open 10am–6pm Wed–Sun. 🅿
🅦 meremuuseum.ee

This 16th-century tower's evocative name derives from the fact that it was the largest part of the city's fortifications, with 4-m- (13-ft-) thick walls. It was originally built to defend the harbour as well as to impress visitors arriving by sea. From the top of the tower, there are good views of the Old Town and Tallinn's harbour and bay. Later, the tower was modified into a prison and was the scene of an outbreak of violence during the 1917 Revolution, when the prison guards were murdered by a mob of workers, soldiers and sailors.

Fat Margaret Tower houses the **Estonian Maritime Museum**, a curious collection of nautical paraphernalia spread out over four storeys. The exhibits include a fascinating insight into ship-building and historical accounts of the country's harbours. There is also a scale model of the *Estonia*, the car and passenger ferry that sank between Tallinn and Stockholm in 1994, killing 852 people on board.

For hotels and restaurants see p120 and p121

⑩ Toompea Castle

Toompea loss

Lossi plats 1a. **Map** B4. **Tel** 631 6357.
🚋 3, 4. **Open** 10am–4pm Mon–Fri.
📷 call in advance. 🚻 ♿
🌐 riigikogu.ee

The unassuming pink façade of Toompea Castle belies the history behind this vital seat of power. The castle now houses the Riigikogu (Estonia's Parliament), but for some 700 years it belonged to various occupying foreign powers. In the 9th century, a wooden fortress stood on the site, which was conquered by the Danes in 1219, who then constructed the stone fortifications around the hill, much of which still survives. The architecturally diverse castle complex features the 50-m (164-ft) Pikk Hermann Tower, above which flies the Estonian flag. The unique-looking Riigikogu, which was built in 1922, is situated in the castle courtyard. Toompea was a town in its own right enjoying its own entitlements and privileges until 1878, when it was merged with the rest of Tallinn below.

⑪ Alexander Nevsky Cathedral

Aleksander Nevski katedraal

Lossi plats 10. **Map** B4. **Tel** 644 3484.
🚋 3, 4. **Open** 8am–7pm daily.
♿ 📷 🌐 orthodox.ee

The imposing Alexander Nevsky Cathedral was built between 1894 and 1900, under orders from Tsar Alexander III.

The manicured ornamental garden of Kadriorg Palace

As intended, the Neo-Byzantine edifice dominates Castle Square (Lossi Plats) with its towering onion domes and golden crosses. A number of icons, mosaics and the bell for the tower were carried all the way from St Petersburg.

Legend has it that the cathedral was built on the grave of the Estonian folk hero Kalev. However, it is named after the sainted Russian Duke Alexander Nevsky (1219–63), who defeated the Livonian knights on the banks of Lake Peipsi in 1242 and conquered a great part of Estonia. Disliked by many Estonians as a symbol of the Russification policies of Alexander III, it was due to be demolished in 1924, but the controversial plan was never carried out.

The extravagant altar is made up of a dazzling display of icons, while the sheer scale of the cathedral's interior is equally impressive.

⑫ Kadriorg Palace

Kadrioru loss

Weizenbergi 37. **Map** F1. **Tel** 606 6400.
Open May–Sep: 10am–5pm Tue–Sun;
Oct–Apr: 10am–5pm Wed–Sun. 📷
🚻 ♿ 📷 📷

Built in 1718 under orders from the Russian Tsar Peter the Great, this palace was meant to serve as a summer residence for the imperial family. The palace was named Kadriorg – which means Catherine's Valley in Estonian – to honour his wife, Empress Catherine. Designed by the famous Italian master architect Nicola Michetti, it was built in Baroque style and made to look like an Italian villa. The main attraction of the palace, however, is the astonishingly ornate Great Hall, which ranks among the finest examples of Baroque exuberance in North Eastern Europe.

Kadriorg Palace today houses the **Museum of Foreign Art** which has an excellent collection of European paintings and sculpture. The palace is also used as a venue for lectures and theatre performances.

Just behind the palace, in the kitchen building, is the **Mikkel Museum** which has some 600 works of foreign art, including a selection of European, Chinese and Russian paintings, donated by Johannes Mikkel (1907–2006). Also worth a visit is the magnificently designed **Kumu Art Museum** near the palace, which shows the diversity of Estonian painting and sculpture.

The austere façade of Toompea Castle

❷ Saaremaa Island

The largest island in Estonia, Saaremaa is the jewel of its archipelago. The capital, Kuressaare, is strikingly picturesque, and its relatively tranquil atmosphere makes it an ideal base from which to explore the island. Sareema has a lot to offer in terms of things to see and do, but its extraordinary natural beauty is the real attraction and the reason why so many people feel compelled to return here. The breathtaking landscape of Vilsandi National Park and the abundance of old churches and fascinating historical relics that dot the island are just some of the highlights.

Art Nouveau lion statues outside the information centre, Kuressaare

Vilsandi National Park
Known for its awe-inspiring landscapes, unspoilt islets and bird sanctuaries, this park was established in 1993 to preserve the ecology of Estonia's coastal areas.

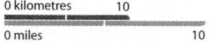

0 kilometres   10

0 miles   10

Mihkli Farm Museum
This museum has one of the most authentic displays of rural architecture and traditional lifestyles in Estonia. Many of the buildings here were built between 1827 and 1856.

For hotels and restaurants see p120 and p121

Vilsandi Island

Tiiga mõisa Peninsula

Vilsandi Island

78

78

Must

Kihelkonna

2

Karla

Lümanda

Saime

Gulf of Riga

77

Sõrve Peninsula

1

Mõntu

Sääre

Key

━━ Major road

══ Minor road

– – Ferry route

– • Park boundary

Angla Windmills

Standing along the main road from Kuressaare to Leisi, the five remaining wooden windmills at Angla are an iconic symbol of Saaremaa Island. In the mid-19th century there were 800 functional windmills on the island.

Hiiumaa Island 18km (11 miles)

Leisi
Triigi

Angla
Karja

Orissaare

Tagavere

Muhu Island

Liiva

Kuivastu

*Virtsu 8 km (5 miles)
Tallinn 145 km (90 miles)*

Laimjala

Kaali
79
10
③
Jpa

Koljala

Kuressaare

Ruhnu Island 75 km (45 miles)
uka

Karja Church

The medieval church is best known for its elaborate stone carvings, which include a relief of the Crucifixion above the side door and some remarkable figures inside depicting saints.

Bishop's Castle

The most important landmark in Kuressaare, the castle has a powerful defence tower and a slender watchtower, both unique features of the architecture of the Teutonic Order. Inside is the Saaremaa Regional Museum.

KEY

① **Sõrve Peninsula** can be explored on a bicycle or by car, and has spectacular scenery unparalled by any other area on the island.

② **Kihelkonna Church**, a splendid 13th-century place of worship, has an impressive steeple that was added in 1897.

③ **Kaarma Church**, which dates from the 13th century, has a striking 15th-century pulpit.

For keys to symbols *see back flap*

❸ Pärnu

Often referred to as Estonia's summer capital, Pärnu has historic buildings, pastel-coloured wooden houses and elegant late-19th-century villas set along leafy streets. With an ultra-modern concert hall and theatre, the town also has a noteworthy cultural scene. All the main sights are within walking distance from the town centre and the Old Town is centred around the pedestrianized Rüütli Street. However, Pärnu's main draw is its beautiful beach where Estonians flock throughout the summer, transforming the town into a thriving holiday spot.

🏛 Town Hall

Uus 4/Nikolai 3. ℹ️

The elegant Neo–Classical building that is now the Town Hall (raekoja) was erected in 1797 as a wealthy merchant's residence. In 1819, the structure was altered to serve as the house for the town's governor and, in 1839, it took on its current function as Pärnu's Town Hall. What makes it worth visiting is the magnificent Art Nouveau extension built in 1911. Its brooding dark exterior is in total contrast to the bright yellow façade of the original structure and provides a fascinating juxtaposition of two radically different architectural styles.

⛪ St Elizabeth's Church

Nikolai 22. **Tel** 443 1381. **Open** Jun–Aug: noon–6pm daily; Sep–May: 10am–4pm Mon–Fri. 🏛

An excellent example of local Baroque architecture, this church (Eliisabeti kirik) has an elegant ochre exterior and a maroon spire towering above the surrounding narrow side streets. It was founded specifically as a Lutheran church in 1747 by the Russian Empress Elizabeth (1709–61). Today, it serves as the largest Protestant place of worship in Pärnu.

The wood-panelled interior is refined and understated, but all the more impressive for it. The church's spire was built by Johann Heinrich Wülbern, who also constructed Rīga's St Peter's Church (see p84). St Elizabeth's Church is also renowned for its organ, one of the best in Estonia, built in 1929 by H Kolbe of Rīga.

Green domes and yellow walls of St Catherine's Church

⛪ St Catherine's Church

Vee 16. **Tel** 444 3198.
Open 9am–5pm daily. 🏛

Built in 1768 for the Pärnu garrison during the reign of Catherine the Great, St Catherine's (Ekateriina kirik) is arguably the finest example of a Baroque-style church in Estonia. With bottle-green domes and lemon-yellow walls, the church boasts an elegant exterior and opulent interior. Intended as an architectural showpiece, St Catherine's had a significant influence on Orthodox churches throughout the region.

🏛 Pärnu Concert Hall

Aida 4. **Tel** 445 5800. **Open** 11am–8pm daily (box office).
🎵 ♿ 🏛 🆆 concert.ee/parnu

Completed in 2002, the Pärnu Concert Hall (kontserdimaja) is a source of great pride for the local people. Designed by three architects – K Koov, K Nõmm and H Grossschmidt – the curvaceous glass and steel building is a strong example of modern Estonian architecture. Its seashell-like shape was intended to symbolize Pärnu's status as a coastal town. The multifunctional building mostly hosts theatre performances and concerts, although it also houses an art gallery and a music school.

🏛 Tallinn Gate

Mere puiestee.

The only trace of the 17th-century ramparts that protected Pärnu at one time, Tallinn Gate (Tallinna värav) still offers a fascinating glimpse of the once impressive fortifications. Until 1710, when Swedish rule came to an end, it was known as Gustav's Gate, named after King Gustav II Adolph of Sweden. Today, the gate's only function is to provide an elegant portal between the Old Town and the area leading to the sea. The cobblestoned passageway offers a relaxed walk.

🏛 Ammende Villa

Mere puiestee 7. **Tel** 447 3888.
🕐 noon–11pm daily.
🆆 ammende.ee

Built in 1905 by a wealthy local merchant for the wedding party

Tallinn Gate, sole remainder of Pärnu's 17th-century ramparts

Art Nouveau carving on the façade of Ammende Villa

Koidula Museum provides a moving testimony to one of Estonia's most revered poets. The museum, which was established in 1945, is situated in the building where her father, Johann Valdemar Jannsen, ran a primary school from 1857 to 1863.

The highlight of the museum is a reconstruction of the bedroom where the 43-year old Koidula died of cancer in 1886 in the Russian naval base of Kronstadt. Although very little of Lydia Koidula's work is available in English, the museum offers an insight into 19th-century Estonian literature.

VISITORS' CHECKLIST

Practical Information
128 km (80 miles) S of Tallinn.
🚇 44,000. 🛈 Uus 4/Nikolai 3,
447 3000. 🎬 Pärnu Film Festival (Jul), Oistrakh Festival (Jul).

Transport
✈ 5 km (3 miles) N of centre.
🚌 Riia mnt 116. 🚌 Pikk tänav. ⛴

of his beloved daughter, Ammende Villa is one of the most impressive examples of Art Nouveau architecture in Estonia. Over the years, it has served as a casino, a health establishment and a library, before two Estonian businessmen renovated it and converted it into a luxury hotel. The villa is located a short walk from the sea and the Old Town.

🏛 Lydia Koidula Museum
J V Jannseni 37. **Tel** 443 3313.
Open Jun–Aug: 10am–6pm, Sep–May: 10am–5pm.. 🅿 📷 call in advance. 🌐 **parnumuuseum.ee**

Situated a short walk across the Pärnu river, the Lydia

Lydia Koidula (1843–86)

Lydia Emilia Florentine Jannsen was a highly influential figure in Estonian history. Although convention forced her to write anonymously under the pseudonym Koidula, meaning "of the dawn", her poetry was ecstatically received. Her *My Country is My Love* became the unofficial national anthem during Soviet times. Some critics believe that Koidula's finest writing was her passionate correspondence with the writer Friedrich Reinhold Kreutzwald, although his wife eventually put an end to it. Koidula married a Latvian doctor whose work took them to Kronstadt in the Gulf of Finland, where she later died, pining for her country to the very end.

Lydia Koidula, Estonia's beloved writer and poet

Pärnu Town Centre

① Town Hall
② St Elizabeth's Church
③ St Catherine's Church
④ Pärnu Concert Hall
⑤ Tallinn Gate
⑥ Ammende Villa

0 metres 200
0 yards 200

❹ Tartu

Home to the venerable Tartu University, the town is frequently referred to as the intellectual capital of Estonia. The university was founded in 1632 by King Gustav II Adolph of Sweden and has played a major role in Estonian history ever since. With the second largest population in Estonia, Tartu has a thriving cultural scene and exciting nightlife, and makes a convenient base from which to explore the southeast of the country.

Town Hall Square, with the Kissing Students Fountain in the centre

🏛 Town Hall Square

Tartu's historic centre is set around this square (Raekoja plats), with the Emajõgi river to the east and Toomemägi hill just behind. Overlooking it from the top is the Town Hall, in front of which stands the **Kissing Students Fountain**

erected in 1998. Most of the square's original medieval architecture burned down in the Great Fire of 1775, and today, the gently sloping cobblestoned square is distinctly Neo–Classical, a look that is in harmony with the rest of the city centre.

🏛 Tartu University Main Building

Ülikooli 18. **Tel** 737 5100.
Open 11am–5pm Mon–Fri.
🐾 ⬜ ♿ 🆆 ut.ee

Completed in 1809, Tartu University Main Building (Tartu ülikooli peahoone), with its impressive Art Museum, is one of Estonia's finest Neo-Classical buildings. The first students registered in this university in 1632 making this only the second in the province of Swedish Livonia. The original graffiti by the students on the walls makes for amusing reading.

🏠 St John's Church

Jaani 5. **Tel** 744 2229. **Open** Jun–Aug: 10am–7pm Mon–Sat; Sep–May: 10am–7pm Tue–Sat. 🐾 🏠
🆆 eelk.ee/tartu.jaani

Dating from 1330, this church (Jaani kirik) was severely damaged by bombing during World War II. Despite extensive renovations and the addition of a new spire in 1999, the church remains one of Northern Europe's best examples of brick Gothic architecture. Hundreds of elaborate terracotta figures, dating from the Middle Ages, adorn its interior and exterior. Originally there were more than 1,000 figures but some have been destroyed over time.

Tartu Town Centre

① Town Hall Square
② Tartu University Main Building
③ St John's Church
④ Tartu Art Museum
⑤ Father and Son Statue

Leaning building in which the Tartu Art Museum is housed

Tartu Art Museum

Raekoja plats 108. **Tel** 744 1080.
Open noon–6pm Wed–Sun, till 9pm Thu. free last Fri of month. call in advance. **W** tartmus.ee

Housing one of the finest collections in the country, Tartu Art Museum (Tartu kunstimuuseum) features the works of prominent Estonian artists such as Elmar Kits (1913–72), Ülo Sooster (1924–70) and Marko Mäetamm (b. 1965). A thorough and captivating overview of Estonian painting, sculpture and drawing, which spans the 19th century through to the present, is also provided. The museum's building conspicuously leans to one side and belonged to the famous Russian Field Marshal Barclay de Tolly, who successfully led the Russian Army against Napoleon in 1812.

Father and Son Statue

Küüni (close to Poe).
Originally planned for Tallinn, this delightful little statue by Ülo Õun (1940–88) was conceived in 1977. It was cast in bronze in 1987, purchased by the Tartu town government in 2001 and finally unveiled on Children's Day (1 June) in 2004. The father figure is modelled after the sculptor, and the child after his son Kristjan, when he was around one-and-a-half years old. Interestingly, both father and son are the same size in this highly unusual and extremely poignant monument.

KGB Cells Museum

Riia 15b. **Tel** 746 1717.
Open 11am–4pm Tue–Sat.
W linnamuuseum.tartu.ee

Formerly situated in the basement of the regional headquarters of the KGB/NKVD, the KGB Cells Museum (KGB kongid) is a grim testimony to the nightmare of the Soviet occupation. Some of the former cells have been turned into exhibition spaces, while others have been restored to their original condition to provide a picture of what so many Estonians suffered under the Soviet regime. Much attention is paid to the mass deportations that took place between 1940 and 1949, including the official plans to carry them out. There are gut-wrenching artifacts from the Gulags, the notorious correction camps where thousands of Estonians died.

A desk in the KGB Cells Museum, with Stalin's portrait on the wall

Estonian National Museum

Kuperjanovi 9. **Tel** 742 1311.
Open 11am–6pm Tue–Sun. free on Fri. call in advance.
W erm.ee

Estonia's most important ethnological centre, the Estonian National Museum (Eesti rahva muuseum) boasts over one million artifacts collected over the last 100 years. Dedicated to the great Estonian folklorist and linguist Jakob Hurt (1839–1907), the museum highlights Estonian and other Finno-Ugric cultures, and its collection covers every imaginable aspect of life in this country. From chairs made of gnarled birch wood to warped wooden beer tankards, the displayed objects eloquently attest to a way of life that seems quaintly anachronistic in modern times.

In addition, there are vast photographic and documental archives and a collection of costumes, including a punk jacket (c.1982–85). The museum occasionally holds temporary exhibitions that encompass themes from furniture to photography.

Karl Ernst von Baer (1792–1876)

A Baltic-German biologist, Karl Ernst von Baer was one of the founders of embryology. His pioneering work in this area was recognized by Darwin, although Baer himself was extremely critical of the Theory of Evolution. Baer studied at Tartu University and later taught at Königsberg and the St Petersburg Academy of Sciences, before living out his last years in Tartu. A statue of him sitting pensively atop a large plinth has pride of place on Toomemägi. A rather endearing tradition takes place every year on the eve of St Philip's Day (1 May), when Tartu University students wash Baer's bronze hair.

Statue of Karl Ernst von Baer on Toomemägi

Practical & Travel Information

Estonia has a well-developed network of visitor information centres, even in small towns. There is an abundance of useful literature to help visitors get the best out of their trip. Several major international carriers from many European cities provide links to Estonia's capital, Tallinn. The country is also well served by both domestic and international ferries, with regular services to Tallinn and the popular island of Saaremaa.

When to Visit

The best time to visit Estonia is from May to September when it is pleasantly warm. July and August are the warmest months. Winter, between October and March, is cold, dark and damp but very atmospheric when forests are laden with snow. January, the coldest month, is best avoided, as is the rainy month of April, when the snow melts and turns sludgy.

Documentation

Citizens of EU member-states, the US, Canada, Australia and New Zealand can enter Estonia for a period of up to 90 days in a half-year period on presentation of a valid passport. Those wishing to stay beyond 90 days will need to apply for a national long-term visa or a residence permit. Visitors from other countries should enquire at their local Estonian embassy or consulate to check visa requirements before travelling. The official website of the Estonian Ministry of Foreign Affairs offers information on visa regulations. EU citizens are not subject to customs regulations, provided they

adhere to EU guidelines. All visitors should check for any customs duty or special permission required to export a cultural object, before buying it. For detailed information on all these guidelines, entrance regulations and visa charges, it is advisable to visit the official website of the European Commission.

Visitor Information

The network of information centres in the country is supported by an equally advanced structure of tourism websites. Most towns have a tourist information office located in or close to the town square. There are no tourist offices at the land borders or at Tallinn airport but there is one at the Tallinn harbour. Offices are generally open from 9am to 6pm on weekdays and for shorter hours on Saturdays; many are also open on Sundays. The staff are friendly and speak English. Free brochures listing local sights and events are available at these offices, which also sell maps and guidebooks. Estonia's official tourism website has a list of all the tourist information offices in the country.

Health and Security

Estonian *haigla* (hospitals) are generally in excellent condition and offer emergency treatment free of charge to everyone. It is safe for visitors to drink tap water.

Using common sense is the best way to ensure personal safety. Visitors should never accept drinks from strangers and avoid disreputable-looking nightclubs. It is wise not to carry any luxury items.

Facilities for the Disabled

Although there has been a significant improvement in recent years, Estonia is not very well equipped in providing facilities for the disabled. In Tallinn, there are several steep winding cobblestoned streets. Trolleybuses, trams and trains do not provide wheelchair access and only a few buses do.

Banking and Currency

In Estonia, banks are usually open from Monday to Friday between 9am and 6pm. Major banks stay open on Saturdays from 9am to 2pm. Exchange bureaus are widespread and have better exchange rates than hotels. ATMs are found everywhere, including petrol stations. In 2011 Estonia introduced the euro, and the former currency, the kroon, was withdrawn.

Communications

Estonia's communications infrastructure is very efficient. All phone lines are digital, ensuring high-quality connections. Mobile phone usage is particularly high. The post offices offer a range of express delivery options. Free Wi-Fi is available in most places.

Arriving by Air

The sleek-looking **Lennart Meri Tallinn Airport** is the main Estonian airport with regular scheduled flights. In recent years the airport has become a regional hub, serviced by

---

The Climate of Estonia

From May to September there is little risk of cold weather, but winters are freezing, with temperatures dipping to -12° C (10° F). Rain comes in brief, sharp outburst throughout the year. Days are short in December and January, with 18 hours of darkness, but between March and October, the long 12-hour days are excellent for outdoor activities.

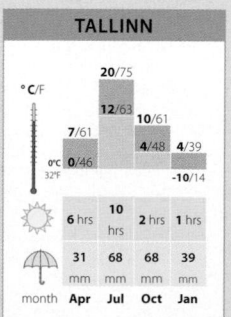

TALLINN			
°C/F	**20**/75		
	12/63	**10**/61	
	7/61	**4**/48	**4**/39
0°C **0**/46			
32°F			**-10**/14
6 hrs	**10** hrs	2 hrs	1 hrs
31 mm	68 mm	68 mm	39 mm
month **Apr**	**Jul**	**Oct**	**Jan**

approximately 15 airlines including major carriers such as **Finnair**, **airBaltic**, **Lufthansa** and **SAS**.

Founded in 1991, **Estonian Air** is the country's national carrier. Based in Tallinn, it offers a good standard of service in both business and economy class. The airline has direct links with several major European destinations as well as many Estonian cities and islands. Visitors from outside Europe need to catch a connecting flight from cities such as London, Copenhagen, Helsinki or Stockholm.

As a consequence of the EU "open-skies" policy, which was implemented in 2004, several economical carriers, such as **easyJet**, now provide daily flights to Tallinn from London.

Arriving by Sea

Estonia is very well served by ferry, with Tallinn's **Passenger Port** (*reisisadam*) handling about 7 million passengers a year. The main line **Tallink** has routes to Helsinki (Finland), Rostock (Germany) and Stockholm (Sweden), while other carriers such as **Viking Line** and **Eckerö Line** are accessible from Helsinki and Stockholm. Travellers from Helsinki are spoilt for choice, with a range of catamarans,

ferries and even a hydrofoil making the crossing at regular intervals. The Passenger Port is within walking distance of Tallinn's Old Town and a taxi ride should cost between €4-5. Tallinn also features on an increasing number of Baltic Sea cruise itineraries, although these normally only allow for a day's stopover.

Rail Travel

Tallinn's main railway station, **Balti Jaam**, is a short walk away from the Old Town. The only international link is a nightly train to Moscow. There is no longer a service to St Petersburg. Tickets should be pre-booked, since Russian visa specifications insist on dates of entry and exit. In 2012, a direct train link from Tartu to Riga was laid, avoiding the need to change trains in Valga.

Travelling by Coach

International coach routes to Estonia are provided by **Eurolines** and **Ecolines**, which operate connections between Tallinn and Berlin, Munich, Kaliningrad, Warsaw and St Petersburg, among others. International coaches arrive at the **Tallinn Bus Station**

(*bussijaam*). From there, it is a short taxi ride into the city centre, or one can catch tram number 2 or 4, or bus number 17, 17a or 23. Passengers travelling to Tallinn by bus from Riga or Vilnius can get off at the more central Viru väljak bus stop. There are also limited international coach connections to Pärnu and Tartu. The coach network is efficiently run and cheap, and services are clearly posted in bus stations. Timetables and fares for international routes are available on the carriers' websites.

Travelling by Car

Since 2007, when the Baltic States agreed to the Schengen Agreement (under which systematic border controls were abolished between Schengen countries), there are no border restrictions for Schengen visa holders. Crossing the border from Latvia is easy, especially for EU passport holders. The border crossing with Russia is slower and border guards are likely to scrutinize all documents. Visitors bringing their own car into Estonia are required to show the Vehicle Registration document, an international driving permit and a valid Green Card insurance policy.

DIRECTORY

Documentation
[w] vm.ee
[w] ec.europa.eu

Visitor Information
[w] visitestonia.com

Embassies

Canada
Toomkooli 13, Tallinn. **Tel** 627 3311. [w] canada.ee

United Kingdom
Wismari 6, Tallinn. **Tel** 667 4700. [w] ukinestonia.fco.gov.uk

United States
Kentmanni 20, Tallinn. **Tel** 668 8100. [w] estonia.usembassy.gov

Emergency Numbers

Ambulance
Tel 112.

Fire
Tel 112.

Police
Tel 112.

Arriving by Air

airBaltic
[w] airbaltic.com

easyjet
[w] easyjet.com

Estonian Air
[w] estonian-air.ee

Finnair
[w] finnair.com

Lennart Meri Tallinn Airport
Tel 605 8888.
[w] tallinn-airport.ee

Lufthansa
[w] lufthansa.com

SAS
[w] flysas.com

Arriving by Sea

Eckerö Line
[w] eckeroline.fi

Passenger Port
Sadama 25, Tallinn.
Tel 631 8550.
[w] portoftallinn.com

Tallink
[w] tallink.ee

Viking Line
[w] vikingline.fi

Rail Travel

Balti Jaam
Toompuiestee 37, Tallinn.
Tel 3721 447.
[w] baltijaam.ee

Arriving by Coach

Ecolines
[w] ecolines.ee

Eurolines
[w] eurolines.ee

Tallinn Bus Station
Lastekodu 46, Tallinn.
Tel 3721 2550.

Shopping & Entertainment

Traditional handicrafts and souvenirs can be found all over Estonia. There are plenty of stores and market stalls that specialize in art, antiques, jewellery and knick-knacks, and Tallinn's Old Town is one of the best places in the capital for gift shopping and souvenir hunting. The country also has an eclectic entertainment scene. The larger towns and cities such as Tartu and Pärnu have a crowded cultural calendar as well as splendid nightlife. Tallinn's many classical music and opera performances are a major draw.

Opening Hours

Most shops are open from 10am to 6 or 7pm on weekdays, from 10am to 4pm on Saturdays, and are closed on Sundays. Shopping centres usually open from 10am to 8 or 9pm daily. In small towns and villages, opening hours are more erratic at weekends, with many shops staying closed or only opening for half a day. Grocery stores normally keep longer hours. However, there are several 24-hour convenience stores in Tallinn.

Markets

Just about every Estonian town has a *turg* (market), although they often sell only fruit, vegetables, household goods and everyday items. Tallinn's main market, the open-air Central Market, offers a glimpse into the everyday life of the city's inhabitants. The market selling knitwear at the corner of Viru and Müürivahe Streets covers a stretch of the Old Town wall and is a great place to find a gift. Uus Käsitööturg, a popular stall in this market, has a good selection of traditional handicrafts and souvenirs. The Christmas Market in Town Hall Square *(see pp104–105)*, which runs through December, features everything from knitwear to marzipan.

Handicrafts

Towns and villages are good places to find local specialities, including textiles, ceramics and ornaments. Marble is used to make carved ashtrays, and pestles and mortars. The use of dolomite, a translucent mineral, is unique to Saaremaa Island *(see pp110–11)*.

Pärnu *(see pp112–13* is known for its handwoven linen.

Tallinn abounds with a variety of handicrafts. Wooden toys and utensils are common, as are traditionally woven rugs with beautiful and elaborate patterns and a wide range of ceramics. **Bogapott**, an exclusive ceramics studio, and **Galerii Kaks**, with its wide range of textiles, are worthy of a visit. **Nukupood** stocks handmade toys as well as dolls in traditional folk costumes. In **Katariina Gild**, craftsmen can be seen at work on handicrafts, jewellery and ceramics. **A-Galerii** has a great selection of local handmade jewellery.

Art and Antiques

Tallinn's contemporary art scene offers plenty of galleries and small shops that stock a variety of attractive oil paintings, graphic art, sculpture, textiles and off-beat ceramics. **Navitrolla Galerii** sells both originals and prints. The city also has many antique stores, selling everything from Soviet-era paraphernalia to exorbitantly priced Russian icons. Special permission is needed to take some objects out of the country, so check with the shop's manager before buying. With stunning bronze items, silverware and crystalware, **Reval Antiik** and **Shifara Art & Antiques**, are among Tallinn's best antique stores.

Food and Drink

Estonian food products can be bought in any supermarket. Rye bread is a local staple, as are sprats, smoked fish and cheese. Try **Kaubamaja** and **Stockmann**, two of the country's largest department stores, for a variety. Chocolate- lovers should try the brand Kalev, Estonia's oldest confectionary producer and, in Tallinn, the handmade delicacies at **Anneli Viik**. There are also numerous bakeries selling delicious pastries and cakes.

Estonia's national drink is a sweet brown liqueur called Vana Tallinn, but in terms of consumption, beer is the most popular tipple. Saku Original, Tartu Alexander and A Le Coq are all popular brands. Locally made as well as quality imported vodka is cheaper here than in other European countries. Saare Dzinn, a gin flavoured with berries from the Estonian islands, is good too. **Liviko**, one of Estonia's leading alcohol producers, has stores all over Tallinn.

Nightlife

Tallinn's Old Town is packed with bars and pubs of every size and description. There are several popular Irish and English-style pubs, including **Molly Malone's** and **Scotland Yard**, as well as stylish lounge bars such as **Déjà Vu** and the extravagant **Lounge 24**. There are also a number of quieter, cosier pubs scattered around the Old Town. **Hell Hunt**, contrary to its name, is a relaxing spot for a chat and a drink. Most of the good clubs are situated in or within walking distance of the Old Town. Many, such as **Bonnie and Clyde**, are equally popular with locals and visitors. **Club Privé** and **BonBon** are the most exclusive hangouts, while serious clubbers can try the port-side **Oscar**.

Elsewhere, Tartu has an impressive range of lively places. One of the best-known nightclubs is **Atlantis**, while the most exclusive is **Illusion**. Another favourite is the **Maailm**. Occasional live performances take place at the **Genialistide Klubi**.

Pärnu also has an active nightlife. **Lime Lounge** is a stylish place for a drink, while **Postipoiss** is a restaurant-cum-pub with frequent live music. Among the clubs, **Mirage** is often packed, while **Bravo** is the slickest.

Music, Theatre and Dance

Lovers of live music are spoilt for choice in Tallinn. **Café Amigo** attracts the biggest local rock, pop and blues bands. **Von Krahl Baar** is one of the best places in the city to experience the local alternative scene, while **Rock Café** offers everything from blues to funk. **No99** hosts jazz concerts on Fridays and Saturdays.

Estonia has an outstanding tradition of classical music. Tallinn's **National Symphony Orchestra** regularly puts on sell-out performances. Concerts also take place in churches and in the **Estonian Music Academy**. **Kanuti Gildi Saal** usually hosts the best

of contemporary Estonian and international dance.

The best place for serious theatre lovers is the **Von Krahl Theatre** (though English translations are rare) and the **Tallinn Linnateater**, which specializes in contemporary works.

In Tartu, the main concert venue, **Vanemuine**, stages theatre, classical music, ballet and other shows while in Pärnu, the town's Concert Hall hosts a wide range of concerts and events.

Eesti Muusikafestivalid has a list of nationwide music festivals and *The Baltic Times* and *In Your Pocket* offer information on arts and entertainment. Bookings for

cultural events can be made at the venue or through ticketing agencies such as **Piletilevi**.

Folk Festivals

A major part of Estonia's cultural life revolves around folk festivals. Among the most important, the **Folkloorifestival** in Võru is one of the biggest, while the **Hiiu Folk Festival** in Hiiumaa has a particularly authentic ambience created by its rustic setting. The splendid **Narva Historic Festival** involves a re-enactment of the Great Northern War, while Obinitsa hosts several festivals celebrating Setu culture.

DIRECTORY

Handicrafts

A-Galerii
Hobusepea 2, Tallinn.
Tel 646 4101.

Bogapott
Pikk jalg 9, Tallinn.
Tel 631 3181.

Galerii Kaks
Lühike jalg 1, Tallinn.
Tel 641 8308.

Katariina Gild
Vene 12, Tallinn.
Tel 644 5365.

Nukupood
Raekoja plats 18, Tallinn.
Tel 644 3058.

Art and Antiques

Navitrolla Galerii
Pikk tanav 36, Tallinn.
Tel 631 3716.

Reval Antiik
Harju 13, Tallinn.
Tel 644 0747.

Shifara Art & Antiques
Vana-posti 7, Tallinn.
Tel 644 3536.

Food and Drink

Anneli Viik
Pikk 30, Tallinn.
Tel 644 4530.

Kaubamaja
Gonsiori 2, Tallinn.
Tel 667 3100.

Liviko
Mere pst 6, Tallinn.
Tel 683 7745.

Stockmann
Liivalaia 53, Tallinn.
Tel 633 9539.

Nightlife

Atlantis
Narva mnt 2, Tartu.
Tel 738 5485.

BonBon
Mere pst 6e, Tallinn.
Tel 661 6080.

Bonnie and Clyde
Olümpia Hotel, Liivalaia 33, Tallinn. **Tel** 682 3000.

Bravo
Hommiku 3, Pärnu.
Tel 444 1847.

Club Privé
Harju 6, Tallinn.
Tel 631 0545.

Déjà Vu
Sauna 1, Tallinn.
Tel 645 0044.

Genialistide Klubi
Lai 37, Tartu.
Tel 5348 5530.

Hell Hunt
Pikk 39, Tallinn.
Tel 681 8333.

Illusion
Raatuse 97, Tartu.
Tel 742 4341.

Lime Lounge
Hommiku 17, Pärnu.
Tel 449 2190.

Lounge 24
Radisson Blu Hotel Tallinn, Rävala pst 3.
Tel 682 3424.

Maailm
Rüütli 12, Tartu.
Tel 742 9099.

Mirage
Rüütli 40, Pärnu.
Tel 447 2404.

Molly Malone's
Mündi 2, Tallinn.
Tel 631 3016.

Oscar
Sadama 6, Tallinn.
Tel 661 4721.

Postipoiss
Vee 12, Pärnu. **Tel** 446 4864.

Scotland Yard
Mere pst 6e, Tallinn.
Tel 653 5190.

Music, Theatre and Dance

Café Amigo
Hotel Viru, Viru väljak 4, Tallinn. **Tel** 680 9380.
Ⓦ amigo.ee

Eesti Muusikafestivalid
Ⓦ festivals.ee

Estonian Music Academy
Rävala 16, Tallinn.
Tel 667 5700.
Ⓦ ema.edu.ee

Kanuti Gildi Saal
Pikk 20, Tallinn.
Tel 646 4704. Ⓦ saal.ee

National Symphony Orchestra
Ⓦ erso.ee

No99
Sakala 3, Tallinn.
Tel 668 8798.

Piletilevi
Ⓦ piletilevi.ee

Rock Café
Tartu mnt. 80d, Tallinn.
Tel 681 0878.
Ⓦ rockcafe.ee

Tallinn Linnateater
Lai 23, Tallinn.
Tel 665 0800.
Ⓦ linnateater.ee

Vanemuine
Vanemuise 6, Tartu.
Tel 744 0165.
Ⓦ vanemuine.ee

Von Krahl Baar
Rataskaevu 10/12, Tallinn.
Tel 626 9090.
Ⓦ vonkrahl.ee

Von Krahl Theatre
Rataskaevu 10, Tallinn.
Tel 626 9090.
Ⓦ vonkrahl.ee

Folk Festivals

Folkloorifestival
Ⓦ werro.ee

Hiiu Folk Festival
Ⓦ hiiufolk.ee

Narva Historic Festival
Ⓦ narvamuseum.ee

Where to Stay

Tallinn

Hotel G9 €
B&B Map F1
Gonsiori 9, 10117
Tel *626 7130*
W hotelg9.ee
Strikingly decorated, decent rooms located on the third floor of an office building that is a ten-minute walk from the Old Town and conveniently close to several restaurants, theatres, bars and casinos.

The Monk's Bunk €
Hostel Map C5
Tatari 1, 10116
Tel *636 3924*
W themonksbunk.com
Located just 5 minutes outside the Old Town, this smart hostel with a friendly buzz has a bar and plenty of social areas including some that are used to project films.

Old House Guesthouse
and Hostel
B&B €
Uus 26, 10111 Map E2
Tel *641 1281*
W olhouse.ee
Excellent-value accommodation located in the Old Town with nice rooms and a communal kitchen. Dorm-style accommodation for backpackers is also available, just a few doors away on the same street.

Merchant's House Hotel €€
Design Map C3
Dunkri 4/6, 10123
Tel *697 7500*
W merchantshousehotel.com
A chic, medieval-meets-modern hotel in a tastefully adapted 14th-century building, just off the Town Hall Square.

Pirita Cloister Guesthouse €€
B&B Map F1
Merivälja tee 18, 11911
Tel *605 5000*
W piritaklooster.ee
Close to Pirita's long, sandy beach and next to the ruins of medieval Pirita Abbey, this is an award-winning modern guesthouse.

Schlössle €€€
Luxury Map D3
Pühavaimu 13/15, 10123
Tel *699 7700*
W schloesslehotel.com
The splendid medieval-style interiors of this elegant hotel in the heart of the Old Town,
perfectly complement the lavishly furnished rooms. Its restaurant is outstanding.

DK Choice

Three Sisters €€€
Historic Map E1
Pikk 71, 10133
Tel *630 6300*
W threesistershotel.com
The three tall, narrow, 14th-century merchants' houses at the corner of Pikk and Tolli have long been a Tallinn landmark. Renovated to form a luxury hotel, The Three Sisters offers 23 individually furnished rooms and suites. Original features, from timber beams to wall frescoes that have been left intact, add considerable charm.

Von Stackelberg €€€
Luxury Map F1
Toompuiestee 23, 10137
Tel *660 0700*
W vonstackelberghotel.com
Once the residence of a Baltic baron; has warm and stylish rooms that are equipped with state-of-the-art facilities.

Rest of Estonia

PÄRNU: Rannahotell €€
Resort
Ranna puiestee 5, 80010
Tel *443 2918*
W rannahotell.ee
A modernist masterpiece dating from 1937, the hotel offers stylish rooms with balconys in a beachside building that looks like an ocean liner.

Flags adorn the entrance of the Schlössle in Tallinn

PÄRNU: Ammende Villa €€€
Historic
Mere puiestee 7, 80010
Tel *447 3888*
W ammende.ee
In a glorious Art Nouveau house built in the early 1900s, this luxurious hotel has features rooms in authentic period style.

SAAREMAA: Linnahotell €€
Spa
Lasteala, Kuressaare, 93819
Tel *453 1888*
W linnahotell.com
Despite its rather minimalist exterior, Linnhotell offers neat and comfortable rooms. Just off the town's historic centre.

SAAREMAA: Georg Ots
Spa Hotel €€€
Spa
Tori 2, Kuressaare, 93810
Tel *455 0000*
W gospa.ee
Warm and intimate hotel known for its excellent swimming pool and spa.

TARTU: Villa Margaretha €
B&B
Tähe 11/13, 50108
Tel *731 1820*
W margaretha.ee
Gorgeous Art Nouveau villa with atmospheric rooms, many with original Art Nouveau-style decoration. A contemporary annexe has split-level suites.

TARTU: Pallas €€
Design
Riia 4, 51004
Tel *730 1200*
W pallas.ee
Rooms with big windows and great city views, each decorated in the style of an artist who passed through Tartu's famous Pallas Art School.

TARTU: London €€€
Luxury
Rüütli 9, 51007
Tel *730 5555*
W londonhotel.ee
With classically decorated rooms and attentive staff right in the centre of town, this is among Tartu's best business-class hotels.

Where to Eat and Drink

Tallinn

African Kitchen €
African   **Map** E2
Uus 34, 10111
Tel *644 2555*
The vibrant, lively interior matches the excellent food served here. Great selection of spicy, but delicious African recipes. Also, offers plenty of vegetarian choices.

Olde Hansa €€
Estonian   **Map** D4
Vana turg 1, 10140
Tel *627 9020*
Go on a journey through Tallinn's golden age at this immensely enjoyable restaurant that has a medieval twist to its meaty fare served on large tables in a candlelit hall, by staff dressed in period costumes.

Vanaema Juures €€
Estonian   **Map** C3
Rataskaevu 10, 10123
Tel *626 9080*
There are few better places than 'At Grandma's', for splendidly presented, rustic Estonian meat, game and fish dishes. Located in an intimate little cellar.

Von Krahli Aed €€
Estonian   **Map** C3
Rataskaevu 8, 10123
Tel *626 9088*
Contemporary Estonian cuisine – local ingredients prepared with a Mediterranean touch, served in an urban-meets-rustic setting.

Bocca €€€
Italian   **Map** D2
Olevimägi 9, 10123
Tel *611 7290*
Favoured by Tallinn's trendy crowd for quality seafood, exciting pasta-and-sauce combinations and classic meats with a Mediterranean influence.

DK Choice

Bordoo €€€
French   **Map** E1
Pikk 71, 10133
Tel *630 6300*
Located in the luxurious Three Sisters Hotel, Bordoo oozes class. The seasonally-changing, primarily French menu, includes classic meat and seafood mains in addition to the multi-course tasting menus. Dine in the charming summer courtyard.

Art Deco interior at Gloria, one of Tallinn's most popular restaurants

Gloria €€€
French   **Map** C4
Müürivahe 2, 10146
Tel *640 6804*
An Art Deco interior and a menu of fine French preparations marks Gloria as one of Tallinn's classic dining venues.

Kohvik Moon €€€
Estonian
Võrgu 3, 10415
Tel *631 4575*   **Closed** *Sun*
In up-scale, well-designed interiors north of the Old Town, Kohvik Moon serves traditional Estonian fare with a contemporary twist.

Rest of Estonia

PÄRNU: Postipoiss €
Russian
Vee 12, 80011
Tel *446 4864*
At an old postal inn, this Russian-themed restaurant has a vast menu that features *blini* (pancakes), *pelmeni* (dumplings) and *solianka* (meat and vegetable soup).

PÄRNU: Steffani €
Italian
Nikolai 24, 80011
Tel *443 1170*
Eternally popular pizzeria on the route from Old Town to the beach, serving a big choice of thin-crust pies alongside pastas, salads and a few Mexican-inspired dishes. Gets busy.

SAAREMAA: Veski €€
Estonian
Pärna 19, Kuressaare, 93814
Tel *453 3776*

Price Guide
Prices are based on a three-course meal for one, half a bottle of wine, including cover charge, service and tax.

€	under €25
€€	€25 to €50
€€€	over €50

An imposing windmill in the centre of Kuressaare is the setting for this pub-restaurant that serves traditional Estonian pork-and-sauerkraut dishes, local seafood and game.

SAAREMAA: Rose Restaurant €€€
International
Tallinna 15, Kuressaare, 93811
Tel *666 7000*
Elegant restaurant in the Grand Rose Spa Hotel, serves Estonian–European fare with local fish and game the specialities. Excellent selection of wines.

TARTU: Genialistide Klubi €
Vegetarian
Magasini 5, 51007
Tel *5657 1545*
Alternative club with a bohemian atmosphere and excellent daytime café serving tasty, healthy and inexpensive fare.

TARTU: Ülikooli Kohvik €
Estonian
Ülikooli 20, 51007
Tel *737 5405*
Spread over two floors of a historic house, this relaxing café offers order-at-the-counter Estonian food.

TARTU: Dolce Vita €€
Italian
Kompanii 10, 51007
Tel *740 7545*
Pizzas, pastas and much more besides, in this quality Italian restaurant that is decorated with posters advertising Fellini films.

Diners enjoying a hearty meal in Olde Hansa, Tallinn

MOSCOW AND ST PETERSBURG

From her 12th-century origins as an obscure defensive outpost, Moscow has come to govern one sixth of the globe. The story of her rise is laced with glory and setbacks, including the two centuries when St Petersburg was the capital of Russia and Moscow lived as a dignified dowager. Today, both cities symbolize the "New Russia".

The Russian Federation, or Russia as it is commonly known, stretches from the Baltic to the Pacific and is the world's largest country. Moscow, the capital, lies at the heart of European Russia, while St Petersburg is situated at its northwest corner. Till the end of 1991, Russia was part of the Soviet Union, but Mikhail Gorbachev's policies of glasnost (openness) and perestroika (restructuring) led to changes that saw the end of the USSR. There have been social problems over the years, however the standard of living is improving. Today, Russia is a member of the CIS, a commonwealth of former Soviet republics.

History

First mentioned in the *Ipatievskaya Chronicles* of 1147, when Kiev was the capital of Russia, Moscow has endured wars, revolutions and drastic social changes. Over four centuries it was transformed from an isolated kremlin (fortress), built in 1156, into a thriving capital. Ironically, Moscow's pre-eminence in Russia came about as a result of the 250-year domination by the Mongols, who invaded in 1137. In the 14th century they chose Moscow's grand prince, Ivan I, to collect tribute from subjugated principalities. However, this sealed their fate and they were defeated in the Battle of Kulikovo

The ornate interior of the Church on Spilled Blood, St Petersburg

◀ The pretty central passageway of the Summer Garden, flanked by statues

Painting of Lenin leading the Russian Revolution, 1917

transformed medieval Russia into a modern European state. He built the city of St Petersburg and declared it the capital in 1712. For most of the 18th century Russia was ruled by women, of whom the most significant was Catherine II.

Napoleon's unsuccessful invasion of Moscow in 1812 and his defeat turned Russia into a major European power. Towards the end of the century, however, the country was on the verge of breakdown. Economic unrest and the urgent need for social reform led to the 1905 Revolution. The outbreak of World War I brought about a surge of patriotism, but wartime losses provoked a series of strikes, the tsar's abdication and the establishment of a provisional government. This was the signal for exiled revolutionaries, such as Vladimir Ilyich Lenin, to organize an uprising in October 1917, heralding more than 70 years of Soviet rule. In 1918, Moscow was reinstated as the capital of the country.

The Germans invaded the Soviet Union in 1941, subjecting St Petersburg (then Leningrad) to a 900-day siege, but Moscow was never taken; Hitler had underestimated both the harshness of the Russian winter and the willingness of the people to fight.

The USSR ceased to exist in 1991. Since then, Russia has tried to reinvent itself as a modern democratic nation. Vladimir Putin succeeded Boris Yeltsin as president in 2000. In 2008, after two terms as president, Putin became prime minister.

In March 2012, Putin became the president of Russia for the third time.

(1380), and the Russian nation was reborn. During the long reign of Ivan III the Great (r. 1462–1505), Moscow's prestige increased and continued under his grandson Ivan the Terrible (r. 1533–84), the first to be called "Tsar of All the Russias". Yet, his reign ended in disaster, leading to the so-called Time of Troubles. To end this strife, in 1613, Moscow's citizens chose Mikhail Romanov to be tsar, thus initiating the 300-year Romanov rule. His grandson, Peter the Great,

KEY DATES IN RUSSIAN HISTORY

863 Missionaries Cyril and Methodius create the Cyrillic alphabet

1147 Moscow is founded

1380 Mongols defeated at the Battle of Kulikovo

1613 Mikhail Romanov becomes first tsar of the Romanov Dynasty

1682 Peter the Great ascends the throne

1703 St Petersburg is founded

1712 Seat of government moves to St Petersburg

1762 Catherine II seizes the throne

1812 Napoleon invades Moscow but has to retreat

1861 Emancipation of serfs

1906 Inauguration of the Duma (parliament)

1917 The Russian Revolution

1918 Civil War starts. Capital moves to Moscow

1953 Death of Stalin

1991 Dissolution of the USSR

1955 Warsaw Pact is established

2000 Putin becomes president of Russia

2008 Medvedev elected president of Russia

2012 Former president Medvedev becomes Prime Minister. Putin elected President of Russia.

Language and Culture

Russian is the official language of the people of Moscow and St Petersburg and Cyrillic is the alphabet used. Classical music is the central theme of a large number of festivals attracting performers from all over the world. Christmas masquerades and the Spas Yablochni Medovy harvest celebration are popular folk festivals.

Exploring Moscow and St Petersburg

The city of Moscow offers a wide variety of sights, ranging from the historic and architectural treasures enclosed within the walls of the Kremlin, to galleries housing spectacular collections of Russian and Western art. Public transport in Moscow is abundant and efficient and an ideal way to explore the city. St Petersburg's short history is reflected in many of its museums such as the Hermitage, which displays Catherine the Great's fine art collection. The most enjoyable way to get around St Petersburg is on foot.

Engraved doors in St Isaac's Cathedral, St Petersburg

Sights at a Glance

❶ *Moscow pp126–41*
❷ *St Petersburg pp142–59*

Petrozavodsk

Lake Onega

M18

Onega

Helsinki, Lübeck, Stockholm, Tallinn

Lake Ladoga

❷ St Petersburg

Volkhov

Belozersk

M11

Kolpino

Gatchina

Cherepovets

Vologda

M20

Novgorod

M10

Yaroslavl

Volga

0 km   100
0 miles   100

Tver

M8

Key

— Motorway

— Major road

— Railway

M9   *Zelenograd*   *Vladimir*

M7

MOSCOW ❶   *Elektrostal*

M1   *M5*

M2

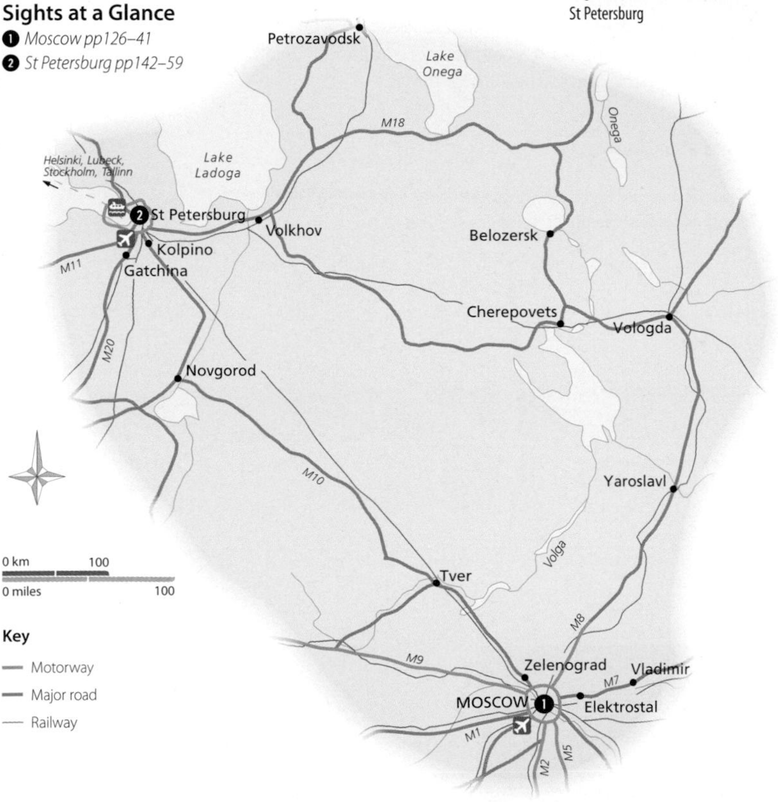

Great Kremlin Palace viewed from the Kremlin embankment, Moscow

❶ Moscow

With a population of over ten million, the Russian capital is now a place where past and present combine to captivate and charm. Most of Moscow's sights are situated in the city centre, within the area bounded by the Garden Ring (Sadovoye Koltso) and the Boulevard Ring (Bulvarnoye Koltso). From the gleaming onion domes of its churches to the graves of Soviet heroes, reminders of the city's past appear in almost every corner. At the heart of the city lies the Kremlin – a source of wealth and power that has dominated Russian life for over 800 years – comprising an impressive complex of buildings from the 15th to the 20th centuries.

Sixteenth-century frescoes in the Cathedral of the Assumption

Sights at a Glance

① Trinity Tower
② Ivan the Great Bell Tower
③ Cathedral of the Assumption
④ Cathedral of the Archangel
⑤ Cathedral of the Annunciation
⑥ State Armoury
⑦ Resurrection Gate
⑧ Red Square
⑨ Lenin Mausoleum
⑩ St Basil's Cathedral pp134–5
⑪ GUM
⑫ Melnikov House
⑬ Pushkin House-Museum
⑭ Pushkin Museum of Fine Arts
⑮ Cathedral of Christ the Redeemer
⑯ Tretyakov Gallery pp140–41
⑰ Gorky Park
⑱ Novodevichiy Convent

Ivan the Great Bell Tower, with the Tsar Bell in the foreground

Getting Around

Moscow's centre is quite spread out and not easily covered on foot. However, the area within the Boulevard Ring contains many sights and is good for walking. The city's vast metro network is the most reliable way of getting around, and trolleybuses are a good option in the city centre. Taxis are the most flexible, but the most expensive way of getting around. River cruises are pleasant and pass several major sites of interest.

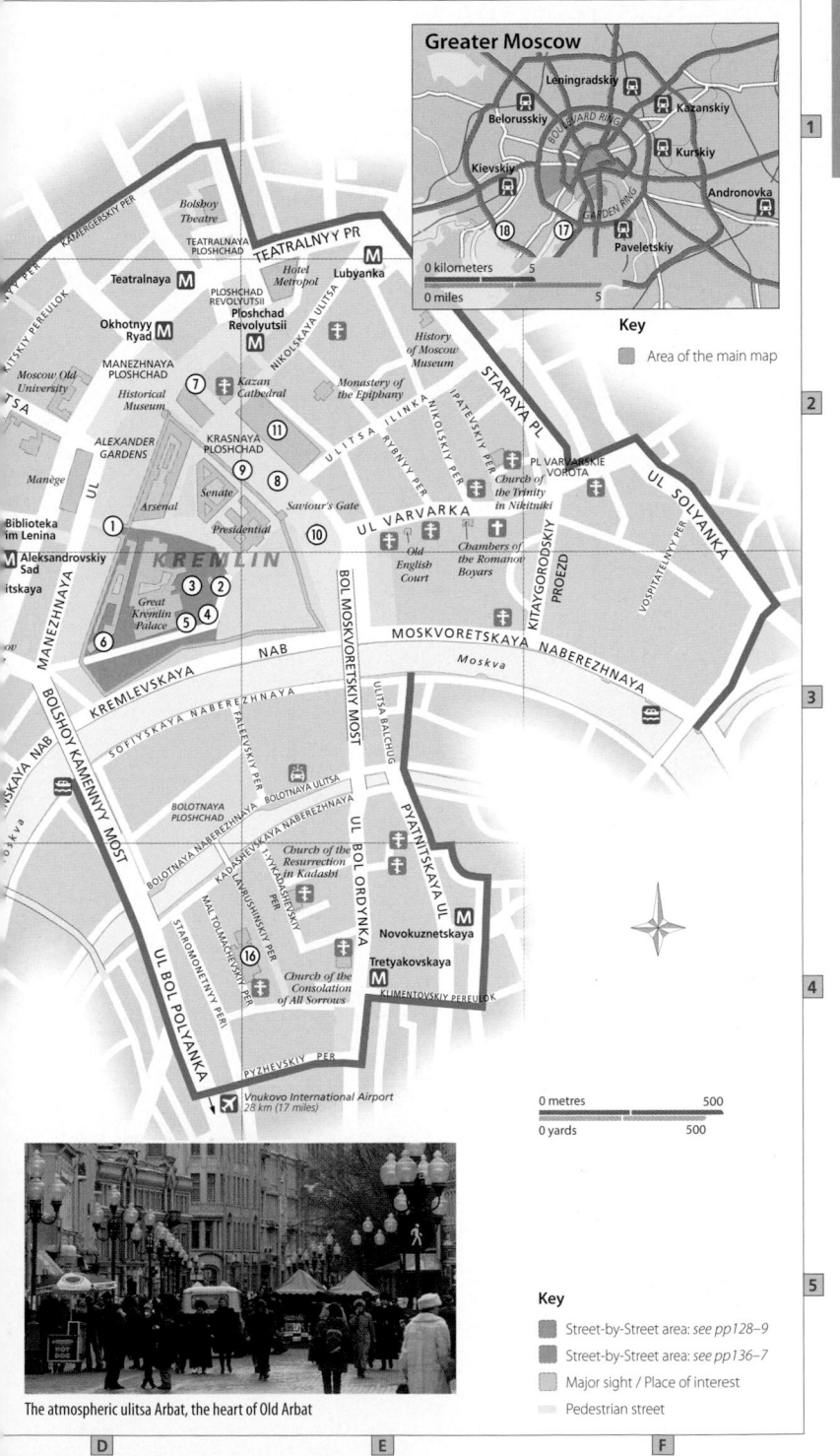

Greater Moscow

Leningradskiy
Belorusskiy
Kazanskiy
Kievskiy
Kurskiy
Andronovka
Paveletskiy

0 kilometers 5
0 miles 5

Key

◼ Area of the main map

Bolshoy Theatre
TEATRALNAYA PLOSHCHAD
TEATRALNYY PR
Hotel Metropol
Teatralnaya Ⓜ
Lubyanka Ⓜ
PLOSHCHAD REVOLYUTSII
Okhotnyy Ryad Ⓜ
Ploshchad Revolyutsii Ⓜ
NIKOLSKAYA ULITSA
History of Moscow Museum
STARAYA PL
Moscow Old University
MANEZHNAYA PLOSHCHAD
Historical Museum
⑦ ✝ Kazan Cathedral
Monastery of the Epiphany
ALEXANDER GARDENS
Manege
KRASNAYA PLOSHCHAD ⑪
ULITSA ILINKA
NIKOLSKY PER
IPATEVSKY PER
PL VARVARSKIE VOROTA
UL SOLYANKA
Church of the Trinity in Nikitniki ✝
Biblioteka im Lenina
⑨ ⑧
RYBNYY PER
UL VARVARKA
✝ ✝
Aleksandrovskiy Sad
itskaya
Arsenal
Senate
Saviour's Gate
Presidential
⑩
Old English Court
Chambers of the Romanov Boyars
VOSPITATELNYY PROEZD
KITAYGORODSKIY PROEZD
KREMLIN
③ ②
Great Kremlin Palace ⑤ ④
⑥
KREMLEVSKAYA NABEREZHNAYA
MANEZHNAYA
BOLSHOY KAMENNYY MOST
SOFIYSKAYA NABEREZHNAYA
NAB
BOL MOSKVORETSKIY MOST
✝
MOSKVORETSKAYA NABEREZHNAYA
Moskva
🚇
FALEEVSKY PER
ULITSA BALCHUG
BOLOTNAYA ULITSA
BOLOTNAYA PLOSHCHAD
BOLOTNAYA NABEREZHNAYA
KADASHEVKSAYA NABEREZHNAYA
1-Y KADASHEVSKY PER
LAVRUSHINSKY PER
MAL TOLMACHEVSKY PER
STAROMONETNYY PER
Church of the Resurrection in Kadashi ✝
UL BOL ORDYNKA
PYATNITSKAYA UL
✝ ✝
Novokuznetskaya Ⓜ
⑯ ✝
Church of the Consolation of All Sorrows
Tretyakovskaya Ⓜ
KLIMENTOVSKY PEREULOK
UL BOL POLYANKA
PYZHEVSKIY PER
↙ Vnukovo International Airport 28 km (17 miles)

0 metres 500
0 yards 500

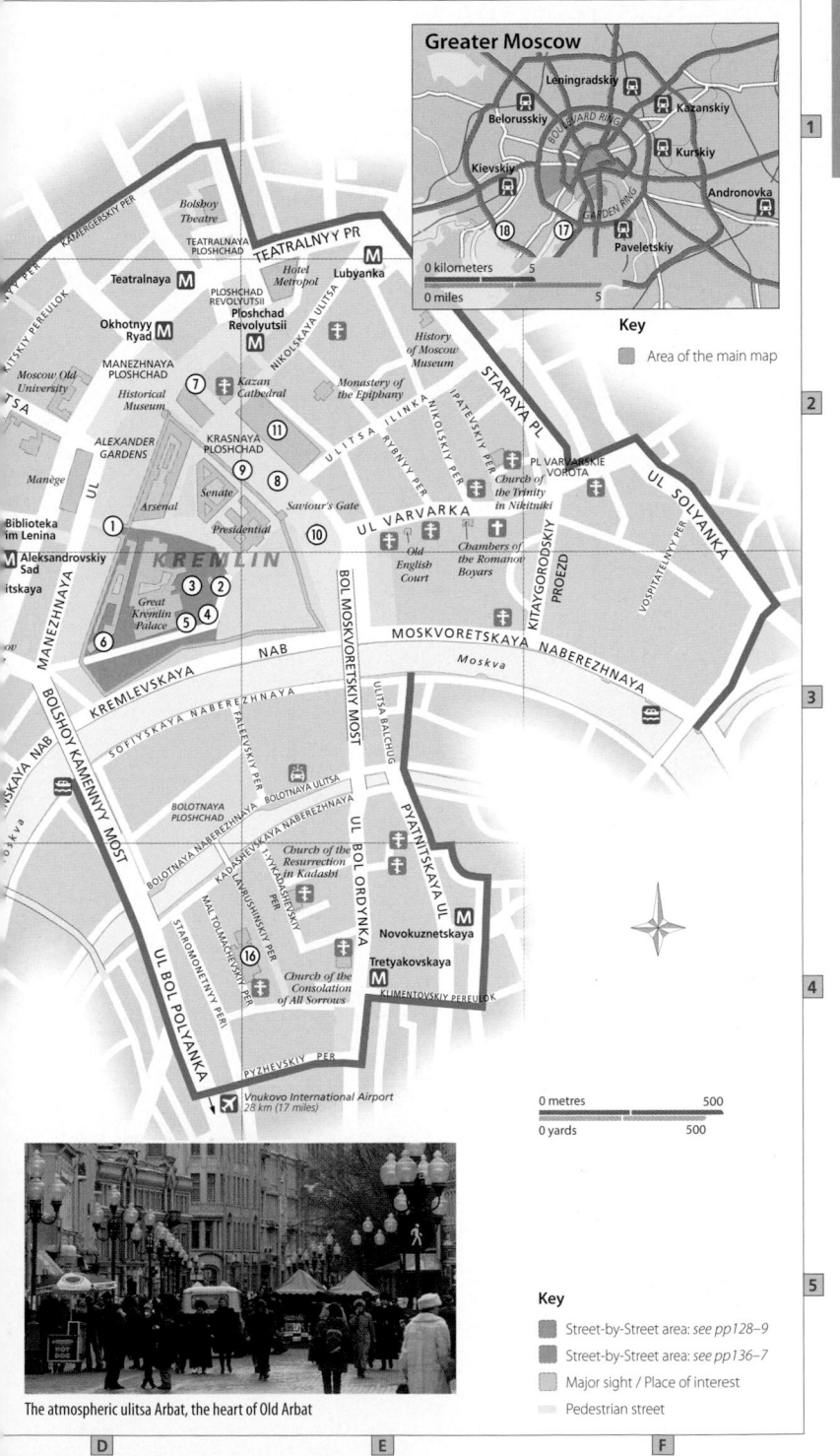
The atmospheric ulitsa Arbat, the heart of Old Arbat

Key
◼ Street-by-Street area: see pp128–9
◼ Street-by-Street area: see pp136–7
◼ Major sight / Place of interest
— Pedestrian street

D E F

For keys to symbols see back flap

Street-by-Street: The Kremlin

The Kremlin is home to the Russian president and the seat of his administration. As a result less than half of it is accessible to the public, but highlights including the State Armoury, the Patriarch's Palace and the churches in Cathedral Square (Ivanovskaya ploshchad) are open to visitors. Christians have worshipped on this site for more than eight centuries, but their early stone churches were demolished in the 1470s to make way for the present magnificent ensemble of cathedrals. In imperial times, these were the setting for great state occasions such as coronations, baptisms and burials.

Ticket office

① **Trinity Tower** was the gate Napoleon used to enter the Kremlin after his triumph in 1812. He left after his defeat a month later.

Great Kremlin Palace
The palace contains several vast ceremonial halls. The splendid stuccowork of St George's Hall provides a magnificent backdrop for state receptions. Its marble walls are inscribed with the names of military heroes.

0 metres 50
0 yards 50

Key

— Suggested route

⑥ ★ **State Armoury**
The State Armoury was designed to complement the Great Kremlin Palace. Constructed in the 19th century, it is now a museum. It houses the imperial collections of decorative and applied art and the State Diamond Fund.

Terem Palace has a chequered roof and 11 golden cupolas topped by crosses – the only visible part of this hidden building.

For hotels and restaurants see p164 and p165

Patriarch's Palace
An imposing palace, rebuilt for Patriarch Nikon between 1652 and 1666, now houses the Museum of 17th-century Life and Applied Art.

VISITORS' CHECKLIST

Practical Information
Map D2 & D3. **Tel** 679 0349.
Open 10am–5pm Fri–Wed. 🎟 tickets sold at the Kremlin entrance and separately at some sights. 🎧 English (book in advance on 697 4115). 🅰 complex, but not buildings. 📷
Ⓦ **kreml.ru**

Transport
Ⓜ Biblioteka imeni Lenina, Borovitskaya. 🚌 6, K.
🚎 1, 2, 12, 33.

The Tsar Cannon, cast in 1586, weighs a massive 40 tonnes (44 tons).

② **Ivan the Great Bell Tower** became the tallest building in Russia after a third storey was added to this beautiful octagonal structure in 1600.

③ ★ **Cathedral of the Assumption**
This 12th-century painting of St George the Warrior is one of the oldest surviving Russian icons. It forms part of the iconostasis in the cathedral's richly decorated interior.

Cathedral Square

Faceted Palace
was constructed by two Italian architects, Marco Ruffo and Pietro Solario, between 1485 and 1491.

④ **Cathedral of the Archangel**
has many elaborate tombs including that of Tsarevich Dmitry, son of Ivan the Terrible, who died as a child in 1591.

⑤ **Cathedral of the Annunciation**
Frescoes cover the walls and ceiling of this cathedral. In the dome above the iconostasis is a painting of Christ Pantocrator, above tiers of pictures of angels, prophets and patriarchs.

The striking red-brick Trinity Tower, with its contrasting conical spire

① Trinity Tower
Троиукая Аашня
TroitsAaya bashnya

The Kremlin. **Map** D2.

This tower takes its name from the Trinity Monastery of St Sergius, which once ran a mission nearby. The tower's Trinity Gate used to be the entrance for patriarchs and the tsars' wives and daughters. It is one of the only two towers – the other being Borovitskaya Tower, to the southwest – of the Kremlin walls' 19 towers that admit visitors into the complex.

At 76 m (249 ft), the seven-storey Trinity Tower is the Kremlin's tallest. It was built between 1495 and 1499 and in 1516 it was linked by a bridge over the Neglinnaya river to the Kutafya Tower. The river now runs under-ground and the Kutafya Tower is the sole survivor of the circle of towers that were originally built to defend the Kremlin walls.

In September 1812, Napoleon triumphantly marched his army into the Kremlin through the Trinity Gate. They left just a month later when Muscovites set fire to their city and fled, leaving the French Army without shelter or provisions.

② Ivan the Great Bell Towey
Колокоуьня Авана Великогу
KolokolnyA Ivana Velikovo

The Kremlin. **Map** D3.

Built to a design by Marco Bon Friazin, the 16th-century bell tower takes its name from the Church of St Ivan Climacus, which stood on the site in the 14th century. The "Great" in its name is derived from the height of the tower. In 1600 it became the tallest building in Moscow when Tsar Boris Godunov added a third storey, extending it to 81m (266 ft). The 16th-century four-storey Assumption Belfry was built beside the bell tower by Petrok Maliy. It holds 21 bells, the largest of which is the 64-tonne (71-tons) Assumption Bell. A museum on the first floor displays the story of the Kremlin. The annexe next to the belfry was commissioned in 1642 by Patriarch Filaret. Outside the bell tower is the **Tsar Bell**. The largest in the world, it weighs over 200 tonnes (221 tons). When it fell from the tower and shattered in a fire in 1701, the fragments were used in a bell ordered by Tsarina Anna. This bell was still in its casting pit when the Kremlin caught fire in 1737. As a result, a large piece broke off as water was poured over the bell.

Frescoes on the entrance to the Cathedral of the Assumption

③ Cathedral of the Assumption
Успенсуий собор
UspenskAy sobor

The Kremlin. **Map** D3.

From the early 14th century, the Cathedral of the Assumption was Moscow's most important church, where princes were crowned and the metropolitans and patriarchs of the Orthodox church buried. In the 1470s, Ivan the Great decided to build a more imposing cathedral and summoned Italian architect Aristotele Fioravanti to Moscow. Inspired by the spirit of the Renaissance, the cathedral is a spacious masterpiece. It houses superb iconostasis and frescoes, including *Scenes from the Life of Metropolitan Peter* by

The Tsar Bell, with the hole left by the section that broke off

For hotels and restaurants see p164 and p165

the famous 15th-century artist, Dionysius, painted on the southern wall of the cathedral.

④ Cathedral of the Archangel

Архангельский собор

ArkhanAelskiy sobor

The Kremlin. **Map** D3.

This was the last of the great cathedrals to be built in the Kremlin. Commissioned by Ivan III and designed by Aleviz Novy in 1505, it is a combination of early-Russian and Renaissance architecture.

This site was the burial place for Moscow's princes and tsars from 1340. The tombs of the tsars, white stone sarcophagi with bronze covers inscribed in Old Slavonic, are in the nave. The tsars, with the exception of Peter II, who died in 1730, were no longer buried here after the capital was moved to St Petersburg in 1712. The walls, pillars and domes of the cathedral are covered with spectacular frescoes painted by a team of artists led by Semen Ushakov, the head of the icon workshop in the State Armoury.

There are more than 60 full-length portraits of Russian rulers and a few striking images of the Archangel Michael, the protector of the rulers of early Moscow. The cathedral's four-tiered iconostasis was constructed between 1680 and 1681, but the Icon of the Archangel Michael on the lowest tier dates from the 14th century.

⑤ Cathedral of the Annunciation

Благовещенский собор

Blagoveshchenskiy sobor

The Kremlin. **Map** D3.

Unlike the other cathedrals in the Kremlin, which were created by Italian architects, the Cathedral of the Annunciation is a wholly Russian affair. Commissioned by Ivan III in 1484 as a royal chapel, it stands beside the Faceted Palace, which is all that remains of a large palace built for Ivan III.

Tiers of frescoes on the central cupola of the Cathedral of the Archangel

The cathedral, built by architects from Pskov, had three domes and open galleries on all sides but, after a fire in 1547, the corner chapels were added and the galleries enclosed. On the south façade is the Groznenskiy Porch, added by Ivan the Terrible *(see p124)* when he contravened church law by marrying for the fourth time in 1572. Barred from attending religious services, he could only watch through a grille in the porch.

The interior of the cathedral is painted with frescoes. The artwork around the iconostasis was painted in 1508 by the monk Feodosius, son of the icon painter Dionysius. The warm colours of the frescoes create an atmosphere of intimacy and the vertical thrust of the pillars draws the eye upwards to the cupola and its awe-inspiring painting of Christ Pantocrator.

The Cathedral of the Annunciation, crowned by golden onion domes

Three of the greatest masters of icon painting in Russia contributed to the iconostasis. Theophanes the Greek painted the images of Christ, the Virgin and the Archangel Gabriel in the Deesis Tier, while the Icon of the Archangel Michael on this tier is attributed to Andrey Rublev. Several of the icons in the Festival Tier were also painted by Rublev. Most of the other icons in this tier are the work of Prokhor Gorodetskiy.

⑥ State Armoury

Оружейнау палата

OruzheinayA palata

The Kremlin. **Map** D3.

The collection of the State Armoury represents the wealth accumulated by Russian princes and tsars over many centuries. The first written mention of a state armoury occurs in 1508, but there were forges in the Kremlin as early as the 13th century. Later, gold- and silver-smiths, workshops producing icons and embroidery, and the Office of the Royal Stables all moved into the Kremlin. The original armoury was demolished in 1960 to make way for the State Kremlin Palace. The current State Armoury was built as a museum by Tsar Nicholas I (r. 1825–55). It was designed by Konstantin Ton in 1844 and completed in 1851. It is home to the State Diamond Fund.

⑦ Resurrection Gate

Воскресенские ворота
Voskresenskie vorota

Krasnaya ploshchad. **Map** D2.
Ⓜ Okhotnyy Ryad, Ploshchad
Revolyutsii.

Rebuilt in 1995, this gateway,
with its red twin towers topped
by green tent spires, is an exact
copy of the original completed
on this site in 1680. The first
gateway was demolished in 1931
on Stalin's orders. There are
mosaic icons on the gate, one of
which depicts Moscow's patron
saint, St George, slaying a dragon.
   Within the gateway is the
equally colourful Chapel of the
Iverian Virgin, originally built in
the late 18th century to house
an icon. Whenever the tsar
came to Moscow, he would
visit this shrine before entering
the Kremlin (see pp128–9).
Visitors should try to see the
gate at night, when it is
impressively lit up.

Resurrection Gate, housing the Chapel of
the Iverian Virgin

⑧ Red Square

Красная площадь
Krasnaya ploshchad

Map E2. Ⓜ Ploshchad Revolyutsii,
Okhotnyy Ryad. Historical Museum:
Tel 692 4019. **Open** 10am–6pm Mon,
Wed & Fri–Sun, 11am–8pm Thu. 🅿
🎫 ♿ 💻 🆆 shm.ru

Towards the end of the 15th
century, Ivan III gave orders for
houses in front of the Kremlin to
be cleared to make way for this
square. It originally served as a
market, locally called the *torg*,

The vast expanse of Red Square, with the Historical Museum at the far end

but the wooden stalls burnt
down so often that the area
later became popularly known
as Fire Square. The current name
dates from the 17th century
and is derived from the Russian
word *krasnyy*, which originally
meant "beautiful" but later came
to denote "red". The association
between the colour red and
Communism is coincidental.
   Red Square, which is almost
500 m (1,600 ft) in length,
was also the setting for public
announcements and executions.
At its southern end, in front of
St Basil's Cathedral (see pp134–
5), there is a small circular dais.
Called **Lobnoe Mesto**, this is
the platform from which the
tsars and patriarchs would
address the people. In 1606
the first "False Dmitry", a usurper
of the throne, was killed by a
hostile crowd. His body was
finally left at Lobnoe Mesto.
Six years later, a second
pretender to the throne, who
like the first "False Dmitry"
was backed by Poland, took
power. He was expelled from
the Kremlin by an army led
by the Russian heroes Dmitriy
Pozharskiy and Kuzma Minin,
who proclaimed Russia's
deliverance at Lobnoe Mesto.
In 1818, a statue was erected
in their honour which now
stands in front of St Basil's.
   Red Square has also long
been a stage for pageants
and processions. Before the
1917 Revolution, the patriarch
would ride a horse dressed
like a donkey through Saviour's
Gate to St Basil's each Palm
Sunday to commemorate

Christ's entry into Jerusalem.
Religious processions were
abolished in the Communist
era. Military parades took their
place and were staged each
year on May Day and on the
anniversary of the Revolution.
Rows of grim-faced Soviet
leaders observed them from
outside the Lenin Mausoleum.
They, in turn, would be keenly
studied by professional
kremlinologists in the West
trying to work out the current
pecking order.
   Today, the square is used for
a variety of concerts, firework
displays and cultural events. The
red-brick building facing St Basil's
Cathedral was constructed by
Vladimir Sherwood in 1883 in
the Russian-Revival style. It
houses the Historical Museum,
which boasts over four million
exhibits covering the rise and
expansion of the Russian state.
In front of the museum on
Manezhnaya ploshchad is

Lobnoe Mesto, the platform from which
the tsars would speak

a statue of Marshal Georgiy Zhukov, one of the heroes of World War II. This statue, sculpted by Vyacheslav Klykov (1939–2006), was unveiled in 1995 to mark the 50th anniversary of the end of World War II.

⑨ Lenin Mausoleum
Мавзолей В.И. Ленина
Mavzoley V.I. Lenina

Krasnaya ploshchad. **Map** E2.
Tel 623 5527. Ⓜ Ploshchad Revolyutsii, Okhotnyy Ryad.
Open 10am–1pm Tue–Thu, Sat–Sun. ✉

Following Lenin's death in 1924, and against his wishes, it was decided to preserve the former Soviet leader's body for posterity. The body was embalmed and placed in a temporary wooden mausoleum in Red Square. Once it became clear that the embalming process had worked, Soviet architect Aleksey Shchusev designed the current mausoleum as a pyramid of cubes cut from red granite and black labradorite.

Paying one's respects to Lenin's remains was once akin to a religious experience, and queues used to trail all over Red Square. In 1993, however, the goose-stepping guard of honour was replaced by a lone militiaman and now the mausoleum attracts mostly tourists. There are rumours that Lenin's body will soon be moved elsewhere or buried.

Behind the mausoleum, at the foot of the Kremlin Wall, are the graves of other famous Communists. They include Lenin's successors, Joseph Stalin, who at one time was laid beside Lenin in the mausoleum, Leonid Brezhnev and Yuriy Andropov. Lenin's wife and sister are also buried here, as are the first man in space, Yuriy Gagarin, writer Maxim Gorky and American journalist John Reed. The latter was honoured as the author of *Ten Days that Shook the World*, published in 1919, an account of the October Revolution, when Bolshevik forces took control of St Petersburg.

Lenin Mausoleum, just outside the walls of the Kremlin

⑩ St Basil's Cathedral
Собор Василия Блаженного
Sobor Vasiliya Blazhennovo

See pp134–5.

⑪ GUM
ГУМ GUM

Krasnaya ploshchad 3. **Map** E2.
Tel 788 4343. Ⓜ Ploshchad Revolyutsii, Okhotnyy Ryad. **Open** 10am–10pm daily. ♿ ⃞ gum.ru

Before the 1917 Revolution, this building was known as the Upper Trading Rows after the covered market that used to stand on the site. In fact, lines of stalls used to run all the way from here to the Moskva river. GUM has three separate arcades, which are still called "lines". The store's name, Gosudarstvennyy Universalnyy Magazin, dates from its nationalization in 1921. The glass-roofed structure is considered the largest department store in Russia. The building was designed by Aleksandr Pomerantsev between 1889 and 1893 in the fashionable Russian-Revival style. Its archways, wrought-iron railings and stuccoed galleries inside are especially impressive when sunlight streams through the glass roof.

There were once more than 1,000 shops located in GUM, selling goods ranging from furs and silks to items of everyday use such as candles. For a period, however, during the rule of Stalin starting from 1924 and ending only with his death in 1953, GUM's shops were requisitioned as offices. Nowadays, Western brands such as Benetton, Estée Lauder and Christian Dior dominate the prestigious ground floor along with a variety of Western-style cafés and restaurants, and even the branch of a bank.

The glass-roofed interior of Russia's largest department store, GUM

⑩ St Basil's Cathedral

Собор Василия Блаженного

Sobor Vasiliya Blazhennovo

Commissioned by Ivan the Terrible to mark the capture of the Mongol stronghold of Kazan in 1552 and completed in 1561, this cathedral is reputed to have been designed by Postnik Yakovlev. According to legend, Ivan had him blinded so he could never design anything as exquisite again. Officially, it was called the Cathedral of the Intercession since the final siege of Kazan began on the Feast of the Intercession of the Virgin. However, it gets its popular name from the "holy fool" Basil the Blessed whose remains are interred here. Its design was inspired by Russian timber architecture and is a riot of gables, roofs and domes.

★ Domes
Destroyed by fire in 1583, these multi-faceted onion domes replaced the original helmet-shaped cupolas. The domes have been colourfully painted since 1670, but at one time St Basil's was white with golden domes.

Chapel of St Cyprian
This is one of eight main chapels commemorating the campaigns of Ivan the Terrible against the town of Kazan, east of Moscow. It is dedicated to St Cyprian.

Minin and Pozharskiy

This statue by Ivan Martos depicts two heroes from the Time of Troubles (1598–1613), Kuzma Minin and Prince Dmitriy Pozharskiy who raised a force to defeat the invading Poles in 1612. The statue was erected in 1818 and originally placed in the centre of the Red Square facing the Kremlin. It was moved in front of St Basil's during the Soviet era.

Monument to Minin and Prince Pozharskiy

Entrance to the cathedral

Central Chapel of the Intercession
Light floods in through the windows of the 61-m (200-ft) high tent-roofed central church.

★ **Main Iconostasis**
The Baroque-style iconostasis in the Central Chapel of the Intercession dates from the 19th century. However, some of the icons inside were painted much earlier.

★ **Gallery**
Running around the outside of the Central Chapel, the gallery connects it to the other eight chapels. It was roofed over at the end of the 17th century and the walls and ceilings were decorated with floral tiles in the late 18th century.

VISITORS' CHECKLIST

Practical Information
Krasnaya ploshchad 2.
Map E2. **Tel** 698 3304.
✝ religious hols. **Open** May–Nov: 11am–6pm Wed–Mon; Dec–Apr: 11am–5pm daily.
📷 🎧 English. 🔲 **saintbasil.ru**

Transport
Ⓜ Okhotnyy Ryad, Ploschad Revolyutsii. 🚌 25. 🚊 8.

KEY

① The Chapel of St Basil

② Chapel of the Three Patriarchs

③ Chapel of the Trinity

④ Bell Tower

⑤ Chapel of St Nicholas

⑥ Chapel of St Varlaam of Khutynskiy

⑦ Tiered gables

⑧ The Chapel of the Entry of Christ into Jerusalem was used as a ceremonial entrance during the annual Palm Sunday procession. On this day the patriarch rode from the Kremlin to St Basil's Cathedral on a horse dressed up to look like a donkey.

⑨ Chapel of Bishop Gregory

Street-by-Street: Old Arbat

In the 19th century, Old Arbat was the haunt of artists, musicians, poets, writers and intellectuals. Some of their homes have been preserved and opened as museums, and are among the district's many houses of that era that have been restored and painted in pastel shades of blue, green and ochre. At the heart of Old Arbat is the pedestrianized ulitsa Arbat. It is lined with antique shops, boutiques, souvenir stalls, pavement cafés and a variety of restaurants – from pizzerias and hamburger joints to traditional Russian pubs. Today, pavement artists, buskers and street poets give it a renewed bohemian atmosphere.

Spaso House is a grand Neo-Classical mansion. It has been the residence of the US ambassador since 1933.

This small garden contains a statue of Alexander Pushkin.

Novyy Arbat ↑

⑬ ★ **Pushkin House-Museum**
The poet Alexander Pushkin lived here just after his marriage in 1831. The interior of the house has been carefully renovated.

Ulitsa Arbat
This 19th-century street was pedestrianized in 1985. Its lively shops, restaurants and cafés are now popular with Muscovites and visitors to the city alike.

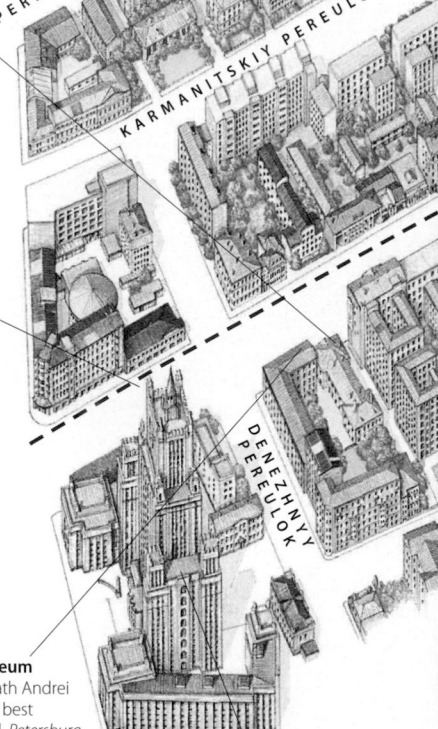

PEREULOK KAMENNOY SLOBODY

SPASOPE PEREUL

KARMANITSKIY PEREULOK

DENEZHNYY PEREULOK

Bely House-Museum
Influential polymath Andrei Bely (1880–1934), best known for a novel, *Petersburg*, and his memoirs, lived in this flat for the first 26 years of his life. Now a museum, its exhibits include this photo of Bely with his wife and his fascinating Symbolist illustration, *Line of Life*.

The Foreign Ministry is one of the seven Stalinist-Gothic skyscrapers in Moscow.

For hotels and restaurants see p164 and p165

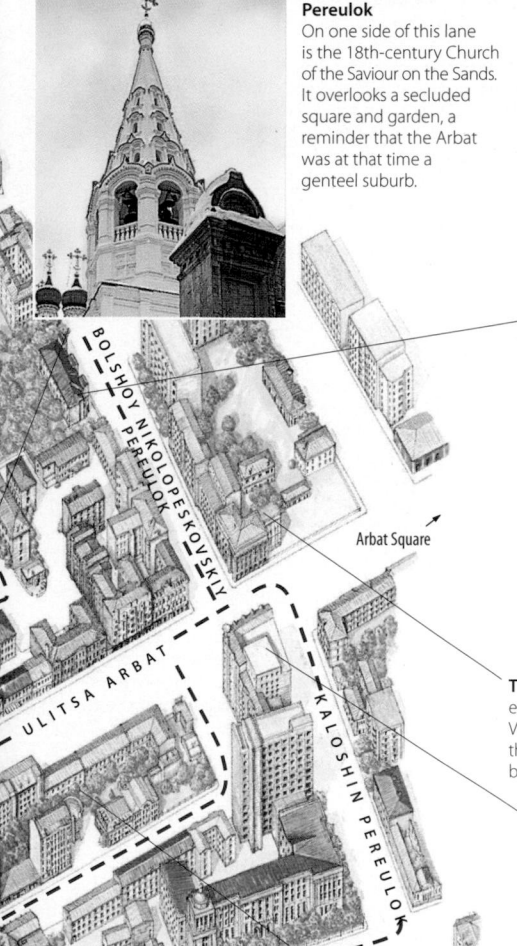

Spasopeskovskiy Pereulok
On one side of this lane is the 18th-century Church of the Saviour on the Sands. It overlooks a secluded square and garden, a reminder that the Arbat was at that time a genteel suburb.

★ Skryabin House-Museum
This apartment has been preserved as it was between 1912 and 1915 when experimental composer Aleksandr Skryabin (1872–1915) lived here. The furniture in the rooms is Style Moderne and the lighting is dim, since Skryabin disliked direct light.

Arbat Square

The Vakhtangov Theatre was established here in 1921 by Yevgeniy Vakhtangov, one of Moscow's leading theatre directors. The current theatre building dates from 1947.

Pre-Revolution apartments, designed for wealthy Muscovites, are decorated with fanciful turrets and sculptures of knights.

Pushkin Museum of Fine Arts

| 0 metres | 100 |
| 0 yards | 100 |

Herzen House-Museum
was the home of the radical writer Aleksandr Herzen from 1843 to 1846.

⑫ Melnikov House
Built in the 1920s by Constructivist architect Konstantin Melnikov, who lived here until his death in 1974, this unusual cylindrical house is now dwarfed by the apartments on ulitsa Arbat

Key

— Suggested route

⑫ Melnikov House

Дом Мельуикова

Dom MelniAova

Krivoarbatskiy pereulok 10. **Map** B3.
Ⓜ Smolenskaya.

This unique house was designed by Konstantin Melnikov (1890–1974), one of Russia's greatest Constructivist architects, in 1927. Made from brick overlaid with white stucco, the house consists of two interlocking cylinders. These are studded with rows of hexagonal windows, creating a curious honeycomb effect. A spiral staircase rises through the space where the cylinders overlap, linking the light, airy living spaces.

Melnikov's house was built for his family, but it was also to have been a prototype for future housing developments. However, his career was blighted when Stalin encouraged architects towards a new monumental style. In spite of this, Melnikov was one of the very few allowed to live in a privately built dwelling in central Moscow. His son, Viktor, had a studio in the house until his death in 2006.

Viktor Melnikov's light-filled art studio in the Melnikov House

⑬ Pushkin House-Museum

Музей-квартира А.С. Пушкину

Muzey-kvArtira A.S. Pushkina

Ulitsa Arbat 53. **Map** B3. **Tel** 241 9295.
Ⓜ Smolenskaya. **Open** 10am–6pm Wed–Fri & Sun; also noon–9pm Thu. **Closed** last Fri of month. 🎨 📷 🎫 English (book in advance).

Alexander Pushkin rented this elegant, blue and white Empire-style flat for the first three months of his marriage to society beauty Natalya Goncharova. They were married in the Church of the Great Ascension on Bolshaya Nikitskaya ulitsa in February 1831. However, by May 1831 Pushkin had tired of Moscow, and the couple moved to St Petersburg, where a tragic fate awaited him. Gossip began to claim that Pushkin's brother-in-law, a French officer called d'Anthès, was making advances to Natalya. Upon receiving letters calling him "Grand Master to the Order of Cuckolds", Pushkin challenged d'Anthès to a duel, dying of his wounds two days later.

The ground floor exhibition gives an idea of what the city would have been like when Pushkin was growing up, before the Great Fire of 1812. Among the artworks there are some unusual wax figures of a serf orchestra that belonged to the Goncharova family.

Pushkin and Natalya lived on the first floor. There are very few personal possessions here, although the poet's writing bureau and some family portraits are displayed. The atmosphere resembles a shrine more than a museum, an indication of the special place Pushkin has in the hearts of Russians.

⑭ Pushkin Museum of Fine Arts

Музей изобразительных искусств имени А.С. Пушкину

Muzey izoArazitelnykh iskusstv imeni A.S. Pushkina

Ulitsa Volkhonka 12. **Map** C3. **Tel** 697 9578. Ⓜ Kropotkinskaya. 🚌 1, 2, 16, 33. **Open** 10am–7pm Tue–Sun. 🎨 📷 🎫 🔊 English. 🌐 museum.ru/gmii

Founded in 1898, the Pushkin Museum of Fine Arts houses several excellent French Impressionist and Post-Impressionist paintings. These reflect the tastes of many private collectors, whose holdings were nationalized by the Soviet government. The most important of these belong to two outstanding connoisseurs, Sergey Shchukin and Ivan Morozov. Shchukin had over

A portrait of Pushkin's wife, Natalya Goncharova

220 paintings by French artists, including Cézanne, and had also champi-oned Matisse and Picasso when they were relatively unknown. Morozov also collected these two painters along with pictures by Renoir, van Gogh and Gauguin. Highlights include *Nude* by Renoir, *The Great Buddha* by Gauguin and *Goldfish* by Matisse.

Following the collapse of the Soviet Union, the curators admitted that they had countless works of art hidden away for ideological reasons. Some of these are now on display, including paintings by Russian-born artists Vasily Kandinsky and Marc Chagall. There is an enviable collection of Old Masters and art from ancient civilizations, such as the Treasure of Troy display, with gold artifacts excavated from the famous city in the 1870s.

⑮ Cathedral of Christ the Redeemer

Храм Христа Суасителя

Khram Khrista SpasAtelya

Ulitsa Volkhonka 15. **Map** C4.
Ⓜ Kropotkinskaya.

Rebuilding this cathedral, blown up on Stalin's orders in 1931, was the most ambitious construction project by the enterprising mayor of Moscow, Yuriy Luzhkov. The basic structure of the new cathedral was built between 1994 and 1997. Before this, the site was used as a swimming pool. The

Cathedral of Christ the Redeemer, rebuilt in the 1990s at huge cost

rebuilding project was controversial from the start, on the grounds of taste and cost. In 1995 a presidential decree declared that no public money should be spent on it. Funds were to come via donations from the public, the Russian Church and foreign donors. Much of the US$200 million spent, however, came from the state budget, at a time when Muscovites were suffering extreme poverty.

The original cathedral was built to commemorate the deliverance of Moscow from Napoleon's Grande Armée in 1812. Begun in 1839, but not completed until 1883, it was designed by Konstantin Ton, who also designed the State Armoury. The cathedral was Moscow's tallest building then, the gilded dome rising to a height of 103 m (338 ft) and dominating the skyline for

miles. With a floor area of 9,000 sq m (97,000 sq ft), it could accommodate more than 10,000 worshippers.

⑯ Tretyakov Gallery
Третьяковскуя уалерея
TretyakovskayA GAlercya

See pp140–41.

⑰ Gorky Park
Парк культуры и отдыха имени М. Горукого
Park Kultury i otAykha imeni M. Gorkovo

Krymskiy val 9. **Map** F1. **Tel** 237 0707. Ⓜ Park Kultury, Oktyabrskaya. **Open** 10am–10pm daily *(pleasure park open May–Oct)*. 🅿️ ♿ 🖥️

Moscow's most famous park is named in honour of the writer Maxim Gorky (1868–1936) and extends for more than 120 ha (297 acres) along the Moskva river. Opened in 1928 as the Park of Culture and Rest, it incorporates the Golitsyn Gardens, laid out by Matvey Kazakov (1738–1812) in the late 18th century, and a 19th-century pleasure park.

The park was immortalized in the opening scenes of Michael Apted's film *Gorky Park*. However, due to the tense political climate of 1983, the film was shot in Finland. During the Soviet era, loudspeakers across the park delivered speeches by Communist leaders. Today, the highlights

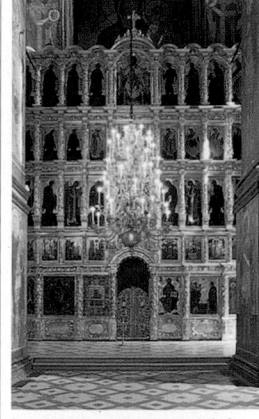

Five-tier iconostasis in the cathedral of Novodevichiy Convent

include fairground rides, woodland walks, boating lakes, a 10,000-seat outdoor theatre and, in winter, an ice rink.

⑱ Novodevichiy Convent
Новодевичий мунастырь
Novodevichiy monAstyr

Novodevichi proezd 1. **Map** E1. **Tel** 246 8526. Ⓜ Sportivnaya. 🚌 64, 132. 🚊 5, 15. **Open** 10am–5:30pm Wed–Mon. 🅿️ 📷 book in advance. ♿ grounds only. 🚻 📷

Considered one of the most beautiful of the semi-circle of fortified religious institutions to the south of Moscow, Novodevichiy Convent was founded by Basil III in 1524 to commemorate the capture of Smolensk from the Lithuanians. The Cathedral of the Virgin of Smolensk was built at this time though the five-tier iconostasis, frescoes and onion domes were added in the 17th century. Most of the other buildings were also added in the late 17th century by Peter the Great's half-sister, the Regent Sophia. In 1812, Napoleon's troops tried to blow up the convent but, according to one story, it was saved by the nuns. The cemetery here is the final resting place of several famous Russians, such as the writer Nikolai Gogol and the composer Dmitry Shostakovich.

Outdoor ice-skating in Gorky Park, a popular activity in the winter months

⑯ Tretyakov Gallery

Третьяковская галерея

Tretyakovskaya galereya

The gallery was founded in 1856 by Pavel Tretyakov, a wealthy merchant, who presented it to the city in 1892. It continued to expand after the Revolution as numerous private collections were nationalized. Today it has the largest collection of Russian art in the world – with more than 100,000 works on display. The building has a striking façade, with a bas-relief of St George and the dragon at its centre. A new wing was added in 1930. Many of the early 20th-century works are now in the New Tretyakov Gallery, an annexe to the main building.

Stairs down to ground floor

Portraits by Ivan Kramskoy

First floor

The Appearance of Christ to the People is by the 19th-century Romantic artist, Aleksandr Ivanov.

The Rooks Have Come (1871)
This bleak winter scene by Aleksey Savrasov contains a message of hope – rooks are taken by Russians as a sign of the coming spring.

Stairs from basement

Portraits by Ilya Repin (1844–1930)

Portrait of Arseny Tropinin, the Artist's Son (c. 1818)
This portrait is by Vasiliy Tropinin, who was a serf for 47 years before gaining his freedom and finding success as a painter.

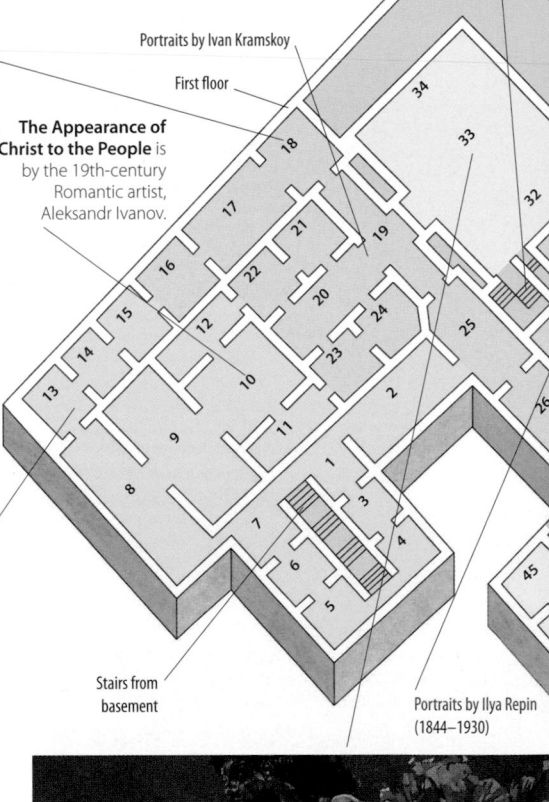

★ **Demon Seated** (1890)
This is one of several innovative paintings by Mikhail Vrubel, who adopted a new, strikingly modern style. They are inspired by Mikhail Lermontov's Symbolist poem, *The Demon* (1839), with which Vrubel became obsessed.

Religious Procession in Kursk Province (1880–83)
Ilya Repin, a socially committed artist, painted this to contrast
the religious devotion of the peasants with the cold hypocrisy
of the rich.

**The Morning of
the Execution
of the Streltsy** is
by Vasiliy Surikov.

Ground
floor

28

39

38

41

42

40

37

36

35

61

62

60

56

59

55

51 52 53 54

57

58

Exit

Main entrance

Russian
jewellery

★ The Trinity (1420s)
This beautiful icon was
painted by Andrey Rublev
for the Trinity Monastery of
St Sergius, where he had
been a novice monk.
He dedicated it to the
monastery's founder,
St Sergius of Radonezh.

Gallery Guide

*There are 62 rooms on two
main floors. Visitors first go to
the basement ticket office, then
head to the first floor. Paintings
are hung in rooms 1–54: visitors
come down to the ground floor
after viewing room 34. Rooms
56–62 contain ancient Russian
art; room 55 features collections
of jewellery, precious stones
and icons.*

Main Façade
The gallery's façade was
designed in 1902 by Viktor
Vasnetsov. An example of
the Russian-Revival style, it
has a frieze inspired by
medieval manuscripts.

Key

▢ 18th and early 19th centuries

▢ Second half of the 19th century

▢ Late 19th and early 20th centuries

▢ Drawings and watercolours of the
18th–20th centuries

▢ Icons and jewellery

▢ Non-exhibition space

❷ St Petersburg

Once Russia's capital and known as its "Window on the West", St Petersburg was built on the marshy lands where the Neva river joins the Gulf of Finland. With a population of just under five million, it is Russia's second largest city. The southern bank of the Neva, Palace Embankment, is lined with glorious palaces. To the east is Gostinyy Dvor, the commercial hub of the city, with bars and restaurants lining Nevskiy Prospekt. To the southwest lies Sennaya Ploshchad, combining tree-lined canals with decrepit reminders of the 19th-century life decribed in Fyodor Dostoevsky's novels. Vasilevskiy Ostrov, the city's largest island, celebrates St Petersburg's naval heritage with its scholarly institutions and museums. Petrogradskaya, to the north, is dominated by the Peter and Paul Fortress.

Getting Around

The most enjoyable way to explore the city is on foot or by taking a boat cruise along its waterways. Metro lines, tram, bus and trolleybus routes radiate out from Nevskiy Prospekt, criss-crossing the city with a network of rail tracks. These can be crowded during the day, particularly at rush hour, but are still the best way to make short trips around the city centre. The metro is used mainly to get to and from the outer districts of the city.

For hotels and restaurants see p164 and p165

Sights at a Glance

① *Peter and Paul Fortress pp140–41*
② Menshikov Palace
③ The Bronze Horseman
④ The Admiralty
⑤ St Isaac's Cathedral
⑥ St Isaac's Square
⑦ Malaya Morskaya Ulitsa
⑧ Palace Square
⑨ *The Hermitage pp148–55*
⑩ Summer Palace
⑪ Summer Garden
⑫ Pushkin House-Museum
⑬ Church on Spilled Blood
⑭ Russian Museum
⑮ Arts Square
⑯ Nevskiy Prospekt
⑰ Mariinskiy Theatre

Key

▦ Major sight / Place of interest
▦ Pedestrian street

0 metres 500
0 yards 500

View of the city and the gilded spire of the Admiralty

① Peter and Paul Fortress

Петропавловская крепость

Petropavlovskaya krepost

The building of the Peter and Paul Fortress, ordered on 27 May 1703 by Peter the Great, is considered to mark the founding of St Petersburg. First built in wood it was later replaced in stone by Domenico Trezzini between 1706 and 1740. Its history is gruesome, since hundreds of forced labourers died while building the fortress and its bastions were later used to guard and torture many political prisoners. The prison cells are open to the public, along with a couple of museums and the magnificent cathedral, which houses the tombs of the Romanovs.

↑ Artillery Museum

KEY

① **Neva Gate** is also known as "Death Gateway".

② **The Naryshkin Bastion** is where the noon cannon is fired. The tradition began in 1873, stopped after the Revolution and was resumed in 1957.

③ **Commandant's House** is an attractive Baroque House which was the scene of interrogations and trials of political prisoners for 150 years. It now houses a museum with a ground-floor exhibition on medieval settlements in the region.

④ **The Mint**, founded in 1724, still produces ceremonial coins, medals and badges.

⑤ **The Archives of the War Ministry** occupy the site of the "Secret House", a prison for political criminals in during 18th and 19th centuries.

⑥ **The Boat House** is now a ticket office and souvenir shop.

⑦ **Golovkin Bastion**

⑧ **The Grand Ducal burial vault** is the last resting place of several grand dukes shot by the Bolsheviks in 1919 and of Grand Duke Vladimir who died in exile.

⑨ **Ivan Gate**, in the outer wall, was constructed between 1731 and 1740.

⑩ **Peter I Bastion**

⑪ **Statue of Peter the Great** by Mikhail Chemiakin (1991).

Trubetskoy Bastion
From 1872 to 1921, the dark, damp, solitary-confinement cells in this bastion served as a grim prison for enemies of the state.

0 metres	100
0 yards	100

The Beach
During summer, the beach is full of sunbathers. In winter, it is the haunt of "The Walruses", a group of people who break through the ice to dip into the waters beneath.

★ Cathedral of SS Peter and Paul
This magnificent cathedral was designed by Domenico Trezzini in 1712. Within is the iconostasis, a masterpiece of gilded woodcarvings, designed by Ivan Zarudnyy and executed by Moscow craftsmen in the 1720s.

VISITORS' CHECKLIST

Practical Information
Petropavlovskaya krepost.
Map C2. **Tel** 230 6431.
English.
Trubetskoy Bastion: **Open** 10am–6pm Thu–Mon, 11am–5pm Tue.
Commandant's House: **Open** 10am–6pm Thu–Mon, 11am–5pm Tue. Cathedral: **Open** 10am–6pm Thu–Mon, 11am–5pm Tue.
Engineer's House: **Open** 11am–6pm Thu–Mon, 11am–5pm Tue.
W **spbmuseum.ru**

Transport
M Gorkovskaya.

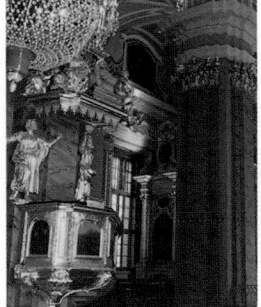

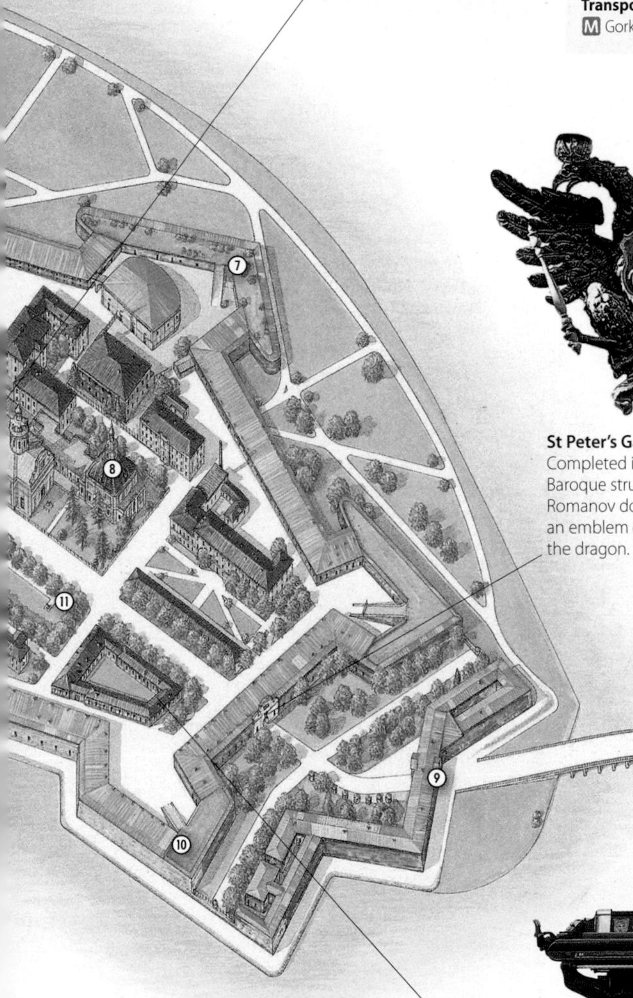
7
8
9
10
11
Kamennoostrovskiy Prospekt, Gorkovskaya Metro and Trinity Bridge

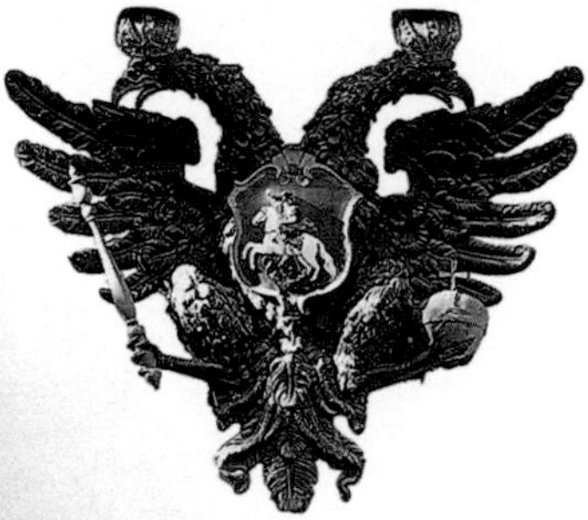

St Peter's Gate
Completed in 1718, this ornate Baroque structure features the Romanov double eagle with an emblem of St George and the dragon.

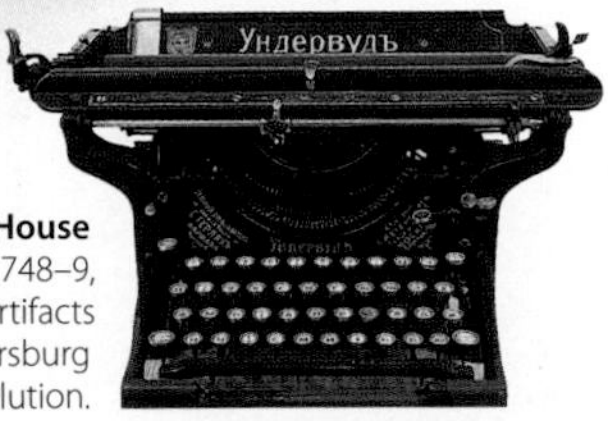
Ундервудъ

Engineer's House
This building, dating from 1748–9, houses temporary exhibitions of artifacts used in everyday life in St Petersburg before the Revolution.

Ochre-painted southern façade of Prince Menshikov's 18th-century palace

② **Menshikov Palace**
Меншиковский дворец

Menshikovskiy dvorets

Universitetskaya naberezhnaya 15. **Map** B3. **Tel** (812) 323 1112. 7, 47, K-47, K-187, K-209, K-298. 6. 1, 11. **Open** 10:30am–6pm Tue–Sat, 10:30am–5pm Sun. compulsory (English, French, German available).

Completed in 1720, this Baroque palace was one of the earliest stone buildings in St Petersburg. It was designed by Giovanni Fontana and Gottfried Schädel for Prince Menshikov, friend and advisor to Peter the Great. Menshikov entertained here, often on behalf of Peter the Great, who adopted the palace as a pied-à-terre. Now a branch of the Hermitage *(see pp148–55)*, it houses exhibitions on early 18th-century Russian culture, revealing the extent to which the court was influenced by Western tastes. Peter and Menshikov often received guests in the Walnut Study. The Great Hall decorated in gold is where balls and banquets were held. Upstairs, rooms are decorated with 17th- century Dutch engravings of Leyden, Utrecht and Krakow.

③ **The Bronze Horseman**
Медный Всадник

Mednyy Vsadnik

Ploshchad Dekabristov. **Map** B3. 3, 10, 22, 27. 5, 22.

The statue of Peter the Great, known as *The Bronze Horseman* after Pushkin's famous poem,

was unveiled in Decembrists' Square (Ploshchad Dekabristov) in 1782, as a tribute from Catherine the Great. The French sculptor, Etienne Falconet, spent over 12 years overseeing the project. The pedestal weighs 1,625 tonnes (1,791 tons) and was hewn from a block of granite, which was hauled from the Gulf of Finland. It bears the inscription "To Peter I from Catherine II" in Latin and Russian. A serpent, beneath the horse's hooves, symbolizes treason.

The Bronze Horseman, Tribute to Peter the Great

④ **The Admiralty**
Адмиралтейство

Admiralteystvo

Admiralteyskaya naberezhnaya 2. **Map** C3. 7, 10, K-187, K-209. 1, 5, 7, 10, 17, 22.

Built as a shipyard between 1704 and 1711 by Peter the Great, the Admiralty's purpose was to gain access to the sea

Tower and spire of the Admiralty, built between 1806 and 1823

and dominance over Sweden. Rebuilt in 1806 by architect Andrey Zakharov, the façade, adorned with sculptures, documents the glory of the Russian fleet. Zakharov retained some of the original features, including the spire, which he recast in the Neo-Classical style.

⑤ **St Isaac's Cathedral**
Исаакиевский собор

Isaakievskiy sobor

Isaakievskaya ploshchad 4. **Map** C4. **Tel** (812) 315 9732. 3, 10, 22, 27, K-169, K-190, K-289. 5, 22. **Open** May–Sep: 10am–11pm Thu–Tue; Oct–Apr: 11am–7pm.

One of the world's largest cathedrals, St Isaac's, was designed in 1818 by architect Auguste de Montferrand. The engineering operation needed to erect the cathedral was, at the time, of an almost unprecedented scale. Opened in 1858, it was designated a museum of atheism during the Soviet era. Officially still a museum today, the church is filled with hundreds of impressive 19th century works of art. The gilded dome, adorned with angels, offers views across the city. Inside, ringed by gilded stucco mouldings and white marble, the ceiling is decorated with a painting of the *Virgin in Majesty* (1847) by Karl Bryullov. The iconostasis has three rows of icons that surround the royal doors. Pyotr Klodt's sculpture, *Christ in Majesty* (1859), rests above the doors, while splendid malachite and lapis lazuli columns frame the pretty iconostasis.

⑥ **St Isaac's Square**
Исаакиевская площадь

Isaakievskaya ploshchad

Map C4. 3, 10, 22, 27. 5, 22.

Dominated by St Isaac's Cathedral, this square was created during the reign of Nicholas I (r. 1825–55), although

St Isaac's Cathedral and the statue of Nicholas I, St Isaac's Square

a few of its earlier buildings date from the 18th century. The monument to Nicholas I at its centre was designed by Montferrand. Erected in 1859 and sculpted by Pyotr Klodt, it depicts the tsar in the uniform of one of Russia's most prestigious regiments, the Kavalergardskiy guards. The pedestal is embellished with allegorical sculptures of his daughters and wife, who represent faith, wisdom, justice and might.

To the west lies the Myatlev House, a Neo-Classical mansion dating from the 1760s. French encyclopedist, Denis Diderot, stayed here between 1773 and 1774. In the 1920s it became the premises of the State Institute of Artistic Culture where some of Russia's most influential avant-garde artists including Kazimir Malevich and Vladimir Tatlin worked. The former German embassy, designed by Peter Behrens, lies alongside. The southern end of the square is dominated by the Mariinskiy Palace which now houses the city hall.

⑦ Malaya Morskaya Ulitsa
Малая Морская улица
Malaya morskaya ulitsa

Map C4. 🚌 3, 10, 22, 27. 🚎 5, 22.

From 1902 to 1993 Malaya Morskaya ulitsa was named ulitsa Gogolya after the great writer, Nikolai Gogol, who lived at No. 17 between 1833 and 1836. It was here that Gogol wrote *The Diary of a Madman* and *The Nose*, two biting satires

on the archetypal Petersburg bureaucrat. The composer, Pyotr Tchaikovsky, died in the apartment at No. 13 shortly after the completion of his *Pathétique* symphony in 1893. It is believed that he committed suicide, after an alleged homosexual affair.

Famous novelist Fyodor Dostoevsky lived in No. 23. He was arrested here for his participation in the socialist Petrashevsky circle. Today, the street continues to exude a 19th-century feel despite the many shops and businesses.

⑧ Palace Square
Дворцовая площадь
Dvortsovaya ploshchad

Map C3. 🚌 7, 10, K-47, K-169, K-190, K-209. 🚎 1, 7, 10.

The Palace Square has played a unique role in Russian history. It was the setting for military parades before the Revolution. In January 1905, it was the scene of the massacre of "Bloody Sunday", when gathered

troops fired on thousands of unarmed demonstrators. Then, on 7 November 1917, Lenin's Bolshevik supporters secured the Revolution by attacking the Winter Palace *(see pp154–5)* from the square. It still remains a popular venue for political meetings, rallies and events such as rock concerts.

The resplendent square is the work of the architect Carlo Rossi, the city's last great exponent of Neo-Classicism. On the southern side of the square is Rossi's magnificent **General Staff Building**, the headquarters of the Russian Army. The two graceful, curving wings – the eastern one now a branch of the Hermitage – are connected by a double arch leading to Bolshaya Morskaya ulitsa. The arch is crowned by the sculpture, *Victory in her Chariot* (1829). To the eastern side of this ensemble is the Guards Headquarters, designed by Aleksandr Bryullov in the 19th century.

To the west lies The Admiralty. The **Alexander Column** in the centre of the square is dedicated to Tsar Alexander I for his role in the triumph over Napoleon. On the pedestal are inscribed the words "To Alexander I, from a grateful Russia". The red granite pillar is balanced by its 600-tonne (661-ton) weight, making it the largest free-standing monument in the world. The column, designed by Montferrand, was erected between 1830 and 1834. It is topped by a bronze angel, and together they stand 47-m (154-ft) high.

The Alexander Column and the General Staff Building, Palace Square

⑨ The Hermitage

Эрмитаж

Ermitazh

One of the most famous museums in the world, the Hermitage occupies a grand ensemble of buildings. The most impressive is the Winter Palace (*see pp154–5*), to which Catherine the Great added the more intimate Small Hermitage. In the 18th century, she built the Large Hermitage to house her collection of art. The Theatre was built in the 18th century, the New Hermitage between 1839 and 1851. The New and Large Hermitages were opened by Nicholas I in 1852 as a museum. From 1918 to 1939 the Winter Palace was incorporated into the museum. The Neo-Classical General Staff Building was added in the late 1990s. Mid- and late-19th-century collections are in the process of being moved there.

Atlantes
Ten 5-m (16-ft) tall granite Atlantes hold up what used to be the public entrance to the Hermitage museum from 1852 until after the Revolution.

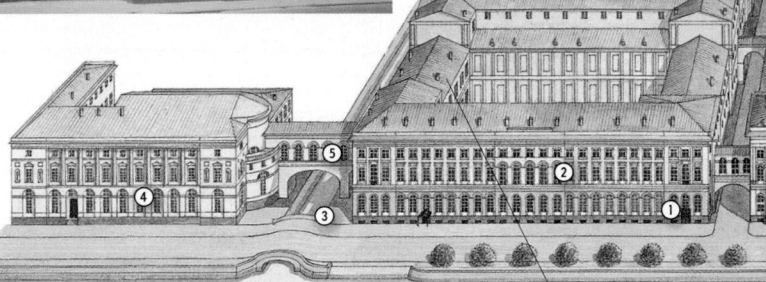

KEY

① **Court ministries** were located here until the 1880s.

② **The Large Hermitage** was designed by Yuriy Velten to house Catherine's paintings.

③ **The Winter Canal**

④ **Quarenghi's Theatre** held regular performances during Catherine's reign. Today, it hosts exhibitions and concerts.

⑤ **A gallery** spanning the canal connects the Theatre to the Large Hermitage and forms the theatre foyer.

⑥ **The New Hermitage** was designed by Leo von Klenze to form a coherent part of the Large

Hermitage. It is the only purpose-built museum within the whole complex.

⑦ **The Small Hermitage**, built between 1764 and 1775, by Vallin de la Mothe and Yuriy Velten, served as Catherine's retreat from the bustle of the court.

⑧ **Palace Square**

⑨ **River Neva** adds to the grandeur of the Hermitage, which is situated on its banks.

⑩ **The Winter Palace** was the official residence of the imperial family until the 1917 Revolution.

★ **Raphael Loggias**
Catherine was so impressed by engravings of Raphael's frescoes in the Vatican that in 1787 she commissioned copies to be made on canvas.

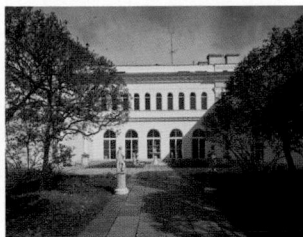

Hanging Gardens
This unusual, raised garden is decorated with statues and fountains. During the Siege of Leningrad in 1941, Hermitage curators grew vegetables here.

VISITORS' CHECKLIST

Practical Information
Dvortsovaya ploschad 2.
Map C3. **Tel** (812) 710 9079.
Open 10:30am–6pm Tue–Sat, 10:30am–5pm Sun. (last admission one hour before closing). English (571 8446).

Transport
7, 10, 24, K-187, K-209, K-252.
1, 7, 10.

Winter Palace Façade
Rastrelli embellished the palace façades with 400 columns and 16 different window designs.

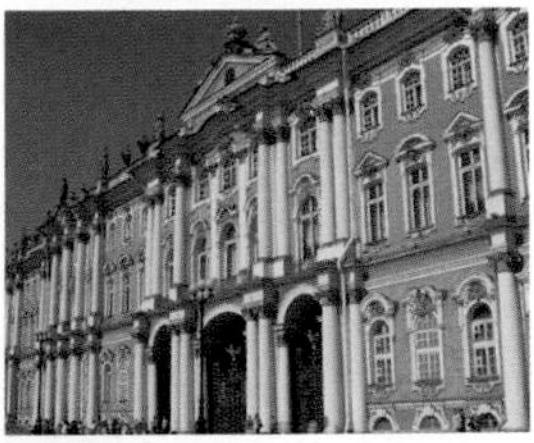

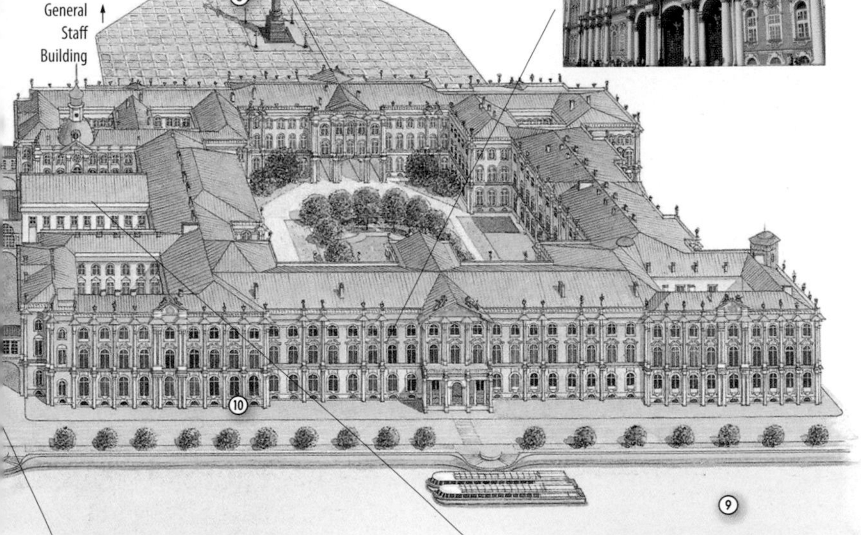
Main entrance via courtyard
General Staff Building
8
10
9

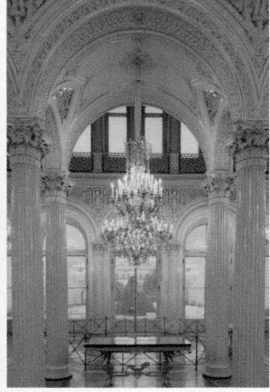

★ Pavilion Hall
Andrey Stakenschneider's white marble and gold hall replaced Catherine's original interior. The hall houses Englishman James Cox's famous Peacock Clock, which was once owned by Catherine's secret lover, Prince Grigory Potemkin.

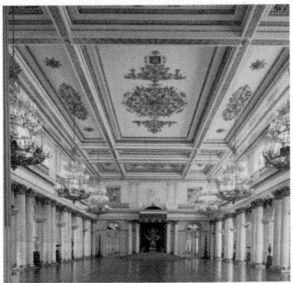

★ Winter Palace State Rooms
The tsars spared no expense in decorating rooms such as the Hall of St George. These rooms were not intended for private life, but were used for state ceremonies.

The Hermitage Collections

Catherine the Great purchased some of Western Europe's best collections between 1764 and 1774, acquiring over 2,500 paintings, 10,000 carved gems, 10,000 drawings and a vast amount of silver and porcelain with which to adorn her palaces. None of her successors matched the quantity of her remarkable purchases. After the Revolution, the nationalization of both royal and private property brought more paintings and works of applied art, making the Hermitage one of the world's leading museums.

The Knights' Hall is used for displays of armour and weapons from the former imperial arsenal.

Stairs to ground floor

Skylight rooms

Raphael Loggias *(see p148)*

First floor

The Gallery of Ancient Painting is decorated with scenes from ancient literature. It houses a display of 19th-century European sculpture.

Ground floor

European Gold Collection

The Litta Madonna (c. 1491)
One of two works by Leonardo da Vinci here, this was much admired by his contemporaries.

Gallery Guide

Individual visitors enter via Palace Square, then cross the main courtyard; group tours use other entrances by arrangement. Visitors can start with the interiors of the Winter Palace State Rooms on the first floor to get an overview of the museum. For 19th- and 20th-century European Art, it is best to use either of the staircases on the Palace Square side of the Winter Palace. However, some collections may move.

The Hall of Twenty Columns

Main entrance

Ticket Office

Entrance for tours and guided groups

★ Abraham's Sacrifice (1635)
In the 1630s Rembrandt painted religious scenes in a High Baroque style, using dramatic and striking gestures rather than detail to convey his message.

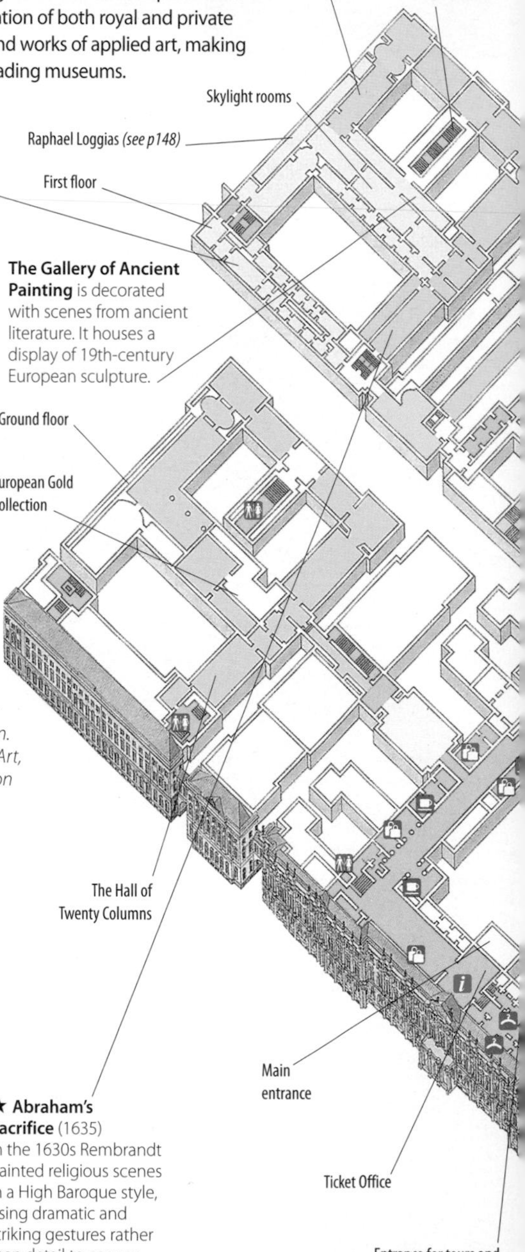

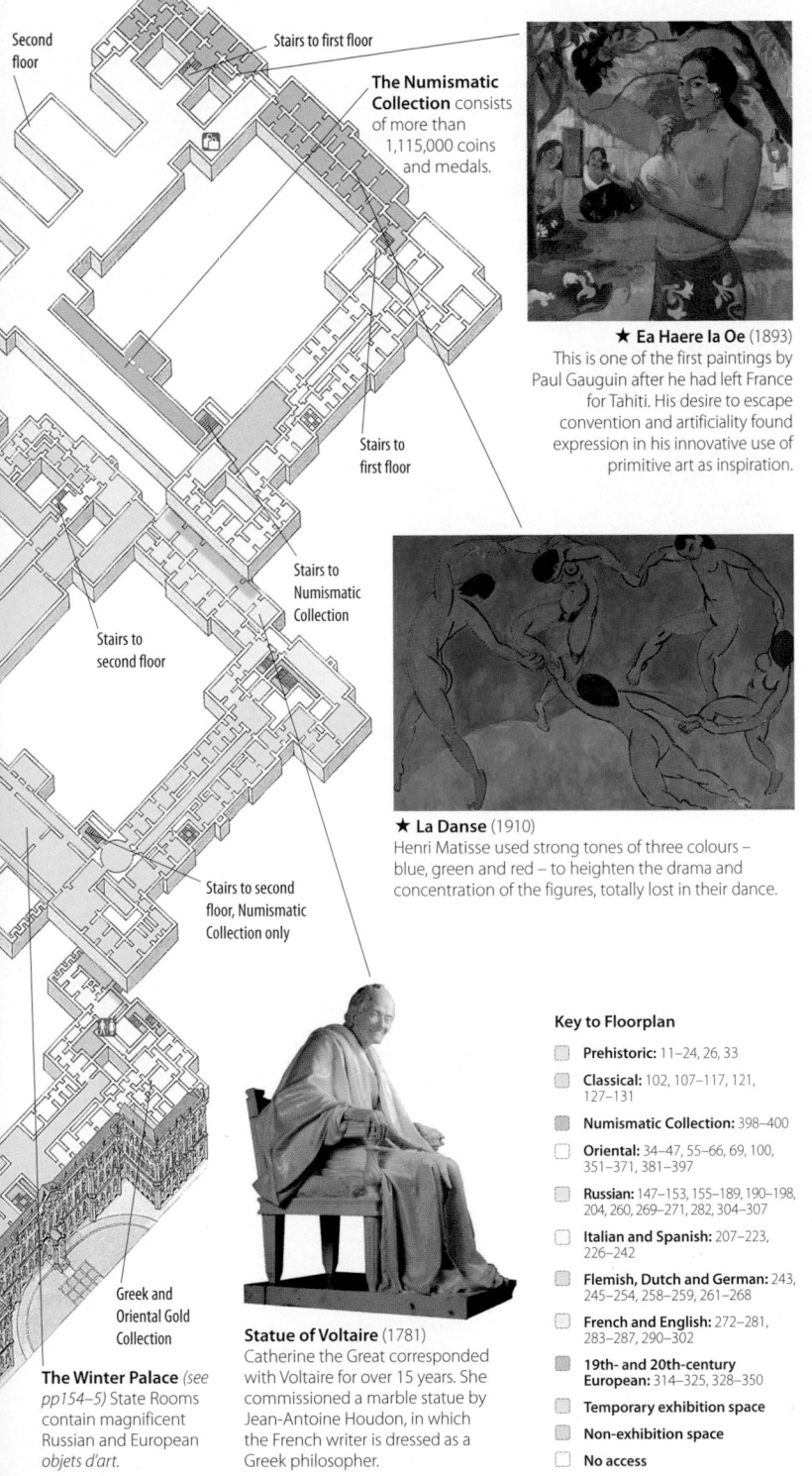

Second floor

Stairs to first floor

The Numismatic Collection consists of more than 1,115,000 coins and medals.

★ **Ea Haere la Oe** (1893)
This is one of the first paintings by Paul Gauguin after he had left France for Tahiti. His desire to escape convention and artificiality found expression in his innovative use of primitive art as inspiration.

Stairs to first floor

Stairs to Numismatic Collection

Stairs to second floor

★ **La Danse** (1910)
Henri Matisse used strong tones of three colours – blue, green and red – to heighten the drama and concentration of the figures, totally lost in their dance.

Stairs to second floor, Numismatic Collection only

Greek and Oriental Gold Collection

Statue of Voltaire (1781)
Catherine the Great corresponded with Voltaire for over 15 years. She commissioned a marble statue by Jean-Antoine Houdon, in which the French writer is dressed as a Greek philosopher.

The Winter Palace *(see pp154–5)* State Rooms contain magnificent Russian and European *objets d'art.*

Key to Floorplan

- Prehistoric: 11–24, 26, 33
- Classical: 102, 107–117, 121, 127–131
- Numismatic Collection: 398–400
- Oriental: 34–47, 55–66, 69, 100, 351–371, 381–397
- Russian: 147–153, 155–189, 190–198, 204, 260, 269–271, 282, 304–307
- Italian and Spanish: 207–223, 226–242
- Flemish, Dutch and German: 243, 245–254, 258–259, 261–268
- French and English: 272–281, 283–287, 290–302
- 19th- and 20th-century European: 314–325, 328–350
- Temporary exhibition space
- Non-exhibition space
- No access

Exploring the Hermitage Collections

It is not possible to absorb the Hermitage's encyclopedic collection in one or even two visits. Whether it be Scythian gold, antique vases and cameos, or Iranian silver, every room has something that catches the eye. The furniture, applied art, portraits and rich clothing of the imperial family make up the Russian section, which also includes the superb state rooms. The collection of European paintings was put together largely according to the personal taste of the imperial family while most of the 19th- and 20th-century European art, notably the Impressionists, Matisse and Picasso, came from private collections after the Revolution.

Eighth-century fresco of a wounded warrior from Tajikistan

Comb with a naturalistic scene of Scythians in battle

Prehistoric Art

Prehistoric artifacts found all over the former Russian Empire include pots, arrow heads and sculptures from Palaeolithic sites nearly 24,000 years old, as well as gold items from the time of the Scythian nomads living in the 7th–3rd centuries BC. Peter the Great's Siberian collection and the European Gold Collection showcase gold objects. Greek masters worked for the Scythians, and from the Dnepr region comes a late 5th-century decorative comb. Unusually well-preserved items from 2,500-year-old burial sites, uncovered during excavations in the Altai between 1927 and 1949, are also on display.

Classical Art

The Graeco-Roman marble sculptures range from the famous Tauride Venus of the 3rd century BC to Roman portrait busts. The smaller objects, however, are the real pride and joy of the Classical department. The collection of red-figured Attic vases from

the 6th–4th centuries BC is unequalled anywhere in the world, while the tiny terracotta figurines from Tanagra, dating back to the 4th and 3rd centuries BC, are exquisite. Other stunning exhibits include the 10,000 carved gems collected by Catherine the Great, the Gonzaga Cameo, presented to Tsar Alexander I, and intricate 5th-century gold jewellery made by Athenian craftsmen.

Third-century BC Gonzaga Cameo, made in Alexandria

Oriental Art

This selection of artifacts covers a wide range of cultures from ancient Egypt and Assyria, through Byzantium, India, Iran, China and Japan, to the marvels of Uzbekistan and Tajikistan. The most complete sections are where excavations were conducted by the Hermitage, mainly in China and Mongolia before the Revolution, and in Central Asia during the Soviet period.

An array of objects, ranging from Buddhist sculptures, fabrics, paintings, utensils,

traditional Persian miniatures and carpets are on display, along with some marvellous 8th-century frescoes from Uzbekistan and Tajikistan. Rare Mughal jewelled vessels, Iranian weapons and Chinese gold objects are displayed in the Greek and Oriental Gold Collection.

Russian Art

Although major Russian works of art were transferred to the Russian Museum (see p158) in 1898, everything else that had belonged to the imperial family was nationalized after the Revolution. Later, the department also began acquiring medieval Russian art, including icons and church utensils.

The tsars from Peter the Great onwards invited foreign craftsmen and artists to train locals. Peter studied with them and his fascination for practical things is reflected in his large collection of sundials, instruments and wood-turning lathes, which includes the universal sundial by Master John Rowley. Russian artists were soon combining traditional art forms with European skills to create intricate marvels. The gunsmiths of Tula, located south of Moscow, perfected their technique to such an extent that they began producing unique furniture in steel inlaid with gilded bronze. The state interiors are the pride of the Russian department, revealing the work of Russian and foreign craftsmen from the mid-18th to the early 20th century. The discovery of stone deposits led to rooms filled with malachite and marble.

Italian and Spanish Art

The fine display of Italian art begins with some early works revealing the rise of the Renaissance in the 14th and 15th centuries. The merits of the later Florentine and Venetian schools can be seen in the masterpieces by da Vinci, Michelangelo, Titian and Raphael, while the Baroque style is represented by the vast canvases of Luca Giordano and other artists. Elegant sculptures by Antonio Canova stand in the Gallery of Ancient Painting.

The Spanish collection is more modest, but Spain's greatest painters can all be seen, from El Greco's *The Apostles Peter and Paul*, to Ribera, Murillo, and Zurbarán with *St Lawrence*. The portrait of a courtier, *Count Olivares*, (c. 1640) by Velázquez, contrasts with a much earlier genre scene of a peasant's breakfast (1617–18).

Flemish, Dutch and German Art

The small collection of early paintings from the Netherlands includes a *Madonna and Child* (1430s) by the Master of Flemalle. Over 40 works by Rubens cover religious subjects and scenes from Classical mythology, as well as landscapes and portraits. The Dutch section is rich in Rembrandts. Among the many small-genre paintings is Gerard Terborch's *Glass of Lemonade* from the mid-17th century, in which all the usual elements of a genre scene are imbued with psychological tension and heavy symbolism.

In the German collection, it is the works of Lucas Cranach the Elder that captivate the viewer. His *Venus and Cupid* (1509), the stylish *Portrait of a Woman in a Hat* (1526) and the tender *Virgin and Child Beneath an Apple Tree* reveal the varied aspects of his talent.

French and English Art

French art was *de rigueur* for collectors in the 18th century. Major artists of the 17th century, including Louis Le Nain and the two brilliant and contrasting painters Claude Lorrain and Nicolas Poussin, are well represented. Antoine Watteau's *Embarrassing Proposal* (c. 1716), *Stolen Kiss* (1780s) by Jean Honoré Fragonard and François Boucher's far-from-virtuous heroines represent the more wicked side of 18th-century taste, but Catherine the Great preferred didactic or instructional works. She also patronized sculptors and English artists. Catherine purchased works by Etienne-Maurice Falconet, Jean-Antoine Houdon, Sir Godfrey Kneller and Sir Joshua Reynolds. However,

Stolen Kiss (1780s), by French artist Jean Honoré

her most daring purchase was of works by the still largely unknown Joseph Wright of Derby. *The Iron Forge* (1773) is a masterpiece of artificial lighting, but *Firework Display at the Castel Sant'Angelo* (1774–5) is a truly romantic fiery spectacle. She provided much work for English cabinet-makers and carvers of cameos and was one of Wedgwood's most prestigious clients, ordering the famous Green Frog Service.

19th- and 20th-Century European Art

Although the royal family did not patronize the new movements in art in the 19th century, there were far-sighted private individuals whose collections were nationalized and entered the Hermitage after the 1917 Revolution. The Barbizon school is well represented by works from Camille Corot and French Romanticism by two richly coloured Moroccan scenes of the 1850s by Delacroix. Nicholas I acquired works by the German Romantic painter Caspar David Friedrich. Collectors Sergey Shchukin and Ivan Morozov brought the museum its fine array of Impressionist and Post-Impressionist paintings including pieces by Monet, Renoir and Pissarro and several pastels by Degas. Works by Van Gogh, such as his *Women of Arles* (1888), and those by Gauguin, Cézanne, Matisse and Picasso show the changes in colour and technique introduced over a period of time. The bold innovation of Picasso's Cubist period of 1907–12 fills a whole room.

Women of Arles (1888), painted by Vincent Van Gogh

The Winter Palace

Зимний дворец

Zimniĭ dvorets

The existing Winter Palace, built between 1754 and 1762, is a great example of Russian Baroque. Created for Tsarina Elizabeth, this opulent winter residence was the finest achievement of Bartolomeo Rastrelli. Though the exterior has changed little, the interiors were largely restored after a fire gutted the palace in 1837. After the assassination of Alexander II in 1881, the imperial family rarely lived here. During World War I, a field hospital was set up in the Nicholas Hall and other state rooms. In July 1917, the provisional government took the palace as its headquarters, which led to its storming by the Bolsheviks.

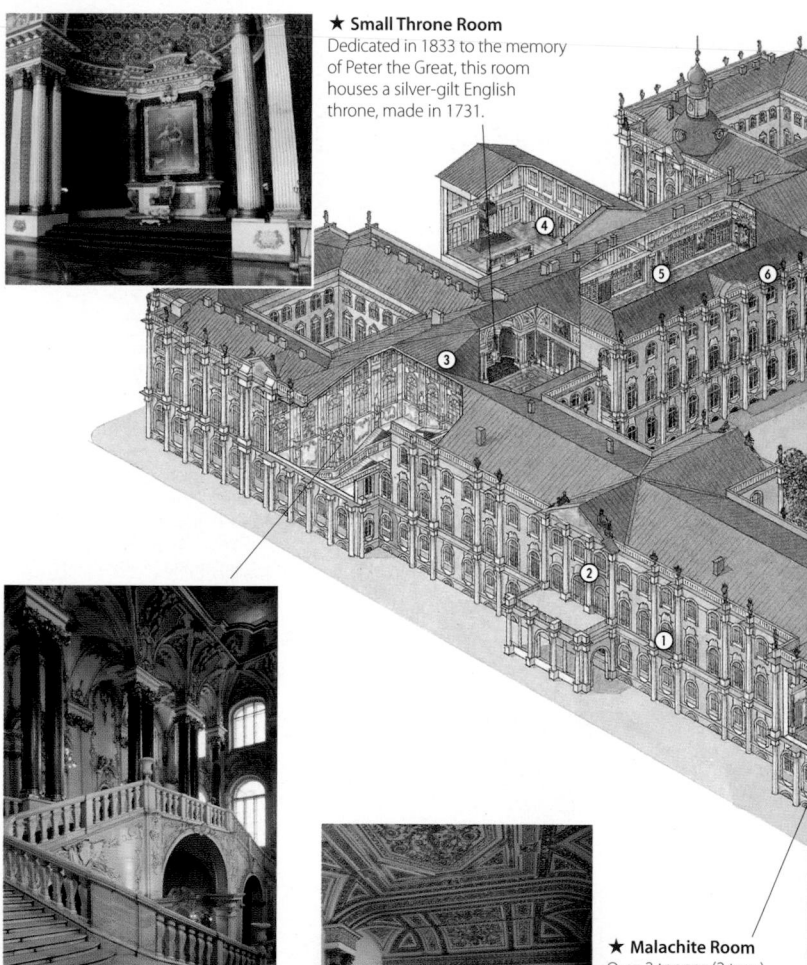

★ Small Throne Room
Dedicated in 1833 to the memory of Peter the Great, this room houses a silver-gilt English throne, made in 1731.

★ Main Staircase
This vast, sweeping staircase was Rastrelli's masterpiece. It was from here that the imperial family watched the Epiphany ceremony of baptism in the Neva river, which celebrated Christ's baptism in the Jordan.

★ Malachite Room
Over 2 tonnes (2 tons) of ornamental stone was used in this room, which is decorated with malachite columns and vases, gilded doors and ceiling, and rich parquet flooring.

For hotels and restaurants see p164 and p165

Alexander Hall
Architect Aleksandr Bryullov employed a mixture of Gothic vaulting and Neo-Classical stucco bas-reliefs of military themes in this reception room of 1837.

Bartolomeo Rastrelli (1700–71)

Bartolomeo Rastrelli

The Italian architect Bartolomeo Rastrelli came to Russia with his father in 1716 to work for Peter the Great. His rich Baroque style became very fashionable and he was appointed Chief Court Architect in 1738. During Elizabeth's reign, Rastrelli designed several buildings, including his magnum opus, the Winter Palace, the dazzling Palace of Tsarskoe Selo and the fine Smolnyy Convent, all in areas around St Petersburg. Unlike Elizabeth, Catherine the Great preferred Classical simplicity and Rastrelli retired in 1763, after she came to power.

Dark Corridor
The tapestries here include the 17th-century *Marriage of Emperor Constantine*, made to designs by Rubens.

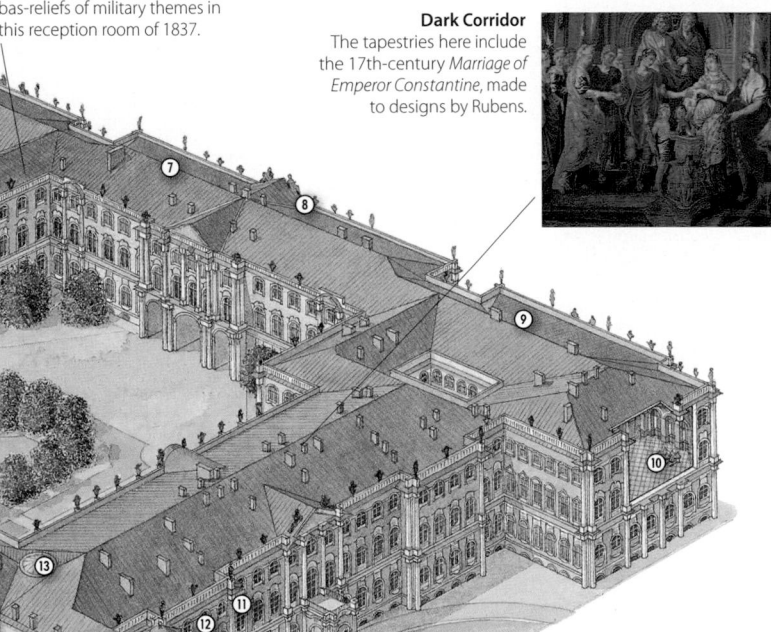

KEY

① **North façade overlooking the Neva river**

② **The Nicholas Hall**, the largest room in the palace, was always used for the first ball of the season.

③ **The Field Marshals' Hall** was the reception room where the devastating fire broke out in 1837.

④ **The Hall of St George** has monolithic columns and wall facings of Italian Carrara marble.

⑤ **The 1812 Gallery** has portraits of Russian military heroes of the Napoleonic Wars, most by English artist George Dawe.

⑥ **The Armorial Hall**, with its vast gilded columns, covers over 800 sq m (8,600 sq ft). Hospital beds were set up in this cavernous room during World War I.

⑦ **The French Rooms**, designed by Bryullov in 1839, house a collection of 18th-century French art.

⑧ **South façade on Palace Square**

⑨ **The White Hall** was decorated for the wedding of Alexander II in 1841.

⑩ **The Gold Drawing Room** was created in the 1850s. This room was decorated in the 1870s with all-over gilding of walls and ceiling. It houses

a display of Western European carved gems.

⑪ **West Wing**

⑫ **The Gothic Library** and other rooms in the northwest part of the palace were adapted to suit Nicholas II's bourgeois lifestyle. This wood-panelled library was created by Meltzer in 1894.

⑬ **The Rotunda** connected the private apartments on the west side with the state apartments on the north side.

⑩ Summer Palace
Летний дворец

Letniy dvorets

Naberezhnaya Kutuzova.
Map D2. **Tel** 314 0374. 🚌 46, 49.
Open May–Nov: 10am–6pm Wed–
Mon. **Closed** last Mon of each month.
🖼 ✅

The remarkable stove in the Summer Palace's tiled kitchen

Built for Peter the Great, the modest two-storey Summer Palace is the oldest stone building in the city. Designed in the Dutch style by Domenico Trezzini, it was completed in 1714. The Prussian sculptor Andreas Schlüter created the delightful maritime bas-reliefs as an allegorical commentary on Russia's naval triumphs under Peter the Great's stewardship.

Grander than his wooden cabin, located on Petrogradskaya across the Neva river, Peter's second St Petersburg residence is still by no means comparable to the magnificent palaces built by his successors.

On the ground floor, the reception room has portraits of the tsar and his ministers and contains Peter's oak Admiralty Chair. The tsar's bedroom has its original four-poster bed with a coverlet of Chinese silk, and an 18th-century ceiling fresco showing the triumph of Morpheus, the god of sleep. Next door is the turnery that contains some original Russian lathes as well as a carved wooden meteorological instrument, designed in Dresden in 1714.

The palace boasted the city's first plumbing system with water piped directly into the kitchen. The original black marble sink can still be seen, along with the beautifully tiled kitchen stove and an array of early 18th-century cooking utensils. The kitchen opens onto the exquisite dining room, imaginatively refurbished to convey an atmosphere of domesticity. It was used only for small family gatherings since major banquets were held at the Menshikov Palace *(see p146)*.

A lavish suite on the first floor was used by Peter's second wife, Catherine, while the throne in the aptly named Throne Room is ornamented with Nereides and other sea deities. The glass cupboards in the Green Room once displayed Peter's lovely collection of curiosa before it was moved to the Kunstkammer on Vasilevskiy Ostrov.

⑪ Summer Garden
Летний сад

Letniy sad

Letniy Sad. **Map** D3. 🚌 46, 49.
Open 10am–10pm daily.
Closed Apr. ♿ 📷

In 1704, Peter the Great commissioned this beautiful garden, which was among the first in the city. Designed by a Frenchman in the style of Versailles, the allées were planted with imported elms and oaks and adorned with fountains, pavilions and some 250 Italian statues dating from the 17th and 18th centuries. A flood in 1777 destroyed most of the Summer Garden, and the English-style garden, which exists today, is largely the result of Catherine the Great's tastes. A splendid feature is the fine filigree iron grille along the Neva embankment, created by architects Yuriy Velten and Pyotr Yegorov.

For a century the Summer Garden was an exclusive preserve of the nobility. When the garden was opened to the public by Nicholas I, two Neo-Classical pavilions, the Tea House and the Coffee House, were erected overlooking the Fontanka. These are now used for temporary art exhibitions by local artists.

Nearby, the bronze statue of Ivan Krylov, Russia's most famous writer of fables, is a favourite with children. Sculpted in 1854 by Pyotr Klodt, with charming bas-reliefs on the pedestal, it depicts animals from Krylov's fables.

Ivan Krylov's statue amidst autumn foliage in the Summer Garden

⑫ Pushkin House-Museum
Музей-квартира А. С.

Пушкина Muzey-kvartira A.S. Pushkina

Naberezhnaya reki Moyki 12.
Map C3. **Tel** 571 3531. **Open** 10:30am–6pm Wed–Mon. **Closed** last Fri of each month.
w museumpushkin.ru

Pushkin was born in Moscow in 1799 *(see p138)*, but spent many years of his life in St Petersburg. From the autumn of 1836 until his death in 1837, Pushkin lived in this fairly opulent apartment overlooking the Moyka, with his wife Natalya and other family members. It was here that he bled to death after his fateful duel with d'Anthès.

Some half a dozen rooms on the first floor have been refurbished in the Empire style of the period. The most evocative is Pushkin's study, which is arranged exactly as it was when he died. On the writing table is an ivory paper knife given to the poet by his sister, a bronze hand-bell and an inkstand. Embellished with the figure of an Ethiopian boy, the inkstand is a reminder of Pushkin's great grandfather, Abram Hannibal. Bought as a slave in Constantinople in 1706, Hannibal served as a general under Peter the Great and was the inspiration for Pushkin's unfinished novel *The Negro of Peter the Great*.

On the wall in front of Pushkin's desk is a Turkish sabre presented to him in the Caucasus, where he had been exiled in 1820. It was there that he began his most famous work, *Eugene Onegin*, a novel in verse written between 1823 and 1830. The apartment's most impressive feature is the poet's library, which contains more than 4,500 volumes in a staggering 14 European and Oriental languages. Among these are works by Byron, Shakespeare and Dante.

⑬ Church on Spilled Blood
Храм Спаса-на-Крови

Khram Spasa-na-Krovi

Naberezhnaya Kanala Griboyedova 2b.
Map D3. **Tel** 315 1636. **M** Gostinyy Dvor, Nevskiy Prospekt. **Open** May–Sep: 10am–11pm Thu–Tue; Oct–Apr: 11am–7pm Thu–Tue.
w cathedral.ru

Also called the Resurrection Church of Our Saviour, this church was built on the spot where Tsar Alexander II was assassinated on 1 March 1881. In 1883, his successor, Alexander III, launched a competition for a permanent memorial. The winning design, favoured by the tsar himself, was by Alfred Parland and Ignatiy Malyshev. The Russian Revival style of the exterior provides a dramatic contrast to the Neo-Classical and Baroque architecture which dominates the centre of St Petersburg. The foundation stone was laid in 1883.

A riot of colour, the overall effect of the church is created by the imaginative juxtaposition of materials. Mosaic panels showing scenes from the New Testament adorn the exterior. They were based on designs by artists such as Viktor Vasnetsov and Mikhail Nesterov. The 144 mosaic coats of arms on the bell tower represent the regions, towns and provinces of the Russian Empire. They were intended to reflect the grief shared by all Russians in the wake of Alexander II's assassination. The perimeter of the lower wall has 20 dark-red plaques made of Norwegian granite, which illustrate key events of the 25-year reign of Alexander II.

Inside, more than 20 types of minerals, including jasper, rhodonite, porphyry and Italian marble, are lavished on the mosaics of the iconostasis, icon cases, canopy and floor. The interior reopened in 1998 after more than 20 years of restoration work.

Mosaic tympanum at the Church on Spilled Blood

Personal effects in Pushkin's study, Pushkin House-Museum

Colourful exterior of the Church on Spilled Blood

Russian Museum, in the Neo-Classical Mikhaylovskiy Palace

⑭ Russian Museum
Русский Музей

Russkiy Muzey

Inzhenernaya ulitsa 4. **Map** D3.
Tel 595 4248. Ⓜ Nevskiy Prospekt,
Gostinyy Dvor. 🚍 3, 7, 22, 27, K-169,
K-187, K-289. 🚎 1, 5, 7, 10, 22.
Open 10am–6pm Mon, Wed, Fri–Sun,
1–9pm Thu (last ticket an hour before
closing). 🎧 📷 English. 🔊 English.
♿ call for details. 📱 📷
Ⓦ **rusmuseum.ru**

Housing one of the greatest
collections of Russian art, the
Russian Museum was opened
to the public for the first time
in 1898. When the museum
was nationalized after the 1917
Revolution, art was transferred
to it from palaces, churches and
private collections. The museum
is housed in the Mikhaylovskiy
Palace, one of Carlo Rossi's
finest Neo-Classical creations,
which was built between 1819
and 1825 for Grand Duke
Mikhail Pavlovich.

The chronologically arranged
exhibition starts on the first
floor. The exhibition continues
on the ground floor of the main
building and Rossi Wing, then
the first floor of the Benois Wing,
which was added between
1913 and 1919. The museum's
exhibits range from 12th–17th
century Russian icons to avant-

garde painting by Kandinsky
and Malevich. Highlights of
the exhibition are the works
of Russia's first-known portrait
painters, Ivan Nikitin and Andrey
Matveev and the brooding
canvases of 19th- and 20th-
century artist Mikhail Vrubel,
who combined Russian themes
with an international outlook.
Other leading artists, including
Marc Chagall, El Lissitskiy and
Alexander Rodchenko, are
also well represented in the
museum. Exhibitions are
changed regularly.

The museum also has a
selection of folk art, which
is wonderfully diverse and
includes painted ceramics
and exquisitely embroi-
dered textiles.

⑮ Arts Square
Площадь Искусств

Ploshchad Iskusstv

Map D3. Ⓜ Nevskiy Prospekt,
Gostinyy Dvor.

Several of the city's leading
cultural institutions are located
on this imposing Neo-Classical
square; hence its name. The
attractive square was designed
by Carlo Rossi in the early 19th
century. Opposite the Russian
Museum is the Great Hall of

the St Petersburg Philharmonia,
also called the Shostakovich
Hall. The Philharmonic
Orchestra has been based
here since the 1920s. Among
the works that premiered
here were Beethoven's
Missa Solemnis in 1824 and
Pathétique by Tchaikovsky
in 1893. On the square's
western side is the Mikhailovsky
Theatre. In the centre of the
square is a sculpture of one
of Russia's greatest literary
figures, Alexander Pushkin.

⑯ Nevskiy Prospekt
Невский проспект

Nevskiy prospekt

Map C3. Ⓜ Nevskiy Prospekt,
Gostinyy Dvor.

Russia's most famous street,
Nevskiy prospekt, is also
St Petersburg's main thoroughfare. In the 1830s, the novelist
Nikolai Gogol declared with
pride: "There is nothing finer
than Nevskiy Avenue in
St Petersburg it is everything
is there anything more gay,
more brilliant, more resplendent than this beautiful street
of our capital?" Not much has
changed as the street's intrinsic
"all-powerful" atmosphere
still prevails.

Laid out in the early days
of the city, it was first known
as the Great Perspective Road,
and ran 5 km (3 miles) from
the Admiralty *(see p146)* to the
Alexander Nevsky Monastery.
In spite of roaming wolves and
uncontrollable flooding from
the Neva, which made the

Pushkin's statue located in the centre of
Arts Square

avenue navigable in 1721, fine mansions, such as the Stroganov Palace, soon started to appear. Shops and bazaars, catering for the nobility, and inns for travelling merchants followed. By the mid-18th century the avenue had become the place to meet for gossip, business and pleasure.

Many of the city's sights are close to the stretch between the Admiralty and Anichkov Bridge. Some of the best shops *(see pp162–3)* can be found around Gostinyy dvor and Passazh arcade. Nevskiy prospekt also offers a wealth of cultural interest: the Small Philharmonia Concert Hall, the Russian National Library, Beloselskiy-Belozerskiy Palace and a wide variety of museums, theatres, churches, including the Church of St Catherine, shops, cinemas and eateries.

One of Russia's most important cultural institutions, the Mariinskiy Theatre

View along the bustle of Nevskiy prospekt, the hub of St Petersburg

⑰ Mariinskiy Theatre
Мариинский театр

Mariinskiy teatr

Teatralnaya ploshchad 1. **Map** B5.
Tel 326 4141. 🚌 3, 22, 27.
🚊 5, 22. 🎭 📷 🛒 🎭 ✉
w mariinsky.ru

Often still known internationally by its Soviet title, the Kirov, this theatre was originally named after Tsarina Maria Alexandrovna, Alexander II's wife, and has now reverted to its first name. Erected in 1860 by the architect who designed Moscow's Bolshoy Theatre, Albert Kavos, it stands on the site of an earlier theatre that was destroyed by fire. Between 1883 and 1896, Viktor Schröter remodelled the Neo-Renaissance façade and added most of the ornamental detail. The pale blue and gold auditorium, where so many illustrious dancers have made their debuts, creates a dazzling impression. Its architectural decoration of twisted columns, atlantes, cherubs and cameo medallions has remained unchanged since the theatre's completion, and the imperial eagles have been restored to the royal box. The ceiling fresço of dancing girls and cupids by Italian artist Enrico Franchioli dates from c.1856, while the superb stage curtain was added during Russian ballet's golden age in 1914. Equally remarkable is the glittering foyer, decorated with fluted pilasters, bas-reliefs of Russian composers and mirrored doors. One of the country's leading opera houses, this theatre was where most of Russia's great 19th-century operas premiered. These include Mussorgsky's *Boris Godunov* (1874), Tchaikovsky's *Queen of Spades* (1890) and Shostakovich's controversial opera *Lady Macbeth of Mtsensk* (1934).

The Ballets Russes

An early 20th-century Ballets Russes programme

The legendary touring company that revolutionized ballet between 1909 and 1929 was the brainchild of the impresario and art critic Sergey Diaghilev (1872–1929). His choreographer Mikhail Fokine shared his vision of a spectacle that would fuse music, ballet and decor in a seamless artistic whole. Diaghilev had the pick of the dancers from Mariinskiy Theatre and, in 1909, he took his Ballets Russes to Paris. His company had a remarkable impact on the contemporary art world. The ballets of Fokine, in particular, prepared audiences for greater innovation and experimentation. Exciting contributions from costume and set designers Léon Bakst and Alexandre Benois, the composer Igor Stravinsky and the dancers Vaslaw Nijinsky, Anna Pavlova and Tamara Karsavina all played a part in expanding artistic frontiers. After Diaghilev's death in 1929, the Ballets Russes fragmented, but its ethos and traditions have been preserved in many of today's leading companies.

Practical & Travel Information

Moscow is not as difficult for visitors to find their way around as it may seem at first. Although tourist facilities are fairly basic, there is an excellent metro system, and passers-by and people working in hotels, restaurants and shops will usually be helpful. In St Petersburg, conventional tourist offices do not exist and information points are often concentrated in hotels and other areas frequented by foreigners. In recent times the city has started putting up English signs pointing out major sights and shops. However, it is a good idea for visitors to familiarize themselves with the Cyrillic alphabet in order to decipher signs.

When to Visit

The best time to visit Moscow and St Petersburg is during the peak tourist season that lasts from May to late August. Winters in Moscow are bitterly cold and best avoided. January is a good time to visit St Petersburg, when the days are sunny.

Documentation

Visitors from almost all countries, including the Baltic States, will need a visa to visit Moscow and St Petersburg. Only citizens of the other CIS member-states are exempt. Independent tourist visa applications must be supported with appropriate documentation as well as proof of pre-booked hotel accommodation or an invitation (visa support) from a tour company, business or private individual in Russia. Anyone intending to reside in Russia for longer than three months is advised to register with their own embassy or consulate in Moscow. Officially, all foreigners are supposed to register with **OVIR**, the Visa and Registration Department, within three days of their arrival; hotels do this for their guests.

All visitors have to fill out a customs declaration form on arrival. Valuables such as jewellery and computers should be declared on entry, otherwise duty may be payable.

Visitor Information

There are no conventional tourist information offices in Moscow or St Petersburg, so hotels are the main source of guidance for visitors. Upmarket hotels in Moscow are the most helpful. Smaller hotels have a service bureau offering similar services, but advice can be indifferent.

VisitRussia.com Ltd., DenRus and the **MIR Travel Company** in St Petersburg provide tourist assistance including information on booking accommodation and entertainment options.

Health and Security

Most hotels have their own doctor, and this should be the first port of call for anyone who falls ill. There are several companies, notably the **European Medical Centre** and the **International Clinic MEDSI** in Moscow, and **MEDEM** and **Euromed** in St Petersburg, which deal with medical emergencies. Medical insurance, however, is essential.

Despite media reports worldwide about the activities of the mafia, Moscow and St Petersburg are relatively safe cities. Petty crime should be the only concern for visitors, and even this can be avoided with the usual precautions. It is advisable to make copies of your passport and visa, and to make a note of traveller's cheque and credit card numbers.

Banking and Currency

The official currency of Moscow and St Petersburg is the rouble. Roubles cannot be obtained outside Russia, but there are numerous exchange bureaus all over Moscow, including at the airports. Banks are open from 9am to 6pm and accept a variety of currencies and credit cards as well as traveller's cheques.

Communications

Russia's phone system has rapidly been brought up to date, with direct dialling worldwide. Blue Comstar satellite phone boxes are installed at airports, in business centres, most hotel

---

The Climate of Moscow and St Petersburg

Moscow experiences warm summers with temperatures reaching 23° C (73° F). Winters are long and cold with temperatures dropping as low as −16° C (3° F). In St Petersburg, summers are mild at 20° C (68° F), while winters are less bitter than in Moscow, with temperatures down to −13° C (9° F).

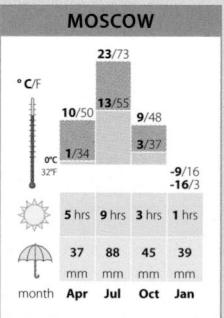

MOSCOW			
°C/F		23/73	
	10/50	13/55	9/48
0°C 32°F	1/34	3/37	-9/16
			-16/3
5 hrs	9 hrs	3 hrs	1 hrs
37 mm	88 mm	45 mm	39 mm
month Apr	Jul	Oct	Jan

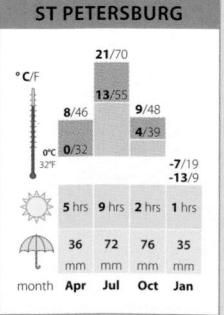

ST PETERSBURG			
°C/F		21/70	
	8/46	13/55	9/48
0°C 32°F	0/32		4/39
			-7/19
			-13/9
5 hrs	9 hrs	2 hrs	1 hrs
36 mm	72 mm	76 mm	35 mm
month Apr	Jul	Oct	Jan

foyers and some restaurants. These accept credit cards or phone cards, which are sold in most major hotels, restaurants and clubs, but calls are expensive.

Moscow's **Main Post Office** and St Petersburg's **Westpost** and **Post International** offer ordinary, express, courier and *poste restante* services.

Arriving by Air

There is a reasonable choice of flights to Moscow from the UK. **British Airways**, **Aeroflot** and **Transaero** operate direct flights, while **SAS**, **KLM** and **Austrian Airlines** run flights via various destinations. The international terminal is **Domodedovo**. Transaero and Aeroflot operate flights from the US, Australia and Canada. Transaero is considered a good alternative to Aeroflot.

Direct flights from the UK to St Petersburg run daily on British Airways and three days a week on **Rossiya**, while those from Ireland, Canada, South Africa, Australasia and the US are limited. The modernized international **Pulkovo Airport**, meets international standards.

Arriving by Sea

Arriving by boat can be one of the most exciting ways to approach St Petersburg. However, ferries and cruises operate irregularly, so it is best to check with a travel agent for details. Ferries from Scandinavia usually dock at the **Maritime Passenger Terminal**. Trolleybus No. 10 and bus No. 7 run from here to the centre or, heading in the other direction, to Primorskaya metro station.

Luxury cruise ships from the US, London and elsewhere arrive at St Petersburg's cargo port, 5 km (3 miles) southwest of the centre. Ships have their own coaches to carry tourists into town and back.

Rail Travel

Rail is a relatively inexpensive way to travel within Russia. Moscow can be reached by train from Paris, Brussels, Berlin and several other European capitals, while St Petersburg is connected to Moscow, Helsinki and London. Travellers should be prepared for a lengthy wait at the Russian border while all

of the train's wheels are changed to fit the wider Russian tracks.

Travelling by Coach

It is possible to get to Moscow by coach, but it is usually only worth it if visitors are travelling from a neighbouring country or are on a tight budget. There are coach routes to Moscow from the Czech Republic, Poland, Hungary and Slovakia. **Ecolines** coaches offer a more affordable alternative to trains.

Travelling Between Moscow and St Petersburg

The most popular form of transport between the two cities is the train, of which there are ten or more a day. Prices vary according to the class of the train – the Red Arrow being the most expensive – and the choice of seat.

Regular commercial flights run by Aeroflot, Rossiya and Transaero also connect the two cities. Prices are modest and tickets are available from the airport or the Central Air Communication Agency.

DIRECTORY

Documentation

W petersburgcity.com

OVIR
Tel (499) 238 6400.

Visitor Information

DenRus
W denrus.ru

MIR Travel Company
Tel (812) 325 2595.
W mir-travel.com

VisitRussia.com Ltd.
W visitrussia.com

Embassies

Australia
W russia.embassy.gov.au

Canada
W canadainternational.gc.ca/russia-russie/

Ireland
W embassyofireland.ru

New Zealand
W nzembassy.com

United Kingdom
W ukinrussia.fco.gov.uk/en

United States
W usembassy.ru

Emergency Numbers

Ambulance
Tel 03, 112.

Fire
Tel 01, 112.

Police
Tel 02, 112.

Health and Security

Euromed
Tel (812) 327 0301.

European Medical Centre
Tel (495) 933 6655.

International Clinic MEDSI
Tel (495) 933 7700.

Medem
W medem.ru

Communications

Main Post Office
Myasnitskaya ulitsa 26,
Moscow.
Tel (495) 624 0250.

Post International
Tel (812) 309 0990.

Westpost
Nevskiy prospekt 86,
St Petersburg.
Tel (812) 275 0784.

Arriving by Air

Aeroflot
W aeroflot.ru

Austrian Airlines
W aua.com

British Airways
W britishairways.com

Domodedovo
Tel (495) 933 6666.

KLM
W klm.com

Pulkovo Airport
W pulkovoairport.ru

Rossiya
Tel (812) 647 0647.
W rossiya-airlines.com

SAS
W sas-airlines.com

Transaero
W transaero.ru

Arriving by Sea

Maritime Passenger Terminal
Tel (812) 322 6052.

Rail Travel

W rzd.ru

Travelling by Coach

Ecolines
W ecolines.ru

Shopping & Entertainment

It is easy to find interesting and beautiful souvenirs in Moscow and St Petersburg. A wide range of goods is available, from enamelled badges to hand-painted Palekh boxes and samovars. Traditional crafts were encouraged by the state in the former Soviet Union and many items are still made by artisans using age-old methods. Moscow and St Petersburg also offer an impressive and varied choice of entertainment, from theatre, opera and ballet to lively nightlife venues. St Petersburg has many rock and jazz clubs, bars, art cafés, discos, nightclubs and casinos. Moscow's street performers are additional attractions.

Opening Hours

Shops in Moscow and St Petersburg usually open from 10am to 8pm. In Moscow, shops are open all day on Saturdays, and for shorter hours on Sundays. In St Petersburg, department stores and other large shops remain open on Sundays; smaller places may close at weekends in summer.

Markets

The markets in Moscow and St Petersburg cater more to the daily needs of locals than to visitors. However, there are a number of souvenir and flea markets. **Izmaylovo Market** in Moscow has all the usual souvenirs on sale, including Soviet memorabilia and painted Russian *matryoshka* dolls.

The official souvenir market in St Petersburg, near the Church on Spilled Blood (*see p157*), sells the best and cheapest selection of *matryoshka* dolls. Visitors are also likely to find handmade chess sets, watches, fur hats, old cameras and military paraphernalia.

Handicrafts

Handmade goods are cheaper in Moscow and St Petersburg than in the West, and they make interesting souvenirs to take home. The best places to shop in Moscow are Izmaylovo Market and the souvenir shops on ulitsa Arbat. Elsewhere in the city, a good range of arts and crafts is available at **Russkiye Uzory**. For more unusual souvenirs, **Dom**

Farfora sells hand-painted tea sets and Russian crystal and the **Salon of the Moscow Cultural Fund** offers samovars, old lamps and sculptures.

In St Petersburg, there are good gifts to be found in the **Souvenir Market** and **Gostinyy Dvor**. Local porcelain is available in the **Imperial Porcelain Factory**.

Art and Antiques

Both Moscow and St Petersburg have a host of treasure-filled art and antique shops worth exploring. Ulitsa Arbat, in Moscow, has many of the best antique shops. **Serebryaniy Ryad** offers a good selection of icons, silver, jewellery and china, while **Ivantsarevich** has a variety of interesting Soviet porcelain. **The Foreign Book Store**, though principally a bookshop, also sells furniture, china and lamps.

Most shops in St Petersburg are very expensive, but **Tertia** is an exception, with readily exportable items to suit all pockets. The **Antique Centre** is a veritable treasure trove. It is worth visiting **Anna Nova** or **S.P.A.S.** to see the paintings on sale. The **Union of Artists** has exhibitions by local artists, while the **Pushkinskaya 10** artists' colony stages shows at weekends, some with works for sale.

Food and Drink

Russia is the best place in the world to buy vodka and caviar. Caviar should not be bought on the street and it is advisable to buy it in tins rather than jars.

Popular vodkas such as Stolichnaya and Moskovskaya are available in supermarkets such as **Sedmoi Kontinent**.

Gostinyy Dvor and **Passazh** are the most central and reliable places for both vodka and caviar in St Petersburg. For something sweet, the **Krupskaya Fabrika** chocolate factory has long been famous across the Soviet Union, while the **Chocolate Museum** sells novelties such as famous buildings crafted in chocolate.

Nightlife

Nightlife in Moscow is booming. For mainstream pop and disco, there are large clubs in Moscow such as **Soho Rooms**. Foreign DJs often perform at **Propaganda** and **Fabrique**. House music is blended with more up-tempo Latin beats at **Karma Bar**, while **Kult** offers more urban grooves. **Secret Bar** and **Dorffman** cater to the "new-rich", with prices and cover charges to match.

St Petersburg's nightclubs offer mostly techno and mainstream pop. **Metro** plays house, techno and Russian dance music. **Cuba libre** has DJ parties and offers a wide choice of cocktails, while **Tribunal** is purely mainstream. Smaller, more diverse clubs, such as the underground **Griboedov**, are still very much of the alternative culture trend, playing a variety of the latest hits from Europe.

Music, Theatre and Dance

In Moscow, many famous foreign acts, as well as the best in local talent, play at clubs such as **ESSE Jazz Club** and **Sixteen Tons**. The **Tchaikovsky Concert Hall** and the **Moscow Conservatory** stand out among the classical music venues, while opera and ballet are performed at the **Bolshoy Theatre**. The city's theatre scene is vibrant and the **Taganka Theatre** and **Mossoviet Theatre** are among the city's best, staging excellent productions of Russian classics. The **Moscow Arts Theatre**, the **Lenkom Theatre** and **Malyy Theatre** stage musicals and plays by contemporary Russian writers, while performances at the **Gypsy Theatre** consist of gypsy dancing and singing.

In St Petersburg, gig venues include **Pyatnitsa**, which features punk bands. The **Great Hall of the Philharmonia**, the **Small Hall of the Philharmonia** and the **Academic Capella** are the historic venues that are used for classical concerts. Opera and ballet are performed at the **Mikhailovsky Theatre**. The **Mariinskiy Theatre** is the epitome of the best in Russian ballet and opera while the **Alexandriinskiy Theatre** is the oldest in Russia.

DIRECTORY

Markets

Izmaylovo Market
Izmaylovskoe Shosse, Moscow.

Handicrafts

Dom Farfora
Leninskiy prospekt 36, Moscow.
Tel (499) 995 6023.

Gostinyy Dvor
Nevskiy prospekt 35, St Petersburg.
Tel (812) 710 5408.

Imperial Porcelain Factory
151 Obukhovskoy Oborony prospekt, St Petersburg.
Tel (812) 560 8544.

Russkiye Uzory
Ul Petrovka 16, Moscow.
Tel (495) 923 1883.

Salon of the Moscow Cultural Fund
Pyatnitskaya ul 16, Moscow.
Tel (495) 951 3302.

Souvenir Market
Naberezhnaya Kanala Griboedova, St Petersburg.

Art and Antiques

Anna Nova
Ul Zhukovskovo 28, St Petersburg.
Tel (812) 275 9762.

Antique Centre
3-ya Sovetskaya ul 36/5, St Petersburg.
Tel (812) 327 8271.

The Foreign Book Store
Malaya Nikitskaya ul 16/5, Moscow.
Tel (495) 290 4082.

Ivantsarevich
Ul Arbat 4, Moscow.
Tel (495) 291 7444.

Pushkinskaya 10
Ligovskiy prospekt 53, St Petersburg.
Tel (812) 764 5371.

Serebryaniy Ryad
Arbat 18, Moscow.
Tel (495) 691 7308.

S.P.A.S.
Naberezhnaya Reki Moyki 93, St Petersburg.
Tel (812) 571 4260.

Tertia
Italyanskaya ul 5, St Petersburg.
Tel (812) 710 5568.

Union of Artists
Bolshaya Morskaya ul 38, St Petersburg.
Tel (812) 314 3060.

Food and Drink

Chocolate Museum
Nevskiy prospekt 17, St Petersburg.
Tel (812) 315 1348.

Krupskaya Fabrika
Ul Vosstaniya 15, St Petersburg.
Tel (812) 346 5532.

Passazh
Nevskiy prospekt 48, St Petersburg.
Tel (812) 571 1426.

Sedmoi Kontinent
Bolshaya Gruzinskaya ul 63, Moscow.
Tel (495) 721 3862.

Nightlife

Cuba libre
Sadovaya 7-9-11, St Petersburg.
Tel (812) 983 5526.

Dorffman
Taganskaya pl 12/2, Moscow.
Tel (495) 679 8688.

Fabrique
Kosmodamianskaya Naberezhnaya 2.
Tel (963) 687 8888.

Griboedov
Voronezhskaya ul 2A, St Petersburg.
Tel (812) 764 4355.

Karma Bar
Pushechnaya ul 3, Moscow.
Tel (495) 624 5633.

Kult
Ul Yauzskaya 5, Moscow.
Tel (495) 917 5706.

Metro
Ligovskiy prospekt 174.
Tel (812) 766 0204.

Propaganda
Bolshoy Zlatoustinskiy pereulok 7, Moscow.
Tel (495) 624 5732.

Secret Bar
Stoleshnikov pereulok 6/3, Moscow.
Tel (495) 921 0750.

Soho Rooms
Savvinskaya naberezhnaya 12/8, Moscow. **Tel** (495) 988 7474.

Tribunal
Karavannaya ulitsa 26, St Petersburg.
Tel (812) 314 2423.

Music, Theatre and Dance

A2
Medikov prospekt 3, St Petersburg.
Tel (812) 309 9922.

Academic Capella
Nab Reki Moyki 20, St Petersburg.
Tel (812) 314 1058.

Alexandriinskiy Theatre
Ploshchad Ostrovskovo 2, St Petersburg.
Tel (812) 710 4103.

Bolshoy Theatre
Teatralnaya pl 1,
Tel (495) 250 7317
(Moscow). Nab Reki Fontanki 65,
Tel (812) 310 9242 (St Petersburg).

ESSE Jazz Club
Pyatnistkaya ulitsa 27/3a, Moscow.
Tel (495) 951 6404.

Great Hall of the Philharmonia
Mikhaylovskaya ul 2, St Petersburg.
Tel (812) 710 4290.

Gypsy Theatre
Leningradskiy prospekt 32/2, Moscow.
Tel (495) 251 8522.

Lenkom Theatre
Ul Malaya Dmitrovka 6, Moscow.
Tel (495) 699 0708.

Malyy Theatre
Ul Rubinsteyna 18, St Petersburg.
Tel (812) 713 2078.

Mariinskiy Theatre
Teatralnaya pl 1, St Petersburg.
Tel (812) 326 4141.

Mikhailovsky Theatre
Pl Iskusstv 1, St Petersburg.
Tel (812) 595 4305.

Moscow Arts Theatre
Kamergerskiy Pereulok 3, Moscow.
Tel (495) 629 8760.

Moscow Conservatory
Bolshaya Nikitskaya Ul 13/6, Moscow.
Tel (495) 629 9401.

Mossoviet Theatre
Bolshaya Sadovaya 16, Moscow. **Tel** (495) 699 2035.

Sixteen Tons
Presnenskiy Val 6, Moscow.
Tel (495) 253 5300.

Small Hall of the Philharmonia
Nevskiy prospekt 30, St Petersburg.
Tel (812) 312 4585.

Taganka Theatre
Zemlyanoy Val 76, Moscow.
Tel (495) 915 1015.

Tchaikovsky Concert Hall
Triumfalnaya ploshchad 4/31, Moscow.
Tel (495) 299 3681.

Where to Stay

Moscow

DK Choice

Hotel Metropol ⓇⓇⓇ
Luxury Map E2
Teatralnyy proezd 2
Tel *(499) 501 7800*
Ⓦ metmos.ru
A wonderful example of
Style-Moderne, the Metropol
boasts spectacular interiors
adorned with mosaics,
golden chandeliers and
stained glass.

**Marco Polo Presnya
Hotel** ⓇⓇ
Business Map C2
Spiridonevskiy pereulok 9
Tel *(495) 660 0606*
Ⓦ presnja.ru
Quiet and comfortable
hotel in a lovely residential
area, a short walk from
Red Square.

Peking Hotel ⓇⓇ
Historic
Ulitsa Bolshaya Sadovaya 5
Tel *(495) 650 0900*
Ⓦ hotelpeking.ru
Towering Empire-style building
with rooms ranging from basic
to luxurious. Free Wi-Fi.

**Ararat Park Hyatt
Moscow** ⓇⓇⓇ
Luxury Map F1
Neglinnaya ulitsa 4
Tel *(495) 783 1234*
Ⓦ moscow.park.hyatt.com
Housed in a former Stalinist
ministry, this hotel offers superb
views from its terrace. There's
a health club with lounging
areas, a sauna and a big
Roman bath.

Hotel National ⓇⓇⓇ
Historic Map D2
Mokhovaya ulitsa 15/1
Tel *(495) 258 7000*
Ⓦ national.ru
Lenin stayed here before
moving into the Kremlin.
Rooms are well-appointed.
Free Wi-Fi.

The Ritz-Carlton ⓇⓇⓇ
Business/chain Map D2
Tverskaya ulitsa 3
Tel *(495) 225 8888*
Ⓦ ritzcarlton.com
Indulge in the spa and pool
at this grand hotel opposite
Red Square.

DK Choice

**Hotel Baltschug
Kempinski** ⓇⓇⓇ
Business Map E3
Ulitsa Balchug 1
Tel *(495) 287 2000*
Ⓦ kempinski-moscow.com
Located by the Moskva river, this
elegant hotel offers magnificent
views of the Kremlin and St Basil's
Cathedral from its rooms on the
riverside. Facilities include a
business centre, spa and beauty
centre. Taxi services are available
from the hotel's fleet of luxury cars.

St Petersburg

Petro Palace Hotel ⓇⓇ
Business Map C4
Malaya Morskaya ulitsa 14
Tel *(812) 571 2880*
Ⓦ petropalacehotel.com
Grand interiors and extensive facil-
ities, including a gym and Jacuzzi.

DK Choice

Casa Leto ⓇⓇⓇ
Historic Map C4
Bolshaya Morskaya ulitsa 34
Tel *(812) 600 1096*
Ⓦ casaleto.com
Ultra-chic family-owned
boutique hotel – reached by
a grand stairwell – with light-
filled rooms and a superb central
location. Completely non-
smoking, with many complimentary extras such as fresh fruit
and refreshments. Free Wi-Fi.

Polikoff Ⓡ
Guesthouse Map D4
Karavannaya ulitsa 11/64, apt 24–26
Tel *(812) 995 3488*
Ⓦ polikoff.ru
Mini-hotel with bright, cosy rooms.
Centrally located. Buffet breakfast.

DK Choice

Grand Hotel Europe ⓇⓇⓇ
Historic Map D4
Mikhaylovskaya ulitsa 1/7
Tel *(812) 329 6000*
Ⓦ grandhoteleurope.com
In a superb location beside
Nevskiy prospekt, the Europe
is close to all the main sights.
It boasts a wonderful decor,
especially the Art Nouveau
Caviar Bar. Suites are furnished
with antiques.

Price Guide

Prices are based on one night's stay in
high season for a standard double room,
inclusive of service charges and taxes.

Ⓡ	under 3,000 rouble
ⓇⓇ	3,000 to 6,500 rouble
ⓇⓇⓇ	over 6,500 rouble

**Kempinski Hotel
Moika 22** ⓇⓇⓇ
Luxury Map C3
Naberezhnaya Reki Moyki 22
Tel *(812) 335 9111*
Ⓦ kempinski.com
Great views of the Hermitage
from some rooms. The restaurant
offers international cuisine.
Indulge in the Turkish bath.

DK Choice

B&B Randhouse Ⓡ
Guesthouse Map C4
Pereulok Grivtsova 11, apt 83
Tel *(812) 310 7005*
Ⓦ randhouse.ru
Named after Ayn Rand, this
loft-based mini-hotel has open
fireplaces, bare-brick walls and
king-size duvets. Some rooms
have private bathrooms, others
share facilities. Great location.

Hotel Columb ⓇⓇ
Guesthouse Map C4
Kazanskaya ulitsa 41
Tel *(812) 315 7093*
Ⓦ columbhotel.com
Quiet, comfortable hotel near the
metro. Free parking and Wi-Fi.

Hotel St Petersburg ⓇⓇ
Business/chain
Lermontovskiy prospekt 43/1
Tel *(812) 740 2640*
Ⓦ azimuthotels.com
Over 1,000 budget rooms
with stunning views of
Fontanka river.

Sophisticated bedroom at the Grand Hotel
Europe, St Petersburg

Where to Eat and Drink

Moscow

Jagannath ®
Vegetarian
Ulitsa Kuznetskiy Most 11
Tel *(495) 628 3580*
Stylish café serving tasty Indian, Mexican, Thai, Chinese and European vegetarian dishes. No alcohol is served but the ginger beer is divine.

Montalto ®
Pizzeria
Ulitsa Sadovaya-Kudrinskaya 20
Tel *(495) 234 3487*
Thick-crust pizzas cooked in a wood-fired oven. Toppings come with an original twist – try the pear, goat's cheese, fennel and pistachio or spicy sausage.

Champagne Café ®®
European **Map** F1
Bolshaya Nikitskaya ulitsa 12
Tel *(495) 629 5913*
On tables laid out in Venetian-style halls, this eatery serves dishes such as *foie gras* with berry sauce and beef stroganoff.

Central House of Writers ®®®
Russian **Map** F1
Ulitsa Bolshaya Nikitskaya 53
Tel *(495) 691 1515*
Lovely carved-oak wood decor, fireplaces, live music and tasty traditional dishes. Uniquely atmospheric, especially for devotees of Russian literature.

Cutty Sark ®®®
Seafood **Map** F1
Novinskiy bulvar 12
Tel *(495) 691 3350*
Designed to resemble the British clipper ship, Cutty Sark serves fresh seafood from all over the world, and has separate oyster and sushi bars.

DK Choice

Suliko ®®
Georgian **Map** D5
Ulitsa Bolshaya Polyanka 42/1
Tel *(499) 238 2888*
With its mini-fountains, figurines and fake plants, and evening entertainment provided by a choir, Suliko is a fun place to enjoy high-quality Georgian cuisine. There are no Georgian wines on the menu, but you can try Georgian *chacha* (grape vodka).

Oblomov ®®®
French/Russian **Map** E4
1-y Monetchikovskiy pereulok 5
Tel *(495) 953 6828*
While the café on the first floor serves home-roasted coffee, the Eastern Room on the third floor has *hookah* and live belly dancing.

St Petersburg

Demyanova Ukha ®
Russian/seafood **Map** C2
Kronverkskiy prospekt 53
Tel *(812) 232 8090*
"Demyanova's Fish Soup", the city's oldest specialist fish restaurant, serves traditional Russian dishes. Enjoy live music in the evenings.

DK Choice

Salkhino ®®
Georgian **Map** C1
Kronverkskiy prospekt 25
Tel *(812) 232 7891*
Generous, top-notch home cooking at this eatery run by two Georgian women. The *khachapuri* is the best in town. Gorge on aubergines stuffed with walnuts, bite into roast beef or try the delicious fish in white sauce.

Austeria ®®®
Russian **Map** C2
Peter and Paul Fortress
Tel *(812) 716 1373*
Impressive Dutch-style decor, and a menu of 17th-century Russian dishes. Choose from a wide range of flavoured vodkas.

Elegantly laid out tables at the Caviar Bar and Restaurant, St Petersburg

The stylish L'Europe Restaurant in St Petersburg

1913 ®®
Russian **Map** C4
Voznesenskiy prospekt 13
Tel *(812) 315 5148*
Named after the last year of Russian imperial greatness, 1913 serves delicious regional dishes.

Literary Café ®
Russian **Map** D4
Nevskiy prospekt 18
Tel *(812) 312 6057*
The former Wolff and Beranger Café serves rather delicious meat dishes in rich sauces.

Caviar Bar and Restaurant ®®®
Russian **Map** D3
Mikhaylovskaya ulitsa 1/7
Tel *(812) 329 6000*
Dine on elegantly served caviar and fish at this bar-restaurant, with a fountain in the tiny interior.

L'Europe ®®®
European/Russian **Map** D3
Mikhaylovskaya ulitsa 1/7
Tel *(812) 329 6000*
Lobster soup and steak tartare are served in an Art Nouveau hall with a stained-glass ceiling at this restaurant in Grand Hotel Europe.

Russkaya Ryumochnaya No.1 ®®
Russian **Map** B4
Konnogvardeiskiy bulvar 4
Tel *(812) 570 6420*
An olde-world-style dining room serving modern interpretations of classic Russian dishes.

CENTRAL
EASTERN
EUROPE

Central Eastern Europe at a Glance

At the geographical heart of mainland Europe, Hungary, Poland and the Czech Republic have witnessed a huge surge in visitor numbers since the end of Communism in the late 1980s and early 1990s. Major cities such as Budapest, Krakow and Prague have been painstakingly restored after the ravages of two world wars and offer a stunning variety of art, historic architecture and rich culture. The region is also abundant in natural attractions, with forest-cloaked mountains in the northern reaches of the Czech and Slovak republics, the farmstead-dotted flatlands of the eastern Hungarian plain, and the dramatic Tatra Mountains. Despite fast-growing tourism, the unique cultural identity of these once little-known countries remains well preserved.

České Švýcarsko *(see pp262–3)*, otherwise known as "Bohemian Switzerland", in the Czech Republic, is an area of extraordinary sandstone formations, with weathered pillars of rock towering above dense green forests. The landscape is best characterized by Pravčicka Brána – the largest natural rock bridge in Central Europe.

Koszali

Szczecin

P

Zielona Góra

V

Cheb Prague

Hradec Králové

Plzeň **CZECH REPUBL**
(see pp222–285)

Písek Jih

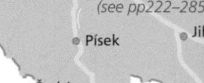

Český Krumlov

VIENNA
(see pp380-391)

Szombat

Nagy

Vienna *(see pp380–91)*, the capital of Austria, is a beautiful city with a rich architectural heritage, exquisite art collecions and an illustrious musical tradition. Its Naturhistorisches Museum *(see p385)* has one of the finest collections of its kind in Europe. The star attraction is its much-visited dinosaur hall.

◀ View of the Chain Bridge at sunset with Parliament in the background, Budapest, Hungary

Krakow *(see pp184–99)*, in southern Poland, has historic monuments spanning hundreds of years, and has been declared a UNESCO World Heritage Site. Its most impressive building, the Cloth Hall *(see p187)*, dominates the Main Market Square. Dating from the 16th century, it is a lively example of Renaissance architecture.

Gdańsk

Olsztyn

Bydgoszcz

Toruń

Białystok

Ostrołęka

POLAND
e pp170–221)

Warsaw

Biała Podlaska

Łódź

Radom

Kielce

pole

Zamość

towice

Tarnów

Kraków

Przemyśl

Ostrava

uc

Žilina

Prešov

SLOVAKIA
(see pp286–319)

Košice

ava

Miskolc

r

Budapest

Debrecen

HUNGARY
(see pp320–379)

Szolnok

Szekszárd

Szeged

Pécs

0 km   100

0 miles   100

Tatra Mountains *(see pp306–307)*, the spectacular mountain range on the border of Poland and Slovakia, are among the highest in Central Europe, with several peaks above 2,500 m (8,202 ft).

Pécs *(see pp362–3)*, Hungary's finest town, after Budapest, is famous for its architectural legacy, ranging from Roman tombstones and Ottoman mosques to medieval fortifications and Baroque churches. The highlight is St Peter's Cathedral *(see p362)*, an imposing Neo-Romanesque structure in the heart of the town.

POLAND

Located between Russia and Germany, Poland has always been a fiercely contested land. Released from the Eastern Bloc in 1989, the country is now developing rapidly, especially the cities of Warsaw, Krakow, Gdańsk and Wrocław. Monuments attest to a stormy history, but Poland is famed for its virtues, especially the generosity of its people and the excellence of its vodka.

Poland has an extremely varied landscape. Alpine scenery predominates in the Tatra Mountains to the south, while the north is dominated by lakes. The country's inhabitants, who number almost 39 million, all but constitute a single ethnic group, with minorities accounting for less than 4 per cent of the population. The largest minority groups are Germans, who are concentrated mainly around the city of Opole in Silesia, and Belarusians and Ukrainians, who inhabit the east of the country. The majority of Poles are Catholic, but large regions of the country, such as Cieszyn in Silesia, have a substantial Protestant population. In the east there are also many Orthodox Christians.

History

The origins of the Polish nation go back to the 10th century, when Slav tribes living in the area of Gniezno united under the Piast Dynasty, which ruled Poland until 1370. Mieszko I (c. 922–92) converted to Christianity in 966, thus bringing his kingdom into Christian Europe, and made Poznań the seat of Poland's first bishopric. After this dynasty died out, the great Lithuanian Grand Duke Jagiełło took the Polish throne and founded a new dynasty. The Treaty of Krewo in 1385 initiated a long process of consolidation between Poland and Lithuania, culminating in 1569 with the signing of the Union of Lublin and the formation of the Commonwealth of the Two Nations (Rzeczpospolita Obojga Narodów). In 1572, the Jagiełłonian Dynasty ended, after which the Polish authorities introduced elective kings, though only the nobility had the right to vote. The 17th century was dominated

The imposing Stalinist Neo-Baroque Palace of Culture and Science, Warsaw

◀ Church of Sts Peter and Paul in the Old Town district of Krakow

Solidarity demonstrators at a mass rally in 1987

by wars with Sweden, Russia and the Ottoman Empire, and although the country survived, it was considerably weakened, and its period of dominance was over.

In 1795, the republic was partitioned by Russia, Prussia and Austria, and was wiped off the map for more than 100 years. Attempts to wrest independence by insurrection were unsuccessful,

---

KEY DATES IN POLISH HISTORY

AD 966 Adoption of Christianity under Mieszko I

1025 Coronation of Bolesław the Brave, first king of Poland

1320 The unification of the Polish state

1385 Poland and Lithuania agree on dynastic union under the Treaty of Krewo

1569 The Union of Lublin creates the Polish-Lithuanian Commonwealth of the Two Nations

1596 The capital moves from Krakow to Warsaw

1655 Beginning of the "Deluge" (the Swedish occupation); it ends in 1660

1772–1918 Poland divided three times between Russia, Prussia and Austria. The final partition (1795) is made after a Polish uprising led by Tadeusz Kościuszko

1918 Poland regains independence

1939 Invasion by German, then Soviet forces

1940 Auschwitz-Birkenau concentration camp established; over one and a half million Poles and Jews are gassed here during the war

1945 Communist government takes control

1980 Solidarity formed, led by Lech Wałęsa

1989 First free postwar elections are held. Lech Wałęsa wins the presidency by a landslide

1999 Poland joins NATO

2004 Poland becomes a member of the EU

2010 President Lech Kaczyński and 95 others killed in air crash; Poland goes to polls

---

and Poland did not regain its sovereignty until 1918. The arduous process of rebuilding and uniting the nation was still incomplete when, at the outbreak of World War II, a six-year period of German and Soviet occupation began. The price that Poland paid was very high: millions of people were murdered, including virtually the entire Jewish population. The country suffered devastation and huge territorial losses, which were only partly compensated by the Allies' decision to move the border westwards.

After the war, the Soviet Union subjugated Poland, but the socialist economy proved ineffective. The formation of Solidarity (Solidarność), the first Independent Autonomous Trades Union, in 1980, led by Lech Wałęsa, accelerated the pace of change. This was completed when Poland regained its freedom after the June 1989 elections.

In 1999, Poland became a member of NATO, and in 2004 it joined the European Union (EU).

Language and Culture

Polish is a West Slavic language closely related to Slovak and Czech. Many of its words are borrowed from Latin, although German, Italian and English words are also common.

The legacy of more than 100 years of partition rule is still visible in Poland's cultural landscape. Russian, Prussian and Austrian administrations left their mark not only on architecture, but also on the customs and outlook of the people.

The Poles have a deep reverence for religious symbols and rituals, and the presence of the church can be seen everywhere, either in the form of Baroque shrines or in images of the Black Madonna.

Exploring Poland

Bordering the Baltic Sea, Poland is one of the largest countries of Central Europe. Warsaw, its capital, is in the centre of the country and is an ideal base for visiting other cities, such as Krakow, the ancient royal capital; Gdańsk, the Hanseatic city and Poznań, one of the oldest Polish cities. Declared a World Heritage Site in 1978, Krakow, with a host of historical monuments, is one of the most beautiful cities in Europe.

Zygmunt Chapel at Krakow
Cathedral, Krakow

Key

― Motorway

‐ ‐ Motorway under construction

― Major road

⎯ Railway

▪ ▪ International border

0 km   100

0 miles   100

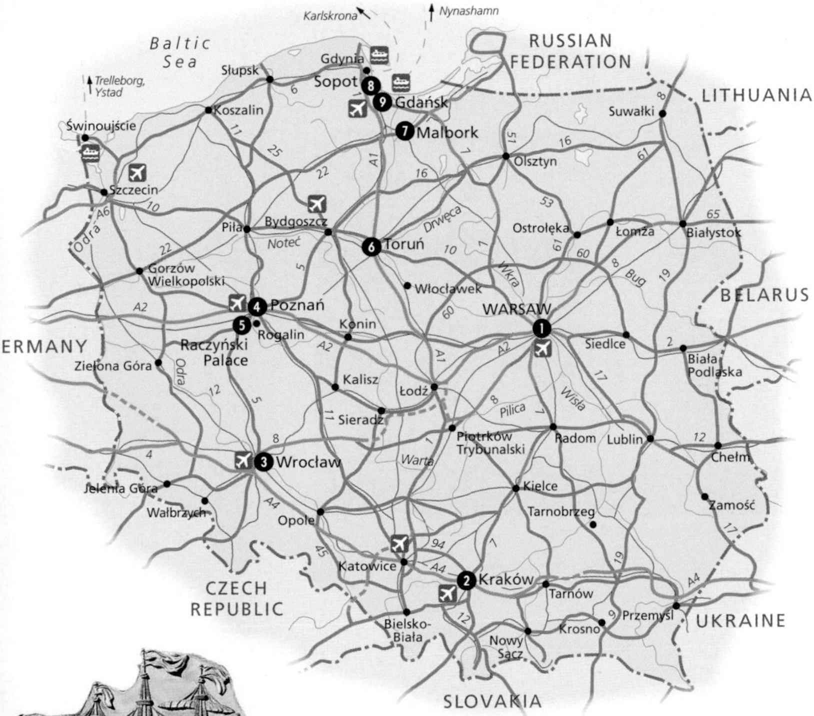

Karlskrona   ↑ Nynashamn

Baltic Sea

↑ Trelleborg, Ystad

RUSSIAN FEDERATION

LITHUANIA

Świnoujście

Gdynia

Słupsk

Sopot ⑧

⑨ Gdańsk

Koszalin

⑦ Malbork

Suwałki

Szczecin

Olsztyn

Piła

Bydgoszcz

Noteć

Ostrołęka

Łomża

Białystok

Gorzów Wielkopolski

⑥ Toruń

Włocławek

WARSAW ①

BELARUS

ERMANY

④ Poznań

⑤ Rogalin

Raczyński Palace

Konin

Siedlce

Biała Podlaska

Zielona Góra

Kalisz

Łódź

Łowicz

Sieradz

Piotrków Trybunalski

Radom

Lublin

Chełm

③ Wrocław

Jelenia Góra

Warta

Kielce

Tarnobrzeg

Zamość

Wałbrzych

Opole

Katowice

② Kraków

Tarnów

Przemyśl

UKRAINE

CZECH REPUBLIC

Bielsko-Biała

Nowy Sącz

Krosno

SLOVAKIA

Traditional house decoration, Warsaw

Sights at a Glance

① *Warsaw pp174–83*

② *Krakow pp184–99*

③ *Wrocław pp200–203*

④ *Poznań pp204–207*

⑤ *Raczyński Palace*

⑥ *Toruń pp208–209*

⑦ *Malbork*

⑧ *Sopot*

⑨ *Gdańsk pp210–15*

For keys to symbols *see back flap*

❶ Warsaw

Warsaw is believed to have been founded in the late 13th century, when Duke Bolesław of Mazovia built a castle here overlooking the Vistula river. It became the capital of Poland in 1596, making it one of Europe's youngest capital cities, with a population of nearly two million. Most places of interest are located in the historic centre, the geographical heart of the city, which has now been declared a UNESCO World Heritage Site. The Old Town (Stare Miasto), partially surrounded by medieval walls, is the oldest district in Warsaw. Next to it is the more recent New Town (Nowe Miasto), which became a separate urban entity in 1408. Almost completely destroyed during World War II, the reconstruction of these two districts was an undertaking on a scale unprecedented in the whole of Europe. Today, they are the most popular tourist destinations in Warsaw.

The elaborate ballroom of the Royal Castle

Sights at a Glance

① Zygmunt's Column
② Royal Castle
③ Cathedral of St John
④ Old Town Market Square
⑤ Monument to the Warsaw Uprising
⑥ St Hyacinth Church
⑦ Ulica Freta
⑧ *Krakowskie Przedmieście pp180–81*
⑨ Pac Palace
⑩ Monument to the Heroes of the Ghetto
⑪ Umschlagplatz Monument
⑫ Pawiak Prison
⑬ Palace of Culture and Science
⑭ National Museum

Key

■ Street-by-Street area: *see pp176–7*
■ Street-by-Street area: *see pp180–81*
□ Major sight / Place of interest
━ Pedestrian street

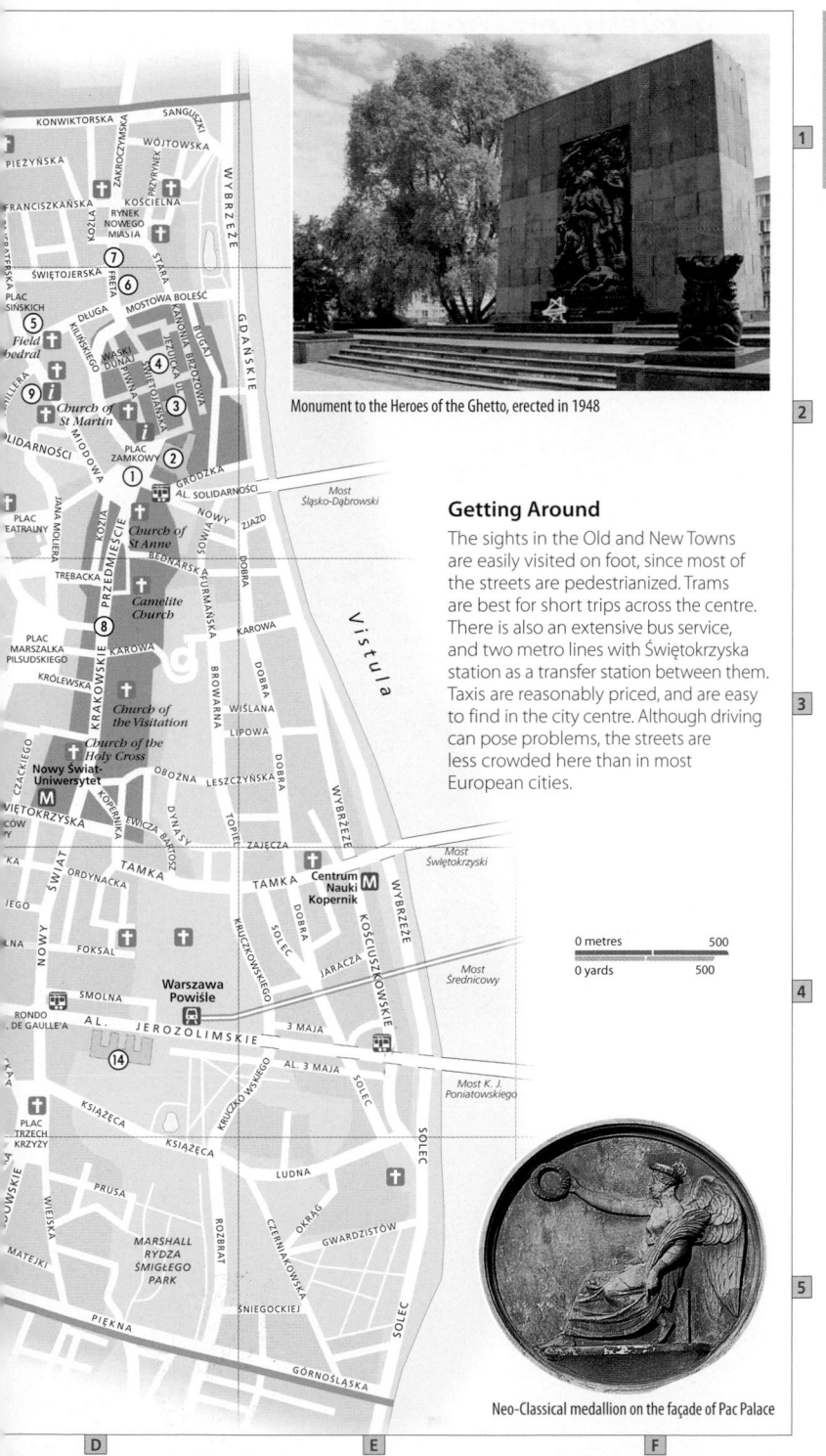

Monument to the Heroes of the Ghetto, erected in 1948

Most Śląsko-Dąbrowski

Vistula

Getting Around

The sights in the Old and New Towns are easily visited on foot, since most of the streets are pedestrianized. Trams are best for short trips across the centre. There is also an extensive bus service, and two metro lines with Świętokrzyska station as a transfer station between them. Taxis are reasonably priced, and are easy to find in the city centre. Although driving can pose problems, the streets are less crowded here than in most European cities.

| 0 metres | 500 |
| 0 yards | 500 |

Most Świętokrzyski

Most Średnicowy

Most K. J. Poniatowskiego

Neo-Classical medallion on the façade of Pac Palace

Street-by-Street: The Old Town

The oldest district in Warsaw, the Old Town is today one of the most attractive places in the city. Partially surrounded by medieval walls, it was almost completely destroyed during World War II but reconstructed on a scale unprecedented in Europe. The pride of the historic Old Town is the Old Town Square (Rynek Starego Miasta), surrounded by townhouses, also rebuilt after World War II. Of great interest here are the Cathedral of St John and the Royal Castle. On the square and in nearby streets, especially Piwna, there are many restaurants and bars that are reputed to be the best in Warsaw.

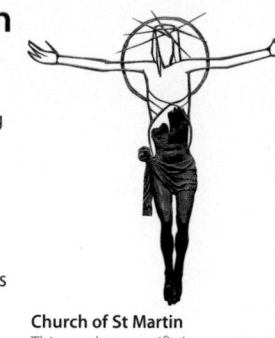

Church of St Martin
This modern crucifix incorporates a fragment of a figure of Christ that was burnt during the 1944 Warsaw Uprising.

③ ★ **Cathedral of St John**
After suffering damage during World War II, the cathedral was rebuilt in the Gothic style.

Jesuit Church, a Baroque-Mannerist sanctuary of Our Lady of Mercy, the patron saint of Warsaw, was rebuilt after World War II.

① **Zygmunt's Column**
is the oldest secular monument in Warsaw.

② ★ **Royal Castle**
This former royal residence, rebuilt in the 1970s, is today the symbol of Polish independence.

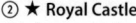

The Palace Under the Tin Roof
Built in 1720, this palace was the first in Warsaw to have a tin, rather than tiled, roof.

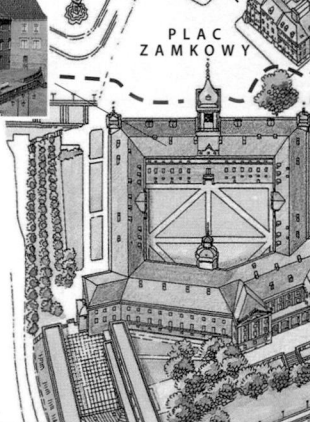

For hotels and restaurants see p220 and p221

Barbican and City Walls
This impressive brick fortification, constructed between the 14th and 16th centuries, once protected the northern approach to the city.

The Museum of Warsaw
(see p178) occupies the north side of Old Town Market Square.

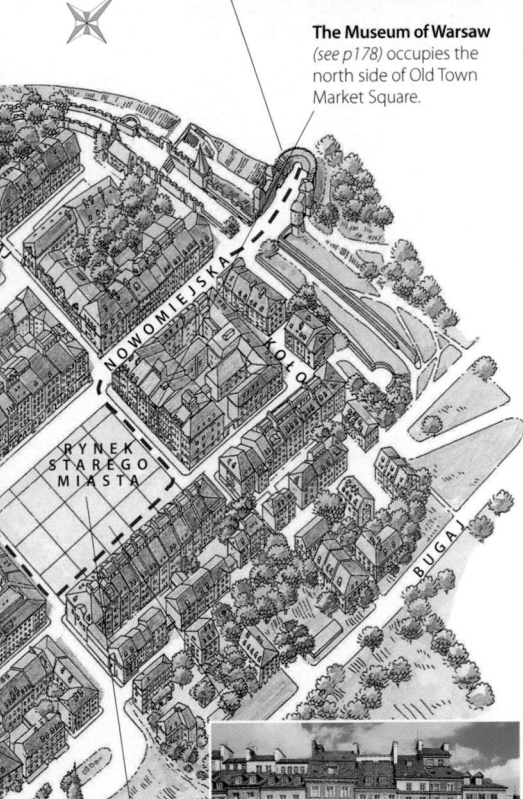

RYNEK STAREGO MIASTA

④ ★ **Old Town Market Square**
One of the most beautiful sights of Warsaw, this square pulsates with life until late in the evening.

Statue of the Mermaid

0 metres	100
0 yards	100

Key

— Suggested route

Statue of Zygmunt III Waza at the top of Zygmunt's Column

① Zygmunt's Column

Kolumna Króla Zygmunta

Plac Zamkowy. **Map** D2.
🚌 116, 175, 178, 180, 190, 222, 503, N44 (stop-on-request night bus).
🚊 4, 23, 26.

Placed in the centre of Plac Zamkowy, King Zygmunt's Column is the oldest secular statue in Warsaw. It was erected in 1644 by Zygmunt III Waza's son, Władysław IV. This monument, which stands 22 m (72 ft) high, consists of a striking Corinthian granite column supported on a tall plinth and topped by a bronze statue of the ruler, who is depicted with a cross in his left hand and a sword in his right. The figure was created by Clemente Molli, and the monument was designed by Augustyn Locci the Elder and Constantino Tencalla, two Italian architects working for the king. The monument glorifies the ruler in a manner which had until then been reserved for saints and other religious figures. Despite repeated damage and repairs, the statue retains its original appearance. However, the column on which it stands has already been replaced twice. An older, fractured shaft can be seen on the terrace near the south façade of the Palace Under the Tin Roof.

A painting in the Senators' Room, Royal Castle

② Royal Castle

Zamek Królewski

Plac Zamkowy 4. **Map** D2. **Tel** (022) 355 5170. 🚌 116, 175, 178, 180, 190, 222, 503, N44. 🚋 4, 23, 26. **Open** 10am–4pm Tue–Sat, 11am–4pm Sun; May–Sep: till 6pm daily. **Closed** public hols. 🎟 free on Sun. Ⓦ **zamek-krolewski.pl**

Warsaw's Royal Castle stands on the site of an original castle built here by the Mazovian dukes in the 14th century. It was transformed between 1598 and 1619 by King Zygmunt III Waza, who asked Italian architects to restyle the castle into a polygon. The king chose this castle as his royal residence in 1596, after the *Sejm* (Parliament) had moved here from Krakow in 1569. In the 18th century, King Augustus III remodelled the east wing in Baroque style and King Stanisław August Poniatowski added a library.

In 1939, the castle was burnt, and then blown up by the Nazis in 1944. Funded by public donations, it was rebuilt between 1971 and 1988.

The castle's fascinating interiors are the result of its dual role: being a royal residence as well as the seat of Parliament. It houses royal apartments as well as the Chamber of Deputies and the Senate. Some of the woodwork and stucco is original, as are many of the furnishings and much of the art. The coats of arms of all the administrative

regions of the country are depicted on the walls. Among the paintings are 18th-century works by Bellotto and Bacciarelli. The Lanckoroński Gallery collection includes two paintings by Rembrandt – *Portrait of a Young Woman* and *Scholar at his Desk*.

③ Cathedral of St John

Katedra św Jana

Świętojańska 8. **Map** D2. **Tel** (022) 831 0289. 🚌 116, 175, 178, 180, 222, 503. 🚋 4, 23, 26. **Open** 10am–noon, 4–6pm daily.

Completed in the early 15th century, the Cathedral of St John was originally a parish church. Gaining collegiate status in 1406, it was not until 1798 that it became a cathedral. The coronation of Poland's last king, Stanisław August Poniatowski, in 1764, and the swearing of an oath by the deputies of the *Sejm* to uphold the 1791 Constitution took place here.

After World War II, various elaborate 19th-century additions were removed from the façade, and the cathedral was restored to its Mazovian Gothic style. The interior features religious art, richly carved wooden stalls and ornate tombs, including those of Gabriel Narutowicz (1865–1922), Poland's first president, assassinated two days after taking office, and Nobel Prize-winning novelist Henryk Sienkiewicz (1846–1916). In a chapel founded by the Baryczka family hangs a

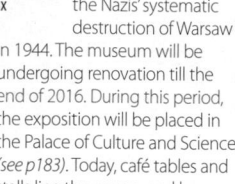

Baryczkowski Crucifix

16th-century crucifix, which is credited with several miracles.

④ Old Town Market Square

Rynek Starego Miasta

Map D2. 🚌 116, 175, 180, 503. 🚋 4, 23, 26. Museum of Warsaw: **Tel** (022) 531 3802. **Open** 11am–6pm Tue, Thu, 10am–3:30pm Wed, Fri, 10:30am–4:30pm Sat–Sun. **Closed** Mon, public hols & one weekend a month. 🎟 free on Sun. 🎦 Note: A 20-min English-language film about Warsaw is screened at noon daily.

Painstakingly restored after World War II, the Old Town Market Square was the centre of Warsaw public life until the 19th century, when the focus of the growing, modern city moved. The tall, ornate, and colourful houses, which lend the square its unique character, were built by wealthy merchants in the 17th century.

The houses on one side form the **Museum of Warsaw** (Muzeum Warszawy). This displays the city's history through paintings, photographs, sculpture and archaeological finds. There is also a film show, with footage of the Nazis' systematic destruction of Warsaw in 1944. The museum will be undergoing renovation till the end of 2016. During this period, the exposition will be placed in the Palace of Culture and Science *(see p183)*. Today, café tables and stalls line the square, and horse-drawn carriages offer tours of the Old Town.

The Historical Museum of Warsaw in the Old Town Square

The sombre Monument to the Warsaw Uprising

⑤ Monument to the Warsaw Uprising

Pomnik Powstania Warszawskiego

pl. Krasińskich. **Map** D2. 116, 178, 180, 222, 503, N44. 18, 23, 26, 35, 36.

This monument, unveiled in 1989, commemorates the heroes of the 1944 Warsaw Uprising. It consists of sculptures by Wincenty Kućma placed in an architectural setting by Jacek Budyń. The sculptures show soldiers – one group defending the barricades, the other going down into the sewers, which were used by the insurgents to move around the city during the uprising. The entrance to one such sewer can be seen nearby.

It was in front of this monument, during the 50th anniversary celebrations of the event, that the then president of Germany, Roman Herzog, apologized to the Polish nation for the Third Reich's unleashing of World War II and the bloody suppression of the Warsaw Uprising.

⑥ St Hyacinth Church

Kościół św Jacka

ul. Freta 10. **Map** D2. **Tel** (022) 635 4700. 116, 178, 180, 222, 503, N44. **Open** 7am–5pm daily. **Closed** mass.

At the beginning of the 17th century, while the Jesuits were building a Baroque church in the Old Town, the Dominicans started work on a Gothic chancel for St Hyacinth Church. They returned to the Gothic style partly because of the conservatism of Mazovian buildings and partly in an attempt to endow the church with the appearance of age. This was done to create an illusion of the age-old traditions of the order – which had in fact only been set up in Warsaw in 1603. When work was interrupted by a plague that raged in Warsaw in 1625, the few remaining monks listened to confessions and gave communion through openings drilled in the doors. The work was completed in 1639. The largest monastery in Warsaw was constructed next to it. Features inside the church, which was rebuilt after World War II, include vaulting above the aisles, a Gothic chancel decorated with stuccowork of the Lublin type and 17th-century tombstones. The Baroque tomb of Adam and Małgorzata Kotowski, by the Dutch architect Tylman van Gameren, is also noteworthy. The domed chapel in which it stands is decorated with portraits of the donors, who became prosperous and were ennobled despite their humble origins.

Façade of the St Hyacinth Church seen from ulica Freta

⑦ Ulica Freta

Map D1 & D2. 116, 178, 180, 222, 503, N44. Maria Skłodowska-Curie Museum: **Tel** (022) 831 8092. **Open** 8:30am–4pm Tue, 9:30am–4pm Wed–Fri, 10am–4pm Sat, 10am–3pm Sun. W **muzeum-msc.pl**

The main road in the New Town, ulica Freta developed along a section of the old route leading from Old Warsaw to Zakroczym, which is to the northeast of the city. At the end of the 1300s, buildings began to appear along it, and in the 15th century it came within the precincts of New Warsaw (Nowa Warszawa).

Several antique shops and cafés line this street. The house at No. 16, where Marie Curie was born, is now the **Maria Skłodowska-Curie Museum** (Maria Skłodowska-Curie Muzeum) dedicated to her. Films about her life and the history of chemistry are presented to groups on request.

Maria Skłodowska-Curie (1867–1934)

Maria Skłodowska was 24 years old when she left Warsaw to study in Paris. Within a decade she had become famous as the co-discoverer of radioactivity. Together with her husband, Pierre Curie, she discovered the elements radium and polonium. She was awarded the Nobel Prize twice: the first time in 1903, when she won the prize for physics jointly with her husband – becoming the first woman Nobel laureate – and the second in 1911 for chemistry.

Marie Curie, the famous physicist

⑧ Street-by-Street: Krakowskie Przedmieście

Rebuilt after World War II, Krakowskie Przedmieście is one of the most beautiful streets in Warsaw. Lined with trees, green squares and statues of distinguished Poles, the street is dominated by several palaces such as the Presidential Palace (Pałac Namiestnikowski). Some of these now house government departments. On weekdays, this is one of the liveliest streets, as two great institutions of higher education – the University of Warsaw and the Academy of Fine Arts – are situated here. Numerous restaurants, bars and cafés line the street.

Carmelite Church
This Baroque church was built for the order of the Discalced Carmelites between 1661 and 1682.

Presidential Palace
was rebuilt in the Neo-Classical style for the tsar's governor. It is now the president's residence.

★ Church of St Anne
This Gothic church was built for the Bernardine Order in the second half of the 15th century. The Neo-Classical façade was a later addition.

The statue of Adam Mickiewicz, the Romantic poet, was unveiled in 1898 on the centenary of his birth.

Hotel Bristol
This hotel, which overlooks the Presidential Palace, is the most luxurious, as well as the most expensive hotel in Warsaw.

| 0 metres | 100 |
| 0 yards | 100 |

For hotels and restaurants see p220 and p221

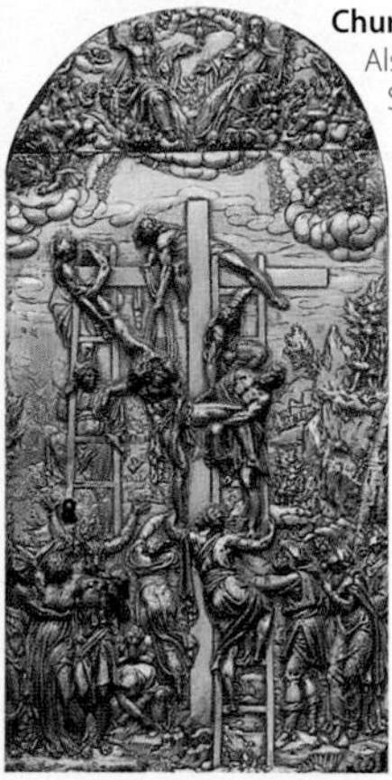

Church of the Visitation
Also known as the Church of St Joseph, this is one of the few churches in Warsaw that was not destroyed during World War II. Its interior features remain intact.

VISITORS' CHECKLIST

Practical Information
Map D2 & 3.
Church of St Anne: **Tel** (022) 826 8991. **Open** 6:30am–7:30pm Mon–Sat, 8am–10:30pm Sun. **Closed** mass. Church of the Holy Cross: **Tel** (022) 556 8820. **Open** 9am–5pm, daily. University of Warsaw: **Tel** (022) 552 0000.

Transport
E-2, 111, 116, 125, 160, 175, 180, 190, 222, 503.
4, 23, 26.

Statue of Nicolaus Copernicus, the Polish astro nomer, was removed by the Germans for scrap during World War II but was later returned to its original site.

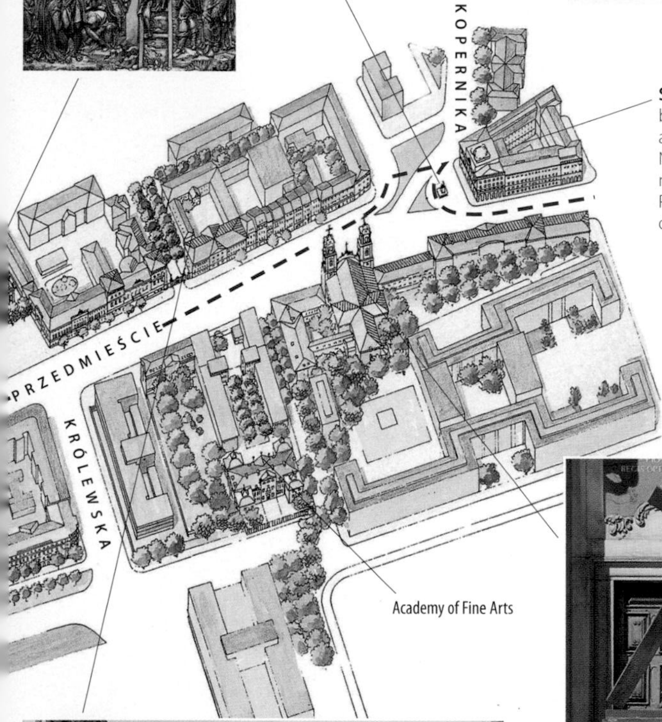
KOPERNIKA
PRZEDMIEŚCIE
KRÓLEWSKA

Staszic Palace, built between 1820 and 1823 in the late Neo-Classical style, now houses the Polish Academy of Sciences.

Academy of Fine Arts

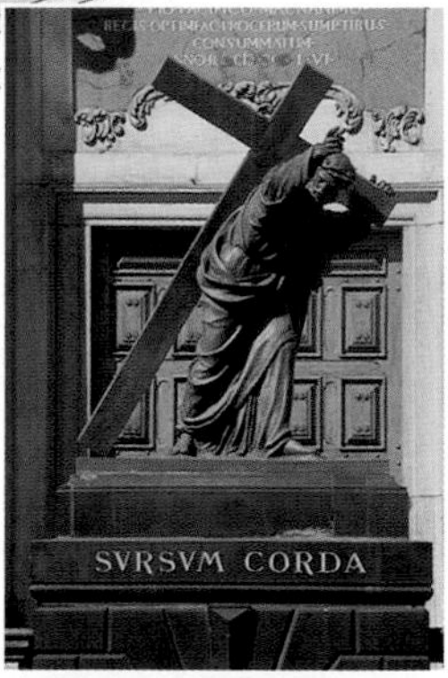
SVRSVM CORDA

★ **Church of the Holy Cross**
This church has urns containing the hearts of composer Frédéric Chopin and novelist Władysław Reymont, awarded the Nobel Prize in 1924.

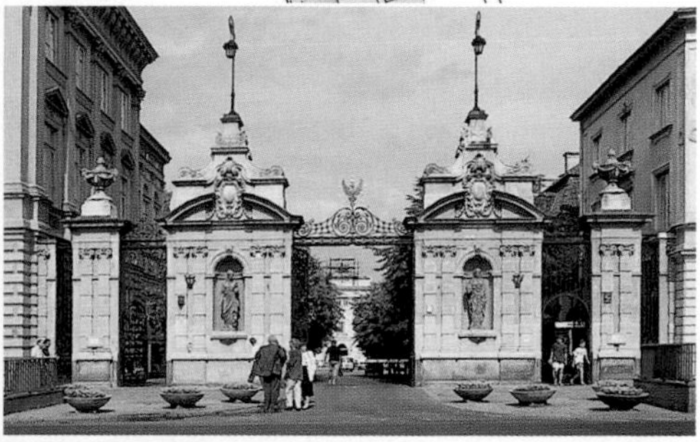

★ **University of Warsaw**
The university is the largest educational institution in Poland but only some of the faculties are situated at its main site on Krakowskie Przedmieście.

Key
— Suggested route

Nineteenth-century Gothic interior of the Pac Palace

⑨ Pac Palace

Pałac Paca

ul. Miodowa 15. **Map** D2.
Tel (022) 634 9600. 🚌 116, 175, 180.
Open occasionally.

This Baroque palace, formerly the residence of the Radziwiłł family, was designed and built between 1681 and 1697 by Dutch-born architect Tylman van Gameren. One of the palace's 19th-century owners, Ludwik Pac, commissioned the architect Henryk Marconi to redesign it; work was completed in 1828. The interiors were decorated in the Gothic, Renaissance, Greek and Moorish styles, and the façade remodelled in the Palladian manner. The palace gate was modelled on a triumphal arch and adorned with Classical bas-relief sculptures – the work

Detail from the Monument to the Heroes of the Ghetto

of Ludwik Kaufman, a pupil of the celebrated Italian Neo-Classical sculptor Antonio Canova. Today, the palace houses the Ministry of Health.

⑩ Monument to the Heroes of the Ghetto

Pomnik Bohaterów Getta

ul. Zamenhofa. **Map** C1. 🚌 111, 180, 227.Museum of the History of Polish Jews: ul. Mordechaja Anielewicza 6.
Closed Tue & public hols.

The city of Warsaw still lay in ruins when the Monument to the Heroes of the Ghetto was erected in 1948. Created by the sculptor Natan Rapaport and the architect Marek Suzin, it symbolizes the heroic defiance of the Ghetto Uprising of 1943, which was planned not as a bid for liberty but as an honourable way to die. The daring revolt lasted for one month.

Reliefs on the monument depict men, women and children struggling to flee the burning ghetto, together with a procession of Jews being driven to death camps under the threat of Nazi bayonets.

On 7 December 1970, Willy Brandt, the then chancellor of West Germany, knelt in front of this monument, to pay homage to the murdered victims. Today, people come here from all over the world to remember the heroes. The **Museum of the History of Polish Jews** (Muzeum Historii Żydów Polskich) is located near the monument, within the former ghetto area of the city.

Between the Monument to the Heroes of the Ghetto and the Umschlagplatz Monument runs the **Path of Remembrance**, opened in 1988. It is marked by a series of 16 granite blocks bearing inscriptions in Polish, Hebrew and Yiddish. The nearby Bunker Monument, on the site where the Uprising commanders blew themselves up, has been specially marked. Each block is dedicated to the 450,000 Jews murdered in the Warsaw Ghetto between 1940 and 1943, to the heroes of the Ghetto Uprising of 1943 and to certain key individuals from that time.

⑪ Umschlagplatz Monument

Pomnik na Umschlagplatz

ul. Stawki. **Map** C1. 🚌 157, 510.
🚃 17, 33, 35.

Unveiled in 1988, the Umschlagplatz Monument marks the site of a former railway siding on ulica Dzika. It was from here that some 300,000 Jews from the Warsaw Ghetto and elsewhere were loaded onto cattle trucks and dispatched to extermination camps. Among them was Janusz Korczak, Polish-Jewish author and pediatrician, and his group of Jewish orphans. Living conditions in the ghetto were indescribably inhumane, and by 1942 over 100,000 of the inhabitants had died. The monument, on which the architect Hanna Szmalenberg and the sculptor Władysław Klamerus collaborated, is made of blocks of black-and-white marble bearing the names of hundreds of Warsaw's Jews.

One of the granite blocks marking the Path of Remembrance

⑫ Pawiak Prison
Więzienie Pawiak

ul. Dzielna 24/26. **Map** C2.
Tel (022) 831 9289. 🚌 107, 111, 180.
🚊 17, 23, 33. **Open** 9:30am–5pm
Wed–Fri, 10am–4pm Sat & Sun.
Closed Mon, Tue. 📷 ♿ 📷

Built between 1829 and 1835
by Polish architect Henryk
Marconi, this prison was initially
used as a transfer camp during
the 1863 Uprising for political
prisoners to be deported to
Siberia. Pawiak got its name
from ulica Pawia, the street
where it was located. The prison
became notorious during the
Nazi occupation, when it was
used to imprison Jews and
Poles arrested by the Germans.
Many of those who were at the
prison were either executed,
tortured or sent to concentration camps.
   Blown up by the Germans in
1944, the prison was partially
reconstructed to house this
poignant museum. The opening
of the museum in 1965 was
a hugely emotional event,
attracting crowds of former
inmates and their families.

Tree with obituary notices in front of
Pawiak Prison

⑬ Palace of Culture and Science
Pałac Kultury i Nauki

pl. Defilad 1. **Map** C4. **Tel** (022) 656
7600. 🚌 several routes. 🚊 4, 7, 8, 9,
18, 22, 24, 25, 35. Ⓜ Centrum.
Viewing Terrace: **Open** 9am–6pm
daily. 📷 🌐 pkin.pl

This monolithic building – a
gift for the people of Warsaw
from the nations of the USSR –

The 30-storey high Palace of Culture
and Science

was built between 1952 and
1955 to the designs of Russian
architect, Lev Rudniev. The
palace resembles Moscow's
Socialist Realist tower blocks,
and although it has only 30
storeys, with its spire it is 231 m
(757 ft) high. Its volume is over
800,000 cubic m (28 million
cubic ft) and it contains 40
million bricks. It incorporates
various architectural and decorative elements requisitioned
from Poland's historic
stately homes.
   The tower now provides
office space and the Congress
Hall is used for concerts and
festivals. The palace remains a
cultural centre in other ways,
with the Theatre of Dramatic
Art, a cinema, puppet theatre,
technology museum and a
sports complex. It also offers
the best view of Warsaw
from its **Viewing Terrace**.
   Not far away is the **Warsaw
Rising Museum**. The museum
pays tribute to the struggle
that took place in 1944 when
the Polish Home Army tried
to liberate the city from
the Nazis.

🏛 Warsaw Rising Museum
ul. Grzybowska 79. **Open** 8am–6pm
Mon, Wed, Fri, 10am–8pm Thu,
10am–6pm Sat & Sun. 📷

⑭ National Museum
Muzeum Narodowe

al. Jerozolimskie 3. **Map** D4.
Tel (022) 629 3093. 🚌 111, 117,
158, 517, 521. 🚊 7, 8, 9, 22, 24, 25.
Open 10am– 6pm Tue–Sun,
till 9pm Thu. **Closed** Mon, pub hols.
📷 free Tue. Military Museum:
Tel (022) 629 5271. **Open** 10am–5pm
Wed, 10am–4pm Thu–Sun. 📷 📷
♿ 📷 📷 🌐 mnw.art.pl

Originally established in 1862
as the Fine Arts Museum, the
National Museum was created
in 1916. Despite wartime losses,
today it has a large collection of
works of art covering all periods
from antiquity to modern times.
The collections are arranged
over three floors. On the ground
floor are the Galleries of Ancient
Art, with their displays of
Egyptian, Greek and Roman
artifacts, the Faras Collection
of early Christian art and the
Gallery of Medieval Art. The
first floor houses a collection of
Polish art which includes two
paintings – Jan Matejko's *Battle
of Grünwald* (1878) and the
Polish Hamlet, a portrait of
the aristocrat and politician
Aleksander Wielopolski, painted
by Jacek Malczewski in 1903
in the style of the Polish
Symbolist school. The foreign
art collection is displayed on
the first and second floors and
includes the *Virgin and Child*
(c. 1465) by Sandro Botticelli
and *The Raising of Lazarus* (1643)
by Carel Fabritius, a pupil of
Rembrandt. The **Military
Museum**, in the building's east
wing, illustrates the history of
Polish firearms and armour.

Fresco of St Anne from the 10th century,
National Museum

❷ Krakow

For nearly six centuries, Krakow was the capital of Poland and the country's largest city. Polish rulers resided at Wawel Royal Castle until the court and parliament moved to Warsaw in 1596. Even then, Krakow continued to be regarded as the nation's spiritual heart and rulers were still crowned and buried in the cathedral on Wawel Hill. Most places of interest are located in its fairly compact historic centre. A good place to start is Wawel Hill with its imposing castle and Gothic cathedral. North of Wawel Hill lies the Old Town, with an attractive market square, the Church of St Mary and the picturesque Cloth Hall. To the south of the hill is the Kazimierz district, with its preserved Jewish quarter. Today, the city has 750,000 inhabitants, and in recent years many buildings and monuments have been restored to their former glory.

Sights at a Glance
① Cloth Hall
② City Hall Tower
③ Ulica Floriańska
④ *Church of St Mary pp188–9*
⑤ Czartoryski Museum
⑥ Church of Sts Peter and Paul
⑦ Szołaysky House
⑧ Fortifications on the Wawel
⑨ Cathedral Museum
⑩ "Lost Wawel" Exhibition
⑪ *Krakow Cathedral pp192–3*
⑫ Wawel Royal Castle
⑬ *Kazimierz District pp194–5*
⑭ *Auschwitz pp196–9*

Spectacular high altar at Krakow Cathedral

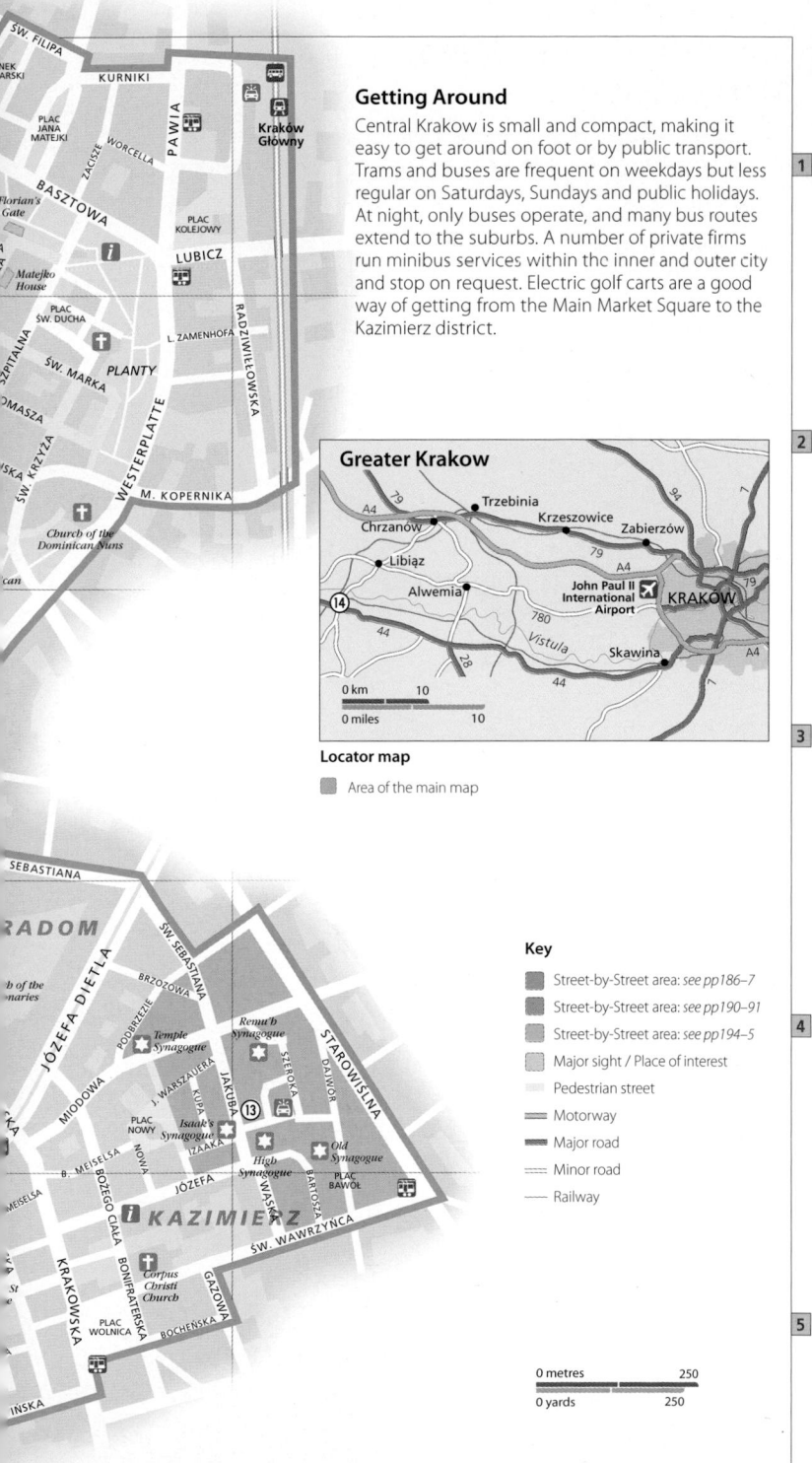

Getting Around

Central Krakow is small and compact, making it easy to get around on foot or by public transport. Trams and buses are frequent on weekdays but less regular on Saturdays, Sundays and public holidays. At night, only buses operate, and many bus routes extend to the suburbs. A number of private firms run minibus services within the inner and outer city and stop on request. Electric golf carts are a good way of getting from the Main Market Square to the Kazimierz district.

Greater Krakow

Locator map

Area of the main map

Key

Street-by-Street area: *see pp186–7*

Street-by-Street area: *see pp190–91*

Street-by-Street area: *see pp194–5*

Major sight / Place of interest

Pedestrian street

Motorway

Major road

Minor road

Railway

0 metres — 250

0 yards — 250

0 km — 10

0 miles — 10

Street-by-Street: Main Market Square

The huge Main Market Square (Rynek Główny) was laid out when Krakow received its new municipal charter in 1257. One of the largest squares in Europe, it brims with life all year round. In summer, pedestrians negotiate the maze of café tables that fill the lively square, along with a host of shops, antique dealers, restaurants, bars and clubs. There are also numerous interesting museums, galleries and historic sights, including some splendid Renaissance and Baroque houses and mansions.

④ ★ **Church of St Mary**
The façade of this church, with its two impressive towers, is one of the finest Gothic structures in Poland.

③ **Ulica Floriańska** is one of the busiest streets in Krakow.

St Adalbert's Church
This is a small but splendid Romanesque church. It predates the planning of the vast Main Market Square and is all but lost in it now.

② **City Hall Tower**
The Gothic tower is the only remaining part of the former City Hall. A café has been opened in the basement.

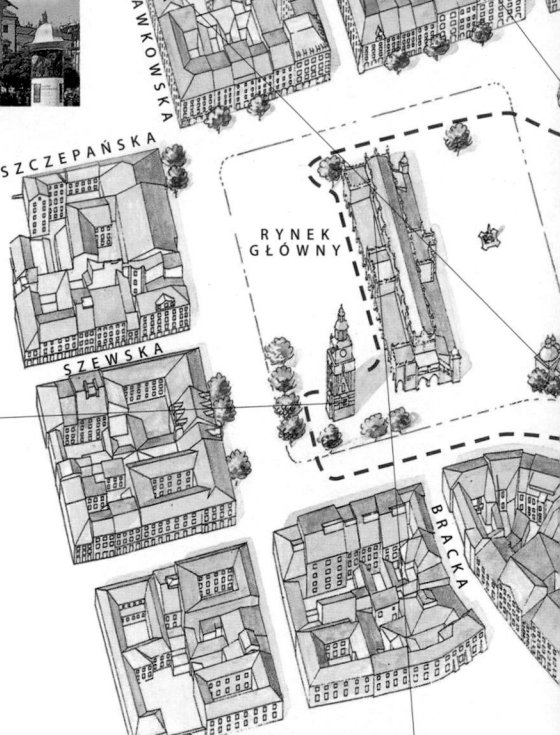

SŁAWKOWSKA

FLORIAŃSKA

SZCZEPAŃSKA

RYNEK GŁÓWNY

SZEWSKA

BRACKA

① ★ **Cloth Hall**
This beautiful Renaissance building replaced an earlier Gothic market hall. The upper floor houses a branch of the National Museum.

For hotels and restaurants see p220 and p221

Church of St Barbara
Dating from the late 14th century, this church contains many treasures, including a 15th-century Gothic pietà. It was the principal Polish church in Krakow during Austrian rule.

Merchant's House, also known as "At a Sign of the Lizard", gets its name from the relief of lizards carved in stone above the main portal. It is now a pub and cultural centre.

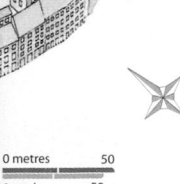

0 metres 50
0 yards 50

Key

— Suggested route

Frenzy, by Władysław Podkowiński, Cloth Hall

① Cloth Hall
Sukiennice

Rynek Główny 1/3. **Map** C2.
152, 502. 3, 4, 8, 10, 14, 18, 20. Museum of 19th Century Art:
Tel (012) 433 5400. **Open** 10am–8pm Tue–Sun. muzeum.krakow.pl

Set in the centre of the Main Market Square, the Cloth Hall replaced an earlier Gothic trade hall dating from the late 14th century. Destroyed in a fire then rebuilt by Giovanni Maria Padovano, it owes part of its present appearance to Tomasz Pryliński's Romantic-style restoration between 1875 and 1879. Today, the ground floor is filled with a selection of souvenir shops and cafés. The **Musuem of 19th Century Art**, a branch of the National Museum, is located on the upper floor. It has a collection of 19th-century paintings by renowned artists, including Jan Matejko and Henryk Siemiradzki.

② City Hall Tower
Wieża Ratuszowa

Rynek Główny 1. **Map** C2. 152, 502. 2, 4, 8, 10, 13, 14, 18, 20. Historical Museum: **Tel** (012) 426 4334. **Open** Apr–Oct: 10:30am–6pm daily. **Closed** 1, 3 May & 15 Aug.

The Gothic tower, crowned by a Baroque cupola, which dominates the Main Market Square is the only remaining vestige of the City Hall, built in the 14th century and pulled down in the 19th century. Today, it houses a branch of the **Historical Museum**.

Aspects of the city's history can be seen in the Museum of the History of the Market, in the crypt of the neighbouring St Adalbert's Church.

③ Ulica Floriańska

Map D2. 152, 352, 502. 2, 4, 8, 10, 14, 18, 20. Matejko House: **Tel** (012) 422 5926. **Open** 10am–6pm Tue–Sat, 10am–4pm Sun. **Closed** Mon. free on Sun. Jama Michalika: **Open** 9am–10pm Sun–Thu, 9am–11pm Fri, Sat.

This charming street in the Old Town is full of restaurants, cafés and shops. It leads from the Main Market Square to the **Florian Gate** and was once part of the Royal Route, along which rulers would ride on their way from Warsaw to their coronation in Krakow.
   Matejko House (Dom Matejki), at No. 41, is the birth-place of the painter Jan Matejko. He spent most of his life here. On display is a collection of his paintings and his studio, full of artist's materials.
   A little further on, at No. 45, is **Jama Michalika**, a café that was very fashionable in the late 19th to early 20th centuries. The fine Art Nouveau decor by Karol Frycz can still be seen. The **Florian Gate** at the end of the street is one of the few surviving remnants of the city's medieval fortifications, along with a section of the city wall.

Medieval Florian Gate at the end of ulica Floriańska

④ Church of St Mary

Kościół Mariacka

The imposing Church of St Mary was built by the citizens of Krakow to rival the Krakow Cathedral on Wawel Hill *(see pp190–91)*. Construction began in 1355, and continued until the mid-15th century; the lower tower was not completed until the early 16th century. Inside, Neo-Gothic paintings cover the walls. This great basilica, with its rows of side chapels, contains an exceptional number of works of art.

★ Crucifix
The large sandstone crucifix by Veit Stoss is a fine example of 15th-century sculpture.

Hejnał Tower
The famous trumpet call – the Hejnał – is sounded hourly from the watchtower. As per legend, the call is unfinished, in memory of a medieval trumpeter, shot while sounding the alarm. The Hejnał is broadcast live on Polish radio daily at noon.

Main entrance

Baroque Porch
The exuberant pentagonal porch was built in the mid-18th century to a design by Francesco Placidi.

Ciborium
This intricately constructed ciborium in the form of a Renaissance church was made by Giovanni Maria Padovano around 1552.

Gothic stained-glass window

Visitors' entrance

★ **Altar of the Virgin**
Carved by sculptor Veit Stoss between 1477 and 1489, this great Gothic polyptych altarpiece is 12 m (39 ft) long and 11 m (36 ft) high.

Leonardo da Vinci's *Lady with an Ermine*, Czartoryski Museum

⑤ Czartoryski Museum

Muzeum Książąt Czartoryskich

ul. św Jana 19. **Map** D1. **Tel** (012) 422 5566. 🚌 152, 304, 502. 🚊 2, 4, 14, 20, 24. **Open** Tue–Sun. 🚻 free on Sun for permanent exhibitions. 🛒

This museum has one of Poland's most varied art collections. Assembled in Puławy at the end of the 18th century by Princess Izabella Czartoryska, it was the private collection of the Czartoryski family. The collection was later taken to Paris and then to Krakow, where it was put on public view. It includes examples of handicrafts, but most significant are the paintings – among them are Leonardo da Vinci's *Lady with an Ermine* (c. 1485) and Rembrandt's *Landscape with Good Samaritan* (1638).

⑥ Church of Sts Peter and Paul

Kościół św Piotra i św Pawła

ul. Grodzka 52a. **Map** C3. **Tel** (012) 422 6573. 🚊 1, 8, 10, 18. **Open** 9am–7pm Mon–Sat, 1:30–5:30pm Sun. 🚻

This twin-domed church is one of the most beautiful examples of early-Baroque architecture in Poland. It was built for the Jesuits after their arrival in Krakow in the 1580s, but after a structural disaster in 1605, the church was almost completely rebuilt

to the designs of an unknown architect.

The church is enclosed by railings topped with the figures of the apostles dating between 1715 and 1722. The interior contains fine stuccowork by Giovanni Battista Falconi. The high altar and organ screen, designed by Kacper Bażanka, are also noteworthy.

Among the many funerary monuments the 17th-century marble tomb of Bishop Andrzej Tomicki is most striking. Standing in front of the church is the statue of Piotr Skarga, a Jesuit preacher and champion of the Counter-Reformation, erected in 2001. He died in 1612 and was buried in the crypt below the high altar.

Baroque façade of the Jesuit Church of Sts Peter and Paul

⑦ Szołaysky House

Kamienica Szołayskich

Plac Szczepański 9. **Map** C2. **Tel** (012) 433 5450. 🚌 152, 502. 🚊 2, 4, 8, 10, 14, 24. **Open** 10am–6pm Tue–Sat, 10am–4pm Sun. 🚻 free on Sun. 🛒

This museum houses permanent and temporary exhibitions, including works by Krakow's foremost Art Nouveau artist, Stanisław Wyspiański. Exhibits of interest here include stage designs, textiles, pastels and portraits of friends and family. The stained-glass windows he produced for the Franciscan church display his ingenuity.

The ground floor of the museum features an information centre, museum shop, café and multi-purpose hall.

Street-by-Street: The Wawel

In about 1038 Kazimierz the Restorer made the citadel on Wawel Hill the seat of Polish political power. In the 16th century the Jagiełłonian rulers transformed the Gothic castle into a magnificent Renaissance palace. Once the site of coronations and royal burials, the cathedral is regarded as a shrine by Poles. The Wawel Royal Castle beside it is a symbol of national identity.

⑫ ★ **Wawel Royal Castle**
Once home to the Jagiellonian kings, the Wawel Royal Castle has survived without major damage. It incorporates the walls of older Gothic buildings

⑧ **Fortifications on the Wawel** have been demolished and renewed several times since the Middle Ages – right up to the 20th century

Monument of Tadeusz Kościuszko

⑪ ★ **Krakow Cathedral**
The Gothic cathedral, lined with royal burial chapels from different ages, has some extraordinarily valuable furnishings

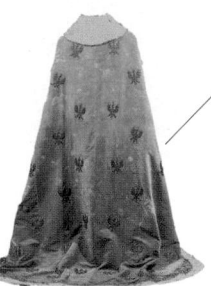

⑨ **Cathedral Museum**
On display are religious and royal regalia from the cathedral treasury, including the magnificent robe of Stanisław August Poniatowski *(see p178)*

0 metres	50
0 yards	50

Key

— Suggested route

Thieves' Tower

For hotels and restaurants see p220 and p221

The Crown Treasury and Armoury situated in the historic Gothic rooms of the castle were used for storing the Polish coronation insignia and Crown Jewels. Memorabilia of the Polish monarchs and objects from the former treasury are also on display here.

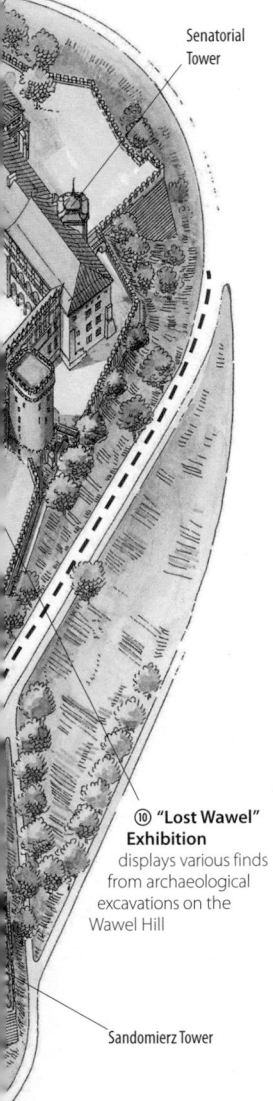

Senatorial Tower

⑩ "Lost Wawel" Exhibition displays various finds from archaeological excavations on the Wawel Hill

Sandomierz Tower

Fortified walls

⑧ Fortifications on the Wawel

Fortyfikacje, Mury Obronne

Wawel. **Map** C4. 🚌 1, 3, 8, 10, 18, 22.

The Wawel Hill was fortified from early times but today only fragments of the oldest Gothic fortifications remain. However, three towers raised in the second half of the 15th century still survive – the Senatorial Tower, the Thieves' Tower and the Sandomierz Tower. Of the fortifications dating between the 16th and 17th centuries the most interesting is the Vasa Gate. The monument to the national hero Tadeusz Kościuszko, leader of the failed insurrection of 1794, on the Władysław Bastion is another highlight. The Wawel continued to play a defensive role into the 19th century, and a system of fortifications dating from the late 18th and mid-19th centuries can still be seen.

Sandomierz Tower, one of three towers of the Wawel fortifications

⑨ Cathedral Museum

Muzeum Katedralne

Wawel 3. **Map** C4. **Tel** (012) 429 3321. 🚌 3, 8, 10, 18, 22. **Open** Oct–Mar: 9am–4pm Mon–Sat; Apr–Sep: 9am–5pm Mon–Sat. **Closed** 1 Jan, Easter, 15 Aug & 25 Dec. 🖼

This museum is located in buildings near the cathedral and contains a valuable collection of pieces from the cathedral treasury. Among the finest liturgical vessels and vestments is the chasuble of Bishop Piotr Kmita, which dates

Embroidered hood of Bishop Trzebicki's cope, Cathedral Museum

from 1504 and has quilted embroidery depicting scenes from St Stanisław's life. Some fascinating pieces of royal memorabilia are also on display at the museum.

⑩ "Lost Wawel" Exhibition

Wawel Zaginiony

Wawel 5. **Map** C4. **Tel** (012) 422 5155. 🚌 3, 8, 10, 18. **Open** Apr–Oct: 9:30am–5pm Tue–Fri, 9:30am–1pm Mon, 10am–5pm Sat–Sun; Nov–Mar: 9:30am–4pm Tue–Sat, 10am–4pm Sun. **Closed** public hols. 🖼 free Nov–Mar: Sun; Apr–Oct: Mon. 🌐 wawel.krakow.pl

For anyone interested in archaeology, this exhibition is a real delight. The display charts the development of the Wawel over a long period of time, and includes a virtual image of the Wawel buildings as they existed in the early Middle Ages, archaeological finds from Wawel Hill and a partially reconstructed early Romanesque chapel dedicated to the Blessed Virgin. Built at the turn of the 11th century, the chapel was discovered during research work in 1917.

Chapel of the Blessed Virgin, part of the "Lost Wawel" exhibition

⑪ Krakow Cathedral

Królewska Katedra na Wawelu

Krakow Cathedral, which stands on the Wawel *(see pp190–91)*, is one of the most important churches in Poland. Before the present cathedral was erected (1320–64), two churches stood on the site. The cathedral has many features, including a series of chapels founded by bishops of which the most beautiful is the Renaissance Zygmunt Chapel. There are royal tombs in the cathedral and the Crypt of St Leonard, a remnant of the Romanesque Cathedral of St Wacław.

Zygmunt Bell
Constructed in 1520, this is the largest bell in Poland. Weighing almost 11 tonnes (24,251 lbs), it has a diameter of over 2 m (6 ft).

★ Tomb of Kazimierz the Jagiełłonian
Completed in 1492, this royal tomb in the Chapel of the Holy Cross is one of the last commissions that the German sculptor Veit Stoss fulfilled in Poland.

Main entrance

Shrine of St Stanisław
The silver coffin containing the relics of St Stanisław, the bishop of Krakow to whom the cathedral is dedicated, was built between 1669 and 1671 by Pieter van der Rennen, a goldsmith from Gdańsk.

KEY

① **The top** of the clock tower is decorated with statues of saints.

② **High Altar**

Stalls
The early Baroque oak stalls in the chancel were built around 1620.

VISITORS' CHECKLIST

Practical Information
Wawel 3. **Map** C4. **Tel** (012) 422 5155. **Open** Apr–Sep: 9am–5pm Mon–Sat, 12:30–5pm Sun; Oct–Mar: 9am–4pm Mon–Sat, 12:30–4pm Sun. 🗝 Royal Tombs & Zygmunt Bell. 🎫 ♿

Transport
🚌 103, 502. 🚊 8, 10, 18, 20.

Room in the Hen's Foot Tower, Wawel Royal Castle

⑫ Wawel Royal Castle

Zamek Królewski na Wawelu

Wawel Hill. **Map** C4. **Tel** (012) 422 1697. 🚌 103, 502. 🚊 8, 10, 18, 40. **Open** Nov–Mar: 9:30am–4pm Tue–Sat; Apr–Oct: 9:30am–5pm Tue–Fri, 10am–5pm Sat & Sun. 🗝 Nov–Mar: Sun. 🎫 Royal Private Apartments. 🌐 wawel.krakow.pl

One of Central Europe's most magnificent Renaissance residences, the Wawel Royal Castle was built for King Zygmunt I the Old, the penultimate ruler of the Jagiellonian Dynasty. The four-winged palace, built between 1502 and 1536, incorporated the remains of a 14th-century building that stood on the site. Italian architects Francisco Fiorentino and Bartolomeo Berrecci designed and constructed it. One of the highlights of the castle is the impressive Renaissance-style courtyard that was built in the 16th century. The rooms in the **Hen's Foot Tower** are among the most beautiful in the castle. The tower was rebuilt after it was damaged by fire in the 16th and 17th centuries.

After the royal court was transferred from Krakow to Warsaw, the palace fell into neglect, and during the era of the partitions it served as barracks. At the beginning of the 20th century, the castle was given to the city of Krakow, which started a restoration programme and turned it into a museum.

★ **Zygmunt Chapel**
The chapel with the tombs of the last two Jagiellonian kings is the jewel of Italian Renaissance art in Poland. The tomb of Zygmunt I the Old was made by Bartolomeo Berrecci after 1530, while that of Zygmunt August was built between 1574 and 1575 by Santi Gucci.

②

Royal Tombs
These Baroque sarcophagi were made for members of the royal Vasa Dynasty. The cathedral is the final resting place of most of the Polish kings, as well as national heroes such as Tadeusz Kościuszko *(see p191)* and several revered poets.

⓭ Street-by-Street: Kazimierz District

Narrow streets lined with low buildings make up the district of Kazimierz. Founded in 1335 by Kazimierz the Great, it soon developed a thriving Jewish population. Czech and German refugees came here to join Jews displaced from Krakow in the late 15th century, and the area bears witness to centuries of co-existence between Jews and Poles. The Jewish quarter, located in the district's eastern part, was concentrated around Szeroka ulica, later known as New Square. Many synagogues, bathhouses and cemeteries were established and Kazimierz became a centre of Judaic culture and learning. During World War II, much of the quarter was destroyed in the Nazi invasion, but recently many galleries, cafés and bars have opened here.

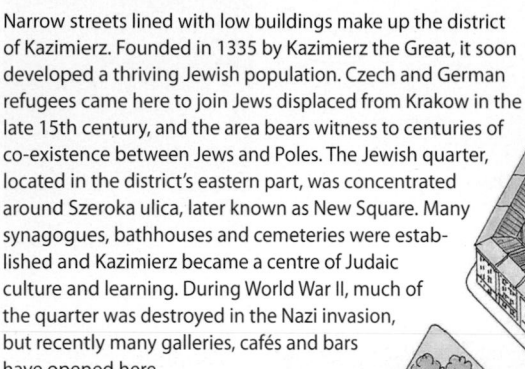

Temple Synagogue
The decoration of this synagogue, built in the Neo-Renaissance style, was influenced by Moorish art.

Key

— Suggested route

0 metres   50
0 yards   50

Jewish Tombs

The signs carved on Jewish tombs have symbolic value. The grave of a rabbi is indicated by hands joined in prayer. Those of Levites are distinguished by basins and jugs for the ritual ablution of hands. Three interlaced snakes feature on the grave of a physician, and a crown of knowledge on that of a learned man. A lion or a six-pointed Star of David signifies a descendant of Judah.

Intricately carved symbolic motifs on Jewish tombs

Kupa Synagogue
Built in the 17th century, this synagogue, financed by the Kahal, the municipality of Kazimierz, was also used for non-religious purposes. It has recently been converted into a Jewish cultural centre.

★ **Remu'h Cemetery**
This evocative Jewish cemetery contains a Wailing Wall which commemorates the tragic fate met by Krakow's Jews during World War II.

VISITORS' CHECKLIST

Practical Information
Map E4.
i ul. Józefa 7, (012) 422 0471.
Remu'h Cemetery: ul. Szeroka 40, (012) 422 1274. **Open** 9am–4pm Mon–Fri. Old Synagogue: ul. Szeroka 24, (012) 422 0962.
⊡ Festival of Jewish Culture (late Jun).

Transport
⊞ 11, 13, 24.

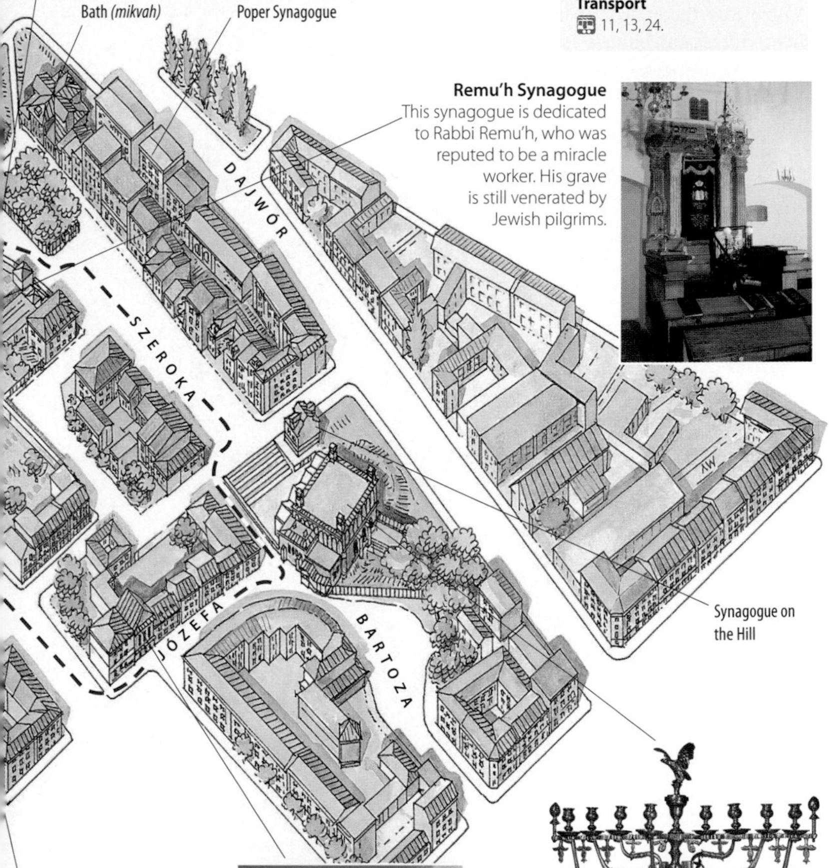

Bath *(mikvah)*   Poper Synagogue

Remu'h Synagogue
This synagogue is dedicated to Rabbi Remu'h, who was reputed to be a miracle worker. His grave is still venerated by Jewish pilgrims.

DAJWOR

SZEROKA

JÓZEFA   BARTOZA

Synagogue on the Hill

Isaak's Synagogue is named after its founder, Isaak Jakubowicz, a Jewish elder.

High Synagogue
Designed in Gothic style, the High Synagogue is one of Krakow's most attractive synagogues.

★ **Old Synagogue**
Although destroyed by the Nazis, Poland's oldest synagogue has been painstakingly restored. This menorah is among its many treasures.

⑭ Auschwitz I

Oświęcim

For most people, Auschwitz represents the ultimate horror of the Holocaust. The Nazis began the first mass transportation of European Jews to Auschwitz in 1942 and it soon became the centre of extermination. Over the next three years, more than one and a half million people, a quarter of those who died in the Holocaust, were killed at Auschwitz and the neighbouring Birkenau camp *(see pp198–9)*, also known as Auschwitz II. Today, Auschwitz is a UNESCO World Heritage Site and the camp has been preserved as a poignant memorial. The prison blocks have been turned into a museum charting the history of the camps and of persecution in Poland.

Exhibitions
The daily horrors of life in the camp are displayed in some of the barracks.

The Camp

Auschwitz I opened in 1940 on the site of former Polish Army barracks. Originally built to incarcerate only Polish political prisoners, further buildings were added in the spring of 1941 as the number of prisoners drastically increased. Camp administration was also based here.

Gas Chambers and Crematoria
The entire Auschwitz complex had seven gas chambers and five crematoria. Four of the gas chambers were in Birkenau but the first was at Auschwitz, operating from 1941.

The Two Camps

Although part of the same camp complex, Auschwitz and Birkenau are in fact 3 km (2 miles) apart. The small Polish town of Oświęcim was commandeered by the Nazis and renamed Auschwitz. Birkenau was opened in March 1942 in the village of Brzezinka, where the residents were evicted to make way for the camp. There were an additional 47 sub-camps in the surrounding area.

Aerial view of Auschwitz I and Birkenau taken by the Allies in 1944

KEY

① **"Arbeit Macht Frei",** the infamous words above the entrance to Auschwitz translate as "Work makes you free". This was certainly not the case for the prisoners transported here, who were often worked to death.

② **Guard house and office of the camp supervisor**

③ **Block 11, the central jail** was where the first experiments with gas were carried out in 1941.

④ **Store containing the poison,** Zyklon B, used to kill prisoners.

⑤ **Camp kitchen**

⑥ **Information Centre for visitors**

For hotels and restaurants see p220 and p221

The "Wall of Death"
This is a reconstruction of the wall near Block 11 used for summary executions carried out by a firing squad. It now serves as a place of remembrance.

Maksymilian Kolbe
This Franciscan priest, who was later canonized, chose to die to save another inmate's life here. He was sentenced to death by starvation.

Roll Call Square
Roll call took place up to three times a day and could last for hours. Eventually, due to the large number of prisoners, roll call was taken in front of individual barracks.

1939 1 Sep, Hitler invades Poland.	**1940** First deportation of German Jews into Nazi-occupied Poland.	**1941** Hitler reported to have ordered the "Final Solution". **1942** First section of Birkenau camp completed.	**1944** As the Soviet Army closes in on Auschwitz, the SS begin destroying all evidence of the camp.	**1945** 27 Jan, Soviet soldiers liberate the few remaining prisoners at Auschwitz.
1939	**1940**	**1941**	**1942**	**1943**	**1944**	**1945**
1940 Oświęcim chosen as the site of the Nazis' new concentration camp.	**1941** Himmler makes first visit to Auschwitz and orders its expansion.	**1941** First gas chamber goes into operation.	**1942** Beginning of mass deportation to Auschwitz.	**1943** Four gas chambers built for mass murder. **1945** 18 Jan, 56,000 prisoners evacuated on "Death March".	**1945** 7 May, Germany finally surrenders to the Allies.

Auschwitz II–Birkenau

Oświęcim-Brzezinka

Birkenau was primarily a place of execution. Over one million people were killed in its four gas chambers, 98 per cent of whom were Jewish. Victims included Poles, Russian prisoners of war, gypsies and Czech, Yugoslav, French, Austrian and German citizens. Birkenau was also an enormous concentration camp, housing 90,000 slave labourers by mid-1944 and providing labour for many of the factories and farms of southwestern, Nazi-occupied Poland. The gas chambers were quickly destroyed by the Nazis shortly before the Soviet Army liberated the camp in January 1945.

Hell's Gate
In 1944, the numbers arriving at the camp began to increase dramatically. A railway line was extended into the camp. The entrance gate through which the trains passed was known as "Hell's Gate".

Visiting Birkenau
There is little left of the camp today; its main purpose is for remembrance. Most visitors come to pay their respects at the Monument to the Victims of the Camp, on the site of the gas chambers.

The Unloading Ramp
This was possibly the most terrifying part of the camp. It was here that SS officers separated the men from the women and children, and the SS doctors declared who was fit for work. Those declared unfit were taken immediately to their death.

Women's Barracks
The conditions in the living quarters at the camps were terrible. With little or no sanitation, poor nutrition and no medical care, diseases such as typhus and cholera spread rapidly. This image shows the women's barracks at Birkenau shortly after liberation.

KEY

① **Towers and barbed wire** isolated the camps from the outside world

② **Gas chamber and crematorium**

③ **Area of expansion**, nicknamed "Mexico", was never completed.

④ **Men's barracks**, with about 500 to 600 people living in each building.

⑤ **Hell's Gate**

For hotels and restaurants see p220 and p221

Kanada

This was the nickname of the barracks where property stolen from prisoners was stored. It was the preferred place to work at Auschwitz II-Birkenau as it offered opportunities for inmates to pilfer items to barter for food or medicine later.

The Sauna

New arrivals selected for work were deloused and disinfected in this building, which became known as the "sauna". Periodic disinfection of existing prisoners was also carried out here.

The Ash Pond

Tonnes of ash – the remains of hundreds of thousands of Auschwitz victims – were dumped in ponds and troughs dug around the outskirts of the camp.

The Camp Reconstruction

In 1944, Birkenau had more than 90,000 prisoners, the majority of whom were exterminated. It was the largest concentration camp in Nazi-occupied Europe. From the unloading ramp to the gas chambers, the crematoria to the ash dumping grounds, the whole process of murder was carried out systematically and on a huge scale. This reconstruction shows the camp at its peak in 1944, when as many as 5,000 people were killed every day.

The Liberation of the Camps

With the war all but lost, in mid-January 1945 the Nazi authorities gave the order for all the camps to be destroyed. However, only a part of Birkenau could be destroyed before the collapse of the German Army. Between 17 and 21 January, more than 56,000 inmates were evacuated by the Nazis and forced to march west, but many died en route. When the Soviet Army entered the camps on 27 January 1945, they found just 7,000 survivors.

Survivors of Auschwitz II-Birkenau, filmed by Soviet troops

❸ Wrocław

The beautiful city of Wrocław bears the stamp of several cultures. It was founded by Duke Vratislav of Bohemia in the 10th century and a Polish bishopric was established here in AD 1000. Later it became the capital of the Duchy of Silesian Piasts, and then came under Czech rule in 1335. In 1526, with the whole Czech state, it was incorporated into the Habsburg Empire, and in 1741 was transferred to Prussian rule. The fierce defence that German forces put up here at the end of World War II left almost three quarters of Wrocław in ruins but the city has now been painstakingly reconstructed.

Baroque *pietá* in the University Church of the Blessed Name of Jesus

Ostrów Tumski

Cathedral of St John the Baptist: pl. Katedralny 18. **Open** 10am–4pm Mon–Sat, 2–4pm Sun.
Ⓦ katedra.archidiecezja.wroc.pl

Once an island in the Odra river, Ostrów Tumski is where the history of Wrocław began. In the 19th century, the northern arm of the Odra was filled in and Tumski ceased to be an island. Ostrów Tumski's principal landmark, the **Cathedral of St John the Baptist** (Katedra św Jana Chrzciciela), has a fine interior despite having suffered the ravages of World War II. Other highlights include the two-tiered Church of the Holy Cross, established in 1288 by Henry IV, the Pious and the Archdiocesan Museum, a rich repository of Gothic art built between 1519 and 1527. A walk through the narrow streets can be followed by a visit to the Botanical Gardens.

🏛 Wrocław University

pl. Uniwersytecki 1. **Tel** (071) 375 2215. Assembly Hall: **Open** 10:30am–3:30pm Mon, Tue & Thu, 11am–5pm Fri–Sun. 🖼

Established as an academy by Emperor Leopold I in 1702, Wrocław University (Uniwersytet Wrocławski) was given its current status in 1811. The university has produced eight Nobel Laureates including the nuclear physicist Max Born. Since 1945 it has been a Polish centre of learning.

The highlight of this Baroque building is the **Assembly Hall** (Aula Leopoldina) whose interior includes stuccowork, gilding by Franz Josef Mangoldt

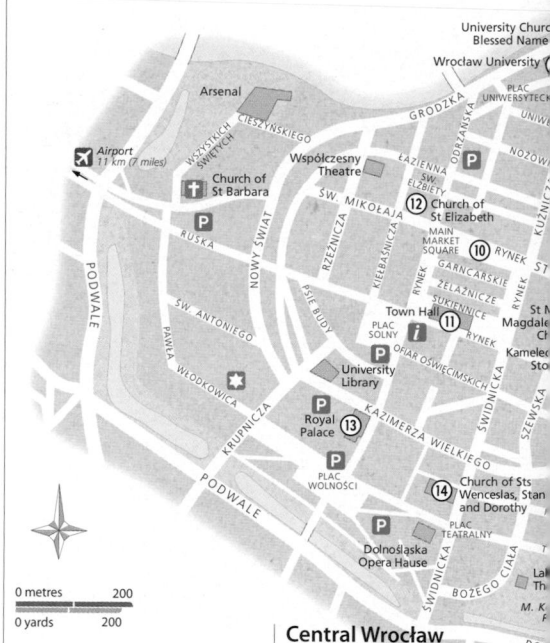

and paintings by Christoph Handke glorifying Wisdom, Knowledge and Science, and the founders of the academy.

The richly ornamented interior of Wrocław University's Assembly Hall

Central Wrocław

① Ostrów Tumski
② Wrocław University
③ University Church of the Blessed Name of Jesus
④ Nankiera Bishop's Square
⑤ National Museum
⑥ Panorama of Racławice
⑦ Bernadine Church and Monastery
⑧ St Mary Magdalene's Church
⑨ Kameleon Store
⑩ Main Market Square
⑪ Town Hall
⑫ Church of St Elizabeth
⑬ Royal Palace
⑭ Church of Sts Wenceslas, Stanisław and Dorothy

🏛 University Church of the Blessed Name of Jesus

pl. Uniwersytecki 1.
Tel (071) 343 6382. 🏛

Built for the Jesuits in 1689–98, this church (Uniwersytecki Kościoł Najświętszego Imienia Jesuza) exemplifies Silesian Baroque church architecture. The interior was built by Krzyszt of Tausch in 1722–34. The vaulting was decorated by the Viennese artist Johann Michael Rottmayer in 1704–6.

The Gothic Church of St Vincent with Hochberg Chapel in front

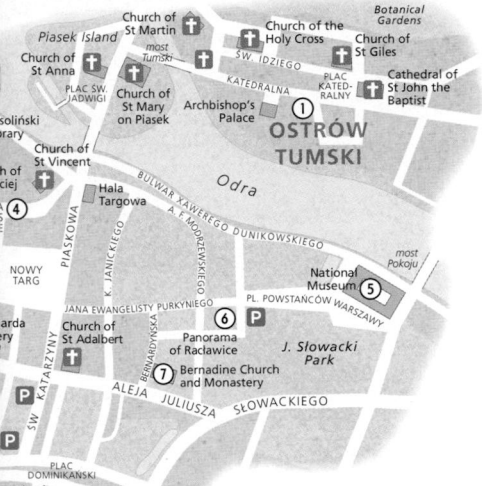

🏙 Nankiera Bishop's Square

The buildings in this square (Plac Biskupa Nankiera) date from various periods. The Gothic **Church of St Vincent** (Kościół św Wincentego), at No. 5, was erected in the 13th to 15th centuries. At No. 16, the 17th-century Baroque monastery, Old Order of St Clare, now hosts a post elementary school. The group of Baroque monastic buildings at No. 16 also encloses the small 3th-century **Church of St Clare** (Kościół św Klary).

The church, used by the Piasts as a mausoleum, still contains Gothic Ducal tombs. Next door, at No. 17, is the Gothic **Church of St Maciej** (Kościół św Macieja), which was once owned by the Knights Hospitallers of the Red Star. The pavilion of the gallery at No. 8, on the opposite side of the square, contains the 13th-century walls of the **House of the Nuns of Trebnica** (Dom Sióstr Trebnica), the oldest surviving secular building in the city.

🏛 National Museum

pl. Powstańców Warszawy 5. **Tel** (071) 343 5643. **Open** Apr–Sep: 10am–5pm Wed–Fri & Sun, 10am–6pm Sat; Oct–Mar: 10am–4pm Wed–Fri, 10am–5pm Sat & Sun. 🎟 free on Sat, limited availability. 🌐 **mnwr.art.pl**

The ground floor of the National Museum (Muzeum Narodowe) contains examples of Silesian and Gothic art, including the tombstone of Henry IV the

Good, dating from 1300. The first floor has 16th- and 17th-century paintings, including works by the Silesian artist Michael Willmann (1630–1706) and wooden sculptures by Thomas Weissfeldt (1630–1712). The second floor is devoted to contemporary Polish works.

Façade of the National Museum

Panorama of Racławice

ul. Purkyniego 11. **Tel** (071) 344 1661.
Open winter: 9am–4pm Tue–Sun; summer: 9am–5pm daily. 📷 ♿

The Panorama of Racławice (Panorama Racławicka) depicts the Battle of Racławice of 4 April 1794, when the Poles defeated the Russians. It is 120 m (400 ft) long and 15 m (46 ft) high and took artists Wojciech Kossak and Jan Styka nine months to paint. Unveiled in 1894 in Lviv, in Ukraine, it was brought to Poland in 1946 and was put on display in Wrocław in 1985.

Rotunda containing the Panorama of Racławice

Wrocław: Old Town

For those who enjoy exploring on foot, the Old Town (Stare Miasto) of Wrocław is a delightful place. The restored buildings located around the large Main Market Square have been given over to an assortment of bars, restaurants and cafés with alfresco seating, while the nearby churches contain a wealth of religious art and ecclesiastical furnishings. The impressive Gothic Town Hall has a finely decorated interior. On summer evenings, this bustling square comes alive as locals as well as visitors gather here to attend the concerts and many cultural events that are held in the square.

The façade of the House of the Seven Electors, Main Market Square

Late-Gothic portal of the Bernadine Church and Monastery

⬆ Bernadine Church and Monastery

ul. Bernardyńska 5. Architecture Museum: **Tel** (071) 344 8279. **Open** 10am–8pm daily.
🔲 free for permanent exhibitions.
W ma.wroc.pl

This impressive group of monastic buildings (Kościół i Klasztor pobernardyński) was constructed by Bernadine monks between 1463 and 1502. Rebuilt from their wartime ruins, they now house the **Architecture Museum** (Muzeum Architektury). The monastery is of interest for its late-Gothic cloisters and the Church of St Bernard of Siena, a towering Gothic basilica with a typically Baroque gable.

⬆ St Mary Magdalene's Church

ul. św Marii Magdaleny. **Tel** (071) 344 1904. **Open** 9am–noon, 4–6pm daily.
The great Gothic St Mary Magdalene's Church (Kościół św Marii Magdaleny) was erected between 1330 and

the mid-15th century, incorporating the walls of a 13th-century church that had previously stood on the site. Inside the basilica is a Gothic stone tabernacle, a Renaissance pulpit made between 1579 and 1581 by Friedrich Gross and tombstones of various periods. The portal on the north side is a superb example of late 12th-century Romanesque sculpture. It was taken from a demolished Benedictine monastery in Olbina and added in 1546.

The tympanum, depicting the Dormition of the Virgin, is now on display in the National Museum *(see p201)*.

Detail on a relief in St Mary Magdalene's Church

🏬 Kameleon Store

ul. Szewska 6–7.
The Kameleon Store (Dom Handlowy Kameleon) is an unusual building on the corner of ulica Szewska and ulica Oławska. It was built by the German architect Erich Mendelsohn as a retail store for Rudolf Petersdorf between 1927 and 1928. Its semicircular bay, formed of rows of windows, juts out dramatically. Nearby, at the intersection of ulica Łaciarska and Ofiar

Oświęcimskich, an office building built between 1912 and 1913 by renowned architect Hans Poelzig is another interesting example of Modernist architecture.

🏬 Main Market Square

Rynek.
Wrocław's Main Market Square is the second largest in Poland, after the one in Krakow. In the centre stand the Town Hall and a group of buildings separated by alleys. The houses around the square date from the Renaissance to the 20th century. Some still have their original 14th- and 15th-century Gothic vaults. The west side of the square is the most attractive with the late-Baroque **House of the Golden Sun**, at No. 6, built in 1727 by Johann Lucas von Hildebrandt, as well as the **House of the Seven Electors**, its paintwork dating from 1672. Also to the south is **Under the Griffins** (Pod Gryfami), at No. 2, built between 1587 and 1589. It has a galleried interior courtyard. On the east side, at No. 31 and No. 32, is **Feniks Store** of 1904 and, at No. 41, **Under the Golden Dog** (Pod Złotym Psem), a rebuilt town house of 1713. The north side was reconstructed after World War II. Just off the corner of the Main Market Square, in front of the Church of St Elizabeth (Kościół św Elżbiety), are two small acolytes' houses, the Renaissance Jaś of around 1564, and the 18th-century Baroque Małgosia.

⊞ Town Hall

ul. Sukiennice 14/15. Museum of City
Art: **Open** 11am–5pm Wed–Sat,
10am–6pm Sun. 🅿 Ⓦ **muzeum.
miejskie.wroclaw.pl**

Wrocław's Town Hall (Muzeum
Miejskie Wrocławia) is one of
the most important examples
of Gothic architecture in Eastern
and Central Europe. Its present
appearance is the result of
extensive rebuilding that took
place between 1470 and 1510.

The building's southern
façade was embellished with
Neo-Gothic stone carvings
around 1871. Inside are impressive
vaulted halls, the largest being
the triple-aisled Grand Hall on
the ground floor that served as
an important venue for public
meetings and receptions. There
are also a number of late-Gothic
and Renaissance doorways. The
building houses the **Museum of
City Art** (Muzeum Sztuki
Mieszczańskiej).

A plaque outside the entrance
to the Town Hall commemorates
the prominent poet and writer
Aleksander Fredro (1793–1876),
who acquired fame with his
comedies about the Polish upper
classes. The plaque was made
in 1879 by Leonard Marconi
and transferred to Wrocław
from Lviv in 1956.

Gothic gables of the east façade of the
Town Hall

⊡ Church of St Elizabeth

ul. św Elżbiety. **Tel** (071) 343 1638.
Open 8am–6pm Mon–Sat,
1–6pm Sun.

The tower dominating the Main
Market Square is that of the
Church of St Elizabeth (Kościół
św Elżbiety), one of the largest
churches in Wrocław. The Gothic
basilica was built in the 14th
century on the site of an earlier
church. However, the tower was
not completed until 1482. It
became a Protestant church in
1525 and has been a garrison
church since 1946.

The church suffered damage
from a succession of wars
and accidents. A fire in 1976
destroyed the roof and the fine
Baroque organ. Fortunately,
more than 350 epitaphs and
tombstones have survived,
forming a display of Silesian
stone-carving from Gothic
to Neo-Classical periods.

Church of St Elizabeth with Jaś and
Małgosia, acolytes' houses

⊞ Royal Palace

ul. Kazimierza Wielkiego 35.
Archaeology Museum: ul.
Cieszyńskiego 9. **Tel** (071) 347 1696.
Open 11am–5pm Wed–Sat,
11am–6pm Sun. 🅿 Ethnographic
Museum: ul. Traugutta 111/113.
Tel (071) 344 3313. **Open** 10am–4pm
Tue, Wed, Fri–Sun, 9am–4pm Thu.
🅿 free on Sat. ⬩

This Baroque palace (Pałac
Królewski) with Classical details,
enclosed by a court of annexes,
was built in 1719. After 1750, when
Wrocław was under Prussian rule,
it became a residence for the
Prussian kings. On the side facing
Plac Wolności, only a side gallery
remains of the Neo-Renaissance
palace built between 1843
and 1846.

The Royal Palace contains
two interesting collections:
the **Archaeology Museum**
and **Ethnographic Museum**,
the latter illustrating Silesian
art and folk history, including
a large collection of dolls in
traditional garments.

Church of Sts Wenceslas, Stanisław
and Dorothy

⊡ Church of Sts Wenceslas, Stanisław and Dorothy

ul. Świdnicka. **Tel** (071) 343 2721.

Dedicated to three saints, the
Czech St Wenceslas, the Polish
St Stanisław and the German St
Dorothy, this Franciscan church
(Kościół św Wacława, Stanisława
i Doroty) was built in 1351 to
strengthen relations between
Wrocław's three nationalities.

The church's unusually
narrow interior is Gothic. The
beautiful Rococo tombstone
of Gottfried von Spaetgen
(c. 1725–1753) stands in
the nave.

The Ossolineum

The National Ossoliński
Institute was founded by
Count Józef Maksymilian
Ossoliński (1748–1829) in
Vienna in 1817. In 1827 it
moved to Lwów (later Lviv),
where it assembled collections of manuscripts, prints,
etchings and drawings,
promoted scientific research
and engaged in publishing.
After World War II, most of the
collections were transferred
to the National Museum
(see p201) in Wrocław, while
the manuscripts were housed
in the Baroque monastery of
the Knights Hospitallers of the
Red Star in Wrocław.

The Baroque monastery that houses
the Ossolineum

❹ Poznań

Poznań is the capital of Wielkopolska, a historical region in west-central Poland, and is its largest city. A stronghold by the name of Polan stood here in the 8th century and it became the capital of the emerging Polish state in the 10th century. It was declared the seat of the first bishopric in Poland in 968. Today, Poznań is Poland's second financial centre after Warsaw and a centre of commerce. Annual trade fairs have been held here since 1921. The city has many historic buildings, the finest of which are its cathedral and those in the Old Town (Stare Miasto). A stroll around the attractive late 19th-century quarter is worthwhile.

banks, cafés and restaurants. From spring to autumn, the square bustles with life; local artists display their paintings, and the outdoor cafés are permanently busy. The square also serves as a venue for cultural events. Some of the houses here were destroyed during the battles for Poznań in 1945 and were rebuilt after World War II, but others escaped any serious

Interior of the Church of the Most Sacred Heart of Jesus

🏛 Church of the Most Sacred Heart of Jesus

ul. Szewska 18. **Tel** (061) 852 5076/ 853 3359.

This magnificent church (Kościół Serca Jezusowego), built in the 13th century, is the oldest in the Old Town. It was a Dominican church until 1920, when it was passed to the Jesuits. During the German occupation in World War II, a repository was set up here for Polish books removed from the libraries in Poznań.

🏛 Church of Sts Mary Magdalene and Stanisław

ul. Gołębia 1. **Tel** (061) 852 6950. Construction work on this Baroque church (Kościół św Marii Magdaleny i św Stanisław), began in 1651 and continued for more than 50 years. Several architects, craftsmen and artists, including Tomasso Poncino, Jan Catenaci and Bartołomiej Wąsowski, had a role in the project.

The most impressive aspect of the church is its monolithic interior. Gigantic columns lead towards the high altar, which was designed and constructed in

1727 by Pompeo Ferrari. Over this is a painting illustrating a legendary episode from the life of St Stanisław. Then a bishop, he was accused by the Polish King Bolesław III Wrymouth (1085–1138) of not paying for a village he had incorporated into his territory. In order to prove his innocence, St Stanisław is believed to have resurrected the deceased former owner of the land to testify on his behalf.

The Baroque buildings of a former Jesuit monastery and college stand close to the church, built for the brotherhood between 1701 and 1733. Today, they are used by the city council for secular purposes.

🏛 Old Town Square

The Old Town Square (Stary Rynek) is the heart of the Old Town. It is surrounded by town houses with colourful façades, among which stands the Renaissance Old Town Hall. The centrepiece of the square is the Baroque Proserpine Fountain of 1766, depicting the abduction of the ancient Roman goddess of fertility, Proserpine. Nearby, a 20th-century fountain commemorates 18th-century Catholic settlers from Bamberg, in southern Germany. The ground floors of the buildings around the square are filled by

damage. They include Mielżyński Palace, which dates from 1796–8, and Działyński Palace, both in Neo-Classical style.

🏛 Old Town Hall

Stary Rynek 1. Historical Museum of Poznań: **Tel** (061) 856 8193. **Open** 9am–3pm Tue–Thu, noon–9pm Fri, 11am–6pm Sat, Sun. 🎫 free on Sat. 🔗 mnp.art.pl

Poznań's Old Town Hall (Ratusz) is one of the finest municipal buildings in Europe. It was built between 1550 and 1560 by the Italian architect Giovanni

For hotels and restaurants see p220 and p221

Poznań City Centre

① Church of the Most Sacred Heart of Jesus
② Church of Sts Mary Magdalene and Stanisław
③ Old Town Square
④ Old Town Hall
⑤ Działyński Palace
⑥ Przemysław Castle
⑦ National Museum
⑧ Raczyński Library
⑨ St Adalbert's Hill
⑩ Ostrów Tumski
⑪ Archdiocese Museum
⑫ Poznań Cathedral

Battista di Quadro. The façade has three tiers of arcades, topped by a grand attic and a large tower, and decorated with portraits of the kings of Poland. The clock tower is an attraction in its own right. At noon each day, two clockwork goats emerge from doors 12 times to butt heads. The building now houses the **Historical Museum of Poznań** (Muzeum Historii Miasta Poznania). The Renaissance Hall on the first floor is lavishly decorated to reflect the affluence of the city's municipal leaders. The coffered ceiling is covered with an intricate series of paintings.

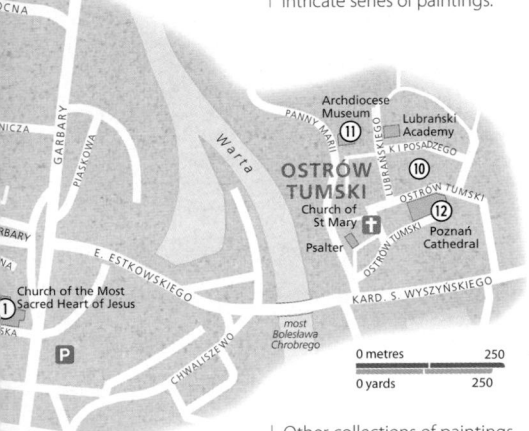

Other collections of paintings can be seen in the Royal Hall and the Court Hall.

🔲 Działyński Palace
Stary Rynek 78. **Tel** (061) 852 0950.
This palace (Pałac Działyńskich) was built in the late 18th century for Władysław Gurowski, Grand Marshal of Lithuania.

Poznań's colourful Old Market Square

VISITORS' CHECKLIST

Practical Information
319 km (175 miles) W of Warsaw.
🚉 560,000. 🛈 Stary Rynek 59, (061) 852 6156. 🚪 Poznań International Trade Fair (all year). 🎭 Malta International Theatre Festival (Jun). 🖥 poznan.pl

Transport
✈ 7 km (4 miles) W of centre.
🚆 Dworzec Główny ul. Dworcowa 1.

Façade of the magnificent Działyński Palace

The Neo-Classical façade is crowned with a large eagle and set with figures of Roman soldiers made by Anton Höhne between 1785 and 1787. The columned Red Room is worth a visit. The building is now used as a library, theatre and concert hall.

🔲 Przemysław Castle
Góra Przemysła 1. **Tel** (061) 856 8186.
Open 9am–3pm Tue–Thu, noon–9pm Fri, 11am–6pm Sat & Sun. 🎟 free on Sat. 🖥 mnp.art.pl

Little remains of the castle (Zamek Przemysława) built by Przemysław II in the 13th century, once the largest in Poland. The reconstructed castle that now stands on the site houses the **Applied Arts Museum** (Muzeum Sztuk Użytkowych), which holds a collection of everyday objects, decorative artifacts and religious items dating from the Middle Ages to the present. The Baroque Franciscan Church on ulica Góra Przemysła dates from the early 18th century. Frescoes by the Franciscan painter Adam Swach decorate the nave.

For keys to symbols see back flap

🏛 National Museum
al. Marcinkowskiego 9. **Tel** (061) 856 8000. **Open** 9am–3pm Tue–Thu (11am–5pm summer), noon–9pm Fri, 11am–6pm Sat & Sun. 🎨 free on Sat.
W mnp.art.pl

The National Museum (Muzeum Narodowe) is housed in what was originally the Prussian Friedrich Museum, a Neo-Renaissance building from 1900–1903. Its fine collections of Polish paintings include medieval art of the 12th to the 16th centuries and 17th- to 18th-century coffin portraits. Canvases by Jacek Malczewski are the best examples of painting by the Young Poland Movement. The Gallery of European Art contains works from various collections, including that belonging to Atanazy Raczyński, brother of Count Edward Raczyński. The most outstanding paintings are those by Dutch and Flemish artists including Joos van Cleve and Quentin Massys. Italian, French and Spanish painters are also represented.

🏛 Raczyński Library
pl. Wolności 19. **Tel** (061) 885 8900. **Open** 9am–8pm Mon–Fri.
W bracz.edu.pl

Architecturally, Raczyński Library (Biblioteka Raczyńskich) is one of the most distinguished buildings in the city. Its columned façade combines grandeur with elegance, and it cannot be

Statue of Hygeia, Greek goddess of health, outside the Raczyński Library

compared with any other building in Poznań. The idea for a library was initiated by Count Edward Raczyński in 1829. The aim of this visionary aristocrat was to turn Poznań into a "New Athens". The library was to be a centre of culture. Although the library's architect is unknown, it is thought to have been built by the French architects and designers Charles Percier and Pierre Fontaine.

A seated statue of Hygeia, the ancient Greek goddess of health, with the features of Konstancja z Potockich, Edward Raczyński's wife, was installed in front of the library in 1906.

St Adalbert's Hill
This hill (Wzgórze św Wojciecha) is believed to be the spot where 1,000 years ago, St Adalbert gave a sermon before setting off on his campaign to evangelize the

Prussians. On the summit, two churches face each other across a small square. One is the Discalced Carmelites' Church of St Joseph, built by Cristoforo Bonadura the Elder and Jan Catenaci between 1658 and 1667. It contains the tomb of Mikołaj Jan Skrzetuski on whom novelist Henryk Sienkiewicz based the hero of his historical saga *With Fire and Sword (Ogniem i Mieczem)*. The other is the Gothic Church of St Adalbert, forming a pantheon with the same function as the Pauline Church on the Rock in Krakow. The crypt contains the remains of eminent local figures, including Józef Wybicki, who wrote the Polish national anthem.

Ostrów Tumski
The oldest part of Poznań, Ostrów Tumski was the site of one of the first capital cities of the Polish state in the 10th century. Today, it is dominated by the Gothic towers of Poznań Cathedral, which contains many fine works of art.

Near the cathedral stands the small Gothic **Church of St Mary** (Kościół Najświętszej Marii Panny), which was built between 1431 and 1448 for Bishop Andrzej Bniński by Hanusz Prusz, a pupil of the prominent late medieval architect Heinrich Brunsberg. Down the road from the church is the **Lubrański Academy**, the first institute of

The Neo-Renaissance façade of the National Museum

For hotels and restaurants see p220 and p221

higher education to be established in Poznań. Founded in 1518 by Bishop Jan Lubrański, it acquired its greatest renown in the early 16th century. Among its alumni was Jan Struś, a physician during the Polish Renaissance.

In the gardens on the other side of ulica Ks.I. Posadzego stand a number of charming houses, one of which holds the collections of the **Archdiocese Museum**. The late Gothic **Psalter**, built around 1520 by Bishop Lubrański, is distinguished for its stepped and recessed gables.

🏛 Archdiocese Museum

ul. Lubrańskiego 1. **Tel** (061) 852 6195. **Open** 10am–5pm Tue–Fri, 9am–3pm Sat. **Closed** public hols. 🐾 🎫

The outstanding collection of religious art on display in the Archdiocese Museum (Muzeum Archidiecezjalne) includes medieval painting and sculpture, pieces of Gothic embroidery and some fine *kontusz* (silk sashes). The most important pieces are the *Madonna of Ołobok*, a Gothic-Romanesque statue dating from around 1310–29, and a fascinating group of coffin portraits, painted on metal plates.

♜ Poznań Cathedral

Ostrów Tumski 17. **Tel** (061) 852 9642. **Open** Mar–Oct: 9am–6pm Mon–Sat, 2–6pm Sun; Nov–Feb: 9am–4pm Mon–Sat, 2–6pm Sun.

In 966, shortly after Poland adopted Christianity, a pre-Romanesque basilica was built on this site and Poland's first rulers were buried here. Between 1034 and 1038, the basilica was destroyed during pagan uprisings, but it was rebuilt in the Romanesque style. It was remodelled in the Gothic and Baroque periods, and after suffering war damage was restored to its Gothic form. Vestiges of the pre-Romanesque and Romanesque churches can be seen in the crypt. Among the highlights of the interior is Golden Chapel, built between 1834 and 1841. Here lie the tombs of two of Poland's first rulers, Mieszko I and Bolesław II the Bold, whose statues were carved by Chrystian Rauch.

The 16th-century tomb of Bishop Benedykt Izdbieński is the work of Jan Michałowicz of Urzędow, the celebrated sculptor of the Polish Renaissance.

Monument to the Victims of June 1956

⊞ Former Kaiser District

After the Second Partition of Poland in 1793, Poznań came under Prussian rule. In the second half of the 19th century, Prussia heightened its policy of Germanization in the region. One of its instruments was the German Union of the Eastern Marches (Deutscher Ostmarkenverein), which the Poles called the "Hakata" colonization commission from the acronym of the initials of its founders. When the city's ring of 19th-century fortifications was demolished, a decision was made to use the space for government buildings. Designed by German town planner Josef Stübben, the buildings were built between 1903 and 1914 and today stand amidst gardens, avenues and the royal academy. Dominating the scene is the Kaiserhaus Castle by Franz Schwechten, although little survives of its original splendour. Renamed the Zamek, it now houses the Zamek Cultural Centre. The **Monument to the Victims of June 1956**, which stands beside it in Plac Mickiewicza, takes the form of two large crosses. It was unveiled in 1981 to commemorate the victims of the Poznań's Workers' Uprising in 1956.

❺ Raczyński Palace

Pałac Raczyńskich

330 km (205 miles) W of Warsaw. Palace Museum: **Tel** (061) 813 8030. **Open** May–Sep: 9:30am–4pm Tue–Sat, 10am–6pm Sun; Oct–Apr: 9:30am–4pm Tue–Sun. **Closed** Mon. 🏛 free on Wed. 🎫 Ⓦ mnp.art.pl

Located in the village of Rogalin, Raczyński Palace is one of the most magnificent buildings in the region. The seat of many Polish nobles, it was begun around 1770 for Kazimierz Raczyński, Palatine of Wielkopolska and Grand Marshal of the Crown.

Although designed in the Baroque style, architectural ornamentation was abandoned during construction. The main building, however, retains its late Baroque solidity. Between 1782 and 1783, colonnades were added and complemented by annexes in the classic Palladian style. A drawing room and grand staircase designed by royal architect Jan Chrystian Kamsetzer were added between 1788 and 1789. A pavilion built between 1909 and 1912 contains a collection of Polish and European paintings dating from about 1850 to the early 20th century, including works by Jacek Malczewski and Jan Matejko.

The grounds contain formal gardens as well as one of the largest areas of protected oak woodland in Europe. The palace's Mausoleum Chapel, designed in the style of a Classical temple, contains the tombs of members of the Raczyński family.

Protected oak trees, Raczyński Palace grounds

❻ Toruń

Founded by the Teutonic knights in 1233, Toruń quickly became a major centre of trade. In 1454, when its citizens rebelled against the knights' rule, it passed to the kings of Poland. Famous as the birthplace of the astronomer Nicolaus Copernicus (1473–1543), the city is also renowned for its architecture. Picturesquely situated on the banks of the Vistula river, the Old Town of Toruń retains its medieval street plan, and has a rare calm, since most of the streets are closed to traffic.

A room in the 15th-century Copernicus House

The elaborate east end of the Gothic St Mary's Church

🎭 Wilam Horzyca Theatre

pl. Teatralny 1. **Tel** (056) 622 5022.
This delightful theatre, in the Art Nouveau style with Neo-Baroque elements, was built in 1904 by the Viennese architects Ferdinand Fellner and Hermann Helmer. The Kontakt Theatre Festival, held here each year, brings together performers from all over Europe drawing a large number of enthusiastic audiences to its performances.

⛪ St Mary's Church

ul. Marii Panny. **Tel** (056) 622 2603.
The Gothic St Mary's Church (Kościół Mariacki) was built for Franciscan monks between 1270 and 1300. It has a richly ornamented east gable. Late 14th-century wall paintings are in the southern aisle, while in the northern aisle is a 16th-century Mannerist organ loft, the oldest in Poland. By the presbytery is the mausoleum of Anna Vasa, sister of Zygmunt III, made in 1636. Although of royal blood, she could not be buried at Wawel Royal Castle (*see p193*) as she was of the Protestant faith.

🏛 Old Market Square

The Old Market Square (Stary Rynek) is the heart of the historic district. The centrepiece is the Town Hall. On the south side, at No. 7, is the Meissner Palace, built in 1739 for Jakob Meissner, the mayor of Toruń, and given a Neo-Classical façade in 1798. Star House, built in 1697 with an ornamented façade, is to the east. In the centre stands a monument to Nicolaus Copernicus, made by Friedrich Tiecek in 1853, and a fountain with the figure of a raftsman.

🏛 Town Hall

Rynek Staromiejski 1. Regional Museum: **Tel** (056) 660 5612.
Open Oct–Apr: 10am–4pm, Tue–Sun; May–Sep: 10am–6pm, Tue–Sun.
Closed Mon. 🄯 (ground floor free on Wed). Tower: **Open** May–Oct: 10am–8pm. 🄯

The Town Hall (Ratusz) was built between 1391 and 1399 as a two-storey edifice. In the 17th century, architect Antonis van Opbergen added the third floor and gave the building its Mannerist appearance. It now houses the **Regional Museum** of Gothic art and its **Tower** commands fine views.

🏛 Copernicus House

ul. Kopernika 15/17. **Tel** (056) 660 5683. **Open** May–Sep: 10am–6pm Tue–Sun; Oct–Apr: 10am–4pm Tue–Sun. 🄯 🆆 **muzeum.torun.pl**

These two neighbouring Gothic town houses from the 15th century are outstanding examples of Hanseatic merchants' houses. The painted façades and fine carving of the arched gables bear witness to the city's former wealth. The house at No. 17 was where Mikołaj Kopernik, Copernicus's father, lived. Although it may not be the house in which the astronomer Copernicus was born, it is now a museum (Muzeum Kopernika).

🏛 Crooked Tower

ul. Pod Krzywą Wieżą 1.
One of Toruń's greatest attractions, this tower (Krzywa Wieża) is part of the town's old fortification system, and was probably built in the first half of the 14th century. Although it leans significantly from the perpendicular, the floors that were added later are perfectly level – so that beer glasses in the pub that it now houses can be set down.

St Mary's Church, as viewed from the top of the Town Hall Tower

Castle of the Teutonic Knights

ul. Przedzamcze 3.

Little more than ruins remain of the castle that the Teutonic Knights began building in Toruń during the 13th century. Before the castle was built at Malbork, Toruń was the knights' capital. The castle was extended in the 14th century, however, it was destroyed in 1454 when the people rose in rebellion against the knights. Only the latrine tower – a tower overhanging a stream that acted as a sewer – was left standing, although part of the cellars and cloisters still survive.

The Gothic house that was built on the site in 1489, probably with materials scavenged from the castle, was the meeting house of the Brotherhood of St George.

New Market Square

The New Town emerged as a separate civic entity in 1264. Although it does not have as many historic buildings as the Old Town, it has a lively atmosphere. In summer, the Market Square (Rynek Nowomiejski) is filled with fruit and vegetable stalls. In the centre is a former Protestant church, built in 1824, probably by the German architect Karl Friedrich Schinkel. It has been converted into a gallery of contemporary art. Fine houses, some with ornate façades like that of the Baroque house at No. 17 surround the square. On the corner of ulica Królowej Jadwigi is the Golden Lion pharmacy, originating in the 15th century.

Malbork Castle, the great fortress on the Nogat river

ⓐ Malbork

316 km (196 miles) NW of Warsaw.
40,000. ul. Kościuszki
54, (055) 647 4747. **Open** summer.
zamek.malbork.pl

Malbork, the castle of the Teutonic knights, was begun in the 13th century. In 1309, it was made the capital of an independent state established by that order. The first major phase of building was the Assembly Castle, a fortified monastery later known as the Upper Castle. The Middle Castle was built after 1310, and includes the Palace of the Grand Master, a structure almost without equal in medieval Europe, built between 1382 and 1399 by Konrad Zöllner von Rotenstein (c. 1335–90), the 23rd Grand Master of the Teutonic Order. The Summer Refectory and Winter Refectory are alongside. The Upper Castle's inner courtyard is surrounded by slender Gothic arches with

Towering granite central column, Summer Refectory, Malbork

triangular vaulting. The partly reconstructed farm buildings in the Lower Castle, abutting the former Chapel of St Lawrence, have been converted into a hotel.

ⓑ Sopot

394 km (245 miles) NW of Warsaw.
38,000. ul. Dworcowa
4, (058) 550 3783. International
Festival of Song (Aug). sopot.pl

The most popular resort town on the Baltic coast, Sopot was established as a sea-bathing centre in 1824 by Jean Georges Haffner, a physician in the Napoleonic Army. Since the 17th century, Sopot has been favoured by the wealthy burghers of Gdańsk for their mansions. In the interwar years, it attracted some of the richest people in Europe. The pier is a continuation of the main street, colloquially known as Monciak. Considered the longest pier in Europe, it is 512 m (1,680 ft) long with a bench running all the way around it. Filled with bars and restaurants, the pier is a pleasant place to enjoy a beer and the sea air. Visitors also flock to the Art Deco Sofitel Grand Hotel *(see p220)*, built between 1924 and 1927, which overlooks the beach.

In the hills behind the town is the Opera in the Woods (Opera Leśna), built in 1909 and the venue for the International Festival of Song. Founded in 1961, this was once regarded as Eastern Europe's answer to the Eurovision Song Contest.

❾ Gdańsk

Among the finest cities of northern Europe, Gdańsk has a history that goes back more than 1,000 years. One of the wealthiest cities in Poland, it was completely destroyed during World War II, but a postwar rebuilding programme has restored many of its grand buildings. Most of the historic buildings are located along the pedestrianized ulica Długa and Long Market (Długi Targ) in the city centre. Despite severe war damage, the Old Town (Stare Miasto) retains a handful of churches, the most remarkable of which is the medieval Church of St Mary, dating back to the 14th century.

Sights at a Glance

① Monument to the Fallen
   Shipyard Workers
② Old Town Hall
③ Great Mill
④ Church of St Catherine
⑤ Gdańsk Crane
⑥ Church of St Mary
⑦ Great Armoury
⑧ Uphagen House
⑨ Main Town Hall
⑩ Artus Court
⑪ Central Maritime
⑫ National Museum

The Upland Gate, part of the fortifications of 1571–6

Key

▨ Major sight / Place of interest

▨ Pedestrian street

| 0 metres | 200 |
| 0 yards | 200 |

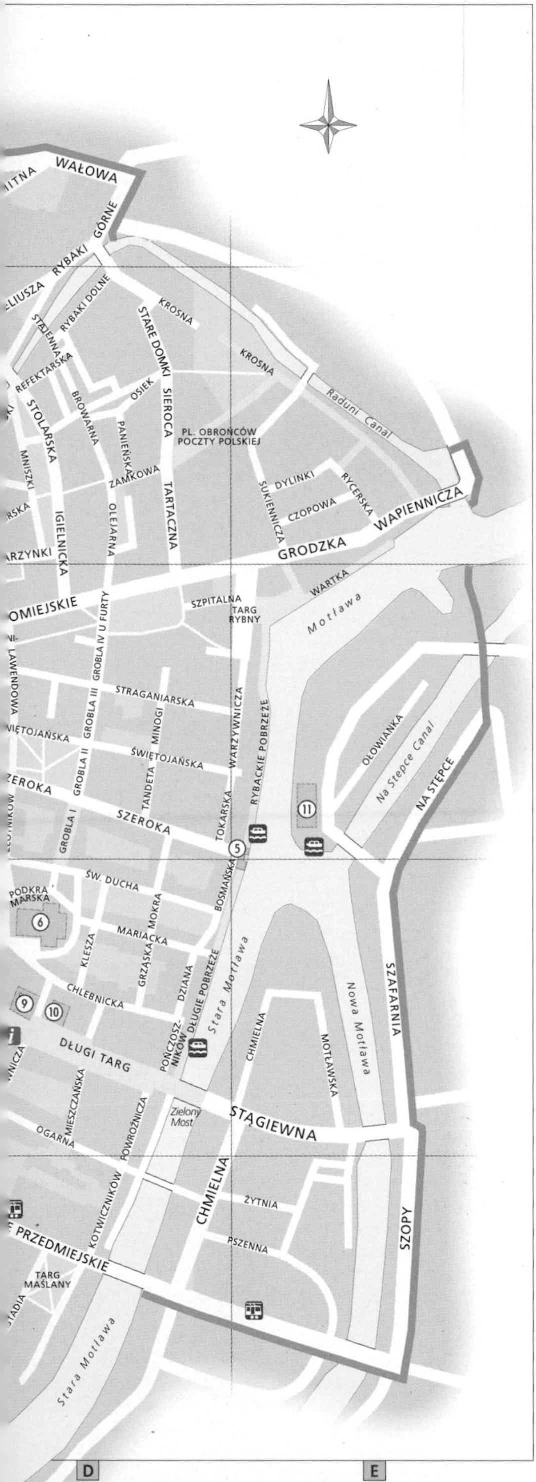

① Monument to the Fallen Shipyard Workers

Pomnik Poległych Stoczniowców

plac Solidarności. **Map** C1.

This monument was built a few months after the Gdańsk Shipyard workers' strike of 1980 and the creation of the first Independent Solidarity Trades Union *(see p172)*. Erected in honour of the shipyard workers who were killed during the first strike and demonstrations of December 1970, it stands 30 m (100 ft) from the spot where the first three victims fell. Its three stainless steel crosses, 42 m (130 ft) high, were intended both as a warning against such tragedies in the future, and as a symbol of hope and remembrance. The monument was designed by the shipyard workers along with a group of artists including Bogdan Pietruszka, Robert Pepliński, Wiesław Szyślak and Elżbieta Szczodrowska. It was built by a team of shipyard workers. In the 1980s, the cross was the rallying point for Solidarity demonstrations.

The towering Monument to the Fallen Shipyard Workers

The impressive façade of Great Mill

② Old Town Hall

Ratusz Starego Miasta

ul. Korzenna 33/35. **Map** C3.
Tel (058) 301 1051.

Built by Antonis van Opbergen between 1587 and 1595, the Old Town Hall is an outstanding example of Dutch Mannerist architecture. A compact building with no distinctive ornamentation, it is equipped with a strong defence tower. The stone door-way was probably made by artist Willem van der Meer at the end of the 16th century. Beneath each bracket are two distorted masks personifying Vice, and two smiling, chubby masks, representing Virtue.

Even though very little is left of the original decorative scheme of 1595, the paintings, sculptures and furniture within the Town Hall are fascinating. Of particular interest is the painted ceiling in one of the rooms by Hermann Hahn, a 17th-century artist from Pomerania. It was removed from a house at ulica Długa 39 and transferred to this building some time after 1900. The theme of the ceiling paintings are allegorical: the central one depicts The Lord's Blessing and the Polish King Zygmunt III also appears in the painting. Today, the building houses the Baltic Sea Culture Centre (Nadbałtyckie Centrum

Kultury). The main room on the ground floor houses a changing series of exhibitions devoted to local, regional, cultural and historical themes. In the main hall is the bronze figure of Jan Hevelius, a Polish astronomer and city councillor.

③ Great Mill

Wielki Młyn

ul. Wielkie Młyny 16. **Map** C2.
Open 10am–6pm Mon–Fri, 10am–3pm Sat.

The seven-storey Great Mill is regarded as one of the largest industrial buildings in medieval Europe. Construction began during the rule of the Teutonic Knights, who seized the town in 1308, and was completed around 1350. Built in brick, it is crowned by a tall and steeply pitched roof. The mill consisted of a two-storey bakery with a chimney set against its gable that reached the height of its roof. Also part of the mill were 12, later 18, large poles to which millstones were attached for grinding various types of grain. The mill was destroyed by fire in 1945, but was restored after World War II. This remarkably old edifice has now been con-verted into a modern shop-ping centre although traces of the original building still exist.

④ Church of St Catherine

Kościół św Katarzyny

ul. Profesorska 3. **Map** C2.
Tel (058) 301 1595.

The Church of St Catherine, or "Katy" as locals call it, was built between 1227 and 1239 by the dukes of Gdańsk-Pomerania. Regarded as the oldest and most important parish church in the Old Town, it underwent major rebuilding in the 14th century.

The 76-m (250-ft) high Baroque tower of the church was added in 1486. It also houses an impressive 49-bell carillon. A major landmark, the tower was demolished in 1944 and then rebuilt. It is well worth climbing to the top of the tower; the effort is rewarded by wonderful views of the city. The presbytery on the east side of the church has a fine late-Gothic gable. Most of the Gothic, Baroque and Mannerist furnishings that the church once contained were pillaged or destroyed in 1945 at the end of World War II. The most notable surviving pieces are paintings by Anton Möller and Izaak van den Blocke, the Baroque memorials to various townspeople and the tombstone of the Polish astronomer Jan Hevelius and his family, dating from 1659.

Gothic tower of the Church of St Catherine

Iconic Gdańsk Crane, a unique
medieval structure

⑤ Gdańsk Crane

Żuraw

ul. Szeroka 67/68. **Map** D3. Central
Maritime Museum: **Tel** (058) 301 6938.
Open 10am–4pm Tue–Sun (Jul & Aug:
to 6pm). **Closed** public hols.
🖼 W **nmm.pl**

One of the city's iconic
buildings, the Gdańsk Crane
was built in the 14th century
and renovated between 1442 and
1444. Its present appearance
combines the functions of a city
gate and a port crane.

The crane, a huge wooden
structure, is set between two
circular brick towers. It was
operated by men working the
huge treadmills within, and was
capable of lifting weights of up
to 2 tonnes (2 tons) to a height
of 27 m (90 ft). It was originally
used not only to load and unload
goods but also to fit masts to
ships. The Gdańsk Crane was
destroyed by fire in 1945. As part
of the rebuilding programme
after World War II, it was repaired
and reconstructed together
with its internal mechanism.
It is now part of the collection
of the **National Maritime
Museum** *(see p215)*.

The Crane Tower looks
out over ulica Długie Pobrzeże,
which runs alongside the
Motława river. The tower, once
known as the Long Bridge, was
originally a wooden footbridge
that functioned as a quay where
ships from all over the world
were moored. Today, yachts
offering trips around the port
of Gdańsk are moored here.

⑥ Church of St Mary

Kościół Mariacki

ul. Podkramarska 5. **Map** D4.
Tel (058) 301 3982. **Open** 9am–
6:30pm Mon–Sat, 1–6:30pm Sun (5pm
in winter). Tower: **Open** 9am–5pm
Mon–Sat, 1–5pm Sun. 🖼
W **bazylikamariacka.pl**

The Church of St Mary is the
largest medieval brick-built
church in Europe. Building
work began in 1343 and took
150 years to complete. The final
stage of construction, involving
the 100-m (325-ft) long nave,
was carried out by Henryk
Hetzel. From 1529 to 1945,
when it was destroyed, it was
a Protestant church. Like many
other parts of Gdańsk, it was
rebuilt after World War II. The
interior has Gothic, Mannerist
and Baroque furnishings. It
also contains several memorial
tablets to prominent local
families. The Tablet of the
Ten Commandments (1480–90)
depicts each of the commandments in two scenes, illustrating
obedience to and disregard of
the laws. The Tablet of Charity,
an ornate panel made in 1607
by Anton Möller, was used to
encourage churchgoers to
be generous. The memorial
tablet dedicated to Valentyn
von Karnitz of around 1590,
has many Dutch Mannerist
features. The centre painting
depicts the biblical tale of
the Lamentation of Abel.

The church has a number of
unique features, including the
Gothic sacrarium, which is in

Finely decorated façade of the monumental
Great Armoury

Anton Möller's decorative Tablet of Charity,
Church of St Mary

the shape of an open work
tower, decorated with pinnacles
and over 8 m (26 ft) high.
Also notable is the 15th-century
Madonna of Gdańsk, by an
unknown artist, in the church's
Chapel of St Anne. Another
attraction is the Astronomical
Clock made by Hans Durunger
between 1464 and 1470. It shows
the hour and also the day, dates
of moveable feasts and phases of
the moon. At noon, a procession
of figures representing Adam and
Eve, the Apostles, the Three Kings
and Death appears. The church's
402 steps leading to its 82-m
(270-ft) high **Tower**, offer
panoramic views of the city.

⑦ Great Armoury

Wielka Zbrojownia

ul. Targ Węglowy 6. **Map** C3. Academy
of Fine Arts: W **asp.gda.pl**

One of the finest examples of
the Dutch Mannerist style in
Gdańsk, the Great Armoury
was built, probably to plans
by Antonis van Opbergen in
collaboration with architect Jan
Strakowski, between 1600 and
1609. Today, the ground floor
of the former weapons and
ammunition store is filled with
shops, while the upper storeys
are occupied by the **Academy
of Fine Arts**. The building has
a façade with 17th-century
decorative carvings by
Wilhelm Barth.

The ornate Rococo doorway of Uphagen House

⑧ Uphagen House

Dom Uphagena

ul. Długa 12. **Map** C4. **Tel** (058) 301 2371.
Open 9am–1pm Mon, 9am–4pm Tue–Thu, 10am–6pm Fri & Sat, 10am–4pm Sun. 🎟 free on Mon. 🌐 mhmg.gda.pl

The house that originally stood here was acquired by Johann Uphagen, a town councillor, in 1775. He had it demolished, and a new residence was built in its place. The architect Johann Benjamin Dreyer completed the project in 1787. The result was an attractive building combining Baroque, Rococo and early Neo-Classical features. The sole ornamentation of the restrained façade is the Rococo decoration to the door, which is inscribed with the initial "A", for Abigail, the owner's wife.

⑨ Main Town Hall

Ratusz Głównego Miasta

ul. Długa 46/47. **Map** D4. Museum of the History of Gdańsk: **Tel** (058) 767 9100. **Open** 9am–1pm Mon, 9am–4pm Tue–Thu, 10am–6pm Fri & Sat, 10am–4pm Sun. 🎟 free on Mon. 🌐 mhmg.gda.pl

The city's first Town Hall was built after 1298 on the orders of Świętopełk II, Duke of Gdańsk-Pomerania. It functioned as an office of the Hanseatic League, a union of trading cities from the Baltic States to the North Sea.
   Work on the current building began in 1327. A tower was added between 1486 and 1488, during one of several phases of

rebuilding. After a fire in 1556, the Gothic structure was remodelled in the Mannerist style. The interior was lavishly decorated from 1593–1608 by prominent painters and craftsmen of the day, including Hans Vredeman de Vries, Izaak van den Blocke and Simon Herle. Their combined genius produced one of the finest town halls in all of northern Europe, proof of the city's wealth and power. It also served as a royal residence.
   The highlight of the Town Hall is the Red Room, which was once the Great Council Chamber. The Renaissance fireplace is by Willem van der Meer and the centrepiece of the ceiling paintings, the *Apotheosis of Gdańsk* (1608), by Izaak van den Blocke.
   After it was destroyed in 1945, it was rebuilt and many furnishings were reconstructed. It now houses the **Museum of the History of Gdańsk**.

⑩ Artus Court

Dwór Artusa

ul. Długi Targ 44. **Map** D4. **Open** 9am–1pm Mon, 9am–4pm Tue–Thu, 10am–6pm Fri & Sat, 10am–4pm Sun. 🎟 free on Mon. 🌐 mhmg.gda.pl

Originally established in the 14th century, Artus Court was a meeting place for the wealthy burghers of Gdańsk, who were inspired by the chivalrous traditions of King Arthur and the knights of the Round Table. Similar fraternities were set up throughout Europe, and they were particularly fashionable

St George killing the Dragon (1485) carving in Artus's Court

in the cities of the Hanseatic League. Visitors came to discuss the issues of the day and to enjoy the unlimited supply of fine beer that was served there.
   The original building was destroyed by fire in 1477 and reconstructed by 1481. Its rear elevation preserves the building's original Gothic style, but the façade was rebuilt twice – first in 1552 and again from 1616–17 by the architect and sculptor Abraham van den Blocke (1572–1628). Despite wartime destruction, reconstruction has succeeded in re-creating something of the court's historic atmosphere. One of the highlights of the interior is the intricately decorated 12-m (40-ft) high, 16th-century Renaissance tiled stove. The furnishings were changed several times, funded mainly by individual fraternities, who would gather for meetings on benches along the walls of the court.

The Red Room in the Main Town Hall

⑪ National Maritime Museum

Narodowe Muzeum Morskie

ul. Ołowianka 9–13. **Map** E3.
Tel (058) 301 8611. 🚌 106, 111, 138.
Open 10am–6pm Tue–Sun (to 4pm winter). **Closed** public hols. ♿
Ⓦ nmm.pl

In the 17th century, Poland strove to be "master of the Baltic Sea" and her seafarers were dedicated to maintaining the country's maritime presence. The themes of the displays in the National Maritime Museum are Gdańsk's seafaring traditions and navigation on the Vistula river. Exhibits include a reconstruction of scenes from a sailor's life aboard the Swedish ship *Solen*, sunk at the Battle of Oliwa in 1627 and raised from the seabed in the Gulf of Gdańsk in 1970.

The museum consists of buildings on both sides of the Motława river. The two sections are connected by a ferry that goes from one bank to another at regular intervals. On the west bank is the Gdańsk Crane *(see p213).* Period Gdańsk, a reconstruction of a merchant's office in the Harbour Town Life exhibition, is one of the highlights here. The adjoining Skład Kolonialny contains an interesting collection of boats from distant parts of the world. The main museum is in a series of grain houses on the east bank. The naval weapons on display here include 17th-century Polish cannons, as well as ones taken from the Swedish warship *Solen*. The exhibits in the adjacent granaries are dedicated to the naval presence of Poland and Gdańsk from the Middle Ages to the present day, and include waxworks depicting Polish sailors. *Sołdek*, the first Polish ocean-going ship to be constructed after World War II, was built in the Gdańsk Shipyard. It is permanently anchored in Motława river and its holds are now used for exhibitions.

Sołdek, used as an exhibition space by the Central Maritime Museum

⑫ National Museum

Muzeum Narodowe

ul. Toruńska 1. **Map** C5. **Tel** (058) 301 6804. 🚌 111, 112, 120, 166, 178, 186. 🚋 8, 13. **Open** May–Sep: 10am–5pm Tue–Sun; Oct–Apr: 9am–4pm Tue–Fri, 10am–5pm Sat, Sun. ♿ free on Fri.
Ⓦ muzeum.narodowe.gda.pl

The National Museum is laid out in a former Gothic Franciscan monastery from 1422–1522. It was set up due to the efforts of Rudolf Freitag, a lecturer at the Royal School of Fine Arts, in 1872. It was closed during World War II and was reopened as the City Museum after the war. The impressive museum was also known as the Pomeranian Museum till 1952 before being elevated to the rank of National Museum in 1972. The museum contains a wealth of artifacts, from wrought-iron grilles to

The Griffin's Talons on display in the National Museum

sculpture, painting, ceramics, gold jewellery, goldwork, metalwork and furniture. Exhibits are spread over three floors. Gothic art and gold jewellery are displayed on the ground floor and paintings on the first. The upper floor holds temporary exhibitions.

The museum's most prized piece is *The Last Judgement*, by the Flemish painter Hans Memling (c. 1430–94). The central panel of the triptych depicts the Last Judgement, while the panel on the left represents the Gates of Heaven and the one on the right portrays the Torments of Hell. In 1473, it was plundered by privateers from Gdańsk from a ship bound for Italy. Other fascinating exhibits are *The Griffin's Talons*, a 15th century bison-horn cup belonging to a sailing fraternity, and the Longcase Clock. This Rococo clock, made in around 1750, is decorated with scenes from the biblical story of Tobias and the Raising of the Copper Snake.

The Last Judgement (1467) by Hans Memling, National Museum

Practical & Travel Information

Since the fall of Communism in 1989, tourism in Poland has greatly increased. Foreign visitors are drawn to the country for its history, folk culture, great architecture and unique scenic beauty. The quality of service has improved, especially in banks. New hotels have sprung up, many of which are cheaper than those in Western Europe. The best-equipped hotels and restaurants are, however, expensive.

When to Visit

The best time to travel to Poland is late spring or early autumn, when temperatures are usually pleasantly warm and the coastal, lakeside and mountain resorts are not too crowded. The big cities, by contrast, are noticeably quieter in summer; this is also when theatres close for the holiday season. However, other events such as festivals take place during summer. After the summer season, many guest-houses, hotels, clubs and restaurants in coastal resorts and other popular lakeside spots close. The skiing season runs from the end of November to mid-March.

Documentation

Citizens of all European Union (EU) countries, Canada, New Zealand and Australia can stay in Poland without a visa for up to 90 days. Beyond that, it is necessary to apply for a residence permit. Visitors of other nationalities should contact the Polish Embassy in their respective country for entry requirements.

Visitor Information

Information centres can be found in most towns and cities. Travel agencies such as **Polish National Tourist Office** can advise on tickets, trains and accommodation. Information is also available at train stations. Hotel employees are often very helpful.

Health and Security

Citizens of the EU and the European Economic Area (EEA) are entitled to free medical treatment in Poland provided they have their European Health Insurance Card (EHIC). For citizens of other countries, transport to hospitals is provided free of charge in case of emergencies, but treatment of serious health problems may incur a fee. Visitors are advised to take out full medical insurance before arriving and always carry policy documents and passport for identification at the hospital during medical emergencies. An ambulance service is available 24 hours a day from any private clinic.

Polish cities suffer from the same security problems and crime as most European capitals, so visitors should stay alert for petty thefts and pick-pockets. They should take extra care of their belongings in busy railway stations, especially in Warsaw. Theft in overnight trains is an increasing menace so it is important to keep compartment doors locked.

Banking and Currency

The official Polish currency is the *złoty*, which is divided into 100 *groszy*. Money can be changed at *kantor* (exchange bureaus), many of which offer better rates than banks. Most banks will cash traveller's cheques, although the transactions are time consuming. The majority of banks are open from 8am to 6pm. ATMs can be found in most towns and cities and accept most international credit cards.

Communications

The most inexpensive way to make international calls is on pre-paid phone cards, which can be bought at most kiosks. Another option is to call from one of the phone-card-operated machines. For long-distance calls, rates are highest between 8am and 6pm. Local calls are cheapest from 10pm to 6am. Poczta Polska, the Polish post office, is open from 8am to 8pm on weekdays. GSM mobile phones have coverage all over Poland; it is best to buy a pre-paid SIM card from local operators. There are also Internet cafés and free WiFi areas all over the country, but connections outside the capital tend to be slow.

Facilities for the Disabled

Poland has a poor record for providing for disabled people but this is changing rapidly. All renovated and new public buildings have ramps or lifts built into them, and special taxis are also available. Nevertheless, many traditional sites of interest may still be poorly equipped. For general advice or information about sites, contact the **Disabled People's National Council**.

The Climate of Poland

Poland's climate is influenced by cold polar air from Scandinavia and sub-tropical air from the south. Polar-continental fronts dominate in winter, bringing crisp, frosty weather and snow. Winters in the north can be particularly cold. In contrast, late summer and autumn (the most popular times to visit) offer plenty of warm sunny days.

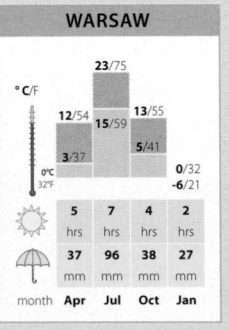

WARSAW			
°C/F	23/75		
	12/54	15/59	13/55
	3/37		5/41
0°C 32°F			0/32 -6/21
5 hrs	7 hrs	4 hrs	2 hrs
37 mm	96 mm	38 mm	27 mm
month **Apr**	**Jul**	**Oct**	**Jan**

Arriving by Air

International flights from some 90 cities in 40 countries arrive in Warsaw. The airports at Gdańsk, Katowice, Szczecin, Poznań, Wrocław, and Krakow also have international flights, linking Poland with Western Europe as well as Bucharest, Budapest, Prague, Sofia and the capitals of the former Soviet Bloc. Some 25 airlines, including **British Airways**, **Air France**, **SAS** (Scandinavia) and **Lufthansa** (Germany), operate from **Warsaw Okęcie Airport**, which also has direct connections with Canada, the US, Israel and Thailand. Most cities including Krakow and Gdańsk are served by budget airlines such as **Ryanair**, **easyJet** and **Wizzair**.

Rail Travel

Poland is covered by a dense network of railway lines. International train services run between all major Polish and European cities. The journeys by fast train from Warsaw to Prague and Berlin take just 6 and 9 hours respectively. Most big cities are connected by express lines. The **Polish Rail Network** (PKP) operates a range of trains, out of which **InterCity** and express trains are the fastest and are usually punctual. InterCity trains are the most comfortable and expensive, but also serve snacks on board. InterCity trains have special compartments for women with children and the disabled. Ordinary trains, such as Osobowy and Tanie Linie Kolejowe, are reasonable. Express trains and sleeping cars are expensive. Tickets can be booked through InterCity's website. The official website **Rozkład** offers information on timetables and fares.

Suburban routes are served by electric trains, some of which are open-plan, double-decker carriages. Tickets can be booked at railway stations. The main station in the capital is **Warsaw Central**.

Travelling by Bus

Polish Motor Transport, Polska Komunikacja Samochodowa (PKS), serves most of Poland's long-distance routes. Local buses are sometimes the only means of getting to smaller towns and villages. These services are generally efficient, although before 8am and in the afternoon, they may be crowded. Tickets are usually bought in advance from the bus station's *kasa* (ticket offices).

Travelling by Car

There are very few motorways, and those that exist are generally in poor condition, but each year new routes are added to the promised network of highways spanning the entire country.

When driving, always carry your passport, car insurance, Green Card, licence and, if applicable, rental contract. If using a foreign car, the international symbol of its country of origin must be displayed. Seat belts need to be fastened at all times; use of mobile phones while driving is illegal. Follow speed limits and switch on headlights even during the day. All the major international car rental companies, including **Avis** and **Hertz**, operate out of Warsaw and Krakow.

Arriving by Ferry

Poland's main port is the **Gdańsk Ferry Terminal** and ships from Scandinavian countries dock here. There are ferries between Gdynia's port and Kaelskrona, Sweden. Information can be found through the agency Polish National Tourist Office.

DIRECTORY

Documentation

w visitpoland.com

Embassies

Australia
ul. Nowogrodzka 11, Warsaw.
Tel (022) 521 3444.
w poland.embassy.gov.au

Canada
ul. Matejki 1/5, Warsaw.
Tel (022) 584 3100.
w canada.pl

New Zealand
al.Ujazdowskie 51, Warsaw.
Tel (022) 521 0500.
w nzembassy.com/poland

United Kingdom
ul. Kawalerii 12, Warsaw.
Tel (022) 311 0000.
w ukinpoland.fco.gov.uk

United States
al. Ujazdowskie 29/31, Warsaw.
Tel (022) 504 2000.
w poland. usembassy.gov

Visitor Information

Orbis
w poland.travel

Emergency

Ambulance, Fire and Police
Tel 112.

Road Emergencies
Tel 981.

Facilities for the Disabled

Disabled People's National Council
ul. Andersa 13, Warsaw.
Tel (022) 530 6570.

Arriving by Air

Air France
w airfrance.com

British Airways
w britishairways.com

easyJet
w easyjet.com

Lufthansa
w lufthansa.com

Ryanair
w ryanair.com

SAS
w flysas.com

Wizzair
w wizzair.com

Warsaw Okęcie Airport
Tel (022) 650 4220.

Rail Travel

InterCity
w intercity.pl

Polish Rail Network
w pkp.pl

Rozkład
w rozklad.pkp.pl

Warsaw Central
Tel (022) 94 36.

Travelling by Car

Avis
Tel (012) 629 6108.
w avis.pl

Hertz
Tel (012) 429 6262.
w hertz.com.pl

Arriving by Ferry

Gdańsk Ferry Terminal
Tel (058) 343 1887.

Shopping & Entertainment

Poland is a great place to pick up memorable souvenirs. These range from handicrafts to beautiful silver and amber jewellery, and hand-embroidered tablecloths, porcelain and ceramic items. Thick, hand-knitted woollen sweaters and ornamented leather slippers can be found in local markets around the country. Vodka, the national drink, is available in various flavours. The country has a vibrant cultural life and there are plenty of jazz clubs, nightclubs, casinos, theatres, opera venues, cinemas and concert halls in all the big cities. In summer, many smaller resorts host folk music festivals or jousting tournaments.

Opening Hours

Shops are open from 10am to 6pm Monday to Friday and 10am to 2pm on Saturdays. In the larger cities, shops usually close at 7pm, with most of the department stores staying open for an extra hour until 8pm. All shops are closed on public holidays, with the exception of some pharmacies and food shops.

Markets and Malls

The majority of Poles buy fruit, vegetables and delicatessen products from markets such as **Stary Kleparz** in Krakow and **Hala Targowa** in Gdańsk. Household goods and fashionable clothes are increasingly sold in big shopping malls situated just outside city centres. Among the largest malls are **Złote Tarasy**, next to Warsaw's central station, and **Galeria Krakowska** near Krakow's main station.

Art and Crafts

Many visitors to Poland return home with contemporary paintings, prints and posters, which are available at very reasonable prices. Paintings on glass, with traditional or modern designs, are sold in many galleries around the country. Galleries in Warsaw include **Zapiecek** and **Art Gallery ZPAP** (Union of Polish Artists and Designers), while in Krakow there is **Kocioł Artystyczny**. The range of folk art and handicrafts in Poland is truly impressive and almost every region has its own speciality. Painted Easter eggs and Christmas

tree ornaments are distinctive examples of folk art. All these items, as well as hand-woven tapestries, embroidered tablecloths and doilies and leather goods are sold in outlets of the **Cepelia** chain found in Warsaw and other big cities.

Antiques

In most towns throughout Poland, antiques and collectables are sold in *Desa* shops (auction houses). In Wrocław, **Antykwariat Daes** also sells antique products.

Gifts and Souvenirs

Some of the best Polish souvenirs are porcelain and pottery products. The most renowned make is Ćmielów porcelain, which is available all over the country. Traditional ceramics are also popular, especially the white and navy-blue crockery decorated with circles and small stylized flowers. **Bolesławiec** and Cepelia are good places to find them. Also worth shopping for is Poland's high-quality modern glass and traditional cut glass or crystal. A variety of designs is available, hand-cut on perfectly transparent glass.

Jewellery

Silver jewellery is a speciality of Polish craftsmen. It is relatively cheap and comes in a variety of sophisticated, modern designs. Amber jewellery is also extremely popular. This is sold at a range of outlets, but to avoid the risk of buying a fake it is best to go to

an established shop. Most Polish amber comes from the Gulf of Gdańsk, and the Old Town has several reliable outlets, including **Bursztynowa Komnata** and **Nord Amber Gallery**.

Food and Drink

A good souvenir from Poland could be a jar of dried *ceps* (porcini mushrooms), honey, smoked eel or dried sausage. The best places to buy such items are bazaars and markets such as Hala Mirowska near Plac Mirowski in Warsaw, Stary Kleparz in Krakow, Plac Wielkopolski in Poznań or in the market halls of Wrocław and Gdańsk. Polish sweets are of a high quality, and chocolates made by the Warsaw firm **Wedel** and the Krakow firm **Wawel** are particularly esteemed. Polish liquor is internationally renowned, especially the pure vodka, which is available in a bewildering array of varieties. Another popular spirit is *żubrówka*, a vodka with an unusual herbal flavour. Polish mead is equally distinctive. Made with honey according to traditional recipes, it is the accompaniment to dessert.

Nightlife

Warsaw is a major nightlife destination with a host of clubs offering live music or DJ-driven dance events. **Hybrydy** has been hosting a well-balanced mixture of gigs and club nights for over 45 years. Krakow is bursting with nightlife activity with a host of characterful bars and clubs grouped around the main square. Elsewhere, Poznań's Przemysław Castle's boiler room makes for a unique jazz venue, the **Blue Note Club**.

In Your Pocket guide provides up-to-date listings on their website.

Theatre

Poland has over 80 theatres scattered across its cities. In Warsaw, the most popular theatre is the **Ateneum**, which specializes in comedy shows. The **Teatr Żydowski** (Jewish Theatre) presents spectacles in Yiddish and is the only such place in the country. In Krakow, **Teatr Stary** is considered one of the country's best theatres. In Warsaw, information about advance booking for cultural events can be found at **Kasy ZASP**. In Krakow, tickets can be bought in advance at the **Cultural Information Centre**. Local tourist information offices can also provide information on shows and booking procedures.

Musicals, Opera and Ballet

Musicals, opera and ballet can provide the best form of entertainment even for those who do not speak Polish. Operettas and musicals are performed at **Opera i Operetka** in Krakow and at **Roma** in Warsaw. For opera-lovers, the productions of the **Great Theatre** (Teatr Wielki) in Warsaw are recommended. There are also opera houses in Gdańsk, Wrocław, Poznań and Krakow. Poland's two best ballet companies perform in the **Teatr Wielki** in Warsaw and Poznań.

Classical and Folk Music

There are over 20 classical orchestras in Poland and they perform in almost all of its big cities. Particularly renowned are the **National Philharmonic Orchestra** (Filharmonia Narodowa) in Warsaw, the **Filharmonia Bałtycka** in Gdańsk and the **Poznań Philharmonia**, which performs in the University Hall. Classical music shows are held in museums, churches and palaces throughout the year. In the rest of the country, many bands perform the traditional folk music of individual regions, but it can be difficult to track down their concerts. The best chance of seeing them is at various music festivals in the summer. Many folk groups also perform in concerts organized by hotels or tourist agencies. Tickets can be bought from the Cultural Information Centre.

Festivals

Poland hosts several local and international festivals. A major theatre festival is the Malta International Drama Festival, held from late June to early July in the streets and theatres of Poznań. In Warsaw, the Street Theaters Festival runs throughout the summer. Opera festivals, such as the Mozart Festival in Warsaw, and Poznan's ballet festivals are also popular. For those interested in religious music, the Wratislava Cantans are held in September in Wrocław. Jazz festivals are also quite renowned in Poland and major events include the Warsaw Jazz Jamboree, Jazz on the Oder in Wrocław (May) and Jazz All Souls' Day in Krakow (early November).

DIRECTORY

Markets and Malls

Galeria Krakowska
ul. Pawia 5, Krakow.
Tel (012) 428 9900.

Hala Targowa
ul. Pańska, Gdańsk.

Stary Kleparz
Rynek Kleparski, Krakow.

Złote Tarasy
ul. Złota 59, Warsaw.
Tel (022) 222 2200.

Art and Crafts

Art Gallery ZPAP
ul. Krakowskie Przedmieście 17, Warsaw.
Tel (022) 828 5170.

Cepelia
W cepelia.pl

Kocioł Artystyczny
ul. Sławkowska 14 (1st floor), Krakow.
Tel (012) 429 1797.

Zapiecek
ul. Zapiecek 1, Warsaw.
Tel (022) 831 9918.

Antiques

Antykwariat Daes
pl. Kościuszki 15, Wrocław.
Tel (071) 343 7280.

Gifts and Souvenirs

Bolesławiec
ul. Prosta 2/14, Warsaw.
Tel (022) 624 8408.

Jewellery

Bursztynowa Komnata
ul. Długie Pobrzeże 1, Gdańsk.
Tel (058) 346 2717.

Nord Amber Gallery
ul. Mariacka 44/45, Gdańsk.
Tel (058) 305 5550.

Food and Drink

Wedel
ul. Szpitalna 8, Warsaw.
Tel (022) 827 2916.

Wawel
Rynek Główny 33, Krakow.
Tel (012) 423 1247.

Nightlife

Blue Note Club
W bluenote.poznan.pl

Hybrydy
W hybrydy.com.pl

In Your Pocket
W inyourpocket.com

Theatre

Ateneum
ul. Jaracza 2, Warsaw.
Tel (022) 625 2421.

Cultural Information Centre
ul. św Jana 2, Krakow.
W karnet.krakow.pl

Kasy ZASP
al. Jerozolimskie 25, Warsaw.
Tel (022) 621 9454.

Teatr Stary
pl. Szczepański 1, Krakow. **Tel** (012) 422 4040.

Teatr Żydowski
pl. Grzybowski 12/16, Warsaw.
Tel (022) 620 6281.

Musicals, Opera and Ballet

Opera i Operetka
ul. Lubicz 48, Krakow.
Tel (012) 296 6100.

Roma
ul. Nowogrodzka 49, Warsaw.
Tel (022) 628 7071.

Teatr Wielki
pl. Tatralny 1, Warsaw.
Tel (022) 692 0200.

Classical and Folk Music

Filharmonia Bałtycka
ul. Ołowianka 1, Gdańsk.
Tel (058) 320 6262.

National Philharmonic Orchestra
ul. Sienkiewicza 10, Warsaw.
Tel (022) 551 7111.

Poznań Philharmonia
ul. św Marcin 81, Poznań.
Tel (061) 852 4708.

Where to Stay

Warsaw

Chmielna Guesthouse ⓩ
B&B **Map** D4
ul. Chmielna 13, 00-021
Tel *(022) 828 1282*
Ⓦ www.chmielnabb.pl
Small, but charming rooms (some
with shared facilities) grouped
around a common lounge.

DK Choice

Rialto ⓩⓩ
Design
ul. Wilcza 73, 00-670
Tel *(022) 584 8700*
Ⓦ hotelrialto.com.pl
Within walking distance of
the central station, this elegant
hotel has an Art Deco theme.
Every detail down to the light
fittings, faithfully reproduces
the "Roaring Twenties". Modern
amenities and helpful staff.

Sofitel Victoria ⓩⓩ
Business **Map** C3
ul. Królewska 11, 00-065
Tel *(022) 657 8011*
Ⓦ sofitel.com
Facing central Warsaw's lush
Saxon Gardens, Sofitel offers well-
furnished rooms with all amenities.

Hotel Bristol ⓩⓩⓩ
Historic **Map** D3
Krakowskie Przedmiescie 42/44, 00/325
Tel *(022) 551 1000*
Ⓦ hotelbristolwarsaw.pl
Luxurious *fin de siècle* building
with a guest list that spans
presidents and rock stars.

Rest of Poland

GDAŃSK: Happy Seven ⓩ
Hostel **Map** E2
ul. Grodzka 16, 80-841
Tel *(058) 320 8601*
Ⓦ happyseven.com
Centrally located in a medieval
building offering a mix of private
singles, doubles, triples and dorms.

GDAŃSK: Wolne Miasto ⓩⓩ
Historic **Map** D4
ul. Św. Ducha 2, 80-834
Tel *(058) 322 2442*
Ⓦ hotelwm.pl
A row of reconstructed tenement
buildings that hide well-equipped
rooms. The accommodation
captures the spirit of pre-War
Danzig, with sepia photos of
the city in its heyday.

Art Deco interior at the Rialto
in Warsaw

GDAŃSK: Podewils ⓩⓩⓩ
Boutique **Map** E4
ul. Szafarnia 2, 80-755
Tel *(058) 300 9560*
Ⓦ podewils.pl
Full of antiques and oil paintings, this
Baroque-style old-world residence
overlooks Gdańsk's marina.

KRAKOW: Mundo Hostel ⓩ
Hostel **Map** D5
ul. Sarego 10, 31-047
Tel *(012) 422 6113*
Ⓦ mundohostel.eu
Comfortable boutique hostel
with ethnic textiles and *objets
d'art*. Offers private double rooms.

KRAKOW: Pollera ⓩⓩ
Historic **Map** D5
ul. Szpitalna 32, 31-024
Tel *(012) 422 1044*
Ⓦ pollera.com.pl
An Art-Nouveau classic, Pollera
was opened in 1834 and has
welcomed guests with style
and grace ever since.

DK Choice

KRAKOW: Hotel Stary ⓩⓩⓩ
Luxury **Map** D5
ul. Szczepańska 5, 31-011
Tel *(012) 384 0808*
Ⓦ stary.hotel.com.pl
Once a merchant's residence, the
hotel retains many of the original
features that include high ceilings
and plenty of exposed brick and
stone. There is a swimming pool
in an arched red-brick basement.
The hotel also offers facilities for
saunas and has a spa centre that
features salt inhalation among
its treatments.

Price Guide

Prices are based on one night's stay in
high season for a standard double room,
inclusive of service charges and taxes.

ⓩ	under 200 zloty
ⓩⓩ	200 to 400 zloty
ⓩⓩⓩ	over 400 zloty

MALBORK: Stary Malbork ⓩⓩ
Historic
ul. 17 Marca 26, 82-200
Tel *(055) 647 2400*
Ⓦ hotelstarymalbork.com.pl
A 19th-century Roman-Gothic
building with comfortable
rooms, many with big half-
moon windows. It also boasts
a small bar, restaurant and
cosy fireplace.

POZNAŃ: IBB Andersia ⓩⓩⓩ
Design
Plac Andersa 3, 61-894
Tel *(061) 667 8000*
Ⓦ andersiahotel.pl
Located in Poznań's tallest
building, the Andersia Tower,
this superbly-equipped hotel
offers minimalist rooms with
great views.

SOPOT: Villa Baltica ⓩⓩ
Luxury
ul. Emiliii Plater 1, 81-777
Tel *(058) 555 2800*
Ⓦ villabaltica.com
Chic rooms, some with sea
views, in a historic building
that also boasts of a modern
spa centre, which offers
a full range of luxury
beauty treatments.

TORUŃ: Petite Fleur ⓩⓩ
Boutique
Piekary 25, 87-100
Tel *(056) 621 5100*
Ⓦ petitefleur.pl
Intimate Old-Town hotel
with smart en suites, attention-
to-detail service and a
good restaurant.

WROCŁAW: Stop Wrocław ⓩ
B&B
ul. Sienkiewicza 31, 50-349
Tel *519 115 075*
Ⓦ stopwroclaw.pl
Pretty 19th-century town house
near the Botanical Garden, with
small, characterful rooms.

WROCŁAW: Granary ⓩⓩⓩ
Design
Mennicza 24, 50-057
Tel *(071) 395 2600*
Ⓦ thegranaryhotel.com
Lovingly restored red-brick
granary that has luxurious
suites, each with a kitchenette.

For map references *see pp174–5 (Warsaw), 184–5 (Krakow) & 210–11 (Gdańsk)*

Where to Eat and Drink

Warsaw

Browarmia ㉵㉵
Brewery Restaurant **Map** D3
ul. Królewska 1, 00-065
Tel *(022) 826 5455*
Busy beer hall with copper brewing vats at the back that has great grilled meats that go well with Browarmia's own brew.

Papaya ㉵㉵㉵
Asian fusion **Map** D4
ul. Foksal 16, 00-372
Tel *(022) 826 4851*
Über-cool restaurant serving imaginative oriental meat and seafood dishes.

Sekret ㉵㉵㉵
Polish **Map** D2
ul. Jezuicka 1/3, 00-272
Tel *(022) 635 7474*
Stylish restaurant close to the Royal Castle and set in a maze of 16th-century cellars; has a vast menu of traditional roast meat and game dishes.

Rest of Poland

GDAŃSK: A la Francaise ㉵㉵
French **Map** E4
ul. Spichrzowa 24/1, 80-750
Tel *(058) 765 1112*
Delightful café-restaurant, which features soups, baguette sandwiches, pancakes and delicious pastries and eclairs on the menu.

DK Choice

GDAŃSK: Kubicki ㉵㉵
Polish **Map** E3
ul. Wartka 5, 80-841
Tel *(058) 301 0050*
Run by the same family since 1919, this legendary eatery is full of vintage furniture. The food reflects traditions of Poland's Baltic cities and includes meaty specialities like *golonka* (roast pork knuckle) as well as halibut, herring and sole. Traditional desserts such as such as *sernik* (cheesecake) are worth a try.

GDAŃSK: Pod Lososiem ㉵㉵㉵
Gourmet **Map** C3
ul. Szeroka 52/54, 80-835
Tel *(058) 301 7652*
Opulent restaurant with classic seafood and game. Frequented by celebrities.

KRAKOW: Zapiecek ㉵
Polish **Map** C1
ul. Sławkowska 32, 31-015
Tel *(012) 422 7495*
Something of a temple for Polish *pierogi*, or stuffed dumplings, which are served in a range of fillings, with savoury, sweet and baked versions well represented.

KRAKOW: Zazie Bistro ㉵
French **Map** D4
ul. Józefa 34, 31-056
Tel *500 410 829*
Busy bistro serving everything from onion soup to bouillabaisse and mussels with fries.

KRAKOW: Studio
Qulinarne ㉵㉵㉵
Gourmet **Map** D5
ul. Gazowa 4, 30-060
Tel *(012) 430 6941*
Original menu conjured through an inventive blend of Polish ingredients, Mediterranean style and Oriental spices.

MALBORK: Gothic ㉵㉵
International
Starościńska 1, 80-200
Tel *(055) 647 0889*
Located in the Teutonic Castle, Gothic serves a combination of varied international and Polish cuisine with elements of traditional medieval cooking.

POZNAŃ: Petit Paris ㉵
Café/Patisserie
ul. Polwiejska 32, 61-888
Tel *(061) 667 1555*
Serves delicious baguette sandwiches, soups, salads, quiche, pastries and more from its location inside the Stary Browar mall.

POZNAŃ: Zagroda
Bamberska ㉵㉵
Polish
ul. Kościelna 43, 60-534
Tel *(061) 842 7790*

The bar at Studio Qulinarne, Krakow

Traditional regional dishes such as roast duck with cranberry sauce in a 19th-century farm-style building.

POZNAŃ: Nowa
Bażanciarnia ㉵㉵㉵
Polish
Stary Rynek 94, 61-772
Tel *(061) 855 3358*
Elegant restaurant serving superb Polish fare including rabbit, pheasant and roast duck.

SOPOT: Tropikalna Wyspa ㉵
Café Restaurant
Sopot beach; end of
ul. Traugutta, 81-769
Tel *(058) 692 8833*
Summer-season cafe-restaurant right on the beach, serving pork-and-sauerkraut staples, fried or baked Baltic fish together with a tempting array of alcoholic drinks.

TORUŃ: Restaurant 1231 ㉵㉵
International
Przedzamcze 6, 87-100
Tel *(056) 619 0917*
Refined Polish and Italian fare, with good steaks and excellent freshwater and Mediterranean fish.

WROCŁAW: Machina Organika ㉵
Vegetarian
Ruska 19, 50-101
Tel *534 088 360*
Choose from the wide range of soups, mains and fruit-cocktails served under a timber ceiling.

WROCŁAW: Akropol na
Solnym ㉵㉵
Greek
plac Solny 18/19, 50-063
Tel *511 421 440*
Contemporary restaurant that offers grilled meats, lamb roasts and lots of Aegean seafood with style and imagination.

WROCŁAW: Mosaiq
㉵㉵㉵
International
św. Mikołaja 12, 50-001
Tel *530 306 605*
French-Polish-Italian fare including steaks, seafood and pasta. Excellent wine list.

CZECH REPUBLIC

The Czech Republic is one of Europe's youngest states. In the years after World War II, foreign visitors to what was then Czechoslovakia rarely ventured further than the capital, Prague. Today, the country's beautifully preserved medieval towns, palaces and castles, which were neglected during the Communist era, are attracting an ever-increasing number of visitors.

Landlocked in Central Europe, the Czech Republic is divided into two regions – Bohemia and Moravia. Rolling plains and lush, pine-clad mountains, dotted with medieval châteaux and 19th-century spa resorts characterize the landscape of southern and western Bohemia. However, much of northern Bohemia has been given over to mining and other heavy industries, with devastating effects on the local environment. Moravia has orchards and vineyards in the south, and a broad industrial belt in the north of the region. Prague, Bohemia's largest city and the capital of the Czech Republic, is a thriving cultural and commercial centre. Its wealth of great architecture, spanning over 1,000 years, has withstood the ravages of two world wars in the last century.

History

From 500 BC, the area now known as the Czech Republic was settled by Celtic tribes, who were later joined by Germanic peoples. The first Slavs, the forefathers of the Czechs, came to the region around AD 500. Struggles for supremacy led to the emergence of a ruling dynasty, the Přemyslids, at the start of the 9th century. The Přemyslids were involved in many family feuds and in 935 Prince Wenceslas was murdered by his brother, Boleslav. Later canonized, Wenceslas became Bohemia's best-known patron saint.

The reign of Holy Roman Emperor Charles IV in the 14th century heralded a Golden Age for Bohemia. Charles chose Prague as his imperial residence and founded many institutions there, including Central Europe's first university.

Ruins of a castle on top of a hill, a common sight in the Czech Republic

◀ Lavishly decorated interior of Prague Castle

In the early 15th century, Central Europe lived in fear of an incredible fighting force – the Hussites, followers of the reformer Jan Hus, who attacked the corrupt practices of the Catholic church. Hus's execution in 1415 led to the Hussite Wars.

At the start of the 16th century, the Austrian Habsburgs took over the region and went on to rule for almost 400 years. Religious turmoil led, in 1618, to the Protestant revolt and the Thirty Years' War. The 19th century saw a period of Czech national revival and the burgeoning of civic pride. However, it was not until 1918 and the collapse of the Habsburg Empire that the independent

Engraving showing the reformer Jan Hus being burnt at the stake

republic of Czechoslovakia was declared. World War II brought German occupation, followed by four decades of Communism. In 1968, a programme of liberal reforms (the Prague Spring) was introduced, but it was swiftly quashed by Soviet leaders. The overthrow of Communism did not come until November 1989, when a protest rally against police brutality led to the Velvet Revolution – a series of mass demonstrations and strikes that resulted in the resignation of the existing regime. In 1993, the peaceful division of Czechoslovakia resulted in the creation of two independent states – Slovakia and the Czech Republic.

Language and Culture

Under the Habsburgs, Czech identity was largely suppressed and the Czech language became little more than a dialect. In the 19th century, however, Austrian rule relaxed, and the Czechs began rediscovering their own culture. Czech was re-established as an official language, thanks to the historian František Palacký, who also wrote the first history of the Czech nation.

Since the Golden Age of the 14th century, Prague has prided itself on its reputation as a flourishing cultural centre. In the early 20th century, the city hosted an interesting Cubist movement that rivalled the one in Paris. The Czech Republic has also produced writers, artists and musicians of world renown.

KEY DATES IN CZECH HISTORY

500 BC Celts settle in Bohemia and Moravia. Joined by Germanic tribes in 1st century AD

AD 500–600 Slavs settle in the region

870 Přemyslids build Prague Castle

1333 Charles IV makes Prague his home, marking the start of the city's Golden Age

1415 Jan Hus executed for heresy; start of the Hussite Wars

1526 Habsburg rule begins with Ferdinand I

1583 Accession of Habsburg Emperor Rudolf II

1618 Protestant revolt leads to the Thirty Years' War

1627 Beginning of Counter-Reformation committee in Prague

1916 Czechoslovak National Council created in Paris

1918 Foundation of Czechoslovakia

1948 Communist Party assumes power

1989 Year of the Velvet Revolution; Communist regime finally overthrown

1993 Czechoslovakia ceases to exist; creation of the new Czech Republic

2004 Czech Republic joins the EU

2007 New centre-right coalition forms a government

2013 Miloš Zeman wins the country's first direct presidential election

Exploring the Czech Republic

One of Europe's most beautiful capital cities, Prague is the highlight of a visit to the Czech Republic. However, the Bohemian countryside is home to dozens of well-preserved castles and historic towns such as České Budějovice. Most of these sights can be visited on a day-trip from Prague, and are easily reached by good public transport. Slightly further afield, Český Krumlov merits at least a couple of days' exploration.

Beautifully restored house, Český Krumlov

Sights at a Glance

The magnificent Town Hall on Horní náměstí, Olomouc

0 km   100
0 miles   100

Key

— Motorway

- - Motorway under construction

— Major road

— Railway

–·– International border

For keys to symbols *see back flap*

❶ Prague

The capital of the Czech Republic, Prague has a population of just over one million. In the late Middle Ages, during the reign of Charles IV, Prague's position at the crossroads of Europe led it to evolve into a magnificent city, larger than Paris or London. In the 16th century, it was taken over by the Austrian Habsburgs, who built many of the Baroque palaces and gardens that delight visitors today. Some of these now house important museums. The fascinating Jewish Quarter has a handful of synagogues and a cemetery that remarkably survived the Nazi occupation. Despite neglect under Communist rule, the historic centre of the city has been preserved, making Prague one of the most beautiful and interesting of all European capitals.

The Three Fiddles, an old house sign in Nerudova ulice

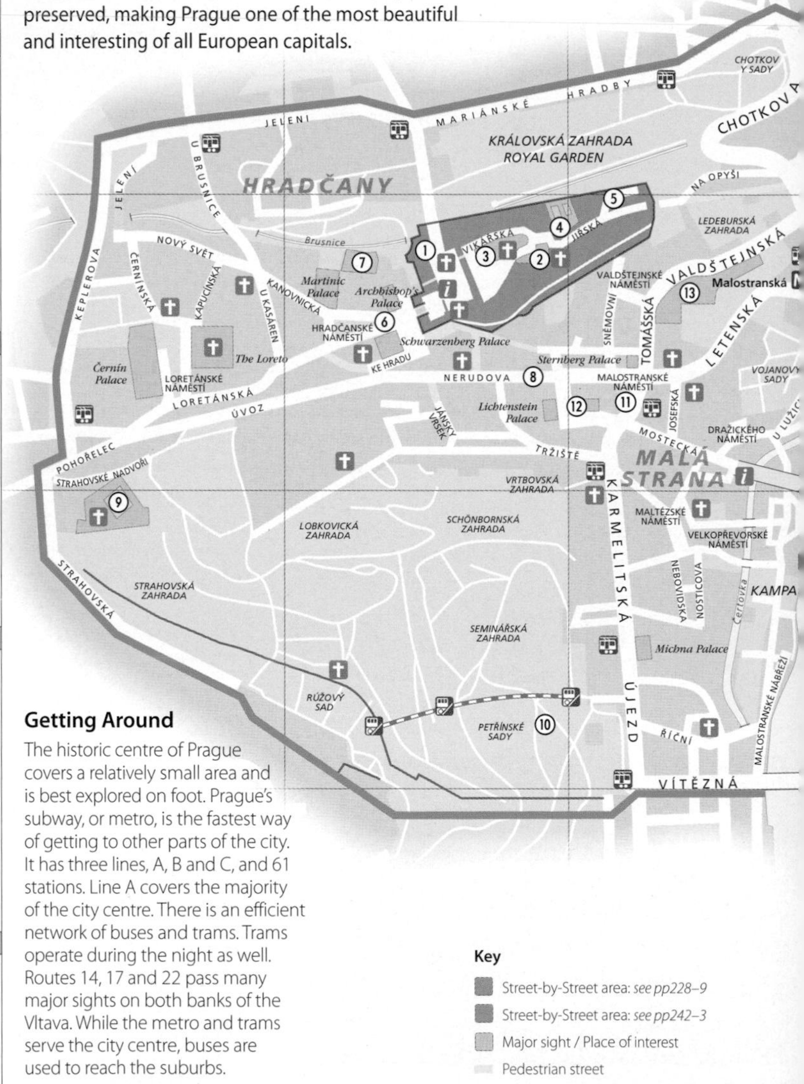

Getting Around

The historic centre of Prague covers a relatively small area and is best explored on foot. Prague's subway, or metro, is the fastest way of getting to other parts of the city. It has three lines, A, B and C, and 61 stations. Line A covers the majority of the city centre. There is an efficient network of buses and trams. Trams operate during the night as well. Routes 14, 17 and 22 pass many major sights on both banks of the Vltava. While the metro and trams serve the city centre, buses are used to reach the suburbs.

Key

▨ Street-by-Street area: see pp228–9

▨ Street-by-Street area: see pp242–3

▢ Major sight / Place of interest

　 Pedestrian street

Sights at a Glance

① Prague Castle Picture Gallery
② Old Royal Palace
③ *St Vitus's Cathedral pp232–3*
④ St George's Basilica and Convent
⑤ Zlatá ulička
⑥ Castle Square
⑦ *Sternberg Palace pp234–5*
⑧ Nerudova ulice
⑨ Strahov Monastery
⑩ Petřín Hill
⑪ Little Quarter Square
⑫ *Church of St Nicholas pp238–9*
⑬ Wallenstein Palace and Gardens

⑭ *Charles Bridge pp240–41*
⑮ *Old Town Hall pp244–5*
⑯ Celetná ulice
⑰ Church of Our Lady before Týn
⑱ Church of St James
⑲ Convent of St Agnes
⑳ Spanish Synagogue
㉑ *Old New Synagogue pp248–9*
㉒ Jewish Town Hall
㉓ Maisel Synagogue
㉔ Old Jewish Cemetery
㉕ Pinkas Synagogue
㉖ Museum of Decorative Arts
㉗ Karlova ulice
㉘ Church of St Giles

㉙ Estates Theatre
㉚ *Municipal House pp252–3*
㉛ Wenceslas Square
㉜ Church of Our Lady of the Snows
㉝ National Museum
㉞ Mucha Museum
㉟ Charles Square
㊱ U Fleků
㊲ National Theatre

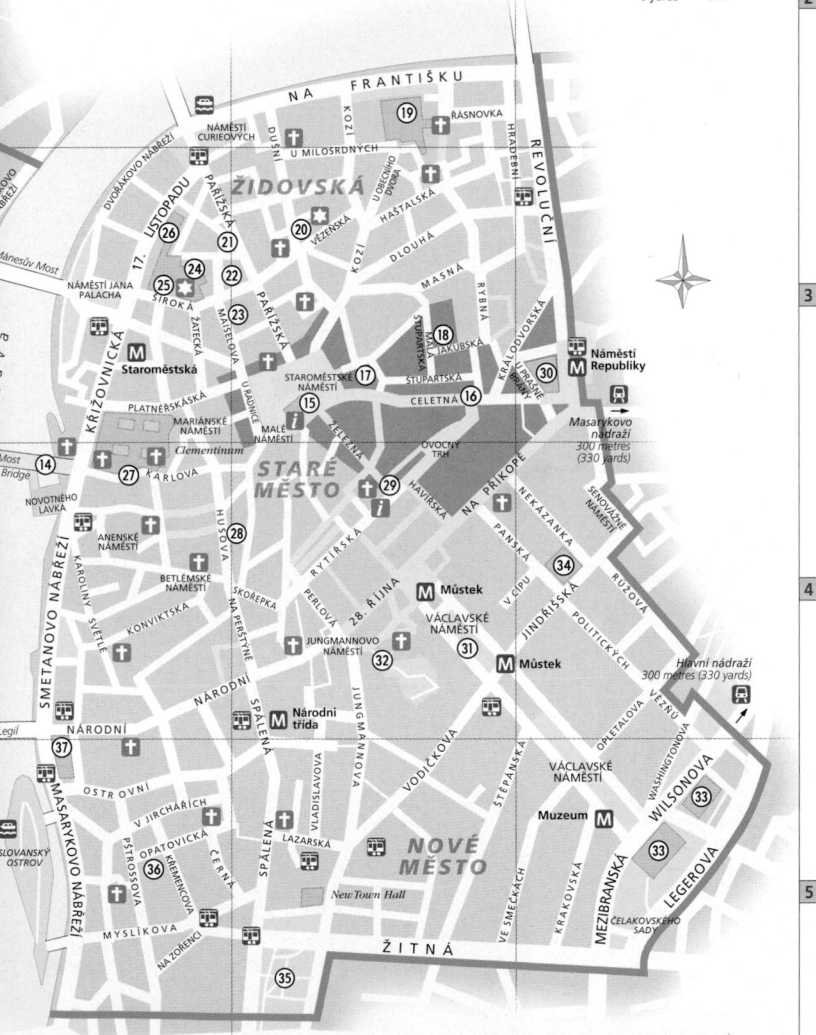

0 metres 200
0 yards 200

Street-by-Street: Prague Castle

The history of Prague began with the foundation of Prague Castle in the 9th century. Despite fires and invasions, the castle has retained churches, chapels and towers from every period of its history, from the Gothic splendour of St Vitus's Cathedral (see pp232–3) to the 16th-century Renaissance additions. The courtyards date from 1753–75, when the whole area was rebuilt in the late-Baroque and Neo-Classical styles. The castle became the seat of the Czechoslovak president in 1918 and the current president of the Czech Republic has an office here.

③ ★ **St Vitus's Cathedral**
This relief in the Gothic St Vitus's Cathedral decorates the Golden Portal.

The Powder Tower, used in the past for storing gunpowder and as a bell foundry, is now a museum.

President's Office

To Royal Garden

① **Prague Castle Picture Gallery** Renaissance and Baroque paintings hang in the restored stables of the castle.

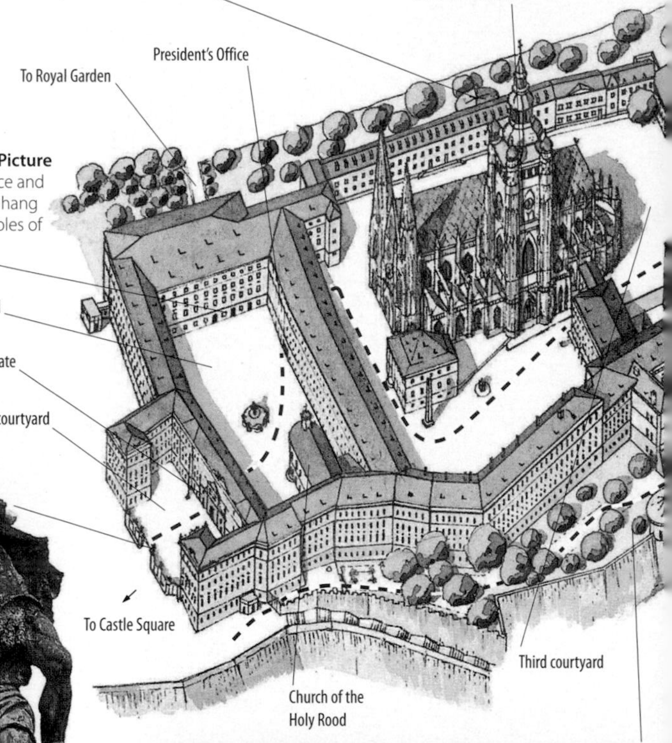

Second courtyard

Matthias Gate

First courtyard

To Castle Square

Third courtyard

Church of the Holy Rood

Castle Gates
The gates of the castle are crowned by copies of 18th-century statues called *Fighting Giants* by Ignaz Platzer.

South Gardens
Here 18th-century statues stand along the old ramparts.

④ ★ St George's Basilica
The superb vaulted chapel of the royal Bohemian martyr St Ludmila is decorated with 16th-century paintings.

⑤ ★ Zlatá Ulička
The picturesque artisans' cottages along the inside of the castle wall were built in the late 16th century for the castle's guards and gunners.

White Tower

JIŘSKÁ

Old Castle steps down to Malostranská Metro

Dalibor Tower takes its name from the first man to be imprisoned in it.

Lobkowicz Palace houses works of art from the Lobkowicz family's private collection. It is also a venue for concerts.

④ St George's Convent
The convent houses 19th-century Czech art such as a piece titled *Summer Countryside with Chapel* by Adolf Kosárek.

② ★ Old Royal Palace
The uniform exterior of the palace conceals many Gothic and Renaissance halls. Coats of arms cover the walls and ceiling of the Room of the New Land Rolls.

| 0 metres | 60 |
| 0 yards | 60 |

Key

— Suggested route

Rib vaulting in the Vladislav Hall, Old Royal Palace

① Prague Castle Picture Gallery

Obrazárna pražského hradu

Prague Castle, second courtyard.
Map B3. **Tel** 224 373 531. 22.
Malostranská, Hradčanská.
Open Apr–Oct: 9am–6pm daily;
Nov–Mar: 9am–4pm daily.
W kulturanahrade.cz

This gallery was created in
Prague Castle in 1965 to
display, among other works,
what remains of the great art
collection of the Habsburg
Emperor Rudolph II (r. 1576–
1612). Though many works of
art were looted by the occupying Swedish Army in 1648,
some fine paintings remain,
including works by artists Hans
von Aachen and Bartolomeus
Spranger. Paintings from the
16th to the 18th centuries make
up the bulk of the gallery's
collection. Highlights include
Rubens *The Assembly of the
Olympic Gods,* featuring Venus
and Jupiter, Tintoretto's
Flagellation of Christ and Titian's
The Toilet of a Young Lady. Master
Theodoric, Paolo Veronese and
the Czech Baroque artists Jan
Kupecký and Petr Brandl are
among the other painters
represented. The sculptures
include a bust of Rudolph II
by Adriaen de Vries.

Visitors can also see the
remains of the castle's first
church, the 9th-century Church
of Our Lady, believed to have
been built by Prince Bořivoj,
the first Přemyslid prince to
be baptized a Christian.

② Old Royal Palace

Starý královský palác

Prague Castle, third courtyard.
Map B3. **Tel** 224 373 102. 22.
Malostranská, Hradčanská.
Open Apr–Oct: 9am–5pm daily;
Nov–Mar: 9am–4pm daily.
W hrad.cz

From the time Prague Castle
was first fortified in the 11th
century, the Old Royal Palace
was the seat of a long line of
Bohemian kings.

The vast palace complex
consists of three different
architectural layers. A Romanesque
palace, built around 1135, forms
the basement of the present
structure. Over the next 200
years, two further palaces were
built above this – the first by
Přemysl Otakar II in 1253, and
the second by Charles IV in
1340. On the top floor is the
massive Gothic Vladislav Hall,
with its splendid rib vaulting.
Designed for King Vladislav

Titian's *The Toilet of a Young Lady* in Prague
Castle Picture Gallery

Jagiello, it was completed in
1502. The Rider's Staircase, just
off the hall, is a flight of steps
with a magnificent Gothic rib-
vaulted ceiling. It was used by
knights on horseback to get
to jousting contests.

Under Habsburg rule, the palace
housed government offices,
courts and the old Bohemian
parliament. The Bohemian
Chancellery, the former royal
offices of the Habsburgs, is
the site of the famous 1618
defenestration. In 1619 the
Bohemian nobles deposed
Emperor Ferdinand II as king
of Bohemia, electing in his
place Frederick of the Palatinate.
This led to the first major
battle of the Thirty Years'
War *(see p224).*

③ St Vitus's Cathedral

See pp232–3.

④ St George's Basilica and Convent

Bazilika a klášter sv Jiří

Jiřská náměstí. **Map** B3.
Tel 224 371 111. 22.
Malostranská, Hradčanská.
Open Apr–Oct: 9am–5pm daily;
Nov–Mar 9am–4pm daily.
Concerts: **Open** Apr–Sep:
call for timings. **W** hrad.cz

St George's Basilica was
founded by Prince Vratislav in
920 and is the best preserved
Romanesque church in Prague.
The huge twin towers and
austere interior have been
restored to give an idea of the
church's original appearance.

The interior contains the
10th-century tomb of Vratislav I,
located opposite the presbytery.
Also buried in the church are
Prince Boleslav II, who died
in 992, and Princess Ludmila
(grandmother of St Wenceslas),
who was murdered in 921 and
is revered as the first Bohemian
saint. Her 14th-century tombstone is located in the Gothic
side chapel. Other points
of interest include a rare
early 13th-century painting,

New Jerusalem, in the choir vault. The double staircase to the chancel is a remarkable late-Baroque addition and now provides a perfect stage for chamber music concerts. Outside, the south portal of the church features a 16th-century relief depicting St George and the dragon.

The adjacent former Benedictine nunnery is the oldest convent building in Bohemia. It was founded in 973 by Princess Mlada, sister of Boleslav II. Throughout the Middle Ages, the convent and St George's Basilica formed the heart of the castle complex. Rebuilt several times, the convent and its religious functions finally ceased in 1782.

The convent building was formerly home to a collection of the National Gallery's 19th-century Czech art. However, it is now closed and there are presently no plans for any future exhibitions.

⑤ Zlatá Ulička

Map C3. 22. Malostranská, Hradčanská.

Named after the goldsmiths who lived here in the 17th century, Golden Lane (Zlatá ulička) is one of the prettiest lanes in Prague. One side of the lane is lined with tiny, brightly painted houses built right into the arches of the castle walls. These were constructed in the late 16th century for Rudolph II's 24 castle guards. A century later, the goldsmiths moved in and modified the buildings. However, by the 19th century

Picturesque 16th-century cottages in Zlatá ulička

the area had degenerated into a slum and was populated by Prague's poor and the criminal communities. In the 1950s, all the remaining residents were moved and the area was restored to something like its original state. Most of the houses were converted into shops selling books, Bohemian glass and other souvenirs for visitors, who now flock to this narrow lane.

Despite the street's name, Rudolph II's alchemists never produced gold here. Their laboratories were in Vikářská, the lane between St Vitus's Cathedral and the Powder Tower (Mihulka).

Zlatá ulička has, however, been home to well-known writers such as Franz Kafka *(see p35)*, who stayed at No. 22 with his sister around 1916–17 and Jaroslav Seifert, the Nobel Prize-winning Czech poet.

⑥ Castle Square

Hradčanské náměstí

Map B3. 22. Malostranská, Hradčanská. Schwarzenberg Palace: **Tel** 233 081 716. **Open** 10am–6pm Tue–Sun. **ngprague.cz**

The vast, grand square in front of Prague Castle was once lined by workshops and artisans' houses, but after the devastating fire of 1541, they were replaced by a series of imposing palaces. These were built by Czech and foreign noblemen, eager to live close to the court of the Habsburgs.

On the south side stands the 16th-century **Schwarzenberg Palace** (Schwarzenberský palác), a beautiful Renaissance building with graceful attics and magnificent *sgraffito* that gives the impression that the façade is clad in Italian-style diamond-point stonework. The western end of the square is taken up by the Thun-Hohenstein Palace (Thun-Hohenšteinský palác), built between 1689 and 1691 and crowned with statues by Ferdinand Brokof. To the north lies the Archbishop's Palace (Arcibiskupský palác), a 16th-century building with a Rococo façade in pink and white, added in the 1760s. The Renaissance Martinic Palace (Martinický palác), at the corner of Castle Square, has *sgraffito* depicting scenes from the Bible. Its high terrace provides views of the city.

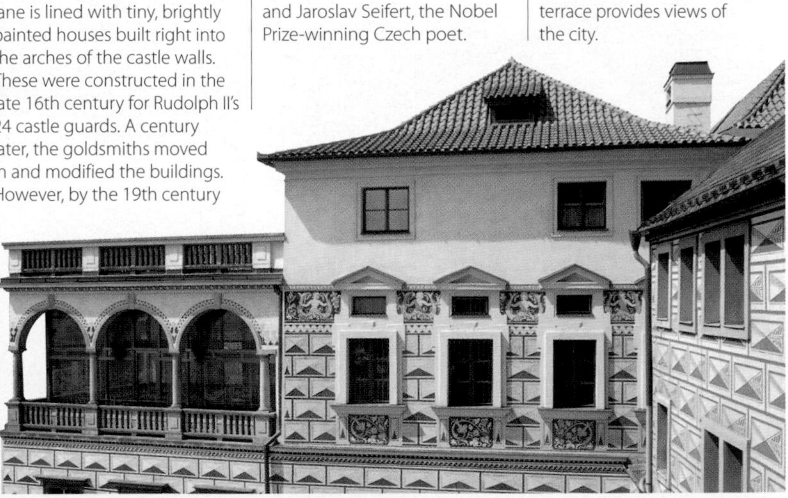

Schwarzenberg Palace in Castle Square, notable for its *sgraffito* decoration

③ St Vitus's Cathedral
chrám sv Víta

Work began on St Vitus's Cathedral, Prague's most distinctive landmark, in 1344. Architect Peter Parler was largely responsible for the grandiose Gothic design, though the building was not completed for another 600 years. The cathedral contains the tomb of Good King Wenceslas and some fine works of art including an exquisite Alfons Mucha window.

Window by Alfons Mucha
The beautiful glass window was painted by Alfons Mucha in Czech Art Nouveau style.

Rose Window
Designed by František Kysela in the 1920s, the window above the portals depicts scenes from the biblical story of the Creation.

Gargoyles
On the ornate west front, gutter spouts are given their traditional disguise as gargoyles.

Main entrance

Bust of Peter Parler on triforium

c.925 Rotunda of St Vitus built by St Wenceslas

1359 Masterbuilder Peter Parler summoned to continue work on the cathedral

1619 Calvinists take over cathedral as house of prayer

1929 Consecration of completed cathedral, nearly 1,000 years after death of St Wenceslas

1000	1200	1400	1600	1800

1060 Building of triple-aisled basilica begins on orders of Prince Spytihněv

1344 King John of Luxembourg founds Gothic cathedral. French architect Matthew of Arras begins work

1421 Hussites occupy St Vitus's

1589 Royal tomb completed

1872 Joseph Mocker begins work on west nave

1770 New steeple added to tower after fire

★ Flying Buttresses
The slender buttresses that surround the exterior of the nave and chancel, supporting the vaulted interior, are richly decorated.

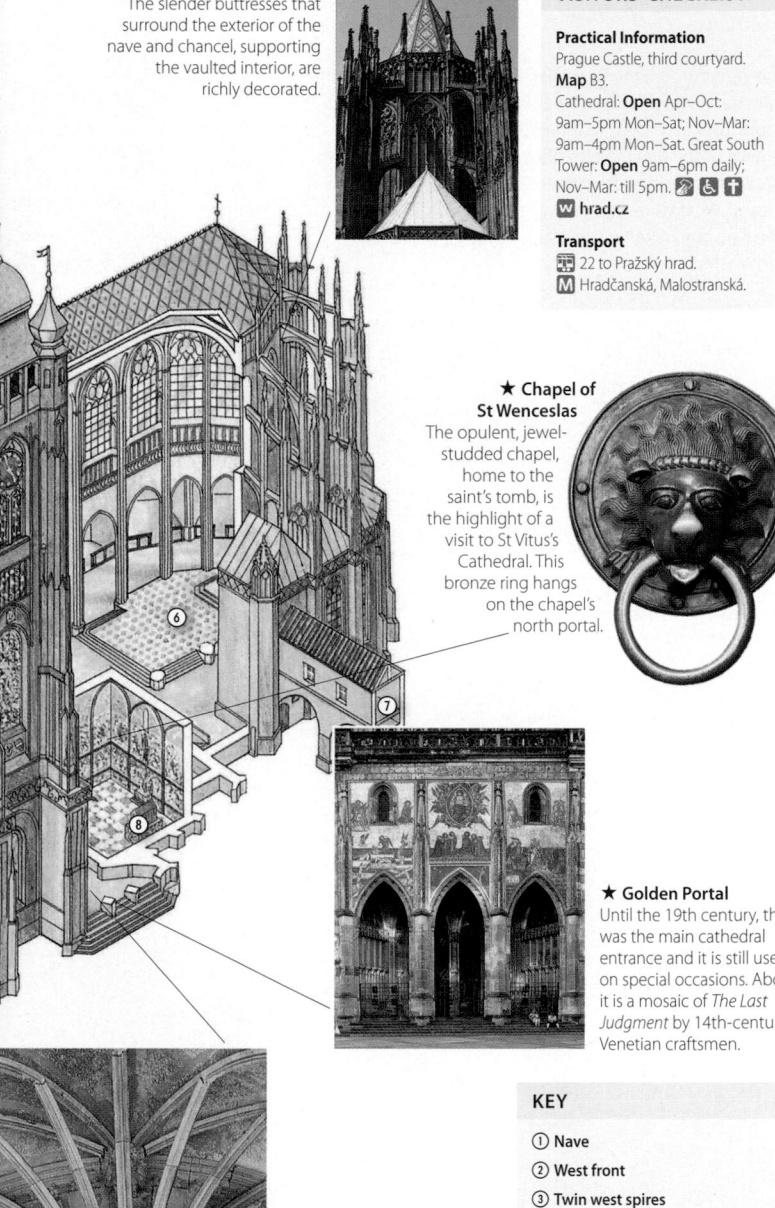

VISITORS' CHECKLIST

Practical Information
Prague Castle, third courtyard.
Map B3.
Cathedral: **Open** Apr–Oct:
9am–5pm Mon–Sat; Nov–Mar:
9am–4pm Mon–Sat. Great South
Tower: **Open** 9am–6pm daily;
Nov–Mar: till 5pm. 🚻 ♿ 🚹
W hrad.cz

Transport
🚊 22 to Pražský hrad.
Ⓜ Hradčanská, Malostranská.

★ Chapel of St Wenceslas
The opulent, jewel-studded chapel, home to the saint's tomb, is the highlight of a visit to St Vitus's Cathedral. This bronze ring hangs on the chapel's north portal.

★ Golden Portal
Until the 19th century, this was the main cathedral entrance and it is still used on special occasions. Above it is a mosaic of *The Last Judgment* by 14th-century Venetian craftsmen.

KEY

① Nave

② West front

③ Twin west spires

④ Triforium

⑤ **The Renaissance bell tower**
is capped with a Baroque "helmet".

⑥ Chancel

⑦ **To Old Royal Palace** *(see p230)*

⑧ **The tomb of St Wenceslas**
is connected to an altar, decorated with semi-precious stones.

Gothic Vaulting
The skills of architect Peter Parler are clearly seen in the delicate fans of ribbing that support the three Gothic arches of the Golden Portal.

⑦ Sternberg Palace

šternberský palác

The 18th-century Sternberg Palace has been home to the National Gallery's collection of European art since 1949. Franz Josef Sternberg founded the Society of Patriotic Friends of the Arts in Bohemia in 1796. Fellow noblemen would lend their finest sculptures and pictures to the society, which had its headquarters in the Sternberg Palace. The Baroque building has a superb range of works by Old Masters.

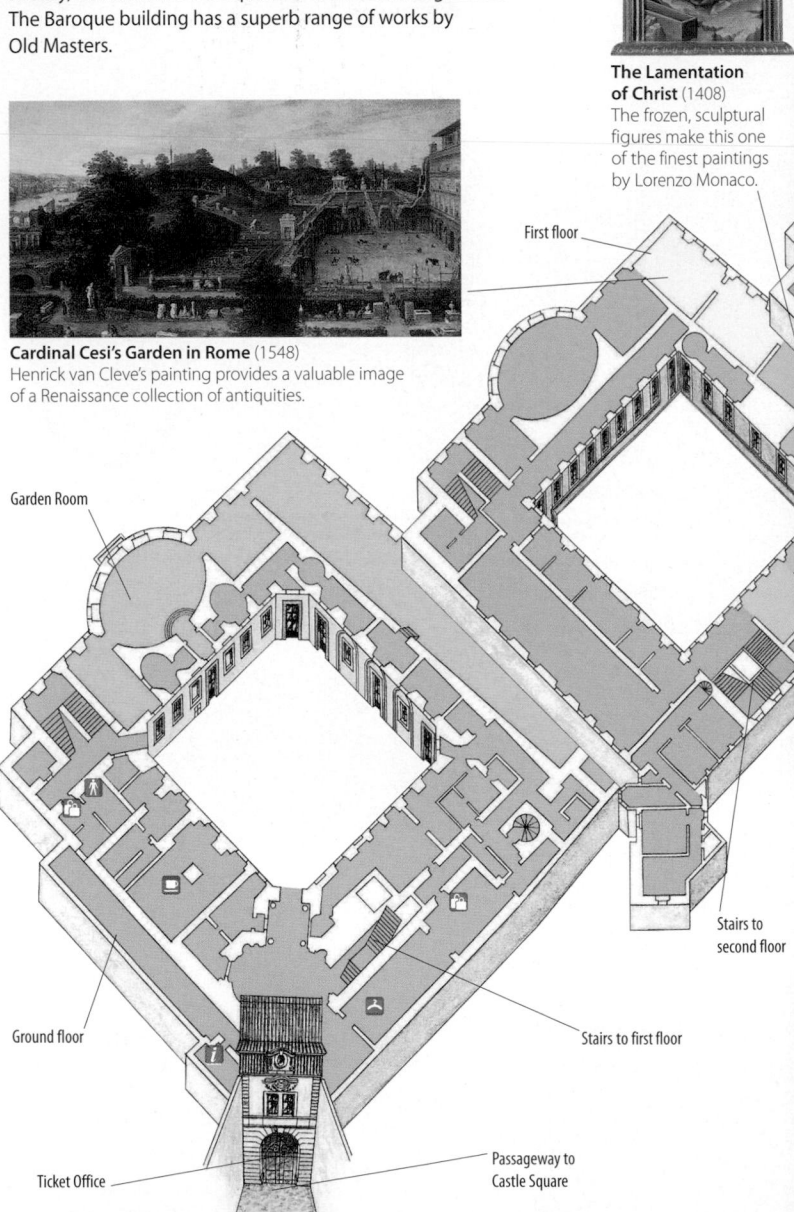

The Lamentation of Christ (1408)
The frozen, sculptural figures make this one of the finest paintings by Lorenzo Monaco.

First floor

Cardinal Cesi's Garden in Rome (1548)
Henrick van Cleve's painting provides a valuable image of a Renaissance collection of antiquities.

Garden Room

Stairs to second floor

Ground floor

Stairs to first floor

Ticket Office

Passageway to Castle Square

★ **Scholar in his Study** (1634)
Rembrandt used keenly observed detail to convey wisdom in the face of the old scholar.

VISITORS' CHECKLIST

Practical Information
Hradčanské náměstí 15.
Map B3. **Tel** 233 090 570.
Open 10am–6pm Tue–Sun.
📷 🖼 💻 🌐 **ngprague.cz**

Transport
🚊 22. Ⓜ Malostranská, Hradčanská.

Chinese Cabinet

The Garden of Eden (1618)
Roelandt Savery studied the animals in the menagerie of Rudolph II. He liked to include them in his biblical and mythological works.

Second floor

Stairs down to other floors and exit

★ **Head of Christ**
Painted by El Greco in the 1590s, this portrait emphasizes the humanity of Christ. At the same time the curious square halo gives the painting the qualities of an ancient icon.

Gallery Guide

The gallery is arranged on three floors around the central courtyard of the palace. The ground floor, reached from the courtyard, houses German and Austrian art from the 15th to 19th centuries. The stairs to the upper floors are just beyond the ticket office. The first and second floors have works of art from various European countries.

Key

- ☐ German and Austrian Art 1400–1800
- ☐ Flemish and Dutch Art 1400–1600
- ☐ Italian Art 1400–1500
- ☐ Roman Art
- ☐ Flemish and Dutch Art 1600–1800
- ☐ French Art 1600–1800
- ☐ Icons, Classical and Ancient Art
- ☐ Venice 1700–1800 and Goya
- ☐ Spanish Art 1600–1800
- ☐ Naples and Venice 1600–1700
- ☐ Italian Art 1500–1600
- ☐ Non-exhibition space

★ **The Martyrdom of St Thomas** (1636)
This magnificent work is by Peter Paul Rubens, a Flemish Baroque painter from the 17th century.

⑧ Nerudova Ulice

Map B3. 🚃 12, 20, 22.
Ⓜ Malostranská.

A picturesque narrow street leading up to Prague Castle, Nerudova ulice is bustling, noisy and crowded by day, but becomes deserted at night – over time, souvenir shops and offices have replaced the ordinary residents. The street is named after the poet and journalist Jan Neruda, who wrote many stories set in this part of Prague. He lived in the house called At the Two Suns (No. 47) between 1845 and 1857.

Until the introduction of house numbers in 1770, the city's dwellings were distinguished by signs. Nerudova ulice's houses have a splendid selection of these, featuring symbols, emblems and heraldic beasts made of stone, stucco or metal, which were usually painted or carved. They often indicate a profession or special interest of the former occupants.

Proceeding up Nerudova's steep slope, signs of particular interest include the Red Eagle (No. 6), the Three Fiddles (No. 12), the Old Pharmacy Museum (No. 32) and the Golden Horseshoe (No. 34). There are also many Baroque buildings, most of which have become embassies. Among them are the Thun-Hohenstein Palace (No. 20, now the Italian Embassy), whose entrance is framed by an imposing portal with two spread-wing eagles by Matthias Braun, and Morzin Palace (No. 5, the Romanian Embassy). The façade of the latter has two vast statues of Moors (a pun on the name Morzin) supporting the semicircular balcony on the first floor sculpted by Ferdinand Brokof. Another impressive façade is that of the Church of Our Lady of Unceasing Succour (Kostel Panny Marie Ustavičné Pomoci), the church of the Theatines, an order founded in the Counter-Reformation.

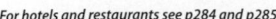

Sign of Jan Neruda's house, 47 Nerudova Street

The magnificent Philosophical Hall, within the Strahov Monastery

⑨ Strahov Monastery
Strahovský klášter

Královská Kanonie Premonstrátů na Strahově, Strahovské nádvoří 1/132, Strahovská. **Map** A4. **Tel** 233 107 730. 🚃 22. **Open** 9am–noon, 1–5pm daily. Church of Our Lady, Philosophical Hall, Theological Hall, Picture Gallery: **Open** 10–11:30am, noon–5pm daily. **Closed** Easter Sun, 24 & 25 Dec. ⊘ 📷 🅦 **strahovskyklaster.cz**

When it was founded by Vladislav II in 1140 to serve an austere religious order, the Premonstratensians, Strahov rivalled Prague Castle *(see pp228–9)* in size. Burnt down in the 13th century, then rebuilt, it acquired its present Baroque form in the 18th century. In 1783, during the reign of Joseph II, the monastery managed to escape dissolution by declaring itself an educational establishment, citing its vast library. The monks were finally driven out in 1950 by the Communists. After the Velvet Revolution (1989) *(see p224)*, the monastery resumed its original function, and monks can sometimes be seen going about their business.

The abbey courtyard is entered via a Baroque gateway sporting a statue of St Norbert, the founder of the Premonstratensian Order. The main monastery church is the **Church of Our Lady** (Nanebevzetí Panny Marie), featuring statues by Johan Anton Quitainer on its façade. The restored Baroque interior is dazzlingly opulent. Besides the magnificent altars and furnishings, the frescoes are particularly striking, covering the ceiling and walls above the arcades.

Inside the monastery, the two Baroque libraries are among the most beautiful in Europe. The first of these, the **Philosophical Hall** (Filosofický sál) was built to house the books and bookcases from Louca monastery in Moravia, dissolved by Joseph II. The vault is decorated with a 1782 fresco depicting mankind's quest for truth. The second library is the **Theological Hall** (Teologický sál), dating from the 16th century. It is equally impressive, with a number of 17th-century astronomical globes and frescoes. The **Picture Gallery** (Obrazárna), in the nearby 17th-century Church of St Roch, is one of the finest art galleries in Prague, focusing on the interpretation of the works of masters such as Dali and Chagall.

⑩ Petřín Hill
Petřínské sady

Map B4. 🚋 6, 9, 12, 20, 22, then take the funicular railway from Újezd.

Petřín Hill, to the west of Little Quarter (Malá Strana), is the highest of Prague's nine hills at 61 m (200 ft). A path winds up its slopes, offering fine views of Prague, but visitors can also take the funicular from Újezd, which lies to the south of Little Quarter. At the top, there are many paths to explore and several attractions, including a version of the Eiffel Tower (Rozhledna), built in 1891 as a tribute to the city's strong cultural and political links with Paris at that time. A mini Gothic castle (Bludiště), containing a hall of distorting mirrors, is particularly popular with children.

⑪ Little Quarter Square
Malostranské náměstí

Map C3. 🚋 12, 20, 22. Ⓜ Malostranská.

This sloping square, busy with trams and people stopping for a drink or a bite to eat, has been the centre of activity in Little Quarter since its foundation in 1257. It began as a marketplace in the outer bailey of Prague Castle. Most of the houses here have a medieval core, but all were rebuilt during the Baroque and Renaissance periods.

The square is dominated by the Church of St Nicholas, regarded as the best example of High Baroque in the city. Opposite the church is the vast Neo-Classical façade of

Baroque Church of St Nicholas in Little Quarter Square

Lichtenstein Palace. Other important buildings include the Town Hall, with its fine Renaissance façade, and Sternberg Palace, built on the site of the outbreak of the 1541 fire, which destroyed most of the district.

⑫ Church of St Nicholas
See pp238–9.

⑬ Wallenstein Palace and Gardens
Valdštejnský palác a zahrada

Valdštejnské náměstí 4. **Map** C3. 🚋 12, 18, 20, 22. Ⓜ Malostranská. **Tel** 257 075 707. Palace: **Open** 10am–4:30pm Sat & Sun (Apr–Oct to 5pm). ♿ from Valdštejnské náměstí. ✉ Gardens: **Open** Apr–May & Oct: 10am–6pm daily; Jun–Sep: 10am–7pm daily. ♿ from Valdštejnské náměstí. 🖥 🌐 senat.cz

The first important secular building of the Baroque era in Prague, the Wallenstein Palace stands as a monument to the ambitions of military chief

Albrecht von Wallenstein. His string of victories over the Protestants in the Thirty Years' War made him vital to Emperor Ferdinand II. However, when Wallenstein started to covet the crown of Bohemia and also dared to negotiate with the enemy, he fell out of favour and was assassinated on the emperor's orders.

Wallenstein spent only 12 months in the palace that he had built for himself between 1620 and 1630. It was designed by Italian architect Andrea Spezza. The main hall has a ceiling fresco of Wallenstein himself, portrayed as Mars, the god of war, riding in a triumphal chariot. Today, the palace is home to the Czech Senate. The restored gardens are laid out as they were when Wallenstein dined in the huge garden pavilion that looks out over the Fountain of Venus (1599) and rows of bronze statues.

Fountain of Venus in front of the Wallenstein Palace

Albrecht von Wallenstein

Wallenstein, politician and commander

Albrecht von Wallenstein (Valdštein) was born in Bohemia in 1583. He studied in Italy and later converted to Catholicism. He joined Rudolph II's Army and rose in prominence to lead the imperial armies in Europe. During the Thirty Years' War he had several victories over the Protestants. In 1630, he negotiated secretly with the Protestants and then joined them. For this, he was killed in 1634 by mercenaries acting on Emperor Ferdinand II's orders.

⑫ Church of St Nicholas

Kostel sv Mikuláše

The Church of St Nicholas divides and dominates the two sections of Little Quarter Square. Construction began in 1703 and the last touches were put to the glorious frescoed nave in 1761. It is recognized as the masterpiece of father-and-son architects Christoph and Kilian Ignaz Dientzenhofer, Prague's greatest exponents of High Baroque, though neither lived to see the church's completion. The statues, frescoes and paintings inside are by leading Baroque artists and include the fine *Passion Cycle* (1673) by Karel Škréta. Renovation in the 1950s dealt with the damage caused by 200 years of leaky cladding.

Altar Paintings
The side chapels hold many works of art. This painting of St Michael is by Francesco Solimena.

★ Pulpit
Dating from 1765, the ornate pulpit by Richard and Peter Prachner is lavishly adorned with golden cherubs.

Baroque Organ
A fresco of St Cecilia watches over the superb organ, built in 1746 by Tomás Schwarz. There were originally three Schwarz organs here.

KEY

① Chapel of St Catherine

② Chapel of St Anne

③ **Entrance from west side of Little Quarter Square**

④ **The dome** was completed by Kilian Ignaz Dientzenhofer in 1751, shortly before his death.

⑤ **The belfry**, added in 1751 and 1756, was the last part to be built. Visitors can climb up it to admire the view.

Façade
St Paul, by John Frederick Kohl, is one of the statues that grace the curving façade. It was completed in 1710 by Christoph Dientzenhofer, who was influenced by Italian architects Borromini and Guarini.

For hotels and restaurants see p284 and p285

★ Dome Fresco
Franz Palko's superb fresco, *The Celebration of the Holy Trinity* (1753–4), fills the 70-m (230-ft) high dome.

High Altar
A copper statue of St Nicholas by Ignaz Platzer (1717–87) surmounts the high altar. Below it is the painting of St Joseph by Johann Lukas Kracker.

★ Statues of the Eastern Church Fathers
The impressive statues of the church fathers, which stand at the four corners of the crossing, are the work of Ignaz Platzer.

The Dientzenhofer Family

Christoph Dientzenhofer (1655–1722) came from a family of Bavarian master builders. His son Kilian Ignaz (1689–1751) was born in Prague and educated at the Jesuit Clementinum. Together, they were responsible for the greatest treasures of Jesuit-influenced Prague Baroque architecture. The Church of St Nicholas, their last work, was completed by Kilian's son-in-law, Anselmo Lurago.

Kilian Ignaz Dientzenhofer

⑭ Charles Bridge

Karlův most

Prague's most familiar monument was built by Peter Parler
(see p232) for Charles IV in 1357 after the Judith Bridge was
destroyed by floods. It connects the Old Town (Staré Město)
with the Little Quarter (Malá Strana) and was the only bridge
across the Vltava until 1741.

Malá Strana

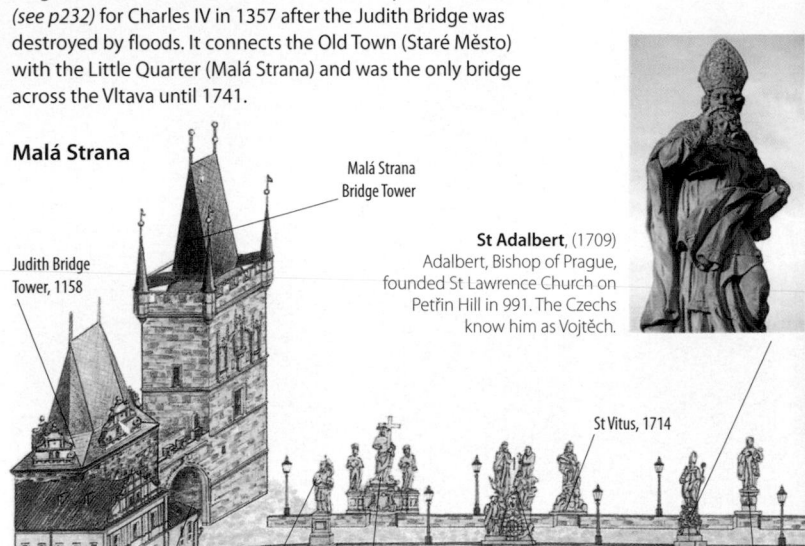

Malá Strana
Bridge Tower

Judith Bridge
Tower, 1158

St Adalbert, (1709)
Adalbert, Bishop of Prague,
founded St Lawrence Church on
Petřin Hill in 991. The Czechs
know him as Vojtěch.

St Vitus, 1714

Tower entrance

St Wenceslas, 1859

Christ between St Cosmas
and St Damian, 1709

St John de Matha,
St Felix de Valois and
the Blessed Ivan, 1714

St Philip
Benizi, 1714

Stare Město

Thirty Years' War
In the last hours of
this war, Staré Město
was saved from the
Swedish Army. The
truce was signed in
the middle of the
bridge in 1648.

**St Cyril and
St Methodius** (19
The saints are wid
acknowledged
as the two who
introduced
Christianity
to the region.

St Norbert, St Wenceslas and
St Sigismund, 1853

St Christopher,
1857

St Anne, 1707

St Francis Borgia, 1710

St John the Baptist, 1855

St Francis Xavier

St Joseph with
infant Jesus, 1854

★ **St Luitgard**, (1710)
The most artistically remarkable statue on the bridge, sculpted by Matthias Braun, shows the crucified Christ appearing to the blind Cistercian nun.

VISITORS' CHECKLIST

Practical Information
Map C4 & D4.
Staré Město Bridge Tower:
Open 10am–6pm daily (Apr–Sep: till 10pm; Mar & Oct: till 8pm).
Malá Strana Bridge Tower:
Open 10am–6pm daily (Apr–Sep: to 10pm; Mar & Oct: to 8pm).

Transport
12, 20, 22 to Malostranské náměstí.

★ **St John Nepomuk**, (1683)
Reliefs on the bridge depict the martyrdom of St John Nepomuk. People walking on the bridge touch the reliefs for good luck.

St Cajetan, 1709

St Augustine, 1708

St Nicholas Tolentino, 1708

St Vincent Ferrer and St Procopius, 1712

St Jude Thaddaeus, 1708

St Anthony of Padua, 1707

St Ludmilla with Little Wenceslas, 1720

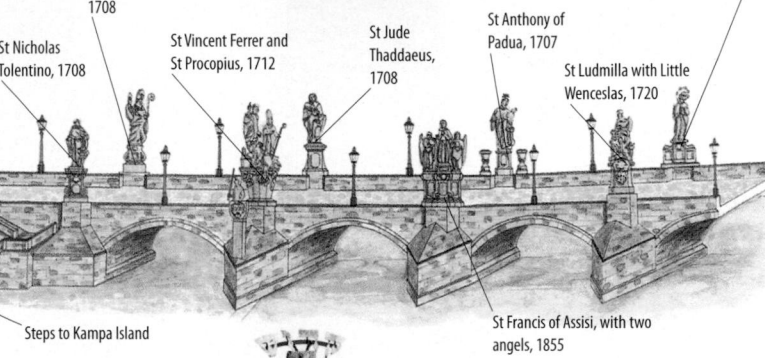

Steps to Kampa Island

St Francis of Assisi, with two angels, 1855

Crucifix
For 200 years this crucifix stood alone on the bridge. The gilded Christ dates from 1629 and the Hebrew words "Holy, Holy, Holy Lord" were paid for by a Jew as punishment for blasphemy.

Madonna and St Bernard, 1709

St Ivo, 1711

Tower entrance

Pietà, 1859

Madonna, St Dominic and St Thomas, 1708

St Barbara, St Margaret and St Elizabeth, 1707

★ **Staré Město Bridge Tower**
This fine Gothic tower was an integral part of the old town's fortifications. The sculptures, like the tower, are by Peter Parler.

Street-by-Street: Old Town

In the 11th century, the settlements around Prague Castle (see pp228–9) grew manifold and the Old Town (Staré Město) was created. Free of traffic and ringed with historic buildings, the Old Town Square (Staroměstské náměstí) ranks among the finest public spaces in any city. In summer, café tables spill out on to the cobblestoned streets, and the area draws visitors in droves. Prague's colourful history comes to life in the buildings around the square.

⑰ **Church of Our Lady before Týn**
The church's Gothic steeples are the Old Town's most distinctive landmark.

Kinský Palace
The palace, built by Kilian Ignaz Dientzenhofer, has a stucco façade crowned with statues of the four elements.

The Jan Hus Monument was erected in 1915 on the 500th anniversary of Jan Hus's (see p224) burning at the stake.

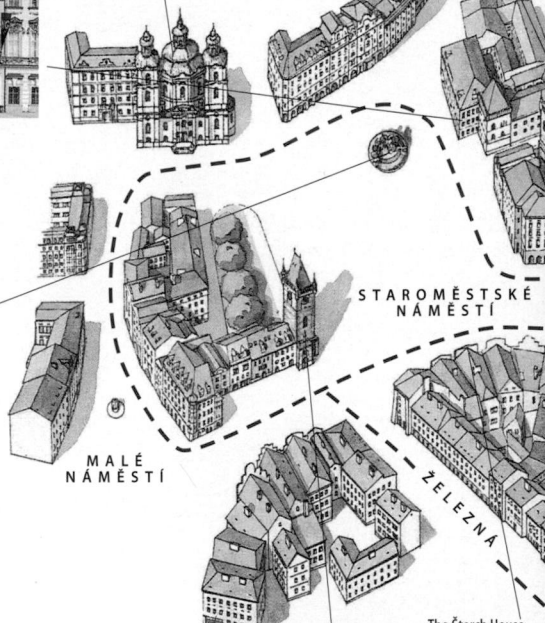

Church of St Nicholas

STAROMĚSTSKÉ NÁMĚSTÍ

MALÉ NÁMĚSTÍ

ŽELEZNÁ

The Štorch House

The Štorch House
Based on designs by Mikoláš Aleš, the façade has a painting of St Wenceslas on horseback.

The House at the Two Golden Bears has a carved Renaissance portal which is the finest of its kind in Prague.

⑮ ★ **Old Town Hall**
Located in the Old Town Square, the Town Hall's famous astronomical clock dates from the early 1400s. A procession of wooden statues moves at the top of the clock every hour.

Key

— Suggested route

For hotels and restaurants see p284 and p285

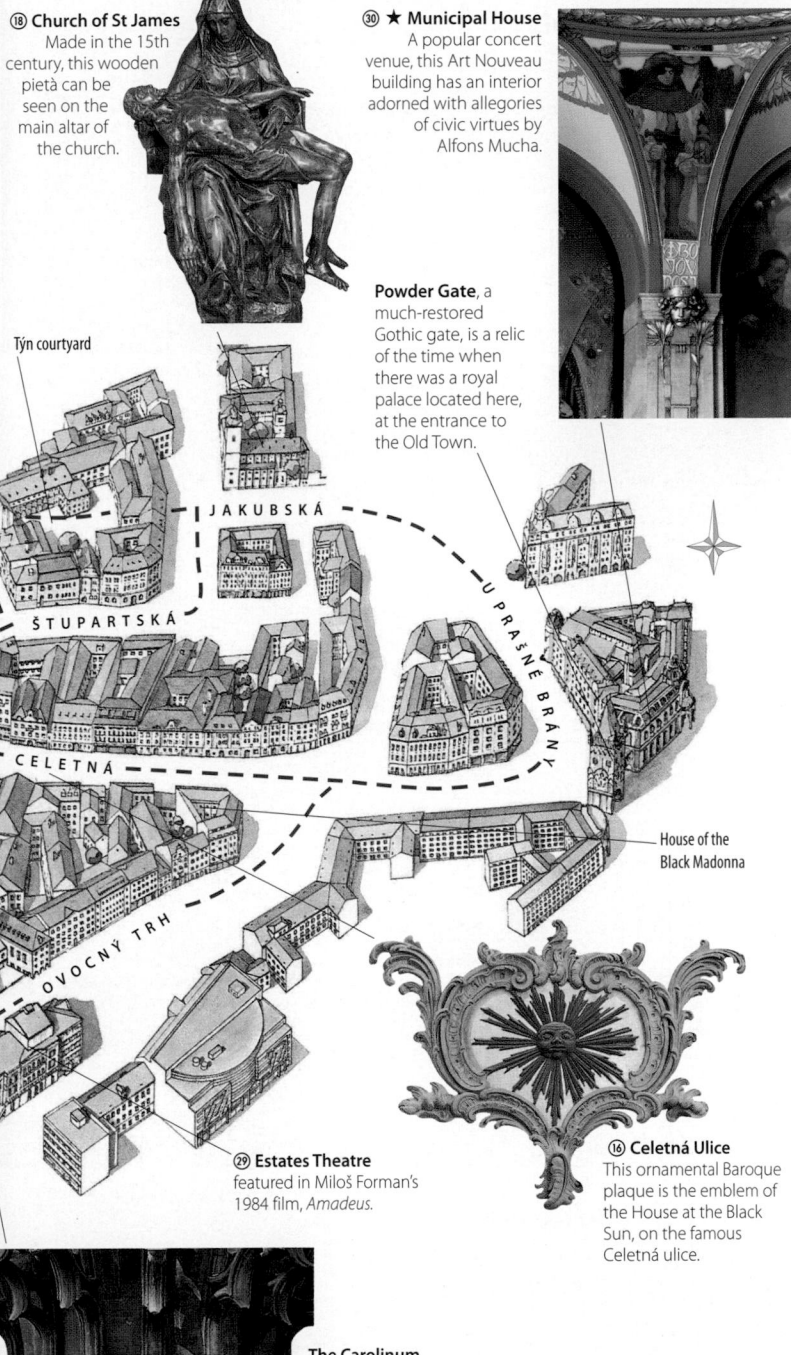

⑱ **Church of St James**
Made in the 15th century, this wooden pietà can be seen on the main altar of the church.

㉚ ★ **Municipal House**
A popular concert venue, this Art Nouveau building has an interior adorned with allegories of civic virtues by Alfons Mucha.

Powder Gate, a much-restored Gothic gate, is a relic of the time when there was a royal palace located here, at the entrance to the Old Town.

Týn courtyard

JAKUBSKÁ

ŠTUPARTSKÁ

CELETNÁ

OVOCNÝ TRH

U PRAŠNÉ BRÁNY

House of the Black Madonna

㉙ **Estates Theatre**
featured in Miloš Forman's 1984 film, *Amadeus*.

⑯ **Celetná Ulice**
This ornamental Baroque plaque is the emblem of the House at the Black Sun, on the famous Celetná ulice.

The Carolinum
This was the heart of the university founded by Charles IV in 1348. A carved Oriel window projects from the oldest surviving part.

0 metres	100
0 yards	100

⑮ Old Town Hall

Staroměstská radnice

One of the most striking buildings in Prague, the Old Town Hall was established in 1338 by King John of Luxemburg. Over the centuries, several nearby houses were knocked together as the Town Hall expanded, and it now consists of a row of colourful Gothic and Renaissance buildings. Most of these have been restored after damage inflicted by the Nazis in 1945. The 69-m (228-ft) high tower offers a great view.

Oriel Chapel
The original stained-glass windows on the five-sided chapel were destroyed in the last days of World War II, but were replaced in 1987.

Old Town Coat of Arms
Above the inscription, "Prague, Head of the Kingdom", is the coat of arms of the Old Town, which was adopted in 1784 for the whole city.

Executions in the Old Town Square

A bronze tablet below the Oriel Chapel records the names of the 27 Protestant leaders who were executed here by order of Emperor Ferdinand II on 21 June 1621. This was the result of Czech Army's humiliating defeat at the Battle of the White Mountain, which was the first battle of the Thirty Years' War in 1620. It led to the emigration of Protestants unwilling to give up their faith, a Counter-Reformation drive by the Catholic Church and a campaign of Germanization.

An illustration depicting the execution of the Protestant leaders

★ Old Town Hall Tower
In 1364, the tower was added to
the private house of Wolflin of
Kámen. Its gallery provides a
fine view of the city.

★ Astronomical Clock
Mechanical figures
perform above
the zodiac signs
in the upper
section; the
lower section
is a calendar.

KEY

① Temporary art exhibitions

② Tourist information and
entrance to tower

③ Prague Tourist Information
Service; 🌐 praguewelcome.cz

④ **Old Council Hall** features a
19th-century engraving on the well-
preserved 15th-century ceiling.

⑤ **The house of Wolflin of Kámen**
was purchased by the authorities
in 1338.

⑥ Viewing Gallery

⑦ Steps to gallery

⑧ Oriel Chapel

⑨ Calendar

Entrance hall decorated
with mosaics

Gothic Door
The late-Gothic main
entrance to the Town Hall
and tower was carved by
Matthias Rejsek. The
entrance hall is filled with
wall mosaics after designs
by the Czech painter
Mikoláš Aleš.

⑯ Celetná Ulice

Map E3. **M** Náměstí Republiky, Můstek.

One of the oldest streets in Prague, Celetná ulice follows an old trading route from eastern Bohemia. Its name comes from the plaited bread rolls that were first baked here in the Middle Ages. In the 14th century, it gained prestige as a section of the Royal Route which linked the Royal Court and Prague Castle via Old Town Square; it was used for coronation processions.

Most of the houses along Celetná ulice date from the Middle Ages. The foundations of Romanesque and Gothic buildings can be seen in some of the cellars, but the majority, with their striking signs, are the result of Baroque remodellings. At No. 34, the **House of the Black Madonna** (Dům U Černé Matky Boží), is a fine example of Cubist architecture. The building was designed by Josef Gočár in 1911 and is home to the historic Grand Café Orient, the only surviving Cubist café in the world. The building hosts temporary exhibitions. The distinctive polychrome figure of the Madonna with Child comes from an earlier house that stood on this site. It is also home to Cubist paintings, sculptures, furniture and architectural plans. The 1759 Pachts' Palace, across the street, has a balcony that rests on the shoulders of four miners and soldiers sculpted by Ignaz Platzer.

The most impressive example of Baroque architecture is the Hrzánský Palace at No. 558, whose façade features busts, gargoyles and stuccoes, as well as a portal with caryatids. A popular venue for state dinners, the palace has been visited by numerous important heads of state. Today, most of Celetná's shops veer towards the chic side of the Czech market, making it a popular place for shopping.

Towering nave of the Church of Our Lady before Týn

⑰ Church of Our Lady before Týn

Kostel matky boží před týnem

Staroměstské náměstí 14. **Map** E3. **Tel** 222 318 186. **M** Můstek, Staroměstská. **Open** 10am–1pm, 3–5pm Tue–Sat, 10am–noon Sun. **Closed** Mon. 🎫 ⛪

Dominating the Old Town Square are the multiple steeples of this historic church, a source of Czech national pride. The present Gothic building was started in 1365 and soon became associated with the reform movement in Bohemia. From the early 15th century until 1620, Týn was regarded as the main Hussite church in Prague. It was taken over by the Jesuits in the 17th century and they were responsible for the Baroque renovation inside, which jars with the Gothic style of

Statue, House of the Black Madonna

the original church. On the northern side is an entrance portal, built in 1390, decorated with scenes of the Christ's Passion. The interior has several notable features, including Gothic sculptures of *Calvary*, a pewter font and a 15th-century Gothic pulpit. The Danish astronomer Tycho Brahe (1546–1601), court astronomer to Rudolf II, is buried here.

⑱ Church of St James

Kostel sv jakuba

Malá Štupartská. **Map** E3. **Tel** 224 828 816. **M** Můstek, Náměstí Republiky. **Open** 9:30am–noon, 2–4pm Tue–Sat, to 3:30pm Fri, 2–4pm Sun. ⛪

This attractive Baroque church was originally the Gothic presbytery of a Minorite monastery. The order, a branch of the Franciscans, was invited to Prague by King Wenceslas I in 1232. The Baroque reconstruction occurred after a fire in 1689, allegedly started by agents of French king Louis XIV. More than 20 side altars were added, decorated with works by painters such as Jan Jiří Heinsch and Petr Brandl.

The tomb of Count Vratislav of Mitrovice, designed by Johann Bernhard Fischer von Erlach and with sculptures by Maximilian Brokof of Prague, is the most beautiful Baroque tomb in Bohemia. The count is believed to have been buried alive by accident; his corpse was later found sitting up in the tomb. There is an equally macabre tale regarding a 400-year-old

Baroque organ in the Church of St James

Třeboň altarpiece, Convent of St Agnes

mummified forearm to be found hanging on the right side of the church entrance. According to legend, when a thief tried to steal the jewels from the Madonna on the high altar, the Virgin grabbed his arm and held on so tightly that it had to be cut off.

The acoustics in the lengthy nave are excellent and concerts are often held here. The splendid organ dates from 1702.

⑲ Convent of St Agnes

Klášter sv anežky české

U Milosrdných 17. **Map** E2. **Tel** 224 810 628. 🚃 17 to Law Faculty (Právnická fakulta), 5, 8, 14 to Dlouhá třída. 🚌 207 to Nemocnice na Františku. Ⓜ Staroměstská, Náměstí Republiky. **Open** 10am–6pm Tue–Sun. 🅿 🅲 🅰 ✉ 🆆 ngprague.cz

The Convent of the Poor Clares, founded by Princess Agnes in 1234, was one of the first Gothic buildings in Bohemia. It functioned as a convent until 1782, when the Order was dissolved by Joseph II.

Following a painstaking restoration, the premises now houses a magnificent collection of medieval art belonging to Prague's National Gallery. Among its most precious exhibits are works by two Czech artists of the 14th century: the Master of the Vyšší Brod Altar and Master Theodoric. The latter's splendid series of panels for Charles IV's chapel at Karlštejn Castle *(see pp256–7)* are the unmissable works in the gallery. These larger-than-life portraits of saints and church fathers are full of intense expression and rich colours. Other interesting works include the moving *Crucifixion* from Prague's Na Slovanech Monastery, 14th-century panels by the Master of Třeboň, and an anonymous sculpture of the Madonna and Child, much influenced by the famous Krumlov *Madonna*, now in a museum in Vienna.

The early 16th century is represented with works by the Master of Litoměřice. These include a Holy Trinity triptych and the stunning *Visitation of the Virgin Mary*.

⑳ Spanish Synagogue

Španělská synagóga

Vězeňská 1. **Map** E3. **Tel** 221 711 511. 🚃 17, 18. 🚌 207. Ⓜ Staroměstská. **Open** Apr–Oct: 9am–6pm Sun–Fri; Nov–Mar: 9am–4:30pm Sun–Fri. **Closed** Jewish hols. 🅿 🅰 🆆 jewishmuseum.cz

This is the site of Prague's first synagogue, known as the Old School (Stará škola). In the 11th century, the Old School was the centre of the Sephardic Jewish community; they lived strictly apart from the Ashkenazi Jews, who were concentrated around the Old-New Synagogue *(see pp248–9)*. The present Moorish building dates from the second half of the 19th century. The ornate exterior gives way to an even more fantastically decorative and gilded interior. The rich stucco decorations are reminiscent of the Alhambra palace in Spain, hence the name. Once closed to the public, the Spanish Synagogue is now home to an interesting permanent exhibition dedicated to the history of Prague's Jews of Bohemia, from the time of the 1848 Jewish emancipation.

㉑ Old-New Synagogue

See pp248–9.

㉒ Jewish Town Hall

Židovská radnice

Maiselova 18. **Map** E3. **Tel** 222 319 002. 🚃 133. 🚃 17, 18. Ⓜ Staroměstská. **Closed** to the public. 🅿

At the core of this attractive pink and white building is the original Jewish Town Hall, built between 1570 and 1577 by the rich mayor, Mordechai Maisel. This is one of the few buildings to survive the Holocaust. It acquired its flowery late-Baroque image in 1763 and further alterations were made in the early 20th century.

Permission for constructing the belfry, a small wooden clock tower with a distinctive green steeple, was granted by Ferdinand III. It has a clock on each of its four sides, one of which has Hebrew figures and so turns in an anti-clockwise direction. The building is now the seat of the Council of Jewish Religious Communities.

Belfry of the Jewish Town Hall, with two of its clocks in view

㉑ Old-New Synagogue
Staronová synagóga

Built around 1270, this is the oldest synagogue in Europe and one of the earliest Gothic buildings in Prague. The synagogue has survived fires, the slum clearances of the 19th century and many Jewish pogroms. Residents of the Jewish Quarter have often had to seek refuge within its walls and it is still the religious centre for Prague's Jews. It was originally called the New Synagogue until another synagogue, which was later destroyed, was built nearby.

Right-hand Nave
The glow from the chandeliers provides light for worshippers, who sit in the seats lining the walls.

★ Jewish Standard
The historic banner of Prague's Jews is decorated with a Star of David, within which the hat that had to be worn by Jews in the 14th century is depicted.

★ Five-rib Vaulting
Two massive octagonal pillars inside the hall support the five-rib vaults: one rib was added to the traditional four ribs.

KEY

① **The cantor's platform** (*bima*) is surrounded by a Gothic wrought-iron grille.

② **Candlestick holder**

③ **These windows** formed part of the 18th-century extensions built to allow women a view of the service.

④ **Fourteenth-century stepped brick gable**

⑤ **The tympanum** above the Ark is decorated with 13th-century leaf carvings.

⑥ **The interior** is dim since the small windows do not allow much light in.

Entrance

Entrance Portal
The tympanum above the door in the south vestibule is decorated with bunches of grapes and vine leaves.

For hotels and restaurants see p284 and p285

East Façade
The east and west façades possess an austerity that is in contrast with the Gothic interior.

VISITORS' CHECKLIST

Practical Information
Červená. **Map** D3 & E3.
Tel 224 800 812. **Open** Apr–Oct:
9:30am–6pm Sun–Fri; Nov–Mar:
9:30am–5pm. **Closed** Jewish
hols. ⚡ ♿ ✦ 7:30am Mon–Fri,
9am Sat. W synagogue.cz

Transport
🚊 17, 18 to Staroměstská, 17 to
Law Faculty. M Staroměstská.

Exterior of Maisel Synagogue, rebuilt in Gothic style

★ Rabbi Löw's Chair
A Star of David marks the chair of the Chief Rabbi, placed where Rabbi Löw once sat. A 16th-century scholar, he was Prague's most revered Jewish sage.

㉓ Maisel Synagogue

Maiselova synagóga

Maiselova 10. **Map** E3.
M Staroměstská. 🚊 17, 18. 🚌 207.
Open Apr–Oct: 9am–6pm Sun–Fri;
Nov–Mar: 9am–4:30pm Sun–Fri.
Closed Jewish hols. ⚡ ♿ ♿
W jewishmuseum.cz

When it was first built, in the late 16th century, Maisel Synagogue was a private house of prayer for use by mayor Mordechai Maisel and his family. It was the most richly decorated synagogue in the city. Maisel, who made a fortune lending money to Rudolph II, funded the extensive Renaissance reconstruction of the ghetto.

The original building was destroyed in a fire that also devastated the Jewish Town Hall in 1689, and a new synagogue was built in its place. Its present Gothic aspect dates from the early 20th century. The synagogue now houses a superb collection of Jewish silver and other metal-work dating from Renaissance times. It includes early examples of items used in the Jewish service, such as Torah crowns and finials, used to decorate the rollers that hold the text of the Torah, shields (hung on the mantle draped over the Torah) and pointers (used by readers to follow the text). Most were brought by the Nazis from synagogues all over Bohemia and Moravia.

The Ark
This is the holiest place in the synagogue as it holds the sacred scrolls of the Torah (the five books of Moses) and of the books of the Prophets.

㉔ Old Jewish Cemetery

Starý židovský hřbitov

Široká 3. **Map** D3. **Tel** 222 749 464 (reservations); 222 749 211 (Jewish Museum). 🚌 207. 🚋 17, 18. Ⓜ Staroměstská. **Open** Apr–Oct: 9am–6pm Sun–Fri; Nov–Mar: 9am–4:30pm Sun–Fri (last adm 30 mins before closing). 🚻 ♿ 🌐 **jewishmuseum.cz**

Founded in 1478, this historic site was, for over 300 years, the only burial ground permitted to Jews. An estimated 100,000 people are believed to have been buried here; due to lack of space they were buried on top of each other, up to 12 layers deep. Today, over 12,000 gravestones exist in this cemetery. The last burial took place in 1787.

From the late 16th century onwards, the tombstones were decorated with symbols denoting the background, family name or profession of the deceased. The tomb of writer and astronomer David Gan (1541–1613) is adorned with symbols representing his name – a Star of David and a goose.

The most visited tomb in the cemetery is that of Rabbi Löw *(see p249)*, a 16th-century philosopher and scholar who was believed to possess magical powers. Visitors place a pebble on his grave as a mark of respect. Elsewhere, fragments of 14th-century Gothic tombstones can be seen embedded in the wall, bought from an older Jewish cemetery in Staré Město.

Near the entrance to the cemetery stands the Klausen Synagogue. It has a rich display of religious objects in its fine, barrel-vaulted interior.

㉕ Pinkas Synagogue

Pinkasova synagóga

Široká 3. **Map** D3. **Tel** 222 326 660. 🚌 207. 🚋 17, 18. Ⓜ Staroměstská. **Open** Apr–Oct: 9am–6pm Sun–Fri; Nov–Mar: 9am–4:30pm Sun–Fri. 🚻 ♿ 🌐 **jewishmuseum.cz**

Regarded as the second oldest synagogue in Prague, Pinkas Synagogue was founded in 1479 by Rabbi Pinkas and expanded in 1535 by his great-nephew Aaron Meshulam Horowitz. Since then, it has been rebuilt several times. Excavations have revealed fascinating relics of life in the medieval ghetto, including a *mikva* (ritual bath).

Stained-glass window inside the Museum of Decorative Arts

The core of the present building is a hall with Gothic vaulting. The gallery for women was added in the early 17th century.

The synagogue now serves as a memorial to all the Jewish Czechoslovak citizens who were imprisoned in the Terezín concentration camp and later deported to various Nazi extermination camps. The names of the 77,297 Czech Jews who went missing during the Holocaust are inscribed on the walls. There is also a haunting display of children's drawings from the Terezín camp.

㉖ Museum of Decorative Arts

Uměleckoprůmyslové muzeum

17 Listopadu 2. **Map** D3. **Tel** 251 093 111. 🚌 207. 🚋 17, 18. Ⓜ Staroměstská. **Open** 10am–6pm Wed–Sun, 10am–7pm Tue. 🚻 ♿ 🌐 **upm.cz**

The museum's collection of glass is one of the largest in the world, but space constraints mean that only a fraction of it is on display. Pride of place goes to the Bohemian glass, of which there are many fine Baroque and 19th- and 20th-century pieces. Other exhibits include Meissen porcelain, Gobelin tapestries, costumes, textiles, photographs and some exquisite furniture.

View across the Old Jewish Cemetery to the Klausen Synagogue

For hotels and restaurants see p284 and p285

㉗ Karlova Ulice

Map D4. Ⓜ Staroměstská.

Dating back to the 12th century, this narrow, winding street was part of the Royal Route, along which coronation processions passed on the way to Prague Castle *(see pp228–9)*. Many original Gothic and Renaissance houses remain, although most have been converted into shops to attract tourists.

A café at No. 18, in the House at the Golden Snake, was established in 1714 by an Armenian, Deodatus Damajan, who handed out slanderous pamphlets from here. It is now a restaurant. Also noteworthy is At the Golden Well at No. 3, which has a magnificent Baroque façade and stucco reliefs of saints including St Roch and St Sebastian, who are believed to offer protection against plague.

㉘ Church of St Giles

Kostel sv Jiljí

Husova 8. **Map** D4. **Tel** 224 220 235.
🚋 6, 9, 17, 18, 22. Ⓜ Národní třída.
Open by appt. 🚻

Despite a beautiful Gothic portal on its south side, the inside of this church is essentially Baroque. Founded in 1371 on the site of a Romanesque church, it became a Hussite parish church in 1420. Following the Protestant defeat in 1620, Ferdinand II gave the church to the Dominicans,

Estates Theatre, a mecca for
Mozart fans

Baroque sculpture of an angel on the altar, Church of St Giles

who built a huge friary on its southern side. The monks were evicted in the Communist era, but they have since been able to return.

The vaults are decorated with stunning frescoes by the painter Václav Vavřinec Reiner, who is buried in the nave. The main fresco, a glorification of the Dominicans, shows St Dominic and his friars helping the pope defend the Catholic Church from non-believers.

㉙ Estates Theatre

Stavovské divadlo

Ovocný trh 1. **Map** E4. **Tel** 224 901 448. Ⓜ Můstek. **Open** for performances. ♿ 🅦 **narodni-divadlo.cz**

Built in 1783 by the German-speaking Count Nostitz Rieneck, the Estates Theatre is one of the finest examples of Classical elegance in Prague. Its white, gold and blue auditorium resembles a luxury chocolate box. Until 1920, the main language used on stage

was German, with occasional performances given in Czech or Italian.

The theatre is renowned for its premieres of operas by Mozart. On 29 October 1787, the public was treated to the world premiere of *Don Giovanni*, with the composer himself conducting from the piano. Acknowledging the connection between Mozart and the theatre, the interior was used by Miloš Forman in his famous Oscar-winning film *Amadeus* (1984).

In 1834, the theatre witnessed the first performance of *Fidlovačka*, a comic opera by Josef Kajetán Tyl. One of its songs, *Kde domov můj?* ("Where is My Home?"), later became the Czech national anthem. More than a century later, in the spirit of the national revival, the theatre was renamed after Tyl, though it has since reverted to its original name.

The Carolinum, opposite, is the core of Prague University, founded by Charles IV. In the 15th and 16th centuries, the university led the movement to reform the church.

㉚ Municipal House
Obecní dům

Prague's most prominent Art Nouveau building was built between 1905 and 1911 on the site of the former royal palace. On 28 October 1918, the Municipal House was the scene of the proclamation of the new independent state of Czechoslovakia. The flamboyant interior, decorated with works by leading Czech artists, including Alfons Mucha, is well worth visiting. It includes Prague's top concert venue, as well as other smaller halls, a restaurant and café.

★ **Mayor's Salon**
This splendid room has furniture by J Krejčuk and murals depicting Czech heroes by Alfons Mucha – a Czech master of Art Nouveau.

★ **Mosaic by Karel Špillar**
The façade has a vast semicircular mosaic depicting *Homage to Prague* by noted artist Karel Špillar.

Main Hall
Lifts in the main hall have beautiful Art Nouveau details and ornaments.

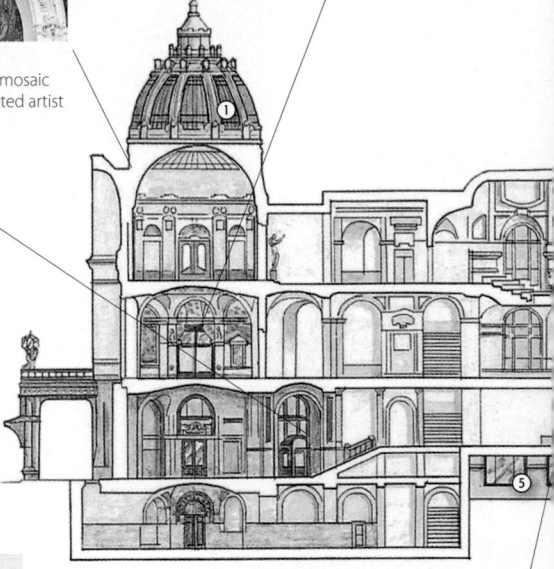

KEY

① **The Glass Dome** towers above Hollar's Hall, a circular room next to the exhibition rooms.

② **Magnificent glass dome**

③ **Figures** seen on all sides of the building are by Czech artists who combined historic and Classical symbols with modern motifs.

④ **The wing** facing U Obecního Domu ulice includes four dining rooms with original panelling, mirrors and clocks.

⑤ **Shops**

★ **Smetana Hall**
The auditorium, seating 1,500, is occasionally used as a ballroom. The box to the left of the stage is reserved for the president of the Republic; the one to the right, for the Mayor.

Side Portal
Here, caryatids and cherubs demonstrate the Art Nouveau era's love of classical motifs.

Decorative Detail
The Mayor's Salon has this delightful detail in one of its columns.

Bronze statue of St Wenceslas, Wenceslas Square

㉛ Wenceslas Square

Václavské náměstí

🚊 3, 9, 14, 24. **Map** E4.
Ⓜ Můstek, Muzeum.

Originally a horse market, today Wenceslas Square remains an important commercial centre. The square has witnessed many key events. It was here that the student Jan Palach burnt himself to death in 1969 in protest against the Soviet-led invasion of 1968, and in November 1989, a protest rally against police brutality led to the Velvet Revolution and the overthrow of Communism *(see p224)*.

At one end of the square is the National Museum, which was completed in 1890. In front of the museum is a huge equestrian statue of St Wenceslas by the late sculptor Josef Myslbek, erected in 1912. At the foot of the pedestal there are statues of Czech patron saints. A memorial near the statue commemorates the victims of the former regime.

Walking down the square from the monument, there are several buildings of interest. To the left, down a passage, is Lucerna Palace, built in the early 20th century by Václav Havel, father of the former Czech president. It is now a shopping and entertainment complex. On the opposite side of the square is the Art Nouveau Grand Hotel Europa.

Decorative Elements
Lavish stucco decoration covers all sides of the Municipal House; including floral motifs typical of the Art Nouveau style.

㉜ Church of Our Lady of the Snows

Kostel Panny Marie Sněžné

Jungmannovo náměstí 18. **Map** E4. **Tel** 222 246 243. Ⓜ Můstek. **Open** 9am–6pm daily. ⬤ ⬤

Founded in 1347 by Charles IV to mark his coronation, this remarkable church was once regarded as one of the great landmarks of Wenceslas Square *(see p253)*. According to legend, the church owes its name to a 4th-century miracle in Rome, when the Virgin Mary appeared to the pope in a dream telling him to build a church on the spot where snow fell in August. Charles IV envisaged the church to be over 100 m (330 ft) long, but it was never completed. The building that exists today was the presbytery of the projected church.

The church had a checkered history. It suffered damage in the Hussite Wars *(see p224)* and was left to decay until 1603, when it was restored by the Franciscans. The intricate net vaulting of the ceiling dates from this period. Most of the interior decoration is in Baroque style, including the splendid three-tiered gold-and-black altar, crowded with statues of saints.

㉝ National Museum

Národní muzeum

Václavské náměstí 68. **Map** F5. **Tel** 224 497 111. Ⓜ Muzeum. Temporary exhibitions also at Vinohradská 1. **Open** 10am–6pm Sun–Fri, 10am–8pm Sat. **Closed** first Tue of month. ♿ Ⓦ **nm.cz**

The vast and magnificent Neo-Renaissance building at one end of Wenceslas Square houses the National Museum. Designed by Bohemian architect Josef Schulz as a triumphal affirmation of the Czech National Revival, the museum was completed in 1890. On closer inspection of the façade, there are visible pockmarks left by shells from Warsaw Pact tanks used during the invasion of Prague in 1968. The entrance is reached by a ramp flanked by allegorical statues; seated by the door are the figures of History and Nature. In front there is a fountain symbolizing the Czech nation and the Czech rivers.

Inside, a monumental staircase lit by grand brass candelabras leads to the Pantheon, a dome-topped hall. This contains statues and busts of the most prominent figures in Czech political,

The lavishly decorated staircase in the National Museum

intellectual and artistic life. The vast room, with windows overlooking Wenceslas Square, has four huge paintings by Czech artists Václav Brožík and František Ženíšek. The exquisite gilt-framed glass cupola overhead fills the space with light.

The rich marbled decoration is impressive, while the museum's displays are devoted mainly to mineralogy, archaeology, anthropology, numismatics and natural history.

The building is undergoing extensive renovation until 2015. During renovations, temporary exhibitions are being housed in an adjacent building.

㉞ Mucha Museum

Muchovo muzeum

Panská 7. **Map** F4. **Tel** 224 216 415. 🚋 3, 9, 14, 24, 26. Ⓜ Můstek, Náměstí Republiky. **Open** 10am–6pm daily. 🎬 📷 ♿ Ⓦ **mucha.cz**

The 18th-century Kaunicky Palace is home to the Mucha Museum, dedicated to Alfons Mucha (1860–1939), the Czech master of Art Nouveau. The exhibits include personal memorabilia, paintings, drawings, photographs – some taken by Mucha – and also a documentary film. The artist's time spent in Paris is well documented. During summer, the museum's central courtyard is converted into a café.

The towering Church of Our Lady of the Snows

㉟ Charles Square
Karlovo náměstí

Map E5. 🚋 3, 4, 6, 10, 16, 18, 21, 22, 24. Ⓜ Karlovo náměstí.

In the southern part of New Town, built around Wenceslas Square and Senovážné Square, lies Prague's biggest square, Charles Square. The public garden in the square was laid out in the mid 19th-century and offers a peaceful and welcome retreat. The statues in the park are of various figures from Czech history.

Charles Square was created when Charles IV was establishing Nové Město in 1348. A wooden tower was built at its centre, where the coronation jewels were put on display once a year. In 1382, the tower was replaced by a chapel. It was from here that, in 1437, the historic document informing the Czechs about the concessions granted to the Hussites by the pope was read out for the first time.

Until the 19th century, the square was used mainly as a cattle market and for selling firewood and coal. On its north side stands the New Town Hall, one of Prague's finest Gothic buildings, embellished with steep, triangular gables. On the south side is the magnificent **Church of St Ignatius**, built by Italian architect Carlo Lurago in the 1660s. The superb façade is topped by a statue of the church's patron saint, St Ignatius of Loyola. At the time, the church's rules allowed only Christ and the Virgin Mary to be represented in this fashion, but the Jesuits succeeded in obtaining an exemption from the Pope on this occasion. Inside, the profusion of gilt is truly dazzling.

㊱ U Fleků

Křemencova 11. **Map** D5. 🚋 6, 9, 18, 22. Ⓜ Národní třída, Karlovo náměstí. **Tel** 224 930 511. 🌐 **ufleku.cz**

A short walk northwest of Charles Square is one of the most famous beer halls in Prague, U Fleků. Records indicate that beer was brewed

A spectacular ceiling fresco inside the National Theatre

U Fleků, Prague's finest and best known beer hall

here as early as 1459. The owners of this archetypal beer hall have kept up the tradition of brewing; the present brewery, the smallest in the capital, produces and serves a special strong, dark beer, sold exclusively on the premises.

㊲ National Theatre
Národní Divadlo

Národní 2. **Map** D5. **Tel** 224 901 448. 🚋 6, 9, 18, 21, 22 to Národní Divadlo. Ⓜ Národní třída. Auditorium: **Tel** 221 714 152. **Open** only during performances (box office open 8am–6pm). 🎭 ♿ 🌐 **narodnidivadlo.cz**

This gold-crested theatre is a cherished symbol of the Czech cultural revival. The original Neo-Renaissance building was designed by Czech architect Josef Zítek and construction began in 1868. Just days before the official opening it was completely destroyed by fire. Josef Schulz was given the job of rebuilding the theatre and all the best Czech artists of the period contributed towards its lavish decoration. During the late 1970s and early 80s, the theatre underwent restoration and the New Stage (Nová Scena) was built.

The beautiful **Auditorium** has an elaborately painted ceiling by František Ženíšek, adorned with allegorical figures representing the arts. Equally impressive are the gold and red stage curtains. There is also a stunning ceiling fresco in the theatre's lobby. The final part of a triptych, painted by František Ženíšek in 1878, depicts the golden age of Czech art.

The theatre's vivid sky-blue roof is covered with stars and is believed to represent the sky – the summit all artists should aim for.

Stately façade of the National Theatre on the Vltava river

❷ Karlštejn Castle

hrad Karlštejn

This Gothic castle is one of the most visited historic sites in the country. It was built for the Holy Roman Emperor Charles IV in 1348 as a royal residence and a treasury where the imperial insignia and crown jewels as well as documents, works of art and holy relics were stored. In the 16th century, Karlštejn was remodelled in the Renaissance style. The castle was restored in the 19th century by Josef Mocker, who returned the building to its original appearance.

★ Holy Cross Chapel
The walls of the Holy Cross Chapel are hung with a unique collection of 129 portraits of saints and monarchs – the work of Master Theodoric, court painter to Charles IV.

Voršilka Tower
The Voršilka Tower was once the castle's main entrance. Now the entrance is via the gate below the tower, and along the former moat.

The Well Tower
The Well Tower is situated at the lowest point of the castle complex. Inside is an old wooden treadwheel for hauling water, which was operated by two people.

For hotels and restaurants see p284 and p285

★ Church of St Mary
One of the paintings in the Church of St Mary depicts Charles IV receiving two thorns from the crown of Jesus from the French dauphin, Charles.

VISITORS' CHECKLIST

Practical Information
25 km (16 miles) SW of Prague.
Tel 311 681 617.
Open Mar–Nov: Tue–Sun.
🚫 interiors. Holy Cross Chapel:
Open Jun–Oct: Tue–Sun
(reservations required for some routes). 🚫 📷
W hradkarlstejn.cz

Transport
🚃 from Prague.

St Catherine's Chapel
Used as a place of meditation by Charles IV, this tiny chapel has walls that are richly decorated with paintings and semi-precious stones.

Madonna Statue
The 14th-century marble statue of the Madonna, in the royal bedchamber, belonged to King Charles IV.

KEY

① **The first floor of the Grand Tower** features two rooms, which in the 19th century were turned into a museum with a collection of paintings of Karlštejn and other castles.

② **Grand Tower**

③ **The Imperial Palace's** first floor was used by courtiers; the second by the emperor for private and official functions.

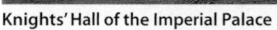

Knights' Hall of the Imperial Palace
A striking feature of the Knights' Hall is the late-Gothic altarpiece from St Palmatius's Church in the village of Budňany at the foot of Karlštejn Castle.

❸ Kutná Hora

A rich source of silver between the 13th and 18th centuries, Kutná Hora was the second most important town in Bohemia, after Prague. Its wealth funded many beautiful buildings, including St Barbara's Cathedral (sv Barbora); the Italian Court (Vlašský Dvůr), which housed the royal mint and later the Town Hall; the 14th-century Church of St James (sv Jakub) and the 15th-century Stone House (Kamenný Dům). Since 1995 the historic centre of Kutná Hora has been on the UNESCO Cultural Heritage List. Located to the northeast of the centre is the suburb of Sedlec, home to an extraordinary ossuary where bones accumulated over centuries were put together by carver František Rint in 1870 to form crosses, a coat of arms and a chandelier.

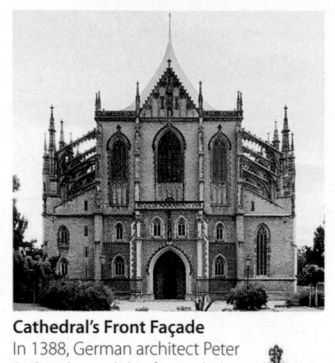

Cathedral's Front Façade
In 1388, German architect Peter Parler planned this five-aisled building, with three tented spires.

★ Vault
The central nave, with its magnificent geometric vaulted ceiling, was designed in the early 16th century by Benedikt Ried. It incorporates coats of arms from local crafts guilds.

Organ
The Baroque organ case dating from 1740–60 hides a much newer mechanism installed in the early 20th century by local organ maker Jan Tuček.

St Barbara's Cathedral

Dedicated to the patron saint of miners, St Barbara's Cathedral is one of Europe's most spectacular Gothic churches. Both the interior and exterior are richly ornamented, and the huge windows ensure it is filled with light. Many of the side chapels are decorated with interesting frescoes, some of which depict miners at work and men striking coins in the mint, reflecting the sources of the town's wealth.

Pulpit
The pulpit dating from 1655 is decorated with four stone reliefs, depicting the four Evangelists. It was produced in 1566 by Master Leopold.

VISITORS' CHECKLIST

Practical Information
70 km (45 miles) E of Prague.
🚹 21,000. 🅹 Palackého náměstí 377, 327 512 378.
Cathedral: **Open** 9am–6pm daily.
🕙 Ossuary: **Open** daily. 🕙
🆆 **kutnahora.cz**

Transport
🚆 🚌 from Prague.

Oak Stalls
The late 15th-century stalls, originally designed for St Vitus's Cathedral in Prague, feature Gothic spired canopies and carved balustrades.

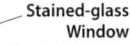

Stained-glass Window
The Art Nouveau stained-glass windows designed by František Urban were added in the early 20th century.

★ **High Altar**
The central scene of the Neo-Gothic high altar (1901–5), a replica of the original, depicts the Last Supper.

Balustrade
The stone balustrade of the presbytery includes the initials of King Vladislav Jagiello ("W") and his son Ludwig ("L").

❹ Hradec Králové

Located at the confluence of the Labe and Orlice rivers, Hradec Králové is one of the most beautiful cities in Bohemia. It first appeared in historical records in 1225 and later became an important Hussite and then Counter-Reformation centre. In the 20th century, the town acquired a new face when architects Jan Kotěra and Josef Gočár built many Modernist structures outside the medieval centre. The New Town (Nové Město) was developed between 1920 and 1930 by the two architects.

Old Town Hall and White Tower in Big Square

🏛 Big Square

The historic sights of the Old Town (Staré Město) are clustered around its former market square (Velké náměstí). One of the most opulent buildings here is the Old Town Hall (radnice). This Gothic edifice, erected before 1418, was remodelled in the late 16th century in the Renaissance style and the two clock towers were added in 1786. The hall served as a prison during the late 16th century.

On the southern side of the square is the Bishop's Palace, one of the town's finest Baroque buildings. It was designed by Giovanni Santini, a Bohemian architect of Italian origin who also created its magnificent entrance portal. Adjacent is the small-scale Baroque Špulak House (Dům U Špuláků). It was remodelled in 1750 by local architect F Kermer. The 20-m (66-ft) column in the square was erected in 1717 in thanksgiving for sparing the town from the plague of the previous year. The monument is probably by sculptor and architect GB Bullo. Adjoining the square to the northeast is the medieval Small Square (Malé náměstí).

🏛 Cathedral of the Holy Ghost

Velké náměstí.

This Gothic cathedral (Katedrála sv Ducha), founded in 1307, is proof of the town's wealth. In 1424, the church was the temporary burial site of Jan Žižka, leader of the Hussite movement. Striking features of its plain interior are the late-Gothic, 15th-century high altar, and in the south aisle, the Baroque altarpiece with a painting of St Anthony by Petr Brandl. The pewter baptismal font, dating from 1406, is one of the oldest in Bohemia.

Relief from the house opposite the cathedral

🏛 White Tower

Franušova 1. **Tel** 495 512 542. **Open** Apr–Sep: 9am–noon, 1–5pm daily.

The 72-m (235-ft) tall Renaissance belfry next to the cathedral was erected in 1589. The white stone used as the building material gave the structure its name: White Tower (Bílá věž), though the stone is now grey. The replacement clock fitted in 1829 can be misleading – the small hand points to the minutes and the large one to the hours.

🏛 Church of the Assumption of the Virgin Mary

Velké náměstí.

This church (Kostel Nanebevzetí Panny Marie) was built for the Jesuit Order by Carlo Lurago in the mid-17th century. A century later, the church burned down and only the chapel of St Ignatius Loyola, with its wall paintings and a picture by Petr Brandl of the glorification of the saint, was spared. The present façade, with its two towers, dates from 1857. The former Jesuit College, the long building to the right of the church, dates from the late 17th century.

🏛 Modern Art Gallery

Velké náměstí 139/140. **Tel** 495 514 893. **Closed** for renovation until spring 2015. 🅿 ♿ 🆆 galeriehk.cz

The striking five-storey Art Nouveau building of the Modern Art Gallery (Galerie moderního umění) was designed in 1912 by Osvald Polívka. Inside is an extensive collection of works by the finest Czech artists, including Jan

Interior of the Church of the Assumption of the Virgin Mary

For hotels and restaurants see p284 and p285

Impressive entrance hall of the Modern Art Gallery

Zrzavý, Jan Preisler, Josef Váchal, Václav Špála, Josef Čapek and Jiří Kolář.

🔲 Former Synagogue

Československé armády.

This distinctive building (synagoga) has a magnificent dome overlaid with sheet copper. It was completed in 1905 to a design by Václav Weinzettel, in the Art Nouveau style, with some Oriental elements. Apart from the prayer hall it also included the domestic quarters of the rabbi, the shammash and the caretaker; there was also a meeting room and space for the archives. The building served the Jewish community until World War II. After 1960 it was acquired

and renovated by the Hradec Králové Research Library, and it remains a library today.

🏛 Museum of Eastern Bohemia

Elíščino nábřeží 465. **Tel** 495 512 391. **Open** 9am–5pm Tue–Sun. 🦽 ♿ **W muzeumhk.cz**

The building of the Museum of Eastern Bohemia (Muzeum východních Čech) is one of the prime examples of Bohemian Modernism. It was built between 1909 and 1912 to a design by Jan Kotěra. Inside are some interesting exhibits – in particular, a scale model of the town from 1865, complete with all of its fortifications.

🚌 Prague Bridge

The 60-m (200-ft) long bridge (Pražský most) was designed by

Jan Kotěra in 1910. It replaced the oldest bridge in Hradec Králové, dating from 1796. Between 1910 and 1912, Kotěra added four pavilions to house shops. The architect also gave it distinctive fairy lighting and masts with the town's emblem. The bridge leads into the section of the New Town across the Labe.

View of the Labe river from the Prague Bridge

Hradec Králové Town Centre

① Big Square
② Cathedral of the Holy Ghost
③ White Tower
④ Church of the Assumption of the Virgin Mary
⑤ Modern Art Gallery
⑥ Former Synagogue
⑦ Museum of Eastern Bohemia
⑧ Prague Bridge

0 metres 200
0 yards 200

❺ České Švýcarsko

Famous for its extraordinary natural beauty, České Švýcarsko is a landscape of forests and fantastically shaped sandstone rocks, criss-crossed by gorges and ravines. Attracting visitors as early as the 19th century, a section of the region was designated a national park in 2000. Spread over an area of 79 sq km (30 sq miles) the geological park contains some of the area's most spectacular natural treasures and is a haven for wildlife.

Pravčická Brána
This is the largest natural rock bridge in Central Europe, at 26 m (85 ft) long, 7–8 m (25 ft) wide, and rising to a height of 16 m (52 ft).

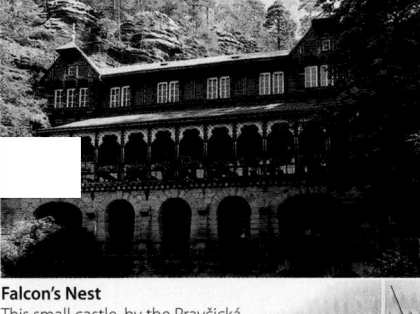

Falcon's Nest
This small castle, by the Pravčická Brána, belonged to the Clary-Aldringen family. It now houses a restaurant and the National Park Museum.

A hiking trail from Mezní Louka leads to the stone bridge of Pravčická brána, 6.5 km (4 miles) away. From here, hikers can continue for another 2.5 km (2 miles) on the same trail to Hřensko.

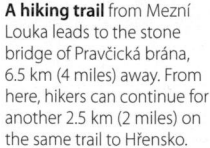

Mezní Louka

Hřensko
Děčín
12km (7 miles)

Mezná

Kamenice

Kamenic Stráň

Tichá Soutěska
Known as the "quiet gorge", this section of Kamenice Gorge stretches for 960 m (3,150 ft).

Kamenice Gorge
This narrow gorge runs between vertical walls of rocks, 50–150 m (165–500 ft) high. Boat trips go up- or downstream. The footpath along its banks was built in the 19th century by Italian workers.

Wildlife in the National Park
České Švýcarsko National Park is home to a range of animal species including the European beaver, river otter and lynx, which settled here in the 1930s, as well as the Alpine chamois, introduced in 1907.

VISITORS' CHECKLIST

Practical Information
144 km (89 miles) N of Prague.
ℹ️ Hřensko 82, 412 554 286.
National Park Museum: Falcon's Nest. **Tel** 604 238 209. **Open** Apr–Oct: 10am–6pm daily; Nov–Mar: 10am–4pm daily.
W pbrana.cz

Transport
🚌 from Děčín.

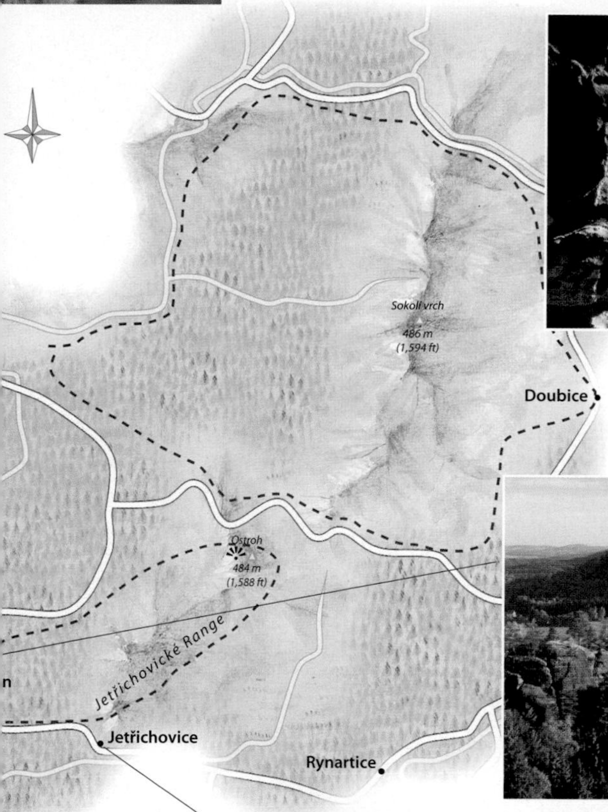

Sokolí vrch
486 m
(1,594 ft)

Doubice

Ostroh
484 m
(1,588 ft)

Jetřichovické Range

Jetřichovice

Rynartice

Trails
A network of clearly signposted hiking and cycling trails covers the entire area of the park.

Šaunštejn
This high rock platform, which was once the site of the small Šaunštejn Castle, can be reached by a series of vertical stepladders.

Jetřichovice
This scenic village, whose timber houses provide accommodation to many walkers, makes a good base for forays into the Jetřichovické Range.

0 km   1
0 miles   1

Key
═══ Road
--- Trail
△ Summit

For keys to symbols *see back flap*

❻ Karlovy Vary

World famous for its mineral springs, the town of Karlovy Vary was founded by Charles IV in the mid-14th century. Legend has it that he discovered it when his dog fell into a hot spring (*vary* means "hot spring") when out hunting. Since the 18th century, the rich and the famous have flocked here to take the waters. All the springs, the historic colonnades and architectural sights are located along the Teplá river. The town is also known for its porcelain and for Moser glassware.

The lovely wooden Market Colonnade and Castle Tower

🛁 Imperial Baths
Mariánskolázeňská 2.
The Imperial Baths (Císařské lázně), looking more like a theatre than a medical establishment, was once the most opulent structure in Karlovy Vary. Built between 1892 and 1895, it features a Neo-Renaissance façade and Art Nouveau decorations.

🏛 Karlovy Vary Museum
Nová louka 23. **Tel** 353 226 252.
Open 9am–noon, 1–5pm Wed–Sun. 🅿
The museum (Karlovarské Muzeum), established in 1853, has collections relating to the region's history and its natural environment; also on display are glass and porcelain items and handicrafts. Besides permanent displays, there are also topical exhibitions organized throughout the year.

🎭 Karlovy Vary Theatre
Divadelní náměstí 21.
Tel 353 225 621.
The Karlovy Vary Theatre (Městské divadlo), built between 1884 and 1886, is the work of Viennese architects Ferdinand Fellner and Hermann Helmer, who designed many theatre buildings all over Europe. It is worth stepping inside to see the grand interior decor, which includes paintings by Gustav Klimt, his brother Ernst and Franz Matsche. A collective work of all three 19th-century artists is the stage curtain, on which they painted their joint self-portrait. Following many years of reconstruction, the theatre was opened again in 1999.

Detail above Karlovy Vary Theatre entrance

⛪ Church of St Mary Magdalene
Kostelní náměstí.
Dating from 1732, and among the best work of the Bohemian architect Kilian Ignaz Dientzenhofer, this church (Kostel sv Máří Magdalény) is one of the finest examples of Baroque architecture in the region.
The single-aisled church with an oval floor plan has an impressively spacious interior with fine decor. The high altar features an image of Mary Magdalene from 1752. It is flanked by Jakob Eberle's 1759 sculptures of Saints Augustine, Jerome, Peter and Paul. It is also worth taking a closer look at the lavishly decorated side altars, the dome and the splendid galleries high up. The wavy façade of the church, with two towers, features a semi-circular stairway.

🛁 Market Colonnade
Tržiště.
This lovely white wooden colonnade (Tržni kolonáda), designed in Swiss style by architects Ferdinand Fellner and Hermann Helmer, was built between 1883 and 1884 on the site of a former Town Hall, which was demolished in 1879.
The colonnade contains two springs. Between 1991 and 1992 it underwent a thorough reconstruction, although it has retained its original appearance.

🛁 Mill Spring Colonnade
Mlýnské nabřeží.
Built between 1871 and 1881 by architect Josef Zítek, creator of the National Theatre *(see p255)* in Prague, the Mill Spring

---

Spa Resorts

Karlovy Vary in 1891

Clustered in the western part of the country, spa resorts began to emerge and flourish in the 18th century. Crowds of patients and prominent figures visited spas, initially to take medicinal baths, and later to drink spring waters in truly exclusive company and opulent surroundings. During the Communist era, spa cures were open to all who needed them, and spa treatments remain popular in the Czech Republic today. The spa towns continue to attract numerous German, Austrian and Russian visitors, and during the past 20 years many have been restored to their former glory.

Columns of the Mill Spring Colonnade

Colonnade (Mlýnská kolonáda) is the largest of the town's colonnades, and one of its most opulent.

The Neo-Renaissance gallery, 132-m (430-ft) long and 13-m (43-ft) wide, has a coffered ceiling resting on 124 columns with Corinthian capitals. Inside are five springs, with water temperatures exceeding 50º C (120º F). Statues at each end represent the 12 months of the year.

🏛 Park Spring Colonnade
Dvořákovy sady.

Right at the centre of town, stands Park Spring Colonnade (Sadová kolonáda), a beautiful, painted wrought-iron structure made of columns decorated with sculptures, terminating in two pavilions. The colonnade was designed by Ferdinand Fellner and Hermann Helmer between 1880 and 1881. It is located in the Dvořákovy sady gardens.

🏛 Church of Sts Peter and Paul
Krále Jiřího. **Open** 10am–5pm daily.
This church (Kostel sv Petra a Pavela) was built between

Gilded domes of the Church of Sts Peter and Paul

1893 and 1897 by architect G Wiedermann, and is among the world's largest Russian Orthodox churches. It was built for the Russian aristocracy, who flocked to Karlovy Vary in the 19th century.

⚜ Diana Viewpoint
Funicular. **Open** 9am–5pm daily (till 6pm Apr, May, Oct; till 7pm Jun–Sep).

Behind the Grandhotel Pupp, at the southern end of Stará Louka, is the lower station of the funicular, which runs to the top of the Hill of Friendship. Built in 1912, the funicular rises 167 m (550 ft).

At the top is the Diana Viewpoint (rozhledna Diana), providing a great view over the resort.

Karlovy Vary Town Centre

① Imperial Baths
② Karlovy Vary Museum
③ Karlovy Vary Theatre
④ Church of St Mary Magdalene
⑤ Market Colonnade
⑥ Mill Spring Colonnade
⑦ Park Spring Colonnade
⑧ Church of Sts Peter and Paul
⑨ Diana Viewpoint

0 metres   200
0 yards   200

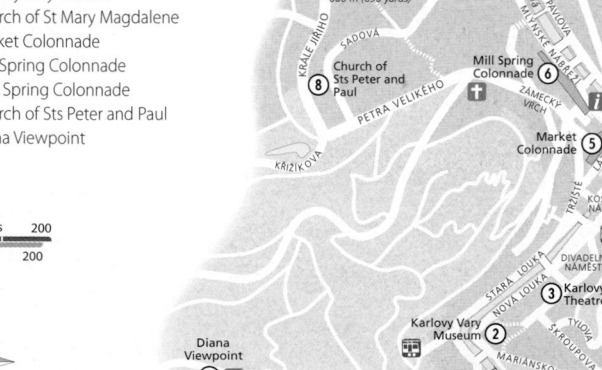

For keys to symbols *see back flap*

❼ Plzeň

West Bohemia's capital was established in 1295 by Wenceslas II at the crossroads of the main trading routes between Saxony, Bohemia and Bavaria. Today, the city is famous for its two main industries – Pilsner Urquell beer, produced here since 1842, and the large Škoda factory that has made armaments and cars since the late 19th century. Most of Plzeň's historic sites, including the Republic Square (Náměstí Republiky) and the Town Hall, are found on the left bank of the Radbuza.

The distinctive Plague Column on Náměstí Republiky

🏛 Republic Square

The market square of Plzeň, (Náměstí Republiky) is one of the largest in the Czech Republic, covering an area of 2.5 ha (6.5 acres). Standing at its centre is the Cathedral of St Bartholomew. The square is fringed by a number of beautiful houses, with the best-preserved along the southern side. Particularly striking is the Red Heart House (U červeného srdce), built in 1894 and sporting magnificent *sgraffito*. Painted by Mikuláš Aleš, the wall decoration shows two mounted knights in full tournament gear. The Bhishoprie (Biskupství) is located on the west side of the square. A market is occasionally held in the square.

🏛 Cathedral of St Bartholomew
See pp268–9.

A statue on Císařský dům

🏛 Town Hall
Náměstí Republiky.
Open 8am–6pm daily.

The lovely Renaissance Town Hall (Stará radnice) was designed by Italian architect Giovanni de Statio. This four-storey edifice with its spectacular gables was built between 1554 and 1559. The interesting *sgraffito* decorations on the façade are the work of J Koul, produced between 1907 and 1912. Standing in front of the Town Hall is the Plague Column built in 1681. It was erected to give thanks for the relative mildness of the epidemic suffered at that time.

🏛 Imperial House
Náměstí Republiky 41.

Located to the west of the Town Hall, this Renaissance edifice (Císařský Dům), dating from 1606, played host to Emperor Rudolph II twice. Today, it houses the tourist information office. The adjacent Pechlátovský House (Pechlátovský dům) was created by combining two Renaissance buildings and adding a Neo-Classical façade to them.

✡ Great Synagogue
Sady Pětatřicátníků 11.
Tel 377 235 749. **Open** Apr–Oct: 10am–6pm Sun–Fri. **Closed** Jewish festivals.

The world's third largest sacred Jewish building, after the synagogues in Jerusalem and Budapest (see p341), the Great Synagogue (Velká synagóga) was built in the 1890s. It was funded by donations from the Plzeň Jewish community. Its architect, Rudolf Štech, designed it in a Moorish-

Romanesque style. The synagogue could accommodate 2,000 worshippers, and the high balcony, intended for women, could take up to 800 people. After World War II, the building and its furnishings, including the unique organ located above the Torah, suffered gradual deterioration. In 1998, it was reopened after restoration.

Onion-domed twin towers of the Great Synagogue

🎭 Tyl Theatre
Smetanovy sady 16.
Tel 378 038 070. **W** djkt-plzen.cz

This theatre (divadlo JK Tyla) is named after Josef Kajetan Tyl, Czech playwright and novelist, and a champion of national culture in the 19th century. This Neo-Classical-style building was erected in 1902 and, like the National Theatre (see p255) in Prague, its design was intended to symbolize and reinforce Czech patriotism. The figures on the theatre's façade are allegories of opera and drama. The beautiful stage curtain was painted by Augustin Němejc.

⛪ Franciscan Monastery and Church of the Assumption
Františkánská.

This early-Gothic monastery (Františkánský klášter s kostelem Nanebevzetí) is one of the oldest buildings in the city. Off the lovely cloisters is the 13th-century Chapel of St Barbara; the chapel is decorated with frescoes from around 1460. The monastery's Church of the Assumption has a

Frescoes in the Franciscan Monastery

main altarpiece painting of the Annunciation, a copy of Rubens work. The Gothic Madonna, below the painting, is from the late 14th century.

🏛 Museum of West Bohemia
Kopeckého sady 2. **Tel** 378 370 111.
Open 10am–6pm Tue–Sun. 🅿
W **zcm.cz**
This museum (Západočeské muzeum) is in a Neo-Baroque building with a grand Art Nouveau interior dating from 1898. The reliefs on the staircase and the Art Nouveau library furnishings are impressive. Exhibits include the armoury of Charles IV, and a glass and porcelain collection in the vast, stately Jubilee Hall.

🏛 Brewery Museum
Veleslavínova 6. **Tel** 377 235 574.
Open Jan–Mar: 10am–5pm daily;
Apr–Dec: 10am–6pm daily.
Appropriately housed in an old malt house, this museum

Beautiful façade of the Museum of West Bohemia

(Pivovarské muzeum) traces the history of brewing in Plzeň with a fascinating range of beer-related exhibits.

🍺 Pilsner Urquell Brewery
U Prazdroje 7. **Tel** 377 062 888.
Open Apr–Sep: 8am–6pm daily; Oct–Mar: 8am–5pm daily. 🅿 🎫
The opulent brewery building, with its imposing Empire-style gate, is a 1917 work of the architect H Zapala. The attractions here – besides tasting Pilsner Urquell (Plzeňský Prazdroj) beer – include the chance to explore the interesting 10-km (6-mile) long cellars, used between 1838 and 1930 to store the fermenting brew.

Plzeň City Centre

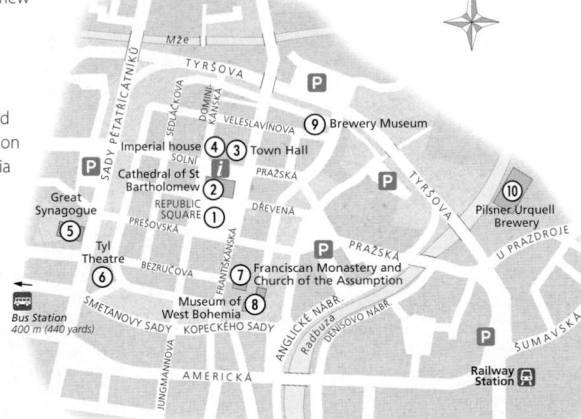

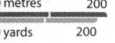

0 metres   200
0 yards   200

Plzeň: Cathedral of St Bartholomew

Chrám sv Bartoloměje

The Gothic Cathedral of St Bartholomew dominates Plzeň's Market Square *(see p266)* from its position in the centre. Its 102-m (335-ft) spire can be seen from all over the city, and was used in the 19th century by the imperial land surveyors in laying out transport routes around Plzeň. Construction of the church started in the late 13th century and continued until 1480. The Sternberg Chapel, adjoining the south wall of the presbytery, is an early 16th-century addition featuring an unusual keystone at the centre of the vault and Renaissance paintings.

★ **Cathedral Tower**
Originally the cathedral had two towers. One collapsed when struck by lightning in 1525.

Sculptures in the Cathedral
The church houses a large number of sculptures, including the figures of saints Barbara, Katherine and Wenceslas, on the pillars of the main nave.

Stained-glass Windows
The striking elongated stained-glass windows in the aisles and the presbytery, which provide the church interior with beautiful light, were fitted in the early 20th century.

KEY

① **Main door**

② **The tower** has a balcony at the top, which is open to the public.

③ **This small tower** is over the main nave.

④ **The presbytery** was given its present form in around 1360.

Pulpit
The sandstone Gothic pulpit as well as the grand traceried canopy above it, date from around 1360, the same period as the rood arch figures.

★ Plzeň Madonna
The statue of the Virgin Mary set at the centre of the main altarpiece dates from around 1390 and is an outstanding example of the International Gothic style.

Pendant Boss, Sternberg Chapel
This unusual hanging keystone in the vault of the chapel is a unique late-Gothic detail.

★ Sternberg Chapel
The Sternberg family founded this chapel in the early 16th century. It has a beautiful altar and marvellous Renaissance paintings.

Entrance

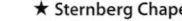

Rood Arch
Standing on the beam of the rood arch are figures in a Calvary scene. The crucifix was made in the 1470s by the Bohemian Master of Plzeň.

❽ České Budějovice

Founded in 1265, the town of České Budějovice had two magnificent churches and mighty town walls from as early as the 13th and 14th centuries. Spared by the Thirty Years' War, it was destroyed by the Great Fire of 1641. Today, the town is the political and commercial capital of southern Bohemia and is renowned for its Budvar Brewery. The town's well-preserved historic centre has maintained its original layout, with a central square and surrounding streets in a grid pattern.

České Budějovice's Town Square, one of Europe's largest squares

🔲 Town Square

The Town Square (Náměstí Přemysla Otakara II) bears the name of the town's founder, Přemysl Otakar II. Measuring 133 m (436 ft) on each side, the square is surrounded by arcaded houses, built mostly during the Middle Ages, that now have Baroque and Renaissance façades because of the numerous alterations made by their German owners. At the square's centre stands Samson's Fountain, built in 1727, with a sculpture of Samson and the Lion. Made by Josef Dietrich, it was for some time the only source of water for the town's population. The cobblestones were laid in 1934 in a distinctive square pattern.

Coat of arms on the Town Hall

🔲 Town Hall

Náměstí Přemysla Otakara II.
Tel 386 801 401. **Open** Jul & Aug: 10am, 2pm, 4pm Mon–Fri, 10am, 2pm Sat, Sun; May, Jun, Sep: 2pm daily.
🔲 ✔

The southwest corner of the Town Square is occupied by the Baroque three-towered, white-and-blue Town Hall (radnice) built by Antonio Martinelli between 1727 and 1730 to replace a Renaissance building. Allegorical statues of Justice, Providence, Wisdom and Honesty stand on the roof.

On top of the tallest tower is a statue of the Czech lion, and on the left side is the medieval standard ell measure (the forearm), used when measuring cloth. The Debating Hall features *The Judgement of Solomon* (1730) by Jan Adam Schöpf.

🏛 Dominican Monastery and Church of the Sacrifice of the Virgin

Piaristické náměstí.
Open 10am–5pm daily.

This former monastery (Kostel Obětování Panny Marie) was built at the same time as the founding of České Budějovice in 1265 and was altered by Peter Parler in the 14th century. Inside the monastery's church, cross-rib vaulting can be seen. The furnishing is mostly Neo-Gothic, but there is also a spectacular Rococo pulpit dating from 1759, and 17th-century organs. The Gothic cloister also has two original tracery windows that are fine examples of medieval stonemasonry work.

The large stone amphibian carved on the side wall by the church entrance, is a reminder of the local legend about the creature. It was believed to have been guarding a treasure that was hidden here, and had tried to prevent the construction of the church.

🔲 Butchers' Market

Krajinská 13.

The Renaissance Butchers' Market (Masné krámy) is now home to one of the most famous restaurants, Masné krámy, in České Budějovice. The building has three stone masks and the year of its construction, 1531, on its façade.

🔲 Black Tower

U Černé věže. **Tel** 386 352 508.
Open Apr–Jun, Sep, Oct: 10am–6pm Tue–Sun; Jul, Aug: 10am–6pm daily. 🖼

The Gothic-Renaissance Black Tower (Černa věž), dating from 1577, stands next to St Nicholas's Cathedral. It formerly served as a belfry and the town's observation tower. In 1723, two bells were placed in the belfry; a third bell, Budvar, was added in 1995. It was presented to the town by the nearby Budvar brewery. Visitors get a fine view of the town after climbing the 225 winding stairs to the top at a height of 72 m (236 ft).

The three-towered façade of the Town Hall

Black Tower with Samson's Fountain in the foreground

🔼 St Nicholas's Cathedral

U Černé věže.

On a small plot at the northeastern corner of the Town Square is St Nicholas's Cathedral (Chrám sv Mikuláše). This triple-aisled edifice started as a church in the 13th century. The original Gothic building burnt down in 1641 and was rebuilt a few years later in the Baroque style. The pulpit, a painting in the south chapel *Death of the Virgin Mary* (1740) and the main altarpiece (1791) by Leopold Huber are truly fascinating.

🏛 South Bohemia Museum

Dukelská 1. **Tel** 391 001 531.
Open 9am–5pm Tue–Sun.
W muzeumcb.cz

Established in 1887, this museum (Jihočeské muzeum) is the oldest of its kind in the region. It houses a natural science collection, regional exhibits and 16th–18th century art.

🔳 Iron Maiden

Zátkovo nábřeží.

Iron Maiden (Železná Panna), erected in the 14th century, was once a prison and torture chamber. The tower is named after the instrument of torture (and death) that was used here, the shape of which resembled a woman.

The 14th-century Iron Maiden, standing on the bank of the Malše

🏛 Motorcycle Museum

Piaristické náměstí. **Tel** 723 247 104.
Open Apr–Oct: 10am–6pm Tue–Sun.

The Motorcycle Museum (Motocyklové muzeum) housed in the former Salt House has numerous well-preserved old Czech machines and some Harley-Davidsons.

Environs

Located just north of the centre is the state-owned **Budvar Brewery** (Budějovický Budvar) where beer has been made since the 19th century. Visits can be arranged directly or via the tourist information office.

🔳 Budvar Brewery

Karolíny Světlé 4. **Tel** 387 705 347.
Open 9am–5pm daily (Jan–Feb: Tue–Sat). 📷 🎦 **W** visitbudvar.cz

Česke Budějovice Town Centre

① Town Square
② Town Hall
③ Dominican Monastery and Church of the Sacrifice of the Virgin
④ Butchers' Market
⑤ Black Tower
⑥ St Nicholas's Cathedral
⑦ South Bohemia Museum
⑧ Iron Maiden
⑨ Motorcycle Museum

0 metres   200
0 yards   200

❾ Český Krumlov

A well-preserved medieval town, Český Krumlov is one of the most-visited places in the Czech Republic. Founded in the 13th century, it belonged to the Rožmberk Dynasty between 1302 and 1602. It was added to the UNESCO World Cultural Heritage List in 1992. The historic town centre is situated on the rocky banks of the sharply meandering Vltava river. The Inner Town (Vnitřní Město), with its market square, Town Hall and Church of St Vitus, is located on the right bank.

🏛 Egon Schiele Centre

Široká 71. **Tel** 380 704 011.
Open 10am–6pm. **Closed** Mon.

A former brewery building, not far from Concord Square, this centre (Egon Schiele Centrum) now houses a gallery devoted to Austrian artist Egon Schiele (1890–1918), who lived in Český Krumlov in 1911. On display are watercolours and drawings, including several famous male and female nudes which in Schiele's day caused a scandal. He was driven out of the town for employing young local girls to pose for him. There are also temporary exhibitions of contemporary works on display.

🏛 Concord Square

The most imposing building in this market square (Náměstí Svornosti) is the Town Hall (radnice). It was created in the mid-16th century by combining two Gothic houses. The Marian Plague Column at the centre of the square was erected in 1716 as a thanksgiving for sparing the town from an outbreak of plague in 1682. Matthäus Jäckel, a Prague sculptor, placed a statue of the Madonna at the top of the column. At the foot of the column, in one of the niches, is a figure of St Roch, the saint invoked for protection against this disease.

Coat of arms on the Town Hall

🏛 Church of St Vitus

ulice Horní.

The Church of St Vitus (Chrám sv Víta) provides a visual counterbalance to the lofty tower of the Krumlov Castle. Dating from the early 15th century, and built on the site of an earlier church, this triple-aisled Gothic edifice has one of the oldest examples of net vaulting in Europe. The sanctuary by the north wall of the presbytery is a splendid example of stonemasonry dating from about 1500. The early-Baroque high altar, made between 1673 and 1683, has paintings depicting St Vitus and the coronation of the Virgin Mary. The late-Gothic porch has an unusual vault in the shape of octagonal stars. Gothic wall paintings dating from 1430 including *St Elizabeth with a beggar, St Katherine, The Crucifixion, St Veronica* and *Mary Magdalene*, can be seen on the north wall of the side aisle. The church once housed the *Krumlov Madonna* (1393), regarded by many as the finest example of the International Gothic style. It is now displayed in the Art History Museum in Vienna. Its 15th-century replica can be seen in the National Gallery in Prague.

The imposing nave of the Church of St Vitus

🏛 Ulice Horní

Regional Museum: Horní 152.
Open 9am–5pm Tue–Sun.
🌐 muzeumck.cz

Located off the market square, ulice Horní was once terminated by a town gate that was demolished in 1839. At No. 159 is the chaplaincy that was built between 1514 and 1520, with a beautiful Gothic gable and Renaissance window jambs. At No. 155 is the former prelature, built in the 14th century and remodelled several times since. Adjoining it is the former Jesuit College at No. 154, designed by Baldassare Maggi and now a hotel. At No. 152, the **Regional Museum** (Regionální muzeum) has a scale model of the town in 1800.

🏛 Latrán

The old quarter of Latrán was once a village inhabited by craftsmen and merchants, who provided services for the Krumlov Castle. It is linked to

Part of the façade of the former Jesuit College in ulice Horní

For hotels and restaurants see p284 and p285

The arcaded bridge linking Krumlov Castle with Castle Theatre

🏰 Krumlov Castle
Zámek 59. **Tel** 380 704 721.
Open Apr–Oct: 9am–5pm Tue–Sun (Jun–Aug: to 6pm). 2 routes.
Castle Theatre: **Tel** 380 704 721.
Open May–Oct: 10am–4pm (every hour, last adm 3pm) Tue–Sun.

This castle (Státní hrad a zámek Český Krumlov) is second only to Prague Castle in terms of its size with a total of 300 rooms. The most breathtaking are the Rožmberk Rooms, completed in 1576, with wooden vaults and Renaissance wall frescoes. The Hall of Masks, which is decorated with some extraordinary trompe l'oeil paintings depicting carnival scenes. A 17th-century tiered bridge (Plášťový most), complete with statues, links the Upper Castle

with **Castle Theatre** (Zámecké divaldo). Built in 1767, the theatre has a well-preserved interior, costumes and stage machinery. It was refurbished in the 20th century and offers a glimpse of theatrical life in the 18th century.

VISITORS' CHECKLIST

Practical Information
177 km (110 miles) S of Prague.
13,600. ℹ Náměstí Svornosti 2, 380 704 622. Five-Petalled Rose Celebration (mid-Jun), Int. Music Festival (mid-Jul–Aug).
🌐 ckrumlov.info

Tansport
🚉 Třída Míru 1 (1 km/0.5 mile N of Krumlov). Nemocniční.

the Inner Town by a bridge over the Vltava river.

All that remains today of the former village is a complex of late-Gothic and Baroque buildings, including the Minorite Monastery, the Convent of the Poor Clares and a church. The entire complex was linked with the castle by a covered walkway running over Latrán. Close by is the Renaissance Budějovice Gate, the only one left of the eight original town gates. It was built between 1598 and 1602 by the Italian architect Dominik Cometta.

Entrance to the Minorite Monastery in Latrán

Český Krumlov Town Centre

① Egon Schiele Centre
② Concord Square
③ Church of St Vitus
④ Ulice Horní
⑤ Latrán
⑥ Krumlov Castle

0 metres   100
0 yards   100

For keys to symbols *see back flap*

⑩ Telč

161 km (100 miles) SE of Prague.
🏙 5,600. 🚉 🚌 ℹ Náměstí
Zachariáše z Hradce 10, 567 112 407.
🅦 **telc.eu**

The turning point for Telč came in 1530, when a fire devastated the town. Lord Zachariáš, the governor of Moravia, brought in Italian master builders and architects to rebuild the town's castle. In the end, they rebuilt almost all the houses in the Renaissance style, endowing the town with a striking architectural uniformity that has survived to this day. Telč was added to the UNESCO World Heritage List in 1992.

The Main Square (Náměstí Zachariáše z Hradce), is lined with pastel-coloured houses with a breathtaking variety of gables and pediments, some 250 years old. At the narrow western end of the square is the **Telč Chateau** (Zámek Telč), a Renaissance building devised by Lord Zachariáš. Inside, the highlights are the rooms with stunning coffered ceilings, such as the Knight's Chambers. It also has a fine collection of arms and porcelain.

Modern Telč is separated from the Old Town by two fishponds, which almost surround the tiny historic centre.

🏠 **Telč Chateau**
Tel 567 243 943.
Open Apr–Oct: 9am-6pm.
🚫 📷 🅦 **zamek-telc.cz**

Telč Chateâu seen beyond the town's fishponds

⑪ Třebíč

163 km (101 miles) SE of Prague.
🏙 37,800. 🚉 🚌 ℹ Karlovo náměstí 47, 568 847 070.
🅦 **visittrebic.eu**

The industrial town of Třebíč is best known for the **Basilica of St Procopius** (Bazilika sv Prokopa) and its historic Jewish quarter. The church once belonged to a monastery, founded in 1101 by the Czech Royal Dynasty, the Přemyslids. It was transformed into a castle in the 1600s. The 13th-century church was restored in the Baroque period but retains its Romanesque portal, with floral and geometric patterns. Notable features include the rosette window in the apse and the unusual "dwarfs' gallery" running outside. The enormous crypt features 50 columns, each with a different capital. The restored Jewish quarter, Zámostí, between the Jihlava river and Hrádek Hill, is on UNESCO's World Heritage List. Třebíč's Jewish population peaked at the end of the 18th century but subsequently dwindled due to the impact of the Holocaust. With many original buildings intact, the quarter is evocative of the old ghetto. In particular, the colourful Leopold Pokorný ulice and richly frescoed Rear/ New Synagogue (Zadní/Nová synagóga) are worth a visit.

🏠 **Basilica of St Procopius**
Zámek 1. **Tel** 568 610 022. **Open** daily.
🚫 📷 (book in advance).

⑫ Znojmo

205 km (128 miles) SE of Prague.
🏙 34,100. 🚉 🚌 ℹ Obroková 10, 515 222 552. 🅦 **znojmocity.cz**

Above the Dyje river lies Znojmo, one of Moravia's oldest towns, with a network of small streets at its heart. The best of its historic sights is the Romanesque Rotunda of St Catherine (sv Kateřiny), located inside the **Znojmo Castle** (Znojemský hrad), which has striking frescoes and portraits of Přemyslid princes. A large part of the castle is now a brewery. The lane of Velka Mikulasska leads to the Gothic Cathedral of St Nicholas (sv Mikuláš), which has a globe-shaped Baroque pulpit.

🏠 **Znojmo Castle**
Přemyslovců 8. **Tel** 515 222 311.
Open Apr: 9am–5pm Sat & Sun; May–Sep: 9am–5pm Tue–Sun.
🚫 ♿ limited access.

Panoramic view of Znojmo, one of Moravia's oldest towns

⑬ Mikulov

251 km (156 miles) SE of Prague.
7,000. Náměstí 1, 519 510 855. mikulov.cz

Built on a hillside close to the Austrian border east of Znojmo, Mikulov is a picture-postcard town with delightful streets and some fine Renaissance and Baroque houses. **Mikulov Castle** (zámek Mikulov), originally 13th-century but much altered, was used by the Gestapo, the secret state police of Nazi Germany, to hoard confiscated art objects. It was burnt down in the final days of World War II. Rebuilt in the 1950s, it now houses the local museum and has a large collection of portraits of Habsburg royalty and cardinals. It also has fine vaults, which were used for centuries to store locally made wine.

In the mid-19th century Mikulov was home to the second-largest Jewish community in the Czech region. Its once thriving Jewish quarter, with a renovated 16th-century synagogue, lies to the west of the castle. Round the corner on Brněnská ulice, a rugged path leads to a medieval Jewish cemetery that has over 4,000 graves and finely carved marble tombstones dating back to 1605.

Mikulov Castle
Zámek 1. **Tel** 519 309 019.
Open Apr, Oct: 9am–4pm Tue–Sun; Jul, Aug: 9am–6pm Tue–Sun; May, Jun, Sep: 9am–5pm Tue–Sun.
rmm.cz

Sumptuous furnishings in the Imperial Room, Archbishop's Palace, Kroměříž

⑭ Brno

See pp276–7.

⑮ Kroměříž

271 km (169 miles) SE of Prague.
29,100. kromeriz.eu

The historic town of Kroměříž, with its lovely gardens and architecturally appealing buildings, has survived the Communist period relatively unscathed. The main square, Velké náměstí, has been carefully restored and is one of the prettiest in Moravia.

The main attraction, just north of the square, is the magnificent UNESCO-listed **Archbishop's Palace** (Arcibiskupský zámek), the seat of the Bishops of Olomouc between the 12th and the 19th centuries. This vast Baroque fortress has some splendidly furnished rooms and houses the impressive art collection of the Liechtenstein family, with works by Titian, Van Dyck, Veronese and Cranach.

Among the highlights is the Assembly Hall, where talks were once held by the exiled Austrian Imperial Parliament from 1848–9, during which they drafted a new constitution. The Imperial Room includes portraits of Franz Joseph I, who went hunting here with Tsar Alexander III. Their trophies can be seen in the Hunting Hall. Above the main entrance, the Vassals' Hall (Mansky sál) has a magnificent ceiling fresco (1759) by the Viennese artist F A Mauelbertsch, while the library houses 90,000 volumes dating from the 16th and 17th centuries.

Archbishop's Palace
Sněmovní náměstí 1. **Tel** 573 502 011.
Open Apr, Oct: 9am–4pm Sat & Sun; May, Jun, Sep: 9am–5pm Tue–Sun; Jul, Aug: 9am–6pm Tue–Sun (or by appt).
3 routes.

Mikulov Castle, set above the red rooftops of the pretty town of Mikulov

⑭ Brno

The second largest city in the Czech Republic, Brno occupies the site of what was in the 9th century the main settlement in the Great Moravian Empire. Located on the confluence of the Svitava and Svratka rivers, the city developed at the foot of Petrov Hill. In 1641 it became the new capital of Moravia but did not develop significantly until the 19th century. World War II devastated the city and despite being totally rebuilt, Brno has never quite regained its former lustre. However, its buoyant theatre life and museums have made Brno a major cultural centre. The city's Old Town is focused around two squares – Zelný Square and Freedom Square.

Sculptures by Anton Pilgram on the Old Town Hall's doorway

View of the Cathedral of Sts Peter and Paul

⛪ Cathedral of Sts Peter and Paul

Petrov Hill. **Open** 8:15am–6:30pm daily. ⛪

This cathedral (Katedrála sv Petra a Pavla) was built on the site where Brno's first castle probably stood in the 11th and 12th centuries. Originally Romanesque, the church acquired a Gothic appearance in the 1200s, but countless subsequent alterations eventually obliterated its original shape. It was restored to its Gothic form in the late 1800s. Of great interest inside is the crypt of the original church.

⛪ Church of the Holy Cross

Kapucínské náměstí. 5. Crypt: **Open** 9am–noon, 2–4pm Tue–Sat (also May–Sep: Mon), 11–11:45am, 2–4:30pm Sun.

The austere façade of the Church of the Holy Cross (Kostel sv Kříže), near the foot of Petrov Hill, is typical of Capuchin churches elsewhere in Europe. The rather macabre attraction of the church are the mummified monks in the **Crypt**.

🏛 Zelný Square

This square (Zelný trh), meaning cabbage market, has served as a vegetable market for the locals since the Middle Ages, and has retained its original, sloping shape. Its main adornment is the Parnassus Fountain. Made to a design by Fischer von Erlach in the 1690s, it combines the best traits of Baroque naturalism, trompe-l'oeil and theatrics. Among the buildings around the square is the home of the Reduta theatre. This is the oldest theatre building in Brno. The Dietrichstein Palace (Dietrichsteinský palác), built in 1700 at the square's southern end, is home to the Moravian Museum, devoted to Brno's early history.

🏛 Old Town Hall

Radnická 8. **Open** Apr–Sep: 9:30am–6pm daily. **Tel** 542 427 106.

Just off Zelný trh, the Old Town Hall (Stará radnice) is the oldest secular building in Brno, dating from 1240. In 1510, a doorway was cut into the tower on Radnická and framed by a superb Gothic portal. This work by Anton Pilgram is decorated at the lower level with figures of knights and, above, with statues of the city's aldermen. At the centre is the allegorical figure of Blind Justice. A pinnacle above the statue is deliberately twisted, said to be Pilgram's revenge for being underpaid for his work. The main tourist office is located here.

🏛 New Town Hall

Dominikánské náměstí 1.

The New Town Hall (Nová radnice), the seat of the city council, dates mainly from the 1700s. It was built inside a former Dominican monastery; the Dominican **St Michael's Church** stands nearby. Gothic cloisters survive inside the Town Hall.

🏛 Freedom Square

Brno's main square (Náměstí Svobody) buzzes with life – its restaurants and cafés are popular meeting places. The architecture around the square spans 400 years. Its finest buildings include the Schwartz House (Schwarzův palác), with a 16th-century façade decorated with *sgraffito*, and the 20th-century House of the Four Mamlases (Dům u Čtyř Mamlasů), whose four comical Atlas figures strain to support the building. The chief landmark is the Plague Column.

Sculpture outside St Michael's Church, New Town Hall

🏛 Moravian Gallery

Husova 18. **Tel** 532 169 111.
Open 10am–6pm Wed, Fri–Sun,
10am–7pm Thu. 🅿

The Moravian Gallery
(Moravská Galerie) is spread
over three premises. Out of
the three, the most spectacular
complex is **Jurkovič House**.
Located at Jana Nečase 2,
Jurkovič House is a splendid
example of architecture created
in Brno around the beginning
of the 20th century.

🏰 Špilberk

Špilberk. **Tel** 542 123 611. Dungeons:
Open 10am–5pm Tue–Sun (to 6pm
May–Sep). 🅿 🌐 **spilberk.cz**

A hilltop castle was built
on this site by the Moravians
in the 13th century, but
Špilberk gained the status
of a royal residence only
400 years later, when it was
transformed into a mighty
Baroque fortress. Its **Dungeons**,
a maze of dark subterranean
corridors, were transformed,

VISITORS' CHECKLIST

Practical Information
206 km (128 miles) SE of Prague.
🅰 384,000. ℹ Stará radnice,
Radnická 8, 542 427 150.
🎟 Moto Grand Prix (Aug).
🌐 ticbrno.cz

Transport
✈ 10 km (6 miles) S of Brno.
🚉 Hlavní Nádraží. 🚌 Zvonařka.

during the reign of Emperor
Joseph II, into a series of
gruesome prisons. These
prisons were later used by
the Nazis. Displays inside
relate to Brno and the castle.

⛪ Augustinian Monastery

Mendlovo náměstí. **Tel** 543 424 010.
Museum: **Open** 10am–6pm Tue–Sun
(to 5pm Nov–Mar). 🅿 ♿

The Augustinian monastery
(Augustiniánský klášter) has
a fine Gothic church, but it is
famous above all as the place
where Gregor Mendel (1822–
84) discovered and formulated
his theory of genetics. A **Museum**,
known as the Mendelianum
and dedicated to his work,
is located in the monastery's
west wing.

Brno's Freedom Square, with its Baroque Plague Column

Brno City Centre

① Cathedral of Sts Peter and Paul
② Church of the Holy Cross
③ Zelný Square
④ Old Town Hall
⑤ New Town Hall
⑥ Freedom Square
⑦ Moravian Gallery
⑧ Špilberk

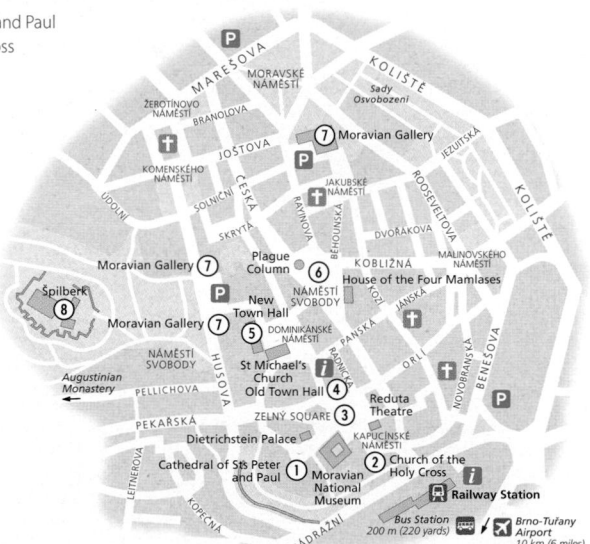

0 metres   250
0 yards   250

⑯ Olomouc

According to legend, Olomouc, one of Moravia's oldest towns, was founded by Julius Caesar. However, the town did not actually come into existence until the 7th century, when it grew into a major power centre. In 1063 it was made a bishopric and in 1187, the capital of Moravia; from 1655 it became a military stronghold. Today, Olomouc is a prosperous and vibrant university city. The oldest part of the historic town centre, surrounded by a ring of parks, is centred on the Main Square (Horní náměstí). This part of the town is fascinating to explore for its lively atmosphere and beautiful religious buildings.

Stained-glass window, Church of St Maurice

⛪ Church of St Maurice
8. května. **Open** 7am–6pm daily. 🎟
Tower: **Open** May–Oct: 9am–5pm
Mon–Sat, noon–5pm Sun. 📷

The 15th-century Church of St Maurice (sv Mořice), with two asymmetrical towers, resembles a medieval fortress. Outside, it has a highly unusual architectural detail in the form of an external staircase enclosed within a round cage. The Gothic interior is impressive, with stained-glass windows and a vast 1505 wall painting. The church also houses the largest organ in Central Europe, made by the esteemed organ maker Michael Engler, in 1745. The church's **Tower** provides panoramic views of the Main Square.

🏛 Main Square
The Main Square (Horní náměstí) has at its centre the grand 13th-century **Town Hall** (radnice), which was greatly extended in the 15th century, when it acquired an exquisite astronomical clock. A finely vaulted Gothic Debating Hall and a chapel dedicated to St Jerome were also added during the renovation. The huge Holy Trinity Column (sousoší Nejsvětější Trojice) in front of the Town Hall was added to the UNESCO World Heritage List in 2000. This unique example of Baroque sculpture was erected between 1716 and 1717. Its three tiers are decorated with historical figures and saints and crowned by figures representing the Holy Trinity. Olomouc has seven fountains, three of which are located in this square. The largest of them, made by local architect Jan J Schauberger in 1725, is the **Caesar Fountain**, sporting an equestrian statue of Gaius Julius Caesar, the legendary founder of the town. The other two are the Arion Fountain, depicting the ancient poet Arion, and the Hercules Fountain, portraying the famed Greek hero holding a white eagle – the official symbol of the town.

Top of the Holy Trinity Column

⛪ Church of St Michael
Žerotínovo náměstí.
Open 10am–noon, 2:30–3:30pm Wed, 2:30–3:30pm Fri. 🎟

The Dominicans, who arrived in Olomouc in about 1240, soon began to build a monastery and the Church of St Michael (sv Michala) on the town's most elevated site. In the 14th and 15th centuries it was destroyed by fire, and in the 17th century it suffered damage during the Thirty Years' War. Between 1673 and 1699 it was rebuilt in Baroque style by the architect Giovanni Pietro Tencalla, who designed the first three-domed edifice in Moravia. Most of the furnishings, including the organs, date from the Baroque period. In 1829, the main façade of the building was decorated with fine statues of the Virgin Mary and Christ, produced by Ondřej Zahner.

Sculptures in the cloister of the Church of St Michael

⛪ St Jan Sarkander Chapel
Na Hradě. **Tel** 603 282 975.

This chapel (sv Jana Sarkandera) is a Neo-Baroque building designed by E Sochor between 1909 and 1912. Dedicated to Jan Sarkander, a 17th-century preacher who was canonized by Pope John Paul II in 1995, it was erected on the site of the town prison.

⛪ Church of Our Lady of the Snows
Denisova. **Open** 10am–5pm daily. 🎟
Built between 1712 and 1722 by Olomouc Jesuits, this church (Panny Marie Sněžné) served, until 1778, as the university church. Over the years it has undergone a thorough restoration. The main features of its façade are the monumental portal including four columns and a balustraded balcony. The lavishly decorated interior includes superb Baroque paintings.

Sculptures on the dome of St Jan
Sarkander Chapel

▥ Olomouc Art Museum

Denisova 47. **Tel** 585 514 111.
Open 10am–6pm Tue–Sun.
▨ ♿

This art gallery (muzeum
umění) is located in a
modernized historic building.
It has a wide collection of
paintings by Italian artists
ranging from the 14th
century onwards, as well
as an excellent collection of
20th-century Czech works.

⛪ St Wenceslas Cathedral

Václavské náměstí. **Open** daily.
Not many traces remain of the
Romanesque church that was
originally built here in 1107. The
present church (sv Václav) was
a result of the initiative of Archbishop Bedřich Fürstenberg, who
ordered its reconstruction between
1883 and 1892 in Neo-Gothic style.

⛪ Přemyslid Palace

Václavské náměstí. **Tel** 585 514 174.
Open May–Sep: 10am–6pm Tue–Sun.
Olomouc Archdiocesan Museum:
Open Tue–Sun. ▨ ♿

This palace (Přemyslovský
palác) is one of Olomouc's

Decorative motifs on the pillars inside
St Wenceslas Cathedral

most picturesque buildings. It
was built after 1126 by Bishop
Jindřich Zdík and was one
of the most excellent works
of residential architecture in
Europe. The bishop's rooms,
with their carved Romanesque
windows and columns, are
considered to be the best
in the country.

The **Olomouc Archdiocesan
Museum** was opened in 2006,
with some fine paintings
collected by the Olomouc
bishops. The building also
houses the Mozarteum
concert hall.

Olomouc Town Centre

① Church of St Maurice
② Main Square
③ Church of St Michael
④ St Jan Sarkander Chapel
⑤ Church of Our Lady of the Snows
⑥ Olomouc Art Museum
⑦ St Wenceslas Cathedral
⑧ Přemyslid Palace

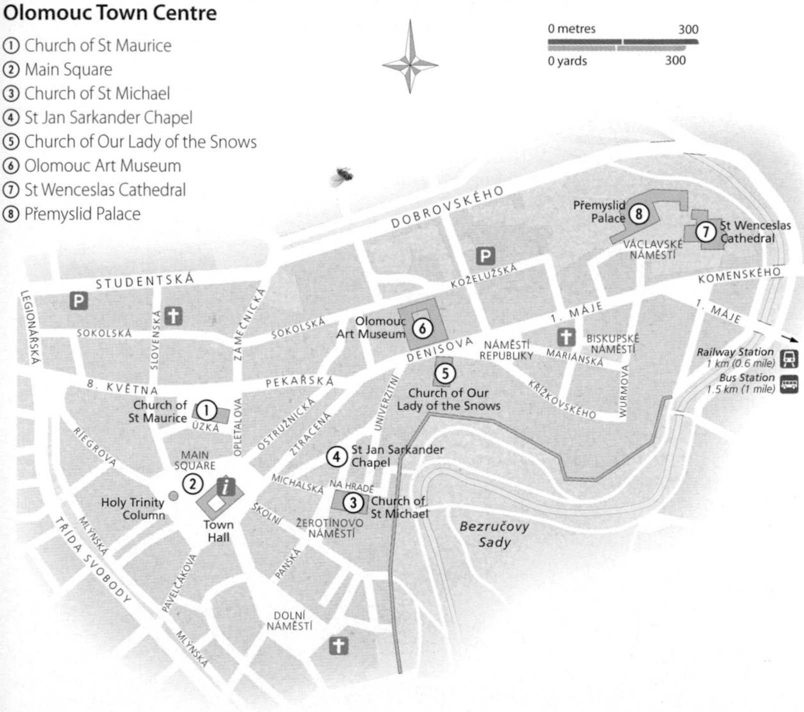

0 metres   300
0 yards   300

Map of Olomouc Town Centre showing streets including DOBROVSKÉHO, STUDENTSKÁ, KOZELUŽSKÁ, KOMENSKÉHO, SOKOLSKÁ, T. MÁJE, PEKAŘSKÁ, DENISOVA, NÁMĚSTÍ REPUBLIKY, 8. KVĚTNA, ŘÍGROVA, MAIN SQUARE, Holy Trinity Column, Town Hall, Bezručovy Sady, and numbered sites 1–8

Practical & Travel Information

Since the Velvet Revolution of 1989 *(see p224)*, the Czech Republic has become far more open to visitors. The country has responded well to the huge influx of tourists, and facilities such as communications, public transport, banks and information centres have improved considerably. Travelling by train is a great way to explore the country at leisure, although buses tend to be cheaper and faster. Remote places are most easily visited by car.

When to Visit

The best time to visit the country is between May and September. During these months the warm weather makes for pleasant outdoor excursions such as camping and mountain trekking. The busiest months are August and September, although Prague can also be very crowded in July. While the main sights are often packed at these times, the crowds lend a festive atmosphere, which can make a visit all the more enjoyable. Late September is a good time to visit Moravia to catch the grape harvest season. Many sights are closed between the end of October and the beginning of April.

Documentation

Citizens of EU countries do not need a visa to travel to the Czech Republic; they are simply required to carry a passport that is valid for at least 6 months, or an ID card. New Zealand, Australian and US citizens need a valid passport to enter the country and can stay for up to 90 days. UK citizens are entitled to stay for up to 180 days without a visa. For more information, consult the nearest Czech Embassy or the Foreign Affairs Ministry's website.

Visitor Information

The Czech Republic has a very efficient network of tourist information offices, which can be found in almost every town, village and resort. They are usually run by the local council and are open from 9am to 5pm (7pm in Prague). Many employ English-speaking staff and offer a variety of English-language publications, maps and guides. The **Prague Information Service (PIS)** is the best source of tourist information for visitors to the capital. It has three offices located in the city centre, providing information in several languages.

Health and Security

There is a reasonable standard of health care in the Czech Republic. EU nationals are entitled to receive free medical treatment, but in all other cases medical help has to be paid for. It is advisable to take out travel insurance to cover any medical costs incurred abroad. For prescription and non-prescription medicines, it is advisable to visit a *lékárna* (pharmacy). Pharmacies are found in large towns and are open on weekdays from 8am until 6pm, and on Saturdays until 2pm.

Violent crime against tourists is rare in the Czech Republic. The main problem, especially in Prague, is petty theft from cars, hotel rooms and pockets. Visitors are advised to carry their passports with them and to keep a separate photocopy.

Facilities for the Disabled

Despite some improvements, the country is not very easy for disabled travellers to negotiate. In Prague, however, hotels, restaurants and historic sights have made efforts to improve access. A number of railway stations, trains and some of the capital's metro stations now provide wheelchair access. Disabled travellers seeking advice on transport, accommodation and sightseeing tours should contact the **Prague Organization of Wheelchair Users**.

Banking and Currency

The Czech unit of currency is the Czech crown (Kč). Banking hours are generally 9am to 5pm Monday to Friday, with some branches closing for lunch. Private exchange bureaus add higher commission charges, and the rate of exchange is often much less favourable than that offered by banks. Traveller's cheques can only be changed in banks. Credit cards are becoming more widely accepted.

Communications

Telephone and postal services in the Czech Republic are very efficient. Every town and village has a post office and public telephones. Card-operated

The Climate of the Czech Republic

The Czech Republic enjoys long, warm days in summer, with June, July and August the hottest months. Winter can be bitterly cold, with temperatures often dropping below freezing; heavy snow is not uncommon. The wettest months are October and November, but frequent, light showers occur in the summer months as well.

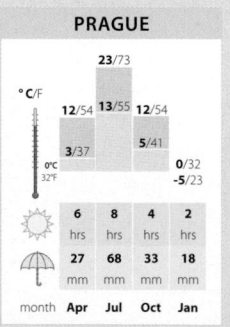

PRAGUE			
		23/73	
°C/F	12/54	13/55	12/54
	3/37		5/41
0°C 32°F			0/32 -5/23
6 hrs	8 hrs	4 hrs	2 hrs
27 mm	68 mm	33 mm	18 mm
month Apr	Jul	Oct	Jan

public phone booths are found all over the country. *Telefonní karta* (phone cards) are available at post offices and newsstands. International calls can be made from public phones, post offices or hotels, although the latter option is expensive. Most post offices are open from 8am to 6 or 7pm, Monday to Friday, and on Saturday morning. *Známky* (stamps) can be purchased at most newsstands as well as post offices. All towns have at least one Internet café. Many hotels also offer Internet access.

Arriving by Air

The country's biggest air transport hub for both international and domestic flights is Prague's **Ruzyně Airport**, which is about 20 km (12 miles) from the city centre. The main Czech carrier is **Czech Airlines (ČSA)**, although Prague is also served by most major European airlines as well as a number of low-cost carriers, including **easyJet**, **Jet2.com** and **Wizzair** from the UK.

Those travelling from Australia, New Zealand and Canada will need to fly to another European capital and take a connecting flight to Prague. A number of carriers, including **Lufthansa**, operate flights from the US via another European city.

Čedaz runs an inexpensive minibus service from Prague's Ruzyně Airport to the city centre. Taxis are also available from the airport to Prague.

Rail Travel

Prague is connected by rail to all the major capitals of Europe. Nearly all international trains arrive at and depart from Hlavní Nádraží, the city's biggest and busiest station.

The rail network is run by Czech Railways, **České Dráhy (ČD)**, which operates several types of domestic routes. Express trains *(rychlík)* stop only at major towns and cities and it is best to reserve a *místenka* (seat) on these. Slower, cheaper trains, or *osobní*, stop at every station and run on local routes. Czech railway stations are well equipped. Detailed information on train services, fares and timetables is available on the ČD website.

Travelling by Bus

Travelling by bus between Prague and other European cities is significantly less expensive than rail or air travel. It is advisable, especially in summer, to book well in advance. **Eurolines** and Student Agency are the main operators of international bus routes to Prague.

Within the Czech Republic, there is an extensive network of inter-city bus routes operated by a variety of national and regional companies. Travelling by bus is cheaper than by train, and sometimes it is faster.

The main bus terminal in Prague is Florenc Station, which serves international and long-distance domestic routes.

Travelling by Car

Well-maintained roads and long sections of motorway make driving one of the best methods of exploring the country. Visitors driving on Czech roads must carry a valid International Driving Permit and an ID card. To travel on the motorways, visitors are required to purchase a *dálniční známka* (tax disc). These are valid for either 10 days or a month and are available from post offices and petrol stations.

Most of the major car rental firms, including **Avis** and **Budget**, have offices in Prague and at Ruzyně Airport, but hiring is relatively expensive.

DIRECTORY

Documentation

W mzv.cz

Visitor Information

W czechcentres.cz

Prague Information Service
Tel 221 714 444.
W praguewelcome.cz

Embassies

Australia
Klimentská 10, Prague.
Tel 221 729 260.

Canada
Muchova 6, Prague.
Tel 272 101 800.
W canada.cz

New Zealand
Malé náměstí 1, Prague.
Tel 23 47 84 777.

United Kingdom
Thunovská 14, Prague.
Tel 257 402 111.
W britain.cz

United States
Tržiště 15, Prague.
Tel 257 022 000.
W usembassy.cz

Emergency Numbers

Ambulance
Tel 112 or 155.

Fire
Tel 112 or 150.

Police
Tel 112 or 158.

Facilities for the Disabled

Prague Organization of Wheelchair Users
Benediktská 6, Prague.
Tel 224 827 210.

Arriving by Air

Czech Airlines (ČSA)
W csa.cz

easyJet
W easyjet.com

Jet2.com
W jet2.com

Lufthansa
W lufthansa.com

Ruzyně Airport
W prg.aero

Wizzair
W wizzair.com

Rail Travel

České Dráhy (ČD)
Tel 840 112 113.
W cd.cz

Travelling by Bus

Eurolines
W eurolines.co.uk

Travelling by Car

Avis
Klimentská 46, Prague.
Tel 221 851 225.
W avis.cz

Budget
Ruzyně Airport, Prague.
Tel 235 325 713.
W budget.cz

Shopping & Entertainment

Shopping in the Czech Republic is undergoing great changes, with malls springing up in towns and international chains opening branches. In Prague an eclectic range of Western goods is on offer, as well as typical Czech products such as crystal, wooden toys, antiques and Czech gemstones, particularly garnets. The country also offers a wide variety of entertainment with something for every taste. Those looking for nightlife will get the most from Prague, with its scores of nightclubs, theatres and music venues. Outside Prague, most towns and cities have a lively cultural scene. Many towns organize rock concerts featuring local and international artists.

Opening Hours

Most shops are open from 9am to 6pm, Monday to Friday. On Saturdays shops close at 1 or 2pm. However, many tourist shops are open every day until 7 or 9pm. Supermarkets and large shopping centres are usually open to 9 or 10pm daily, and some in larger cities are open 24 hours. On Sundays in small towns and villages all shops remain closed, or open for just a few hours in the morning.

Markets

Prague has several famous markets. Its Christmas and Easter markets in the Old Town Square and Wenceslas Square *(see p253)* are filled with festive and traditional goods. There are also two permanent markets. The central, open-air **Havel Market** sells fruit and vegetables as well as toys and ceramics; it is open all year round. The indoor Prague Market (Pražská tržnice) sells consumer goods and is also open year round.

Outside Prague there are local markets in most towns and cities selling produce and crafts.

Glass and Ceramics

Bohemia is famous for its high-quality lead crystal and ornamental glass and almost every town has a shop specializing in glass and crystalware. The Old Town quarter *(see pp242–3)* in Prague has scores of them with **Erpet Bohemia**, **Dana-Bohemia**, **Moser** and

Česky Porcelán among the best known. Interesting souvenirs include gilded and hand-painted crystal wine glasses and traditional earthenware beer tankards decorated with the Czech brewery logo.

Handicrafts

Czech craftsmen have kept up the tradition of making handicrafts and the range of souvenirs on offer includes ceramics, wooden vessels and toys. The largest selection of such goods can be found at local markets, but gift and souvenir shops may also stock some interesting items.

Antiques

The Czech Republic is rich in antiques. During the 1990s specialist antique shops, called *starožitnosti*, opened and are now to be found in almost every town. Some of the well-known dealers in Prague's Old Town include **Antikvariát Pražský Almanach**, **Dorotheum** and **Pražské Starožitnosti**, stocking old books, antique furniture, paintings and porcelain. The prices are often more reasonable than in Western Europe.

Food and Drink

Czech chocolates are quite famous, and range from boxed chocolates to *tyčinky* (bars) and wafers. Spa hotels and speciality shops often sell spa wafers. The country is also known for

producing excellent cheese. Try the long strings of smoked cheese available in delicatessens, or *olomoucké tvarůžky*, an oval cheese with a distinct flavour. Department stores, found in almost every large town, are a good bet for food shopping.

The famous Czech beers Pilsner Urquell *(Plzeňský Prazdroj)* and Budvar, which make excellent presents, can be bought in almost every food store. Czech liquors, including the famous Becherovka, are also available throughout the country. Absinthe and *slivovice* (plum brandy) are other popular Czech spirits. As for wine, those from southern Moravia are the country's finest and are well worth taking back home. In Prague, a good selection of alcoholic drinks is available in the **Jan Paukert Delicatessen and Wine Bar**.

Cinema

There are cinemas throughout the country, even in small towns. One of the biggest multiplexes in Prague is the **Cinema City Flora** complex. The annual International Film Festival is the largest Czech cinema event, held in early July in Karlovy Vary *(see pp264–5)*.

Classical Music, Theatre and Opera

Classical music has a long tradition in the Czech Republic and the country has produced some well-known composers, including Bedřich Smetana, Antonín Dvořák, Leoš Janáček and Bohuslav Martinů. Their works figure in the repertoires of local orchestras all year round. Although most orchestras and concert halls close over the summer holiday season, this is when numerous classical music concerts are staged in churches, castles and palaces. Many churches in Prague and several other large cities organize concerts of Baroque music year round. The **Rudolfinum** in Prague is home to the Czech Philharmonic Orchestra, while the Prague Symphony Orchestra is based at **Municipal House** *(see pp252–3)*. Brno *(see pp276–7)* also has an active classical music scene with the **National Theatre** another superb venue for concerts.

Theatre has played an important role in the cultural development of the Czech Republic. Most large towns have a theatre, often a historic building with a beautiful interior. Prague's **National Theatre** is the city's main drama venue, but there are many mainstream and fringe theatres, such as the **Laterna Magika** and the **Komedie Theatre**, both of which stage more avant-garde productions. Tickets for the National Theatre can be purchased on the Internet, with group tickets to the most popular performances available well in advance.

As a rule, theatres display the plays that are currently in their repertoire on the front of the building. Few productions outside Prague are performed in English. During the 20th century, opera became popular in Prague and there are now two major opera

companies in the city: the **State Opera** and the **Estates Theatre**. Both stage first-class operas and ballets. The State Opera presents all its performances in the language in which they are written, usually Italian.

Music Festivals

Czech music festivals are one of the country's greatest attractions for music lovers. Of these the most famous is the **Prague Spring International Music Festival**. Prague Castle also stages **Strings of Autumn**, a traditional music festival held from October to December.

Nightlife

Every large Czech town has a music club, although Prague naturally has the greatest number. The best-known cultural centre in the capital is the **Palace Akropolis** complex, including a theatre, concert hall, exhibition space,

café and restaurant. It attracts many world music artists. **Agharta Jazz Centrum** is Prague's best jazz club. **Karlovy lázně** (Charles Spa) is a famous three-storey club close to the Charles Bridge entrance, with five stages offering different kinds of music from house to R&B. There are a number of rock venues hosting a variety of groups, **Roxy** is one of the most popular. Prague also has a lively gay and lesbian scene; **Friends** is one of the most popular gay bars.

Most cities and larger towns have venues with live music at night, mainly performed by local bands and musicians. Techno and dance is very popular throughout the country.

Information on events in Prague can be found in the weekly English-language *Prague Post*. Other sources of information are the leaflets and posters in the local area. For information on gigs and clubs outside Prague, check the posters around town.

DIRECTORY

Where to Stay

Luxuriously furnished rooms at the Grandhotel Pupp in Karlovy Vary

Prague

LITTLE QUARTER:
Design Hotel Sax ⓚ
Boutique **Map** B3
Jánský vršek 328/3, Praha 1
Tel *257 531 268*
Ⓦ hotelsax.cz
Comfortable and charming hotel attractively furnished in vintage style.

LITTLE QUARTER:
Domus Henrici ⓚⓚ
Boutique **Map** A3
Loretánská 11, Praha 1
Tel *220 511 369*
Ⓦ domus-henrici.cz
Housed in a historical building equipped with all the amenities.

NEW TOWN: Anna ⓚ
Value
Budečská 17, Praha 2
Tel *222 513 111*
Ⓦ hotelanna.cz
Stay in Art Nouveau rooms at this hotel with a lovely breakfast room and a quiet location.

NEW TOWN: Icon ⓚⓚ
Boutique **Map** E5
U Jámé 6, Praha 1
Tel *221 634 100*
Ⓦ iconhotel.eu
Hip hotel with wonderful rooms, all-day breakfasts, and efficient staff. Spa and lounge bar, too.

NEW TOWN: Le Palais ⓚⓚ
Luxury
U Zvonarky 1, Praha 2
Tel *234 634 111*
Ⓦ palaishotel.cz
A *belle époque* hotel with plush, bright rooms, attentive staff, and a great wellness centre.

NEW TOWN: Carlo IV ⓚⓚⓚ
Luxury **Map** F4
Senovážné náměstí 13, Praha 1
Tel *224 593 111*
Ⓦ prague.boscolohotels.com
Stylish rooms, Italian opulence and impressive spa facilities.

OLD TOWN: Fusion ⓚⓚ
Boutique **Map** F4
Panská 9, Praha 1
Tel *226 222 800*
Ⓦ fusionhotels.com
A quirky hotel with industrial-chic rooms and a rooftop terrace.

DK Choice

OLD TOWN: Josef ⓚⓚ
Boutique **Map** E3
Rybná 20, Praha 1
Tel *221 700 111*
Ⓦ hoteljosef.com
A beautiful, modern hotel that features lots of white surfaces and lovely, colour-coordinated rooms, with interiors designed by Eva Jiřičná. Other perks include a truly outstanding breakfast, a small but well-equipped gym on the top floor, and multilingual staff.

OLD TOWN: Kempinski
Hotel Hybernska ⓚⓚⓚ
Luxury
Hybernská 12, Praha 1
Tel *226 226 111*
Ⓦ kempinski-prague.com
A beautifully reconstructed hotel with large rooms, abundant amenities, and a lovely garden.

OLD TOWN: Paříž ⓚⓚⓚ
Luxury **Map** F3
U Obecního domu 1, Praha 1
Tel *222 195 195*
Ⓦ hotel-pariz.cz
The beautiful rooms and *fin-de-siècle* decor at Paříž, in the Old Town, contribute to the creation of an ultra luxurious ambience.

Rest of the Czech Republic

BRNO: Holiday Inn ⓚⓚ
Luxury
Křížkovského 20, 603 00
Tel *543 122 111*
Ⓦ hibrno.cz
Large rooms in warm colours and consistently high standards of service. Located near the city's trade-fair grounds.

Price Guide

Prices are based on one night's stay in high season for a standard double room, inclusive of service charges and taxes.

ⓚ	under 3,000 Kč
ⓚⓚ	3,000 to 6,000 Kč
ⓚⓚⓚ	over 6,000 Kč

ČESKY KRUMLOV: Leonardo ⓚ
Boutique
Soukenická 33, 381 01
Tel *380 725 911*
Ⓦ hotel-leonardo.cz
Situated in a 16th-century building, the Leonardo features lovely wooden ceilings and a Baroque staircase.

KARLSBAD (KARLOVY VARY):
Grandhotel Pupp ⓚⓚ
Luxury
Mírové náměstí 2, 360 91
Tel *353 109 111*
Ⓦ pupp.cz
The 18th-century Pupp offers luxurious rooms with mod cons, and a Neo-Baroque concert hall.

KUTNÁ HORA:
U Vlašského Dvora ⓚ
Historic
28 října 511, 284 01
Tel *327 514 618*
Ⓦ vlasskydvur.cz
In a 15th-century building, with well-appointed rooms that have views over the Old Town.

OLOMOUC: Arigone ⓚ
Boutique
Univerzitní 20, 779 00
Tel *585 232 351*
Ⓦ arigone.cz
This stylish hotel in the historic centre has Romanesque stonework and en-suite rooms.

Neo-Gothic façade of the stately hotel, Paříž in the Old Town

Where to Eat and Drink

Seating at the well-reviewed Kampa Park in the Little Quarter

Price Guide
Prices are based on a three-course meal for one, half a bottle of wine, including cover charge, service and tax.

Ⓚ under 250 Kč
ⓀⓀ 250 to 500 Kč
ⓀⓀⓀ over 500 Kč

Prague

LITTLE QUARTER:
Café Lounge Ⓚ
Café
Plaská 615/8, Praha 1
Tel *257 404 020*
A beautiful café with a secret courtyard. The great coffee and creative menu make this a go-to place from morning till night.

LITTLE QUARTER:
La Terrassa ⓀⓀ
Spanish
Janáčkovo nábřeží – Dětský ostrov, Praha 5
Tel *725 161 616*
Enjoy tapas and other Spanish fare on a beautifully renovated boat. Attentive staff and a good wine list ensure a stream of regular customers.

DK Choice
LITTLE QUARTER:
Lehká Hlava ⓀⓀ
Vegetarian **Map** D4
Boršov 2/280, Praha 1
Tel *220 665*
One of the best vegetarian restaurants in Prague, with a creative take on its extensive menu – ranging from Asian to Mexican to Lebanese. The Thai red curry with tofu is a real treat, and the burrito will probably force diners to skip dessert. Hip ambience and cool interiors.

LITTLE QUARTER: SaSaZu ⓀⓀ
Asian
Bubenské nábřeží 13, Praha 7
Tel *284 097 455*
Classic Indonesian, Thai, and Vietnamese dishes are prepared with flair and served in Oriental-palace surroundings. There is also

a popular nightclub in the same building, so stay after dinner for a fun night out.

LITTLE QUARTER:
Kampa Park ⓀⓀⓀ
Fusion **Map** C3
Na Kampě 8b, Praha 1
Tel *296 826 102*
The place for modern fusion cuisine with a focus on seafood, served up in extravagantly decorated rooms on Kampa Island, on the Vltava river.

NEW TOWN: Nota Bene ⓀⓀ
Czech
Mikovcova 4, Praha 2
Tel *721 299 131* **Closed** *Sun*
A rotating beer list and authentic Czech fare make Nota Bene one of the hottest places around. Head to the basement beer hall for beer and snacks.

OLD TOWN: Lokál Ⓚ
Czech **Map** E3
Dlouhá 33, Praha 1
Tel *222 316 265*
This old-style pub serves Czech classics and lots of refreshing Pilsner Urquell beer. Modern lighting and long wooden tables create a cozy but cool ambience.

OLD TOWN: Sansho ⓀⓀ
Fusion
Petrská 25, Praha 1
Tel *222 317 425* **Closed** *Sun & Mon*
Quality Asian-influenced fusion cuisine in a casual living-room space. The menu depends on what is fresh at the local market.

OLD TOWN:
Grosseto Marina ⓀⓀⓀ
Italian **Map** D3
Alšovo nábřeží, Praha 1
Tel *605 454 020*
Enjoy superb service, beautiful river views, and excellent Italian

food – pasta dishes, pizzas, and fabulous desserts – on a boat. The top deck is a great place to have a drink.

OLD TOWN:
La Degustation ⓀⓀⓀ
International **Map** E3
Haštalská 18, Praha 1
Tel *222 311 234*
Step into La Degustation for the ultimate Prague dining experience. Expect several courses of imaginative dishes prepared with skill and verve.

OLD TOWN: Plzeňská ⓀⓀⓀ
Czech **Map** F3
Náměstí republiky 5, Praha 1
Tel *222 002 770*
An enjoyable evening is in store at this restaurant with fabulous Art Nouveau interiors, friendly staff, and authentic Czech dishes.

Rest of the Czech Republic

ČESKY KRUMLOV:
Pivovar Eggenberg ⓀⓀ
Czech
Latrán 27, 381 01
Tel *380 711 917*
Beer sets the tone at this eatery, located in the cooling rooms of a former brewery. It is a good place to enjoy hearty Czech fare that can be washed down with local light and dark beers.

KARLSBAD (KARLOVY VARY):
Lázně 5 ⓀⓀⓀ
International
Smetanovy sady 1145/1, 360 01
Tel *602 266 088*
Located in a historic spa building, this elegant restaurant offers traditional Czech fare as well as Mediterranean cuisine. Lázně 5 is justly famous for its steaks.

OLOMOUC:
Svatováclavský Pivovar ⓀⓀ
Czech
Mariánská 4, 779 00
Tel *585 207 517*
A centrally located restaurant with a huge range of own-brewed beers, daily specials, and a long menu of meat and dumplings.

SLOVAKIA

A province of the kingdom of Hungary for nine centuries and part of Czechoslovakia for 70 years, Slovakia has had a tumultuous past. It gained independence in 1993 and is now one of Europe's youngest countries. With diverse topography, beautifully preserved architecture and rich folk culture, the country holds a great appeal for visitors.

Landlocked at the heart of Central Europe, Slovakia combines a dynamic economy with a wealth of natural assets – mountains, lakes, unspoilt valleys and spectacular ice caves. Beautiful churches ranging from the Romanesque to Art Nouveau, are a feature of its towns and cities, while numerous castles and ruined fortresses stand testimony to the region's turbulent history. Slovakia, nevertheless, remains a relatively little-known country, with few visitors.

History

During the 5th and 6th centuries the Slavs arrived in the Danube Lowlands, but they were later conquered by the nomadic Avars. In 795 the Avars were beaten by Charlemagne (r. 742–814),

at the head of an alliance of Franks and Moravians. This cleared the way for the establishment of two Slavic principalities, out of which grew the Great Moravian Empire. By 885, this incorporated parts of present-day Slovakia, Germany and Poland, as well as Bohemia and Moravia. The Moravian Empire was destroyed in the 9th century by the invading Magyars, who took control of the Danube Lowlands, including much of modern-day Slovakia. From this period the Czechs and Slovaks were exposed to different cultural and political influences. In 1025, the Slovak Lands became part of the kingdom of Hungary. The turning point in Slovakia's history came with the Battle of Mohács (1526), when the invading

vintage tourist bus in Bratislava's Old Town

◀ The romantic turreted Bojnice Castle, one of Slovakia's greatest attractions

Ottoman Army crushed the forces of King Louis II Jagiełło, then ruler of Hungary and the Czech lands. Slovakia came under Habsburg rule and due to its position between Christian Europe and the Muslim Ottoman Empire, it was repeatedly ravaged by raids and military campaigns. Homegrown troubles also surfaced, thanks to the Reformation and resistance to the Habsburgs' centralist policies. The Enlightenment reforms of the 18th century resulted in the codification of the Slovak language and the stirrings of nationalism. By 1848, revolutions had broken out all over Europe, including within the Habsburg Empire. The leader of the Slovak Nationalist Movement, L'udovit Štúr, demanded self-determination for Slovakia in vain. After suppressing the revolution, Emperor Franz Joseph II restored absolute monarchy. The situation worsened after the creation of the Austro-Hungarian Empire in 1867, when Slovakia was placed

Hungarians entering former Czech territory

in the Hungarian-ruled half of the monarchy. Slovak politicians forged links with Czech activists and, in 1918, the Czechoslovak Republic was declared Czech politicians rejected Slovakia's bid for autonomy however, steadfastly promulgating the concept of a single country. When Hitler took the Sudetenland in 1938, the Slovaks declared independence, but the country became little more than a Nazi puppet state. The democratic state of Czechoslovakia was reborn in 1945, only to fall under the control of the Communist Party three years later. Not until the Velvet Revolution of 1989 was the Communist government finally overthrown.

On 1 January 1993, the sovereign Slovak Republic was proclaimed, and its position within the international community was confirmed when, in 2004, Slovakia joined NATO and the European Union.

KEY DATES IN SLOVAKIAN HISTORY

5th–6th centuries Slav tribes colonize Danube Lowlands

833 Foundation of the Great Moravian Empire

1000 St Stephen crowned king of Hungary

1241–42 Mongol invasion

1536 Bratislava (Pressburg) becomes capital of the kingdom of Hungary

1683 Ottoman Turks defeated at the Battle of Vienna

1840s L'udovit Štúr becomes leader of the Slovak Nationalist Movement

1867 Creation of Austro-Hungary Monarchy

1918 Czechs and Slovaks proclaim the creation of Czechoslovakia

1938 Parliament proclaims the Slovak Republic

1944 Slovak National Uprising

1948 Communists take control of Czechoslovakia

1993 Creation of the Slovak Republic

2004 Slovakia joins NATO and becomes an EU member

2007 Slovakia signs the Schengen Agreement

2014 Andrej Kiska, entrepreneur and philanthropist, becomes president

Language and Culture

Slovakian is the official language of Slovakia, although there is a sizeable Hungarian minority in the south. There is a full calendar of cultural events and folk festivals are one of the country's main attractions. Slovakia is also rich in religious traditions: Catholic feasts are celebrated throughout the country while Orthodox rituals are mainly observed in the east.

Exploring Slovakia

Slovakia surprises visitors with its diverse scenery and cultural wealth. The majority of the historic sights in the capital city of Bratislava can be found in its compact Old Town centre. Western Slovakia boasts the city of Trnava, with its many magnificent Gothic, Renaissance, Baroque and Neo-Classical buildings. Central Slovakia, regarded as the country's true heart, is primarily a mountainous region, encompassing the High Tatra Mountains. Eastern Slovakia's towns of Spiš and Levoča are treasure-houses of the country's history, while Košice enjoys a well-deserved reputation as its cultural centre. The country's well-developed network of public transport can be used for exploring the region.

Tablet in the Church of St James, Levoča

Sights at a Glance

Winter landscape in the Tatra Mountains

0 km 50
0 miles 50

Key

— Motorway

– – Motorway under construction

— Major road

— Railway

—·– International border

For keys to symbols *see back flap*

① Bratislava

Founded by the Celts in the 2nd century BC, Bratislava is Slovakia's administrative centre and has long been the focus of the country's social and cultural life. Most of the historic sights are located in the Old Town centre on the left bank of the Danube (Dunaj) river. Some of the finest buildings, such as the Mirbach Palace and the Old Town Hall, can be seen around Franciscan Square (Františkánské námestie). The landmark Bratislava Castle is on a hill above the city. The views from the open-air observation decks here, or from the restaurant on SNP Bridge (Slovenské Národné Povstanie), are breathtaking.

Detail of the elegant altarpiece in St Anne's Chapel, St Martin's Cathedral

Sights at a Glance

① Old Town Hall
② Primatial Palace
③ Franciscan Church
④ Mirbach Palace
⑤ Michael's Gate
⑥ Bratislava Castle
⑦ House at the Good Shepherd
⑧ *St Martin's Cathedral pp296–7*
⑨ Slovak National Theatre
⑩ Reduta
⑪ Slovak National Gallery
⑫ SNP Bridge
⑬ Devín Castle
⑭ Red Stone Castle

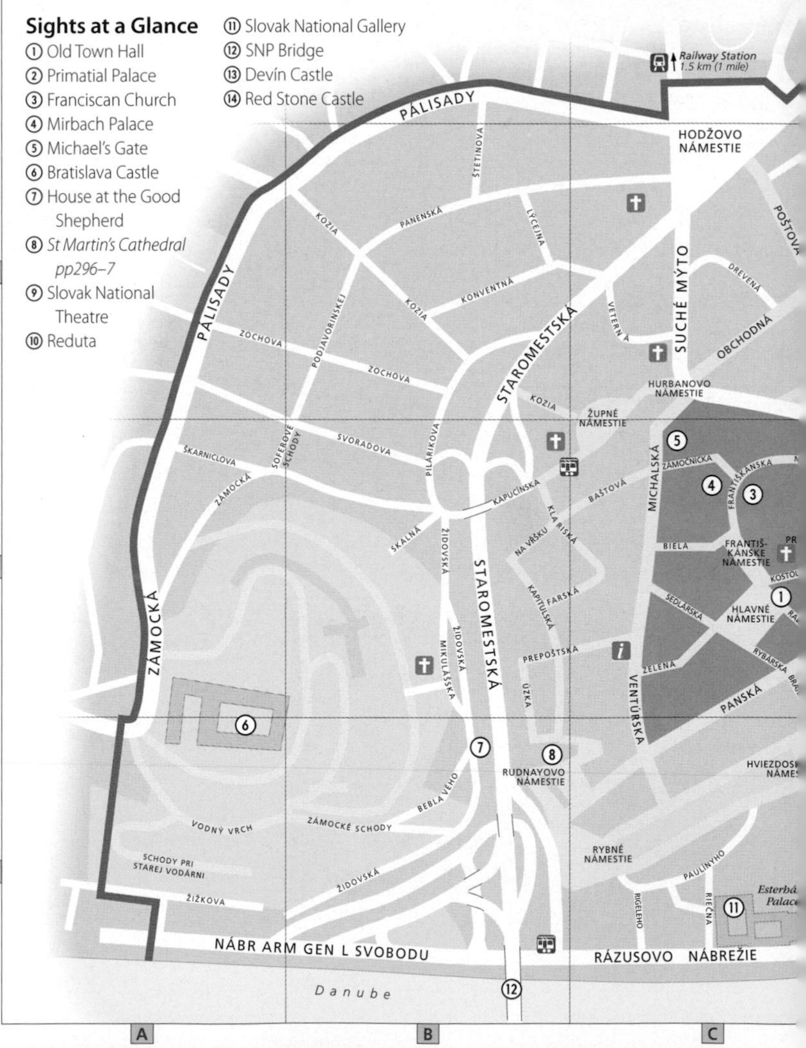

Railway Station
1.5 km (1 mile)

PÁLISADY
HODŽOVO NÁMESTIE
ŠTEFÁNIKOVA
POŠTOVÁ
KOZIA
PANENSKÁ
LYCEJNÁ
DREVENÁ
PALISADY
PODJAVORINSKEJ
KOZIA
KONVENTNÁ
VETERNÁ
SUCHÉ MÝTO
OBCHODNÁ
ŽOCHOVA
ŽOCHOVA
STAROMESTSKÁ
HURBANOVO NÁMESTIE
ŠKARNICLOVA
SOLÉ OVÉ SCHODY
SVORADOVA
PILÁRIKOVA
ŽUPNÉ NÁMESTIE
MICHALSKÁ
ZÁMOČNÍCKA
⑤
④ ③ FRANTIŠKÁNSKA
ZÁMOCKÁ
ZÁMOCKÁ
KAPUCÍNSKA
KLÁ RISKÁ
BAŠTOVÁ
SKALNÁ
NA VRŠKU
ŽIDOVSKÁ
BIELA
FRANTIŠ-KÁNSKE NÁMESTIE
KOSTOL
PR
STAROMESTSKÁ
KAPITULSKÁ
FARSKÁ
SEDLÁRSKA
HLAVNÉ NÁMESTIE
①
RYBÁRSKA BRÁ
MIKULÁŠSKA
ŽIDOVSKÁ
PREPOŠTSKÁ
UZKÁ
ZELENÁ
VENTÚRSKA
PANSKÁ
⑥
⑦
⑧
RUDNAYOVO NÁMESTIE
HVIEZDOSL NÁMES
VODNÝ VRCH
ZÁMOCKÉ SCHODY
BEBLA VÉHO
RYBNÉ NÁMESTIE
SCHODY PRI STAREJ VODÁRNI
ŽIDOVSKÁ
ŽIŽKOVA
RIGELEHO
PAULÍNYHO
RIEČNA
Esterbá Palace
⑪
NÁBR ARM GEN L SVOBODU
RÁZUSOVO NÁBREŽIE
⑫
Danube

A **B** **C**

Getting Around

The historic centre of Bratislava is mostly pedestrianized, so the best way to explore it is on foot. For longer trips within the city and into its environs, there is a quick and efficient network of buses, trams and trolleybuses. These also run at intervals throughout the night, starting from Námestie SNP. Drivers should be aware that it can be difficult to get a parking space, and that leaving a car illegally parked could incur a heavy fine. From April to October ferries and sightseeing boats operate from a jetty on the Danube at Fajnorovo Nábrežie.

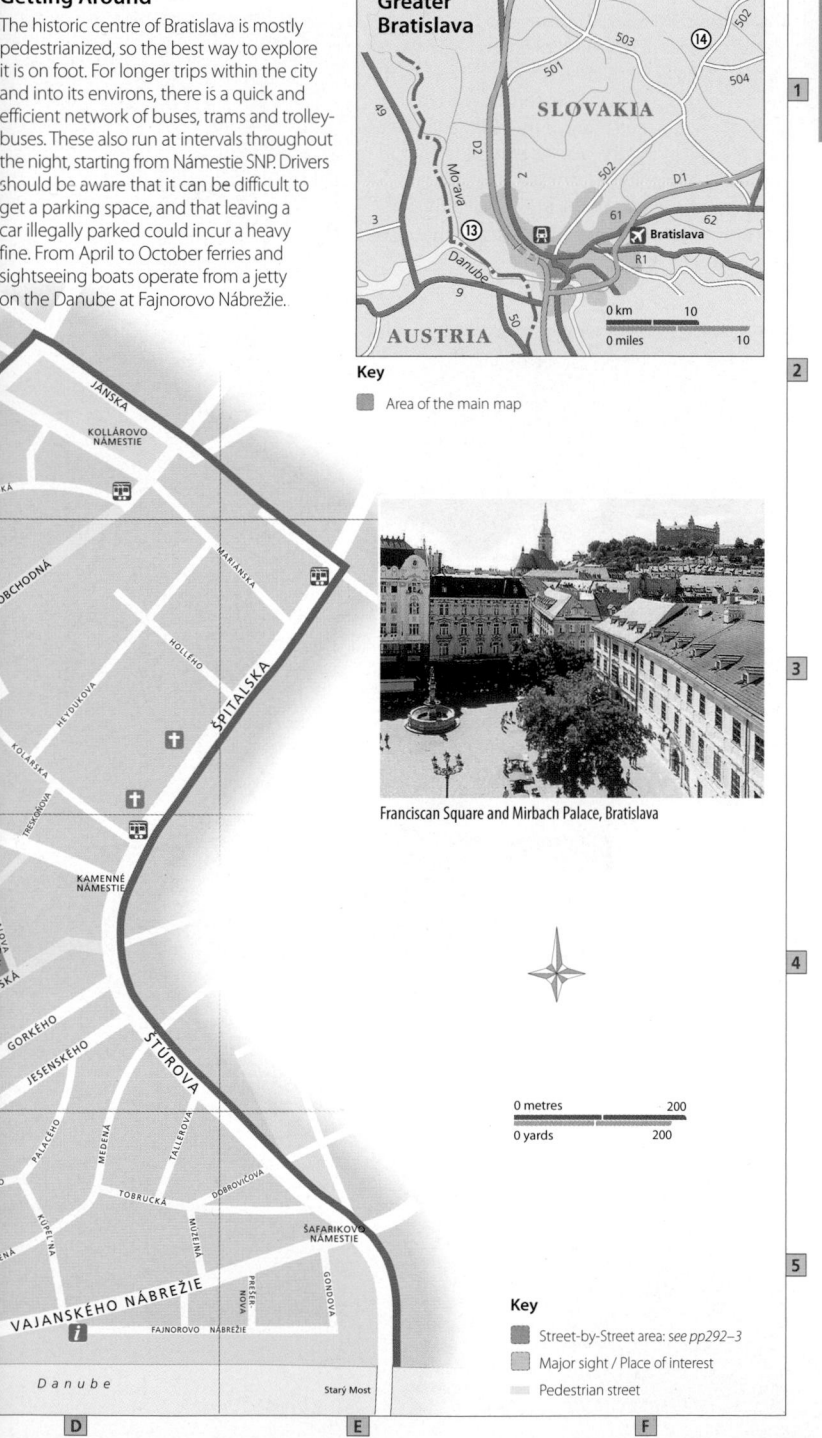

Greater Bratislava

SLOVAKIA

AUSTRIA

Bratislava

0 km   10

0 miles   10

Key

Area of the main map

Franciscan Square and Mirbach Palace, Bratislava

0 metres   200

0 yards   200

Key

Street-by-Street area: *see pp292–3*

Major sight / Place of interest

Pedestrian street

Street-by-Street: Old Town

The centre of Bratislava's historic Old Town (Staré Mesto) consists of two interlinked squares: Hlavné námestie and Františkánské námestie. The first has the distinctive Old Town Hall. This square also lay along the coronation route of the Hungarian kings, now marked by golden crowns embedded in the pavement. The pride of Františkánské námestie, apart from its lovely trees, is the Marian Column, erected in 1657. With attractive cafés, both squares are popular meeting places.

⑤ Michael's Gate
This is the only gate that remains from the medieval fortifications. In the 18th century it was topped with a statue of the Archangel Michael.

④ Mirbach Palace
One of Bratislava's finest architectural relics, this Rococo palace now houses the City Gallery.

Marian Column

Statue of Napoleon's Soldier
This is one of several life-sized figures in the Old Town. Others include a paparazzo and a worker poking his head out of a manhole.

ZAMOČNÍCKA

FRANTIŠKÁNS

BIELA

FRA
KÁN
NÁM

SEDLÁRSKA

ZELENÁ

HLA
NÁME
RYB

Hlavné Námestie
At the centre of the main square is the 1572 Maximilian Fountain, designed by Andreas Luttringer, from where Roland, a medieval French knight adopted as patron by the locals, surveys the square.

For hotels and restaurants see p318 and p319

③ ★ **Franciscan Church**
Bratislava's oldest religious building, the Franciscan Church, was erected in the 13th century. Remodelled several times, it acquired its Baroque form in the 18th century.

The Jesuit Church was built between 1636 and 1638 by Protestants. Its greatest treasure is its pulpit by Ľudovit Gode.

② ★ **Primatial Palace**
One of the city's finest Neo-Classical structures, this palace was built between 1778 and 1781 by architect Melchior Hefele for Archbishop Josef Batthyány, the head of the Hungarian church.

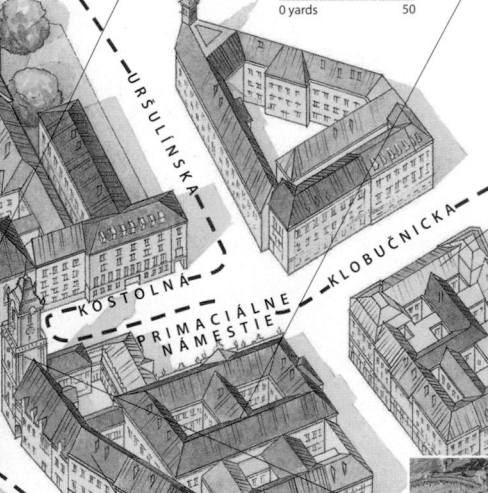

0 metres 50
0 yards 50

URŠULINSKÁ

KOSTOLNÁ

KLOBUČNÍCKA

PRIMACIÁLNE NÁMESTIE

RADNIČNÁ

Museum of Music
The birthplace of Johann Nepomuk Hummel, a celebrated composer and pianist, this Renaissance house has displays about his life and works, as well as the history of music in Bratislava.

Key

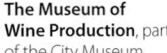— Suggested route

The Museum of Wine Production, part of the City Museum, displays wooden grape presses that are over 200 years old.

① **Old Town Hall**
Remodelled and rebuilt many times since the 13th century, the Old Town Hall is now home to the impressive City Museum, which houses exhibits related to the history of Slovakia.

① **Old Town Hall**
Stará Radnica

Hlavné námestie. **Map** C4. City Museum: **Tel** (02) 3218 1312. **Open** 10am–5pm Tue–Fri, 11am–6pm Sat & Sun. 🖼

The charming Old Town Hall, in Hlavné námestie, was created in the 15th century by combining a number of residential houses. At the turn of the 16th century, it was rebuilt in the Renaissance style. In the 18th century, its much older corner tower was remodelled in Baroque style; excellent views can be had from the top. On the lower section of the tower is a plaque marking the level of flood waters recorded in February 1850. Higher up, to the left of the Gothic window, is another historical relic – a cannonball embedded in the wall during the 1809 siege of Bratislava by Napoleon's Army. It is worth taking a look at the unusual colourful roof of the building on the side of Primaciálne námestie.

The Town Hall houses the popular **City Museum** (Mestské múzeum). Displayed within its splendid vaulted interiors are exhibits associated with the history of Bratislava, including an unusual collection of 17th–19th century painted shooting targets.

Opposite the Town Hall stands the Jesuit Church of the Holy Saviour. It was built between 1636 and 1638 for Bratislava's Protestant community, which explains its plain façade. Its Baroque furnishings include a richly decorated black and gold Rococo pulpit with gilded tassels.

An ornate fountain in the courtyard at the Primatial Palace

② **Primatial Palace**
Primaciálny Palác

Primaciálne námestie 1. **Map** C4. **Tel** (02) 5935 6394. **Open** 10am–5pm Tue–Sun. 🖼

The most beautiful palace in Bratislava, Primatial Palace was built between 1778 and 1781 to a design by architect Melchior Hefele, for Jozef Batthyány, the primate of Hungary and archbishop of Esztergom. Its lovely Neo-Classical pink-and-gold façade features a magnificent pediment that is crowned with the archbishop's coat of arms and topped with a giant-sized cardinal's hat. The figures of angels on the façade hold the letters I and C, a reference to the motto in the cardinal's coat of arms – Iusticia (Justice) and Clementia (Mercy). The palace, now the seat of the town's mayor, is partly open to the public. The most opulent room is the Hall of Mirrors, where in 1805, the Peace Treaty of Pressburg was signed between Napoleon and Francis I, after the French victory at the Battle of Austerlitz. Other first-floor rooms are occupied by a branch of the Municipal Gallery, with a modest collection of paintings and six unique English tapestries dating from 1632, depicting the love story of Hero and Leander. The strikingly bright tapestries were discovered in a hidden compartment during building works in the early 20th century.

③ **Franciscan Church**
Františkánsky Kostol

Františkánska 2. **Map** C4. **Open** 10:30am–5pm Mon–Fri.

The oldest religious building in Bratislava stands behind an inconspicuous Baroque façade. Built in the 13th century, the church was consecrated in 1297 in the presence of King Andrew II. Subsequent remodelling obliterated its original Gothic form, but it is still possible to see the medieval rib vaulting above the presbytery. Particularly impressive is the two-tier 14th-century chapel of St John the Evangelist. During coronation pageants, the church was used for knighting ceremonies, in which the new monarch appointed Knights of the Golden Spur. This prestigious honour was bestowed on those who distinguished themselves through feats of bravery.

Statue in the Franciscan Church

The church's elaborate furnishings, mainly Baroque in style, date from the 17th and 18th centuries. The 15th-century Pietà, in a side altar, is a highlight.

Imposing façade of Bratislava's eclectic Old Town Hall

④ Mirbach Palace
Mirbachov Palác

Františkánske námestie 11. **Map** C4. City Gallery: **Tel** (02) 5443 1556. **Open** 11am–6pm Tue–Sun. 🎨 Ⓦ **gmb.sk**

The Rococo Mirbach Palace, opposite the Franciscan Church, has a beautiful façade with stuccoes and a triangular pediment. The building was erected between 1768 and 1770 by a rich brewer, Martin Spech. Its subsequent owner, Count Karol Nyary, ordered his family crest to be placed in the tympanum. The last owner, Emil Mirbach, bequeathed the building to the city.

Now an art gallery, the palace currently holds the main collection of Bratislava's **City Gallery** (Galéria mesta Bratislavy), including examples of 17th- and 18th-century Baroque paintings. Two of the first-floor halls have walls almost entirely covered with colourful 18th-century engravings set in wood panelling.

⑤ Michael's Gate
Michalská Brána

Michalská ulica 24. **Map** C4. Museum of Weapons and Town Fortifications: **Tel** (02) 5443 3044. **Open** 10am–5pm Tue–Fri, 11am–6pm Sat & Sun. 🎨 Ⓦ **muzeum.bratislava.sk**

Built in the first half of the 14th century, Michael's Gate is the only surviving gateway to the medieval city. In the 18th century, its Gothic tower was

Michael's Gate with its striking Baroque cupola

Bratislava Castle perched above the Danube river

raised to its present height of 51 m (167 ft) by the addition of a Baroque cupola, and the statue of the Archangel Michael on top. The tower now houses the captivating **Museum of Weapons and Town Fortifications** (múzeum zbraní a mestského opevnenia), which throws light on the history and fortifications of the town.

The viewing terrace affords a stunning panorama of the city and beyond. Next to the gate stands Bratislava's oldest pharmacy, the Baroque At the Red Lobster (U červeného raka).

⑥ Bratislava Castle
Bratislavský hrad

Bratislavský hrad. **Map** A5. Slovak National Museum: **Tel** (02) 2048 3111. **Open** 9am–5pm Tue–Fri, 10am–6pm Sat & Sun (last adm 45 mins before closing). 🎨 Ⓦ **bratislava-hrad.sk**

The Bratislava Castle, first mentioned in written accounts in 907, is perched on a large, rocky hill above the scenic Danube. It was strategically located at the crossing of ancient trade routes including the ancient Amber Route. Fortified in the 11th and 12th centuries, the castle was rebuilt in Gothic style in the 15th century, and between 1552 and 1560 remodelled into a superb Renaissance residence. Between 1750 and 1760 it acquired beautiful Rococo furnishings. In 1811, the castle burnt down; it was rebuilt in the 1950s. The castle and all exhibitions are now open to the public after going through

a complete reconstruction to restore both the building and its surroundings to their original Baroque splendour. There are still ongoing exterior reconstructions on the north terrace of the castle. The castle hill is now the domicile of the Slovak parliament.

The area outside the castle has been developed into a beautiful park with amazing views over the city, and there is also a restaurant and children's playground.

⑦ House at the Good Shepherd
Dom U Dobrého Pastiera

Židovska 1. **Map** B5. **Tel** (02) 5441 1940. Museum of Clocks: **Open** 10am–5pm Mon–Fri, 11am–6pm Sat & Sun.

One of the city's finest examples of Rococo architecture can be seen at the House at the Good Shepherd, named after the statue of the Good Shepherd on its corner. Built between 1760 and 1765, it is one of the few remaining 18th century houses in the area. It is colloquially referred to as the "house like an iron", because of its tall, flat wedge shape, dictated by the plot on which it was erected. It is believed to be the narrowest building in Europe, and contains only one room on each floor. Inside is the **Museum of Clocks** (múzeum hodín), a branch of the City Museum located in the Old Town Hall. The exhibits date from the 17th to the 20th centuries and are mostly the works of Bratislava's clockmakers.

⑧ St Martin's Cathedral

Dóm sv Martina

This imposing Gothic edifice, with a wide nave flanked by two aisles, was built in 1452 on the site of an earlier 14th-century Romanesque church. Between 1563 and 1830, 11 Hungarian kings and 8 queens were crowned in the cathedral. From here it is possible to walk the former coronation route through the Old Town by following a series of golden crowns embedded in the pavement. In the 19th century, the church was rebuilt in Neo-Gothic style by architect Jozef Lippert and its interior refurbished along more purist lines.

Structure of the Cathedral
Vibrations from heavy traffic on the road to SNP Bridge *(see p298)* have damaged the cathedral, which often has to undergo restoration.

Presbytery
After completing the hall the builders realized that the section by the altar was too small, and added a presbytery with a fine net vault. The coat of arms on the vault is that of the Hungarian King Mátyás Corvinus *(see p321)*.

★ Sculpture of St Martin
Originally made for the main altar, this statue of St Martin (1734) by sculptor Georg Raphael Donner depicts St Martin in Hungarian dress, cutting his cloak to share it with a beggar.

①

Chapel of St John the Almsgiver
In 1732 Georg Raphael Donner built the side chapel of St John the Almsgiver at the request of Archbishop Esterházy.

For hotels and restaurants see p318 and p319

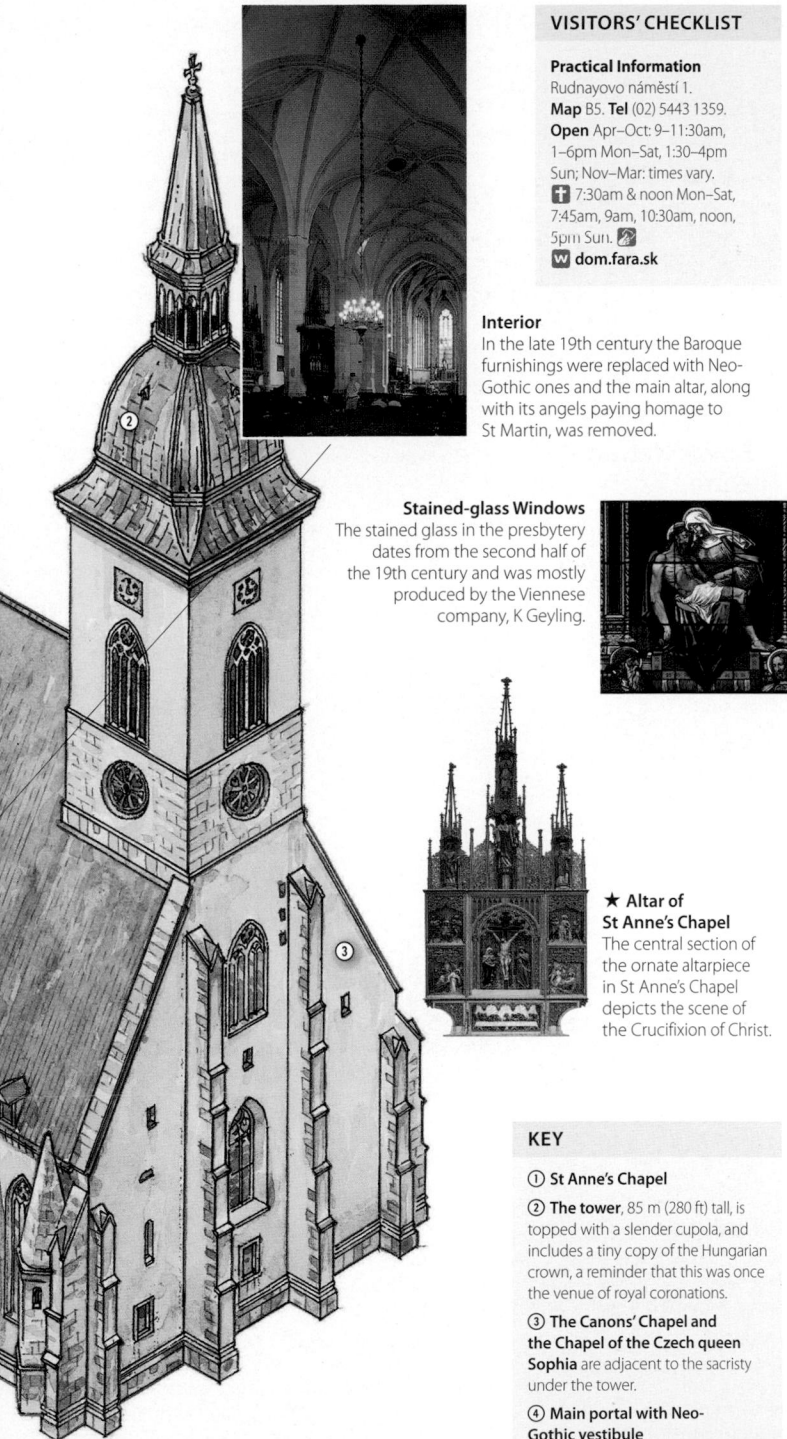

Interior
In the late 19th century the Baroque
furnishings were replaced with Neo-
Gothic ones and the main altar, along
with its angels paying homage to
St Martin, was removed.

Stained-glass Windows
The stained glass in the presbytery
dates from the second half of
the 19th century and was mostly
produced by the Viennese
company, K Geyling.

**★ Altar of
St Anne's Chapel**
The central section of
the ornate altarpiece
in St Anne's Chapel
depicts the scene of
the Crucifixion of Christ.

KEY

① **St Anne's Chapel**

② **The tower**, 85 m (280 ft) tall, is
topped with a slender cupola, and
includes a tiny copy of the Hungarian
crown, a reminder that this was once
the venue of royal coronations.

③ **The Canons' Chapel and
the Chapel of the Czech queen
Sophia** are adjacent to the sacristy
under the tower.

④ **Main portal with Neo-
Gothic vestibule**

Impressive façade of the Neo-Renaissance Slovak National Theatre

⑨ Slovak National Theatre
Slovenské Národné Divadlo

Hviezdoslavovo námestie 1. **Map** C5.
Tel (02) 2047 2289/297. **Open** 8am–
5:30pm Mon–Fri, 9am–1pm Sat.
W snd.sk

The Neo-Renaissance Slovak National Theatre, on the east side of Hviezdoslavovo námestie, was built between 1884 and 1886 by Viennese architects Ferdinand Fellner and Hermann Helmer, who specialized in theatres. The façade is decorated with busts of Goethe and Shakespeare, among others. At the centre of the tympanum is a sculptural group including the muse of comedy, Thalia. The theatre stages performances of ballet and opera, and attending one of these is the only way to see the interior. In front of the theatre is a fountain made in 1880 by sculptor V. Tilgner. It depicts the Trojan youth Ganymede flying on the back of Zeus, who is disguised in the form of an eagle.

⑩ Reduta

Palackého 2. **Map** C5. **Tel** (02) 2047
5233. **Open** 1–7pm Mon, Tue, Thu, Fri;
8am–2pm Wed. **W** filharm.sk

Near the Slovak National Theatre stands the imposing building of the Reduta. Built between 1913 and 1918, with a grand lobby and staircase, it used to stage social and artistic events, symphony concerts and theatre performances. Today the Reduta is home to the Slovak Philharmonic, and every autumn it is the venue for the Bratislava Music Festival. A section of the building, on the side of Mostova ulica, houses a casino and a restaurant.

The Reduta, home to the acclaimed Slovak Philharmonic

⑪ Slovak National Gallery
Slovenská Národná Galéria

Riečna 1. **Map** C5. **Tel** (02) 2047 6111.
Open 10am–5:30pm Tue–Sun.
Closed 1 Jan, Easter Fri, 24 & 25 Dec.
🖼 **W** sng.sk

Established in 1948, the Slovak National Gallery occupies a building that was created by combining two structures – the four-wing 18th-century Baroque naval barracks, designed by G Martinelli and F Hildebrandt, and architect V Dědeček's house. In 1990, the gallery's collections were also placed in the neighbouring Neo-Renaissance Esterházy Palace. Designed by I Feigler Jr and built between 1870 and 1876, Esterházy Palace is reminiscent of an Italian Renaissance town palace.

The gallery boasts a number of works of art. The finest are the 13th- and 14th-century Slovak art collections, including altarpieces and statues from churches in the Spiš region in eastern Slovakia. The most compelling works in the Baroque section are those by sculptor Franz Xaver Messerschmidt. Some significant 16th–18th-century European works are on display in the adjoining naval barracks.

Modern Slovak art is also well represented, with models of buildings, photographs, ceramics, jewellery and posters giving an eclectic overview of the country's creative output over the last 100 years.

As well as Slovak artists, the collection includes works by a number of acclaimed foreign artists including Rubens, Caravaggio, Manet and Picasso.

⑫ SNP Bridge
Slovenské Národné Povstanie Most

Staromestská. **Map** B5.

Also known as the Bridge of the Slovak National Uprising (SNP), this steel construction was built between 1967 and 1972. It officially opened on 26 August 1972, as the second bridge over the Danube. This feat of engineering is suspended from one pylon on the south bank of the Danube. The sheer size of this single, open suspension bridge is impressive; it is 431 m (1,414 ft) high and weighs 7,537 tonnes (8,308 tons). At the top of the pylon is a restaurant, whose saucer-like shape is reminiscent of the Starship Enterprise from *Star Trek*. From here there are beautiful sweeping views of the city on the north bank, and of the vast housing estates of Petržalka on the south. Built by the Communists, this estate houses more than 150,000 of the city's inhabitants.

The construction of SNP Bridge and the Staromestská Highway, which cuts through the city and over the bridge, involved the complete destruction of the former Jewish quarter at the foot of Bratislava Castle *(see p295)*.

⑬ Devín Castle
Hrad Devín

8 km (5 miles) W of Bratislava. **Map** E2. **Tel** (02) 6573 0105. 🚌 29. 🚢 from Central Bratislava. **Open** 10am–5pm Tue–Sun (May–Sep: until 7pm Sat & Sun). ♿

At the confluence of the Morava and the Danube rivers lie the ruins of Devín Castle, perched on a high rock. The rock was once the site of a Celtic settlement. Later, the Romans built a fortress here and in the 9th century, Prince Rastislav, king of Great Moravia between 846 and 870, chose it for his stronghold. It changed hands many times until 1809, when it was blown up by the

Coat of arms from the well in the courtyard of Red Stone Castle

French Army during the Napoleonic Wars. In the 19th century, during the period of national rebirth, the castle became a symbol in the shaping of Slovak national identity, promoted by Ľudovít Štúr, the leader of the Slovak Nationalist Movement *(see p288)*.

During the 1980s the castle area, separated from Austria by the Danube, was closed to the public. Now, it is a popular recreational spot for Bratislavans. One section of the castle has been reconstructed, and features the remains of a Roman fortress and an archaeological museum.

⑭ Red Stone Castle
hrad Červený Kameň

155 km (96 miles) N of Bratislava. **Map** F1. **Tel** (033) 690 5803. 🚌 **Open** May–Sep: 9am–5pm daily; Oct–Apr: 9:30am–3:30pm Tue–Sun. ♿ 📷 🎦 Historic Fencing festival (May).
🌐 hradcervenykamen.sk

The remarkable Red Stone Castle is regarded as one of the best-preserved castles in Slovakia. A mighty edifice with four corner towers, it was acquired in the 16th century by a German banking family, the Fuggers. Anton Fugger, one of the richest men in 16th-century Europe, converted the original 13th-century fort into a Renaissance castle. When the Pálffy family took it over in 1580, they converted it into a Baroque residence.

The castle's interior includes finely preserved porcelain and furnishings while the castle chapel has lavishly decorated walls and marble altars. An unusual feature is the 1656 *sala terrena*, an artificial grotto with trompe l'oeil paintings and stuccoes. The castle also houses collections from the Slovak National Museum, including a gallery of paintings with portraits of the Habsburgs and Pálffy family members.

Environs
Častá, about 1 km (0.6 mile) east of Red Stone Castle, has been a centre of wine-making for centuries and several cellars offer tastings. Its 15th-century Gothic Church of St Imre has interesting medieval paintings.

The ruins of Devín Castle, high above the Danube river

❷ Trnava

One of Slovakia's oldest towns, Trnava was granted town privileges in 1238. In the 16th and 17th centuries, it was the seat of the Hungarian primate and the headquarters of the Church of Hungary. Known as the "Slovak Rome", the town acquired numerous churches and monasteries. The historic town centre is enclosed within old walls, forming an almost complete square. The main Holy Trinity Square is at its heart. The chief attractions of the town are its religious buildings and relaxed ambience.

Baroque column of St Joseph, St Nicholas's Square

🏛 Holy Trinity Square

The town's main square, Trojičné námestie, sports the lofty Municipal Tower dating from 1574, with a viewing gallery and a cupola crowned with a golden statue of Our Lady. There is also an 18th-century Plague Column. Close by is the 1831 **Municipal Theatre** (Trnavské divadlo), the oldest theatre building in Slovakia. Just north of the square, the **Holy Trinity Church** (now known as Jezuitský kostol in Slovakian) was built in the early 18th century by the Trinitarian monks. It has been used by the Jesuits since 1853. To the west of the square is the single-towered **Church of St Jacob** (sv Jakub), built in 1640 and given a Baroque remodelling in 1712.

Plague Column, Holy Trinity Square

were given their present shape after a fire in 1676. They are still not identical; the southern tower is slightly narrower. Inside, the main attraction is the octagonal chapel of the Virgin Mary, added in 1741 to the left aisle of the church. It contains the miraculous picture of the Trnava Madonna, which is particularly revered in Slovakia. The gilded Renaissance-Baroque main altarpiece dates from 1639. Built into the side walls of the chapels are a number of interesting Renaissance and Baroque tombstones.

🏛 St Nicholas's Square

This spindle-shaped square (námestie sv Mikuláša) by the old city walls was the focus of the town in the Middle Ages. At its centre is the 1731 Baroque column of St Joseph, surrounded by chapter buildings. Among these is the **Archbishop's Palace** (Arcibiskupský palác), built by

⬆ Cathedral of St John the Baptist

See pp302–303.

⬆ Church of St Nicholas

Námestie sv Mikuláša. ⬆

The twin towers of the Church of St Nicholas (sv Mikuláš), with their distinctive bell-shaped cupolas, are one of Trnava's chief landmarks. The church, dedicated to the patron saint of merchants, was built in the 11th century. The original structure was demolished in the 14th century to make way for the new Gothic church built between 1380 and 1421. Its outside walls are supported by mighty buttresses, particularly imposing in the presbytery. The towers, initially of unequal size,

The twin towers of Church of St Nicholas

the Italian masters Pietro and Antonio Spazzi in 1562. During the 16th and 17th centuries, this Renaissance edifice was the seat of the Hungarian primates, whose residence in Esztergom had been appropriated by the Ottomans. It was also the headquarters of the Church of Hungary at the height of the Ottoman threat. The archbishops went back to Esztergom in 1820, but a Slovak archbishopric was re-established here in 1990.

🏛 Music Museum

M S Trnavského 5. **Tel** (033) 551 4421. **Open** 9am–5pm Tue–Fri, 11am–5pm Sat & Sun. 🈲

The Music Museum (Dom hudby) occupies a building called Dom hudby, which used to be the home of one of Trnava's most famous citizens – the composer Mikulas Schneider Trnavský (1881–1958). It displays objects and mementos associated with the musician and serves as a concert venue.

✡ Synagogue

Halenárska 2. **Tel** (033) 551 4657. **Open** 10am–6pm Tue–Fri (Oct–Apr: 9am–5pm), 1–6pm Sat & Sun. 🈲
🌐 snm.sk

This imposing edifice in Byzantine-Moorish style was built in the 19th century to a design by Viennese architect Jakub Gartner. Today, it houses a centre of modern art and the Museum of Jewish Culture, and is also an exhibition and concert hall. Standing in front of the Synagogue (Synagoga) is a marble monument, designed by architect Artur Szalatnai-Slatinský, dedicated to the memory of Trnava's Jews, murdered in the Holocaust.

Nineteenth-century synagogue in Byzantine-Moorish style

🏛 Museum of West Slovakia

Muzejné námestie 3. **Tel** (033) 551 29 13. **Open** 8am–5pm Tue–Fri, 11am–5pm Sat & Sun.

One of the biggest in the country, the Museum of West Slovakia (Západoslovenské múzeum) is housed in the 13th-century convent next to the Church of the Assumption of the Virgin Mary. Following administrative restructuring of

the empire's institutions carried out during the reign of Joseph II in the late 18th century, the building became a military hospital, and later, a warehouse. In 1954 it became a museum, with the aim of continuing Trnava's museum traditions.

The collections, spread over two floors, include archaeological discoveries, an exhibition of religious art, ethnography, natural history displays and eight rooms of folk ceramics as well as a unique collection of bells.

🏛 Church of the Assumption of the Virgin Mary

Muzejné námestie.
The Order of the Poor Clares settled in Trnava during the Middle Ages. This church (Nanebovzatia Panny Márie) was built for the nuns in the 13th century as an aisleless Romanesque structure. Following a fire in the 17th-century it was extended and remodelled in the Baroque style. Original features of the interior include the early 18th-century high altar and three side altars.

🏛 Church of St Helen

Dolné Bašty.
Trnava's oldest church, sv Helena, dates from the

VISITORS' CHECKLIST

Practical Information
46 km (28 miles) NE of Bratislava.
🚋 68,300. 🛈 Trojičné námestie 1,
(033) 323 6440. 🎭 International
Folk Music Festival (end Jul),
Traditional Folk Handicraft Fair
(2nd weekend Sep)
W trnava.sk

Transport
🚌 Kollárova. 🚆 Stanična.

Interior of the Church of the Assumption of the Virgin Mary

14th century. Adjoining its north façade is the original tower with Gothic windows. There are statues of saints above the portal.

Trnava Town Centre

① Holy Trinity Square
② Cathedral of St John the Baptist
③ Church of St Nicholas
④ St Nicholas's Square
⑤ Music Museum
⑥ Synagogue
⑦ Museum of West Slovakia
⑧ Church of the Assumption of the Virgin Mary
⑨ Church of St Helen

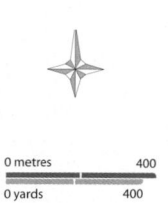

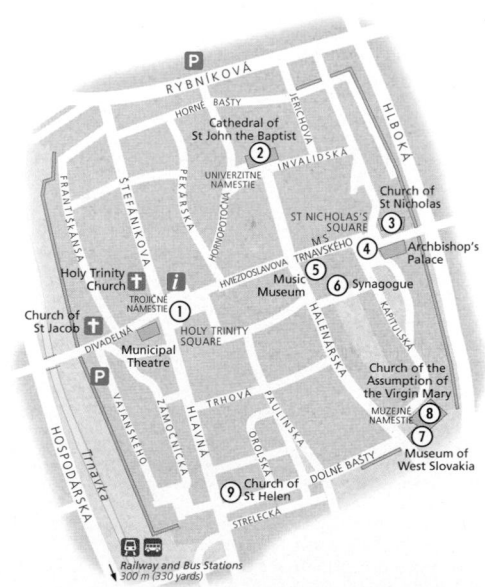

0 metres 400
0 yards 400

Railway and Bus Stations
300 m (330 yards)

For keys to symbols see back flap

Trnava: Cathedral of St John the Baptist

Katedrálny Chrám sv Jána Krstiteľa

The first monumental Baroque structure in Slovakia and one of the largest and most impressive religious buildings, the Cathedral of St John the Baptist was constructed between 1629 and 1637. The building, intended as a church for the Jesuit-run university, was founded by Count Miklós Esterházy. It has an ornamented Italianate interior with oval frescoes and wooden altarpieces. From 1777, when the university was moved to Buda in Hungary, the church was used by war veterans.

Main Façade
The impressive twin towered façade, divided by protruding cornices, is decorated with statues of various saints, including saints Joachim, Anna, and Elizabeth.

Main Portal
The inscription in Latin above the entrance refers to Count Miklós Esterházy, the cathedral's founder.

Main entrance

Interior
The walls, windows and vault are decorated with stucco ornamentation – figurative, floral and geometric – by artists Giovanni Rossi and Tornini.

For hotels and restaurants see p318 and p319

St John's Pulpit
This Baroque pulpit, decorated with figures depicting the Fathers of the Church, was built by artisans B Kniling and V Stadler in 1640.

VISITORS' CHECKLIST

Practical Information
Univerzitne námestie.
Tel (033) 551 4586.
Open May–Oct: 10am–noon, 2–5pm & 30 min before each mass. 🕆 7:30am daily, 9:30 & 11:30am Sun. 📷

★ **The High Altar**
This lavish Baroque gilded wooden altarpiece (1640) depicts the scene of Christ's baptism.

Ornate Door
Above the richly carved wooden door leading to the sacristy is an ornate metal grille with gilded elements.

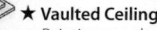

★ **Vaulted Ceiling**
Paintings on the arched vaulting of the presbytery ceiling depict scenes from the life of St John the Baptist.

KEY

① **Figures of the apostles** were placed in niches on the south side of the church.

② **Pilasters** decorate the façade.

❸ Bojnice Castle

Zámok Bojnice

Originally built in the 12th century, the romantic Bojnice Castle is one of Slovakia's greatest attractions. In the 13th century, it passed into the hands of the most powerful Hungarian warlord of the time, Matúš Čák. In 1527, the Thurzo family converted the castle into a comfortable Renaissance residence and in the 19th century, its last owner, Count Ján Pálffy, remodelled it into a stately residence resembling the Gothic castles of France's Loire Valley.

Chapel
The chapel, with its stuccoed and painted vault, was built in the 17th century, in a former bastion.

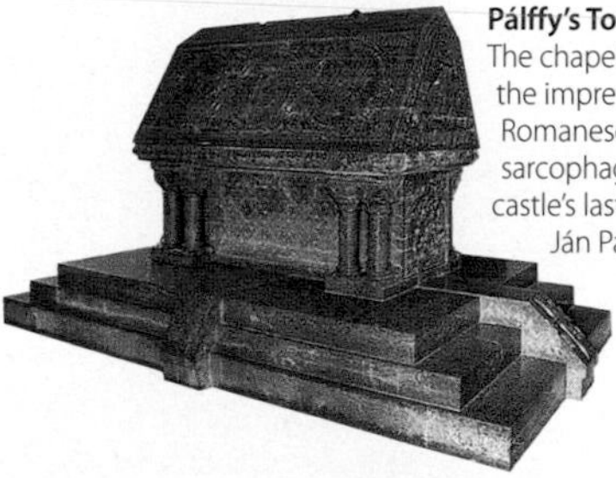

Pálffy's Tomb
The chapel crypt contains the impressive Neo-Romanesque marble sarcophagus of the castle's last owner, Ján Pálffy.

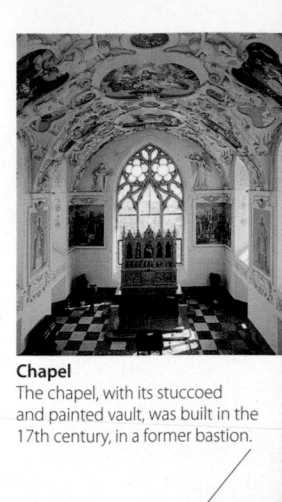

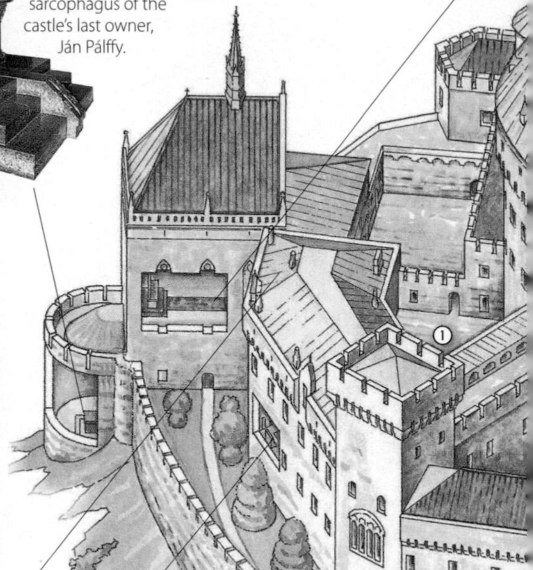

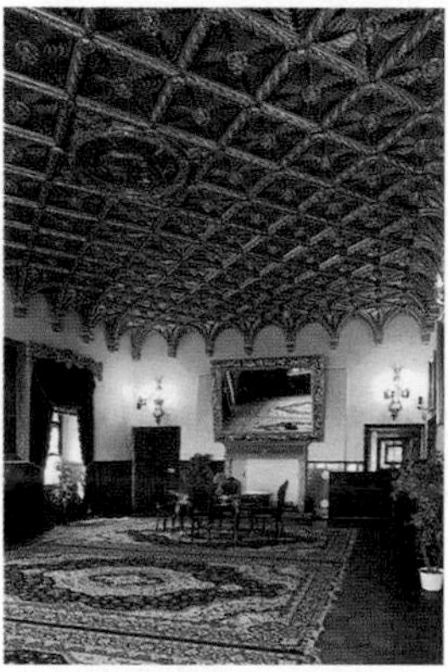

★ Golden Hall
The hall's spectacular vault, made of pine and covered with gold leaf, was modelled on the interior of the Venetian Academy of Fine Arts.

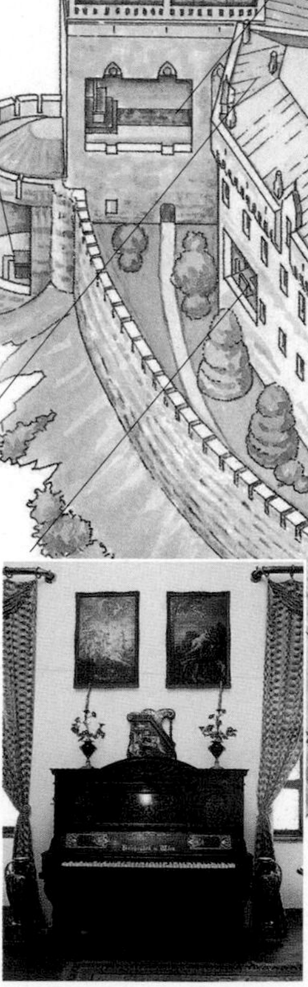

Music Room
The present Music Room was once Count Ján Pálffy's bedroom. It now houses a beautiful piano made in Vienna in 1884.

For hotels and restaurants see p318 and p319

Castle Grounds
Bojnice is located in a large park with many rare species of trees, including what is claimed to be the oldest lime tree in Slovakia. In summer, various events are staged in the grounds.

VISITORS' CHECKLIST

Practical Information
181 km (123 miles) NE of Bratislava. **Tel** (046) 543 0633.
Open May: 9am–5pm Tue–Sun; Jun–Sep: 9am–5pm daily; Oct–Apr: 10am–3pm daily. 🅿
W bojnicecastle.sk

Transport
🚉 🚌 from Bratislava.

Central Castle
The rooms of the Central Castle are furnished in Gothic style. The top floor is the Knights' Hall, with 14- to 17th-century weapons.

Entrance Tower and Gate

Well in the Fourth Courtyard
Standing in the smallest of the castle's courtyards, this decorative well was once linked to an old thermal spring. Its ornate grille was made in 1895.

②

★ Bojnice Altarpiece
The altarpiece, painted by Italian painter Nardo di Cione, is the only complete surviving work by the artist. Painted in the mid-14th century, using tempera paint on a wooden panel, it is the most important piece from Ján Pálffy's collection.

KEY

① Castle courtyards

② Neo-Gothic gallery

Narodna Street, leading to the market square in Banská Bystrica

❻ Banská Bystrica

208 km (130 miles) NE of Bratislava.
🏙 82,100. 🚉 🚍 🛈 Námestie SNP 14, (048) 415 5085.

One of the oldest towns in Slovakia, Banská Bystrica (Neusohl) was granted royal privileges associated with the mining of gold, silver and copper in 1255. In 1944 it became the centre of the Slovak National Uprising (Slovenské národné povstanie).

The historic sights are concentrated along the pedestrianized Dolna, the large market square námestie SNP, and Horna. The central square is flanked by buildings of the old castle complex. Of these, the parish **Church of the Ascension of the Virgin Mary** (Nanebovzatia Panny Márie), has magnificent Baroque furnishings. Its greatest treasures are the Gothic Altar of St Barbara, and the Side Altar, which contains a fine 15th-century Gothic triptych of St Mary Magdalene. The castle complex also includes the Church of the Holy Cross, the Matthias House and the Town Hall as well as remnants of the old fortifications. Nearby, the striking concrete **SNP Museum** (SNP múzeum) is dedicated to Slovak history, with an emphasis on the 1944 Uprising against the Nazis and the fate of Slovak Jews.

🏛 **Church of the Ascension of the Virgin Mary**
Námestie Š Moyzesa. **Tel** (048) 412 4531. **Open** during mass. ✉

🏛 **SNP Museum**
Námestie SNP. **Tel** (048) 412 3258. **Open** May–Sep: 9am–6pm Tue–Sun; Oct–Apr: 9am–4pm Tue–Sun. 📷 🎫

❺ Tatra Mountains

Slovakia's Northern Tatra Mountains consist of three ranges: the Western Tatras (Západné Tatry), the High Tatras (Vysoké Tatry) and the small area of Eastern Tatras (Belianske Tatry), a protected reserve that is closed to the public. All of them are within the Tatra National Park. The most spectacular range, the High Tatras, is a major draw for hikers.

View from around Zuberec
The village of Zuberec, at the mouth of the Roháčska Valley, offers magnificent views of Rohače, the start of the Western Tatras.

Habovka

Osobi
1687
(5535

Zuberec

ROHAČE

Salatín
2050 m
(6726 ft)

584

Baranec
2184 m
(7165 ft)

Jaloveck ý P.

Smerčianka

Liptovský Mikuláš
This town, set in a valley surrounded by peaks, is an interesting and convenient base for the Low Tatras.

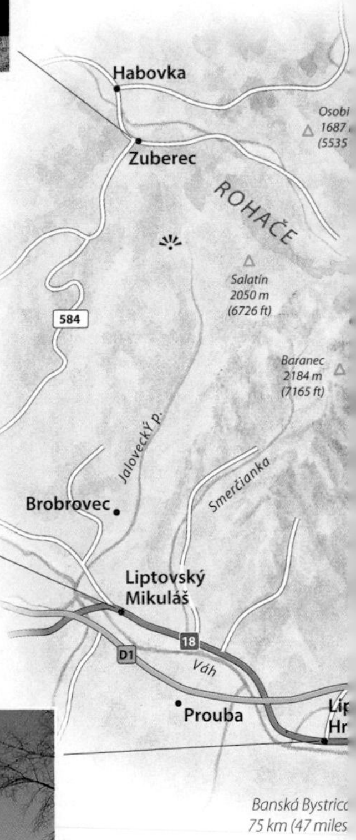

Brobrovec

Liptovský Mikuláš

D1

Váh

18

Prouba

Líp
Hr

*Banská Bystrica
75 km (47 miles*

Liptovský Hrádok
This town is famous for its ruined 14th-century castle, later extended into a Renaissance palace. The palace now houses an Ethnography Museum dating from the 19th century.

Gerlachovský Štít
The highest peak of the Tatras range, the 2,654-m (8,707-ft) high Gerlachovský Štít can only be climbed with the help of a professional guide.

VISITORS' CHECKLIST

Practical Information
339 km (210 miles) NE of Bratislava. *i* Starý Smokovec, Štrbské Pleso, Tatranská Lomnica, Tatranská Kotlina (052) 442 3440.
Open Oct–Apr: 8:30am–4pm daily; May–Sep: 8am–6pm daily.
w tanap.org

Transport
✈ Poprad-Tatry. 🚌 from Poprad to Tatranská Lomnica, Starý Smokovec, Štrbské Pleso.

Lomnický Štít
The second highest peak, at 2,632 m (8,635 ft), it is accessible by cable car.

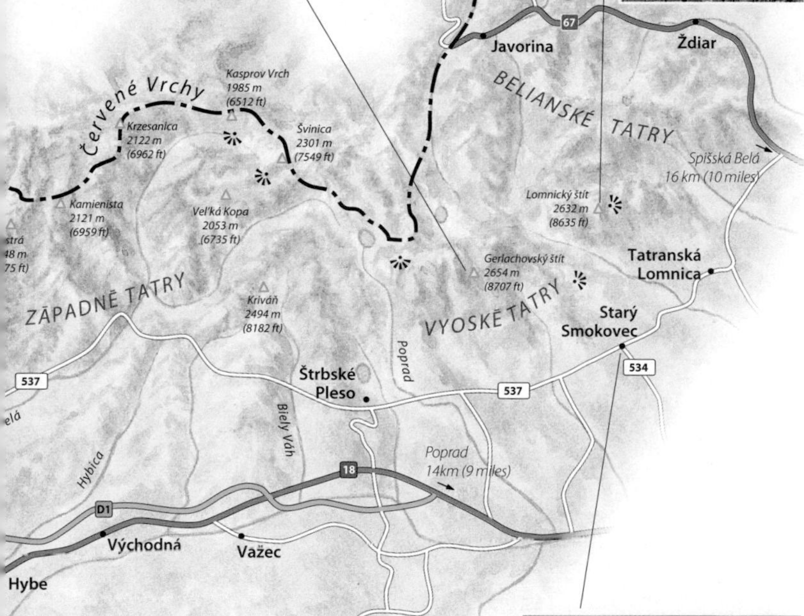

Bukowina Tatrzanska 10 km (6 miles)

Javorina

Ždiar

67

BELIANSKE TATRY

Červené Vrchy

Kasprov Vrch 1985 m (6512 ft)

Krzesanica 2122 m (6962 ft)

Svinica 2301 m (7549 ft)

Spišská Belá 16 km (10 miles)

Kamienista 2121 m (6959 ft)

strá 48 m 75 ft)

Veľká Kopa 2053 m (6735 ft)

Lomnický štít 2632 m (8635 ft)

Tatranská Lomnica

Gerlachovský štít 2654 m (8707 ft)

ZÁPADNÉ TATRY

Krivaň 2494 m (8182 ft)

VYOSKÉ TATRY

Starý Smokovec

537

Štrbské Pleso

537

534

Biely Váh

Poprad

Poprad 14km (9 miles)

18

D1

Hybica

Východná

Važec

Hybe

Starý Smokovec
This attractive spa complex has several hotels, pensions and restaurants that blend well with their woodland surroundings.

Key
▬▬ Motorway
▬▬ Major road
═══ Minor road
–·– International border
△ Summit

0 km — 5
0 miles — 3

For keys to symbols *see back flap*

The striking Renaissance Thurzo House in the old centre of Levoča

❻ Levoča

396 km (246 miles) NE of Bratislava.
🚶 14,000. 🏠 🚌 ℹ️ Námestie Majstra Pavla 58, (053) 451 3763.
🌐 **levoca.sk**

The former capital of the Spiš region, a historic province populated by Saxon settlers, Levoča is situated between the High Tatras and the Slovenské Rudohorie Mountains. The town has a well-preserved historic centre, full of magnificent Gothic, Baroque, Renaissance and Neo-Classical buildings. Its main square, námestie Majstra Pavla, features the Gothic **Church of St James** (sv Jakub), containing a set of 18 altarpieces and a splendid collection of medieval and Renaissance sacred art. The main altarpiece, 18.6 m (61 ft) high, is the world's tallest Gothic altar. The tall statues of the Madonna, St James and St John the Evangelist are by Master Pavol of Levoča, an outstanding sculptor of the late-Gothic period. To the south of the church lies the former **Town Hall**.

The most striking historic houses around the main square are the **Thurzo House** (Thurzov dom), crowned with a Renaissance attic, and the **House of Master Pavol of Levoča**, now a museum devoted to the sculptor's life and works. At the edge of the historic district, the 14th-century **Old Minorites' Church** (Starý kláštor minoritov) has a dazzling Baroque interior.

🏛️ **House of Master Pavol of Levoča**
Námestie Majstra Pavla 20.
Tel (053) 451 3496. **Open** 9am–5pm daily (by appt Mon). ♿ 🌐 **snm.sk**

Levoča: Town Hall
Radnica

One of Levoča's most distinguished buildings, the Town Hall was erected in 1550 in Gothic style, replacing an earlier building that had been destroyed by fire. In the early 17th century it was remodelled along Renaissance lines. The bell tower dates from 1656–61, with Baroque decorations added in the 18th century. The Neo-Classical pediments were added in the 19th century. The Town Hall is still used for civic functions, and it also houses the main branch of the Spiš Museum on the first floor, with exhibits on regional history.

★ **Arcades**
The original Town Hall did not have any galleries. The two-tier arcades were added to the central part of the building in 1615.

Cage of Disgrace

The infamous 16th-century Cage of Disgrace

The wrought-iron cage by the south wall of the Town Hall is the 16th-century Cage of Disgrace, in which women, who had committed minor crimes, were locked up and put on public display. It used to stand in a park belonging to the Probstner family, who gave it to the town in 1933.

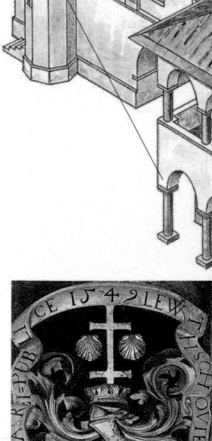

Town's Coat of Arms
The town's striking coat of arms consists of a red shield with a double cross supported by two lions.

Main Hall
The main hall's vaulted ceiling bears witness to the Gothic origin of the Town Hall.

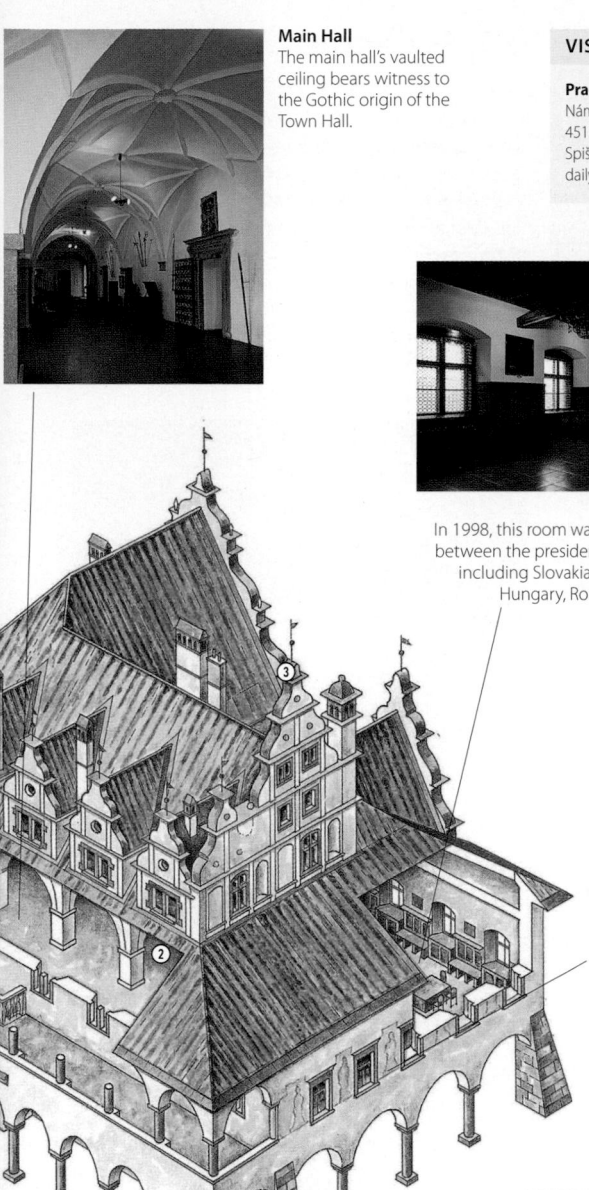

VISITORS' CHECKLIST

Practical Information
Námestie Majstra Pavla. **Tel** (053) 451 2449. **Open** 9am–5pm daily. Spiš Museum: **Open** 9am–5pm daily. 🚻 🆆 **snm.sk**

★ Council Chamber
In 1998, this room was used for a summit meeting between the presidents of 11 European countries, including Slovakia, Poland, the Czech Republic, Hungary, Romania, Bulgaria and Slovenia.

PRVDENTIA EST VIRTVS ACCVRATE
RESPICIENS ID QVOD IN VNA
QVAQVE ACTIONE DECET.

★ Wall Paintings
The impressive Renaissance wall paintings on the south elevation of the building depict the civic virtues of restraint, courage, justice and patience.

KEY

① **Coat of arms**

② **The Spiš Museum**, on the first floor, contains several important historical artifacts as well as an exhibition on the town's history.

③ **The Neo-Classical** pediments date from the 19th century.

④ **Corner column buttresses** were added in the 19th century to protect the arches from structural failure.

Impressive Church of the Holy Spirit in Žehra near Spišská Kapitula

❼ Spišská Kapitula

400 km (249 miles) NE of Bratislava.

The walled, one-street town of Spišská Kapitula is located on a ridge, west of Spišské Podhradie. Since 1776 it has been the seat of the Spiš bishopric and the ecclesiastical capital of the Spiš region. Dominating the town is the late-Romanesque, twin-towered **St Martin's Cathedral**, (katedrála sv Martina) dating from 1245–75, with two Romanesque portals and the statue of a white lion at the entrance. The interior has unique medieval frescoes in the central nave. The interesting burial chapel of the Zápolya family, by the south wall, dates from the 15th century.

Further along the street stand the imposing Baroque Bishop's Palace with a clock tower, and a row of Gothic canon houses. Spišská Kapitula has been on the UNESCO World Cultural Heritage list since 1993.

Environs
The village of **Žehra** lies 6 km (4 miles) southeast of Spišská Kapitula. It features the historic UNESCO-protected 13th-century Romanesque Church of the Holy Spirit (sv Duch), a white building with a tower and a bell, topped with onion-shaped wooden cupolas. Inside, 13th–15th-century frescoes cover the presbytery and a wall of the nave, and there is a 13th-century stone font.

🏛 **St Martin's Cathedral**
Open May–Oct: 10am–4:30pm daily, 1–4:30pm Sun. 🅿 📷

❽ Spiš Castle
Spišský hrad

The ruins of Spiš Castle are part of a historic complex, along with the small town of Spišské Podhradie (*podhradie* means "below the castle") and Spišská Kapitula to the northwest; all three are on the UNESCO World Cultural Heritage list. Spiš Castle was the administrative capital of the Spiš region, a historic province populated by Saxon settlers. Its oldest parts date from between the 11th and 12th centuries. In 1780, the castle burned down, but it is now gradually being restored. Most impressive from a distance, it is nonetheless worth a visit for its spectacular views.

Fortress
Occupying an area of 4 ha (10 acres), Spiš Castle is the remains of the largest fortress complex in Central Europe. In the 17th century it had 2,000 inhabitants.

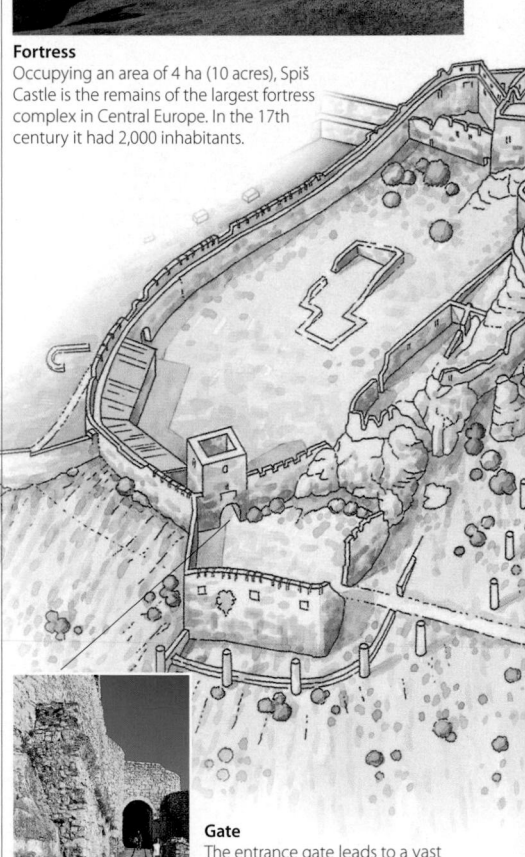

Gate
The entrance gate leads to a vast lower courtyard, nearly 300 m (985 ft) long and 115 m (380 ft) wide.

★ Castle Chapel
Six wooden statues of saints adorn the interior of the 15th-century Gothic chapel of the Zápolya family. The chapel was completely renovated in 2003.

VISITORS' CHECKLIST

Practical Information
405 km (252 miles) NE of Bratislava. **Tel** (0) 904 564 290. **Open** May–Sep: 9am–6pm daily; April & Oct: 10am–6pm daily; Nov: 10am–3pm daily. **Closed** Dec–Mar. 🎟 Sat evening tours in Jul & Aug.
w spisskyhrad.sk

Transport
🚌 🚏 from Spišské Podhradie.

Walls
The Zápolya family, who owned the castle in the 15th and 16th centuries, had the defensive walls rebuilt, reinforced and equipped with new gun positions.

★ Upper Castle
Situated at the highest point on the hill, the Upper Castle, with its Romanesque palace and tower, was built in the 13th century. Burnt down in 1780, it was not rebuilt.

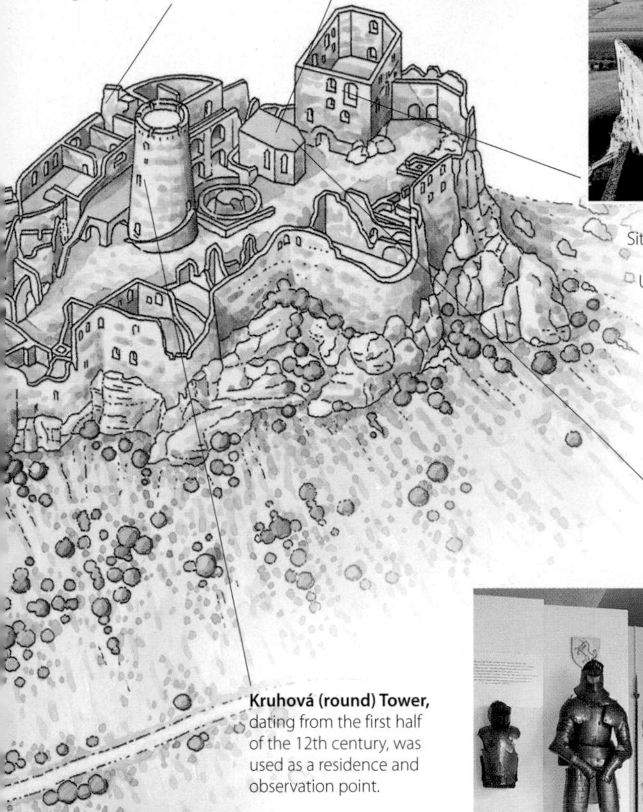

Kruhová (round) Tower, dating from the first half of the 12th century, was used as a residence and observation point.

Tournaments
During summer, colourful historical pageants and tournaments are held in the castle courtyards, featuring men dressed as knights.

★ Museum
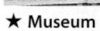
The museum has a range of exhibits, including pieces from the castle kitchens, bedrooms and bathrooms as well as from the medieval torture room and castle armoury.

❾ Košice

Slovakia's second largest city, Košice has roots reaching back to the 12th century. At the crossroads of major trade routes, it was granted the same town privileges as the then capital of Hungary, Buda, in 1347. In 1369, King Louis the Great gave the town its coat of arms, making it the first town in Europe to receive this by royal decree. Due to its proximity to the Hungarian border, Košice has always had a large Hungarian population. The most interesting sights in the city are clustered within its large and superbly restored historic centre.

The Plague Column and beautiful houses in Hlavná

🏛 Hlavná

This lovely avenue, full of shops and cafés, makes for an enjoyable stroll. The most striking of its buildings are the Gothic Levoča House (Levočský dom) and the Old Town Hall, its façade deco-rated with sculptures of ancient heroes by Anton Kraus (1705–1752). Built between 1722 and 1723, the Plague Column is Košice's most beautiful piece of Baroque sculpture.

🏛 State Theatre

Hlavná 58. **Tel** (055) 622 1231.
Open performances only. **W** sdke.sk
The imposing building of the State Theatre (Štátné divadlo)

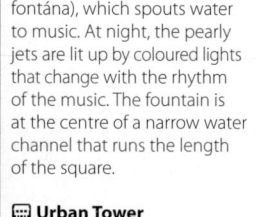

The Singing Fountain in front of the ornate State Theatre

was built between 1897 and 1899, to a design by Hungarian architect Adolf Lang. Its lofty dome is topped with the torch-bearing figure of Dawn. The interior, with its beautiful auditorium and lyre-shape floor plan, features a magnificent ceiling with paintings of scenes from Shakespeare's works. The foyer and the rest of the theatre are richly decorated with stuccoes.

🏛 Singing Fountain

Hlavné námestie.
In the square between the theatre and St Elizabeth's Cathedral is the Singing Fountain (Spievajúca fontána), which spouts water to music. At night, the pearly jets are lit up by coloured lights that change with the rhythm of the music. The fountain is at the centre of a narrow water channel that runs the length of the square.

🏛 Urban Tower

Hlavná. **Tel** (055) 832 4576.
Open noon–4pm Tue–Sun.
The 14th-century Urban Tower (Urbanova veža) is dedicated to

St Urban, the patron saint of viniculture, as wine production has always been a source of Košice's wealth. St Urban's bell was cast in 1557 and installed inside the tower; the tower itself was remodelled in Renaissance style in 1628.

⬆ St Elizabeth's Cathedral

Hlavná 28. **Tel** (055) 622 1555.
Open 9am–5pm, daily. 🏛 📷
W dom.rimkat.sk
The largest church in Slovakia, St Elizabeth's Cathedral (Dóm sv Alžbety) dominates the main square. Begun in 1378, the church is an achievement of the popular European Gothic style. The main, western façade was meant to have two towers, but by 1477 only one had been built. In 1508 work was completed on the beautifully vaulted presbytery. Not until 1775 was the second tower of the cathedral built, topped with an impressive Rococo copper cupola.

The present form of the church is the result of the intricate reconstruction that began in the late 19th century, when it was restored to its former appearance, close to the original design. Inside, the spectacular main altarpiece has 48 panels. The relief work over the north and west doors is also impressive.

Detail from
St Elizabeth's Cathedral

⬆ St Michael's Chapel

Hlavná 26.
Open 9am–5pm, daily. 🏛
The chapel of St Michael (sv Michal) was built in the 14th century, on the site of a cemetery south of St Elizabeth's Cathedral. The lower section of the building served as an ossuary, while the upper section was used to celebrate masses for the souls of the dead. During the 16th century, the chapel was converted into a storehouse for weapons and ammunition when the Turks threatened to invade. In the early 20th century, 17 old tombstones from the cemetery were built into the chapel walls. Highlights of the interior include the altarpiece depicting

St Michael the Archangel, the lovely stone tabernacle, and above the sacristy door, the oldest coat of arms of Košice.

✦ Former Synagogue
Puškinova.

The Former Synagogue was built between 1926 and 1927. In 1992, a bronze memorial plaque was added to the front of the building to commemorate over 12,000 Jews who were taken from Košice to concentration camps in 1944.

⊞ Executioner's Bastion
Hrnčiarska 7. **Open** 9am–5pm Tue–Sat.

The bastion (Katova bašta) takes its name from a nearby house, which was once the home of the city's hangman. This semicircular structure was built around 1500 and served defence purposes, with eight cannon chambers set in its walls. The lower section of the bastion is reinforced with slanting buttresses.

⊕ Jesuit Church
Junction of Hlavná & Univerzitna.

One of the finest remaining Baroque structures in the city,

Bas-relief from the Jesuit Church's façade

this church (Univerzitný kostol šv Trojice) was built in 1681 by the Jesuit order. Its austere, early-Baroque façade, bearing traces of the Renaissance style, hides a lavishly furnished interior, which includes a 17th-century pulpit and stalls and a 19th-century main altar. The central nave and side chapels are beautifully decorated with magnificent trompe l'oeil paintings.

▥ East Slovak Museum
Hviezdoslavova 3. **Tel** (055) 622 0309. **Open** 9am–5pm Tue–Sat, 9am–1pm Sun. ⏿ **W** vsmuzeum.sk

One of Slovakia's oldest museums, the East Slovak Museum (Východoslovenské múzeum) was established in 1872 as the Upper Hungary Museum. Its vast collections, numbering half a million exhibits, are displayed in an early 20th-century Neo-Renaissance building. The impressive façade is decorated with the town's coat of arms and carved figures of Perseus and Vulcan. The museum's greatest attraction

VISITORS' CHECKLIST

Practical Information
445 km (277 miles) NE of Bratislava. ⌖ 240,000. ℹ Hlavná 59, (055) 625 8888. **W** kosice.sk

Transport
✈ 6 km (4 miles) SE of centre.
🚊 Staničné námestie.
🚌 Staničné námestie.

is the "golden treasure of Košice" – a huge find of nearly 3,000 gold coins dating from the 15th to the 17th centuries.

The Neo-Renaissance building housing the East Slovak Museum

Košice City Centre

① Hlavná
② State Theatre
③ Singing Fountain
④ Urban Tower
⑤ St Elizabeth's Cathedral
⑥ St Michael's Chapel
⑦ Former Synagogue
⑧ Executioner's Bastion
⑨ Jesuit Church
⑩ East Slovak Museum

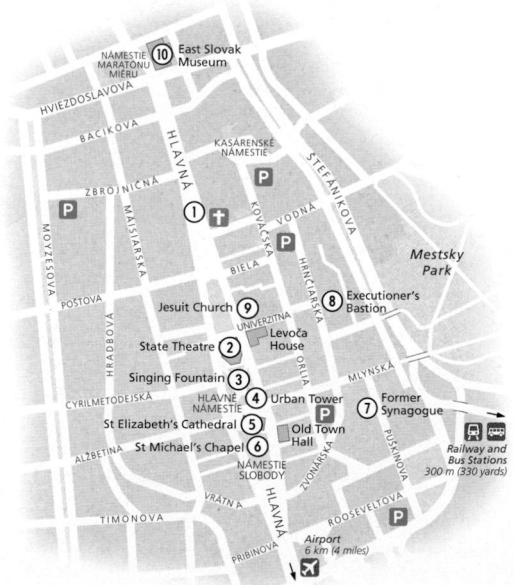

0 metres 300
0 yards 300

For keys to symbols *see back flap*

Practical & Travel Information

Slovakia is a visitor-friendly destination. Numerous historic sights, good roads, efficient internal transport, tasty local food and a wide choice of accommodation options have contributed to the steadily growing number of visitors to the country. A good network of tourist information offices, found in almost every town and village, also helps to provide invaluable information and assistance to travellers.

When to Visit

Slovakia can be visited throughout the year. Spring and autumn are good times for nature enthusiasts to visit – ideal for mountain hikes, bike tours and cave exploration. Summertime is excellent for swimming in the numerous pools and bathing centres, and indulging in water sports on its many artificial lakes. In winter, Slovakia tempts visitors with its excellent ski slopes as well as more unusual attractions such as swimming in outdoor thermal pools.

Documentation

Nationals of EU countries may enter Slovakia on presenting a valid passport or ID card, but if they intend to stay in the country for more than 90 days, they are required to report to the police and apply for a resident's permit. Australian, New Zealand, US, Canadian and Japanese citizens can stay in the country without a visa for a period of 90 days.

Foreigners entering the country have to carry €56.40, or the equivalent in any convertible currency, in the form of traveller's cheques, cash or credit cards, for each day of their intended stay (this also applies to children). This rule is, however, applied to EU citizens only in exceptional circumstances. The sum may be reduced on presentation of documents confirming advance payment for some services, such as hotel bookings or car hire.

Customs regulations do not apply to visitors from within the EU as long as they stay within the EU guidelines for personal use.

Visitor Information

Local tourist information centres provide details on accommodation and the region's attractions, as well as popular cultural and sporting events. The most reliable information can be obtained from the **Asociácia Informačných Centier Slovenska** (AICES) affiliated offices.

Many places also have their own information centres providing similar services. These may also sell parking permits and local discount cards to tourists and exchange foreign currency. In some of these centres (although very few) it is even possible to book accommodation. The **Bratislavská Informačná Služba** (BIS) in Bratislava is specifically set up to help visitors, providing maps and booking information.

However, almost none of the maps, guidebooks and information brochures that can be obtained from tourist information offices are free of charge; the best visitors can hope to be given for free are a few pamphlets.

Tourist information offices are usually open from 9am to 5pm, although some of them close for an hour at lunchtime. On Saturdays many offices close at 1pm, and many remain closed on Sundays. The staff usually speak English and German.

Health and Security

In emergencies and life-threatening situations, EU nationals with an EHIC (European Health Insurance Card) are entitled to free medical treatment, but in all other cases, hospitalization or medical help has to be paid for. *Lekareň* (pharmacies) can be found in all towns and villages and are open from 8am to 6pm. Large towns also have 24-hour pharmacies.

Visitors to Slovakia do not require any immunizations or vaccinations. Drinking water is safe but mineral water is also widely available.

In Slovakia, crime directed at visitors remains relatively rare. Slovaks would usually prefer to resolve disagreements by way of negotiation rather than open confrontation. The best way for visitors to protect themselves against losing documents, cash or other valuables is for them to take a few basic precautions to safeguard belongings, particularly in crowded places.

Facilities for the Disabled

Facilities for the disabled are limited in Slovakia, although buildings are gradually being adapted to their needs. Most trains have wheelchair access

The Climate of Slovakia

Slovakia has a continental climate with warm summers and cold winters. Temperatures in summer, between June and August, can reach 20° C (68° F), and fall to -2° C (28° F) in winter, between November and February. Spring and autumn usually experience mild and pleasant weather.

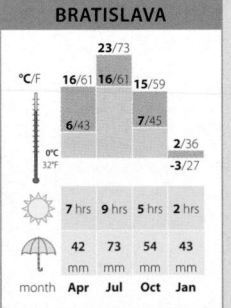

BRATISLAVA

°C/F	Apr	Jul	Oct	Jan
	16/61	23/73	15/59	
		16/61		
	6/43	7/45		2/36
				-3/27
Sun	7 hrs	9 hrs	5 hrs	2 hrs
Rain (mm)	42	73	54	43
month	Apr	Jul	Oct	Jan

to at least one carriage, but it is often difficult to get through the station to reach the carriage.

Banking and Currency

The national currency of Slovakia is the euro. Most Slovak banks are open from 8am to 5pm and accept traveller's cheques, which can also be cashed in exchange bureaus. An increasing number of services and retail outlets now accept credit card payments. It is easy to find a bank for exchanging or withdrawing money in towns and tourist resorts. The most common are branches of large banks such as **Slovenská Sporiteľňa**, **VÚB** and **Tatra Banka**. Slovak banks are generally open from 8am to 5pm.

Communications

Slovak telephone and postal services are widely available and efficient and are usually open from 8am to 5pm. Public phones are mostly in good working order, and making a local or international call is fairly easy. Payphones in Slovakia are both coin- and card-operated. The service is quick and efficient, but not all public telephones allow international calls. Those that do not allow outgoing calls to international and mobile numbers are marked with an orange sticker. Post offices can be found in all towns and larger villages. A poste restante service is available in the main post office in every major town and city.

Arriving by Air

Bratislava's **M R Štefánika Airport** is served by airlines from all over Europe, but the most popular are **Air Slovakia**, **Czech Airlines**, **Austrian Airlines**, **Ryanair**, **Aeroflot**, **Lufthansa** and **KLM**. Visitors to southern Slovakia can fly to Vienna's **Schwechat International Airport**, less than 50 km (30 miles) from the border, while those heading for northern Slovakia can consider taking a flight to Krakow in Poland, which is closer than Bratislava, and head south from there.

Low-cost airlines offer a good range of deals on flights to Prague, Brno, Bratislava and Krakow in Poland, and the number of routes is steadily increasing. Bratislava's airport is 12 km (7 miles) from the city centre. Vienna's airport also operates a bus service to Bratislava.

Rail Travel

Trains in Slovakia are run by **ŽSR** (Železnice Slovenskej Republiky). Travelling by train is more comfortable than by coach, but it should be stressed that standard fares on international train routes are usually very high – so travelling by air might not cost much more. Discounted fares may be available on advance bookings or with concessions. Slovakia's principal station is the **Bratislava Main Train Station**.

Travelling by Coach

Visitors can travel to Slovakia by coaches operated by international carriers. These run scheduled services between **Autobusová Stanica Bratislava** and major European cities. Travelling by coach is generally less expensive than by air, but it may be less comfortable, and takes much longer. The coaches on international routes are well equipped with air conditioning.

DIRECTORY

Documentation
[w] slovakia.org
[w] ec.europa.eu

Visitor Information
[w] slovakia.travel

Asociácia Informačných Centier Slovenska
[w] aices.sk

Bratislavská Informačná Služba
[w] bkis.sk

Embassies

United Kingdom
Panská 16, 814 99, Bratislava.
Tel (02) 5998 2000.

United States
Hviezdoslavovo námestie 4, 811 02, Bratislava.
Tel (02) 5443 3338.

Emergency Numbers

Ambulance
Tel 155, 112.

Fire
Tel 150, 112.

Police
Tel 158, 112.

Banking and Currency

Slovenská Sporiteľňa
Nám Snp 18, Bratislava.
[w] slsp.sk

Tatra Banka
Hodžovo námestie 3, Bratislava.
[w] tatrabanka.sk

VÚB
Mlynské Nivy 1, 82990, Bratislava.
[w] vub.sk

Arriving by Air

Aeroflot
[w] aeroflot.ru

Austrian Airlines
[w] astrian.com

Czech Airlines
[w] czechairlines.com

KLM
[w] klm.com

Lufthansa
[w] lufthansa.com

M R Štefánika Airport
[w] letiskobratislava.sk

Ryanair
[w] ryanair.com

Schwechat International Airport
[w] viennaairport.com

Rail Travel

Bratislava Main Train Station
Predstaničné námestie 1, Bratislava.
Tel (02) 18 188.

ŽSR
[w] slovakrail.sk

Travelling by Coach

Autobusová Stanica Bratislava
Mlynské Nivy 31, 821 09, Bratislava.
Tel (02) 18 211, (02) 5542 2734.
[w] slovaklines.sk

Shopping & Entertainment

Shops in Slovakia range from small local outlets and stalls in bazaars and markets to department stores and supermarkets belonging to large international chains. The country is famed for its handcrafted goods such as traditional clothing, tablecloths, lace, wooden or china figurines, sculptures, ceramics and paintings. Slovakia also has wide-ranging cultural entertainment that should satisfy most visitors. There are scores of theatres, cinemas, clubs, concert halls, art galleries and museums. Visitors can catch world-class artistes in larger cities, or traditional folk festivals in provincial areas.

Opening Hours

Shops in Slovakia are generally open from 9am to 6pm, although some food stores open as early as 6am and do not close until 8 or 9pm. Some shops are open on Saturdays and Sundays, usually till 1pm. Most shops no longer close for lunch and remain open all day.

Markets

In many Slovak towns and villages the traditional market day is Saturday. This is the best opportunity to buy fresh local fruit, vegetables and meat. The most famous Christmas market takes place in Hlavné námestie and Františkánské námestie *(see pp292–3)*, the twin central market squares in Bratislava.

Slovak markets are also a great place to taste local delicacies, such as *lokša* (potato pancakes) and *langoš* (fried garlic cakes) and sample local wines.

Handicrafts

Slovakia is rich in culture and traditions, most of which have been carefully preserved by the conscientious people.

Typical crafts include handmade dolls dressed in traditional costume, embroidered tablecloths, carved wooden figurines, painted Easter eggs, dolls made of dried corn leaves or wire, and secular or religious paintings on glass, wood or ceramic. Slovak artists are also renowned for their woodcarvings, mostly depicting nativity figures and saints. Hand-carved nativity scenes are quite expensive but

make superb and unique souvenirs that last for decades. Traditional arts and crafts products can be bought relatively easily in larger towns and tourist resorts at shops such as **Folk – Folk** (*see* Art and Antiques) in Bratislava. **UL'UV Stores** (Centre for Folk Art Production) is a chain of stores specializing in Slovak handicrafts that has branches in Bratislava, Banská Bystrica and Trnava.

Art and Antiques

Slovakia is renowned for its colourful ceramicware. Majolica from Modra (western Slovakia) is sold in most towns, although the best selection is available in **Benekit v.o.s.**, **Corvus**, **Folk – Folk** and **LÚČ Vydavatelské Družstvo** in Bratislava.

Starožitnosti (antique shops) are found in most towns, and there are many interesting items that can be picked up for a good price. **U Žofky** in Bratislava also offers an array of antiques.

Food and Drink

Shops sell a variety of traditional local food products, including a varied and delicious range of cheeses and a wide variety of wines, beers and spirits.

Sheep cheeses to try include *bryndza*, smoked *oštiepky* and steamed *parenica*. Those who enjoy good liquor might like to bring home a few bottles of local wine, liqueurs, the famous plum brandy *slivovica* or cognac. They are all

relatively inexpensive. The bottled Slovak Zlatý bažant beer is excellent.

Nightlife

Bratislava pulsates with life around the clock. From April until early October countless outdoor bars and music venues spring up around the city. The focus of social life in the evenings is the bars and pubs in Korzo, on the outskirts of the Old Town. Visitors interested in partying can venture into a fashionable discotheque or visit one of the capital's music clubs housed, for example, in post-Communist nuclear shelters. The flourishing nightlife is encouraged by the relatively low prices of drinks.

The best-known and most popular clubs and discos in Bratislava include: **17's Bar** and **Harley Davidson** for rock, **Café Kút** for reggae, **Jazz Café** for jazz, **Subclub** or **Trafo** for disco, **Casa del Havana** for a salsa party and **Randal** for punk and rock n' roll.

Nightlife is not limited to the capital city – those who enjoy spending their time in clubs can also find something to their liking in Košice, Trnava and in the foothills of the Tatras, although the entertainment on offer is rather modest compared with that in Bratislava. Inevitably, Bratislava offers the most vibrant gay and lesbian nightlife. Two established gay clubs there are **D4** and **Apollon Gay Club**.

Music and Theatre

The main establishments associated with classical music, opera and ballet have their homes in the capital, Bratislava. The **Slovak Philharmonic Orchestra** is housed in the Neo-Baroque Reduta *(see p298)* building, while the country's best opera and ballet theatre is the **Slovak National Theatre**.

Of the 24 national theatres in Slovakia, a few, such as the **Hungarian Theatre** and **Romany Theatre** in Košice, give performances in foreign languages, however, there are not many performances in English. The contemporary **Astorka Theatre** in Bratislava is marvellous. Other theatres there include **Radošin Naive Theatre**, **GUnaGU** and **Aréna**. Slovakia also hosts a number of international theatre festivals, including the biennial **Bábkarska Bystrica** (festival of puppet theatres), held during March–April in Banská Bystrica, and the annual **Divadelná Nitra**, held in Nitra in September.

Numerous music events and festivals also take place throughout Slovakia. The most prominent are the **Bratislava Music Festival** and **Bratislava Jazz Days**, both held in the

autumn. The best-known Slovak festival of popular music is Bratislava Lyre, which was one of the flagship national entertainment events under Communist rule, and is now a nationwide song festival. The Jewish folklore music group **Pressburger Klezmer Band** often perform at festivals.

The free English-language weekly *The Slovak Spectator* and the monthly magazine *What's on – Bratislava & Slovakia* are good sources of information about the events in the capital and around the country, and contain some good reviews.

Visitors are advised to visit tourist offices for the most up-to-date information.

Folk Festivals

Most folk festivals take place in summer. The **International Historic Fencing Festival** in Trenčín (Jul–Aug), Červený Kameń Castle (May), Levice (Jun) and Banská Bystrica (Sep), draws the biggest crowds. The **Janošíkove Dni** (Janosik's Days) folklore festival, held in July–August in Terchova, is also popular, with art, theatre and book presentations as well as music.

DIRECTORY

Handicrafts

UL'UV Stores
Main store: Obchodná 64, 816 11 Bratislava.
Tel (02) 5273 1351.

Other branches:
Dolná 14, 974 01 Banská Bystrica.
Tel (04) 8412 3657.

Hlavná 5, 917 00 Trnava.
Tel (03) 3551 3684.
W uluv.sk

Art and Antiques

Corvus
Europalia 24, 945 01 Komárno, Bratislava.
Tel (02) 9035 72125.

Folk – Folk
Obchodná 24, 811 01 Bratislava.
Tel (02) 5443 4874.

I.N.A. Business
Obchodná 60, Bratislava.

LÚČ Vydavatelské Družstvo
Špitalská 7, 813 59 Bratislava.
Tel (02) 6042 1233.

U Žofky
Michalska 5, 811 01 Bratislava.
Tel (02) 5443 1994.

Nightlife

17's Bar
Hviezdoslavovo námestie 17, 811 22 Bratislava.
Tel (09) 0363 7038.

Apollon Gay Club
Panenská 24, 820 00 Bratislava.
Tel (02) 9154 8031.
W apollon-gay-club.sk

Café Kút
Zámočnická 11, 811 03 Bratislava.
Tel (02) 5443 4957.

Casa del Havana
Pod Michalskou Bránou, Bratislava.
Tel (02) 9107 97222.

D4
Jedlíkova 9, 811 06 Bratislava.

Harley Davidson
Rebarborová 1, 821 07 Bratislava.
Tel (02) 4319 1094.

Jazz Café
Ventúrska 5, 811 01 Bratislava. **Tel** (02) 5443 4661. W jazz-cafe.sk

Randal Club
Karpatská 2, Bratislava.
Tel (02) 9077 49413.
W randalclub.eu

Subclub
NábrArm. Gen. L. Svobodu, Bratislava.
Tel (02) 5411 1183.
W subclub.sk

Trafo
Venturska 1, Bratislava.
Tel (02) 2092 2744.
W trafo.sk

Music and Theatre

Aréna
Viedenská Cesta 10, 851 01 Bratislava.
Tel (02) 6720 2557.

Astorka Theatre
Nám Snp 33 Bratislava.
Tel (02) 5441 2245.
W astorka.sk

Bábkarska Bystrica
Marionet's Festival
W BDNR.sk

Bratislava Jazz Days
W bjd.sk

Bratislava Music Festival
Michalská 10, 811 03 Bratislava.
Tel (02) 5443 0378.
W bhsfestival.sk

Divadelná Nitra Festival
W nitrafest.sk

GUnaGU
Na Františkánskom námestie 7, Bratislava.
Tel (02) 5443 3335.

Hungarian Theatre
Thalia Mojmirova 3, 04001 Košice.
Tel (055) 622 5866.
W thaliaszinhaz.sk

Pressburger Klezmer Band
W klezmer.sk

Radošin Naive Theatre
Škultétyho 5, 831 04 Bratislava.
Tel (02) 5556 3508.

Romany Theatre
Stefanikova 4, 040 01 Košice.
Tel (055) 622 4980.
W romathan.sk

Slovak National Theatre
Hviezdoslavovo Nám 1, 811 02 Bratislava.
Tel (02) 2047 2111.
W snd.sk

Slovak Philharmonic Orchestra
Palackého 2, 811 02 Bratislava.
Tel (02) 5920 8233.
W filharm.sk

Folk Festivals

Jánošíkove Dni (Jánošik's Days)
W janosikovedni.sk

International Historic Fencing Festival
W serm.sk

Where to Stay

Bratislava

Hostel Blues €
Hostel **Map** E3
Špitálska 2, 811 08
Tel *905 204 020*
Ⓦ hostelblues.sk
This centrally located hostel has bunk-bed dorms, private doubles, comfortable social areas and live blues or jazz concerts in its bar.

Arcadia €€
Historic **Map** C4
Františkánska 3, 811 01
Tel *(02) 5949 0500*
Ⓦ www.arcadia-hotel.sk
High ceilings, rich textiles and old-school furnishings characterize this plush *pied-a-terre* in the Old Town.

Loft €€
Boutique
Štefánikova 864/4, 811 05
Tel *(02) 5751 1000*
Ⓦ lofthotel.sk
Loft combines a modern and a 19th-century building through a central atrium and offers sleek modern rooms. Located close to the city centre.

Tatra €€
Historic **Map** C2
Nám. 1 Mája, 811 06
Tel *(02) 5927 2111*
Ⓦ hoteltatra.sk
Located centrally, this 1930s hotel offers modern rooms, many with views of the presidential palace on Hodžovo námestie.

Mamaison Sulekova €€
Luxury
Šulekova 20, 811 06
Tel *(02) 5910 0200*
Ⓦ mamaison.com
Close to the Bratislava Castle, the Mamaison offers well-equipped apartments with modern kitchens and swish bathrooms.

Park Inn €€
Luxury **Map** C5
Rybné námestie 1, 811 02
Tel *(02) 5934 0000*
Ⓦ parkinn.com/hotel-bratislava
Located in the central pedestrianized zone, the ParkInn has plush rooms, fitness centre, indoor pool and meeting facilities.

Tulip House €€
Historic **Map** D4
Štúrova 15/10, 811 02
Tel *(02) 3217 1819*
Ⓦ tuliphousehotel.com
In an Art Nouveau building that has a tulip design on the facade,

this modern hotel carries the theme inside with retro furnishings and inspired decor.

DK Choice

Marrol's Boutique €€€
Boutique **Map** D5
Tobrucká 4, 811 02
Tel *(02) 5778 4600*
Ⓦ hotelmarrols.sk
One of the most exclusive hotels of the city, Marrol's is located close to the exit from the Old Bridge. It offers ultra-modern conveniences, and impeccable service. Rooms and apartments have retro-styled furnishings and come in a variety of sizes. Outstanding restaurant, well-equipped gym and business facilities.

Rest of Slovakia

BOJNICE: Kaskada €
Resort
Jánošíková 1301/24, 972 01
Tel *(046) 518 3010*
Ⓦ www.kaskada.sk
A modern hotel with its own aquapark, Kaskada offers plush fully equipped rooms and a wide range of facilities.

KOŠICE: Bankov €€
Boutique
Dolny Bankov 2, 040 01
Tel *(055) 632 4522*
Ⓦ hotelbankov.sk
Situated beside the woods on the outskirts of the town, Bankov is a romantic retreat with plush rooms, a stylish restaurant and a spa centre.

Spacious and comfortable bedroom at Bankov, Košice

Price Guide
Prices are based on one night's stay in high season for a standard double room, inclusive of service charges and taxes.

€	under €70
€€	€70 to €120
€€€	over €120

KOŠICE: Yasmin €€
Boutique
Tyršovo nábrežie 1, 040 01
Tel *(055) 795 1100*
Ⓦ hotel-yasmin.sk
Stylish ten-storey hotel with a modern design and pleasing interiors. It offers comfortable, spacious rooms, a wellness centre and is well-equipped for holding large conferences.

LEVOČA: Arkada €
Historic
Námestie Majstra Pavla 26, 054 01
Tel *(053) 451 2372*
Ⓦ arkada.sk
Bright and airy en suites on Levoča's evocative Town Square, in a lovely building that dates back to the late Middle Ages.

SPIŠSKÉ PODHRADIE: Hotel Kapitula €
Historic
Spišská Kapitula 15, 053 04
Tel *(053) 454 2581*
Ⓦ hotelkapitula.eu
In a 15th-century historic Gothic building in the immediate vicity of several cultural monuments; offers spacious well-styled en suites and facilities for events and conferences.

STARY SMOKOVEC: Grand Hotel Stary Smokovec €
Luxury
Stary Smokovec 38, 062 01
Tel *(052) 478 0000*
Ⓦ www.grandhotel.sk
The Grand occupies a lovely, Carpathian-style half-timbered 1904 building right in the heart of the Stary Smokovec mountain resort. The interior retains many original Art Nouveau fittings and the rooms are richly furnished. Spa facilities on site.

TRNAVA: Penzion u Mami €
B&B
Jeruzalemská 3, 917 01
Tel *(033) 535 4216*
Ⓦ penzionumami.sk
Located on a quiet street near the Cathedral of St John the Baptist, this hotel offers 11 comfortably furnished rooms as well as a few apartments.

Where to Eat and Drink

Bratislava

Bistro St Germain €
French
Rajská 7, 811 08
Tel *911 331 999*
Bistro-by-day and café-by-night,
the cosy St Germain is popular
for its sandwiches, burgers and
salads. Live music at weekends.

**Bratislavsky Mestiansky
Pivovar** €
Brewery Restaurant **Map** D4
Dunajska 21, 811 06
Tel *948 710 888*
A large beer hall with a spacious
garden, serves meaty goulash,
steaks and grilled sausages.
Wash them down with their
own brew: the Bratislavsky
Ležiak pilsener beer.

Modra Hviezda €€
Slovak **Map** B5
Behlavého 11, 811 01
Tel *948 703 070*
Enjoy traditional poultry, rabbit or
game dishes and local wines in a
brick cellar environ or beside the
cobbled Behlavého Lane.

DK Choice

Pivnica u Zlatej Husy €€
Slovak
Pezinská 2, Slovensky Grob, 900 26
Tel *905 525 417*
The village of Slovensky Grob
is famous for the roast goose
served at its rustic inns of which
the 'Golden Goose Tavern' is
one of the most famous. The
goose is usually served whole
(sufficient for a group), although
you can also order individual
cuts. *Lokša* (potato pancakes)
is the traditional side-order.

FouZoo €€€
Fusion
Ševčenkova 34, 851 01
Tel *901 747 477*
Japanese fusion restaurant
serving top class sushi and an
appetizing variety of steak or
seafood mains. Arty interiors
influencesd by contemporary
and retro science-fiction.

Messina €€€
International **Map** D5
Tobrucká 4, 811 02
Tel *(02) 5778 4600*
Warm colours and chandeliers
set the tone for creative cuisine
that changes seasonally. Expect
the best cuts of meat and

Spectacular location of UFO at the top of
Nový Most, Bratislava

poultry, served with inventive
combinations of spices
and vegetables.

Le Monde €€€
French **Map** C4
Rybárska Brána 8, 811 01
Tel *(02) 5441 5411*
Situated in a historic house in
the Old Town that offers fantastic
views from the terrace, Le Monde
serves sophisticated French
cuisine with an innovative
contemporary angle.

UFO €€€
Fusion
Nový Most, 851 01
Tel *(02) 6252 0300*
Located at the top of the pylon
on Nový Most (New Bridge), the
stylish UFO offers Mediterranean–
Asian fusion cuisine, cocktails and
delicious desserts. Breathtaking
views too.

Rest of Slovakia

**BANSKA BYSTRICA: Hotel
Šactička** €
Slovak
Šachtičky 34, 974 01
Tel *(048) 414 1911*
Overlooking wooded mountain
slopes, this hotel restaurant is a
great place to enjoy freshwater
fish, lamb, game, dumpling-
dishes and other Slovak staples.

KOŠICE: Golem €
Brewery Restaurant
Dominikánske námestie 15, 040 01
Tel *(055) 728 9102*
Choose between the wood-
floored beer hall and the summer
garden for traditional Slovak
pub food: smoked beef tongue,
grilled pork and chicken backed
by locally brewed ales.

Price Guide

Prices are based on a three-course meal
for one, half a bottle of wine, including
cover charge, service and tax.

€	under €15
€€	€15 to €30
€€€	over €30

DK Choice

KOŠICE: Med Malina €€
Slovak
Hlavná 81, 040 01
Tel *(055) 622 0397*
Perfect for sampling East Slovak
specialities, Med Malina has
a dining room that looks like
granny's parlour, complete
with wooden sideboards and
hanging clumps of garlic. Try
the *pirohy:* pastry parcels stuffed
with meat, potato, cabbage or
cottage cheese. Dishes like
bigos (meat and cabbage stew)
and *zurek* (rye soup) betray the
influence of nearby Poland.

**LEVOČA: Reštaurácia u 3
Apoštolov** €
Slovak
Námestie Majstra Pavla 11, 054 01
Tel *(053) 451 4352*
This elegant restaurant in the
centre of town, offers traditional
Slovak cuisine, a vast selection of
freshwater fish as well as a choice
of vegetarian dishes.

**SPIŠSKÁ NOVA VES:
Nostalgie** €€
International
Letná 49, 052 01
Tel *(053) 441 4144*
A historic restaurant with a
contemporary global menu,
Nostalgie offers Mexican, Italian
and Creole options together with
local freshwater fish and poultry.
Be sure to save room for dessert.

**STARY SMOKOVEC:
Lefevre** €€€
International
Stary Smokovec 25, 062 01
Tel *(052) 478 0000*
With high ceilings and a classy
air, this elegant restaurant in the
Grand Hotel, serves traditional
Slovak and European–Asian
fusion cuisine.

TRNAVA: Patriot €€
International
Jeruzalemska 12, 917 01
Tel *(033) 551 2511*
This homely bar-restaurant offers
bistro fare that includes Italian
pastas, risottos, juicy steaks, roast
fowl and Slovak dumpling dishes.

HUNGARY

Unique to Central Europe, Hungary is peopled by descendants of Magyars, a race from Central Asia who settled here in the 9th century. In recent times, the country has fought against Ottoman, German, Austrian and Soviet occupiers, yet its indigenous culture remains intact. In 1989 Hungary became the first Eastern Bloc country to embrace Western-style democracy.

Hungary has a varied landscape, with forests and mountains dominating the north and a vast plain covering the rest of the country. The Tisza river and its tributaries shape the eastern regions, while the west has Lake Balaton, one of the largest lakes in Europe. The mighty Danube flows through the heart of the country, bisecting the capital, Budapest, where one-fifth of the population lives.

History

In AD 100 the Romans established the town of Aquincum near modern-day Budapest, and ruled the area, then called Pannonia, for three centuries. They withdrew completely following the arrival of the Huns in the early 5th century. After the death of Attila the Hun in 453, the area was ruled by the Goths, the Lombards and the Avars. The ancestors of the modern Hungarians, the Magyars, migrated from the Urals in 896, under the leadership of Prince Árpád, whose dynasty lasted until 1301, when King András III died without leaving an heir. The throne then passed to a series of foreign kings, but the country flourished, and during the reign of Mátyás Corvinus (r. 1458–90) it became the greatest monarchy in Central Europe. The Ottomans won a major victory at the Battle of Mohács in 1526. They returned to capture Buda in 1541, which became the capital of Ottoman Hungary. To quell their advance, the Austrians, under Ferdinand of Habsburg, occupied western Hungary, while the central plains stayed under Ottoman control; the eastern region, including Transylvania, became

View from Castle Hill across the Danube, with the Parliament visible beyond Elizabeth Bridge, Budapest

◀ The popular Szechenyi thermal baths

a semi-autonomous land, tied to the Ottomans. Christian armies led by the Habsburgs finally defeated the Ottomans in 1686. Economic prosperity came with Austrian rule, but nationalism was suppressed, which led to a major uprising in 1848. After crushing the rebellion, Emperor Franz Joseph I sought to unite the two nations, and so created the Dual Monarchy of Austro-Hungary in 1867. Following World War I, the Habsburg Empire was dismantled, and Hungary lost two-thirds of its territory to the "successor states" of Yugoslavia, Czechoslovakia and Romania. It was to regain these territories that Hungary backed Germany in World War II, but in 1945 Budapest was occupied by the Soviets. The subsequent Communist rule

Mátyás Corvinus (1440–90), King of Hungary

was ruthlessly upheld, most visibly in 1956 when demonstrations were crushed by Soviet tanks. Nevertheless, free elections took place in 1989, resulting in victory for the democratic opposition. Since then, the country has invested in tourism, which is now a major source of income.

Language and Culture

Modern Hungarian derives from a language originally spoken by the Finno-Ugric tribes of the Urals. Traditional peasant culture was all but destroyed in the 20th century, but folk songs and dances still survive.

Musically, the country has produced several famous composers, including Franz Liszt and Béla Bartók, while in literature, powerful voices include

Exploring Hungary

Located in the heart of Central Europe, Budapest is the perfect base for exploring Hungary. Szentendre, with its Serbian religious art, is a short drive north. Pécs, a treasure trove of European history, lies to the south, while the popular town of Eger in the wine-producing area is to the east. The country has an excellent rail network, fares are reasonable and the road infrastructure has expanded in recent years.

Sights at a Glance

Folk dancers performing at a wine festival, Tihany

Tibor Déry and István Örkény.
Hungary is also known for its
wine and meat-based dishes,
the latter spiced with paprika,
the country's most
famous export.

KEY DATES IN HUNGARIAN HISTORY

c. AD 100 Romans establish Aquincum

c. 410 Huns overrun the region

896 Magyar tribes arrive

1001 Coronation of Stephen I (István), Hungary's first king

1300s Angevin rule begins

1458–90 Reign of Mátyás Corvinus

1526 Ottomans win the Battle of Mohács

1526–41 Ottomans conquer Buda three times

1541 Start of Ottoman rule

1686 Habsburg troops enter Buda, ending Turkish rule in Hungary

1848 Hungarian Nationalist Uprising

1867 Compromise with Austria gives Hungary independence in internal affairs

1873 Buda and Pest become Budapest

1918 With the break-up of the Austro-Hungarian Empire, Hungary gains independence after nearly 400 years of foreign rule

1941 Hungary enters World War II

1945 Soviet Army takes Budapest

1956 The Soviets repress a nationalist uprising

1989 Hungary proclaimed a democratic republic

2004 Hungary becomes a member of the EU

2014 Viktor Orbán's Fidesz party re-elected

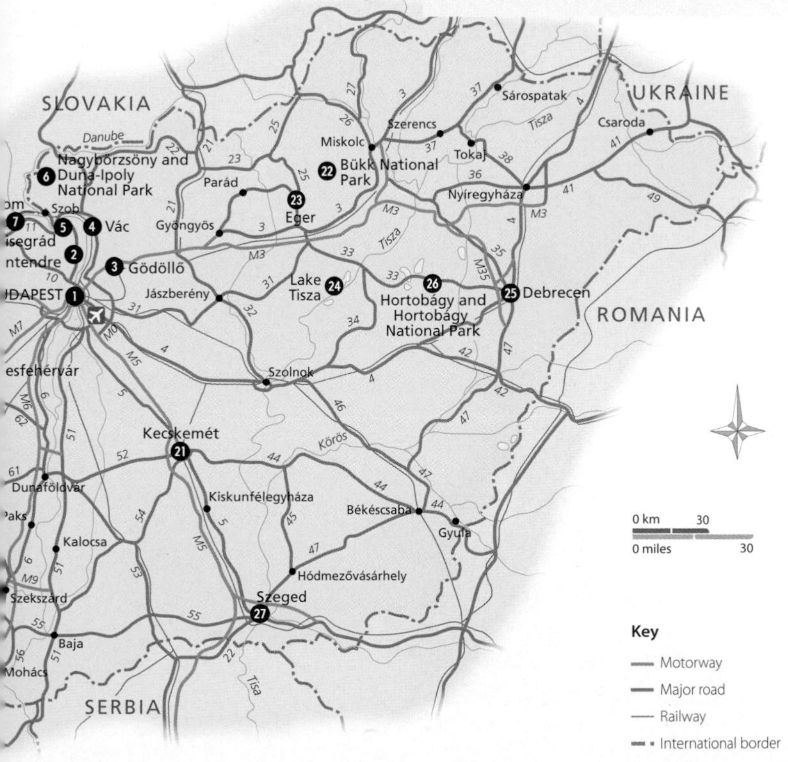

Key

— Motorway

— Major road

— Railway

— · International border

For keys to symbols *see back flap*

❶ Budapest

Budapest was founded in 1873 after the unification of three separate towns – Buda and Obuda on the west bank of the Danube, and Pest on the east. All three towns developed in the second half of the 12th century; Buda became the seat of Hungary's rulers in 1247. A period of Turkish rule from 1541 to 1686 left few traces, except for the city's wonderful bathhouses. Now home to two million people, Budapest is considered one of the most beautiful cities in Europe. Many of the historic sights lie along the banks of the Danube, including the Neo-Classical Parliament, Neo-Gothic Mátyás Church and the Hungarian National Museum.

Sights at a Glance

1. Hungarian National Gallery
2. Budapest History Museum
3. Mátyás Fountain
4. Holy Trinity Square
5. Mátyás Church see pp330–31
6. Gellért Hill see pp332–5
7. Parliament see pp336–7
8. Roosevelt Square
9. St Stephen's Basilica
10. State Opera House
11. Vigadó Square
12. Váci Utca
13. Inner City Parish Church
14. University Church
15. Museum of Applied Arts
16. Hungarian National Museum
17. Great Synagogue
18. Jewish Quarter
19. Heroes' Square
20. Museum of Fine Arts
21. Városliget
22. Széchenyi Baths
23. Vajdahunyad Castle
24. Margaret Island

Sculpture at the foot of Liberation Monument, Gellért Hill

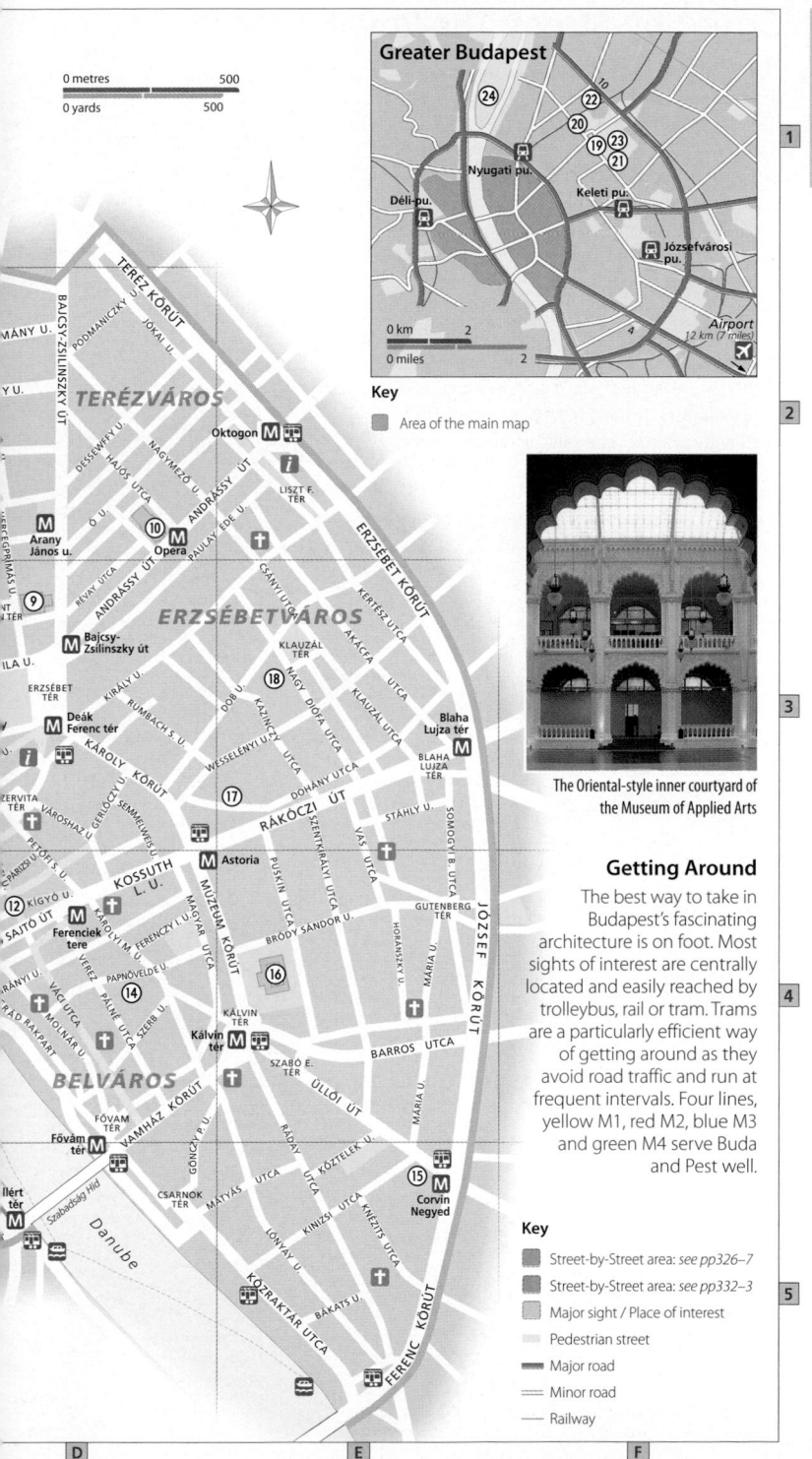

Greater Budapest

㉔ ㉒ ㉓ ㉑ ㉓ ㉑ ㉕ 10 20 19

Nyugati pu.

Déli-pu.

Keleti pu.

Józsefvárosi pu.

Airport
12 km (7 miles)

0 km 2
0 miles 2

Key
▢ Area of the main map

0 metres 500
0 yards 500

TERÉZ KÖRÚT

BAJCSY-ZSILINSZKY ÚT

MÁNY U.

Y U.

TERÉZVÁROS

Oktogon Ⓜ 🚊
ⓘ
LISZT F. TÉR

Ⓜ Arany János u.

⑩ Opera Ⓜ
✝

⑨

ERZSÉBETVÁROS

Ⓜ Bajcsy-Zsilinszky út

KLAUZÁL TÉR

⑱

ERZSÉBET TÉR

Ⓜ Deák Ferenc tér
ⓘ 🚊

ZERVITA TÉR
✝

KÁROLY KÖRÚT

⑰

RÁKÓCZI ÚT

Blaha Lujza tér Ⓜ
BLAHA LUJZA TÉR

✝

Ⓜ Astoria

⑫ KÍGYÓ U.

Ⓜ Ferenciek tere
✝

KOSSUTH L. U.

⑭

⑯

KÁLVIN TÉR

Kálvin tér Ⓜ 🚊

SZABÓ E. TÉR

ÜLLŐI ÚT

BELVÁROS

FŐVÁM TÉR

Fővám tér Ⓜ
🚊

llért tér Ⓜ

Szabadság Híd

Danube

KÖZRAKTÁR UTCA

⑮ Corvin Negyed Ⓜ 🚊

FERENC KÖRÚT

JÓZSEF KÖRÚT

The Oriental-style inner courtyard of the Museum of Applied Arts

Getting Around

The best way to take in Budapest's fascinating architecture is on foot. Most sights of interest are centrally located and easily reached by trolleybus, rail or tram. Trams are a particularly efficient way of getting around as they avoid road traffic and run at frequent intervals. Four lines, yellow M1, red M2, blue M3 and green M4 serve Buda and Pest well.

Key
▨ Street-by-Street area: see pp326–7
▨ Street-by-Street area: see pp332–3
▢ Major sight / Place of interest
▢ Pedestrian street
▬ Major road
═ Minor road
— Railway

Street-by-Street: The Royal Palace

The Royal Palace has experienced many incarnations over the centuries. Even now it is not known exactly where, in the 13th century, King Béla IV began building his castle, though it is thought to be near the site of Mátyás Church *(see pp330–31)*. The Holy Roman Emperor Sigismund of Luxembourg built a Gothic palace on the present site, from which today's castle began to evolve. After the Ottoman occupation, the Habsburgs built a monumental palace here in the 18th century. The current form dates from the rebuilding of the 19th-century palace after its destruction in February 1945. During the renovation, the remains of the 15th-century Gothic palace were exposed and archaeologists decided to showcase the defensive walls and royal chambers in the reconstruction.

Sándor Palace

Ornamental Gateway
Dating from 1903, this gateway leads to the Habsburg Steps and the Royal Palace. Nearby, a bronze sculpture of the mythical *turul* bird guards the palace.

③ ★ **Mátyás Fountain**
In the northern courtyard of the Royal Palace stands the Mátyás Fountain. It was designed by Alajos Stróbl in 1904 and depicts King Mátyás Corvinus and his beloved Ilonka.

Lion Gate
This gate, leading to the rear courtyard of the palace, gets its name from the four lions that watch over it. These sculptures were designed by János Fadrusz in 1901.

1200	1400	1600	1800
1255 First written document, a letter by King Béla IV, refers to building a fortified castle	**c.1400** Sigismund of Luxembourg builds an ambitious Gothic palace on this site	**1541** After capturing Buda, the Ottomans use the Royal Palace to stable horses and store gunpowder	**1719** The building of a small palace begins on the ruins of the old palace, to a design by Hölbling and Fortunato de Prati	**1881** Architect Miklós Ybl begins a programme to rebuild and expand the place
c.1356 Louis I builds a royal castle on the southern slopes of Castle Hill		**1686** The assault by Habsburg soldiers leaves the palace razed to the ground	**1849** Royal Palace is destroyed again, during an unsuccessful attack by Hungarian insurgents	
1458 A Renaissance palace evolves under King Mátyás		**1749** Maria Theresa builds a vast palace comprising 203 chambers		

Turul bird

Dome of the Royal Palace
The original Neo-Baroque dome,
designed by Alajos Hauszmann,
was destroyed in the razing
of the palace during World
War II; it was later rebuilt
in Neo-Classical style.

Statue of Prince Eugene of Savoy
Unveiled in 1900, this statue by József Róna
commemorates the 1697 Battle of Zenta,
which was a turning point in the Turkish War.
The bas-reliefs on the base depict scenes
from the battle.

① ★ Hungarian National Gallery
Works of art illustrating Hungary's turbulent
history are displayed here. Periods of both foreign
domination and patriotic home rule are brought
to life through the gallery's extensive collection.

**② Budapest
History Museum**

Key

— Suggested route

National Széchényi Library

0 metres   50
0 yards   50

Building the Royal Palace

In the early 15th century, a Gothic Royal Palace
was built on the site. This was rebuilt in the
Renaissance style by King Mátyás in 1458. After
the Ottoman occupation, it was razed and built on
a smaller scale. The palace was further developed
by Queen Maria Theresa and was rebuilt again
after World War II, to a design conceived in 1905.

☐ 15th century   ☐ 1749
☐ 1719   ☐ 1905

The Visitation (1506) by Master MS,
Hungarian National Gallery

① Hungarian National Gallery

Magyar Nemzeti Galéria

Royal Palace, Szent György tér 2.
Map C3. **Tel** (01) 439 7325. 🚌 5, 16,
78, Várbusz. **Open** 10am–6pm Tue–
Sun. 🅿 🖥 📷 **W** mng.hu

Established in 1957, the Hungarian National Gallery houses a comprehensive collection of Hungarian art from medieval times to the 20th century. Gathered by various groups and institutions since 1839, these works were previously exhibited at the Hungarian National Museum *(see p340)* and the Museum of Fine Arts *(see p342)*. The collection was moved to the Royal Palace *(see pp326–7)* in 1975.

The gallery houses six permanent exhibitions, comprising the most valuable and critically acclaimed Hungarian art in the world. Highlights include religious artifacts spanning several centuries, Gothic altarpieces as well as Renaissance and Baroque art.

The collection is spread over three floors. On the ground floor are early stone and Gothic exhibits, including sculptural and architectural fragments discovered during the reconstruction of the Royal Palace. Among the star exhibits are a carved stone head of King Béla III, from c. 1200, the *Madonna of Bártfa* (1465–70) and the *Madonna of Toporc* (c. 1420). Originally crafted for

a church in Spiš (now part of Slovakia), it is a fine example of medieval wood sculpture in the Gothic style.

Late-Gothic, Renaissance, Baroque and 19th-century artifacts share the first floor. *The Visitation* (1506) by Master MS, a fragment of a folding altarpiece from a church in modern-day Slovakia, is a delightful example of late-Gothic Hungarian art. Several works by Mihály Munkácsy, widely regarded as Hungary's greatest artist, show the development of 19th-century historicist art and the influence of Impressionism. *The Woman Bathing* (1901), by Károly Lotz, better known for his frescoes, is one of the best examples of Neo-Classical painting in Hungary. The painting reflects Lotz's fascination with the work of the French painter Ingres. Another impressive work of art is the elaborately decorated folding St Anne altarpiece (c. 1520) from Kisszeben.

Works from the 20th century, including paintings and exhibits from the Art Nouveau era as well as the Expressionist, Surrealist and avant-garde movements, are all showcased on the second floor. Those by painter Tivadar Kosztka Csontváry give a unique, idiosyncratic vision of the world. Temporary exhibits are housed on the third floor.

② Budapest History Museum

Budapesti Történeti Múzeum

Royal Palace, Szent György tér 2.
Map C3. **Tel** (01) 487 8800. 🚌 5, 16,
78, Várbusz. **Open** Mar–Oct: 10am–
6pm Tue–Sun; Nov–Feb: 10am–4pm
Tue–Sun. 🅿 🦽 ♿
W btm.hu

The Budapest History Museum, also known as Castle Museum, is situated in the Royal Palace and holds an interesting collection of artifacts relating to the city's development.

The Royal Palace was damaged during World War II and during its reconstruction, chambers dating from the Middle Ages were uncovered in the south wing. These remarkable rooms, including a prison cell and a chapel, have been recreated in the basement and provide an insight into the character of a much earlier castle within today's Habsburg reconstruction. They now house an exhibition on the palace's medieval history, with weapons, seals and other early artifacts.

The museum also has an interesting display on Budapest in the Middle Ages, illustrating the evolution of the town from its Roman origins to a 13th-century settlement, and one on Budapest in modern times tracing the city's history from 1686 to the present.

Fifteenth-century majolica floor, Budapest History Museum

Buda's Old Town Hall, crowned with an onion-shaped dome, on Holy Trinity Square

③ Mátyás Fountain

Mátyás Kút

Royal Palace. **Map** C3.
🚌 5, 16, 78, Várbusz.

The ornate fountain in the northernmost courtyard of the Royal Palace was designed by Hungarian sculptor and artist, Alajos Stróbl in 1904. Decorated with bronze sculptures, this flamboyant fountain is dedicated to the great Renaissance king, Mátyás Corvinus who is the subject of many popular legends and fables.

The design of the bronze figures takes its theme from a 19th-century ballad by the poet Mihály Vörösmarty (1800–55). According to the legend, King Mátyás met a peasant girl, Ilonka, while on a hunting expedition. The two fell in love but their love was doomed. This representation shows the king dressed as a hunter, standing proudly with his kill. He is accompanied by his chief hunter and several hunting dogs in the central part of the fountain. Below the columns on the left, is the statue of Galeotto Marzio, an Italian court poet, with a hawk in his hand. The striking figure of the young Ilonka, with a doe, is below the columns on the right. In keeping with the romantic reputation of King

Mátyás, a new tradition is gaining popularity with visitors, who throw coins into the fountain in the belief that this will ensure their safe return to Budapest in the future.

Statue of King Mátyás with his hunting trophy, Mátyás Fountain

④ Holy Trinity Square

Szentháromság tér

Map B3. 🚌 Várbusz from Moszkva tér.

This square, located close to the Royal Palace, is the central point of the Old Town. It takes its name from the Baroque Holy Trinity Column in the middle of the square, which was originally sculpted by Philipp Ungleich between 1710 and 1713 and restored in 1967.

The column was commissioned by the Buda Council after the outbreak of the second plague in the city. It commemorates the dead of two outbreaks of the plague, which struck the inhabitants of Buda in 1691 and 1709. The pedestal of the column is decorated with bas-reliefs by Anton Hörger depicting the horrific fate Buda's citizens suffered during those epidemics. Further up the ornate column are statues of holy figures, while at the summit is a superb composition of the figures of the Holy Trinity. The central section of the column is decorated with beautiful angelic figures surrounded by clouds.

Buda's Old Town Hall, a large Baroque building with two courtyards, was also built on the square at the beginning of the 18th century. It was designed by the 17th-century imperial court architect, Venerio Ceresola, whose architectural scheme incorporated the remains of medieval houses. In the 18th century an east wing was built and bay windows and a stone balustrade with Rococo urns, by Mátyás Nepauer, were also added. The corner niche, opposite Mátyás Church, houses a small statue of the Greek goddess Pallas Athene by Carlo Adami.

⑤ Mátyás Church

Mátyás templom

The Parish Church of Our Lady Mary was built on this site between the 13th and 15th centuries. Some of the architectural style dates from the reign of Sigismund of Luxembourg, but the church was named after King Mátyás Corvinus, one of the greatest Hungarian rulers. Much of the original detail was lost when the Ottomans converted the church into the Great Mosque in 1541. The liberation of Buda saw the church almost totally destroyed, but it was rebuilt in the Baroque style by the Franciscan friars. It sustained further damage in 1723 but was restored in the Neo-Gothic style between 1873 and 1896 by the architect Frigyes Schulek. The crypt houses the Museum of Ecclesiastical Art.

Rose Window
Architect Frigyes Schulek faithfully reproduced, in stone, the medieval stained-glass window to its original Gothic style.

Béla Tower
Named after the church's founder, King Béla IV, this tower has retained several of its original Gothic features.

★ **Baroque Madonna**
According to legend, the original statue was set into a wall of the church during the Ottoman occupation. When the church was destroyed in 1686, the statue miraculously appeared. The Ottomans took this as an omen of defeat.

Main Portal
Below the arches of the west entrance is an impressive 19th-century bas-relief by sculptor Lajos Lantai showing the Madonna and Child seated between two angels.

KEY

① **The roof** is decorated with multicoloured glazed tiles.

② **The main altar** was created by Frigyes Schulek and based on Gothic triptychs.

★ Tomb of King Béla III and Anne de Châtillon

The remains of this royal couple were transferred from Székesfehérvár Cathedral to Mátyás Church in 1860. They lie beneath an ornamental stone canopy in the Trinity Chapel.

VISITORS' CHECKLIST

Practical Information
Szentháromság tér 2.
Map B2.
Tel (01) 489 0716.
Open 9am–5pm Mon–Fri,
9am–1pm Sat, 1–5pm Sun.
Museum: **Open** 9am–5pm Sun–Fri.
W **matyas-templom.hu**

Transport
Várbusz.

Pulpit

The richly decorated pulpit of the church includes the intricately carved stone figures of the four Holy Fathers of the Church and the four Evangelists.

Stained-glass Windows

This beautiful 19th-century stained glass depicting Christ the Lamb, is from one of the three arched windows on the south elevation.

★ Mary Portal

This depiction of the Assumption of the Blessed Virgin Mary is the most magnificent example of Gothic stone carving in Hungary. Frigyes Schulek reconstructed the portal from fragments.

---

c.1387 Church redesigned as Gothic hall-church by Sigismund of Luxembourg

1458 Thanksgiving mass following the coronation of Mátyás Corvinus

1541 Ottomans convert church into a mosque

1686 After liberation of Buda from Turkish rule, church is almost destroyed. New church built with a Baroque interior

Holy figures on the pulpit

1250	1350	1450	1550	1650	1750	1850	1950

1309 Coronation of the Angevin king Charles Robert

1255 Church originally founded by King Béla IV after the Mongol invasion

1526 Cathedral burnt in the first attack by Turks

1470 Mátyás Tower rebuilt after its collapse in 1384

1896 Frigyes Schulek completes the reconstruction of the church in Neo-Gothic style

1945 Church is severely damaged by German and Soviet armies

1970 Final details are completed in post-war rebuilding programme

⑥ Street-by-Street: Gellért Hill

Rising steeply beside the Danube, Gellért Hill is one of the city's most attractive areas. It is named after Bishop Gellért, who converted the pagan Magyars to Christianity at the behest of King Stephen (István), the first king of Hungary. In the 11th century, Prince Vata, brother of King Stephen, incited a heathen rebellion here that resulted in the death of the bishop. Under the Ottomans, a stronghold was built on the hill to protect Buda, and in 1851, the Habsburgs placed their own intimidating Citadel at the summit. It was not until the end of the 19th century that Gellért Hill became a venue for picnickers. In 1967, the area around the Citadel was made into an attractive park.

Queen Elizabeth Monument
Close to the entrance of Elizabeth Bridge stands this statue of Habsburg Emperor Franz Joseph's wife, Elizabeth, who was popular with the Hungarians.

Elizabeth Bridge

Gellért Hill's reservoir

HEGYALIA ÚT

★ **Statue of St Gellért**
The statue of Bishop Gellért, blessing the city with his uplifted cross, overlooks Elizabeth Bridge. He is regarded as the patron saint of Budapest.

Citadel
Once a spot that inspired terror, the Citadel now hosts a hotel, restaurant and lounge bar, where people can relax and enjoy the splendid view.

Key

— Suggested route

Liberation Monument
Designed by Hungarian sculptor Zsigmond Strobl, the monument commemorates the liberation of Budapest by the Soviet Army in 1945.

For hotels and restaurants see p378 and p379

Rudas Baths, with decorative Ottoman cupolas, are famous Turkish baths that date from the 16th century.

Observation Terraces
The observation terraces on Gellért Hill offer spectacular views of the southern part of Buda and the whole of Pest.

The Reservoir

In 1978, a new reservoir was built near Uránia Observatory to the northwest of Gellért Hill to supply the capital with drinking water. The surface of the reservoir is covered over and provides a point from which to observe the Royal Palace *(see pp326–7)* to the north. A sculpture by Márta Lesenyei decorates the structure.

Sculpture by Márta Lesenyei on Gellért Hill's reservoir

Rock Church
This church was established in 1926 in a holy grotto. Under the Communists, the Pauline Order of monks was forced to abandon the church, but it was reopened in 1989.

0 metres		500
0 yards		500

SZENT GELLÉRT RAKPART

Liberty Bridge

★ **Gellért Hotel and Baths Complex**
One of a number of bath complexes built at the beginning of the 20th century, this impressive spa hotel *(see pp334–5)*, with its thermal pool, was built to exploit the natural hot springs here.

Gellért Hotel and Baths Complex
Gellért Szálló és Fürdo

Located at the foot of Gellért Hill, this hotel and spa was built between 1912 and 1918 in the Modernist Art Nouveau style by architects Ármin Hegedűs, Artúr Sebestyén and Izidor Sterk. The earliest reference to the existence of healing waters at this spot dates from the 13th century. During the reign of King András II in the Middle Ages, a hospital stood on the site. Baths built here by the Ottomans were mentioned by the renowned 17th-century Turkish travel writer, Evliya Çelebi. Destroyed during World War II, the hotel was later rebuilt and modernized. Today it also houses several restaurants and cafés. The baths complex includes an institute of water therapy, set within Art-Nouveau-era interiors, but with modern facilities.

Outdoor Wave Pool
Built in 1927, this swimming pool with a wave mechanism is situated at the back of the complex, providing a view of Gellért Hill.

★ Baths
Two separate baths, one for men and another for women, are identically arranged. In each there are three plunge pools – with water at different temperatures – a sauna and a steam bath.

Balconies
The balconies fronting the hotel rooms have fanciful Art Nouveau balustrades decorated with lyre and bird motifs.

★ Entrance Hall
Like the baths, the interior of the hotel has kept its original Art Nouveau decor, with elaborate mosaics, stained-glass windows and statues.

For hotels and restaurants see p378 and p379

Sun Terraces
Situated in the sunniest spot, these terraces are a popular place for drying off in summer.

VISITORS' CHECKLIST

Practical Information
Szent Gellért tér.
Tel (01) 889 5500.
♿ ⊠ ⁄ ▭ ⌂
Baths: Kelenhegyi út.
Open 6am–8pm daily. ♨ ♿ ⊠
ⓦ gellertbath.com

Transport
🚌 7, 7A, 86. 🚊 18, 19, 47, 49.

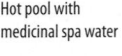

Hot pool with
medicinal spa water

Eastern-Style Towers
The towers and turrets of the hotel were designed in characteristically Oriental cylindrical form.

Main Staircase
The landings of the main staircase have stained-glass windows by Bozó Stanisits, added in 1933. They illustrate an ancient Hungarian legend about a magic stag, referred to in the poetry of János Arany.

Restaurant Terrace
This first-floor terrace offers diners a pretty view of Budapest. The ground and first floors of the hotel house a total of four cafés and restaurants.

★ Main Façade
Behind the hotel's façade are attractive recreational facilities and a health spa that is also open to non-guests. The entrance to the baths is around to the right from the main entrance, on Kelenhegyi út.

⑦ Parliament

Parlamentnek

The largest building in the country, Hungary's Parliament has become a symbol of Budapest. A competition, held to choose its design, was won by Hungarian architect Imre Steindl, who based his plans on the Houses of Parliament in London, built by Charles Barry in the mid-19th century. Steindl's Neo-Gothic masterpiece, constructed between 1885 and 1904, is 96 m (315 ft) high and has 691 rooms.

Lateral View
The magnificent dome marks the central point of the Parliament building. Although the façade is elaborately Neo-Gothic, the ground plan follows Baroque conventions.

★ **Domed Hall**
Adorning the massive pillars that support Parliament's central dome are figures of some of Hungary's rulers.

★ **Deputy Council Chamber**
Formerly the lower house, this is where the National Assembly now convenes. Paintings by Hungarian artist Zsigmond Vajda (1860–1931) hang on either side of the Speaker's lectern.

Gables
Almost every corner of the Parliament building features gables with pinnacles based on Gothic sculptures.

Lobbies
Magnificent corridors, adorned with stained-glass windows, are the venue for many political discussions.

For hotels and restaurants see p378 and p379

Dome
The ceiling of the 96-m (315-ft) high dome is covered in an intricate design of Neo-Gothic gilding combined with heraldic decoration.

Tapestry Hall
This room, on the Danube side of the Domed Hall, has a tapestry depicting Prince Árpád with seven Magyar leaders under his command, as he signs a peace treaty and takes an oath.

Old Upper House Hall
This vast hall is virtually a mirror image of the Deputy Council Chamber. Both halls have public galleries running around a horseshoe-shaped interior.

The main entrance on Kossuth Lajos tér

Main Staircase
The best contemporary artists were invited to decorate the Parliament's interior. The sumptuous main staircase features ceiling frescoes by painter Károly Lotz and sculptures by György Kiss.

KEY

① **South wing**

② **Danube façade**

③ **North wing**

④ **The Royal Insignia**, excluding the Coronation Mantle (see p340), are kept in the Domed Hall.

⑧ Roosevelt Square

Roosevelt tér

Map C3. 🚌 16. 🚃 2.

Known by different names over the years – Unloading Square and Franz Joseph Square among others – Roosevelt Square received its current title in 1947. It leads into the Pest side of the **Chain Bridge**, the city's first permanent bridge over the Danube river. A major feat of engineering, the bridge was designed by Englishman William Tierney Clark and built by the Scot, Adam Clark, between 1839 and 1849.

At the beginning of the 20th century, the square was lined with hotels, the Diana Baths and the Lloyd Palace, designed by József Hild. The only building from the 19th century still standing today is the Hungarian Academy of Sciences. All other buildings were demolished and replaced by the Gresham Palace and the Bank of Hungary, on the corner of József Attila utca. There is a statue to Baron József Eötvös, a reformer of public education, in front of the InterContinental Budapest.

In the centre of the square are monuments to two famous politicians: Count István Széchenyi, the leading social and political reformer of his age, and Ferenc Deák, who was instrumental in the Compromise of 1867, which led to the Dual Monarchy of Austria-Hungary.

⑨ St Stephen's Basilica

Szent István Bazilika

Szent István tér. **Map** D3. **Tel** (01) 311 0839. Ⓜ Deák Ferenc tér. **Open** 9am–5pm Mon–Sat, 2–5pm Sun. 🅿 ♿ ✝ Ⓦ **bazilika.biz**

Dedicated to St Stephen (István), the first Hungarian Christian king, this church was designed by József Hild in the Neo-Classical style, using a Greek cross floor plan. Construction began in 1851 and was taken over in 1867 by the great Hungarian architect, Miklós Ybl.

Impressive exterior of the St Stephen's Basilica

He added the Neo-Renaissance dome after the original collapsed in 1868. József Kauser completed the church in 1905. It received the title of Basilica Minor in 1938, the 900th anniversary of St Stephen's death.

A marble statue of the saint stands on the main altar, and scenes from his life are depicted behind it. A painting to the right of the main entrance shows St Stephen, who was left without an heir, dedicating Hungary to the Virgin Mary. His mummified forearm is kept in the Chapel of the Holy Right Hand.

The outer colonnade at the back of the church has the figures of the 12 Apostles. The dome is decorated with superb mosaics by Károly Lotz and it reaches 96 m (315 ft) and is visible all over Budapest. The basilica has two towers, one of which houses a bell weighing 9 tonnes (10 tons). This was funded by German Catholics to compensate for the loss of the original bell, which was looted by the Nazis in 1944.

⑩ State Opera House

Magyar Állami Operaház

Andrássy út 22. **Map** D2. **Tel** (01) 332 7914, 353 0170 (box office). Ⓜ Opera. 🅿 🎟 3pm & 4pm daily. ♿ ✉ 🎧 Ⓦ **opera.hu**

Opened in September 1884, the State Opera House was built to rival those in Paris, Vienna and Dresden. Its beautiful architecture and interior decor were the life's work of architect Miklós Ybl.

The façade celebrates musical themes, with statues of Hungary's most prominent composers, including Ferenc Liszt. The interior contains ornamentation by Hungarian artists, including Alajos Strobl and Károly Lotz.

The opulence of the foyer, with its chandeliers and vaulted ceilings, is echoed in the grandeur of the sweeping main staricase and the three-storey auditorium. During its lifetime, the opera house has seen some influential musical directors, including Franz Erkel, composer of the Hungarian opera *Bánk Bán*, Gustav Mahler and Otto Klemperer.

The imposing façade of the State Opera House

⑪ Vigadó Square

Vigadó tér

Map C3. 🚌 2.

The square is dominated by the Vigadó Concert Hall, with its mix of eclectic forms. Built to designs by architect Frigyes Feszl between 1859 and 1864, it replaced an earlier building destroyed by fire during the uprising of 1848–9. The façade has arched windows and includes features such as folk motifs, dancers on columns and busts of former monarchs, rulers and other Hungarian personalities. An old Hungarian coat of arms is also visible in the centre.

The Budapest Marriott Hotel, located on one side of the square, was designed by József Finta in 1969. It was one of the first modern hotels to be built in the city.

On the Danube promenade is a statue of a childlike figure on the railings, *Little Princess*, by László Marton. Vigadó Square also has craft stalls, cafés and restaurants.

⑫ Váci Utca

Map D4. Ⓜ Ferenciek tere.

Once two separate streets which were joined at the beginning of the 18th century, the two ends of Váci utca still have distinctly different characters.

Today, part of the southern section is open to traffic, but the northern end is pedestrianized and has long been a popular commercial centre. Most of the buildings lining the street date from the 19th and early 20th centuries, although new banks, modern department stores and shopping arcades have now sprung up along the street among the older original buildings.

The street has a number of famous buildings, notable for their architecture or for their place in local history. Philantia, an Art-Nouveau-style florist's shop opened in 1905, now occupies part of the Neo-Classical block at No. 9, built in 1840 by József Hild. The same block also houses the Pest Theatre,

Thonet House, with Zsolnay tile decoration, Váci Utca

which stages classic plays by Russian playwright Anton Chekhov, among others. The building was once occupied by the "Inn of the Seven Electors" which had a large ballroom and concert hall, and it was here that a 12-year-old Ferenc (Franz) Liszt performed in 1823.

Built by Ödön Lechner and Gyula Pártos, the Thonet House, at No. 11, is most notable for the Zsolnay tiles from Pécs *(see pp362–3)* that adorn its façade. The oldest building on Váci utca, No. 13, was built in 1805. In contrast, the Post-Modern Fontana department store at No. 16 was constructed in 1984. Outside there is a bronze fountain with a figure of the Greek god Hermes, dating from the mid-19th century.

Crest of Pest, Inner City Parish Church

The Nádor Hotel once stood at No. 20 and featured a statue of Archduke Palatine József. Today, the Taverna Hotel, designed by József Finta and opened in 1987, stands here. It has a popular coffee shop.

In a side street off Váci utca, at No. 13 Régiposta utca, stands a Modernist-style building. An unusual sight in the city, this striking Bauhaus-influenced building dates from 1937 and is by Lajos Kozma.

⑬ Inner City Parish Church

Belvárosi Plébánia Templom

Március 15 tér 2. **Map** D4.
Tel (01) 318 3108. Ⓜ Ferenciek tere.
Open 9am–7pm daily. 🚻
🅦 belvarosiplebania.hu

Built in the 11th century, this is the oldest building in Pest. It was first established during the reign of St Stephen, on the burial site of the martyred St Gellért, who played a major role in converting Hungary to Christianity. In the 12th century it was replaced by a Romanesque church of which a wall fragment remains in the façade of the South Tower.

In the 14th century, it became a Gothic structure and subsequently a mosque – a small prayer niche, a reminder of the Ottoman occupation, can be seen beside the altar.

Damaged by the Great Fire of 1723, the church was partly rebuilt in the Baroque style by György Paur between 1725 and 1739. The interior also contains Neo-Classical elements by János Hild, as well as some 20th-century works such as the main altar, which replaced the original in 1948. The altar was painted by Károly Antal and Pál Molnár. On the south side of the church is a tabernacle bearing the Crest of Pest.

The Baroque nave of the Inner City Parish Church

Magnificent sculptures decorating the pulpit in the University Church

⑭ University Church

Egyetemi templom

Papnövelde utca 7. **Map** D4. **Tel** (01) 318 0555. **M** Kálvin tér. **Open** 7am–6pm Mon–Sat, 8am–7:30pm Sun. **W** kpi.hu

This single-aisle church, built between 1725 and 1742, is considered one of the most impressive Baroque churches in Budapest. It is believed to have been designed by local architect András Mayerhoffer and the tower was added in 1771. The church was built for the Pauline Order, which was founded by Canon Euzebiusz in 1263; it was the only religious order to be founded in Hungary.

The superb exterior features a tympanum and a row of pilasters that divide the façade. Figures of St Paul and St Anthony flank the emblem of the Pauline Order, which crowns the exterior. The carved-wood interior of the main vestibule is also worth seeing.

Inside the church, a row of side chapels stand behind unusual marble pilasters. In 1776, Bohemian artist Johann Bergl painted the vaulted ceiling with frescoes depicting scenes from the life of Mary, though these are now in poor condition. The main altar dates from 1746, and the carved statues behind it are the work

of József Hebenstreit. Above the altar is a copy of the famous Polish painting *The Black Madonna of Częstochowa* (c. 1720). The balustrade of the organ loft, the confessionals and the carved pulpit are the work of the Pauline monks.

⑮ Museum of Applied Arts

Iparművészeti múzeum

Üllői út 33–7. **Map** E5. **Tel** (01) 456 5107. **M** Ferenc körút. **Open** 10am–6pm Tue–Sun. **W** imm.hu

Opened in 1896 by Emperor Franz Joseph I as part of the Millennium Celebrations, this museum is housed within an outstanding Art Nouveau building designed by Gyula Pártos (1845–1916) and Ödön Lechner (1845–1914). The exterior incorporates elements inspired by the Orient as well as the Zsolnay ceramics characteristic of Lechner's work. Damaged in 1945 and again in 1956, the building was recently restored to its original magnificence.

The building is set around a glorious, arcaded courtyard, surrounded by cloisters and designed in an Indian-Oriental style. The museum, established in 1872, comprises many superb examples of arts and crafts workmanship.

Among the permanent collections are furniture from the 14th to the 20th centuries,

A 17th-century dress in the Museum of Applied Arts

including fine French pieces, Thonet bentwood furniture, and a large collection of ceramics. The metalwork collection comprises watches, jewellery and other items made by foreign and Hungarian craftsmen. The textiles section includes silks from the 13th and 14th centuries and also traces the history of traditional lacemaking.

The museum holds regular temporary exhibitions. The library, dating from 1872, contains around 50,000 books, making it one of the largest in Hungary.

Gothic painting of *Saint Martin of Tours*, Hungarian National Museum

⑯ Hungarian National Museum

Magyar Nemzeti múzeum

Múzeum körút 14–16. **Map** E4. **Tel** (01) 338 2122. 9, 15. 47, 49. **M** Kálvin tér, Astória. **Open** 10am–6pm Tue–Sun. **W** hnm.hu

Housed in a Neo-Classical edifice built by Mihály Pollack, the Hungarian National Museum was founded in 1802. It was started when Count Ferenc Széchényi bequeathed his collection of coins, books and documents to the nation. The museum's expanding collection of art stretches from the 11th century to the present day and offers the richest source of art and artifacts relating to the country's history.

Among the star exhibits are a textile masterpiece made of Byzantine silk, which became the Coronation Mantle in the 12th century, a 6th-century BC figure of a Golden Stag and a 13th-century golden funeral crown, discovered on Margaret Island *(see p343)*.

⑰ Great Synagogue

Zsinagóga

Dohány utca 2. **Map** E3. **Tel** (01) 342 8949. Ⓜ Astoria. 🚌 74. Jewish Museum: **Open** Mar–Oct: 10am–6pm Sun–Thu, 10am–4pm Fri; Nov–Feb: 10am–4pm Sun–Thu, 10am–2pm Fri. 🅿 📷 🌐 **zsidomuzeum.hu**

The Great Synagogue is the largest in Europe. Built in a Byzantine-Moorish style between 1854 and 1859 by the Viennese architect Ludwig Förster, it has three naves and, in accordance with Orthodox tradition, separate galleries for women. Together the naves and galleries can accommodate up to 3,000 worshippers. Some features, such as the position of the reading platform, reflect elements of Judaic reform. The interior has valuable decorative fittings, such as those on the Ark of the Law,

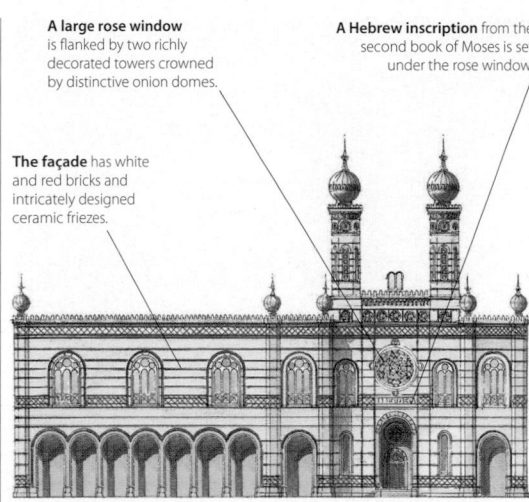

A large rose window is flanked by two richly decorated towers crowned by distinctive onion domes.

A Hebrew inscription from the second book of Moses is set under the rose window.

The façade has white and red bricks and intricately designed ceramic friezes.

by Frigyes Feszl. In 1931, a **Jewish Museum** was established here with a vast collection of historical relics, devotional and everyday objects from ancient Rome to the present, including the book of Chevra Kadisha from 1792. There is also a Holocaust Memorial Room.

⑱ Jewish Quarter

Zsidó Negyed

Király utca, Rumbach Sebestyén utca, Dohány utca & Akácfa utca. **Map** E3. Ⓜ Deák Ferenc tér.

Jews first came to Hungary in the 13th century, initially settling in Buda and Óbuda and, later, in the 19th century, establishing a larger community outside the Pest city boundary. In the late 19th century, three synagogues were built and many Jewish shops and workshops were established. Kosher businesses were a common

Detail of the Orthodox Synagogue, Jewish Quarter

feature of the area. The Jewish community became well integrated into Hungarian society until, in 1941, a series of anti-Semitic laws were passed. In 1944, a ghetto was created in the area around the Great Synagogue and the deportation of thousands of Jews to camps, including Auschwitz *(see pp196–9)*, was implemented.

In total, 600,000 Hungarian Jews were victims of the Holocaust. A plaque on the Orthodox Synagogue in Rumbach utca commemorates the thousands of Jews sent from Budapest. Today, the Jewish Quarter is recovering its pre-ghetto character, and shops are being rebuilt.

⑲ Heroes' Square

Hősök tér

Király utca, Rumbach Sebestyén utca, Dohány utca & Akácfa utca. **Map** F1. Ⓜ Hősök tere.

Heroes' Square is a relic of a proud age in Hungary's history – it was here that the Millennium Celebrations opened in 1896. This marked a high point in the development of Budapest and

Millennium Monument, Heroes' Square

in the history of the Austro-Hungarian monarchy. The city underwent a huge programme of modernization, with the construction of hundreds of civic buildings and palaces as well as the introduction of gas lighting and Europe's first underground transport system. The square is surrounded by monuments including the Museum of Fine Arts, the Széchenyi Baths and the Vajdahunyad Castle *(see p343)* built in Városliget.

Dominating the square is the **Millennium Monument**, featuring statues of prominent Hungarian leaders. The famous *Statue of Anonymous* (1903), by Miklós Ligeti, stands in front of the castle.

Magnificently decorated ceiling at the Museum of Fine Arts

⑳ Museum of Fine Arts

Szépművészeti Múzeum

Dózsa György út 41. **Map** F1. **Tel** (01) 469 7100. 4, 20, 30, 105. 75, 79. Hősök tere. **Open** 10am–5pm Tue–Sun. **w** szepmuveszeti.hu

The origins of the Museum of Fine Arts date from 1870, when the state bought a spectacular collection of paintings from the aristocratic Esterházy family. The museum's collection was further enriched by donations and acquisitions. In 1906, it moved to its present location, a Neo-Classical building with Italian Renaissance influences, designed by Hungarian architects Albert Schickedanz and Fülöp Herzog. The tympanum crowning the portico is supported by eight Corinthian columns. It depicts the Battle of the Centaurs and Lapiths, and is copied from the Temple of Zeus at Olympia, Greece.

The museum's collection encompasses a wide range of art from antiquity to the 20th century. Among the Egyptian artifacts, most of which were unearthed by Hungarian archaeologists during 19th century excavations, the collection of bronze figures from the New Kingdom of Ptolemy is the most fascinating.

The collection of Greek vases is the highlight of the classical artifacts, along with the famous Grimani jug, which dates from the 5th century BC. In the sculpture gallery, a small bronze figure by Leonardo da Vinci stands out, while the rich collection of Dutch and Flemish art features the sublime *St John the Baptist's Sermon* (1566), by Pieter Bruegel the Elder. There are Italian and Spanish works, including some by Raphael, El Greco and Goya and drawings and graphics by one of the best-known German painters, Albrecht Dürer. Also on view are stunning 19th- and 20th-century works by Pablo Picasso as well as gems by French Impressionists.

㉑ Városliget

Városliget

Városliget. **Map** F1. Hősök tere, Széchenyi Fürdő.

Városliget, also known as City Park, was once an area of marshland used as a royal hunting ground. Drained and planted during the reign of Queen Maria Theresa, the park was laid out in the English style in the late 19th century. Városliget was the centre for the Millennium Celebrations in 1896, when the Museum of Fine Arts, Vajdahunyad Castle and the Heroes' Square Monument *(see p341)* were built. Among its attractions is a lake, Varosligetito, which serves as an ice rink in winter and a boating lake in summer. The park is also home to the Széchenyi Baths, Budapest's zoo and the 110-year-old Gundel Restaurant.

㉒ Széchenyi Baths

Széchenyi Strandfürdő

Állatkerti körút 11. **Map** F1. 72. **Tel** (01) 363 3210. Széchenyi fürdő. Swimming Pool: **Open** 6am–10pm daily. Thermal Pool: **Open** 6am–7pm daily. **w** spasbudapest.hu

The largest complex of spa baths in Europe, Széchenyi Baths also has the deepest and hottest baths in Budapest; the water here reaches the surface at a temperature of about 75° C (180° F). The spa, housed in an attractive Neo-Baroque building by Győző Czigler and Ede Dvorzsák, was constructed between 1909 and 1913. At the main entrance stands a statue of geologist Vilmos Zsigmondy, who discovered a hot spring here while drilling a well in 1879. In 1926, three open-air swimming pools were added; these are popular throughout the year due to the heat of the water. The springs are known for their alleged healing properties and are recommended for treating rheumatism, disorders of the nervous system, joints and muscles.

An outdoor pool at Széchenyi Baths

㉓ Vajdahunyad Castle
Vajdahunyad Vára

Városliget. **Map** F1. **Tel** (01) 363
1973. 🚋 70, 72, 75, 79. 🚌 4, 20, 30.
Ⓜ Széchenyi fürdő. Museum of
Agriculture: **Tel** (01) 422 0765.
Open Apr–Oct: 10am–5pm Tue–
Sun; Nov–Mar: 10am–4pm
Tue–Sun. 🐾 📷 ♿
Ⓦ **mmgm.hu**

Located at the edge of
the lake in Városliget, this
fairytale castle is a complex
consisting of several buildings
reflecting various architectural
styles. Designed by architect
Ignác Alpár for the Millennium
Celebrations in 1896, it illustrates the history of architecture in Hungary. Originally
intended as temporary
exhibition pavilions, the castle
proved so popular with the
public that, between 1904
and 1906, it was rebuilt
using brick to create a
more permanent structure.

The pavilions are grouped
chronologically in style, with
individual styles linked to
give the impression of a single,
cohesive design. Each one
uses authentic details copied
from Hungary's most important historic buildings, or is
the interpretation of a style
inspired by a specific architect
of that period. The medieval
period, often considered a
glorious time in Hungary's
history, is emphasized, while
the controversial Habsburg
era is not. The Romanesque
complex features a copy
of the portal from a
rural village as well
as a monastic cloister
and palace. The

details on the Gothic
pavilion stem from castles
such as that in Segesvár,
now in Romania. The famous
Austrian architect Josef
Emanuel Fischer von Erlach
(see p384) inspired the
Renaissance and Baroque
complex. The façade copies
part of the Bakócz chapel
in the lovely Esztergom
Basilica *(see p348)*.

The popular **Museum of
Agriculture**, in the Baroque
section, has interesting
exhibits on wine-making,
cattle-breeding, hunting
and fishing.

㉔ Margaret Island
Margitsz viget

Margitsziget. **Map** F1.
🚌 26 from Nyugati Station.

Inhabited as far back as
Roman times, Margaret
Island is a tranquil oasis in
the middle of the Danube
river. The 2.5-km (1.5-mile)
long island was also known
as the Island of Rabbits, as it
served as a popular hunting
ground for medieval kings.
Monks, too, were drawn to
its peaceful setting. During
Ottoman rule it was used
as a harem. In the 1200s,
Princess Margaret (1242–70),
daughter of King Béla IV after
whom the island is named,
spent most of her life as a
recluse in a convent here.
It has been open to the
public since 1869.

Today, Margaret Island
still offers the perfect

The delightful Japanese Garden,
Margaret Island

escape after sightseeing
in the busy city. Besides
its lovely green spaces,
swimming pools and play-
grounds, notable attractions
include the Centenary
Monument, a unique water
tower and a serene Japanese
Garden. Designed by István
Kiss, the Centenary Monument
was erected in 1973 to celebrate
a century of the merger of
the cities of Buda, Pest
and Óbuda.

At the centre of the
island, the 57-m (187-ft)
high water tower, built in
1911, offers great views
from its lookout gallery.
The relaxing Japanese
Garden, one of three lovely
landscaped parks, features
a wide range of flora as
well as beautiful rock
gardens, ponds, waterfalls
and playgrounds.

Gothic and Renaissance sections of Vajdahunyad Castle, seen across the lake in Városliget

❷ Szentendre

With its Baroque architecture, Orthodox churches, cobbled streets and riverside setting, Szentendre makes for an idyllic visit. It is also known for its museums, which document the history of the region. Originally founded by the Romans in the 4th century, the town was settled by Serbian refugees in the 14th century. They fled here first from the Ottoman Turks after the Battle of Kosovo in 1389, and again after the Battle of Belgrade in 1690, ushering in a period of great prosperity. In the 1920s, many Serbs moved away to be replaced by artists who were attracted by the town's air and light. It remains popular with them today.

Entrance to the fascinating Charles Ferenczy Museum

🏛 Fő Square

Szentendre Gallery: **Tel** (026) 310 244. **Open** 10am–4pm Tue–Sun. 🖼 János Kmetty Memorial Museum: **Tel** (026) 310 244. **Open** Apr–Oct: 10am–2pm Wed–Sun. 🖼 📷 ♿

At the heart of Szentendre lies the bustling Fő Square (Fő tér), which is packed with hawkers and street artists in summer. A wrought-iron cross was raised here in 1763 by the survivors of the last major outbreak of bubonic plague.

On the Danube side of the square is the Orthodox Blagoveštenska Church, built between 1752 and 1754 and designed by András Mayerhoffer (1690–1771). Its elegantly curved balcony and tall, split-level belfry are fine examples of late-Baroque simplicity. Inside, frescoes of the Roman emperor, Constantine, a fine choir and a colourful iconostasis depicting the Annunciation vie for attention.

Opposite the church is the **Szentendre Gallery**, featuring the work of local artists. The building was originally a terrace formed by six identical merchants' houses; it was converted into a gallery in 1987.

Opposite, in an early-19th-century Saxon-style house, is the **János Kmetty Memorial Museum**, devoted to the life and works of the painter János Kmetty (1889–1975), a pioneering Cubist who lived here for 45 years.

🏛 Charles Ferenczy Museum

Fő tér 6. **Tel** (026) 310 244. **Open** 10am–4pm Tue–Sun. 🖼 📷 ♿
W femuz.hu

This art museum (Károly Ferenczy muzeum), northeast of the Blagoveštenska Church, houses the work of Hungarian Impressionist painter Károly Ferenczy (1862–1917), who lived in Szentendre between 1889 and 1906. Rooms here also display the works of his wife, painter Olga Fialka, and their three children: a painter, a sculptor and a weaver.

Although most of Ferenczy's best works are on display at the Hungarian National Gallery *(see p328)*, the lucid and comic *Acrobats* (1912) and his serene *Portrait of Mrs Sándor Ernst* (1916) can be seen here. The museum's fine arts collection has some 8,000 works by local artists.

🏛 Templom Square

Czóbel Museum: **Tel** (026) 312 721. **Open** 10am–4pm Tue–Sun. 🖼 📷 ♿

This walled square (Templom tér), at the top of a hill above Fő Square, stands on the site of the original Roman fort of Ulcisia. The square was the centre of the town in the Middle Ages and is popular today for the views it offers of the streets below.

The Catholic church in the middle of the square was first built in Romanesque style in the 14th century and renovated in Baroque style in the 18th century. A few original features remain, including the sundial on the right-hand side.

Opposite the church is a charming building housing the **Czóbel Museum**. It is dedicated to painter Béla Czóbel, famous for his landscapes and nudes. He lived in Szentendre from 1946 until his death in 1976.

🏛 Belgrade Church and Museum of Serbian Orthodox Ecclesiastical Art

Pátriárka utca 5. **Tel** (026) 312 399. **Open** Apr–Oct: 10am–4pm Wed–Sun; Nov–Mar: 10am–4pm Fri–Sun. 🖼 ♿

Constructed by Serbs but often known as the Greek Church, the Belgrade Church (Szerb Ortodox Egyházművészeti Gyűjtemény, Könyvtár és Levéltár) is the Hungarian seat of the Serbian Orthodox Patriarch, and is

Wrought-iron cross amid pretty, colourful houses in Fő Square

For hotels and restaurants see p378 and p379

therefore, officially a cathedral. Built between 1756 and 1764, it is a mix of Baroque and Rococo styles, its clock tower topped by a tall spire. Inside, it contains icons of Orthodox saints by Vasili Ostoic and a red marble altar.

In the garden outside the church, the Museum of Serbian Orthodox Ecclesiastical Art has a collection of around 2,000 Icons, vestments, treasures and art objects brought here in the last 150 years after the closure of their original host churches.

Icons of Orthodox saints in the Belgrade Church

🏠 Bogdányi Utca

Imre Ámos/Margit Anna Museum: **Open** Apr–Oct: 10am–2pm Tue–Sun.

Winding its way north from Fő Square, Bogdányi utca is a lively thoroughfare lined with historical buildings, and packed with many shops, stalls and portrait painters.

The **Imre Ámos/Margit Anna Museum** at No. 10 commemorates the life and works of well-known painters Imre Ámos and Margit Anna, who married in 1936, and moved to Szentendre in 1937. Ámos, a Jew, was taken to a labour camp in Vojvodina in 1940, where he continued to paint. He was deported to Germany in 1944, where he died, probably in a concentration camp. His wife Margit lived until 1991. Her Cubist paintings are on the ground floor, while Ámos's works, including his account of life in the camp, are displayed on the first floor. A cross on the corner of Bogdányi utca and Lázár tér stands where the body of the

A wine barrel sign in Bogdányi utca

legendary Serb ruler Prince Lázár once lay in a church. He was killed by a traitor at the Battle of Kosovo Polje in 1389. His body was taken back to Serbia in the 1800s, and the church was later destroyed in a fire.

Built between 1741 and 1746, **Preobraženska Church**, is another fine Baroque Serbian Orthodox church. It is also famous for the annual Serb Folk Festival that takes place here on 19 August.

Szentendre Town Centre

① Fő Square
② Charles Ferenczy Museum
③ Templom Square
④ Belgrade Church and Museum of Serbian Orthodox Ecclesiastical Art
⑤ Bogdányi Utca
⑥ Margit Kovács Ceramics Collection
⑦ Barcsay Collection

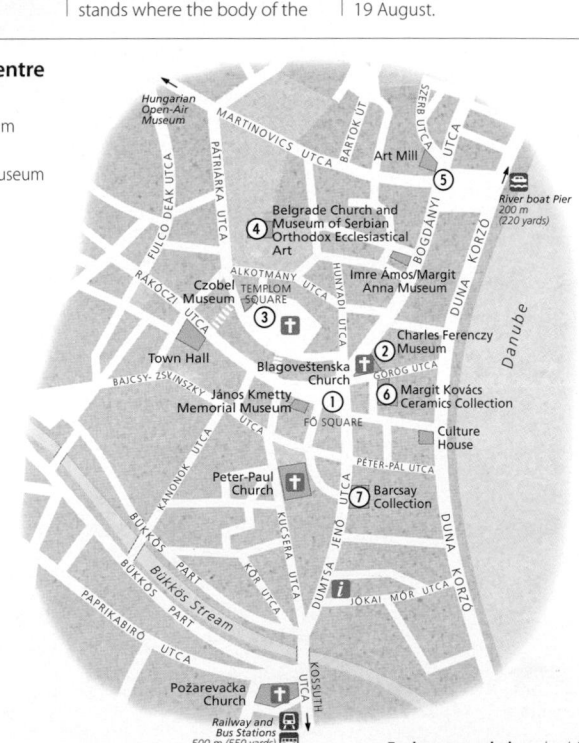

0 metres 100
0 yards 100

For keys to symbols *see back flap*

🏛 Margit Kovács Ceramics Collection

Vastagh György utca 1. **Tel** (026) 310 244. **Open** 10am–6pm daily. 🎫 ⑤

This striking 18th-century building (Kovács Margit Kerámiagyűjtemény) was originally a salt storage facility, and later became a vicarage for the Blagoveštenska Church. Since 1973 it has been devoted to the work of ceramic artist Margit Kovács (1902–77). Kovács attended Budapest's School of Applied Arts before learning the fundamentals of pottery in the workshop of artist Herta Bücher in Vienna. She developed her skills further in the State School for Applied Arts in Munich before returning to Hungary. *Nursing* (1948) is an example of Kovács's obsession with the Madonna, a common theme in many of her early works, while the *Bread Cutter* (1962) is a witty satire on the idealized peasant woman from a feminist perspective.

Plaque, Margit Kovács Ceramics Collection

🏛 Barcsay Collection

Dumtsa Jenő utca 10. **Tel** (026) 310 790. **Open** Apr–Oct: 10am–6pm Wed–Sun. 🎫

Barcsay Collection (Barcsay Gyűjtemény), located in a 19th-century Saxon house, is dedicated to Jenő Barcsay (1900–88), who settled in Szentendre in 1926 after studying art in Budapest and Paris, teaching art and anatomy here from 1931–45. Regarded as the first Hungarian Constructivist,

he strongly influenced his contemporaries. His finest works, including *Landscape at Szentendre* (1934) and *Street at Szentendre* (1932), are displayed here.

🏛 Hungarian Open-Air Museum

Sztaravodai út. **Tel** (026) 502 500. 🚌 7. **Open** 9am–5pm Tue–Sun. 🎫 🅲 ⑤ 🆆 skanzen.hu

Hungary's largest and best open-air village museum (Szabadtéri Néprajzi Múzeum) is 4 km (2 miles) from Szentendre. The museum, opened in 1967, is spread over 55 ha (136 acres) and features a reconstructed village from each of Hungary's five historic regions. Each of the villages is complete and self-contained, comprising houses, churches, schools, mills, wine presses, forges and stables. In particular, it is worth seeing the three huge outdoor ovens in the village of the Great Plain, brought to the museum from the village of Kisbodak; the roadside crucifixes in the central Transdanubian village; and the flintstone walls of the Bakony region houses.

All the buildings in the museum are open to the public, and some are working museums, with artisans demonstrating traditional skills from pottery to wine-making. Special courses in traditional skills are also on offer at various times of the year.

The façade of the Baroque Royal Palace at Gödöllő

❸ Gödöllő

35 km (22 miles) NE of Budapest. 🅼 29,000. 🚊 HÉV from Budapest. 🛈 Tourinform, Királyi Kastély, (028) 415 402.

Once the summer residence of the Habsburgs, Gödöllő is most famous for the **Royal Palace**, built in 1741. The enchanting Baroque palace was commissioned by the flamboyant aristocrat Antal Grassalkovich I and designed by Andras Meyerhoffer. Home to a long line of Hungarian rulers from Emperor Franz Joseph to Admiral Horthy, the palace has been restored to its full glory. Elegant rooms and extravagant furnishings offer a glimpse into the lives of the rulers who lived here.

The oldest building in the town, dating from 1661, was once the home of local land-owner Ferenc Hamvay. Today, it houses the excellent **Gödöllő Town Museum**. Besides displays that tell the story of the town and its greatest patron, Antal Grassalkovich, there is an exhibition focusing on the works of the Gödöllő Artists' Colony, a group of artists active between 1901 and 1920, who pursued ideals of communal rural living.

🏛 Royal Palace

Királyi Kastély. **Tel** (028) 420 331 **Open** Apr–Oct: 10am–6pm daily; Nov–Mar: 10am–5pm Tue–Sun. 🎫 🅲 ⑤ 🅿 🎫 🆆 kiralyikastely.hu

🏛 Gödöllő Town Museum

Szabadság tér 5. **Tel** (028) 422 002. **Open** 10am–6pm Tue–Sun (to 4pm Nov–Feb). 🎫 🅲 Hungarian only.

A thatched building in the Hungarian Open-Air Museum

❹ Vác

40 km (25 miles) N of Budapest.
🗺 33,000. 🚊 from Budapest.
🚌 from Budapest. 🛈 Tourinform,
Március 15 tér 17, (027) 316 160.
🏛 daily, behind Március 15 tér.

Founded in the year 1000, Vác
is situated on the eastern bank
of the Danube river. The town
was rebuilt in the late 17th
century after being destroyed
by war. Its central square, around
Március 15 tér, dates from the
18th century and was a thriving
marketplace until 1951. The
market itself survives, although
it is now hidden behind the
Town Hall, a Baroque masterpiece from 1680. The superb
façade, with two Corinthian half-
columns guarding the entrance,
is adorned with an intricate
wrought-iron balcony. The Sisters
of Charity Chapel and Hospital,
built in the 17th century and still
a functioning hospital to this day,
is located next door.

On the southern side of the
square stands the **Dominican
Church of Our Lady of Victory**,
the construction of which
began in 1699. Due to the War
of Independence, however,
work on the interior only began
in 1755. As a result the façade
is sober, while the interior is
rich in Rococo artwork.

At the northernmost end of
the Old Town, on Köztársaság
út, stands the only triumphal
arch in Hungary. This was built
in 1764, ostensibly to honour
Queen Maria Theresa.

❺ Visegrád

40 km (25 miles) N of Budapest.
🗺 1,700. 🚊 from Budapest.
🚌 from Budapest. 🚢 from Budapest,
Esztergom; from Szentendre (summer
only). 🖥 **visegrad.hu**

Set on the narrowest stretch
of the Danube, the village of
Visegrád is a popular tourist
destination that is surrounded
by its spectacular ruined citadel.
Built in the 13th century by King
Béla IV (1206–70), this was once
one of the finest royal palaces
in Hungary. The massive outer
walls are still intact, and offer
superb views. Halfway down

The Dominican Church in Vác, with its rich
Rococo ornamentation

the hill, in the Solomon Tower,
is the fascinating **Mátyás Király
Museum**, a collection of items
excavated from the ruins of
the **Royal Palace**.

Built by King Béla IV
at the same time as
the citadel, this lovely
palace was renovated
two centuries later
by King Mátyás
Corvinus (r. 1458–90),
in magnificent
Renaissance style. It
fell into dereliction in
the 16th century after
the Turkish invasion and
was then buried in a
mud slide. The ruins
were not rediscov-
ered until 1934, when
excavations took place.

Signpost in Duna-Ipoly
National Park

🏛 **Mátyás Király Museum**
Salamon-Torony utca. **Tel** (026) 597
010. **Open** May–Oct: 9am–5pm Tue–
Sun. 🎦 🖥 **visegradmuzeum.hu**

🏛 **Royal Palace**
Fő utca 23. **Tel** (026) 398 026.
Open 10am–4pm Tue–Sun. 🎦 🗐

❻ Nagybörzsöny and Duna-Ipoly National Park

72 km (45 miles) N of Budapest.
🚌 from Szob (to Nagybörzsöny).
🖥 **dinpi.hu**

Home to the fine 14th-century
stone Romanesque Church
of St Stephen, a working mid-
19th-century water mill (open
to the public) and a mining
museum, Nagybörzsöny is best
known as the gateway to the
Duna-Ipoly National Park, one
of the largest in the country.
The Buda Hill caves and the
Sas-hegy nature trail outside
Budapest are also within the
park's boundaries.

The park is home to more
than 70 protected plants
and more than half of
Hungary's native bird species,
including black-and-white-
backed woodpeckers.

A narrow-gauge railway
runs at weekends
from Nagybörzsöny
to Nagyirtás across the
Börzsöny Hills, from
where well-marked
hiking trails fan
out across the
park. There is also
a long trail starting
from the town of
Nagybörzsöny itself,
leading up to Nagy
Hideg Hegy peak,
which offers views
across to Slovakia.

A second narrow-gauge
railway, from Kismaros to
Királyrét, opens up the southern
part of the park. There are
hiking trails from Királyrét
across the hills, and on to
Nógrád, where there is a
spectacular castle in ruins.

The magnificent ruins of the citadel, towering over Visegrád

❼ Esztergom

Esztergom is the seat of the Archbishop of Hungary and the most sacred city in the country. St Stephen, Hungary's first king, was baptized in the city and crowned here on Christmas Day in the year AD 1000. Almost completely destroyed by the Mongol invasion 250 years later, the city was gradually rebuilt during the 18th and 19th centuries. Although it is dominated by the huge Esztergom Basilica, the city has much to offer besides its mighty cathedral, including the remains of a 10th-century castle, a picturesque Old Town, the fascinating Danube Museum and Hungary's finest collection of ecclesiastical art.

🏛 Esztergom Basilica
Szent István tér 1. **Tel** (033) 402 354.
Open 6am–6pm daily. 🅿 🅲 ♿ 🖼
treasury, crypt. 🖉 **w** bazilika-esztergom.hu

Rising above the Danube, its bright blue cupola visible from afar, Esztergom Basilica (Esztergomi bazilika) has been a symbol of Hungary for a millennium, since St Stephen was crowned here. Hungary's largest cathedral, the present structure dates from the 19th century and was built over a 47-year period from 1822 to 1869. Its interior has a copy of Titian's *Assumption of the Virgin* (1853–4), the largest single-canvas painting in the world. Other highlights include the Treasury, which holds the country's most valuable collection of liturgical and royal art.

🏰 Royal Palace and Castle Museum
Szent István tér 1. **Tel** (033) 402 354.
Open Apr–Oct: 10am–6pm Tue–Sun;
Nov–Mar: 10am–4pm Tue–Sun.
🖼 🅲 **w** varmegom.hu

Opposite the Basilica stands the Royal Palace (Vár), parts of which date back to the 10th century. From 1256 it served as the palace of Esztergom's archbishops until it was sacked during the Ottoman invasion. Much of the palace survived, and is open today as the Castle Museum (Vármúzeum). The only way to see it is on a guided tour, which takes in the study of King Mátyás's tutor, with Renaissance-style ceiling frescoes, and the 12th-century Royal Chapel, with an original rose window and 13th-century portraits of the Apostles.

To the south and north are well-preserved remains of the ramparts and steps back into the town. The Esztergom Castle Festival takes place in the palace grounds in summer.

🏠 Víziváros
Berényi utca.
A district of mainly Baroque buildings, Víziváros (Watertown), has narrow streets, single-storey houses and tiny well-kept gardens. The area was developed during the regeneration of Esztergom after the withdrawal of the Ottomans. Víziváros Parish Church, consecrated by Jesuits in 1728, is a perfect example of the Baroque architecture of the time, with its rounded façade and high nave. The twin spires were added in the middle of the 19th century. The Baroque interior was lost during World War II. A bridge behind the church leads to the island of Prímás Sziget, from where another bridge crosses the river into Slovakia.

The intricately carved Lord's Coffin of Garamszentbenedek

🏛 Christian Museum
Mindszenty tér 2. **Tel** (033) 413 880.
Open Mar–Oct: 10am–6pm Tue–Sun;
Nov–Feb: 11am–3pm Tue–Sun. 🖼
🅲 **w** christianmuseum.hu

The Roman Catholic Primate of All Hungary, János Simor, moved into this grand Neo-Renaissance palace after it was completed in 1882 and immediately opened the palace and its vast collection of paintings, including works by early Italian Renaissance artists Migazzi and Bertinelli, to the public. The building has been a dedicated museum (Keresztény múzeum) since 1924, and its collection of church art, bolstered by many subsequent purchases, is now the finest in Hungary. Tamás Koloszvári's *Ascension* (1427), is considered the most outstanding example of Hungarian Gothic art.

The splendid, wheeled Lord's Coffin of Garamszentbenedek (1480), now in Slovakia, decorated with carved figures, is

View of the imposing Esztergom Basilica

used in Easter processions. Though called a coffin, its purpose has always been symbolic; it is believed not to contain any human remains. The room devoted to altarpieces, some of which are 700 years old, is stunning in its colour and historical import. Besides the picture gallery, there are equally superb sculpture and icon galleries.

🏛 Bálint Balassa Museum

Mindszenty tér 5. **Tel** (033) 500 175.
Open May–Oct: 9am–5pm Tue–Sun; Nov–Apr: 9am–5pm Wed–Sun.
📷 🎫 Hungarian only.
🌐 **balassamuzeum.hu**

Named after a Renaissance poet who died in 1594 while fighting the Turks, the Bálint Balassa Museum (Bálint Balassa múzeum) focuses primarily on life in Esztergom during the Middle Ages and the Ottoman era. It also includes some archaeological finds from the Royal Palace.

The two-storey museum building, with its huge, tunnellike entrance, dates from 1860 and was originally a boys' school.

The Danube Museum, devoted to the famous river

🏛 Danube Museum and Lower Esztergom

Kölcsey utca 2. **Tel** (033) 500 250.
Open May–Oct: 10am–6pm Wed–Mon; Nov–Dec, Feb–Apr: 10am–4pm Wed–Mon. 🎫 ♿
🌐 **dunamuzeum.org.hu**

The role of the Danube in the history and development of Esztergom is given due importance in this excellent museum (Duna múzeum) close to the city centre. The building itself is a gem, originally built in Baroque style in the 18th century and fully renovated in 1973, when the museum moved here from its previous

location. The museum houses all sorts of hydraulic equipment from the 20th century, as well as exhibits devoted to damming the Danube and navigation. There is a collection of engineering tools, as well as a history of water management since Roman times. There are several hands-on displays aimed at children.

A five-minute walk south along Vörösmarty utca leads to Széchenyi tér, centre of the Lower Town and surrounded on all sides by a mixture of Baroque and Neo-Classical houses, many of which are now cafés. Its focal point is the Town Hall, an immaculately preserved Rococo building from 1729.

Esztergom City Centre

① Esztergom Basilica
② Royal Palace and Castle Museum
③ Víziváros
④ Christian Museum
⑤ Bálint Balassa Museum
⑥ Danube Museum and Lower Esztergom

0 metres 150
0 yards 150

For keys to symbols see back flap

❽ Székesfehérvár

60 km (37 miles) SW of Budapest.
🏛 105,000. 🚉 from Budapest.
🚌 from Budapest. Piac tér.
ℹ Tourinform, Piac tér 12–14, (022)
312 818. 🛍 Piac tér, daily.

Settled by the Magyar chieftan
Arpad in the 9th century,
Székesfehérvár was the first
permanent settlement on the
Székesferhérvár plain. Arpad's
descendants, Prince Geza and
St Stephen, erected a castle and
a vast basilica respectively. The
walled city that grew around
them was the site of Hungary's
Diet, or Parliament, until the
Turkish occupation in 1543.
Although much of the city was
destroyed in World War II, the
Old Town was spared, and its
cobbled streets are packed with
historically and religiously
significant buildings.

On the main square,
Városház tér, the
Baroque **Bishop's
Palace**, designed by
Jakob Riedler, was
built in 1801 using
stone from the Royal
Basilica. Across the
square, behind the
18th-century Town
Hall, is the 15th-cen-
tury St Anne's
Chapel, the only part
of the medieval city
to have survived the
Ottoman occupation. Behind
it is **St Stephen's Cathedral**,
founded by Bela IV, where
parts of the original Hungarian
coronation ceremony once
took place. Renovated in

Pannonhalma Abbey's great library housing ancient manuscripts

Baroque style, the entrance
features statues of St Stephen,
Laszlo and Imre. The **Carmelite
Monastery** features colourful,
dramatic frescoes by
Viennese artist Franz
Anton Maulbertsch,
while the 18th-century
altar fresco in the
Cistercian Church
was painted by local
artists. Opposite this
stands the Black Eagle
Pharmacy Museum,
adorned with hun-
dreds of old medicine
bottles and an
amazing frescoed
ceiling. The town's
most visited site,
however, is the **Bory Castle**,
built by Jeno Bory (1879–1959).
Part Roman forum, part Gothic
castle, it houses sculptures and
artworks by Bory and his wife.

**Entrance to St Stephen's
Cathedral**

❾ Pannonhalma Abbey

Pannonhalmi Főapátság

100 km (62 miles) W of Budapest.
Tel (096) 570 191. 🚉 🚌 Abbey &
Arboretum: **Open** 22 Mar–Apr & Oct:
9am–4pm Tue–Sun; May–Sep: 9am–
5pm daily; Nov–21 Mar: 10am–3pm
Tue–Sun. Library: **Tel** (096) 570 142.
🎨 📷 ♿ ✉ Abbey ⚲ 🏠

The story of Pannonhalma Abbey
is as old as Hungary itself. A
UNESCO World Heritage Site since
1996, there has been an abbey
here since 1002, the same year
St Stephen brought Christianity
to the Magyars. The original

abbey burnt down in 1137,
and was replaced with a
Romanesque construction
that itself was superseded by
the late-Romanesque basilica
still in existence today. The
Western Tower, added in 1832,
is one of the abbey's most
prominent features.

The basilica's main portal of
receding arches is one of the
most important surviving examples of a *porta speciosa* extant in
Hungary. Though now hemmed
in by extensions to the complex,
it is an outstanding example of its
kind – an ornamental portal held
in red marble with rich wood
carvings. Inside, the stained-glass
window, added in 1860, depicts
the popular Roman Catholic saint,
Martin of Tours, who was born at
Szombathely in western Hungary.

The Neo-Classical **Library** holds
330,000 volumes, including the
Tihany Manuscript, the earliest
written Hungarian text. On the
far side of the basilica, Our Lady's
Chapel has three Baroque altars
and a tiny organ. All the abbey's
monks are buried here. The abbey
also houses a treasury that is
home to a rich collection of
ecclesiastical art and historical
artifacts. The abbey's Benedictine
grammar school, founded in 1802,
is one of the finest in Hungary.
The abbey's **Arboretum**, on
the eastern slope, is the site of
hundreds of rare tree and shrub
species that have grown wild in
its grounds. The abbey also boasts
a smart new visitor's center, with
a café and gift shop selling wine
made on the grounds.

Stunning 18th-century Town Hall
in Székesfehérvár

⑩ Győr

120 km (74 miles) W of Budapest.
🚆 125,000. 🚍 from Budapest.
🚌 from Budapest. **ℹ** Tourinform,
Árpád utca 32, (096) 311 771. 🛒 daily
flower market, Arany János utca.
🎭 Győr Spring Festival (Mar).
W gyor.hu

Located halfway between
Budapest and Vienna, where
the Danube, Rába and Rábca
rivers meet, Győr has long been
a place where empires met, and
clashed. During the Ottoman
Wars it became home to the
most impregnable fortress in
Hungary. Today it is a modern,
vibrant city, full of monuments
that tell of its eventful past.

Founded in the 11th century,
Győr Cathedral was rebuilt in
Gothic style between 1257 and
1267; its Baroque interior dates
from after the Ottoman period,
when the altarpieces and superb
frescoes by Franz Anton
Maulbertsch were added.
It houses the remains of
St Laszlo, one of Hungary's
most sacred relics, and a miraculous painting of the Virgin
Mary, one of its most significant pilgrimage sites.

The imposing **Bishop's Palace**,
next door, saw most of its fortifications added in the 16th century,
to keep out the Ottomans. Nearby,
the Diocesan Treasury and
Library and Lapidary houses a
treasure trove of manuscripts
and liturgical items, including
an illuminated manuscript once
belonging to King Mátyás.

Up Apaca utca to the north,
the Margit Kovács Exhibition
houses a vast collection of

Győr's Bishop's Palace, built as a defence
against Ottoman invaders

Magnificent interiors of a bedroom in the Esterházy Palace in Fertőd

ceramics by Hungary's leading
20th-century abstract sculptor
(see p346), while to the south,
Szechényi tér, once the city's
market place, is ringed by
splendid buildings, many
housing museums.

⑪ Fertőd

184 km (114 miles) W of Budapest.
🚆 3,400. 🚍 from Szombathely.
🚌 from Sopron. **ℹ** Tourinform,
Joseph Haydn utca 3, (099) 370 544.
🎭 Haydn Festival (Jun–Sep).

The small town of Fertőd
was created in 1950, when
two former estates belonging
to the Esterházy family, Süttör
and Esterháza, were merged.
For three centuries the
Esterházy family was one of
the richest and most powerful
in Hungary. They flourished
under the Habsburgs, under
whom family members served
in a variety of political and
military offices.

Originally constructed as
a hunting lodge in 1720, the
Esterházy Palace is the result
of vast extensions by architect
Melchior Hefel in the 1770s.

The Neo-Baroque French
gardens were laid out at the
same time, though these
were remodelled along English
ideas of garden design at the
beginning of the 20th century.

The palace is approached
through a grand wrought-iron
entrance gate, with its Rococo-
stone-vase separating columns.
Although the palace was badly
damaged during World War II,
the main ballrooms and drawing
rooms have been restored
to their glorious best, filled
with priceless French furniture,
Venetian mirrors and
Flemish tapestries.

Joseph Haydn's presence at
the palace, from 1766 to 1790,
is celebrated by the annual
Haydn Festival, with concerts
showcasing the Austrian composer's work. The emphasis is
on his chamber music, which
is performed by outstanding
musicians in the Grand Gallery
and the beautiful gardens.

🏛 **Esterházy Palace**
Joseph Haydn utca 2. **Tel** (099) 537
640. **Open** Nov–Mar: 10am–4pm Fri–
Sun; Apr–Oct: 10am–6pm daily. 🎫
🅿 ♿ **W** eszterhaza.hu

⓬ Fertő-Hanság National Park

Fertő-Hanság Nemzeti Park Igazgatósága

195 km (121 miles) W of Budapest. 🚃 from Sopron, Győr. 🚌 from Zalaergeszeg. 🛈 Rév-Kócsagvár, Sarród (Park Administration), (099) 537 620. 📷 🛢 ♿ 🅦 **fertohansag.hu**

Located in northwest Hungary near the Austria-Hungary border, the Fertő-Hanság National Park, set around Lake Fertő, was once one of the most heavily guarded sections of the Iron Curtain. Now a designated nature reserve, it is regarded as one of Europe's most significant water habitats and was included on UNESCO's list of World Heritage Sites in 2001.

Lake Fertő is shallow – in most places less than 1-m (3-ft) deep – and is famous for its vast expanse of tall reeds. Its main sources of water are rainfall and two streams. More than 200 species of birds nest here, including the Hungarian ibis, spoonbill, heron and egret, and there are also numerous rare plant species.

With the eastern Alps as its backdrop, the lake is encircled by one of Europe's best cycle paths, which takes in superb scenery in both Hungary and Austria. Favourable, frequent winds also make the lake a popular place for sailing, while the shallow waters are regarded as good swimming spots. The main resort on the Hungarian side, Fertőrákos, is popular

Frozen Lake Fertő in the picturesque Fertő-Hanság National Park

both as a sailing spot and for its grassy beaches and attractive nature walks.

Many parts of the park can only be visited with a special permit or on organized guided tours. Information about visits and tours is available from the park's administration office in the small village of Sarród, located southwest of the park.

The Firewatch Tower, a striking landmark in Sopron

⓭ Sopron

209 km (130 miles) W of Budapest. 🚊 56,000. 🚃 from Győr, Vienna. 🚌 from Győr. 🛈 Tourinform, Liszt Ferenc utca 1, (099) 517 560. 🍴 Csarnok utca, daily. 🎫 Early Music Days (Jun), Sopron Festival Weeks (Jun–Jul), Volt Pop Festival (Jul), Sopron Jazz (Sep), Christmas Market (Dec).

A border town of the Pannonia province, Sopron is regarded as one of Hungary's most attractive towns. Its proximity to Austria is evident in the street signs and shops with German-speaking staff that dominate the town. The country's oldest cultural centre, Sopron has remains of Roman edifices, and city walls as well as grand medieval buildings, including both churches and a synagogue. Among its other attractions are a Pharmacy

Museum and an outstanding art collection.

The town is built around the magnificent Belváros – the Inner Town. Centred around Fő tér, an impressive central square that acts as a focal point, Belváros contains most of the town's main sights. Built between 1861 and 1864, the former Ursuline Convent houses a fine collection of ecclesiastical art, owned and managed by Sopron's Catholic Convent. Most of the items on display date from the Baroque period but there is also a collection from the early 1800s. Sopron's largest church, the **Benedictine Church**, on Fő tér, was built by Franciscan monks in 1280 and displays remnants of medieval frescoes. It is also known as the Goat Church, as it is believed that a goatherd financed it from the treasure found by his flock. Opposite the Benedictine Church, the Storno House is a grand house built in the 1400s, which was home to King Mátyás between 1482 and 1483.

Originally a Renaissance building, it was remodelled in the Baroque style in 1720. It displays a collection of art and period furniture.

Sopron also has a wealth of fine Art Nouveau architecture including the **Firewatch Tower**, from where superb views unfold. In 1921, the townspeople voted to stay in Hungary, rather than join Austria and the Gate of Loyalty, at the foot of the tower, was added in 1928 to honour the result of that plebiscite.

Also worth visiting is the medieval Synagogue, one of the oldest in Europe, believed to have been built around 1300. Abandoned in 1526, when the Jews were expelled from the town, many of its original features remain intact, including a replica of the Ark of the Covenant.

🏛 **Benedictine Church**
Templom utca 1, Fő tér. **Tel** (099) 523 768. **Open** 8am–6pm daily. 📷 ♿

🏰 **Firewatch Tower**
Fő tér. **Open** May–Aug: 10am–8pm Tue–Sun; Apr, Sep–Oct: 10am–6pm Tue–Sun. 📷

⓮ Kőszeg

219 km (136 miles) W of Budapest.
👥 12,000. 🚂 from Szombathely.
🚌 from Sopron. 🛈 Tourinform,
Rajnis József utca 7, (094) 563 120.

Nestled in lowland hills just minutes from the Austrian border, Kőszeg is a small, quiet town. Spared during World War II, it is regarded as one of the prettiest towns in the region. The town preserves the memory of Captain Miklós Jurisics, who led the Hungarians against the Turks. Its main square, castle and museum are named after him. **Jurisics Castle** is on the site where Miklós Jurisics and 450 soldiers held Turkish forces at bay for 25 days in August 1532; the bells of the town toll every day at 11am in his honour.

Crest above the gate to
Jurisics Castle

A fire destroyed parts of the castle in 1777; however, the interior arcades were built after the blaze. The Castle Museum has displays on the town's history, including various depictions of the siege. In the heart of Kőszeg's Old Town stands the elegant Miklós Jurisics tér, surrounded by churches and museums. The impressive entrance to the square, the Heroes' Gate, was erected to commemorate the 400th anniversary of the Turkish siege. The **Jurisics Museum** has a fine collection of memorabilia belonging to the artisans and tradesmen who inhabited the town. Set in a Baroque house on Jurisics tér, the **Golden Unicorn Pharmaceutical Museum**, contains a superb late 18th-century wooden apothecary counter with old medicine bottles. Nearby, the Gothic **Church of St James**, completed in 1407, but reconstructed in the 18th century, has served Jesuit, Protestant and Roman Catholic congregations. Inside, the faded frescoes by an unknown artist portraying the Magi date from 1403. An original statue of the Madonna from the Gothic period is also noteworthy. Built between 1892 and 1894 to designs by Austrian architect Otto Kott, the fantastical Neo-Gothic **Jesus's Heart Church**, on Fő tér, is famous for its stained-glass altar windows depicting Sts Stephen, Imre and Elizabeth.

⓯ Sárvár

212 km (132 miles) W of Budapest.
👥 16,000. 🚂 from Szombathely.
🚌 from Szombathely. 🛈 Tourinform,
Várkerület 33, (095) 520 178.

Located on the banks of the Rába river, this town was originally the site of Roman and Celt fortifications. Sárvár (mud castle) derives its name from the castle of mud that was built here by the Magyars in the 10th century.

The Sárvár Castle that now attracts visitors is, however, a distant relation to its muddy ancestor, having been built in the 16th century. Its illustrious patrons were the Nádasdy family, who bought the town in 1534.

Superb frescoes depicting battle scenes,
Sárvár Castle

Patriarch Tamás Nádasdy brought in Italian architects to create a genuine Renaissance masterpiece. This, with various additions including a palatial interior, has remained intact until the present day. Much of the castle is devoted to the captivating **Ferenc Nádasdy Museum**, which has exhibitions on the history of the family and the town, regional folk art and period furniture. Highlights include two series of frescoes: 17th-century works showing the Hungarians in battle with the Turks, and scenes from the Old Testament painted by artist István Dorffmaister in 1769.

In 1961, the search for oil led to the discovery of hot springs in Sárvár. Since then the development of spas has added to the town's appeal as a tourist destination. The famous **Sárvár Spa and Wellness Centre** has grown to become one of the largest and most modern bath complexes in Hungary. It comprises indoor and outdoor pools, leisure and splash pools, a sauna and a treatment centre offering various therapies.

🏛 **Ferenc Nádasdy Museum**
Várkerület 1. **Tel** (095) 320 158.
Open 9am–5pm Tue–Sun; Jul–Aug:
9am–9pm Tue–Sun. 🗱 🖊

🏊 **Sárvár Spa and Wellness Centre**
Vadkert utca 1. **Tel** (095) 523 600.
Open 8am–10pm daily. 🗱 🖊 ♿

Heroes' Gate in Miklós Jurisics Square, Kőszeg

⑯ Veszprém

The site of the nation's first bishopric, and for centuries the seat of the Queen of Hungary's household, Veszprém is one of Hungary's great historic towns. It was all but razed by the Turks as they fled Hungary in the 1600s. Spread over five hills, the most picturesque part of the city is its Castle District (Vár), with its delightful mixture of medieval and Baroque buildings. The twin towers of St Michael's Cathedral, visible from afar, are a symbol of Veszprém. Many sights are at the top of long staircases or at the end of steep, cobbled streets. Down below, the lower city also offers some fine Baroque architecture, great museums and quaint streets.

Dazzling golden interior of
St Michael's Cathedral

⬆ St Michael's Cathedral

Vár utca 27. **Tel** (088) 426 088.
Open May–mid-Oct: 10am–5pm.

There was a church here as early as 1001, when St Stephen created a bishopric, but the cathedral's (Szent Mihály Érseki Székesegyház) present appearance dates back to 1908, when it was extensively rebuilt in Neo-Romanesque style. Remains of earlier styles include the Gothic undercroft and the crypt's vaulting, both from 1380. The towers were built in 1723, and many older features of the cathedral have recently been restored.

⬆ Gizella Chapel

Vár utca 18. **Tel** (088) 426 088.
Open May–mid-Oct: 10am–5pm
Tue–Sun. 🅿 ♿ ✉

This 13th-century Gothic chapel (Gizella Kápolna) commemorates the life of Gizella, wife of Stephen and first queen of Hungary. The chapel was lost and only rediscovered in the 1760s, during building work. It retains original Byzantine frescoes of the apostles on its walls.

▦ Archbishop's Palace

Vár utca 16–18. **Tel** (088) 426 088.
Open May–Oct: 10am–5pm Tue–Sun
(only a few rooms are open to the
public). 🅿 ♿

Veszprém's finest building, this (Érseki Palota) is a brilliant example of Baroque design by Jakab Fellner, built in 1764 with his trademark rounded four-columned loggia. Used to house the archbishop's archive, it also has a fine collection of Baroque furniture and frescoes.

▦ Castle Gate and Museum

Vár utca. **Tel** (088) 426 088. Museum:
Open Apr–Sep: 9am–3pm daily.
🅿 ♿

Although it looks medieval, this gate (Várkapu) is a replica of the original castle gate that was built in 1938 to commemorate the Hungarian dead of World War I. The tower affords good views of the city from the top.

▦ Óváros Square

Óváros tér.
Veszprém's former market square, Óváros Square (Óváros tér) is surrounded by some

fine houses, many of which have been turned into cafés. The Pósa House at No. 3 was built for a local merchant, Endre Pósa, in 1783. Its showy decoration, especially the two cherubs below the roof, was intended to offset the linearity of the building. The contours of the Art Nouveau house next door are gentler. Opposite is the Neo-Classical **Town Hall**, built in 1896 as church offices, but renovated and converted in 1990. Behind the Town Hall, up a flight of stairs, is Lenke Kiss's fountain *Girl with a Jug*, affectionately known as "Zsuzsi" by locals.

A late-Art Nouveau stained-glass window
in the Petőfi Theatre

▦ Petőfi Theatre

Óváry Ferenc utca 2. **Tel** (088) 424 235.
♿ 🖥 **petofiszinhaz.hu**

This late-Art Nouveau municipal theatre building, set in well-kept gardens, is named after revolutionary playwright and poet Sándor Petőfi. The theatre (Petőfi Színház) was designed in 1908 by István Medgyaszay, who studied in Vienna. It has intricate folk motifs on the façade, typical of the later Art Nouveau buildings.

Façade of the Neo-Classical Town Hall, built in 1896

🏛 **Laczkó Dezső Museum**

Erzsébet Sétány 1.
Tel (088) 564 330. **Open** 10am–6pm
Tue–Sun. 🎫

Designed by the local architect
István Medgyaszay, the Country
Museum (Laczkó Dezső múzeum)
was opened in 1922. It displays
local artifacts and folk costumes
dating back to Celtic times.
Most of the collection was
donated by local Piarist monks,
after whose leader, Laczkó
Dezső, the museum was named.
It also housed Hungary's first
public library, still a leading
research facility.

🏛 **Bakony Regional Folk House**

Erzsébet Sétány 3. **Tel** (088) 564 310.
Open Jun–Sep: 10am–6pm Tue–Sun.
🎫 🎫

Hungary's first ethnographic
museum, the Bakony House
(Bakonyi Ház) was created in
1935, and modelled on the
19th-century houses of a
nearby town. The house is
built on high foundations
and has a covered terrace.
A staircase leads to a single
door. Inside, items on show
date to 1700.

St István Viaduct, designed by the
Hungarian architect Róbert Folly

🚇 **St István Viaduct**

Szent István völgyhíd.
Stretching over the Fejes
valley, from Dózsa György
utca to the St László Church,
the St István Viaduct
(Szent István
Völgyhíd) was built
in 1938, a major
engineering achievement
at the time. Designed by a
Hungarian, Róbert Folly, it
rises 50 m (164 ft) above
the Séd river at its
highest point. It offers
magnificent views of
the castle and the
Bakony Mountains
to the north.

🦒 **Veszprém Zoo**

Kittenberger Kálmán út 15–17.
Tel (088) 566 140. **Open** May–Sep:
9am–6pm daily; Apr, Oct: 9am–5pm
daily; Mar, Nov: 9am–4pm daily; Dec–
Feb: 9am–3:30pm daily. 🎫 🎫 ♿
Ⓦ veszpzoo.hu

Hungary's best zoo
(Kittenberger Kálmán Növény
És Vadaspark) is named after
19th-century biologist and
natural historian Kálmán
Kittenberger (1881–
1958). Spread over
13 ha (32 acres) in
the lovely Fejes valley,
it is home to 120
species, including
Sumatran tigers,
Kamchatka bears
and wonderful
exotic birds.

A giraffe in
Veszprém Zoo

Veszprém City Centre

① St Michael's
   Cathedral
② Gizella Chapel
③ Archbishop's Palace
④ Castle Gate
   and Museum
⑤ Óváros Square
⑥ Petőfi Theatre
⑦ Laczkó Dezső Museum
⑧ Bakony Regional
   Folk House

0 metres   200
0 yards   200

Marina in Siófok, departure point for pleasure cruises and water sports

ⓗ Siófok

88 km (54 miles) SW of Budapest.
🚹 23,000. 🚌 🚆 from Budapest.
🚢 from Balatonalmádi, Tihany.
ℹ️ Tourinform, Viztorony, Szabadság tér (084) 310 117. 🎪 Golden Cockle Folklore Festival (Jul).
🌐 **siofoktourism.com**

The largest and liveliest resort on Lake Balaton's southern coast, Siófok stretches along the shore for 17 km (11 miles). It is popular with weekenders from Budapest, many of whom have holiday homes here. The main attraction is the beach. It is split into two parts – Golden Shore (Aranypart) to the north, and Silver Shore (Ezüstpart) to the south – by the Sió canal, which was originally built by the Romans in AD 276. Like all of Lake Balaton's resorts, Siófok offers mainly grass beaches. The resort's marina is at the head of the canal, from where pleasure cruisers and ferries depart for the nearby Tihany Peninsula, Hungary's first conservation area. The port is a good place to hire sailing boats, and to organize a variety of other water sports.

On summer evenings, Siófok comes alive with tens of thousands of young people looking for a good time in the resort's innumerable bars, discos and nightclubs, many of which are in the open air. Visitors looking for a quiet night may prefer to go to one of the smaller resorts along the coast.

ⓘ Lake Balaton Tour

Spread over an area of 596 sq km (230 sq miles), Lake Balaton is the largest freshwater lake in Central Europe. It is often referred to as Budapest-on-Sea and attracts thousands of holidaymakers every summer. Most of the southern side of the lake is very shallow, with an average depth of just 4 m (13 ft), and the waters are fairly warm, making this the most popular shore with bathers and families. The southern shore is, therefore, the most developed, with sandy beaches and a wide choice of accommodation.

⑪ Kis-Balaton
The Kis-Balaton Nature Reserve at the mouth of the Zala river covers an area of 40 sq km (15 sq miles). It is home to many rare plants and animals.

⑩ Balatonberény
One of the first resorts on the lake to become popular, Balatonberény retains a late-19th-century charm, most apparent in its delightful lakeside cottages and rural houses.

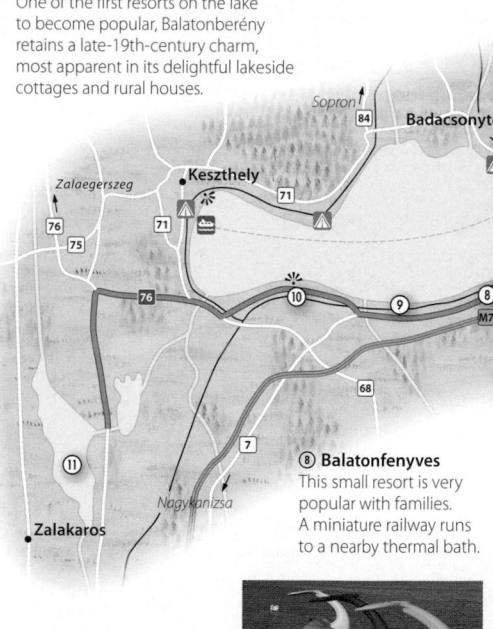

⑧ Balatonfenyves
This small resort is very popular with families. A miniature railway runs to a nearby thermal bath.

⑨ Balatonmáriafürdő
This lively resort attracts water sports enthusiasts and those looking for a good range of bars and restaurants.

① Zamárdi
A world away from noisy Siófok, Zamárdi is home to some fine thatched cottages, including this arcaded house on Fő utca, now the village's museum.

② Balatonföldvár
This town owes its name to Iron Age fortifications called *földvár*, remains of which can still be seen. The village's leafy promenade is generally considered the finest on the south shore.

③ Kőröshegy
A short detour south of Balatonföldvár is Kőröshegy, with a well-preserved Gothic fortified church dating from 1460.

Tips for Drivers

Length: 87 km (54 miles).
Stopping-off points: All the resorts along the shore have a wide range of restaurants. For a quieter ambience, there are many small places in Buzsák. The most panoramic lake views are from the top of Bokros-hegy, above Balatonberény.
W balaton-tourism.hu

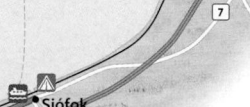

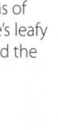

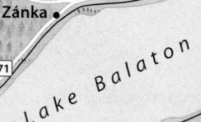

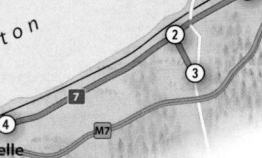

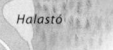

④ Balatonszemes
This quiet resort has a Postal and Carriage Museum. Its tree-lined streets are ideal for a stroll and there is an aquapark nearby.

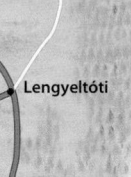

⑤ Somogyvár
Somogyvár is well worth the detour south from Buzsák – the impressive ruins of the Benedictine monastery here date back to the 11th century.

0 kilometres — 10
0 miles — 5

⑦ Fonyód
Unremarkable as a resort, Fonyód sits at the foot of the largest hill on the southern shore, the 233-m (764-ft) high Várhegy, an extinct volcano.

⑥ Buzsák
The Living Museum of Arts and Crafts at Buzsák is the best place around Balaton to learn about the traditions of the lake and its people. Fine cloth, pottery and garments are still made here.

Key

━━━ Motorway
━━━ Tour route
═══ Minor road
—— Railway
– – Ferry route

⑲ Keszthely

Keszthely is the oldest and largest of the towns that line the shores of Lake Balaton *(see pp356–7)*. Many of its elegant streets evocatively preserve the small-town atmosphere of the 19th century, when it was the property of the Festetics family. Their Baroque family seat, Festetics Palace *(see pp360–61)*, is one of Hungary's finest stately homes. The town possesses one of the lake's few sandy beaches and serves as Balaton's cultural hub, hosting the annual Balaton Festival. Since the conversion in 2006 of a nearby former Soviet airfield into the Hévíz-Balaton Airport, Keszthely is transforming itself into one of the most visited places in Hungary.

The Town Hall, one of many attractive buildings on Fő Square

🏛 Fő Square and Town Hall
Fő tér.

At the heart of Keszthely is the bustling Fő Square (Fő tér), dominated on its northern side by the attractive late-Baroque, pastel-pink Town Hall (Polgármesteri Hivatal). This was built in 1790, although the façade was extensively remodelled in the 1850s. Erected earlier, in 1770, the Baroque Trinity Column, in the centre of the square, looks its best in early summer when it is surrounded by bedding flowers of every colour.

🏛 Franciscan Church
Fő tér 5. **Tel** (083) 314 271.

This grand building, towering over the southern side of the square, is the Franciscan Church and former monastery (Magyarok Nagyasszonya Templom), built in the 14th century. Its tall Neo-Gothic tower with a 10-m (33-ft) spire was added in the 18th century. The crypt holds the tomb of György Festetics *(see p361)*,

the patriarch of the Festetics family and uncle of István Széchenyi, one of Hungary's social and political reformers.

The church was originally built in Gothic style using stone taken from an old Roman settlement nearby. During restoration work

Stained-glass window in the Franciscan Church

in 1974, remains of captivating 14th- and 15th-century frescoes were discovered. Lost during the Ottoman occupation, when the church served as a fortress and was connected to Lake Balaton by a canal, these represent the largest collection of Gothic frescoes remaining in Hungary. The fine rose window above the eastern portal is also an original 14th-century feature.

🏛 Kossuth Utca

Keszthely's main thoroughfare was built to allow the Festetics family easy access from their castle to the lake. Undoubtedly the widest street in the older part of the town, it is lined with some fine houses. The oldest, at No. 22, is the birthplace of the Hungarian-Jewish pianist Karl Goldmark. With its porticos and covered upper-level loggia, the house has a Mediterranean feel. Just behind, in a leafy courtyard, is Keszthely's well-preserved Neo-Renaissance synagogue. Originally dating from 1780, it was entirely rebuilt between 1851 and 1852.

🏛 Balaton Museum
Múzeum utca 2. **Tel** (083) 312 351.
Open Check website for timings. 🐾
♿ 📷 🌐 **balatonimuzeum.hu**

The mustard-yellow Neo-Baroque Balaton Museum (Balatoni múzeum) building was erected in the 1920s to a design by Dénes Györgyi, and is worth seeing in its own right.

The exhibitions inside are equally interesting and include a fascinating look at life around Lake Balaton in pre-Roman times. There are displays showing the development of fishing on the lake as well as a more sombre display explaining the effects of pollution on life in the lake. Models of sailing ships, streamers and paddleboats that once traversed the lake are also on view.

There is also a collection of outstanding Roman stoneware from the region and an original milestone to Aquincum, a Roman town 69 km (43 miles) from Keszthely, whose remains were excavated at the end of the 19th century.

Excavated fishing equipment on display at the Balaton Museum

VISITORS' CHECKLIST

Practical Information
187 km (116 miles) SW of
Budapest. 🏘 10,000.
ℹ️ Tourinform, Kossuth utca 28,
(083) 314 144. 🎷 Balaton Festival
(May), Helikon Chamber Music
Festival (May). 🌐 keszthely.hu

Transport
✈️ 10 km (6 miles) S of centre.
🚌 Kazinczy utca. 🚆 Kazinczy
utca. 🚍 Kazinczy utca.

🏛 Georgikon Farm Museum

Bercsényi Miklós utca 65–7.
Tel (083) 311 563. **Open** May–Oct:
10am–5pm Tue–Sat, 10am–6pm Sun.

Europe's first Academy of
Agriculture was set up here
by György Festetics in 1797. It
was converted into a museum
(Georgikon Majormúzeum) in
1972, and exhibitions focus on the
history of Hungarian agriculture
from Celtic times to the present
day. There are separate displays on
wine production in the Balaton
area and domestic farming in
southern Transdanubia, a region
along the border between
Hungary and Austria. A
selection of antique agricultural
equipment ranges from Bronze
Age tools to steam ploughs,
including an early motor tractor.

🏛 Doll and Waxwork Museum

Kossuth Lajos utca 11. **Tel** (083) 318
855. **Open** 10am–5pm Mon–Sun. 🎷
🌐 babamuzeum-keszthely.hu

This museum (Történelmi
Panoptikum) is actually three
museums in one. The first
contains a collection of 700
porcelain dolls. Each doll wears
the traditional costume of a
particular Hungarian village,
and was handmade there.

The dolls are complemented
by a display of local village
architecture, with more than
200 scale models, including
houses, stables and churches.
The second part of the museum
holds waxworks, featuring
500 life-size figures of eminent
Hungarians, from Prince
Árpád to Imre Nagy.

The third section is a 7-m
(23-ft) long model of Hungary's
Parliament, which was made by
Ilona Miskei from more than four
million sea-snail shells.

🏛 Festetics Palace
See pp360–61.

Keszthely Town Centre

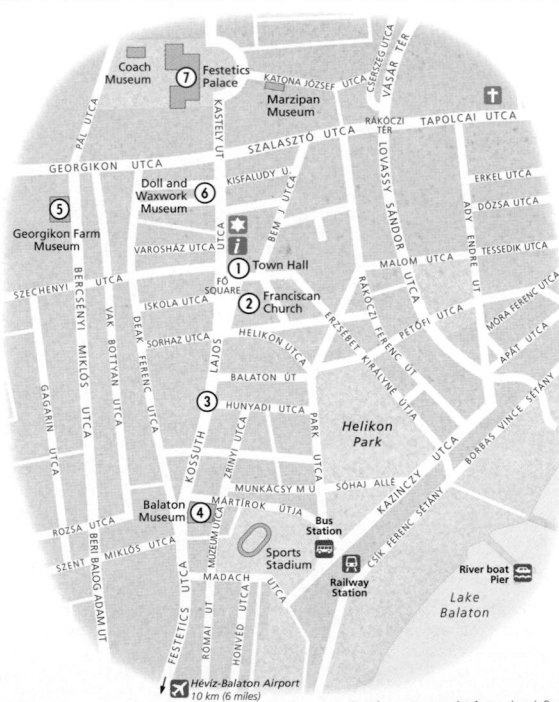

For keys to symbols *see back flap*

Keszthely: Festetics Palace

Festetics Palota

Originally the home of the Festetics family, the stately Neo-Baroque Festetics Palace is the magnum opus of little-known architect Viktor Rumpelmayer, who redesigned the palace in the 1880s. It was requisitioned by the Soviet Army in 1944. Today, the palace houses the Helikon Palace Museum, which is a popular day trip from Lake Balaton *(see p356–7)*. More than half of the palace's 101 rooms are open to the public, and feature fine examples of exotic art, furniture and arms gathered on the family's many foreign expeditions. The palace is famous for its 100,000-volume library and its fine English gardens, which cover over 42 ha (104 acres).

★ **Baroque Tower**
This Neo-Baroque façade is based on the French stately homes of the same era. The central tower's dome, however, evokes an earlier Baroque style.

Main entrance

English Gardens
English stately homes were the inspiration for the beautiful palace gardens. These were laid out by the English landscape artist Edward Miller.

Carriage Museum
In the palace's former stables, the Carriage Museum is home to a priceless collection of hunting and parade coaches and carriages from the 18th and early 19th centuries.

KEY

① **Weapons display**

② **Each room** is decorated in a different colour scheme and features priceless artifacts.

The World of Islam
The Festetics family filled the mansion with treasures brought back from their travels to North Africa and the Middle East. The collection has been enhanced with loans from the Tareq Rajab Museum, Kuwait.

★ **Mirror Room**
Adorned with Venetian mirrors and English furniture, the striking Mirror Room, also known as the Main Hall, regularly hosts chamber music concerts and operettas.

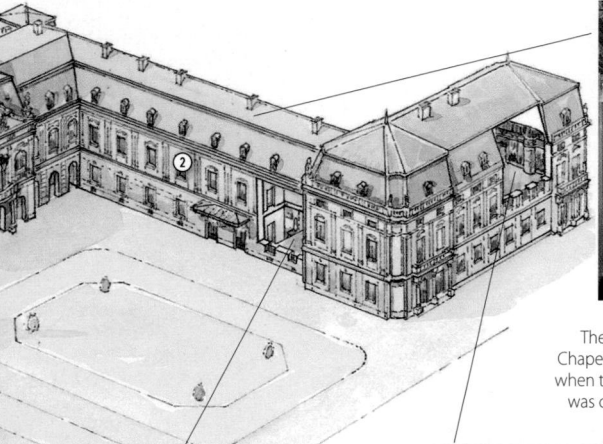

Chapel
The small, private Festetics Chapel was built in the 1880s, when the extent of the palace was considerably expanded.

★ **Library**
The Rococo Helikon Library holds over 100,000 volumes on its oak shelves. Hungary's literary elite gathered here in the 19th century.

Portrait Gallery
Beautiful portraits of almost every member of the Festetics family, as well as prominent members of Hungarian and Viennese society, line the palace's walls.

György Festetics

A polymath who combined a love for agriculture and the arts with the progressive ideals of the Enlightenment, György Festetics (1755–1819) was the grandson of Kristóf Festetics, who had been given the Helikon Estate in 1743 by the Habsburgs. György is best known for founding Europe's first agricultural college, the Georgikon *(see p359)* at Keszthely in 1797. A great explorer, he went on to become a generous patron of the arts and organized poetry and music festivals at the palace.

Statue of György Festetics

⑳ Pécs

Cosmopolitan Pécs calls itself "Hungary's Mediterranean city", as the sun shines here for more than 200 days a year. Many of the city's streets also have an Oriental feel to them. Pécs was founded by the Romans, who called the place Sopianae, in the 3rd century AD. It served as the capital of Valeria Province and was an early centre of Roman Christianity – as evidenced by the 4th-century tombs on Apáca utca. It was the Ottoman Turks, however, 1,000 years later, who left the deepest marks on the city's landscape. Széchenyi tér, the bustling heart of the city, is dominated by the former Gazi Kasim Pasha mosque, the largest surviving original Islamic construction in Hungary. The city also boasts excellent galleries, museums and great examples of Islamic architecture.

Impressive sculpture outside the Modern Hungarian Gallery

🏠 St Peter's Cathedral and Bishops' Palace

Dóm tér. **Tel** (072) 513 050.
Open Apr–Oct: 9am–5pm Tue–Sat, 1–5pm Sun; Nov–Mar: 10am–4pm Tue–Sat, 1–4pm Sun. 🎨 🖼

The historic centre of Pécs, Dóm tér, is dominated by St Peter's Cathedral (Szent Péter Székesegyház), first built as a Neo-Romanesque church in 1009 when St Stephen made Pécs a bishopric. The original church, which burnt down in 1064, was replaced by a Baroque cathedral built over nearly 200 years. Badly damaged by the Mongols, it was almost entirely rebuilt as a Gothic church in the 15th century. The current edifice dates from 1891, and is the work of Viennese architect Friedrich Schmidt. The interior is impressive, especially the frescoes in the chapel by Károly Lotz and the reliefs in the crypt by György

Zala. A bronze statue of Janos Pannonius, a leading humanist, stands in front of the cathedral.

Opposite is the deep red, 19th-century Neo-Renaissance Bishops' Palace (Püspöki Palota). It has a statue of Hungary's most prominent musician Franz Liszt in a raincoat, on the southern balcony. The palace is home to one of Hungary's largest libraries.

🏛 Modern Hungarian Gallery

Káptalan utca 4. **Tel** (072) 514 040.
Open 10am–6pm Tue–Sun. 🎨 🖼 🖼 **w** jpm.hu

One of the finest collections of 20th-century Hungarian art in the country with more than 10,000 pieces, this gallery (Modern Magyarképtár) features works by every major artist of the age, including József Rippl-Rónai, Lajos

Gulácsy and Farkas Molnár. In the garden there is a collection of large granite statues by Budapest-born sculptor Pierre Szekely. Outdoor events are also staged here in summer.

🏛 Csontváry Museum

Janus Pannonius utca 11.
Tel (072) 310 544. **Open** 10am–4pm Tue–Sun. 🎨 🖼 🖼

A tortured soul and former pharmacist turned artist, Tivadar Kosztka Csontváry (1853–1919) produced most of his work between 1903 and 1909, after which he moved to Naples. Most of Kosztka Csontváry's master-pieces, including the startling *View of the Dead Sea from the Temple Square in Jerusalem* (1905), have been on display in this Neo-Renaissance building since 1973.

🏛 Apáca Utca and Early Christian Mausoleum

Christian Burial Site Apáca utca 14:
Tel (072) 224 755. **Open** by appt only; book in advance. 🎨 🖼 Early Christian Mausoleum: Szent István tér 4. **Open** Apr–Oct: 10am–5:30pm Tue–Sun; Nov–Mar: 10am–3:30pm Tue–Sun. 🎨 🖼

Four graves at Apáca utca 14, all from AD 390, mark one of the earliest Christian burial sites in Europe. The bodies are buried under a chapel, and not in sarcophagi. Nearby, the **Early Christian Mausoleum** (Ókeresztény Mauzóleum), below an excavated chapel, is even older, dating from AD 275. It is decorated with biblical frescoes. These and two further burial chambers at Pécs were declared UNESCO World Heritage Sites in 2000.

St Peter's Cathedral, with its distinctive corner towers

For hotels and restaurants see p378 and p379

🏛 Archaeological Museum

Széchenyi tér 12. **Tel** (072) 312 719.
Open May–Oct: 10am–2pm Tue–Sat;
Nov–Apr: 10am–3pm Mon–Fri by
appt only. ♿

This 18th-century building
(Régészeti múzeum) was
converted into a museum in
1922. The highlight is the story
of Pécs in Roman times. The
museum also features artifacts
left behind by Goths, Huns,
Tatars and Visigoths and a
bust of Marcus Aurelius.

☪ Gazi Kasim Pasha Mosque/ Inner City Parish Church

Széchenyi tér. **Tel** (072) 321 976.
Open mid-Apr–mid-Oct: 10am–4pm
Mon–Sat; mid-Oct–mid-Apr: 10am–
noon Mon–Sat. 🗺 ♿

Built in 1579 for Gazi Kasim
Pasha, this lovely mosque (Gazi
Kasim Pasha Dzámi/Belvárosi
Templom) was the largest in
Hungary, and remains its most
important Ottoman monument.
   Converted into a Christian
church in the late 1600s,
calligraphy at the entrance
and a prayer niche are reminders
of its origins.

🏛 Király Utca

Largely pedestrianized,
Király utca is an architectural
showcase. Art Nouveau façades
can be seen at No. 5 – Palatinus
hotel – as well as at Nos. 8, 10,
19 and the National Theatre.
The St Pauline Church at No. 44
is in Baroque style.

✡ Synagogue

Kossuth tér. **Open** May–Sep:
10am–5pm Sun–Fri.
🗺 ♿

This grand Neo-Renaissance
synagogue (Zsinagóga),
built in the 1860s, indicates
the high standing that the
5,000-strong Jewish
community had in Pécs
society. They lived in
Pécs until 1944, when
the anti-Semitic Arrow
Cross government
sent them to camps
in Auschwitz *(see
pp196–9)*. A memorial
commemorates
those who were killed.
Services take place in
the smaller prayer hall
at the side.

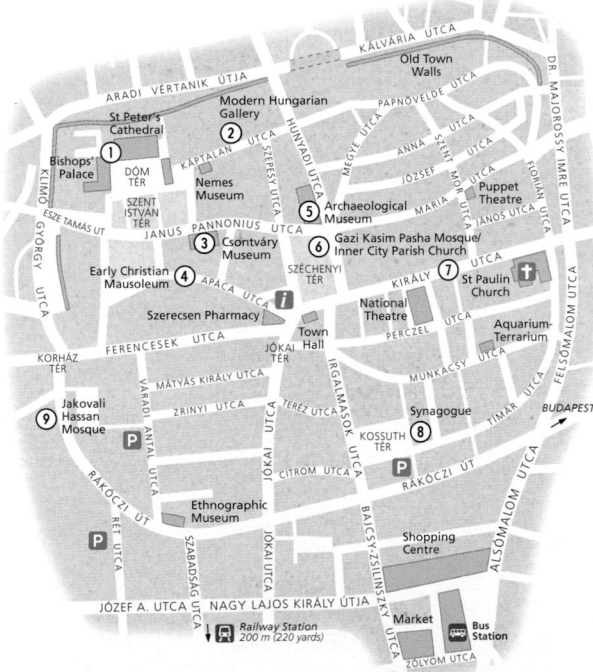

Façade of Pécs
Synagogue

☪ Jakovali Hassan Mosque

Rákóczi út. 2. **Tel** (072) 313 853.
Open Apr–Sep: 10am–6pm Tue–Sun.
🗺 📷

This 16th-century mosque
(Jakovali Hassan Dzámi)
was converted into a
Catholic church in 1714,
but its 23-m (75-ft) high
minaret remains intact.
Since 1975 it has been a
museum documenting
the Ottoman occupa-
tion of Pécs. Many exhi-
bits were donated by
the Turkish government as a
mark of friendship in the 1990s.

Pécs City Centre

① St Peter's Cathedral and
   Bishops' Palace
② Modern Hungarian Gallery
③ Csontváry Museum
④ Apáca Utca and Early
   Christian Mausoleum
⑤ Archaeological Museum
⑥ Gazi Kasim Pasha Mosque/
   Inner City Parish Church
⑦ Király Utca
⑧ Synagogue
⑨ Jakovali Hassan Mosque

0 metres   100
0 yards   100

For keys to symbols *see back flap*

⑳ Kecskemét

The city of Kecskemét dates back to 1368, though little remains from that era. Kecskemét benefited from self-government during Ottoman rule, and the Habsburgs encouraged the development of agriculture in the region, which is often called the "Garden of Hungary". The local plums are the source of a delicious brandy. An earthquake in June 1911 shook the city, but the outstanding Baroque and Art Nouveau city centre was mercifully spared. Home to some great museums, Kecskemét is a superb place to explore.

🏛 Piarist Church and School
Jókai tér. Church: **Open** 11am–2pm daily.

The Piarists were a relatively progressive and scientific Catholic Order founded in Rome in 1597 by St Joseph Calasanctius. They arrived in Kecskemét in 1715 and founded the school on Jókai tér. The present school building (Rendház), however, was built in the late 1940s. The Baroque church (Piarista Templom) opposite the school was erected between 1729 and 1765, to designs by Andras Mayerhoffer. St Calasanctius is represented by one of four statues in front of the building, alongside the Virgin Mary and St Stephen and St László.

🏛 Ornamental Palace
Rákóczi utca 1. **Tel** (076) 480 776. **Open** 10am–5pm Tue–Sat, 1:30–5pm Sun. 🅿 ♿

This masterpiece (Cifra Palota), completed in 1902, was the work of architect Géza Markus. An art gallery since World War II, the palace holds over 10,000 works and exhibitions on the Art Nouveau architects Tóth and Glücks. The green and orange tiled roof is outstanding.

🏛 Hungarian Photography Museum
Katona József tér 12. **Tel** (076) 483 221. **Open** noon–5pm Wed–Sun. 🅿 ♿
🌐 fotomuzeum.hu

This museum (Magyar Fotográfiai múzeum), is housed in a former synagogue that retains many of its original features. The museum displays the works of every great Hungarian photographer, including André Kertész and László Moholy-Nagy. There are regular exhibitions by international artists. A photography bookshop is attached to the museum.

🏛 József Katona Theatre and Holy Trinity Monument
Katona József tér 5. **Tel** (076) 328 420. **Open** 10am–2pm Tue–Sat. ♿ 📷

Resembling a jewellery box, this theatre (Katona József Színház) was the creation of Austrian architects Ferdinand Fellner and Hermann Helmer. Completed in 1896, it was named after playwright József Katona. It is worth attending a performance to see the ceiling alone.

The superb Holy Trinity Monument (Szentharomsag Szobor) in front of the theatre was erected after the end of the most recent outbreak of plague, in 1742.

🏛 Great Catholic Church
Nagytemplom
Kossuth tér 2. **Open** 9am–7pm daily; spire and viewing platform summer only. 🅿 ♿

The gigantic Great Catholic Church was built in 1772–96. Its spire rises to 73 m (240 ft), offering superb views. The Baroque exterior features statues and reliefs of figures from Hungarian history. Grand steps lead to the pulpit in an otherwise plain interior.

Room in the Museum of Medicinal and Pharmaceutical History

🏛 Museum of Medicinal and Pharmaceutical History
Kölcsey utca 3. **Tel** (076) 329 964. **Open** May–Oct: 10am–2pm Tue–Sun. 🅿 ♿

Although this museum (Orvos És Gyógyszerészettörténeti Kiállítás) houses only a small collection, consisting mainly of colourful old medicine bottles, intricate old surgical instruments, a weighing chair and various reference works, it is worth a visit if only to see the superb building, which was once a pharmacy.

🏛 Museum of Hungarian Naïve Art
Gáspár András utca 11. **Tel** (076) 324 767. **Open** Mar–Oct: 10am–5pm Tue–Sun; Nov–Feb: by appt only. 🅿 📷

This charming museum (Magyar Naiv Művészek Múzeuma) is devoted to local Naïve artists who produced some stunning work. Unique in Hungary, the museum provides a thorough survey of the genre. There are more than 2,500 exhibits, with the collection of small animal sculptures a special highlight.

The Art Nouveau Ornamental Palace

Mechanical toys in the Toy Museum and Workshop

🏛 Szórakaténusz Toy Museum and Workshop

Gáspár András körát 11.
Tel (076) 481 469. **Open** Mar–Oct: 10am–5pm Tue–Sun; Nov–Feb: by appt only. 🔗 🏠

Next to the Museum of Hungarian Naïve Art is this children's paradise, housed in a specially built wooden building (Szórakaténusz Játékmúzeum És Műhely). There is a wide array of Hungarian toys from the 18th century to the present, with dolls and wooden toys taking pride of place. Among them are some relatively clumsy mechanical toys that were considered state of the art in the 1950s. There are also interactive toy workshops for children during summer.

🏛 Zwack Fruit Brandy Distillery and Exhibition

Matkói utca 2. **Tel** (076) 487 711.
Open Mon–Fri, by appt only.
🔗 🎟 compulsory.

Zwack Unicum Company is the Hungarian market leader in plum brandy, and its factory offers a fascinating insight into the world of alcohol distillation. Visitors can see how the brandy is made – before tasting it – and learn about the life of the Zwack family. The plant is open only to group tours; Tourinform provides information on where and when to join one.

🏛 Museum of Applied Folk Art

Serfőző utca 19. **Tel** (076) 327 203.
Open 10am–4pm Tue–Sat.
Closed 17 Dec–10 Jan. 🔗 🎟
Hungarian only. ♿

This vast and enchanting building (Népi Iparművészeti múzeum) and garden, formerly a brewery for nearly 200 years, is

VISITORS' CHECKLIST

Practical Information
86 km (53 miles) SE of Budapest.
🗺 105,000. ℹ Tourinform, Kossuth tér 1, (076) 481 065.
🚌 daily. 🎭 Spring Festival (last two weeks of Mar), Zoltan Kodály Classical Music Festival (last week of Jun to last week of Aug).
🌐 kecskemet.hu

Transport
🚊 Kodály Zoltán tér; Narrow Gauge, Széchenyi tér. 🚌 Kodály Zoltán tér.

a fascinating place to visit. Opened to the public in 1984 as the Museum of Popular Folk Art, the permanent collection now covers woodcarving, pottery, embroidery and weaving. Visitors can access on-site workshops to watch the artisans at work and then try embroidering a waistcoat or tablecloth themselves; an interactive kitchen produces local specialities in traditional ovens. However, the workshops and kitchen are open only on selected days in the summer.

Kecskemét City Centre

① Piarist Church and School
② Ornamental Palace
③ Hungarian Photography Museum
④ József Katona Theatre and Holy Trinity Monument
⑤ Great Catholic Church
⑥ Museum of Medicinal and Pharmaceutical History
⑦ Museum of Hungarian Naïve Art
⑧ Szórakaténusz Toy Museum and Workshop

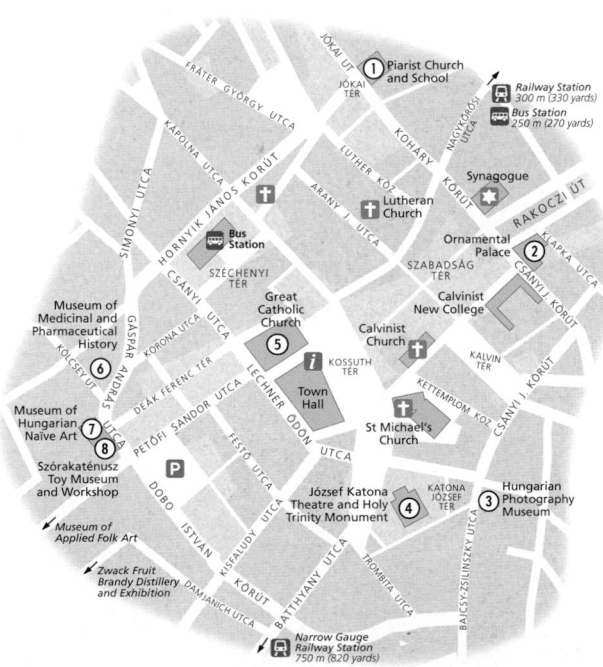

㉒ Bükk National Park

Bükki Nemzeti Park

Since 1977, most of the Bükk Mountain region in northern Hungary has been classified as a national park. It extends from Eger *(see pp368–9)* in the south to Mályinka, 61 km (38 miles) to the north. An area of outstanding natural beauty, Bükk, meaning "beech", is renowned for its beech forests and steep cliffs, riddled with more than 800 caves. There is some skiing in winter at Felső-Borovnyák, but the main activities are hiking and climbing. Routes of all grades and lengths criss-cross the range, linking the main towns in the region.

Lipizzaners in Szilvásvárad Horse Museum
The famous Lipizzaner horses were brought here from Lipica, in Slovenia, in the 16th century.

Fátyol Waterfall
Staggered limestone steps make this 17-m (56-ft) long waterfall one of the most attractive in Hungary. The steps grow a little every year as the water deposits more lime.

Vineyards in Felsőtárkány
The pretty town of Felsőtárkány, surrounded by vineyards and parks, is one of the best gateways to Bükk National Park.

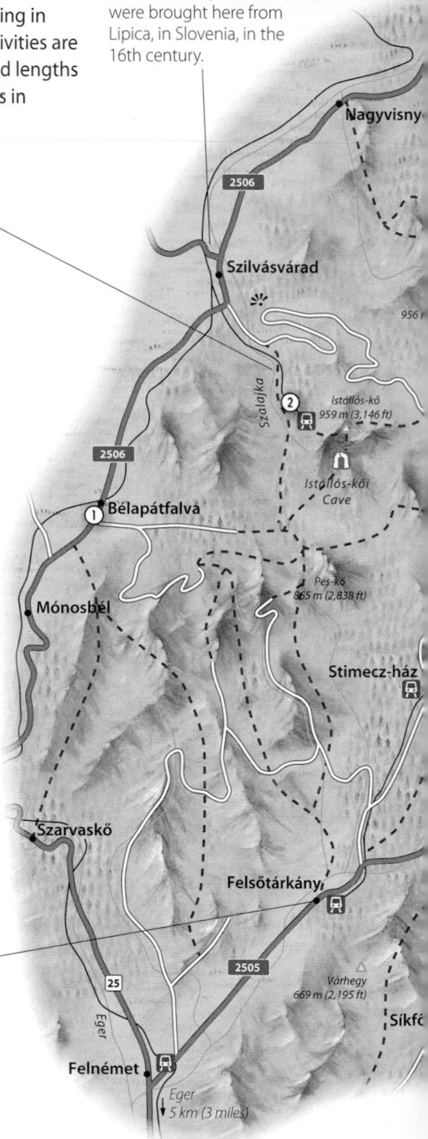

Nagyvisny

2506

Szilvásvárad

956 r

Szalajka

② Istállós-kő
959 m (3,146 ft)

Istállós-kői
Cave

2506

① Bélapátfalva

Pes-kő
665 m (2,838 ft)

Mónosbél

Stimecz-ház

Szarvaskő

Felsőtárkány

25

2505

Várhegy
669 m (2,195 ft)

Síkfő

Eger

Felnémet

Eger
↓ 5 km (3 miles)

KEY

① **Romanesque Bélapátfalva**, erected by Cistercian monks in the 1200s, is the best preserved abbey in Hungary.

② **The Szalajka Narrow Gauge Railway** runs along the entire length of the Szalajka Valley during summer.

For hotels and restaurants see p378 and p379

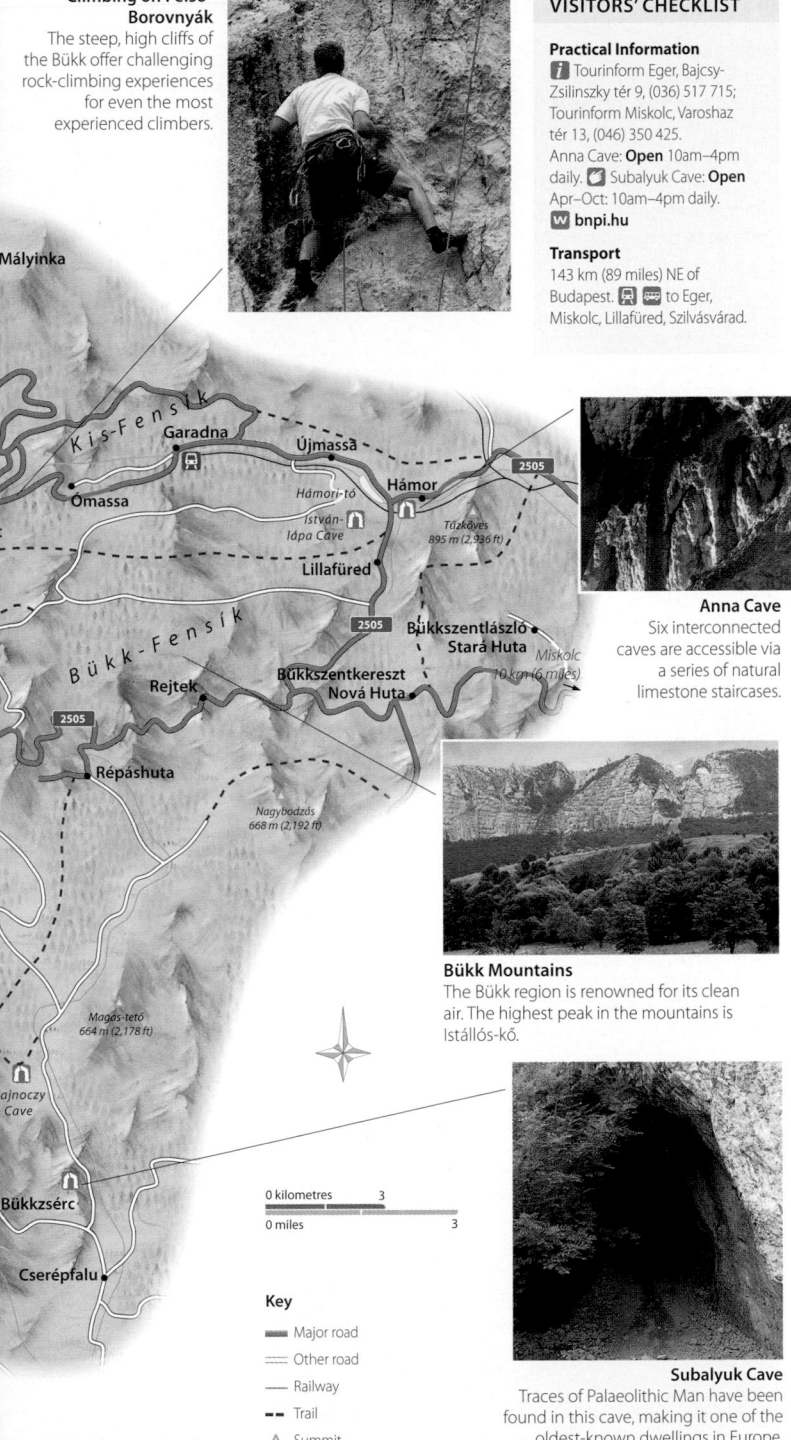

Climbing on Felső-Borovnyák
The steep, high cliffs of the Bükk offer challenging rock-climbing experiences for even the most experienced climbers.

VISITORS' CHECKLIST

Practical Information
Tourinform Eger, Bajcsy-Zsilinszky tér 9, (036) 517 715; Tourinform Miskolc, Varoshaz tér 13, (046) 350 425.
Anna Cave: **Open** 10am–4pm daily. Subalyuk Cave: **Open** Apr–Oct: 10am–4pm daily.
bnpi.hu

Transport
143 km (89 miles) NE of Budapest. to Eger, Miskolc, Lillafüred, Szilvásvárad.

Anna Cave
Six interconnected caves are accessible via a series of natural limestone staircases.

Bükk Mountains
The Bükk region is renowned for its clean air. The highest peak in the mountains is Istállós-kő.

Subalyuk Cave
Traces of Palaeolithic Man have been found in this cave, making it one of the oldest-known dwellings in Europe.

Key
- Major road
- Other road
- Railway
- Trail
- △ Summit

0 kilometres 3
0 miles 3

For keys to symbols see back flap

㉓ Eger

Situated off the main road from Budapest to the east of Hungary, Eger is a sleepy, provincial town dominated by its castle *(see pp370–71)* and the legend of the great siege of 1552. Eger has been rebuilt twice, almost from scratch, by the church. After destruction by the Mongols in 1241, it was reconstructed with money from the Minorite and Franciscan Orders. After the withdrawal of the Ottomans in 1687, the local bishopric revived the town by commissioning many of the Baroque masterpieces that remain today, including the cathedral, the Lyceum and the Bishop's Palace. Nowadays, Eger is also known for its Bull's Blood wine *(see p371)* and its university.

🏛 Eger Cathedral
Pyrker János tér 1. **Tel** (036) 515 725. **Open** 8am–8pm daily. ♿ 🏛

The second largest church in Hungary, Eger Cathedral (Főszékesegyház – Szent János Apostol És Evangélista Szent Mihály Főangyal) is the most astonishing sight in the town, though its mixture of Neo-Classical and Neo-Romanesque styles, in bright yellow, may not be to everyone's taste. It was built between 1831 and 1837 to a design by the architect József Hild, who would later design the even larger and more stunning basilica at Esztergom *(see p348)*.

The cathedral is unique in Hungary, with a cupola, which at 40 m (131 ft) is shorter than the two western towers, which measure 44 m (144 ft). At the other end of the building, three gargantuan statues loom over the colonnaded Neo-Classical façade. These represent Faith, Hope and Charity, and were the work of the Italian sculptor Marco Casagrande. The cathedral's interior is sombre, brightened primarily by Viennese artist Johann Kracker's ceiling frescoes of the *Kingdom of Heaven* on the inside of the cupola. The cathedral is also home to Hungary's largest organ, which is played every Sunday after morning mass at 12:45pm.

🏛 Bishop's Palace
Széchenyi utca 1. **Tel** (036) 517 589. **Open** 9am–5pm Tue–Sat.

The second element of central Eger's ecclesiastical architectural triumvirate is the former Bishop's Palace (Római Katolikus Érseki Palota). It was built in Baroque style to the designs of 18th-century architect Jakab Kellner and completed in 1766.

The palace houses the Ecclesiastical Collection of the Eger Bishopric, and the coronation cloak of Habsburg Empress Maria Theresa among other priceless objects.

🏛 Lyceum
Eszterházy Károly tér 1. **Tel** (036) 520 400. **Open** 9:30am–1pm Sat–Sun. 📷 📹 ♿

Founded in 1765 by Bishop Károly Eszterházy as a Catholic university, this university (Líceum, Eszterházy Károly Főiskola) was relegated to the ranks of a lyceum by the imperial authorities who opposed the idea of a church university. The highlight is the library, which holds over 150,000 volumes, including the first book ever printed in Hungary, in 1473. The library boasts Johann Kracker's fresco of 132 figures, depicting the meeting of the Council of Trent (1545–63). The tower is Hungary's leading centre of astronomy, with a collection of astronomical items and a 19th-century camera obscura.

Façade of the Lyceum, built as a Catholic university

🏛 Kossuth Lajos Utca
The wide boulevard of Kossuth Lajos utca has long been home to Eger's most important administrative and ecclesiastical buildings. At No. 4 is the Vice-Provost's Palace, a pastel-shaded Rococo mansion with a façade of hewn stone dating from 1758. On the same side of the street, at No. 14, is the Franciscan Church and Monastery, a single-nave church built in 1738 on the ruins of a mosque.

Opposite, at No. 9, is the Baroque County Hall, completed in 1758. It is famed for the two grand wrought-iron gates, crafted by the blacksmith Henrik Fazola (1730–79), who moved to Eger from Germany to take the city's waters. He is also responsible for most of

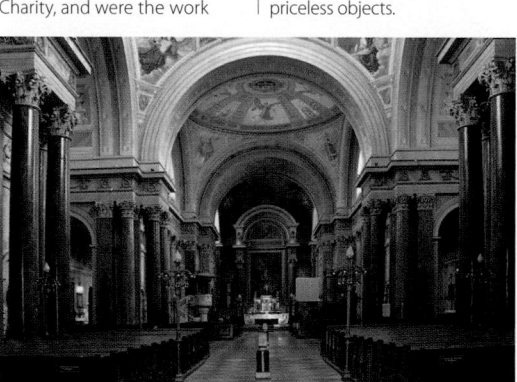

The sombre interior of Eger Cathedral, brightened by ceiling frescoes

Aerial view of Kossuth Lajos utca, Eger's most sought-after address

the ironwork that typifies many of the buildings on Kossuth Lajos utca, as well as the famous Hungarian National Gallery *(see p328)* in Budapest and Festetics Palace in Keszthely *(see pp360–61)*.

Minorite Church

Dobó István tér

Set against the background of the open spaces of Dobó István tér, the ornate exterior of the former Minorite Church (Szent Antonius Minorita Templom) has more aesthetic appeal than the cathedral. The rounded,

tiered façade and twin towers were designed by Bohemian architect Kilian Ignaz Dientzenhofer, but the church was not completed until 1773. It is dedicated to St Anthony of Padova and scenes from the saint's life feature in the ceiling frescoes painted by Márton Raindl. St Anthony is also depicted alongside the Virgin Mary on the altar, in a painting by Johann Kracker.

Main façade of the former Minorite Church, built in the 18th century

VISITORS' CHECKLIST

Practical Information
137 km (85 miles) NE of Budapest.
56,000. Tourinform,
Bajcsy-Zsilinszky tér 9, (036) 517
715. Dobó István tér, daily.

Transport
Vasút utca. Pyrker János
tér. Dobó István tér 9.

Minaret

Knézich Károly utca. **Open** Apr–Oct:
10am–5pm daily.

A relic of the Ottoman regime, Eger's minaret (Minaret) is a classic of its genre. Sleek and perfectly symmetrical, the 14-sided sandstone tower rises on an incline to its needle-like point, 40 m (131 ft) above the street. It is topped with a crescent moon and a cross. Closed for 150 years after the mosque next to it was demolished in 1841, the 17th-century minaret is now open to visitors and offers fine views of the city to those prepared to climb the 97 steps up to the balcony.

Eger Castle

See pp370–71.

Eger Town Centre

① Eger Cathedral
② Bishop's Palace
③ Lyceum
④ Kossuth Lajos Utca
⑤ Minorite Church
⑥ Minaret
⑦ *Eger Castle pp370–71*

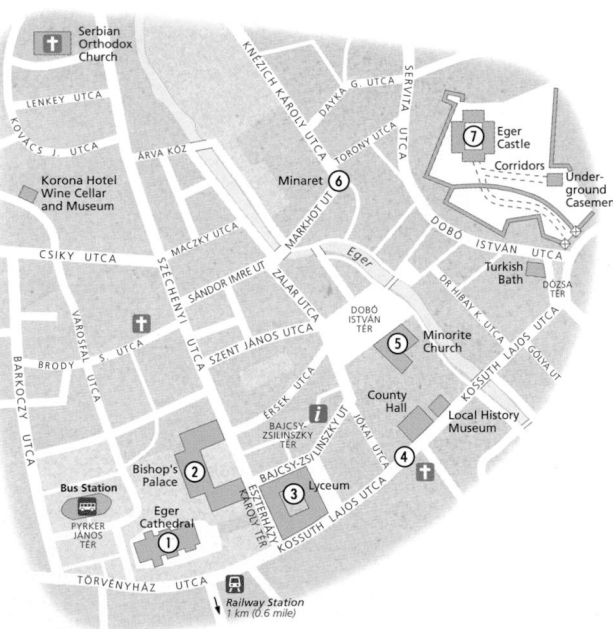

0 metres 100
0 yards 100

Serbian Orthodox Church

LENKEY UTCA

KOVACS J. UTCA

ÁRVA KÖZ

Korona Hotel Wine Cellar and Museum

CSIKY UTCA

KNÉZICH KÁROLY UTCA

DAYKA G. UTCA

SERVITA UTCA

TORONY UTCA

Minaret ⑥

MARKHOT UT

MACZKY UTCA

SZÉCHENYI UTCA

SÁNDOR IMRE UT

ZALÁR UTCA

Eger

Eger Castle ⑦

Corridors

Underground Casemates

DOBÓ ISTVÁN UTCA

Turkish Bath

DR HIBAY K. UTCA

DÓZSA TÉR

VÁROSFAL S. UTCA

BRÓDY UTCA

BARKÓCZY UTCA

SZENT JÁNOS UTCA

DOBÓ ISTVÁN TÉR

⑤ Minorite Church

KOSSUTH LAJOS UTCA

GÓLYA UT

ÉRSEK UTCA

BAJCSY-ZSILINSZKY UT

ESZTERHÁZY KÁROLY TÉR

County Hall

Local History Museum

JÓKAI UTCA

④

Bishop's Palace ②

Bus Station

PYRKER JÁNOS TÉR

Eger Cathedral ①

③ Lyceum

TÖRVÉNYHÁZ UTCA

Railway Station
1 km (0.6 mile)

Eger: Eger Castle
Eger Vár

The site of a legendary siege against the invading Ottomans, Eger Castle is an imposing edifice. Entered by a tiny gate set into 3-m (10-ft) thick walls with the menacing upper fortress in the background, it was here, in 1552, that the greatest rearguard action in Hungarian military history was carried out. The castle, defended by a garrison of just 2,000 soldiers and ably assisted by the women of the town, held out against a formidable Ottoman force five times that size for six weeks. The Ottomans eventually retreated, but took the castle 44 years later, only for much of it to be destroyed in 1702 by the Habsburgs.

★ Bishop's Palace
The names of all those who defended the castle in 1552 are engraved in a marble tablet on the main hall.

Fold Bastion Waxworks
A great collection of lifelike wax figures, displayed over three levels of the bastion, recreates scenes from the siege.

Art Gallery
The Art Gallery hosts an unrivalled collection of Hungarian Baroque paintings and sculptures, including this bas-relief above the entrance.

KEY

1. Round Tower
2. Ticket Office
3. Cannon Hill
4. Three Crosses Hill
5. Tomb of Gárdonyi

Dobó Bastion
The bastions and walls were fortified from the mid-1500s under István Dobó, who led the defenders during the siege.

★ **Ruins of Romanesque Cathedral**
Among the ruins of a 10th-century baptistry in the inner courtyard stands the grave of Eger's first bishop, Buldus.

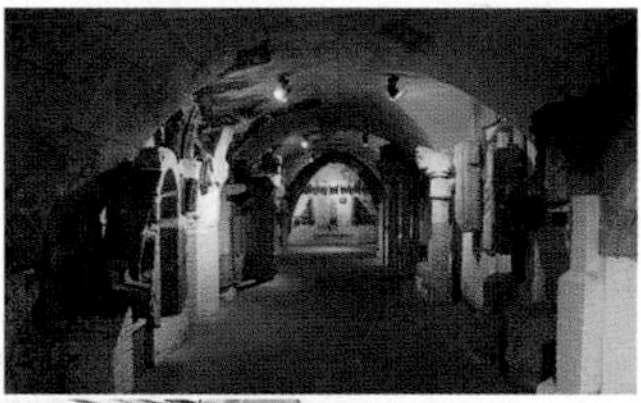

★ **Underground Corridors**
Castle Hill is a warren of underground chambers and paths, dug by the Ottomans in order to attack the castle from below. Some 200 m (656 ft) are open to the public.

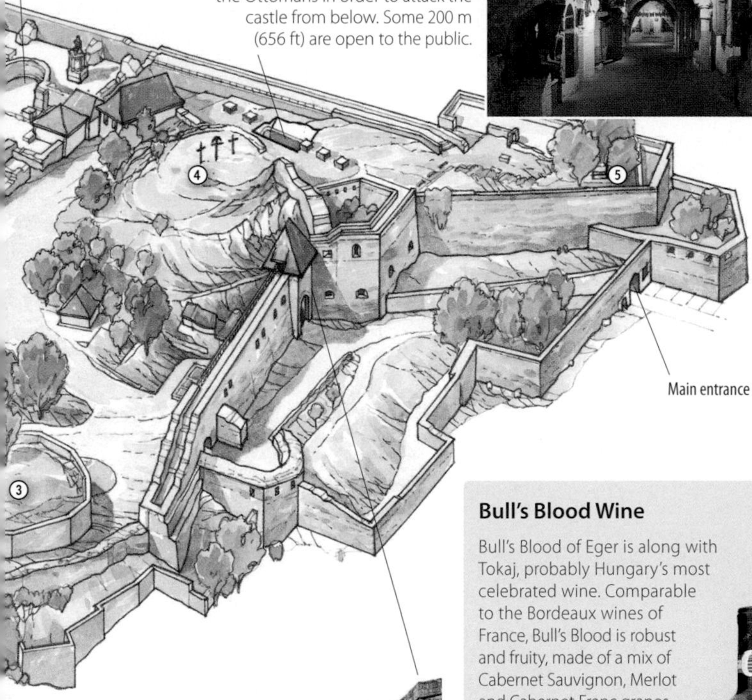

Main entrance

Ippolito Gate and Bornemissza Bastion
This striking castle gate is named after an Italian cardinal, Ippolito d'Este, who became the Archbishop of Esztergom.

Bull's Blood Wine

Bull's Blood of Eger is along with Tokaj, probably Hungary's most celebrated wine. Comparable to the Bordeaux wines of France, Bull's Blood is robust and fruity, made of a mix of Cabernet Sauvignon, Merlot and Cabernet Franc grapes. During the Siege of Eger, copious amounts of the wine were drunk by the defending soldiers, and word was put about that their bravery was based on the blood of bulls that had been added to the wine. The stories were almost certainly false, but they impressed the superstitious Ottomans, and played a minor role in their defeat and retreat.

Hungary's Bull's Blood wine

㉔ Lake Tisza
Tisza-tó

199 km (124 miles) E of Budapest. ▣ from Debrecen. ▣ from Debrecen.

Although it is considered one of the natural wonders of Hungary, Lake Tisza is, in fact, an artificial lake. It was created in the early 1970s, when the Tisza river was dammed for the irrigation of the Great Plain, which covers about 56 per cent of the country. Covering 127 sq km (49 sq miles), the lake is second in size only to Lake Balaton (*see p356–7*), and is increasingly challenging its famous neighbour as the summer holiday destination of choice. Most of the northern part of the lake is a protected nature reserve. Much loved by bird-watchers, the reserve is accessible only with a guide. Almost 200 species can be seen here, including peregrine falcons, which enjoy the microclimate generated by the lake waters.

Peregrine falcons at Lake Tisza

The largest resort on Lake Tisza is the bustling town of **Tiszafüred**, which has many grass beaches, boat launches and one of Hungary's oldest regional museums, **Pál Kiss House Museum**. Housed in a Neo-Classical villa, the museum was founded in 1877 and displays painted furniture, pottery and an archaeology exhibition with Roman coins and mosaics. Named after Pál Kiss, a general in the revolution of 1848, it is also a major bird-watching centre.

The family-oriented resort of Kisköre is home to the lake's best beaches. The town of **Tiszaderzs**, set back from the shores of the lake, has a 13th-century Romanesque church rebuilt in the 1600s and an 18th-century Baroque Reformed Church. South of Tiszaderzs, the water park at **Abádszalók** is one of the lake's most popular attractions. It is also known for water sports. On the western shore, the village of Sarud, has many 18th- and 19th-century thatched cottages as well as a great shallow beach. North of Sarud rowing boats are available for hire at the village of Poroszló and there is also a nature trail that meanders around the surrounding countryside.

🏛 **Pál Kiss House Museum**
Tel (059) 352 106. **Open** 9am–noon, 1–5pm Tue–Sat.

Abádszalók
ℹ (059) 535 346.

㉕ Debrecen

220 km (137 miles) E of Budapest. 🚌 200,000. ▣ from Budapest. ▣ from Budapest. Railway Station, Múzeum utca. ℹ Tourinform, Piac utca 20, (052) 412 250. 🛏 daily. 🎭 Spring Festival (Mar), Jazz Days (Mar), Summer Theatre (Aug), Flower Carnival (Aug). 🌐 **debrecen.hu**

Famous for its Calvinist Reformed College and Calvinist Church, the pretty town of Debrecen is Hungary's second largest. It has always been an important market town and,

Imposing Great Reformed Church and fountain, Debrecen

during the revolution of 1848, it served as Hungary's capital. Today it is celebrated for its grand thermal bath complex and excellent university.

Debrecen's defining landmark, the **Great Reformed Church**, towers above the town from the top of its main street, Piac utca. Built between 1819 and 1823, on the site of an earlier church to designs by Mihaly Pechy, this is where Hungary's parliament met between 1848 and 1849, and where its secession from the Habsburg Empire was declared. Across the square is the Civis Aranybika Hotel, an Art Nouveau master-piece designed by Alfred Hajos, Hungary's first Olympic champion. Piac utca leads into the central square, Kalvin tér, which is home to the **Calvinist Reformed College**, founded by Dominican monks in 1538. Rebuilt twice, the present building was designed by Mihaly Pechy. It was in the Oratory here that Hungary's provisional parliament met in 1944 while Budapest was under siege.

Nearby stands the excellent **Deri Museum**, built between 1926 and 1928, to house local industrialist Frigyes Deri's art collection. It has a rich collection of antiquities from Egypt and Ancient Greece as well as displays on Debrecen's history, ethnography and art.

Debrecen's famous thermal bath complex lies just north of the centre, with an extensive range of pools and baths and a vast water-therapy treatment centre.

The popular water park at Abádszalók, Lake Tisza

For hotels and restaurants see p378 and p379

㉖ Hortobágy and Hortobágy National Park

Hortobágyi Nemzeti Park

183 km (114 miles) E of Budapest. 🚌 ℹ️ Pásztormúzeum, Petőfi tér 1, Hortobágy, (052) 589 000. Hortobágy National Park: **Tel** (052) 589 170. **Open** 8am–4pm daily. 🐾 📷 ♿ 🚻 🏪 🏛️ 🌐 hnp.hu

Established in 1973, this was the first national park in Hungary and remains the largest, stretching over 820 sq km (317 sq miles) from Lake Tisza to Debrecen. It was added to UNESCO's World Heritage List in 1999. The vast plain, known locally as the *puszta*, meaning "emptiness", is the nesting site of as many as 152 bird species, including great bustards, herons, storks and spoonbills. Up to 342 different bird species have been spotted here in migration, including tens of thousands of screeching cranes, which can be seen in late September.

The park is also home to cattle, horses, buffalo, and Hungarian long-haired sheep, which continue to be herded by semi-nomadic farmers as they have been for centuries.

The 300-year-old **Hortobágy Máta Stud Farm** riding centre, located inside the park, is Hungary's best. It organizes riding performances by the *Csikós* (Hungarian cowboys), as well as riding lessons for visitors throughout the summer.

While much of Hortobágy National Park is open to visitors all year round, some parts have limited access. The park's administration and visitors'

centre is in the tiny but charming village of Hortobágy itself.

Here, the 17th-century Hortobágy Csárda restaurant serves Hungary's national dish, goulash (gulyásleves), which originated in the *puszta*. A small **Shepherds' Museum** (Pásztormúzeum) offers a fascinating insight into the life of the *puszta* shepherd.

The unique Nine-Arch Bridge (Kilenclyukú Híd), built between 1827 and 1833 to designs by Ferenc Povolny, crosses the Hortobágy river and once formed part of the main road from Budapest to Debrecen.

Hortobágy Máta Stud Farm
Czinege J utca 1, Hortobágy. **Tel** (052) 589 369. **Open** 8am–8pm daily. 🐎 📷 riding lessons.

🏛️ **Shepherds' Museum**
Petőfi tér 1, Hortobágy. **Tel** (052) 589 321. **Open** Mar–Apr: 10am–4pm daily; May–Sep: 9am–6pm daily; Oct–Dec: 10am–2pm daily. **Closed** Jan–Feb. 📷

㉗ Szeged

170 km (105 miles) SE of Budapest. 🚆 97,000. 🚌 from Budapest. 🚉 Roosevelt tér. ℹ️ Tourinform, Dugonics tér 2, (062) 488 690. 🎭 Szeged Open Air Theatre Festival (mid-Jul–Sep). 🌐 szeged.hu

The fourth largest city in the country, Szeged straddles the Tisza river less than 20 km (12 miles) from the point where Hungary, Serbia and Romania meet. Completely destroyed by the spring floods in 1879, Szeged was entirely remodelled and its avenues, squares and variety of architectural styles are testimony to enlightened town

Twin-towered Neo-Romanesque Votive Church, Szeged

planning. Today, the city is an important centre for the salami and paprika trades.

Constructed between 1913 and 1930, the grand Neo-Romanesque **Votive Church** on Dom tér contains several ornate frescoes and the third largest organ in Europe. In front of it stands the Demetrius Tower, built between the 12th and 13th centuries, while behind it is the single-towered Serbian Orthodox Church. Founded by Serb immigrants in the 1700s, it contains a magnificent iconostasis engraved in pear wood.

To the west, beyond the university, are two notable Art Nouveau buildings. The elaborate **Reok Palace**, was designed by Ede Magyar Oszadszki for local merchant Istvan Reok in 1907. In the Jewish Quarter, the New Synagogue, built between 1900 and 1903, has a grand dome and a marble tabernacle covered with gold leaf.

Szechenyi tér, has a pond commemorating the devastating 1879 flood. Further away is the Neo-Baroque **National Theatre** on Déak Ferenc utca, which stages ballets, opera and performances by the Philharmonic Orchestra. The Old Synagogue, in the Jewish Quarter, bears a plaque displaying the level of the flood waters. The Art Nouveau-style New Synagogue, built between 1900 and 1903, has a grand dome with a marble tabernacle covered with gold leaf.

A pair of storks in Hortobágy National Park, Hortobágy

Practical & Travel Information

In recent years, tourism has become an important part of the Hungarian national economy and as a result there have been vast improvements in communications, banking facilities and public transport. The biggest problem visitors face is the formidable language barrier. However, staff at many tourist offices, hotels and major attractions speak English or German.

When to Visit

The best time to visit Hungary is between April and the end of June, and from the middle of August until October. July is usually hot and Budapest can become quite uncomfortable, although away from the capital the heat is less severe. From November until March, many museums have shorter opening hours and may close altogether.

Documentation

Citizens of the US, Canada, Australia, New Zealand, and the European Union (EU) simply require a valid passport to visit Hungary for up to 90 days. For more information about visas and extended visits, visitors should check the website of the Hungarian Ministry of Foreign Affairs.

Visitor Information

Visitors can obtain various information leaflets and maps from the **Hungarian National Tourist Office**, which has branches worldwide.

Within Hungary, there are tourist information offices in most large towns. In Budapest,

visitors can get advice on sightseeing, accommodation and cultural events from the offices of **Tourinform Budapest**. The official website also provides brochures and maps, all of which can be downloaded for free in various formats. The **BTH Tourinform** sells entry tickets to most major attractions in Budapest and organizes specialist tours.

The Budapest Card entitles card holders, along with one child under 14, to unlimited use of the city's public transport system, free entry to 60 museums, the zoo and the funfair, a 50 per cent discount on guided tours and 10–20 per cent discount on selected cultural events and restaurants.

Health and Security

Hungary has long been a world leader in medical research and development. No special vaccinations are required to visit the country. However, visitors with allergy problems and breathing difficulties who intend to visit Budapest should be aware of the summer smog conditions, which are particularly acute in Pest. Those with

heart ailments should seek medical advice before using Hungary's thermal baths. For minor ailments, it is advisable to visit a *patika* or *gyógyszertár* (pharmacy). If the nearest store is closed, it usually displays a list of 24-hour emergency pharmacies.

Hungary has a relatively low crime rate. However, as in most cities that attract a large number of visitors, pickpockets operate in Budapest, targeting crowded metro stations, buses and shopping malls.

Facilities for the Disabled

The country's transport system, museums and other major attractions are gradually being renovated to make them wheelchair-friendly, although access problems can still occur. Those seeking advice on transport and sightseeing tours for the disabled should contact the **Hungarian Disabled Association**.

Banking and Currency

The Hungarian currency is the forint (HUF or Ft). Banks are open from 10am to 5pm, Monday to Friday and closed on weekends; exchange bureau and ATMs, however, remain open all week. Since banks and exchange bureau offer the best rates, it is always advisable to change money there.

Credit cards are more widely accepted now, but are still not as commonly used as elsewhere in Europe, so it is a good idea to carry sufficient cash.

Communications

The Hungarian telephone system used to be notoriously bad, but improvements are slowly being made. Phone cards, which are available from tobacconists, post offices, petrol stations and newspaper kiosks, are the best option when using public phones, although some booths still accept coins. Mobile phone coverage is almost total, with only a few remote areas of

The Climate of Hungary

Hungary enjoys some of the best weather in Europe, with an average of eight hours of sunshine a day in summer. June, July and August are the hottest months. In winter, temperatures can fall well below freezing point and there may also be snow. The country has comparatively low rainfall. June usually gets the most rain, while autumn is the driest season.

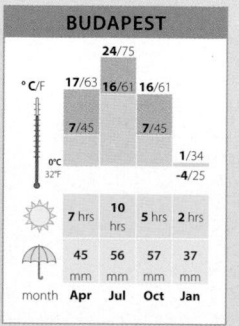

BUDAPEST			
	24/75		
°C/F	17/63	16/61	16/61
	7/45	7/45	
0°C 32°F			1/34
			-4/25
☀ 7 hrs	10 hrs	5 hrs	2 hrs
☂ 45 mm	56 mm	57 mm	37 mm
month	Apr	Jul	Oct	Jan

the Northern Highlands not benefiting from the presence of at least one of the networks. Post offices are open from 8am to 6pm Monday to Friday and on Saturday mornings. Visitors should be prepared to wait as service is slow and there are often long queues.

Arriving by Air

Budapest's international airport is **Ferenc Liszt Airport**, located 16 km (10 miles) from the city centre. **British Airways** operates three daily scheduled flights from London. Many low-cost airlines also operate daily flights from London.

Other major airlines flying from the US and Canada to Hungary include **Air France**, British Airways, **KLM**, **Lufthansa** and **Delta Airlines**, although services entail a transfer or touch down at another European city.

The Airport Minibus Shuttle takes passengers from the airport to any address in the capital. Taxis are also a quick and comfortable way of getting into the city.

Rail Travel

The Hungarian national rail network is efficient, reliable and punctual. Budapest has direct rail links to 25 other capital cities, with **Keleti Pu Station** handling the majority of international traffic. High-speed trains to Vienna, the main communications hub for Western Europe, depart every 3 hours approximately and take about 3 hours to get there.

Almost all trains within Hungary are operated by **Magyar Államvasutak (MÁV)**, a state-owned company that offers excellent value for money. There are different types of local trains, each categorized according to its speed: *személy* (slow), *sebes* (speedy) or *gyors* (fast).

There are also modern Intercity services between Budapest and the larger cities. A number of concessionary fares are available for those planning extensive rail travel within the country. **European Rail Passes (Eurail)** are also valid.

Travelling by Bus

Buses to all European destinations depart from **Népliget Station**. Within Hungary, the state-owned **Volánbusz** company operates an extensive network of buses to most cities and towns.

Travelling by Car

Although the government has recently invested in a new motorway network, many towns are still only connected by single-lane roads. To hire a car, visitors should be aged 21 or over and they must have held a valid driving license for at least a year. An international driving licence is also useful. Most of the international car hire firms have offices at the airport in Budapest, and rent-als can also be arranged through travel agencies and at hotels.

DIRECTORY

Documentation

W mfa.gov.hu

Visitor Information

BTH Tourinform
Liszt Ferenc tér 11, Budapest.
Tel (01) 322 4098.

Hungarian National Tourist Office
W tourinform.hu

Tourinform Budapest
Sütő utca 2, Budapest.
Tel (01) 438 8080.
W tourinform.hu

Embassies

Canada
1027 Ganz út 12–14, Budapest.
Tel (01) 392 3360.

United Kingdom
1051 Harmincad utca 6, Budapest.
Tel (01) 266 2888.

United States
1054 Szabadság tér 12, Budapest. **Tel** (01) 475 4400. W hungary.usembassy.gov

Emergency Numbers

Ambulance
Tel 104.

Fire
Tel 105.

Police
Tel 107.

Facilities for the Disabled

Hungarian Disabled Association
1032 San Marco utca 76, Budapest. **Tel** (01) 388 2388. W meosz.hu

Arriving by Air

Air France
Tel (01) 483 8800 (Hungary). **Tel** 800 237 2747 (US).

British Airways
Tel (01) 411 5555 (Hungary).
Tel 0845 773 3377 (UK). **Tel** 877 428 2228 (US).

Delta Airlines
Tel (01) 301 6680 (Hungary).
Tel 888 750 3284 (US).

Ferenc Liszt Airport
Tel (01) 296 9696.

KLM
Tel (01) 373 7737 (Hungary).
Tel 800 374 7747 (US).

Lufthansa
Tel (01) 411 9900 (Hungary).
Tel 800 645 3880 (US).

Rail Travel

European Rail Passes (Eurail)
W raileurope.com

Keleti Pu Station
Kerepesi út 2/6, Budapest.
Tel (01) 313 6835.
W mav-start.hu

Magyar Államvasutak
Kerepesi út 3, Budapest.
Tel (01) 313 7214.
W mav.hu

Travelling by Bus

Népliget Station
Üllői út 131, Budapest.
Tel (01) 219 8080.

Volánbusz
Üllői út 131, Budapest.
Tel (01) 219 8063 (reservations).
W volanbusz.hu

Shopping & Entertainment

Shopping in Hungary has changed dramatically in recent years. The choice of places to shop ranges from small, family-owned shops selling inimitable trinkets and luxuries to flea markets packed with the bizarre and the beautiful. Souvenir hunters are spoilt for choice and those looking for something typically Hungarian have a variety of Zsolnay porcelain, vintage Tokaji wine and paprika to choose from. The range of cultural events and entertainment is also richly varied. Even the smallest of towns has its own orchestra, dance company and theatre.

Opening Hours

Shops in Budapest are open from 10am to 6pm Monday to Friday and 10am to 1pm on Saturday. Many stay open until 8 or 9pm on Thursday. In the rest of the country an increasing number of shops and outlets remain open on Saturdays and Sundays. Supermarkets are open seven days a week, until 8pm. Shops are also open on public holidays with the exception of Christmas and New Year's Day.

Markets

Markets are an essential aspect of life in Budapest. The most spectacular are the cavernous late 19th-century market halls dotted around the city, of which the largest is the three-level **Central Market Hall** (Nagy Vásárcsarnok) on Fővám tér. This is open from 7am to 6pm Monday to Friday and 7am to 1pm on Saturday.

Many other cities also organize open-air craft and folk art markets. The Debrecen city craft fair is held during August in Kossuth tér.

Folk Art

Hungarian folk art items such as embroidered peasant blouses and wooden carvings are still made in many rural areas, and many are sold in the capital. These can be found at flea markets around Parliament (see pp336–7). Handmade items are available at **Folkart Kézműveshaź** and machine-made products at **Folkart Centrum**. Other local goods worth looking out for include carpets, especially rugs with plain, naïve designs and wooden toys including soldiers in Habsburg-era uniforms.

Porcelain, Crystal and Antiques

Hungary has a long tradition of producing high-quality porcelain, with the **Herend** name carrying a worldwide reputation. Herend porcelain is famous for its decorative and colourful designs; the factory shop in the small town of Herend, north of Lake Balaton, stocks a small selection. The Zsolnay porcelain factory has a shop located in Pécs. Ajka crystal, made near the town of Veszprém has been recognized as Hungary's finest for more than 150 years. **Ajka Crystal** in Budapest is a good place to pick up this excellent work of art.

Antique shops in Budapest are concentrated in the Vár and Víziváros areas and are good places to purchase domestic items from the 18th and 19th centuries. The tiny shop **Moró Antik** specializes in 18th-century weapons, while the **Nagyházi Gallery** sells everything from jewellery to furniture.

Food and Drink

Paprika – as a condiment – can be bought in all colours and varieties. Along with a wide variety of spicy salamis, it is available in many supermarkets and smaller delicatessens scattered all around the country. Cheese is another popular delicacy. The best sort is smoked, such as *sonkás*, an excellent cheese flavoured with ham. Visitors must be sure to buy – and sample – Hungary's regional wines, including the golden Tokaji, which is available in Budapest. Locally made apricot and plum liqueurs and *palinka* (brandy) can be purchased in Budapest at **House of Palinka**.

Cinema

Most major Hungarian cities have a multiplex cinema usually housed within the main shopping centre. Almost all foreign films are dubbed and subtitled in Hungarian, allowing cinema-goers to choose which version they prefer. Non-Hungarian speakers should opt for the *angol nyelvű* (English soundtrack) version. Films may even be shown in English with no subtitles at all – these are advertised as *angol nyelvű, felirat nélkül* (English language, no subtitles).

Music, Opera and Dance

The **Ferenc Liszt Academy of Music** in Budapest is one of Europe's finest classical music venues. The **Palace of Art** is a recent addition among the capital's music venues, while organ or choral music are performed at **Mátyás Church** (see pp330–31) and **St Stephen's Basilica** (see p338). The standard of opera in Budapest is very high. Both the **State Opera House** (see p338) and the **Erkel Theatre** have a mainly classical repertoire. Famous names in rock and pop play at the modern **Papp László Budapest SportArena**. For live rock, the party boat **A38** is also popular.

Elsewhere in the country, Veszprém is known for its music and small-scale chamber concerts in the Castle District courtyard, the highlight of all summer visits here. Pécs also has a rich cultural heritage, with renowned opera and dance companies, as well as the Pannon Philharmonic Orchestra, all of which perform at the **Pécs National Theatre**. The best way of securing a seat for concerts at the Ferenc

Liszt Academy of Music or major opera productions is via the **Cultur-Comfort Central Ticket Office** based in Budapest. Tickets for plays and concerts can be purchased in advance by contacting the box office at the relevant venue.

Music Festivals

Music festivals – from Baroque to jazz – feature regularly on the international arts calendar. Prominent events include the annual **Debrecen Jazz Festival** and the **Sopron Early Music Days**. For fans of rock and pop, the biggest event is the seven-day **Sziget Festival** held in August.

Nightlife

There is no doubt, Budapest is a party town, there are plenty of nightspots in the region. One extreme is a popular international club such as **Dokkoló**, where the beautiful people are regularly out in force.

Outside the capital, the university cities of Szeged and Győr are among the liveliest, with a wide range of pubs and clubs. In the town of Veszprém, the **Expresszó Club** is the busiest venue, while the **Mythos Music Club** features live acts or international DJs on weekends. During the summer almost all of Lake Balaton's resorts thump to the beat of Euro-pop. Siófok's **Palace Disco** is one of the country's largest, only a 15-minute walk out of the town centre.

The country is also home to a number of classy casinos attracting gamblers from all over Europe and the Middle East. Those in Győr and Sopron are housed in glorious historical buildings. At any of Hungary's casinos – most of which are operated by one Austrian company – players can try their hand at roulette, blackjack, poker and the wheel of fortune. Most stay open 24 hours a day, and require visitors to dress smartly. Presentation of a passport is also required.

DIRECTORY

Markets

Central Market Hall
Vámház körút 1–3
Fövám tér,
Budapest.
Tel (01) 366 3300.

Folk Art

Folkart Centrum
Váci út 58,
Budapest.
Tel (01) 318 5840.

Folkart Kézműveshá
Régposta út 12,
Budapest.
Tel (01) 318 5143.

Porcelain, Crystal and Antiques

Ajka Crystal
Jozsef Attila 7, Budapest.
Tel (01) 317 8133.

Herend
Andrásst út 16,
Budapest.
Tel (01) 374 0006.

Moró Antik
Falk Miksa út 13,
Budapest.
Tel (01) 311 0814.

Nagyházi Gallery
Balaton út 8,
Budapest.
Tel (01) 475 6000.

Food and Drink

House of Palinka
Rákóczi út 17, Budapest.
Tel (01) 338 4219.

Music, Opera and Dance

A38
Pázmány Péter Sétány
3–11, Budapest.
Tel (01) 464 3940.

Cultur-Comfort Central Ticket Office
Paulay Ede út 31,
Budapest.
Tel (01) 322 0000.

Erkel Theatre
Köztársaság tér 30,
Budapest.
Tel (01) 333 0540.

Ferenc Liszt Academy of Music
Üllői út 25, Budapest.
Tel (01) 462 4600.

Mátyás Church
Szentháromság tér 2.
Tel (01) 355 5657.

Palace of Art
Komor Marcell út 1,
Budapest.
Tel (01) 555 3300.

Papp László Budapest SportArena
Stefánia út 2, Budapest.
Tel (01) 422 2600.

Pécs National Theatre
Preczel Miklós út 17, Pécs.
Tel (072) 512 675.

St Stephen's Basilica
Szent István tér 2,
Budapest.
Tel (01) 318 9159.

State Opera House
Andrássy út 22, Budapest.
Tel (01) 332 7914.

Music Festivals

Debrecen Jazz Festival
Ⓦ debrecen.hu

Sopron Early Music Days
Ⓦ prokultura.hu

Sziget Festival
Ⓦ szigetfestival.com

Nightlife

Dokkoló
Hajogyari Sziget 122,
Budapest.
Tel 0630 535 2747.

Expresszó Club
Brusznyai út 2,
Veszprém.
Tel (020) 938 0411.

Mythos Music Club
Szabadsag tér 1,
Veszprém.

Palace Disco
Deák Ferenc
Sétány 2, Siófok.
Tel (084) 350 698.

Where to Stay

Budapest

BUDA: Abel Panzió ⓦ
Value
Ábel Jenő utca 9, 1113
Tel *(01) 209 2537*
Ⓦ abelpanzio.hu
This restored family villa in a leafy
street in Buda offers charming
rooms and good service.

BUDA: BI & BI Guesthouse ⓦ
Value
Retek utca 16, 1024
Tel *(01) 786 0955*
Ⓦ bibipanzio.hu
Stay in neat rooms and enjoy a
decent breakfast at this friendly
guesthouse close to the Castle
District and a metro station.

BUDA: Burg ⓦⓦ
Value   Map B2
Szantháromság tér 7, 1014
Tel *(01) 212 0269*
Ⓦ burghotelbudapest.com
The Burg provides small but
comfortable en-suite rooms,
several of which boast fabulous
views of the Mátyás Church.

DK Choice

BUDA: Gellert ⓦⓦⓦ
Luxury   Map D5
Szent Gellért tér 1, 1111
Tel *(01) 889 5500*
Ⓦ danubiushotels.com
Visited by Hungarian high
society since World War I, this
legendary spa hotel has both
indoor and outdoor pools fed
by healing spring waters. The
rooms are opulently decorated,
and the social areas feature Art
Nouveau decor. Massages and
other wellness treatments are
available. Wonderful views
across the Danube.

PEST: Leo Panzió ⓦ
Pension   Map D4
Kossuth Lajos utca 21a, 1053
Tel *(01) 266 9041*
Ⓦ leopanzio.hu
A superb pension in the heart of
Pest, Leo Panzió offers exemplary
service and good value for money.

PEST: Astoria ⓦⓦ
Boutique   Map D4
Kossuth Lajos utca 19–21, 1053
Tel *(01) 889 6000*
Ⓦ danubiushotels.com
In a predominantly Art Nouveau
building, the Astoria has spacious
rooms, an elegant café, and a lovely
Neo-Baroque breakfast room.

For map references *see pp324–5*

PEST: Cotton House ⓦⓦ
Boutique   Map D2
Jókai út 26, 1066
Tel *(01) 354 2600*
Ⓦ cottonhouse.hu
This atmospheric hotel has
some of the best-decorated
rooms in Hungary, each themed
on a famous stage or screen star.

PEST: K & K Opera ⓦⓦⓦ
Boutique   Map D3
Révay utca 24, 1065
Tel *(01) 269 0222*
Ⓦ kkhotels.com
Located close to the Opera House,
this hotel offers comfortable
rooms behind a splendid façade.

**PEST: Kempinski
Corvinus** ⓦⓦⓦ
Luxury   Map D3
Erzsébet tér 7, 1051
Tel *(01) 429 3777*
Ⓦ kempinski.com
An exclusive hotel popular
with visiting heads of state,
the Corvinus has luxurious rooms
and a host of excellent facilities.

**PEST: Mamaison
Hotel Andrassy** ⓦⓦⓦ
Boutique
Andrassy út 111, 1063
Tel *(01) 462 2100*
Ⓦ mamaison.com
Situated in a Bauhaus-style
building, the Andrassy offers
elegance, intimacy, superb
service, and a touch of romance.

Rest of Hungary

EGER: Senator-ház ⓦⓦⓦ
Modern
Dobó tér 11, 3300
Tel *(036) 411 711*
Ⓦ senatorhaz.hu

Price Guide

Prices are based on one night's stay in
high season for a standard double room,
inclusive of service charges and taxes.

ⓦ	under 15,000 HUF
ⓦⓦ	15,000 to 35,000 HUF
ⓦⓦⓦ	over 35,000 HUF

In an atmospheric building from
1753, this hotel enjoys a main-
square location; neat, attractive
rooms, many with castle views.

KESTHELY: Helikon ⓦⓦ
Luxury
Balaton-part 5, 8360
Tel *(083) 889 600*
Ⓦ hotelhelikon.hu
The modern high-rise Helikon
offers plush rooms, many with
superb views across the water.

PECS: Palatinus ⓦⓦ
Boutique
Király utca 5, 7621
Tel *(072) 889 400*
Ⓦ danubiushotels.com
Palatinus is decorated with a
mixture of Art Nouveau and Art
Deco styles. Sumptuous rooms
and a basement spa centre.

PECS: Patria ⓦⓦⓦ
Boutique
Rákóczi utca 3, 7621
Tel *(072) 889 500*
Ⓦ danubiushotels.com
The wonderfully designed Patria
is a modernist masterpiece. The
rooms are bright and colourful.

**SIÓFOK: Janus
Boutique Hotel & Spa** ⓦⓦⓦ
Boutique
Fő út 93–95, 8600
Tel *(084) 312 516*
Ⓦ janushotel.hu
Individually designed rooms with
varied themes ranging from
Japanese to Gothic.

The classy Cotton House hotel in Pest

Where to Eat and Drink

Budapest

BUDA: Régi Sipos ⓦ
Seafood
Lajos utca 46, 1036
Tel *(01) 250 8082*
Set apart from the tourist
trail, Régi Sipos serves up fish
specialties such as *pontypörkölt*
(carp goulash) and *harcsapaprikás*
(catfish stew), with cheesy
lasagne-like noodle sheets.

**BUDA: Alabárdos
Etterem** ⓦⓦⓦ
Hungarian **Map** B2
Országház út 2, 1014
Tel *(01) 356 0851* **Closed** *Sun*
Set in an outstanding Gothic
building, Alabárdos serves classic
cuisine from days gone by.
Everything, from the service to the
presentation, exudes elegance.

**BUDA: Búsuló
Juhász Etterem** ⓦⓦⓦ
Hungarian **Map** C5
Kelenhegyi út 58, 1118
Tel *(01) 209 1649*
There are spectacular views
from this restaurant on the
slopes of Gellért Hill. Expect
traditional Hungarian specialties
and live gypsy music.

BUDA: Fekete Holló ⓦⓦⓦ
Hungarian **Map** B2
Országház út 10, 1014
Tel *(01) 356 2367*
Located on Buda Hill, this
is a gem of a traditional
restaurant, where the kitsch
medieval decor fails to detract
from the excellent food. It
can get very busy.

PEST: Bohém Tanya ⓦ
Hungarian **Map** E2
Paulay Ede út 6, 1061
Tel *(01) 267 3504*
Savour hearty Hungarian food
in pleasant surroundings. Diners
are seated in wooden alcoves
large enough for eight, and that
might mean sharing a table
with others.

PEST: Café Kör ⓦ
European **Map** D3
Sas út 17, 1051
Tel *(01) 311 0053*
A popular, good-value bistro
that serves Hungarian and
European mains, as well as
fine salads and a handful of
vegetarian dishes. Originally
a wine bar, Kör is also a good
place to enjoy wine, spirits
and liquers.

The 1960s retro-style Menza café
in Pest

PEST: Vakvarjú ⓦ
International **Map** E2
Paulay Ede út 7, 1061
Tel *(01) 268 0888*
Providing excellent views
of one of Budapest's busiest
streets, this lively restaurant
offers an extensive menu
of interesting inexpensive
international fare.

PEST: Károlyi Etterem ⓦ
Hungarian **Map** D4
Kárlyi Mihály utca 16, 1053
Tel *(01) 328 0240*
Enjoy elegant, sophisticated
dining in the courtyard of the
Kárloyi Palace, with a traditional
menu of Hungarian classics.
Popular with wedding parties
at weekends.

PEST: Kárpátia ⓦⓦ
Hungarian **Map** D4
Ferenciek tere 7–8, 1053
Tel *(01) 317 3596*
Ostentatiously decorated
with Transylvanian folk
motifs, the 19th-century
Kárpátia is a long-established
favourite. The goulashs
remain of unimpeachably
high quality.

PEST: Soul Café ⓦⓦ
International **Map** E4
Ráday út 11–13, 1092
Tel *(01) 297 6986*
An intimate restaurant
on a thriving street, Soul
Café offers diners well-
prepared international
and Hungarian cuisine.
There is plenty of choice
for vegetarians.

Price Guide
Prices are based on a three-course meal
for one, half a bottle of wine, including
cover charge, service and tax.

ⓦ	under 3,000 HUF
ⓦⓦ	3,000 to 5,000 HUF
ⓦⓦⓦ	over 5,000 HUF

DK Choice

PEST: Bock Bisztró ⓦⓦⓦ
Hungarian **Map** E2
Erzsébet körút 43–49, 1073
Tel *(01) 321 03 40* **Closed** *Sun*
With an interior that is lined
with cookery books and wine
magazines, Bock Bisztró has
made old-school Hungarian
cooking attractive again. Serves
traditional mains such as
borjúpaprikás and veal *paprikash*
are served alongside European
and East–West fusion dishes.
Also a wine shop, so diners get
good advice on wine pairings.

PEST: Menza ⓦⓦⓦ
Hungarian **Map** E2
Liszt Ferenc tér 2, 1061
Tel *(01) 413 14 82*
Classic Hungarian dishes are
made with fresh produce and
a postmodern twist. The 1960s
decor provides a fitting backdrop.

Rest of Hungary

**EGER: Fehérszarvas
Vadásztanya** ⓦⓦ
European
Klapka út 8, 3300
Tel *(036) 411 129*
Eger's silver-service restaurant is
a little way from the centre but
well worth the trek. Feast on
game and freshwater fish in a
cellar filled with hunting trophies.

**KECSKEMÉT: Kecskeméti
Csárda és Borház** ⓦⓦ
Hungarian
Kölcsey 7, 6000
Tel *(076) 488 686*
One of the best-regarded
eateries in the country, this
place specializes in the paprika-
rich cuisine of the great plain.

PECS: Cellarium ⓦⓦ
International
Hunyadi János út 2, 7621
Tel *(072) 314 596*
Housed in catacombs that once
provided shelter from invading
Ottomans, Cellarium offers
delicious local specialties and
classic international dishes.

VIENNA

Originally a Celtic settlement, Vienna's location on the edge of the Hungarian plains made it vulnerable to attacks, and Barbarian invasions reduced the town to ruins by the early 5th century. In the 10th century, the German Babenberg Dynasty acquired Vienna and it became a major trading centre. Later, in the 13th century, Vienna came under the control of the prosperous Habsburgs, who remained in power until 1918. In the 16th century, the threat of Ottoman invasion hindered its progress, and it was not until 1683, with the final defeat of the Ottoman Turks, that Vienna was able to flourish. In the mid-19th century, the city's defences were demolished and the Ringstrasse, a wide circular boulevard, was built, linking new political and cultural institutions. Today, Vienna is an architectural delight, with its magnificent palaces, imposing churches and world-class museums. The city's rich cultural scene and vibrant nightlife add to its appeal.

Sights at a Glance

1 *The Hofburg Complex pp382–4*
2 Kunsthistorisches Museum
3 MuseumsQuartier Wien
4 Naturhistorisches Museum
5 Burgtheater
6 Stephansdom
7 Staatsoper
8 Secession Building
9 Karlskirche
10 Austrian Museum of Applied Arts
11 Freud Museum

GETTING AROUND

Vienna's city centre is easily explored on foot. Trams 1 and 2, 71 and D trams take visitors along part of the Ringstrasse, past many of the important sights. *Fiakers* (horse-drawn carriages) are a novel way to get around. Hopper buses serve the city centre while larger buses run to the outer suburbs, which are also served by the U-Bahn (subway) service.

Key

Major sight / Place of interest
Pedestrian street

0 metres 500
0 yards 500

◀ Pretty interiors of the Karlskirche, a Baroque masterpiece

❶ The Hofburg Complex

What began as a small fortress in 1275 grew over the centuries into a vast palace, the Hofburg. It was the seat of Austrian power for over six centuries, and successive rulers were all anxious to leave their mark. The various buildings range in style from Gothic to late 19th-century Neo-Renaissance. The Hofburg is particularly impressive when seen from Heldenplatz. This is one of Vienna's most lively areas, both by day and at night, when the rooms of the palace serve as a theatre and concert halls.

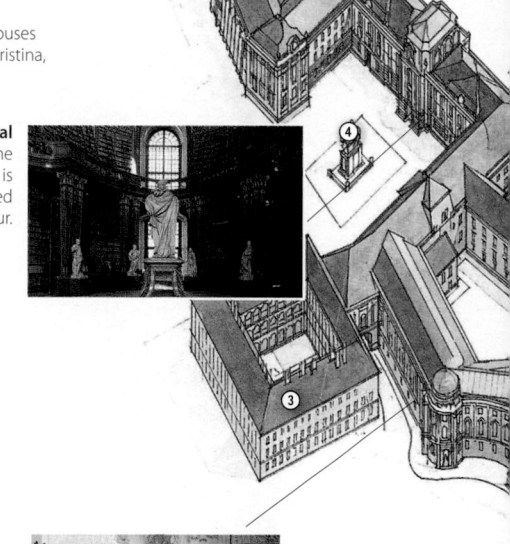

★ **Augustinerkirche**
The Habsburgs' former parish church houses the late 18th-century tomb of Maria Christina, Maria Theresa's daughter.

Prunksaal
The showpiece of the Austrian National Library is the grand, wood-panelled Prunksaal, or Hall of Honour.

KEY

① **Michaelertor** is the gate through which visitors reach the older parts of the palace.

② **Schatzkammer** (the treasury) is housed in the Alte Burg.

③ **Stallburg**

④ **Statue of Joseph II (1806) in Josefsplatz**

⑤ **Albertina**, built in 1781, now houses one of the finest collections of graphic art in Europe.

⑥ **Burggarten**

⑦ **The Burgtor**, or outer gate, was built to a design by Peter Nobile between 1821 and 1824.

⑧ **Monument to Eugene of Savoy (1865)**

⑨ **Heldenplatz**

⑩ **Hofburgkapelle**, the Hofburg chapel, is where the famous Vienna Boys' Choir performs.

★ **Spanish Riding School**
The gracious interior of the riding school is lined with 46 columns and adorned with elaborate plasterwork, chandeliers and a coffered ceiling.

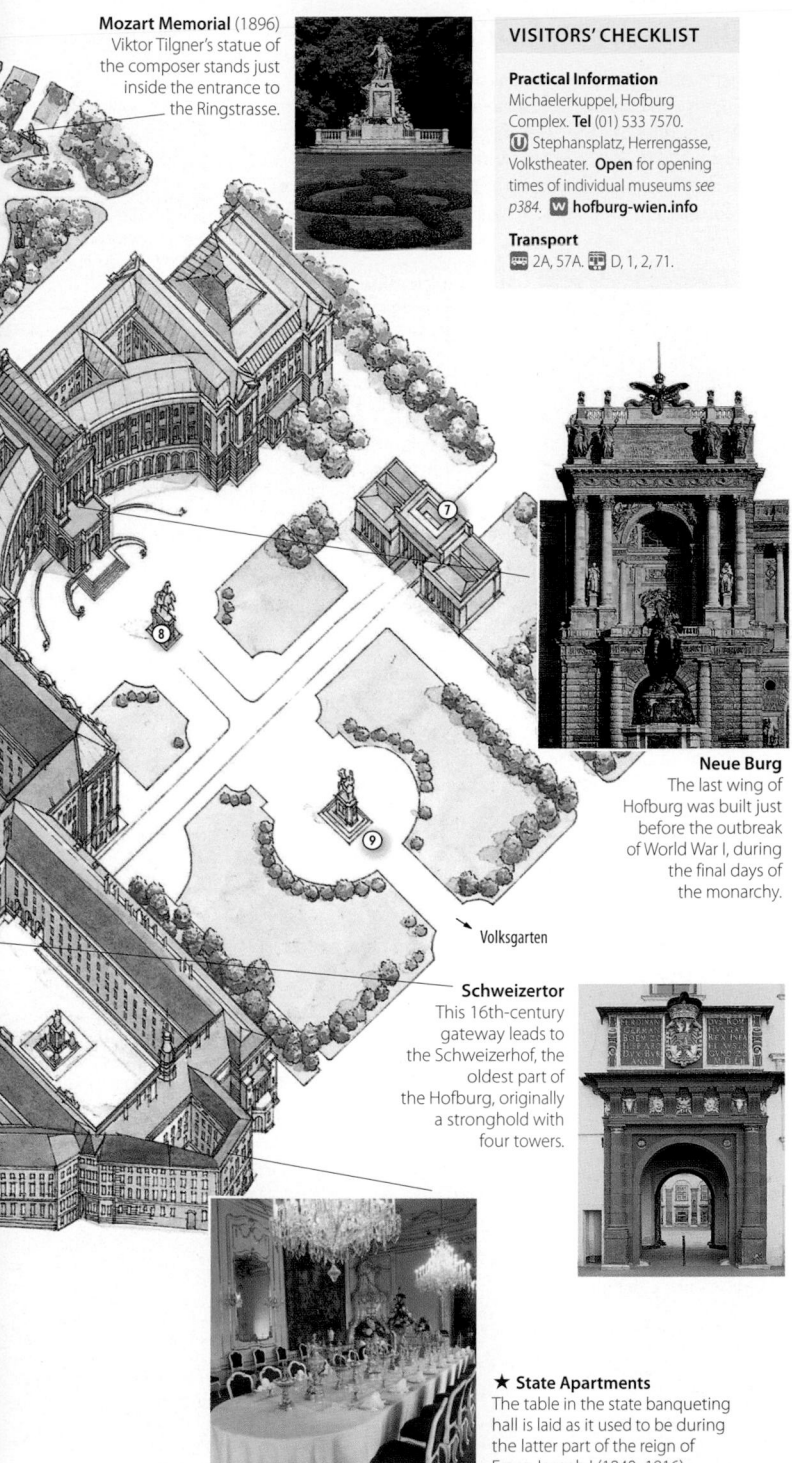

Mozart Memorial (1896)
Viktor Tilgner's statue of the composer stands just inside the entrance to the Ringstrasse.

VISITORS' CHECKLIST

Practical Information
Michaelerkuppel, Hofburg Complex. **Tel** (01) 533 7570.
Ⓤ Stephansplatz, Herrengasse, Volkstheater. **Open** for opening times of individual museums see p384. Ⓦ **hofburg-wien.info**

Transport
🚌 2A, 57A. 🚊 D, 1, 2, 71.

Neue Burg
The last wing of Hofburg was built just before the outbreak of World War I, during the final days of the monarchy.

Volksgarten

Schweizertor
This 16th-century gateway leads to the Schweizerhof, the oldest part of the Hofburg, originally a stronghold with four towers.

★ **State Apartments**
The table in the state banqueting hall is laid as it used to be during the latter part of the reign of Franz Joseph I (1848–1916).

Exploring the Hofburg Complex

The vast Hofburg complex contains the former imperial apartments and treasuries (Schatzkammer) of the Habsburgs, several museums, a chapel, a church, the Austrian National Library, the Winter Riding School and the offices of the president of Austria. The entrance to the imperial apartments and treasuries is through the Michaelertor on Michaelerplatz.

Tenth-century crown of the Holy Roman Empire, Schatzkammer

Elisabeth of Bavaria, Empress of Austria (1865) by Winterhalter

Neue Burg

Heldenplatz. **Tel** (01) 52524 4031. **Open** 10am–6pm Wed–Sun. **Closed** 1 Jan, 6 Apr, 25 May, 2 Nov. Weltmuseum Wien: **Open** 10am–6pm daily, except Tue. **welt museumwien.at** **khm.at**

The massive curved building, Neue Burg, was added to the Hofburg between 1881 and 1913. The Ephesus Museum houses archaeological finds from Ephesus, while pianos that belonged to Haydn, Schubert and Beethoven are kept in the musical instruments museum – the Sammlung alter Musikinstrumente. The collection of weapons in the Hofjagd und Rüstkammer is one of the finest in Europe. There is also a fine ethnological collection, the **Weltmuseum Wien**.

Augustinerkirche

Augustinerstrasse 3. **Tel** (01) 5330 9470. **augustinerkirche.at**

One of the oldest parts of the Hofburg complex, the church has one of the city's best-preserved 14th-century Gothic interiors. The Loreto Chapel here has a series of silver urns that contain the hearts of the Habsburg family. The church is also celebrated for its music, with masses by Schubert or Haydn performed here on Sundays.

State Apartments

Michaelerkuppel-Feststiege. **Tel** (01) 533 7570. **Open** Sep–Jun: 9am–5pm daily; Jul & Aug: 9am–6pm daily. **hofburg-wien.at**

The State Apartments (Kaiserappartements) in the Reichskanzleitrakt (1726–30) and the Amalienburg (1575) include the rooms occupied by Franz Joseph I from 1857 to 1916, those of Empress Elisabeth from 1854 to 1898 and those where Czar Alexander I lived during the Congress of Vienna in 1815.

Spanish Riding School

Tel (01) 533 9031. **Open** for performances; Morning training sessions: 10am–noon Tue–Fri. **Closed** public hols. some areas. **srs.at**

The Spanish Riding School is believed to have been founded by the Habsburgs in 1572 to cultivate the classic skills of *haute école* horsemanship. Today, 80-minute shows take place in the building known as the Spanish Riding School, built between 1729 and 1735, to a design by Josef Emanuel Fischer von Erlach.

Schatzkammer

Schweizerhof. **Tel** (01) 525 240. **Open** 10am–5:30pm Wed–Mon. **Closed** public hols. **khm.at**

Sacred and secular treasures amassed during centuries of Habsburg rule are displayed in 21 rooms known as the treasuries (Schatzkammer). They include relics of the Holy Roman Empire, the crown jewels and liturgical objects of the imperial court, and in addition dazzling gold, silver and porcelain that were once used at state banquets.

Hofburgkapelle

Schweizerhof. **Tel** (01) 533 9927. **Open** 10am–2pm Mon & Tue, 11am–1pm Fri. **Closed** public hols. Vienna Boys' Choir: Sep–Jun: 9:15am Sun (book by phone). **hofburgkapelle.at**

Originally built in 1296, the Hofburgkapelle was renovated in the 1440s by Friedrich III; it contains Gothic statues in canopied niches. Every Sunday, visitors can hear performances by the renowned Vienna Boys' Choir (Wiener Sängerknaben).

Burggarten and Volksgarten

Burgring/Opernring/Dr-Karl-Renner-Ring. **Open** daily.

Some of the space left around the Hofburg after Napoleon's invasion was transformed by the Habsburgs into gardens. The Volksgarten opened in 1820, but the Burggarten remained the palace's private garden until 1918.

Ornamental pond in the Volksgarten, with Burgtheater in the background

For hotels and restaurants see p390 and p391

Hunters in the Snow (1565) by Pieter Bruegel the Elder

❷ Kunsthistorisches Museum

Maria Theresien-Platz. **Tel** (01) 52524 4031. 🚋 D, 1, 2, 71. 🚌 57A. Ⓤ Volkstheater, MuseumsQuartier. **Open** 10am–6pm Tue, Wed, Fri–Sun; 10am–9pm Thu. 🐾 ⬛ ♿ Ⓦ khm.at

Built in the style of the Italian Renaissance, the Museum of Art History houses a collection amassed over the centuries by generations of Habsburg monarchs. The public was given access to these art treasures when the museum opened in 1891 in Ringstrasse, built to designs by Karl von Hasenauer (1833–94) and Gottfried Semper (1809–79). The museum's lavish interior complements its exhibits perfectly and attracts more than a million people each year.

The collection focuses on Old Masters from the 15th to the 18th centuries. Due to links between the Habsburgs and the Netherlands, Flemish art is also well represented.

Highlights are about half the surviving works by Pieter Bruegel the Elder, including his *The Tower of Babel* and most of the cycle of *The Seasons*, all from the mid-16th century. Among the other outstanding works are Dutch paintings from genre scenes of great charm to magnificent land-scapes. *The Artist's Studio* (1665), an enigmatic allegorical painting by Vermeer (1632–75), is believed by some to be a self-portrait of the artist at work. The most interesting

Spanish works are by Velasquez (1599–1660), who immortalized the eight-year-old Margarita Teresa, the future wife of Emperor Leopold I (1640–1705), in *Infanta* (1659).

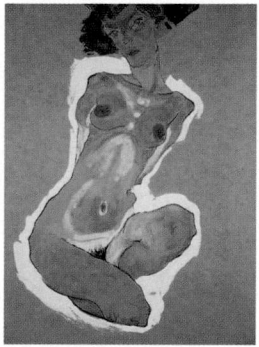

Schiele's *Kneeling Female Nude*, (1917) MuseumsQuartier Wien

❸ MuseumsQuartier Wien

Museumsplatz 1. **Tel** (01) 523 5881. 🚋 1, 2, 49, 71, D, J. 🚌 48A. Ⓤ MuseumsQuartier, Volkstheater. Visitor Centre: **Open** 10am–7pm daily. Ⓦ mqw.at. KUNSTHALLE wien: **Open** 10am–7pm Fri–Wed, 10am–10pm Thu. 🐾 ♿ Leopold Museum: **Open** 10am–6pm Wed, Fri–Mon, 10am– 9pm Thu; Jun–Aug: open daily. 🐾 Museum of Modern Art Ludwig Foundation Vienna: **Open** 2–2pm Mon, 10am–7pm Tue–Sun.

Once home to the imperial stables and carriage houses, the MuseumsQuartier Wien is one of the largest cultural centres in the world. It houses a diverse range of facilities from art museums to venues for film, theatre, architecture, dance and new media.

The complex includes **KUNSTHALLE wien**, Vienna's main showcase for international and contemporary art exhibitions. It focuses on transdisciplinary work, including photography and film, as well as modern-art retrospectives. To the left of Kunsthalle is the **Leopold Museum**, home to over 5,000 works of Austrian art of which the highlights are major works by Gustav Klimt and the world's largest Egon Schiele collection. The **Museum of Modern Art Ludwig Foundation Vienna (MUMOK)** contains one of the largest European collections of modern art ranging from Pop Art to Viennese Actionism.

❹ Naturhistorisches Museum

Maria Theresien-Platz. **Tel** (01) 52177 276. 🚋 1, 2, 46, 49, 71, D. 🚌 48A. Ⓤ Volkstheater. **Open** 9am–6:30pm Thu–Mon, 9am–9pm Wed. **Closed** 1 Jan, 1 May, 1 Nov, 25 Dec. 🐾 ♿ ⬛ 🎥 Ⓦ nhm-wien.ac.at

Almost a mirror image of the Kunsthistorisches Museum, the Natural History Museum was designed by the same architects and opened in 1889. Both were built under the reign of Franz Joseph I.

The Natural History Museum is home to one of the richest and most wide-ranging collections in the world. It includes archae-ological, anthropological, mineralogical, zoological and geological displays. Besides casts of dinosaur skeletons, it also has the world's oldest collection of meteorites. In addition, it includes prehistoric sculptures, Bronze Age items and extinct birds and mammals as well as Europe's most comprehensive exhibition of gems. The archaeological section includes the celebrated *Venus of Willendorf*, a 25,000-year-old Paleolithic fertility figurine.

Splendid grand staircases gracing the side wings of the Burgtheater

❺ Burgtheater

Universitätsring 1. **Tel** (01) 51444 4140. 🚃 1, 2, 71, D. Ⓤ Schottentor. **Open** for performances and guided tours. **Closed** Good Fri, 24 Dec. 📷 📷 3pm daily. ♿ 🖥 burgtheater.at

The impressive Burgtheater is one of the most prestigious stages in the German-speaking world. The original theatre, built under Maria Theresa's reign, was replaced in 1888 by the present Italian Renaissance-style building by architects Karl von Hasenauer and Gottfried Semper. It closed for refurbishment in 1897 after it was discovered that several seats had no view of the stage. A bomb devastated the building at the end of World War II, leaving only the side wings containing the grand staircases intact. It has since been restored to wide acclaim.

❻ Stephansdom

Stephansplatz 1. **Tel** (01) 51552 3526. 🚃 1A, 2A. Ⓤ Stephansplatz. **Open** 6am–10pm daily. 📷 10:30am, 3pm Mon–Sat, 3pm Sun & pub hols; tours in English daily 3:45pm Apr–Oct. 📷 ♿ 📷 Organ concerts: May–Nov: 7pm Wed. 🖥 stephanskirche.at

The Stephansdom, with its magnificent glazed-tile roof, is the heart and soul of Vienna. A church has stood on the site for over 800 years, but all that remains of the original 13th-century Romanesque structure are the Heathen Towers and

Giant's Doorway. Severely damaged during World War II, the cathedral was later restored to its former glory. Its interior contains an impressive collection of art spanning several centuries. Highlights are the Baroque high altar and Pilgram's pulpit, decorated with portraits of the Four Fathers of the Church. The 15th-century, 137-m (450-ft) Steffl or South Spire, is the striking symbol of the city.

❼ Staatsoper

Opernring 2. **Tel** (01) 51444 2250. 🚃 59A. 🚃 1, 2, 71, D. Ⓤ Karlsplatz. 🖥 **wiener-staatsoper.at**

Vienna's Opera House, the Staatsoper, was the first of the grand Ringstrasse buildings to be completed. It opened

Superb sculptures adorn Singer Gate, Stephansdom

on 25 May 1869, to the strains of Mozart's *Don Giovanni*. Built in Neo-Renaissance style, the Staatsoper did not appeal to Emperor Franz Joseph, who compared it to a "railway station" leading Eduard van der Null, its Austrian architect, to commit suicide. Yet, when the Opera House was hit by a bomb in 1945 and largely destroyed, the event was seen as a symbolic blow to the city.

With a new state-of-the-art auditorium and stage, the Opera House reopened on 5 November 1955, with a performance of Beethoven's *Fidelio*. Gustav Mahler, Richard Strauss and Herbert von Karajan are among the illustrious composers who have conducted here. Each year, on the last Thursday of Carnival, the stage is extended to create a vast dance floor for the Vienna Opera Ball.

The imposing façade of Vienna's Opera House, Staatsoper

❽ Secession Building

Friedrichstrasse 12. **Tel** (01) 587 5307. 🚃 59A. Ⓤ Karlsplatz. **Open** 10am–6pm Tue–Sun. 📷 🖥 **secession.at**

Designed by Joseph Maria Olbrich in 1898, the unusual Secession Building was a showcase for the Secession movement's artists such as Gustav Klimt, Kolo Moser and Otto Wagner. The almost windowless building, with its filigree globe of entwined laurel leaves on the roof, is a squat cube with four towers. The motto of the founders,

...lden filigree dome adorning the ...cession Building

...n the façade, states: "To every ...ge its Art, to Art its Freedom". ... The Secession Building's ...est-known exhibit is Klimt's ...ethoven Frieze. This 34-m (110-ft) ...ainting is regarded as one of ...e masterpieces of Viennese ...t Nouveau. Designed in 1902 ...d covering three walls, the ...eze was carefully restored in ...e 1970s. It shows interrelated ...oups of figures thought to be ...commentary on Beethoven's ...nth Symphony.

Karlskirche

...rlsplatz 8. **Tel** (01) 505 6294.
...4A. 1, 2, 71, D. Karlsplatz.
...pen 9am–6pm Mon–Sat, 12–
...5pm Sun & public hols.
...karlskirche.at

...uring Vienna's plague
...pidemic of 1713, Emperor
...arl VI vowed that as soon as
...e city was delivered from
...s plight he would build a
...urch dedicated to St Charles
...orromeo (1538–84), a former
...chbishop and patron saint
...plague victims. He announced
...competition to design the
...urch, which was won by
...ohann Bernhard Fischer von
...lach's (1656–1723), architect
...many of Vienna's finest
...uildings. His eclectic Baroque
...asterpiece has a gigantic
...eo-Classical dome and portico
...orrowed from classical Greek
...d Roman architecture,
...anked by two minaret-
...ke towers.
... One of the most striking
...atures is the frescoes in the

cupola painted by Johann
Michael Rottmayr between
1725 and 1730, depicting
the *Apotheosis of St Charles
Borromeo*. It was the painter's
last commission. Others include
the typically Baroque high
altar featuring a stucco relief
by Albert Camesina, which
shows St Charles Borromeo
being taken to heaven on a
cloud filled with angels and
putti, and the two intricate
columns, inspired by Trajan's
Column in Rome. These feature
scenes from the life of the
saint, illustrating his qualities
of steadfastness and courage.

Stucco relief on the Baroque high
altar, Karlskirche

⑩ Austrian Museum of Applied Arts

Stubenring 5. **Tel** (01) 711 360.
2. 3A, 74A. Stubentor,
Landstrasse. Wien Mitte.
Open 10am–10pm Tue, 10am–6pm
Wed–Sun. free on Tue. **mak.at**

The Austrian Museum of
Applied Arts (Museum für
angewandte Kunst or MAK),
founded in 1864, was the first
of its kind in Europe and
exercised a strong influence
on the development of the
applied arts for some time.
 The renovated museum
acts both as a showcase for
Austrian decorative arts and
as a repository for fine objects
from around the world. Originally
founded in 1864 as a museum
of art and industry, it expanded

and diversified over the years
to include objects representing
new artistic movements. The
permanent collection, presented
according to periods from the
Gothic to the present, includes
world-famous works by the
Wiener Werkstätte, an arts and
crafts cooperative workshop
from 1870 to 1956. Furniture,
textiles, glassware, and fine
Renaissance jewellery are also
on display. A number of rooms
are devoted to the Art
Nouveau period.

⑪ Freud Museum

Berggasse 19. **Tel** (01) 319 1596.
37, 38, 40, 41, 42, D. 40A.
Schottentor, Schottenring.
Open 9am–5pm daily.
freud-museum.at

Berggasse No. 19, a typical
20th-century Viennese town
house, is now one of the city's
most famous addresses. The
father of psychoanalysis,
Sigmund Freud (1856–1939),
lived, worked and received
patients here from 1891 till
1938, when he was forced to
leave the city, where he had
lived almost all his life, by the
Nazis. Although abandoned
by Freud in a hurry, the flat
still preserves an intimate
atmosphere with most of
his belongings still in place.
 The room in which Freud
received patients is on the
mezzanine floor. There are at
least 420 items of memorabilia
on display, including his letters
and books. His frayed hat and
travel trunk can be seen in the
small, dark lobby. A cabinet
contains some archaeological
objects collected by Freud. The
world-famous couch is now in
the Freud Museum in London.

Beautifully restored patients' waiting room
in the Freud Museum

Practical & Travel Information

Vienna is well equipped for both winter and summer tourism. The public transport system is clean, efficient and easy to use and banking and currency exchange facilities are widely available in the city. The official language is German but English is widely spoken throughout the city.

Documentation

Citizens of the US, Canada, Australia and New Zealand need just a passport to visit Vienna. No visa is required for visitors who intend to stay for three months or less. Most European Union (EU) citizens require only a valid identity card to enter the country.

Visitor Information

Austria has a wide network of local tourist offices. In Vienna, the **Wiener Tourismusverband** (Vienna Tourist Board) is very helpful, especially with regard to forthcoming events and booking accommodation.

Visitors can also plan their trip to Vienna by contacting travel agencies or the representatives of **Österreich Werbung** (the Austrian National Tourist Office) in their native country. For information on cheap accommodation, youth hostels and tickets for concerts, the multilingual staff at **Jugendinformation Wien** (Vienna Youth Information Office) can provide assistance and leaflets.

Health and Security

Hospitals in Vienna are of a high standard. In case of medical emergencies, visitors should call an ambulance or the local doctor on call. For minor ailments or injuries, it is best to go to a pharmacy. All pharmacies are marked with a distinctive red "A" sign, and when closed, display the address of the nearest open one.

Although visitors are unlikely to encounter any violence in Vienna, it is always advisable to be cautious when out walking. The police and emergency services are easy to contact if the need arises.

Banking and Currency

The official currency of Austria is the euro. Banks are the best place to change money and are open Monday to Friday from 8am to 12:30pm and from 1:30 to 3pm. Some, generally those at main train stations and airports, stay open longer and do not close for lunch. Major credit cards are accepted at large stores, hotels and restaurants, but visitors are advised to carry some cash as

well. However, traveller's cheques are the safest way to carry large sums of money and can be exchanged in most banks in Vienna. *Bankomats* or ATMs are found everywhere in the city, even railway stations and airport, most are closed after midnight.

Communications

The telecommunications network in Vienna is run by **Telekom Austria**. Public phones are slowly being phased out, however you can make long-distance phone calls from all major post offices. The mobile phone network is well developed and SIM cards can be obtained at the airport, major train stations and throughout the city. The postal service in the city is very reliable and post offices are open Monday to Friday between 8am and noon and 2 and 6pm.

Facilities for the Disabled

Public awareness of the needs of the disabled is growing in Austria. Wiener Tourismusverband has a good online information service with details of wheelchair access points at tourist sights, hotels and public toilets.

Arriving by Air

Vienna's **Schwechat International Airport** is 19 km (12 miles) from the city centre. There are direct flights from the

---

DIRECTORY

Visitor Information

Jugendinformation Wien
 jugendinfowien.at

Österreich Werbung
 austria.info

Wiener Tourismusverband
 wien.info

Embassies

Australia
Tel (01) 506 740.
 australian-embassy.at

Canada
Tel (01) 531 383 000.
 kanada.at

United Kingdom
Tel (01) 716 130.
 britishembassy.at

United States
Tel (01) 313 39.
 usembassy.at

Emergency Numbers

Ambulance
Tel 144.

Fire
Tel 122.

Police
Tel 133.

Communications

Telekom Austria
 telekom.at

Arriving by Air

Austrian Airlines
 aua.com

British Airways
 britishairways.com

Delta Airlines
 delta.com

Fly Niki
 flyniki.com

Ryanair
 ryanair.com

Schwechat International Airport
 viennaairport.com

Rail Travel

Rail Enquiry
 oebb.at

Arriving by Coach

Busterminal Erdberg
Erdbergstrasse 200A.

Eurolines
 eurolines.com

hited States on **Delta Airlines**
om New York and Orlando.
ustrian Airlines flies from New
ork, Chicago and Washington,
hile **Fly Niki** operates flights to
veral US destinations. There are
veral flights a day from Gatwick
d Heathrow airports in London.
ritish Airways and **Ryanair** also
ffer regular flights to Vienna.

ail Travel

s of 2015, the Hauptbahnhof
ien, located on Südtiroler Platz,
ill be Vienna's most important
ain station serving all interna-
onal rail travel as well as local
estinations going to the south
d east. The Westbahnhof will
rve local destinations only and
e Franz-Josephs-Bahnhof will
ontinue to run train services
ping north. Check www.oebb.
: and www.hauptbahnhof-

The Climate of Vienna

Summers (June–August)
in Vienna can be quite hot
with temperatures sometimes
as high as 30° C (86° F)
between June and August.
Spring (March–May) and
autumn (September–October)
are very pleasant. Winters
(November–March) are very
cold with regular snowfall,
temperatures usually dip
to as low as -4° C (25° F).

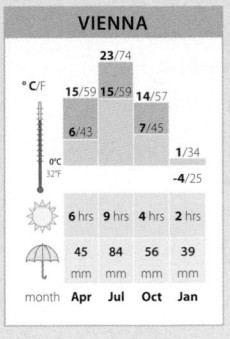

VIENNA			
	23/74		
15/59 15/59		14/57	
6/43		7/45	
			1/34
			-4/25
6 hrs	9 hrs	4 hrs	2 hrs
45 mm	84 mm	56 mm	39 mm
month Apr	Jul	Oct	Jan

wien.at for up-to-date information.
Information about train schedules
is available on the official website.

Arriving by Coach

International coach services
arrive at **Busterminal Erdberg**

in the east of the city, right
beside the U3 Erdberg
underground station. The Old
Town is a short six-stop journey
from here. **Eurolines** operates
daily services from Busterminal
Erdberg to most Eastern
European cities.

hopping & Entertainment

hopping in Vienna can be expensive, but it is a good place
 buy traditional goods such as Loden coats, porcelain and
lass. Famous for its coffee shops, Christmas markets, world-
ass opera and orchestras, Vienna is also the centre of
ntertainment in Austria.

ood and Drink

ustria is justly famous for
s cakes and pastries. Visitors
nould try the buttery *advent
ollen* (Christmas cake), stuffed
ith fruit and nuts and dusted
vith icing sugar, available
om the **Meinl am Graben**
elicatessen. Specialist choco-
te shops such as **Altmann &
ühne** are also worth a visit,
oth for the chocolates and
eir unusual packaging.

ouvenirs

etit-point embroidery, which
dorns elegant handbags,
owder compacts and similar
rticles, is a Viennese speciality.
 wide range of these goods is
vailable at **Petit Point** and
aria Stransky. *Trachten*
Austrian costumes) shops sell
ypical hats, pretty children's
resses, jackets and blouses.
 & L. Lobmeyr is the best
lace for glassware.

Theatre and Music

Viennese theatre enjoys a
high reputation and the
Burgtheater *(see p386)* is the
city's leading theatrical venue.
The **Volkstheater** puts on modern
plays while the **Ronacher**
produces lavish musicals.

At the **Staatsoper** *(see p386)*,
operas are normally performed
in the original language whereas
at most other theatres, they are
sung in German. The principal
venues for classical music are
the **Musikverein** and the concert
halls of **Konzerthaus**.

The city supports two
great orchestras, the Wiener
Philharmoniker and the Wiener
Symphoniker. Seasonal events
include the **Vienna Festival** in
May and June, and Impulstanz,
a festival for contemporary
dance and performance.
Seasonal opera, drama and
concert performances take
place throughout the city in
late July and August.

DIRECTORY

Food and Drink

Altmann & Kühne
Tel (01) 533 0927.
W altmann-kuehne.at

Meinl am Graben
Tel (01) 532 3334.
W meinlamgraben.at

Souvenirs

J. & L. Lobmeyr
Tel (01) 512 0508. W lobmeyr.at

Maria Stransky
Tel (01) 533 6098.
W maria-stransky.at

Petit Point
Tel (01) 512 4886.
W petitpoint.eu

Theatre and Music

Burgtheater
W burgtheater.at

Konzerthaus
W konzerthaus.at

Musikverein
W musikverein.at

Ronacher W musicalvienna.at

Staatsoper W staatsoper.at

Vienna Festival
W festwochen.at

Volkstheater
W volkstheater.at

Where to Stay

Vienna

Hotel Post €
Boutique
Fleischmarkt 24, 1010
Tel *(01) 515 830*
W hotel-post-wien.at
Uniquely designed rooms at this 6-storey hotel, most with a private bathroom. Great on-site restaurant.

DK Choice

Hollmann Beletage €€
Boutique
Köllnerhofgasse 6, 1010
Tel *(01) 961 1960*
W hollmann-beletage.at
With its sleek tangerine and granite decor and 25 spacious rooms boasting an array of gadgets, this hotel is an absolute gem. Mammoth breakfasts, friendly staff and a sauna are just a few of the many perks of this family-run boutique hotel.

Hotel Am Parkring €€
Boutique
Parkring 12, 1015
Tel *(01) 514 800*
W schick-hotels.com
The city views from this privately-owned hotel are stunning. It has modern, comfortable rooms.

Hotel Am Stephansplatz €€
Boutique
Stephansplatz 9, 1010
Tel *(01) 534 050*
W hotelamstephansplatz.at
This hotel is popular with both business and leisure guests and features paintings by famous artists such as Patricia Karg.

Hotel Capricorno €€
Boutique
Schwedenplatz 3–4, 1010
Tel *(01) 5333 1040*
W schick-hotels.com

Lively metropolitan hotel located close to the city's nightlife. Hearty breakfast spread for late risers.

Kaiserin Elisabeth €€
Luxury
Weihburggasse 3, 1010
Tel *(01) 515 260*
W kaiserinelisabeth.at
Visit this traditional hotel with 63 non-smoking rooms and a host of in-room amenities.

Pension Aviano €€
Pension
Marco-d'Aviano-Gasse 1, 1010
Tel *(01) 512 8330*
W aviano-pension-vienna.h-rez.com/
Traditional Viennese decor at this non-smoking, pet-friendly pension.

Palais Coburg €€€
Luxury
Coburgbastei 4, 1010
Tel *(01) 518 180*
W coburg.at
Opulence complements history beautifully at this exclusive hotel. Grand rooms and stunning service.

Palais Hansen Kempinski Vienna €€€
Luxury
Schottenring 24, 1010
Tel *(01) 236 1000*
W kempinski.com
Elegant rooms and suites with all high-tech facilities. Great location.

Altstadt Vienna €
Boutique
Kirchengasse 41, 1070
Tel *522 66 66*
W altstadt.at
Choose from 42 exquisitely decorated rooms that blend period character and exotic modernity.

Harmonie €
Boutique
Harmoniegasse 5–7, 1090
Tel *(01) 317 6604*
W bestwestern-ce.com

Famous for its huge breakfast buffet, this hotel also has a lovely café and a well-stocked bar.

Pension Schottentor
Pension
Hörlgasse 4, 1090
Tel *(01) 319 1176*
W tinyurl.com/l4b2hho
Family-run three-star pension with neat rooms and all basic amenities.

The Levante Parliament €
Boutique
Auerspergstrasse 9, 1080
Tel *(01) 228 280*
W thelevante.com
Unwind in the gorgeous courtyard of this hotel with an eye-catching glass bar and a Finnish sauna.

Hotel am Konzerthaus
Boutique
Am Heumarkt 35–37, 1030
Tel *(01) 716 160*
W mgallery.com/Vienna
This 211-room hotel attracts a sophisticated clientele with sumptuous breakfasts, an excellent restaurant and high-tech rooms.

Imperial €€
Luxury
Kärntner Ring 16, 1015
Tel *(01) 501 100*
W imperialvienna.com
Stately 1800s hotel with exquisite rooms. Butlers serve the suites.

The spacious, inviting library at Hollmann Beletage

Where to Eat and Drink

Vienna

Café Prueckel €
Café
Stubenring 24, A-1010
Tel *(01) 512 6115*
A much-loved Viennese café
with 50s-style, kitschy decor
offering excellent coffee, meals
and pastries. This place always
attracts a cool and arty crowd.

Gasthaus Poschl €
Gasthaus
Weihburggasse 17, 1010
Tel *(01) 513 5288*
Sit down with a crisp chicken
schnitzel with parmesan
potatoes and a glass of Austrian
beer in this friendly restaurant.

Griechenbeisl €
Austrian
Fleischmarkt 11, A-1010
Tel *(01) 533 1977*
Enjoy a schnitzel meal and a few
drinks in Vienna's oldest inn.
Excellent beef fillet and an exten-
sive wine list. Framed autographs
of such figures as Beethoven and
Schubert add gravitas.

Konditorei Gerstner €
Austrian
Kärntner Strasse 11–15, 1010
Tel *(01) 512 4630*
One of the city's greatest pastry
makers and chocolatiers, Gerstner
is a favourite with tour groups.
Ask for the scrumptious
poppy pie.

Beaulieu €€
Mediterranean
Herrengasse 14/18, 1010
Tel *(01) 532 1103*
The seafood risotto with saffron
is a popular draw at Beaulieu.
Or go for a plate of delectable
Austrian cheese and breads.

DK Choice

Ilona Stuberl €€
Austrian
Bräunerstrasse 2, 1010
Tel *(01) 533 9029*
Founded in 1957, this family-
run Austro-Hungarian restaurant
is a well-respected part of Vienna's
culinary scene. A menu in eight
languages covers veal, pork, fish,
beef and vegetarian dishes. The
restaurant also serves salads,
pastas, soups and hearty desserts.
The waiters are well versed in the
1867 unification history of Austria
and Hungary under Franz Josef.

Dining room of the Vestibul with marble
pillars and arches

Lebenbauer €€
Vegetarian
Teinfaltstrasse 3, 1010
Tel *(01) 533 5556*
Closed *Sat & Sun*
One of Vienna's most upmarket
vegetarian restaurants,
Lebenbauer boasts a creative,
meat-free menu. Recipes use
mainly organic produce and
are cooked without fat, eggs
or flour. Do not miss the
pumpkin risotto.

Ofenloch €€
Austrian
Kurrentgasse 8, 1010
Tel *(01) 533 8844*　　　　**Closed** *Sun*
Traditional menu with all
the usual soups, potato
dumplings and schnitzels.
The service is a cut above
the rest.

Le Siècle €€
Mediterranean
Weihburggasse 32, 1010
Tel *(01) 515 173 440*
Serving a delectable array
of international dishes, this
award-winning restaurant is
renowned for decadent dining.
Le Siècle serves everything
from caviar and suckling pig
to herb-rubbed roasted lamb
and chateaubriand.

Teahouse Haas & Haas €€
International
Stephansplatz 4, 1010
Tel *(01) 512 2666*
A 25-year-old institution,
this friendly teahouse is known
for its inviting courtyard. It
expertly delivers a wide selection
of Germanic dishes for brunch,
lunch and afternoon tea.

Price Guide
Prices are based on a three-course meal
for one, half a bottle of wine, including
cover charge, service and tax.

€	under €35
€€	€35 to €65
€€€	over €65

Wrenkh €€
Vegetarian
Bauernmarkt 10, 1010
Tel *(01) 533 1526*　　　**Closed** *Sun*
Simple, no-frills menu that
lays an emphasis on regional
food and healthy vegetarian
dishes. Try the mango and
quinoa salad.

Palmenhaus €€€
European
Burggarten 1, 1010
Tel *(01) 533 1033*
One of Vienna's plushest
venues with a menu to match.
Opt for a *carpe diem* breakfast –
fresh pineapple, mint, honeycracker,
rye breads, goats cheese
omelette and rolls with jam.

Plachutta €€€
Austrian
Wollzeile 38, 1010
Tel *(01) 512 1577*
The Plachutta Wollzeile
plays host to numerous
Austrian soap stars and other
celebrities. Savour Viennese
dishes such as the famous
tafelspitz (boiled beef).

DK Choice

Vestibul €€€
Austrian
Universitätsring 2, 1010
Tel *(01) 532 4999*　　　**Closed** *Sun*
This accolade-winning
kitchen specializes in seasonal,
wholesome ingredients with
everything made from scratch,
be it home-made stock or
elderberry juice. Great food,
reliable service and superb
location, just a stone's throw
away from Vienna's fine
cultural venues.

Zum Schwarzen Kameel €€€
Austrian
Bognergasse 5, 1010
Tel *(01) 533 812 511*　　　**Closed** *Sun*
Step inside this century-
old Viennese Jugendstil
building and be wowed
by an 800-strong wine list.
Choose from dozens of cheeses
on a first-class menu. The
wild boar with red wine is
particularly good.

SOUTH EASTERN EUROPE

South Eastern Europe at a Glance

One of the most diverse areas of the European continent, South Eastern Europe is where the cultural traditions of Central Europe, the Mediterranean and the Balkans come together. So it is not uncommon to see Catholic churches, Orthodox monasteries and Muslim holy sites in the same region. The region's island-scattered Adriatic coast and the golden-hued sands of Romania and Bulgaria offer ample opportunities to relax on the beach. Inland, rugged mountain regions, rich in wildflowers and woodland, provide the perfect backdrop for exhilarating hikes.

Mount Triglav *(see pp418–19)*, the highest peak in Slovenia, stands at the heart of a national park filled with jagged summits, evergreen woodland and glacier-carved lakes.

Zagreb *(see pp466–73)*, capital of Croatia and an important regional cultural centre, boasts a fine collection of museums and galleries and a year-round supply of top-quality music and theatre.

Jajce *(see pp494–5)*, the medieval Bosnian capital, is a picturesque hilltop town famous for its thundering waterfall and water-powered mills.

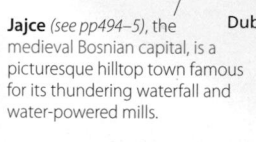

Ostrog Monastery *(see pp512–13)*, one of the highlights of Montenegro, is a popular pilgrimage site. Its painted rock churches are among the most beautiful religious buildings in the Balkans.

◄ Aerial view of the popular town, Cavtat, near Dubrovnik, Croatia

Peleş Castle *(see pp558–9)* is nestled in the Transylvanian Alps. Its fairy tale spires and turrets reflect the romantic tastes of its high-living first resident, German-born King Carol I of Romania.

0 km   100

0 miles   100

Satu Mare   Suceava

Oradea   Iaşi

Cluj-Napoca   Târgu Mureş

ROMANIA *(see pp542–573)*   Bârlad

Arad

Deva   Braşov   Galaţi

Buzău

...grade   Târgu Jiu   Piteşti

Pożarevac   Bucharest   Constanţa

SERBIA *see pp520–541)*   Craiova

Paraćin   Calafat   Ruse

Niš   Montana   Pleven   Varna

Grdelica   Veliko Tûrnovo

Sofia   **BULGARIA** *(see pp574–611)*   Burgas

Kyustendil   Plovdiv   Haskovo

Sofia *(see pp578–85)*, capital of Bulgaria, is rich in Roman remains, medieval treasures and Orthodox churches. The cavernous Neo-Byzantine Aleksandûr Nevski Memorial Church serves as the city's graceful centrepiece.

Belgrade *(see pp524–31)*, the Serbian capital, centres on the sprawling Kalemegdan Fortress, overlooking the Danube river. With its crumbling bastions built by former conquerors, it is now a tranquil park laced with flowerbeds and tree-shaded promenades.

SLOVENIA

Despite being one of Europe's smallest nations, Slovenia offers magnificently varied scenery and splendid architecture. Since 1991, it has re-established itself as a major holiday destination for outdoor pursuits, high-quality health spas and ski resorts. Economic growth has helped sustain tourism, and the lively people make Slovenia a welcoming place to visit.

Few countries in South Eastern Europe pack as much variety into such a small geographical area as Slovenia. The landscape changes swiftly between the Alps and limestone plateaus, dense forests and Mediterranean coastline, all within a very short distance of each other. At the heart of the country is Ljubljana, a city combining graceful architecture with an exuberant lifestyle.

The population is relatively homogenous with 83 per cent of its two million inhabitants ethnically Slovene. Small but significant minorities include Albanians, Bosnians, Croats and Serbs, who came to live and work in Slovenia during the Yugoslav period.

History

The Slovene nation has its origins in the great migrations of the 6th century, when Slav tribes from the Carpathian basin settled in the Drava and Sava valleys. A Slav tribal state known as Carantania came into existence in the territory of present-day Slovenia and southern Austria, but this soon came under the control of more powerful German-speaking rulers.

In the medieval period, the country was governed by feudal landowners, including the Babenbergs, the Spannheims and the Counts of Celje. Ultimate authority was also wielded at various times by Hungarian kings, German emperors and the Austrian Habsburg family, who established control over most of Slovenia by the 15th century.

Around the same time, the Ottoman Turks mounted attacks deep into Central Europe, turning Slovenia into the front line in the region's defence.

Pavement café on Old Square, Ljubljana's oldest medieval square

◀ View of the picturesque Bled Castle

Guards carrying Tito's coffin at his funeral in 1980

Throughout the Habsburg period, the predominant language was German, with Slovene spoken only among the peasantry. However, a brief period of French rule (1809–1813) introduced Slovene-language schooling and a new generation of educated Slovenes rose to promote national culture. Following the collapse of the Habsburg Empire in 1918, Slovenia entered the newly created kingdom of Serbs, Croats and Slovenes, later renamed Yugoslavia. This multi-ethnic state was invaded by Hitler in April 1941 and Slovenia was divided between Nazi Germany and Fascist Italy.

After World War II, Slovenia became a federal republic within a reconstituted, Communist-ruled Yugoslavia. The Yugoslav Federation functioned successfully under the leadership of President Tito. However, with the death of Tito and the onset of economic problems, the union began to disintegrate.

Slovenia declared independence from Yugoslavia on 25 June 1991. The Ten Day War (27 June–6 July) with Yugoslavia followed, in which the Yugoslav People's Army was outmanoeuvred by Slovenia's defence forces.

Slovenia went on to establish itself as one of the economic and political successes of the new Europe, joining NATO and the European Union in 2004.

KEY DATES IN SLOVENIAN HISTORY

AD 591 Slavs arrive in the upper Drava region

1282 The Habsburg Dynasty establishes its first feudal holdings in Slovene lands

1573 Peasant Uprising ends with the defeat of the rebels and bloody retribution by the nobility

1813 A brief period of Napoleonic rule is followed by a return to Habsburg control

1918 Slovenia joins other south Slav peoples to form the kingdom of Serbs, Croats and Slovenes

1921 Vidovdan Constitution establishes a constitutional monarchy; Belgrade is the capital

1938 Josip Broz Tito appointed leader of the Communist Party of Yugoslavia

1941 Slovenia divided between Fascist Italy, Nazi Germany and Miklós Horthy's Hungary

1974 The 1974 Constitution gives each republic greater responsibility for its internal affairs

1980 Yugoslavia enters a period of crisis following the death of Tito

1991 Slovenia declares independence from Yugoslavia

2004 Slovenia joins NATO

2007 Euro introduced in Slovenia

Language and Culture

Modern Slovene belongs to the Slavic family of languages and is closely related to Croatian and Serbian. Centuries of Austrian rule has left a profound imprint on the language and many colloquial expressions are of German origin.

The Austrian influence also extended to architecture, with Alpine farmhouses and onion-domed churches scattered across parts of the country.

Slovenia was predominantly a peasant country until the early 20th century and folk music and village festivals are still an integral part of national life.

During the 1970s and 80s, Slovenia emerged as a centre of contemporary art and popular music and Slovenian culture retains a modern outlook.

Exploring Slovenia

A delightful destination in its own right, Ljubljana is also a good base from which to explore the rest of the country. The city lies at the centre of Slovenia's road and rail network and many regional attractions are within a couple of hours' drive. To the north are the grand Julian Alps, towering above Lakes Bled and Bohinj. To the west, routes cross the cave-studded karst region before descending towards the coast, characterized by Venetian-style architecture and lush vegetation.

Sights at a Glance

1. *Ljubljana pp400–407*
2. *Postojna Cave pp408–409*
3. Predjama Castle
4. Škocjan Caves
5. Koper
6. Piran
7. Portorož
8. Hrastovlje
9. Lipica
10. Idrija
11. *Soča Valley Tour p413*
12. Kobarid
13. Bovec
14. Kranjska Gora
15. *Bled pp416–17*
16. *Triglav National Park pp418–21*
17. Velika Planina
18. Logarska Dolina
19. *Maribor pp422–23*
20. Ptuj

Traditional Alpine farmhouses along a stream, Lake Bohinj

The Plague Column in the town of Maribor

0 kilometers   40

0 miles   40

Key

— Highway

— Major road

— Railway

–·– International border

For keys to symbols *see back flap*

❶ Ljubljana

Slovenia's capital, Ljubljana, began life as the Roman colony of Emona, a major trading centre that was sacked by the Huns in AD 452. Reoccupied by Slavs in the 7th century, the focus of the settlement was moved to the east bank of the Ljubljanica river, where both Ljubljana Castle and the Old Town are located today. With a population of two hundred and eighty thousand, it is one of Europe's smallest capital cities. The Prešeren Square (Prešernov trg) is a good base from which to explore the main sights. On the right bank of the river is the fascinating Old Town (Stari Grad), with its Baroque architecture and several ancient churches. Important museums and galleries, such as the Museum of Modern Art and National Gallery, as well as the sprawling Tivoli Park, are located on the left bank.

Sights at a Glance

① Ljubljana Castle
② St Nicholas's Cathedral
③ Market
④ Prešeren Square
⑤ National Gallery of Slovenia
⑥ Tivoli Park
⑦ Museum of Modern Art
⑧ National Museum of Slovenia
⑨ National and University Library
⑩ Plečnik House

0 metres		500
0 yards		500

Key

■ Street-by-Street area: *see pp402–403*
■ Major sight / Place of interest
■ Pedestrian street

Sequin Castle

TIVOLI PARK

Tivoli Castle

JAKOPIČEVO SPREHAJAL

TIVO

The Triple Bridge spanning the Ljubljanica river, designed by leading architect Jože Plečnik

A   B   C

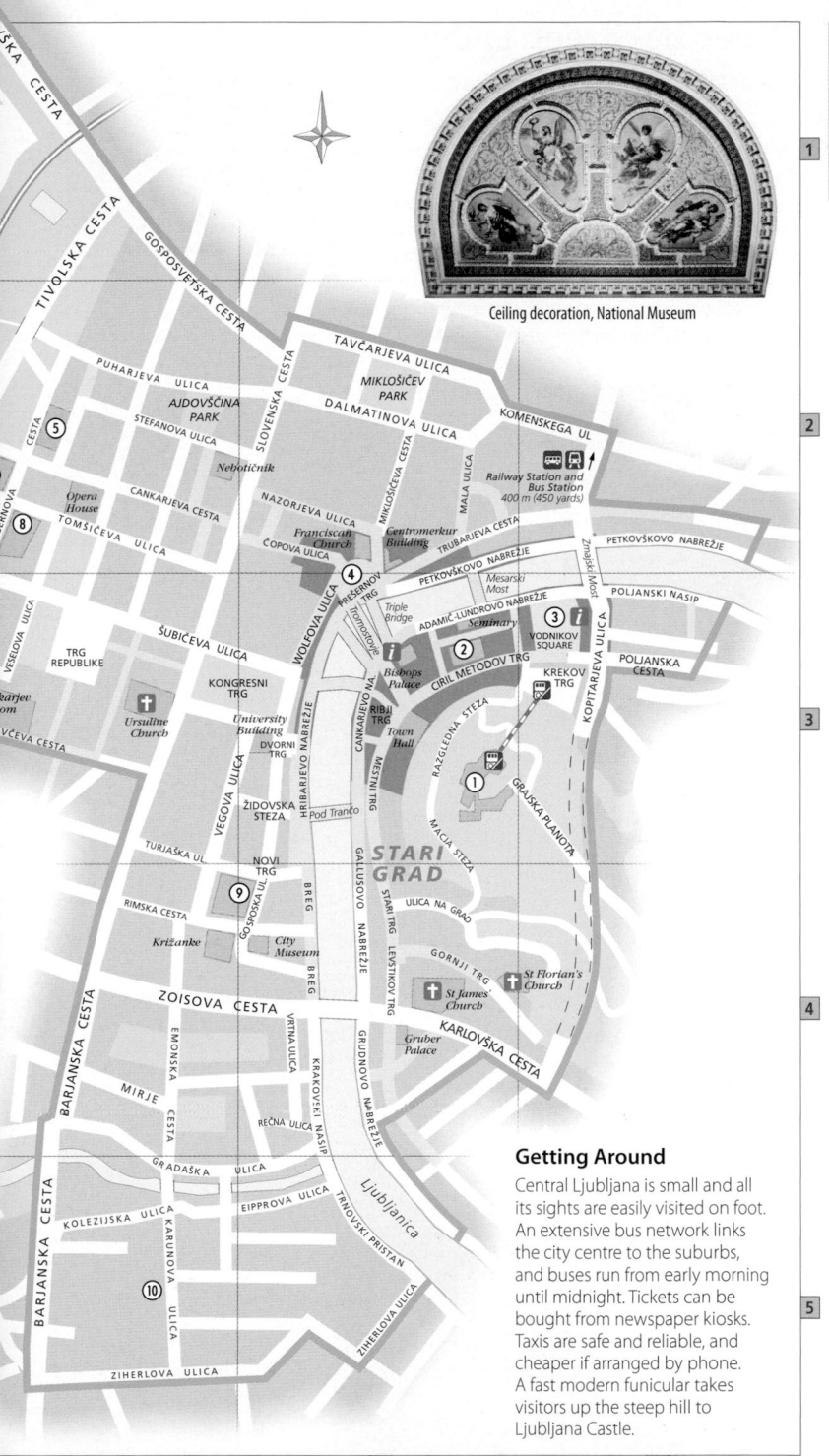

Ceiling decoration, National Museum

Getting Around

Central Ljubljana is small and all its sights are easily visited on foot. An extensive bus network links the city centre to the suburbs, and buses run from early morning until midnight. Tickets can be bought from newspaper kiosks. Taxis are safe and reliable, and cheaper if arranged by phone. A fast modern funicular takes visitors up the steep hill to Ljubljana Castle.

For keys to symbols *see back flap*

Street-by-Street: Ljubljana Old Town

Located between the medieval castle and the leafy banks of the Ljubljanica river, Ljubljana's Old Town contains one of the best-preserved ensembles of Baroque buildings in South Eastern Europe. Arcaded 18th-century houses, domed churches and fountain-studded piazzas add to its elegant character. Narrow cobbled alleys such as Stari trg and Mestni trg, lined these days with swanky cafés and upmarket shops, provide a vibrant introduction to the Slovene capital.

③ ★ **Market**
Ljubljana's lively outdoor market is known for its fresh herbs and dried mushrooms alongside every kind of local produce.

Statue of Valentin Vodnik

VODNIKOV SQUARE

ADAMIČ-LUNDROVO NABREŽJE

② **St Nicholas's Cathedral**
The cathedral's bronze doors, decorated with scenes from the history of Christianity in Slovenia, were created in 1996 to commemorate the visit of Pope John Paul II to Ljubljana.

The Market Colonnade, an elongated pavilion built by architect Jože Plečnik in 1939, houses food shops and a fish market.

The Triple Bridge (Tromostovje) was designed for pedestrians by Jože Plečnik in 1932 as part of the renovation of the riverbank area.

Key

 Suggested route

Franciscan Church of the Annunciation
Ljubljana's most attractive Baroque church, with a single nave and two rows of lateral chapels, contains a splendid 18th-century altar by Italian sculptor Francesco Robba, richly adorned with spiral columns and figurines.

The Prešeren Statue, one of Ljubljana's best-known landmarks, honours Romantic poet and national icon France Prešeren.

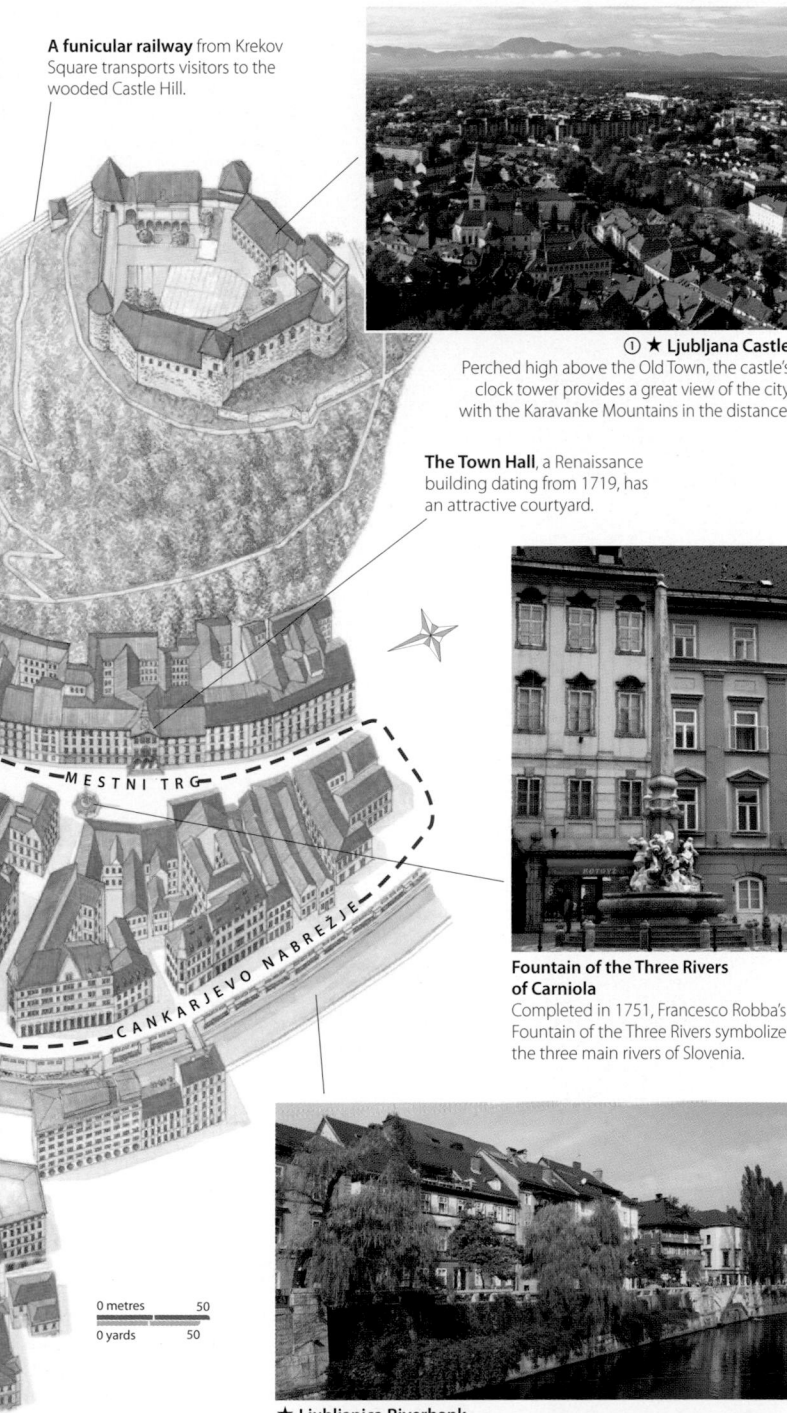

A funicular railway from Krekov Square transports visitors to the wooded Castle Hill.

① ★ **Ljubljana Castle**
Perched high above the Old Town, the castle's clock tower provides a great view of the city with the Karavanke Mountains in the distance.

The Town Hall, a Renaissance building dating from 1719, has an attractive courtyard.

MESTNI TRG

CANKARJEVO NABREŽJE

Fountain of the Three Rivers of Carniola
Completed in 1751, Francesco Robba's Fountain of the Three Rivers symbolizes the three main rivers of Slovenia.

0 metres   50
0 yards   50

★ **Ljubljanica Riverbank**
The east bank of the river is lined with willow trees, orange- and red-roofed townhouses and fabulous terrace cafés and restaurants.

Exterior of St Nicholas's Cathedral, dominated by its twin towers

① Ljubljana Castle
Ljubljanski grad

Grajska planota 1. **Map** E3. **Tel** (01) 306 4293. **Open** May–Sep: 9am–11pm daily; Oct–Apr: 10am–9pm daily. Virtual Museum: **Open** May–Sep: 9am–9pm; Oct–Apr:10am–6pm daily. 🅿

Looming above the Old Town, Ljubljana Castle dates from the 11th century when the Spannheims adopted the city as their feudal power base. Following Ljubljana's absorption by Austria in 1355, the castle became the property of the Habsburg family. It went on to serve as army barracks, a refuge for the poor and a prison. Now an immaculate building with

A section of Ljubljana's medieval castle, high above the Old Town

manicured lawns, the castle has several points of interest grouped around its irregular courtyard. Built in 1848 to serve as a viewing platform, the spectacular **Clock Tower** provides a wonderful view of the city, with the Karavanke Mountains visible to the north.

On the western side of the courtyard, the remarkable 15th-century Gothic **Chapel of St George** has a ceiling decorated with the coats of arms of the Carniola province's leading feudal families. The nearby **Virtual Museum** (Virtualni muzej) showcases the history of the city through an impressive 20-minute audio-visual presentation.

② St Nicholas's Cathedral
Stolnica sv Nikolaja

Dolničarjeva ulica. **Map** E3. **Tel** (01) 234 2690. **Open** 6am–noon & 3–7pm daily.

Built on the site of an earlier church by leading Jesuit architect Andrea Pozzo in 1707, this Baroque cathedral is dedicated to St Nicholas, patron saint of fishermen and sailors. The cathedral's exterior has two doors, built for Pope John Paul II's visit in 1996, each decorated with expressive bronze reliefs. The west door is adorned with scenes from the history of Slovene Christianity; it portrays the baptism of the Slovene nation at the bottom, with Pope

John Paul II shown peering from a window at the top. The south door depicts the tall mitred profiles of six of Slovenia's 20th-century bishops, praying at the tomb of Christ.

Inside, the cathedral has a rich sequence of side chapels and a nave dominated by an Illusionist ceiling painting of the Crucifixion by Giulio Quaglio (1610–58).

Down a side street brightened by flower stalls is the 18th-century portal of Ljubljana's seminary, framed by a pair of titans carved by Angelo Putti. The seminary's library is decorated with frescoes by Quaglio and can be visited by contacting the Ljubljana tourist information office in advance (see p425).

Local produce in Ljubljana's bustling Market

③ Market
Glavna tržnica

Adamič-Lundrovo nabrežje. **Map** F3. **Open** 7am–4pm Mon–Fri, 7am–2pm Sat (Colonnade); 6am–6pm Mon–Fri, 6am–4pm Sat & in winter (stalls).

The northern end of Ljubljana's Old Town has long been the site of the city's large and lively market. Running along the curving bank of the Ljubljanica river is the Market Colonnade, a Classical-inspired structure built by Jože Plečnik in 1942 to provide shelter for a row of delicatessen stalls. Built into the riverbank itself, the colonnade's lower storey is home to a fish market filled with glistening heaps of octopus, squid and lobster from the Adriatic Sea. The lower storey also has a simple seafood snack bar and an arcaded terrace looking out on to the river.

Outside the colonnade are stalls selling souvenirs, herbs and speciality foods. Just east of this area is the main fruit and vegetable section of the market, where trestle tables fill the broad expanse of Vodnikov Square. At the southern end of the square is a statue of Valentin Vodnik, the priest and poet whose works helped to shape the modern Slovene language.

Marking the eastern end of the market is the Dragon's Bridge (Zmajski most), named after the personable bronze dragons – a traditional symbol of the city – adorning each of its four corners. Built to mark the 40th anniversary of the reign of Austrian Emperor Franz Josef in 1901, the bridge also features ornate Art Nouveau lampposts.

Statue of Romantic poet France Prešeren, Prešeren Square

Centromerkur Building, topped by a statue of Mercury, the Roman god of commerce, was built as a department store in 1903. On the opposite side of the square is the angular **Hauptman House**, decorated with multicoloured tiles. Just behind the house, the building at Wolfova No. 4 features a relief of the 19th-century beauty Julija Primic, peering from a first-floor window. Primic was the object of France Prešeren's unrequited love and the inspiration behind many of his poems.

Dragon sculpture, Dragon's Bridge, Market

A short walk north along Miklošičeva cesta leads to the most vivacious of Ljubljana's buildings, the Cooperative Bank built by architect Ivan Vurnik in 1922. Covered in bright red, yellow and blue chevrons, it is a unique mixture of Art Deco and folk art influences.

④ **Prešeren Square**
Prešernov trg

Map E2 & 3.

Standing at the junction between Ljubljana's Old Town and the 19th-century districts on the west bank of the Ljubljanica river, Prešeren Square is the symbolic heart of the city. It is named in honour of France Prešeren, the Romantic poet whose patriotic verses were central to the development of a Slovene national consciousness. Prešeren is commemorated by a monument in the centre of the square, portraying the poet with a book in hand, accompanied by a muse. Opposite the statue is the Franciscan Church, containing a fine 18th-century high altar by famous Italian sculptor Francesco Robba.

Around the square are some of the finest Art Nouveau structures in Ljubljana. On the northeastern corner, the

⑤ **National Gallery of Slovenia**
Narodna galerija Slovenije

Prešernova 24. **Map** D2. **Tel** (01) 241 5418. **Open** 10am–6pm Tue–Sun. 🅿 🗐 🛗 W **ng-slo.si**

Slovenia's national art collection occupies an elegant 19th-century building with stucco ceilings and ornate chandeliers. A modern annexe was added in 2001. A tall atrium holds Francesco Robba's original Fountain of the Three Rivers of Carniola, which was completed in 1751 and symbolizes the meeting of the Sava, Krka and Ljubljanica rivers. The fountain initially stood in the Old Town, but was replaced by a replica in 2006.

The gallery's Slovene collection is particularly rich in Gothic statuary; highlights include a 13th-century Madonna on Solomon's Throne, carved by the little-known Master of the Solčava Maria. There is also an outstanding collection of work by Slovene Impressionists such as Rihard Jakopič, Matija Jama and Matej Sternen, whose canvases exalt the Slovene landscape in the years before World War I.

The European galleries contain an impressive cross-section of Flemish still life and genre paintings, a rich collection of Baroque altar pieces, and Max Reichlich's early 16th-century carving *Killenberg Triptych*, in which the Virgin Mary and St Anne nurse the infant Jesus.

Superb interior of the National Gallery of Slovenia

The green expanses of Ljubljana's Tivoli Park

⑥ Tivoli Park
Park Tivoli

Celovska cesta. **Map** C1 & C2. **Open** Nov–Mar: 8am–3pm Mon–Sat; Apr–Oct: 8am–5pm Mon–Sat. International Centre of Graphic Arts: Grad Tivoli, Pod turnom 3. **Tel** (01) 241 3800. **Open** 10am–6pm Tue–Sun. 🖼 **mglc-lj.si.** National Museum of Contemporary History: Celovška cesta 23. **Tel** (01) 300 9611. **Open** 10am–6pm Tue–Sun. 🖼 **muzej-nz.si.** Cankar Memorial Room: Cankarjev vrh 1. **Tel** (01) 241 2506. **Open** Apr–Oct: 11am–6pm Sat & Sun. **Closed** Nov–Mar. 🖼

To the west of the National Gallery *(see p405)* stretches Tivoli Park, a well-tended expanse of lawns and trees much loved by locals and visitors alike. The park's main avenue, Jakopičevo sprehajališče, is lined with display stands that regularly show art and photography exhibitions. At the end of the avenue stands Tivoli Castle (Tivolski grad), an 18th-century villa that now houses the excellent **International Center of Graphic Arts** (Mednarodni grafični likovni center). As well as organizing the Ljubljana Biennale of Graphic Arts, held in autumn every odd-numbered year, the centre also hosts exhibitions of posters, prints and drawings.

On the northern edge of the park is the stately Baroque Sequin Castle (Cekinov grad), housing the **National Museum of Contemporary History** (Muzej novejše zgodovine Slovenije). The museum chronicles the history of 20th-century Slovenia in multimedia form, using film footage to bring each period to life.

Rising above the western end of the park is a series of wooded hills, including the 391-m (1,283-ft) high Rožnik Hill. Reached by a network of well-signposted tracks, the hill is topped by the Church of St Mary's Visitation.

Downhill from the church is the Pri Matiji Inn, once the home of famous novelist Ivan Cankar (1876–1918). The nearby **Cankar Memorial Room** (Spominska soba Ivana Cankarja) displays his writing desk and personal possessions.

⑦ Museum of Modern Art
Moderna galerija

Tomšičeva 14. **Map** D2. **Tel** (01) 241 6800. **Open** 10am–6pm Tue–Sun. **mg-lj.si**

The Museum of Modern Art contains the national collection of 20th-century art, along with paintings and sculptures from several other former Yugoslav republics. Slovenia was at the forefront of Modernism in the years following World War I and the movement is represented here by the Constructivist works of artist Avgust Černigoj and his poet collaborator Srečko Kosovel. More fascinating still is the work of the contemporary group Irwin, who mix avant-garde art and extreme political symbolism to create a series of ironic statements on the nature of national identity.

⑧ National Museum of Slovenia
Narodni muzej Slovenije

Prešernova 20. **Map** D2. **Tel** (01) 241 4400. **Open** 10am–6pm daily (until 8pm Thu). 🖼 🖼 **nms.si**

The National Museum of Slovenia was founded in 1821. Housed since 1888 in the grand Rudolfinum building, the museum features an impressive staircase overlooked by beautiful frescoes of cavorting muses.

The ground floor contains an extensive collection of expressively carved funerary monuments from the Roman settlement of Emona, together with a gilded bronze statue of a young male aristocrat. Ancient Egypt is represented by an intriguing 7th-century BC coffin of the priest Isahta, decorated with brightly painted hieroglyphs. Also on the ground floor is the numismatic collection, displaying ancient coins and bronze ingots as well as modern currency.

The upstairs galleries display Stone Age pottery, Copper Age vessels and implements from the Ljubljana marshes, along with Celtic weaponry and jewellery. The most valued

Magnificent staircase of the National Museum of Slovenia

em on display is the Vače
itula, a 30-cm (12-inch)
igh bronze bucket from
he 6th century BC that once
erved as a ritual drinking
essel. Its outer surface has
tunning frieze-like reliefs
epicting a parade of horse-
nen, a drinking party and a
ne of antelope-like animals
eing stalked by a big cat.

The museum's department
f History and Applied Arts
in a separate building at
Metelkova 25 and displays
bjects from the 14th century
o the present.

Plečnik House, residence of Slovenia's most influential architect

⑨ National and University Library
Narodna in univerzitetna knjižnica

urjaška 1. **Map** E4. **Tel** (01) 200 1188.
pen 8am–8pm Mon–Fri, 9am–2pm
at. 🅿 📷

et back from the west bank
f the Ljubljanica river on
he site of a former palace,
he National and University
ibrary is considered to be
he masterpiece of Jože
lečnik, the architect
esponsible for the
ppearance of
nodern Ljubljana.

Completed in
940, the landmark
uilding is typical of
lečnik's work, combining
ne straight lines
opular in the archi-
ecture of the period
with inspired decorative
etails. The exterior is a
atchwork of different hues,
nixing grey hunks of Slovene

granite with terracotta-
coloured brickwork. Inside, a
dark stairway of polished black
limestone leads to the brightly
lit first floor reading rooms,
symbolizing the transition
from ignorance to knowledge.
The exquisite doorknobs, table
lamps and chandeliers were all
designed by Plečnik himself,
fusing Art Deco with folk-
influenced motifs to create
a highly personalized style.

Immediately south of the
library is **Križanke**, a medieval
monastery complex
renovated by Plečnik and
turned into an outdoor
concert venue.

A major venue for rock
concerts in summer,
Križanke also hosts
several classical
music events as
part of the popular
Ljubljana Summer
Festival *(see p426)*, held
between July and August
every year.

Detail of library door handle

⑩ Plečnik House
Plečnikova hiša

Karunova 4. **Map** D5. **Tel** (01) 241
2500. **Closed** for restoration until May
2015. 🅿 📷 🆆 mgml.si

Present-day Ljubljana would
be unimaginable without the
work of Jože Plečnik, the
architect and town planner
responsible for the Triple
Bridge, Market Colonnade
(see p402) and the Ljubljanica
riverbank area, as well as the
National and University Library.
Plečnik's work was in many
ways a precursor of Post-
Modernism, combining pure
forms of modern architectural
style with ornamental details
drawn from Egypt, Classical
Greece and Central European
folk art.

The house where Plečnik
lived from 1921 until his death
in 1957 exemplifies his extraordinary commitment to the
world of architecture. With
each room having its own
design scheme, the house
now serves as an intimate
and absorbing museum of
his work. Visitors can view the
sunny, cylindrical annexe he
built to serve as a work space,
filled with furniture he
designed himself. Most of his
original plans, photographs
and models of his major works
are preserved here. Most
famous among his unfinished
projects is the Slovene
Acropolis, a monumental
parliament building originally
intended for Ljubljana's
Castle Hill.

erial view of the imposing National and University Library

❷ Postojna Cave
Postojnska jama

Slovenia's most popular natural attraction, Postojna Cave constitutes the longest subterranean system in the country, with over 20 km (12 miles) of chambers and tunnels. It was formed by the seeping waters of the Pivka river and its tributaries, which carved out several levels of underground galleries over a period of roughly three million years. The cave was first opened to visitors in 1819, with Austrian Emperor Francis I as the guest of honour. The site currently receives just under half a million people a year, making it one of the most-visited natural attractions in Europe. Inside, magnificent formations of stalactites and stalagmites seem to stretch endlessly in all directions.

Visitors outside the main entrance to Postojna Cave

Tracks and Walkways
Guided tours, lasting 90 minutes, begin with visitors riding an electric train into the heart of the cave, before embarking on a walking tour through a series of halls encrusted with intricate rock formations.

Stalactites, formed by constantly dripping water, hang from the ceiling of the cave.

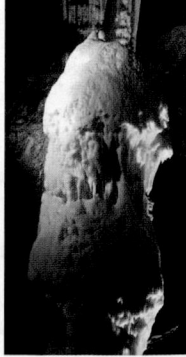

★ The Diamond
This huge stalagmite, also called "Brilliant", on account of its dazzling white surface and peculiar shape, is one of the highlights of the spectacular Winter Chamber.

Russian Bridge
Built by Russian prisoners during World War I, the Russian Bridge leads to the Macaroni Hall, which is covered with stunning pure-white stalactites.

For hotels and restaurants see p428 and p429

Big Mountain
This 45-m (147-ft) high rocky mound was created when the ceiling collapsed.

Predjama Castle, built into a natural rock arch on a hill slope

❸ Predjama Castle

Predjamski grad

50 km (31 miles) S of Ljubljana.
🚌 from Ljubljana. **Open** Jan–Mar,
Nov–Dec: 10am–4pm; Apr &
Oct: 10am–5pm; May, Jun & Sep:
9am–6pm; Jul & Aug: 9am–7pm. 🎦
📷 🎿 Erasmus Jousting Tournament
(Aug). 🌐 **postojnska-jama.eu**

The Vivarium
The cave is the natural habitat of this rare worm-like amphibian, known as the human fish. It can be seen in the Vivarium, where visitors can learn about species of the underground world.

★ **White Passage**
One among a series of chambers collectively known as Beautiful Caves, the White Passage is crammed with impressive stalagmites and stalactites.

There are few fortresses more dramatically situated than Predjama Castle, which stands halfway up a hillside at the mouth of a cave. The site was fortified as early as the 13th century. However, most of what remains today is the result of a 16th-century renovation by the then owner Ivan Kobencl.

The castle museum has several fascinating rooms containing period furnishings and weaponry. Several exhibits recall its 15th-century owner Erazem Lueger, a Robin Hood figure who, according to legend, was killed by a cannon ball that hit the castle. Inside the chapel is a delicately carved Gothic pietá dating from 1420.

Steep passageways descend into the **Cave** below the castle, an interesting, atmospheric underground chamber that can be visited only by guided tour.

🏠 Cave
🎦 📷 May–Sep: 11am, 1pm,
3pm & 5pm daily. 🌐 **postojnska-jama.eu**

★ **Concert Hall**
Visitors finally emerge into the Concert Hall, a vast space where orchestral performances are occasionally held, before returning by train to the cave entrance.

❹ Škocjan Caves
Škocjanske jame

80 km (51 miles) SW of Ljubljana.
🚉 from Divača. 🚌 ℹ️ Matavun, (05)
708 2110. **Open** check website for
timings. 🅿️ ♿ 🚻 🏛️ 📷 🚾 **park-skocjanske-jame.si**

Located in rolling countryside
just outside the town of Divača,
the Škocjan Caves are one of
Slovenia's most spectacular karst
features and a UNESCO World
Heritage Site. The labyrinthine
complex of passages and
collapsed valleys is believed to
be the world's largest network
of subterranean chambers and
remains only partially explored
to this day. About half of the
5 km (3 miles) of underground
passageways are open to the
public, accessible by a 90-minute
guided tour. Tickets are available
at the tourist information centre
in the village of Matavun, a short
distance from the cave entrance.
Highlights of the tour include
the 15-m (49-ft) long stalactites
of the Great Hall and the underwater river in the canyon-like
Murmuring Cave. The temperature
underground is a constant 12° C
(53° F), so warm clothing is
recommended.

❺ Koper

120 km (75 miles) SW of Ljubljana.
🏙️ 24,000. 🚉 🚌 ⛴️ ℹ️ Titov trg 3,
(305) 664 6403. 🚾 **koper.si**

Now Slovenia's main port, Koper
started off as a small Roman
settlement known as Goat Island
(Insula Caprea). It became a
major trading centre under the
Venetian Empire (1278–1797),

Main altar of the Cathedral of Mary's
Assumption, Koper

leaving its attractive Old Town
rich in Venetian-influenced
architecture. Koper was home
to a largely Italian-speaking
community until it became
part of Slovenia in 1954; the
town still bears traces
of its Italian heritage, with
bilingual street signs and
many locals speaking
both languages.

Central Koper is an
enjoyable warren of
narrow, pedestrian-only
streets, most of which meet at
Tito Square (Titov trg).
Its most enduring symbol, the
Praetorian Palace (Pretorska
palača), is a striking example of
Venetian Gothic architecture
with fancy tooth-like crenellations.
Embedded in the façade are
several coats of arms belonging
to distinguished families from
Koper. Opposite the palace
stands the town loggia, with

a beautifully proportioned
ground floor arcade. Also on
the square is the 12th-century
Cathedral of Mary's Assumption
(Stolna cerkev Marijinega
vnebovzetja), which contains
the ornate medieval sarcophagus
of local protector St Nazarius
behind the main altar. On the
right side of the transept is an
animated *Madonna with Child on
the Throne and Saints* attributed
to the Venetian painter Carpaccio
(1460–1526), who is believed
to have lived in Koper for a
time. Behind the cathedral is
a 12th-century rotunda that
originally served as the baptistry,
bearing a faded relief of St John
the Baptist above the door.

A short walk west of Tito
Square, the **Regional Museum**
(Pokrajinski muzej) houses a rich
collection of archaeological
finds and medieval stonework.
East of the square, the
Ethnographic Collection
(Etnološka zbirka) fills a
restored Gothic house
with a display of domestic
utensils, farmers' tools and
local costumes.

Stair detail,
Praetorian Palace

🏛️ **Regional Museum**
Kidričeva 19. **Tel** (05) 663
3570. **Open** 9am–5pm Tue–
Fri, 11am–5pm Sat (till 10pm May–
Aug), 11am–3pm Sun. 🅿️

🏛️ **Ethnographic Collection**
Gramscijev trg 4. **Tel** (05) 663
3586. **Open** 8am–4pm Mon–
Fri. 🅿️

❻ Piran

124 km (77 miles) SW of Ljubljana.
🏙️ 4,600. 🚌 ℹ️ (05) 673 4440.
🚾 **portoroz.si**

A jumble of pastel-coloured
houses on a small peninsula,
Piran is coastal Slovenia's most
charming town. The town
centres around Tartini Square
(Tartinijev trg), named after local
violinist and composer Giuseppe
Tartini (1692–1770); Antonio dal
Zotto's statue of Tartini occupies
the centre. The most striking
building on the square is the
14th-century wine-red Venetian
House (Benečanka hiša), with
delicate Gothic windows and
balustraded balconies. Nearby,

Breathtaking stalactites in a chamber in the Škocjan Caves

For hotels and restaurants see p428 and p429

Panoramic view of the coastal town of Piran, centred on Tartini Square

st Peter's Church (Cerkev sv Petra) contains a 14th-century crucifix that shows Jesus on a fork-shaped cross, thought to symbolize the Tree of Life. Tucked away in a small plaza behind the church, **Tartini House** (Tartinijeva hiša) honours the composer with a collection of heirlooms, including one of his violins.

Uphill from the square, narrow streets wind towards st George's Cathedral (Stolna Cerkev sv Jurja), a single-nave structure paired with a Venetian-style campanile. The small Parish Museum (Župnijski muzej) displays the church silverware, including an 18th-century statuette of St George studded with semi-precious stones. To the west of Tartini Square, the **Aquarium** (Akvarij) has a selection of fish and crustaceans indigenous to the Adriatic Sea. On the opposite side of the

harbour, the **Sergej Mašera Maritime Museum** (Pomorski muzej Sergej Mašera) recounts the history of Piran as a trading town.

Tartini House
Tartinijev trg. **Tel** (05) 663 3570. **Open** Jun–Aug: 9am–noon & 6–9pm daily; Sep–May: 11am–noon & 5–6pm daily.

Aquarium
Kidričevo nabrežje 4. **Tel** (05) 673 2572. **Open** mid-Jun to Aug: 9am–10pm daily; Sep–mid-Nov & mid-Mar–mid-Jun: 9am–7pm daily; mid-Nov–mid-Mar: 9am–5pm daily.

Sergej Mašera Maritime Museum
Cankarjevo nabrežje 4. **Tel** (05) 671 0040. **Open** Sep–Jun: 9am–5pm Tue–Sun; Jul–Aug: 9am–noon & 5–9pm Tue–Sun. **W pommuz-pi.si**

❼ Portorož

125 km (76 miles) SW of Ljubljana. ⌂ 13,000. 🚌 ℹ️ Obala 16, (05) 674 2220. **W portoroz.si**

Strung along the sun-bathed sweep of Piran Bay, Portorož is Slovenia's biggest beach resort. Apart from the grand Habsburg-era hotel – the Kempinski Hotel built in 1911 – most of the modern cafés, hotels and casinos bordering the palm-lined main boulevard date from the post-World War II period.

Portorož is a popular spa resort busy throughout the year thanks to a warm microclimate and the therapeutic qualities of the seawater. The large crescent beach, with its seaside park, has tennis and volleyball courts.

❽ Hrastovlje

104 km (65 miles) SW of Ljubljana. ⌂ 120. 🚉

Located in the arid hills above the coast, the rustic village of Hrastovlje is home to one of Slovenia's most outstanding medieval treasures. Crowning a hillock slightly apart from the rest of the village is the Romanesque **Holy Trinity Church** (Cerkev sv Trojice), its interior covered from floor to ceiling with dazzling frescoes painted by local artist John of Kastav in 1490. The most famous of the friezes is the *Dance of Death* on the southern wall, in which a group of skeletons leads people old and young, rich and poor alike, towards the grave. Many other scenes feature stories from the Bible. The main characters are clad in 15th-century attire, providing an insight into the lifestyle of late-medieval Slovenia.

Holy Trinity Church
Hrastovlje 6275. **Tel** (05) 664 6403 (Koper Tourist Office). **Open** 9am–noon & 1–5pm daily. **Closed** Tue.

Multistorey hotels along the tree-lined waterfront in Piran

The stone tower and walls of Holy Trinity Church, Hrastovlje

❾ Lipica

85 km (53 miles) SW of Ljubljana.
🅰 50. 🚌 🚐 🆆 lipica.org

Located near the Italian border in the hills above Trieste, the village of Lipica is synonymous with the Lipizzaner horses bred here since 1580. Established by the Habsburg Archduke Charles II of Styria, the **Lipica Stud Farm** crossed Spanish, Italian and Arab horses with local steeds, resulting in the uniquely graceful white Lipizzaner. The breed found favour with the Spanish Riding School *(see pp382–3)* in Vienna and has since been considered an aristocrat in the equine world.

Tours of the stables allow visitors to see the horses at close quarters, while the **Classical Riding School** stages shows in which the horses perform complex routines. The morning "Experience the Lipizzaner" session gives insight into the training of the Lipizzaners and their riders.

Riding courses and carriage trips can be arranged all year round. Riding courses must be booked in advance. The stable complex also contains Lipikum – museum of the Lipizzaner and an art gallery devoted to August Černigoj (1898–1985), the avant-garde painter who spent his final years in Lipica.

Lipica Stud Farm

Lipica 5. **Tel** (05) 739 1580.
🔵 Jan–Mar & Nov–Dec: 10am–3pm daily; Apr–Oct: 10am–5pm daily. 🚫 8 tours of the Lipica stables take place on the hour.

Classical Riding School

🔵 Apr–Oct: 3pm Tue, Fri & Sun; Experience the Lipizzaner: Apr–Oct: 10am–noon Tue–Sun. 🚫 🖥 📷
🆆 lipica.org

The colourful walls of Gewerkenegg Castle, Idrija

❿ Idrija

60 km (37 miles) W of Ljubljana.
🅰 6,500. 🚌 from Bovec. 🅸 Mestni trg 2, (05) 374 3916.
🆆 **visit-idrija.si**

One of the largest mercury mining centres in the world, Idrija once provided 13 per cent of the global output. Since active mining came to a halt in 2008, the town has begun to develop into a major centre of industrial heritage tourism.

The best way to get a feel of Idrija's mining past is to take the tour of **Anthony's Shaft** (Antonijev rov), a network of tunnels excavated in 1500. The tour starts with a video presentation about the history of the mine. Visitors are then led down the shaft, where mining techniques of the past are demonstrated. The **Town Museum** (Mestni muzej), housed in the 16th-century Gewerkenegg Castle, contains an exhibition on mining

history as well as an interesting display on Idrija lace-making – a household industry. Several industrial monuments are located around the town centre. The pavilion at St Francis' Shaft (Jašek Frančiške) contains a display of mining machinery, while the reconstructed 19th-century Miner's House (Rudarska hiša) shows how miners' families used to live.

Environs

Some 25 km (16 miles) north of Idrija is the **Franja Partisan Hospital**, a timber-built field hospital used by Slovene resistance fighters during World War II. Active from December 1943 until the end of the war, the hospital was damaged by floods in 2007 but is now restored.

🏛 Anthony's Shaft

Kosovelova 3. **Tel** (05) 377 1142.
🚫 📷 10am & 3pm Sat & Sun.

🏛 Town Museum

Prelovčeva 9. **Tel** (05) 372 6600.
Open 9am–6pm Mon–Fri. 🚫 📷

The Soča Front (Isonzo Front)

Portraits of World War I heroes in the Kobarid Museum *(see p414)*

During World War I, Italy declared war on Austria-Hungary in 1915, believing that victory would lead to territorial gains in the northern Adriatic Sea. The Soča Front, extending from north of Bovec through Kobarid to north of Trieste, Italy, served as the front line for almost three years. The Austrians used the mountainous terrain to their advantage, hurling back 12 successive Italian offensives. In 1917, the Italians were forced to retreat in the 12th battle, known as the Battle of Caporetto. Memories of the Soča Front are poignant for the Slovenes, who fought and died alongside Croats and Czechs, in defence of an Austro-Hungarian Empire that collapsed in 1918.

⓫ Soča Valley Tour

Famous for its turquoise Alpine waters, the Soča river, also known by its Italian name, Isonzo, rises in the Triglav National Park *(see pp418–21)* and flows south towards the Gulf of Trieste. The Soča valley has many features typical of the Slovene karst, including waterfalls, limestone gorges and rock formations. Several monuments recall the battles of World War I, when Italian and Austro-Hungarian forces fought for control of the valley.

Tips for Drivers

Starting point: Bovec. Highway number 203 from Bovec to Kobarid, and number 102 from Kobarid to Tomlin, run alongside the Soča river.
Length: 40 km (25 miles).
Stopping-off points: There are several restaurants along the route, especially in Kobarid; most serve traditional cuisine.

② Boka Waterfall
This tumbling waterfall in the hills west of Bovec is a popular tourist spot.

*Trenta
15 km
(9 miles)*

203 206

②

40 ● Žaga

203

Soča

● Drežnica

③

Robič Vrsno

102

102

Soča Valley

ITALY

⑤

④

103

Most na Soči

*Idrija
25 km
(15.5miles)*

102

① Bovec
The main town of the northern Soča valley, Bovec is Slovenia's leading resort for adventure sports.

0 kilometres 5
0 miles 5

③ Kobarid
The town of Kobarid witnessed the bloodiest battles of World War I. The town museum documents the suffering of the soldiers.

④ Tolmin
The museum in Tolmin sheds light on the costumes, trades and lifestyles of the valley's inhabitants.

Key
▬ Tour route
— Other road
— Railway
▬• International border

⑤ Tolminka Gorge
Northeast of Tolmin lies the steep Tolminka gorge, with a walking route running precariously above it. The Tolmin–Čadrg road crosses the gorge at the Devil's Bridge (Hudičev most).

Interior of the fascinating Kobarid Museum, Kobarid

⓬ Kobarid

118 km (73 miles) NW of Ljubljana.
🚗 4,500. 🚌 from Ljubljana.
ℹ️ Trg svobode 16, (05) 380 0490.
🌐 dolina-soce.com

A pleasant town characterized by a mix of Alpine and Italianate architecture, Kobarid (Caporetto in Italian) is famous as the site of the Battle of Caporetto (see p412), which saw Austro-Hungarian and German units rout their way through Italian lines in 1917. The **Kobarid Museum** (Kobariški muzej) poignantly documents the battle through a 20-minute film and mocked-up trenches. The museum's Black Room conveys the horrors of war through a distressing series of photographs.
East of the town centre lies **Charnel House**, a memorial for fallen Italian soldiers. It was opened in 1938, with Mussolini in attendance, when much of western Slovenia belonged to Italy. Inside the huge ossuary are the remains of soldiers killed on the Soča Front. The nearby Church of St Anthony, set on three tiers of arcaded octagonal

platforms, dominates the landscape of the lower Soča valley (see p413). A walking route heads north from the Charnel House on to the surrounding hillsides, where World War I trench positions can still be seen. The Kozjak waterfall nearby is well worth seeing.

🏛 **Kobarid Museum**
Gregorčičeva 10. **Tel** (05) 389 0000. **Open** Apr–Sep: 9am–6pm daily; Oct–Mar: 10am–5pm daily. 🅿️
📷 🌐 kobariski-muzej.si

⓭ Bovec

132 km (82 miles) NW of Ljubljana.
🚗 1,700. 🚌 ℹ️ Trg Golobarskih žrtev, (05) 384 1919.
🌐 bovec.si

Nestling on the eastern side of the Triglav massif, Bovec occupies the broad plain formed by the confluence of the Koritnica and Soča rivers. A paradise for

adrenalin junkies and nature lovers, the area offers numerous summer and winter sports activities and natural wonders. The stretch of the Soča river to the south and west of Bovec is regarded as prime white-water terrain, with numerous sports agencies offering rafting, kayaking and canoeing trips during the high season from April to September. However, the most popular attraction in these parts is the breathtaking **Boka Waterfall**, which tumbles from the karst some 6 km (4 miles) southwest of Bovec.

⓮ Kranjska Gora

85 km (53 miles) NW of Ljubljana.
🚗 5,500. 🚌 from Jesenice.
ℹ️ Kolodvorska ulica 1c, (04) 580 9440. 🌐 kranjska-gora.si

Set in the mountain-fringed Upper Sava valley, the Alpine town of Kranjska Gora is Slovenia's premier winter holiday resort. Most of the skiing trails are located on the slopes of the 1,555-m (5,102-ft) high Vitranc Mountain, southwest of the town. There are also ski slopes at Podkoren resort, 3 km (2 miles) up the valley.
Located alongside the lovely parish church is **Liznjek House**, Kranjska Gora's main urban attraction. A beautiful balconied 18th-century building, it was the property of a wealthy local farmer and once served as a

Skiing

The mountains of northern and western Slovenia provide a wealth of winter sports opportunities. The season runs from mid-December to late March and almost all ski cen-tres are equipped with snowmobiles. The largest resort, Kranjska Gora, has 20 km (13 miles) of ski trails. The Mariborsko Pohorje resort, outside Maribor (see p422), is Slovenia's largest ski area, with a wide range of intermediate runs and good facilities. Another favourite is Mount Vogel, accessible by cable car from Lake Bohinj (see pp420–21). Several ski centres can be visited on a day-trip from Velika Planina.

Winter sports enthusiasts skiing on the slopes of Velika Planina

The evocative Charnel House in Kobarid

Alpine houses with pretty window boxes, Kranjska Gora

country inn. Inside is a wonderful display of folk crafts and traditional furnishings including wooden beds, wardrobes, folk-painted trousseau chests and grandfather clocks painted with bright floral designs.

In summer, Kranjska Gora is a popular base for hiking in Triglav National Park *(see pp418–21)*. Starting at Mojstrana, 13 km (8 miles) east of Kranjska Gora, the Triglavska Bistrica walking trail runs up the ruggedly beautiful Vrata valley before reaching the forbidding north face of Mount Triglav, Slovenia's highest mountain.

For visitors wishing to explore the area by car, Kranjska Gora stands at the intersection of several scenic mountain routes. North of the town, a road winds dramatically across the Würzen pass towards the city of Villach in Austria. To the south are the hairpin bends of the Vršič pass, high among the peaks of Triglav National Park. A major feat of engineering, the road over the pass was built by Russian Prisoners of War during World War I, to send supplies to Habsburg armies defending the Soča Front.

To the west of Kranjska Gora lies Planica valley, the site of one of the world's highest ski jumps. Ski jumps in Planica are symbols of Slovene prowess in winter sports and annually host the famous ski-jumping World Cup.

⓯ Bled

See pp416–17.

⓰ Triglav National Park

See pp418–21.

⓱ Velika Planina

30 km (19 miles) NE of Ljubljana.
🚠 🔲 velikaplanina.si

Literally meaning "Big Mountain", Velika Planina is one of the most popular destinations in the Kamnik Alps. Reached by cable car from the Kamniška Bistrica valley, at 1,666 m (5,466 ft) it is a relatively smooth mountain, covered in highland pastures where dairy herds graze during the summer. Scattered across the mountain are wooden huts topped by broad shingle roofs and surrounded by wooden stockades. A unique form of traditional architecture, they were built by local shepherds as seasonal sleeping quarters.

In winter, Velika Planina is a popular out-of-town destination for skiers, offering a choice of downhill and cross-country runs. It is also busy during summer, when its well-marked paths become busy with hikers. Many choose to walk up the mountain without taking the cable car, an exhilarating hike that begins in the village of Stahovica.

⓲ Logarska Dolina

100 km (62 miles) NE of Ljubljana. Taxi from Ljubljana. 🔲 logarska-dolina.si

Hidden away on the northern side of the Kamnik Alps, the Logarska Dolina valley is one of the most beautiful spots in northern Slovenia. It is a typical example of a glacier-carved valley, with a level green valley floor dotted with dairy farms and steep sides where dense forests give way to bare cliffs. The relatively isolated valley can be entered via the village of **Solčava**, which is accessed by road from the regional centre of Velenje, a mining town located 50 km (31 miles) northeast of Ljubljana. Solčava itself is famous for the splendid 13th-century Solčava Madonna, a Romanesque statuette housed in the local parish church.

About 2 km (1 mile) beyond Solčava is the starting point of the landscape park, Logarska Valley hiking route, which runs for 6 km (4 miles) along the valley floor to reach the charming Rinka Waterfall, surrounded by grizzled grey mountain peaks.

Running parallel to Logarska Dolina to the west is **Matkov Kot**, another stunning glacial valley. The main target for hikers here is the famous Matk's Tub (Matkov Škaf), a dramatic circular hollow gouged out of bare rock by a seasonal waterfall.

Distinctive conical, shingled wooden huts on Velika Planina

⑮ Bled

With its placid lake, fairy-tale island church, clifftop castle and girdle of grey mountains, Bled has become a visual trademark for the Slovene tourist industry. Although it emerged as a popular spa resort in the mid-19th century, Bled's key attractions today consist of boat trips to the island church and excursions into the Alpine surroundings. Offering plenty of good hotels, Bled also makes a good base for exploring nearby places of interest such as the enchanting Lake Bohinj and Triglav National Park *(see pp418–19)*. In winter, buses connect Bled with the skiing and snowboarding centre at Mount Vogel, near Lake Bohinj.

Boats moored on the forested lakeshore, Bled

🎋 Lake Bled

Just over 2 km (1 mile) long, 2 km (1 mile) wide and 30 m (98 ft) deep, Lake Bled (Blejsko jezero) fills a hollow gouged out by retreating glaciers towards the end of the last Ice Age. With wooded hills surrounding the lake and Alpine peaks in the distance, it is nothing less than truly entrancing. The best way to soak in the landscape is to walk along the path which leads right around the lake, a circuit that takes about an hour to complete. The most stunning views are from the western end, with the church spire on Bled Island set against the stupendous backdrop of the snow-capped Karavanke Alps.

On the southern shore of the lake, visitors can stop by the gardens of Vila Bled, built for Yugoslav strongman Josip Broz Tito in 1947 and now converted into an upmarket hotel.

🏰 Bled Castle

Tel (04) 572 9782. **Open** 8am–6pm daily (until 8pm Apr–Oct). 🅿️ 🚫 📷 ♿ 🅦 blejski-grad.si

Dramatically located on a sheer cliff overlooking the lake's eastern end, Bled Castle (Blejski grad) began as the 11th-century stronghold of the Bishops of Brixen, who ruled over the area until 1803. Rebuilt by various owners over the years, the castle now houses an absorbing museum and a restaurant.

The former features an imaginative audio-visual display, detailing both the history of the castle and the development of tourism in the region. Replicas of historical costumes recall the Slavs who first settled in the area in the 6th century, while a natural history section exhibits the 5th-century skeleton of an elk. The wine cellar and printing works are also worth a visit.

Outside, the castle terrace commands an outstanding view, with the lake directly below and the Karavanke mountain range looming in the distance.

Bled Island

Open May–Sep: 9am–7pm daily; Nov–Mar: 9am–4pm; Apr & Oct: 9am–6pm. 🚫 📷 ♿ 🅦 blejskiotok.si

Perched atop the hummock-shaped Bled Island (Blejski otok), the creamy-ochre Church of the Assumption (Cerkev Marijinega vnebovzetja) occupies a site that has been sacred for centuries.

The island initially served pagan Slavs as a shrine, inspiring a famous episode in France Prešeren's epic poem "Baptism at the Savica" ("Krst pri Savici"), in which the Slovene prince, Črtomir, falls in love with the beautiful Bogomila, daughter of the island shrine's guardian.

After the region's conversion to Christianity, the island became a focus of Catholic pilgrimage. It has been associated with the cult of the Virgin Mary since the early Middle Ages, when a wooden chapel stood on the site of the current church. Pilgrimages

Bled Castle, perched on a rock above the town

For hotels and restaurants see p428 and p429

Church of the Assumption on Bled Island

rainy days) or by traditional canopied rowing boat (*pletna*). Visitors disembark at the bottom of a 99-step staircase, which leads to the front door of the church. Inside are the fragmentary remains of some 15th-century frescoes illustrating the lives of the Virgin Mary and Jesus Christ.

Hanging from a small tower above the nave is the 15th-century Wishing Bell, which was presented to the church by a wealthy pilgrim whose prayers had been answered. Among the various legends surrounding it, it is believed that the original bell sank in a shipwreck and had to be replaced by one donated by the Pope. It is also believed that those who ring the bell to honour the Blessed Virgin will have their wishes granted.

People used to walk across the ice to the church during harsh winters, although ice is a rare occurrence nowadays.

boomed during the Baroque era, when the church was expanded and redecorated. Today, the island remains a popular place for pilgrimages on the Marian feast days, notably the Ascension and the Birth of the Virgin. These are traditionally all-night affairs with participants arriving late in the evening and celebrating mass at 4am. The island is open to visitors throughout the year and can be reached either by electrical boats (in winter or on

Vintgar Gorge

Tel (04) 572 5266. **Open** Apr–Oct:
8am–7pm daily. 🏃 🚻

Located 4 km (2 miles) north of Bled, Vintgar gorge (Soteska Vintgar) is a 2-km (1-mile) long ravine carved by the rushing waters of the Radovna river. In 1893, the locals decided to construct wooden walkways and galleries to make the ravine accessible to visitors, turning it into a major attraction. Visiting the gorge is an exhilarating experience as the trail winds its way beneath sheer cliffs, passing gurgling rapids and whirlpools on the way. The walkway culminates at the 16-m (52-ft) high Šum Waterfall, which marks the northern end of the gorge. The waterfall is at its most impressive in spring, when it throws up clouds of steam.

Bled Town Centre

① Lake Bled
② Bled Castle
③ Bled Island

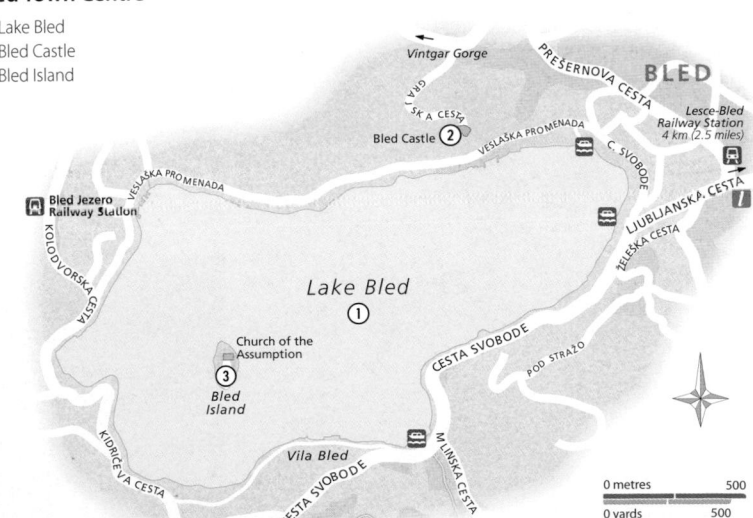

For keys to symbols *see back flap*

⓰ Triglav National Park

Triglavski narodni park

Established in 1961, Slovenia's only national park is centred on the country's highest mountain, the 2,864-m (9,396-ft) high Mount Triglav. Starkly beautiful outcrops of bare limestone characterize the higher altitudes of the park, while its lower reaches encompass forests of spruce and beech, which are home to a fantastic range of flora and fauna. An outstanding network of picturesque trails, valleys, deep blue lakes and peaks makes Triglav National Park one of the most visited places in the country.

Alpinium Juliana
This lush botanical garden on the southern approaches of the Vršič Pass showcases the diverse flora of the Slovene Alps. About 600 botanical species can be found here.

Soča Trail
This 20-km (12-mile) long trail runs along the Soča river as it carves its way through the pine-fringed Trenta valley to the tiny hamlet of Kršovec.

0 kilometres   5

0 miles   5

Valley of the Triglav Lakes
This sequence of seven glacial lakes, surrounded by boulders and spruce trees, constitutes one of the park's most captivating sights.

Key

===== Minor road

▬ ▬ Walking trail

– ▬ Cycle route

▬ ▬ Park boundary

– – International border

△ summit

For hotels and restaurants see p428 and p429

Vrata Valley
A classic glacial valley on the northern side of Mount Triglav, Vrata valley is overlooked by towering limestone rock formations.

VISITORS' CHECKLIST

Practical Information
ℹ️ Bled: Ljubljanska cesta 27, (04) 578 0200; Trenta: Na Logu, (05) 3889 330; Mojstrana: Pocar Farm, Zgornja Radovna 25, (04) 578 0200. 📷 🚻 on Lake Bohinj and in Bled and Kranjska Gora, just outside the park. 🇼 **tnp.si**

Transport
60 km (37 miles) NW of Ljubljana. 🚌 from Bled.

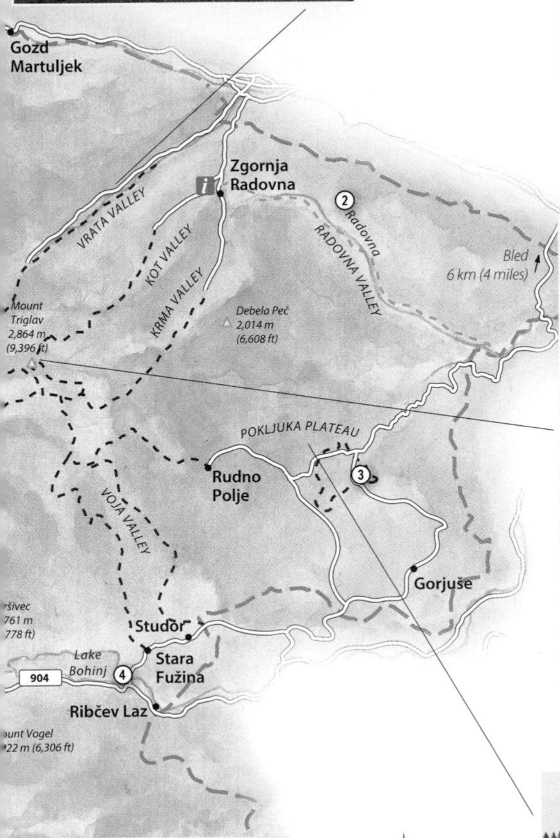

Gozd Martuljek

VRATA VALLEY

Zgornja Radovna ℹ️

KOT VALLEY

KRMA VALLEY

② Radovna

RADOVNA VALLEY

Bled 6 km (4 miles)

Mount Triglav 2,864 m (9,396 ft)

Debela Peč 2,014 m (6,608 ft)

POKLJUKA PLATEAU

VOJA VALLEY

Rudno Polje

③

Gorjuše

Ršivec 761 m 778 ft)

Lake Bohinj

904

④

Studor

Stara Fužina

Ribčev Laz

unt Vogel 22 m (6,306 ft)

Mount Triglav
Slovenia's highest peak, Mount Triglav is a national symbol; its three-peaked silhouette appears on the national flag.

KEY

① **Vršič Pass**, a spectacular mountain road cutting through the heart of the park, features an exhilarating sequence of hairpin bends.

② **The Radovna cycle route** leads visitors through verdant farmland dotted with traditional villages.

③ **The Goreljek Peat-Bog Nature Trail** passes through unspoilt wetlands, rich in cranberries, bilberries and the insect-devouring sundew plant.

④ **Lake Bohinj** (see pp420–21) is the largest water body in Slovenia.

Pokljuka Plateau
This unspoilt area of pine forests and pastures is criss-crossed by nature trails. The highlight is the Pokljuka Gorge, which burrows through the plateau's northern flanks.

Triglav National Park: Lake Bohinj

Tucked into the southeastern corner of Triglav National Park, Lake Bohinj is a beautiful expanse of water, fed by clear mountain streams and with high mountains on almost all sides. Surrounded by some of Slovenia's best-preserved rustic villages, it is ideal for swimming and kayaking and an excellent base from which to explore the region's hiking trails. In winter, Mount Vogel, to the south of the lake, is a popular spot for skiing and snowboarding, while the frozen lake provides a great opportunity for ice skating.

Visitors canoeing near Ribčev Laz, at the eastern end of Lake Bohinj

Slap Savica
A popular walking trail west from Ukanc leads to Slap Savica, a pair of waterfalls surrounded by high cliffs. Their waters feed the Sava river, which flows southeast to meet the Danube at Belgrade in Serbia.

*Slap Savica
1.5km (1mile)*

Savica

Ukanc

*Mount Vogel
1.5 km (1 mile)*

Ukanc
The small village of Ukanc, at the lake's western end, has pebbly beaches and is surrounded by the peaks of Pršivec and Komna.

Mount Vogel
At an altitude of 1,800 m (5,906 ft), Mount Vogel is a paradise for skiers in winter and hikers in summer. The cable car from the shores of Lake Bohinj ascends to a plateau from where there are breathtaking views of the Triglav massif to the north.

Stara Fužina
With charming Alpine farmhouses, Stara Fužina is one of the best-preserved traditional villages in western Slovenia. The 13th-century St Paul's Church, in the outskirts of the village, is also worth a visit.

VISITORS' CHECKLIST

Practical Information
Ribčev Laz 48, (04) 574 6010.
Zlatorog campsite, (04) 572 3482. **bohinj.si** Mount Vogel Cable Car: **Open** May–mid-Oct: 8am–6pm daily. Cable car runs every half hour in peak season, hourly at other times. Church of St John: **Open** Jul & Aug: 9am–noon daily.

Transport
82 km (51 miles) NW of Ljubljana. from Lesce-Bled and Ljubljana. from Bled and Ljubljana.

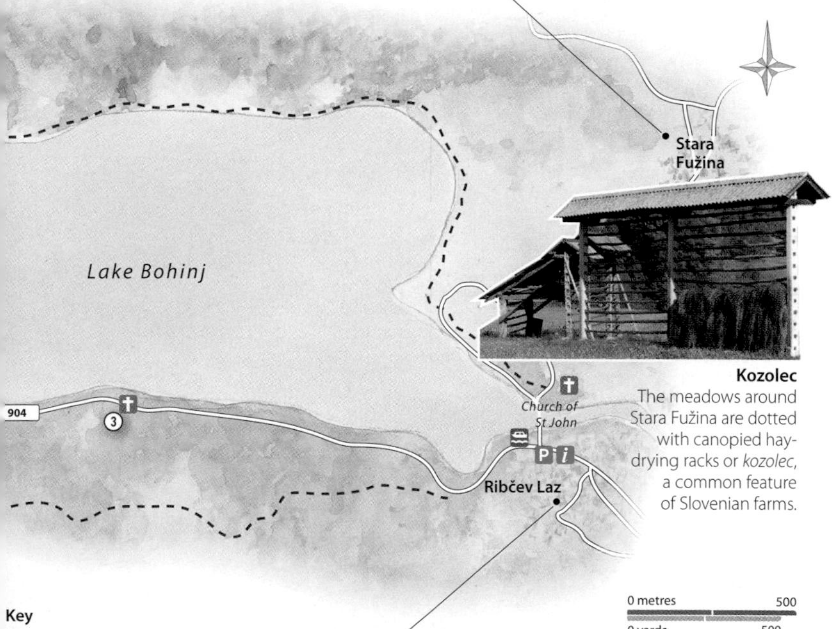

Lake Bohinj

Stara Fužina

Kozolec
The meadows around Stara Fužina are dotted with canopied hay-drying racks or *kozolec*, a common feature of Slovenian farms.

Church of St John

Ribčev Laz

0 metres   500
0 yards   500

Key

═══ Minor road

▬ ▬ Trail

KEY

① **The cable car to Mount Vogel** begins from the southern shores of Bohinj.

② **A World War I Cemetery** holds the graves of about 300 soldiers buried between 1915 and 1917.

③ **The Church of the Holy Spirit** (Cerkev sveti Duh) has a fine bell tower and contains a number of notable 15th- and 16th-century frescoes.

★ **Ribčev Laz**
The main settlement at the eastern end of Lake Bohinj, Ribčev Laz is famous for its dainty parish Church of St John (sveti Janez), which contains some late-Gothic frescoes.

For keys to symbols *see back flap*

⑲ Maribor

Slovenia's second largest city, Maribor occupies a strategic location on the Drava river. Settled by Slavs in the early Middle Ages, the city became an important trading centre. However, with the expansion of the Ottoman Empire, it turned into a border fortress and trade declined. The city's fortunes improved with the construction of the Vienna–Trieste railway in 1846. Today, it has a mix of old and new architecture; the riverside quarter of Lent has the most attractive Baroque buildings.

Ornate west wing façade of the 15th-century Maribor Castle

🏛 Maribor Castle and Regional Museum

Grajski trg 4. **Tel** (02) 228 3551. **Open** 9am–1pm & 4–7pm Tue–Sat, 9am–2pm Sun. ♿ 🖥 **pmuzej-mb.si**

Dominating the northern end of Castle Square (Grajski trg), Maribor Castle (Mariborski grad) was built in 1478 to protect Maribor from Ottoman attacks. Once the Turkish threat receded, the castle became an aristocratic residence. Today, it is home to the Regional Museum (Pokrajinski muzej), which displays folk costumes, military uniforms, furniture spanning several eras and Gothic and Baroque religious art. The building's 18th-century Rococo staircase, adorned with statues, is remarkable.

🏛 Cathedral

Slomškov trg. **Tel** (02) 251 8432. **Open** dawn–dusk daily.

Just southwest of the castle, Maribor's medieval cathedral (Katedrala) is predominantly Gothic in style, although a characterful Renaissance bell tower was added in 1601. The interior decorations date mostly from the Baroque period, although some exquisitely carved medieval stone stalls remain in the choir. A chapel to the left of the main altar is dedicated to Bishop Anton Slomšek, who promoted the Slovenian language at a time when Maribor was ruled by a German-speaking elite.

🏛 Main Square

The town's long, rectangular Main Square (Glavni trg) took shape in the 13th century, when Maribor was emerging as a major commercial centre in the region. On its northern side is the Town Hall (Rotovž), with an onion-domed clock tower and an arcaded Renaissance courtyard at the back. In the

Baroque Plague Column on the Maribor's Main Square

Maribor City Centre

① Maribor Castle and Regional Museum
② Cathedral
③ Main Square
④ Lent
⑤ The Jewish Quarter

[Map of Maribor City Centre showing streets including GREGORČIČEVA, ULICA, GRAJSKA ULICA, TRUBARJEVA ULICA, SLOVENSKA, PARTIZANSKA CESTA, GRAJSKI TRG, VOLKMERJEV PREHOD, ULICA SKORA MAKSIMILIANA DREŽENIKA, SLOMŠKOV TRG, OROŽNOVA ULICA, POŠTNA ULICA, LEKARNIŠKA UL, ROTOVŠKI TRG, GOSPOSKA ULICA, JURČIČEVA UL, OB JARKU, VETRINJSKA ULICA, KOROŠKA CESTA, ŽIDOVSKA ULICA, DRAVSKA, GLAVNI MOST, USNJARSKA ULICA, ULICA SLOVENSKE OSAMOSVOJITVE, PRISTAN. Landmarks: Maribor Castle and Regional Museum ①, Bus and Railway Stations 550 m (600 yards), Cathedral of St John the Baptist ②, Town Hall, Main Square ③, Plague Monument, St Alosius's Church, Old Vine, Lent ④, The Jewish Quarter ⑤, Synagogue, Water Tower, Judgement Tower, Drava river]

0 metres 200
0 yards 200

Old Vine adorning the Drava riverfront in the Lent quarter

centre of the square is an ornate Baroque Plague Column (Kužno znamenje), raised in 1743 to commemorate all the people from the city who died during the Great Plague of the 17th century.

🏛 Lent

Downhill from the city centre is the charming riverside quarter of Lent, which was once a busy port from where rafts laden with local timber began their journey south along the Drava and Danube rivers.

Today, Lent is a bustling neighbourhood, its well-preserved Baroque houses home to modern art galleries, cafés and bars. Growing along the façade of one of the waterfront houses is the famous 400-year-old Old Vine (Stara trta), the oldest vine in the world. Marking Lent's

western boundary is the **Judges' Tower** (Sodni stolp), a barrel-shaped medieval structure with a curious mansard roof. To the east is the rather peculiar 16th-century **Water Tower** (Vodni stolp) featuring a pentagonal ground plan and a tall, tapering roof.

🏛 The Jewish Quarter
Synagogue Židovska 4. **Tel** (02) 252 7836. **Open** 8am–4pm Mon–Fri. 🅦 sinagogamaribor.si

Standing on a terrace immediately inland from the Water Tower is the Jews' Tower (Židovski stolp), a quadrangular red-brick structure attached to a short stretch of the surviving city wall. The narrow lanes beside the tower were once home to Maribor's Jewish community, who were an important presence in the city from the 13th century until their extermination by the Nazis during World War II. The beautifully restored 14th-century Synagogue (Sinagoga) now houses an exhibition devoted to local Jewish heritage.

Period furnishings at the Regional Museum, Ptuj Castle

⑳ Ptuj

135 km (84 miles) NE of Ljubljana.
🚏 11, 000. 🚆 🚌 🛈 Slovenski trg 5, (02) 779 6011. 🎭 Ptuj Carnival (late Feb/early Mar). 🅦 ptuj.info

Set on the banks of the Drava river, the charming rural town of Ptuj is one of the oldest in Slovenia. During the Roman period, it served as a legionary base and the centre of local trade. Ptuj's most revered sight is the 2nd-century **Orpheus Monument** (Orfejev spomenik), the carved tombstone of a Roman administrator, which depicts the scene of Orpheus playing the lyre and taming a group of wild animals. This stands on Slovenski Square (Slovenski trg), in the town centre. Slightly uphill from the monument, **St George's Church** (Cerkev sv Jurij) is a treasure trove of Gothic religious art, with a famous statue of St George near the main entrance. The grand attraction of the town, however, is the fortified **Ptuj Castle** (Ptujski grad), dating from the 10th century. Expanded several times, the most important renovation occurred under Walter Leslie, Baron of Balquhane, in the 1650s. The castle is now home to the Regional Museum, which boasts an extensive archaeological collection, furniture acquired through the ages and a section on local ethnography.

🏰 Ptuj Castle
Tel (02) 748 0360. **Open** May–mid-Oct: 9am–6pm daily; mid-Oct–Apr: 9am–5pm daily. 🎨 🖥

Water Tower on the banks of the calm Drava river, Maribor

Practical & Travel Information

With Slovenia's popularity as a holiday destination growing rapidly, standards in the travel industry here have improved greatly. Slovenia is one of the better-developed countries in South Eastern Europe and travelling is a pleasant experience. The extensive road network is in good condition and public transport is efficient and well organized. The country also has a modern communications network, making it easy to keep in touch by telephone, post or Internet. Many young Slovenes speak fluent English, and Italian and German are also widely spoken.

When to Visit

Slovenia's vibrant capital city, Ljubljana, is a year-round destination. Elsewhere in the country, April to October is the best time to visit as many museums and tourist attractions have restricted opening hours, or close altogether, for the rest of the year. July and August can be hot in lowland areas and along the coast, but in other parts of the country, cool Alpine breezes create the perfect conditions for summer hiking.

Mountain resorts are at their liveliest during the winter sports season, which lasts from mid-December until March.

Documentation

Citizens of the European Union (EU) can enter Slovenia on presentation of a valid identity card. Citizens of the US, Canada, Australia and New Zealand require a valid passport to visit Slovenia and can stay for up to 90 days. The official website of the **Slovene National Tourist Office** offers guidance on visa regulations and extended visits.

Visitor Information

The **Slovene Tourist Information Centre** provides brochures and information leaflets on tours and transportation. The **Ljubljana Tourist Information Centre** also maintains a website in English. Most towns have their own information centres. The staff, most of whom speak English, are usually proficient in several foreign languages and helpful in providing information on accommodation and events.

Health and Security

High standards of hygiene and health care are maintained in Slovenia and no special vaccinations are required for a visit to the country. Most town centres have a pharmacy (*lekarna*) with trained staff, most of whom speak English. These are open from 8am to 7pm, Monday to Friday, and for a few hours on Saturday mornings. In Ljubljana, there are pharmacies that stay open all night.

Slovenia has a very low crime rate and is considered extremely safe. The threat posed by petty thieves and pickpockets is relatively minor, but visitors should still be on their guard, particularly in crowded buses and busy shopping centres.

Banking and Currency

Banks are open from 8:30am to 5pm, Monday to Friday and from 8:30 to 11am on Saturday mornings. Credit cards are widely accepted and ATMs are easy to find throughout the country. On January 1 2007, Slovenia officially adopted the euro. It is advisable to exchange foreign currency at banks and bureaus rather than hotels as they offer better exchange rates.

Communications

Postal and telephone services in Slovenia are problem free. Public phones use *telekartice* (phone cards), which can be purchased from post offices, tobacco shops and newspaper kiosks. However, for long distance and international calls it is best to go to the post office. The Slovene postal service is well developed. Post offices are open from 8am to 7pm, Monday to Friday and from 8am to 1pm on Saturdays. Internet cafés are common in several city centres and most hotels now offer Wi-Fi Internet connection to guests.

Facilities for the Disabled

There has been a significant improvement in recent years with regard to the needs of the disabled traveller. The **Paraplegics Association of Slovenia** gives advice on the facilities available. Public transport offers wheelchair facilities while ramps feature in a number of train stations. High-end hotels have at least one room equipped for wheelchair users, however, this is less common in the lower-category hotels.

The Climate of Slovenia

Slovenia has a continental climate characterized by warm, dry summers and fairly cold winters. In summer, daytime temperatures reach 20° C to 25° C (68° F to 77° F). The weather is best from May to September, when the days are warm and the nights cool. January is the coldest month with temperatures frequently falling below freezing point.

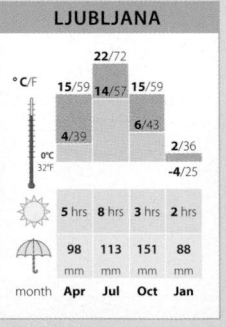

LJUBLJANA			
°C/F	**22/72**		
	15/59 **14/57** 15/59		
4/39		6/43	
0°C 32°F			2/36
			-4/25
5 hrs	8 hrs	3 hrs	2 hrs
98 mm	113 mm	151 mm	88 mm
month **Apr**	**Jul**	**Oct**	**Jan**

Arriving by Air

The easiest way to reach Slovenia is to fly. The Slovene national airline, **Adria Airways**, has direct scheduled flights from London's Gatwick Airport to **Ljubljana Airport** at Brnik, situated 26 km (16 miles) north of the capital. In addition, budget airline **easyJet** flies several times a week from London's Stansted airport to Ljubljana. There are no direct flights from the US and Canada to Slovenia, but there are several one-stop options involving a change of flight in Amsterdam, Frankfurt or London. A regular bus service runs daily from the Brnik airport to Ljubljana bus station until around 8pm. A privately operated minibus shuttle service is also available, which runs till slightly later.

Rail Travel

The Slovene railways run a smooth service. Ljubljana stands at the centre of the rail network, offering fast and punctual services to destinations such as Maribor, Postojna, Koper, Ptuj and Bled. Mountainous areas such as the Triglav National Park (see pp418–21) and the Soča valley (see p413) are not served by train; however, they are well connected by bus.

Within Slovenia, trains fall into three categories. InterCity Slovenia (ICS) operate on the Ljubljana-Maribor-Ljubljana route. In the summer and on Saturdays, Sundays and public holidays, ICS trains also operate along the Maribor-Ljubljana-Koper route and back. EuroCity (EC) operate along major international routes and connect important economic and tourist hubs in Slovenia and Europe. EuroNight (EN) are international night trains, which include sleepers and couchettes. Regional (RG) and other passenger (potniški) trains (LV) connect Slovenian towns on shorter and longer routes. These are intended primarily for daily journeys to and from work or school.

Ljubljana is a good starting point for onward travel to Central Europe, with daily trains from the **Ljubljana Train Station** to Vienna, Budapest, Zagreb and Belgrade.

Travelling by Bus

The **Ljubljana Bus Station** serves most destinations in Slovenia. Major towns and cities have frequent departures, although smaller destinations may only have one or two buses a day. Timetable information regarding bus services is available on the bus station's website.

Buses are comfortable and ticket prices reasonable. International services also run daily to Belgrade and Sarajevo.

Travelling by Car

Slovenia's well-surfaced roads are uncrowded and well signposted. In order to drive here each vehicle must display a windscreen sticker or vinjeta (vignette), which can be bought from petrol stations and newspaper kiosks. A weekly vignette for a car costs €15.

Ljubljana's central location means that a drive from here to anywhere else in the country can be completed in two hours or less. Two-lane highways run southwest from Ljubljana to the Adriatic coast, and east to Maribor.

Note that mountain roads, especially the Predel pass and the Vršič pass in the Triglav National Park, may be closed in winter due to harsh weather conditions.

DIRECTORY

Documentation

Slovene National Tourist Office
w slovenia.info

Visitor Information

Free telephone Information line
Tel 080 1900.

Ljubljana Tourist Information Centre
Adamič-Lundrovo nabrežje 2, Ljubljana.
Tel (01) 306 1215.
w visitljubljana.com

Slovene Tourist Information Centre
Krekov trg 10, Ljubljana.
Tel (01) 306 4575.
w slovenia.info

Embassies

Australia
Železna cesta 14.
Ljubljana.
Tel (01) 234 8675.
w dfat.gov.au

Canada
Linhartova cesta 49a, Ljubljana.
Tel (01) 252 4444.

United Kingdom
Trg Republike 3, Ljubljana.
Tel (01) 200 3910.
w ukinslovenia.fco.gov.uk

United States
Prešernova 31, Ljubljana.
Tel (01) 200 5500.
w slovenia.usembassy.gov

Emergency Numbers

Ambulance
Tel 112.

Fire
Tel 112.

Police
Tel 113.

Facilities for the Disabled

Paraplegics Association of Slovenia
Štihova 14, Ljubljana.
Tel (01) 432 7138.
w zveza-paraplegikov.si

Arriving by Air

Adria Airways
Tel 080 1300 (Slovenia),
(01) 369 1010 (call UK)
w adria.si

Easyjet
w easyjet.com

Ljubljana Airport
Brnik.
Tel (04) 206 1981.
w lju-airport.si

Rail Travel

Ljubljana Train Station
Trg Osvobodilne fronte 4.
Tel (01) 291 3391.
w slo-zeleznice.si

Travelling by Bus

Ljubljana Bus Station
Trg Osvobodilne fronte, Ljubljana.
Tel 1991.
w ap-ljubljana.si

Shopping & Entertainment

Slovenia has a lively and varied shopping culture that embraces old-style outdoor markets as well as modern malls. A wide range of handmade goods is available including crystal, black pottery and fine lace. Food items are also of particularly high quality. As for entertainment, the Slovenes are outgoing people. They enjoy spending time in the country's cafés and bars and the capital city, Ljubljana, has a vibrant clubbing scene. Theatres and concert venues can be found in all the country's cities. Several interesting local events, such as excellent traditional music and art festivals are also held in most big cities and towns.

Opening Hours

Shops are mostly open from 8am to 7pm Monday to Friday and from 8am to 2pm on Saturday. Only a handful of food shops stay open on Saturday afternoons and Sundays.

Markets

The area around Ljubljana's Slovenska cesta offers the most choice in the way of high-street shops and department stores, while the nearby Old Town is the best place for luxury goods, gifts and souvenirs. At the northern end of the Old Town, Ljubljana's colourful main market offers a variety of fresh fruit and vegetables as well as delicates-sen products, dried herbs and craft items. The Sunday morning antiques and bric-a-brac market on the Ljubljanica riverbank is full of potential discoveries. Most towns have their own markets selling fruits, vegetables and home-cured meats.

Crafts and Souvenirs

Slovenia is renowned for its traditional handicrafts. Quality crystal from the town of Rogaška in the east of the country can be found at **Galerija Rogaška** in Ljubljana's Old Town. The delightfully intricate lace made by the women of Idrija is available at **Galerija Idrijske Čipke**, also in the Old Town. An especially typical form of folk art is the decoration of beehives with scenes depicting village life or wild animals. Painted boards displaying beehive motifs and

black pottery are exhibited in museums, but are also sold in most souvenir shops, including **Etnogalerija Skrina** in Ljubljana.

Lavishly illustrated books on Slovene architecture, the natural landscape and folk traditions are sold at bookshops. **Mladinska Knjiga Konzorcij** in Ljubljana is one of the bigger outlets where these books can be purchased.

Food and Drink

Many of Slovenia's delicatessen products make ideal gifts, with *pršut* (home-cured ham) of the karst region topping the list. Other gourmet delights include *klobase* (farmhouse sausages), *med* (honey) and *bučno olje* (pumpkin seed oil).

Most food shops and supermarkets stock a wide selection of Slovene wines. Alongside excellent Merlots, Sauvignons and Rieslings, there are a handful of outstanding indigenous wines: the dry white šipon from eastern Slovenia; rich red teran from the karst region; and the gentler red refosk from the coast. Strong *viljamovka* (Williams pear brandy), the splendid *brinjevec* (Juniper brandy) and delicious *slivovka* (plum brandy) are among the most popular local spirits.

Pubs and Bars

Most places in Slovenia have a downtown area with cafés and bars. The Old Town in Ljubljana and the Lent riverside area in Maribor are two of the liveliest places for bar hopping. Clubbing

and live music are major features of Ljubljana's nightlife, although venues change from one year to the next. Fans of live rock should head to **Metelkova Mesto**, a former Yugoslav Army barracks that has been taken over by several alternative cultural organizations and transformed into a variety of bar and club venues.

Classical Music

Slovenia offers a diverse musical repertoire. The **Slovene National Theatre**, **Opera and Ballet** and the **Slovene Filharmonic** are among the best of their kind in Central Europe.

Located in the heart of Ljubljana, **Cankarjev Dom** can claim to be one of Europe's finest cultural venues frequently hosting top international performances.

Tickets for concerts are available from the box offices of the venues themselves.

Festivals

Festivals form an integral part of Slovenian cultural life. The popular **Ljubljana Summer Festival** embraces classical music, jazz, opera and folk and usually takes place from July to mid-September.

Other well-known annual festivals include **Druga Godba**, featuring ethnic music from around the world, which takes place in Ljubljana during May. Tickets for both the Summer Festival and Druga Godba can be obtained from the Ljubljana Summer Festival box office opposite the Križanke concert venue. The noted **Lent Festival**, which covers everything from pop to classical music on outdoor riverside stages, takes place in Maribor from late June to early July.

Slovenia also has firmly rooted seasonal traditions, as evidenced by its famous Pust Festival. Held in February each year, this is regarded as the most famous of Slovenia's pre-Lent carnivals and involves riotous displays of masked revelry.

Sports Activities

Dominated by one of Europe's most stunning mountain ranges, the Julian Alps, Slovenia is an excellent outdoor destination and a major centre for activity holidays. The country's picturesque mountains, beautiful rivers and lakes offer unlimited opportunities to indulge in a wide range of adventure sports including hiking and skiing, whitewater rafting or kayaking in the Soča valley *(see p413)* and cycling through the majestic hills of Dolenjska. The Slovene coast offers some of the best windsurfing in Europe while scuba diving and sailing are also popular.

Hiking

Hiking has been a popular pursuit in Slovenia for well over a century and a half. There is a wide variety of trails to suit the recreational rambler as well as the serious mountain climber, and routes are well kept with frequent signposts. Hiking maps are widely available and there is an established network of mountain huts offering refuge to the long-distance trekker.

Cycling

The popularity of cycling has grown in recent years. Slovenia's varied topography presents many opportunities for cyclists. There is a broad range of well-marked mountain biking trails in the north and west of the country including the mountain trails in Triglav National Park *(see pp418–21)*. There are also several well-organized recreational routes in the lowlands.

Cycling is permitted on all roads except motorways. Local tourist information centres are well equipped to advise visitors about cycling routes. Mountain bikes are available for hire in the main resort centres.

Rafting

Slovenia offers various water sports, from boating for relaxation to adrenaline-inducing white water descents over steep waterfalls and rapids. The fast-flowing Alpine rivers are perfect for rafting, canoeing and kayaking, with many agencies offering trips on the Soča river. Among these are **Maya**, **Soča Rafting** and **Bled Rafting** in the towns of Tolmin, Bovec and Bled respectively. The same agencies also arrange adventure sports such as canyoning and bungee jumping.

Skiing

In winter, visitors flock to Slovenia's wonderful ski slopes. Snowboarding and downhill skiing are popular in the Alpine parts of Slovenia. Kranjska Gora and Mariborsko Pohorje are the largest and best-equipped ski resorts, although there are several smaller destinations to choose from, many of which are only an hour's drive from the capital, Ljubljana. Since Slovenia's split from Yugoslavia in 1991, many Slovenes have achieved tremendous success in winter sports. The most notable event in the Slovenian sporting calendar is the World Ski-Jumping Championships, held in Planica in March.

Other winter pleasures include snowmobile rides – in Kranjska Gora – and organized sled runs outside the ski centres. Depending on the weather, the ski season usually lasts from December to March.

DIRECTORY

Crafts and Souvenirs

Etnogalerija Skrina
Breg 8, Ljubljana.
Tel (01) 425 5161.
🅦 skrina.si

Galerija Idrijske Čipke
Mestni trg 17, Ljubljana.
Tel (01) 425 0051.
🅦 idrija-lace.com

Galerija Rogaška
Mestni trg 22, Ljubljana.
Tel (01) 241 2701.
🅦 steklarna-rogaska.si

Mladinska Knjiga Konzorcij
Slovenska cesta 29, Ljubljana.
Tel (01) 241 0657.
🅦 mladinska.com

Food and Drink

Čokoladnica Cukrček
Mestni trg 11, Ljubljana.
Tel (01) 421 0453.
🅦 cukrcek.si

Kraševka
Ciril Metodov trg 10, Ljubljana.
Tel (01) 232 1445.
🅦 krasevka.si

Pubs and Bars

Metelkova Mesto
Metelkova ulica, Ljubljana.
🅦 metelkovamesto.org

Classical Music

Cankarjev Dom
Prešernova cesta 10, Ljubljana.
Tel (01) 241 7100.
🅦 cd-cc.si

Slovene Filharmonic
Kongresni trg 10, Ljubljana.
Tel (01) 241 0800.
🅦 filharmonija.si

Slovene National Theatre, Opera and Ballet
Župančičeva 1, Ljubljana.
Tel (01) 241 5900.
🅦 opera.si

Festivals

Druga Godba
Ljubljana.
Tel (01) 241 7299.
🅦 drugagodba.si

Lent Festival
Maribor.
Tel (02) 229 4000.
🅦 festival-lent.si

Ljubljana Summer Festival
Ljubljana.
Tel (01) 241 6026.
🅦 ljubljanafestival.si

Rafting

Bled Rafting
Cesta svobode 4, Bled.
Tel (040) 955 955.
🅦 bled-rafting.si

Maya
Padlih borcev 1, Tolmin.
Tel (051) 312 972.
🅦 maya.si

Soča Rafting
Trg Golobarskih žrtev 14, Bovec. **Tel** (05) 389 6200.
🅦 socarafting.si

Where to Stay

Ljubljana

DK Choice

Celica €
Hostel
Metelkova 8, 1000
Tel *(01) 230 9700*
W hostelcelica.com
Making full creative use of the
former Yugoslav military police
station, 'The Cell' is an interior-
design classic — each room
decorated by a different team
of international artists. It offers
bunk-bed dorms as well as
double rooms. Basic breakfast is
included. Book well in advance.

Vila Veselova €
Hostel **Map** D3
Veselova 14, 1000
Tel *(059) 926 721*
W v-v.si
In a grand-looking 19th-century
villa at the edge of Tivoli Park this
simple but friendly hostel-cum-
pension offers self-contained 4-,
6- and 8-bed dorms.

Allegro €€
Historic **Map** E4
Gornji trg 6, 1000
Tel *(059) 119 620*
W allegrohotel.si
Rooms with reproduction
furniture and loud fabrics but
crisp modern bathrooms mark
out this intimate hotel set in a
historic house in the Old Town.

City Hotel €€
Business **Map** E2
Dalmatinova 15, 1000
Tel *(01) 239 0000*
W cityhotel.si
This popular mid-range hotel

Plush interiors of the Vila Bled
in Bled

with spacious and well-equipped
rooms, is conveniently located
mid-way between the Old Town
and the train and bus stations.

Maček €€
B&B **Map** E3
Krojaška 5, 1000
Tel *(041) 827 815*
W sobe-macek.si
On the banks of the river
and right above the popular
Maček café-bar, this friendly and
informal B&B has bright and
cheerfully coloured en suites
with laminated wooden flooring.

Antiq Hotel €€€
Boutique **Map** E4
Gornji trg 3, 1000
Tel *(01) 421 3560*
W antiqhotel.eu
Boutique hotel with a lovely
location in the heart of the Old
Town, with rooms ranging from
snug 'economy' doubles with
shared facilities to regular rooms
with en suite bathrooms.

Grand Hotel Union €€€
Historic **Map** E2
Miklošičeva 1, 1000
Tel *(01) 308 1270*
W union-hotels.eu
Handsome Art Nouveau building
near the Tromostovje bridge.
'Executive' rooms in the main
building are spacious and stylish;
while 'business' rooms in the
modern annexe are more contemporary in style. There are several
on-site cafés and restaurants.

**Best Western Premier
Hotel Slon** €€€
Luxury **Map** E2
Slovenska cesta 34, 1000
Tel *(01) 470 1100*
W hotelslon.com
Right on the main shopping street,
minutes away from the Old Town,
Slon offers fully-equipped modern
rooms. Slon meaning 'Elephant'
refers to a Habsburg emperor
who once stayed at an inn at this
site with an elephant.

Rest of Slovenia

BLED: Vila Bled €€€
Historic
Cesta svobode 26, 4260
Tel *(04) 575 3710*
W vila-bled.si
Now a luxury hotel with spacious
rooms and modern bathrooms,
the Vila Bled was originally
President Tito's holiday home.

Price Guide

Prices are based on one night's stay in
high season for a standard double room,
inclusive of service charges and taxes.

€	under €75
€€	€75 to €150
€€€	over €150

KRANJSKA GORA: Kotnik €€
Resort
Borovška cesta 75, 4280
Tel *(04) 588 1564*
W hotel-kotnik.si
Rooms at this intimate and
friendly family-run hotel come
with Internet connection,
minibar and a hairdryer too.

LAKE BOHINJ: Hotel Jezero €€
Resort
Ribčev Laz 51, 4265
Tel *(04) 572 9100*
W hotel-jezero.si
Lakeside location, pool and
modern rooms that have
balconies. Jezero is also
well-managed.

MARIBOR: Orel €€
Business
Volkmerjev prehod 7, 2000
Tel *(02) 250 6700*
W hotel-orel.si
Located in the heart of Maribor's
pedestrian zone, this combined
hotel and hostel offers three-star
hotel rooms as well as simply
decorated doubles and triples.

PIRAN: Max €
B&B
Ulica IX. Korpusa 26, 6330
Tel *(05) 673 3436*
W maxpiran.com
On a stepped street near Piran's
cathedral, Max offers cosy en
suites, squeezed into a tall thin
house that has a steep and
narrow staircase.

PORTOROŽ: Riviera €€€
Luxury
Obala 33, 6320
Tel *(05) 692 6020*
W lifeclass.net
Among the best-equipped of the
many four-star hotels grouped
along the Portorož seafront,
Riviera offers spacious bedrooms
as well as on-site spa facilities.

PTUJ: Kurent €
Hostel
Osojnikova 9, 2250
Tel *(02) 771 0814*
A smart hostel with a choice
of cosy double rooms with or
without shower, and 6-person
dorms with bunk beds. Breakfast
and Internet access are included.

Where to Eat and Drink

Homely and relaxed ambience at Špajza in Ljubljana

Ljubljana

Cafe Romeo $
International　　　　　Map E4
Stari trg 6, 1000
Tel *(040) 706 070*
This popular café offers a reasonably priced lunch of pastas, tortillas, sandwiches and salads in a pop-art environment.

Celica Café $
International
Metelkova 8, 1000
Tel *(01) 230 9700*
Rather popular for its inexpensive but filling fare with a choice of vegetarian options, this café at the Celica hostel also has a daily menu which is a real bargain.

Le Petit Café $
Café-Patisserie　　　　Map D4
Trg francoske revolucije 4, 1000
Tel *(01) 251 2575*
French-style café with terrace looking towards the Ilyrian Monument, best known for its fresh pastries and croissants.

Pri Škofu $$
Slovene　　　　　　　Map E4
Rečna 8, 1000
Tel *(01) 426 4508*
Enjoy a traditional Slovene meal at this delightful suburban restaurant, where the waiter tells you of the choices available.

Shambala $$
Asian　　　　　　　　Map E4
Križevniška 12, 1000
Tel *031 843 833*
An exquisite selection of Asian dishes with Thai curries, spicy grilled fish and Chinese stir-fries. The fixed-price lunch is excellent value.

Gostilna AS $$$
International　　　　　Map E3
Čopova 5A, 1000
Tel *(01) 425 8822*
This smart but not overly formal restaurant has long been a favourite among local gourmets. The blend of Mediterranean and central European cuisine makes full use of local ingredients.

Pri Vitezu $$$
International　　　　　Map E4
Breg 20, 1000
Tel *(01) 426 6058*
'At the Knight's Place', located in a 300-year-old inn on the banks of the Ljubljanica, offers upscale dining in a pleasing barrel-vaulted environ. Adriatic seafood and meat dishes from central Europe form the backbone of the menu.

DK Choice

Špajza $$$
Slovene　　　　　　　Map E4
Gornji trg 28, 1000
Tel *(01) 425 3094*
Experience relaxed dining in an interior comprising a cluster of small rooms decorated with folksy bric-a-brac. The menu includes fresh fish from the Adriatic as well as inland Slovenian classics such as breast of duck, horsemeat fillets and game. The 4- to 5-course set lunches are worth trying.

Rest of Slovenia

BLED: Okarina $$
International
Ljubljanska cesta 8, 4260
Tel *(04) 574 1458*
Quality fusion restaurant with a menu that spans Adriatic seafood, Balkan-style grilled meats, and spicy Indian dishes with several vegetarian options. There is also a good list of Slovene wines.

DK Choice

KOBARID: Hiša Franko $$$
Slovene
Staro Selo 1, 5222
Tel *(05) 389 4120* **Closed** *Mon*
This homely family-run restaurant that has quickly established itself as a cult destination for creative cuisine. Fish and game, the main ingredients here, are garnished with organic vegetables from the restaurant's own garden.

Price Guide
Prices are based on a three-course meal for one, half a bottle of wine, including cover charge, service and tax.

€　　　　　under €40
€€　　　　　€40 to €80
€€€　　　　　over €80

KRANJSKA GORA: Miklič $$
International
Vitranška 13, 4280
Tel *(04) 588 1635*
Highly regarded hotel restaurant with a balanced menu of meat, game and Adriatic seafood. Specialities include delicious pasta dishes dressed with Istrian truffles.

MARIBOR: Gril Ranca $
Balkan Grill
Dravska 10, 2000
Tel *(02) 252 5550*
Balkan grilled food including *ćevapčiči* (grilled minced-meat rissoles), *pljeskavice* (hamburger-style patties) and *vešalice* (skewer-grilled chunks of pork). The riverside location is a major plus.

PIRAN: Neptun $$
Seafood
Županičeva 7, 6330
Tel *(05) 673 4111* **Closed** *Tues*
Very popular with tourists, this excellent seafood restaurant occupies a quiet street just a few steps away from the main square. Great place to sample fresh Adriatic fish, expertly grilled. Reservations are recommended.

PORTOROŽ: Santa Lucia $$$
Seafood
Obala 26, 6320
Tel *(05) 677 9104*
One of the few bar-restaurants clustered around Portorož's tennis club, Santa Lucia offers the best in Adriatic seafood, with some excellent oven-baked fish recipes alongside shellfish and squid.

PTUJ: Gostilna Ribič $$
Seafood
Dravska ulica 9, 2250
Tel *(02) 749 0635* **Closed** *Mon*
The menu at this traditional riverside inn with a big outdoor terrace includes a good choice of freshwater fish, delicous seafood and seasonal specials, notably game.

CROATIA

Situated between Eastern and Western Europe, Croatia has long served both as a land of passage and a point of contact between different worlds and cultures. Though small, it has great ethnic, historical and architectural diversity as well as a variety of landscapes. The beautiful Adriatic coast is an outstanding attraction and the largely unspoilt interior has great rural charm.

Croatia forms a meeting point between the Mediterranean, Central Europe and the Balkans. The north of the country has a Viennese look; while to the west, the Adriatic coast boasts a great deal of Italian-style architecture. The 1991–5 war which followed the break-up of Yugoslavia had a disastrous effect on Croatia's economy but the country has regained its reputation as a popular holiday destination.

History

Croatia has been home to human civilization since the Neolithic era. Illyrian tribal states established themselves throughout the region during the 1st millennium BC. They were, however, no match for the Romans, who conquered present-day Croatia in the 2nd century BC.

Slav tribes, including the Croats, settled in South Eastern Europe from the early 6th century onwards. Croats on the Adriatic coast accepted the rule of Byzantium, which had inherited Roman possessions in Eastern Europe. Croats living inland carved out an independent territory of their own. In the 9th century, invading Hungarians were pushed back by Croatian rulers strengthening their hold over northern and eastern Croatia. Over the next 200 years, the Croats extended their territories towards the Adriatic, allowing a Christian Slav culture to flourish.

The last Croatian king died childless in 1091, and the crown was claimed by the Hungarians. Hungarian monarchs ruled over Croatia until 1526, when their armies were destroyed by the Ottoman Turks. Croatia turned to the Habsburg Empire

Ruins of the Roman Amphitheatre in Pula, dating from the 3rd century AD

◀ A breathtaking view of Plitvice Lakes National Park

Marshal Josip Tito, the first president of Yugoslavia

for protection, and became a front line state in the Habsburgs' wars against the Ottomans.

The Ottoman threat had receded by the 19th century, and patriotic Croats began to demand political and cultural autonomy from the Habsburgs. These calls were left unanswered until the end of World War I, when the Habsburgs were defeated and began to disintegrate. Croatia declared its independence in October 1918, and entered into a political union with the neighbouring kingdom of Serbia, creating the kingdom of Serbs, Croats and Slovenes. The kingdom was renamed Yugoslavia in 1929. However, the Croats and Serbs could not agree on how power was to be shared in the new state, and Yugoslavia remained an unstable unit with frequent political crises.

Yugoslavia was invaded by Germany and Italy in 1941, breaking up the country and re-establishing Croatia as a pro-Nazi puppet state. Resistance to the Nazis was led by the partisan movement created by local Communist leader Josip Broz Tito.

At the end of World War II, Tito re-established Yugoslavia as a Communist federation composed of six equal republics. Following Tito's death in 1980, tensions between Yugoslavia's republics re-emerged, leading to a disintegration of central authority. Slovenia and Croatia declared their independence in 1991. Serbs living in Croatia launched a rebellion, supported by the Yugoslav People's Army. Fighting continued for four years, and was finally brought to an end by Croatian military victories in August 1995. Croatia has since developed into a modern European democracy, becoming a member of NATO in 2009 and an EU member in 2013.

KEY DATES IN CROATIAN HISTORY

1200 BC Illyrian settlement in the Balkans

229 BC The Roman Army destroys Illyrian forts, and rules Illyria for the next three centuries

AD 7 Croats settle in Pannonia and Dalmatia

899 Hungarians enter the Balkans but are pushed back by the Croats

901 Prince Tomislav defeats the Hungarians and forces them beyond Sava river

1091 Hungarian King Ladislas seizes the Croatian crown

1526 Hungary is defeated by the Ottomans; Croatia turns to the Habsburg Empire for support

1918 Croatia proclaims independence after the fall of the Habsburg Empire

1945 The Yugoslav Federal State is founded with Croatia, Serbia, Macedonia, Montenegro, Slovenia and Bosnia and Herzegovina as members

1980 Yugoslavia's President Tito dies, leaving the state without a firm leader

1991 Croatia declares independence; Serb forces occupy large parts of the country

1995 Croatian forces recapture occupied territory

2009 Croatia joins NATO

2013 Croatia joins EU

Language and Culture

The official language of Croatia is Croatian, although many dialects are spoken in its regions. Croatia is a devoutly Catholic country and colourful religious festivals take place throughout the year. During the summer, traditional songs and dances are performed at folk festivals.

Exploring Croatia

Croatia is a fascinating country made up of a wide variety of landscapes. Its capital, Zagreb, is a delight, with plenty of galleries and museums. The country's coast and islands are spectacular, with several national parks to preserve their natural charm. The rest of Croatia features rolling fields and hills covered with vineyards. The country also benefits from an efficient transport system with excellent connections between the mainland and the islands.

The Korzo, an avenue lined with 19th-century buildings, Rijeka

Key

— Motorway

— Major road

— Railway

▪ ▪ International border

- - Ferry route

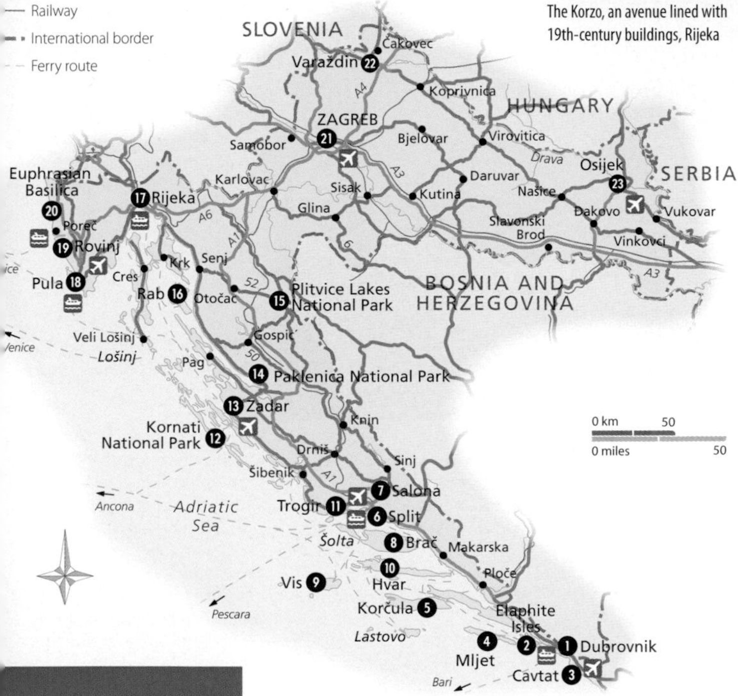

SLOVENIA

HUNGARY

SERBIA

BOSNIA AND HERZEGOVINA

Adriatic Sea

0 km 50
0 miles 50

Pedestrianized street in Dubrovnik's Old Town

Sights at a Glance

For keys to symbols *see back flap*

❶ Dubrovnik

Located on the Adriatic coast, the city of Dubrovnik is renowned for the beauty of its monuments and its magnificent walls. It was founded by refugees from Roman Epidaurum, now Cavtat *(see p441)*, in the 7th century. Dubrovnik (or island of Ragusa as it was called) came under Byzantine, Venetian and then Hungarian suzerainty, although by the late 14th century, it was a de facto self-governing city-state. In the 15th and 16th centuries, its fleet exceeded 500 ships. Artistically it flourished, and its wealth increased due to its privileged access to the trade routes of the Ottoman Empire. Much of the Old Town centre dates from the rebuilding that took place after the earthquake of 1667. A UNESCO World Heritage Site, Dubrovnik has been restored to its former glory after the seige in the 1990s by Serb and Montenegrin forces.

The Big Fountain of Onofrio, dating from 1438–44

A superb view from the impressive city walls

🏛 Walls

Access to the walls near the Franciscan Monastery in Poljana Paška Miličevića, the large square behind Pile Gate, and near the Dominican Monastery. 🛈 (020) 324 641. **Open** Jun & Jul: 8am–7:30pm; Apr, May, Aug & Sep: 8am–6:30pm; Oct: 8am–5:30pm; Nov–Mar: 10am–3pm.

A symbol of Dubrovnik, the walls (Gradske zidine) offer splendid views from their parapets. They were built in the 10th century, with modifications completed in the 13th century, and then reinforced over the years by architects such as Michelozzo Michelozzi (1396–1472), Juraj Dalmatinac (c. 1400–73) and Antonio Ferramolino (c. 1490–1550).

The walls and ramparts are 1,940 m (6,363 ft) long and reach a height of 25 m (82 ft) in some parts. Those facing inland are up to 6 m (20 ft) wide and strengthened by an outer wall with ten semi-circular bastions. Other

towers and the Fort of St John defend the section facing the Adriatic Sea and the Old Port. Completing the defences to the east and west are two fortresses, the Revelin and the Lovrijenac.

🏛 Pile Gate

The main entrance to the old fortified centre is through the

Pile Gate, leading to the Old Town

imposing Pile Gate (Gradska vrata Pile). The stone bridge leading to the gate dates from 1537, and crosses a moat which is now a garden. The gate is a strong defensive structure built on different levels. Above the ogival arch stands a statue of St Blaise, the patron saint of Dubrovnik, by Ivan Meštrović *(see p471)*. Between the inner and outer walls is a Gothic portal.

🏛 Big Fountain of Onofrio

In the square which opens out immediately beyond the Pile Gate is the Big Fountain of Onofrio (Velika Onofrijeva fontana), one of the best-known monuments in the city. It was built between 1438 and 1444 by the Neapolitan architect, Onofrio della Cava, who was responsible for designing the city's water supply system. He decided to draw water from the Dubrovačka river for this purpose. The fountain once had two storeys, but the upper level was destroyed in the earthquake of 1667, which killed thousands of people and destroyed countless buildings. Tucked between the city walls and the Franciscan Monastery, opposite the fountain, is the **Church of St Saviour** (sv Spas), built after an earlier earthquake of 1520. Its façade is an example of Venetian-Dalmatian Renaissance architecture.

🏛 Franciscan Monastery

Placa 2. **Tel** (020) 321 410. **Open** summer: 9am–6pm daily; winter: 9am–5pm daily. Franciscan Museum: **Open** Apr–Oct: 9am–6pm daily; Nov–Mar: 9am–5pm daily. 🖼

Construction of the Franciscan Monastery (Franjevački samostan) began in 1317 and was completed in the following century. It was almost entirely rebuilt after the earthquake in 1667. However, the Venetian Gothic south door, dating from 1499, along with a 15th-century marble pulpit and the cloister, escaped undamaged.

One side of the cloister leads to the Pharmacy (Stara Ljekarna), in use since 1317, lined with shelves of alembics, measuring apparatus and jars. The capitular room of the monastery is home to the **Franciscan Museum** (Muzej Franjevačkog samostana), with religious art, pharmaceutical instruments and a library.

Stradun or Placa, the busy main street of Dubrovnik

🏛 Stradun

The street that crosses the city from east to west between two city gates is known as Stradun or Placa. It was constructed in the 12th century by filling in the channel that separated the island of Ragusa from the mainland. The street was paved in 1468 and stone houses were built after the earthquake of 1667. Today,

VISITORS' CHECKLIST

Practical Information
600 km (375 miles) SE of Zagreb. 🅜 43,000. 🛈 Local: Brsalje 5, (020) 323 887; Regional: (020) 324 999. 🎭 Dubrovnik Summer Festival (Jul–Aug).
🌐 **experience.dubrovnik.hr**

Transport
✈ 20 km (12 miles) NE of centre.
🚌 Obala Pape Ivana Pavla II 44a.
⛴ Obala Stjepana Radića 37.

its lively shops and cafés are popular with locals and visitors.

🏛 Minčeta Tower

The most visited of the walls' defensive structures, this tower (Tvrđava Minčeta) was designed by Michelozzo Michelozzi in 1461 and completed by Juraj Dalmatinac in 1464. The semi-circular tower is crowned by a second tower with embrasures at the top.

Dubrovnik City Centre

① Walls
② Pile Gate
③ Big Fountain of Onofrio
④ Franciscan Monastery
⑤ Stradun
⑥ Minčeta Tower
⑦ Square of the Loggia
⑧ Church of St Blaise
⑨ Rector's Palace
⑩ Cathedral and Treasury
⑪ Fort of St John
⑫ Sponza Palace
⑬ Ploče Gate
⑭ Dominican Monastery

Key

▮ Street-by-Street area: see pp436–7

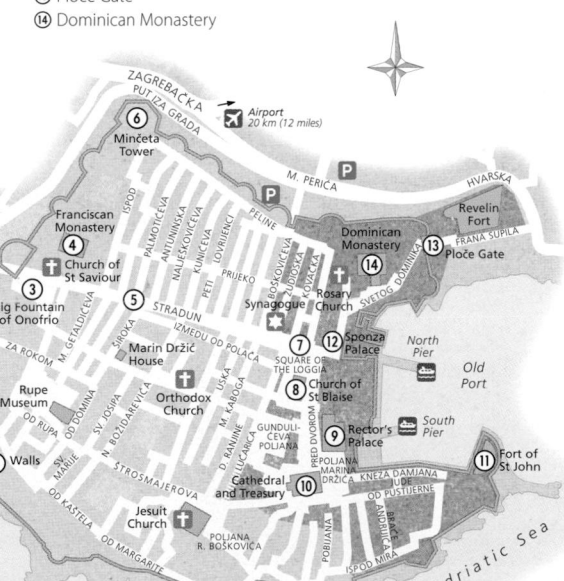

Street-by-Street: Old Town

In 1991, the peaceful city of Dubrovnik was the target of heavy shelling by Serb and Montenegrin troops. This period saw some of the most significant symbols of Dalmatian culture badly damaged. The war also sent the city's economy, especially tourism, into decline. Only after the Erdut Agreement of 1995 did life begin to return to normal. UNESCO and the European Union set up a special commission for the reconstruction of the city and the damage was repaired in a remarkably short period of time. Dubrovnik has now regained its former splendour and tourism is flourishing once again. Besides its magnificent walls, the city has several churches, monasteries and museums that throw light on an eventful history.

★ **Rector's Palace**
Considered the political centre of the city, this originally served as the rector's residence and now houses the city's history museum.

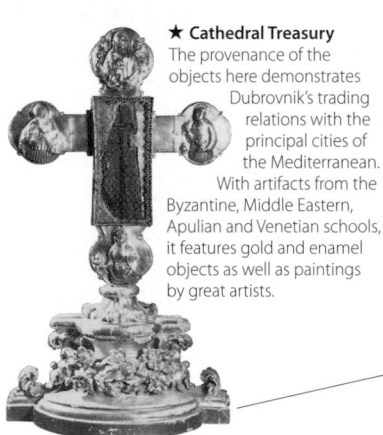

★ **Cathedral Treasury**
The provenance of the objects here demonstrates Dubrovnik's trading relations with the principal cities of the Mediterranean. With artifacts from the Byzantine, Middle Eastern, Apulian and Venetian schools, it features gold and enamel objects as well as paintings by great artists.

Key

— Suggested route

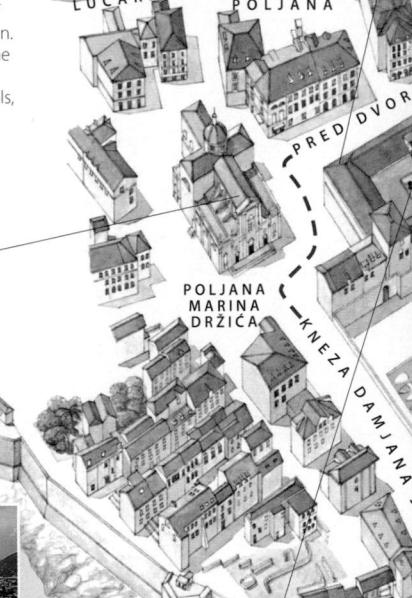

LUCARICA   GUNDULIĆEVA POLJANA

PRED DVOR

POLJANA MARINA DRŽIĆA

KNEZA DAMJANA J

View of Dubrovnik
Spectacular views of the entire city can be enjoyed from the car park, situated about 2 km (1 mile) south along the beautiful coast.

The Church of St Blaise, originally a 16th-century church, was redesigned in the 18th century by Marino Groppelli.

For hotels and restaurants see p482 and p483

Sponza Palace

Built in the 16th century, this palace features Renaissance arches and Venetian Gothic windows. A Latin inscription in the courtyard refers to the public scales that once stood here. Today, it houses the State Archives.

★ Dominican Monastery

Since its foundation in 1315, the monastery has played a leading role in the cultural activities of the city. Important sculptors and architects played a part in its construction.

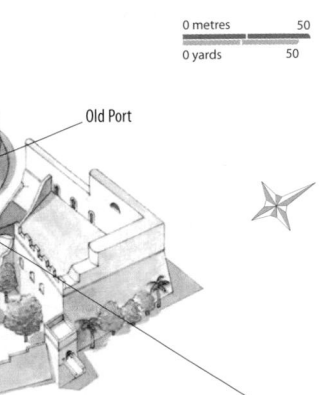

The outer city walls

Old Port

| 0 metres | 50 |
| 0 yards | 50 |

Ploče Gate

Next to the Dominican Monastery is the Ploče Gate, which leads to the suburb of Ploče. From there goods arrived from, and were sent to, every port in the Mediterranean.

Fort of St John

This imposing fortress was one of many bulwarks built to make the city impregnable. It now houses an interesting museum devoted to the city's maritime past.

🏛 Square of the Loggia
Luža.

The political and economic heart of Dubrovnik, the Square of the Loggia is situated at the eastern end of Stradun and surrounded by important buildings.

On the eastern side of the square is a delightful **Clock Tower** (Gradski zvonik), which was restored in 1929. The nearby **Loggia of the Bell**, with four bells, dates from 1463. The bells were rung to alert the citizens whenever danger threatened. Next to this stands the **Main Guard House**, rebuilt in 1706, after the earthquake of 1667. It has a large Baroque doorway and, on the first floor, Gothic mullioned windows, reminiscent of the earlier building constructed on this site in the late 15th century.

Today, the square is a popular meeting place, particularly around **Orlando's Column**, which was built by Croatian sculptor Antonio Ragusino in 1418.

⛪ Church of St Blaise
Luža. **Tel** (020) 323 887. **Open** 8am–noon & 4:30–7pm daily.

The pretty Church of St Blaise (Crkva sv Vlaha) was rebuilt at the beginning of the 18th century according to a 17th-century design and contains many Baroque works of art.

On the main altar stands a 15th-century statue of St Blaise, the patron saint of Dubrovnik. It depicts the saint holding a model of the city in the Middle Ages.

The 18th-century Baroque façade of the Church of St Blaise

Rector's Palace, the administrative centre of Dubrovnik

🏛 Rector's Palace
Pred Dvorom 3. **Tel** (020) 321 422. **Open** Apr–Oct: 9am–6pm daily; Nov–Mar: 9am–4pm daily.

For centuries, the Rector's Palace (Knežev dvor) was the political and administrative centre of Ragusa (see p434). It housed the Upper Council, as well as the rector's quarters and rooms for diplomatic meetings and audiences. The early 15th-century building was constructed on the site of a medieval fortress and designed by Italian architect Onofrio della Cava. The portico, by Petar Martinov from Milan, was added in 1465. The Gothic works are by the 15th-century architect and sculptor Juraj Dalmatinac. Concerts are held in the courtyard during the Dubrovnik Summer Festival.

The rooms of the palace house the interesting **Cultural Historical Museum** (Kulturno-povijesni muzej)), which displays 13 collections of over 15,000 art and craft items, paintings and sculptures created in Europe between the 16th and 20th centuries.

An authentic jail space and court have been preserved on the ground floor while the mezzanine floor holds coins, stamps and an inventory of the state pharmacy, Domus Christi. Also of interest are the portraits of illustrious personalities who were born or lived in Dubrovnik, whose histories are narrated through commemorative medals and heraldic coats of arms.

Among the paintings are the 16th-century *Venus and Adonis* by Paris Bordon and *Baptism of Christ*

(1509) by Mihajlo Hamzić. Next door is the Neo-Renaissance **Town Hall** (Vijećnica), designed and built by Emilio Vecchietti in 1863. It is also home to Gradska kavana, a charming café, and the prestigious Civic Theatre.

Impressive dome of Dubrovnik's Baroque Cathedral

⛪ Cathedral and Treasury
Kneza Damjana Jude 1. **Open** Apr–Oct: 8am–5pm Mon–Sat, 11am–5pm Sun; Nov–Mar: 8am–noon & 3–5pm Mon–Sat, 11am–noon, 3–5pm Sun. Cathedral Treasury: **Tel** (020) 323 459. **Open** as cathedral.

The elegant Cathedral (Velika Gospa) was built after the earthquake of 1667, following designs by Italian architects Andrea Buffalini and Paolo Andreotti. Inside, there are three aisles enclosed by three apses. Paintings by Italian and Dalmatian artists from the 16th and 18th centuries decorate the side altars, while the *Assumption*

c. 1513) by Titian dominates the main altar. Alongside the church is the Cathedral Treasury (Riznica katedrale), famous for its collection of about 200 reliquaries. It includes the arm of St Blaise, which dates from the 13th century, and the Holy Cross, which contains a fragment of the cross on which Jesus is said to have been crucified. The tondo *Virgin of the Chair* (c. 1513) is thought to have been painted by Raphael and is a copy of the masterpiece which is now in Florence.

The treasury also has an extraordinary collection of sacred objects in gold, including a pitcher and basin with decoration showing the flora and fauna of Dubrovnik.

Fort of St John

Maritime Museum: **Tel** (020) 323 904. **Open** Apr–Oct: 9am–6pm Tue–Sun; Nov–Mar: 9am–2pm Tue–Sun. Aquarium: **Tel** (020) 323 978. **Open** Jun–Sep: 9am–8pm daily; Oct–May: 9am–1pm Mon–Sat.

The imposing Fort of St John (Tvrđa sv Ivana) was once the city harbour's main defence, a part of a chain that stretched to the Tower of St Luke (Kula sv Luke), along the walls.

The upper areas of the fort house the **Maritime Museum** (Pomorski muzej), where the seafaring history of the city is told through displays of model ships, prints, diaries and

Sponza Palace and Clock Tower

portraits. On the lower level is an **Aquarium** (Akvarij) with an assortment of Mediterranean marine life, including sea horses. At the top is the circular **Bokar Fort** (Tvrđava Bokar), built by Michelozzo Michelozzi.

Sponza Palace

Tel (020) 321 032. **Open** May–Oct: 9am–10pm daily; Nov–Apr: 10am–3pm daily.

To the left of the Square of the Loggia stands the splendid Sponza Palace (Palača Sponza), remodelled between 1516 and 1522. It has an elegantly sculpted Renaissance loggia on the ground floor, a Venetian Gothic three-mullioned window on the first floor – evidence of its 14th-century origins – and a statue of St Blaise on the upper floor. Once the city's custom house, it was the Mint in the

14th century and now houses the State Archives.

Ploče Gate

Luža.

To the northeast of the Sponza Palace is the Ploče Gate (Vrata od Ploča), which faces a small port and is preceded by the polygonal Asimov Tower. Dating from the 1300s, the gate is a complex structure with a double defence system, reached by a stone bridge. A moat separates it from the **Revelin Fort** (Tvrđava Revelin). Designed in 1538 by Antonio Ferramolino, the fort was the last of the defences to be built. Based on a pentagonal ground-plan, it has walls enclosing three large rooms and a terrace. Such was its strength that the city's art treasures were brought here for safe-keeping during times of trouble.

Dubrovnik's tiled roofs as seen from Ploče Gate

Church of St Dominic, in the Dominican Monastery

⬆ Dominican Monastery

Sv Dominika 4. **Tel** (020) 321 423.
Open May–Oct: 9am–6pm daily;
Nov–Apr: 9am–5pm daily.

Located in the eastern part of Dubrovnik, near the Ploče Gate, the Dominican Monastery (Dominikanski samostan) was first built in 1315, but it soon became clear that because of the size of the complex, the city walls would have to be enlarged. The monastery was later rebuilt after the earthquake of 1667.

A long flight of steps with a stone balustrade leads up to the church. The elaborate door, by Bonino of Milan, is decorated with a Romanesque statue of St Dominic. The interior has a wide single nave; hanging from the central arch is a splendid gilded panel – *Crucifix and Symbols of the Evangelists* – by 14th-century painter Paolo Veneziano.

The various rooms of the monastery, arranged around a superb 15th-century Gothic Renaissance cloister by sculptor Maso di Bartolomeo, house the **Dominican Museum** (Muzej dominikanskog samostana). It contains an extraordinary collection of works of art from the Dubrovnik school, including a beautiful triptych and an Annunciation by Niccolò Ragusino, from the 16th century. There are also works of art from the Venetian school, including *St Blaise, St Mary Magdalene*, and *The Angel Tobias and the Purchaser* by Titian, as well as precious reliquaries and objects in gold and silver.

Environs

The serene island of **Lokrum**, 700 m (2,296 ft) across the water from Dubrovnik, is a nature reserve set up to protect the exotic plants found there. Its scenic beauty makes it a popular tourist destination.

The first inhabitants of the island were the Benedictines, who founded an abbey here

Statue of Neptune overlooking the pond in Trsteno's arboretum

in 1023. This was rebuilt in the 14th century but destroyed by the 1667 earthquake. In 1859, the Habsburg Archduke Maximilian (1832–67) built a palace here and renovated the cloister, which later became the Natural History Museum. The fort, built by the French in 1808, provides sweeping views of the island.

In **Trsteno**, 20 km (12 miles) northwest of Dubrovnik, is an arboretum. Begun in 1502, it is in a park surrounding a villa built by a noble, Ivan Gučetić (1451–1502), and has the typical layout of a Renaissance garden with grottoes and ruins. In the middle of the park is an attractive lily pond, filled with fish and overlooked by an impressive statue of the god Neptune.

Above the park beside the main road are two huge plane trees, thought to be over 400 years old.

❷ Elaphite Isles

3 km (2 miles) N of Dubrovnik.
2,000. from Dubrovnik (020) 324 999.

The beautiful Elaphite Isles (Elafitski otoci) were named after the fallow deer said to roam here by the natural historian Pliny the Elder (AD 23–79). The islands became a part of the Dubrovnik Republic in the 14th century. Only three of them are inhabited – **Šipan, Lopud** and **Koločep** – while Jakljan is devoted to farming. The islands are characterized by woods of maritime pines and cypresses, beautiful beaches and bays frequented by pleasure boats. They have long been popular with the aristocracy of Dubrovnik, who built villas here. Many of the churches date from the pre-Romanesque period, although few remain intact. Some islands had monasteries, which were suppressed with the arrival of French troops in 1808.

The island nearest to Dubrovnik, Koločep, has been a popular summer retreat since

Aerial view of Šipan, the largest of the Elaphite Isles

the 16th century. A large part of the island is covered in subtropical undergrowth and maritime pines. The churches of St Anthony and St Nicholas have pre-Romanesque origins, while the Parish Church dates from the 15th century.

Lopud, covering 4.6 sq km (1.7 sq miles), has a fertile valley sheltered from the cold winds by two ranges of hills. Most of the inhabitants live in the village of Lopud, strung around a wide, curving bay. The Franciscan Monastery dates from 1483. The monastery church, St Mary of the Rocks (sv Marija od Špilica), contains several works of art including a polyptych (1520) by Pietro di Giovanni, triptychs by Nikola Božidarević and Girolamo di Santacroce depicting the Virgin and Child, and a carved choir from the 15th century.

In the southeast of the island, **Šunj** draws visitors to its sandy beach, but its church is also worth visiting for many intriguing works of art, including a painting by Venetian artist Palma il Giovane and a polyptych by Matej Junčić.

The largest of the Elaphite Isles, Šipan, covering 15 sq km (6 sq miles), has just two settlements, Šipanska Luka and Suđurađ. Šipanska Luka has the pre-Romanesque Church of St Michael and the ruins of a Benedictine monastery, while the village of Suđurađ has the ruins of a bishop's palace and a castle.

❸ Cavtat

20 km (12 miles) S of Dubrovnik.
🏠 2,500. 🚌 from Dubrovnik. 🚢
ℹ️ Zidine 6, (020) 478 025. 🎭 Jul–Aug in Cavtat, Epidaurus Festival (Sep).
ⓦ visit.cavtat-konavle.com

The pretty coastal town of Cavtat is the Croatian name for Civitas Vetus, the site of the ancient Roman town of Epidaurum, destroyed in the 7th century by the Avars. Occasional excavations have revealed the remains of a theatre, several tombs and also parts of a road. The present-day village attracts visitors for the beauty of the area, its beaches, luxuriant vegetation and interesting monuments. Much of Cavtat's charm is encapsulated in the

Old Town located behind the waterfront. The 16th-century Rector's Palace houses the impressive Baltazar Bogišić collection. It was assembled and donated by Bogišić (1834–1908), a cultural activist and jurist of the 19th century who spent a lifetime promoting literature and learning. Several books from Bogišić's collection are displayed here. The works of well-known painter Vlaho Bukovac (1855–1922) are also displayed inside the palace, including his depiction of the local carnival celebrations in 1901.

At the end of the seafront stand the Church of Our Lady of Snow (Gospa Snježna) and a Franciscan monastery, both dating from the end of the 15th century. On the hilltop is the **Račić Mausoleum**, built by Ivan Meštrović (see p471) for a local ship-owning family in 1922. The Byzantine-inspired domed structure is decorated with Greek angels and ornate gargoyles. Eagles and Neo-Assyrian winged lambs adorn the elaborate cupola.

A pair of fine shingle and sandy beaches lie about 1 km (0.6 miles) east of the town centre in an area known as Žal, literally meaning "beach". Visitors throng the beaches in spring and summer.

A panoramic view of the seafront and port of Cavtat

❹ Mljet

The island of Mljet, called Melita by the Romans and
Meleda by the Venetians, covers an area of 98 sq km (37 sq
miles). It is mountainous, with two limestone depressions
in which there are two saltwater lakes linked by a channel.
In Roman times, Mljet was a holiday resort for the wealthy
of Salona *(see pp450–51)*, who built villas here. In 1151,
Duke Desa, Grand Prefect of Zahumlje, in Herzegovina,
gave the island to the Benedictines of Pulsano in Gargano,
Italy, who founded a monastery here. Two centuries later,
Stjepan, Governor of Bosnia, gave it to Dubrovnik *(see
pp434–40)*. In 1960, the western end, which covers an area
of 31 sq km (12 sq miles) and is entirely forested, was
declared a national park.

Roman Palatium
Near Polače lie the ruins of a
Roman settlement named Palatium.
It includes the remains of a large villa
and an early Christian basilica.

Pomena •   Goveđari •   Polače   Mljet National Park   • Kozarica   •Soline   •Blato

Monastery of St Mary
In the centre of Veliko jezero is a small island
with a 12th-century Benedictine monastery,
remodelled in the 1500s. It features colourful
altarpieces carved from local stone.

Veliko jezero
Covering about 145 ha (358 acres) Veliko jezero (Big
Lake) reaches a depth of 46 m (150 ft). A channel links
the lake to the sea and another links it to a smaller lake,
Malo jezero.

Mljet National Park
The national park was created
to save the forest of Aleppo
pine and Holm oak. In the 19th
century, mongooses were introduced here to kill snakes.

0 kilometres   3
0 miles   3

For hotels and restaurants see p482 and p483

Marine Life
Dozens of species of fish, including grouper, inhabit the underwater ravines and caves along the coast. The endangered monk seal, protected in these waters, is highly valued.

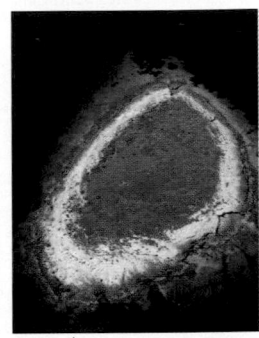

Uninhabited Islands
Nature is left undisturbed on these islands, with woods of pine, Holm oak and oak stretching down to the rocky shore.

Sobra Prožura Okuklje
Babino Polje Korita
Maranovići

Key

— Major road

= Minor road

- - Park boundary

Fishing Villages
The island's ancient stone villages are inhabited mainly by farmers and fishermen. Along with the delightful bays and surrounding coves, these villages are lovely places to visit and spend time.

KEY

① **The village of Babino Polje** was founded around the middle of the 10th century by a group of refugees from the mainland. The governor's residence was built in 1554, when the island became part of the Republic of Ragusa, now Dubrovnik.

② **Saplunara** lies at the southernmost tip of the island. It boasts the most beautiful beach in the area and has been declared a nature reserve for its greenery and lush vegetation.

❺ Korčula

At a length of 47 km (29 miles), Korčula is one of the largest islands in the Adriatic Sea. Mountains run the length of the island, reaching an altitude of 560 m (1,837 ft) at their peak, and dense forests of Aleppo pine, cypress and oak are found all over. Inhabited since prehistoric times, the island was named Korkyra Melaina by the Greeks. After AD 1000, it was fought over by Venice and the Croat kings, and later by the Genoese and the Ottoman Turks. In the 1298 naval battle between Genoa and Venice, the Genoese captured Marco Polo said to be a native of the island. Today, Korčula is a popular holiday spot for its beaches, scenic villages and the eponymous town.

Land Gate, the main entrance to Korčula's Old Town

Korčula Town

This enchanting town is perched on a peninsula and surrounded by strong 13th-century walls, which were reinforced with towers and bastions by the Venetians after 1420. The **Land Gate** (Kopnena vrata), the main entrance to the Old Town, was fortified by a huge tower, which overlooked a canal dug by the Venetians to isolate the town. Narrow streets branching off the main road were designed to lessen the impact of the strong Bora wind common in this area.

Facing the central square, Strossmayerov Square, is the 13th-century **Cathedral of St Mark** (Katedrala sv Marka), built in pale, honey-coloured stone. The skill of Korčula's sculptors and stone masons is evident in its ornate door. On the left stands an imposing bell tower, while inside the church are large columns with elaborately decorated capitals and several important sculptures, including the tomb of Bishop Toma Malumbra. The paintings include Venetian artist Tintoretto's impressive *St Mark with St Jerome and St Bartholomew* (1550). On a wall are trophies recalling the Battle of Lepanto of 1571.

Next to the cathedral, in the Bishop's Palace, now the Abbot's House, is the **Abbey Treasury** (Opatska riznica). It is particularly known for its Dalmatian and Venetian art, including a polyptych by Blaž of Trogir, two altar paintings by Pellegrino of San Daniele, a *Sacred Conversation* and an *Annunciation* by Titian and *Portrait of a Man* by Vittore Carpaccio. To the left of the cathedral, a door by Bonino of Milan decorates the Gothic Church of St Peter (sv Petar). Facing the church are the Gothic Arneri Palace and the 16th-century Renaissance Gabriellis Palace. The latter has been the **Town Museum** (Gradski muzej) since 1957 and contains documents on Korčula's seafaring history, an interesting archaeo-logical section covering the period from prehistoric to Roman times and other works of art.

Along the seafront is the **All Saints' Church** (Svi Sveti), built in 1301 and remodelled in the Baroque style; it belongs to the oldest confraternity on the island. Inside is an 18th-century wooden *Pietà* by the Austrian artist George Raphael Donner, and a 15th-century polyptych by Blaž of Trogir. In the nearby quarters of the brotherhood is the **Icon Collection** (Zbirka ikona), famous for its range of

Proizd

Hvar
41 km (25 miles)

Vela Luka

Potirna

Blato

Prigradica

Prižba

Brna

The beautiful rocky coastline of Korčula

Byzantine icons from the 13th to the 15th centuries. Outside the walls are the **Church and Monastery of St Nicholas** (Sv. Nikola), from the 15th century, with paintings by Italian artists.

🏛 Abbey Treasury
Trg sv Marka. ℹ (020) 711 049.
Open call for information. 🎭

🏛 Town Museum
Trg sv Marka. **Tel** (020) 711 420.
Open Jul–Sep: 9am–9pm Mon–Sat; Apr–Jun: 10am–2pm Mon–Sat; Oct–Mar: 10am–1pm Mon–Sat; Sun: by appt.

🏛 Icon Gallery
Trg Svih Svetih. ℹ (020) 711 306, (091) 593 1281. **Open** summer: 10am–2pm & 5–8pm Mon–Sat; Winter & Sun: by appt.

Lumbarda
Thought to have been founded by Greeks, the village of Lumbarda lies 6 km (4 miles) southeast of Korčula town. In the 16th century, it became a holiday resort for the nobles of Korčula. Some inscriptions from the Greek period are now kept in the Archaeological Museum of Zagreb (see p473). Today, the village is the only centre of production for Grk, a liqueur-like white wine made from grapes of the same name. The nearby beaches are famous for their golden sands.

Blato
The central square of the village of Blato, towards the western end of the island, has an 18th-century Baroque loggia, the **Arneri Castle**, where the Civic Museum documents the local history of the town and displays archaeological finds from the surrounding area. **All Saints' Church** (Svi Sveti), of medieval origin, was enlarged and rebuilt in the 17th century. The church has an altarpiece of the *Virgin with Child and Saints* (1540) on the main altar by Girolamo di Santacroce and, in the chapel, the relics of the local focus of veneration, the martyr St Vincenza. The cemetery church of the **Holy Cross** and that of **St Jerome** date from the 14th century. Every April, the central square plays host to St Vincenza's Day, which is celebrated with Kumpanjija dance and drum music.

Vela Luka
Situated about 45 km (28 miles) west of Korčula town is Vela Luka, known as "the oldest and the newest town", because it was built at the beginning of the 19th century on the Neolithic site of Vela Spilja. One of the largest towns on the island, it has a number of industries that coexist with attractive bays and islands. The surrounding hills shelter the town from the winds from the north and south. Vela Luka is also the main port on the island and there are regular ferry services to Split (see pp446–9).

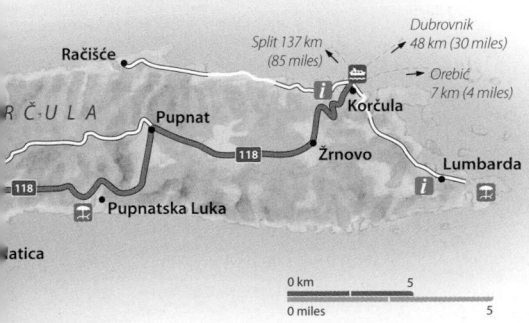

Račišće — Split 137 km (85 miles) — Dubrovnik 48 km (30 miles) — Orebić 7 km (4 miles)
Pupnat — Korčula
Žrnovo
118 — Lumbarda
Pupnatska Luka
atica

0 km 5
0 miles 5

Town of Korčula, on a peninsula on the northeast coast of the island

❻ Split

Built on the remains of an imperial Roman palace, Split is a fascinating and vibrant Mediterranean city, featuring palm-lined avenues and bustling pavement cafés. At its heart is the Palace of Diocletian, a 3rd-century structure that was abandoned by the Romans before being settled by sanctuary-seeking locals. Adapted to the needs of a growing city, the palace area is nowadays a labyrinth of atmospheric alleyways with exciting architectural discoveries at every corner. During the Middle Ages, a steadily growing Slav population turned Split into a centre of Croatian language and culture. Almost four centuries of Venetian rule (1409–1797) filled the city with Italianate art and architecture. During the 20th century, Split became the biggest ferry terminal on the Adriatic, and remains the main gateway to Croatia's seductively beautiful islands.

View of the port and the seafront in Split

🏛 Palace of Diocletian
See pp448–9.

🏛 Braće Radić Square
This medieval square (Trg braće Radić) is on the southwest corner of the Palace of Diocletian. The tall **Hrvoje's Tower** (Hrvojeva kula) is the only evidence of the imposing castle built here by the Venetians in the second half of the 15th century to strengthen the city's sea-facing defences. Built on an octagonal groundplan, it stands on the southern side of the square.

On the northern side of the square is the Baroque **Milesi Palace**, from the 17th century, and at its centre is a striking bronze statue dedicated to Marko Marulić (1450–1524), the writer and scholar who composed the first epic poem in the Croatian language. His statue, by sculptor Ivan Meštrović,

is inscribed with verses by another famous Croatian poet, Tin Ujević.

🏛 People's Square
The busy People's Square (Narodni trg/Pjaca) was Split's centre of business and admin-istration during the 15th century,

The 15th-century Hrvoje's Tower on Braće Radić Square

and the nobility erected prestigious buildings here. Examples include the Venetian Gothic Cambi Palace and the Renaissance **Town Hall** (Vijećnica), built in the first half of the 15th century, which has a loggia with three arches on the ground floor and a Gothic window on the upper floor.

🏛 Church of St Francis
Trg Republike. 🛈 (021) 348 600.
Open by appt.
The pretty Church of St Francis (Sv. Frane) has been rebuilt in recent times, but the Romanesque-Gothic cloister, with thin columns enclosing a flower garden, is original.

The church, with mainly Baroque furnishings, has a 15th-century crucifix by Blaž Jurjev Trogiranin (c. 1412–48). It also houses the tombs of the city's illustrious citizens, including that of Archdeacon Toma, the first Dalmatian historian, writer Marko Marulić and the well-known composer Ivan Lukačić.

🏛 Museum of Croatian Archaeological Monuments
Stjepana Gunjace bb. **Tel** (021) 323 901. **Open** Jul–Aug: 9am–1pm & 5–8pm Mon–Fri, 9am–2pm Sat; Sep–Jun: 9am–4pm Mon–Fri, 9am–2pm Sat. 🈁 🌐 mhas-split.hr

Set up in 1975, this museum (Muzej hrvatskih arheoloških spomenika) houses finds from the area around Split dating from the early Middle Ages. The collection also includes the works of early Croat sculptors, from AD 800. The stone fragments, salvaged from castles and churches, consist mainly of tombs, capitals, altar fronts, ciboria and windows. Highlights include Prince Višeslav's 9th-century hexagonal baptis-mal font and the striking 10th-century sarcophagus of Queen Jelena discovered in Solin, near the ancient Roman city of Salona (*see pp450–51*).

🏛 Meštrović Gallery
Šetalište Ivana Meštrovića 46.
Tel (021) 340 800. **Open** May–Sep: 9am–7pm Tue–Sun; Oct–Apr: 9am–4pm Tue–Sat, 10am–3pm Sun. 🈁

Distant Chords (1918) by Ivan Meštrović, Meštrović Gallery

Regarded as one of the most important sculptors of the 20th century, Ivan Meštrović *(see p470)* himself designed the Meštrović Gallery (Galerija Meštrović) building, which was his residence in the early 1930s. His sculptures decorate the garden and the interior, and part of the building still preserves the artist's apartments. Further down the road is the **Kaštelet**, a 17th-century residence that belonged to the Capogrosso-Kavanjin family and was bought by Meštrović in 1932 to set up an exhibition hall. It can be visited with the same ticket. He also built a church here to exhibit a series of reliefs.

🏛 Archaeological Museum

Zrinsko Frankopanska 25. **Tel** (021) 329 340. **Open** Jun–Sep: 9am–2pm & 4pm–8pm Mon–Sat; Oct–May: 9am–2pm & 4–8pm Mon–Fri, 9am–2pm Sat. 🈳 🎟 ♿

Considered Croatia's oldest museum, the Archaeological Museum (Arheološki muzej) was founded in 1820 and moved to its present location in 1914. It contains a fine collection of finds from the Roman, early Christian and medieval periods that are exhibited in rotation. Of particular interest are the finds from the ruins of Salona including sculptures, capitals, sarcophagi, jewellery, coins and small objects in glazed terracotta and ceramic.

🏔 Marjan Peninsula

Rising to the west of central Split is the Marjan Peninsula, a hilly, densely wooded area criss-crossed by attractive footpaths. The best way to reach Marjan is to walk through the Varos district immediately west of the Old Town, taking a flight of steps which gradually ascends Marjan's flanks. Near the top, fine views of Split's port, along with the islands of Brač *(see p452)* and Hvar *(see pp454–5)* to the south are clearly visible. Paths along the southern edge of the peninsula lead past a sequence of medieval chapels. The best beaches in Split are in this area.

VISITORS' CHECKLIST

Practical Information
210 km (131 miles) NW of
Dubrovnik. 🚗 178,000.
ℹ Peristil bb, (021) 345 606.
🎉 St Domnius Feast (7 May),
Split Summer (Jul–Aug),
Split Film Festival (Sep).
🌐 visitsplit.com

Transport
✈ 20 km (12 miles) N
of centre. 🚉 Obala kneza
Domagoja. 🚌 Obala kneza
Domagoja. ⛴ Jadrolinija.

Split Town Centre

① Palace of Diocletian
② Braće Radić Square
③ People's Square
④ Church of St Francis

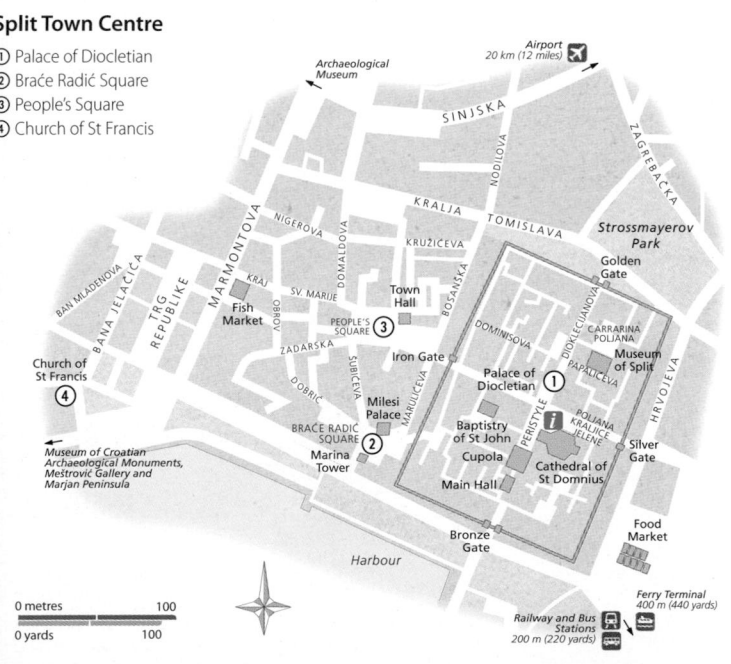

Split: Palace of Diocletian

Dioklecijanova palača

Split's main attraction is the Old Town centre, a fantastic architectural jumble built on what remains of the once-magnificent Palace of Diocletian, now a World Heritage Site. Believed to be a native of Salona, Diocletian became emperor of Rome in 284. After governing for 20 years, he retired from public life and in 305 moved into the palace in the bay of Split. The corners of the palace were marked by four square towers. Four further towers were set along each of the north, east and south sides, while the side facing the sea had a loggia with arches. After Diocletian's death, the palace was used as an administrative centre and also housed the governor's residence. In 615, refugees from Salona found shelter here after the destruction of their city by the Avars.

Iron Gate and the Clock Tower
The best preserved gate leads to the Church of Our Lady of the Belfry, with a 12th-century bell tower next to it.

★ Temple of Jupiter
Consecrated in the 6th century, the Temple of Jupiter had an atrium with six columns, while the main building had a coffered vault resting on a crypt. In the early Middle Ages, it was turned into the Baptistry of St John.

KEY

① **Bronze Gate**

② **The Temples of Venus and Cybele** were circular outside and had a hexagonal ground plan inside. A colonnaded corridor ran around the outside.

③ **Temple of Cybele**

④ **The Cardo** was the main street of the complex.

⑤ **The Decumanus**, a transverse path, divided the complex into two halves.

⑥ **The Silver or Eastern Gate** was a simpler version of the Golden Gate.

★ Peristyle
Near the crossroads where the Cardo and Decumanus intersected, the peristyle gave access to the sacred area of the palace. On one side were the temples of Venus and Cybele and, further back, that of Jupiter, now the Baptistry of St John.

Golden Gate

The main entrance to the palace, the Golden Gate, facing Salona *(see pp450–51)*, was the most imposing of the gates, with twin towers and numerous decorations.

VISITORS' CHECKLIST

Practical Information
Cathedral of St Domnius:
Open Jun–Aug: 8am–sunset;
Sep–May: 9am–noon &
4:30–7:30pm daily.
Temple of Jupiter: **Open** summer
only (8am–8pm).

Transport
Palace Basement.

Diocletian's Emblem

After reorganizing the empire, Emperor Diocletian sought the spiritual unification of its citizens. The state religion, personified by the emperor, grew steadily in importance and temples were constructed bearing his image.

Reconstruction of Diocletian's Palace

The spectacular palace, shown here in its original form, was laid out in the same way as a Roman military camp. It was 215-m (705-ft) long and 180-m (590-ft) wide and was enclosed by very thick walls, at times 28-m (92-ft) high. The four-sided stronghold was reinforced with towers on the north, east and west sides. There is a gate on each side, connected by two roads corresponding to the Roman Cardo and Decumanus.

★ Cathedral of St Domnius

Originally Emperor Diocletian's mausoleum, the cathedral was consecrated in the 7th century when the sarcophagus containing the emperor's body was removed. The superb interior features Roman columns and fine Romanesque carvings.

❼ Salona

The ancient town of Salona, 5 km (3 miles) from Split, is famous for its Roman ruins, scattered among meadows, olive groves and vineyards. The name Salona derives from the salt works in the area, the Latin for salt being *sal*. Originally an Illyrian settlement, it later came under Greek control, but only became an important centre when the Romans built a town next to the Greek city. Under the rule of Augustus, it became a Roman colony called Martia Julia Salonae, and in due course was made capital of the Dalmatian province. In the 1st century AD, the Romans built theatres, temples, town walls, towers and an amphitheatre, and Salona became the richest and most populous town in the mid-Adriatic. In 614, it was destroyed by the Avars and Slavs; the buildings were stripped and the stone used for new structures.

Main road leading to Salona

Ruins of the town walls and triangular tower

Exploring Salona
At the end of the 19th century, excavations began to bring to light the buried remains of this ancient settlement. The work revealed that the town had two districts dating from different periods: the original, Old Town (Urbs Vetus) and a later part which dates from the Augustan-era (Urbs Nova Occidentalis and Urbs Nova Orientalis). The excavations have uncovered only a part of the layout of the **Outer Walls**, which were frequently reinforced over the centuries. However, the foundations and the remains of the towers, with triangular or rectangular bases, are still visible.

The tour usually begins from the site closest to the entrance, the **Necropolis of Manastirine**, a burial area just outside the walls, north of the town. In the 4th century, a religious building

was constructed here to house the relics of the Salonian saints, victims of Emperor Diocletian's persecution of Christians. The ruins of the necropolis and the basilica are well preserved.

Located near Manastirine is the **Tusculum**, a villa with interesting sculptures embedded in the walls and the garden. It was built for the distinguished archaeologist Frane Bulić (1846–1934) to enable him to study the ruins of Salona. A scholar and director of the Archaeological Museum (*see p447*) in Split, Bulić devoted much of his life to researching the ancient city. The building is now a small museum, but the most interesting finds are now housed in the Archaeological Museum in Split.

Further on is the richest area of ruins with the foundations

of baths, the **Caesarea Gate** and early-Christian basilicas. The **Baths** were built in the 1st century when the town became the capital of the province of Dalmatia.

In the early Christian period, the buildings were probably transformed into religious buildings such as those in the **Bishop's Complex** in the northeastern part of ancient Salona. This comprised basilicas, a baptistry and the bishop's residence. Before Christianity became widespread, several early Christian martyrs were slayed here, including St Domnius (patron saint of Split), and Sts Venantius and Anastasius.

The foundations of two basilicas have been excavated: the Urban Basilica, and Honorius's Basilica, which had a Greek cross plan. This is also the site of what remains of the impressive Caesarea Gate, which features arches flanked by two octagonal towers, displaying the advanced

Excavated remains of the Necropolis of Manastirine

For hotels and restaurants see p482 and p483

The Basilica Urbana in the Bishop's Complex

building techniques used by the Romans in the imperial era.

Moving west along the walls, visitors reach the **Necropolis of Kapljuč**, another early Christian burial site, and then the imposing ruins of the **Amphitheatre**, in the westernmost part of the settlement.

The amphitheatre, in brick, was probably covered in stone and stood in the newer part of the town on the northwest edge of the Old Town (Urbs Vetus) close to the walls. According to historians, it could seat 20,000 people. The foundations and a part of the lower tribune have been excavated and the discovery of a network of underground channels has led to the theory that simulated naval battles were held in the arena. The amphitheatre's construction date was controversial for a long time, but it has now been dated to the second half of the 2nd century AD. From the amphitheatre, another path leads to the **Theatre** at the edge of the Old Town. This was built in the first half of the 1st century AD and part of the stage and the foundations of the stalls have been excavated. Next to the theatre is the **Forum**, the political and commercial heart of the town. Unlike the forum in Zadar *(see p458)*, the paving was dismantled and only the foundations remain. In the Roman era, some of the most important buildings stood around the Forum, which began to be built in the 1st century AD and were subsequently modified.

The best-preserved Roman construction from ancient Salona is the aqueduct, built to bring water from the Jadro river to the town, and extended during the reign of Diocletian to reach his palace *(see pp448–9)* in Split. Repair work was carried out at the end of the 19th century and the southern part of the aqueduct is still in use. Alongside the walls it is possible to see some parts of the aqueduct – more evidence of the great skill of Roman civil engineers.

From the theatre, visitors return to the Necropolis of Manastirine. North of this stands the **Necropolis of Marusinac**, built outside the ancient town around the tomb of St Anastasius.

VISITORS' CHECKLIST

Practical Information
255 km (158 miles) NE of Dubrovnik. *i* (021) 211 538. Ruins: **Open** Apr–Sep: 7am–7pm Mon–Fri, 9am–7pm Sat, 9am–1pm Sun; Oct–Mar: 9am–3:30pm Mon–Fri, 9am–2pm Sat. **W** solin-info.com

Transport
from Split.

The Amphitheatre, of which only a part of the lower tribune remains

The Ruins of Salona

① Necropolis of Manastirine
② Tusculum
③ Baths
④ Bishop's Complex
⑤ Caesarea Gate
⑥ Necropolis of Kapljuč
⑦ Amphitheatre
⑧ Theatre
⑨ Forum
⑩ Necropolis of Marusinac

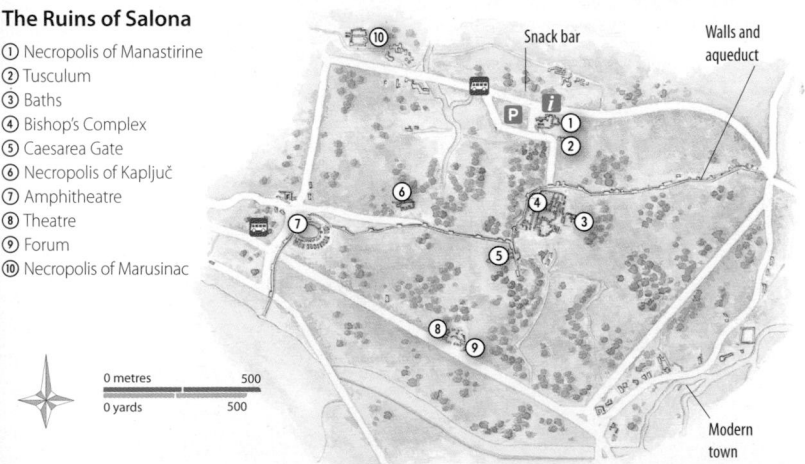

Snack bar

Walls and aqueduct

Modern town

0 metres 500
0 yards 500

For keys to symbols *see back flap*

❽ Brač

175 km (109 miles) NW of Dubrovnik.
🏔 14,000. ✈ 🚌 🚢 to Supetar from
Split. Supetar: ℹ Porat 1, (021) 630
551. 🌐 **supetar.hr** Bol: ℹ Porat
bolskih pomoraca bb, (021) 635 638.
🌐 **bol.hr**

The third largest island in the
Adriatic, Brač has an interesting
geological structure. In some
areas, the limestone hills have
sinkholes and are cut by deep
ravines and gorges. In others
a white, hard stone prevails,
which has been quarried since
ancient times. Extensive woods
cover some parts of the island,
while other parts are cultivated.

Although Brač has always
been inhabited, it was first ruled
by Salona *(see pp450–51)* and
the rich Salonians built villas
and sought refuge here when
their town was attacked by the
Avars. It was later ruled by Split
(see pp446–9). However, both
Split and Brač came under
Byzantine and then Venetian
rule (1420–1797).

Ferries departing from Split
on the mainland dock to the
Old Town of **Supetar**, which
has some good beaches. **Škrip**
is probably the site of the first
settlement on the island and
the presumed birthplace of Helen,
mother of Emperor Constantine,
the first Christian Roman emperor.
The church and a painting by
Palma il Giovane *(see p454)* on
its main altar are dedicated to
Helen. A fortified house in Škrip
is home to the **Brač Museum**,
which displays archaeological
finds from the area. To the
southwest lies **Milna**, which
was founded at the beginning

Zlatni rat, Bol's famous beach which changes with the seasons

of the 18th century and faces
a sheltered bay. The exterior of
the Church of the Annunciation
of Mary (Gospa od Blagovijesti)
is Baroque, with a Rococo
interior. In the centre of the
island, **Nerežišća** was Brač's
main town for a long period.
The governor's palace, the
loggia and a pedestal with
the lion of St Mark are signs
of its former status.

The major attraction at **Bol**,
on the southern coast, is its
famous long beach, Zlatni rat,
meaning Golden Horn – a
triangular spit of shingle which
reaches out into the sea and
changes shape with the
seasonal winds. It is
a popular spot
for windsurfing.

A Dominican
monastery, founded
in 1475, stands on a
headland at the edge
of the village. The
beautiful church here
is decorated with
paintings, including a
Virgin with Saints (1563)
attributed to Tintoretto.

A rich treasury includes
liturgical objects. From Bol,
visitors can make the 2-hour
climb up the 778-m (2,552-ft)
high **Vidova gora**, the highest
peak in the Dalmatian islands,
near which a fortified monastery,
Blaca Hermitage (Pustinja Blaca),
clings to the rocks. In **Pučišća**,
to the northeast, quarrymen
can be seen at work and the
old Roman quarries can also
be visited. Similarly charming
is **Sumartin**, further east, which
was founded by refugees from
the coastal region of Makarska,
when they fled the Turks in
1645. There is a fine Franciscan
monastery, the foundations of

The town of Pučišća on the island of Brač

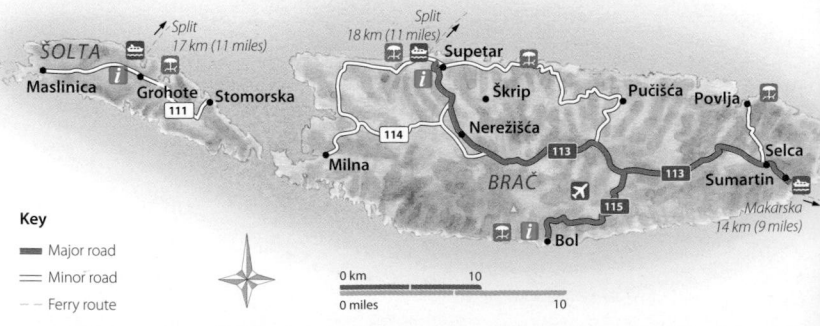

Key

▬ Major road
═ Minor road
--- Ferry route

0 km   10
0 miles   10

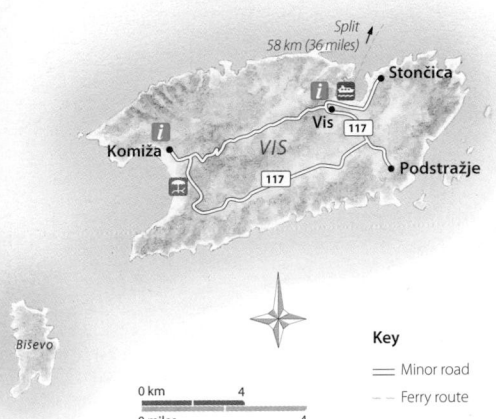

Key

═══ Minor road

- - - Ferry route

0 km   4

0 miles   4

The façade of the Church of Our Lady of Spilica, Vis

which were laid by the poet Andrija Kačić Miošić (1704–60).

Environs

The long island of **Šolta**, to the northwest of Brač, was a holiday resort for the nobility of Roman Salona. After the attack on Salona in 614, some of the refugees fled and established villages. It was later abandoned in favour of Split and left uninhabited for over a century due to frequent Turkish raids. Traces of defence towers can be seen, as well as the ruins of Roman villas.

🏛 Brač Museum

Škrip. *i* (021) 637 092.
Open summer: 8am–8pm Mon–Sat; winter: by appt.

❾ Vis

220 km (137 miles) NW of Dubrovnik. 🚍 4,300. 🚢 from Split. *i* Šetalište Stare Isse 5, (021) 717 017. Komiža: *i* (021) 713 455.

Further out to sea than the other Dalmatian islands, Vis was a military base until 1989 and closed to tourism. Now gradually being rediscovered by intrepid travellers, it has a jagged coastline with beaches, and an inland mountain chain with Mount Hum reaching a height of 587 m (1,925 ft).

The island was chosen by Dionysios of Syracuse as a base for Greek domination of the Adriatic. The Greeks founded the town of Issa here. The island was later ruled by the Romans, the

Byzantines and, from 1420, the Venetians. Vis played a key role during World War II – in 1944, Marshal Tito used it as a base for partisan military operations.

The main town of **Vis** has Venetian Gothic buildings and the Renaissance church of Our Lady of Spilica (Gospa od Spilica), with a painting by Girolamo di Santacroce (1516–84). In the town of **Komiža**, on the western coast, there is a tower built by the Venetians.

Environs

The island of **Biševo**, to the southwest of Vis, has a Blue Grotto (Modra Spilja), where, at midday, the water takes on beautiful colours. Day-trips by boat depart from Komiža and Vis in the mornings. The ruins of a monastery, built around AD 1000, can be seen; it resisted raids by pirates and Saracens for 200 years.

Beautiful coastline near Komiža, on the island of Vis

⑩ Hvar

Art treasures, a mild climate, good beaches and fields of scented lavender make this island one of the gems of the Adriatic. Limestone hills form the central ridge. Hvar's story begins in the 4th century BC when Greeks from Paros founded Pharos and Dimos, present-day towns of Stari Grad and Hvar. Traces have been left by the Romans, the Byzantines, the Croatian sovereigns and the Venetians, who ruled from 1278 until 1797. After 1420, defences were built, and the capital was moved from Pharos to Hvar. In 1886, under Austria-Hungary, the Hvar Hygienic Society began to promote the town as a health resort. Crucially for Croatian literature, Hvar was the native island of Renaissance poets Hanibal Lucić and Petar Hektorović, both of whom wrote lyrically about the people and landscapes of the Adriatic.

Main square of Hvar, with the Cathedral of St Stephen

A peaceful bay on the island of Hvar

Hvar Town

This beautiful town is one of the most visited on the eastern coast of the Adriatic Sea, thanks to the treasures within its 13th-century walls. During Venetian rule, local nobles and governors decided to make the town a safe harbour for the fleets going to, or returning from, the Orient. They also transferred the bishopric and built monasteries there.

Hvar has a long tradition of art and culture. It is home to one of the first theatres ever built in Europe. The town was also the birthplace of the Renaissance poet Hanibal Lucić (c. 1485–1553) and the playwright Martin Benetović (c. 1550–1607).

The town's most important buildings stand on three sides of the main square, the fourth side is open to the sea. The Renaissance **Cathedral of St Stephen** (Katedrala sv Stjepana) has a trefoil pediment and a 17th-century bell tower standing to one side. The interior contains many works of art including

Virgin and Saints (1627) by Palma il Giovane (1544–1628), *Pietà* (c. 1520) by Juan Boschetus, *Virgin with Saints* (1692) by Domenico Uberti and a fine 16th-century wooden choir.

The Clock Tower, the civic Loggia below and **Hektorović Palace** (Hektorovićeva palača), recognizable by the beautiful Venetian Gothic mullioned window, all date from the 15th century.

On the south side of the square is the **Arsenal**, which dates from the late 16th century. A theatre was built on the first floor in 1612. This was the first "public theatre" in the Balkans; people of all classes could come and watch performances here, regardless of their social standing.

Outside the walls of the Old Town are the **Franciscan Monastery** (Franjevački samostan), dating from 1461, and the Church of Our Lady of Charity (Gospa od Milosti), with a relief on the façade by Nikola Firentinac. Inside are *St Francis receiving the Stigmata* and *St Diego* by Palma il Giovane, three polyptychs by Francesco da Santacroce, *Christ on the Cross* by Leandro da Bassano, and six

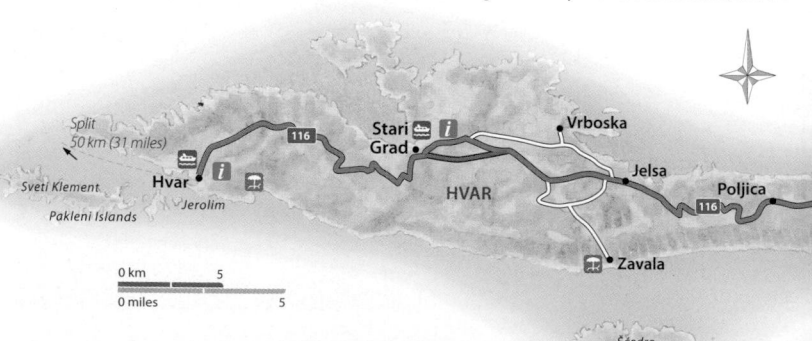

Lavender growing wild on the island of Hvar

scenes inspired by the Passion of Christ by Martin Benetović.

There are also many works of art in the rooms facing the cloister. The painter of the *Last Supper* in the refectory is unknown. The 16th-century Španjola fort and early 19th century Napoleon fort both offer splendid views of the town.

The cloister of the Franciscan Monastery, outside Hvar

Stari Grad

This town was originally called Pharos and was founded by the Greeks in the 4th century BC. Remains of the town can be seen in Ciklopska ulica. Around Pod dolom are the ruins of a Roman villa with mosaic floors.

Stari Grad lies at the end of a long bay and the key sights are situated around the main square. Facing the square are the 17th-century Church of St Stephen (Sv Stjepan) and the Baroque Biankini Palace (Palača Biankini), the home of an archaeological collection.

The heart of the town is dominated by Tvrdalj, the fortified residence of Petar

Hektorović (1487–1572), which houses an Ethnographic Collection and has a seawater fishpond. Hektorović, a poet, built the fort in around 1520. He was the author of the poem "Fishing and Fishermen's Conversation" (*Ribanje i ribarsko prigovaranje*) in which he describes a fishing trip around the islands of Hvar, Brač (*see p452*) and Šolta.

The **Dominican Monastery** (Dominikanski samostan) was founded in 1482. It was rebuilt and fortified after destruction by the Turks and has a rich library and a collection of paintings. The town also has an International School of Painting and Sculpture.

🏠 Dominican Monastery
Tel (021) 765 442. **Open** Jun–Sep: 10am–noon & 4–8pm; Oct–May: by appt.

Tvrdalj, Stari Grad

Vrboska

The road leading to this small village is a marvellous sight in June when the surrounding fields are covered with lavender. Vrboska is home to the

VISITORS' CHECKLIST

Practical Information
165 km (103 miles) NW of Dubrovnik. 🚐 11,500. Hvar: ℹ️ Trg svetog Stjepana bb, (021) 741 059. 🆆 tzhvar.hr Stari Grad: ℹ️ Obala dr F. Tudmana 1, (021) 765 763 🆆 stari-grad-faros.hr. Sućuraj: ℹ️ (021) 717 288. 🆆 tz-sucuraj.hr

Transport
Hvar: 🚢 from Split. Stari Grad: 🚢 from Split; Jadrolinija. Sućuraj: 🚢 from Drvenik.

16th-century Church of St Mary (Sv Marija), fortified in 1575 to provide shelter for villagers in the event of a siege. The Baroque Church of St Lawrence (Sv Lovro) has a polyptych (c. 1570) on the main altar by Paolo Veronese and a *Virgin of the Rosary* by Leandro da Bassano.

Sućuraj

Lying in a sheltered bay at the eastern tip of the island is the village of Sućuraj with the remains of a castle built by the Venetians in around 1630.

Environs

To the west of the island are the **Pakleni Islands**. Facing the town of Hvar, these islands are uninhabited and mostly wooded. Their name derives from the *paklina* (resin) that was once extracted from the pines and used to water-proof boats. During the summer, boat trips to the islands depart from Hvar. The nearest island, Jerolim, is given over to naturism.

The island of **Šćedro**, off the south coast of Hvar, is covered in pines and maquis. Illyrian tombs and parts of a Roman villa have been found here.

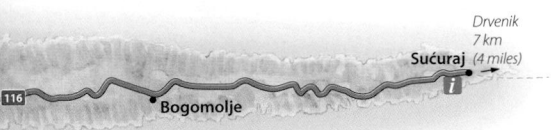

Drvenik 7 km
Sućuraj (4 miles)
116 Bogomolje

Key
— Major road
═ Minor road
-- Ferry route

For keys to symbols *see back flap*

⑪ Trogir

Set on an island joined to the mainland by a bridge, Trogir is one of the jewels of the Dalmatian coast. The Greeks of Issa, now Vis *(see p453)*, first settled here in the 3rd century, when they founded the fortified town of Tragyrion, which became Tragurium under the Romans in AD 48. In 1123, Trogir was attacked and destroyed by the Saracens and abandoned by the surviving inhabitants. It revived again 70 years later and a period of extra-ordinary artistic growth ensued, first under the kings of Hungary and later under Venetian rule. Trogir's buildings display a profusion of architectural styles, evidence of its earlier prosperity and cultural past. In 1997, it was listed as a UNESCO World Heritage Site.

The picturesque seafront at Trogir

🏛 Land Gate

Hrvatskih mučenika.

Rebuilt in the 17th century, the Land Gate (Sjeverna vrata) was made from a tall doorway in pale rusticated stone, with grooves that once supported a drawbridge. On the cornice above the arch is the Lion of St Mark and, above that, on a pedestal, stands a statue of St John of Trogir (Sv. Ivan Trogirski), one of the town's patron saints.

🏛 Civic Museum

Gradska vrata 4. **Tel** (021) 881 406. **Open** May–Oct: 9am–noon & 5–8pm Mon–Sat; Nov–Apr: 9am–2pm by appt.

Through the Land Gate is the lovely Baroque Garagnin Fanfogna Palace, now the Civic Museum (Muzej grada Trogira), with 18th-century furnishings. On display are interesting archaeological collections, books, documents, drawings and antique clothes linked to the town's history.

🏛 Stafileo Palace

Matije Gupca 20. **Closed** to the public.

Built in the late 15th century, the Stafileo Palace (Palača Stafileo) has a series of five windows in Venetian Gothic style on each of its two floors, their openings framed by pillars and carved arches. Around the arches are reliefs of flowers and leaves. The design is attributed to the school of Juraj Dalmatinac *(see p438)*, who worked for many years in Trogir.

🏛 Čipiko Palace

Gradska ulica. **Closed** to the public, except courtyard.

An inscription indicates 1457 as the year of completion of the Čipiko Palace (Palača Čipiko), built for Trogir's most illustrious family. Over a Renaissance doorway, distinguished by its columns, is a shell decoration above a finely worked cornice. The first floor has a beautiful mullioned window with a balustrade in stone; the second floor is similarly designed but lacks the balustrade. A second door, opening onto a side street, has a complex structure with two sculpted lions holding a coat of arms. They are flanked by sculptures of angels.

🏛 Cathedral of St Lawrence

Trg Ivana Pavla II. **Tel** (091) 531 4754. **Open** mid May–Oct: 9am–8pm; Nov–mid May: by appt.

This opulent Cathedral of St Lawrence (Katedrala sv Lovre) stands on the site of an ancient church destroyed by the Saracens. Construction began in 1193, but was prolonged for decades. Its most spectacular feature is the west door, decorated with carved reliefs executed by local stonemason Master Radovan in 1240. His delightful frieze, filled with plants and animals, depicts the changing of the seasons. Inside, there is an octagonal pulpit from the 13th century and a ciborium on the main altar with sculptures depicting the Annunciation.

To the right of the cathedral stands a 14th-century Venetian Gothic bell tower, rebuilt when Trogir became part of the Venetian territory.

🏛 Town Hall

Trg Ivana Pavla II.

On the eastern side of John Paul II Square (Trg Ivana Pavla II) stands the impressive Town Hall (Gradska vijećnica), originating in the 15th century. It has three storeys with open arches and a mullioned window with a balustrade on the upper floor; the façade is decorated with coats of arms. The pretty porticoed courtyard is open to the public.

Exterior of the Čipiko Palace, built for Trogir's most illustrious family

🏛 Loggia and Clock Tower

Trg Ivana Pavla II.

On the southern side of the square is the striking town Loggia (Gradska loža); its roof is supported by six columns with Roman capitals dating from the 14th century. On the wall are two splendid reliefs – *Justice* (1471) by Nikola Firentinac, and *Ban Berislavić* (1950) by Ivan Meštrović. The Clock Tower, to the left of the Loggia, supports a pavilion dome salvaged in 1447.

🏛 Church of St John the Baptist

Trg Ivana Pavla II. **Open** Check at tourist office for timings.

The Romanesque Church of St John the Baptist (Sv. Ivan Krstitelj), built in the 13th century, is the pantheon of the powerful Čipiko family. The church was home to an art gallery (Pinacoteca) with collections of medieval illuminated manuscripts, ornaments, paintings and gold pieces from various churches. However, the collection is currently in the Museum of Sacred Art near the cathedral.

🏛 Church of St Nicholas

Gradska ulica 2. **Tel** (021) 881 631. **Open** Check at tourist office for timings.

The Church of St Nicholas (Sv. Nikola) and Benedictine convent date from the 11th century, but were rebuilt in the 16th century. The convent now houses the Zbirka umjetnina Kairos, an interesting art collection that includes the *Kairos*, a relief of Greek origin dating from the 1st century BC, a Gothic crucifix and a Romanesque statue of *The Virgin with Child*.

🏛 Kamerlengo Castle and St Mark's Tower

Hrvatskog proljeća.

In the southwest corner of the island stands the beautiful Kamerlengo Castle (Kaštel Kamerlengo), at one time the residence of the Venetian governor. Built in around 1430, it stands facing the sea. It was once connected to St Mark's Tower (Kula svetog Marka), also built by the Venetians in 1470 for defence;

artillery was installed at the top of the castle for defence purposes.

Imposing St Mark's Tower, built for defence in 1470

Trogir Town Centre

① Land Gate
② Civic Museum
③ Stafileo Palace
④ Čipiko Palace
⑤ Cathedral of St Lawrence
⑥ Town Hall
⑦ Loggia and Clock Tower
⑧ Church of St John the Baptist
⑨ Church of St Nicholas
⑩ Kamerlengo Castle and St Mark's Tower

Airport
7 km (5 miles)

JADRANSKA MAGISTRALA
Market
Bus Station

BLAŽA JURJEVA TROGIRANINA

Land Gate ①

Civic Museum ②

RADOVANOV TRG

HRVATSKIH MUČENIKA

ŠUBIĆEVA

Čipiko Palace ④ ⑤ Cathedral of St Lawrence

③ MATIJE GUPCA
Stafileo Palace

TRG IVANA PAVLA II ⑥ Town Hall

⑦ Loggia and Clock Tower 🛈

⑧ Church of St John the Baptist

SINJSKA

AUGUSTINA KAŽOTIĆA

MORNARSKA

OBROV

IVANA DUKNOVIĆA

GRADSKA UL.

⑩ St Mark's Tower

HRVATSKOG PROLJEĆA 1971

MATICE HRVATSKE

VUKOVARSKA

Church of St Dominic

Walls

Church of St Nicholas ⑨

Marmont's Gloriette

⑩ Kamerlengo Castle

OBALA BANA BERISLAVIĆA

OBALA BANA BERISLAVIĆA

0 metres   100
0 yards   100

For keys to symbols *see back flap*

⓬ Kornati National Park

Nacionalni Park Kornati

340 km (213 miles) NW of Dubrovnik. 🚢 from Biograd, Murter, Primošten, Rogoznica, Vodice, Zadar. ℹ️ Butina 2, (022) 435 740. 🖥️ 🌐 **kornati.hr**

The Zadar Archipelago is made up of more than 300 islands surrounded by crystal-clear waters. In 1980, part of the archipelago was designated as Kornati National Park. It is 36 km (22 miles) long and 6 km (4 miles) wide and is made up of 89 islands of white stone, which about 20,000 years ago were the peaks of a mountain chain. These include Kornat (for which the National Park is named), Piškera, Lavsa and Mana along with dozens of rocky outcrops. There are no permanent inhabitants; even though the vegetation appears to be sparse, flora and fauna are rich.

Today, they belong to the people of the small island of Murter, who bought these islands around the end of the 19th century for grazing sheep. The park was set up to protect the waters, to allow marine life to flourish. With around 350 plant and 300 animal species, it is a popular destination with scuba divers and sailors. To conserve this diversity, fishing is prohibited in the park's waters. The best way to visit it is by a sailing boat, and there are also organized day-trips from Zadar and Murter, Biograd, Vodice, Primošten and Rogoznica.

Aerial view of the spectacular islands of Kornati National Park

⓭ Zadar

360 km (225 miles) NW of Dubrovnik. 🏙️ 92,000. ✈️ 🚉 from Zagreb. 🚌 from Rijeka, Split, Zagreb. 🚢 Jadrolinija. ℹ️ City: Ilije Smiljanića 5, (023) 212 222. Regional: Sv Leopolda Mandića 1, (023) 315 316. 🎭 Musical evenings at St Donat (Jul & Aug), Summer Theatre. 🌐 **visitzadar.net**

Set on a narrow peninsula on the Adriatic coast, Zadar's present layout dates back to Roman rule when it became an important *municipium*, and a port for the trading of timber and wine. It later enjoyed a spell of prosperity under Venetian rule, when many of its churches and palaces were built. Today, its proximity to the Zadar Archipelago has turned it

Imposing exterior of the Church of St Donat, Zadar

into a major ferry port. The centre of public life is the People's Square – a business district and the site of political debate, it has been the heart of the town since medieval times.

Further away is the Forum, where the main square of the ancient Roman city of Jadera once stood. Little remains of the Forum that once stood here since much of the original stone found its way into the adjacent 9th-century **Church of St Donat** named after its founder Bishop Donat. One of the finest examples of Byzantine architecture, it has a circular groundplan and a women's gallery. It has not been used as a church since 1797, but concerts are often held here. Beside the church is the "**Sea Organ**", a set of pipes built into stairs leading down to the sea, which produces a musical sound when the waves hit the shoreline. Another installation just next to this one is known as "**Greeting to the Sun**" and consists of 300 glass plates that produce interesting light effects.

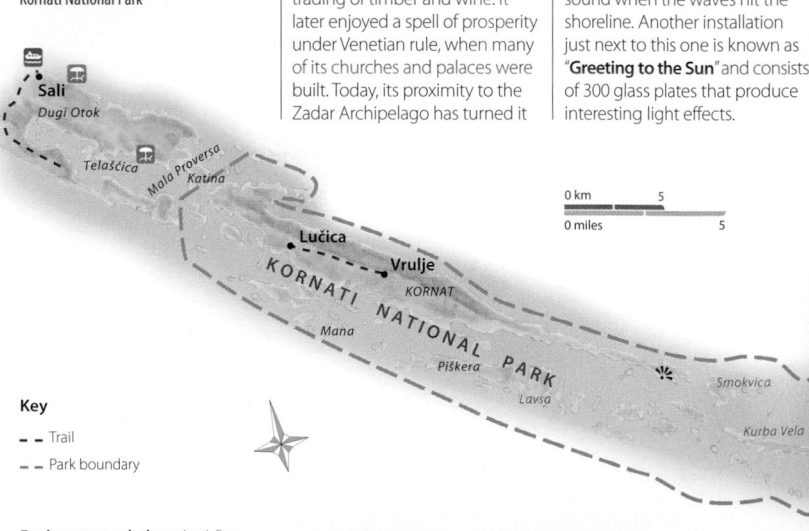

Key

– – Trail

– – Park boundary

For keys to symbols *see back flap*

The superb Romanesque **Cathedral of St Anastasia** is another attraction of the Forum. The interior contains fine Venetian carvings in the 15th-century wooden choir stalls. Beneath the ciborium lies the sarcophagus of St Anastasia, dating from the 9th century. The bell tower that stands to one side of the cathedral was completed in the 19th century by architect Thomas G. Jackson. Housed in a building near the Forum is the **Archaeological Museum**, with collections dating from prehistory to recent times from the entire Zadar area.

Striking Renaissance façade of the Church of St Mary, Zadar

🏛 **Church of St Donat**
Forum. ℹ️ Archaeological Museum, (023) 250 516. **Open** Apr, May & Oct: 9am–5pm daily; Jun–Sep: 9am–9pm daily; Nov–Mar: by appt. ♿

🏛 **Cathedral of St Anastasia**
Forum. **Tel** (023) 251 708. **Open** 8am–noon & 5–7pm daily.

⑭ Paklenica National Park
Nacionalni park Paklenica

370 km (231 miles) NE of Dubrovnik. 🚌 from Zadar. ℹ️ Starigrad Paklenica, (023) 369 202. **Open** Apr–Oct: 6am–8:30pm daily; Nov–Mar: 7am–3pm daily. ♿ 🌐 **paklenica.hr**

Situated in the Velebit massif, Paklenica National Park was founded in 1949. The entire Velebit massif chain is nearly 150 km (93 miles) long. The terrain is made up of limestone karst with many sink holes and plateaus separated by deep fissures. In 1978, UNESCO listed Velebit as a biological reserve with the aim of protecting this wildlife haven, which hosts 2,700 plant species and colonies of large birds of prey. The *kukovi* – rock formations sculpted by wind and water – are also protected.

The park itself covers an area of 95 sq km (37 sq miles), and is formed by two gorges, Big Paklenica (Velika Paklenica) and Small Paklenica (Mala Paklenica), which cut into the limestone mountains. Parts of the canyon walls are more than 400 m (1,312 ft) tall. High up, birds of prey make their nests in a habitat ideal for breeding. Golden eagles and even peregrine falcons can be spotted, while in the forests there are bears, wild boars, foxes and hares. The bare rock faces of Velika Paklenica are popular with rock climbers. The rock is pierced by numerous caves, but they are not easily accessible. Only the Manita Cave is open to visitors, when accompanied by a guide. However, deep within the walls of the canyon is an extensive network of underground tunnels built by the Yugoslav Army. These are currently being renovated for use as a multi-purpose visitor centre.

Hiking and mountain biking are popular activities here. A path in the valley penetrates far into the interior of the park to a cliff edge, which offers magnificent views of the wooded Vaganski vrh, the highest peak in the Velebit chain. In summer, visitors can stay overnight in the mountain hut, on the banks of the Velika Paklenica creek.

One of the forested paths leading to Paklenica National Park

⓯ Plitvice Lakes National Park

Nacionalni park Plitvička jezera

The picturesque Plitvice Lakes National Park, in the heart of Croatia, was founded in 1949. This area of 300 sq km (115 sq miles), covered in lakes and forest, has been on the UNESCO World Heritage Site since 1979. It is particularly known for its spectacular waterfalls. There are 16 lakes within the park, each offering eye-catching scenery; visitors can explore by following the paths along the shores or by using footbridges. There are no towns or villages in the reserve, only hotels. Shuttle buses take people to the starting points of the trails and to the hotels. The largest lake can be toured by electric boat.

A charming shepherd's hut located by the lake shore

Ciginovac

Prošćansko jezero

Okrugljak

STUBICA

Galovac

Footbridges and Boats
Numerous footbridges and environmentally friendly electric boats, that serve the largest lake in the region, enable visitors to move from one lakeshore to another and are a lovely way to explore the lush green fir, pine and beech forests.

Gradinsko jezero

PRIJEKA KOSA

Gliborita draga

Velika Poljana

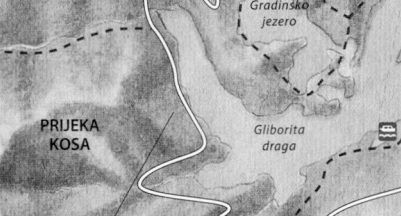

Dense Forests
The forests alongside the waters are home to some of the largest European species of animal, including wolves, lynx, foxes, wild boars, bears, roebucks, wild cats, otters and badgers.

For hotels and restaurants see p482 and p483

Flora
The park flora ranges from waterlilies on the lakes to forests of gigantic trees. The rich undergrowth is also a source of food for the park's wildlife.

VISITORS' CHECKLIST

Practical Information
460 km (288 miles) NW of Dubrovnik.
i (053) 751 015.
Open summer: 8am–sunset daily; winter: 9am–sunset daily.
partly.
w np-plitvicka-jezera.hr

Transport
from Zagreb.

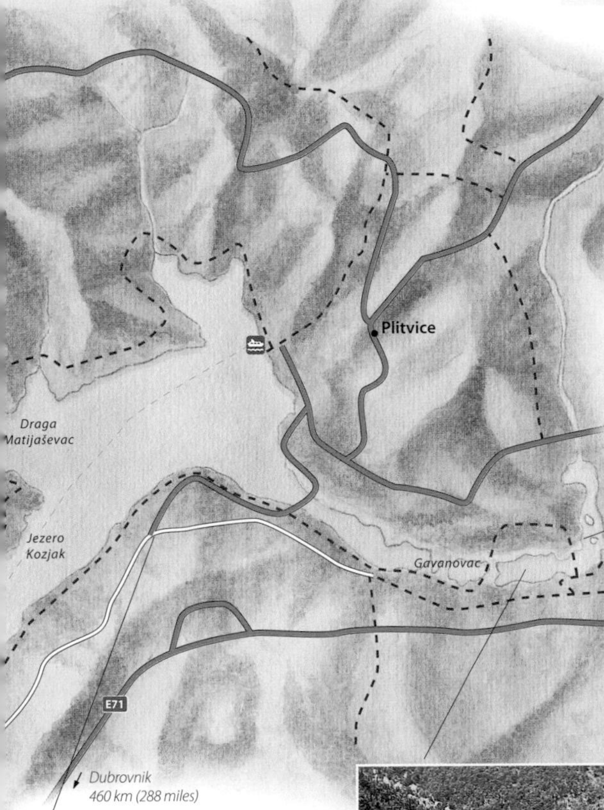

Plitvice

Draga
Matijaševac

Jezero
Kozjak

Gavanovac

Zagreb
160 km
(99 miles)

Entrance 1

E71

Dubrovnik
460 km (288 miles)

Waterfalls
Signposted routes direct visitors to viewpoints to watch the rushing water as it cascades from the lake above.

Special routes are taken by the park's shuttle buses to take visitors around the area.

Key

— Major road

═══ Minor road

- - - Trail

- - - Boat route

View of the Korana River
The lakes drain into the Korana river, one of Croatia's cleanest waterways. The long-winding river flows between steep cliffs amidst spectacular scenery, and is a popular place for kayak and raft trips.

For keys to symbols see back flap

View of the beautiful town of Rab with its four striking bell towers

⑯ Rab

460 km (288 miles) NW of Dubrovnik.
🏙 9,200. 🚌 from Rijeka & Zagreb.
🚢 from Rijeka, Jablanac, Pag, Valbisca
(Krk). 🛈 Trg Municipium Arba 8, (051)
724 064. 🎭 Tournament of Rab (July
25–27), Musical Evenings, Church of the
Holy Cross (Jun–Sep). 🌐 tzg-rab.hr

The Kvarner Gulf region, home
to the enticing island of Rab,
lies parallel to the Velebit
massif. With its sandy beaches
and mild climate, the island is
a popular holiday destination.
The main town, Rab, which
gives its name to the island,
became a bishopric in the
early Christian period and was
inhabited by Slavic people
in the 6th century. The town
came under Venetian rule
between 1409 and 1797 and
has some fine examples of
Venetian architecture, including its four famous bell towers
which make it look like a ship.
The Sea Gate, a tower from the

14th century, leads to the
town square. The heart of Rab,
the square, is graced by the
13th-century Romanesque
Prince's Palace, which was
later rebuilt in Renaissance
style with mullioned windows.
In the courtyard are some
Roman and medieval remains.

The town has many monastic
buildings. Among them, the
fine Romanesque **Cathedral of
St Mary the Great** has a stunning
façade of pink and white stone
with a sculpted *Deposition* by
Petar Trogiranin above the portal.
Inside is a beautiful font, made
by the same sculptor in 1497.
At a height of 70 m (230 ft), the
cathedral's 13th-century bell
tower is the tallest on the island.

Northwest of Rab, set on a
long bay, the village of Kampor
is famous for the Church of
St Bernard, which contains
superb panels. Further north, at
the end of a rocky peninsula, is
the village of Lopar, popular for
its beaches and leisure facilities.

⑰ Rijeka

620 km (388 miles) NW of Dubrovnik.
🏙 130,000. ✈ 🚆 from Zagreb.
🚌 from Pula, Zadar & Zagreb. 🚢
Jadrolinija, Riva 16. 🛈 Korzo 14, (051)
335 882. 🎭 Rijeka Carnival (Feb &
Mar), Rijeka's Summer Nights Arts
Festival (Jun–Jul). 🌐 visitrijeka.hr

Once the Roman city of
Tarsatica, Rijeka came under
the Habsburgs in 1466 and was
declared a free port in 1719.
Today Rijeka is one of Croatia's
main ports and a key rail and
road junction.

The Korzo, a broad avenue
running south of the Old Town,
is the heart of the city and
lined with majestic 19th-cen-
tury buildings. Halfway along
stands the domed Civic Tower,
decorated with the coat of
arms of the city. In the Old
Town is the **Cathedral of
St Vitus**. Built at the top of a
hill between 1638 and 1742,
the interior features a Gothic
crucifix from the 13th century
on the main altar. To the west
stands the late 19th-century
Governor's Palace, which since
1955 has housed the **Maritime
and History Museum of the
Croatian Littoral**. Founded in
1876, the museum documents
the history of navigation
through a collection of seafaring equipment from the 17th
and 18th centuries. East of the
cathedral lies Tito Square, from
where 561 steps lead up to the
Sanctuary of Our Lady of Trsat,
a church and a monastery built
by Martin Frankopan. According
to legend, parts of the Holy
House of Mary of Nazareth were
brought here in 1291, before
being transferred to Italy. To
compensate the local people
for this loss, Pope Urban V
donated a *Virgin with Child* in
1367, painted by St Luke, a copy
of which now stands on the
main altar. Opposite the church
is **Trsat Castle**, built by the
Romans to defend Tarsatica,
parts of which are intact.

In February and March
from the first Sunday after Ash
Wednesday, Rijeka hosts Croatia's
largest carnival celebrations.

The Sea Gate, one of the many entrances
into Rab town

Gothic crucifix in the Cathedral of
St Vitus, Rijeka

For hotels and restaurants see p482 and p483

The Temple of Romae and Augustus, a jewel of Roman architecture, Pula

⑱ Pula

720 km (450 miles) NW of Dubrovnik.
🏔 60,000. ✈ 🚊 from Zagreb. 🚌 from Poreč, Rovinj & Zagreb. 🚢 from Zadar. ℹ️ Forum 3, (052) 219 197.
🎭 Music events in Arena, Pula Amphitheatre (summer), Croatian Film Festival (summer). 🌐 **pulainfo.hr**

The hisoric town of Pula is best known for its magnificent monuments from the Roman era, when it was a colony known as Pietas Julia. It was destroyed by an East-Germanic tribe, the Ostrogoths, but began to flourish again when it became the main base for the Byzantine fleet in the 6th and 7th centuries. In 1150, it came under Venetian rule and in 1856, Austria made it the base for its fleet. Pula continues to be one of the most important naval bases in Croatia and it is also now an important university town.

The **Pula Amphitheatre** is the town's star attraction. Regarded as one of the six largest Roman amphitheatres in the world, it once seated 23,000 spectators. Originally built by Emperor Claudius, it was expanded by Emperor Vespasian in AD 79 for gladiator fights. Today, it is a popular venue for concerts ranging from opera to rock as well as an annual film festival.

To the south of the amphitheatre, two gates mark the entrance to the heart of the town. The single-arched **Gate of Hercules**, with a carving of the head of Hercules at the top, was built in the 1st century BC and is the oldest and best-preserved Roman monument in the town. Just north, towards the harbour, the later **Twin Gate**, with an ornate frieze, leads to the **Archaeological Museum**. On display are finds from Pula and the surrounding area, with collections from Prehistoric times to the Middle Ages. Roman antiquities and architectural remains from medieval times are the other items on exhibit.

In the southeast of the town stands the **Arch of the Sergii**, also known as the Golden Gate. It was erected in the 1st century BC to honour three brothers who held important positions in the Roman Empire. Its frieze has a bas-relief depicting a chariot pulled by horses.

Headless statue, Archaeological Museum

⑲ Rovinj

700 km (438 miles) NW of Dubrovnik.
🏔 13,000. ✈ 🚌 from Pula, Poreč, Rijeka & Zagreb. ℹ️ Obala Pina Budicina 12, (052) 811 566. 🎭 Grisia, International Art Exhibition (2nd Sun Aug); Patron St Euphemia's Day (16 Sep). 🌐 **tzgrovinj.hr**

Originally a port built by the Romans, the pleasant town of Rovinj is situated on what was formerly an island. The strait separating it from the coast was filled in 1763, after which the town expanded on to the mainland. Rovinj was ruled by the Byzantines and Franks, from 1283 until 1797, and then passed into Venetian hands.

The remains of a wall dating back to the Middle Ages can still be seen. In the square in front of the pier is Balbi's Arch, an ancient city gate, as well as a striking late-Renaissance clock tower. The Baroque Califfi Palace is now the **Native Museum**, housing 18th-century art from the Venetian school and works by modern Croatian artists. Dominating the town from its hilltop location is the 18th-century **Cathedral**, dedicated to the third-century martyr St Euphemia. Originating in early Christian times, it was rebuilt in 1736. The saint's remains are preserved in a Roman sarcophagus in the apse of the triple-aisled church. The adjacent bell tower is over 62 m (200 ft) high and was modelled on that of San Marco in Venice. It is crowned by a copper statue of St Euphemia. Along the waterfront, the interesting Institute of Marine Biology, founded in the late 19th century, houses one of the oldest aquariums in Europe.

To the south of the town lies Zlatni rt, an attractive park planted with cedars and cypresses and fringed by rocky beaches.

🏛 Native Museum
Trg m. Tita 11. **Tel** (052) 816 720.
Open summer: 10am–2pm & 6–10pm Tue–Fri, 10am–2pm & 7–10pm Sat & Sun; winter: 10am–1pm Tue–Sat.

The port town of Rovinj, dominated by the cathedral and its bell tower

⑳ Euphrasian Basilica

Eufrazijeva bazilika

Located in the town of Poreč, this 6th-century church is a Byzantine masterpiece decorated with mosaics on a gold background. It was built for Bishop Euphrasius between 539 and 553 by expanding the existing 4th-century Oratory of St Maurus Martyr, patron saint of Poreč. Although the building has undergone many alterations over the centuries, some of the original floor mosaics survive. In December 1997, the basilica was added to the UNESCO World Heritage Site. Classical concerts are held in the church from July to August.

★ **Ciborium**
Dominating the presbytery is a beautiful 13th-century ciborium supported by four marble columns. The canopy is decorated with mosaics.

★ **Apse Mosaics**
Mosaics from the 6th century cover the apse. Christ and the Apostles are depicted on the arch, while the Virgin appears on the vault enthroned with the child and two angels. Bishop Euphrasius himself is shown with a model of the basilica.

Sacristy and Votive Chapel
Past the sacristy's left wall is a triple-apsed chapel with a 6th-century mosaic floor. Here lie the remains of Sts Maurus and Eleuterius.

KEY

① **The Garden is home to the remains** of a 4th-century mosaic floor from the Oratory of St Maurus Martyr.

② **Bell tower**

③ **The Bishop's Residence**, a triple-aisled building dating from the 6th century, now houses paintings by Antonio da Bassano, Palma il Giovane and a polyptych by Antonio Vivarini.

Interior

The entrance leads to a large basilica with a central nave and two side aisles. The 18 Greek marble columns have carved capitals featuring animals, some of Byzantine origin and others Romanesque. All bear the monogram of Euphrasius.

VISITORS' CHECKLIST

Practical Information
710 km (444 miles) NE of Dubrovnik. **Tel** (052) 431 635. *i* Eufrazijeva ulica 22, (052) 429 030. **Open** Apr–Jun & Sep–Oct: 9am–6pm Mon–Sat; Jul & Aug: 9am–9pm Mon–Sat; Nov–Mar: 9am–4pm Mon–Sat. 🚻

Transport
🚌 from Rovinj, Pula & Zagreb.

Baptistry

This octagonal building dates from the 6th century. In the centre is a baptismal font and there are also fragments of mosaics. To the rear is a 16th-century bell tower.

Atrium

The church atrium is composed of a square portico with two columns on each side. Medieval tombstones and archaeological finds are displayed here.

㉑ Zagreb

Croatia's capital since 1991, Zagreb is the heart of the political, economic and cultural life of the country. With a population of almost 800,000, it is also Croatia's largest city. Zagreb is divided into two parts: the Old Town (Gornji grad or Upper Town), which includes the two districts of Gradec and Kaptol, and the modern area (Donji grad or Lower Town). The Upper Town is home to the main centres of religious, political and administrative power. The Lower Town developed after 1830 around a U-shaped series of parks and open spaces known as the "green horseshoe", and the major museums, including the Mimara Museum and Gallery of Old Masters, are all located here, as well as the Croatian National Theatre. Around Governor Jelačić Square (Trg bana Jelačića), where the Upper and Lower towns meet, there are plenty of lively cafés with summer terraces.

Mary with Child, Church of St Mark

Sights at a Glance

① Cathedral of the Assumption of the Blessed Virgin Mary
② Archbishop's Palace
③ Dolac Market
④ Stone Gate
⑤ City Museum
⑥ Meštrović Gallery
⑦ Church of St Mark
⑧ Croatian Museum of Naïve Art
⑨ Lotrščak Tower
⑩ Church of St Catherine
⑪ Croatian National Theatre
⑫ Museum of Arts and Crafts
⑬ Mimara Museum
⑭ Gallery of Old Masters
⑮ Archaeological Museum
⑯ Museum of Contemporary Art

Key

- Street-by-Street area: *see pp468–9*
- Major sight / Place of interest
- Pedestrian street
- — Railway

Greater Zagreb

Granešina
Sesvete
Črnomerec
Maksimir
ZAGREB
🚉 Zagreb
Jarun
Lake Jarun
Sava
⑯
Novi Zagreb
Botinec
✈ Zagreb

0 km ___ 3
0 miles ___ 3

Key

Area of the main map

ILICA
MEDULIĆEVA
FRANKOPANSKA
DALMATINSKA
PRILAZ GJURE DEŽELIĆA
TRG MARŠALA T
⑫
⑪
KLAIĆEVA
ROOSEVELTOV TRG
⑬
TRG BRAĆ MAŽURAN
PERKOVĆEVA
VUKOTINOV
MARULIĆ TRG
SAVSKA
VODNIKOVA
CRNATKOVA
TUŠKAN
STRELJA
DEŽMANOVA

A   B   C

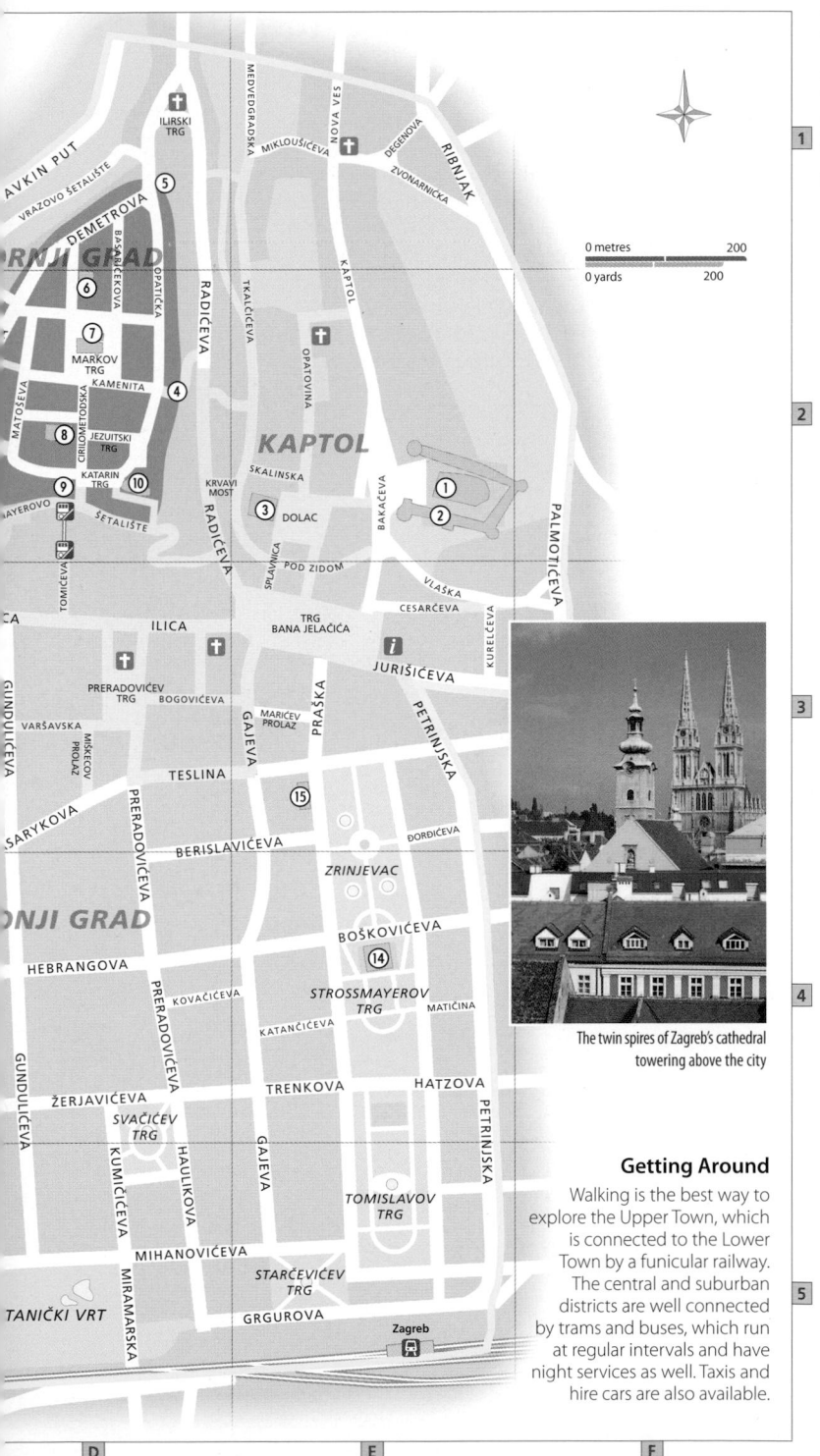

The twin spires of Zagreb's cathedral towering above the city

Getting Around

Walking is the best way to explore the Upper Town, which is connected to the Lower Town by a funicular railway. The central and suburban districts are well connected by trams and buses, which run at regular intervals and have night services as well. Taxis and hire cars are also available.

Street-by-Street: the Upper Town

In the Upper Town (Gornji grad) there are various institutions that have played a significant part in the history of the city and of Croatia. They now house the political and cultural centres of the country: the presidency of the republic, the parliament, the State Audit Court and several government ministries. All of these buildings were restored, repaired or rebuilt after the devastating earthquake of 1880. Some of the ancient noble palaces have been converted into museums. There are also three interesting churches: the ancient Church of St Mark, the Baroque Church of St Catherine, built by the Jesuits, and the Church of Sts Cyril and Methodius. The daily signal to close the city gates was rung from the medieval Lotrščak Tower.

The Natural History Museum, created from three collections, houses most of the finds from Krapina, which date human presence in Croatia back to the Palaeolithic era.

Ban's Palace
The building dates from the 17th century and was built after the city became the seat of the Ban, Governor of Croatia, in 1621. It now houses the presidency of the republic.

Croatian Historical Museum
This museum, housed in the splendid Vojković-Oršić Palace has works of art and documents collected since 1959.

⑧ ★ **The Croatian Museum of Naïve Art**
Over 1,500 works of Naïve art by the founders and followers of the Hlebine school are held here.

The Church of Sts Cyril and Methodius was designed in the early 19th-century by Bartol Felbinger. This Byzantine-style church serves Croatia's Greek Catholic community and has a splendid iconostasis.

⑨ **Lotrščak Tower**
At noon every day a cannon is fired from this tower, which dates from the 12th century.

Museum of Broken Relationships
The museum is dedicated to failed love relationships. Its exhibits include personal objects left behind from former lovers, accompanied by brief descriptions.

For hotels and restaurants see p482 and p483

⑥ ★ Meštrović Gallery
The great Croatian sculptor Ivan Meštrović lived in this 18th-century building from 1922 to 1941. About ten years before his death, he donated his home and all the works of art in it to the state.

Parliament Building
This building dates from 1910, when the provincial administration offices were enlarged. The independence of Croatia was proclaimed from the central window of the building in 1918.

⑦ ★ Church of St Mark
The coloured tiles on the roof of this fine Gothic church form the coats of arms of Croatia, Dalmatia, Slavonia and Zagreb.

The Klovićevi dvori is one of the city's most important art exhibition spaces. Housed in a 17th-century Jesuit monastery, prestigious touring exhibitions are held here throughout the year.

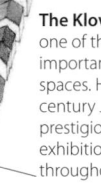

⑩ Church of St Catherine
Built on the site of an ancient Dominican church, this is the city's most fascinating Baroque building.

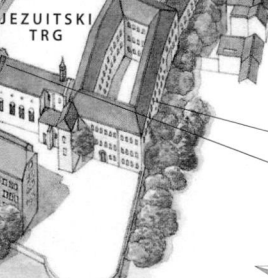

Key

— Suggested route

| 0 metres | | 50 |
| 0 yards | | 50 |

Awe-inspiring central nave of Cathedral of the Assumption of the Blessed Virgin Mary

① Cathedral of the Assumption of the Blessed Virgin Mary
Katedrala Marijina Uznesenja

Kaptol. **Map** E2. **Tel** (01) 481 4727.
Open 10am–5pm Mon–Sat, 1–5pm Sun.

Dedicated to the Assumption and the Blessed Virgin Mary, Zagreb's cathedral is the city's most recognizable landmark. Despite its 11th-century origins, the cathedral owes its present appearance to the reconstruction carried out by Austrian architect Friedrich von Schmidt and Hermann Bollé following the earthquake of 1880.

The imposing Neo-Gothic façade is topped by a slender pair of 105-m (345-ft) high spires. The

Intricate detail on a pillar inside Cathedral of the Assumption of the Blessed Virgin Mary

lofty interior contains a string of Neo-Gothic altars and some impressive earlier tombstones, notably the fine Baroque plaque honouring the warrior-aristocrat Toma Bakac Erdödy. Behind the altar is an effigy of Cardinal Alojzije Stepinac, who was persecuted by the Communist regime and subsequently beatified by Pope John Paul II.

② Archbishop's Palace
Nadbiskupska palača

Kaptol. **Map** E2. **Closed** to the public.

The complex of buildings that forms the Archbishop's Palace encloses three sides of Cathedral Square. It incorporates three of five round towers and one square tower, which were built from 1469 onwards as defence against Ottoman attacks. The present palace dates from 1730, when several buildings were linked and unified by a single, imposing Baroque façade.

In the square in front of the palace stands a fountain crowned by a statue of Mary with four angels, by Viennese sculptor Dominik Fernkorn, in around 1850.

The former moat east of the palace has now been converted into the Ribnjak Park, with various statues, including one called *Modesty* by Antun Augustinčić. A leafy area ideal for strolling, the park also includes a couple of popular cafés.

③ Dolac Market

Dolac. **Map** E2. **Tel** (01) 481 4959.

Overlooking Governor Jelačić Square (Trg bana Jelačića) and west of Zagreb's Cathedral is this picturesque market, which has held this spot since 1930. Local farmers display their colourful produce, while fresh fish from the Adriatic is sold from a pavilion in the market's northwestern corner. Dominating the plaza above Dolac Market is a sculptural ensemble by Vanja Radauš featuring Petrica Kerempuh, a fictional character who figures strongly in Croatian literature.

On the western side of the market is the **Church of St Mary** (Crkva sv Marije), a 14th-century church rebuilt in Baroque style in 1740. Inside is a fine collection of marble altars by 18th-century Slovene stonemason Franjo Rottman.

④ Stone Gate
Kamenita vrata

Kamenita. **Map** D2.

West of Dolac Market, the streets ascend towards Gradec, a well-preserved old quarter, that was once surrounded by defensive walls. Gradec's only surviving gate is the Stone Gate, a 13th-century structure that houses one of the city's most venerated shrines. According to popular belief, a painting of the Virgin Mary, which hangs inside

Baroque façade of the elegant Archbishop's Palace

Sculptures in the garden of the Meštrović Gallery

the gate, miraculously survived a fire in 1731. The painting became the centre of a popular cult, and Zagreb folk still come here to light candles and offer prayers.

On the other side of the gate, on the corner of Habdelićeva and Kamenita, stands **Ljekarna Aligheri**, a pharmacy that has been in existence since 1350. The pharmacy was named after the previous owner, Nicolò Alighieri, great-grandson of Italian poet Dante Aligheri.

⑤ Zagreb City Museum
Muzej grada Zagreba

Opatička ulica 20. **Map** D1. **Tel** (01) 485 1361. **Open** 10am–6pm Tue–Fri, 11am–7pm Sat, 10am–2pm Sun. 🖼 📷 by appt. 🔧 ✉ 🔳 **mgz.hr**

Three historic buildings – the Convent of the Nuns of St Clare dated from around 1650, a 13th-century tower and a granary from the 17th century – combine to form the City Museum. A room-sized floor map depicting the history and culture of Zagreb is on display. The permanent exhibition, which comprises more than 2,500 exhibits, has a thematic approach that helps the visitor to understand the various aspects of the city. It covers 45 diverse topics, ranging from the artistic and the popular to the everyday. On the same street as the museum a 19th-century **Palace** houses part of the

Croatian Academy of Arts and Sciences. Inside is the beautifully decorated Illyrian Hall (Ilirska dvorana). The 19th-century Paravić Palace, with wrought-iron gates, is now the Institute of Historical Studies.

Statues of saints from the main portal of the convent, City Museum

⑥ Meštrović Gallery
Atelje Meštrović

Mletačka 8. **Map** D2. **Tel** (01) 485 1123. **Open** 10am–6pm Tue–Fri, 10am–2pm Sat & Sun. 🖼

This 17th century gallery building was modernized by sculptor Ivan Meštrović and was his residence between 1922 and 1942. It now belongs to the Meštrović Foundation, which also owns the gallery and the Kaštelet in Split *(see p447)* as well as Meštrović's mausoleum. It houses a collection of Meštrović's work. There are almost 300 works on display, including copies of *History of Croatia, Deposition* and *Woman in Agony.*

⑦ Church of St Mark
Crkva sv Marka

Markov trg. **Map** D2. **Tel** (01) 485 1611. **Open** call in advance.

Now the Upper Town's parish church, the Church of St Mark was first mentioned in 1256, when King Bela IV granted permission to hold a fair in front of the church. On the south side of the church is a Gothic portal carved by Ivan Parler between 1364 and 1377. Surrounding the portal are 15 niches containing statues of Jesus, Mary, St Mark and the 12 apostles. The tiles of the church roof portray the coats of arms of Croatia, Dalmatia, Slavonia and the city of Zagreb.

The 20th-century sculptor Ivan Meštrović

Ivan Meštrović

Born in 1883, Ivan Meštrović (1883–1962) is regarded as one of the most important sculptors of the 20th century. He studied sculpture in Split and Vienna before he established himself in Paris in 1908. He worked in various cities, including Split – where he created many of the works now on display in the Meštrović Gallery – and Zagreb. After World War II, he taught at universities in the US, where he died in 1962. He was buried in the mausoleum in Otavice that he designed for himself and his family.

Woodcutters (1959) by Ivan Generalić, Croatian Museum of Naïve Art

⑧ Croatian Museum of Naïve Art

Hrvatski muzej naivne umjetnosti

Čirilometodska ulica 3. **Map** D2.
Tel (01) 485 1911. **Open**
10am–6pm Tue–Fri, 10am–1pm
Sat & Sun. 🖼️ 🎫 🎦 **W** hmnu.org

Since 1994, this 18th-century building, with its Neo-Baroque façade, has housed works from an exhibition of Naïve painters that opened in Zagreb in 1952. Inspired by peasant craft traditions, the paintings are characterized by the use of vivid colour and a strong feeling for narrative. There are paintings by the founders of the Naïve trend, including Ivan Generalić and Mirko Virius; some new works by the Hlebine School of Painting, which originated in the village of Hlebine near the Hungarian border; and works by artists such as Ivan Rabuzin from other regions.

⑨ Lotrščak Tower

Kula Lotrščak

Strossmayerovo šetalište. **Map** D2.
Tel (01) 485 1768. **Open** Apr–Oct:
9am–9pm Mon–Fri, 10am–9pm Sat
& Sun. 🖼️

Dating from the 13th century, the captivating Lotrščak Tower, or Burglars' Tower, is one of the oldest buildings in Zagreb and a remnant of its fortifications. Since the middle of the 19th century, the city's inhabitants have set their clocks at noon by the sound of a cannon fired from this tower, a practice begun in 1877 to coordinate the city's bell-

ringers. Today, the tower houses an art gallery and a gift shop. It is worth climbing the spiral staircase up to the terrace to enjoy the fine views over the red-tiled roofs of the city.

⑩ Church of St Catherine

Crkva sv Katarina

Katarinin trg. **Map** D2.
Tel (01) 485 1950.
Open 8am–8pm daily.

Considered to be one of the most beautiful religious buildings in Zagreb, the Church of St Catherine was built by Jesuits around 1630 on the site of a Dominican building. The white façade has a doorway with four niches for statues and six prominent pilasters. Above is a niche with a statue of the Virgin Mary. The single-nave church has one of the most striking Baroque

interiors in Croatia. Of particular interest are the stucco reliefs covering the walls and ceiling made by Antonio Quadrio. On the ceiling is a medallion depicting *Scenes of the Life of St Catherine* by Franc Jelovšek, while the main altar, dating from 1762, has *St Catherine among the Alexandrian Philosophers and Writers*, by Kristof Andrej Jelovšek.

⑪ Croatian National Theatre

Hrvatsko narodno kazalište

Trg maršala Tita 15. **Map** C4.
Tel (01) 4888 418. **Open** for performances only. **Closed** Mon, 1 Jan, Easter, 1 May, 1 Nov, 25–26 Dec.
W hnk.hr

The Croatian National Theatre stands in the square that marks the beginning of a U-shaped series of parks and squares called the "green horseshoe", the design of engineer Milan Lenuci. Completed in 1895, the theatre was designed by the architects Hermann Helmer and Ferdinand Fellner and is a blend of Neo-Baroque and Rococo styles.

The richly decorated interior is famous for the stage curtain, which features a patriotic scene entitled *The Croatian Renewal* by painter Vlaho Bukovac. In front of the theatre stands a masterpiece by sculptor Ivan Meštrović *(see p471)* called *The Well of Life*, depicting a group of bronze figures huddled around a well.

Stately exterior of the Neo-Baroque Croatian National Theatre

⑫ Museum of Arts and Crafts
Muzej za umjetnost i obrt

Trg maršala Tita 10. **Map** C4.
Tel (01) 488 2111. **Open** 10am–7pm
Tue–Sat, 10am–2pm Sun. 🅿 🅲 🅿
📷 🖥 🅦 muo.hr

This elegant 19th-century building contains the finest collection of applied art in the country, with an extensive display of furniture throughout the ages. Many of the exhibits are by graduates of the Zagreb School of Applied Arts, which has been turning out talented ceramicists, glass-makers and graphic designers since its establishment in 1882. An outstanding collection of photography and poster art is also on display.

The Bather (1868) by Renoir in the Mimara Museum

⑬ Mimara Museum
Muzej Mimara

Rooseveltov trg 5. **Map** C4. **Tel** (01)
482 8100. **Open** Oct–Jun: 10am–5pm
Tue, Wed, Fri & Sat, 10am–7pm Thu,
10am–2pm Sun; Jul–Sep: 10am–7pm
Tue–Fri, 10am–5pm Sat, 10am–2pm
Sun. **Closed** Mon. 🅿 🅲 🅿

In 1972, Ante Topić Mimara, a businessman who was also a collector, painter and restorer, donated his extensive collections to the city of Zagreb, and the Mimara Museum was set up for their display. The museum is housed in a Neo-Renaissance building built by the German architects Ludwig and Hülsner in 1895. The ground floor contains archaeological finds, Oriental carpets and Ming vases. The first floor concentrates on applied art and religious sculpture, including some fine medieval statues. On the top floor, a wide-ranging collection of paintings takes in Byzantine icons, a Rembrandt, a Rubens, a Renoir and some delightful still lifes by Manet.

⑭ Gallery of Old Masters
Galerija starih majstora

Trg Nikole Šubića Zrinskog 11.
Map E4. **Tel** (01) 489 5117.
Open 10am–7pm Tue, 10am–4pm
Wed–Fri, 10am–1pm Sat & Sun.
📷 🅲

In 1880, Bishop Strossmayer of Đakovo, one of the proponents of the pan-Slav movement, had this building constructed to house the Yugoslav Academy of Arts and Sciences. Now called the Croatian Academy of Arts and Sciences, the building houses the Gallery of Old Masters, which contains one of the country's finest picture collections, most of which was donated by Strossmayer himself. The collection features Renaissance art including canvases by Tintoretto and El Greco. In the entrance hall is the 11th-century Baška tablet, bearing one of the oldest-known inscriptions in the Glagolitic script. Glagolitic was used by medieval rulers

St Sebastian, Gallery of Old Masters

until it was replaced by the Roman alphabet.

⑮ Archaeological Museum
Arheološki muzej

Trg Nikole Šubića Zrinskog 19.
Map E3. **Tel** (01) 487 3101.
Open 10am–6pm Tue–Sat (until 8pm
Thu), 10am–1pm Sun. 🅿 🅲 by appt.
🅿 🅦 amz.hr

The Neo-Classical Vraniczany-Hafner Palace has housed this museum since 1945. It contains artifacts from all over Croatia, ranging from prehistoric finds to Greek vases and medieval Croatian jewellery. One of the most captivating objects on display is the Vučedol Dove, a three-legged pouring vessel in the shape of a bird which dates from the Copper Age (c. 2500 BC). Discovered near Vukovar, it is regarded as the emblem of the museum. Among the Egyptian mummies on display is the so-called Zagreb Mummy, dating from the 3rd century BC.

⑯ Museum of Contemporary Art
Muzej suvremene umjetnosti

Avenija Dubrovnik 17. **Map** A5. **Tel** (01)
605 2700. 🚋 14. **Open** 11am–6pm
Tue–Fri & Sun, 11am–8pm Sat. 🅿 🅲
🅰 🅿 🅦 msu.hr

A major centre of avant-garde art in the years following 1945, the museum, which opened in 2009, showcases contemporary Croatian art. Highlights of the display, *Collection in Motion*, include abstract canvases by painters Ivan Picelj, Aleksandar Srnec and Julije Knifer and conceptualist pieces by Mladen Stilinovič, Tomislav Gotovac and Vlado Martek. International acquisitions include artist Carsten Höller's toboggan slides. The building is in itself an attraction, displaying both moving images and abstract light displays on its façade at night.

Susanna and the Old Men, Gallery of Old Masters

㉒ Varaždin

Although traces of the Neolithic Age and the Roman period have been identified around Varaždin Castle, the first documented mention of the town of Varaždin was in 1181, when King Bela III (r. 1172–96) confirmed the rights of the Zagreb Curia to the thermal spas in the area. In 1209, it was declared a free town by King Andrew II (r. 1205–35) and began to develop as a trading centre. From the 16th century onwards, Varaždin was a border fortress defending Habsburg territories from the Ottoman Turks, and the Croatian Parliament began to meet here in 1756. In 1776, a huge fire caused widespread destruction, but left many churches and palaces standing. Today, Varaždin is one of the best-preserved towns in Croatia.

View of Varaždin Castle, home to the Civic Museum

🏛 Varaždin Castle and Civic Museum

Strossmayerovo šetalište 7.
Tel (042) 658 754. **Open** 9am–5pm Tue–Fri, 9am–1pm Sat & Sun.
🐾 💳 ✉

Varaždin Castle (Stari grad i Gradski muzej) has origins in the 12th century, and was rebuilt between the 14th and 19th centuries when an Ottoman attack was imminent. The stout round bastions built at this time are still an impressive sight. The castle was remodelled in the 1560s, when Italian architect Domenico dell'Allio created a Renaissance structure with a beautiful arcaded courtyard. The castle's present look dates from the time of the powerful Erdödy counts, who added bastions and a moat. Now the Civic Museum, it houses collections of weapons, porcelain, handicrafts and an 18th-century pharmacy. Ruins of the wall and the Lisak Tower, to the east of the castle, are the only remaining evidence of the original medieval walls.

🖼 Gallery of Old and Modern Masters

Stančićev trg 3. **Tel** (042) 214 172.
Open 9am–5pm Tue–Fri, 9am–1pm Sat & Sun. 🐾 💳 by appt. ✉

The gallery (Galerija starih i novih Majstora) has a large collection of works from all over Europe, and is particularly rich in landscapes by Flemish and Italian artists as well as portraits by German and Dutch painters.

🏛 Tomislav Square

Town Hall: Trg kralja Tomislava 1.
Tel (042) 402 508. **Open** by appt.
Drašković Palace: Trg kralja Tomislava 3.
Closed to the public.

The charming Tomislav Square (Trg kralja Tomislava) is the heart of the town. Facing the square is the **Town Hall** (Gradska vijećnica), one of the oldest buildings in Varaždin. Built in the 15th century in Gothic style, it has since been altered and a clock tower added. It was a private house until 1523, when its owner Prince George of Brandenburg gave it to the town to serve as the Town Hall. It is guarded in summer by the Purgars, the traditional town guard, who wear 19th-century uniforms and bearskin hats. To the east of the square stands **Drašković Palace** (Palača Drašković), built in the late 17th century with a Rococo façade. The Croat Parliament met here between 1756 and 1776. Opposite stands the Renaissance Ritz House, one of the oldest in the town; the date of construction, 1540, is engraved on its doorway.

🏛 Cathedral of the Assumption

Pavlinska ulica 4. **Tel** (042) 210 688.
Open 9:30am–12:30pm & 4–7pm daily.

The Church of the Assumption (Katedrala Uznesenja Marijina) became a cathedral in 1997. Both the church and the monastery annexed to it were built in the first half of the 17th century by the Jesuits. Later, the Pauline Order took over.

The cathedral's tall façade features pillars, and its interior is in the Baroque style. The main altar occupies the width of the central nave and is a riot of gilded columns, stuccoes and engravings. At the centre is an *Assumption of the Virgin*, reminiscent of Titian's work in Venice. Baroque music concerts are held here on some evenings.

Rich Baroque altar in the Cathedral of the Assumption

🏛 Church of St John the Baptist

Franjevački trg 8. **Tel** (042) 213 166. **Open** 8:30am–noon & 5:30–7pm daily.

Built in 1650 in the Baroque style on the site of a 13th-century church, the Church of St John the Baptist (Crkva sv Ivana Krstitelja) has a Renaissance doorway with a tympanum and statues of St Anthony of Padua and St Francis of Assisi. The interior has eight side chapels and an ornate

Bell tower of the Church of St John the Baptist, Tomislav Square

gilded pulpit from the late 17th century. The bell tower is 54 m (177 ft) high.

In front of the church is a copy of the *Monument of Bishop Gregory of Nin* by Ivan Meštrović. The adjacent former pharmacy has many works of art, among them some allegorical frescoes by the 18th-century painter Ivan Ranger.

Herzer Palace
Franjevački trg 6. **Open** 9am–5pm Tue–Fri, 9am–1pm Sat & Sun. Entomological Museum: **Tel** (042) 658 760.

Built at the end of the 18th century, the late Baroque Herzer Palace (Palača Herzer) has housed the **Entomological Museum** (Entomološki odjel Gradskog muzeja) since 1954. The museum was founded by entomologist Franjo Košćec, who, in 1959, donated his own natural history collection to the town. The museum also hosts occasional themed exhibitions.

Church of the Holy Trinity
Kapucinski trg 7. **Tel** (042) 213 550. **Open** 9am–noon & 6–7pm Mon–Sat, Sun before and after mass.

The Church of the Holy Trinity (Crkva Presvetog Trojstvo) dates from the early 18th century and houses Baroque paintings, furnishings by local masters and an organ with figures of angels playing instruments. The neighbouring monastery is famous for its library, containing manuscripts, parchments and incunabula and some of the oldest documents written in Kajkavski (ancient Croatian).

Croatian National Theatre
Ulica Augusta Cesarca 1. **Tel** (042) 214 688. **Open** for performances only.

Built by Hermann Helmer in 1873, the Croatian National

VISITORS' CHECKLIST

Practical Information
80 km (50 miles) NE of Zagreb. 40,000. Ivana Padovca 3, (042) 210 987. Varaždin Baroque evenings (Sep–Oct), Špancirfest (late Aug).
W tourism-varazdin.hr

Transport
Kolodvorska 17. Zrinskih i Frankopana bb.

Theatre (Hrvatsko Narodno Kazalište) is one of the main cultural centres in the town. Every year during summer and autumn, theatregoers from all over Europe come to attend the performances here.

Municipal Cemetery
Hallerova aleja. **Open** Mar–Apr & Oct: 7am–8pm; May–Sep: 7am–9pm; Nov–Feb: 7am–5pm.

To the west of the castle, this cemetery (Gradsko groblje) is a public garden as well as a place of rest. It was laid out in the early 20th century by cemetery keeper, Herman Haller.

Varaždin Town Centre

① Varaždin Castle and Civic Museum
② Gallery of Old and Modern Masters
③ Tomislav Square
④ Cathedral of the Assumption
⑤ Church of St John the Baptist
⑥ Herzer Palace
⑦ Church of the Holy Trinity
⑧ Croatian National Theatre

0 metres   200
0 yards   200

For keys to symbols *see back flap*

㉓ Osijek

The capital of Slavonia, Osijek sits in the middle of a fertile plain. The city developed in 1786 with the merger of three districts: the Fort (Tvrđa), Lower Town (Donji grad) and Upper Town (Gornji grad). Due to its position on the Drava river, Osijek has always played a strategic role. In 1991, after the declaration of independence by Croatia, the city was bombed by Yugoslav forces and much of the old centre was damaged. Osijek never fell, and emerged from the war to become a prosperous centre. Trvđa, the fortified centre, escaped serious damage during the war and has preserved much of its Baroque architecture. The Upper Town, meanwhile, presents Osijek's modern face with bustling streets, filled with shops, bars and restaurants.

The main square, trg sv Trojstva, in the heart of Tvrđa

🏛 Museum of Slavonia

Trg sv Trojstva 6, Tvrđa. **Tel** (031) 250 730.
Open 9am–7pm Tue, Wed & Fri, 9am–10pm Thu, 5–9pm Sat, 10am–2pm Sun.
📷 🎫 🖼 🕐 Osijek Archaeological
Museum: **Open** 10am–6pm Tue & Wed, noon–8pm Thu, 10am–4pm Fri, 10am–2pm Sat & Sun. **Closed** Mon. 📷 🎫

On the eastern side of Tvrđa is the old Town Hall, which houses the Museum of Slavonia (Muzej Slavonije). The museum has nearly 400,000 registered objects grouped into about 100 collections.

There are nine departments: natural history, archaeology (with prehistoric, antique and medieval sections), numismatics, history, department of arts and crafts, ethnography, the technical department and a collection of old newspapers. There is a rich collection devoted to local folklore, including intricately embroidered traditional costumes from surrounding villages. Local crafts are represented with a range of painted wooden furniture.

The museum also houses the **Osijek Archaeological Museum**, which has displays of statuary and tombstones from the Roman settlement of Mursa, as well as weapons and jewellery belonging to the first Croat settlers.

🏛 Church of the Holy Cross

Franjevačka ulica, Tvrđa. **Tel** (031) 208 177. **Open** 8am–noon & 3–8pm, daily.
Northeast of Trg sv Trojstva, on the site of a sacred medieval building, stands this church (Crkva svetog Križa), built by the Franciscans between 1709 and 1720. Inside is a pretty

Statue from Roman Mursa, Osijek
Archaeological Museum

statue of the Virgin Mary from the 15th century and some liturgical furnishings.

🏛 Church of St Michael

Trg Jurja Križanića, Tvrđa. **Tel** (031) 208 990. **Open** before mass.
The second biggest church in the city, this impressive building (Crkva sv Mihovila) was built by the Jesuits in the first half of the 18th century. The Baroque façade is flanked by two bell towers, and the monastery has a splendid doorway built in 1719. Below street level, the foundations of the 16th-century Kasim-paša Mosque are still visible.

🚌 Europska avenija

This avenue is Osijek's main thoroughfare, linking Tvrđa to the Upper Town. It is famous for the superb row of Art Nouveau houses built for local industrialists at the beginning of the 20th century. It runs through the leafy Park kralja Državislava, which contains the monumental sculpture *Soldier in the Throes of Death* (1894) by Croatian sculptor Robert Frangeš-Mihanović.

Soldier in the Throes of Death, Park kralja
Državislava, Europe Avenue

🏛 Museum of Fine Arts

Europska avenija 9. **Tel** (031) 251 280.
Open Sep–Jun: 10am–6pm Tue–Fri (till 8pm Thu), 10am–1pm Sat & Sun; Jul & Aug: 10am–6pm Mon–Fri. 📷 🎫 by appt.
This gallery (Muzej likovnih umjetnosti), founded in 1954, is housed in an elegant 19th-century house. There are collections of paintings from the 18th

Splendid Neo-Gothic Church of
Sts Peter and Paul

and 19th centuries, as well as
works by popular Croatian artists.
A special section is dedicated to
works of art from the Osijek school.

🔲 Church and Monastery of St James

Kapucinska 41, Gornji grad.
Tel (031) 201 182. **Open** 6:30am–
noon, 4–8pm & by appt, daily.

The medieval Gothic Church
and Monastery of St James
(Crkva i samostan sv Jakova),
with a Capuchin monastery, is
the oldest building in the Upper
Town. In the sacristy are mid-
18th-century paintings on the
life of St Francis.

🔲 Church of Sts Peter and Paul

Trg Marina Držića, Gornji grad.
Tel (031) 310 020. **Open** 2–6:30pm
Mon, 9am–6:30pm Tue–Fri.

This imposing late 19th-century
Neo-Gothic church (Crkva sv
Petra i Pavla) is dedicated to Sts
Peter and Paul. It was designed
by Franz Langenberg. The 40
stained-glass windows and
some sculptures are by the
Viennese artist Eduard Hauser.

🔲 Croatian National Theatre

Županijska 9, Gornji grad.
Tel (031) 220 700.

Osijek has a long and rich
theatre tradition. The Croatian
National Theatre (Hrvatsko
narodno kazalište) was built

in Moorish style in the
19th century, but was badly
damaged during the bombing
by Yugoslav forces in 1991. It
has now been restored and
stages a number of opera and
drama productions from
September to May.

Lavish interior of the Croatian National Theatre

Osijek City Centre

① Museum of Slavonia
② Church of the Holy Cross
③ Church of St Michael
④ Europska avenija
⑤ Museum of Fine Arts
⑥ Church and Monastery of St James
⑦ Church of Sts Peter and Paul
⑧ Croatian National Theatre

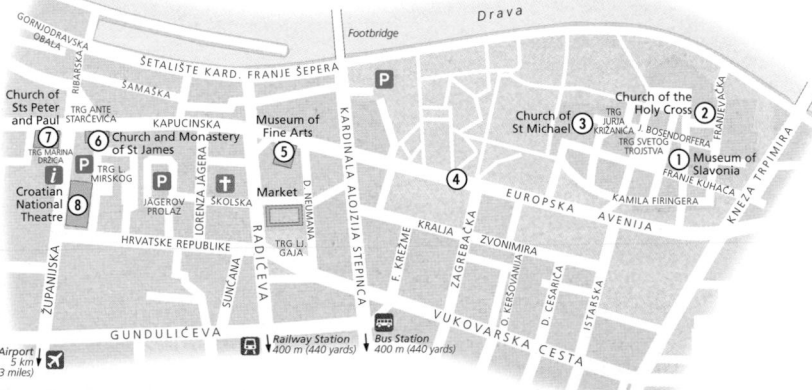

Practical & Travel Information

Croatia is a welcoming country to visit with minimal border formalities, an up-to-date transport network and a well-organized tourist information infrastructure. Modern highways ensure speedy access to the Adriatic coast, while a busy fleet of passenger ferries serves the offshore islands. Public services and tourist facilities are efficient and modern, making the country an increasingly popular holiday destination in South Eastern Europe.

When to Visit

The most popular time to visit Croatia is in summer, during July and August. With its crystal-clear seas, islands and bays offering plenty of opportunities for exploration and swimming, the coast is a major attraction. For a quieter holiday, off-season months such as May, June or September are preferable, when the weather is still fine, resorts are not so crowded and accommodation is cheaper. Cities such as Zagreb, Dubrovnik and Split are enjoyable destinations all year round.

Documentation

Citizens of European Union (EU) countries, the US, New Zealand, Canada and Australia may visit Croatia for up to 90 days without a visa. The **Croatian Ministry of Foreign and European Affairs** website provides a list of countries whose citizens require visas. All foreign visitors must register with the local police within 48 hours of arrival; this is usually arranged by hotel staff. Failure to do so may result in a penalty or even deportation from the country.

Visitor Information

Every town and city has a tourist office, usually called the Turistički Ured, Turistička Zajednica or Turistički Informativni Centar. The staff are usually helpful and speak English. The **Croatian National Tourist Board** has offices in cities throughout the world, including London and Washington, and also runs a useful website.

Opening hours for tourist offices vary depending on the season. In July and August, the tourist offices open daily from 8am to 8pm; in May, June and September hours are shorter. In smaller towns, some tourist offices may be closed altogether between October and April.

Health and Security

Croatian public health services meet the standards of those elsewhere in Europe, and in general visitors run no serious health risks. There are no endemic diseases and the most common ailments are those caused by insect bites and over-exposure to the sun. There are *bolnica* or *klinički*

centar (hospitals and clinics) in all the major towns and health centres and *ljekarna* (pharmacies) in the smaller towns. Visitors need not pay for medical services if the Health Care Convention has been signed between Croatia and their home country. This applies to all countries in the EU including the UK, Ireland and Italy. If not, visitors have to pay for treatment according to a standardized price list.

Croatia has a relatively low crime rate and violent crime is rare. If petty theft occurs, it is most likely to happen on crowded beaches during the summer season, so visitors should be vigilant in these places.

Facilities for the Disabled

Croatia is quite well equipped with facilities for the disabled. Most public places, including trains, buses and toilets, are wheelchair-friendly.

Banking and Currency

The Croatian currency is the kuna. Money can be changed in banks and authorized exchange bureaus as well as post offices and tourist agencies. In cities and major towns, cash can be withdrawn from ATMs using internationally recognized cards.

Communications

Public telephones are found everywhere and are operated using phone cards, which are usually sold in units of 15, 30 and 50 kuna. They can be bought from news kiosks and tobacco shops.

SIM cards from local mobile network providers such as **Tele2**, **T-Mobile** and **Vipnet** are economical, but visitors should check with their own phone service providers for advice on roaming facilities within the country.

Internet facilities are widely available, and it is easy to find Internet cafés with good connections in most places.

The Climate of Croatia

Along the coast, the climate is typically Mediterranean, with mild winters and hot, dry summers; the Dalmatian coast is one of the sunniest parts of Europe. Inland, the weather is continental, with hot summers and cold winters. The mountainous areas have an Alpine climate, with plenty of rain, including thunderstorms and snow in winter.

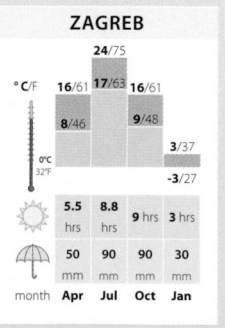

ZAGREB

°C/F	Apr	Jul	Oct	Jan
	16/61	24/75	16/61	3/37
	8/46	17/63	9/48	-3/27
sun (hrs)	5.5 hrs	8.8 hrs	9 hrs	3 hrs
rain (mm)	50 mm	90 mm	90 mm	30 mm
month	Apr	Jul	Oct	Jan

Arriving by Air

The national airline, **Croatia Airlines**, links Croatia's main airports with the rest of Europe. Other European airlines offering scheduled services to Croatia include **Air France**, **Lufthansa** and **Austrian Airlines**. Among the budget airlines, **Wizz Air** flies direct to Zagreb from London Luton airport while **easyJet** and **Ryanair** operate summer season flights from the UK and Ireland to several cities on the Croatian coast. There are no direct flights from North America or Australasia although one or two-stop flights involving a change at a major European airport are easy to arrange.

Croatia has airports at **Zagreb**, **Split**, **Dubrovnik**, Osijek, Pula, Rijeka and Zadar. All are close to their respective city centres and well connected to them by regular bus services.

Arriving by Sea

Several boat companies operate between Croatia and Italy. **Jadrolinija**, the main ferry company, runs between Ancona and Split four times a week all year round. **Blue Line** also runs daily services.

Rail Travel

Croatia is well connected to the rest of Europe by rail, especially Central Europe. Visitors travelling from London to Zagreb should contact **Rail Europe** or see their website for information. Connections from other European cities include Munich and Vienna.

Within Croatia, all the major towns and cities are linked by rail, with the exception of Dubrovnik, where there is no railway station. The hub of the Croatian railway network is in the capital Zagreb, where the head office of **Croatian Railways** is located.

Travelling by Bus

Croatia is also well linked to other countries by bus. International buses connect the country with the bordering states and also with France, Switzerland, Germany, Slovakia, Austria and Italy. Within Croatia, the bus network is comprehensive but can be expensive. Services are divided into Intercity (direct connections between the larger cities) and regional services (with connections to smaller towns and the main cities). For information, visitors can contact or check the website of the main bus station, **Autobusni kolodvor Zagreb**.

Travelling by Car

Travelling to Croatia by car is most popular with visitors from neighbouring countries. Those driving in Croatia need to carry a valid driving licence, the car's log book and a Green Card.

Hiring a car is relatively easy and rental agencies can be found in all the main towns and cities. It is best to hire from big companies such as **Avis** or **Hertz**, which offer competitive prices. One of the advantages of renting a car through these companies is having the option of leaving the car in a different town from the collection point.

DIRECTORY

Documentation

Croatian Ministry of Foreign Affairs
w mvep.hr

Embassies

Australia
Kaptol Centar, Zagreb.
Tel (01) 489 1200.

Canada
Prilaz Gjure Deželića 4, Zagreb.
Tel (01) 488 1200.

New Zealand
Vlaška 50a, Zagreb.
Tel (01) 461 2060.

United Kingdom
I. Lučića 4, Zagreb.
Tel (01) 600 9100.

United States
Ul. Thomasa Jeffersona 2, Zagreb.
Tel (01) 661 2200.
w zagreb.usembassy. gov

Visitor Information

Croatian National Tourist Board
Iblerov trg 10/IV, Zagreb.
Tel (01) 469 9333.
w croatia.hr

Emergency Numbers

Ambulance
Tel 194.

Fire
Tel 193.

General Emergency
Tel 112.

Police
Tel 192.

Communications

Tele2
w tele2.hr

T-Mobile
w hrvatskitelekom.hr

Vipnet
w vipnet.hr

Arriving by Air

Air France
w airfrance.com

Austrian Airlines
w austrian.com

Croatia Airlines
w croatiaairlines.com

Dubrovnik Airport
Tel (020) 773 100.
w airport-dubrovnik.hr

easyJet
w easyjet.com

Lufthansa
w lufthansa.com

Ryanair
w ryanair.com

Split Airport
Tel (021) 203 506.
w split-airport.hr

Wizz Air
w wizzair.com

Zagreb Airport
Pieso bb HR - 10 150, Zagreb. Tel (060) 320 320.
w zagreb- airport.hr

Arriving by Sea

Blue Line
w blueline-ferries.com

Jadrolinija
Riva 16, Rijeka.
Tel (051) 666 111.

Rail Travel

Croatian Railways
Tel (060) 333 444.
w hzpp.hr

Rail Europe
Tel (08448) 484 064.
w raileurope.com

Travelling by Bus

Autobusni Kolodvor Zagreb
Tel (060) 313 333.
w akz.hr

Travelling by Car

Avis
w avis.com.hr

Hertz
w hertz.hr

Shopping & Entertainment

Souvenir-hunters in Croatia will be spoilt for choice, with a range of traditional crafts such as costume dolls, exquisite handmade lace and hand-painted ceramics and jewellery to choose from. Ties and fountain pens, both of which originated in Croatia, also make good purchases. A variety of accessible and engaging entertainment caters for all age groups and tastes, ranging from opera and ballet to folk music festivals and nightclubs. In summer, performances are sometimes held outdoors in places with a particularly pretty setting.

Opening Hours

Shops and department stores are usually open from 8am to 8pm Monday to Friday (sometimes 7am to 9pm) and from 8am to 2 or 3pm on Saturday. It should be noted that smaller shops often close at lunchtime, usually from noon to 4pm. Shops are generally closed on Sundays and holidays, although many remain open in the high season in tourist resorts.

Markets

The street markets of Croatia are colourful, lively places to stroll around. In Zagreb, the **Dolac** is a daily market where food is sold under bright red umbrellas. In Split, a morning market is held every day on Pazar, selling absolutely everything: fruit, vegetables, shoes, flowers, clothes and a vast assortment of souvenirs.

Bigger shopping centres are mainly found in larger towns and cities where most merchandise is sold under one roof, and usually include a department store or supermarket. In Zagreb, the busiest shopping centres are the **Importanne Centar** in the city centre and **Avenue Mall** in the southern suburb of Novi Zagreb.

Handicrafts

Croatia has a long tradition of producing fine handicrafts. In Zagreb, **Širok** has an array of dolls in traditional costume, embroidered items, terracotta, ceramics and wooden objects. In Split, an assortment of souvenirs, including objects inspired by maritime themes is available. Visitors can also find good reproductions of Roman objects in the underground area of Diocletian's Palace (see pp448–9). In Osijek, the most interesting buys are textiles, finely embroidered with gold and silver thread.

A typical Croatian craft is needlework with red geometric patterns stitched on to a white background. This characteristic design, painstakingly sewn by hand, is mostly used to decorate table linen, pillowcases and blouses. The art of lace-making is also widely admired. A centuries-old tradition, the lace was originally used to embellish women's blouses. The patterns produced are the lace-maker's interpretation of designs that have been passed down from generation to generation. Beautiful lace can be bought in many places. **Hrvatska kuća Materina priča** and **Etno butik Mara** sell a variety of handicrafts.

Jewellery

There is one item of jewellery that can only be found in Croatia or, more precisely, in Rijeka. This is the *morčić*, a small figurine in the form of a black Moorish character wearing a turban. It was originally produced as earrings but today tie-pins and brooches can also be found. Considered a symbol of good luck, the item is traditionally made of glazed ceramic, although precious stones may be used to decorate it on request. The best place to buy a *morčić* in Rijeka is the **Mala Galerija**.

Souvenirs

Three good souvenirs from Croatia are ties, fountain pens and lavender. The country can claim to have invented the tie, or cravat, which was originally a scarf used by Croatian cavalrymen to distinguish them from other soldiers during the Thirty Years' War in the 17th century. A good selection can be found in leading clothes stores in Zagreb such as **Boutique Croata**. Another little-known fact is that the inventor of the fountain pen, Eduard Slavoljub Penkala, was an engineer from Zagreb. Pens are available in most department stores in the capital.

The country's best-known natural product is lavender, which is sold dried, in small bags, or as essence, in bottles. It can be found more or less all over Croatia but is particularly linked with the island of Hvar (see pp454–5).

Food

Among Croatia's gastronomic specialities, mustard (in traditional containers), honey and *cukarini* biscuits are particularly worth buying. Truffles from Istria and olive oil from the Dalmatian Islands are highly prized by gourmets. Another valued delicacy is *paški sir*, a mature cheese made from sheep's milk, produced on the island of Pag. Food specialities can be bought from **Zigante Tartufi** in Istria and **Natura Croatica** in Zagreb.

Nightlife

Croatia is never short of nightlife. For an all-night party, however, the capital or the coast are the best places to be. There are lots of lively bars along the pedestrianized Tkalčićeva ulica in Zagreb; while clubs like **Aquarius Club** (house and techno) and **Močvara** (alternative rock) provide plenty in the way of DJ action and live music.

Apart from Zagreb, other places have an equally lively nightlife. Located in the boat, Arca Fiumana on Rijeka's waterfront, **Café-Disco Bar Makina** holds live concerts and plays alternative, rock, funk and indie music. Another good spot for lively alternative rock concerts is **Rock Club Uljanik**, occupying a vacant building above the shipyards in Pula.

Split features clubs with open-air terraces looking out to sea, the best of which are **O'Hara** on the seafront path and **Hemingway** near the yachting marina. The alleyways of Dubrovnik's Old Town are full of café-bars that remain lively until the early hours, while the **Night Club Fuego** is casual and relaxed, and plays a range of music.

Hvar, one of the country's many islands, has developed a reputation as a party island. Early evening activity centres around the harbour in bar-cum-clubs such as **Carpe Diem**, where the dancers warm up before heading up the tree-covered hillside to **Veneranda**, a concert and cultural centre with a Baroque chapel, located close to the main square.

Theatre, Dance and Festivals

Although usually performed in Croatian, high-class stagings of opera and theatre are enjoyable, especially those put on by Zagreb's **Croatian National Theatre**, Rijeka's **Croatian National Theatre Ivan pl. Zajc** and Split's **National Theatre**. For a more unusual form of drama, a visit to the unique Zagreb puppet theatre, **Zagrebačko kazalište lutaka**, can be rewarding. They have performances almost every weekend and tickets can be bought on the spot. Information about programmes is available from the tourist information office or on posters announcing forthcoming events.

Croatia also has many traditional festivals, of which the most famous is the sword dance, enacted in Korčula's town centre twice a week throughout the summer. Any festive occasion incorporates folk dances such as the *poskočica*, where couples weave themselves into intricate configurations. Tickets for performances can be bought in advance from an agency or at the relevant venue.

Folk Music

Croatia has a rich tradition of folk music and folk bands play all along the Adriatic, in open-air concerts and at holiday festivals. Unusual instruments to look out for are the *tamburica*, a mandolin-type instrument of Anatolian origin common in Slavonia and in the extreme east of the country, and the *roženice* (a traditional Istrian woodwind instrument similar to the modern oboe). Visitors will also encounter variations on the folk theme such as *klapa* – five- to ten-part harmony singing, mainly by males – or *linđo*, the most popular dance of Dubrovnik, accompanied by a traditional instrument with three strings called a *lijerica*. The famous **Dubrovnik Summer Festival**, held between July and August, is not to be missed, nor any event at Pula's ancient and stunning **Pula Amphitheatre**.

DIRECTORY

Markets

Avenue Mall
Av Dubrovnik 16, Zagreb.
Tel (01) 652 7645.

Dolac
Tel (01) 481 3199.

Importanne Centar
Starčevićev trg 7, Zagreb.
Tel (01) 457 7076.

Handicrafts

Etno butik Mara
Ilica 49, Zagreb.
Tel (01) 480 6511.

Hrvatska kuća Materina priča
Preradovićeva 31, Zagreb.

Širok
Bakačeva 8, Zagreb.
Tel (01) 481 6552.

Jewellery

Mala Galerija
Užarska 25, Rijeka.
Tel (051) 335 403.

Souvenirs

Boutique Croata
Prolaz Oktogon,
Ilica 5, Zagreb.
Tel (01) 481 2726.

Food

Natura Croatica
Preradovićeva 8, Zagreb.
Tel (01) 485 5076.

Zigante Tartufi
Livade 7, Livade.
Tel (052) 664 030.

Nightlife

Aquarius Club
Aleja Matije Ljubeka bb,
Jarun, Zagreb.
Tel (01) 364 0231.

Café-Disco Bar Makina
Putnička obala bb.

Carpe Diem
Riva, Hvar.

Hemingway
VIII. Mediteranskih igara 5,
Split. **w** hemingway.hr

Močvara
Trnjanski nasip bb, Zagreb.
Tel (01) 615 9667.

Night Club Fuego
Brsalje 8, Near Pile Gate,
Dubrovnik.
Tel (020) 312 870.

O'Hara
Uvala Zenta 3, Split.
w ohara.hr

Rock Club Uljanik
Dobrilina 2, Pula.

Veneranda
On the hill above Riva, Hvar.

Theatre, Dance and Festivals

Croatian National Theatre
Trg maršala Tita 15,
Zagreb. **Tel** (01) 488 8418;
Trg Gaje Bulata 1, Split.
Tel (021) 306 908.

Croatian National Theatre Ivan pl. Zajc
Uljarska 1, Rijeka.
Tel (051) 337 114.

Zagrebačko kazalište lutaka
Ulica baruna
Trenka 3, Zagreb.
Tel (01) 487 8445.

Folk Music

Dubrovnik Summer Festival
w dubrovnik-festival.hr

Pula Amphitheatre
Forum 3, Pula.
Tel (052) 219 197.

Where to Stay

Excellent view from the Hotel Luxe in Split

Zagreb

ZigZag Integrated Hotel
Apartments   Map E3
Petrinjska 9
Tel *(01) 889 5433*
Ⓦ zigzag.hr
Stylish self-catering apartments in a variety of sizes conveniently located at the central Petrinjska address and in nearby streets.

DoubleTree by Hilton Ⓚ Ⓚ
Business
Grada Vukovara 269a
Tel *(01) 600 1900*
Ⓦ hilton.com/zagreb
Modern hotel with excellent service and faciities In the up-and-coming commercial district.

Esplanade Ⓚ Ⓚ Ⓚ
Historic   Map D5
Mihanovićeva 1
Tel *(01) 456 6666*
Ⓦ esplanade.hr
Long established as a haven for celebrities, this uber-stylish and iconic hotel is set in a regal 1920s building combining its Art Deco glamour with every contemporary convenience.

Rest of Croatia

BRAČ: Villa Adriatica Ⓚ Ⓚ
Boutique
Put vele luke 31, Supetar
Tel *(021) 755 010*   **Closed** *Oct–Apr*
Ⓦ villaadriatica.com
A chic and well-equipped family-run hotel, Adriatica is situated in a quiet, peaceful neighbourhood, which is just minutes away from the seafront.

DUBROVNIK: Fresh Sheets B&B Ⓚ Ⓚ
B&B
Bunićeva poljana 6
Tel *091 896 7509*
Ⓦ freshsheetsbedandbreakfast. com
Occupying a unique space behind the Cathedral, Fresh Sheets offers a mix of well-equipped and modern double rooms and apartments, all decorated in bright colours.

DUBROVNIK: Karmen Ⓚ Ⓚ
B&B
Bandureva 1
Tel *(020) 323 433*
Ⓦ karmendu.com
Comfortable apartments in one of the Old-Town's most atmospheric corners, atractively furnished with bric-a-brac and antiques.

DUBROVNIK: Villa Dubrovnik Ⓚ Ⓚ Ⓚ
Luxury
Vlaha Bukovca 6
Tel *(020) 500 300*
Ⓦ villa-dubrovnik.hr
In addition to characteristic comfort, seclusion and high standards of service, expect stunning views at Villa Dubrovnik, nestled beneath cliffs to the east of the Old Town, overlooking the crystal clear waters of the Adriatic.

HVAR: Adriana Ⓚ Ⓚ Ⓚ
Luxury
Obala Fabrika 28
Tel *(021) 750 200*
Ⓦ suncanihvar.com
Smart hotel on the harbourfront with small but stylish rooms, popular top-floor bar and swimming pool.

KORČULA: Lesić-Dimitri Ⓚ Ⓚ Ⓚ
Luxury
Don Pavla Poše 1–6
Tel *(021) 715 560*
Ⓦ lesic-dimitri.com
Luxury apartments occupying a row of restored houses in Korčula's Old Town. Each apartment has a fully-equipped kitchen and contemporary bathroom.

OSIJEK: Waldinger Ⓚ Ⓚ
Historic
Županijska 8
Tel *(031) 250 450*
Ⓦ waldinger.hr
Nineteenth-century city-centre building with neat, burgundy-hued rooms and modern bathrooms.

ROVINJ: Hotel Lone Ⓚ Ⓚ Ⓚ
Boutique
Luje Adamovića 31
Tel *(052) 800 250*
Ⓦ lonehotel.com
This uber-contemporary hotel hovers above Lone Bay like a friendly alien spaceship. The rooms are well appointed and the social areas, grouped around a spiral stairway, a joy to use.

DK Choice

SPLIT: Goli&Bosi Ⓚ
Hostel
Morpurgova poljana 2
Tel *(021) 510 999*
Ⓦ gollybossy.com
A converted department store is home to this innovative design hostel. The hostel provides plenty of accomo-dation options–dorm beds taking the form of semi-private cubicles, en suite doubles and top-floor family rooms. The hostel's cafe-restaurant spreads out into the neighbouring piazza during the summer.

SPLIT: Hotel Luxe Ⓚ Ⓚ
Boutique
Kralja Zvonimira 6
Tel *(021) 314 444*
Ⓦ hotelluxesplit.com
Bright colours and swish design characterize this contemporary hotel located above the port.

TROGIR: Concordia Ⓚ
B&B
Obala Bana Berislavića 22
Tel *(021) 885 400*
Ⓦ concordia-hotel.net
Set in an 18th-century stone house, Concordia offers cosy rooms, many with harbour views.

VARAŽDIN: Pansion Garestin Ⓚ
B&B
Zagrebačka 34
Tel *(042) 214 314*
Ⓦ gastrocom-ugostiteljstvo.com
A 10-minute walk from the town's Baroque centre this B&B offers plain but well-equipped rooms above a popular restaurant.

For map references *see pp466–7*

Where to Eat and Drink

Zagreb

Pauza
International **Map** D4
Preradovićeva 34
Tel *(01) 485 4598* **Closed** *Sun*
Adriatic seafood and Asian spices
are the hallmarks of Pauza's
imaginative menu, although
there's a lot more besides, with
soups, pastas and salads luring
the lunchtime crowds.

Ribice i Tri Točkice (Kn)
Seafood **Map** D3
Preradovićeva 7/1
Tel *(01) 563 5479*
This rather enjoyable restaurantis
bedecked with maritime murals,
and specializes in smartly priced
Adriatic seafood dishes with
fillets of fish, squid, octopus
stews and risottos filling its
extensive menu.

Vinodol (Kn)(Kn)
Croatian **Map** D3
Teslina 10
Tel *(01) 481 1427*
Grilled meats and roast lamb
are the specialities at this popular
restaurant that boasts a large
terrace in a covered courtyard.

Rest of Croatia

BRAČ: Bistro Palute (Kn)
Seafood
Porat 4, Supetar
Tel *(021) 631 730*
With seating right on Supetar's
harbour, Palute serves the best

Grand interiors of the Vinodol
in Zagreb

fresh fish alongside inexpensive
dishes such as hake fillets, pastas
and grilled meats.

DUBROVNIK: Lokanda
Peskarija (Kn)(Kn)
Seafood
Na ponti bb
Tel *(020) 324 750*
With outdoor seating spread
along the Old Port quayside,
this is a reliable choice for grilled
squid, seafood risotto and other
Adriatic staples.

DUBROVNIK: Nishta (Kn)(Kn)
International
Prijeko bb
Tel *(020) 322 088* **Closed** *Sun*
Nishta kicked off something
of a gastro revolution in the fish-
and meat-obsessed Dalmatia by
opening this strictly vegetarian,
vegan and gluten-free restaurant
in the heart of the Old Town. The
menu has Thai, Indian, Mexican
and Mediterranean influences.

DUBROVNIK: Proto (Kn)(Kn)(Kn)
Seafood
Široka 1
Tel *(020) 323 234* **Closed** *Nov–Mar*
Traditional Dalmatian fish
and seafood dishes are
served with care and imagination
in this elegant restaurant
just off the main street in
the Old Town.

HVAR: Kod Kapetana (Kn)(Kn)
Seafood
Fabrika 30
Tel *(021) 742 230*
Occupying a pleasant
spot on Hvar's harbourfront,
'At The Captain's' is popular
among locals for its excellent
fresh fish and squid,
expertly grilled.

DK Choice

HVAR: Macondo (Kn)(Kn)(Kn)
International
Groda bb
Tel *(021) 742 850*
This fine restaurant just uphill
from the main square has long
been regarded as one of the
best places on the island for
seafood served in an informal
and friendly ambience. The
spaghetti with lobster or the
scampi in buzara sauce are well
worth trying; and the wine list
provides a good introduction
to the island's developing
viniculture. Outdoor seating is
in an atmospheric narrow alley.

KORČULA: LD (Kn)(Kn)(Kn)
Gourmet
Don Pavla Poše 1–6
Tel *(020) 715 560*
This classy restaurant with
seating on Korčula's waterfront
promenade, gives an inventive
twist to local meat and fish
dishes. The ideal place to sample
the best of local wines.

OSIJEK: Slavonska kuća (Kn)(Kn)
Croatian
Kamila Firingera 26a
Tel *(031) 369 955*
Decorated to look like a country
kitchen, the 'Slavonian house' is
one of the best restaurants in the
region to sample freshwater fish;
either pan-fried, or stewed as hot
spicy *fiš paprikaš*.

ROVINJ: Wine Vault (Kn)(Kn)(Kn)
French
A. Smareglia 3
Tel *(052) 636 017*
Based in the Monte Mulini Hotel,
Wine Vault is renowned for its
French-influenced cuisine. The
multi-course tasting menus are
intended to last several hours.

SPLIT: Fife (Kn)
Croatian
Trumbićeva obala 11
Tel *(021) 345 223*
Very much a legend of the local
culinary scene, Fife offers large
inexpensive portions of Dalmatian
seafood and stews, and remains
unspoiled by its growing popularity
with in-the-know tourists.

SPLIT: Kadena (Kn)(Kn)(Kn)
Seafood
Ivana pl. Zajca 4
Tel *(021) 389 400*
Occupying a terrace overlooking
the seafront path and yachting
marina, Kadena specializes in
local fish and shellfish, prepared
with haute-cuisine flair.

VARAŽDIN: Verglec (Kn)
International
Silvija Strahimira Kranjčevića 12
Tel *(042) 211 131*
This centrally located restaurant
straddles two culinary cultures
with its fine pizzas and filling
north-Croatian fare. Try the roast
duck or roast pork.

BOSNIA AND HERZEGOVINA

In the light of its tragic history in recent times, it is easy to forget that Bosnia and Herzegovina was one of the most powerful states in Europe in the Middle Ages. Although the country still wears the scars of battle, it nevertheless charms visitors with its breathtaking scenery, atmospheric medieval towns and warm, hospitable people.

Situated in the southwestern Balkans, the mountainous northern part of Bosnia has long been paired with Herzegovina, its smaller neighbour; both regions are bound by centuries of common history. Although the capital, Sarajevo, has recovered from its wartime ordeal, towns such as Mostar are yet to be fully restored, as many settlements still remain abandoned. Despite the danger of landmines, it is still possible to get a flavour of the country's natural treasures, from mountains and lush forests to rivers and dramatic gorges, in the company of experienced local guides. Rafting on Bosnia's world-class rapids is especially popular.

History

The earliest evidence of human settlement in the region dates back to 12,000 BC. However, the first significant records are of the Illyrians, who occupied the western Balkans in the 6th century BC before the Romans conquered it some four centuries later. By the 6th century, attacks by Huns, Goths and Avars had weakened the Romans, and the arrival of Slavic tribes from northeast Europe further added to the region's veritable melting pot of ethnicities. The region was first ruled by the Serbs, then by the Croats, and finally by the Hungarians, before establishing itself as an independent kingdom under King Tvrtko in 1377. Following Tvrtko's death in 1391, the country was absorbed into the expanding Ottoman Empire. When the Austro-Hungarians took over from the Ottomans in 1908, they sought to unite the country's ethnic and religious groups

The pedestrianized Old town market in the capital city, Sarajevo

◀ The landmark single-arch stone bridge on the Neretva river, Mostar

Depiction of the assassination of Archduke Francis Ferdinand and his wife Sophie, Duchess of Hohenberg, at Sarajevo

as loyal Habsburg subjects. However, this attempt at homogeneity was resisted by nationalists seeking independence from Austria, and led the radical Bosnian Serb Gavrilo Princip to assassinate the Austro-Hungarian heir Franz Ferdinand and his wife in Sarajevo in 1914. It was this event

KEY DATES IN THE BOSNIA AND HERZEGOVINA HISTORY

AD 445 The region is conquered by Ostrogoths

1189 Signing of the Kulin Ban Charter trade agreement between Bosnia and Dubrovnik

1377 Bosnia becomes a kingdom under King Tvrtko I

1463 The Ottomans conquer Bosnia and Herzegovina

1908 Austria-Hungary annexes Bosnia and Herzegovina

1914 Archduke Franz Ferdinand is assassinated, sparking World War I

1918 Bosnia and Herzegovina becomes part of the kingdom of Serbs, Croats and Slovenes

1945 Bosnia and Herzegovina becomes part of a new federal Yugoslavia

1990 Collapse of Yugoslav regime

1992 Bosnia and Herzegovina is recognized as an independent country

1995 Dayton peace accord signed by Croatia, Serbia and Bosnia and Herzegovina

2006 Constitutional amendment for EU integration rejected in Parliament

that triggered World War I. Bosnia and Herzegovina joined the newly formed Kingdom of Serbs, Croats and Slovenes in 1918. During World War II, the Nazis established a puppet state in Croatia which grew to include Bosnia and Herzegovina. After the war, the country was reintegrated into Yugoslavia, and enjoyed a peaceful and prosperous period. As the Yugoslav regime slowly collapsed throughout 1990–91, Bosnia and Herzegovina voted for independence, but despite international recognition it soon fell prey to inter-ethnic violence. The republic's largest ethnic group, the Bosnian Muslims, were challenged by ethnic Serbs and later Croats who did not want to become part of an independent Bosnian state. The Bosnian Croats claimed an area of the country for themselves, while the Bosnian Serbs created Republika Srpska (the Serb Republic) within the borders of Bosnia and Herzegovina. The army of the Republika Srpska, and, to a lesser extent, the Croatian army, carried out ethnic cleansing in the form of mass exterminations and deportations. In 1995, the Dayton Agreement brought an end to the conflict by creating a single Bosnian state made up of two entities, a Muslim-Croat federation holding 51 per cent of the country and a Serb republic holding the remaining 49 per cent. Despite sharing a common government, Bosnia's ethnic groups still cooperate poorly.

Language and Culture

There are three official languages spoken in Bosnia and Herzegovina: Bosnian, Croatian and Serbian. With a multi-ethnic composition, the country's cultural heritage is diverse. Orthodox Christianity and Islam have combined with Austro-Hungarian and Catholic traditions to create a unique culture.

Exploring Bosnia and Herzegovina

Bosnia and Herzegovina has a wealth of fascinating towns to explore as well as stunning natural beauty. The capital, Sarajevo, is one of Europe's most lively cities, yet retains an old-world charm. To the south lies Mostar, with its atmospheric medieval centre, while to the northwest Jajce enjoys a picturesque location above two waterfalls. The country's rail network is poorly connected, but its roads are in reasonably good condition. Although most towns are served by buses, car hire provides greater flexibility.

Sights at a Glance

1. Sarajevo pp488–93
2. Travnik
3. Jajce
4. Bihać
5. Mostar pp496–7
6. Međugorje

The well-preserved medieval fortress dominating the town of Travnik

Key

— Motorway

— Major road

— Railway

– • International border

Church of St James in the central square at Međugorje

0 kilometres 50
0 miles 50

For keys to symbols *see back flap*

❶ Sarajevo

Founded by the Ottoman Empire in the 15th century, the vibrant capital of Bosnia and Herzegovina was at the centre of the longest siege in modern European history. Between 1992 and 1995, it lost over 11,000 of its citizens in the Bosnian War. Today, Sarajevo is home to a population of nearly half a million people and a massive reconstruction effort has returned the city to its former glory. Its bustling streets are now lined with designer boutiques, trendy bars and cafés catering to the influx of visitors, while the 16th-century Old Town (Baščaršija) offers laid-back charm. Scattered throughout the city are mosques, synagogues and Catholic and Orthodox churches, a reflection of Sarajevo's complex history and rich cultural diversity.

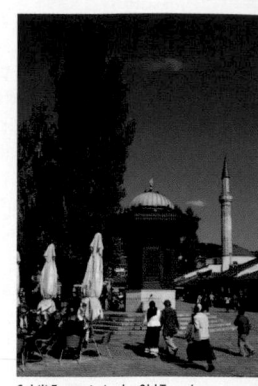

Sebilj Fountain in the Old Town's main market

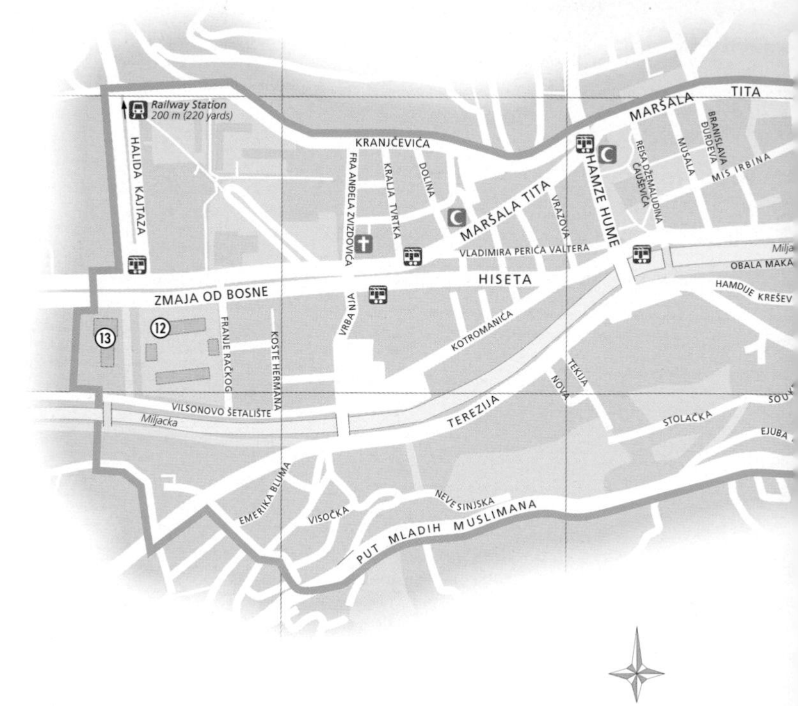

Sights at a Glance

① Old Town
② City Hall and National Library
③ Archangel Michael and Gabriel Orthodox Church and Museum
④ Old Synagogue and Jewish Museum
⑤ Gazi Husrev Bey's Mosque
⑥ Long Bazaar and Brusa Bazaar
⑦ Latin Bridge
⑧ Emperor's Mosque
⑨ Franciscan Church of St Anthony
⑩ Ashkenazi Synagogue
⑪ National Art Gallery
⑫ National Museum
⑬ History Museum

0 metres 200
0 yards 200

Key

Major sight / Place of interest

Pedestrian street

For hotels and restaurants see p500 and p501

Getting Around

The compact city centre and the Old Town are easily visited on foot. The pedestrianized Ferhadija runs through the heart of the city. Efficient tram and bus services cover the whole city and are a reliable way of getting around. Taxis are plentiful and fairly inexpensive; taxi stands can be found all over the city and operate 24 hours a day.

Decorative arch, Ashkenazi Synagogue

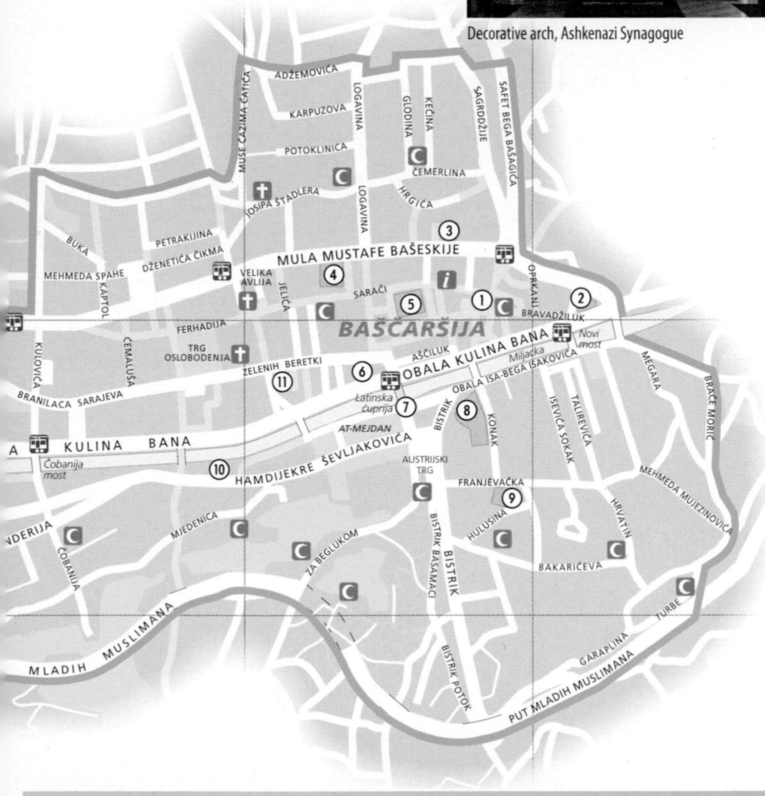

ADŽEMOVIĆA
KARPUZOVA
POTOKLINICA
MUSE ĆAZIMA ĆATIĆA
LOGAVINA
GLODINA
KEČINA
SAFET BEGA BAŠAGIĆA
SAGRDŽIJE
ČEMERLINA
JOSIPA STADLERA
LOGAVINA
HRGIĆA
BUKA
PETRAKIJINA
MEHMEDA SPAHE
DŽENETIĆA ČIKMA
VELIKA AVLIJA
JELIĆA
MULA MUSTAFE BAŠESKIJE
SARAČI
OPRKANJ
BRAVADŽILUK
KULOVIĆA
KAPTOL
ČEMALUŠA
FERHADIJA
TRG OSLOBOĐENJA
ZELENIH BERETKI
BAŠČARŠIJA
Novi most
BRANILACA SARAJEVA
Latinska ćuprija
AŠČILUK
OBALA KULINA BANA
Miljacka
OBALA ISA-BEGA IŠAKOVIĆA
MEGARA
BRAĆE MORIĆ
KULINA BANA
AT-MEJDAN
HAMDIJEKRE ŠEVLJAKOVIĆA
Ćobanija most
KONAK
BISTRIK
ISEVIĆA SOKAK
TAIREVIĆA
MEHMEDA MUJEZINOVIĆA
NDERIJA
ĆOBANIJA
MIEDENICA
ZA BEGLUKOM
AUSTRIJSKI TRG
FRANJEVAČKA
HULUSINA
HRVATIN
BISTRIK BAŠMAČI
BISTRIK
BAKARIĆEVA
TURBE
MLADIH MUSLIMANA
BISTRIK POTOK
GARAPLINA
PUT MLADIH MUSLIMANA

View of Sarajevo, set on the banks of the Miljacka river

D   E   F

For keys to symbols *see back flap*

The atmospheric Old Town market lined with old buildings and shops

① Old Town

Baščaršija

Baščaršija. **Map** E2.

A labyrinth of cobbled streets, the Old Town is known as Baščaršija after its main market, which has been a trading place since the 16th century. In the centre of the market stands the Moorish-style Sebilj Fountain, built in 1753 on the orders of Mehmed Paša Kukavica, governor of Bosnia and patron of fine architecture.

Reminiscent of an Arabian souk, the market's narrow streets, lined with small shops, offer an intriguing choice of authentic souvenirs. Local cuisine can be sampled in any of the grill or pie shops and Turkish-style coffee houses as well as at the Morica Han *(see p501)*, an ancient Ottoman inn with a shaded courtyard.

② City Hall and National Library

Vijećnica

Obala Kulina Bana. **Map** F2.

One of the city's most striking works of architecture, the building that once served as Sarajevo's Town Hall became the National Library after World War II. Damaged during the Bosnian War, this impressive structure underwent

careful restoration over 18 years, largely funded by the EU, and reopened in 2014. When it first opened in 1896, the building was originally designed to resemble a grand palace, featuring elaborate arched windows, a decorative rooftop crenellation and a first floor balcony. The Czech architect Alexander Wittek, responsible for the building's construction, visited Cairo for inspiration but committed suicide before its completion.

Although its magnificent Moorish façade survived the war relatively unscathed, the interior, which housed the National Library, was completely gutted by fire during shelling. The library's irreplaceable repository of Bosnian written culture was almost completely destroyed.

Entrance to the Orthodox Church and Museum, marked by an icon

③ Archangel Michael and Gabriel Orthodox Church and Museum

Stara pravoslavna crkva i muzej

Mula Mustafe Bašeskije 59. **Map** E2. **Open** 8am–5pm daily.

Built below ground level and hidden behind stone walls, the Archangel Michael and Gabriel Orthodox Church is thought to rest on the foundations of a 5th-century church. However, its current appearance dates back to 1734.

The cramped interior is supported by wooden columns and dominated by a wonderful gilt iconostasis. Intricately carved, it features colourful 17th-century icons by local master painters as well as others added in 1734. Religious artworks by 19th-century artists adorn the walls.

The neighbouring museum, opened in 1890, is one of Bosnia's oldest, and displays the church's treasures in smartly renovated surroundings.

Among the exhibits are 17th-century gold- and silver-plated icons by Russian, Greek and Cretan master painters, along with a rare copy of the Sarajevo *Nomocanon* (a book of church and secular laws) and valuable churchware.

④ Old Synagogue and Jewish Museum
Velika avlija i muzej jevreja

Velika Avlija bb. **Map** E2. **Tel** (033) 535 688. **Open** 10am–6pm Mon–Fri (4pm mid-Oct–mid-Apr), 10am–3pm Sun. 🚹 🆆 muzejsarajeva.ba

Built in 1850, the Old Synagogue long served as the centre of Sarajevo's vibrant Jewish community. The majority of Sarajevo's Jews were Sephardis, descended from the Jews of Spain and Portugal who were expelled from the Iberian Peninsula in the 1490s. Bosnia's Ottoman rulers gave them refuge, valuing their expertise in banking and trade.

The interior once featured arched balconies, but the building was plundered during World War II and used as a Jewish prison during the Holocaust, when Sarajevo's Jewish population of 12,000 was reduced by 85 per cent. The synagogue's restoration in 1965 was timed to coincide with the celebration of 400 years of Jewish presence in Bosnia, when it became a museum of Jewish history. It was then badly damaged after repeated shelling during the Bosnian War, but was renovated in 2003.

The museum's collections, which include some rare manuscripts, document the thriving Jewish culture in the region up until the Holocaust.

⑤ Gazi Husrev Bey's Mosque
Gazi Husrev-begova džamija

Sarači 18. **Map** E2. **Tel** (033) 532 144. **Open** 1 May–30 Sep: 9am–noon, 2:30pm–4pm & 5:30pm–7pm daily. **Closed** during Ramadan. 📷 🆆 vakuf-gazi.ba

Regarded as one of the finest examples of Ottoman Islamic architecture in the world, this stunning old mosque with its five-arch porch and multiple domes was commissioned in 1531 by Gazi Husrev Bey, who governed Bosnia between 1521 and 1541. Persian architect

Ornate entrance to Gazi Husrev Bey's Mosque, commissioned in 1531

Adzem Esir Ali was brought in to design what was to be the region's grandest mosque. This was achieved by combining a series of domes with a 45-m (148-ft) minaret, and by illuminating the interior with over 50 windows. Elaborate calligraphic quotations from the Koran adorn the walls and thick Oriental rugs, gifted by visiting rulers, cover the floor.

The mosque's spacious courtyard is dominated by an ancient chestnut tree and contains two domed mausoleums as well as a beautiful marble fountain used by worshippers for their ritual ablutions. The mosque was, however, a key target during the Bosnian War and, despite its 2-m (7-ft) thick walls, suffered extensive damage from shelling, though it has since been restored. Gazi Huzrev Bey also funded the construction of a children's religious *maktab* (school) within the complex and an advanced *madrasa* (school) opposite, with an intricately decorated arched entrance.

The administrative building to the west of the courtyard is notable for its imposing clock tower. Built in 1697, the tower measures lunar time and shows precisely when the sun sets.

⑥ Long Bazaar and Brusa Bazaar
Dugi bezistan i Brusa bezistan

Kundurdžiluk 10, Baščaršija. **Map** E3. **Open** 15 Apr–15 Oct: 10am–6pm (till 4pm mid-Oct–mid-Apr) Mon–Fri, 10am–3pm Sat. 🚹

Sarajevo's largest covered market, the Long Bazaar, was built in 1542 on the orders of Governor Gazi Husrev Bey. The massive stone structure is covered by a vaulted ceiling and once housed 52 shops selling goods imported from all over Europe and the Ottoman Empire. The bazaar lies near Kundurdžiluk Street, which also leads to the Gazi Husrev Bey Mosque commissioned by the governor 12 years earlier.

The nearby Brusa Bazaar was built in 1551 by the Ottoman General Grand Vizier Rustem for trading in Bursa silk from Turkey. Its eight cupolas and rough stone walls were damaged by shelling, but since its reconstruction it has been used as an ethnographic and historical museum.

Hand-decorated shell and mortar cases on sale in the bazaars

The historic Latin Bridge over the Miljacka river

⑦ Latin Bridge
Latinska ćuprija

Obala Kulina Bana. **Map** E3.

Before the Bosnian War drew the world's attention to Sarajevo, the city was best known for a series of events that sparked World War I. On 28 June 1914, the Bosnian Serb nationalist Gavrilo Princip assassinated Archduke Franz Ferdinand and his wife Sofia as they stopped near a bridge over the Miljacka river during an official visit. Princip was considered a national hero by Bosnian Serbs, and his footsteps were marked in the pavement, a memorial was built nearby and the bridge was renamed in his honour, until the recent war when Bosnian Serbs turned against the city.

Today, there is little acknowledgement of Princip's infamous deed other than a brass plaque and an exhibition in the adjacent Sarajevo Museum, with displays of Sarajevo during the Austro-Hungarian period. The historic bridge has now been renamed Latin Bridge.

⑧ Emperor's Mosque
Careva džamija

Obala Isa-bega Isakovića. **Map** E3.
Open 8am–6pm daily.

Built in 1566, during the reign of Suleiman the Magnificent, the Emperor's Mosque is one of Sarajevo's main holy sites and was enlarged in the 19th century under Sultan Abdülmedcid to accommodate the expanding congregation. The interior is decorated with simple floral motifs.

Behind the Emperor's Mosque's imposing stone walls are tranquil gardens and a pleasant courtyard centred around an intricately designed fountain, where worshippers gather for ritual ablutions before prayer.

⑨ Franciscan Church of St Anthony
Franjevački samostan Svetog Ante

Franjevačka 6. **Map** E3. **Tel** (033) 236 107. **Open** 8am–6pm daily. 🚋
W bosnasrebrena.ba

Constructed in 1912 during Austro-Hungarian rule, St Anthony's Church and the neighbouring Franciscan monastery were designed by prominent Czech architects. The church was the last work

Splendidly illuminated exterior of the Emperor's Mosque

of architect Josip Vancaš, while his colleague Karlo Panek built the monastery, which houses a superb collection of ancient religious literature and works of art.

The church's Neo-Gothic façade is dominated by its 43-m (141-ft) tower, while the interior is brightened by colourful stained-glass windows. In 2005, the Archbishop of Canterbury gave an Anglican Eucharist service here as part of an initiative to build bridges between communities of different faiths.

⑩ Ashkenazi Synagogue
Aškenaska sinagoga

Hamdije Kreševljakovića 59. **Map** D3.
Open 8am–7pm daily.

In 1959, most of the functions of the Old Synagogue *(see p491)* were transferred to the Ashkenazi Synagogue, a grand Moorish-style edifice built in the early 20th century. Today, the synagogue is the main cultural and religious centre for the city's 700 remaining Jews.

⑪ National Art Gallery
Umjetnička galerija

Zelenih Beretki 8. **Map** E3.
Open noon–8pm Tue–Sat. 📷

Standing opposite the leafy Alije Izetbegovića park, the eclectic National Art Gallery hosts both permanent and temporary exhibitions and occasional jazz performances. The building's façade is still pockmarked with bullet holes despite its restoration following the Bosnian War.

Founded in 1946, the gallery has over 4,500 works, including some by several prominent 20th-century Bosnian artists, paintings from the early Yugoslavian and Austro-Hungarian periods and a collection by the Swiss painter Ferdinand Hodler. The highlight of the gallery's absorbing icon collection, displayed in the

Monolithic entrance to the History Museum

central foyer, is the striking *Virgin Hodegetria*, painted by Montenegrin iconographer Tudor Vuković in 1568.

⑫ National Museum
Zemaljski muzej

Zmaja od Bosne 3. **Map** A3. **Tel** (033) 668 027. **Closed** for renovations. **W** zemaljskimuzej.ba

First opened in 1888 and located in its current imposing building since 1913, the National Museum is regarded as Bosnia's oldest museum.

Inside, the Archaeology Department has many exhibits from the Stone Age to the Middle Ages. The most intriguing, however, are the *stećci* (tombstones) which adorn the front garden. Bosnia's most legendary symbol, these monumental tombstones first appeared between the 12th and the 15th centuries and thousands are scattered across the country. Many are covered with engravings of animals, plants and obscure symbols linked to the region's early Slavic culture. Other highlights include the priceless Sarajevo Haggadah *(see p35),* a richly illustrated 14th-century book which includes one of the first depictions of the world as a sphere. Also on display is an array of national costumes from the 19th century in the Ethnographic Department. The Natural History collection has been depleted as a result of damage during the Bosnian War.

⑬ History Museum
Istorijski muzej

Zmaja od Bosne 9. **Map** A3. **Tel** (033) 210 416. **Open** summer: 9am–7pm Mon–Fri, 10am–2pm Sat & Sun; winter: 9am–4pm Mon–Fri, 9am–1pm Sat & Sun. 🅿 **W** muzej.ba

The battered façade of this modernist concrete building, with its broken, weed-covered steps and bullet-scarred walls, gives an impression of abandonment that seems like a deliberate historic statement. The museum and its collection were almost completely destroyed during the devastating Bosnian War.

The building is currently open to the public, but its original collection of 400,000 artifacts has been reduced to a one-room display entitled "Bosnia and Herzegovina through the Centuries", consisting mainly of documents and old photographs. The museum's main attraction is the "Surrounded Sarajevo" presentation on the first floor, to which Sarajevans have contributed objects, photographs and documents relating to their personal experience of the war. The result is a powerful yet understated exhibition which gives an invaluable insight into the siege. The struggle for survival is illustrated through homemade weapons used to defend the city, improvised lamps to combat the lack of electricity and editions of the Sarajevo newspaper printed every day to boost people's morale.

Interior of the poignant Tunnel Museum

Tunnel Museum

The nondescript rural home of the Kolar family in Butmir, on the outskirts of Sarajevo, was the scene of the biggest clandestine supply operation during the siege. The house, which was within the free territories (land defended by Sarajevans), is now the Tunnel Museum. It is situated over the entrance to the 800-m (2,625-ft) long tunnel dug under the nearby UN-administered airport in 1993, which was the city's only constant supply route throughout the siege. The tunnel took six months of manual digging to complete and was repeatedly targeted by Bosnian Serb forces. Today, only a section of it remains, but it is enough to give an impression of the cramped and dangerous underground journey an average of 4,000 Sarajevans made daily, each carrying around 50 kg (110 lbs) of food and supplies into Sarajevo. It was also used by the first president of Bosnia and Herzegovina, Alija Izetbegović. Guided tours of the tunnel are available from 9am until 4pm daily.

❷ Travnik

95 km (59 miles) NW of Sarajevo.
🏙 33,000. 🚌

Dwarfed by the lush green mountains to which it owes its name, Travnik is overlooked by the medieval 15th-century **Travnik Fortress** (Travnička tvrdava). It is famous as the birthplace of the Nobel Prize-winning novelist Ivo Andrić, who immortalized the town in his book, *Bosnian Chronicle*. The fortress and the surrounding Old Town, perched on steep slopes with dramatic views, were built and strengthened during the reign of Bosnian kings in the early 15th century. In 1463, the fortress fell to the Ottomans *(see p486)*, who coveted its commanding position and built a mosque, of which only the minaret remains. The interesting Archaeological and Ethnographic Museum in the complex presents an eclectic display of local finds as well as regional costumes. From the heights of the Old Town, the minaret of the **Many Coloured Mosque** (Šarena džamija) is clearly visible. Originally constructed in 1757 and rebuilt after a fire in 1815, the mosque stands above a covered bazaar. Its interior is decorated with floral patterns.

One of the best-developed ski resorts in Bosnia, Babanovac lies 28 km (17 miles) north of the town, on Mount Vlašić.

Detailing on the façade of the Many Coloured Mosque, Travnik

The mountain reaches a height of 1,943 m (6,375 ft) at Paljenik, its highest peak. The surrounding highlands are still populated by shepherds but the threat of landmines means that hiking should not be attempted without experienced local guides.

🏰 **Travnik Fortress**
Old Town. **Open** 8am–8pm daily.
📷 🏛

🕌 **Many Coloured Mosque**
Bosanska ulica. **Open** 8am–7pm daily.

❸ Jajce

137 km (85 miles) NW of Sarajevo.
🏙 31,000. 🚌

The town of Jajce – meaning egg – takes its name from the egg-shaped hill upon which its fortified citadel was founded in the 14th century. It served as the capital of the Bosnian Kingdom before succumbing twice to the Ottomans: first in 1463 and again in 1527. From then on, Jajce remained part of the Ottoman Empire until the Austro-Hungarians took over in 1908.

The idyllic position of this small town on a hillside above the mighty Pliva Waterfalls belies its disturbing recent history. Before the Bosnian War, Jajce was a peaceful multi-ethnic town, but in May 1992, most of its Bosnian Serb residents fled in fear of Croat aggression. In October 1992, the army of Republika Srpska responded by heavily bombarding the town, forcing the Bosnian Croat and Muslim population out. Croat forces recaptured the town in 1995, causing the Serb population to flee once more. Though much of the damage to the town has since been repaired, few of its original Bosnian Serb residents have returned.

One of the town's oldest sights is the ruined **St Mary's Church** (Crkva sv Marije), which dates back to the 12th century and was used as a Franciscan monastery in the 14th century. The last Bosnian queen, Katerina Kotromanić, added St Luke's Tower to the church building but fled with the saint's relics when the Ottomans conquered the region and converted the church

The picturesque town of Travnik, with its towering minarets

into a mosque. Nearby are some catacombs that were carved out in the early 1400s. It is widely believed that they were used as a chapel and crypt for the family of Duke Hrvoje Vucović, a powerful Bosnian feudal leader. Adjoining the church are the remains of a 4th-century Roman temple dedicated to the god Mithras.

Beyond the church looms Jajce's sturdy medieval **Bear Tower** (Medvjed kula). The tower, impenetrable in its day, boasted 6-m (20-ft) thick walls in places and could only be reached by a ladder. In recent years, a ground level entrance has been added. Access to the tower, the catacombs and the Roman temple can be arranged by staff at the nearby information office.

The spectacular 20-m (66-ft) high Pliva Waterfalls, below the town at the confluence of the Pliva and Vrbas rivers, are a popular attraction. The river's superb canyons make it a perfect spot for rafting.

🏠 **St Mary's Church**
Svetog Luke.

🏛 **Bear Tower**
Svetog Luke. **Open** 9am–7pm daily.
🅿 ℹ️ ulica Svetog Luke.

❹ Bihać

281 km (175 miles) NW of Sarajevo.
🔺 78,000. 🚌

Situated on the Una river, the picturesque town of Bihać is renowned for the pleasant fish restaurants that line its river banks. Medieval Bihać was one of the last Bosnian towns to fall into Ottoman hands, finally succumbing in 1592. After spending the next three centuries as a border fortress on the Austrian-Ottoman frontier, Bihać was absorbed into the Austro-Hungarian Empire in 1878. The town was heavily bombarded in World War II after Josip Broz Tito, who later became the president of Yugoslavia, made it the centre of his anti-Fascist movement. Bihać's majority Bosnian Muslim population was subjected to a three-year siege by Serbian

The impressive Pliva Waterfalls, set amidst lush forests below Jajce

forces between 1992 and 1995. The siege was finally broken when Croatian forces participating in Operation Storm pushed forward to join their Bosnian allies.

The **Captain's Tower** (Kapetanova kula), in the Main Square, is one of the town's few remaining medieval fortified buildings. The tower was turned into a prison when the Austro-Hungarians took control and continued to function as such until 1959; since then it has housed the Regional History Museum's well-presented collection. Behind it

stands St Anthony's Church, which was turned into the current **Fethija Mosque** by the Ottomans in the 16th century.

The lovely countryside around Bihać is notorious for being densely mined. Hiking and mountain biking trips, though possible, should not be undertaken without experienced local guides.

🏛 **Captain's Tower**
ulica 5 Korpusa 2.**Tel** (037) 229 743.
Open Mon–Fri 10am–8pm. 🅿

☪ **Fethija Mosque**
ulica 5 Korpusa.
Open 7am–7pm daily.

Whitewater rafting on the rapids of the Vrbas river

Rafting

Stunning mountain landscapes along with captivating waterfalls have made Bosnia a popular destination with adventure sports enthusiasts. The waters of the Vrbas, Drina, Tara, Una and Neretva rivers offer such an extensive range of rafting and kayaking experiences that the World Rafting Championship was held here in May 2009. The remarkable UNESCO-protected Tara river canyon, the second deepest in the world, offers some of the most intense and challenging rafting in Europe.

❺ Mostar

Located on the banks of the Neretva river, Mostar has been the political, cultural and economic cornerstone of Herzegovina since Turkish rule. Once the provincial capital of the Ottoman Empire, the town suffered more severely than any other during the Bosnian War. In 1992, it came under attack from the Yugoslav People's Army, dominated by Serbs. The Croats and Muslims joined forces to expel them, but in 1993, these two ethnic groups turned against each other and occupied opposing sides of the Neretva river, creating a racial divide that still exists. Today, the popular Old Bridge (Stari most), symbolizes Mostar's pre-war glory.

conflict are the souvenir salt cellars fashioned from empty shell cases. In the heart of the Old Town is the 16th century Kriva Ćuprija (crooked bridge), the oldest single-arch stone bridge in Mostar. It was built by the Turkish architect, Ćejvan Ketoda, in 1566. Near Kriva Ćuprija are the Hamam and Tabhana Turkish baths. Despite being severely damaged during the war, the place is still worth visiting, especially for the gorgeous views of the Neretva river and the Old Bridge from its terrace.

The narrow cobbled streets of Mostar's Old Town

🏛 Old Town

A UNESCO World Heritage Site, the historic Old Town (Stari grad) is the main attraction of Mostar with its grand Turkish houses and the Old Bridge. Ideal for a walking tour, the area can easily be explored in a day. The Kujundžiluk Bazaar, with its rambling streets of small shops and cafés, is charming, and the only reminders of the 1990s

🌉 Old Bridge

Mostar's symbolic centrepiece, the elegant stone Old Bridge (Stari most) spans the Neretva river, connecting the two sides of the Old Town. Built by Mimar Hajruddin in the 16th century, during the reign of the Ottoman ruler Suleiman the Magnificent, the bridge reaches a maximum height of 21 m (69 ft). Despite being recognized by UNESCO as a World Heritage Site, the bridge became the focus of target practice for Croatian soldiers during the Bosnian War and was completely destroyed in November 1993. Reconstruction began soon after the war ended and the renovated bridge, which is an

Mostar Town Centre

① Old Town
② Old Bridge
③ Herzegovina Museum
④ Karadjoz-Beg Mosque
⑤ Bišćević House

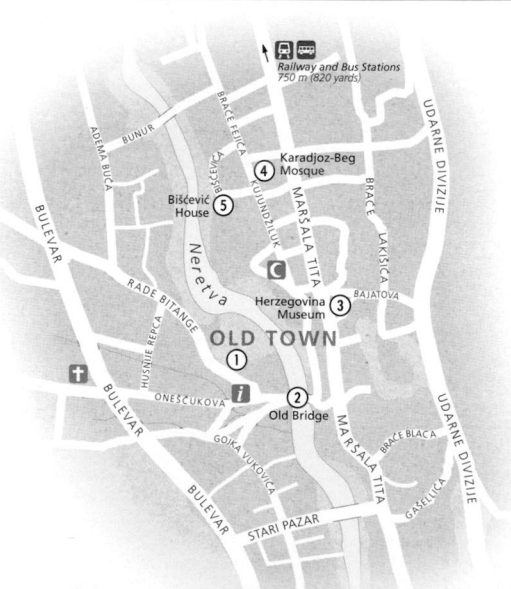

Railway and Bus Stations
750 m (820 yards)

Karadjoz-Beg Mosque ④

Bišćević House ⑤

C

Herzegovina Museum ③

OLD TOWN

①

Neretva

Old Bridge ②

0 metres   300
0 yards   300

exact replica of the original, was opened to the public in July 2004.

The Old Bridge is a popular spot, especially during summer, when visitors jostle for space to catch a glimpse of daring local men who collect money from onlookers before jumping off the bridge. This traditional diving competition is usually held in July.

Mostar's landmark Old Bridge, spanning the Neretva river

🏛 Herzegovina Museum
Bajatova 4. **Tel** (036) 551 602. **Open** 8am–4pm Mon–Fri, 10am–noon Sat. 🗺 🌐 **muzejher cegovine.com**

Founded in 1950, the eclectic Herzegovina Museum (Muzej Hercegovine) is housed in the residence of Džemal Bijedić, former head of the Yugoslav government. Built in an Oriental style with a porch and a courtyard, the building was established to promote the literary and cultural history of Herzegovina. It exhibits a variety of regional costumes

and traditional tools alongside archaeological discoveries and a display outlining Mostar's history.

🄲 Karadjoz-Beg Mosque
Kujundžiluk. **Open** 9am–9pm daily.
On the eastern side of Mostar stands the most significant example of sacred Islamic architecture in Herzegovina. Built in 1557, this mosque (Karadžozbegova džamija) is typical of Ottoman architecture, with a marble fountain and an *madrasa* (Islamic school) in the courtyard. Its interior was once adorned with floral motifs, of which only fragments remain. The slender minaret offers sweeping views over Mostar and its environs.

🏠 Bišćević House
Bišćevića. ℹ️ (036) 580 275.
Open 9am–6pm daily. 🗺
The delightful 17th-century Bišćević House (Bišćevića kuća), is a fine example of Turkish design. Partially supported by tall stone columns, the interior of the house features segregated living quarters and period furnishings. The building enjoys a lofty position on the eastern bank of the Neretva river and offers fine views over the town.

Statue of the Virgin Mary on Apparition Hill, Međugorje

❻ Međugorje
169 km (105 miles) SW of Sarajevo. 🗺 5,000. 🚌 🌐 **medjugorje.org**

The village of Međugorje, in the southern part of Herzegovina, is regarded as Bosnia's most famous Catholic pilgrimage site.

The small parish owes its reputation to a series of reported visions of the Virgin Mary. The "Queen of Peace", as locals refer to her, was initially witnessed in 1981 by six children. Crowds of eager pilgrims gathered to see the apparition, but it was only visible to the children, who were reportedly told ten secrets about the future of the planet. Today, over 20 million people have visited the site and numerous independent sightings have been recorded. However, the Vatican has never acknowledged the apparitions and dismisses the claims. A blue cross stands on the mountain, now called Apparition Hill, where the first sighting took place.

Also worth visiting is the impressive Church of St James, in the heart of the town. Completed in 1969, this is the gathering place for worshippers and holy masses are regularly held here in many languages.

Southwest of the town stands Mount Križevac, on top of which an 8-m (26-ft)high cross was planted in 1934 to commemorate the 1,900th anniversary of Christ's death.

Elegant interior of the Karadjoz-Beg Mosque

Practical & Travel Information

Bosnians are traditionally hospitable people and will often go out of their way to help visitors. Visitor information centres with English-speaking staff are rare outside big towns. With the increasing influx of visitors, accommodation is now readily available in most towns. The country's good network of trains and buses ensures easy travel, although a lack of sleeper carriages means that overnight train journeys can be exhausting. It is most convenient to travel by car but drivers need to be aware of the danger of landmines. Hiking is also a great way to explore the countryside, but not without a guide.

When to Visit

The best time to visit Bosnia and Herzegovina is in summer, when days are warm and evenings pleasant. In general, summer is from June to September, although in Herzegovina, it begins earlier in May. Bosnia experiences severe cold winters, while in Herzegovina they are relatively mild. For skiers, the best time to visit Bosnia is from January to March.

Documentation

All European Union (EU), US and Canadian citizens can enter Bosnia without a visa for up to 90 days, on a valid passport. Other nationalities should apply to their nearest embassy for a visa. Visitors are required to register with the police on arrival, but hotels will arrange this automatically.

Visitor Information

Bosnia's only official tourist information offices with English-speaking staff are in Sarajevo and Mostar. The **Sarajevo Tourist Information Centre** and **Mostar Tourist Information Centre** are well equipped and have brochures covering the whole country. Smaller towns have tourist association offices, but have unreliable opening hours and staff are unlikely to speak English.

Health and Security

Visitors are advised to get vaccinated against tetanus, hepatitis A, diphtheria and polio prior to travel. Public health clinics are best avoided as private clinics offer better medical care. The **Emergency Medical Service** in Sarajevo is open to visitors and has good doctors, while in Mostar, the **Clinical Hospital Mostar** also has good medical care. In case of any emergency it is advisable to contact the relevant embassy.

Crime against visitors is virtually non-existent, although visitors should be wary of pickpockets, especially in trams and trains.

Facilities for the Disabled

Public awareness about the needs of travellers with disabilities is poor in Bosnia and Herzegovina. Only hotels and restaurants in major towns have facilities for the disabled.

Banking and Currency

The official currency of Bosnia is KM (2 KM is approximately €1). Banks will usually exchange traveller's cheques and major currencies. In small towns and villages, credit cards are less likely to be accepted and ATMs are scarce, so visitors should carry enough cash for their journey.

Communications

Many city hotels and coffee shops offer free Wi-Fi to guests. Public telephones require phone cards, which are sold in post offices or newspaper kiosks.

Landmines

One of Bosnia's biggest safety concerns for both locals and visitors are the landmines laid during the Bosnian War, which cover an estimated four per cent of the country. Mine clearance has been ongoing since 1995, but the sheer danger of the work, combined with lack of funding and alleged misappropriation of funds, has unfortunately hampered progress. Although the densely populated areas have been cleared, there is a real danger of unexploded mines in open countryside and isolated buildings. The roads have been largely cleared, but the possibility of roadside mines means that drivers should avoid pulling over on to rough or unmarked ground. Hikers need to take special care and should consult Sarajevo's Tourist Information Centre before setting out and are strongly advised to take a professional guide. Bosnia's **Mine Action Centre** has up-to-date information on the current situation, as does the **UK Foreign Office**.

The Climate of Bosnia and Herzegovina

The south and west of Bosnia as well as Herzegovina, has a Mediterranean climate with long, hot summers and mild, wet winters. In the north and east, much of the country has warm summers and cold winters, with snow at higher altitudes benefiting ski resorts close to Sarajevo and Mount Vlašic. Sarajevo averages 20° C (68° F) in summer and -1° C (30° F) in winter.

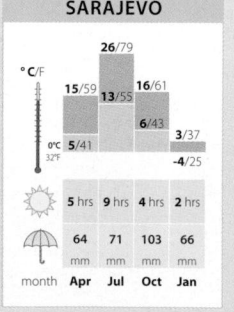

SARAJEVO

°C/F	Apr	Jul	Oct	Jan
high	15/59	26/79	16/61	3/37
low	5/41	13/55	6/43	-4/25
sunshine	5 hrs	9 hrs	4 hrs	2 hrs
rainfall	64 mm	71 mm	103 mm	66 mm
month	Apr	Jul	Oct	Jan

Arriving by Air

Sarajevo International Airport, 12 km (7 miles) southwest of the city, is the only international airport with daily flights. It is worth noting that the airport is prone to fog in winter, which can cause flight cancellations or delays at short notice. Mostar's airport has weekly flights to Dubrovnik in Croatia, and caters to charter flights travelling to Međugorje. **BH Airlines** connects Sarajevo with many European cities such as Amsterdam, Vienna, Frankfurt, Zurich and Copenhagen. **Lufthansa**, **Austrian Airlines**, **Air Serbia**, **Adria Airways**, **Pegasus**, **Scandinavian Airlines** and **Croatia Airlines** have regular flights to Munich, Vienna, Koeln, Zagreb, Stuttgart, Belgrade, Budapest, Ljubljana, Istanbul, and Stockholm.

Rail Travel

Bosnia's rail network suffered severe damage during the Bosnian War. Its services are still limited and journeys are slow, as the routes tend to be circuitous. Mainline connections with neighbouring capitals have been introduced and overnight trains run north from Sarajevo to Zagreb and Ploče in Croatia. The southern line from Sarajevo via Mostar to Ploče, in Croatia, is the country's most scenic route. Bosnia is now accessible with an InterRail ticket, but not yet with Eurail. **Sarajevo Train Station** is easily accessible from the downtown area.

Travelling by Bus

The country has a reliable bus network with daily services covering the whole country. International buses run daily from Sarajevo to Ljubljana, Kotor, Belgrade, Zagreb and Dubrovnik. Eurolines operates coaches from Sarajevo to other European cities through the Bosnian bus company **Centrotrans**. Reservations can be made through Eurolines offices abroad.

Travelling by Car

Travelling by car is the most convenient form of transport in Bosnia. It is safe to drive all around the country, although the usual landmine warnings about not straying off the road apply. Petrol stations are plentiful and often accept credit cards. Major car rental firms at Sarajevo Airport include **Budget, Rent a Car Minell** and **Thrifty**, as well as Hertz, Avis and more. Those travelling in their own car will need registration documents, Green Card insurance and an EU or international driving licence. Snow chains are essential for winter travel. Drivers should ensure that they carry a dual language road map as most of the road signs in Republika Srpska – one of the two main political divisions of the country – are in Cyrillic.

Outdoor Activities

Before Bosnia's natural beauty was marred by landmines, it was a paradise for hiking, mountain biking, climbing and rafting. None of these activities are now recommended without a local professional guide. Both **Green Visions** and the **Encijan Mountain Association** promote sustainable development, providing internationally qualified guides and running organized wilderness trips in areas that are clear of mines.

DIRECTORY

Embassies

United Kingdom
Tina Ujevića 8, Sarajevo.
Tel (033) 444 429.
W ukinbih.fco.gov.uk

United States
1 Robert C. Frasure St,
Sarajevo. **Tel** (033) 704
000. W sarajevo.
usembassy.gov

Visitor Information

Mostar Tourist Information Centre
Tel (036) 580 275.
W hercegovina.ba

Sarajevo Tourist Information Centre
Tel (033) 580 999.
W sarajevo-tourism.com

Emergency Numbers

Ambulance
Tel 124.

Fire
Tel 123.

Police
Tel 122.

Health and Security

Clinical Hospital Mostar
Tel (036) 336 500.

Emergency Medical Service
Kolodvorska 14, Sarajevo.
Tel (033) 611 111.

Landmines

Mine Action Centre
W bhmac.org

UK Foreign Office
W fco.gov.uk

Arriving by Air

Austrian Airlines
W aua.com

Air Serbia
W airserbia.com

Adria Airways
W adria.si

BH Airlines
W bhairlines.ba

Croatia Airlines
W croatiaairlines.com

Lufthansa
W lufthansa.com

Pegasus
W flypgs.com

Sarajevo Airport
W sarajevo-airport.ba

Scandinavian Airlines
W flysas.com

Rail Travel

Sarajevo Train Station
Tel (033) 655 330.

Travelling by Bus

Centrotrans
Tel (033) 464 045.
W eurolines.ba

Travelling by Car

Budget
Tel (033) 766 670; (063)
047 968. W budget.ba

Rent a Car Minell
Tel (033) 881 188.
W rentacarminell.net

Thrifty
Tel (033) 760 645.
W thrifty.ba

Outdoor Activities

Green Visions
W greenvisions.ba

Encijan Mountain Association
W pkencijan.com

Where to Stay

Sarajevo

Hostel Franz Ferdinand
Hostel **Map** E2
Jelića 4, 71000
Tel (033) 834 625
W franzferdinandhostel.com
Smart, crisply decorated hostel on the edge of the Baščaršija, with a choice of cubicle-style dorm beds or comfortable history-themed doubles.

Traveller's Home
Hostel **Map** E3
Ćumurija 4, 71000
Tel 70 242 400
W myhostel.ba
Stylishly restored Austro-Hungarian building with parquet floors, fully equipped kitchen and a good mix of dorms and private rooms.

Garni Hotel Konak
B&B/Guesthouse **Map** E2
Mula Mustafe Bašeskije 54, 71000
Tel (033) 476 900
W konak.ba
Small friendly setup with neat en suite rooms that have wooden floors and contemporary comforts. Centrally located near the pedestrian zone, a short distance from the Old Town.

Mejdan Motel
B&B/Guesthouse
Mustaj-pašin mejdan 11, 71000
Tel (033) 233 563
W mejdanmotel.com
Despite the motel tag, this is an intimate guesthouse in the Old Town offering neat rooms at an attractive price.

Hotel Astra
Business **Map** E3
ul. Zelenih Beretki 9, 71000
Tel (033) 252 100
W hotel-astra.co.ba
Located centrally, this hotel with an impressive interior also has on-site sauna and conference facilities. Efficient staff.

Hotel Colors Inn
Design
Koševo 8, 71000
Tel (033) 276 600
W hotelcolorsinnsarajevo.com
Between the train station and the Old Town is this smart modern place with stylish, contemporary, colour-themed rooms and a bright relaxing breakfast area.

Hotel Safr
B&B/Guesthouse **Map** F2
ul. Jagodića 3, 71000
Tel (033) 475 040
W hotelsafir.ba
Smart intimate hotel just uphill from the Baščaršija offering neat en suites with wooden floors.

Rest of Bosnia and Herzegovina

BIHAĆ: Ada
Resort
Put 5. Korpusa bb, 77000
Tel (037) 318 100
W aduna.ba
Lovely riverside complex with great scenery and comfortable rooms located in the pleasant countryside just outside Bihać.

DK Choice

BIHAĆ: Kostelski Buk
Resort
Kostela bb, 77000
Tel (037) 302 340
W kostelski-buk.com
Located near a popular riverside spot characterized by waterfalls and foaming waters, this hotel offers bright and romantic rooms. Local walks, a modest animal park and riverside restaurant ensure that there's plenty to do.

JAJCE: Stari Grad
Historic
Svetog Luke 3, 70101
Tel (030) 654 006
W jajcetours.com

Impressive façade of the Muslibegović House in Mostar

Built on the ruins of a Turkish bath, in the centre of the Old Town, this hotel offers sauna facilities and smartly-furnished rooms.

MEĐUGORJE: Villa Petra
B&B
Bijakovići Podbrdo bb, 88266
Tel 63 994 499
W villapetra-medjugorje.com
Pleasant family house set in the Herzegovinian countryside, within walking distance of the main pilgrimage sites.

MOSTAR: Pansion Villa Sara
Hostel
Lacina-Šaša Rogina 4, 88000
Tel (036) 555 940
W villasara-mostar.com
Well-run establishment offering a mix of dorms and double rooms, with bathroom and kitchen facilities on each of its four floors.

MOSTAR: Bevanda
Luxury
Stara Ilička bb, 88000
Tel (036) 332 332
W hotelbevanda.com
Sophisticated 5-star hotel with opulently furnished rooms, fitness facilities and a garden restaurant with delightful water fountains.

MOSTAR: Muslibegović House
Historic
Osman Dikića 41, 88000
Tel (036) 551 379
W muslibegovichouse.com
Once home to an Ottoman-era aristocrat, this beautifully preserved building is both a museum and hotel. Its atmospheric rooms provide all modern comforts.

TRAVNIK: ABA Motel
Business
ulica Šumeće 166, 72270
Tel (030) 511 462
W aba.ba
At the foot of forested hills, the recently built ABA offers spotless rooms, good service and sumptuous buffet breakfasts.

Where to Eat and Drink

Sarajevo

Buregdžinica Bosna
Bosnian   Map F2
Bravadžiluk 11, 71000
Tel *(033) 538 426*
This sparsely furnished
fast-food bar excels in the
flaky pastries that occupy an
important place in Bosnian
cuisine. Choose between *burek*
(minced meat), *krumpiruša*
(diced potato), *sirnica* (cheese)
and *zeljanica* (spinach
and cheese).

DK Choice

Ćevabdžinica Željo
Balkan grill   Map E3
Kundurdžiluk 19, 71000
Tel *(033) 447 000*
Full of football-related
memorabilia and named
after the local team Željezničar
(Željo for short), this small
cafe-restaurant is one of the
best places in town to sample
ćevapi, the local fast-food
speciality – small spicy cylinders
of ground lamb and beef, which
are grilled and sandwiched in a
somun (springy flat bread).

Dveri
International   Map E2
Prote Bakovića 12, 71000
Tel *(033) 537 020*
With a vast menu extending
from steak to seafood risottos
and even the odd tandoori,
Dveri is a small and cosy
restaurant artfully decorated
with hanging bunches of
garlic, corn-cobs and
potted plants.

Kibe
Bosnian
Vrbanjuša 164, 71000
Tel *(033) 441 936*
This hillside restaurant
with great views of the city,
is known for its traditional
Bosnian meat menu,
ncluding some hearty
stews and roasts.

Mala Kuhinja
International
Tina Ujevića 13, 71000
Tel *(033) 841 076*
Creative European–Asian
fusion food with menus tailored
to your dietary needs. Great
steak, seafood and wok-fries.
The daily specials are
excellent value.

Unique interiors of Karuzo
in Sarajevo

Sedef
Bosnian   Map D3
Ferhadija 16, 71000
Tel *(033) 200 588*
Excellent family-run eatery
in a warm, atmospheric space,
serving fresh salads, high-quality
grilled meats and traditonal
soups and stews.

Karuzo €€€
Vegetarian/Seafood   Map D2
Dženetića Čikma bb, 71000
Tel *(033) 444 647*
This cosy restaurant with
bench seating and nautical bric-
a-brac has a seasonally changing
menu of creative vegetarian
cuisine as well as sushi
and seafood.

Morica Han
Bosnian   Map E2
Sarači 77, 71000
Tel *(033) 236 119*
Housed in a 16th-century *han*
(merchants' inn), this appealing
restaurant serves traditional
Bosnian meats and stews in a
quiet cobbled courtyard.

Rest of Bosnia and Herzegovina

BIHAĆ: Kostelski Buk
Seafood
Kostela bb, 77000
Tel *(037) 302 340*
The quality menu at this smart
hotel restaurant that has a large
terrace overlooking the Una river,
includes Adriatic seafood, local
freshwater fish and traditional
syrupy desserts.

Price Guide
Prices are based on a three-course meal
for one, half a bottle of wine, including
cover charge, service and tax.

	under 30 KM
	30–60 KM
	over 60 KM

JAJCE: Stari Grad
Bosnian
Svetog Luke 3, 70101
Tel *(030) 654 006*
A cosy hotel restaurant with an
excellent choice of regional
specialities, including spicy stews
and freshwater fish dishes.

MOSTAR: Ćevabdžinica Tima-Irma
Balkan grill
Onešćukova bb, 88000
Tel *062 958 539*
Local staples such as *ćevapi*,
pljeskavice (grilled meat patties)
and *sudžukice* (spicy sausages)
served in a cosy interior or on
the outdoor terrace.

MOSTAR: Hindin Han
Balkan grill/Seafood
Jusovina bb, 88000
Tel *(036) 581 054*
Enjoy large portions of grilled
meats, fresh salads and Adriatic
seafood in a traditional house
that has a balustraded terrace
overlooking the river.

MOSTAR: Kriva Ćuprija
International
Onešćukova 23, 88000
Tel *(036) 360 360*
Choose from dining on the large
terrace or indoors under a ceiling
with wooden beams. The restaurant
has a large menu comprising
roast meats, seafood, freshwater
fish, pizza and pasta.

MOSTAR: Kulluk
Bosnian/International
Kurluk 1, 88000
Tel *(036) 551 716*
Rising above street level with
a cobbled terrace overlooking
the Neretva river, Kulluk serves a
broad range of Bosnian dishes
alongside decent pizza and
Adriatic seafood.

TRAVNIK: Plava Voda
Seafood
Ulica Šumeće bb, 72270
Tel *061 798 040*
Enjoy local trout, grilled meats
and traditional Bosnian desserts
such as *hurmašica* (sticky, syrupy
buns) served on a large riverside
terrace at the eastern end
of town.

MONTENEGRO

Famous for its idyllic Adriatic coastline, Montenegro is enormously popular with those looking to plant beach umbrellas or moor their luxury yachts, though this small and newly independent country has far more to offer. Venetian-flavoured, fortified towns line the coast, while national parks protect the best of its abundant and largely unspoilt natural beauty.

Montenegro's mountains have long provided a buffer between this small country and its neighbours. To the north lies Serbia; to the west, Bosnia and the coastal sliver of Croatia. However, despite an eventful and frequently war-ravaged past, Montenegro has attracted a steady flow of visitors since the 1970s. Its lush forests, glacial lakes, waterfalls and mountains offer rewarding opportunities for rafting, caving, climbing, skiing and hiking.

History

The region now known as Montenegro was settled as early as the Stone Age. However, its complex history begins in the 6th century BC with the Illyrians. During the Illyrian Wars of the 3rd century BC, the Romans conquered much of the territory and maintained a strong presence there until the split of their empire in the 4th century AD, when the Byzantines wrested control of the region. Meanwhile, Slavic Serb and Croat tribes settled in the west and developed a Slavic state, which was recognized by the Byzantine Empire. In 1189, the Serbian ruler Stefan Nemanja conquered Montenegro – known at the time as Duklja – and renamed it Zeta. Upon the collapse of the Serbian Empire in the late 14th century, two powerful local tribes, the Balšić and the Crnojević, took control of Zeta. The Balšić held much of the coast, while the Crnojević occupied the mountainous interior. Under threat from the advancing Ottoman Empire in the 15th century, Stefan Crnojević (r. 1451–65) forged a defensive alliance with the Venetians, who occupied most of the coast. However, by 1496

The serpentine Crnojević river, Lake Skadar National Park

◀ A stretch of Slovenska Beach, one of Budva's most popular attractions

much of the region had succumbed to the Ottomans. At this time Cetinje was established as capital of Crna Gora (Montenegro), the mountainous interior region. Due to the difficult terrain, the Montenegrins were left largely to their own devices, while the Ottomans focused on taking control of strategic coastal towns.

Following an unsuccessful allegiance with Russia against the Ottomans in 1710, Montenegro came under frequent attack by the Turks. Sporadic conflicts continued until 1878, when the Berlin Congress recognized it as an independent state. Allied with Serbia during World War I, Montenegro was soon occupied by Austria-Hungary. In 1918, Montenegro joined the new kingdom of Serbs, Croats and Slovenes, losing much of its identity in the process. During World War II, the country was occupied first by the Italians and then the Germans,

Đukanović supporters holding his portrait, 2006 rally

whose eventual defeat led to the creation of Tito's Federal Republic of Yugoslavia, in which Montenegro was one of six republics.

Following the break up of Yugoslavia (1991–95), Montenegro sided with Serbia in attacks on Bosnia and Croatia. However, in 1996 President Mizo Đukanović began to slowly move away from Serbian tutelage, beginning the move towards full Montenegrin independence.

On 26 May 2006, a referendum finally established Montenegro as a sovereign state.

Language and Culture

Montenegrins speak Serbo-Croatian and officially use both the Latin and Cyrillic alphabets. There is little to culturally differentiate Montenegrins from Serbians as they have been intermarrying for centuries; variations in traditions are most pronounced between the communities of the Ottoman-influenced coast and those of the interior.

Right up until the last century, elaborate regional costume played an important role in the cultural life of the interior communities; it was a custom to be buried in full traditional dress. Colourful festivals are still a regular feature of Montenegrin life.

KEY DATES IN MONTENEGRIN HISTORY

AD 395 Roman Empire divided into two: Serbia and Montenegro are part of Byzantine Empire

1015 Duklja develops into a Serb-controlled principality

1189 Serbian ruler Stefan Nemanja conquers Duklja and renames it Zeta

1496 Cetinje established as the capital of the interior region of Crna Gora (Montenegro)

1667 A devastating earthquake hits the Adriatic coast, destroying Kotor

1800s Prince Petar I seeks Russian support in the struggle against the Ottomans

1876–8 Montenegro wins freedom from a shrinking Ottoman Empire

1918 Montenegro joins the newly formed kingdom of Serbs, Croats and Slovenes, accepting the Serbian royal family as its new monarchs

1941 Mussolini occupies Montenegro with plans to absorb it as an Italian protectorate

2006 Montenegrins vote in a referendum for independence from Serbia

2007 Montenegro signs a membership agreement with the EU

2012 Montenegro begins accession negotiations with the EU

Exploring Montenegro

Montenegro is dominated by towering peaks that provide a stunning backdrop to the sparkling blue Adriatic and the sandy beaches that line the country's coastline. Its capital is the Ottoman-influenced city of Podgorica, dotted with mosques, cafés and restaurants. Among the other cities of interest is Kotor, located on Montenegro's most beautiful bay. Getting around is easy as the bus service is extensive, although sporadic inland. A railway line runs from Bar to Podgorica, and on to Belgrade.

Sights at a Glance

1. Podgorica
2. Lake Skadar National Park
3. Bar
4. Ulcinj
5. Budva
6. Tivat
7. Herceg Novi
8. Kotor
9. Lovćen National Park
10. Cetinje
11. *Ostrog Monastery pp512–3*
12. Durmitor National Park

Venetian buildings along the cobbled streets of the Old Town, Budva

0 kilometres 25

0 miles 25

BOSNIA AND HERZEGOVINA

Gradac

Pljevlja

Mratinje

Durmitor National Park ⑫

Plužine

Trsa

Žabljak

Kovren

Goransko

Đurđevića Tara

SERBIA

Gornja Bukovica

Bijelo Polje

Nedakusi

Šavnik

Ravna Rijeka

Jasenovo Polje

Redice

Mojkovac

Rastovac

Crni Vrh

Berane

Rožaje

Vilusi

Lake Slansko

Nikšić

Ostrog Monastery ⑪

Kolašin

Grahovo

Andrejevica

KOSOVO

CROATIA

Kruševice

Risan

Danilovgrad

Spuž

Gusinje

Plav

Igalo

Tivat ⑥

Medun

Vusanje

Herceg Novi ⑦

Kotor ⑧

 Liješnje

PODGORICA ①

ALBANIA

Lovćen National Park ⑨

Cetinje ⑩

Rijeka Crnojevića

Tuzi

Budva ⑤

Golubovci

Sveti Stefan

Virpazar

Vranjina

Petrovac

Godinje

Lake Skadar National Park ②

Adriatic Sea

Sutomore

Murići

Bar ③

Veliki Ostros

Bari

Valdanos

Krute

Vladimir

Ulcinj ④

Donji Štoj

Key

— Major road

=== Minor road

— Railway

-- • International border

For keys to symbols *see back flap*

Impressive Millennium Bridge over the Morača river, Podgorica

❶ Podgorica

🏔 180,000. ✈ 🚉 🚌 🛈 Slobode 47, (020) 667 535. 🆆 **podgorica.travel**

Podgorica initially developed as an important centre for trade; the first official mention of it was in 1326. The city thrived during medieval times but then succumbed to the Ottomans who occupied it as a defensive citadel for four centuries. In 1878, the city was integrated into Montenegro and it flourished economically and culturally for several decades. Podgorica suffered in the 20th century, however, due to intensive bombing during World War II and severe economic decline during the Yugoslav Wars in the 1990s. Today, Montenegro's capital has a handful of minor sights that can be explored in a day. The most striking structure and a symbol of 21st-century progress is the 140-m (459-ft) long Millennium Bridge (Most Milenijum) across the Morača river. The city's Old Town, south of the Ribnica river, was almost entirely destroyed during World War II. However, some remnants of its Ottoman past remain. In the Old Town Square is the 30-m (98-ft) high 18th-century Turkish Clock Tower (Sahat Kula) while the Muslim quarter houses the renovated 16th-century Glavatovići and Osmanagića mosques.

To the north of the Ribnica river, the New Town's **City Museum** (Muzeji i galerije Podgorice) houses absorbing archaeological and ethnographic collections. Further north is the 11th-century **St George's Church** (Crkva Sv Đorđa), with frescoes depicting the life of St George. Podgorica's finest building, King Nikola's former Winter Palace contains the **Modern Art Gallery** (Centar Savremene Umjetnosti) with a collection of ethnographic art from Africa and Asia among other exhibits. Nearby is the **Orthodox Cathedral of the Resurrection of Christ**, which boasts 17 Russian bells; the largest, at 11 tonnes (12 tons), is the heaviest in the Balkans.

🏛 City Museum
Marka Miljanova 4. **Tel** (020) 242 543. **Open** noon–8pm Tue–Fri, 9am–2pm Sat & Sun. 🎨 📷

⛪ St George's Church
ulica 19 Decembar. **Open** 7am–8pm daily. 🛈

🏛 Modern Art Gallery
Ljubljanska ulica BB. **Tel** (020) 225 043. **Open** 4–9pm Mon–Fri.

⛪ Orthodox Cathedral of the Resurrection of Christ
ulica Georga Vašingtona. **Open** 7:30am–7pm daily. 🛈

❷ Lake Skadar National Park
Skadarsko jezero

25 km (16 miles) S of Podgorica. 🚌 from Podgorica. 🛈 Vranjina Island, close to Virpazar, (020) 879 103; Centre for Protection and Research of Birds in Montenegro, Piperska 370A, (067) 245 006. 🆆 **nparkovi.me**

Located in the Zeta Skadar valley and surrounded by picturesque mountains, the 400-sq-km (154-sq-mile) Lake Skadar is the Balkan Peninsula's largest lake and is split between Albania and Montenegro. In 1983, two-thirds of the lake on the Montenegro side was designated as a national park. The lake is fed by around 50 underwater springs and is home to about 264 bird species, such as great white herons, Caspian terns, black-headed gulls, Griffon vultures, Dalmatian pelicans and white-tailed eagles. It also has about 40 species of fish including mullet, carp, eel and chub. The northern

Dalmatian pelican, Lake Skadar

and eastern shores of the lake are characterized by marshlands which are scattered with yellow water lilies in spring.

The lake's islands are also home to many monasteries and churches, some dating back to the 11th century; there are several ruined medieval fortresses as well.

The visitors' centre in Vranjina can arrange boat trips around the park and to the monasteries as well as fishing permits. It also offers general information on Montenegro's national parks.

The magnificent Lake Skadar National Park, home to numerous species of flora and fauna

For hotels and restaurants see p517 and pp518–9

❸ Bar

70 km (43 miles) S of Podgorica.
🏠 16,000. 🚌 🚍 ⛴ ℹ️ Obala 13
Jul bb, (030) 312 912. 🌐 **bar.me**

The beautiful coastal town
of Bar is the country's only
international port, with ferries
from Italy docking three times
a week.

However, the star attraction is
the Old Town (Stari Bar), situated
4 km (2 miles) inland on a rocky
plateau at the foot of Mount
Rumija. Founded in the 6th
century, the town was ruled by
Byzantines, Serbs and Venetians
before becoming part of the
Ottoman Empire from 1571 to
1878. It was gradually abandoned
in the early 20th century after
being destroyed during the
War of Liberation (1878) and
suffering two catastrophic
explosions in 1882 and 1912.
Archaeological and restoration
work begun in the 1950s was
set back by another earthquake
in 1979 which again devastated
the Old Town.

Today, many of the Old Town's
buildings and sections of its
walls have been restored and are
used as a summer venue for
cultural events. The 12th-century
St George's Church was built
on the ruins of the 9th-century
St Theodor's Church and was
once the Old Town's
largest cathedral. The
Ottomans rebuilt it
as a mosque in the
17th century, but
today only its found-
ations remain. Also
worth visiting is the
restored Church of
St Venerada, used for
music recitals, and the
old Bishop's Palace,
which houses a small
museum of the Old
Town history.

A more compre-
hensive museum collection
can be found in the **Homeland
Museum** (Zavičajni muzej) on
the seafront in the New Town
(Novi Bar). It is located in the
19th-century summer residence
of King Nikola, who used the
mansion to receive guests from
abroad. The town is also famous
for its numerous olive trees.
According to legend, locals
were unable to marry until they
had planted at least ten olive
trees. One, in particular, is
believed to be over 2,000 years
old and can be found near the
Old Town.

The 2,000-year-old olive tree near Bar's Old Town

🏛️ **Homeland Museum**
Šetalište Kralje Nikole.
Tel (030) 314 079. **Open** 9am–2pm &
6pm–8pm daily. 🅿️ 📷

❹ Ulcinj

95 km (59 miles) S of Podgorica.
🏠 11,000. 🚍 ℹ️ ulica 6 Novembra,
(030) 412 595. 📅 Fri. 🌐 **ulcinj.travel**

The southernmost city on the
Montenegrin coast, Ulcinj is
thought to be one of the oldest
trading settlements in the
Adriatic. Its Old Town (Stari grad)
was mentioned as early as the
6th century BC, when it was
home to a Greek colony. Its
naturally defensive position atop
a rocky peninsular made for an
ideal vantage point over the
sheltered harbour and was
reinforced by mighty walls,
rendering it virtually impenetrable to attack over the centuries. However, it succumbed to
the Serbs, then the Venetians,
and, finally, the Ottomans in 1571
before its integration into the
new Montenegrin state in 1880.
Today, the Old Town has been
restored following widespread
damage caused by the 1979
earthquake. The **Old Town
Museum** (Zavičajni muzej) occupies many buildings on Slave's
Square (trg Robova). Its archaeological collection, housed in a
16th-century Renaissance
church, includes marble Turkish
tombstones, medieval coins and
a variety of pottery specimens.
Traditional costumes are on
display in the neighbouring
6th-century Bishop's Palace, while
the 15th-century Balšić Tower is
used for temporary exhibitions.

🏛️ **Old Town Museum**
Stari grad. **Tel** (030) 421 419.
Open May–Sep: 7am–noon &
3pm–8pm daily; Oct–Apr: 7am–2pm
daily. 🅿️ 📷

One of the remote beaches in Ulcinj

Montenegro's Best Beaches

Between Bar and Ulcinj, endless stretches of fine sandy beaches
merge with the clear blue waters of the Adriatic. To the west of Bar,
and only accessible by sea, is the Kraljičina (Queen's) Beach, favoured
by Queen Milena, wife of King Nikola. To the east is the 1-km (0.5-mile)
long Crvena (Red) Beach named after its unusual red sand. The Veliki
Pijesak (Great Sand) Beach between Bar and Ulcinj or the 13-km
(8-mile) long Velika Plaža (Great Beach) east of Ulcinj are the most
isolated beaches. Naturists can also visit the beach at Ada Bojana, a
small island at the end of Velika Plaža.

Budva's walled town with the striking tower of St Ivan's Catholic Church

❺ Budva

67 km (42 miles) SW of Podgorica.
🚹 17,000. 🚌🚢 ⓘ Mediteranska 4,
(033) 402 814. 🌐 **budva.travel**

With its fantastic beaches, islands and bays, the enchanting town of Budva has become extremely popular. One of the oldest urban settlements on the Montenegrin coast, the town was successively conquered by Greeks, Romans, Serbs and various feudal rulers before the Venetians gained control in 1442. They strengthened its existing defences and managed to resist the Ottoman expansion that absorbed the neighbouring towns of Bar, Ulcinj and Podgorica in the 16th

century. Budva stayed under Venetian control until 1797, when it fell into Austrian hands; it did not join Montenegro until the Allied defeat of the Austro-Hungarian Empire in 1918.

Perched on a rocky bluff and overlooked by picturesque mountains, Budva's atmospheric Old Town (Stari grad) still has a distinct Venetian flavour. Devastated by an earthquake in 1979, it has been painstakingly restored. Today, its enchanting alleys open on to charming squares filled with shops, bars and restaurants enlivened by street performers.

The **Budva Museum** (Muzej Budve) on the Old Town Square (Starogradski trg) houses a fascinating display of archaeological artifacts, many of which were uncovered after the upheaval of the 1979 earthquake. They include Roman glassware and an engraved 5th-century Illyrian helmet. Smaller ethnographic and historical exhibitions are displayed on the upper floors of the museum.

Standing next door is **St Ivan's Catholic Church** (Katolička Crkva Sv Ivana), notable for its prominent tower. Dating from the 7th century, this is the town's oldest church, although the design was modified following a severe earthquake in 1667. Its simple façade conceals an interior with a fine array of 17th-century Venetian icons as well as the 12th-century *Madonna of Budva* icon, believed to have miraculous curative powers. The small Franciscan **Church of St Mary** (Crkva Svete Marije), tucked away in the southwest corner of the town, has a distinctive triple-arched bell tower. Founded in the 9th century, it is now used to host occasional cultural events.

Painted arch, Church of St Mary

A short distance out to sea is the sloping St Nikola's Island. Boats shuttle back and forth during the summer allowing visitors to climb to the island's summit at 120 m (395 ft), laze on its sandy beaches or visit the small St Nikola Church.

🏛 **Budva Museum**
Petra I Petrovića 11, Stari grad.
Tel (033) 453 308. **Open** May–Sep:
8am–10pm Tue–Sun; Oct–Apr:
10am–8pm Tue–Fri, 10am–5pm Sat &
Sun. 🅿 📷

🔼 **St Ivan's Catholic Church**
Strarogradski trg.
Open 7am–7:30pm daily. 🔼

🔼 **Church of St Mary**
Stari grad, southeast wall.
Open 8:30am–6pm daily.

Sveti Stefan

Built on a rocky island to the south of Budva, Sveti Stefan appears to float dreamily on the turquoise waters of the Adriatic. The island's natural beauty, combined with ancient stone houses converted into luxury apartments, earned it a reputation in the 1970s and 80s as an exclusive summer resort. Once a haven for medieval pirates and fishermen resisting the Ottomans, it became the summer retreat of royalty, such as Queen Elizabeth II and Hollywood stars such as Sophia Loren and Sylvester Stallone. The Yugoslav Wars abruptly curtailed its popularity. It remained closed for almost 15 years before reopening in 2009 as an exclusive Aman Resort hotel.

The fairy tale island resort of Sveti Stefan

❻ Tivat

80 km (50 miles) W of Podgorica.
🏔 8,000. ✈ 🚌 *i* Palih Boraca 8,
(032) 671324. **W** tivat.travel

Situated on the Bay of Kotor,
Tivat has emerged as a major
tourist attraction, where visitors promenade along the
beachfront beneath palm
trees as expensive yachts
cruise in and out of
the marina.

Wealthy aristocrats from
Kotor were among the first to
build their summer residences
here in the Middle Ages. The
Buća-Luković Summer Palace
(Vila Buća-Luković) on the
seafront was once the seasonal
home of the Bućas, one of the
wealthiest families of Kotor. The
palace's stone tower and small
Baroque church date back to
the 15th century. The
Renaissance building is now
used for cultural performances
and exhibitions throughout
the summer.

North of the town centre,
the Town Park is a pleasant
retreat shaded by cypress,
eucalyptus and oleander trees.
The small Island of Flowers,
connected to the mainland
by a narrow isthmus, is home
to the partially excavated ruins
of the Monastery of Archangel
Michael, founded in the 13th
century by Benedictine monks.

🏛 **Buća-Luković Summer Palace**
Nikole Đurkovića br. 10. **Tel** (032) 674
591. **Open** summer: 8am–1pm &
noon–7pm daily; winter: 8am–1pm &
4pm–11pm Mon–Fri. 🅿 ▯ 🖼

Igalo's Healing Mud

The town of Igalo, close to Herceg Novi, is
famed for the healing *Igaljsko blato* (Igalo
mud) found on its beach. First documented
by an Austro-Hungarian physician in the 19th
century, a spa treatment centre was built
here, which now operates as a spa hotel
(*see p542*). Visitors can also treat themselves
for free by sunbathing on the beach with its
therapeutic mud.

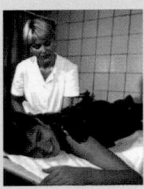

Visitor undergoing mud
therapy

Evening stroll along the broad promenade
in Tivat

❼ Herceg Novi

90 km (56 miles) W of Podgorica.
🏔 11,000. 🚌 *i* Jova Dabovića 12,
(031) 350 820. **W** hercegnovi.travel

Founded in the 14th century
by the Bosnian King Tvrtko,
Herceg Novi fell to the
Ottoman Empire shortly after
1483. Following two centuries
of intermittent battles, the
Venetians took power in
the late 17th century and
stayed until 1797. The Austro-
Hungarians then took over
until 1918, when the town
was finally absorbed into
Montenegro. The 19th-century

Austro-Hungarian Clock
Tower (Sahat Kula) has
been a symbol of the town
ever since.

King Tvrtko left his mark
by constructing the Forte
Mare Castle on the seafront,
while the Ottomans added
to the defences with the
Bloody Tower (Kanli Kula). The
latter gained its gruesome
moniker following its conversion to an infamous prison
during Turkish rule. In the
1950s, part of the tower was
turned into a summer amphitheatre with the Adriatic as
its backdrop.

In the heart of the Old Town
is the **Church of the Archangel
Michael** (Crkva Sv Arhanđela
Milaila), completed in 1911.
It harmoniously combines
Romanesque and Islamic
architectural features,
exemplified by the central
cupola flanked by minaret-
like turrets. Inside is a fine
marble iconostasis made
by Croatian masons.

🏛 **Bloody Tower**
Stari grad. **Open** 8am–8:30pm daily.

🏛 **Church of the
Archangel Michael**
trg Belavista. **Open** 8am–8:30pm daily.

The seaward bastion of Forte Mare Castle, Herceg Novi

Mist covered hills forming a backdrop to Lovćen National Park

⑧ Kotor

69 km (43 miles) W of Podgorica.
🚇 6,000. 🚌 🛈 Stari grad, (032) 325
947. 🅦 tokotor.com

Located amidst breathtaking
mountain scenery at
the tip of Kotor Bay's
furthest inlet, the
medieval town of
Kotor is encircled by
ancient and imposing
walls. Built between
the 9th and 14th cen-
turies, the walls stretch
for 5 km (3 miles) and
are up to 15 m (42 ft)
thick and 20 m (66 ft)
high. Thanks to these
defences, Kotor with-
stood two Ottoman sieges,
in 1537 and 1657.

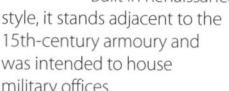

The 17th-century clock
tower in Kotor

During Roman times, the
town (then known as Acruvium)
was so well hidden that it
escaped the devastating
barbarian raids that brought
down the Roman Empire. Its
navy was also a formidable
force; by the 18th century it
had a fleet of 300 ships and
was trading as far afield as
India and northern Europe.
In 1979, after being hit by an
earthquake, Kotor was designated a UNESCO World Heritage
Site. Today, the Old Town (Stari
grad) is filled with
visitors admiring
the labyrinthine
streets that connect
its squares, ancient
churches and
splendid palaces.
Forming part of
the western wall is
the 17th-century
Duke's Palace,
facing the town's
1602 clock tower.
Built in Renaissance
style, it stands adjacent to the
15th-century armoury and
was intended to house
military offices.

The only building to escape
damage by the earthquake was
the single-nave **St Luke's Church**
(Crkva Sv Luke), with both
Orthodox and Catholic altars. Its
brightest features are the Cretan
icons within the small 18th-
century Chapel of St Spiridon.
On the other side of town is
the Romanesque **St Tryphon's
Cathedral** (Katedrala Sv Tripuna),
one of only two Catholic cathedrals in Montenegro. Its most
precious treasure is St Tryphon's
skull, which was brought to Kotor
from Constantinople in 809 and
kept in a silver casket. Other
valuable items include a superb
15th-century engraved silver
altar screen depicting Christ on
a throne surrounded by saints.

🏛 **St Luke's Church**
trg Bokelijske Mornarice, Stari grad.
Open 8am–8pm daily.

🏛 **St Tryphon's Cathedral**
trg Ustanka Mornara, Stari grad.
Tel (032) 322 315. **Open** 9am–
6pm daily.

⑨ Lovćen National Park

Nacionalni park Lovćen

37 km (23 miles) W of Podgorica.
🚌 from Podgorica. 🛈 Bajova 2,
Cetinje, (041) 231 570. 🅦 nparkovi.me

Inaugurated in 1952, Lovćen
National Park is the second
smallest of Montenegro's five
national parks. Covering an area
of 62 sq km (24 sq miles), it
includes protected areas of
ancient pine and beech forests
that are home to over 200
species of birds and about 1,300
species of flora. The park is
dominated by the twin peaks
of Mount Lovćen. At the top of
Jezerski Vrh (1,657 m/5,436 ft),
Mount Lovćen's second-highest
peak, is the mausoleum of the
Montenegrin poet and ruler
Petar II Petrović Njegoš.

Aerial view of Kotor's sea-facing Old Town

For hotels and restaurants see p517 and pp518–9

❿ Cetinje

39 km (24 miles) W of Podgorica.
🏠 16,000. 🚌 ℹ️ (041) 230 250.
🌐 cetinje.travel

Once the capital of Montenegro, Cetinje exudes an inescapable air of faded grandeur. Podgorica replaced the town as capital in 1946 but despite the loss of its official status, it is still considered to be the country's historic centre; it was here that King Ivan Crnojević established the capital of the old Zeta kingdom in the 15th century. Pretty houses line the streets and low rocky hills frame the town on all sides.

The most significant building here, the **Cetinje Monastery** (Cetinjski Manastir), was constructed in 1701 to replace the 15th-century Crnojević Monastery. As the seat of Montenegro's religious leader, Vladika, the monastery attracted the country's influential figures and functioned as the unofficial capital and centre of organized resistance against the Ottomans. Today, the monastery is best known for possessing what is believed to be St John the Baptist's right hand, a tiny fragment of the original Holy Cross, and for its Treasury Museum. Exhibits in the museum include unique religious manuscripts dating back to the 13th century and decorative 16th-century crosses painstakingly carved with miniature biblical scenes.

Next to the monastery is Biljarda, a castle-like, single-storey palace, built in 1838 for Petar II Petrović Njegoš. Surrounded by a wall with towers, the palace now functions as the **Njegoš Museum** (Njegošev muzej), where visitors can see many of the king's personal possessions, including period furniture and a billiard table.

Nearby is the **Montenegrin National History Museum** (Istorijski muzej Crne Gore), housed in the Government House (Zetski Dom), which was built in 1910 to accommodate government offices and the national assembly. On the ground floor is the History Museum, which exhibits a vast array of Turkish war trophies.

Façade of the imposing 18th-century Cetinje Monastery

Highlights include the death mask of the legendary Albanian ruler Karo Mahmud Pasha Busatlija. On the first floor is the museum's absorbing collection of 19th- and 20th-century Montenegrin and Yugoslavian art.

Cetinje Monastery
Cetinje BB. **Tel** (041) 231 021.
Open 8am–6pm daily. 🎨 📷

🏛️ **Njegoš Museum**
trg Kralja Nikole, Biljarda. **Tel** (041) 230 310. **Open** 9am–5pm daily.
🎨 📷

🏛️ **Montenegrin National History Museum**
Novice Cerovića 7, Vladin Dom.
Tel (041) 230 310. **Open** 9am–5pm daily. 🎨 📷

⓫ Ostrog Monastery
Manastir Ostrog

See pp512–3.

⓬ Durmitor National Park
Nacionalni park Durmitor

140 km (87 miles) N of Podgorica.
🚌 from Podgorica. ℹ️ ulica Jovana Cvijića, (052) 360 228.
🌐 nparkovi.me

Designated a national park in 1952 and a UNESCO World Heritage Site in 1980, Durmitor National Park takes in a vast expanse of spectacular scenery. One of the oldest protected areas in Montenegro, it is situated on a 1,500-m (4,920-ft) high plateau, from which numerous peaks rise to heights of about 2,500 m (8,200 ft).

Known for its glacial lakes, waterfalls and crystal-clear rivers, the park has a broad range of flora and fauna, including mountain maple, Bosnian iris, edelweiss, Montenegrin bellflower, and bears, wolves, golden eagles and white-headed vultures. It is also famous for its 400-year-old black pine forest with trees up to 50 m (165 ft) tall.

The superb mountain range around Durmitor National Park

⓫ Ostrog Monastery

Manastir Ostrog

Founded by St Basil in the 17th century, Ostrog Monastery was built into a sheer cliff face high above the Zeta river to guard it from the Ottomans. It comprises two complexes: Lower Monastery, which houses the administrative buildings, including the abbot's residence, and the Upper Monastery, which contains two cave-churches – the Chapel of the Honourable Cross and the Church of the Presentation of the Virgin Mary. Montenegro's most important place of pilgrimage, Ostrog has been associated with many healing miracles, attracting Catholic, Christian and Muslim pilgrims.

St Trinity Church
Part of the Lower Monastery complex, St Trinity Church is over 200 years old. Its barrel-vaulted interior is covered with intricate frescoes in gold and turquoise, which have been restored over time.

★ Upper Monastery
Completely rebuilt in the 1920s following a devastating fire, the Upper Monastery provides accommodation for Ostrog's 15 monks. The narrow corridors are decorated with lovely, colourful icons and mosaics.

Lower Monastery
The 18th-century Lower Monastery stands beside St Trinity Church in the valley below the Upper Monastery.

Lower Monastery
↓

For hotels and restaurants see p517 and pp518–9

★ **St Basil's Relics**
The Church of the Presentation of the Virgin Mary houses St Basil's bones. Pilgrims start gathering here from early in the morning, eager to catch a glimpse of the holy relics and in the hope of witnessing a miracle.

VISITORS' CHECKLIST

Practical Information
40 km (25 miles) NW of Podgorica. **Tel** (020) 811 040.
Open 7am–5pm daily. 🕆 7am daily. ⬛ Note: The Lower Monastery offers small single-sex dorm rooms, while the Upper Monastery offers free accomodation for pilgrims in the courtyard for a maximum of three days.

Transport
🚌 from Podgorica.

★ **Chapel of the Honourable Cross**
Nestled in the rock face above the Church of the Presentation is the Chapel of the Honourable Cross. The walls of the chapel feature splendid frescoes by the 17th-century painter Radul, depicting scenes from the life of Christ and venerated saints.

St Basil's Relics

St Basil

One of the Orthodox Church's most revered saints, St Basil founded the Ostrog Monastery in 1667 and remained here until his death in 1671. It was at Ostrog that he forged his reputation as a miracle-worker – a healer of the physically and mentally afflicted. The saint also assisted in the renovation of numerous monasteries, a practice forbidden by the Turkish rulers of the time.

Portrait of St Basil, patron saint of Ostrog

Vaulted Candle Room
Hundreds of flickering votive candles fill the atmospheric vaulted Candle Room; its frescoes are barely visible beneath the soot.

Practical & Travel Information

With the years of Communism and the recent Yugoslav Wars firmly behind it, tourism has picked up in Montenegro. There are plenty of tourist information centres across the country, although the staff may not be fluent in English. Public transport is good with frequent bus services connecting most towns, and additional minibus shuttles operating along the coast during summer. The country's only passenger railway line runs from Bar to Podgorica, from where it continues north to Belgrade. Those intent on exploring the more remote interior regions and the beautiful countryside are best advised to rent a vehicle.

When to Visit

A good time to visit the country is during spring and autumn: late March to late June, and between September and October. July and August are the best months for those seeking sunshine and crowds, however this is high season, so room prices can be high.

Documentation

Citizens of the European Union (EU), Switzerland, Norway, Iceland, Israel, the US, Canada, Korea, Singapore, Australia and New Zealand can enter Montenegro with a valid passport for up to 90 days without a visa. Those needing visas should apply directly to the Montenegrin Embassy in their respective country.

Visitors are required to register with the police within 24 hours of their arrival; this is usually arranged by the hotel soon after arrival.

Visitor Information

The **National Tourism Organization of Montenegro** is quite helpful, and there are several informative tourist websites, as well as Podgorica's free **In Your Pocket** guide, which also has its own website. There are tourist offices in all the main towns. These offer free maps and brochures and can provide information on hotels and local attractions, although not all staff members speak English. Smaller towns also have good sources of information, but again, not necessarily in English. There is, however, a 24-hour tourist information helpline in English.

Health and Security

Visitors are advised to carry any medical prescription and essential medicines with them when travelling to Montenegro. They also need to be vaccinated against diphtheria, tetanus and polio prior to travel. Generally, public clinics are not open to visitors and it is better to go to private hospitals where the standard of care is high and the doctors speak English. Private clinics and hospitals expect cash payment even for minor treatment; visitors are advised to have their own health insurance. Well-known hospitals in the capital include **As Mediph** and **Kbc**. Pharmacists sell over-the-counter medicines and can advise on minor ailments. People need to be wary of tick bites, especially when camping or hiking, and seek immediate medical assistance if bitten.

Montenegro has a low crime rate and travellers are unlikely to encounter anything more serious than pickpocketing and petty theft. It is safe for women travellers to walk alone at night, but they should exercise caution in lonely spots.

Facilities for the Disabled

There is little public awareness of the needs of the disabled in Montenegro although upmarket hotels and popular beach resorts may cater for travellers with disabilities. In Podgorica, most pedestrian crossings have sloped kerbs and the main crossings are equipped with sound signalling systems.

Banking and Currency

The euro has been the country's official currency since 2002. ATMs can be found in all but the smallest towns. Credit cards are accepted in many large hotels, restaurants, shops and petrol stations. Banks are usually open from 8am to 5pm Monday to Saturday, and will exchange cash and traveller's cheques.

Communications

Public payphones are very rare in Montenegro, so it is best to head to a post office to make a call. Phone cards, such as MonteCards, for use in phone booths, can be purchased

The Climate of Montenegro

The coast of Montenegro enjoys a Mediterranean climate with long, hot summers and short, wet winters. Summer temperatures average 28° C (82° F) and drop to around 8° C (46° F) in winter. Inland, the mountainous regions average 22° C (72° F) in summer and -3° C (27° F) in winter, with heavy snowfall.

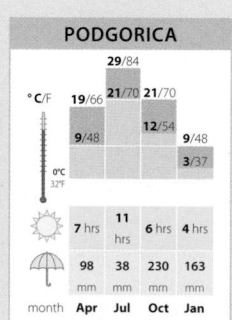

PODGORICA			
29/84			
19/66	**21**/70	**21**/70	
	12/54		
9/48		9/48	
			3/37
7 hrs	11 hrs	6 hrs	4 hrs
98 mm	38 mm	230 mm	163 mm
Apr	**Jul**	**Oct**	**Jan**

°C/F · 0°C 32°F · month

in post offices as well as newspaper kiosks. However, these are usually expensive. Using a local SIM card from mobile phone providers such as T-Mobile, Telenor and M:tel is the cheapest way to stay connected. These can also be bought from kiosks, and work out cheaper than landlines. International calls are best made in post offices. Most towns have Internet cafés and many hotels and restaurants are free Wi-Fi spots.

Arriving by Air

Podgorica and Tivat both have international airports. Tivat is the best choice for those visiting the coast. Visitors can also use Dubrovnik's Čilipi airport, which is only 25 km (16 miles) northwest of Herceg Novi. The Budget airline, **Ryanair**, has flights from Stansted to Podgorica. Montenegro is well served by national carriers. **Montenegro Airlines** offers flights from London to Tivat and thrice weekly direct flights from Podgorica to London. Serbia's **Air Serbia** has indirect flights from Rome, London, Paris, Frankfurt and Budapest to Podgorica and Tivat, while Slovenia's **Adria Airways** offers indirect European

flights to Podgorica. **Croatia Airlines** connects Dubrovnik (Čilipi) to major European cities.

Arriving by Sea

Those with private yachts can head for the marinas at Herceg Novi, Kotor, Budva and Bar, which all offer basic services. **Montenegro Lines** run three ferries daily from Bar to Italy.

Rail Travel

Two trains a day, including a sleeper, make the 11-hour journey from Belgrade to Bar, along what is considered to be one of the most spectacular railway lines in the world. Completed in 1979, the Montenegrin section carries passengers across the Mala Rijeka viaduct, the highest in the world at 200 m (656 ft), through the 6-km (4-mile) Sozina tunnel, and past a succession of dramatic rocky mountains. The railway journey from Belgrade to Podgorica takes 10 hours. Euro Rail also offers trips via Vienna, Budapest and Belgrade to Montenegro. Detailed timetables are available on their website, **Montenegro Railways**.

Travelling by Bus

Public and private transport companies run an efficient network of buses, boosted by minibus shuttles in the summer. Tickets for local buses can be purchased on board. The country's more remote mountainous regions are connected by bus, but services are limited and timetables should be checked in advance. Tourist information offices can provide details of bus routes.

Travelling by Car

Reckless local drivers present the greatest danger on Montenegro's roads. They frequently harass slower vehicles and overtake on blind corners. Lights should be kept on at all times, seat belts should be worn in the front and drunken driving should be avoided. Drivers need to carry an international or EU licence, the registration documents of their vehicle and Green Card insurance. Car hire is available at both Podgorica and Tivat airports as well as through city rental agencies such as **Delta** and **Meridian** – and should be booked in advance during high season.

Taxis, which are metered, are reasonably cheap, and can be ordered by phone. Most companies have English-speaking operators.

DIRECTORY

Documentation

Council of Europe
Novaka Miloševa 6, Podgorica.
Tel (020) 230 819.

Embassies

Croatia
Vladimira Četkovića 2, Podgorica.
Tel (020) 269 760.

United Kingdom
Ulcinjska 8, Podgorica.
Tel (020) 618 010.
w gov.uk/government/world/montenegro

United States
Ljubljanska bb, Podgorica.
Tel (020) 225 417.
w podgorica.usembassy.gov

Visitor Information

National Tourism Organization of Montenegro
Rimski trg 47, Vektra 81000 Podgorica.
Tel (020) 235 155.
w montenegro.travel

In Your Pocket
w inyourpocket.com

Emergency Numbers

Ambulance
Tel 124.

Fire
Tel 123.

Police
Tel 122.

Health and Security

As Mediph
Slobode 4, Podgorica.
Tel (020) 231 800.

Kbc
Podgorica bb, Podgorica.
Tel (020) 412 412.

Arriving by Air

Adria Airways
w adria.si

Air Serbia
w airserbia.com

Croatia Airlines
w croatiaairlines.com

Montenegro Airlines
w montenegroairlines.com

Ryanair
w ryanair.com

Arriving by Sea

Montenegro Lines
w montenegrolines.net

Rail Travel

Montenegro Railways
w zcg-prevoz.me

Travelling by Car

Delta
w rentacar-delta.com

Meridian
w meridian-rentacar.com

Shopping & Entertainment

There is no shortage of things to buy or places to shop in Montenegro. Painted icons, foodstuffs, such as olives and cheeses, and embroidered tablecloths make interesting gifts. The nightlife in Podgorica is vibrant, although it tends to fizzle out in the coastal towns during the off-season. Many festivals take place throughout the year, of which the Carnival of Kotor is perhaps the most colourful. The countryside is perfect for outdoor pursuits such as rafting through some of the world's deepest canyons as well as mountain biking and hiking.

Markets

Most towns have their own fruit and vegetable markets. At the market in Bar, women still dress in traditional outfits. In Kotor, the daily market on the seafront is a great spot to buy fresh vegetables and fish. It is also the place to find inexpensive tablecloths and hand-made lace curtains.

Gifts and Souvenirs

Wooden toys and utensils are sold in the markets of most towns, as is hand-made lace. Colourful icons and other religious knick-knacks can be bought from church and monastery shops. Traditional folk-music CDs make good souvenirs and are available in most gift shops.

Food and Drink

For olive products, it is worth visiting the Olive Museum in Bar's Old Town. Honey from the Durmitor region, where bees graze on heather and wild flowers, is also particularly good.
Montenegro has a thriving wine industry and its red wine, *vranac*, is well known, as are *krstač*, *crmničko*, cabernet and chardonnay. Local brandies such as *šljivovica* (made from plums) and *loza* (made from grapes) are also popular.

Jewellery

Podgorica's Zlatarska (gold) street is lined with several jewellery shops, and the town of Ulcinj is famous for the work of its gold-smiths. Budva's Old Town is crammed with trinket shops. Also, worth buying is delicate silver filigree jewellery.

Theatre

Theatre lovers should check what is on at the **Montenegrin National Theatre**, which hosts international performances. In summer, **Budva City Theatre** organizes drama, exhibitions and poetry readings.

Nightlife

Podgorica has numerous wine bars, clubs and cafés that stay open till late. **Porto Club**, with local DJs, **L'Ombelico**, with great live music, and **Nice Vice**, are some of the most popular. The coastal towns cater to visitors during summer with mainstream clubs and bars; Budva is also known for its all-night club scene.

Festivals

Budva's open-air **Petrovac Jazz Festival** takes place in the last week of August, while Herceg Novi hosts the **Sunčane Skale** pop-music festival in July. Kotor celebrates the **Carnival of Kotor**, a colourful procession of masked troupes through the Old Town, at the end of July.

Outdoor Activities

Numerous agencies organize a wide range of outdoor activities. **Anitra Travel** and **Eco Tours** both arrange hiking, biking, climbing, rafting, jeep safaris, horse riding, skiing and paragliding. The **Pelikan Surf Club** organizes windsurfing on Lake Skadar, while the **Dragon Surf Club** in Ulcinj offers courses in kitesurfing, windsurfing, sailing, skiing, paragliding and snowboarding. The **Diving Association of Montenegro** can provide information for scuba divers.

DIRECTORY

Theatre

Budva City Theatre
13 Jul, Zgrada BSP, Budva.
Tel (033) 402 934.
W gradteatar.me

Montenegrin National Theatre
ulica Stanka Dragojevića br. 18.
Podgorica. **Tel** (020) 664 082.
W cnp.me

Nightlife

L'Ombelico
Hercegovačka 85, Podgorica.
Tel (067) 201 790.
W lombelico.me

Nice Vice
ulica Slobode 82, Podgorica.
Tel (020) 230 394.

Porto Club
ulica Stanka Dragojevića 34,
Podgorica.
Tel (067) 330 888.

Festivals

Carnival of Kotor
W tokotor.com

Petrovac Jazz Festival
W petrovacjazzfestival.tripod.com

Sunčane Skale
W suncaneskale.org

Outdoor Activities

Anitra Travel
Atrium, Njegoševa 12, Nikšić.
Tel (040) 402 598.
W tara-grab.com

Diving Association of Montenegro
Tel (067) 508 009.
W mdiving.org.me

Dragon Surf Club
Ulcinj. **Tel** (069) 640 800.
W dragonproject.net

Eco Tours
Kolasin.
Tel (020) 086 700.
W eco-tours.co.me

Pelikan Surf Club
Tel (069) 077 869.

Where to Stay

Podgorica

Hotel Evropa €
B&B
Orahovoačka 16, 81000
Tel *(020) 623 444*
W hotelevropa.co.me
Many on suites at this pleasant
B&B have a sloping attic ceiling.

Montenegro Hostel €
Hostel
Đečevica 25, 81000
Tel *69 039 751*
W montenegrohostel.com
Conveniently located for bus and
train, Montenegro has comfortable
social areas, doubles and dorms.

Bojatours €€
Value
Kralja Nikole 10, 81000
Tel *(020) 623 349*
W bojatours.me
Elegant rooms with parquet
floors, floral rugs and a minibar.

Hotel Kerber €€
Value
Novaka Miloševa 6, 81000
Tel *(020) 405 405*
W hotelkerber.me
Well-equipped, bright, clean
rooms above a shopping centre.

DK Choice

Hotel Podgorica €€€
Luxury
Svetlane Kane Radević 1, 81000
Tel *(020) 402 500*
W hotelpodgorica.co.me
Built in the 1960s, this stunning
hotel on the riverbank, blends
modern architecture with the
natural environment. Rooms
Stylish furnishings and some
have a terrace facing the river.

Rest of Montenegro

BAR: Hotel Princess €€€
Resort
Jovana Tomaševića 59, 85000
Tel *(030) 300 100*
W hotelprincess.me
Located on a superb beach, this
4-star resort hotel has spacious
and well-equipped rooms,
swimming pool and tennis courts.

BUDVA: Astoria €€
Boutique
Njegoševa 4, Stari Grad 85310
Tel *(033) 451 110*
W budva.astoriamontenegro.com
Chic, intimate hotel with a
fantastic location within the walls
of the Old Town. Elegantly
furnished rooms with superb sea
views.

BUDVA: Šajo €€€
Resort
Jadranski put bb, 85310
Tel *86 460 243*
W sajohotel.com
With high standards of service
Šajo offers plentiful facilities
that include a sauna, gym and
pleasant garden restaurant.

CETINJE: Sport In €
Budget
Obilića bb, 81250
Tel *(041) 234 630*
W hotel-sportin-cetinje.
host22.com
Sparsely furnished neat
en suites as well as triples
and quads in a pre-World War I
stone building.

KOTOR: Old Town Hostel €
Hostel
Stari Grad 284, 85339
Tel *(032) 325 317*
W hostel-kotor.me

This atmospheric hostel, located
in a restored medieval building,
offers dorms, private doubles and
triples and a relaxing café-bar.

KOTOR: Cattaro €€
Historic
Stari Grad 232, 85330
Tel *(032) 311 000*
W cattarohotel.com
Occupying what was once the
Rector's Palace, Old Town Hall and
Town Guard, this 4-star has sea
battle pictures adorning its walls.

KOTOR: Vardar €€€
Boutique
Stari Grad 476, 85 330
Tel *(032) 325 084*
W hotelvardar.com
Intimate hotel combining antique
stonework and modern facilities.

TIVAT: Pine Hotel €€
Resort
Obala Pine bb, 85320
Tel *(032) 671 255*
W htpmimoza.me
The aptly named Pine Hotel is
located on a seafront lined with
pine trees, the large terrace of its
cafe–restaurant facing the sea.
Prim and comfortable rooms.

ULCINJ: Velika Plaža €
Resort
Velika Plaža bb, 85360
Tel *(030) 431 131*
W velikaplaza.com
Located near the beach, Velika
Plaza is a pleasant resort that
offers a choice of hotel rooms
and self-catering bungalows.

ULCINJ: Dvori Balšića €€€
Luxury
Stari Grad, 85360
Tel *(030) 421 457*
W hotel-dvoribalsica-montenegro.
com
This magnificent stone building
that was once a royal palace, has
opulently furnished rooms with
wooden ceilings. Great views of
the sea too.

The pool at the charming Hotel Princess in Bar

Where to Eat and Drink

Podgorica

Carine Centar €
International
Ulica Slobode 43, 81000
Tel *(020) 402 400*
Centrally located, this restaurant is popular with the locals. Choose between indoor and outdoor seating to enjoy the vast inexpensive spread with Balkan grills, pizzas and pastas together with a handful of vegetarian options.

Lanterna €
Italian
Marka Miljanova 41, 81000
Tel *67 069 020*
Pizzas come out of a wood stove, and the pastas and grilled-meat dishes are served in generous portions here. The intimate restaurant, located right in the heart of Podgorica, is in Mediterranean-style with low lighting and exposed stonework.

Per Sempre €€
Italian
Vojvode Maše Đurovića 2/10, 81000
Tel *(020) 220 066*
Upmarket but by no means expensive Italian cuisine, with carpaccio starters, silky risottos and a choice of meat or fish. Attractive lounge–terrace.

Pod Volat €€
Balkan Grill/Montenegrin
Trg Vojvoda Bećira Osmanagića 1, 81000
Tel *69 666 622*
Centrally located stone building with contemporary timber-beam interior and pleasant outdoor seating. Serves an excellent array of grilled and roast meats.

Imanje Knjaz €€€
International
Mareza bb, 81000
Tel *67 765 800*
Elegant out-of-town restaurant with beautiful garden, cooking up lavish meat and fish dishes based on royal-court recipes from Montenegro, Serbia, Russia and beyond.

Three Centuries €€€
International
Bul svetog Petra Cetinjskog 1, 81000
Tel *(020) 402 500*
Stylish restaurant in Hotel Podgorica boasts a Modernist decor, a riverside location, and a well-presented menu of local and Mediterranean dishes.

Rest of Montenegro

BAR: Kaldrma €€
Montenegrin
Stari Bar, 85354
Tel *85 341 744*
Stone house in the hilltop settlement of Stari Bar, serving food typical of inland Montenegro: slow-roast meats, stews and lots of vegetables.

BUDVA: Garden Café €
International
Mediteranska bb, 85310
Tel *(033) 452 090*
Tree-shaded café-restaurant just outside town, featuring plenty of salads, light Montenegrin dishes as well as toasted sandwiches and pastries.

BUDVA: Sambra €
Italian
Trg Palmi, 85310
Tel *(033) 451 308*
Shaded patio in the Old Town serving authentic thin-crust pizzas,

pasta dishes and substantial salads. Decent desserts too.

BUDVA: Hotel Mogren €€
Seafood
Mediteranska 1, 85310
Tel *(033) 451 102*   **Closed** *Nov–April*
Excellent place to sample Adriatic squid, octopus and shells, as well as quality fish grilled or baked to your specifications. On the main square right beside the walls of the Old Town.

BUDVA: Konoba Stari Grad €€
Seafood
Njegoševa 12, 85310
Tel *63 225 410*
Characterful Old Town tavern serving squid risottos, seafood pasta and grilled fish alongside tasty steaks, accompanied frequently by live music.

BUDVA: Lim €€
Balkan Grill/Seafood
Slovenska obala bb, 85310
Tel *69 023 957*
This beachside restaurant with a large terrace shaded by palm trees, serves grilled meats, fresh seafood and classy cocktails.

BUDVA: Jadran Kod Krsta €€€
Balkan Grill/Seafood
Obala bb, 85310
Tel *69 030 180*
Seafront restaurant with almost four decades of experience in serving a vast range of seafood and local grill standards such as *pljeskavice* (various ground meats shaped into a patty), *ćevapčići* (a type of kebab) and liver.

CETINJE: Kole €€
International
Crnogorskih Junaka 12, 81250
Tel *69 035 716*
Just outside the Old Town, this smart restaurant with a big outdoor terrace, provides quality platters of grilled and roast meats as well as Adriatic fish. Vast wine list.

CETINJE: Vinoteka €€
International
Njegoševa 103, 81250
Tel *(041) 679 936*
Local cheeses and hams together with steak, pasta

Tall palms trees outside Hotel Mogren, Budva

and pizza mains at this inviting restaurant that also has a comprehensive selection of local and international wines.

HERCEG NOVI: Kafana pod Lozom €
International
Trg Nikole Đurkovića 18, 85340
Tel *(031) 322 880*
Popular café-restaurant slightly uphill from the seafront. Choose from grilled meats, seafood dishes and traditional stews.

HERCEG NOVI: Konoba Feral €
Seafood
Šetalište 5 Danica 47, 85340
Tel *88 322 232*
With a pleasant stone building, a small shaded terrace and a checked-tablecloth interior, Feral is a perfect setting for inexpensive grilled fresh fish and grilled scampi, and seafood platters.

HERCEG NOVI: Konoba Krušo €€
Seafood
Šetalište 5 Danica, 85340
Tel *(031) 323 238*
Enjoy spicy seafood stews, fresh grilled fish or roast squid at this restaurant that is adorned with fishing nets, maritime memorabilia and offers great views of the sea from its terrace.

HERCEG NOVI: Mali Raj €€€
International
Norveška 21, Igalo
Tel *(031) 331 138*
Located in Igalo, just west of Herceg Novi, the elegant Mali Raj, meaning 'Little Paradise', serves the best of Adriatic seafood, Central European *schnitzels* and Balkan grills and roasts.

KOTOR: Scala Santa €
Seafood
Stari Grad, 85330
Tel *69 290 512*
In a characterful Old Town building featuring exposed stone and quirky bric-a-brac, this restaurant serves quality grilled fish and plenty of Adriatic staples such as seafood risottos and fried squid.

KOTOR: Le Bastion €€€
International
Sari Grad 517, 85330
Tel *(032) 322 116*
This elegant restaurant that is located right in the heart of the Old Town has an atmospheric terrace, which complements the excellent menu comprising Mediterranean salads, grilled meats and fresh fish.

Picturesque setting of the Konoba Ćatovića Mlini, Kotor

KOTOR: Galion €€€
International
Šuranj bb, 85330
Tel *(032) 325 054*
Stylish glass pavilion on Kotor's harbourfront offering refined Mediterranean fare with a strong emphasis on local fish. Great seafood pasta and risotto options too.

KOTOR: Konoba Ćatovića Mlini €€€
Seafood
Morinj bb, 85338
Tel *(032) 373 030*
On the shore between Kotor and Herceg Novi, in an old stone building with a beautiful terrace, this elegant restaurant specializes in fresh fish, home-cured hams and home-grown vegetables. Served with the family's own wine.

LAKE SKADAR: Pelikan €
Seafood
Virpazar, 81305
Tel *(020) 711 107*
Cosy family-run restaurant on the shores of the lake, offering freshly caught fish, smoked carp and roasted eel, accompanied by home-baked breads.

OSTROG: Kolibe Bogetići €€€
Montenegrin
Ostrog, 81400
Tel *67 888 189*
While this rather garish pavilion on the road to Ostrog monastery may not win any prizes for architecture, diners can expect first class food that includes local specialities such as baked veal and lamb.

TIVAT: Konoba Koliba €
Balkan Grill/Seafood
Peraška 6, Seljanovo, 85320
Tel *(032) 671 886*
Using fresh local ingredients, this traditional restaurant offers grilled meats, excellent

seafood and a lot more. Home-baked bread and cakes for sale.

TIVAT: Ponta Veranda €
Balkan Grill/Seafood
Šetalište Seljanovo 9, 85320
Tel *67 563 985*
Friendly family-run place north of town with a vast range of Balkan staples, from grilled meats to bean stew, stuffed peppers and local seafood.

TIVAT: Vino Santo €€
Seafood
Krtoli bb, 85320
Tel *67 851 662*
South of Tivat beyond the airport, this elegant eatery draws gourmets with its superbly baked fish, *fruits-de-mer* and scampi cooked in all manner of delicious guises.

ULCINJ: Durante €€
Seafood
Ada Bojana, 85360
Tel *67 231 620*
Waterside restaurant that makes the most of the local catch. It offers superb fish soup, seafood risottos and mixed-seafood grills.

DK Choice

ULCINJ: Miško €€€
Seafood
Ada Bojana, 85360
Tel *(069) 022 868*
This scenic restaurant on Bojana island, south of Ulcinj, is immensely popular with locals and tourists alike. Locally caught Adriatic fish is the main attraction, prepared many ways – on the open grill, baked in an oven or cooked with wine and herbs. Squid, octopus and shrimp broaden the menu, and there's a good choice of local wines. The pleasant terrace is an ideal spot to laze on over lunch.

SERBIA

Lying at the crossroads of Europe, Serbia's history goes back to the Neolithic era. Settled by Slavs in the 6th century, the country was home to a thriving civilization in the Middle Ages, and many of the surviving churches and monasteries from the period are UNESCO-protected today. Serbia's natural forests, pristine mountain lakes and karst rock formations add to its stunning natural beauty.

Situated at the heart of the Balkan Peninsula, Serbia has played a central role in the history and culture of South Eastern Europe. A turbulent past has produced a nation that seems uncertain about the future, but is rarely lacking in cultural pride.

At the crossroads of history, Serbia's population of just under 7.5 million is composed of various ethnic groups. The majority are Orthodox Christian Serbs, although the northern province of Vojvodina is home to a large number of Catholic Hungarians, alongside small numbers of Slovaks, Romanians and Croats. In addition, there are significant numbers of Muslim Bosnjaks, who are mostly concentrated in the southeast.

History

The establishment of a Serb state dates back to the early 13th century, when the rulers of the Raška region (modern-day Novi Pazar) established a kingdom with an autonomous church. The state reached its zenith under Stefan Dušan (r. 1331–46), who conquered territories in modern-day Macedonia and Greece. However, Serbian power declined with the arrival of the Ottomans in the Balkans. Although the epic Battle of Kosovo (1389) held them at bay for a while, the constant conflict weakened the state and, after 70 years of resistance, Serbia fell to the Ottomans, ushering in four centuries of foreign occupation. In the late 17th century, Habsburg victories

View of the 15th-century Nebojša Kula on the Sava river, Kalemegdan Park, Belgrade

◀ Famous townhall of Subotica town, Serbia.

Massacre of Serbs, First Balkan War, 1912

over the Ottomans persuaded thousands of Serbs to leave their homelands in Kosovo and seek a new life in the Habsburg-controlled region of Vojvodina, in the north of the country. This went on to become the centre of education and culture.

A series of uprisings against the Ottomans in 1830 led to the creation of a Serbian principality. This was upgraded to the status of a kingdom in 1878, and became the focus of the

KEY DATES IN SERBIAN HISTORY

AD 600 Serb tribes settle in the Balkans

1219 Saint Sava establishes the Serbian Orthodox Church

1345 The Serbian Empire under Stefan Dušan reaches its height

1389 Serbs and Ottoman Turks fight at the Battle of Kosovo

1459 Serbia conquered by the Ottoman Empire

1690 Austrian-controlled Vojvodina is settled by Serbs from Kosovo

1804 First Serbian Uprising against the Ottoman Turks

1869 Principality of Serbia gains independence

1912–13 Serbia expands its territory during the Balkan Wars

1918 Serbia becomes part of the kingdom of Serbs, Croats and Slovenes

1945 Serbia becomes part of the Communist-ruled Yugoslav Federation

1980 Serbs campaign to regain Vojvodina and Kosovo

1991 Slovenia and Croatia leave Yugoslavia

1999 NATO bombards Serbia

2008 Kosovo declares its independence from Serbia

aspirations of people throughout the Balkans. The collapse of the Habsburg Empire in 1918 led to the creation of the kingdom of Serbs, Croats and Slovenes (later renamed Yugoslavia). However, the lack of a common Yugoslav identity resulted in the collapse of the country when Germany attacked it in April 1941. In Serbia, resistance groups formed around the Serbian-nationalist Četnik Movement, and the pan-Yugoslav Partisans led by Communist Josip Broz Tito. In 1945, Tito established a federal Yugoslavia composed of six republics. The ethnically mixed Serbian regions of Vojvodina and Kosovo were made into autonomous provinces. After the death of Tito in 1980, Serbians launched a campaign to regain control of these regions. This upsurge of Serbian national sentiment was perceived as a threat by the other Yugoslav republics, and both Slovenia and Croatia chose to break away from Yugoslavia in 1991. In 1999, an Albanian insurgency was answered by a Serbian crackdown, leading to the NATO bombardment of Serbia.

Throughout the 1990s Serbian politics was controlled by the Nationalist-Communist Slobodan Milošević. He fell from power in 2000, leading to a process of democratization. Serbia is currently a parliamentary democracy, with hopes of joining the EU.

Language and Culture

Serbian is a Slavic language, related closely to Bosnian and Croatian and more distantly to Russian, Polish and Czech. It is traditionally written in the Cyrillic script.

Traditional song and dance play an important part in Serbia's rich folk culture. The Roma community has greatly influenced its musical heritage, and visitors may come across their energetic brass bands at weddings and village fêtes throughout the year.

Exploring Serbia

Serbia's lively capital, Belgrade, stands at the centre of the country's transport network. Beyond the capital are a number of impressive cultural monuments as well as picturesque towns. North of Belgrade are the flatlands of Vojvodina, home to the city of Novi Sad and its riverside fortress as well as the border town of Subotica, while to the south are the Sopoćani and Studenica monasteries. Travelling by bus is the preferred choice of transportation; trains are crowded and can get delayed.

Sights at a Glance

❶ Belgrade pp524–31
❷ Novi Sad
❸ Subotica
❹ Despotovac
❺ Studenica Monastery
❻ Niš
❼ Novi Pazar
❽ Sopoćani Monastery

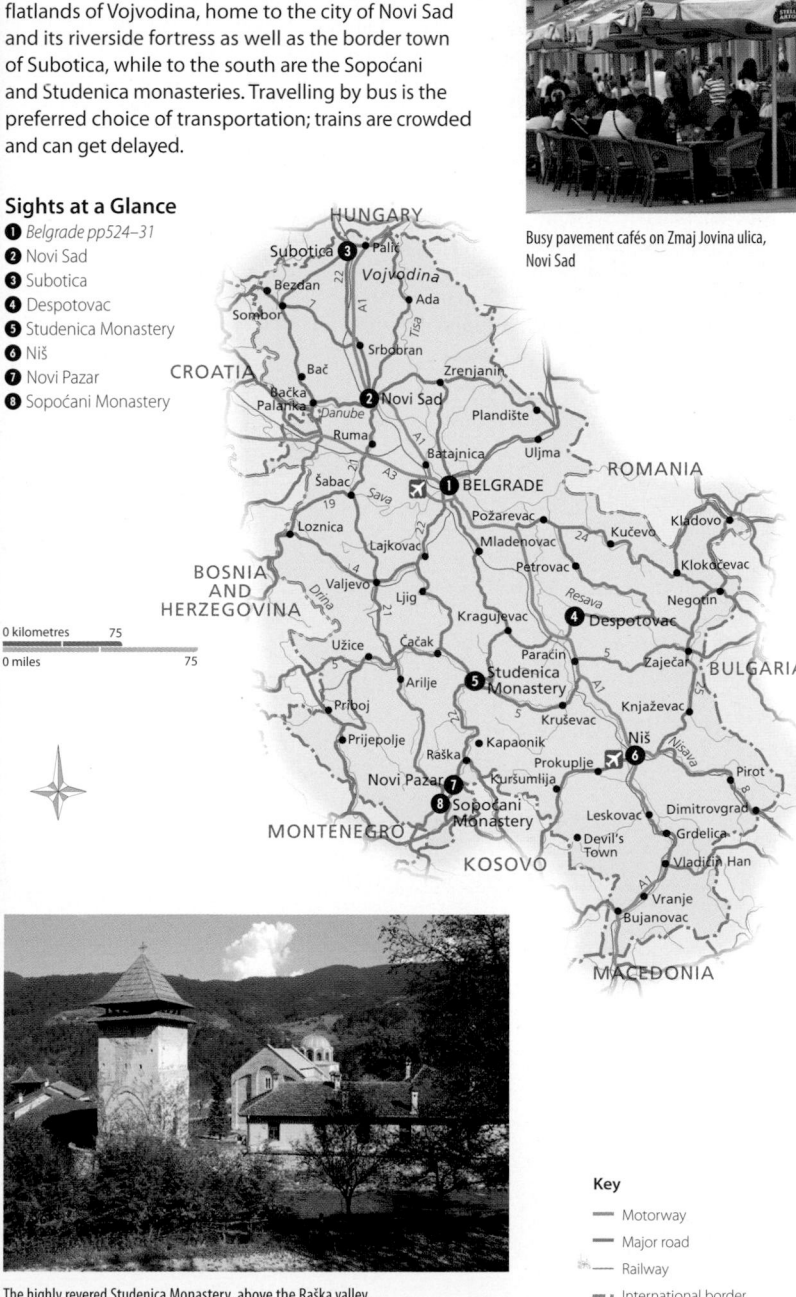

Busy pavement cafés on Zmaj Jovina ulica, Novi Sad

The highly revered Studenica Monastery, above the Raška valley

Key

— Motorway
— Major road
╍ Railway
–•– International border

For keys to symbols *see back flap*

❶ Belgrade

The capital of Serbia since 1840, Belgrade, today with a population of approximately 1.8 million people, has been a site of strategic importance for a succession of imperial rulers. Over the second half of the 19th century it gradually took on the appearance of a modern European metropolis, although the magnificent Kalemegdan Fortress bears eloquent witness to its turbulent past. Situated between the main fortress and Kalemegdan Park is the Old Town (Stari grad), with remnants from Ottoman times. Today, Knez Mihailova is the centre of social and commercial life in the city. A long, pedestrianized street lined with handsome 19th-century buildings, it is busy with shoppers and strollers throughout the day and night.

Sights at a Glance

① *Kalemegdan Fortress pp526–7*
② Fresco Gallery
③ Vuk and Dositej Museum
④ Ethnographic Museum
⑤ Palace of Princess Ljubica
⑥ Orthodox Cathedral
⑦ Skadarlija
⑧ St Mark's Church
⑨ Nikola Tesla Museum
⑩ The Royal Compound
⑪ St Sava's Church
⑫ Museum of Yugoslav History
⑬ Zemun

Key

▢ Major sight / Place of interest
▢ Pedestrian street
━ Motorway
━ Major road
═ Minor road
— Railway

Intricate stonework detail, Fresco Gallery

Getting Around

Central Belgrade is easily explored on foot, with the lively Knez Mihailova serving as the main route from the city centre to the Kalemegdan Fortress. Attractions outside the city centre can be reached by tram, bus or trolleybus. Taxis are reasonably priced, although those booked in advance (hotel receptionists can make the call) are cheaper than those flagged down on the street. Driving in the city can be stressful due to heavy traffic, bad roads and limited parking.

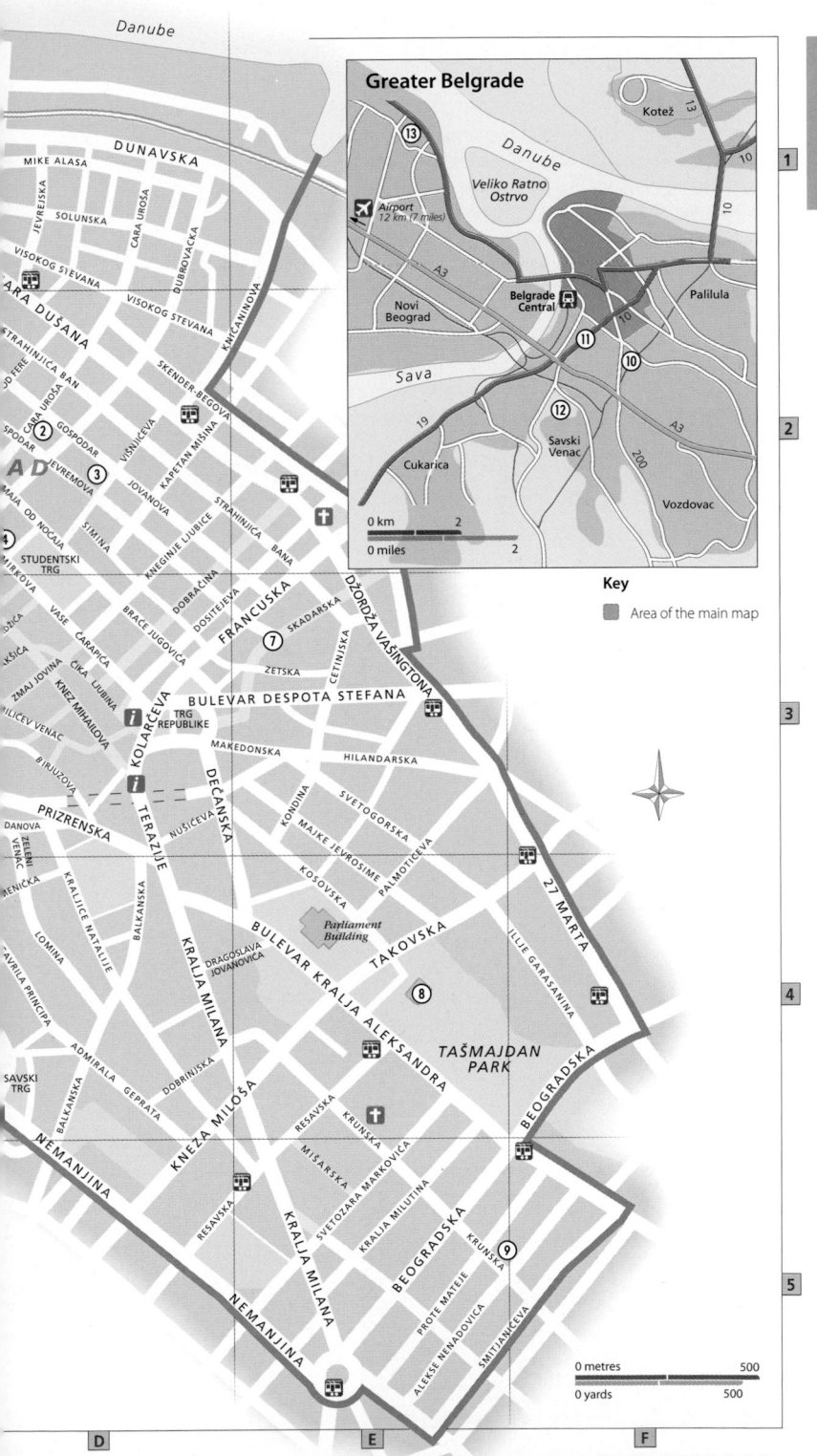

Danube

DUNAVSKA

MIKE ALASA

JEVREJSKA

SOLUNSKA

CARA UROŠA

VISOKOG STEVANA

ARA DUŠANA

VISOKOG STEVANA

DUBROVAČKA

KNIĆANINOVA

STRAHINJIĆA BAN

JD FERE

CARA UROŠA

SPODAR

GOSPODAR

② VIŠNJIĆEVA

③ JEVREMOVA

SKENDER-BEGOVA

KAPETAN MIŠINA

JOVANOVA

STRAHINJIĆA BANA

MAJA OD NOĆAJA

SIMINA

KNEGINJE LJUBICE

④ MIRKOVA

STUDENTSKI TRG

DOBRAČINA

DOSITEJEVA

FRANCUSKA

SKADARSKA

DŽORDŽA VAŠINGTONA

A D

BRAĆE JUGOVIĆA

⑦

CETINJSKA

ŽIĆA

VASE ČARAPIĆA

ZETSKA

AKŠIĆA

ZMAJ JOVINA

ČIKA LJUBINA

BULEVAR DESPOTA STEFANA

ILIĆEV VENAC

KNEZ MIHAILOVA

MAKEDONSKA

HILANDARSKA

B IRUŽOVA

ⓘ TRG REPUBLIKE

KOLARČEVA

DEČANSKA

SVETOGORSKA

KONDINA

PRIZRENSKA

TERAZIJE

NUŠIĆEVA

MAJKE JEVROSIME

PALMOTIĆEVA

DANOVA

ⓘ

KOSOVSKA

ZELENI VENAC

KRALJICE NATALIJE

BALKANSKA

BULEVAR KRALJA ALEKSANDRA

TAKOVSKA

ILIJE GARAŠANINA

ENIČKA

DRAGOSLAVA JOVANOVIĆA

Parliament Building

27 MARTA

LOMINA

KRALJA MILANA

⑧

AVRILA PRINCIPA

ADMIRALA GEPRATA

DOBRINJSKA

TAŠMAJDAN PARK

SAVSKI TRG

BALKANSKA

KNEZA MILOŠA

RESAVSKA

KRUNSKA

BEOGRADSKA

RESAVSKA

MIŠARSKA

SVETOZARA MARKOVIĆA

KRALJA MILANA

KRALJA MILUTINA

BEOGRADSKA

NEMANJINA

KRUNSKA

⑨

PROTE MATEJE

NEMANJINA

ALEKSE NENADOVIĆA

ŠMITIJANJSKIVA

Greater Belgrade

Kotež

Danube

Veliko Ratno Ostrvo

✈ Airport
12 km (7 miles)

Belgrade Central 🚇

Palilula

Novi Beograd

⑪

⑩

⑬

A3

10

10

13

⑫

Savski Venac

19

Cukarica

Sava

A3

200

Vozdovac

0 km   2

0 miles   2

Key

◻ Area of the main map

0 metres   500

0 yards   500

D   E   F

1 2 3 4 5

For keys to symbols *see back flap*

① Kalemegdan Fortress

Kalemegdanska tvrđava

Dominating the confluence of the Sava and Danube rivers, the Kalemegdan Fortress (*kale* meaning "fortress" and *meydan* meaning "field") was one of the most fought-over strategic points in South Eastern Europe. It was first settled by the Celts, then refortified by Serbia's medieval rulers and expanded during the Ottoman and Austrian occupations, evolving into an extensive complex of buildings blending various architectural styles. Today, it is Belgrade's most popular park, offering fine views of the Danube from its bastions.

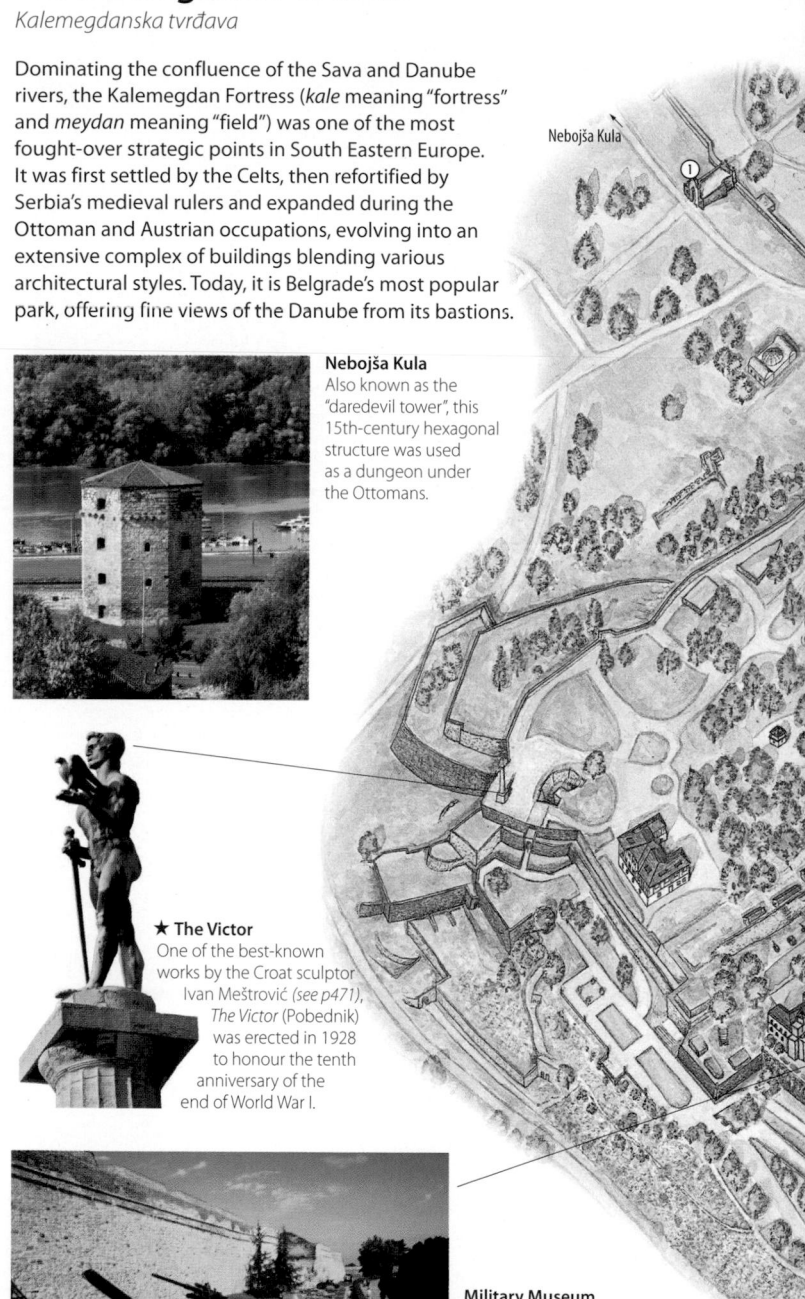

Nebojša Kula

Nebojša Kula
Also known as the "daredevil tower", this 15th-century hexagonal structure was used as a dungeon under the Ottomans.

★ The Victor
One of the best-known works by the Croat sculptor Ivan Meštrović *(see p471)*, *The Victor* (Pobednik) was erected in 1928 to honour the tenth anniversary of the end of World War I.

Military Museum
Built in 1929, the Military Museum resembles a medieval fortress. Tanks, cannons and World War II machinery are on display.

For hotels and restaurants see p539 and pp540–41

★ Chapel of Sveta Petka

Built in 1937, this chapel stands on the site of a sacred spring associated with St Petka, patron saint of families. The spring is believed to have miraculous powers. It is thought that St Petka's relics were kept in a church here during the Middle Ages.

VISITORS' CHECKLIST

Practical Information
Kalemegdan. **Map** C2.
(011) 262 0685.
Military Museum: **Tel** (011) 334
3441. **Open** 10am–5pm Tue–Sun.
Nebojša Kula: **Closed** for
restoration. Sahat Kula: **Open**
10am–5pm daily.
beogradskatvrdjava.co.rs

Transport

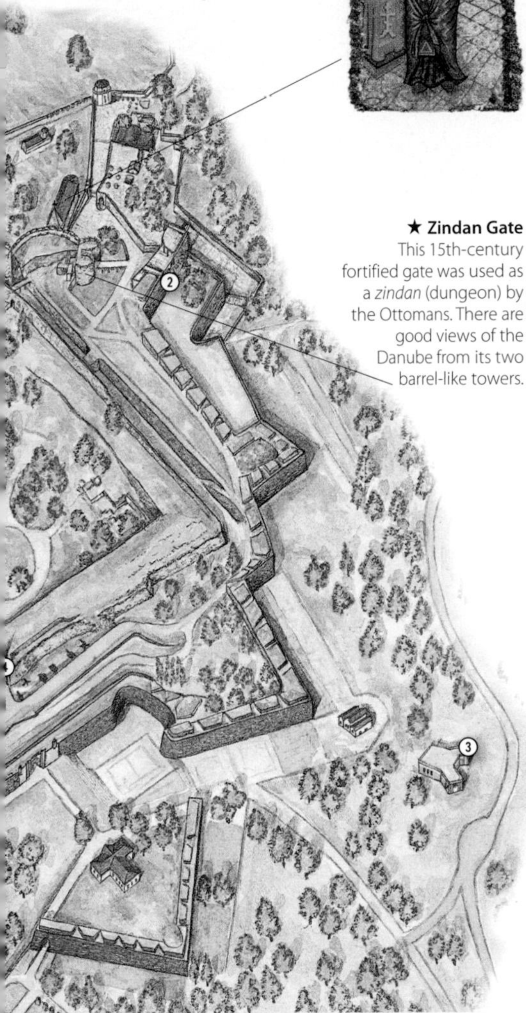

★ Zindan Gate

This 15th-century fortified gate was used as a *zindan* (dungeon) by the Ottomans. There are good views of the Danube from its two barrel-like towers.

KEY

① **Emperor Karl VI Gate**, a triumphal arch, was built by the Austrians to celebrate the capture of Belgrade in 1718.

② **Leopold Gate**, on the east side of the fortress, was built in honour of Austrian Emperor Leopold I, who held Belgrade briefly in the 1680s.

③ **The Cvijeta Zuzoric Art Pavilion**, used for high-profile art exhibitions, was named after a celebrated poet and beauty from 16th-century Dubrovnik.

④ **Sahat Kula**, a distinctive clock tower, was built by the Austrians in the 18th century.

⑤ *Struggle* **by Simeon Roksandić** (1874–1943), a Serbian sculptor, depicts a naked fisherman wrestling with a snake.

Ivan Meštrović's Memorial to France

Meštrović's sculpture, which depicts a bathing figure, was built in honour of the French troops who played a major role in liberating Serbia in 1918.

② Fresco Gallery

Galerija fresaka

Cara Uroša 20. **Map** D2. **Tel** (011) 262 1491. **Open** 10am–5pm Tue, Wed & Fri, noon–8pm Thu & Sat, 10am–2pm Sun.

Displaying copies of some of the remarkable medieval paintings that adorn the churches and monasteries in Serbia, the Fresco Gallery provides a stunning visual introduction to the Orthodox Christian culture that thrived in the region before the Ottoman occupation. In the 14th century, Serbia was at the forefront of religious art, blending traditional Byzantine styles with a new style of realistic, emotional portraiture. In particular, New Testament scenes from the monastery churches of Studenica *(see p534)* and Sopoćani *(see p535)* are reproduced here to great effect. There are also many paintings from the monastery of Kosovo-Metohija and frescoes from the 14th-century foundation at the Orthodox monastery of Dečani. Visitors can also view scale models of many of the churches in which the frescoes can be found, which helps to place the paintings in their architectural context.

③ Vuk and Dositej Museum

Vukov i Dositejev muzej

Gospodar Jevremova 21. **Map** D2. **Tel** (011) 262 5161. 26. **Open** 10am–5pm Tue, Wed & Fri, noon–8pm Thu, 10am–2pm Sun.

The Vuk and Dositej Museum honours two of Serbia's most important language reformers.

Traditional folk costumes on display in the Ethnographic Museum

The museum occupies one of the oldest houses in Belgrade. Featuring oriel windows and terracotta tiles, it is a fine example of the Levantine-style houses that characterized the city in the early 19th century.

The ground floor houses a display devoted to Dositej Obradović (1742–1811), a widely travelled educator who opened Serbia's first high school here in 1808. The first floor holds personal effects and manuscripts relating to Vuk Stefanović Karadžić (1787–1864), who is regarded as one of the most influential figures in modern Serbian history and culture.

Born into a simple, peasant family, Vuk Stefanović Karadžić spent much of his life compiling traditional songs and stories, amassing a huge body of Serbian folk literature that still exerts a profound influence over the nation's culture. He was also a linguist, responsible for standardizing Serbian grammar, and publishing dictionaries and books that set the standard for language teachers in his day.

④ Ethnographic Museum

Etnografski muzej

Studentski trg 13. **Map** D2. **Tel** (011) 328 1888. 31, 28, 29, 41. **Open** 10am–5pm Tue–Sat, 9am–2pm Sun. **W etnografskimuzej.rs**

The Ethnographic Museum offers a colourful and informative introduction to Serbia's rich folk traditions. It is housed in the former Belgrade Stock Exchange, a stark piece of Functionalist architecture built in 1934. The ground floor hosts interesting temporary exhibitions on various themes, often featuring items on loan from foreign museums.

The permanent collection begins on the first floor with a display of traditional Serbian textiles. The highlight here is a collection of vividly coloured woollen carpets from the east Serbian town of Pirot, decorated with a rich repertoire of geometric, floral and zoomorphic symbols. There are also examples of the vertical looms on which such carpets were handwoven, alongside the beautifully carved *preslice* (distaff) used to spin the wool, each adorned with sun and star motifs.

The top floor displays traditional folk costumes as well as examples of 19th-century urban dresses, top hats and umbrellas. There are also intricate scale models of village farmsteads and re-creations of typical urban and rural house interiors.

Reproduction of a fresco from the Orthodox Cathedral, Fresco Gallery

⑤ Palace of Princess Ljubica

Konak Kneginje Ljubice

Kneza Sime Markovića 8. **Map** C3.
Tel (011) 263 8264. **Open** 11am–5pm
Tue, Wed & Fri, 10am–6pm Thu,
11am–8pm Sat, 10am–4pm Sun.

Situated a short distance from
Belgrade's Orthodox Cathedral,
this former royal residence is
the finest surviving example of
Ottoman-Serbian architecture
from the early 19th century.
It was built for Prince Miloš
Obrenović in 1830, but he
preferred his forest-fringed
residence in Topčider Park
southwest of the city centre,
and left this building to his
wife, Princess Ljubica, and
their children Milan and Mihail.

The exterior is Oriental in
appearance, with bay windows
protruding from the upper
floors and slender minaret-like
chimneys emerging from the
roof. Inside is a display
of traditional Balkan
decorations, with the
ground floor *divanhane*
(reception room)
containing a raised
platform carpeted
with brightly coloured
Oriental rugs. Cushioned
benches, charcoal
braziers, Turkish coffee
jugs and tables inlaid
with mother-of-pearl
re-create the semi-
European, semi-Levantine lifestyle
enjoyed by the Serbian elite of
the period. The top-floor rooms
house a collection of 19th-
century furniture and portraits
of the Serbian Royal Family.

Visitors enjoying a stroll through the cobbled streets of Skadarlija

⑥ Orthodox Cathedral

Saborna crkva

Kneza Sime Markovića 3. **Map** C3.
Tel (011) 263 6684. **Open** 7am–8pm
daily.

Built in 1837 on the orders of
Prince Miloš Obrenović and
dedicated to the Archangel
Michael, the
Orthodox Cathedral
is a blend of Neo-
Classical and
Baroque styles.
Inside, the gilded
iconostasis carved
by Dimitrije Petrović
bears several tiers of
icons. In front of it is
a casket containing
the bones of Prince
Lazar, who was killed
during the Battle of

Mosaic, Orthodox
Cathedral

Kosovo in 1389. This battle
ended in stalemate and the
province of Kosovo has held
special importance in Serbian
national consciousness ever
since. Outside the main

entrance lie the tombs of
cultural reformers Dositej
Obradović and Vuk Karadžić.
Opposite the cathedral, on
Kralja Petra, is the **Café of the
Question Mark** (Kafana "?"),
built in 1823 and the oldest
functioning tavern in the city.
It was originally called the
Café at the Cathedral, but the
church authorities objected to
the name, leaving the owner
to hang the "?" sign above the
door as a symbol of protest.

⑦ Skadarlija

Skadarska

Skadarska ulica. **Map** E3.
2, 5, 10, 79.

Centred on a cobbled street,
Skadarlija was early 20th-cen-
tury Belgrade's bohemian quarter, where artists and poets
would gather for a night of
wine and song. Crowded with
cafés and restaurants, it is one
of the city's hot spots for dining
and carousing.

Skadarlija's history as a hub for
nightlife dates back to the 1880s,
when Czech entrepreneur Ignat
Bajloni established a brewery at
the end of the street. A host of
inns opened up in the vicinity
and a regular clientele of artists
and writers began to meet here.
Today, Skadarska ulica is still
atmospheric, with most of
the restaurants retaining their
traditional furnishings.

Further down the street stands
an Ottoman-style fountain, a
replica of the Sebilj Fountain
(see p490) in the Baščaršija
district of Sarajevo.

Oriental façade of the Palace of Princess Ljubica

⑧ St Mark's Church
Crkva Svetog marka

Bulevar Kralja Aleksandra 17.
Map E4. **Tel** (011) 323 1940. 🚌 25, 26, 27, 32. 🚏

Completed in 1940, St Mark's Church is an architectural tribute to Serbia's medieval builders, being largely based on the 14th-century monastery church of Gračanica in Kosovo. With its cluster of green domes and striped red-and-ochre stonework, it is a more exuberant piece of work than the original, and features an angular modern belfry. Laid out beneath a 52-m (171-ft) high cupola, the interior of the church is comparatively bare, which draws attention to a glittering mosaic of the Last Supper set in the iconostasis. Set against the south wall of the nave is the sarcophagus of Serbia's greatest medieval ruler, Tsar Dušan.

Southeast of the church stretches **Tašmajdan Park** (Tašmajdanski park), named after a quarry from the Ottoman period; Tašmajdan means "stone quarry" in Turkish. Today, its leafy promenades attract a lot of visitors. A few steps west of the church is Serbia's **Parliament Building** (zgrada Parlamenta), stormed in October 2000 by protesters demanding the overthrow of the then president, Slobodan Milošević. The entrance to this Classical-style building features striking sculptures of muscular figures wrestling to control struggling horses, the work of the 19th-century Croatian sculptor Toma Rosandić.

Section of the permanent exhibition space inside the Nikola Tesla Museum

⑨ Nikola Tesla Museum
Muzej Nikole tesle

Krunska 51. **Map** F5.
Tel (011) 243 3886. 🚊 7, 12. 🚌 26, 27. **Open** 10am–6pm Tue–Sun. 🚾 🏛 **w** tesla-museum.org

Born to Serb parents in the Lika region of Croatia, Nikola Tesla (1856–1943) was one of the engineering geniuses of the Modern Age, carrying out pioneering work in the fields of X-rays, radio transmission and remote-control devices. One of his greatest achievements was demonstrating how electricity could be transmitted in the form of alternating currents, a system now used around the world.

Tesla is also credited with being one of the co-inventors of the radio, even though his Italian rival Guglielmo Marconi was the first to succeed in demonstrating the technology in action. Despite spending most of his adult life in North America, Tesla requested that his ashes be brought to Belgrade after his death; this memorial museum was established to house them. The display provides an informative overview of Tesla's life and work, with labels in Serbian and English. There are scale models of his laboratories, together with a replica of the remote-control led boat he first demonstrated to the public at Madison Square Gardens in New York in 1898.

⑩ The Royal Compound
Kraljevski dvorovi

Dedinje. **Map** F2. **Tel** (011) 306 4000. 🛈 Makedonska 5. **Open** Apr–Oct: 11am & 2pm Sat & Sun. 🚾 🏛 **w** royalfamily.org

Comprising two palatial villas and a landscaped park, the Royal Compound was built by King Aleksandar of Yugoslavia in the 1920s. It is located in Dedinje, a hilly suburb southwest of the centre. After the monarchy was abolished by a referendum in 1947, the compound was used by the then Yugoslav president Tito, and more recently, by the Serbian Nationalist-Communist leader Slobodan Milošević. After the fall of Milošević, the Royal Family returned to Dedinje, and the compound now serves as their home. The main royal residence has an entrance hall decorated with copies of medieval Serbian frescoes and a splendid dining room decked in Flemish tapestries. The basement is decorated in Muscovite style, with motifs from Russian folk art adorning its vaulted ceilings.

On the other side of the park stands the **White Palace** (Beli Dvor), originally built by Aleksandar for his sons; it now contains the royal art collection. Highlights include paintings by Poussin and Canaletto as well as Rembrandt's *Portrait of a Young Man*.

Detail on the exterior of St Mark's Church

⑪ St Sava's Church

Hram svetog save

Krušedolska 2a. **Map** F2. 🚌 9, 10. 14. 31, 33, 39, 47, 48. **Open** 7am–7pm daily. 🆆 **hramsvetogsave.com**

Dedicated to St Sava, the Serbian prince and holy man who is regarded as the founder of the Serbian Orthodox Church, St Sava's Church is the largest working Orthodox church in the world. It is the result of a Herculean building project that has lasted several decades and is still in the process of completion. The location of the church is considered sacred, as it was here that the saint's remains were ritually burned by the Ottomans in 1595 after being seized from the Mileševa Monastery in southwest Serbia.

Begun in the 1930s, construction was halted midway with the onset of World War II and only resumed in 1984. The basic structure of the church is now in place. It is styled on the Byzantine cross-in-square model, with a central dome flanked by four half-domes. Faced with white-coloured marble plates, it has a luminous appearance. The interior, still unfinished, covers an area of 3,650 sq m (36,288 sq ft) and boasts a capacity of 10,000 worshippers.

⑫ Museum of Yugoslav History

Muzej istorije Jugoslavije

Botićeva 6. **Map** F2. **Tel** (011) 367 1296. 🚌 40, 41. 🚌 94. **Open** 10am–4pm Tue–Sun. 🅿️ ♿ 🆆 **mij.rs**

One museum not to be missed while in Belgrade: the Museum of Yugoslav History actually comprises three entities. The centrepiece of the complex is the House of Flowers (Kuća Cveća), the former president Josip Broz Tito's tomb. Communist leader Tito led partisan forces during World War II and was the architect of the federal Yugoslav state that emerged from the ashes of the war. He served as the dictator of Yugoslavia from 1945 until his death on 4 May 1980. The House of Flowers keeps a fascinating collection of Tito memorabilia, including a range of gifts presented to him by foreign dignitaries. An adjacent building houses the 25th May Museum, where the former leader's Rolls Royce and a collection of batons used in the annual "Relay of Youth", held on Tito's official birthday (25 May), are displayed. The Old Museum houses ethnographical displays from the former Yugoslavia.

Statue of Tito, 25th May Museum

The striking Millennium Tower in Gardoš, Zemun

⑬ Zemun

Map E1. 🚌 15, 84, 704, 706. ℹ️ Zemun Tourist Centre, Zmaj Jovina 14, (011) 219 2904.

Sprawled along the west bank of the Danube, 4 km (3 miles) from central Belgrade, lies the suburb of Zemun. Unlike the rest of Belgrade, Zemun was part of the Austro-Hungarian Empire from the late 17th century until World War I, and retains the pleasant atmosphere of a small central European town.

The most interesting part of Zemun is Gardoš, an area of steep cobbled alleyways on a hillside overlooking the river. Presiding over Gardoš from the top of the hill is the **Millennium Tower** (Milenijumski kula), a red-brick monument built by the Hungarians in 1896 to celebrate the 1,000-year anniversary of the creation of their state. From the foot of the tower, there is a wonderful view of central Belgrade, and key landmarks such as the Kalemegdan Fortress *(see pp526–7)* and St Sava's Church are clearly visible.

Zemun's other attraction is **Kej Oslobođenja** (Freedom Quay), a foot-and-cycle path that runs along the banks of the Danube and is popular with strollers on Sunday afternoons. This is also the heart of Belgrade's nightlife due to the long line of rafts moored here, most of which have been turned into restaurants, bars, pubs and clubs.

Monumental structure of St Sava's Church

Freedom Square, the spacious hub of Novi Sad

❷ Novi Sad

74 km (46 miles) N of Belgrade.
🏠 300,000. 🚉 🚌 ℹ️ Bulevar
Mihajla Pupina 9, (021) 421 811; Ulica
Modene 1, (021) 661 7343. 🎭 EXIT
Festival (Jul). 🅦 **turizamns.rs**

On the north shore of the
Danube river, Novi Sad is the
administrative centre of the
Vojvodina region. The town owes
its existence to the strategically
located Petrovaradin Fortress on
the south bank of the river. Fortified since Roman times, Petrovaradin was turned into an
impregnable garrison by the
Austrians in the 18th century,
and the civilian settlement of
Novi Sad grew up by its side.

Largely populated by Serbs
fleeing from the Ottoman
Empire, the town soon became
a major centre of Serbian
religion, culture and learning.
The first ever Serbian-language
theatre was founded here in
1861, and the key literary and
cultural society, Matica Srpska,
moved here from Budapest in
1864. Modern Novi Sad houses
the cultural institutions of
Vojvodina's Hungarian, Slovak,
Romanian and Rusyn (a
different ethnic group to the
Russians) communities.

🏛 Pedestrian Zone
A cluster of pedestrianized
streets constitutes the centre of
Novi Sad. At their heart is the
Freedom Square (trg Slobode),
dominated by Ivan Meštrović's
statue of Svetozar Miletić, a
19th-century politician and
lawyer who fought for the rights
of Serbs within the Habsburg

monarchy. Looming over the
eastern end of the square is the
Neo-Gothic **St Mary's Cathedral**
(crkva sv Marije), the city's main
Catholic church and the
principal venue for Hungarian
and Croatian-speaking masses.
The church's plain interior
stands in remarkable contrast
to its colourful stained-glass
windows, made by Czech and
Hungarian masters.

Stretching northeast from
the cathedral, Zmaj Jovina
ulica is distinguished by
several two-storey build-
ings painted in pastel hues
of yellow, ochre and
turquoise. At the end
of the street stands the
19th-century Bishop's
Palace, designed by
Vladimir Nikolić in a variety
of architectural styles. Just around
the corner is the Orthodox
Church of St George, dating from
1742, which features a Rococo
iconostasis and vivacious Art
Nouveau stained-glass windows
by local artist Paja Jovanović.

Monument to Serbian statesman Svetozar
Miletić at Freedom Square

St Mary's
Cathedral

🏛 Museum of Vojvodina
Dunavska 35. **Tel** (021) 420 566.
Open 9am–7pm Tue–Fri, 10am–6pm
Sat & Sun. 🅦 **muzejvojvodine.org.rs**

Located in the pedestrian zone,
this museum (Muzej Vojvodine)
displays Neolithic pottery and
tools unearthed in the region.
There is also a wealth of finds
from the Roman city of Sirmium
(now Sremska Mitrovica), just
west of Novi Sad, which served
as Emperor Galerius's capital city
in the late 3rd century. The
ethnographic diversity of
Vojvodina emerges through a
colourful display of Serb,
Hungarian and Slovak cos-
tumes. There are also painted
wooden chests and brightly
decorated ceramics in a range
of traditional folk designs.

🏰 Petrovaradin Fortress
Petrovaradinska tvrđava.
Open 8am–5pm Tue–Sun.
City Museum: **Tel** (021) 643 3145.
🕘 9am–5pm (except Mon).
🅦 **museumns.rs**

A short walk east of central
Novi Sad, Petrovaradin
Fortress (Petrovaradinska
tvrđava) stretches along
the high ground on the
south bank of the Danube
river. Occupied first by the
Romans, then medieval
Hungarians and Ottoman
Turks, the fortress itself
dates from the arrival of
the Austrians in 1692. Eager to
consolidate their rule over
Central Europe, they saw
Petrovaradin as the focal point of
their southern defences and set
about building a fortress so
formidable that the Ottomans
would be dissuaded from ever
taking up arms against Austria
again. The resulting stronghold
comprised a star-shaped pattern
of bastions and trenches, with
over 15 km (9 miles) of underground galleries to house
30,000 defending troops.

Positioned high above the
river, the central citadel offers
magnificent views of Novi
Sad from its ramparts. Inside,
many of the barrack blocks
have now been converted
into artists' workshops and
galleries, with atmospheric
cafés and restaurants.

View of Petrovaradin Fortress across the Danube river, Novi Sad

Petrovardin's former arsenal (topovnjača) is now occupied by the **City Museum** (Gradski muzej), home to a fine collection of period furnishings, porcelain and fine arts. Guided tours of the underground galleries (podzemne vojne galerije) offer the chance to explore a subterranean warren of gun positions and ammunition dumps.

Every July, Petrovaradin becomes the venue for the famous EXIT Festival *(see p538)*, a four-day celebration of rock and pop that draws between 150,000 and 190,000 revellers from all over Europe.

❸ Subotica

178 km (111 miles) N of Belgrade.
🏛 150,000. 🚉 🚌 🛈 trg Slobode 1,
(024) 670 350. 🎬 Palić Film Festival
(mid-Jul). **W** visitsubotica.rs

Located close to the Hungarian frontier, Subotica is a typical multicultural border town with a mixed community of Hungarians, Serbs and Croats. First documented in the late 14th century as a free-trading post, the town is known for its Art Nouveau architecture, of which the monumental Town Hall (Gradska kuća) on the main square is an outstanding example. Designed in 1908 by architects Marcell Komor and Dezső Jakab, it is rich in Hungarian folk motifs, with colourfully patterned roof tiles, oriole windows and decorative floral designs adorning the façade.

North of the main square, at Synaoque square (trg Sinagoge) stands Subotica's Synagogue (Sinagoga), which showcases Komor and Jakab's flamboyant architectural style. Mixing red brick with green and yellow tiling and topped with a cluster of plump domes, it is an extraordinarily striking building. Set in one corner of the synagogue enclosure is a monument honouring Subotica's 4,000-strong Jewish population, transported to Nazi death camps in July 1944.

The nearby **Municipal Museum** (Gradski muzej) houses a colourful ethnographic collection rich in traditional Hungarian and Croatian costumes, and a display of African folk artifacts collected by famous local explorer Oskar Vojnić. East of the main square, the pedestrianized Korzo is full of fine buildings from the pre-World War I period. Most remarkable is the richly decorated apartment house at No. 4. The beehive symbol on its façade reveals its former function as a savings bank. Just round the corner from Korzo, the **Likovni Susret Gallery** (galerija Likovni Susret), covered in brightly coloured tulip motifs is an Art Nouveau gem. Built by architect Ferenc Rajhl to serve as a family home in 1904, it now hosts changing exhibitions of contemporary art.

Environs
Located 8 km (5 miles) east of Subotica, the lakeside settlement of **Palić** was developed as a health resort in the mid-19th century, and is now a popular spot for sunbathing and swimming in summer. Here, too, is an ensemble of buildings designed by Komor and Jakab, blending Art Nouveau style with Hungarian folk motifs. A cone-shaped *vodotoranj* (water tower), attached to a gateway of the lakeside park, is among them. The town's most distinctive building, however, is the Womens' Beach (Ženski štrand), an all-timber waterside pavilion resembling Transylvanian village huts.

🏛 **Municipal Museum**
trg Sinagoge 3. **Tel** (024) 555 128.
Open 10am–6pm Tue–Sat. 🅿

🏛 **Likovni Susret Gallery**
Park Ferenca Rajhla 5. **Tel** (024) 553
725. **Open** 8am–7pm Mon–Fri,
9am–1pm Sat.

Subotica's main square, graced by Art Nouveau buildings

Fortifications at the serene Manasija Monastery, Despotovac

❹ Despotovac

130 km (81 miles) SE of Belgrade. 🏔 33,000. 🚌 from Belgrade. 🛈 Cerska 3, (064) 264 5986. 🆆 **despotovac.rs**

Located in the Resava valley 30 km (19 miles) east of the main Belgrade-Niš Highway, the town of Despotovac is renowned for the spectacular medieval **Manasija Monastery** (manastir Manasija), also known as Resavska after the local river. Founded by Despot Stefan Lazarević in 1418, the monastery is surrounded by forti-fications, including 11 castellated towers. Inside are some of Serbia's finest 15th-century frescoes. The west wall has a portrait of Stefan Lazarević wearing gold-embroidered robes, while the north and south walls are cov-ered with friezes of warrior-saints wielding weapons. Higher up, the walls are

Detail of fresco, Manasija Monastery

decorated with scenes from the gospel, while depictions of Old Testament prophets adorn the cupola.

Environs

The **Resava Cave** (Resavska Pećina), one of Serbia's most dra-matic karst features, is situated 20 km (12 miles) southeast of Despotovac. Formed by seeping water over an estimated 80 million years, the cave features rock formations. An 800 m (2,625 ft) stretch of the cave is accessible via a staircase. Highlights include the Beehive Hall, characterized by beehive-shaped stalagmites, and the Crystal Hall, which takes its name from its chandelier-like stalactites.

🛈 **Resava Cave**
Tel (035) 611 610. **Open** Apr–Nov: 9am–5pm daily. 🎫
🆆 **resavskapecina.rs**

❺ Studenica Monastery

135 km (84 miles) S of Belgrade. **Tel** (036) 536 050. 🚌 from Belgrade. **Open** 5am–8pm daily. 🛈 🆆 **manastirstudenica.rs**

Nestled in a wooded valley, Studenica Monastery is regarded as the spiritual heartland of the Serbian Orthodox church. It was founded in the late 12th century by Prince Stefan Nemanja, founder of the medieval Serb state, who became a monk in 1196. The monastery later served as a base for his son Sava, the first archbishop of the Serbian Church and the nation's patron saint.

Surrounded by a horseshoe-shaped ring of buildings, the main monastery is a Byzantine-style basilica decorated with a profusion of Romanesque details, notably floral swirls and animal motifs. Inside are some of the most splendid frescoes in the Balkans, in which portraits of the holy family, saints and apostles combine Byzantine formality with the realism of Western European art.

On the northern side of the monastery compound stands the smaller **King's Church** (Kraljeva Crkva), built in 1314 by Stefan Nemanja's great-grandson King Uroš II Milutin. Among several brilliantly executed frescoes are a joyous *Birth of the Virgin* on the north wall, and portraits of Serbian rulers in the south chapel.

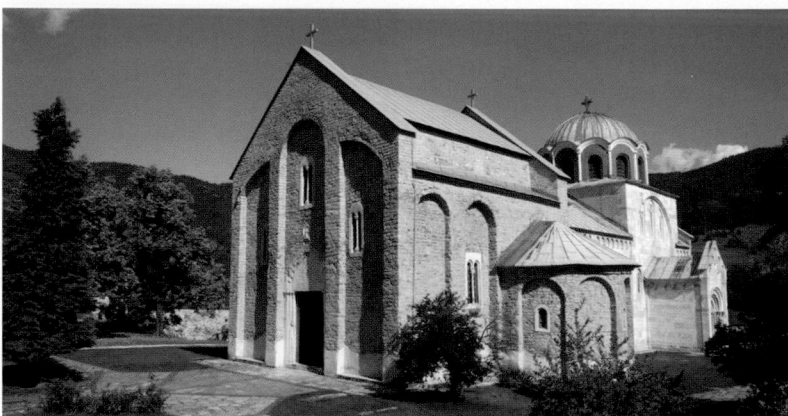

Well-preserved complex of the Studenica Monastery, of special significance to the Serbian Orthodox faith

For hotels and restaurants see p539 and pp540–41

Equestrian monument to the Liberation of 1878, Niš

➏ Niš

235 km (146 miles) SE of Belgrade. 🚇 250,000. 🚉 🚌 ℹ️ Voždova 7 (018) 523 118. **W** visitnis.com

The town of Niš has an ancient pedigree. Believed to be the birthplace of Emperor Constantine the Great, it was also an important Roman trading post. Conquered by the Ottomans in 1386, Niš became a part of the modern Serbian state in 1878. Today it is Serbia's third largest city and centres around the pedestrianized Kralja Milana Square, where there is an equestrian monument dedicated to the liberators of 1878.

North of the square, a bridge leads across the Nišava river towards the 18th-century **Tvrđava** (Fortress) built by the Ottoman Turks, which is now the town park. Entered via the Istanbul Gate (Stambul Kapija), the park contains some Ottoman buildings, including a domed bath house and the 15th-century Mosque of Bali Beg, which now serves as an art gallery.

South of the main square, the Copper-workers' Alley (Kazandžijsko Sokače) preserves some 19th-century craft workshops. About 3 km (2 miles) east of the centre stands the **Tower of Skulls** (Ćele Kula), a gruesome monument dedicated to the origins of the Serbian Uprising of 1809, when insurgents blew themselves up to avoid capture by the Turks. The Ottomans built a tower studded with the victims' heads to serve

as a warning. It originally contained 1,000 skulls, but just 60 remain.

Environs
Djavolja Varoš (Devil's Town), about 90 km (56 miles) west of Niš, is so named for 202 eerie rock formations caused by centuries of erosion.

🏛️ **Tower of Skulls**
Bulevar Dr Zorana Đinđica. **Tel** 822 2228. **Open** 9am–8pm Tue–Sun.

➐ Novi Pazar

270 km (168 miles) S of Belgrade. 🚇 120,000. 🚌 ℹ️ 28 Novembar 27, (020) 338 030. **W** tonps.rs

Situated in mountainous territory in southwest Serbia, Novi Pazar was founded in the mid-15th century as a way-station on the Dubrovnik-Constantinople caravan route. The town centre still has some Ottoman-era buildings and plenty of mosques. Highlights include the many-domed **Isa Beg Hammam** (Isabegov hamam), a 15th-century bath house beside the Raška river. North of the river is the Lejlek Mosque, built a century later, with its arched portico overlooked by a minaret.

The area around Novi Pazar was once the heartland of the medieval Serbian state and is dotted with ancient churches and monasteries. North of the centre stands the 9th-century **St Peter's Church** (Petrova Crkva), the original seat of the bishops of Ras and the oldest surviving church in Serbia.

Detail from the Tower of Skulls

St Peter's Church in Novi Pazar, the oldest church in Serbia

Environs
Around 25 km (16 miles) northeast of Novi Pazar, **Kopaonik National Park** lies in a picturesque plateau surrounded by high mountain peaks, and is popular with skiers and hikers.

➑ Sopoćani Monastery

287 km (178 miles) S of Belgrade. 🚌 from Novi Pazar.

Located on a hill surrounded by mountains, the monastery of Sopoćani was founded in 1263 by King Uroš I, the grandson of Stefan Nemanja. The monastery church is a three-aisled Romanesque basilica made from blocks of stone. The nave is covered with frescoes painted by masters from Constantinople, with a fine *Dormition of the Virgin* filling the west wall. Also in the nave are the tombs of Uroš I and his Venetian mother Anna Dandolo. The narthex contains more frescoes, with superb portraits of Uroš and his son Dragutin.

Evocative fresco of *Dormition of the Virgin*, Sopoćani Monastery

Practical & Travel Information

Serbia has largely missed out on the tourism boom enjoyed by other countries in Eastern and Central Europe, and facilities for visitors are a little less predictable than elsewhere in the region. However, tourist information is available in the most popular destinations, and banks, post offices and public transport ticket offices are efficient. There is a good network of rail and road services reaching all parts of the country, although standards of comfort in trains and buses vary widely.

When to Visit

Serbia has a continental climate that is prone to seasonal extremes. Spring, early summer and early autumn are the best times both for sightseeing and for catching regional festivals. Temperatures can be very high in August, while in mid-winter, they can drop to below freezing for long periods of time. Heavy snow can hamper transport in rural areas. Many museums have shorter opening hours from October until March and may stay closed on weekends. The skiing season is generally from December to March.

Documentation

Citizens of the EU, US, Canada, Australia and New Zealand only need a valid passport to visit Serbia for up to 90 days. For more information about visas or extended stays, visitors should contact the Serbian Embassy or Consulate in their home country before travelling, or check the website of the **Serbian Ministry of Foreign Affairs**.

Visitor Information

The country is still in the process of developing a tourist information infrastructure. Many smaller destinations may lack tourist information of any kind. However, cities such as Belgrade, Niš and Novi Sad, have professional tourist information centres with English-speaking staff. These cities are also well signposted, making it easy to tour the main sights on foot. Most towns in Serbia have official websites with information given in English, though these are not updated regularly. The **National Tourism Organization of Serbia** and the **Tourist Organization of Belgrade** have informative websites.

Health and Security

No special vaccinations are required for visiting Serbia. Minor ailments can be dealt with by visiting a *apoteka* (pharmacy) where over-the-counter medication is available. Each city has one or more centrally located pharmacies that stay open 24 hours. Air quality in the capital, Belgrade, is poor especially in mid-winter and mid-summer. Serbia is generally a safe country in which to travel, and the only likely dangers are petty theft and pickpocketing. Visitors should keep their valuables out of sight in crowded areas or while using public transport services. They should also avoid leaving their bags unattended on trains.

Facilities for the Disabled

Few of Serbia's public transport facilities, museums or tourist attractions have been adapted for wheelchair users. Pavement ramps are being introduced in central Belgrade, but their provision elsewhere in Serbia is erratic. Hotels offering facilities for the disabled are mostly in the four- and five-star bracket and command high prices.

Banking and Currency

Banks and *menjačnica* (exchange bureaus) offer better exchange rates than hotels and travel agencies. Banks are open from 8am to 5pm Monday to Friday and from 8am to 2pm on Saturday.

ATMs are widespread in towns and cities. However, not all accept the full range of plastic cards. If the logo of the card is not displayed on the ATM, the machine will reject the card. Major international credit cards are accepted in central shops as well as restaurants in Belgrade and other bigger cities. If travelling in small towns or rural areas, it is a good idea to carry sufficient cash to cover major items such as hotel bills as well as lesser expenses.

The currency of Serbia, the dinar (RSD or din), is rarely available in banks or exchange bureaus outside the country. However, there are exchange facilities at Belgrade's airport, train and bus stations and at road border crossings.

Communications

Serbia's telephone network is straightforward and easy to use, and there is mobile phone coverage almost everywhere in

---

The Climate of Serbia

Winters are cold and wet with heavy snow. Summers are rarely oppressively hot, although it can get quite humid in Belgrade during August. May, June and September are the perfect months to visit in terms of weather, although May and June are also the wettest. Early to mid-October is still warm, and excellent for cultural and outdoor activities.

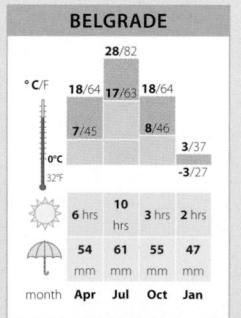

BELGRADE

°C/F	Apr	Jul	Oct	Jan
	18/64	28/82 17/63	18/64	
	7/45		8/46	3/37
0°C 32°F				-3/27
sunshine	6 hrs	10 hrs	3 hrs	2 hrs
rainfall	54 mm	61 mm	55 mm	47 mm
month	Apr	Jul	Oct	Jan

the country. Public telephones use Halo cards (Halo Plus cards for international calls), which can be purchased from newspaper kiosks and post offices. Wi-Fi is readily available everywhere, including most hotels and cafés as well as an increasing number of public spaces, such as the main square in Novi Sad.

Post offices stay open from 8am to 7pm Monday to Friday and from 8am to 3pm on Saturday.

Arriving by Air

Air Serbia, from London Heathrow airport, and **Wizz Air**, from Luton airport, offer direct flights from the UK to Belgrade. There are no direct flights from North America or Australasia to Belgrade, although most travel agents will offer a one- or two-stop flight to Belgrade, changing at a major European airport such as Amsterdam, Frankfurt, London or Vienna.

Belgrade's **Nikola Tesla Airport** is 18 km (11 miles) north of the city at Surčin. Local bus number 72 runs from the airport to the city centre every 30 minutes from about 5am until midnight. There is also the faster, more expensive, A1 line, which runs every 30 minutes up to Slavija Square.

Rail Travel

Rail travel in Serbia is slightly cheaper than bus travel, but journey times are slower and departures less frequent. There is a useful international service from Belgrade to Zagreb, with one departure per day, and to Budapest, with two departures per day. The 10-hour train trip from Belgrade to the Montenegrin capital Podgorica is one of South Eastern Europe's classic journeys, taking in breathtaking mountain scenery and spectacular viaducts. The train for the trip departs twice daily. Train carriages on international services are clean and plush. The rolling stock used on domestic journeys is often old and less comfortable, and toilets may be filthy. As few domestic or

international trains include a buffet car, passengers should purchase provisions before travelling. Both local and Intercity trains are crowded and can be late. Tickets and information on rail travel throughout the country is available on the **Serbian Railways** website.

Travelling by Bus

Bus travel is the most popular form of public transport in Serbia. The **Belgrade Bus Station** is the central bus station that serves most destinations in the country. Fast Intercity services link the main centres as well as rural destinations. Many buses may be old, especially in the rural south of the country, and are unlikely to be air conditioned.

Each town or city has a central bus station with clearly displayed timetables (*polasci* means departures, *dolasci* means arrivals). Tickets should be purchased in advance and usually include a seat reservation. When buying a ticket, passengers are also given a *žeton* (token) which provides access to the relevant departure platform. Both Belgrade and Novi Sad have daily international services to Zagreb, Sarajevo and in the summer months, to Dubrovnik and Split. The Bulgarian capital Sofia can be reached twice a day from Niš.

Travelling by Car

A valid international driving license is required to drive legally in Serbia. Insurance policies from countries that have signed the Vehicle Insurance Convention are valid. However, citizens of other countries must purchase an insurance policy when entering Serbia. The European Green Card vehicle insurance is now valid in Serbia. Well-maintained *autoput* (highways) run from Belgrade to Niš, Novi Sad and Subotica. Tolls are payable on these roads. Cars can be hired from service providers **Budget** and **Hertz**. Headlights should be kept on at all times. The use of mobile phones is forbidden, as is drinking and driving.

Shopping & Entertainment

Serbia's high streets have modern shops selling branded goods, however, traditional open-air markets where an array of fresh foodstuffs and craft items are available are a big draw. The country has a lively outdoor drinking culture, with cafés and alfresco bars particularly popular during the spring and summer months. The capital, Belgrade, has a thriving music and theatre scene with the season usually running from October to June. A busy schedule of music festivals takes over in the summer, with Novi Sad's EXIT festival drawing the biggest crowds.

Crafts and Souvenirs

In Belgrade, the main upmarket shopping area is along Terazije and Knez Mihailova Streets. Open-air stalls along the main avenue in Kalemegdan Park (see pp526–7) in Belgrade display traditional Serbian handicrafts such as carpets, opanke (leather slippers), painted gourds and shoulder bags decorated with folk motifs. A good selection of items is also available at the **Ethnographic Museum**. For postcards, guidebooks, T-shirts and other souvenirs, head for the **Beoizlog** gift shop. The multimedia store **Mamut** has a selection of English-language books and music, and also sells guidebooks and maps.

Food and Drink

The **Zeleni Venac** market in Belgrade is a good place to pick up dried red paprika, scented honey and herbs. The Serbian national drink, rakija (brandy), comes in several varieties although šljivovica (plum brandy) and lozovača (grape brandy) are the most common. Rakija and other spirits can be bought at supermarkets throughout Serbia, although **Rakia Bar and Gift Shop** outlets have a larger range of products.

Music and Festivals

Serbia's national opera and ballet companies are based at the **National Theatre** in Belgrade. The **Belgrade Philharmonic Orchestra** performs most weeks in the Kolarac Hall. **Sava Centre** is the venue for musicals, variety shows and visiting symphony orchestras as well as major rock,

pop and world music acts. The **Belgrade Music Festival** in October brings top classical performers, while the **Belgrade Dance Festival**, held in April, features international dancers. Serbia's biggest summer rock and pop event, the **EXIT Festival**, takes place in Novi Sad's Petrovaradin Fortress (see p532–3). In August, the **Guča Trumpet Festival**, sees Serbia's best brass bands perform. The **Kustendorf Film and Music Festival** in January features top actors and directors.

Theatre

For classical drama in the Serbian language, both the **National Theatre** and the **Yugoslav Drama Theatre** offer quality productions. Novi Sad is the home of the **Serbian National Theatre**, while Subotica has a dedicated Hungarian-language theatre, the **Dezső Kosztolányi Theatre**. The **Belgrade International Theatre Festival (BITEF)**, in September, is the leading festival of contemporary theatre in South Eastern Europe.

Bars and Clubs

Many of Belgrade's fanciest bars are located along Strahinjića Bana. Nearby is Skadarlija (see p529), whose restaurants and cafés preserve the atmosphere of the 1920s and 30s and feature live music. In spring and summer, nightlife shifts to the splavovi (rafts) that line the banks of the Sava and Danube rivers. A popular one is **Povetarac**, which plays rock music. Also famous for electronic music are nightclubs such as **Plastic**.

Where to Stay

Belgrade

Green Studio Hostel
Hostel   Map C4
Karađorđeva 61, 11000
Tel *(011) 218 5943*
W greenstudiohostel.com
Mix of dorm rooms, self-contained doubles and triples opposite Belgrade's train and bus stations.

Palace Hotel
Historic   Map C3
Topličin venac 23, 11000
Tel *(011) 218 5585*
W palacehotel.co.rs
Centrally located elegant hotel with rooms decorated in mood-enhancing creams and reds.

Majestic
Historic   Map D3
Obilićev venac 28, 11000
Tel *(011) 328 5777*
W majestic.rs
Dating from the 1930s, the hotel retains a few Art Deco touches. Good mid-range choice near the cultural and shopping spots.

Moskva
Historic   Map D4
Terazije 20, 11000
Tel *(011) 364 2071*
W hotelmoskva.rs
Landmark hotel blending Art Nouveau details with green Gothic spires, tastefully combines old-style furnishings and modern fittings in its rooms.

Travelling Actor
B&B   Map D2
Gospodar Jevremova 65, 11000
Tel *(011) 323 4156*
W travellingactor.rs
Rooms are small but comfortable and well-equipped in this intimate B&B located in the picturesque Skadarlija district.

Hyatt Regency
Luxury
Milentija Popovića 5, 11070
Tel *(011) 301 1234*
W belgrade.regency.hyatt.com
Expect high levels of comfort and service at this hotel that is located amid the modern blocks of Novi Beograd.

Imposing façade of Square Nine in Belgrade

DK Choice

Le Petit Piaf
Boutique   Map E3
Skadarska 34, 11000
Tel *(011) 303 5252*
W petitpiaf.com
Charming hotel located in the restaurant-packed Skadarlija district, just round the corner from the pubs of Strahinjića bana. Rooms are decorated in warm colours and come with TV, safe and Internet access. The hotel also offers smart two-person suites with living room and kitchenette.

Square Nine
Boutique   Map D2
Studentski trg 9, 11000
Tel *(011) 333 3500*
W squarenine.rs
Centrally located boutique hotel with elegant rooms, swanky bathrooms and spa centre.

Rest of Serbia

NIŠ: My Place
Boutique
Kej 29. Decembar bb, 18000
Tel *(018) 525 555*
W hotelmyplace.com
Striking riverside building with crisp rooms featuring a Jacuzzi.

NOVI PAZAR: Hotel Tadž
Business
Rifata Đurđevića 79, 36300
Tel *(020) 311 904*
W hoteltadznd.com

This conveniently located hotel has comfortable rooms, each with Internet access and reasonable desk space.

NOVI SAD: Hostel Sova
Hostel
Ilije Ognjanovića 26, 21000
Tel *(021) 661 5230*
W hostelsova.com
En suite double rooms and multi-bed dorms in an apartment building near Novi Sad's pedestrianized centre.

NOVI SAD: Ile de France
B&B
Cara Dušana 41, 21000
Tel *(021) 636 2382*
W iledefrance.co.rs
Friendly place with bright rooms that have wooden floors and modern bathrooms. The owner is French-speaking.

NOVI SAD: Leopold I
Historic
Petrovaradinska tvrđava bb, 21000
Tel *(021) 488 7878*
W leopoldns.com
Situated in the heart of the Petrovaradin Fortress, Leopold I comes with plush rooms and bags of period atmosphere.

SUBOTICA: Hotel Gloria
Business
Dimitrija Tucovića 2, 24000
Tel *(024) 672 010*
W hotelgloriasubotica.com
Intimate hotel just off the main square offering chic coffee-and-crimson rooms each with a minibar, desk and free Wi-Fi access.

SUBOTICA: Hotel Patria
Business
Đure Đakovića 1a, 24000
Tel *(024) 552 320*
W hotelpatria.rs
Centrally located 6-storey hotel with tastefully furnished rooms and modern bathrooms.

For map references *see pp524–5*

Where to Eat and Drink

Belgrade

Proleće
Serbian · **Map** D3
Vuka Karadžića 11, 11000
Tel *(011) 263 5436*
Few other restaurants in the city offer so wide a fare at such low prices. Range includes grills, soups, stews and salads. Popular with students from the nearby Fine Arts Academy.

Smokvica
International · **Map** D2
Kralja Petra 73, 11000
Tel *069 446 4056*
With its Minimalist design and retro furniture serving as backdrop, Smokvica offers a global menu of snacks and mains that have Mexican and Mediterranean influences.

To je to
Balkan Grill · **Map** E3
Bul Despota Stefana 21, 11000
Tel *(011) 323 1299*
Simple diner specializing in Sarajevo-style *ćevapi* (grilled minced-meat kebabs), usually served with a *somun* flat-bread bun and a generous helping of *kajmak* (buttery cheese).

Kafana Question Mark
Balkan Grill · **Map** C3
Kralja Petra 6, 11000
Tel *(011) 236 5421*
The oldest café in Belgrade, the Question Mark first opened in 1826 and has changed little in the intervening period, offering simple local standards such as grilled meats served in home-baked bread.

DK Choice

Manjež
International · **Map** E5
Svetozara Markovića 49, 11000
Tel *(011) 362 1111*
Located beside Manjež Park, this comfortable restuarant is popular with both stylish youth as well as intelligentsia from the older generation. It strikes a nice balance between Serbian and international fare. The traditional favourites at include *mućkalica* (meat in a rich and spicy paprika sauce) and *prebranac* (baked beans), although there is plenty by way of fancier fish and steak dishes.

Radost Fina Kuhinjica
International · **Map** C3
Pariška 3, 11000
Tel *060 603 0023*
Artfully restored old house offering creative vegan cuisine featuring Indian, Thai and Mediterranean flavours. Don't miss its delicious desserts, smoothies and shakes.

Salaš
International
Sinđelićeva 34, Zemun, 11080
Tel *(011) 219 0324*
Quaint and cosy restaurant in the Gardoš district, serving a combination of Serbian and Central-European cuisine: the *ćuretina s mlincima* (turkey with baked shards of pasta) is a speciality.

Šaran
Seafood
Kej oslobođenja 53, Zemun, 11080
Tel *(011) 618 235*
Occupying a historic one-storey house beside the Danube footpath, Šaran (The Carp) specializes in local freshwater fish, although there is plenty of Adriatic seafood and Balkan meat dishes on the menu.

Dva Jelena
Serbian · **Map** E3
Skadarska 32, 11000
Tel *(011) 723 4885*
Its location has been a landmark in the bohemian Skadarlija district since 1832. The 'Two Stags' offers classy grilled-meats and steaks in a wood-panelled setting, frequently with live music.

Delicious pasta served at Salaš in Belgrade

El Hispano
Spanish · **Map** D3
Obilićev venac 27/11, 11000
Tel *(011) 262 8685*
Spanish home cooking served with haute-cuisine panache, in an elegant old villa with parquet floors. Seafood is the speciality.

Homa
International
Žorža Klemansoa 19, 11000
Tel *(011) 328 6659*
Creative fusion cuisine with Mediterranean, South American and South Asian elements, and innovative desserts in a modern Minimalist setting.

Ima Dana
Serbian · **Map** E3
Skadarska 38, 11000
Tel *(011) 323 4422*
Choose from a sizeable menu of traditional Balkan dishes at this eatery that is counted amongst the oldest restaurants in the Skadarlija quarter.

Lorenzo & Kakalamba
International · **Map** F4
Cvijićeva 110, 11000
Tel *(011) 329 5351*
Quality cuisine based on the traditions of Tuscany and Eastern Serbia, with pastas, risottos, pizzas, and rustic stews cooked in earthenware pots. The extravagant interior is a colourful mix of Italian and Serbian folk art.

Madera
Serbian · **Map** E4
Bul Kralja Aleksandra 43, 11000
Tel *(011) 323 1332*
Eternally popular restaurant beside Tašmajdan Park exuding old-world elegance. The menu covers the Serbian repertoire from humble *ćevapčići* right up to *Karađorde Steak* (veal stuffed with ham and cheese).

Tri Šešira
Serbian · **Map** E3
Skadarska 29, 11000
Tel *(011) 724 7501*
Named after a shop sign that once hung above the door, 'Three Hats' offers quality grills and roast meats in an elegantly maintained wood-panel interior.

Zaplet (RSD)(RSD)(RSD)
International
Kajmakčalanska 2, 11000
Tel *(011) 240 4142*
With atmospheric lighting and loud music, this restaurant is popular with the affluent and fashionable. Serves global fare, from Serbian grilled snacks to modern European fusion.

Rest of Serbia

NIŠ: Kafana Sinđelić (RSD)
Serbian
Trg republike bb, 18000
Tel *(018) 512 548*
Comfortable restaurant in a 19th-century house with a big garden. Its meat-heavy menu includes lamb, steaks and a delicious *mućkalica* (spicy stew).

NIŠ: Nišlijska Mehana (RSD)
Balkan Grill
Prvomajska 49, 18000
Tel *(018) 511 111*
One of the liveliest places for a night out in Niš, this restaurant features folksy tableware, traditional wallhangings and the Serbian repertoire of grilled meat dishes.

NIŠ: Stara Srbija (RSD)(RSD)
Balkan Grill
Trg republike 12, 18000
Tel *(018) 521 902*
Popular main-square eatery serving grilled mincemeat snacks and skewer kebabs, alongside some more sustantial veal, fish and steak dishes.

NOVI PAZAR: Ras (RSD)
Serbian
Novi Pazar bb, 36300
Tel *(020) 361 578*
Just outside town on the road to Tutin, Ras offers grilled meats and locally caught trout in folksy wooden buildings surrounded by a park.

NOVI SAD: Astal Saren (RSD)
Balkan Grill
Mite Ružića 2, 21000
Tel *(021) 528 004*
Traditional grilled-meat and sausage dishes served in generous portions, over a checked-tablecloth affair in what looks like a rustic living room setting.

NOVI SAD: Kuća Mala (RSD)
Italian
Laze Telečkog 4, 21000
Tel *(021) 422 728*
An intimate, homely place with touches of surreal design inside,

Outdoor seating at Zak in Novi Sad

serving an imaginative range of large-size pizzas. Plenty of choice for vegetarians.

NOVI SAD: Pivnica Gusan (RSD)
Balkan Grill
Zmaj Jovina 4, 21000
Tel *(021) 425 570*
In the basement of what once was a cinema theatre, this enjoyable beer hall serves hearty, simple grilled-meat dishes and substantial salads.

NOVI SAD: Bela Lađa (RSD)(RSD)
International
Kisačka 21, 21000
Tel *(021) 661 6594*
Charmingly old-fashioned restaurant serving hearty grilled-meat dishes with all the trimmings. There is a strong list of wines from southeastern Europe as well as an excellent choice of Serbian brandies.

NOVI SAD: Plava Frajla (RSD)(RSD)(RSD)
International
Sutjeska 2, 21000
Tel *(021) 613 675*
Tucked into the side of a large shopping centre, the eccentrically-decorated "Blue Lady" features checked tablecloths and chairs hanging from the ceiling. The menu covers everything from Serbian grilled-meat dishes to Hungarian-influenced goulashes.

NOVI SAD: Zak (RSD)(RSD)(RSD)
International
Šafarikova 6, 21000
Tel *(021) 447 565*
European–Asian fusion cuisine featuring plenty of seafood and some exquisite desserts, served in a chic interior with live piano music.

SUBOTICA: Majkin Salaš (RSD)
International
Atile Jožefa 79, Palić 24413
Tel *(024) 753 276*
Traditional paprika-flavoured stews served in an old-style farmstead interior filled with vintage furniture, or in the courtyard with a vine trellis.

SUBOTICA: Bosscaffe (RSD)(RSD)
International
Matije Korvina 7–8, 24000
Tel *065 655 1111*
Popular café–restaurant inside a glass-walled pavilion. Serves good pizzas, decent steaks and fish, alongside a tempting array of cakes and pastries.

SUBOTICA: Gostiona Gurinović (RSD)(RSD)
Serbian
Bajski put 32, 24000
Tel *(024) 554 934* **Closed** *Sun*
A 10-minute walk from the main square, this folksy place with a beautiful garden offers quality north-Serbian cuisine, with goulash, roast lamb and duck, and local wines to wash it down.

DK Choice

SUBOTICA: Riblja Čarda (RSD)(RSD)
Seafood
Obala Lajoša Vermeša, Palić, 24413
Tel *(024) 755 040*
Popular out-of-town destination near the shore of lake Palić, ideal for sampling local fish dishes. The house speciality, *riblji paprikaš* (fish stew rich in paprika), is usually served with locally made pasta similar to tagliatelle. Dine in the pretty dining room with exposed timbers, or outdoors on the terrace facing the lake.

ROMANIA

Although the country is unlikely ever to disassociate itself from the myth of Dracula, in recent years Romania has certainly managed to shake off its Communist-era image of grey uniformity. Beyond its prettily restored historic towns and cities lie breathtaking mountains and scenes of rural tranquillity that have changed little for generations.

Bordered by Ukraine to the north, Bulgaria to the south and Serbia and Hungary to the west, Romania has long been torn between its neighbours, particularly during the 18th and 19th centuries when the Russians and Austrians waged war against the Ottoman Empire on Romanian soil.

Despite its turbulent history, Romania has retained much of its traditional culture and a visit there is an extremely rewarding experience. In Transylvania, the country's largest region, medieval castles neighbour modern ski resorts. To the northeast, Bukovina is home to beautiful monasteries, and to the south, Bucharest, the ancient capital of Wallachia, has superb museums and gardens.

History

The earliest evidence of human settlement in Romania is from the Neolithic period around 5,000 BC. Thracian tribes arrived in the first millennium BC, followed by Greeks, who settled along the Black Sea coast in the 7th century BC. The expanding Roman Empire conquered the region in the 1st century AD and named it Dacia.

Subsequent centuries saw Dacia gradually split into three principalities – Transylvania, Moldavia and Wallachia – which were ruled by feudal leaders throughout the Middle Ages. Neighbouring Hungary conquered and controlled Transylvania in the 10th century and by the 13th century the principalities and their neighbours fought together to fend

The spectacular snow-laden Făgăraş Mountains, Transylvania

◀ The popular medieval Bran Castle

off the relentless Ottoman Empire. As the Ottoman grip weakened in the 19th century, Moldavia and Wallachia united to form the independent state of Romania in 1862. Carol I was made king of a constitutional monarchy in 1866 and full independence was declared in 1877.

Fighting with the Allies in World War I brought the reward of unification with Transylvania in 1918, only to be lost again at the beginning of World War II, prompting Romania to take sides with Germany in the hope of regaining its territory. Romania changed sides towards the end of the war, ensuring the final return of Transylvania.

In 1947, the Communist Party, with the support of Soviet troops, forced King Michael I (r. 1927-30, 1940-7) to abdicate and declared Romania a People's Republic. Gheorghe Gheorghiu-Dej (1901–65) was the first leader of the single-party dictatorship; upon his death

Romanians protesting against Nicolae Ceaușescu, 1989

in 1965, he was succeeded by Nicolae Ceaușescu (1918–89). However, Ceaușescu indulged in several grand projects which consumed the nation's resources, leading to a massive economic crisis. In 1989, a series of violent demonstrations culminated in the resignation and subsequent execution of Ceaușescu. Since 1990, the country has been ruled by a succession of democratic governments.

In 2004, Romania joined NATO and on 1 January 2007, it became a member of the European Union.

Language and Culture

Romanian is the country's official language, although Hungarian is spoken by the large Hungarian minority in Transylvania.

The fascinating ethnographic museums scattered around the country provide an insight into Romania's rich cultural heritage.

It has a diverse history of rural traditions involving music, dance and ritual. These are still preserved in towns and villages where most people have practised Orthodox Christianity for centuries, while the large, modern cities are very much on a par with many of their European counterparts.

KEY DATES IN ROMANIAN HISTORY

AD 101 Romans conquer and colonize Dacia

1003 Hungarian king Stephen conquers Transylvania

1456–1476 Vlad the Impaler brutally resists invading Ottoman forces

1526 Transylvania wins independence from Hungary

1600 Michael the Brave unifies Wallachia, Moldavia and Transylvania for a single year

1683 Transylvania is absorbed into the Habsburg Empire

1878 Treaty of Berlin recognizes the principalities of Moldavia and Wallachia as the independent state of Romania

1918 Transylvania is unified with Romania following World War I

1941 Romania joins Germany to fight the Allies under the dictatorship of Marshall Ion Antonescu

1947 Communists force King Michael to abdicate; Romania is proclaimed a People's Republic

1989 Following a bloody revolution, Romania becomes a democratic republic

2004 Romania joins NATO

2007 Romania becomes a member of the EU

Exploring Romania

With plenty of historic sites, Bucharest offers a rich taste of Romanian culture. Just north of the capital, in the foothills of the mighty Carpathian Mountains, are the medieval town of Braşov and Bran Castle, while further north, Suceava makes a good base for the Bucovina Monasteries Tour. The delightful towns of Sighişoara and Sibiu lie to the southwest the Carpathians. An extensive yet slow network of railways connects many main towns and Bucharest has a bus service to most towns and villages across the country. The seaside resorts are best reached by bus or taxi from Constanţa.

The scenic tree-lined drive to Peleş Castle, southeastern Transylvania

Sights at a Glance

1. Bucharest pp546–54
2. Braşov
3. Bran Castle pp556–7
4. Peleş Castle pp558–9
5. Curtea de Argeş
6. Sibiu
7. Timişoara
8. Sighişoara pp562–3
9. Târgu Mureş
10. Cluj-Napoca pp564–5
11. Bucovina Monasteries Tour p566
12. Suceava
13. Constanţa
14. Danube Delta

Carved portal, Old Court Church, Bucharest

Key

— Motorway

— Major road

— Railway

– • – International border

0 kilometres   100

0 miles   100

For keys to symbols *see back flap*

❶ Bucharest

In the Middle Ages, Bucharest served as the summer residence of the Wallachian court, but it gained notoriety as the seat of the brutal Vlad Țepeș (The Impaler) between 1456 and 1476. After periodic attacks by the Austrians and Russians, the city was eventually conquered by the Ottomans in the late 16th century, as a result of which it has a strong Turkish flavour. Heavy bombing in World War II, followed by a devastating earthquake in 1977, caused severe damage, and gave President Nicolae Ceaușescu an excuse to demolish huge swathes of the historic Old Town. However, this bustling, cosmopolitan capital still boasts an abundance of parks, churches, lavish mansions and French-style architecture. Its numerous high-class restaurants and boutiques, combined with a vibrant nightlife, add to its appeal.

Sights at a Glance
1. *Palace of Parliament pp548–9*
2. National History Museum
3. Old Court Church
4. Stavropoleos Church
5. Russian Church
6. Communist Party Headquarters
7. Romanian Athenaeum
8. George Enescu Memorial Museum
9. Royal Palace and National Art Museum
10. Museum of Art Collections
11. Storck Museum
12. Museum of the Romanian Peasant
13. Herăstrău Park and Lake
14. Museum of Old West Art

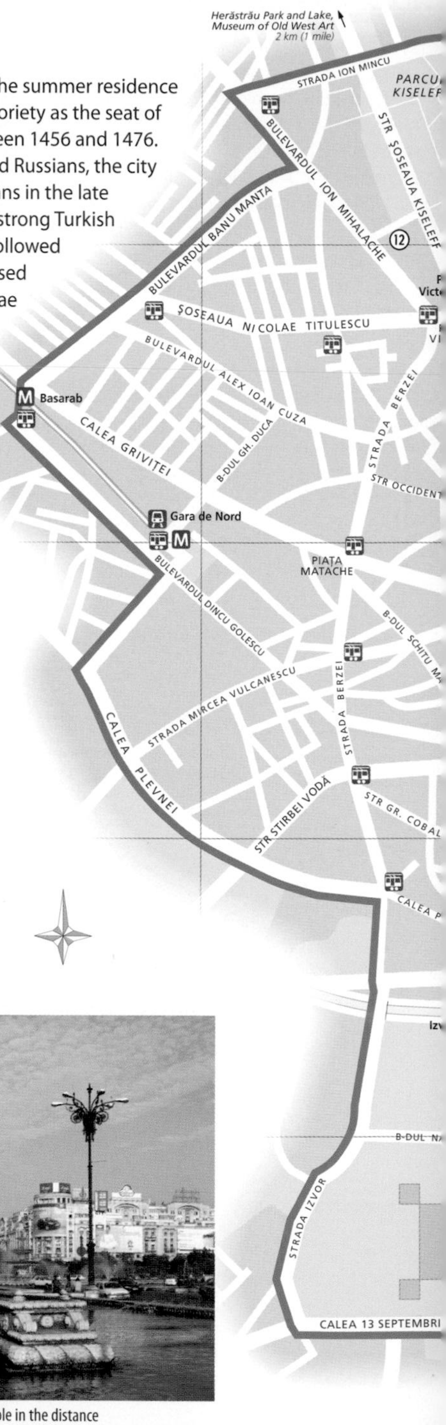

Herăstrău Park and Lake,
Museum of Old West Art
2 km (1 mile)

STRADA ION MINCU
PARCU
KISELEF
BULEVARDUL ION MIHALACHE
STR ȘOSEAUA KISELEF
BULEVARDUL BANU MANTA
Victe
VI
ȘOSEAUA NICOLAE TITULESCU
BULEVARDUL ALEX IOAN CUZA
STRADA BERZEI
M Basarab
CALEA GRIVIȚEI
B-DUL GH. DUCA
STR OCCIDENT
Gara de Nord **M**
PIAȚA
MATACHE
BULEVARDUL DINCU GOLESCU
B-DUL SCHITU M
STRADA BERZEI
CALEA
PLEVNEI
STRADA MIRCEA VULCĂNESCU
STR GR. COBAL
STR ȘTIRBEI VODĂ
CALEA P
Iz
B-DUL NA
STRADA IZVOR
CALEA 13 SEPTEMBRI

Fountains in Unity Square, with the Palace of Parliament visible in the distance

A   B   C

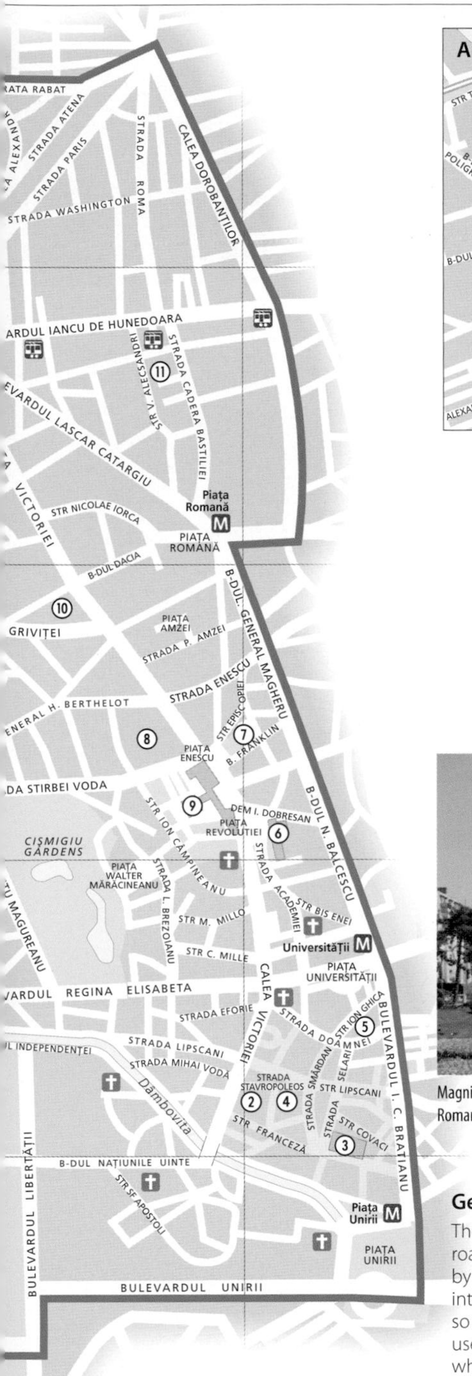

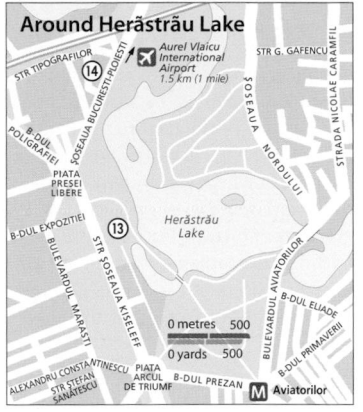

Around Herăstrău Lake

STR TIPOGRAFILOR

Aurel Vlaicu
International
Airport
1.5 km (1 mile)

STR G. GAFENCU

ȘOSEAUA BUCUREȘTI-PLOIEȘTI

⑭

B-DUL
POLIGRAFIEI

ȘOSEAUA NORDULUI

STRADA NICOLAE CARAMFIL

PIAȚA
PRESEI
LIBERE

B-DUL EXPOZIȚIEI

BULEVARDUL MARAȘTI

STR ȘOSEAUA KISELEFF

*Herăstrău
Lake*

⑬

BULEVARDUL AVIATORILOR

B-DUL ELIADE

B-DUL PRIMĂVERII

0 metres   500
0 yards   500

ALEXANDRU CONSTANTINESCU   PIAȚA
STR ȘTEFAN   ARCUL
SANĂTESCU   DE TRIUMF

B-DUL PREZAN

Ⓜ **Aviatorilor**

0 metres   500
0 yards   500

Key

◼ Major sight / Place of interest

◼ Pedestrian street

Magnificent Neo-Classical colonnades of the
Romanian Athenaeum

Getting Around

There is usually heavy traffic on the
roads during the day, making travelling
by car, taxi or bus tortuously slow. Sites of
interest are spread widely across the city,
so rather than walk it is a good idea to
use the comprehensive metro system,
which is clean, cheap and safe. However,
metro maps and signs can be confusing.
Taxis are cheap, but visitors should be
wary of being overcharged.

① Palace of Parliament
Palatul Parlamentului

Towering over the western end of Bulevardul Unirii, the Palace of Parliament is the second-largest administrative building in the world, next to the Pentagon. Covering an area of 33 ha (82 acres), this colossal structure has 15 floors, 5 of which are underground. President Nicolae Ceaușescu ordered its construction in 1983, clearing a large area of historic Bucharest to make way for the project. The Romanian government continued the project after his death and in 1997 moved the Chamber of Deputies there, followed by the Senate in 2005.

The grand chandelier in the Palace Theatre

★ **Alexandra Ioan Cuza Hall**
(Sala Alexandru Ioan Cuza)
One of the palace's many elegant rooms, the auditorium was intended for international meetings. The room opens on to a central balcony with sweeping views of Bulevardul Unirii.

KEY

① **Nicolae Bălcescu Hall**, an imposing conference hall, has pink Transylvanian marble pillars adorned with gilt Corinthian capitals.

② **The 100-m (328-ft) corridor**, the longest in the building, is separated by three sets of enormous sliding wooden doors.

③ **IIC Bratianu Hall**, a venue for international conferences, features floor-to-ceiling marble panelling.

④ **The 137-seat Senate**, Romania's Upper House, was moved here in 2005 from Palatul Senatului in Revolution Square.

⑤ **The National Museum of Contemporary Art** hosts temporary exhibitions of contemporary art from Romania and abroad in its opulent halls.

⑥ **The palace was constructed** exclusively from Romanian building materials, including locally quaried marble.

Nicolae Ceaușescu (1918–1989)

Romania's former president, Nicolae Ceaușescu, joined the Romanian Communist Party at the age of 14. He rose to ministerial level following the Communist takeover in 1947 and succeeded Gheorghe Gheorghiu-Dej as First Secretary of the Party in 1965.

During his leadership, he earned the respect of Western governments, but his megalomaniac vision of development caused immense suffering to the Romanian people. By the 1980s, poverty was rife and food and fuel shortages were crippling the country, giving rise to the Romanian Revolution of December 1989. On 25 December, Ceaușescu and his wife were tried by a military court and executed.

Ceaușescu at his last session of the party congress

★ Unification Hall (Unirii Hall)
The largest room in the building, this hall has walls 15 m (49 ft) high, ornate marble columns and an immense glass ceiling. The two marble panels at either end of the room were intended to contain portraits of Nicolae and his wife Elena.

VISITORS' CHECKLIST

Practical Information
Calea 13 Septembrie 1.
Map C5. **i** (021) 311 3611.
Open 10am–4pm daily. 🖼 📷
🖥 🏛 **W** **cdep.ro** The National
Museum of Contemporary Art:
Tel (021) 318 9137.
Open 10am–6pm Wed–Sun.
📷 **W** **mnac.ro**

Transport
🚌 136, 385.

★ Palace Theatre
(Sala CA Rosetti)
Marble pillars, ornate balconies and a gigantic central chandelier adorn this circular theatre. However, it has only been used for meetings because it lacks a backstage area.

Assembly Hall (Camera Deputaților)
Topped by a stunning glass dome, the Assembly Hall has, since 1997, been home to the 332-seat Chamber of Deputies, Romania's Lower House.

② National History Museum
Muzeul Naţional de Istorie

Calea Victoriei 12. **Map** E4. **Tel** (021) 315 8207. 336, 601. **Open** Apr–Oct: 10am–6pm Wed–Sun; Nov–Mar: 9am–5pm Wed–Sun. **mnir.ro**

Housed in a late 19th-century Neo-Classical building that served as the headquarters of the Romanian Postal Service until 1970, the eclectic National History Museum offers a great introduction to Romania's past. The museum's well-presented exhibitions are spread over 60 rooms. The central hall holds an enormous replica of the original Trajan's Column in Italy. A basement vault houses Romania's National Treasury, with jewellery and gold dating from the 14th century BC. The highlights of this collection are the beautiful gold earrings from the Hellenistic period (3rd–4th century BC) and the legendary Pietroasele Treasure, also known as The Hen and her Golden Brood, discovered by peasants in the Buzău region in 1837. The treasure is thought to have belonged to the Goths. Its 12 surviving pieces include brooches inlaid with semi-precious stones, a sacrificial dish engraved with images of gods, a 12-sided ceremonial goblet and several intricate necklaces.

Ornamental brickwork on the 16th-century Old Court Church

③ Old Court Church
Biserica Curtea Veche

Str Franceza 25–31. **Map** E4. 116. **Open** daily.

The lovely Old Court Church, with its striped brick tower and ornamental niches, is one of Bucharest's oldest churches. Founded in the 16th century, it has undergone several renovations following fires and earthquakes, but has retained its original design. It was here that the Wallachian princes were crowned between the 16th and the 19th centuries. The interior is blackened from years of candle smoke, however, parts of the superb murals and frescoes are still visible.

④ Stavropoleos Church
Biserica Stavropoleos

Str Stavropoleos 4. **Map** E4. **Tel** (021) 313 4747. 336, 601. **Open** daily. **stavropoleos.ro**

Built in 1724 for the first Phanariot ruler, Nicolae Mavrocordat, this church has remained intact ever since, despite renovation work carried out in the 20th century. Four columns support the brilliant Byzantine-style arched porch and a series of framed icons adorn the church's façade. The interior, dominated by an 18th-century gilt iconostasis, features detailed biblical scenes from floor to ceiling.

Next door is a small monastery complex, which was added to the church in the early 20th century and accommodates an active community of nuns today. The nuns maintain a valuable library of Byzantine manuscripts and a museum collection of icons and frescoes. Some of these priceless frescoes were rescued from the numerous churches that were torn down by Communist leader Nicolae Ceauşescu to make way for his grandiose scheme for the rebuilding of Bucharest's centre.

Byzantine motifs and intricate iconography in Stavropoleos Church

Colourful onion domes of the Russian Church

⑤ Russian Church
Biserica Rusă

Str Ion Ghica 9. **Map** E4. 📧 336, 601. **Open** daily.

The imposing Russian Church, with its seven onion domes, has stood opposite Bucharest University since 1909 when it was commissioned by Russian Tsar Nicholas II to serve the Russian Embassy's staff. Its splendid yellow brick façade is decorated with floral motifs and mosaics featuring images of saints. Intricate details such as fish head guttering add to its appeal. A portrait of St Nicholas stands over the entrance. Entered through a narrow passage, the church's interior is lit by candles, which have blackened the murals over the years. In 1992, the church became the official chapel of the academic community, but has remained open to visitors.

⑥ Communist Party Headquarters
Partidul Comunist Român

Piața Revolutiei. **Map** E3. 📧 300.

Closely associated with the downfall of Nicolae Ceaușescu, the General Secretary of the Communist Party, Revolution Square (Piața Revolutiei) is overlooked by buildings which once housed Romania's Communist Party Headquarters. It was from the first floor

balcony of this block that Ceaușescu gave his last speech to a gathering of 80,000 people on 21 December 1989, just a few days after thousands were killed by police in Timișoara *(see p561)*. Surprised by shouts of "murderer" and Timișoara", the dictator famously faltered on live television. The crowd seized on his weakness and tried to storm the building. Ceaușescu's minister of defence, General Vasile Milea, was executed on the spot for refusing to order his troops to open fire on the protestors. Ceaușescu himself fled Bucharest in a helicopter from the roof of the building but was executed shortly thereafter.

Today, a huge marble needle stands opposite the building and forms the centrepiece of a memorial to the thousands killed during the revolution. The only other reminder of the event is the bullet-scarred façade of a building to the left of the square, which now houses government offices.

⑦ Romanian Athenaeum
Ateneul Român

Benjamin Franklin 1–3. **Map** E3. **Tel** (021) 315 0024. 📧 131, 182, 301, 330. **Open** for concerts. Box office: 2–4pm daily. 🅿️

Designed by French architect Albert Galleron and completed in 1888 with the help of public

Façade of the historic Communist Party Headquarters

donations, the impressive Romanian Athenaeum is home to the George Enescu Philharmonic Orchestra. The concert hall is encircled by a 3-m (10-ft) high fresco depicting glorious moments in Romania's history. The auditorium, with plush red velvet chairs beneath a lavish dome featuring stucco sculptures of mythological creatures, can seat up to 600 people.

Detail in the Neo-Classical colonnade of the Roman Athenaeum

⑧ George Enescu Memorial Museum
Muzeul Național George Enescu

141 Calea Victoriei. **Map** D3. **Tel** (021) 318 1450. **Open** 10am–5pm Tue–Sun. 🅿️ 🌐 georgeenescu.ro

The magnificent 20th-century Cantacuzino Palace was the one-time residence of Romania's most illustrious composer, conductor and musician, George Enescu. Enescu resided here briefly after his marriage to Princess Maria Cantacuzino in 1939, but the opulent Baroque palace was too much for him and he chose to live with his wife in the servants' quarters behind the building instead. After his death in 1955, the palace became the George Enescu Memorial Museum. Three of its stunning rooms feature an array of musical scores, manuscripts, photographs and memorabilia related to the musician's life and works.

⑨ Royal Palace and National Art Museum

Palatul Regal şi Muzeul Naţional de Arta

Calea Victoriei 49–53. **Map** D3.
Tel (021) 313 3030. 🚌 178. **Open**
May–Sep: 11am–7pm Wed–Sun; Oct–
Apr: 10am–6pm Wed–Sun. 🅿️ 📷 📱
🌐 mnar.arts.ro

An imperial residence since the mid-19th century, the Royal Palace has undergone several renovations during its lifetime. King Carol I *(see p558)* was responsible for much of the current layout, redesigned in 1906. Further reconstruction took place after a catastrophic fire in 1926 and heavy bombing in World War II. Its location next to Revolution Square led to further damage from gunfire in December 1989.

Housed in the north wing of the palace, the National Art Museum was opened in 1950 to house the royal family's art collection. It closed in 1989 following the revolution when as many as 1,000 artworks were damaged, but reopened after complete renovation. The Gallery of Romanian Art includes sculptures by world-renowned sculptor Constantin Brâncuşi and paintings by artist Nicolae Grigorescu. The European Art Gallery, spread over 15 rooms, boasts works by masters such as Rubens, Rembrandt, El Greco, Tintoretto and Monet.

Visitors at the Royal Palace and National Art Museum

Transylvanian biblical icons on stained glass, Museum of Art Collections

⑩ Museum of Art Collections

Muzeul Colecţiilor de Arta

Calea Victoriei 111. **Map** D3. **Tel** (021)
212 9641. 🚌 **Open** May–Sep:
11am–7pm Wed–Sun; Oct–Apr:
10am–6pm Wed–Sun. 🅿️

Housed in a Neo-Classical mansion with a surprisingly unassuming interior, the Museum of Art Collections has an intriguing variety of exhibits, of which the dazzling 17th-century gilt icon of Jesus Christ is the undisputed highlight. An impressive range of Romanian artwork by masters such as Nicolae Grigorescu, Ştefan Luchian and Nicolae Tonitza occupies the ground floor. On the first floor, a display of traditional glass Transylvanian icons, remarkable for their bright colours and simplicity, can be seen alongside the Oriental collection, comprising 15th-century Chinese porcelain, 19th-century Japanese crockery, statues and a pretty wooden cupboard inlaid with mother-of-pearl, as well as Iranian ceramics and Turkish rugs. The same floor has a selection of antique European treasures which includes Austrian silverware, colourful Bohemian crystal and

Carpet, Museum of Art Collections

19th-century French furniture and tapestries.

⑪ Storck Museum

Muzeul de Arta Frederic Storck şi Cecilia Cutescu-Storck

Str V Alecsandri 16. **Map** D2. 🚌
Open 9am–5pm Tue–Sun. 🅿️

Built in 1913 by sculptor and architect Frederick Storck, this museum contains numerous works of art created or collected by Storck and his wife Cecilia. Delightful murals with floral and feminine motifs cover the walls of the central rooms, which took Cecilia four years to paint. Other pictures by Cecilia include seascapes painted at the family villa in Balchik (now in Bulgaria), portraits and still lifes. Particularly impressive among Storck's sculptures, which are exhibited next to his wife's work, are the bronze pieces inspired by Rodin. Several rooms are furnished with lovely ceramic stoves decorated with floral and bird motifs painted by Karl Storck, Frederick's father, who was the first Romanian teacher of sculpture in the Fine Arts Academy of Bucharest. There is also a small exhibition of

For hotels and restaurants see p572 and p573

medieval religious objects collected during the couple's travels.

⑫ Museum of the Romanian Peasant
Muzeul Țăranului Roman

Str Șoseaua Kiseleff 3. **Map** C1.
Tel (021) 317 9661. 🚌 300.
Open 10am–6pm Tue–Sun. 🎫
🖥 muzeultaranuluiroman.ro

Housed in a red-brick edifice built in 1906, the Museum of the Romanian Peasant was intended as a celebration of the country's traditions at a time when industrialization was beginning to alter the rural face of Romania. With around 100,000 exhibits, the collection covers the regions of Romania. It includes mock-ups of craftsmen's workshops, a 19th-century classroom and numerous colourful traditional costumes. The highlight, however, is an enormous wooden 18th-century windmill, which has been reconstructed on the ground floor alongside a massive spiked *dărstă* (carding comb), which was used to prepare wool for spinning. A room at the back contains a replica of an Orthodox church, hung with icons dating back to the 17th century.

The Communism Exhibition, which has paintings and memorabilia relating to Romania's former Communist leaders, is

Replica of a typical Romanian house at the Village Museum, Herăstrău Park

worth a visit. Also of interest are the handmade wooden chairs collected from villages around the country, displayed on the first floor.

⑬ Herăstrău Park and Lake
Parcul Herăstrău

Str Kiseleff 32. **Map** F1. 🚌 Village Museum: **Tel** (021) 317 9110.
Open 9am–7pm (till 5pm Mon).
🎫 🖥 muzeul-satului.ro

Bucharest's largest park was created in the 1930s under King Carol II after several marshes in the area were drained. Located to the north of the city, the park is popular today with walkers, cyclists, roller-bladers and joggers. Regular boat trips traverse the lake and smaller boats are available for individual hire.

Costume display, Museum of the Romanian Peasant

Herăstrău is also home to one of Europe's oldest museum parks, the **Village Museum**. Inaugurated in 1936, it comprises a wonderful collection of reconstructed rural dwellings and work-shops. The buildings represent architectural styles from all over the country and range from 19th-century wood-tiled houses to wooden windmills and thatched Transylvanian cottages with beautifully painted window frames. There is even a half-buried house, designed to escape

the notice of invading tribes. However, the highlights of the museum are the oak houses from Maramureş county, which have beautifully carved hunting and animal scenes on their gateways. The museum shop stocks an excellent range of souvenirs.

⑭ Museum of Old West Art
Muzeul de Arta Veche Apuseana

Str Dr Minovici 3. **Map** F1.
Tel (021) 665 7334. 🚌
Closed for renovations. 🎫

This charming red-brick Tudor-style house was built in the 1930s for Dumitru Minovici, who made his fortune in the oil industry and became an avid art collector. The house contains a collection of European art dating back to the 16th century and is furnished with antiques and Swiss stained-glass windows.

The grand building of the Museum of the Romanian Peasant

Passenger boat cruising on the calm waters of Herăstrău Lake

Hiking in the Făgăraş Mountains

Part of the Carpathian Mountains, the beautiful Făgăraş range offers some of Romania's most thrilling hiking routes, reaching heights of up to 2,544 m (8,346 ft). A combination of incredible views, glacial lakes, waterfalls, spruce forests, wildlife and hospitable shepherds ensures that a trip here is an unforgettable experience. However, the mountains are notorious for abrupt changes in weather, so inexperienced hikers are advised to join a group or hire a local guide. Severe winters restrict the hiking season to a few months between July and October.

Dianthus alpinus, commonly known as Alpine pinks, bloom in late spring. They can be found growing above 2,000 m (6,561 ft) in the Făgăraş Alpine regions.

Glacial lakes, many at altitudes above 2,000 m (6,561 ft), are scattered throughout the mountains. Balea is the highest at 2,034 m (6,673 ft), and offers panoramic views as well as a lakeside mountain hut.

Mountain huts, or cabanas, are available on the northern side of the Făgăraş ridge, offering crackling log fires, dormitory beds and simple food. However, hikers intending to climb further south will need to carry camping equipment.

Transfăgărăşan, Romania's highest road, crosses the Făgăraş Mountains and connects the regions of Transylvania and Wallachia as well as the towns of Sibiu and Piteşti. The road has five tunnels; the longest is 884 m (2,900 ft).

Moldoveanu is Romania's highest peak at 2,544 m (8,346 ft). The country boasts a total of eight peaks over 2,500 m (8,202 ft).

Hiking routes in this region are well marked and easy to follow. However, all hikers should carry essential items such as maps, a compass, a first-aid kit, adequate food and water supplies, waterproofs and strong walking boots.

❷ Braşov

168 km (104 miles) N of Bucharest.
🏛 253,200. 🚗 🚌 ℹ Piaţa Sfatului,
(0268) 419 078. 🆆 **ghid-brasov.ro**

Founded by German settlers in the 13th century, Braşov quickly grew into one of the region's leading defensive and commercial centres, thanks to its position on the southwestern border of Transylvania. Today, this city is one of the most-visited places in Romania.

Facing the Main Square (Piaţa Sfatului) and built into a line of Baroque buildings is the façade of the intriguing 19th-century **Orthodox Cathedral**. Built in Byzantine style, the church is noteworthy for its beautiful frescoes. In the centre of the square stands the 15th-century Town Hall, which now houses the **History Museum**. It has an excellent collection of archaeological, medieval and modern history exhibits. Dominating the southwestern corner of the square is Transylvania's largest Gothic building, the **Black Church**, built in the 14th century. Originally named St Mary's, it came to be known as the Black Church after a fire in 1689 blackened its walls. The church contains Romania's heaviest bell, weighing 6.3 tonnes (6.9 tons) as well as its biggest organ.

Two streets south of the Black Church is the imposing Viennese and Art Nouveau style **Temple Synagogue**, built in 1899. In the north of the city is the **Art and Ethnographic Museum**,

View of the Gothic Black Church and Tampa Hill, Braşov

displaying traditional costumes from the region and some antique European and Oriental ceramics. This is also the place to see Romania's largest collection of paintings by Nicolae Grigorescu, one of the forefathers of modern Romanian art.

Of the city's ancient fortifications, the most striking is the southeastern Ekaterina Gate, with a pointed central tower surrounded by four corner watch towers. For superb views of Braşov, a cable car ascends to the summit of the forested 995-m (3,264-ft) high Tampa Hill.

🔼 **Orthodox Cathedral**
Piaţa Sfatului 3.
Open 9am–6pm.

🏛 **History Museum**
Piaţa Sfatului.
Open 10am–6pm Tue–Sun.
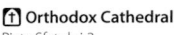

🔼 **Black Church**
Curtea Johannes Honterus 2.
Open 10am–7pm Mon–Sat, noon–7pm Sun (Winter: 10am–3pm Mon–Sat, noon–3pm Sun). 🔲

✡ **Temple Synagogue**
Str Poarta Schei 27.
Open 9am–4pm Mon–Fri.

🏛 **Art and Ethnographic Museum**
B-dul Eroilor 21. **Open** 10am–6pm Tue–Sun (9am–5pm in winter). 🔲
🆆 **muzeulartabv.ro**

❸ Bran Castle

See pp556–7.

❹ Peleş Castle

See pp558–9.

❺ Curtea de Argeş

150 km (93 miles) NW of Bucharest.
🏛 33,000. 🚗 🚌

The small town of Curtea de Argeş began as the 13th-century capital of Argeş county

The Episcopal Church, Curtea de Argeş

and later became the capital of Wallachia. Its most famous building is the **Episcopal Church**, built in 1512 on a 2-m (7-ft) high stone platform within the grounds of Curtea de Argeş Monastery. Its elaborate design features two domes and a pair of cupolas with slanting narrow windows set atop a box-like building adorned with tiers of niches and arabesque motifs.

According to legend, the chief architect, Manole, was forced to entomb his wife in the walls of the church to keep the building from collapsing; popular belief at the time held that ghosts were required to keep buildings from falling down. Upon completion of the building, the church's patron, Radu Negru, left Manole and his fellow workers stranded on the roof to ensure they never built a greater church. The whole group fell to their death attempting to fly using wooden wings made from the roofing shingles.

Not far from the town centre and to the north is one of Wallachia's oldest churches. Built in the 14th century, the **Princely Church** is located within the 13th-century complex of the Court de Argeş. Its original frescoes have been restored.

🔼 **Episcopal Church**
B-dul Basarabilor. **Open** summer: 8am–8pm daily; winter: 8am–5pm.

🔼 **Princely Church**
Court de Argeş. **Open** 8am–6pm daily.

For hotels and restaurants see p572 and p573

❸ Bran Castle

Castelul Bran

Perched on a rocky bluff, Bran Castle was built in the 13th century and first used as a defence against the Ottomans. Although the ruler of Wallachia, Vlad Țepeș, better known as Dracula, never lived here, it is believed that he was briefly imprisoned here by the Hungarians. In more recent times, the castle was the favourite summer residence of Queen Marie (granddaughter of Queen Victoria of England), who refurbished the entire building and had electricity installed. Known today as Dracula's Castle, it is now a museum dedicated to the history of the Romanian Royal Family.

Queen Marie's Music Saloon and Library
Dark wooden floors and rustic furniture create an inviting atmosphere in this attic room. The largest room in the castle, it became Queen Marie's music room and housed her German harmonium.

The Inner Yard Well
Converted into an elevator in 1921, this 60-m (197-ft) deep well led to a passage that opened out into a park in the valley.

KEY

① **The castle's highest tower** was built in the early 20th century as a decorative feature.

② **The dining hall** was used by Queen Marie to entertain royal guests. The massive wooden dining table is ornately carved with mythical images.

★ **Chapel of Prince Mircea**
This chapel is dedicated to Queen Marie's first child, who died of typhus in 1916 at the age of three. The centrepiece is a dazzling gilt iconostasis brought from Mount Athos in Greece.

For hotels and restaurants see p572 and p573

★ Gothic Room

Distinctly Gothic in style, this vaulted room is furnished with sculptures and furniture dating back to the 14th century. Among these is the 16th-century wooden sculpture of St Anne.

VISITORS' CHECKLIST

Practical Information
195 km (121 miles) NW of Bucharest.
Tel (0268) 237 700.
Open Check website for timings.
W bran-castle.com

Transport
from Braşov.

★ Queen Marie's Bedroom

Decorated in Art Nouveau style, the queen's bedroom contains several pieces of furniture she commissioned herself, including a rosewood Italian Baroque bed and an armchair adorned with carved vultures.

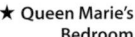

Secret Passages

Some of the castle's 60 rooms are connected by a network of underground passages, which were used either for hasty evacuations or to bring in food supplies in times of siege.

Râşnov Fortress

Situated halfway between the towns of Braşov and Bran, Râşnov Fortress overlooks the small town of Râşnov from a hilltop. Founded in the 13th century by Teutonic knights,

Râşnov Fortress sitting on a hilltop

the fortress served as a refuge for the people of Râşnov during times of seige. The central courtyard contains a 143-m (469-ft) deep well, dug to supply drinking water to the inhabitants. A museum within the complex displays armour and various finds uncovered during excavations, among them a skeleton now encased beneath a glass floor.

❹ Peleş Castle

Castelul Peleş

An extravagant palace built by King Carol I to serve as his summer residence, Peleş Castle is among the most impressive palaces in Europe. Built between 1873 and 1883 and redesigned in 1914, the castle stands in a vast forested park tucked away among the low hills of the Carpathian countryside. The German Neo-Renaissance façade recalls a fairy tale castle with its sharp Gothic profile and decorative woodwork. The interior design of its 170 rooms was overseen by King Carol I's wife Elisabeth and features lavish furnishings, ornate woodcarvings and numerous artworks. One of the last royal palaces to have been built in Europe, it was the first to be supplied with electricity, central heating and a lift.

Statue of King Carol I
A towering statue of King Carol I, by Italian sculptor Raffaello Romanelli, overlooks the park.

KEY

① **The walls of the French Passage** are adorned with two valuable early 20th-century tapestries featuring Cleopatra and Marc Antony.

② **The Renaissance-style dining room** contains an exquisite set of silverware and Rosenthal crockery. Its stained-glass windows are framed by intricately carved columns of walnut and ash.

③ **The abundance of carved woodwork** on the building is typical of the German Neo-Renaissance style.

④ **The Large Armory Hall** has a fascinating collection of over 3,500 items dating back to the 15th century, including weapons from Japan, Persia, India and Turkey.

⑤ **King Carol's office** is lined with walnut panelling and portraits of the royal family.

⑥ **The Music Room** was occasionally used for literary evenings; its teak furniture was a gift from the Maharajah of Kapurthala.

★ **Florentine Hall**
The bright Murano glass chandeliers and Palanazzo marble fireplace provide a wonderful contrast to the dark ebony wall cabinets. Venetian mirrors reflect the ceiling paintings, which are reproductions of works by the Flemish artists van Eyck and Rubens.

★ Theatre Room
Originally designed as a theatre, this room was turned into a cinema in 1906. The highlight is the Art Nouveau wall frieze painted by Gustav Klimt in 1894 and elegantly framed with cream and gilt mouldings.

VISITORS' CHECKLIST

Practical Information
129 km (80 miles) NW of Bucharest. **Tel** (0244) 311 496.
Open summer: 11am–5pm Tue, 9am–5pm Wed–Sun; winter: 11am–5pm Wed, 9am–5pm Thu–Sun.  **W** visit.peles.ro

Transport
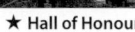 from Bran.

★ Hall of Honour
The castle's main entrance incorporates a striking three-storey display of Viennese walnut carvings that decorate the spiral staircase and arched balconies overlooking the Reception Hall. Light floods into the hall from the 16-m (52-ft) high sliding glass roof.

Library
Among the king's collection of over 10,000 books are 40 novels written by Queen Elisabeth under the pseudonym Carmen Sylva. One of the beautifully carved book cases conceals a secret passage leading to the royal bedroom.

❻ Sibiu

273 km (170 miles) NW of Bucharest.
🏠 154,000. ✈ 🚌 🚐 ℹ Str S.
Brukental 2, (0269) 208 913.
🌐 sibiu.ro

Founded in the 1190s, Sibiu is one of Romania's most charming cities. Its historic centre is filled with medieval, steep-roofed houses with attic windows and the narrow streets lead into wide open squares surrounded by the colourful façades of renovated mansions and churches.

The first recorded mention of the city dates back to the 12th century, when the region received two waves of Saxon settlers who had obtained privileges from the Hungarian rulers controlling Transylvania at the time. In 1241, invading Tatars prompted Sibiu's residents to raise fortifications. Successive centuries saw the city walls enlarged and strengthened, eventually transforming it into an impenetrable citadel. In the 15th century, Sibiu's craftsmen formed some of Europe's first guilds and the city developed into a prosperous trading centre.

In recent years, the Old Town has benefited enormously from European Union (EU) funding, and Sibiu served as European Capital of Culture in 2007. Dominating the vast Large Square (Piaţa Mare) is an imposing Baroque palace built for Samuel von Brukenthal,

Houses and shops lining a street in Sibiu

who governed Transylvania between 1774 and 1787. The grand façade bears Brukenthal's medieval coat of arms above the ornate entrance. The interior, with plush halls, stucco ceilings and embossed wallpaper, now houses Romania's oldest museum – the **National Brukenthal Museum**. This holds Transylvania's finest art collection as well as Romanian and Western works, including some by Romanian artists such as Nicolae Grigorescu *(see p552)*, Theodor Pallady and the Abstractionist Hans Mattis

Teutsch. The palace library holds over 280,000 volumes as well as a priceless collection of manuscripts.

Tiles, Evangelical Cathedral

The nearby **History Museum** is housed in an elegant 15th-century Gothic building that served as Sibiu's Town Hall for 500 years until 1948. The collection was moved here from the Brukenthal Palace in 1984 after the Town Hall's restoration. A secluded gateway leads into its cobbled courtyard overlooked by balconies festooned with colourful flowers. The ancient doors at the museum entrance open on to a surprisingly modern interior with original vaulted ceilings. Smartly lit glass cases display an absorbing collection of old coins, medieval weaponry

and archaeological finds. Just a few streets away on Huet Square (Piaţa Huet) is the five-towered **Evangelical Cathedral**, whose exquisitely tiled spire can be seen from all over town. Constructed over an original 14th-century Roman church, the cathedral has a regal Gothic interior and contains the tombs of local nobles.

Situated in a dense forest just outside Sibiu is the **Museum of Traditional Folk Civilization**, Romania's largest outdoor museum. Over 300 replicas of traditional dwellings are scattered throughout the 101-ha (250-acre) complex, which can be explored either on foot or in the comfort of a horse-drawn carriage. Buildings include Dutch-style windmills, farmhouses, wooden churches and traditional inns.

🏛 **National Brukenthal Museum**
Piaţa Mare 4-5. **Tel** (269) 217 691.
Open 10am–6pm Tue–Sun (Wed–Sun in winter). 🔲 ✅ 📷
🌐 brukenthalmuseum.ro

🏛 **History Museum**
Str Mitropoliei nr 2. **Tel** (269) 218 143.
Open 10am–6pm Wed–Sun. 📷
🌐 brukenthalmuseum.ro

⛪ **Evangelical Cathedral**
Piaţa Huet 1. **Open** 9am–5pm Mon–Sat, 11am–5pm Sun.

🏛 **Museum of Traditional Folk Civilization**
Calea Rasinari. **Tel** (0269) 242 599.
Open 10am–6pm (Winter: 9am–5pm). 🌐 muzeulastra.ro

The cobbled courtyard of the National Brukenthal Museum, Sibiu

For hotels and restaurants see p572 and p573

❼ Timişoara

347 km (216 miles) NW of Bucharest.
🏛 310,000. 🚆 🚌 ℹ️ Str Alba Iulia
2, (0256) 437 973.

Located close to the border of
Serbia and Hungary, Timişoara
claims to have been the first city
in Europe to introduce electric
street lighting, the first in
Romania to have a public water
supply and one of the first in
the world to have had horse-
drawn trams.

In the 14th century, Timişoara
was a part of Hungary and the
heavily fortified town became a
focal point of resistance against
invading Ottoman forces. The
Ottomans conquered it in 1551
and it remained a military
stronghold until the Habsburg
Empire forced them out in 1716.
The town was then completely
rebuilt and the historic centre
owes much of its present-day
appearance to its Austrian conquerors. When Timişoara finally
became part
of Romania in
1920, it was still
dominated by ethnic
Hungarians and
Germans, but most of
them left following the
end of World War II.
Today, Timişoara has a
majority population of ethnic
Romanians and is venerated as
the city that sparked events
leading to the overthrow of
Nicolae Ceauşescu in December
1989 *(see p548)*.

Victory Square (Piaţa
Victoriei), scene of the tragic
events that saw police open fire
on peaceful protesters in 1989,
is now the city's thriving hub.

The Baroque Roman Catholic Cathedral on Unity Square, Timişoara

Nearby is its best museum,
the **Banat Museum**, which has
excellent regional, historical,
archaeological and natural
history exhibitions. Founded
in 1872, it has been located in
Hunyadi Castle (Castelul Huniade)
since 1948. This Venetian-style
castle was constructed in the
15th century and is thought to
be Timişoara's oldest building.
To the south of Victory Square
is the extravagant 20th-century
Orthodox Cathedral,
with 11 towers
of differing sizes,
each covered with
patterned mosaic
tiles. The striped brick-
work is reminiscent of
both Byzantine and
Moldavian church
architecture. A memorial to the
victims of 1989 stands in front
to mark the protests that took
place in and around the church.

To the north of the square
is **Unity Square** (Piaţa Unirii),
an expansive space lined with
elaborate Austro-Hungarian
mansions. In the 18th century,
it was used as a major commercial and ceremonial site. Two

Detail, Banat
Museum

impressive Baroque cathedrals,
both constructed in the late
18th century, stand here; to
the west is the grand Serbian
Orthodox Cathedral; to the
east the Roman Catholic
Cathedral. Located in another
18th-century building, just
off Unity Square, is the
**Memorial Museum of the
1989 Revolution** which documents events around the
uprising with original video
footage, photographs, military
uniforms and newspapers.
The adjoining chapel has
been dedicated to
the revolution.

🏛 **Banat Museum**
Piaţa Huniade 1,
Castelul Huniazilor. **Tel** (0256) 491 339.
Open 10am–4pm Mon–Sat.
📷 🏠 🔲 muzeulbanatului.ro

⛪ **Orthodox Cathedral**
Piaţa Victoriei. **Open** daily.

🏛 **Memorial Museum of the
1989 Revolution**
Str Emanuil Ungureanu 8.
Tel (0256) 294 936.
Open 9am–5pm daily.

The 1989 Revolution

Ecstatic crowds after the
overthrow of the regime

In December 1989, Romania's
Communist regime was toppled by
the most violent revolution in Eastern
Europe at the time. The catalyst was a
minor protest against the eviction of
an ethnic Hungarian anti-Ceauşescu
priest, László Tőkés, on 16 December.
Around 1,000 lives were lost when
police opened fire on demonstrators
and the military was called to suppress
the unrest. It culminated with the execution of Ceauşescu on 25 December.

The 11-spired Orthodox Cathedral near
Victory Square, Timişoara

❽ Sighişoara

Perched high on a hill above the Târnava Mare river, Sighişoara was founded in the 12th century by German merchants and craftsmen who had been invited by the king of Hungary to settle in the region and defend its borders. The settlement grew into a major Transylvanian town but was almost abandoned following a devastating fire in 1676. Most of the buildings today date from the town's subsequent rebuild. The Old Town is one of Europe's few remaining inhabited medieval citadels, and is now a UNESCO World Heritage Site. Sentenced around it are a number of towers, many of which belonged to the town guilds; of the 14 towers originally built, 9 have survived. Clustered behind the fortified walls is an ensemble of 17th-century buildings whose fading façades enhance the citadel's period charm.

The Gothic Venetian House, at the corner of Museum Square

Symbolic wooden figures on the 13th-century Clock Tower

🏛 Clock Tower

Piaţa Muzeului 1. **Tel** (265) 771 108. **Open** 9am–4pm Tue–Sun.

Built over the main gate in the 13th century, the Clock Tower (Turnul cu Ceas) is the dominant feature of the citadel. Designed as a defensive structure, its thick lower stone walls made it difficult for enemies to attack. It housed the town council offices until 1550. The fifth and sixth floors, as well as the clock, were added at the beginning of the 17th century. At midnight every day one of seven wooden figures, symbolizing day and night, emerges from the clock to face the town. The tower was destroyed by the Great Fire of 1676 and rebuilt in subsequent years. Today, it is occupied by the History Museum and a small Museum of Torture, which includes among its exhibits a ladder that was used to roast people alive.

🏛 Monastery Church

Piaţa Muzeului. **Open** daily.

Originally part of a 13th-century Dominican monastery, this Gothic church (Biserica Manastirii Dominicane) has been Lutheran since 1556. Its present appearance dates back to the late 17th century, when it was rebuilt following the Great Fire; the Baroque organ was installed in 1680. Its interior walls are decorated with 300-year-old Anatolian rugs.

🏛 Vlad Dracul's House

Str Cositorarilor 5. **Tel** (265) 771 596. **Open** 10am–3:30pm Tue–Sun. 🍴 10am–11pm daily.

Casa Vlad Dracul (Vlad Dracula's House) is said to be the birthplace of Vlad Tepes, the Wallachian ruler who was notorious for his methods of punishment and an inspiration for Dracula. Some of the murals inside the house, discovered during renovations, depict a figure bearing some resemblance to the infamous ruler.

The ground floor is now an interesting medieval-themed restaurant while the first floor is home to the Museum of Weapons, which is closed on Mondays.

Sign outside Dracul's House

🏛 Venetian House

Piaţa Muzeului.

Located on the corner of Museum Square (Piaţa Muzeului), the Venetian House (Casa Venetian) was once a mayoral residence. Built in the 16th century, it is named for its Venetian Gothic stone window frames, which were added during renovations in the 19th century. Today, the house is used by the German Evangelical parish and the German Democratic Forum, founded in 1989, which represent the town's remaining German residents.

Sighişoara Monastery Church seen across a cluster of rooftops

⊞ Shoemakers' Tower

Str Manastirii.

At the northernmost point of the citadel stands the 16-m (52-ft) high Shoemakers' Tower (Turnul Cizmarilor), built in 1594. The unusual hexagonal structure incorporates a watchtower over the Old Town. There was once an identical watchtower on the tower's opposite side, from where guards could survey the surrounding area. Although it retains much of its original appearance, the tower's main entrance and windows have been modified in recent years to accommodate a radio station and a newspaper office.

Shoemakers' Tower, offering a vantage point over the Old Town

⊞ Tailors' Tower

Str Manastirii.

This twin-arched 14th-century tower (Turnul Croitorilor) is one of three entrances to the citadel. The upper part of the tower was destroyed in the 1676 fire but was restored in 1935. Known as the Rear Gate, it was once defended by massive wooden doors secured with iron bars, and a small army of 30 tailors belonging to Sighişoara's oldest guild.

⊞ Furriers' Tower

Str Manastirii.

The 15th-century Furriers' Tower (Turnul Cojocarilor) is one of the smallest of the nine surviving towers. It is linked to the Butchers' Tower by an ancient gateway through which shepherds once took cattle out to pasture.

⬆ Church on the Hill

Str Scolii. **Open** 10am–6pm daily. 🖼
Reached by a 400-year-old covered wooden staircase, the striking 14th-century Gothic Church on the Hill (Biserica din Deal) stands high above the citadel. Initially a Catholic church, it has since become part of the German Evangelical parish. During renovations between 1992 and 2003, its plain white façade was rebuilt and some

Distinctive arches of the 14th-century Tailor's Tower

of the original interior murals were discovered. The church's centrepiece is the 16th-century altarpiece of St Martin, which depicts scenes from the saint's life. It originally belonged to the Monastery Church and was transferred here after Russian Cossacks stole the original silver altar in 1601.

Sighişoara Town Centre

① Clock Tower
② Monastery Church
③ Vlad Dracul's House
④ Venetian House
⑤ Shoemakers' Tower
⑥ Tailors' Tower
⑦ Furriers' Tower
⑧ Church on the Hill

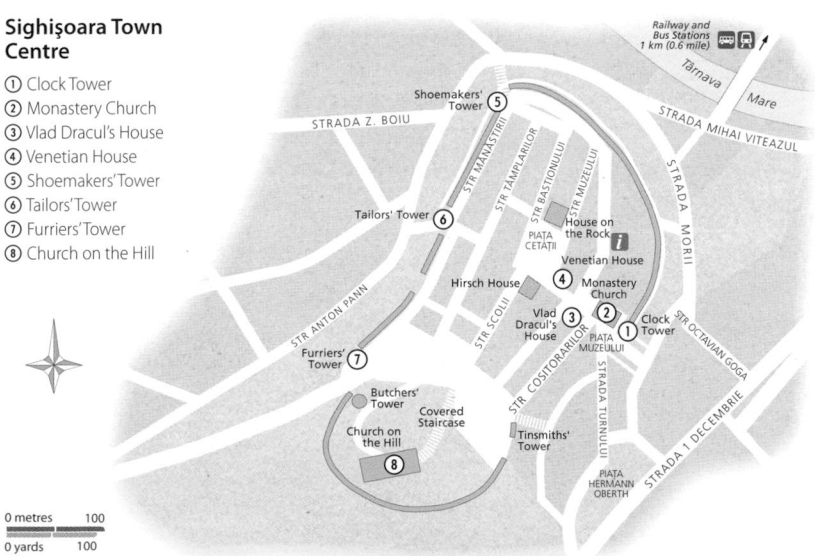

0 metres   100
0 yards   100

❾ Târgu Mureş

341 km (212 miles) N of Bucharest.
🏘 143,939. ✈ 🚉 🚌 🛈 Str G Enescu
2, (0365) 404 934. 🆆 **cjmures.ro**

Although it currently lies
within Romania's borders,
the city of Târgu Mureş has
always had a strong Hungarian
influence and for many centuries
was known by its Hungarian
name Marosvásárhely. It was
ceded to Hungary for four
years during World War II and
for 15 years, was an autonomous
Hungarian province under
Communist rule. Today,
half of its population is
ethnically Hungarian.

Târgu's most striking
building, the **Palace of Culture**,
stands right in the heart of the
city. Built between 1911 and
1913, its main attraction is the
Mirror Hall, with 12 stained-
glass windows depicting
Hungarian folklore. The art
gallery within the palace
exhibits works by famous
Romanian painters. Classical
concerts take place inside
the palace every Thursday.

East of the city centre is the
Teleki-Bolyai Library, where
the Transylvanian chancellor,
Count Samuel Teleki, opened
the region's first library in 1802.
Today, it holds over 200,000
ancient volumes, manuscripts
and other documents.

🏛 **Palace of Culture**
Str G Enescu 2. **Open** 9am–4pm Tue–
Fri, 9am–1pm Sat & Sun. 🎟

🏛 **Teleki-Bolyai Library**
Str Bolyai 17. **Open** 9am–4pm Tue–Fri,
9am–1pm Sat–Sun. 🎟

Broad and attractive pedestrianized streets
in Târgu Mureş

❿ Cluj-Napoca

Now Romania's third largest city, Cluj-Napoca began life as a
Roman colony, although it was abandoned in the 3rd century.
Cluj was refounded in the Middle Ages by the Hungarians, who
brought in Saxon immigrants to boost regional trade. Periods
of Ottoman and Austrian rule followed, and not until 1918 did
the town become part of Romania. In recent history, the 1989
revolution saw violent demonstrations here, resulting in many
deaths. Today, Cluj-Napoca retains an air of small-town charm,
and its wide pedestrianized streets are lined with 19th-century
buildings connected by narrow alleys and courtyards.

Exterior of the Gothic St Michael's Church
on Unity Square

🏛 **Ethnographic Museum
of Transylvania**
Str Memorandumului 21.
Tel (0264) 592 344. **Open** 9am–5pm
Tue–Sun. 🎟 🍴 🆆 **muzeul-
etnografic.ro**

Founded in 1922, this
museum (Muzeul de Etnografie
din Transilvania) features a
large collection of Transylvanian
ethnographic objects. Housed
in the 16th-century Reduta
Palace, exhibits include traditional
costumes, brightly patterned
rugs and agricultural tools and
pottery that date back 300
years. The museum also has an
outdoor section with full-size
replicas of rural dwellings and
village churches.

🔼 **St Michael's Church**
Piaţa Unirii. 🔼
With a spire over 76 m
(249 ft) high, this Gothic
church (Biserica Sfântul
Mihail) towers over the city.
Its austere interior is adorned
with stained-glass windows
featuring a portrait of St
Michael, a graceful cream and
gilt altar and a superbly carved
pulpit decorated with doves,
angels and biblical characters.

🏛 **Art Museum**
Piaţa Unirii 30. **Tel** (0264) 596 952.
Open 10am–5pm Wed–Sun. 🎟
🆆 **macluj.ro**

Housed in the 18th-century
Baroque Bánffy Palace, the
museum's (Muzeul de Arta)
collection is dominated by the
works of French-influenced
artists of the 19th and 20th
centuries. Among them are
Romanian masters Nicolae
Grigorescu, Theodor Pallady
and Ştefan Luchian.

🔼 **Orthodox Cathedral**
Piaţa Avram Iancu.
Open daily. 🔼
Built between 1923 and 1933,
this monumental cathedral
(Catedrala Ortodoxa), with its
massive central dome, dominates Avram Iancu Square. The
highlight of its opulent interior
is a huge gilt iconostasis comprising 18th- and 19th-century
icons illustrating the life of
Christ. In front of the church
is a modernist statue of Avram
Iancu, a 19th-century Romanian
nationalist who led the 1848
revolt against the unification of
Transylvania and Hungary.

Entrance to the Art Museum in the Bánffy
Palace, Unity Square

For hotels and restaurants see p572 and p573

The brightly painted National Theatre and Opera

VISITORS' CHECKLIST

Practical Information
440 km (273 miles) NW of
Bucharest. 305,600.
B-dul Eroilor 6-8, (0264) 452
244. Transylvanian Film
Festival (Jun). **visitcluj.ro**

Transport
7km (4 miles) NE of centre.

National Theatre and Opera

Piaţa Stefan cel Mare 24. **Tel** (0264)
597 175. **operacluj.ro**

Opened in 1906, the National
Theatre and Opera (Teatrul
National si Opera) started as a
Hungarian theatre. The majestic
building was designed by Austrian
architects Ferdinand Fellner and
Hermann Helmer, and it has
been home to the Romanian
theatre and opera since 1918.
Its striking Art Nouveau lobby
leads into a grand auditorium
seating up to 1,200 people.
Regular national and international
performances take place here.

Babeş-Bolyai University

Mihail Kogalniceanu nr1. **Tel** (0264)
405 300. **ubbcluj.ro**

Founded in 1581, this
(Universitatea Babeş-Bolyai)
is the largest university in
Romania. It started off as a
Jesuit Academy but was later
closed down when Romanians
were denied education in their
language and taught in Hungarian
instead. After the country's
liberation, two universities
were established to provide
education in both languages.
In due course, the institutions
were merged and adopted a
name inspired by the Romanian
scientist Babeş and Hungarian
mathematician Bolyai. Today,
the university has a student
population of 45,000 with
21 faculties.

Botanical Gardens

Str Bilaşcu. **Open** 9am–7pm daily.

Opened in 1920, the Botanical
Gardens (Gradina Botanica)
are located just outside the
city centre on a hillside park.
It has six greenhouses filled
with equatorial and tropical
plants, including specimens
from Japan, as well as flora
from all over Romania.

Synagogue

Str Horea 21. **Tel** (0264) 596
600. **Open** varies, call
in advance.

Built in the late 19th century,
this is the city's main synagogue (Sinagogă Neologă),
topped with four silver onion
domes. It has had a chequered
history, first attacked in 1927
by the Romanian fascist
organization, the Iron Guard,
and then during World War II.
It has now been restored to its
original design and serves as a
Holocaust memorial for the
city's small Jewish community.

Cluj-Napoca City Centre

① Ethnographic Museum
  of Transylvania
② St Michael's Church
③ Art Museum
④ Orthodox Cathedral
⑤ National Theatre
  and Opera
⑥ Babeş-Bolyai University
⑦ Botanical Gardens

0 metres   500
0 yards   500

For keys to symbols see back flap

⓫ Bucovina Monasteries Tour

The painted churches of Bucovina, a hilly region in northwestern Moldavia, were the illustrated Bibles of their time. Most were constructed during the reign of Stephen the Great (1457–1504), who welcomed Bulgarian and Serbian Orthodox Christian monks seeking refuge from the Ottoman Empire. After each victory against the Ottomans, Stephen commissioned a church to be built. Petru Rareş, his son, continued the tradition. Their beauty and rarity has earned the monasteries UNESCO World Heritage Site status.

Sucevita Monastery, the last church to be built before the Ottoman invasion

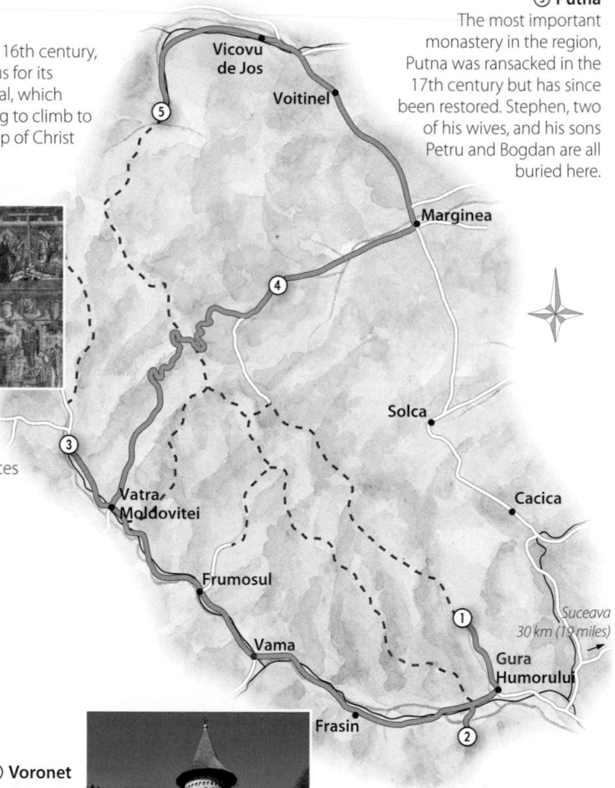

④ Sucevita
Founded in the late 16th century, this church is famous for its *Ladder of Virtue* mural, which depicts monks trying to climb to heaven with the help of Christ and his angels.

⑤ Putna
The most important monastery in the region, Putna was ransacked in the 17th century but has since been restored. Stephen, two of his wives, and his sons Petru and Bogdan are all buried here.

③ Moldovita
Rebuilt in 1532, the painted walls here incorporate references to the encroaching Ottoman Empire.

Key

▬ Tour route
═ Minor road
••• Walking trail
— Railway route

Vicovu de Jos
Voitinel
⑤
Marginea
④
Solca
③
Cacica
Vatra Moldovitei
Frumosul
①
Suceava 30 km (19 miles)
Vama
Gura Humorului
②
Frasin

② Voronet
This fortified monastery was built in 1488 to celebrate a victory against the Turks. The mural of *The Last Judgement* on its southern wall is notable for its skilful incorporation of Moldavian folk motifs.

① Humor
Founded in the 15th century and rebuilt in 1530, the exterior walls of this small church feature impressive murals.

0 km   5
0 miles   5

Tips for Drivers

Starting point: Humor.
Length: 204 km (127 miles).
Getting there: Suceava is 440 km (273 miles) N of Bucharest on the E85 Highway.
The monasteries are generally open from 7am–5pm daily.

🕐 Suceava

440 km (273 miles) N of Bucharest.
🏛 107,000. 🚌 🚍 ℹ️ Str Stefan cel
Mare 23, (0230) 551 241.

Once the powerful capital of
Moldavia, Suceava has long
since faded from glory. Today,
the town serves as a base for
visitors who want to explore
the marvellous monasteries in
the Bucovina region.

Suceava Fortress, on a hill
overlooking the town, is the
most impressive sight here.
Built during the reign of Petru I
Muşat and occupied by a
succession of powerful rulers, it
resisted a number of seiges and
remained unconquered when
the Ottoman Empire ordered its
destruction. Only the ruins of
the citadel are visible today.

Closer to the town centre,
the colourfully tiled
roof of the **Mirăuţi
Church of St George**
can be seen rising
above the surrounding
pine trees. Founded
by Petru I Muşat in
about 1390, this is the
town's oldest church
and was once used for the
coronations of Moldavia's princes.
It was here that Stephen the
Great was crowned as prince of
Moldavia. Some of the original
murals can still be seen.

**Detail in the
Mahmudiye mosque**

🏰 **Suceava Fortress**
Dealul Cetăţii. **Open** 9am–6pm
daily. 📷

🏛 **Mirăuţi Church of St George**
Str Mirăuţi. **Open** daily.

The scattered ruins of ancient Tomis, Constanţa

🕐 Constanţa

223 km (139 miles) E of Bucharest.
🏛 301,200. ✈️ 🚌 🚍 ℹ️ B-dul
Tomis 221, (0241) 488 600.

Romania's main port and fifth
largest city, Constanţa is also one
of the oldest cities in Romania.
Known as Tomis in the 5th century BC, Constanţa
started off as a Greek
colony. It was then con-
quered by the Romans
around 20 BC and was
renamed Constanţa by
the Roman Emperor
Constantine the Great.
Today, all that remains
of the city's glorious past is an
uninspiring array of unmarked
Roman walls, columns and
fragments of statues in the
Archaeological Park on Bulevardul
Republicii. More interesting is
the **Tomis Mosaic Museum**,
housing a colourful 800-sq-m
(9,149-sq-ft) mosaic floor from
Tomis's 4th-century Roman
forum. A short walk from the
museum is **Mahmudiye Mosque**.
Built in 1910 during the reign

of King Carol I, it is Romania's
largest mosque. The plain interior
is brightened by a vast Persian
carpet, a gift from the Ottoman
ruler, Sultan Abdul Hamid. One
of the biggest Turkish carpets in
Europe, it measures 144 sq m
(1,550 sq ft). There are fine views
of the city from the 47-m (154-ft)
high minaret.

🏛 **Tomis Mosaic Museum**
Piaţa Ovidiu 12. **Open** 8am–8pm daily
(10am–6pm in winter). 📷 📷
🌐 ghidulmuzeelor.cimec.ro

☪ **Mahmudiye Mosque**
Str Arhiepiscopiei 5. **Open** 9:30am–
9:30pm daily. 📷 📷

🕐 Danube Delta

223 km (139 miles) E of Bucharest.
🚍 from Tulcea. ℹ️ Str Gariii 26,
Tulcea, (0240) 519 130. 🚤 Navrom
boat tours from Tulcea.
🌐 navromdelta.ro

Covering an area of 4,142 sq km
(1,599 sq miles), the Danube
Delta, a biosphere reserve, is the
largest and best-preserved delta
in Europe. A UNESCO World
Heritage Site, it is home to a
variety of wildlife including wolves,
wild cats and around 300 bird
species and 150 species of fish. The
starting point for exploring
the reserve is Tulcea, located at the
tip of the delta. From here, five
ferries a week make the 3-hour
journey to Sulina, once a
bustling port. The town's old
lighthouse, built in 1870, is
now a history museum detailing
Sulina's heyday as the headquarters of the European Danube
Commission (1856–1938).
Sulina's vast 40-km (25-mile)
beach is also worth a stroll.

The old lighthouse in the coastal town of Sulina, Danube Delta

Practical & Travel Information

Romanians are generally polite and hospitable and will often go out of their way to help, especially in rural areas where foreign visitors are less common. The country's substantial size makes it a formidable area to explore. Public transport is adequate, but slower than using a car and although car hire is reasonably priced and cuts down journey time, it exposes travellers to the perils of Romania's reckless drivers. There are numerous airports around the country and those wishing to see as much as possible in a short space of time should consider taking domestic flights, which connect the most important places of interest.

When to Visit

Spring and autumn are the best seasons to visit Romania, with warm, sunny days and cool nights. The capital, Bucharest, becomes unbearable in summer, when most residents escape to the coast or the hills, where temperatures are 10–15 degrees lower. The months of September and October are the best time to go hiking in Transylvania.

Documentation

Since Romania's accession to the European Union (EU) in January 2007, EU citizens no longer require a visa and can enter the country with a valid passport or identity card. Citizens of the US, Canada, Australia and New Zealand can stay in Romania for up to 90 days without a visa, provided they show a valid passport. Citizens of other countries such as Ukraine, Moldova and South Africa require a visa.

Visitor Information

Most cities have at least rudimentary tourist information centres, but visitors usually tend to rely on guide books, tourist websites or local English-language publications such as **In Your Pocket**, which provides up-to-date listings and is distributed at bars, restaurants and hotels for Bucharest, Brașov and Sibiu. The guide also has a free website. City maps can be found at bookshops, kiosks and petrol stations. Most tourist destinations have privately run travel centres that provide brochures; they can also arrange car rental and hotel reservations.

Health and Security

Although no vaccinations are officially required for travel to Romania, it is recommended that visitors are immunized against tetanus, hepatitis A, diphtheria and typhoid as well as polio. Medical services are free of charge to EU citizens carrying their European Health Insurance Card (EHIC). However, standards are not always high, so visitors are advised to take out medical insurance to cover private treatment. There have been no instances of malaria in Romania, but mosquitoes can be a problem around the Danube Delta in summer; repellent is recommended. Stray dogs are a major problem in all of Romania's cities, and if you are unfortunate enough to be bitten you will need an anti-rabies shot. For medical emergencies, it is best to go to the **Emergency Clinic Hospital** in Bucharest or in Brașov.

Violent crime against visitors is non-existent in Romania, but pickpockets can be a problem on crowded public transport in Bucharest and other cities. Travellers are advised to be vigilant and keep their valuables in a money belt or bag. When travelling on overnight trains, doors to sleeping compartments should always be locked and bags guarded.

Facilities for the Disabled

Public awareness of the needs of the disabled is low, but has improved in recent years. Hotels in bigger cities are more likely to have facilities than smaller hotels.

Banking and Currency

The Romanian currency is the leu. Although most foreign currencies can be exchanged at banks, exchange bureaus and larger hotels, euros and dollars are preferred. Traveller's cheques are accepted only at major banks and hotels in the bigger cities and towns. Banks are open from 9am to 5pm Monday to Friday.

ATMs can be found in most places, but are less common in the more remote areas; visitors to these places are advised to carry sufficient cash. Similarly, credit cards can be relied upon only in larger hotels, restaurants, petrol stations and shops.

Communications

Public telephones can be found across the country,

The Climate of Romania

The country has hot, dry summers with temperatures soaring up to 35° C (95° F) in June and July. Autumn is cool but dry, and beautiful when the fields and trees are colourful. Winters can be bitterly cold, with temperatures dipping as low as -8° C (18° F) in January. Snowfalls usually start in mid-December and continue until March.

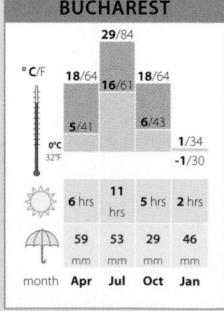

BUCHAREST

month	Apr	Jul	Oct	Jan
°C/F	18/64	29/84 / 16/61	18/64	1/34
	5/41		6/43	-1/30
☀	6 hrs	11 hrs	5 hrs	2 hrs
☂ mm	59	53	29	46

0°C 32°F

and are operated with a Telekom card sold at post offices such as the **Bucharest Main Post Office** and at newspaper kiosks. Mobile phones with roaming will function everywhere, but those visitors staying longer in the country are advised to buy a local prepaid SIM to reduce the cost of calls.

Romania has one of the fastest average internet speeds in the world, and free, fast Wi-Fi is ubiquitous in all venues - from hotels to cafés - in the cities, most towns and even villages.

Arriving by Air

Bucharest's Henri Coandă (Otopeni) airport is located 16 km (10 miles) from the city centre. It is served by a wide range of airlines from all over Europe, but there are no direct flights from destinations such as the US or Canada. Visitors should note that international flights from the UK, Germany and Italy also serve Bacau, Cluj-Napoca, Craiova, Iasi, Sibiu, Targu Mures and Timisoara airports.

Rail Travel

Most international and domestic trains arrive and depart from Bucharest's Gara de Nord, which lies north of the centre. There are three classes of Romanian train – Intercity is the quickest and most comfortable; InterRegio tend to stop more frequently; Regio trains are slow, uncomfortable and best avoided. The first two categories require seat reservations. Domestic train tickets can be bought online in advance at the website bilete.cfrcalatori.ro, run by the Romanian railway company CFR. The Romanian train timetable is online at infofer.ro. Visitors can book international tickets through the agency Wasteels, which has offices in Bucharest and Braşov.

Travelling by Bus

Instead of a central bus station, Bucharest has six smaller bus stations located around the edges of the city. Of these, **Filaret Bus Station** serves Thessaloniki, Athens and southeastern Romania; **Bucureşti Militari** serves northern destinations including Sibiu; **C&I Bus Terminal** serves Braşov

and Târges Mureş. Minibuses also leave for various destinations around the country from opposite Gara de Nord. Tickets for local buses, trams and trolleybuses can be bought at street kiosks and should be validated once on board. In Bucharest, an Activ Card (similar to London's Oyster Card) is required. It can be bought at ticket kiosks next to major stops.

Travelling by Car

Driving in Romania is an unsettling experience, as Romanian drivers are very impatient, relying on tailgating and frequent use of horns to intimidate other road users. In rural areas, horses and carts are a major hazard, particularly at night when they may not have lights. Drivers are required to carry an EU or international licence, Green Card insurance or its equivalent and vehicle registration documents. Car hire is available in most towns and cities. Major rental companies are: **Avis**, **Europcar** and **Hertz.**

Taxis are also plentiful in bigger towns and cities. However, passengers should insist on the meter being used, or agree on a fare in advance.

DIRECTORY

Documentation
W mae.ro/en

Embassies and Consulates

Australia
34e Titu Maioresću St,
Bucharest.
Tel (21) 319 0229.

United Kingdom
24 Jules Michelet,
Bucharest.
Tel (21) 201 7200.

United States
B-dul Liviu Librescu 4–5,
Bucharest.
Tel (21) 200 3300.

Visitor Information
W romaniatourism.
com

In Your Pocket
W inyourpocket.com

Emergencies

Ambulance, Police
Tel 112.

Health and Security

Emergency Clinic Hospital
Calea Floreasca 8,
Bucharest.
Tel (021) 599 2300.
Calea Bucureşti 25-27,
Braşov.
Tel (0268) 320 022.

Communications

Bucharest Main Post Office
St Matei Millo 10,
Bucharest.

Arriving by Air

TAROM
W tarom.ro

Wizz Air
W wizzair.com

Rail Travel

CFR
W cfr.ro

Wasteels
Tel (021) 317 0369.
W wasteels.ro

Travelling by Bus

Bucureşti Militari
Valea Cascadelor 1,
Bucharest.
Tel (0725) 939 939.

C&I Bus Terminal
Splaiul Unirii 60,
Bucharest.
Tel (021) 330 8132.

Filaret Bus Station
1 Gara Filaret Square,
Bucharest.
Tel (021) 336 0692.

Travelling by Car

Avis
B-dul Theodor Pallady 51,
Bucharest.
Tel (21) 210 4344.
W avis.ro

Europcar
Str. Grigore Mora 17,
Bucharest.
Tel (21) 310 1797.
W europcar.ro

Hertz
Piata Montreal 10,
Bucharest.
Tel (21) 407 8200.
W hertz.ro

Shopping & Entertainment

From small, busy markets to upmarket malls, Romania offers great shopping opportunities. Bucharest is by far the best place for most shopping needs. However, towns and villages often sell regional crafts and produce not found elsewhere. Bucharest is also the entertainment capital, hosting a wide range of classical music concerts, theatre, opera and ballet while the ever-expanding number of bars and clubs contribute to a lively nightlife. The country's wealth of natural beauty makes it very attractive to outdoor enthusiasts. Its mountains cater for all hiking levels, with well-marked routes for experienced walkers as well as organized trips.

Opening Hours

Local shops usually open from 9 or 10am to around 6 or 8pm on weekdays. Larger department stores stay open all day on Saturdays, while most shopping malls open from 10am to 10pm daily. Food shops open from 8am to 8pm Monday to Sunday..

Markets

Most towns have daily fruit and vegetable markets which offer an intriguing insight into local life. Bucharest's main markets are at Piaţa Obor and Piaţa Amzei. In rural areas, weekly markets are often colourful affairs, with traders arriving in horsecarts from outlying areas, bringing home-grown produce and, sometimes, crafts such as wooden utensils and embroidered shawls.

Malls

Bucharest has a host of shopping malls ranging from the country's largest, **Afi Palace Cotroceni**, with 300 shops and a 20-screen cinema, to the central **Unirii Shopping Centre**, which was the city's biggest department store during Communist times. These tend to sell well-known clothing brands at prices similar to other European cities. Bigger towns such as Timişoara, Braşov and Constanţa also have large modern malls. **Iulius Mall Timişoara** has an ice rink during winter.

Antiques

The Lipscani area of Bucharest, between Unity Square and University Square, is known for its numerous antique and second-hand shops, and is the best place to hunt for rarities and obscure Communist memorabilia.

Gifts and Souvenirs

Some of the best souvenirs can be found at the outdoor Village Museum and the Museum of the Romanian Peasant (see p553) in Bucharest; both stock a range of original crafts. **Romartizana**, in Bucharest, also has a good selection of crafts, and there are several small shops selling glassware, porcelain and hand-crafted crystal clustered around the courtyard of **Curtea Sticlarilor**. Textile weaving is popular across the country; embroidered rugs, folk costumes, tablecloths and wall hangings are found in most souvenir shops. Reproductions of religious icons are also worth looking out for.

Several high-end jewellery shops such as **Cellini** are located along Bucharest's B-dul Magheru and B-dul Balcescu. The bigger shopping malls also stock jewellery.

Food and Drink

Romanian cuisine is noted for its ciorba (soup), which is traditionally made with ciorba de burta (tripe), ciorba de perisoare (meatballs) or ciorba de legume (vegetables). Main dishes lack variety and tend to consist of grilled meat, but spicy stews such as tocaniţă are worth trying. Sarmale is a delicious dish made of stuffed vine or cabbage leaves, which is found all over the Balkans.

Romania is one of the world's largest producers of plums and turns most of its harvest into the enormously popular, and potent ţuică (plum brandy). Wine is also produced in large quantities; the sweet moldavian grasă and tămâioasă are two of the best wines in the country. Romania has a reputable beer brewing industry. Ciuc and Ursus are the most popular brands.

Books and Music

For English-language books in Bucharest, visitors should head for either **Nautilus**, which has a particularly good range of fiction, or the **Anthony Frost English Bookshop**. Those in search of traditional Romanian folk music should try Bucharest's Village Museum shop or **Muzica** in the city centre. The huge Sony Music Centre in the Unirii Shopping Centre has a good selection of mainstream music.

Listings

Şapte Seri is Bucharest's best free weekly events guide. Written in a mixture of English and Romanian, its website has a full English-language version. **In Your Pocket Bucharest** provides comprehensive entertainment listings. Those who understand Romanian can consult B24.

Nightlife

The country's nightlife is best experienced in Bucharest, where hundreds of clubs and bars cater to every taste and budget. Popular clubs with live music include **Club A** and **Mojo**. Larger towns and cities with a substantial population of students, such as Braşov, Timişoara and Cluj-Napoca, also offer good nightlife. In summer, numerous seasonal clubs and bars open in Constanţa to entertain the influx of both Romanian and foreign visitors to the coast.

Theatre

Bucharest is home to the country's modern **National Theatre** with regular plays in Romanian. Many smaller theatres are scattered around the city and occasionally feature foreign-language productions.

Classical Music and Opera

The **Romanian Athenaeum** in Bucharest is the best place to catch performances by the world class George Enescu Philharmonic Orchestra, which plays most days of the week. Opera fans should visit the **Bucharest National Opera**, **Opera Braşov** or **Cluj-Napoca National Opera**, which stage both opera and ballet. Timişoara and Constanţa also host regular performances.

Festivals

In June every year, Bucharest's Village Museum holds a **Traditional Crafts Fair** with participants from all over the country. **Bucharest of Old**, in July, is a celebration of the city as it was in the 19th century, involving a street procession in traditional costume with horse-drawn carriages.

The atmospheric **Sighişoara Medieval Festival**, which takes place in the last week of July, is certainly worth visiting. Local culture is celebrated at folk festivals throughout August – the Romanian Folk Art Festival is one of the biggest. Sibiu hosts an **International Jazz Festival** in May. If visiting in late October, Halloween in Transylvania, revolving around Count Dracula, is not to be missed.

Outdoor Activities

The country's most popular ski resort, **Poiana Braşov**, is located 12 km (7 miles) south of Braşov. Its runs range from easy to medium levels and ski equipment can be hired on site. The season lasts from December until March.

Romania's abundance of mountainous terrain offers endless possibilities for hikers, who usually head for the well-marked paths in the Făgăraş range. Bird-watchers should visit the Danube Delta, which attracts numerous species of rare birds; bird-watching boat trips can be arranged through various agencies in Tulcea. **Travel Maker** organizes mountain biking, bird-watching, hiking, horse riding, caving and rafting trips all over Romania.

DIRECTORY

Malls

Afi Palace Cotroceni
Bulevardul Vasile Milea 4, Bucharest.

Iulius Mall Timişoara
Str Aristide Demetriade nr. 1, Timişoara.

Unirii Shopping Centre
Piaţa Unirii 1, Bucharest.

Gifts and Souvenirs

Cellini
Bulevardul N Bălcescu 16, Bucharest.
Tel (021) 312 2202.

Curtea Sticlarilor
Str Selari 9–11, Bucharest.
Tel (021) 314 3228.

Romartizana
Calea Victoriei 16–20, Bucharest.
Tel (021) 313 14 65.

Books and Music

Anthony Frost English Bookshop
Calea Victoriei 45, Bucharest.
Tel (021) 311 5138.
W anthonyfrost.ro

Muzica
Calea Victoriei 41–43, Bucharest.
Tel (021) 313 9674.

Nautilus
Str Arh. Ion Mincu 17, Bucharest.
Tel (021) 222 5030.
W nautilus.ro

Listings

In Your Pocket Bucharest
W inyourpocket.com

Şapte Seri
W sapteseri.ro

Nightlife

Club A
Str Blănari 14, Bucharest.
Tel (021) 313 5592.

Mojo
Str Gabroveni 14, Bucharest.
Tel (760) 263 496.

Theatre

National Theatre
Bulevardul Bălcescu 2, Bucharest.
Tel (021) 314 7171.

Classical Music and Opera

Bucharest National Opera
Bulevardul Kogalniceanu 70, Bucharest.
Tel (021) 314 6980.
W operanb.ro

Cluj-Napoca National Opera
Piaţa Ştefan cel Mare 24, Cluj-Napoca. **Tel** (0264) 597 175. W operacluj.ro

Opera Braşov
Str Bisericii Romane Nr. 51, Braşov.
Tel (0268) 419 380.
W opera-brasov.ro

Romanian Athenaeum
Str Franklin 1–3, Bucharest.
Tel (021) 315 2567.
W fge.org.ro

Festivals

Bucharest of Old
W http://ro.earlymusic. ro

International Jazz Festival
W sibiujazz.ro

Sighişoara Medieval Festival
W sighisoara-medieval. ro

Traditional Crafts Fair
W muzeul-satului.ro

Outdoor Activities

Travel Maker
Str. Elena Vacarescu 9, Bucharest.
Tel (021) 232 03 31.
W bucharestcitytour. com

Poiana Braşov
Tel (0268) 417 866.
W poiana-brasov.com

Where to Stay

Lavish lobby at the Athenee Palace, Bucharest

Bucharest

Andy Hotel (lei)
Boutique
Str Witing 2
Tel *(021) 300 30 50*
[W] andyhotels.ro
Smart modern hotel near the railway station with immaculate, well-equipped en suites. Doubles with shared facilities also available.

Funky Chicken (lei)
Hostel **Map** D3
Str Gen. Berthelot 63
Tel *(021) 312 1425*
[W] funkychickenhostel.com
Crammed into several rooms of a residential block, this lively hostel offers dorms and private rooms.

Rembrandt (lei)(lei)
Boutique **Map** E4
Str Smardan 11
Tel *(021) 313 93 15*
[W] rembrandt.ro
Exquisite town house in the old city centre offering luxurious rooms and a great breakfast.

Athenee Palace (lei)(lei)(lei)
Historic **Map** E3
Str Episcopei 1–3, 10092
Tel *(021) 303 3777*
[W] hiltonbucharest.com
Once the hotbed of international espionage, this member of the Hilton chain is as comfortable and well-run as you would expect.

Golden Tulip (lei)(lei)(lei)
Luxury **Map** D3
Calea Victoriei 166, 10096
Tel *(021) 212 5558*
[W] goldentulipbucharest.com
Superbly located on the main boulevard, the hotel offers contemporary rooms. Superb views from the breakfast room on the top floor.

For map references *see pp546–7*

Rest of Romania

BRAŞOV: Casa Wagner (lei)(lei)
Historic
Piaţa Sfatului 5, 500031
Tel *(0268) 411 253*
[W] casa-wagner.com
A 15th-century building in the main square with large rooms featuring exposed beams and period furnishings.

BRAŞOV: Villa Prato (lei)(lei)(lei)
Boutique
Str St O. Josif 2, 500041
Tel *(0268) 473 371*
[W] villaprato.ro
Wonderfully restored villa with well-equipped and spacious rooms. Enjoy views of the Old Town over breakfast served in the conservatory.

CLUJ-NAPOCA: Capitolina (lei)(lei)
Business
Str Victor Babes 35, 400012
Tel *(0264) 450 490*
[W] hotel-capitolina.ro
Smart hotel with spacious and well-equipped rooms, fitness centre and conference facilities just a few minutes from various shopping and cultural sites.

CLUJ-NAPOCA: City Plaza Hotel (lei)(lei)(lei)
Spa
Str Sindicatelor 9–13, 400029
Tel *(0264) 450 101*
[W] cityhotels.ro
In a quiet part of town, this modern hotel offers fully equipped rooms, spa, swimming pool and event facilities.

CONSTANŢA: Hotel Voila (lei)
Boutique
Str Callatis 22, 900744
Tel *(0241) 508 004*
[W] hotelvoila.ro

Close to the seafront, this is a small but delightful hotel. The restaurant terrace overlooks the beach.

SIBIU: Felinarul (lei)
Hostel
Str Felinarului 8, 550183
Tel *(0269) 250 282*
[W] felinarulhostelsibiu.ro
This boutique hostel in a historic house offers two dorms and one double, healthy breakfasts and plenty of genuine hospitality.

DK Choice

SIGHISOARA: Casa cu Cerb (lei)(lei)
Historic
Str Scolii 1, 545400
Tel *(0265) 774 625*
[W] casacucerb.ro
Housed in one of Sighisoara's oldest buildings, the Casa cu Cerb (House of the Stag) is located in the centre of the Old Town. This delightful historic inn features barrel-vaulted ceilings, exposed brick walls, woodwork and plenty of period-style furniture. Rooms are neat and well-equipped. Attic rooms are particularly charming.

SUCEAVA: Continental Suceava (lei)(lei)
Business
Str Mihai Viteazul 4–6, 720042
Tel *(0372) 304 904*
[W] continentalhotels.ro
City centre hotel with comfortable rooms and a good buffet breakfast.

TIMIŞOARA: Timişoara (lei)(lei)
Business
Str Marasesti 1–4, 300086
Tel *(0256) 498 852*
[W] hoteltimisoara.ro
Relaxing, casual hotel in the heart of the city with spacious rooms that offer good views.

TULCEA: Delta (lei)(lei)
Resort
Str Isaccei 2, 820169
Tel *(0240) 514 720*
[W] hoteldelta.eu
With a Danube riverfront location, this tourist complex offers 3-star and 4-star sections.

Where to Eat and Drink

Bucharest

Vatra
International   Map D4
Strada Actor Ion Brezoianu 19, 010131
Tel *(021) 315 8375*
Folksy restaurant near Cismigiu Park with traditional grilled meats, skewer-kebabs and stuffed vine and cabbage leaves. Try the *papanasi* (cottage cheese fritters).

DK Choice

Caru cu Bere
Romanian   Map E4
Str Stavropoleos 5, 30081
Tel *(021) 313 7560*
Built in 1899, the atmospheric Caru cu Bere has retained much of its original appearance, featuring a high-vaulted ceiling, stained-glass windows, ornate wooden balustrades and intricate floral murals. The menu covers everything in the Romanian culinary pantheon from simple grilled snacks to extravagant platters of roast meat. Own-brewed beer is a real treat.

Trattoria il Calcio
Italian   Map E3
Strada B Franklin 1–3, 10287
Tel *(0732) 528 140*
Housed in a delightful 19th-century building opposite the Royal Palace, the trattoria serves an excellent choice of well-prepared pizza and pasta dishes.

The Artist
European   Map E5
Str Nicolae Tonitza 13
Tel *(0728) 31 88 71*
Considered among Romania's leading fine dining restaurants. The seasonal menu features only the best of local produce.

Rossetya
Romanian
Str Dimitrie Bolintineanu 9, 21061
Tel *(031) 805 9199*
Cuisine based on traditional 19th-century Romanian recipe books. The broad-ranging menu covers duck, pork and lamb as well as vegetarian choices.

Rest of Romania

BRAŞOV: Casa Hirscher
French/Mediterranean
Piaţa Sfatului 12–14, 500025
Tel *(0268) 410 533*

Occupying a handsome 16th-century house, this restaurant offers an imaginative choice of Mediterranean and classic French cuisine. Excellent wine list.

CLUJ-NAPOCA: Baracca
Italian
Str Napoca 8a, 400009
Tel *(0732) 155 177*
Italian-leaning international cuisine in a smart restaurant that features exposed brick walls, wooden floors and enormous shell-shaped lampshades.

CLUJ-NAPOCA: Via
International
Str Inocenţiu Micu Klein 6, 400087
Tel *264 593 220*
Quality food fusing local, Asian and Mediterranean influences served in an 18th-century house that blends original features with modern furnishings. Refined desserts and a long wine list.

CONSTANŢA: Manarola
Seafood
Portul Tomis, 900744
Tel *(0722) 100 193*
Superb seafood right by the sea in Constanta's Tomis Harbour. Reserve in advance for a table outside.

SIHGIŞOARA: Casa Vlad Dracul
Romanian
Str Cositorarilor 5, 545400
Tel *(0256) 771 596*
In the 15th-century house, the alleged birthplace of Vlad the Impaler, this straightforward restaurant with a theatrically Gothic flourish serves meaty Romanian staples.

SIBIU: Crama Sibiul Vechi
Romanian
A. Papiu Ilarion Str 3, 550178
Tel *(07380) 210 461*

Price Guide

Prices are based on a three-course meal for one, half a bottle of wine, including cover charge, service and tax.

	under 70 lei
	70–140 lei
	over 140 lei

Reasonably priced restaurant In a 500-year-old wine cellar serving a broad selection of traditional Transylvanian fare, frequently with live music.

SINAIA: Cuţitu' de Argint
Romanian
Aleea Peleşului 2, Sinaia 106100
Tel *(0241) 555 571*
Sit at the long wooden tables of this eatery that resembles a medieval inn, to enjoy hearty portions of the roast meats.

SUCEAVA: Latino
European
Str Curtea Domneasca 9, 720042
Tel *(0230) 523 627*
Good pizza and steaks are the main attractions, although European classics such as *Duck à l'Orange* and *Tafelspitz boiled beef* also feature on the menu.

TARGU MUREŞ:
Concordia
Mediterranean
Piaţa Trandafirilor 43, 540053
Tel *(0265) 260 602*
Refreshingly modern in design and international in its cuisine, Concordia offers superb steaks, and Mediterranean salads.

TIMIŞOARA: Harold's
International
Aleea Studenţilor 17, 540053
Tel *(0256) 496 335*
Classy spot in the student campus area, with wide choice of Chinese, Romanian and Mexican fare.

Diners at Caru Cu Bere in Bucharest

BULGARIA

Bulgaria's stunning scenery and Mediterranean climate have made it one of Europe's best tourist destinations. Though famous for its Black Sea beaches and scintillating ski resorts, it offers the visitor many further rewards through the sheer diversity of its natural beauty spots, archaeological sites and picture-postcard villages.

With its warm climate and fertile soil, Bulgaria has attracted settlers from ancient times and remnants of former civilizations can be found everywhere, from prehistoric burial grounds to Ottoman mosques. Among its natural attributes, its sandy beaches are captivating and the mountains provide scope for hiking and skiing. The country's proud folk heritage contrasts with its recent transformation into a modern European nation, making Bulgaria a vibrant and invigorating destination.

History

Archaeological discoveries have shown that Neolithic people were living in the region as early as 5500 BC. By 1000 BC, South Eastern Europe was falling under the Thracians, who established tribal states across Bulgaria, Romania and northern Greece. By AD 50, however, the Romans had taken control of the region. The Roman Empire was split in the 5th century and Bulgaria became part of the eastern Byzantine half. Migrating Slav tribes were allowed to settle and live peacefully throughout the region.

The Bulgars, a Turkic tribe from Central Asia, crossed the Danube in 681 and soon fused with the Slavs already living there, creating the Bulgarian nation. Bulgarian power reached its peak under Tsar Simeon (r. 893–927), who extended the borders almost as far as Constantinople. However, a Byzantine resurgence halted further expansion.

The colourful Rose Festival celebrations in central Bulgaria

◀ Early spring in Rila National Park

The Ottoman Turks conquered Bulgaria in the 1390s and ruled it for almost 500 years, cutting the country off from Western Europe and weakening its language and culture.

An upsurge of Bulgarian culture known as the National Revival took place in the 19th century, and young patriots planned a revolt. The so-called April Rising began in 1876 but was quashed by the Ottomans. Outraged by the massacre that took place, public support in Russia and Western Europe took up the Bulgarian cause. Russia declared war on the Ottomans in April 1877, resulting in the creation of an independent Bulgarian state. The new Bulgaria was initially intended to include Macedonia as well but this was prevented by the European powers at the Congress of Berlin in 1878.

Eager to force the Ottomans out of Macedonia, Bulgaria was drawn into an alliance with Serbia and Greece. In the First Balkan War of 1912, the three Balkan states defeated the

Bulgarian soldiers during the Second Balkan War, 1913

Ottomans but disagreed on how to divide their conquests. Bulgaria declared war on Serbia and Greece but was defeated in the Second Balkan War of 1913.

In 1941, two years after the outbreak of World War II, Bulgaria joined Germany. However, it switched sides in 1944, hoping in vain to head off an invasion by the Soviet Red Army. Supported by the Soviets, the Bulgarian Communists staged a coup and ruled the country for the next 45 years.

The Communist regime disintegrated in 1989 but economic collapse soon followed. Bulgaria's entry into the EU in 2007 marked a new phase in the country's voyage from post-Communist chaos to political and economic stability.

Language and Culture

The country's official language is Bulgarian, a Slavonic language related to Serbian, Russian and Croatian. It is written in the Cyrillic script, although Roman lettering is sometimes used on public signs.

With heritage playing a highly visible role in Bulgarian society, religious holidays, saints' days and folk festivals form the backbone of Bulgaria's festive calendar.

KEY DATES IN BULGARIAN HISTORY

1000–800 BC The Thracians begin to form powerful tribal states in Bulgaria

AD 50 Thracian lands are captured by the Romans

681 The Bulgars conquer the land south of the Danube

930 Rila Monastery is founded by St Ivan of Rila

1393 The Ottomans seize the capital of Bulgaria

1830 The National Revival gains momentum, bringing with it a flowering of the arts

1876 The April Rising

1877–8 The Russo-Turkish War ends in defeat for the Ottomans

1912–13 First Balkan War against the Ottomans

1913 Second Balkan War

1915–18 Bulgaria joins World War I on the German side

1944 Bulgarian Communists, supported by the Soviet Red Army, seize power

1946 Bulgaria becomes a republic

2004 Bulgaria joins NATO

2007 Bulgaria becomes a member of the EU

Exploring Bulgaria

Few capitals bear the imprint of history as clearly as Sofia, Bulgaria's largest city. Roman masonry juts from the walls of its churches, while fragments of Byzantine fortifications survive in pedestrian subways. To the south of bustling and sophisticated Sofia are fascinating highland villages such as Bansko and Borovets and the monasteries of Rila and Bachkovo; to the east, on the Black Sea, are the coastal towns of Varna and Nesebûr and the Golden Sands resort; while all over the country, medieval fortresses stand as reminders of Bulgaria's illustrious history. The country's rail network links all the major towns and cities, while rural Bulgaria is accessible by local bus. Taxis can also be used for long-distance journeys, if arranged in advance.

Wooden houses along a street in the Old Town, Sozopol

Sights at a Glance

1 Sofia pp578–85
2 Rila Monastery pp586–9
3 Rila National Park
4 Borovets
5 Bansko
6 Melnik
7 Bachkovo Monastery pp592–3

8 Plovdiv pp594–5
9 Koprivshtitsa pp596–7
10 Veliko Tûrnovo pp598–601
11 Varna pp602–603
12 Stone Forest
13 Golden Sands
14 Kaliakra
15 Sunny Beach

16 Nesebûr
17 Burgas
18 Sozopol

The popular beach at Golden Sands near Varna, on the Black Sea coast

0 kilometres   100

0 miles   100

Key

— Motorway

— Major road

⋯ Railway

–•– International border

For keys to symbols *see back flap*

❶ Sofia

With a population of over one million people, Sofia was founded more than 7,000 years ago and has been the capital of Bulgaria since 1879. Today, the city's historic centre bears witness to the diverse cultural influences that have shaped the country. Orthodox churches and an Art Nouveau synagogue are evidence of its rich religious heritage, while Roman, medieval and Ottoman-era buildings serve as reminders of the city's ancient origins. Adding to the city's grandeur are the monumental public buildings from the Communist period, appearing in the downtown squares and junctions. Beyond the city centre, residential suburbs are broken up by attractive swathes of green parkland and the looming presence of Mount Vitosha.

The magnificent Aleksandŭr Nevski Memorial Church

0 metres   200

0 yards   200

Key

▢ Major sight / Place of interest

▢ Pedestrian street

━━━ Motorway

━━━ Major road

═══ Minor road

──── Railway

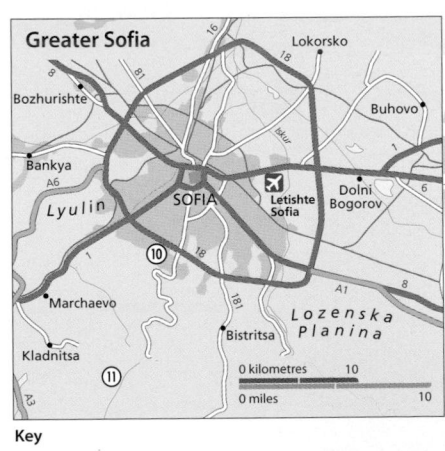

Greater Sofia

Lokorsko

Bozhurishte

Buhovo

Bankya

Lyulin

SOFIA

Letishte Sofia

Dolni Bogorov

Marchaevo

Lozenska Planina

Bistritsa

Kladnitsa

0 kilometres   10

0 miles   10

Key

▢ Area of the main map

(Main map labels:) TSAR SAMUIL · STEFAN STAMBOLOV · BRATYA MILADINOVI · Zhenski Pazar · Railway Station 1 km (0.6 mile) · GEORGE WASHINGTON · MARIA LOUISA · TSAR SIMEON · EKZARH IOSIF · BORIS I · KNYAZ · PIROTSKA · Central Market Hall · Banya F Mosque · BULEVARD KNYAGINYA · BULEVARD TODOR ALEXANDROV · TRAPEZITSA · LOM · Monument to Sveta Sofia · Serdika · PLOSHTA NEZAVISIM · PLOSHTAD SVETA NEDELYA · LAVELE · SVETA SOFIA · Rotunda of Sveti Georgi · SABORN · POZITANO · VITOSHA · TSAR KALOYAN · ALABIN

Sights at a Glance

① Church of Sveta Nedelya
② Sofia Synagogue
③ Archaeological Museum
④ National Art Gallery
⑤ Natural History Museum
⑥ Russian Church
⑦ *Aleksandûr Nevski Memorial Church see pp582–3*
⑧ Church of Sveta Sofia
⑨ National Gallery of Foreign Art
⑩ National History Museum
⑪ Mount Vitosha

Getting Around

The city centre is easy to explore on foot, although visitors may need public transport to reach some outlying museums. An efficient tram network covers the city centre and the inner suburbs, while buses and trolleybuses are a convenient way of reaching Sofia's outer fringes. Taxis are numerous and inexpensive, and the single metro line runs across the city from northwest to southeast, connecting a handful of sites of interest.

For keys to symbols *see back flap*

Church of Sveta Nedelya, one of Sofia's most important places of worship

① Church of Sveta Nedelya

Църква "Света Неделя"

pl. Sveta Nedelya. **Map** C4. **Tel** (02) 987 5748. **Open** 7am–6pm daily. Ⓜ Serdika. 🚋 1, 3, 5, 7, 8, 12, 18. 🖼

Set on an island in central Sofia, the Church of Sveta Nedelya (Tšurkvata Sveta Nedelya) was built on the site of a 10th-century church and has long been one of the city's principal places of worship. It serves as the seat of the bishops of Sofia and has now been given a cathedral status.

During the Ottoman period it was known as the Church of Sveti Kral – the Blessed King – because it held the relics of Stefan Urosh II Milutin, a 14th-century Serbian ruler who defeated the Bulgarian emperor, Mihail Shishman. The bones, believed to have miraculous

Detail of the ornate Moorish exterior of the Sofia Synagogue

healing powers, are kept in a wooden casket beside the iconostasis. The church was rebuilt between 1856 and 1863, but was almost completely destroyed in 1925, when Communist extremists bombed it during a funeral service attended by Tsar Boris III. The arcades on the north side and the gilt iconostasis remain intact. Frescoes executed in the 1970s and a marble floor added in the 1990s give the interior a contemporary look.

② Sofia Synagogue

Софийска Синагога

ul. Ekzarh Iosif 16. **Map** C3. **Tel** (02) 983 5085. 🚋 1, 7, 18, 20, 22. Ⓜ Serdika. **Open** 9am–4pm Mon–Fri, 9am–1pm Sat, call in advance.

One of the largest in Europe, this synagogue (Sofiska sinagoga) can hold as many as 1,300 people. Designed by Austrian architect Friedrich Grünanger and completed in 1909, it has a brass chandelier weighing over 2,000 kg (4,400 lb). The interior also has some exquisite Moorish mosaics, painted pillars and scalloped arches. A Jewish Museum of History tells the history of the Jews in Bulgaria. The museum opens erratically so a visit may not always be possible.

③ Archaeological Museum

Археологически Музей

ul. Saborna 2. **Map** D4. **Tel** (02) 988 2406. 🚋 1, 3, 5, 7, 8, 12, 18. Ⓜ Serdika. **Open** May–Oct: 10am–6pm daily; Nov–Apr: 10am–5pm Tue–Sun. 🈂 🖥 museum annexe. 🆆 **naim.bg**

Many of Bulgaria's finest Thracian, Roman and medieval treasures are preserved in Sofia's Archaeological Museum (Arheologicheski Muzei). The building, once the Grand Mosque (Buyuk Dzhamiya), was built in 1494 and converted into the present museum in 1894. The former prayer hall, a cube-shaped space beneath nine graceful domes, perfectly complements an open-plan display of Greek, Roman and medieval sculpture. The side rooms are devoted to a superb sequence of treasures. Highlights include a finely crafted Golden Burial Mask belonging to a Thracian chieftain of the 5th century BC, a bronze helmet and a delicate golden laurel wreath found near Plovdiv *(see pp594–5)*.

Golden Burial Mask, Archaeological Museum

The ground floor features Roman finds, including finely carved tombs, while the first floor holds a host of valuable medieval icons and lavishly decorated pottery.

④ National Art Gallery

Национална Художествена Галерия

pl. Knyaz Aleksandûr Batenberg 1. **Map** D4. **Tel** (02) 980 3325. 🚋 1, 7, 20, 22. Ⓜ Serdika. **Open** 10am–6pm Tue–Sun. 🈂 Ethnographic Museum: **Tel** (02) 988 4191. **Open** 10am–6pm Tue–Sun. 🈂 📷

The imposing National Art Gallery (Natsionalna Hudozhestvena Galeriya) occupies the west wing of the former royal palace. Built in 1873 for Sofia's Ottoman rulers, it was adapted for the monarchs of independent Bulgaria after 1877. The building's palatial character persists. Many of the exhibition halls have pre-World War I parquet floors and intricate stucco ceilings.

Bulgarian fine art grew out of the icon-painting workshops of the 19th century, and the gallery's exhibition appropriately begins with works by the greatest of all Bulgarian religious artists, Zahari Zograf *(see p586)*. His series of realistic portraits shows great psychological insight and effectively launched Bulgarian painting on a modern European course.

The gallery's collection traces the development of Bulgarian painting. Highlights include a room devoted to the work of local Impressionists, and that of Bulgarian painters of the interwar generation, in which modernist styles are fused with traditional native themes. Foremost among them are Vladimir Dimitrov-Maistora, Zlatyu Boyadzhiev and Tsanko Lavrenov. Exhibitions of contemporary art are often held in the gallery's ground floor rooms.

The **Ethnographic Museum** (Etnografski Muzei) in the east wing has a fascinating collection of traditional Bulgarian costumes. It also mounts temporary exhibitions devoted to aspects of Bulgarian folklore. The museum shop offers a range of traditional craft items.

Entrance to the four-storey Natural History Museum

⑤ Natural History Museum
Национален Природонаучен Музей

bul. Tsar Osvoboditel 1.
Map E4. **Tel** (02) 987 4195. 🚌 9, 94, 280, 306. 🚊 20, 22, 23. Ⓜ Serdika.
Open 10am–6pm daily. **Closed** 1 Jan, 3 Mar, 25 Dec. ♿ 📷
Ⓦ nmnhs.com

The Natural History Museum (Natsionalen Prirodonauchen Muzei) is devoted to European fauna and geology. The display begins by charting the development of rocks and crystals through the ages.

The upper floors exhibit mammals, birds and reptiles, including the Caroline parrot, which is now extinct, as well as bearded vultures, cranes and tamarin monkeys. Live snakes and rodents are kept in glass enclosures on the staircases. The museum shop sells decorative stones and crystals.

⑥ Russian Church
Руска Църква

bul. Tsar Osvoboditel 3. **Map** E4.
Tel (02) 986 2715. 🚊 20, 22, 23.
Ⓜ Sveti Kliment Ohridski.
Open 7:30am–6pm daily. ✉

The Church of St Nicholas the Miracle-Worker (Tsurkva Na Sveti Nikolai Chudotvorets), popularly known as the Russian Church, is the most striking building in Sofia. It was built in 1914 to serve the city's Russian community.

Modelled on 16th-century Muscovite churches, it boasts a cluster of gilt domes, one of which thrusts skywards at the tip of a pea-green spire. The porch, with a steeply pitched roof covered in bright green tiles, exudes a fairy tale charm.

The church's interior, covered with frescoes derived from 17th-century paintings in Moscow and Yaroslavl, reveals the influence of exotic Eastern styles on Russian art. A door on the west side of the church leads down to the crypt, the resting place of Archbishop Serafim, leader of the Russian Church in Bulgaria from 1921 to 1950. Serafim's reputation for anti-Communism and his kindness made him popular with Sofians. Such is his enduring spiritual stature that his tomb is believed to be capable of working miracles. As a result, a regular stream of worshippers can be seen visiting the tomb to place prayers beside his sarcophagus.

Traditionally painted icons in elaborate gilt frames adorning the iconostasis in the Russian Church

⑦ Aleksandûr Nevski Memorial Church

Храм-паметник "Александър Невски"

Crowned with a cluster of gilt domes, the Aleksandûr Nevski Memorial Church (Hram-pametnik Aleksandûr Nevski) was built in stages between 1882 and 1924 to commemorate Russia's military contribution to the War of Liberation of 1877–8. It is named after one of Russia's most revered medieval rulers, Prince Aleksandûr Nevski of Novgorod (1220–63), who defeated the Teutonic knights on the frozen waters of Lake Peipsi in Estonia in 1242. Modelled on Russian Neo-Byzantine churches, it is built in pale Bulgarian limestone. The solemn interior is bathed in amber light, enhanced by the glow of hundreds of flickering candles.

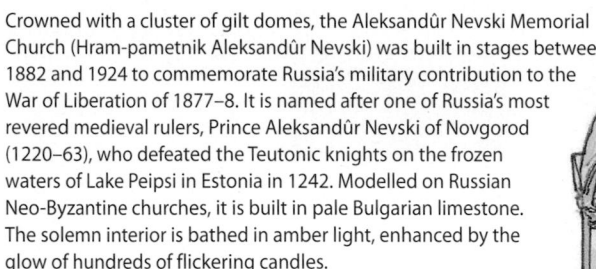

Exterior of the Church
The church's domes are its outstanding feature. While the central dome and belfry are gold-plated, the others are plated with copper, which has developed a green hue.

Entrance to the crypt

★ Icon Gallery in Crypt
With icons dating from the 12th to the 19th centuries and several delicately carved iconostases, this gallery contains the richest collection of religious art in Bulgaria.

Main entrance

KEY

① West window

② Gold-plated dome

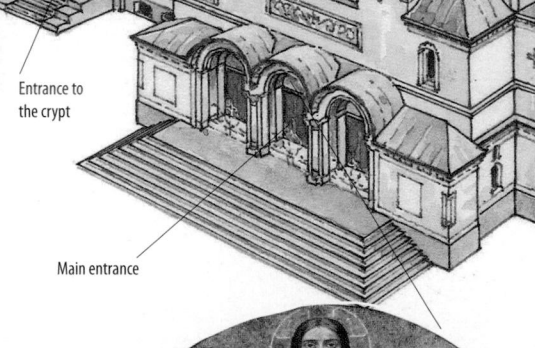

Mosaic of Christ
This mosaic of Christ, with arms outstretched, fills the tympanum over the portal's central arch.

Dome Fresco
The dome fresco depicts God the Creator, with the Christ Child on his knee, looking down on the congregation. The frescoes were painted by Russian and Bulgarian artists.

②

★ Iconostasis
The marble, onyx and alabaster iconostasis features carvings of grapes, palms and peacocks. The icons include portraits of Christ and the Virgin.

Tsar's Throne
Built for Tsar Ferdinand (r. 1887–1918), the throne is guarded by stone lions and crowned by a marble canopy. Behind it is a portrait of the tsar and his wife.

Clusters of Candles
Visitors to the church buy candles at the entrance and light them as a symbol of prayer.

⑧ Church of Sveta Sofia

Църква Света София

pl. Aleksandûr Nevski. **Map** E4.
Tel (02) 987 0971. 🚌 9. 🚋 20, 22, 23.
Open 9am–7pm. ⚿

The origins of Sofia's oldest surviving Christian church go back to the 6th century. It was built on the site of two 4th-century churches outside the city walls. The spot was also the town graveyard of Serdika, as Sofia was known in ancient times. The church remained Sofia's principal cemetery church well into the Middle Ages.

During the Second Bulgarian Kingdom (1185–1396), the church became the seat of the city's bishop. The city itself, known in Bulgarian as Sredets, gradually took the church's name, which means Holy Wisdom. After the Ottoman conquest, the church became a mosque, but was abandoned when an earthquake struck in 1858.

The church takes the form of a three-aisled Byzantine-style basilica. The interior is lofty, calm and peaceful, and the beautiful brickwork of the walls and arches is completely devoid of ornamentation. Some fragments of mosaic from a 4th-century church can be seen on the floor of the south aisle.

Outside the church, beside the south wall, is the Tomb of the Unknown Soldier, which commemorates the thousands of Bulgarian soldiers who died during World War I. The monument is guarded by a stately bronze lion.

⑨ National Gallery of Foreign Art

Национална галерия за чуждестранно изкуство

pl. Aleksandûr Nevski. **Map** F4. **Tel** (02) 980 7262. 🚌 9, 280, 306. 🚋 1, 2, 4, 11. Ⓜ Sveti Kliment Ohridski. **Open** 11am–6pm Mon, Wed–Sun. ⚿ 📷 🖵 **foreignartmuseum.bg**

The pristine white building behind the Aleksandûr Nevski Memorial Church *(see pp582–3)* houses the National Gallery of Foreign Art (Natsionalna Galeriya za Chuzhdestranno Izkustvo). It opened in 1985 and comprises gifts made to the Bulgarian state, either by private

Main entrance to the National Gallery of Foreign Art

individuals or by countries allied to the ruling Communist regime at that time. On the ground floor are outstanding collections of African tribal sculpture and Japanese woodblock prints. Upstairs, a display of 19th- and 20th-century paintings includes a pastel drawing by Renoir, a lithograph by Picasso and some animated sketches by Eugène Delacroix. Thematic exhibitions are often held in the basement, where a barrel-roofed late-Roman tomb is on display.

The building itself is a modern reconstruction of the State Printing House of 1883, one of post-Liberation Bulgaria's finest Neo-Classical buildings, which was destroyed by Allied bombing raids in 1944.

⑩ National History Museum

Национален Исторически Музей

ul. Vitoshko Lale 16, Boyana. **Map** A5. **Tel** (02) 955 4280. 🚌 63, 111. 🚋 2. **Open** Nov–Mar: 9am–5:30pm (last ticket 4:45pm) Tue–Sat; Apr–Oct: 9:30am–6pm (last ticket 5:30pm) Tue–Sat. ⚿ Free last Mon of the month. 📷 🖵 📱 🖵 **historymuseum.org**

Bulgaria's largest collection of historic artifacts is located 7 km (4 miles) from the centre of Sofia. It has a delightful setting in the foothills and showcases remarkable objects. The collections are displayed chronologically over three floors. The building was

Lion guarding the Tomb of the Unknown Soldier, Church of Sveta Sofia

once a Communist Party palace, so touring the vast rooms is interesting in itself, just to see how Communist leaders lived.

On the first floor, the prehistory section features a clay figure called the Earth Mother statue, found near Tûrgovishte in northeastern Bulgaria. Just 14 cm (5.5 in) high, it is believed to be about 6,500 years old. Other highlights include the 3rd-century BC Thracian gold treasures from Panagyurishte in western Bulgaria, which consist of eight richly decorated gold *rhytons* (drinking vessels).

The second floor of the museum includes displays from the 6th millenium BC to the late 19th century AD. Displays cover artifacts from the Neolithic, Chalcolithic and Bronze Ages, jewellery and treasure from the Thracian and Greek settlements as well as manuscripts from the 7th to the 14th centuries, including the richly decorated Tzar Ivan Alexzander's *Gospel*.

The third floor of the museum is devoted to modern history, with military uniforms, hardware and theatrical memorabilia. It also houses a collection of traditional costumes from all over Bulgaria, including metal *pafti* (belt buckles) embossed with animals, figures of saints and abstract designs. Cinema posters and other exhibits taken from the world of entertainment and popular culture are part of the display devoted to 20th-century life.

Fresco of the Last Judgment, National History Museum

Magnificent view of Cherni Vruh, Vitosha's highest point

⑪ Mount Vitosha
Витоша

12 km (7 miles) S of Sofia.
Map A5. 🚌 98 to Dragalevtsi; 122, 123 to Simeonovo: all from Hladilnika Bus Terminus (on tram route no. 10). 🛈 (02) 988 5841.
🅦 **park-vitosha.org**

Rising above Sofia's southern suburbs, the granite massif of Mount Vitosha provides Bulgaria's capital with an easily accessible recreation area. The top of the mountain is relatively smooth, making it the ideal terrain for easy hikes. Acres of beech forest cover the lower slopes, while spruce and pine predominate further up. The mountain's highest point, the 2,290-m (7,500-ft) Cherni Vruh (Black Peak), is surrounded by a plateau covered in grassland, juniper bushes and bogs. Protected since 1934, Vitosha provides a safe, natural habitat for martens, deer, wild boar and, occasionally, brown bears.

Vitosha's main recreational centre, connected to the city by road and within easy reach of the summit, is Aleko. Built in 1924, the mountain hut here is a popular starting point for hikers in summer; in winter, it becomes the centre of a busy ski scene. The pleasant suburbs of Dragalevtsi and Simeonovo, nestling in the foothills, make a good base for exploring the

region. The 14th-century **Dragalevtsi Monastery**, set in deep forest just above the suburbs, contains stunning 15th-century frescoes.

Chairlifts and cable cars run from Dragalevtsi and Simeonovo, providing excellent views over Sofia. The summit of Cherni Vruh is about an hour's walk from Aleko, or a 30-minute walk above the last stop of the highest chairlift, when they are running.

On the western side of Mount Vitosha lies Zlatni Mostove, which features the spectacular Stone River, a popular natural attraction with huge, smooth boulders deposited by a glacier in the last Ice Age.

Unusual Stone River at Zlatni Mostove, Mount Vitosha

❷ Rila Monastery
Рилски манастир

Established in the 10th century by St Ivan of Rila, Rila Monastery (Rilski manastir) is Bulgaria's most impressive example of National Revival architecture. Generously supported by successive kings, the monastery flourished until Ottoman raids destroyed it in the late 15th century. While the Russian Church sponsored its renovation, Rila's monks played a crucial role in preserving Bulgaria's language and history during the most repressive periods of Ottoman rule. Devastated by fire in 1833, the monastery was rebuilt with funding from wealthy Bulgarians intent on cultivating national pride at a time of great hope for liberation from the Ottomans.

Rila Monastery, situated in the northwestern Rila Mountains

Arcades
The murals in the arcades vividly depict sinners thrown into an apocalyptic vision of Hell. This contrasts with the arcades' graceful structure of arches, slender columns and blind cupolas.

Church of the Nativity
The exquisite Church of the Nativity, which stands proudly in the middle of Rila Monastery's courtyard, is the largest monastic church in Bulgaria. Its exterior is a busy but harmonious confection of stripes, curved domes and arches set at different levels. It is worth spending some time exploring the outside before entering the main body of the church.

Entrance to church

★ Murals
Magnificent murals adorn the church walls, illustrating characters and episodes from the Bible. Zahari Zograf, Bulgaria's greatest 19th-century painter, is the only one of the artists responsible to have signed his work.

★ **Holy Relic of St Ivan**
A silver casket holds the nation's holiest relic: the preserved left hand of St Ivan of Rila. In the 16th century, the right hand was taken on a tour of Russia to raise funds for the monastery.

★ **Iconostasis**
This masterpiece was created by a team of woodcarvers working under Atanas Telador between 1839 and 1842. The 10-m (33-ft) wide iconostasis, covered in gold leaf, is elaborately decorated with complex carvings of stylized floral elements, symbolic human and animal images, biblical scenes and wild animals.

Grave of Tsar Boris
The heart of Tsar Boris III, who was allegedly poisoned by the Nazis in 1943 for saving Bulgarian Jews, is buried here.

St Ivan of Rila, patron saint of Bulgaria

St Ivan of Rila

The medieval hermit St Ivan of Rila (880–946) retreated into the Rila Mountains to escape what he believed to be the moral decline of society. He was venerated both for his wisdom and as a healer, and was persuaded by his followers to establish a monastery. After his death, pilgrims came to view his remains, which were believed to possess curative powers.

KEY

① **The arcades** are decorated with some of the finest murals.

② **The three main cupolas** contain murals of the Holy Trinity.

Exploring the Rila Monastery

Deep in the heart of a forest reserve, Rila Monastery has an imposing external presence. The entire complex is ringed by mighty walls, giving it the outward appearance of a fortress. Visitors usually enter through the Dupnitsa (Western) Gate, crossing over ancient stone slabs worn smooth by pilgrims' feet. Several floors of wooden balconies enclose the courtyard and the central Church of the Nativity, with Hrelyo's Tower to one side. To the right of the Dupnitsa Gate is the Treasury Museum, located in the south wing. The north wing, to the left of the gate, contains the old kitchen and leads to the Samokov (Eastern) Gate, which conceals the entrance to the Monastery Farm Museum and leads out to a cluster of restaurants and souvenir shops.

The beautiful intricate carvings on Raphael's cross

Church of the Nativity

Construction of the Church of the Nativity began in 1835, two years after the monastery had been devastated by fire. It was carried out by 19th-century master builder Petûr Ivanovich, who had previously worked on Mount Athos in Greece.

The church's design was intended to be innovative and original, as befitted the National Revival period. For the interior, emphasis was placed on spatiality so as to draw worshippers into the centre of the building. The three large domes were positioned to allow maximum light to fall on the spectacular gilt iconostasis, while keeping the rest of the interior in sombre darkness. The murals on the inner walls are also typical of the period and were executed by the country's

best painters. The biblical scenes that cover the walls are brightly painted and show an attention to detail that was the hallmark of the National Revival movement. Among the many artists responsible were Zahari Zograf and his brother Dimitûr, of the Samokov school of icon painters, which developed in a town near Sofia.

The walls are also filled with delightful displays of icons, some produced by 19th-century artists from Samokov and Bansko *(see p591)*. Others date from much earlier. On the left-hand side of the church, usually hidden away in a wooden drawer, is the serene 12th-century Icon of the Virgin.

A chapel on the right of the church contains a smaller iconostasis and the simple grave of Tsar Boris III, marked with a plain wooden cross.

Treasury Museum

The museum collection includes about 20 miniature crosses, jewelled silver boxes containing ancient Bibles, a ruby-encrusted communion cup and other church silver. The highlight, however, is Raphael's Cross. Just 81 cm (32 in) high, the cross bears a series of biblical scenes carved with needles, each one enclosed in silver-plated frames no larger than a fingernail. The work, completed in 1802, took 12 years and cost the monk Raphael his eyesight.

The lower floor has varied exhibits, including a 2-m (6-ft) long musket and several swords and pistols. Nearby is a collection of books from the monastery library. The oldest dates back to the 10th century and is written on parchment in the Glagolitic script of the old Slavonic languages. Also on display is the Suchava Tetra, a large Bible produced in 1529. Its embossed gold and enamel cover depicts Christ on the cross, with the four evangelists watching from each corner. Several other ancient Bibles are on show below some extravagantly jewelled icons.

A neighbouring glass case is filled with a selection of 19th-century gold church plate. At the far end of the room is a 14th-century ivory-inlaid bishop's throne that belonged to the original monastery church. Alongside

The Church of the Nativity, the courtyard's dominant feature

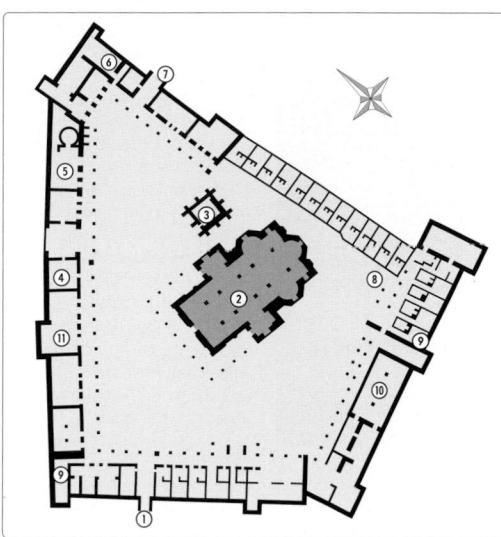

Rila Monastery Plan

① Western Entrance
 (Dupnitsa Gate)
② Church of the Nativity
③ Hrelyo's Tower
④ Monastery Kitchen
⑤ Oven
⑥ Monastery Farm Museum
⑦ Eastern Entrance
 (Samokov Gate)
⑧ Treasury Museum
⑨ Public Toilets
⑩ Icon Exhibition
⑪ Ethnographic Museum

Key

■ See pp586–7

□ Rila Monastery Complex

---

are the skilfully carved original doors from **Hrelyo's Tower** and a pair of 14th-century icons of St Ivan of Rila.

Monastery Complex

In contrast to the monastery's stern exterior, the courtyard is light and open. An elegant tracery of red, white and black striped arches deftly frame more than 300 monks' cells, mirroring the façade of the Church of the Nativity.

Hrelyo's Tower, the monastery's oldest surviving structure, was built by Hrelyo Dragoval, a feudal lord, in 1334. A small chapel on the top floor, with 14th-century frescoes, is occasionally open to the public. Today, access to this mini-fortress is via wooden steps but originally there was a removable stepladder.

An intriguing section of the north wing contains the **Monastery Farm Museum**, which is entered via the old guard house, off Samokov Gate. Here, muskets used by the guards are displayed alongside their red and white uniforms, which have metal breastplates featuring a portrait of St Ivan of Rila and the monastery. Next door is a bare-walled room that houses the monastery's water-powered mill, with a display of

hollow logs once used as sewage pipes. A 19th-century see-saw water pump used for fire fighting demonstrates the precautions taken after the fire that devastated the monastery in 1833. The enormous domed brick oven that takes up most of the next room is an impressive sight. Like the huge pots and cauldrons of the old kitchen, and the giant wooden ladles on display in the adjoining room, the oven's great size was essential to provide sufficient food for the hundreds of monks and pilgrims at the monastery. The kitchen ceiling curves into a huge blackened chimney that tapers elegantly through the four floors of the north wing.

Around Rila Monastery

The **Chapel of St Ivan of Rila** and the dark cave where he spent the last part of his life are an hour's walk north of the monastery and worth visiting to see the surrounding countryside. Visitors can clamber through the narrow opening of the cave ceiling, a challenge once presented to visiting pilgrims: it is said that only the pure of heart can get through.

About 7 km (4 miles) northeast of the monastery is **Kiril Meadow**, an attractive leafy green picnic spot with cafés and a few places offering accommodation.

The 14th-century Hrelyo's Tower, in the monastery courtyard

View of Mount Malyovitsa, Rila National Park

❸ Rila National Park
Национален парк Рила

85 km (53 miles) S of Sofia. 🚌 from Sofia, Samokov. 🏕 campsites, and chalets can be booked via Bulgarian Tourism Union, (02) 987 3409 / 987 6941. 🔲 **panparks.org**

Bulgaria's largest national park is located in the Rila Mountains, the highest range in the Balkan peninsula. The source of several Balkan rivers, the massif derives its name from the Thracian word *rula*, meaning "abundance of water". Its dense forests of spruce, fir and Macedonian pine are home to wolves, bears, boar, Balkan chamois and *suslik* (ground squirrels) as well as the rare wallcreeper and the Alpine chough. No fewer than 57 endemic plant species, including the divine primrose, Rila pansy and Bulgarian avens, also thrive here.

The national park is home to two forest reserves. Created in 2000, the Rila Monastery Forest Reserve covers more than 270 sq km (104 sq miles) around Rila Monastery *(see pp586–9)*. The Parangalitsa Reserve, on the southwestern slopes of the Rila Mountains, was established in 1933 to preserve some of Europe's oldest spruce forests. It is now a protected UNESCO Biosphere Reserve.

A network of hiking trails criss-crosses the park, reaching the spectacular peaks of Musala, at 2,925 m (9,596 ft),

and Malyovitsa at 2,729 m (8,953 ft). One of the most popular hiking trails follows the Seven Lakes – a series of small glacial lakes set amidst beautiful scenery. Formed by melted glaciers, the lakes are set at ascending levels. A set of glacial pools, located below Mount Musala, are also popular with hikers.

❹ Borovets
Боровец

70 km (43 miles) S of Sofia. 🚌 Ⓜ

Located just below the majestic peaks of the Rila Mountains, Borovets is one of Bulgaria's major ski resorts, clustered with large hotel blocks and lines of wooden huts housing bars,

restaurants, ski shops and souvenir stalls. During the winter season, visitors crowd the ski runs and lifts by day, and then move on to the bars and clubs for late-night partying.

The resort also offers a wide range of summer activities, including pony trekking, motorized safaris, hiking and abseiling, most of which can be arranged through the large hotels here. One option is to take the main gondola up to Yastrebets, a peak that rises to the height of 2,369 m (7,775 ft), from where hikers can follow a path to the Musala refuge before climbing to the lofty summit of Musala, the highest peak in the Balkans. Alternatively, the Sitnyakovo Express, a chairlift that operates only on weekends, whisks visitors up to the highest point among the Sitnyakovo ski runs, from where a path leads back down to Borovets.

The resort has one other highlight: the captivating **Bistritsa Palace**. This was built as a hunting lodge for Ferdinand, the prince of Bulgaria in the late 19th century, making Borovets the country's oldest mountain resort. It is sometimes possible to tour the impressive interior, which features luxurious Victorian fittings and elaborate Samokov woodcarving.

🏛 Bistritsa Palace
3 km (2 miles) from central Borovets. **Tel** (0750) 32710. **Open** 9am–4:30pm. 🎟

Ski lesson in Borovets, one of Bulgaria's major ski resorts

Painting with inscription in the Church of Sveta Troitsa, Bansko

❺ Bansko

Банско

160 km (100 miles) S of Sofia.
🏔 8,500. 🚌 🚆 🏛 ℹ pl. Nikola Vaptsarov, (0749) 885 80. 🎭 Pirin Sings (Aug, even years).
🌐 **bansko.bg**

The small mountain town of Bansko lies just below the jagged peaks of the Pirin Mountains. Founded in the 9th century, it remained obscure until the 19th century, when its prospering merchants began to fund the building of churches here. Famous as the birthplace of 19th-century scholar Neofit Rilski, the town is also closely associated with Bulgarian nationalism. Another of its famous sons is Father Paisii, whose seminal work *Slavo-Bulgarian History* provided the impetus for the beginnings of the National Revival.

Bansko's historic centre consists of a labyrinth of cobbled streets running between high stone walls, which conceal 19th-century timber and stone houses. In the Old Town stands the massive **Church of Sveta Troitsa**. Construction began in 1832 but the bell tower was added in 1850. Its carved wood interior contains an intricately designed iconostasis. Behind the church, along ulica Pirin, stands the **Neofit Rilski House-Museum**, former home of Rilski, revered as the founder of modern education in Bulgaria.

The remarkable **Nikola Vaptsarov House-Museum** stands on the corner of a square of the same name. This was the childhood home of Vaptsarov, a poet who was executed for anti-Fascist activities, and the museum contains his possessions.

Bansko's surburbs, mostly filled with hotels, reflect its recent development into a ski resort and weekend retreat.

❻ Melnik

Мелник

182 km (113 miles) S of Sofia. 🏔 385. 🚌 from Sofia. 🌐 **melnik-gb.eu**

Once a thriving centre of wine-making and a major focus of Balkan trade, the enchanting town of Melnik is tucked away in a valley formed by rocky hills crowned with pyramidal sandstone formations.

Wine has been Melnik's major export since the 13th century, when it had tax-free trade with Dubrovnik *(see pp434–40)*. During this period, the despot Aleksei Slav made Melnik the capital of his principality, funding the construction of monasteries and churches in the vicinity. After the Ottoman conquest, Melnik fell into decline, but its fortunes revived in the 19th century, when the town's Greek population began to prosper from exporting wine and tobacco. Much of the town

Bottle of wine from Kordopulov House

of Melnik was destroyed during the Second Balkan War of 1913, however, and its remaining Greek residents left. Today, Melnik is officially Bulgaria's smallest town, but it continues to attract visitors, who come to admire the intriguing rock features and taste the famous wine that is still produced by a few local families.

Most of Melnik's attractions are at the top of a hill overlooking the town. The **History Museum** is housed in a building located right next to the Despot Slav hotel. The museum is a branch of the Regional History Museum of Sandanski. It has a fine collection of exhibits on display including terracotta wine vessels, regional costumes and photographs. Further on is **Kordopulov House**, a superb example of early National Revival architecture in which Western and Oriental motifs are combined on a grand scale. The interior features a central salon and an Ottoman-style raised seating area. Downstairs is a small *mehana* (tavern) connected to a labyrinthine wine cellar.

🏛 **History Museum**
Pashovata Kŭshta.
Open 9am–noon, 1–5pm daily.

🏠 **Kordopulov House**
Kordopulov House.
Open 9am–7:30pm daily.
♿ ✏ 📷

Melnik and its square *konak*, the Town Hall during Ottoman rule

❼ Bachkovo Monastery

Бачковски манастир

At the foot of Rhodope Mountains lies Bachkovo
Monastery (Bachkovski manastir), the second largest
monastery in Bulgaria after Rila Monastery *(see pp586–9)*.
It was founded in 1083 by Grigori and Abbasi Bakouriani,
Georgian brothers who were commanders in the Byzantine
Army. In the 13th century, the monastery was sponsored
by Tsar Ivan Asen II and his successor Ivan Aleksandûr.
Destroyed by the Ottomans in the 16th century, it
was restored by the 17th century. Today, its serene
courtyards are filled with trees and drinking fountains,
and, thanks to its architecture and frescoes, it has
been added to UNESCO's World Heritage List.

The Ossuary
Located away from the main
monastery complex, the ossuary
is the only surviving part of the
11th-century monastery.

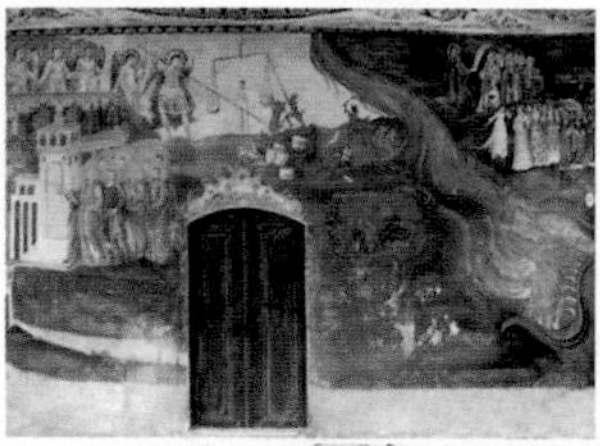

★ Last Judgment
In the porch of the Church of Sveti Nikola
is a fresco of the Last Judgment by Zahari
Zograf, with sinners falling into the
fires of Hell.

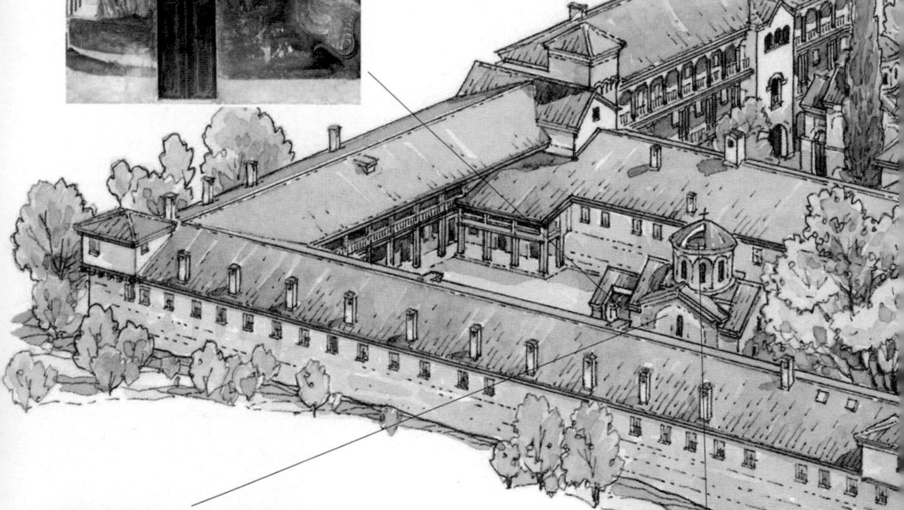

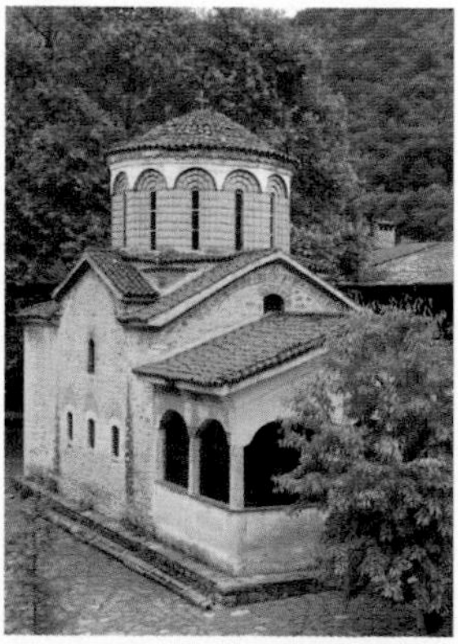

Church of Sveti Nikola
A door to the left of the main
courtyard leads to the Church
of Sveti Nikola, which was
built in 1834. It contains
frescoes by Zahari Zograf and
other renowned painters.

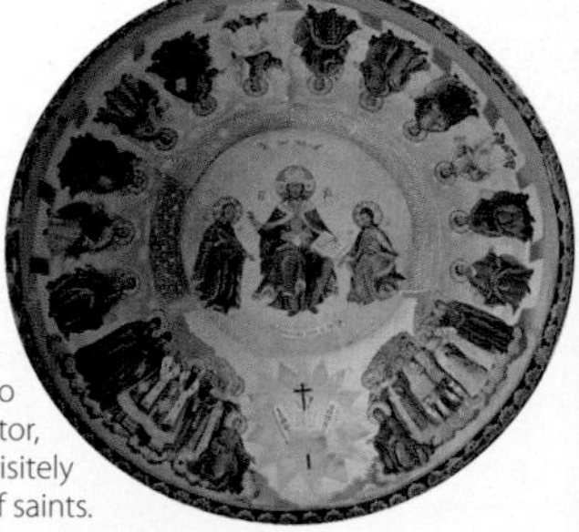

Fresco in the Dome
The dome of the
Church of Sveti Nikola is
decorated with a fresco
of Christ Pantocrator,
encircled by exquisitely
painted portraits of saints.

Church of Sveta Bogoroditsa
This 17th-century church is richly decorated with frescoes. Themes include the Devil addressing Christ from the mouth of a monster, and Death shadowing an angel.

★ Iconostasis
The Church of Sveta Bogoroditsa also contains a highly ornate 17th-century gilt iconostasis, which gleams in the soft light of hundreds of flickering candles.

Devotees gather here to kiss the silver-plated Icon of the Virgin, painted in 1310.

Main entrance

Ayazmoto

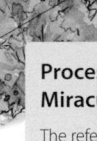

Procession of the Miraculous Icon

The refectory wall on the left of the courtyard bears the largest panoramic wall painting in Bulgaria. Painted by Alexi Atanasov in 1846, it depicts the annual procession of the Icon of the Virgin on 15 August, the day of the Assumption of the Virgin. After Orthodox Easter, the icon is carried to Ayazmoto.

Ayazmoto
The nearby hills shelter a chapel near a locality known as Ayazmoto. The Icon of the Virgin was once hidden here from the Ottomans.

★ Refectory
A solid stone table and wooden benches stretch the length of the 17th-century refectory. The vaulted ceiling is covered with frescoes by pupils of Zahari Zograf.

Procession of the miraculous Icon of the Virgin Mary

❽ Plovdiv
Пловдив

Situated along the two banks of the Maritsa river, Plovdiv is Bulgaria's second largest city after Sofia. Settled as early as the 7th millennium BC, the city was held by the Romans between the 1st and 4th centuries. It rose to economic power in the 14th century under the Ottomans, becoming a centre of the Bulgarian National Revival in the 19th century when wealthy citizens built ornamented houses. In 1885, Plovdiv became part of Bulgaria. Today, it is a pleasant city, with a pedestrianized centre, mosques, churches, Roman ruins and National Revival mansions. An architectural reserve, the Old Town consists of steep cobbled streets lined with museum-houses and galleries all the way up to Nebet Hill, from where there are stunning views over the city.

The well-preserved Roman Theatre, still used for performances

🏛 Roman Stadium
pl. Dzhumaya.

Crumbling marble terraces and columns, oddly incorporated into the concrete foundations of modern Plovdiv, are almost all that remains of the city's once huge Roman stadium. Built in the 2nd century AD, it could seat 30,000 spectators.

⛪ Church of Sveta Marina
ul. Dr Vulkovich 7.

The present church was built in 1783 on the site of a 16th-century church. It is renowned for its iconostasis, which is decorated with tiny figures painted by various artists including Zahari Zograf.

🏛 Roman Theatre
ul. Hemus. **Open** 9am–5:30pm daily. 🖼

This impressive amphitheatre, set in the hillside overlooking the city and the Rhodope Mountains beyond, was discovered during construction work in 1972. It was built in the 2nd century AD, when Roman Plovdiv (Trimontium) was at its height, and formed part of the acropolis. Today, the theatre is used for plays and concerts.

⛪ Church of Sveta Bogoroditsa
ul. Saborna 6. **Open** 7:30am–6:30pm daily. 📷

The imposing Church of Sveta Bogoroditsa has a distinctive pink and blue bell tower which was added with Russian assistance in 1880, after the Liberation. Its murals echo the mood of the late 19th century. They depict Bulgarian Orthodox saints alongside leaders of the Liberation movement.

🏛 Hristo Danov House
ul. Mitropolit Paisii 2. **Open** 9am– noon, 2–5pm Mon–Fri. 📷

Built on Taxim Hill (Taxim Tepe) and approached up steep steps, Hristo Danov House overlooks Plovdiv. Its arched gable is supported by four columns, and trompe l'oeil pillars adorn the façade. The symmetrical interior layout is typical of National Revival architecture. Hristo Danov, founder of organized book publishing in Bulgaria, lived here from 1868 until his death in 1911.

🏛 State Gallery of Fine Arts
ul. Sûborna 14a. **Open** 9:30am–12:30pm, 1–5:30pm Mon–Fri, 10am–12:30pm, 1–5:30pm Sat, Sun. 📷 free on Thu.

This gallery has a vast collection of 19th- and 20th-century Bulgarian paintings. Solemn 19th-century portraits hang alongside idyllic pastoral scenes and some vibrant works by Vladimir Dimitrov-Maistor. Large, bold canvases on the second floor represent more recent Bulgarian painting. Among the works here is *The Fire* (1977) by Svetlin Rusev, in which a figure walks away from a furnace carrying a glowing ember into the darkness.

💊 Hipokrat Pharmacy
ul. Sûborna. **Open** 10am–5pm Mon–Fri.

The fascinating Hipokrat Pharmacy has been preserved virtually as it was when it was a working pharmacy. It is lined with wooden drawers and contains bottles and jars neatly labelled in Latin.

🏛 Icon Museum
ul. Sûborna 22. **Open** 9:30am–12:30pm, 1–5:30pm Mon–Fri, 10am–12:30pm, 1–5:30pm Sat, Sun. 📷 free on Thu.

This interesting museum is home to a valuable array of

The State Gallery of Fine Arts, in an imposing Neo-Classical building

15th- and 16th-century icons collected from churches under threat during the Communist years.

🏛 Hindliyan House

ul. Artin Gidikov 4. **Open** 9am–5pm Mon–Fri. 🖼

This elegant house, its pale blue outer walls decorated with floral motifs, looks on to a peaceful courtyard garden. It was built between 1835 and 1840 for Stepan Hindliyan, a wealthy Armenian merchant. The interior has murals depicting the European cities that he visited. The house also has a

Icon of Sts Cyril and Methodius in the Icon Museum

Room in Nedkovich House, built for a textile trader in 1863

hammam with a marble floor, and a domed ceiling with tiny windows. The first-floor salon has a stunning panelled ceiling and a marble fountain.

🏛 Nedkovich House

ul. Tsanko Lavrenov 3.
Open 8:30am–4:30pm Mon–Fri. 🖼

This grand house is a fine example of National Revival architecture. An interesting feature is the courtyard structure with a window to the street called the *klyukarnik* (gossip room), where the inhabitants could drink tea and chat. The rooms contain many original furnishings, imported from the East and West to blend European and oriental styles.

🏛 History Museum

pl. Sŭedinenie 1. **Tel** (032) 229 409.
Open 9:30am–5pm Mon–Sat (until 6pm Oct–Mar) 🖼 Thu (free entrance). 🖼

Housed in what was intended to be eastern Rumelia's new parliament building, the museum documents the reunification of Plovdiv with Bulgaria in 1885. Exhibits include declarations, weaponry, uniforms and photographs of soldiers.

☪ Imaret Mosque

ul. Han Kubrat.

Dating from 1445, this is one of more than 50 mosques built in Plovdiv during the Ottoman period. *Imaret* means "shelter for the homeless", and this was the mosque's original function. Its square walls support a central dome and a minaret with unusual zigzag brickwork.

Plovdiv City Centre

① Roman Stadium
② Church of Sveta Marina
③ Roman Theatre
④ Church of Sveta Bogoroditsa
⑤ Hristo Danov House
⑥ State Gallery of Fine Arts
⑦ Hipokrat Pharmacy
⑧ Icon Museum
⑨ Hindliyan House
⑩ Nedkovich House
⑪ History Museum
⑫ Imaret Mosque

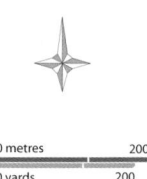

0 metres   200
0 yards   200

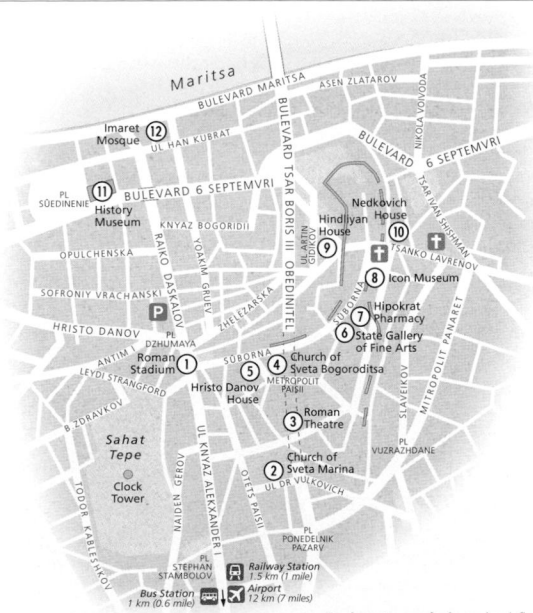

For keys to symbols *see back flap*

❾ Koprivshtitsa
Копривщица

Considered one of Bulgaria's most attractive towns due to its many fine National Revival houses, Koprivshtitsa was founded in the 14th century. It was originally a rich centre of cattle farming. Under Ottoman rule its citizens were granted autonomy in return for collecting taxes on behalf of the Ottoman Empire. In the early 19th century, Koprivshtitsa's prosperity attracted *kûrdzhali* (bandits), who plundered and torched the town on several occasions. It was during the ensuing period of reconstruction that its colourfully painted wood and stone houses were built. Koprivshtitsa was also the home of several of Bulgaria's leading revolutionaries, and it was here that the momentous April Rising of 1876 *(see p576)* was declared.

Kableshkov House, elegant home of the leader of the April Rising

🏠 Debelyanov House
ul. Dimcho Debelyanov. **Tel** (07184) 2077. **Open** May–Oct: 9:30am–5:30pm Tue–Sun; Nov–Apr: 9am–5pm Tue–Sun. 🖼

This delightful house set above the town was the birthplace of the Symbolist poet Dimcho Debelyanov, who was killed in action in World War I. The house contains personal possessions, such as books, photographs and paintings, including a portrait of the poet by Georgi Mashev.

Statue in the garden of Debelyanov House

🏠 Church of Sveta Bogoroditsa
ul. Dimcho Debelyanov 26. **Open** irregular hours. 🏠

The blue-walled Church of Sveta Bogoroditsa played a memorable role in Bulgarian history. On 20 April 1876, its bell rang out to announce the beginning of the April Rising. The church was built in 1817 on the site of an earlier church that was destroyed by the *kûrdzhali*. Surrounded by thick stone walls, it was built slightly sunken into the ground so as to comply with Ottoman regulations governing the height of Christian churches. The three-storey bell tower was added in 1896. The church's interior is plain, but it has a superb iconostasis by wood-carvers of the Tryavna School. Some of its icons were painted by Zahari Zograf. Tragically, the church's original murals were replaced by newly painted icons in the course of misguided renovation.

🏠 Kableshkov House
ul. Todor Kableshkov 8. **Tel** (07184) 2054. **Open** May–Oct: 9:30am–5:30pm Tue–Sun; Nov–Apr: 9am–5pm Tue–Sun. 🖼

This imposing building was the home of Todor Kableshkov, leader of the April Rising. He declared the start of the uprising with his Bloody Letter, written in the blood of the revolutionaries' first Turkish victim. The house was built in 1845 to a symmetrical design, the central salons on both floors flanked by identical rooms. The central bay on the upper floor has stepped windows and a decorated ceiling.

🏠 Bridge of the First Shot
ul. Pûrva Pushka.

A hallowed site in Bulgarian history, this humpbacked bridge in a quiet location southwest of the town centre is the spot where the first Turk was killed during the April Rising.

🏠 Lyutov House
ul. Nikola Belovezhdov 2. **Tel** (07184) 2138. **Open** May–Oct: 9:30am–5:30pm Wed–Mon; Nov–Apr: 9am–5pm Wed–Mon. 🖼

Designed by master craftsmen from Plovdiv in 1854, Lyutov House features a huge curved gable, symmetrical layout and decorative features of Plovdiv architecture. In 1906, it was acquired by Petko Lyutov, a local merchant. The central salon has an elliptical vaulted ceiling edged with murals of the cities that Lyutov visited. The rooms on either side are furnished with Ottoman-style benches and European furniture. On the ground floor is an exhibition of 18th- and 19th-century rugs, made in Koprivshtitsa.

🏠 Oslekov House
ul. Gereniloto 4. 🛈 (0885) 743 657. **Open** 9:30am–5:30pm Tue–Sun (9am–5pm winter). 🖼

This house was built in 1856 for the wealthy merchant, Nincho

The Church of Sveta Bogoroditsa, whose bell proclaimed the April Rising

Oslekov. Due to space restrictions, it is asymmetrical, but is otherwise typical of the National Revival style, with separate winter and summer quarters. Murals depict places Oslekov visited while on business. Views of European cities decorate the façade, while on the walls of the Red Room are paintings of mansions and the original symmetrical plan for the house.

Karavelov House
bul. Hadzhi Nencho Palaveev 39. **Tel** (07184) 2191. **Open** 9:30am–5:30pm Wed–Mon.

Home to one of the National Liberation movement's key ideologists, Karavelov House

The pretty painted façade of the Oslekov House

consists of two separate buildings. The winter quarters were constructed in 1810, while the summer house, built over the main entrance, was added in 1835. Lyuben Karavelov was a prolific writer, publisher and fervent revolutionary, responsible for publishing two newspapers in Bucharest. The printing press is on display here in the winter quarters along with some of the publications he put together with fellow revolutionaries.

Benkovski House
ul. Georgi Benkovski 5. **Tel** (07184) 2030. **Open** 9:30am–5:30pm Wed–Mon (9am–5pm winter).

Georgi Benkovski, who was born as Gavril Hlutev, became a revolutionary in Romania. He returned to Koprivshtitsa in 1875 to form the legendary "winged" cavalry detachment that rallied support from local villages during the April Uprising. This was the Hlutev family home and the rooms contain his revolutionary flag, Winchester rifle and personal photographs. The veranda has a replica of one of the cherry-tree cannons used in the uprising. The granite monument on the hillside

View of Koprivshtitsa from the Benkovski monument

above the house portrays a cloaked Benkovski astride a leaping horse looking over his shoulder to rouse his rebel army.

Koprivshtitsa Town Centre

1. Debelyanov House
2. Church of Sveta Bogoroditsa
3. Kableshkov House
4. Bridge of the First Shot
5. Lyutov House
6. Oslekov House
7. Karavelov House
8. Benkovski House

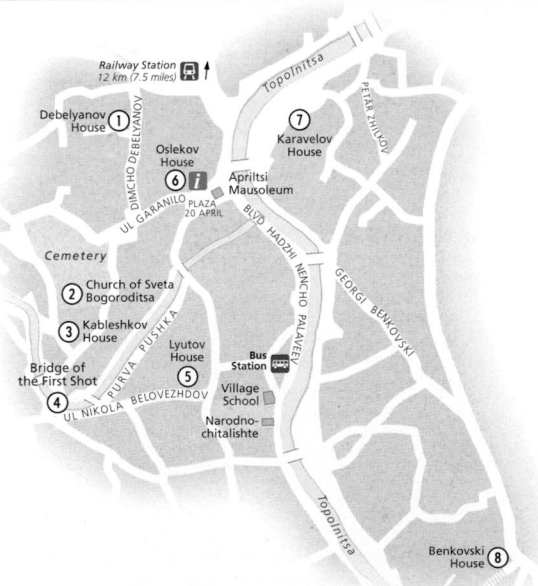

0 metres 100
0 yards 100

For keys to symbols see back flap

⑩ Veliko Tûrnovo
Велико Търново

With a picturesque hillside setting, fine architecture and a wealth of historic sights, Veliko Tûrnovo is one of Bulgaria's most beautiful cities. Tall, narrow houses teeter on sheer cliffs that rise high above the meandering Yantra river, while to the east are the ruins of the majestic fortress of Tsarevets *(see pp600–601)*. The city has a proud history as the mighty capital of the Second Kingdom (1185–1393), and later as the seat of liberated Bulgaria's first National Assembly. By day, Veliko Tûrnovo bustles with a mix of locals, students and visitors. After dark, the focus switches to the city's lively bars and clubs.

🏠 House of the Little Monkey
ul. Vûstanicheska 14. **Closed** to the public.

This house, one of many in Veliko Tûrnovo designed by the great local architect Kolyo Ficheto, dates from 1849. It is set on a hillside, with the ground floor accessible at street level, and entrances to the two upper floors at the rear. It features a pair of bay windows, attractive red-and-white brickwork, and a tiny statue of a monkey that gives the house its name.

🏠 Samovodska Charshiya
Varusha quarter.

In the 19th century, Samovodska Charshiya developed into a thriving bazaar, with stalls, workshops and a caravanserai for visiting merchants. It is located in the pleasant historic Varusha quarter of the city, which rises steeply above the Old Town. The attractive stone houses that line the bazaar's narrow cobbled streets are now occupied by souvenir shops selling local craft items.

An outdoor café in Samovodska Charshiya, Varusha quarter

⛪ Church of Sts Cyril and Methodius
ul. sv sv Kiril i Metodi, Varusha quarter. **Open** 8am–7pm daily. 🏛

Built by Kolyo Ficheto in 1860, this church lost its dome and belfry during an earthquake in 1913. A curved wooden balcony at the back of the church was designed for the segregation of female worshippers.

⛪ Church of Sveti Nikolai
ul. Vûstanicheska 43, Varusha quarter. **Open** 8am–7pm daily. 🏛

Kolyo Ficheto's design for this church features a simple stone exterior and a red-tiled roof. The iconostasis, with dragons, eagles and a central sun motif lighting the church's gloomy interior, is a stunning example of the work of the Tryavna School, Bulgaria's oldest school of icon painting. The bishop's throne has an allegorical carving of a dragon (Turkey) attacking a lion (Bulgaria) that is being suffocated by a snake (the Greek-speaking priesthood).

🏛 Asenevtsi Monument
Asenevtsi Park.

Unveiled in 1985 to mark the 800th anniversary of the founding of the Second Bulgarian Kingdom, this monument features a mighty sword, with the figures of Asen, Petûr, Ivan Asen II and Kaloyan, the four tsars who ruled the kingdom from 1185 to 1241. The monument is an excellent point from which to admire the city's old houses, precariously perched on the cliffs opposite.

🏛 Art Gallery
Asenevtsi Park. **Tel** (062) 938 951. **Open** 10am–6pm Tue–Sun. Nov–Feb: 10am–5pm.

Bulgarian paintings of the 19th and 20th centuries make up this fine collection. Charcoal landscapes by Boris Denev fill much of the ground floor, while the upper rooms hold works by Dimitûr Kazakov, with sharply outlined figures in abstract compositions. Some monumental works are *Veliko Tûrnovo in the Past* (1981) by Naiden Petkov and *People Say Goodbye to Patriarch Evtimii* (1969) by Svetlin Rusev.

🏠 Sarafkina House
ul. Gen. Gurko 88. **Tel** (062) 635 802. **Open** 9am–noon & 1–6pm Tue–Sat.

With stone walls below and whitewashed walls above, shuttered windows and a tiled roof, this house is typical of the city's 19th-century domestic architecture. It was built in 1861

Church of Sveti Nikolai, built by the 19th-century architect Kolyo Ficheto

For hotels and restaurants see p610 and p611

Luxurious interior of Sarafkina House

for Dimitûr Sarafkina, a wealthy banker, and is set on sheer cliffs above the river. The wood-panelled interior displays Western-style furniture as well as family photographs and period outfits.

🏛 Archaeological Museum

ul. Ivanka Boteva 2. **Tel** (062) 601 528.
Open Apr–Oct: 9am–6pm Tue–Sun, noon–6pm Mon; Nov–Mar 9am–5pm Tue–Sun, noon–5pm Mon. 📷

The courtyard of this building is littered with Classical columns and busts. Although several artifacts were stolen in 2006, most of this absorbing collection remains in place. The centrepiece is a replica of a burial site, Kaloyan's Grave. It was discovered in 1972 near the Church of the Forty Martyrs in the Asenova quarter *(see pp600–601)*. On the skeleton

was a gold ring and seal bearing the name Kaloyan, suggesting that these may be the remains of Tsar Kaloyan. The gold seal of Tsar Ivan Asen II is displayed under a magnifying glass in an adjoining room. Downstairs are finds from the Roman city of Nikopolis ad Istrum; the ruins lie 20 km (12 miles) north of Veliko Tûrnovo.

Fine arcades of the grand old Archaeological Museum

🏛 Museum of the National Revival and Constituent Assembly

pl. Sûedenenie 1. **Tel** (062) 629 821.
Open Apr–Oct: 9am–6pm Wed–Mon, noon–6pm Tue; Nov–Mar 9am–5:30pm Wed–Mon, noon–5:30pm Tue. 📷

Built by Kolyo Ficheto for the city's Ottoman governor in 1872, this vast edifice became Bulgaria's first parliament building after the Liberation. It holds a copy of the new state's first constitution, signed in 1879, as well as a huge collection of material relating to the revolt against Ottoman rule.

🏛 Modern History Museum

pl. Sûedenenie 1. **Tel** (062) 623 847.
Open 9am–5pm Mon–Sat. 📷

Housed in a former prison, the museum's exhibits cover the Balkan Wars and Bulgaria's role in World War I. A display recalls the life of one of the most popular Bulgarian prime ministers, Stefan Stambolov, who was born in Veliko Tûrnovo.

Veliko Tûrnovo City Centre

① House of the Little Monkey
② Samovodska Charshiya
③ Church of Sts Cyril and Methodius
④ Church of Sveti Nikolai
⑤ Asenevtsi Monument
⑥ Art Gallery
⑦ Sarafkina House
⑧ Archaeological Museum
⑨ Museum of the National Revival and Constituent Assembly
⑩ Modern History Museum

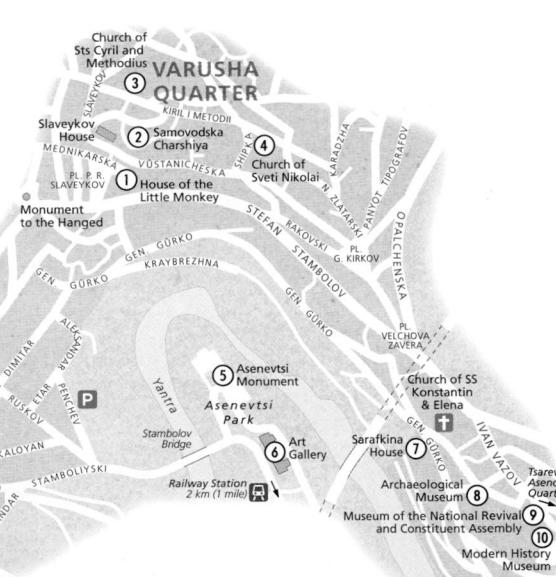

Veliko Turnovo: Tsarevets & Asenova Quarter
Царевец и Асенова Махала

The hilltop fortress of Tsarevets occupies a commanding position on a rocky hill that is almost completely encircled by the Yantra river. It was a sought-after vantage point from the 4th millennium BC and in 1186, Tsar Petûr made it the capital of the Second Bulgarian Kingdom. When the kingdom fell to the Ottomans in 1393, Tsarevets was reduced to rubble. Only a few buildings have been completely restored. Below the walls of Tsarevets and straddling the banks of the river, lies the Asenova Quarter. For centuries it was inhabited by a community of artisans and clerics, but they left after a devastating earthquake in 1913.

★ **Light Show**
A fantastic light show, with a soundtrack, takes place almost every night in summer. Waves of colour light up the fortress, and the spectacle culminates with fireworks and the ringing of bells.

Church of St George
Constructed in 1616, the church contains badly damaged and heavily restored frescoes of Orthodox saints.

To Veliko Tûrnovo

Main Gate

Asenova Gate
Reconstructed in 1976, this three-storey gate tower was used by the inhabitants of the Asenova Quarter.

KEY

① **The Church of the Forty Martyrs**, built in 1230, commemorates Ivan Asen II's victory over the Byzantines.

② **The Church of the Dormition**, dedicated to the Dormition of the Virgin, was built in 1923.

③ **Church of Sts Peter and Paul** dates from the 13th century and is notable for its openwork capitals, frescoes of the two saints, to whom it is dedicated, and a depiction of the *pietà*.

★ **Baldwin's Tower**
Named after Emperor Baldwin of Constantinople, who was held here in the 13th century, this tower guarded the southernmost point of the hilltop. Earlier, it was known as the Frenk Hisar Gate, and defended the merchants' quarter.

For hotels and restaurants see p610 and p611

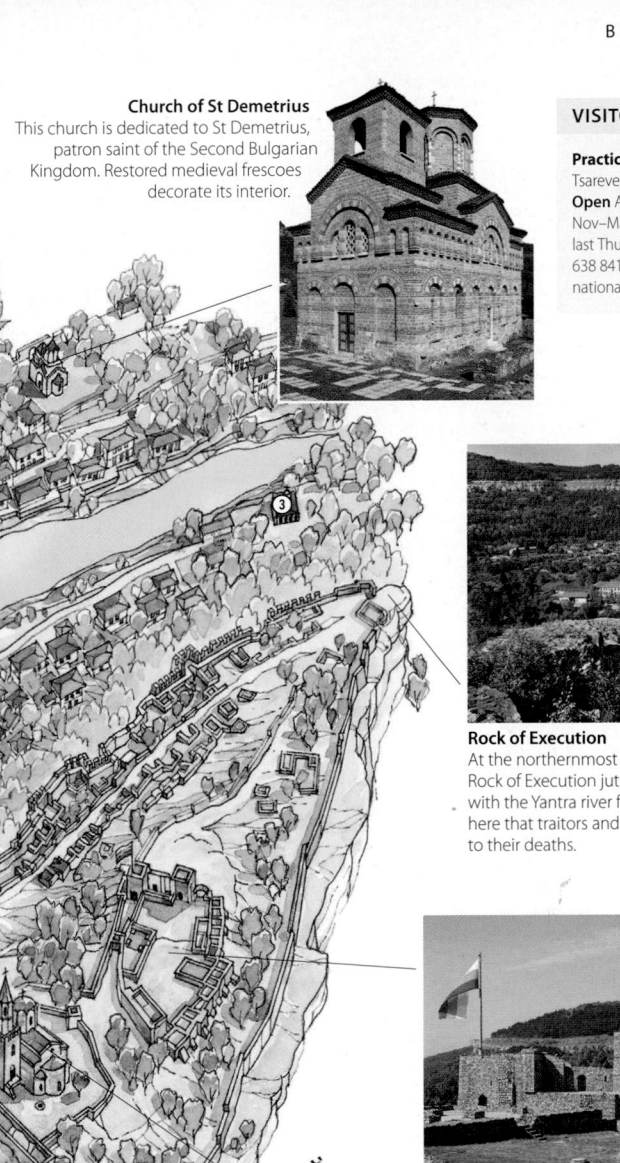

Church of St Demetrius
This church is dedicated to St Demetrius, patron saint of the Second Bulgarian Kingdom. Restored medieval frescoes decorate its interior.

Rock of Execution
At the northernmost point of the fortress, the Rock of Execution juts out above sheer cliffs, with the Yantra river far below. It was from here that traitors and criminals were pushed to their deaths.

★ **Royal Palace**
Built in the 12th century, the Royal Palace was an enclosed complex with a central courtyard. Now partially reconstructed, it has modern concrete staircases enabling visitors to climb up for magnificent views of the surroundings.

Patriarchate
At the hill's highest point is the 13th-century Church of the Patriarchate. Defended by thick walls, it was once part of the patriarch's residential complex. Striking modern murals adorn the interior.

0 metres		50
0 yards		50

⑪ Varna
Варна

With wide pedestrianized boulevards and a sandy beach, Varna has the tranquil air of a coastal resort, despite being a centre of commerce and Bulgaria's third largest city. As Varna's remarkable Archaeological Museum shows, the city's history goes back to the 5th millennium BC. In the 6th century BC, it was settled by Greeks. The thriving colony fell to the Romans in the 1st century BC, but retained its role as one of the Black Sea's key ports. Varna became part of Bulgaria in the 8th century. It was taken over by the Ottomans in 1393, but after the Liberation of 1878 it rapidly grew to become the bustling modern city, port and resort that it is today.

🏛 Archaeological Museum
bul. Maria Luiza 41. **Tel** (052) 681 011. **Open** Summer: 10am–5pm Tue–Sun; Winter: 10am–5pm Tue–Sat. 🎟 ⬛ 🗔 📷 **w** amvarna.com

Over 100,000 ancient artifacts discovered in and around Varna fill this museum. It was founded in 1888 by the Czech archaeologist Karel Škorpil, who pioneered the exploration of Bulgaria's ancient past. The collection is housed in 40 rooms on two floors. The most intriguing section is that devoted to Varna's necropolis, west of the modern city. It contains some stunning gold items. The upper floor has pottery, weaponry and religious art from the medieval period.

Archaeological Museum exhibit

🏛 Cathedral of the Assumption
pl. sv sv Kiril i Metodi. **Tel** (052) 613 005. **Open** 8am–6pm daily. 🕇 📷

The second-largest place of Christian worship in Bulgaria after the Alexandŭr Nevski Memorial Church in Sofia (*see pp582–3*), this cathedral was built to commemorate the Russian soldiers who died in the fight for liberation from Ottoman rule. Funded by Varna's citizens and designed by Russian architect Maas, it was completed in 1886. The interior is covered with over-life-size murals painted under Russian supervision in 1949, and the vast iconostasis and splendid bishop's throne are the work of master craftsmen from Macedonia.

🏛 Ethnographic Museum
ul. Panagyurishte 22. **Tel** (052) 630 588. **Open** May–Oct: 10am–5pm daily; Nov–Apr: 10am–5pm Tue–Sat. 🎟 📷

Housed in a fine 19th-century National Revival-style house, this is one of Bulgaria's largest ethnographic museums. The ground floor is devoted to farming, with a wide array of tools for harvesting, beekeeping and viniculture.

Upstairs, traditional costumes are on display, along with the re-creation of a typical farmer's house used by the Gagauz, a Turkish-speaking Christian people who settled on the Black Sea coast in the 12th century.

🕇 Church of the Assumption
ul. Han Krum 19. **Tel** (052) 633 925. **Open** 7:30am–6pm Mon–Sat, 10am–6pm Sun. 🕇

This small church, built in 1602, is set below ground level, in accordance with the orders given by the Ottoman rulers that churches should be no higher than a man on horseback, lest they outshine mosques. The attractive wooden bell tower was added after the Liberation. The church contains Varna's oldest icon, a brilliant 13th-century depiction of the Virgin.

A surviving section of the Roman Thermae baths complex

🕇 Roman Thermae
ul. Han Krum. **Tel** (052) 600 059. **Open** May–Oct: 10am–5pm Tue–Sun; Nov–Apr: 10am–5pm Mon–Fri. 🎟

A monument to the ingenuity of Roman architects, this massive public baths complex covers over 7,000 sq m (75,000 sq ft). It was built in the 2nd century AD for what was then the Roman city of Odessos. Although in ruins, enough of the complex is intact to give an idea of Roman bathing habits. The exorbitant amount spent on the baths caused their steady decline in the 3rd and 4th centuries.

🏛 City History Museum
ul. 8 Noemvri 3. **Tel** (052) 632 677. **Open** 10am–5pm Tue–Sun. 🎟

Constructed in 1851, this building is one of Varna's oldest surviving houses. The museum

Iconostasis made by Macedonian craftsmen, Cathedral of the Assumption

The torpedo boat, *Drûzhki* at the entrance of the Navy Museum, Varna

traces the history of Varna from the late 18th century, when it was a neglected coastal town, to the mid-20th century, when it became a major port and popular seaside resort.

Navy Museum
bul. Primorski 2. **Tel** (052) 632 018.
Open Summer: 10am–6pm
Wed–Sun; Winter: 9am–5:30pm
Tue–Sat.

The prize exhibit of the Navy Museum is the torpedo boat *Drûzhki* (Intrepid) displayed outside the museum. In 1912, during the First Balkan War, the *Drûzhki* secured the Bulgarian navy's only victory in the conflict when it sank a large Turkish cruise ship.

The museum itself holds exhibits relating to navigation on the Black Sea starting from the 6th century BC.

Sea Gardens
Aquarium: **Tel** (052) 632 066.
Open May–Sep: 9am–8pm daily;
Oct–Apr: 9am–5pm daily.
aquariumvarna.com
Planetarium: **Tel** (052) 684 441. **Open**
Mar–Oct: 5pm, 6pm Tue–Sat, Nov–Feb:
5pm Tue–Fri. shows for pre-booked
groups only. Dolphinarium: **Tel** (052)
302 199. shows during summer
at 10:30am, noon, 3:30pm, 5pm.
dolphinarium.festa.bg

Begun in 1862, this urban park was designed by Czech landscape architect Anton Novak, with trees and plants from Bulgaria and around the Mediterranean. Among its flowerbeds and shaded paths are several family-friendly attractions, including an **Aquarium** with stingrays, a **Planetarium** and a **Dolphinarium** with regular shows conducted in four languages. Stretching out

below the Sea Gardens is Varna's long, sandy beach. Lined with outdoor restaurants, cafés and bars, it is ideal for lazy days of swimming and sunbathing. After dark, the beach is one of the Black Sea's liveliest spots, with clubs open until the small hours.

Evksinograd Palace
Tel (052) 393 140. **Open** 10am–3pm
Mon–Fri, only for pre-booked groups
of 5 or more. **Closed** July & Aug.

Located 8 km (5 miles) from central Varna, the spectacular Evksinograd Palace, built for Prince Aleksandûr Batenberg I, was completed in 1886, and served as the summer residence for Bulgarian royalty until the Communists came to power in 1944. It was designed by famous Viennese architect Rumpelmeyer and its gardens were laid out by French landscape designers in the 19th century. Today, the palace is still a state property.

Varna Town Centre

1. Archaeological Museum
2. Cathedral of the Assumption
3. Ethnographic Museum
4. Church of the Assumption
5. Roman Thermae
6. City History Museum
7. Navy Museum
8. Sea Gardens

0 metres   300
0 yards   300

⓬ Stone Forest
Побитите камъни

420 km (260 miles) E of Sofia. 🚌

As the name suggests, the famous Stone Forest (Pobiti kamûni) is a cluster of tree-like stone columns. Spread over a barren landscape, they stand together in 7 groups of more than 300 each. Some of them are 6 m (20 ft) high and up to 9 m (30 ft) in circumference.

The stones are believed to be 50 million years old and their origins have long been the subject of scientific speculation. Among the numerous theories advanced by experts, it is generally agreed that they were formed when separate layers of chalk merged through a layer of sand. Some scientists, however, still support the theory that they are fossilized remnants of an ancient forest.

Massive tree-like pillars of the 50-million-year-old Stone Forest

⓭ Golden Sands
Златни пясъци

455 km (283 miles) E of Sofia. 🚌 from Varna. 🏨 🖥 goldensands.bg

Bulgaria's second largest coastal resort after Sunny Beach, Golden Sands (Zlatni pyasâtsi) certainly lives up to its name. Wooded hills, which are part of the Golden Sands Nature Park, slope down towards the sea, rimmed by an almost continuous line of newly built hotels. The beach itself is an unbroken 3.5-km (2-miles) long stretch of fine white sand. The areas behind the beach feature well-tended gardens, outdoor pools and

Beach at Golden Sands, one of Bulgaria's most popular resorts

sports facilities for children. The resort has a wide range of restaurants and bars and offers a variety of water sports.

Environs
About 7 km (4 miles) inland from Golden Sands is the **Aladzha Monastery**. The hermits who settled here in the 6th century cut dozens of cells and chambers into the limestone cliff, and evidence of Stone Age dwellers has also been discovered. The caves are now linked by sturdy metal steps, but the monks accessed them by scrambling up and down perilous ledges, using footholds that are still visible in the cliff face.

A museum at the entrance displays earlier models of the monastery, alongside ancient relics, including artifacts dating from around 5000 BC discovered in a Chalcolithic necropolis on the outskirts of Varna.

⓮ Kaliakra
Калиакра

520 km (323 miles) E of Sofia. 🚌 from Varna. **Open** 10am–7pm daily. 🚲 ⛵ 🚢 🏛

Meaning "fine nose" in Greek, Kaliakra is a rocky promontory that extends 2 km (1 mile) into the sea. Locals attribute the reddish colour of its limestone cliffs to the blood of the many people who died in battles for control of this strategic point. Kaliakra is now an extensive archaeological site, occupied by the ruins of a grand fortress dating back to the 4th century BC. It was successively held by Greeks, Romans, Bulgarians and Ottomans. According to legend, 40 maidens tied their hair together and jumped into the sea here to escape a worse fate at the hands of invading Ottoman soldiers. The spot affords stunning views of the imposing cliffs around the coast.

Ruins of the 4th-century BC fortress at Kaliakra

⓯ Sunny Beach
Слънчев бряг

430 km (267 miles) E of Sofia.
🚌 from Burgas. 🏨
🌐 sunnybeach.bg.com

Established in the 1960s, Sunny Beach (Slûnchev Bryag) was one of Bulgaria's first coastal resorts. It is now the country's largest, and it continues to expand in all directions. Palatial hotels, apartment blocks and Socialist-era leisure complexes stretch out behind a beach 8 km (5 miles) long.

Sunny Beach has earned Blue Flag status in view of its high environmental standards and is particularly popular with families and visitors on package holidays. The resort offers a range of water sports, as well as a multitude of shops.

⓰ Nesebûr
Несебър

435 km (270 miles) E of Sofia.
🏨 8,700. 🚌 from Sunny Beach, Burgas and Varna (in summer). 🚢 daily.

Set on a rocky peninsula, Nesebûr was first settled by Thracians, but it was in the 13th and 14th centuries that it reached its commercial and cultural zenith. Today, it is a UNESCO World Heritage Site, and tends to become very crowded in summer.

The beautiful Old Town is packed with historic houses and attractive churches, many in Byzantine style. Among the churches, the **Old Metropolitan Church**, founded in the 5th century, is the largest and oldest. Although it is in ruins, it is still the focal point of the Old Town, and a popular meeting point and concert venue. In the 15th century, it was supplanted by the **New Metropolitan Church**, which has a breathtaking interior densely covered in 16th- to 18th-century frescoes, as well as an ornate bishop's throne and a wooden pulpit. The **Archaeological Museum** provides a fascinating insight into Nesebûr's long history, with fine Thracian and medieval collections, including an

Ruins of the Old Metropolitan Church, Nesebûr

outstanding array of icons, gold jewellery and architectural elements. There is also an Ethnographic Museum.

⓱ Burgas
Бургас

403 km (250 miles) E of Sofia.
🏨 200,300. ✈ 🚉 🚌 🚍 🚢 daily.
🌐 burgas.bg

Burgas had its heyday in the 19th century, when it enjoyed an economic boom based on craftsmanship and the export of grain. It has benefited from recent refurbishment and has several fine churches and museums.

The **Church of Sts Cyril and Methodius** was designed by Ricardo Toskanini, an Italian architect who strongly influenced Burgas's architecture in the early 20th century.

Nearby, the Ethnographic Museum contains a good collection of traditional costumes, while the Archaeological Museum has a small but captivating display of items dating back 10,000 years. The town's Art Gallery has some fine 18th- and 19th-century icons as

Elegant façade of the Church of Sts Cyril and Methodius, Burgas

well as works by modern Bulgarian painters, including local artists.

Environs
Outside Burgas is **Lake Poda**, a haven for rare birds and plants. Managed by the Bulgarian Society for the Preservation of Birds, the lake and its environs are internationally important.

⓲ Sozopol
Созопол

435 km (270 miles) E of Sofia.
🏨 5,750. 🚌 from Burgas. 🏨
🚢 daily. 🎭 Apollonia Arts Festival (first 10 days in Sep). 🌐 sozopol.com

With sandy bays to the north and south, Sozopol stands on a peninsula jutting out into the Black Sea, its cobbled streets lined with pretty old houses. One of the First Bulgarian Kingdom's major ports, it remained an important centre of shipbuilding, commerce and fishing until it was overtaken by Burgas in the 19th century.

The collections in the Archaeological Museum document Sozopol's long history, including Greek pottery and some fascinating figurines from the ancient Greek necropolis. Most of the town's medieval churches were destroyed in the Ottoman period, but later examples remain, including the 15th-century Church of Sveta Bogoroditsa, with elaborate wooden iconostases, and the Church of Sveti Zosim, with icons by the famous artist Dimitar of Sozopol. Sozopol also hosts the Apollonia Arts Festival, one of Bulgaria's foremost cultural events.

Practical & Travel Information

With fine cities, beautiful beaches and ski resorts, Bulgaria is a mecca for sun-seekers and winter sports enthusiasts alike. Travelling to the country is relatively easy, with frequent flights and trains from most European countries. Although domestic travel may not be as quick and easy as in other European destinations, there are no serious obstacles, and Bulgarians are helpful and courteous towards foreign visitors.

When to Visit

Bulgaria is an attractive destination all year round. On the Black Sea coast, the main holiday season runs from May to September, peaking in July and August when temperatures are at their highest and the beaches fill with holidaymakers. Bulgaria's historic cities, with their churches, museums and art galleries, are rewarding places to visit at any time of the year.

Documentation

To enter Bulgaria, citizens of European Union (EU) countries do not need a visa but must show a valid passport or ID card. Citizens of Australia, Canada, New Zealand and the US do not need a visa for a stay of less than 90 days. Nationals of other countries should check current regulations with the Bulgarian Embassy or consulate in their country.

Visitor Information

The availability of visitor information in Bulgaria differs greatly from one region to another. A useful resource is the National Information and Publicity Centre in Sofia, which is run by the **Bulgarian Tourism Authority** and provides information on the whole country. There are also some privately run regional information centres, mostly in those areas popular with hikers and skiers, and in towns such as Bansko (see p591) and Koprivshtitsa (see pp596–7), which attract visitors on account of their historic and cultural interest. Visitor information centres in such places sell maps of the local area and can offer advice on accommodation in the vicinity.

Surprisingly, given its popularity with holiday-makers, there are very few tourist information centres on the Black Sea coast.

For details of local attractions and tourist excursions, and advice on local restaurants, visitors should enquire at the reception desks of their hotels, or go to a privately run travel agency in the nearest town or city.

Health and Security

Basic medical advice is available at pharmacies but, as hospitals are underfunded, visitors should make sure that they have adequate medical insurance for private care in case of more serious problems. Every major town has a duty pharmacy with an emergency counter that is open 24 hours a day. However, it may be difficult to find one with English-speaking staff.

Although Bulgaria has a low crime rate, petty theft can be a problem in major towns and cities and in tourist spots. To minimise the risk of being targeted, take basic precautions and keep documents, money and credit cards hidden from view at all times; keep valuables in the safe in your hotel room and beware of pickpockets in crowded areas.

Facilities for the Disabled

Few public buildings, shops and visitor attractions in Bulgaria are adapted for wheelchair users. Pavements everywhere are uneven and unramped, many museums are in older buildings without lifts, and access to archaeological sites is also very difficult.

Most of Sofia's five-star hotels are wheelchair-accessible, and they all also have rooms that have been specially adapted for use by disabled guests.

Banking and Currency

Bulgarian towns and cities are well serviced by banks, and automatic cash machines can be found outside most major high-street branches. Credit cards are increasingly accepted in high-end hotels, restaurants and luxury shops, but are not widely used elsewhere. Most transactions, from paying for a stay in a hostel to buying souvenirs, are usually made in cash.

The currency of Bulgaria is the *lev*, which is divided into 100 *stotinki*. As *leva* are not widely available outside Bulgaria, visitors will need to withdraw currency on their arrival to the country.

The Climate of Bulgaria

Bulgaria lies in two overlapping climate zones – continental and Mediterranean – characterized by warm, dry summers and cold winters. Temperatures in summer, between June and September, average between 17° C (63° F) and 24° C (75° F). In winter, between December and February, they rarely rise above 6° C (43° F) but may drop to - 1° C (30° F).

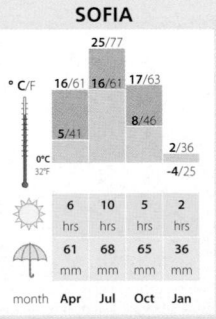

SOFIA

month	Apr	Jul	Oct	Jan
°C/F	16/61	25/77	17/63	
	5/41	16/61	8/46	2/36
				-4/25
	6 hrs	10 hrs	5 hrs	2 hrs
	61 mm	68 mm	65 mm	36 mm

0°C 32°F

Communications

Bulgaria's national telephone and postal systems are reasonably efficient, although the postal service is a little slower than in some Western European countries. Visitors will have no trouble finding an Internet café, even in small towns.

Visitors can avoid high call charges by buying a pre-paid SIM card from a Bulgarian mobile phone operator, enabling them to make calls to local numbers at Bulgarian rates during their stay.

Arriving by Air

Sofia is well served by direct flights from other European countries. **Bulgaria Air**, the national carrier, has daily scheduled flights to Sofia from **Gatwick Airport** in London, Amsterdam, Paris and other European capitals. **British Airways** also provides scheduled flights to Sofia from **Heathrow Airport** in London. The low-cost airlines **easyJet** and **Wizz Air** offer flights to Sofia, Varna and Burgas from the UK and parts of Central Europe. Direct flights to Bulgaria from North America and other non-European countries are rare. Most intercontinental routes involve flying to either London, Amsterdam or Frankfurt, then taking a connecting flight to Bulgaria.

Bulgaria's largest airport is **Sofia Airport**, which serves the capital. It has convenient transport connections with the city centre, which is about 10 km (6 miles) to the west. Much of western and central Bulgaria is easily accessible from Sofia. For visitors heading for the Black Sea coast, there are budget flights to **Varna Airport** and **Burgas Airport**.

Rail Travel

The total cost of travelling to Bulgaria by train is likely to be higher than by air. It may also be difficult to buy one ticket all the way from Western Europe to Bulgaria. From Continental Europe, the main routes to Bulgaria are from Budapest to Sofia via Belgrade or Bucharest. The country's rail network is operated by the **Bulgarian State Railways** (Bulgarska durzhavna zheleznitsa, or BDZ). Train tickets can be purchased at station ticket offices. Reservations are advisable for visitors travelling between Sofia and the Black Sea coast during summer. The best sources of information on train travel to Bulgaria are **Rail Europe** and **Trainseurope**.

Travelling by Bus

Bus services in Bulgaria are operated by several national and regional bus companies. Most towns and villages are accessible by bus. Intercity bus routes connecting Sofia with major towns and cites depart several times a day. Buses on these routes are modern, with comfortable seats and air conditioning.

Tickets can be bought from counters at bus stations, but not on the buses themselves. On intercity routes, advance reservations are advisable. Tickets and information on bus travel throughout Bulgaria is available from **Sofia Central Bus Station**.

Travelling by Car

Exploring Bulgaria by car is an attractive option, as it gives greater freedom and allows visitors to explore more remote areas of the country that may not be well served by public transport. However, visitors should bear in mind that motorways are few, and that road conditions often leave much to be desired. Road signs on main intercity trunk roads are in Cyrillic and Roman scripts. Cars can be hired from reliable service providers such as **Avis**, **Budget** and **Europcar**.

DIRECTORY

Documentation
w **mfa.bg/en**

Embassies and Consulates

United Kingdom
ul. Moskovska 9, Sofia.
Tel (02) 933 9222.
w **ukinbulgaria.fco. gov.uk**

United States
ul. Kozyak 16, Sofia.
Tel (02) 937 5100.
w **bulgaria.usembassy. gov**

Visitor Information

Bulgarian Tourism Authority
w **bulgariatravel.org**

Emergency Numbers

Ambulance
Tel 150.

Emergency Calls
Tel 112.

Fire
Tel 160.

Police
Tel 166.

Arriving by Air

British Airways
w **britishairways.com**

Bulgaria Air
w **air.bg**

Burgas Airport
w **burgas-airport.com**

easyJet
w **easyjet.com**

Gatwick Airport
w **gatwickairport.com**

Heathrow Airport
w **heathrowairport.bg**

Sofia Airport
w **sofia-airport.bg**

Varna Airport
w **varna-airport.bg**

Wizz Air
w **wizzair.com**

Rail Travel

Bulgarian State Railways
w **bdz.bg**

Rail Europe
w **raileurope.com**

Trainseurope
w **trainseurope.co.uk**

Travelling by Bus

Sofia Central Bus Station
w **centralnaavtogara. bg**

Travelling by Car

Avis
Tel (02) 826 1100.
w **avis.bg**

Budget
Tel (02) 870 0001.
w **budget.bg**

Europcar
Tel (02) 981 4626.
w **europcar.bg**

Shopping & Entertainment

Bulgaria has a wealth of shops, malls, open-air markets and stalls selling everything from Bulgarian-made soaps to *rakiya* (fruit brandy). In every town centre there is a market, its stalls stacked with fruit, vegetables and flowers, and street kiosks with meticulously arranged trays of dried fruit, nuts and sweets. The country's classical music, ballet and theatre season runs from the beginning of October to the end of June, when orchestras, opera and ballet companies perform at venues in Sofia and other major towns, and theatre companies stage productions of classical and contemporary plays. Bulgaria's summer folk festivals also provide an opportunity to see the country's vigorous folk culture.

also carry a wide selection of Bulgarian wines. While Bulgarian Merlot and Cabernet Sauvignon are on a par with red wines from elsewhere in Europe, domestic varieties, such as Melnik from the southwest, have a much more distinctive character. The highest quality wines are those produced by leading wineries such as **Todoroff** and **Damyanitza**. These are available in stores throughout the country. Bottles of *rakiya* (grape or plum brandy) make very good gifts. Bottles marked *otlezhala* (matured) are likely to be of superior quality.

Opening Hours

In major towns, cities and holiday resorts, shops open from 10am to 8pm from Monday to Saturday, and often later during the summer season. In Sofia and towns along the Black Sea coast, shops also open on Sundays, closing at various times between 2 and 6pm.

Markets

Every town in the country has an open-air market, where fresh fruit and vegetables and a great variety of Bulgarian cheeses and sausages are sold.

Several of Bulgaria's most picturesque outdoor markets sell not only fresh produce, clothing and household goods but also handicrafts. The liveliest of these are the daily **Zhenski Pazar** in Sofia, the daily market in Varna and the Sunday morning market in Bansko.

The daily **Bric-à-Brac Market** in front of the Aleksandûr Nevski Memorial Church in Sofia is the best place for antiques, old postcards, and Communist-era medals and militaria.

Handicrafts

High-quality craft items are abundant at Bulgaria's souvenir stalls, with ceramics, embroidery and traditional textiles among the most popular tourist buys. Pottery from the central Bulgarian town of Troyan, decorated with flowing patterns in bright colours, is a favourite Bulgarian souvenir, and is available throughout the country.

Traditional Bulgarian textiles include vividly patterned *kilims* (carpets) hand-woven on vertical looms by the womenfolk in highland villages. Other highland crafts include *guberi* (fleecy rugs), and *kozyatsi* (tufted goat-hair rugs). Brightly coloured blouses, delicately embroidered with folk motifs, are usually also of high quality.

Bulgaria is a major producer of attar of roses, an essential oil extracted from the damask rose, which is used all over the world in perfumes and beauty products. Locally made soaps, skin creams and eau de cologne made from Bulgarian attar are available from pharmacies and supermarkets throughout the country. Other items to look out for include traditional copper pots and coffee sets, and hand-painted copies of Orthodox icons.

Souvenirs can be found in market stalls and small shops in tourist resorts across the country. Specialist outlets selling fine handicrafts include the **Ethnographic Museum Shop** in Sofia. Shops in Veliko Tûrnovo are also good places to pick up good-quality items made by local crafts workshops.

Food, Wine and Rakiya

The most famous Bulgarian speciality is yogurt, considered very healthy due to a rare bacteria found only in Bulgaria. *Sirene* (salty white cheese) and *kashkaval* (cheese made from cow's milk) are also some good buys available in most supermarkets. Most food shops

Nightlife

Central Sofia is packed with clubs and bars, many of which have designer interiors and attract an equally style-conscious clientele. **Motto**, which serves cocktails and food in a trendy lounge-bar atmosphere, is typical of Sofia's contemporary bar scene. There is also a growing number of pubs, of which **McCarthy's** is one of the longest-established.

Dance clubs are informal and inexpensive, with long-standing venues such as **Yalta** and **Mascara** attracting international DJs and a young crowd.

Music, Theatre and Dance

Bulgaria has a fine tradition of classical music and tickets for concerts are very reasonably priced. The Bulgarian Philharmonic Orchestra, which performs weekly at the **Bulgaria Concert Hall** in Sofia, is the country's most prestigious orchestra. Plovdiv, Varna and Burgas also have good symphony orchestras. Many of Bulgaria's best ensembles and soloists perform at **Varna Summer International Festival** in July.

Local bands playing rock and jazz standards are a frequent feature of bars and clubs in the cities and holiday resorts. Rock and pop stars perform at the **National Palace of Culture** in Sofia. International jazz musicians gather for the **Varna International Jazz Festival** in early August, and the **Bansko Jazz Festival** in mid-August.

Every sizeable town and city in Bulgaria has at least one theatre. Sofia's leading theatre, the **Ivan Vazov National Theatre**, is the base for Bulgaria's best actors and directors. Modern plays are also put on by the **Sofia Drama Theatre**, the **Aleko Konstantinov Satirical Theatre**, and **Tears and Laughter**, Sofia's oldest theatre.

The **Sfumato Theatre Workshop** is well known internationally for putting on contemporary and avant-garde plays. However, the main festival for challenging modern drama is **Scene at the Crossroads**, which takes place in Plovdiv in mid-September. Modern drama also forms part of **Sozopol's Arts Festival**, in early September. For visitors from other countries, the main disadvantage is that almost all performances are in Bulgarian with simultaneous

translations seldom provided. However, many are based on improvisation and movement rather than text, so they are accessible even to non-Bulgarian speakers.

The leading opera and ballet companies in the country operate under the aegis of the **National Opera and Ballet Sofia**. The **Plovdiv Opera and Philharmonic Society**, **Stara Zagora Opera** and **Varna Opera and Philharmonic Society** are the best regional companies.

Information and tickets for most cultural events in Sofia are available from the National Palace of Culture.

Cinema

New Hollywood blockbusters and other international films reach Bulgaria a month or two after their release elsewhere. They are screened in their original language, with subtitles

in Bulgarian. Modern multiplex cinemas with comfortable seats and high-quality sound are common in Sofia. Outside the capital, cinemas tend to be old-fashioned and badly ventilated. Both in Sofia and elsewhere, cinema tickets are inexpensive.

Folk Festivals

Performances of traditional folk music and dancing are an important feature of the Bulgarian calendar. The leading folk festival, held in Koprivshtitsa, is the **International Folk Festival**, at which folk dancers and musicians from all over Bulgaria perform. This takes place every five years on a meadow outside the village.

The **Folklore Days Festival**, a smaller gathering featuring local folk singers and dancers, is held in central Koprivshtitsa in mid-August each year.

DIRECTORY

Markets

Bric-à-Brac Market
pl. Aleksandŭr Nevski, Sofia.

Zhenski Pazar
bul. Stefan Stambolov, Sofia.

Handicrafts

Ethnographic Museum Shop
pl. Aleksandŭr Batenberg 1, Sofia. **Tel** (02) 989 5010; 989 6416.

Food, Wine and Rakiya

Damyanitza
W damianitza.bg

Todoroff
W todoroff-wines.com

Nightlife

Mascara
bul. G. S. Rakovski 113, Sofia. **Tel** 886 272 272.

McCarthy's Irish Pub
ul. Alabin 29A, Sofia. **Tel** (89) 995 3243.

Motto
ul. Aksakov 18, Sofia. **Tel** (02) 987 2723.
W motto-bg.com

Yalta
bul. Tsar Osvoboditel 20, Sofia. **Tel** (02) 980 1297.
W yaltaclub.com

Music, Theatre and Dance

Aleko Konstantinov Satirical Theatre
ul. Stefan Karadzha 26, Sofia. **Tel** (02) 988 1060.

Bansko Jazz Festival
Vaptsarov Square, Bansko.
W bansko-jazz.com

Bulgaria Concert Hall
ul. Aksakov 1, Sofia. **Tel** (02) 987 7656.

Ivan Vazov National Theatre
ul. Dyakon Ignatii 5, Sofia. **Tel** (02) 811 9227.
W nationaltheatre.bg

National Opera and Ballet Sofia
Dondukov Bul. 30, Sofia. **Tel** (02) 987 1366.
W operasofia.bg

National Palace of Culture
pl. Bulgaria 1, Sofia, **Tel** (02) 916 6300. W ndk.bg

Plovdiv Opera and Philharmonic Society
Tel (032) 625 553.
W ofd-plovdiv.org

Scene at the Crossroads
Tel (032) 630 476.
W scenatepe.com

Sfumato Theatre Workshop
ul. Dimitar Grekov 2, Sofia.
Tel (02) 944 0127.
W sfumato.info

Sofia Drama Theatre
bul. Y Sakuzov 23a, Sofia.
Tel (02) 944 2485.
W sofiatheatre.eu

Sozopol's Arts Festival
Tel (02) 980 7833.
W apollonia.bg

Stara Zagora Opera
M M Kussev 30, Stara Zagora. **Tel** (042) 622 431.
W stateopera-starazagora.com

Tears and Laughter
ul Rakovski 127, Sofia.
Tel (02) 987 5895.

Varna International Jazz Festival
Chaika 50-D-47, Varna.
Tel (052) 302 322.
W vsjf.com

Varna Opera and Philharmonic Society
pl. Nezavisimost 2, Varna.
Tel (052) 665 022.
W operavarna.bg

Varna Summer International Festival
W varnasummerfest.org

Folk Festivals

Folklore Days Festival
W folklore-bg.com

International Folk Festival
W varnafolk.org

Where to Stay

Sofia

Art Hostel €
Hostel
ul. Angel Kanchev 21a
Tel *(02) 987 0545*
W art-hostel.com
Full of art with a charming
garden and communal kitchen.
There's even a bar-gallery
for exhibitions.

Bulgari €€
Value   **Map** B3
ul. Pirotska 50
Tel *(02) 831 0060*
Located in one of Sofia's
oldest shopping areas. Rooms
are neatly decorated and have
TV and desk space.

Scotty's Boutique Hotel €€
Boutique   **Map** C3
ul. Ekzarh Yosif 11
Tel *(02) 983 6777*
W scottyshotel.biz
Elegantly transformed block that
has themed rooms decorated in
bright colours and kitschy fabrics.

Grand Hotel Sofia €€€
Luxury   **Map** D5
ul. Gûrko 1
Tel *(02) 811 0801*
W grandhotelsofia.bg
Leading full-service hotel with
majestic rooms and efficient service.

Sheraton Sofia Hotel
Balkan €€€
Luxury   **Map** C4
pl. Sveta Nedelya 5
Tel *(02) 981 6541*
W sheratonsofia.com
Sheer opulence, complete
with chandeliers, grand
rooms with plush furnishings
and more.

Sofia Plaza €€€
Luxury
bul. Hristo Botev 154
Tel *(02) 813 7912*
W hotelsofiaplaza.com
Conveniently located for the city's
historic and cultural sites. Chic
rooms and apartment suites.

Rest of Bulgaria

BACHKOVO: Djamoura €
Guesthouse
ul. Osvobozhdenya 74
Tel *(03327) 2320*
W djamura.com
Cosy rooms and suites in a
restored house, next to Bulgaria's
second-largest monastery.

BANSKO: Kempinski Grand
Hotel Arena €€€
Luxury
ul. Pirin 96
Tel *(0749) 88888*
W kempinski-bansko.com
Plush five-star hotel with
service matching its fantastic
mountain views. Perfect for
ski-lovers.

BOROVETS: Rila €€€
Luxury
Tel *(07503) 2295*
W rilaborovets.com
Bulgaria's largest ski hotel
right next to the slopes,
offers elegant rooms and
superb facilities.

MELNIK: Litova Kûshta €€
Guesthouse
Tel *(07437) 2313*
W litovakushta.com
Hotel built upon an ancient
wine cellar; rooms with
hand-painted borders and
wood ceilings.

DK Choice

PLOVDIV: Renaissance €€
Guesthouse
pl. Vuzrazhdane 1
Tel *(032) 266 966*
W renaissance-bg.com
Decorated in traditional 19th-
century style, this hotel on the
fringes of the Old Town offers
rooms with period furniture
and hand-painted walls.

KOPRIVSHTITSA:
Tryanova Kûshta €
Guesthouse
ul. Gereniloto
Tel *(07184) 3057*
All-wooden house with comfortable
rooms that feature traditional
fabrics and pine furniture.

VELIKO TÛRNOVO:
Hikers Hostel €
Hostel
ul. Rezervoarska 91
Tel *(0889) 691 661*
W hikers-hostel.org
Quirky wooden furniture. The
summer terrace has great views.

BURGAS: Bulgaria €€
Boutique
ul. Aleksandrovska 21
Tel *(056) 841 291*
W bulgaria-hotel.com
Sophisticated 17-storey building
with fantastic views of Burgas.

SOZOPOL: Orion €€
Guesthouse
ul. Vihren 28
Tel *(0550) 23193*
W hotel-orion.net
A modest establishment with ten
rooms and six apartments.

DK Choice

VARNA: Graffit Gallery €€€
Boutique
bul. Knyaz Boris I 65
Tel *(052) 989 900*
W graffithotel.com
This stylish building holds four
floors of chic rooms, each floor
in a different colour. Luxurious
rooms and bathrooms, spa
centre and gym.

Picturesque setting of the luxurious Kempinski Grand Hotel Arena in Bansko

For map references see pp578–9

Where to Eat and Drink

Sofia

Boyansko Hanche €
Bulgarian
pl. Sborishte 1
Tel *(02) 856 3016*
A folk-style restaurant offering
the full range of Bulgarian cuisine
and a sprinkling of international
steak and chicken dishes.

DK Choice

Pod Lipite €€
Bulgarian
ul. Elin Pelin 1
Tel *(02) 866 5053*
Just across the road from the
Borisova Gradina Park, "Under the
Limes" perfectly re-creates the
atmosphere of a 19th-century
country tavern with its wood-
beamed interior and delicious
home cooking. The emphasis is
on grilled and oven-baked meats.

Sushi Bar €€
Japanese
ul. Ivan Denkoglu 18
Tel *(02) 981 8442*
Chic, but by no means too formal,
Sushi Bar offers a huge choice of
expertly prepared sushi.

Gioia €€€
Italian **Map** D3
ul. Tsar Samuil 60
Tel *(02) 986 0854*
Exquisite Italian fare in an intimate
setting. Excellent fresh pasta, veal
cutlets and a list of fine fish dishes.

L'Etranger €€€
French **Map** D3
ul. Tsar Simeon 78
Tel *(02) 983 1417*
Upscale family-run bistro serving
well-made dishes, from simple
quiches to full meals.

Maraia Fusion €€€
International
ul. G.S. Rakovski 123
Tel *(02) 980 6260*
Mixing the informality of a diner
with haute cuisine standards, this
upscale option serves an imaginative
range of European-Asian dishes
alongside excellent sushi.

Shades of Red €€€
International **Map** D5
ul. Gûrko 1
Tel *(02) 811 0811*
Classy restaurant attached to the
Grand Hotel Sofia, offers a wide
variety of Mediterranean and
French dishes.

Sidoniya €€€
International
ul. Slavovitsa 51a
Tel *(0893) 688 884*
Imaginative fusion of modern
European and Bulgarian cuisine,
with the menu changing regularly.

The Chefs €€€
International
Lake Pasarel
Tel *(0896) 723 222* **Closed** *Mon,
Tue, Wed, Thu*
Award-winning, weekend-only
restaurant, 17 km (10.5 miles)
southeast of town. Offers European
cuisine combining inventiveness
and flair. Menu changes daily.

Rest of Bulgaria

BACHKOVO: Djamoura €
Bulgarian
ul. Osvobozhdenie 74
Tel *(03327) 2320*
Great place for grilled meats,
excellently cooked local trout
and vegetarian dishes.

**BANSKO: Obetsanova
Mehana** €€
Bulgarian
pl. Vazrazhdane 1
Tel *(0878) 555 611*
Converted from an old National-
Revival-style house into a tavern.
Serves Bansko specialities.

MELNIK: Mencheva Kûshta €
Bulgarian
Tel *(07437) 339*
An old house with a distinct
character; the perfect place to
sample traditional dishes.

PLOVDIV: Veda House €
Vegetarian
ul. Georgi Benkovski 50
Tel *(032) 622 760*
Two-storey café–restaurant known
for tasty vegetarian dishes, leaf
teas and home-made biscuits.

DK Choice

**PLOVDIV: Art Café
Filipopolis** €€€
International
ul. Suborna 29
Tel *(032) 624 851*
More of a restaurant, this café
has an elegant interior and an
oudoor terrace with sweeping
views of modern Plovdiv. The
mains menu has competently
handled steaks, duck and
freshwater fish.

Casual and comfortable seating at Veda
House, Plovdiv

**RILA MONASTERY:
Drushliavitsa** €€
Bulgarian
Tel *(0888) 278 756*
With hearty Bulgarian dishes and
freshly caught trout dominating
its menu, this restaurant offers a
fine dining experience.

**KOPRIVSHTITSA:
Dyado Liben** €€
Bulgarian
ul. Hadzhi Nencho Palaveev 47
Tel *(07184) 2109*
This romantic restaurant in a
beautifully restored mansion
offers a short but excellent menu
of grilled meats.

VELIKO TÛRNOVO: Yantra €€€
International
ul. Opalchenska 2
Tel *(062) 600 607*
One of the town's best, this
capacious restaurant offers an
excellent choice of Bulgarian
and international cuisine.

SOZOPOL: Rusalka €€
Seafood
ul. Milet 36
Tel *(0550) 23047*
Waves crash against rocks directly
below Rusalka, which offers
amazing seafood, pasta and pizza.

VARNA: Garibaldi €€
Italian
ul. Tsar Osvoboditel 9
Tel *(052) 604 080*
This majestic restaurant is just the
place for great Italian cuisine.

General Index

Acknowledgments

Dorling Kindersley would like to thank the following people whose contributions and assistance have made the preparation of this book possible.

Main Contributors

Jonathan Bousfield was born in the UK and has been travelling in Central and Eastern Europe for as long as he can remember. A student of East European history and languages, Jonathan has lived at various times in Belgrade, Sofia, Zagreb, Rīga, Vilnius and Cracow. His first travel-writing job involved researching a guide to the former Yugoslavia in 1989. Since then he has authored the Dorling Kindersley *Eyewitness Travel Guide to Bulgaria*, Rough Guides to Croatia and the Baltic States, and co-authored the Rough Guides to Austria, Poland and Bulgaria. He has also been a magazine editor, feature writer and rock critic.

Matt Willis first encountered Central and Eastern Europe during an overland trip to Iran from his home town of Malvern, UK, in 1996. Since then, he has returned repeatedly to explore the region and has worked there both as a journalist and travel guide writer. He is the author of Dorling Kindersley *Top 10 Travel Guide to Moscow* and co-author of Dorling Kindersley *Eyewitness Travel Guide to Bulgaria*.

Additional Contributors

Stephen Brook, Tomasz Darmochwał, Božidarka Boza Gligorijević, Howard Jarvis, Jerzy S Majewski, John Oates, Tim Ochser, Małgorzata Omilanowska, Marek Pernal, Catherine Phillips, Chistopher Rice, Melanie Rice, Marek Rumiński, Jakub Sito, Neil Taylor, Craig Turp, Teresa Czerniewicz-Umer, Barbara Sudnik-Wójcikowska.

Fact Checkers

Višnja Arambašić, Talis Saule Archdeacon, Andrei Bogdanov, Joel Dullroy, Irena Jamnikar, Michal Jareš, Tomáš Kleisner, Brigita Pantelejeva, Petya Milkova, Marko Mirović, Karolina Montygierd, Natasa Novakovic, Jonathan Smith, Craig Turp.

Proofreader

Debra Wolter.

Indexer

Cyber Media Services Ltd.

Design and Editorial

Publisher Douglas Amrine
List Manager Vivien Antwi
Editorial Consultant Justine Montgomery, Hugh Thompson
Senior Cartographic Editor Casper Morris
Managing Art Editor (jackets) Karen Constanti
Jacket Design Kate Leonard
Senior DTP Designer Jason Little
Senior Picture Researcher Ellen Root
Production Controller Louise Daly

Editorial Assistance

Vicki Allen.

Revisions and Relaunch Team

Zora Groholova, Cincy Jose, Adil Kaan Kızıltuğ, Scarlett O'Hara, Melanie Nicholson-Hartzell, Mohammad Hassan, Sumita Khatwani, Piotr Kozlowski, Ana Krsmanovic, Darren Longley, Carly Madden, Deepak Mittal, Helen Partington, Animesh Kumar Pathak, Filip Polonsky, Azeem Siddiqui, Beverly Smart, Susana Smith, Selma Stevanovich, Neil Taylor, Priyansha Tuli, Vinita Venugopal, Scott Alexander Young, Tanveer Zaidi.

Cartographic Assistance

The map on page 488–9 is derived from © www.openstreetmap.org and contributors, licensed under CC-BY-SA, see www.creativecommons.org for further details.

DK Picture Library

Rose Horridge, Emma Shepherd, Romaine Werblow.

Additional Photography

Gabor Barka; Demetrio Carrasco; Jiri Dolezal; John Heseltine; Nigel Hudson; Dorota and Mariusz Jarymowicz; Dave King; Beata Kowalewska; Jiri Kopriva; Krzysztof Kur; Jamie Marshall; Stanislaw Michta; Frantisek Preucil; Rough Guides: Jon Cunningham, Eddie Gerald, Michelle Grant; Lucio Rossi; Tony Souter; Jonathan Smith; James Tye; Peter Wilson; Linda Whitwam; Gregory Wrona; Leandro Zoppe.

Special Assistance

Dorling Kindersley would like to thank the following for their assistance: Alex Priscu at Bran Castle Museum, Roxana Lozneanu at Palace of Parliament, Protopresbyter Radomir Nikcevic and Nada at SPC Mitropolija Crnogorsko Primorska, Elena Obuhovich at The State Hermitage Museum, Anna Kotlyar at Tretyakov Gallery.

Photography Permissions

Dorling Kindersley would like to thank the following for their assistance and kind permission to photograph at their establishments: Lea Ferjan at Bled Castle Museum; Ethnographic Museum, Belgrade; Fresco Gallery, Belgrade; Jože Šerbec at Kobarid Museum; Marta Kovac at The National Gallery, Slovenia; Veronica Leca at The National Museum of Art of Romania and The Museum of Art Collections; National Museum of Contemporary History; Irena Ribic at Postojna Caves; The Plečnik House. Works of art have been reproduced with the kind permission of the following copyright holders; *La Danse* © Succession H Matisse/DACS 2009 151cr

Picture Credits

Placement Key- a=above, b=below/bottom, c=centre, f=far, l=left, r=right, t=top.

The Publishers are grateful to the following individuals, companies and picture l ibraries for permission to reproduce their photographs:

4Corners Images: Pavan Aldo 503b, 513tc; Simeone Giovanni 42-43; Kaos03 222; Panayiotou Paul 321b; SIME/ Schmid Reinhard 320.

akg-images: 36ca, 197cra; 129cr,/ Erich Lessing 48tl, 248cla, 249bc.

Alamy Images: Vladimir Alexeev 27br; Arco Images GmbH 27cb; Peter Barritt 1c; Pat Behnke 423tr; Gary Cook 91bl; Danita Delimont/Walter Bibikow 362tr,/Inger Hogstrom 130tl,/Janis Miglavs 75b; Don Davis 554cla; Diomedia 535br,/Snezana Negovanovic 37br; Sindre Ellingsen 61tl; I Capture Photography 557cra; James Davis Photography 382bc; johnrochaphoto 34clb; Ladi Kirn 409ca; Stan Kujawa 554bl; Kuttig - Travel 449tl; Yadid Levy 154bc; Nikreates 594br; PBstock 558cl; PhotoEdit 495cb; Nicholas Pitt 37clb; PjrFoto/Phil Robinson 564bl; Profimedia International s.r.o./Michaela Dusíková 249tr, 271c; Alex Segre 154cla; Snappdragon 493c; Ilian Stage 594cl; TTL Images 511br; Ivan Vdovin 535tr; Jan Wlodarczyk 26tr; Sven Zacek 110cla.

Archaeological Museum, Zagreb: 36bl.

Archives Matisse: 151cr.

Auschwitz - Birkenau Memorial & Museum: 196tr, 196cl, 196bl, 196br, 197tc, 198cl, 199tl, 199tr, 199cb, 199br,/ Ryszard Domasik 197crb.

Szabolcs Baranyai: 352bl.

Bran Castle Museum: 556bc, 557tc.

The Bridgeman Art Library: Torun, Poland (engraving) (b/w photo), German School, (17th century)/Private Collection 25ca, Holy Roman Emperor Charles IV (colour litho), French School/Private Collection/The Stapleton Collection 38ca, Matthias I, Hunyadi (oil on paper),/ Kunsthistorisches Museum, Vienna, Austria 322tc, The Visitation, 1506, Master M.S., (16th century)/Hungarian National Gallery, Budapest, Hungary 328tl, ureus (obverse) of Diocletian (AD 284-AD 305) cuirassed, wearing a laurel wreath. (gold) Inscription: IMP C C VAL DIOCLETIANVS P F AVG, Roman (4th century AD)/Private Collection 449cra.

Corbis: Atlantide Phototravel 34cla; The Art Archive/ Alfredo Dagli Orti 38bl, 340cra; Bettmann 40cla, 100tr, 398tl; Tibor Bognar 34-35c; EPA 198bl; Owen Franken 561bl; The Gallery Collection 382tr, 383tl; E.O. Hoppé 471br; Hulton-Deutsch Collection 40tr, 76tl, 288tl, 432tl, 576tr; JAI/Ivan Vdovin 128cla; Barry Lewis 323tl, 335tl; The Picture Desk Limited/Gianni Dagli 159br; Carmen Redondo 198tr, 198cla; Roman Soumar 331cr; Rudy Sulgan 293cra; Sygma/Bernard Bisson & Thierry Orban 41tl/Pascal Le Segretain 544tr; Paul Thompson 187br, Peter Turnley 41tr, 172tl.

The Croatian Museum of Naïve Art: 472tl.

Croatian National Tourist Board Archives: 436cl, 440bc, 441tl, 441br, 442cr, 442bl, 443tl, 445br.

Danita Delimont Stock Photography: Russian Look 131tr.

DK Images: Gabor Barka 330c, 331tl, 336cl, 337tl, 337cra, 337crb, 337bc.

European Central Bank: 19 (all images).

Ethnographic Open-Air Museum: 85cla, 85clb.

Getty Images: AFP 593br,/Dimitar Dilkoff 504tr,/ Gerard Fouet 548bl,/Stringer 34bc, 130tr; Bettmann 35br; Hulton Archive/Handout 37tr,/ Imagno 35bl; Stringer/Valentina Petrova 36cb; The Image Bank/Peter Aºdams 8-9; Time & Life Pictures/Ben Martin 35bc.

The Granger Collection, New York: 9c, 34tr, 39ca, 39bl, 124tl, 167ca, 224tc, 393ca, 486tl; Rue des Archives 522tl.

High Tatras Tourism Association: 307br.

Igalo Spa: 509tr.

Igor Jeremic: 510br.

Jewish Culture Festival Society: *Mizrah* designed by Zbigniew Prokop, paper-cutting by Marta Gołąb 35cb.

KGB Cells Museum: 115c.

Klaipeda Clock Museum: 64crb.

Lonely Planet Images: Richard I'Anson 129tc.

Erica Martinetti: 513br.
Mary Evans Picture Library: 43ca.

Masterfile: Mike Dobel 467cr; Lloyd Sutton 223b.

National Geographic Stock: H. M. Herget 37bl; James L. Stanfield 36tr, 588tr.

Naturhistorisches Museum: 168bl.

Nikola Tesla Museum: 530tr.

Old Masters Gallery: 473c, 473bc.

Protopresbyter Radomir Nikcevic: 513cla, 513bl.

Palace of Parliament: 548tr, 548cl, 549tl, 549crb, 549bc.

Igor Palmin:137bc, 138clb.

Peleş Castle: 558clb, 559tl, 559cra, 559br.

Photo Tresor: 578tr, 593cra, 595cl.

Photolibrary: César Lucas Abreu 194bl; Alamer 33crb; Richard Ashworth 392-393; Henry Ausloos 506c; Gonzalo Azumendi 98, 383bc, 387br; Walter Bibikow 26clb, 166-167, 170, 307br, 398, 485b, 492tl, 502, 506tl; Barbara Boensch 287b; Sebastien Boisse 15cr; The Bridgeman Art Library 384cla; Wojtek Buss 44br, 47b, 66cl, 74, 574, 586cl, 593bl; The British Library 35tr; Wendy Connett 175tr; JD. Dallet 412tl; Peter Dawson 1-2; Cécile DéGremont 442tr; Günter Flegar 442cl; Raymond Forbes 445tl, 459tr; Kevin Galvin 431b; Gilsdorf Gilsdorf 380; Sylvain Grandadam 154clb; Gavin Hellier 24-25, 32clb; Hi Pix 555bl; 26br, 245tc; John Warburton-Lee Photography/Christian Kober 533br; Jon Arnold Travel/Russell Young 99b; JTB Photo 29br, 46, 575b; Henryk T Kaiser 239cra, 286; Frank Krahmer 413br; Dinu Lazar 543b; Paolo Lazzarin 520; Günter Lenz 44cla; Holger Leue 434tr; Sheldon Levis 444cl; Lonely Planet Images/Grant Dixon 419cra; Oleksiy Maksymenko 122; Mary Evans Picture Library 37tl; Gotin Michel 35tl; Rainer Mirau 418bc, 430; Graham Monro 274bl; Don Mckinnell 39crb; S. Nicolas 588bl; Jose Fuste Raga 171br, 463br; Rolf Richardson 592br; Robert Harding Travel/Ken Gillham 443br; Martin Siepmann 386cr, 419bc; Witold Skrypczak 474cla; Frédéric Soreau 458cl; Dimitar Sotirov 589br; Egmont Strigl 484; Yoshio Tomii 123b; Wolfgang Weinhäupl 487bl.

Photoshot: Hemis 443cra.

Pictures Colour Library: Simon Heaton 590br.

Prague Castle Picture Gallery: 230bc.

Private Collection: 35cra, 39tr, 38br, 39tc, 113cr, 155tr, 244br.

The State Hermitage Museum, St Petersburg: 148cla, 148clb, 148br, 149tl, 149cra, 149bl, 149br, 150cla, 150bc, 151tr, 151bc, 152c, 152cla, 153tr, 153bl.

Dusan Timotijevic: 521b.

Tretyakov Gallery: 140cla, 140clb, 140br, 141tl, 141cra, 141bc.

Velika Planina: 414br, 415br.

Wikipedia, The Free Encyclopedia: Public Domain 39tl.

Front Endpaper: 4 Corners Images: Kaos03 ftl, SIME/ Schmid Reinhard crb; **Photolibrary**: Gonzalo Azumendi fcr; Walter Bibikow tc, fcl, bl; Wojtek Buss fcr (Riga), fbr; Gilsdorf Gilsdorf tl; JTB Photo cr; Henryk T Kaiser ftl (Mountain); Paolo Lazzarin br; Oleksiy Maksymenko tr; Rainer Mirau cl; Egmont Strigl fbl.

Cover Picture Credits

Front– Photolibrary: Jose Fuste Raga main;
Back – Alamy Images: Paul Thompson Images/Chris Ballentine tl; **AWL Images:** Gavin Hellier bl; **Dorling Kindersley:** Dorota i Mariusz Jarymowiczowie clb; **Photolibrary:** Superstock Inc. cla; S**pine – Photolibrary:** Jose Fuste Raga t.

All other images © Dorling Kindersley
For further information see: www.dkimages.com

Eastern and Central Europe's Rail Network

The quality and density of the railway network varies greatly from one part of Central and [Eas]tern Europe to another. The Austrians, in [par]ticular, were great railway builders and the [?] countries of the former Austro-Hungarian [Em]pire, such as the Czech Republic, Slovakia, [Hu]ngary, Slovenia, Croatia, eastern Romania and [nor]thern Serbia, are still connected by a compre[hen]sive web of well-run railway lines. In Central [Eur]ope, the rail network is the main means of [inter]city travel, while in South Eastern Europe, [trai]ns are frequently slow and uncomfortable. [Thi]s map is not a guide to the frequency or type [of r]ail services; details of rail travel in individual [cou]ntries are given in the Practical Information [sec]tions of each country chapter.

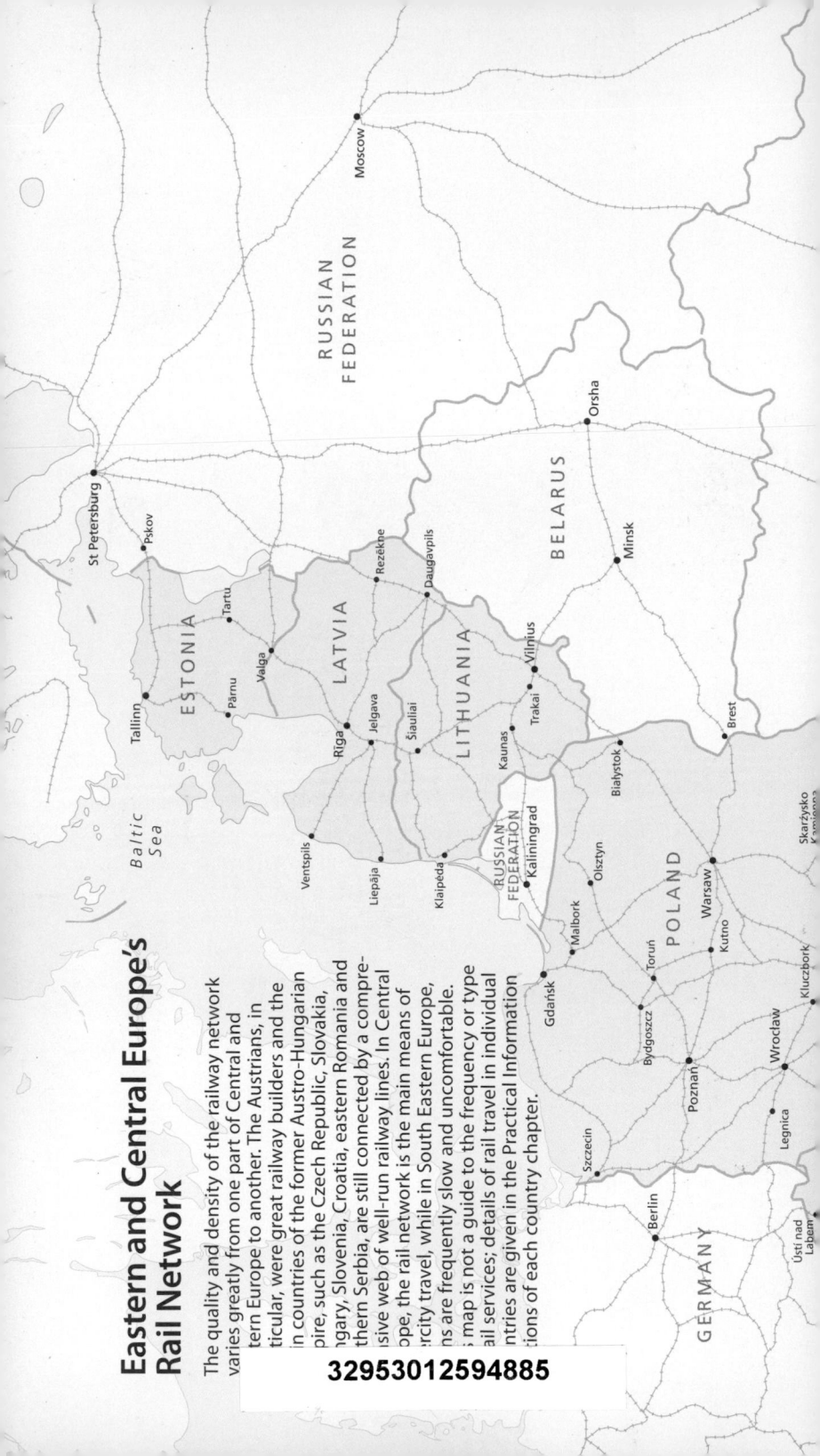

32953012594885